The Gospel of
LUKE

JOEL B. GREEN

WILLIAM B. EERDMANS PUBLISHING COMPANY
GRAND RAPIDS, MICHIGAN / CAMBRIDGE, U.K.

© 1997 Wm. B. Eerdmans Publishing Co.
255 Jefferson Ave. S.E., Grand Rapids, Michigan 49503 /
P.O. Box 163, Cambridge CB3 9PU U.K.
All rights reserved

Printed in the United States of America

10 09 08 07 06 05 04   11 10 9 8 7 6 5 4

Library of Congress Cataloging-in-Publication Data

ISBN 0-8028-2315-7

THE NEW INTERNATIONAL COMMENTARY
ON THE
NEW TESTAMENT

General Editors

NED B. STONEHOUSE
(1946-1962)

F. F. BRUCE
(1962-1990)

GORDON D. FEE
(1990-   )

CONTENTS

EDITOR'S PREFACE

This replacement commentary (the eighth) represents another milestone for the New International Commentary on the New Testament, in that it replaces the first commentary to appear in the original series, that by Norval Geldenhuys in 1951. For that volume, the first editor, Ned Stonehouse, wrote a general foreword introducing the series, while F. F. Bruce, who would eventually succeed Stonehouse as its second editor, wrote a foreword to Geldenhuys's commentary in particular. Reading these two forewords can be instructive with regard to the evolution of the series.

That the proposed seventeen- (now nineteen-)volume series would "appear with some regularity" is our yet-to-be-realized hope, which now looks to the turn of the century for final realization (Matthew, the Pastoral Letters, and 2 Peter/Jude are outstanding but in process). Whereas the international scope of the series has been maintained, its original Dutch and South African flavor has, with the present volume, now been lost. So also under Bruce's editorship the intentionally Reformed perspective of the series envisioned by Stonehouse began to wane. The present volume, the second in the series by a Methodist (along with I. Howard Marshall's *Johannine Epistles*) is another indication of the cooperative, broadly based, cross-confessional dimension of the evangelical tradition that has emerged in the second half of the twentieth century. But the goal of the series has been maintained throughout all of this evolution: "to provide earnest students of the New Testament with an exposition that is thorough and abreast of modern scholarship and at the same time loyal to Scripture as the infallible Word of God" (Stonehouse, p. 3 in Geldenhuys's *Luke*).

Two further reflections from those first forewords are of interest regarding the present volume: the pointedly pastoral dimension of the Geldenhuys volume, and its way of being "abreast of modern scholarship." The first matter, very frankly, disappeared from most of the succeeding volumes until it was reintroduced in my *First Corinthians* (1987); and I have urged current authors to work hard at maintaining this dimension of the series. The present commentary happily does so, although not in the more fixed form that Geldenhuys (or Fee) did.

The second matter is the more significant one regarding the present volume; for in some ways Geldenhuys and Green, at the midpoint and the end of the present century respectively, represent two considerably different approaches to these matters, while in both cases going against the grain of the atomistic approach to Synoptic studies that has so long held sway. In his foreword Professor Bruce noted that Geldenhuys maintained a "healthy scepticism" toward "some parts of the critical stock-in-trade" of the academy, which made it look a bit obscurantist for its time, despite Bruce's demurrer to the contrary.

The present commentary is anything but obscurantist. But it is different from most Synoptic commentaries in its approach to the evangelist Luke, showing very little concern for traditional form-critical and redaction-critical issues. Professor Green is fully aware of these matters, but leaves the reader to consult other commentaries for their details. His concern, and it is a refreshing and exciting concern, is that the reader capture Luke's narrative of Jesus on its own right. Here at last is a commentary on Luke that tries to help the reader to see how the narrative "works," how Luke's own obvious concerns drive the narrative from beginning to end (including Acts), how one should read Luke as its first reader would have read it — without cross-referencing to Matthew or Mark. Thus I am pleased to commend this superb reading of Luke to both the primary audience of the series — the working pastor and teacher, as well as students — and its secondary audience in the academy. Read it and learn — and enjoy,

Also belonging to the newer generation of evangelical scholars (see my preface to Doug Moo's *Romans*), Joel Green is especially well-equipped for this task. Since the completion of his Ph.D. in New Testament in 1985 (from Aberdeen, Scotland), he has maintained a vigorous schedule of publications, especially on Luke-Acts (see the entries in his bibliography), as well as serving as editor (or co-editor) for a whole variety of projects (*Catalyst*, a quarterly for seminarians; the *Dictionary of Jesus and the Gospels* [IVP]; the I. Howard Marshall *Festschrift*; and others). He also already has a distinguished teaching career at New College (Berkeley) and the American Baptist Seminary of the West (Berkeley). As of the publication of this volume (Fall 1997) he begins his appointment as Professor of New Testament Interpretation at Asbury Theological Seminary, Wilmore, Kentucky. However, throughout all of his academic life, both as a student and teacher, he has also maintained an active pastoral life in the church. This combination of passion for scholarship and the life of the church has come to a splendid fruition with the present commentary.

GORDON D. FEE

AUTHOR'S PREFACE

If the name of Hans Conzelmann is associated with the massive shift in Lukan studies characterizing the decades reaching from the 1950s to the publication of Joseph Fitzmyer's two-volume commentary on the Third Gospel in the 1980s, any survey of more recent exploration of the Gospel of Luke would highlight the work of such scholars as Robert Tannehill and Luke Johnson on the literary side, and Halvor Moxnes and Philip Esler on the social-scientific. My own introduction to serious study of Luke coincided with this latter shift, marked by the waning of the hegemony of historical study (historical criticism, tradition criticism, redaction criticism, and the rest) and the blooming of so-called "newer" approaches (e.g., new literary criticism, narrative criticism, new historicism, and the like). At the time, even the idea of writing a commentary seemed to present too many problems of method and presentation; indeed, more than one person pronounced a plague on all commentary writing! My decision to undertake this project was grounded in my belief that those involved in the church's ministry continue to be helped most by commentaries on whole books, written from the perspective of a fundamental reverence for the biblical text and from a position of critical engagement with academic biblical studies and active involvement in the life of the church. I also believed that discussion about method in the study of the Gospels need not lead necessarily into a cul-de-sac, and that recent innovations in method had as their natural outcome the possibility of making the Gospel of Luke and its message come even more alive for contemporary readers.

How I have navigated the sometimes difficult, always exciting waters of interpretive method will become clear to any who actually(!) read the Introduction. It will become equally clear that, in spite of the size of this volume, I have made no attempt to address the whole spectrum of questions that might possibly be put to the Gospel of Luke. This has never really been possible, and it is even less so today. This is not for me a cause of despair, but rather reason to rejoice, and to reflect on the multivalency of the Gospel, which can address in so many ways the diverse needs of the historic and global church.

A project of this magnitude is not brought to completion without a crowd of witnesses and participants. Above all, I want to record my gratitude for the encouragement and support of Pamela, Aaron, and Allison — my family; no doubt they will welcome the publication of this commentary as a harbinger of future conversations in our home that do *not* turn so quickly to Luke! I have benefited greatly from my students and research assistants Gilles Bekaert, Meagan Howland, Kevin Anderson, and Michael McKeever, and from many others who have participated in my various courses on the Third Gospel — first at New College Berkeley, then more recently at the American Baptist Seminary of the West and Graduate Theological Union, Berkeley. Much of my perspective on the Gospel of Luke has been developed in the context of sermons and seminars in local churches and conferences — especially among friends at St. Luke's United Methodist Church, Richmond, California, and at Redwood Christian Park, Boulder Creek, California. New College Berkeley and the American Baptist Seminary of the West each afforded me time for intensive work on the Gospel of Luke with sabbaticals. I am grateful to the University of Durham for appointing me as Visiting Fellow in the Department of Theology in Spring 1992, and especially to Jimmy and Meta Dunn for their numerous acts of hospitality during that period of study. My research was supported financially not only through these periods of sabbatical leave, but also through the Catholic Biblical Association, which awarded me a Young Scholar's Fellowship for my project "Toward a Unified Hermeneutic: The Application of Discourse Theory and Sociological Analysis to the Gospel of Luke" (1991-92); and through the Graduate Theological Union, which provided research assistance and additional funding in the form of a Henry Mayo Newhall Fellowship for Student-Faculty Partnership, for the project "Luke-Acts and the Jewish People." Of course, I am also grateful to Fred Bruce, who extended the initial invitation to me to contribute a commentary on the Gospel of Luke for the NICNT; and to his replacement as series editor, Gordon Fee, whose patience, encouragement, insight, and willingness to allow me to follow a different sort of interpretive path have been greatly appreciated.

Originally, the NICNT was to have used the American Revised Version (1901); this has since given way both to translations generated by the authors of the various commentaries and to the use of other translations. Not wishing to proliferate the number of translations, and in the hope of using a text that is readily available and widely used in churches, I have chosen to employ the NRSV in this commentary. For the most part, I have refrained from discussing text-critical alternatives, though from time to time I have indicated in my editing of the NRSV where my own thinking departs from the translation committee on both text-critical and translation issues.

JOEL B. GREEN
HOLY WEEK 1997

x

INTERPRETIVE ASIDES

FIGURES

ABBREVIATIONS

1. General Abbreviations

§(§)	paragraph(s) or section(s)
κτλ	καὶ τὰ λοιπά, and the remainder
a.k.a.	also known as
Aq.	Aquila
B.C.E.	Before the Common Era (B.C.)
ca.	*circa,* about (with dates)
C.E.	Common Era (A.D.)
cf.	*confer,* compare
ch(s).	chapter(s)
ed.	edition; editor(s), edited by
e.g.	*exempli gratia,* for example
et al.	*et alii,* and others
esp.	especially
ET	English translation
fr(s).	fragment(s)
i.e.	*id est,* that is
LXX	Septuagint
mss.	manuscripts
MT	Masoretic Text
n(n)	note(s)
n.d.	no date given
n.s.	new series
NT	New Testament
OT	Old Testament
QL	Qumran Literature
rev.	revised
Theod.	Theodotion
v(v)	verse(s)
vol(s).	volume(s)

2. Ancient Literature

2.1. Biblical Books and the Apocrypha

Gen	Genesis
Exod	Exodus
Lev	Leviticus
Num	Numbers
Deut	Deuteronomy
Josh	Joshua
Judg	Judges
Ruth	Ruth
1-2 Sam	1-2 Samuel
1-2 Kgs	1-2 Kings
1-2 Chr	1-2 Chronicles
Ezra	Ezra
Neh	Nehemiah
Esth	Esther
Job	Job
Ps(s)	Psalm(s)
Prov	Proverbs
Eccl	Ecclesiastes
Cant	Song of Solomon
Isa	Isaiah
Jer	Jeremiah
Lam	Lamentations
Ezek	Ezekiel
Dan	Daniel
Hos	Hosea
Joel	Joel
Amos	Amos
Obad	Obadiah
Jonah	Jonah
Mic	Micah
Nah	Nahum
Hab	Habakkuk
Zeph	Zephaniah
Hag	Haggai
Zech	Zechariah
Mal	Malachi
Add Esth	Additions to Esther
Bar	Baruch

Bel	Bel and the Dragon
1-2 Esdr	1-2 Esdras
4 Ezra	4 Ezra
Jdt	Judith
Ep Jer	Epistle of Jeremiah
1-4 Macc	1-4 Maccabees
Pr Azar	Prayer of Azariah
Pr Man	Prayer of Manasseh
Sir	Sirach (Ecclesiasticus)
Sus	Susannah
Tob	Tobit
Wis	Wisdom of Solomon
Matt	Matthew
Mark	Mark
Luke	Luke
John	John
Acts	Acts
Rom	Romans
1-2 Cor	1-2 Corinthians
Gal	Galatians
Eph	Ephesians
Phil	Philippians
Col	Colossians
1-2 Thess	1-2 Thessalonians
1-2 Tim	1-2 Timothy
Tit	Titus
Phlm	Philemon
Heb	Hebrews
Jas	James
1-2 Pet	1-2 Peter
1-3 John	1-3 John
Jude	Jude
Rev	Revelation

2.2. Pseudepigrapha and Early Christian Writings

Apoc. Abr.	*Apocalypse of Abraham*
2 Apoc. Bar.	Syriac *Apocalypse of Baruch*
3 Apoc. Bar.	Greek *Apocalypse of Baruch*
As. Mos.	*Assumption of Moses*
Did.	*Didache*

1 Enoch	Ethiopic *Enoch*
2 Enoch	Slavonic *Enoch*
Ep. Arist.	*Epistle of Aristeas*
Gos. Pet.	*Gospel of Peter*
Jos. As.	*Joseph and Aseneth*
Jub.	*Jubilees*
Mart. Isa.	*Martyrdom of Isaiah*
Pss. Sol.	*Psalms of Solomon*
Sib. Or.	*Sibylline Oracles*
T. Abr.	*Testament of Abraham*
T. Ben.	*Testament of Benjamin*
T. Dan	*Testament of Dan*
T. Iss.	*Testament of Issachar*
T. Job	*Testament of Job*
T. Jos.	*Testament of Joseph*
T. Jud.	*Testament of Judah*
T. Lev.	*Testament of Levi*
T. Mos.	*Testament of Moses*
T. Reub.	*Testament of Reuben*
T. Sim.	*Testament of Simeon*
T. Sol.	*Testament of Solomon*
T. Zeb.	*Testament of Zebulun*

2.3. Dead Sea Scrolls and Related Texts

CD	Cairo (Genizah text of the) *Damascus Document/Rule*
1Q28b	*Rule of the Blessings* from Qumran Cave 1
1Q34	*Festival Prayers* from Qumran Cave 1
1QapGen	*Genesis Apocryphon* from Qumran Cave 1
1QH	*Hôdāyôt* or Thanksgiving Hymns from Qumran Cave 1
1QIsaᵃ	Isaiah (first copy) from Qumran Cave 1
1QM	*Milḥāmāh* or War Scroll from Qumran Cave 1
1QpHab	*Pesher on Habakkuk* from Qumran Cave 1
1QS	*Serek hayyaḥad* or Rule of the Community or Manual of Discipline from Qumran Cave 1
1QSa	Appendix A, *Messianic Rule,* to 1QS (= 1Q28a)
4Q246	*Aramaic Apocalypse* from Qumran Cave 4
4Q416	*Sapiential Work A$_b$* from Qumran Cave 4
4Q504	*Words of the Luminaries* from Qumran Cave 4
4Qapocr Josephᵃ	*Apocryphon of Josephᵃ* from Qumran Cave 4 (= 4Q372)
4QFlor	*Florilegium* from Qumran Cave 4 (= 4Q174)
4QMess ar	*Elect of God* (= 4Q534)

4QMMT	*Miqsat Ma'aseh ha-Torah (Halakhic Letter)* from Qumran Cave 4
4QpIsa^a	*Pesher on Isaiah* (first copy) from Qumran Cave 4 (= 4Q161)
4QPrNab ar	*Prayer of Nabonidus* (= 4Q242)
4QTest	*Testimonia* from Qumran Cave 4 (= 4Q175)
11QMelch	*Melchizedek* from Qumran Cave 11 (= 11Q13)
11QApPs^a	*Apocryphal Psalms^a* from Qumran Cave 11 (= 11Q11)
11QTemple	*Temple Scroll* from Qumran Cave 11

2.4. Targumim

Tg. Onq.	*Targum Onqelos*
Tg. Ps.-J.	*Targum Pseudo-Jonathan*

2.5. Rabbinic Literature and Tractates

b.	Babylonian Talmud
Bek.	*Bekorot*
Ber.	*Berakot*
Giṭ.	*Giṭṭin*
Ḥag.	*Ḥagigah*
Kelim	*Kelim*
m.	Mishna
Menaḥ	*Menaḥot*
Nid.	*Niddah*
Qidd.	*Qiddušin*
Pesaḥ.	*Pesaḥim*
Rab.	*Rabbah*
Šabb.	*Šabbat*
Sanh.	*Sanhedrin*
Tamid	*Tamid*
Yoma	*Yoma*

2.6. Other Ancient Authors and Writings

Aristotle
Nic. Ethics	*Nicomachean Ethics*
Rhetoric	*Art of Rhetoric*

Augustine
   De cons.   *De consensu evangelistarum*

Bede
   Luc.   *Im Lucam*

Demosthenes
   Third Phil.   *Third Philippic*

Dionysius
   De orat.   *De oratoribus antiquis*
   Rom. Ant.   *Roman Antiquities*

Euripides
   Rhes.   *Rhesus*

Eusebius
   Hist. eccl.   *Historia ecclesiastica*
   Psalms   *Commentary on the Psalms*

Galen
   Diff. feb.   *De differentiis febrium*

Herodotus

Josephus
   Ag. Ap.   *Against Apion*
   Ant.   *Jewish Antiquities*
   J.W.   *Jewish War*
   Life   *Life of Flavius Josephus*

Justin
   1 Apol.   *First Apology*
   Dial.   *Dialogus cum Tryphone Judaeo*

Lucian
   De Hist.   *Quomodo Historia conscribenda sit*
     Conscrib.

Origen
   Con. Cel.   *Contra Celsus*
   Hom. in Luc.   *Homilia in Lucam*
   Quinta   *Quinta*

Philo
Abr.	*De Abrahamo*
Agr.	*De agricultura*
Flacc.	*In Flaccum*
Leg. Gai.	*De Legatione ad Gaium*
Praem.	*De Praemiis et Poenis*
Quaest. Exod.	*Quaestiones in Exodum*
Quod omn.	*Quod omnis probus liber sit*
Spec. Leg.	*De specialibus legibus*
Virt.	*De virtutibus*
Vita Cont.	*De vita contemplativa*
Vita Mos.	*De vita Mosis*

Plato
Rep.	*Republic*

Pliny (the elder)
Nat. Hist.	*Naturalis Historia*

Pliny (the younger)
Ep.	*Epistolae*

P.Oxy.	The Oxyrhynchus Papyri

Prot. Jas.	*Protevangelium of James*

Ps.-Phoc.	*Pseudo-Phocylides*

Quintilian
Inst. orat.	*Institutio oratoria*

Seneca
Ep.	*Epistulae Morales*

Tacitus
Ann.	*Annals*

Xenophon
Mem.	*Memorabilia Socratis*

2. Modern Literature

A1CS	The Book of Acts in Its First Century Setting
AASFDHL	Annales Academiae Scientiarum Fennicae Dissertationes Humanarum Litterarum
AB	Anchor Bible
ABD	*Anchor Bible Dictionary.* Edited by David Noel Freedman
ABRL	Anchor Bible Reference Library
AGSU	Arbeiten und Geschichte des Spätjudentums und Urchristentums
AMTBBB	Athenäum^s Monografien: Theologie; Bonner Biblische Beiträge
AnBib	Analecta Biblica
AnGreg	Analecta Gregoriana
ANRW	*Aufstieg und Niedergang der römischen Welt: Geschichte und Kultur Roms im Spiegel der Neueren Forschung.* Edited by Hildegard Temporini.
AS	Advances in Semiotics
ATR	*Anglican Theological Review*
AUS	American University Studies
AusBR	*Australian Bible Review*
AUSDDS	Andrews University Seminary Doctoral Dissertation Series
AUSS	*Andrews University Seminary Studies*
BAGD	Arndt, William F., and F. Wilbur Gingrich. *A Greek-English Lexicon of the New Testament and Other Early Christian Literature.* A Translation and Adaptation of the Fourth Revised and Augmented Edition of Walter Bauer's *Griechisch-Deutsches Wörterbuch zu den Schriften des Neuen Testaments und der übrigen urchristlichen Literatur.* 2d ed. Revised and augmented by F. Wilbur Gingrich and Frederick W. Danker from Walter Bauer's 5th ed., 1958.
BBB	Bonner Biblische Beiträge
BBET	Beiträge zur biblischen Exegese und Theologie
BBR	*Bulletin of Biblical Research*
BC	The Beginnings of Christianity
BDF	Blass, F., and A. Debrunner. *A Greek Grammar of the New Testament and Other Early Christian Literature.* Translated and revised by Robert W. Funk.
BECNT	Baker Exegetical Commentary on the New Testament
BES	Biblical Encounter Series
BETL	Bibliotheca ephemeridum theologicarum lovaniensium
BGU	Ägyptische Urkunden aus den Museen zu Berlin. Griech. Urkunden I-VIII (1895-1933).

Bib	*Biblica*
BibLeb	*Bibel und Leben*
BibTod	*The Bible Today*
BJRL	*Bulletin of the John Rylands University Library of Manchester*
BJS	Brown Judaic Studies
BTB	*Biblical Theology Bulletin*
BTF	*Bangalore Theological Forum*
BWANT	Beiträge zur Wissenschaft vom Alten und Neuen Testament
BZ	*Biblische Zeitschrift*
BZNW	Beihefte zur *ZNW*
CahRB	*Cahiers d'archéologie biblique*
CBQ	*Catholic Biblical Quarterly*
CCWJCW	Cambridge Commentaries on Writings of the Jewish and Christian World, 200 BC to AD 200
CEP	Contemporary Evangelical Perspectives
CHCL	*Cambridge History of Classical Literature*
ConBNT	Coniectanea biblica, New Testament
CRTP	Critical Readers in Theory and Practice
CSHSMC	Comparative Studies of Health Systems and Medical Care
CSS	Cistercian Studies Series
CTL	Cambridge Textbooks in Linguistics
CThM	Calwer theologische Monographien
CurTM	*Currents in Theology and Mission*
DJG	*Dictionary of Jesus and the Gospels.* Edited by Joel B. Green and Scot McKnight.
DPL	*Dictionary of Paul and His Letters.* Edited by Gerald F. Hawthorne et al.
DRev	*Downside Review*
EDNT	*Exegetical Dictionary of the New Testament.* 3 vols. Edited by Horst Balz and Gerhard Schneider.
EH	Europäische Hochschulschriften
EKKNT	Evangelisch-Katholischer Kommentar zum Neuen Testament
EMar	*Ephemerides Mariologicae*
EPROER	Études préliminaires aux religions orientales dans l'empire romain
ErFor	Erträge der Forschung
ESCK	Eidos: Studies in Classical Kinds
ESEC	Emory Studies in Early Christianity
ET	*Eglise et Théologie*
ETL	*Ephemerides theologicae lovanienses*

ETS	Erfurter theologische Studien
EvQ	*The Evangelical Quarterly*
ExpT	*Expository Times*
FB	Forschung zur Bibel
FCCGRW	First-Century Christians in the Graeco-Roman World
FF	Foundations and Facets
FF:LF	Foundations and Facets: Literary Facets
FilNT	*Filologia Neotestamentaria*
FMA	Foundations of Modern Anthropology
ForFasc	Forum Fascicles
FRLANT	Forschungen zur Religion und Literatur des Alten und Neuen Testaments
GBS	Guides to Biblical Scholarship
GBT	Gender and the Biblical Tradition
GELNT	*Greek-English Lexicon of the New Testament Based on Semantic Domains.* 2 vols. Edited by Johannes P. Louw and Eugene A. Nida.
GELS	*A Greek-English Lexicon of the Septuagint.* Part 1. Compiled by J. Lust, E. Eynikel, and K. Hauspie, with the collaboration of G. Chamberlain.
GNS	Good News Studies
GP	Gospel Perspectives
HCPE	Health Care Policy and Ethics
HeyJ	*Heythrop Journal*
HNT	Handbuch zum Neuen Testament
HSM	Harvard Semitic Monographs
HTKNT	Herders theologischer Kommentar zum Neuen Testament
HTR	*Harvard Theological Review*
HTSSup	Hervormde Teologiese Studies Supplementum
IBS	*Irish Biblical Studies*
ICC	International Critical Commentary
IDB	*The Interpreter's Dictionary of the Bible.* 4 vols. Edited by George Arthur Buttrick.
IDBSup	*The Interpreter's Dictionary of the Bible, Supplementary Volume.* Edited by Keith Crim.
Int	*Interpretation*
ISBL	Indiana Studies in Biblical Literature
ITQ	*Irish Theological Quarterly*
ITS	*Indian Theological Studies*
JBL	*Journal of Biblical Literature*
JerP	*Jerusalem Perspectives*
JETS	*Journal of the Evangelical Theological Society*
JLT	*Journal of Literature and Theology*

JPC	*Journal of Psychology and Christianity*
JPTSup	Journal for the Study of Pentecostal Theology Supplement Series
JQR	*Jewish Quarterly Review*
JR	*Journal of Religion*
JRS	*Journal of Roman Studies*
JSF	*Journal of Spiritual Formation*
JSNT	*Journal for the Study of the New Testament*
JSNTSup	Journal for the Study of the New Testament Supplement Series
JSOTSup	Journal for the Study of the Old Testament Supplement Series
JSPSup	Journal for the Study of the Pseudepigrapha Supplement Series
JTC	*Journal for Theology and the Church*
JTS	*Journal of Theological Studies*
JTSA	*Journal of Theology for Southern Africa*
KKNT	Kritisch-exegetischer Kommentar über das Neue Testament
LB	*Linguistica Biblica*
LCBI	Literary Currents in Biblical Interpretation
LCL	Loeb Classical Library
LEC	Library of Early Christianity
LF	Literary Facets
LLL	Longman Linguistics Library
LS	Language in Society
LT	Liberation and Theology
MHT	Moulton, James Hope, Wilbert Francis Howard, and Nigel Turner. *A Grammar of New Testament Greek.* 4 vols.
MM	Moulton, James Hope, and George Milligan. *The Vocabulary of the Greek Testament: Illustrated from the Papyri and Other Non-literary Sources.*
MS	*Marian Studies*
NA^{26}	*Novum Testamentum Graece.* 26th ed.
NAB	New American Bible
NAC	New American Commmentary
NCV	New Century Version
NEBNT	Neue Echter Bibel: Neuen Testament
NDCEPT	*New Dictionary of Christian Ethics and Pastoral Theology.* Edited by David Atkinson, David F. Field, Arthur Holmes, and Oliver O'Donovan.
Neot	*Neotestamentica*
NIDNTT	*New International Dictionary of New Testament Theology.* 3 vols. Edited by Colin Brown.

NIGTC	New International Greek Testament Commentary
NIV	New International Version
NovT	*Novum Testamentum*
NovTSup	Novum Testamentum, Supplements
NRSV	New Revised Standard Version
NRT	*La nouvelle revue théologique*
NTAbh	Neutestamentliche Abhandlungen
NTD	Das Neue Testament Deutsch
NTS	*New Testament Studies*
NTT	New Testament Theology
ÖBS	Österreichische Biblische Studien
OBT	Overtures to Biblical Theology
OGIS	*Orientis graeci inscriptiones selectae.* 2 vols. Edited by W. Dittenberger.
ÖTKNT	Ökumenischer Taschenbuch-Kommentar zum Neuen Testament
OTP	*The Old Testament Pseudepigrapha.* 2 vols. Edited by James H. Charlesworth.
PFES	Publications of the Finnish Exegetical Society
PGM	*Papyri graecae magicae.* Edited by K. Preisendanz.
PIP	Pontifical Institute Publications
PRCS	Parallax Re-visions of Culture and Society
PRS	*Perspectives in Religious Studies*
PS	The Passion Series
PTMS	Pittsburgh Theological Monograph Series
PTS	Paderborner theologische Studien
QD	Quaestiones Disputatae
REB	Revised English Bible
RefTRev	*Reformed Theological Review*
ResQ	*Restoration Quarterly*
RevExp	*Review and Expositor*
RGRW	Religions in the Graeco-Roman World
RST	Regensburger Studien zur Theologie
RSV	Revised Standard Version
SANT	Studien zum Alten und Neuen Testament
SBF	Studium Biblicum Franciscanum
SBLDS	Society of Biblical Literature Dissertation Series
SBLMS	Society of Biblical Literature Monograph Series
SBLSS	Society of Biblical Literature Semeia Series
SBS	Stuttgarter Bibelstudien
SBT	Studies in Biblical Theology
SCL	Sather Classical Lectures
SEÅ	*Svensk exegetisk årsbok*

SGKA	Studien zur Geschichte und Kultur des Altertums
SHM	Studies in the History of Missions
SJLA	Studies in Judaism in Late Antiquity
SJT	*Scottish Journal of Theology*
SNT	Studien zum Neuen Testament
SNTA	Studiorum Novi Testamenti Auxilia
SNTSMS	Society of New Testament Studies Monograph Series
SNTU	Studien zum Neuen Testament und seiner Umwelt
SNTW	Studies of the New Testament and Its World
SO	*Symbolae osloenses*
SS	Studies in Scripture
ST	*Studia theologica*
Str-B	H. Strack and P. Billerbeck. *Kommentar zum Neuen Testament*
StBTh	*Studia Biblica et Theologica*
STTAASF	Suomalaisen Tiedeakatemian Toimituksia Annales Academiæ Scientiarum Fennicæ
TDNT	*Theological Dictionary of the New Testament.* 10 vols. Edited by Gerhard Kittel and Gerhard Friedrich.
TEV	Today's English Version
Thayer	*A Greek-English Lexicon of the New Testament.* Translated and revised by Joseph Henry Thayer. Corrected ed. 1886.
TheolRev	*Theologische Revue*
THNT	Theologischer Handkommentar zum Neuen Testament
TI	Theological Inquiries
TJT	*Toronto Journal of Theology*
TLNT	*Theological Lexicon of the New Testament.* 3 vols. By Celsas Spicq.
TPINTC	Trinity Press International New Testament Commentary
TR	Theology and Religion
TrinJ	*Trinity Journal*
TS	*Theological Studies*
TU	Texte und Untersuchungen zur Geschichte der altchristlichen Literatur
TynB	*Tyndale Bulletin*
TZ	*Theologische Zeitschrift*
UCP:NES	University of California Publications: Near Eastern Studies
VBAG	Vestigia: Beiträge zur alten Geschichte
VE	*Vox Evangelica*
VGSup	Supplements to Vigiliae Christianae
VT	*Vetus Testamentum*
WBC	Word Biblical Commentary
WTJ	*Westminster Theological Journal*

WUNT	Wissenschaftliche Untersuchungen zum Neuen Testament
WW	*Word and World*
ZNW	*Zeitschrift für die Neutestamentliche Wissenschaft*
ZSNT	Zacchaeus Studies: New Testament
ZWKB	Zürcher Werkkommentare zur Bibel

BIBLIOGRAPHY

1. Commentaries on Luke

Commentaries are cited with reference to the author's name only.

Bock, Darrell L. *Luke.* 2 vols. BECNT. Grand Rapids: Baker, 1994/96.

Bovon, François. *Das Evangelium nach Lukas.* Vol. 1. EKKNT 3:1. Zürich: Benziger; Neukirchen-Vluyn: Neukirchener, 1989.

Caird, G. B. *Saint Luke.* Pelican. Harmondsworth: Penguin, 1963.

Danker, Frederick W. *Jesus and the New Age: A Commentary on St. Luke's Gospel.* Rev. ed. Philadelphia: Fortress, 1988.

Evans, C. F. *Saint Luke.* TPINTC. London: SCM; Philadelphia: Trinity, 1990.

Fitzmyer, Joseph A. *The Gospel according to Luke.* 2 vols. AB28-28A. Garden City, NY: Doubleday, 1981/85.

Godet, F. *A Commentary on the Gospel of St. Luke.* 2 vols. 5th ed. Edinburgh: T. & T. Clark, n.d.

Goulder, Michael D. *Luke: A New Paradigm.* 2 vols. JSNTSup 20. Sheffield: JSOT, 1989.

Grundmann, Walter. *Das Evangelium nach Lukas.* THNT 3. Berlin: Evangelische, 1971.

Johnson, Timothy Luke. *The Gospel of Luke.* Sacra Pagina 3. Collegeville, MN: Liturgical, 1991.

Klostermann, Erich. *Das Lukasevangelium.* 2d ed. HNT 5. Tübingen: J. C. B. Mohr (Paul Siebeck), 1929.

Kremer, Jacob. *Lukasevangelium.* NEBNT 3. Würzburg: Echter, 1988.

Marshall, I. Howard. *The Gospel of Luke: A Commentary on the Greek Text.* NIGTC. Grand Rapids: Wm. B. Eerdmans, 1978.

Nolland, John. *Luke.* 3 vols. WBC 35A-C. Dallas, TX: Word, 1989-93.

Plummer, Alfred. *A Critical and Exegetical Commentary on the Gospel according to S. Luke.* 5th ed. ICC. Edinburgh: T. & T. Clark, 1901.

Petzke, Gerd. *Das Sondergut des Evangeliums nach Lukas.* ZWKB. Zürich: Theologischer, 1990.

Rengstorf, Karl Heinrich. *Das Evangelium nach Lukas.* NTD 3. Göttingen: Vandenhoeck & Ruprecht, 1965.

Sabourin, Leopold. *The Gospel according to St. Luke: Introduction and Commentary.* Bombay: St. Paul, 1984.

Schneider, Gerhard. *Das Evangelium nach Lukas.* 2 vols. ÖTKNT 3. Gerd Mohn: Gütersloher; Würzburg: Echter, 1977.

Schürmann, Heinz. *Das Lukasevangelium.* Vol. 1. 3d ed. Vol. 2. 1st ed. HTKNT 3. Freiburg: Herder, 1984/94.

Schweizer, Eduard. *The Good News according to Luke.* Atlanta: John Knox, 1984.

Stein, Robert H. *Luke.* NAC 24. Nashville: Broadman, 1992.

Talbert, Charles H. *Reading Luke: A Literary and Theological Commentary on the Third Gospel.* New York: Crossroad, 1988.

2. Other Works

Throughout the commentary, items are referred to by short titles.

Abel, E. L. "The Genealogies of Jesus O XPICTOC." *NTS* 20 (1973-74) 203-10. "Genealogies."

Abogunrin, S. O. "The Three Variant Accounts of Peter's Call: A Critical and Theological Examination of the Texts." *NTS* 31 (1985) 587-602. "Three Variant Accounts."

Abraham, M. V. "Good News to the Poor in Luke's Gospel." *Bible Bhashyam* 14 (1988) 65-77. "Good News."

Achtemeier, Paul J. "The Lucan Perspective on the Miracles of Jesus: A Preliminary Sketch." *JBL* 94 (1975) 547-62. "Lucan Perspective."

Adam, A. K. M. "The Sign of Jonah: A Fish-Eye View." *Semeia* 51 (1990) 177-91. "Sign of Jonah."

Aichinger, Hermann. "Zur Traditionsgeschichte der Epileptiker-Perikope (Mk 9,14-29 par Mt 17,14-21 par Lk 9,37-43a)." In *Probleme der Forschung,* edited by Albert Fuchs, 114-43. SNTU A3. München: Herold Wien, 1978. "Epileptiker-Perikope."

Albertz, Rainer. "Die 'Antrittspredigt' Jesu im Lukasevangelium auf ihrem alttestamentlichen Hintergrund." *ZNW* 74 (1983) 182-206. "Antrittspredigt."

Alexander, Loveday. "Luke's Preface in the Context of Greek Preface-Writing," *NovT* 28 (1986) 48-74. "Luke's Preface."

———. *The Preface to Luke's Gospel: Literary Convention and Social Con-*

text in Luke 1.1-4 and Acts 1.1. SNTSMS 78. Cambridge: Cambridge University, 1993. *Preface.*

——. "The Preface to Acts and the Historians." In *History, Literature and Society in the Book of Acts,* edited by Ben Witherington III, 73-103. Cambridge: Cambridge University, 1996. "Preface to Acts."

Allison Jr., Dale C. *The End of the Ages Has Come: An Early Interpretation of the Passion and Resurrection of Jesus.* Philadelphia: Fortress, 1985. *End of the Ages.*

——. "The Eye Is the Lamp of the Body (Matthew 6.22-23 = Luke 11.34-36)." *NTS* 33 (1987) 61-83. "Eye Is the Lamp."

——. " 'The hairs of your head are all numbered'." *ExpT* 101 (1989-90) 334-36. "Hairs of Your Head."

——. "Jesus and the Covenant: A Response to E. P. Sanders." *JSNT* 29 (1987) 57-78. "Jesus and the Covenant."

——. "Matt. 23:39 = Luke 13:35b as a Conditional Prophecy." *JSNT* 18 (1983) 75-84. "Conditional Prophecy."

——. "Mountain and Wilderness." In *DJG,* 563-66.

Alter, Robert. *The Art of Biblical Narrative.* New York: Basic, 1981. *Art.*

——. "How Convention Helps Us Read: The Case of the Bible's Annunciation Type-Scene." *Prooftexts* 3 (1983) 115-30. "Annunciation Type-Scene."

Anderson, Janice Capel. "Mary's Difference: Gender and Patriarchy in the Birth Narratives." *JR* 67 (1987) 183-202. "Mary's Difference."

Annen, Franz. "λεγίων." In *EDNT,* 2:345-46.

Archer, Léonie J. *Her Price Is beyond Rubies: The Jewish Woman in Graeco-Roman Palestine.* JSOTSup 60. Sheffield: Sheffield Academic, 1990. *Her Price Is beyond Rubies.*

Argyle, A. W. "The Greek of Luke and Acts." *NTS* 20 (1973-74) 441-45. "Greek of Luke."

Ascough, Richard S. "Rejection and Response: Peter and the People in Luke's Passion Narrative." *Bib* 74 (1993) 349-65. "Rejection and Response."

Atkins Jr., Robert A. *Egalitarian Community: Ethnography and Exegesis.* Tuscaloosa: University of Alabama, 1991. *Egalitarian Community.*

Auffret, Pierre. "Note sur la structure littéraire de Lc 1,68-79." *NTS* 24 (1977-78) 248-58. "Lc 1,68-79."

Aune, David E. *The New Testament in Its Literary Environment.* LEC 8. Philadelphia: Westminster, 1987. *Literary Environment.*

——. "Magic in Early Christianity." In *ANRW* 2.23.2 (1980) 1507-57.

——. "The Problem of the Genre of the Gospels: A Critique of C. H. Talbert's *What Is a Gospel?*" In *Gospel Perspectives,* vol. 2: *Studies of History and Tradition in the Four Gospels,* edited by R. T. France and David Wenham, 9-60. Sheffield: JSOT, 1981. "Genre of the Gospels."

———. *Prophecy in Early Christianity and the Ancient Mediterranean World.* Grand Rapids: Wm. B. Eerdmans, 1983. *Prophecy.*

Austin, Michael R. "The Hypocritical Son." *EvQ* 57 (1985) 307-15. "Hypocritical Son."

Avalos, Hector. *Illness and Health Care in the Ancient Near East: The Role of the Temple in Greece, Mesopotamia, and Israel.* HSM 54. Atlanta: Scholars, 1995. *Illness and Health Care.*

Baarlink, Heinrich. "Ein gnädiges Jahr des Herrn — und Tage der Vergeltung." *ZNW* 73 (1982) 204-20. "Gnädiges Jahr."

Bachmann, Michael. *Jerusalem und der Tempel: Die geographisch-theologischen Elemente in der lukanische Sicht des jüdischen Kultzentrums.* BWANT 9. Stuttgart: W. Kohlhammer, 1980. *Jerusalem und der Tempel.*

Badian, E. *Publicans and Sinners: Private Enterprise in the Service of the Roman Republic.* Rev. ed. Ithaca, NY: Cornell University, 1983. *Publicans.*

Bailey, F. G. "The Peasant View of the Bad Life." In *Peasant and Peasant Societies: Selected Readings,* edited by Teodor Shanin, 284-99. 2d ed. Oxford: Basil Blackwell, 1987. "Peasant View."

Bailey, James L. "Genre Analysis." In *Hearing the New Testament: Strategies for Interpretation,* edited by Joel B. Green, 197-221. Grand Rapids: Wm. B. Eerdmans, 1995.

Bailey, Kenneth E. "Informal Controlled Oral Tradition and the Synoptic Gospels." *Themelios* 20 (2, 1995) 4-11. "Oral Tradition."

———. "The Manger and the Inn: The Cultural Background of Luke 2:7." *TheolRev* 2 (1979) 33-44. "Manger."

———. *Poet and Peasant.* Grand Rapids: Wm. B. Eerdmans, 1976.

———. *Through Peasant Eyes.* Grand Rapids: Wm. B. Eerdmans, 1980.

Bajard, J. "La structure de la péricope de Nazareth en Lc., IV,16-30: Propositions pour une lecture plus cohérente." *ETL* 45 (1969) 165-71. "Péricope de Nazareth."

Bakhtin, Mikhail. "Heteroglossia in the Novel," in *Bakhtinian Thought: An Introductory Reader,* edited by Simon Dentith, 195-224. CRTP. London/New York: Routledge, 1995. "Heteroglossia."

Bal, Mieke. *Narratology: Introduction to the Theory of Narrative.* Toronto: University of Toronto, 1985. *Narratology.*

Balch, David L. "Rich and Poor, Proud and Humble in Luke-Acts." In *The Social World of the First Christians: Essays in Honor of Wayne A. Meeks,* edited by L. Michael White and O. Larry Yarbrough, 214-33. Minneapolis: Fortress, 1995. "Rich and Poor."

Balz, Horst. "γαζοφυλάκιον." In *EDNT*, 1:232.

―――. "ἑπτάκις." In *EDNT*, 2:48.

―――. "κατηγορέω." In *EDNT*, 2:272.

―――. "μετεωρίζομαι." In *EDNT*, 2:420.

Balz, Horst, and Günther Wanke. "φοβέω κτλ." In *TDNT*, 9:189-219.

Bammel, Ernst. "The Baptist in Early Christian Tradition." *NTS* 18 (1971-72) 95-128. "Baptist."

―――. "The *titulus.*" In *Jesus and the Politics of His Day*, edited by Ernst Bammel and C. F. D. Moule, 353-64. Cambridge: Cambridge University, 1984.

―――. "The Trial before Pilate." In *Jesus and the Politics of His Day*, edited by Ernst Bammel and C. F. D. Moule, 415-51. Cambridge: Cambridge University, 1984. "Trial."

Banks, Robert J. "Narrative Exegesis." In *DJG*, 570-71.

Barbour, Robin S. "Gethsemane in the Tradition of the Passion." *NTS* 16 (1969-70) 231-51. "Gethsemane."

Barnett, Paul W. "ἀπογραφή and ἀπογράφεσθαι in Luke 2:1-5." *ExpT* 85 (1973-74) 377-80. "ἀπογραφή."

―――. "The Jewish Sign Prophets — A.D. 40-70: Their Intentions and Origin." *NTS* 27 (1980-81) 679-97. "Jewish Sign Prophets."

Barr, David L., and Judith L. Wentling. "The Convention of Classical Biography and the Genre of Luke-Acts: A Preliminary Study." In *Luke-Acts: New Perspectives from the Society of Biblical Literature Seminar*, edited by Charles H. Talbert, 63-88. New York: Crossroad, 1984. "Classical Biography."

Barrett, C. K. *The Acts of the Apostles.* Vol. 1. ICC. Edinburgh: T. & T. Clark, 1994. *Acts.*

―――. *Luke the Historian in Recent Study.* London: Epworth, 1961. *Luke the Historian.*

―――. "Theologia Crucis — in Acts?" In *Theologia Crucis — Signum Crucis: Festschrift für Erich Dinkler zum 70. Geburtstag,* edited by C. Andersen and G. Klein, 73-84. Tübingen: J. C. B. Mohr (Paul Siebeck), 1979. "Theologia Crucis."

Bartchy, S. Scott. "Community of Goods in Acts: Idealization or Social Reality?" In *The Future of Early Christianity: Essays in Honor of Helmut Koester,* edited by Birger A. Pearson et al., 309-18. Minneapolis: Fortress, 1991. "Community of Goods."

―――. "Table Fellowship." In *DJG*, 796-800.

Barth, Markus. *Das Mahl des Herrn: Gemeinschaft mit Israel, mit Christus und unter den Gästen.* Neukirchen-Vluyn: Neukirchener, 1987. *Das Mahl.*

―――. *Rediscovering the Lord's Supper: Communion with Israel, with*

Christ, and among the Guests. Atlanta: John Knox, 1988. *Lord's Supper.*

Bartolomé, Juan J. "Comer en común: Una costumbre tipica de Jesus y su proprio comentario Lc 15." *Salesianum* 44 (1982) 669-712. "Comer en común."

―――. "ΣΥΝΕΣΘΕΙΝ en la obra lucana: Lc 15,2; Hch 10,41; 11,3: A propósito de una tesis sobre la essencia del Christianismo." *Salesianum* 46 (1984) 269-88. "ΣΥΝΕΣΘΕΙΝ."

Barton, Stephen C. *The Spirituality of the Gospels.* London: SPCK; Peabody, MA: Hendrickson, 1992. *Spirituality.*

Batey, Richard A. "Jesus and the Theatre." *NTS* 30 (1984) 563-74.

Bauckham, Richard. "Hades, Hell." In *ABD,* 3:14-15.

―――. *Jude and the Relatives of Jesus in the Early Church.* Edinburgh: T. & T. Clark, 1990. *Jude.*

―――. "The Rich Man and Lazarus: The Parable and the Parallels." *NTS* 37 (1991) 225-46. "Rich Man and Lazarus."

Bauer, David R. "Son of David." In *DJG,* 766-69.

Bauer, J. "ΠΟΛΛΟΙ." *NovT* 4 (1960) 263-66. "ΠΟΛΛΟΙ."

Bauer, Johannes B. "καρδιογνώστης, Ein Unbeachteter Aspekt (Apg 1,24; 15,8)." *BZ* 32 (1988) 114-17.

Bauernfield, Otto. *Kommentar und Studien zur Apostelgeschichte.* WUNT 22. Tübingen: J. C. B. Mohr (Paul Siebeck), 1980. *Apostelgeschichte.*

Baum, Armin Daniel. *Lukas als Historiker der letzten Jesusreise.* Wuppertal: R. Brockhaus, 1993. *Lukas als Historiker.*

Bayer, Hans F. *Jesus' Predictions of Vindication and Resurrection: The Provenance, Meaning and Correlation of the Synoptic Predictions.* WUNT 2:20. Tübingen: J. C. B. Mohr (Paul Siebeck), 1986. *Jesus' Predictions.*

Beasley-Murray, George R. *Jesus and the Kingdom of God.* Grand Rapids: Wm. B. Eerdmans, 1986. *Kingdom of God.*

Beck, Brian E. *Christian Character in the Gospel of Luke.* London: Epworth, 1989. *Christian Character.*

―――. "The Common Authorship of Luke and Acts." *NTS* 23 (1976-77) 346-52. "Common Authorship."

―――. "*Imitatio Christi*' and the Lucan Passion Narrative." In *Suffering and Martyrdom in the New Testament: Studies Presented to G. M. Styler by the Cambridge New Testament Seminar,* edited by William Horbury and Brian McNeil, 28-47. Cambridge: Cambridge University, 1981. "Imitatio Christi."

Bede. *Commentary on the Acts of the Apostles.* Translated and edited by Lawrence T. Martin. CSS 117. Kalamazoo, MI: Cistercian, 1989. *Acts.*

—————. *Homilies on the Gospels.* 2 vols. Translated and edited by Lawrence T. Martin and David Hurst. CSS 110-11. Kalamazoo, MI: Cistercian, 1991. *Homilies.*

Behm, Johannes. "καρδία κτλ." In *TDNT,* 3:605-14.

Bekaert, Gilles. "The Literary Unity of Luke 16: Almsgiving and Friendship with the Poor." M.A. thesis, Graduate Theological Union, 1996. "Literary Unity."

Bellah, Robert N., et al. *The Good Society.* New York: Alfred A. Knopf, 1991. *Good Society.*

Bemile, Paul. *The Magnificat within the Context and Framework of Lukan Theology: An Exegetical, Theological Study of Lk 1:46-55.* RST 34. Frankfurt am Main: Peter Lang, 1986. *Magnificat.*

Benko, Stephen. "The Magnificat: A History of the Controversy." *JBL* 86 (1967) 263-75. "Magnificat."

Benoit, Pierre. "L'enfance de Jean-Baptiste selon Luc 1." *NTS* 3 (1957) 169-94. "L'enfance de Jean-Baptiste."

Berger, Klaus. "Das Canticum Simeonis (Lk 2:29-32)." *NovT* 27 (1985) 27-39. "Canticum Simeonis."

Berger, P. R. "Lk 2:14: ἄνθρωπος εὐδοκίας. Die auf Gottes Weisung mit Wohlgefallen beschenkten Menschen." *ZNW* 74 (1983) 129-44. "Lk 2:14."

Berger, Peter L., and Thomas Luckmann. *The Social Construction of Reality: A Treatise in the Sociology of Knowledge.* New York: Doubleday, 1966. *Social Construction of Reality.*

Betori, Giuseppe. "Luke 24:47: Jerusalem and the Beginning of the Preaching to the Pagans in the Acts of the Apostles." In *Luke and Acts,* edited by Gerald O'Collins and Gilberto Marconi, 103-20. New York/ Mahwah, NJ: Paulist, 1993. "Luke 24:47."

Betz, Hans Dieter. "The Cleansing of the Ten Lepers (Luke 17:11-19)." *JBL* 90 (1971) 314-28. "Cleansing."

—————. *Essays on the Sermon on the Mount.* Philadelphia: Fortress, 1985. *Sermon on the Mount.*

—————. "Matthew vi.22f. and Ancient Greek Theories of Vision." In *Text and Interpretation: Studies in the New Testament Presented to Matthew Black,* edited by E. Best and R. McL. Wilson, 43-56. Cambridge: Cambridge University, 1979. "Greek Theories."

Bivin, David. "The Miraculous Catch: Reflections on the Research of Mendel Nun." *JerP* 5 (2, 1992) 7-10. "Miraculous Catch."

Black, Matthew. " 'Not Peace but a Sword': Matt 10:34ff; Luke 12:51ff." In *Jesus and the Politics of His Day,* edited by Ernst Bammel and C. F. D. Moule, 287-94. Cambridge: Cambridge University, 1984. "Not Peace."

Blomberg, Craig L. *Interpreting the Parables.* Downers Grove, IL: InterVarsity, 1990. *Parables.*

———. "The Law in Luke-Acts." *JSNT* 22 (1984) 53-80. "Law."

———. "Midrash, Chiasmus, and the Outline of Luke's Central Section." In *Studies in Midrash and Historiography,* edited by R. T. France and David Wenham, 217-59. GP 3. Sheffield: JSOT, 1983. "Luke's Central Section."

———. " 'Your Faith Has Made You Whole': The Evangelical Liberation Theology of Jesus." In *Jesus of Nazareth: Lord and Christ. Essays on the Historical Jesus and New Testament Christology,* edited by Joel B. Green and Max Turner, 75-93. Grand Rapids: Wm. B. Eerdmans, 1994. "Your Faith Has Made You Whole."

Böcher, Otto. "Βεελζεβούλ." In *EDNT,* 1:211-12.

———. "δαιμόνιον, δαίμων." In *EDNT,* 1:271-74.

Bock, Darrell. *Proclamation from Prophecy and Pattern: Lucan Old Testament Christology.* JSNTSup 12. Sheffield: JSOT, 1987. *Proclamation.*

———. "The Son of Man in Luke 5:24." *BBR* 1 (1991) 109-21. "Son of Man."

———. "The Son of Man Seated at God's Right Hand and the Debate over Jesus' 'Blasphemy.' " In *Jesus of Nazareth: Lord and Christ,* edited by Joel B. Green and Max Turner, 181-91. Grand Rapids: Wm. B. Eerdmans, 1994. "Jesus' Blasphemy."

Boff, Leonardo. *The Maternal Face of God: The Feminine and Its Religious Expressions.* San Francisco: Harper & Row, 1979. *Maternal Face.*

Böhl, Felix. "Das Fasten an Montagen und Donnerstagen: Zur Geschichte einer pharisäischen Praxis (Lk 18,12)." *BZ* 31 (1987) 247-50.

Booth, Wayne C. *The Rhetoric of Fiction.* 2d ed. Harmondsworth: Penguin, 1983. *Rhetoric of Fiction.*

———. *A Rhetoric of Irony.* Chicago: University of Chicago, 1974. *Rhetoric of Irony.*

Borg, Marcus. "Luke 19:42-44 and Jesus as Prophet?" *Forum* 8 (192) 99-112. "Luke 19:42-44."

Borse, Udo. "ἄγω." In *EDNT,* 1:24-25.

Bösen, Willibald. *Jesusmahl, eucharistisches Mahl, Endzeitmahl: Ein Beitrag zur Theologie des Lukas.* SBS 97. Stuttgart, Katholisches, 1980. *Jesusmahl.*

Botha, J. "Iser's Wandering Viewpoint: A Reception-Analytical Reading of Luke 12:35-48." *Neot* 22 (1988) 253-68. "Wandering Viewpoint."

Bourdieu, Pierre. *Language and Symbolic Power.* Cambridge, MA: Harvard University, 1991.

———. *The Logic of Practice.* Stanford, CA: Stanford University, 1990. *Logic of Practice.*

Bovon, François. *Luke the Theologian: Thirty-three Years of Research (1950-1983)*. PTMS 12. Allison Park, PA: Pickwick, 1987. *Luke the Theologian.*

Bowen, Clayton Raymond. "The Meaning of Συναλιζόμενος in Acts 1,4." *ZNW* 13 (1912): 247-59. "συναλιζόμενος."

Brandon, S. G. F. *The Trial of Jesus of Nazareth.* New York: Stein and Day, 1968. *Trial of Jesus.*

Braun, Willi. *Feasting and Social Rhetoric in Luke 14.* SNTSMS 85. Cambridge: Cambridge University, 1995. *Feasting and Social Rhetoric.*

Braund, David C. *Augustus to Nero: A Sourcebook on Roman History. 31 B.C.–A.D. 68.* London: Crook Helm, 1985. *Augustus.*

Brawley, Robert L. *Centering on God: Method and Message in Luke-Acts.* LCBI. Louisville, KY: Westminster/John Knox, 1990. *Centering on God.*

———. *Luke-Acts and the Jews: Conflict, Apology, and Conciliation.* SBLMS 33. Atlanta: Scholars, 1987. *Luke-Acts.*

———. *Text to Text Pours Forth Speech: Voices of Scripture in Luke-Acts.* ISBL. Bloomington: Indiana University, 1995. *Text to Text.*

Brindle, Wayne. "The Census and Quirinius: Luke 2:2." *JETS* 27 (1984) 43-52. "Census."

Brodie, Thomas Louis. "The Departure for Jerusalem (Luke 9,51-56) as a Rhetorical Imitation of Elijah's Departure for the Jordan (2 Kgs 1,1–2,6)." *Bib* 70 (1989) 96-109. "Departure for Jerusalem."

———. "Not Q but Elijah: The Saving of the Centurion's Servant (Luke 7:1-10) as an Internalization of the Saving of the Widow and Her Child (1 Kings 17:1-16)." *IBS* 14 (1992) 54-71. "Not Q but Elijah."

———. "Towards Unravelling Luke's Use of the Old Testament: Luke 7.11-17 as an *Imitatio* of 1 Kings 17.17-24." *NTS* 32 (1986) 247-67. "Luke 7.11-17."

Brooten, Bernadette J. *Women Leaders in the Ancient Synagogue.* BJS 36. Atlanta: Scholars, 1982. *Women Leaders.*

Broughton, T. R. S. "The Roman Army." In *The Acts of the Apostles,* edited by F. J. Foakes Jackson and Kirsopp Lake, vol. 5: *Additional Notes to the Commentary,* edited by Kirsopp Lake and Henry J. Cadbury, 427-45. BC 5. London: Macmillan, 1933; reprint ed., Grand Rapids: Baker, 1979. "Roman Army."

Brown, Colin. "ἀσφάλεια." In *NIDNTT,* 1:663.

Brown, Gillian, and George Yule. *Discourse Analysis.* CTL. Cambridge: Cambridge University, 1982.

Brown, Raymond E. *The Birth of the Messiah: A Commentary on the Infancy Narratives in the Gospels of Matthew and Luke.* 2d ed. ABRL. Garden City, NY: Doubleday, 1993. *Birth.*

———. *The Death of the Messiah: From Gethsemane to the Grave. A Com-*

mentary on the Passion Narratives in the Four Gospels. 2 vols. ABRL. Garden City, NY: Doubleday, 1994. *Death of the Messiah.*

————. "Gospel Infancy Narrative Research from 1976 to 1986: Part II (Luke)." *CBQ* 48 (1986) 660-80. "Gospel Infancy Research."

Brown, Robert McAfee. *Unexpected News: Reading the Bible with Third World Eyes.* Philadelphia: Westminster, 1984. *Unexpected News.*

Brown, Schuyler. *Apostasy and Perseverance in the Theology of Luke.* AnBib 36. Rome: Pontifical Biblical Institute, 1969. *Apostasy and Perseverance.*

————. "The Role of the Prologues in Determining the Purpose of Luke-Acts." In *Perspectives on Luke-Acts,* edited by Charles H. Talbert, 99-111. *PRS.* Edinburgh: T. & T. Clark, 1978. "Prologues."

Browning, Iain. *Jerash and the Decapolis.* London: Chatto & Windus, 1982. *Jerash.*

Bruce, F. F. "Canon." In *DJG,* 93-100.

————. "Render to Caesar." In *Jesus and the Politics of His Day,* edited by Ernst Bammel and C. F. D. Moule, 249-63. Cambridge: Cambridge University, 1984.

Brueggemann, Walter. "Gabriel." In *IDB,* 2:332-33.

————. "An Exposition of Luke 3:1-4." *Int* 30 (1976) 404-9. "Luke 3:1-4."

Bruners, Wilhelm. *Die Reinigung der zehn Aussätzigen und die Heilung des Samariters Lk 17,11-19: Ein Beitrag zur lukanischen Interpretation der Reinigung von Aussätzigen.* FB 23. Stuttgart: Katholisches, 1977. *Reinigung der zehn Aussätzigen.*

Brutscheck, Jutta. *Die Maria-Marta-Erzählung: Eine redaktionskritische Untersuchung zu Lk 10,38-42.* BBB 64. Frankfurt am Main: Peter Hanstein, 1986. *Maria-Marta-Erzählung.*

Büchele, Anton. *Der Tod Jesu im Lukasevangelium: Eine redaktionsgeschichtliche Untersuchung zu Lk 23.* FTS (Frankfurter theologische Studien) 26. Frankfurt-am-Main: Knecht, 1978. *Tod Jesu.*

Büchsel, Friedrich. "δέω (λύω)." In *TDNT,* 2:60-61.

————. "παραδίδωμι." In *TDNT,* 2:169-73

Buck, Edwin. "The Function of the Pericope 'Jesus before Herod' in the Passion Narrative of Luke." In *Wort in der Zeit: Neutestamentliche Studien. Festgabe für Karl Heinrich Rengstorf zum 75. Geburtstag,* edited by Wilfrid Haubeck and Michael Bachmann, 165-78. Leiden: E. J. Brill, 1980. "Jesus before Herod."

Bühner, Jan-Adolf. "παῖς." In *EDNT,* 3:5-6.

————. "σκηνή." In *EDNT,* 3:251-52.

Bultmann, Rudolf. "The Concept of Life in Judaism." In *TDNT,* 2:855-61. "Concept of Life."

Burge, Gary M. "Glory." In *DJG,* 268-70.

Burger, Christoph. *Jesus als Davidssohn: Eine traditionsgeschichtliche Untersuchung.* FRLANT 98. Göttingen: Vandenhoeck & Ruprecht, 1970. *Jesus als Davidssohn.*

Burridge, Richard A. *What Are the Gospels? A Comparison with Graeco-Roman Biography.* SNTSMS 70. Cambridge: Cambridge University, 1992. *What Are the Gospels?*

Busse, Ulrich. *Das Nazareth-Manifest Jesu: Eine Einführung in das lukanische Jesusbild nach Lk 4,16-30.* SBS 91. Stuttgart: Katholisches Bibelwerk, 1978. *Nazareth-Manifest.*

————. *Die Wunder des Propheten Jesu: Die Rezeption, Komposition und Interpretation der Wundertradition im Evangelium des Lukas.* FB 24. Stuttgart: Katholisches, 1977. *Wunder.*

Buth, Randall. "Hebrew Poetic Tenses and the Magnificat." *JSNT* 21 (1984) 67-83. "Magnificat."

————. "That Small-fry Herod Antipas, or When a Fox Is Not a Fox." *JerP* 40 (1993) 7-9, 14. "Herod Antipas."

Byrne, Matthew. "No Room for the Inn." *Search* 5 (2, 1982) 37-40. "Inn."

Caba, José. "From Lukan Parenesis to Johannine Christology: Luke 9:23-24 and John 12:25-26." In *Luke and Acts,* edited by Gerald O'Collins and Gilberto Marconi, 48-71. New York/Mahwah, NJ: Paulist, 1991. "Lukan Parenesis."

Cadbury, Henry J. "Commentary on the Preface of Luke." In *The Acts of the Apostles,* edited by F. J. Foakes Jackson and Kirsopp Lake, vol. 2: *Prolegomena II: Criticism,* 489-510. BC 1. Grand Rapids: Baker, n.d. "Commentary."

————. "Dust and Garments." In *The Acts of the Apostles,* edited by F. J. Foakes Jackson and Kirsopp Lake, vol. 5: *Additional Notes to the Commentary,* edited by Kirsopp Lake and Henry J. Cadbury, 269-77. BC 1. Grand Rapids: Baker, n.d.

————. "The Knowledge Claimed in Luke's Preface." *Expositor* 8, 24 (1922) 401-20. "Knowledge Claimed."

————. "Lexical Notes on Luke-Acts — II: Recent Arguments for Medical Language." *JBL* 45 (1926) 190-206. "Medical Language."

————. "Lexical Notes on Luke-Acts — III: Luke's Interest in Lodging." *JBL* 45 (1926) 305-22. "Lodging."

————. *The Making of Luke-Acts.* London: Macmillan, 1927. *Making of Luke-Acts.*

————. " 'We' and 'I' Passages in Luke-Acts." *NTS* 3 (1956-57) 128-32.

————, F. J. Foakes Jackson, and Kirsopp Lake. "The Greek and Jewish Traditions of Writing History." In *The Acts of the Apostles,* edited by F. J. Foakes Jackson and Kirsopp Lake, vol. 2: *Prolegomena II: Criticism,* 7-29. BC 1. Grand Rapids: Baker, n.d. "Greek and Jewish Traditions."

Caird, George B. "The Transfiguration." *ExpT* 67 (1955-56) 291-94.

———. "Uncomfortable Words — II. Shake off the Dust from Your Feet (Mk 6:11)." *ExpT* 81 (1969-70) 40-43. "Uncomfortable Words."

Callan, Terrance. "The Preface of Luke-Acts and Historiography." *NTS* 31 (1985) 576-81. "Preface."

Caragounis, Chrys C. "Kingdom of God/Kingdom of Heaven." In *DJG*, 417-30. "Kingdom of God."

———. "Kingdom of God, Son of Man and Jesus' Self-Understanding (II)." *TynB* 40.2 (1989) 223-38. "Son of Man."

Carlson, Richard P. "The Role of the Jewish People in Luke's Passion Theology." In *Society of Biblical Literature 1991 Seminar Papers,* edited by Eugene H. Lovering Jr., 82-102. Atlanta: Scholars, 1991. "Jewish People."

Carroll, John T. "Luke's Crucifixion Scene." In *Reimaging the Death of the Lukan Jesus,* edited by Dennis D. Sylva, 108-24, 194-203. AMTBBB 73. Frankfurt am Main: Anton Hain, 1990.

———. "Luke's Portrayal of the Pharisees." *CBQ* 50 (1988) 604-21. "Luke's Portrayal."

———. *Response to the End of History: Eschatology and Situation in Luke-Acts.* SBLDS 92. Atlanta: Scholars, 1988. *End of History.*

Carroll, John T., and Joel B. Green. *The Death of Jesus in Early Christianity.* Peabody, MA: Hendrickson, 1995. *Death of Jesus.*

Carroll R., M. Daniel. "La cita de Isaías 58:6 en Lucas 4:18: Una nueva propuesta." *Kairos* 11 (1992) 61-78. "Isaías 58:6 en Lucas 4:18."

Carson, D. A. "Matthew 11:19b/Luke 7:35: A Test Case for the Bearing of Q Christology on the Synoptic Problem." In *Jesus of Nazareth: Lord and Christ. Essays on the Historical Jesus and New Testament Christology,* edited by Joel B. Green and Max Turner, 128-46. Grand Rapids: Wm. B. Eerdmans, 1994. "Matthew 11:19b/Luke 7:35."

Carter, Warren. "Zechariah and the Benedictus (Luke 1,68-79): Practicing What He Preaches." *Bib* 69 (1988) 239-47. "Zechariah."

Cassidy, Richard J. *Jesus, Politics, and Society: A Study of Luke's Gospel.* Maryknoll, NY: Orbis, 1978. *Jesus, Politics, and Society.*

———. "Luke's Audience, the Chief Priests, and the Motive for Jesus' Death." In *Political Issues in Luke-Acts,* edited by Richard J. Cassidy and Philip J. Scharper, 146-67. Maryknoll, NY: Orbis, 1983. "Luke's Audience."

———. *Society and Politics in the Acts of the Apostles.* Maryknoll, NY: Orbis, 1987. *Society and Politics.*

Catchpole, David R. "Q and 'The Friend at Midnight' (Luke xi.5-8/9)." *JTS* 34 (1983) 407-24. "Friend at Midnight."

———. "The Son of Man's Search for Faith (Luke xviii.8b)." *NovT* 19 (1977) 81-104. "Son of Man's Search."

Catchpole, David R. "The 'Triumphal' Entry." In *Jesus and the Politics of His Day,* edited by Ernst Bammel and C. F. D. Moule, 319-34. Cambridge: Cambridge University, 1984. "Triumphal Entry."

Champion, James. "The Parable as an Ancient and a Modern Form." *JLT* 3 (1989) 16-39. "Parable."

Chance, J. Bradley. *Jerusalem, the Temple, and the New Age in Luke-Acts.* Macon, GA: Mercer University, 1988. *Jerusalem.*

————. "The Jewish People and the Death of Jesus in Luke-Acts: Some Implications of an Inconsistent Narrative Role." In *Society of Biblical Literature 1991 Seminar Papers,* edited by Eugene H. Lowering Jr., 50-81. Atlanta: Scholars, 1991. "Jewish People."

Charlesworth, James H. "Paradise." In *ABD,* 5:154-55.

Chatman, Seymour. *Story and Discourse: Narrative Structure in Fiction and Film.* Ithaca, NY: Cornell University, 1978. *Story and Discourse.*

Chilton, Bruce D. "Announcement in Nazara: An Analysis of Luke 4:16-21." In *Gospel Perspectives,* vol. 2: *Studies in History and Tradition in the Gospels,* edited by R. T. France and David Wenham, 147-72. Sheffield: JSOT, 1981. "Announcement in Nazara."

————. *A Galilean Rabbi and His Bible: Jesus' Use of the Interpreted Scripture of His Time.* GNS 8. Wilmington, DE: Michael Glazier, 1984. *Galilean Rabbi.*

————. "Jesus and the Repentance of E. P. Sanders." *TynB* 39 (1988) 1-18. "Jesus and the Repentance."

Clifford, James. "Partial Truths." In *Writing Culture: The Poetics and Politics of Ethnography,* edited by James Clifford and George E. Marcus, 1-26. Berkeley: University of California, 1986.

Clayman, Charles, ed. *The American Medical Association Encyclopedia of Medicine.* New York: Random House, 1989. *Encyclopedia of Medicine.*

Cloete, G. D., and D. J. Smit. "Exegesis and Proclamation: 'Rejoicing with God . . .' (Luke 15:11-32)." *JTSA* 66 (1989) 62-73. "Exegesis and Proclamation."

Cohen, Shaye J. D. *From the Maccabees to the Mishnah.* LEC 7. Philadelphia: Westminster, 1987. *From the Maccabees.*

Cohn-Sherbok, D. M. "An Analysis of Jesus' Arguments concerning the Plucking of Grain on the Sabbath." *JSNT* 2 (1979) 31-41. "Jesus' Arguments."

Coleridge, Mark. *The Birth of the Lukan Narrative: Narrative as Christology in Luke 1–2.* JSNTSup 88. Sheffield: Sheffield Academic, 1993. *Birth.*

Combrink, H. J. B. "The Structure and Significance of Luke 4:16-30." *Neot* 7 (1973) 27-47. "Luke 4:16-30."

Conrad, Edgar W. "The Annunciation of Birth and the Birth of the Messiah." *CBQ* 47 (1985) 656-68. "Annunciation."

Conzelmann, Hans. "Luke's Place in the Development of Early Christianity." In *Studies in Luke-Acts,* edited by Leander E. Keck and J. Louis Martyn, 298-316. Nashville: Abingdon, 1966. "Luke's Place."

————. *The Theology of St. Luke.* London: Faber & Faber, 1960; reprint ed., London: SCM, 1982. *Luke.*

Cook, Albert. *History/Writing: The Theory and Practice of History in Antiquity and in Modern Times.* Cambridge: Cambridge University, 1988. *History/Writing.*

Cooper, John W. *Body, Soul, and Life Everlasting: Biblical Anthropology and the Monism-Dualism Debate.* Grand Rapids: Wm. B. Eerdmans, 1989. *Body, Soul, and Life Everlasting.*

Coote, Robert Allan. "What Is a Person Worth? The Good Samaritan Problem Reexamined." *Listening* 3 (1988) 198-213. "What Is a Person Worth?"

Corbo, Virgilio C. "Golgotha." In *ABD,* 2:1071-73.

Corley, Kathleen E. *Private Women, Public Meals: Social Conflict in the Synoptic Tradition.* Peabody, MA: Hendrickson, 1993. *Private Women.*

Cortés, Juan B., and Florence M. Gatti. "On the Meaning of Luke 16:16." *JBL* 106 (1987) 247-59. "Luke 16:16."

Cosgrove, Charles H. "The Divine Δεῖ in Luke-Acts." *NovT* 26 (1984) 168-90. "Divine Δεῖ."

Cotterell, Peter, and Max Turner. *Linguistics and Biblical Interpretation.* London: SPCK; Downers Grove, IL: InterVarsity, 1989. *Linguistics.*

Craig, Kerry M. and Margret A. Kristjansson. "Woman Reading as Men/ Women Reading as Women: A Structural Analysis for the Historical Project." *Semeia* 51 (1990) 119-36. "Women Reading."

Creech, Robert R. "The Most Excellent Narratee: The Significance of Theophilus in Luke-Acts." In *With Steadfast Purpose: Essays on Acts in Honor of Henry Jackson Flanders, Jr.,* edited by Raymond H. Keathley, 107-26. Waco, TX: Baylor University, 1990. "Theophilus."

Crockett, Larrimore C. "Luke 4:25-27 and Jewish-Gentile Relations in Luke-Acts." *JBL* 88 (1969) 177-83. "Luke 4:25-27."

Crossan, John Dominic. "Parable and Example in the Teaching of Jesus." *Semeia* 1 (1974) 63-104. "Parable and Example."

Crown, Alan D., ed. *The Samaritans.* Tübingen: J. C. B. Mohr (Paul Siebeck), 1989. *Samaritans.*

Crump, David. *Jesus the Intercessor: Prayer and Christology in Luke-Acts.* WUNT 2:49. Tübingen: J. C. B. Mohr (Paul Siebeck), 1992. *Jesus the Intercessor.*

————. "Jesus, The Victorious Scribal-Intercessor in Luke's Gospel." *NTS* 38 (1992) 51-65. "Scribal-Intercessor."

Culler, Jonathan. *The Pursuit of Signs: Semiotics, Literature, Deconstruction.* London: Routledge & Kegan Paul, 1981. *Pursuit of Signs.*

Cullmann, Oscar. *Prayer in the New Testament.* OBT. Minneapolis: Fortress, 1994. *Prayer.*

Culpepper, R. Alan. "Seeing the Kingdom of God: The Metaphor of Sight in the Gospel of Luke." *CurTM* 21 (1994) 424-33. "Seeing the Kingdom of God."

Dahl, Nils A. "The Story of Abraham in Luke-Acts." In *Studies in Luke-Acts,* edited by Leander E. Keck and J. Louis Martyn, 139-58. Philadelphia: Fortress, 1966. "Abraham."

Dalman, Gustaf. *Arbeit und Sitte in Palästina.* 7 vols. Hildesheim: Georg Olms, 1964 (1928-42).

Danker, Frederick W. *Benefactor: Epigraphic Study of a Graeco-Roman and New Testament Semantic Field.* St. Louis, MO: Clayton, 1982. *Benefactor.*

Darr, John A. *On Character Building: The Reader and the Rhetoric of Characterization in Luke-Acts.* LCBI. Louisville, KY: Westminster/John Knox, 1992. *Character Building.*

Daube, David. "Responsibilities of Master and Disciples in the Gospels." *NTS* 19 (1972-73) 1-15. "Responsibilities."

Dauer, Anton. "Zur Authentizität von Lk 24,12." *ETL* 70 (1994) 294-318. "Lk 24,12."

Dautzenberg, Gerhard. "ἀγών, ἀγωνίζομαι." In *EDNT,* 1:25-27.

Davids, Peter H. "Rich and Poor." In *DJG,* 701-10.

Davidson, Maxwell J. "Angels." In *DJG,* 8-11.

Davies, J. G. "The Prefigurement of the Ascension in the Third Gospel." *JTS* 6 (1955) 229-33. "Prefigurement."

———. *He Ascended into Heaven: A Study in the History of Doctrine.* London: Lutterworth, 1958. *He Ascended.*

Davis III, Charles Thomas. "The Literary Structure of Luke 1–2." In *Art and Meaning: Rhetoric in Biblical Literature,* edited by David J. A. Clines et al., 215-29. JSOTSup 19. Sheffield: JSOT, 1982. "Literary Structure."

Dawsey, James M. "Confrontation in the Temple: Luke 19:45–20:47." *PRS* 11 (1984) 153-65. "Confrontation in the Temple."

———. "Jesus' Pilgrimage to Jerusalem." *PRS* 14 (1987) 217-32. "Jesus' Pilgrimage."

———. "The Literary Unity of Luke-Acts: Questions of Style — A Task for Literary Critics." *NTS* 35 (1989) 48-66. "Literary Unity."

———. *The Lukan Voice: Confusion and Irony in the Gospel of Luke.* Macon, GA: Mercer University, 1986. *Lukan Voice.*

———. "The Origin of Luke's Positive Perception of the Temple." *PRS* 18 (1991) 5-22. "Luke's Positive Perception."

———. "What's in a Name? Characterization in Luke." *BTB* 16 (1986) 143-47. "Characterization."

de Beaugrande, Robert. "Discourse Analysis." In *The Johns Hopkins Guide to Literary Theory and Criticism,* edited by Michael Groden and Martin Kreiswirth, 207-10. Baltimore: Johns Hopkins University Press, 1994.

de Certeau, Michel. *The Writing of History.* New York: Columbia University, 1988. *Writing of History.*

Deissler, Alfons. "The Spirit of the Lord's Prayer in the Faith and Worship of the Old Testament." In *The Lord's Prayer and Jewish Liturgy,* edited by Jakob J. Petuchowski and Michael Brocke, 3-17. New York: Seabury, 1978. "Spirit of the Lord's Prayer."

de Jonge, Hank J. "Sonship, Wisdom, Infancy: Luke II.41-51a." *NTS* 24 (1977-78) 317-54. "Sonship."

de Jonge, M., and A. S. van der Woude. "11Q Melchizedek and the New Testament." *NTS* 12 (1965-66) 301-26. "11QMelchizedek."

de la Potterie, Ignace. "Κεχαριτωμένη en Lc 1,28: Étude exégétique et théologique." *Bib* 68 (1987) 480-508. "Étude exégétique."

—————. "Κεχαριτωμένη en Lc 1,28: Étude philologique." *Bib* 68 (1987) 357-82. "Étude philologique."

DeLeers, Stephen Vincent. "The Road to Emmaus." *BibTod* 24 (1986) 100-107.

Delling, Gerhard. "τρεῖς, τρίς, τρίτος." In *TDNT,* 8:216-25. "τρεῖς."

Delobel, J. "L'onction par la pécheresse: La composition littéraire de Lc., VII, 36-50." *ETL* 42 (1966) 415-75. "L'onction."

de Meeûs, X. "Composition de Lc., XIV et genre symposiaque." *ETL* 37 (1961) 847-70. "Composition."

Denney, James. "The Word 'Hate' in Luke xiv.26." *ExpT* 21 (1909-10) 41-42. "Hate."

Derrett, J. Duncan M. "Christ and Reproof (Matthew 7.1-5/Luke 6.37-42)." *NTS* 34 (1988) 271-81. "Christ and Reproof."

—————. "'ΗΣΑΝ ΓΑΡ ἈΛΙΕΙΣ (MK. 1.16): Jesus's Fishermen and the Parable of the Net." *NovT* 22 (1980) 108-37. "Jesus's Fishermen."

—————. "Fresh Light on St. Luke XVI: The Parable of the Unjust Steward." *NTS* 7 (1960-61) 198-219. "Fresh Light."

—————. "The Friend at Midnight: Asian Ideas in the Gospel of St. Luke." In *Studies in the New Testament,* vol. 3: *Midrash, Haggadah, and the Character of the Community,* 31-41. Leiden: E. J. Brill, 1982. "Friend at Midnight."

—————. "Further Light on the Narratives of the Nativity." In *Studies in the New Testament,* vol. 2: *Midrash in Action and as a Literary Device,* 4-32. Leiden: E. J. Brill, 1978. "Further Light."

—————. "Getting on Top of a Demon (Luke 4:39)." *EvQ* 65 (1993) 99-109.

—————. "Gratitude and the Ten Lepers (Luke 17,11-19)." *DRev* 113 (391, 1995) 79-95. "Gratitude."

————. "James and John as Co-Rescuers from Peril (Lk. V.10)." *NovT* 22 (1980) 299-303. "James and John."

————. *Law in the New Testament.* London: Darton, Longman, and Todd, 1970.

————. "Law in the New Testament: The Parable of the Unjust Judge." *NTS* 18 (1971-72) 178-91. "Unjust Judge."

————. "Law in the New Testament: The Syro-Phoenician Woman and the Centurion of Capernaum." *NovT* 15 (1973) 161-86. "Law."

————. "The Manger at Bethlehem: Light on St. Luke's Technique from Contemporary Jewish Religious Law." In *Studies in the New Testament,* vol. 2: *Midrash in Action and as a Literary Device,* 39-47. Leiden: E. J. Brill, 1978. "Manger at Bethlehem."

————. "The Manger: Ritual Law and Soteriology." In *Studies in the New Testament,* vol. 2: *Midrash in Action and as a Literary Device,* 48-53. Leiden: E. J. Brill, 1978. "Manger."

————. *New Resolutions to Old Conundrums: A Fresh Insight into Luke's Gospel.* Shipston-on-Stour: Peter I. Drinkwater, 1986. *New Resolutions.*

————. "The Parable of the Profitable Servant (Luke xvii.7-10)." In *Studies in the New Testament,* vol. 4: *Midrash, the Composition of Gospels, and Discipline,* 157-66. Leiden: E. J. Brill, 1986. "Profitable Servant."

————. "Positive Perspectives on Two Lucan Miracles." *DRev* 104 (1986) 272-87. "Two Lucan Miracles."

————. "The Rich Fool: A Parable of Jesus concerning Inheritance." In *Studies in the New Testament,* vol. 2: *Midrash in Action and as a Literary Device,* 99-120. Leiden: E. J. Brill, 1978. "Rich Fool."

Derrida, Jacques. *Given Time: 1. Counterfeit Money.* Chicago: University of Chicago, 1992. *Given Time.*

Dibelius, Martin. *From Tradition to Gospel.* Cambridge: James Clarke, 1971.

————. "Jungfrauensohn und Krippenkind: Untersuchungen zur Geburtgeschichte Jesu im Lukas-Evangelium." In *Botschaft und Geschichte: Gesammelte Aufsätze,* vol. 1: *Zur Evangelienforschung,* edited by Günther Bornkamm, 1-78. Tübingen: J. C. B. Mohr (Paul Siebeck), 1953. "Jungfrauensohn."

Dietrich, Wolfgang. *Das Petrusbild der lukanischen Schriften.* BWANT 94. Stuttgart: W. Kohlhammer, 1972. *Petrusbild.*

Dihle, Albrecht. "Die Evangelien und die griechische Biographie." In *Das Evangelium und die Evangelien: Vorträge vom Tübinger Symposium 1982,* edited by Peter Stuhlmacher, 383-411. WUNT 28. Tübingen: J. C. B. Mohr (Paul Siebeck), 1983. "Evangelien."

Dillon, George L. "Discourse Theory." In *The Johns Hopkins Guide to Literary Theory and Criticism,* edited by Michael Groden and Martin Kreiswirth, 210-12. Baltimore: Johns Hopkins University, 1994.

Dillon, Richard J. "Easter Revelation and Mission Program in Luke 24:46-48." In *Sin, Salvation, and the Spirit,* edited by Daniel Durken, 240-70. Collegeville: Liturgical, 1979. "Easter Revelation."

―――. *From Eyewitnesses to Ministers of the Word: Tradition and Composition in Luke 24.* AnBib 82. Rome: Biblical Institute, 1978. *Eyewitnesses.*

―――. "Previewing Luke's Project from His Prologue (Luke 1:1-4)." *CBQ* 43 (1981) 205-27. "Luke's Project."

Dixon, Suzanne. *The Roman Mother.* Norman: University of Oklahoma, 1988. *Roman Mother.*

Dockery, David S. "Baptism." In *DJG,* 55-58.

Dodd, C. H. "The Fall of Jerusalem and the 'Abomination of Desolation.'" *JRS* 37 (1947) 47-54. "Fall of Jerusalem."

Dominic, A. Paul. "Lucan Source of Religious Life." *ITS* 23 (1986) 273-89. "Lucan Source."

Donahue, John R. *The Gospel in Parable: Metaphor, Narrative, and Theology in the Synoptic Gospels.* Philadelphia: Fortress, 1988. *Gospel in Parable.*

―――. "A Neglected Factor in the Theology of Mark." *JBL* 101 (1982) 563-94. "Neglected Factor."

―――. "Tax Collectors and Sinners: An Attempt at Identification." *CBQ* 33 (1971) 39-61. "Tax Collectors."

―――. "Two Decades of Research on the Rich and Poor in Luke-Acts." In *Justice and the Holy: Essays in Honor of Walter Harrelson,* edited by Douglas A. Knight and Peter J. Paris, 129-44. Atlanta: Scholars, 1989. "Two Decades."

Doran, Robert. "Luke 20:18: A Warrior's Boast?" *CBQ* 45 (1983) 61-67. "Luke 20:18."

Douglas, Mary. *How Institutions Think.* Syracuse, NY: Syracuse University, 1986. *Institutions.*

―――. *Implicit Meanings.* London: Routledge and Kegan Paul, 1975.

―――. *Purity and Danger: An Analysis of the Concepts of Pollution and Taboo.* London: Routledge and Kegan Paul, 1966. *Purity and Danger.*

―――. *Risk and Blame: Essays in Cultural Theory.* London/New York: Routledge, 1992. *Risk and Blame.*

Downing, F. Gerald. "The Ambiguity of 'The Pharisees and the Toll-collector' (Luke 18:9-14) in the Greco-Roman World of Late Antiquity." *CBQ* 54 (1992) 80-99. "Pharisee and Toll-collector."

D'Sa, Thomas. "The Emmaus Narrative: A Missionary Journey." *Vidyajyoti* 57 (1993) 147-56. "Emmaus Narrative."

Dumm, Demetrius R. "Luke 24:44-49 and Hospitality." In *Sin, Salvation, and the Spirit,* edited by Daniel Durken, 231-39. Collegeville, MN: Liturgical, 1979.

Dunn, James D. G. *Baptism in the Holy Spirit: A Re-examination of the New Testament Teaching on the Gift of the Spirit in Relation to Pentecostalism Today.* Philadelphia: Westminster, 1970. *Baptism.*

————. *Christology in the Making: A New Testament Inquiry into the Origins of the Doctrine of the Incarnation.* Philadelphia: Westminster, 1980. *Christology in the Making.*

————. "Demythologizing the Ascension — A Reply to Professor Gooding." *IBS* 3 (1981) 15-27. "Ascension."

————. "Demythologizing — The Problem of Myth in the New Testament." In *New Testament Interpretation: Essays on Principles and Methods,* edited by I. Howard Marshall, 285-307. Grand Rapids: Wm. B. Eerdmans, 1977. "Demythologizing."

————. *Jesus and the Spirit: A Study of the Religious and Charismatic Experience of Jesus and the First Christians as Reflected in the New Testament.* Philadelphia: Westminster, 1975. *Jesus and the Spirit.*

————. "Pharisees, Sinners, and Jesus." In *The Social World of Formative Christianity and Judaism: Essays in Tribute to Howard Clark Kee,* edited by Jacob Neusner et al., 264-89. Philadelphia: Fortress, 1988.

————. "Prayer." In *DJG,* 617-25.

————. *Romans.* 2 vols. WBC 38. Dallas, TX: Word, 1988.

————. "Spirit-and-Fire Baptism." *NovT* 14 (1972) 81-92.

Du Plessis, I. I. "Once More: The Purpose of Luke's Prologue (Luke 1:1-4)." *NovT* 16 (1977) 259-71. "Luke's Prologue."

Du Plessis, I. J. "Contextual Aid for an Identity Crisis: An Attempt to Interpret Luke 7:35." In *A South African Perspective on the New Testament: Essays by South African New Testament Scholars Presented to Bruce Manning Metzger during His Visit to South Africa in 1985,* edited by J. H. Petzer and P. J. Martin, 112-27. Leiden: E. J. Brill, 1986. "Contextual Aid."

du Plessis, J. G. "Why Did Peter Ask His Question and How Did Jesus Answer Him? or: Implicature in Luke 12:35-48." *Neot* 22 (1988) 311-24. "Implicature."

du Plooy, Gerhardus Petrus Viljoen. "The Narrative Acts in Luke-Acts from the Perspective of God's Design." Th.D. diss., University of Stellenbosch, 1986. "God's Design."

Dupont, Jacques. "Béatitudes egyptiennes." *Bib* 47 (1966) 185-22.

————. "Die individuelle Eschatologie im Lukasevangelium und in der Apostelgeschichte." In *Orientierung an Jesus: Zur Theologie der Synoptiker,* edited by Paul Hoffman, 37-47. Freiburg: Herder, 1973. "Individuelle Eschatologie."

————. "Le Magnificat comme discours sur Dieu." *NRT* 102 (1980) 321-43. "Magnificat."

Dupriez, Bernard. *A Dictionary of Literary Devices.* New York: Harvester Wheatsheaf, 1991. *Literary Devices.*

Earl, Donald. "Prologue-form in Ancient Historiography." In *ANRW* 1.2:842-56. "Prologue-form."

Easterling, P. E. "Books and Readers in the Greek World: The Hellenistic and Imperial Periods." In *CHCL,* 1:16-41. "Books and Readers."

Eco, Umberto. *The Limits of Interpretation.* AS. Bloomington: Indiana University, 1984. *Limits.*

———. *The Role of the Reader: Explorations in the Semiotics of Texts.* AS. Bloomington: Indiana University, 1979. *Role of the Reader.*

———. *Semiotics and the Philosophy of Language.* AS. Bloomington: Indiana University, 1984. *Semiotics.*

Edwards, Richard Alan. *The Sign of Jonah in the Theology of the Evangelists and Q.* SBT 2:18. London: SCM, 1971. *Sign of Jonah.*

Egelkraut, Helmuth L. *Jesus' Mission to Jerusalem: A Redaction Critical Study of the Travel Narrative in the Gospel of Luke, Lk 9:51–19:48.* EH 23: Theologie 80. Frankfurt am Main: Peter Lang, 1976. *Jesus' Mission.*

Ehrman, Bart D., and Mark A. Plunkett. "The Angel and the Agony: The Textual Problem of Luke 22:43-44." *CBQ* 45 (1983) 401-16. "Angel and Agony."

Eilberg-Schwartz, Howard. *The Savage in Judaism: An Anthropology of Israelite Religion and Ancient Judaism.* Bloomington, IN: Indiana University, 1990. *Savage in Judaism.*

Elias, Jacob W. "The Furious Climax in Nazareth (Luke 4:28-30)." In *The New Way of Jesus: Essays Presented to Howard Charles,* edited by William Klassen, 87-99. Newton, KS: Faith and Life, 1980. "Furious Climax."

Elliot, John H. "Patronage and Clientism in Early Christian Society." *Forum* 3 (1987) 39-48. "Patronage."

———. "Temple Versus Household in Luke-Acts: A Contrast in Social Institutions." In *The Social World of Luke-Acts: Models for Interpretation,* edited by Jerome H. Neyrey, 211-40. Peabody, MA: Hendrickson, 1991. "Temple Versus Household."

Elliott, J. K. "Anna's Age (Luke 2:36-37)." *NovT* 30 (1988) 100-102. "Anna's Age."

Eltester, Walther. "Israel im lukanischen Werk und die Nazarethperikope." In *Jesus in Nazareth,* edited by Walther Eltester, 76-147. BZNW 40. Berlin: Walter de Gruyter, 1972. "Israel."

Epp, Eldon Jay. "The Ascension in the Textual Tradition of Luke-Acts." In *New Testament Textual Criticism: Its Significance for Exegesis,* edited by Eldon Jay Epp and Gordon D. Fee, 131-45. Oxford: Clarendon, 1981. "Ascension."

Ernst, Josef. "Gastmahlgespräche: Lk 14,1-24." In *Die Kirche des Anfangs: Festschrift für Heinz Schürmann zum 65. Geburtstag,* edited by Rudolf Schnackenburg, Josef Ernst, and Joachim Wanke, 57-78. ETS 38. Leipzig: St. Benno, 1977. "Gastmahlgespräche."

――――. *Johannes der Täufer: Interpretation, Geschichte, Wirkungsgeschichte.* BZNW 53. Berlin: Walter de Gruyter, 1989. *Johannes der Täufer.*

Esler, Philip Francis. *Community and Gospel in Luke-Acts: The Social and Political Motivations of Lucan Theology.* SNTSMS 57. Cambridge: Cambridge University, 1987. *Community and Gospel.*

Evans, Craig A. "The Function of the Elisha/Elijah Narratives in Luke's Ethic of Election." In *Luke and Scripture: The Function of Sacred Tradition in Luke-Acts,* by Craig A. Evans and James A. Sanders, 70-83. Minneapolis: Fortress, 1993. "Luke's Ethic of Election."

――――. " 'He Set His Face': Luke 9,51 Once Again." *Bib* 68 (1987) 80-84. "Luke 9,51 Once Again."

――――. " 'He Set His Face': A Note on Luke 9,51." *Bib* 63 (1982) 545-48. "He Set His Face."

――――. "Luke 16:1-18 and the Deuteronomy Hypothesis." In *Luke and Scripture: The Function of Sacred Tradition in Luke-Acts,* by Craig A. Evans and James A. Sanders, 121-39. Minneapolis: Fortress, 1993. "Luke 16:1-18."

――――. "Luke's Use of the Elijah/Elisha Narratives and the Ethic of Election." *JBL* 106 (1987) 75-83. "Elijah/Elisha Narratives."

――――. "Prophecy and Polemic: Jews in Luke's Scriptural Apologetic." In *Luke and Scripture: The Function of Sacred Tradition in Luke-Acts,* by Craig A. Evans and James A. Sanders, 171-211. Minneapolis: Fortress, 1993. "Prophecy and Polemic."

――――. *To See and Not to Perceive: Isaiah 6.9-10 in Early Jewish and Christian Interpretation.* JSOTSup 64. Sheffield: Sheffield Academic, 1989. *Isaiah 6.9-10.*

Evans, John K. *War, Women and Children in Ancient Rome.* London: Routledge, 1991. *War, Women and Children.*

Eyben, Emiel. "Fathers and Sons." In *Marriage, Divorce, and Children in Ancient Rome,* edited by Beryl Rawson, 114-43. Oxford: Oxford University, 1991.

Falkenroth, Ulrich, and Colin Brown. "Punishment, Vengeance." In *NIDNTT,* 3:92-97.

Farrell, H. K. "The Structure and Theology of Luke's Central Section." *TrinJ* 7 (1986) 33-54. "Structure and Theology."

Farris, Stephen. *The Hymns of Luke's Infancy Narratives: Their Origin, Meaning and Significance.* JSNTSup 9. Sheffield: JSOT, 1985. *Hymns.*

Fasold, Ralph. *The Sociolinguistics of Language.* Vol. 2. LS 6. Cambridge: Basil Blackwell, 1990. *Sociolinguistics.*

Fee, Gordon D. " 'One Thing Is Needful?' Luke 10:42." In *New Testament Textual Criticism: Its Significance for Exegesis,* edited by Eldon J. Epp and Gordon D. Fee, 61-75. Oxford: Clarendon, 1981. "One Thing Is Needful?"

Feldman, Louis H. *Jew and Gentile in the Ancient World: Attitudes and Interactions from Alexander to Justinian.* Princeton, NJ: Princeton University, 1993. *Jew and Gentile.*

Fernández Marcos, N. "La unción de Salomón y la entrada de Jesús en Jerusalén: 1 Re 1,33-40/Lc 19,35-40." *Bib* 68 (1987) 89-97. "La unción de Salomón."

Finegan, Jack. *Encountering New Testament Manuscripts: A Working Introduction to Textual Criticism.* Grand Rapids: Wm. B. Eerdmans, 1974. *NT Manuscripts.*

Finkel, A. "Jesus' Sermon at Nazareth (Luk. 4,16-30)." In *Abraham unser Vater: Juden und Christen in Gespräch über die Bibel. Festschrift für O. Michel zum 60. Geburtstag,* edited by Otto Betz, Martin Hengel, and Peter Schmidt, 106-15. AGSU 5. Leiden: E. J. Brill, 1963. "Sermon at Nazareth."

Finley, M. I. *The Ancient Economy.* SCL 43. Berkeley: University of California, 1973. *Ancient Economy.*

Firmage, Edwin. "Zoology (Fauna)." In *ABD,* 6:1109-67.

Fishwick, Duncan. *The Imperial Cult in the Latin West: Studies in the Ruler Cult of the Western Provinces of the Roman Empire.* 2 vols. EPROER. Leiden: E. J. Brill, 1987-92. *Imperial Cult.*

Fitzer, Gottfried. "σκιρτάω." In *TDNT,* 7:401-2.

Fitzmyer, Joseph A. "The Composition of Luke, Chapter 9." In *Perspectives on Luke-Acts,* edited by Charles H. Talbert, 139-52. Edinburgh: T. & T. Clark, 1978. "Composition."

————. "The Contribution of Qumran Aramaic to the Study of the New Testament." *NTS* 20 (1973-74) 382-407. "Contribution of Qumran Aramaic."

————. "Further Light on Melchizedek from Qumran Cave 11," in *Essays on the Semitic Background of the New Testament,* 245-67. London: Geoffrey Chapman, 1971. "Melchizedek."

————. *Luke the Theologian: Aspects of His Teaching.* New York/Mahwah: Paulist, 1989. *Luke the Theologian.*

————. " 'Peace upon Earth among Men of His Good Will' (Lk 2:14)." In *Essays on the Semitic Background of the New Testament,* 101-4. London: Geoffrey Chapman, 1971. "Peace upon Earth."

————. "The Virginal Conception of Jesus in the New Testament." In *To*

Advance the Gospel: New Testament Studies, 41-78. New York: Crossroad, 1981. "Virginal Conception."

Fleddermann, Harry. "The Householder and the Servant Left in Charge." In *Society of Biblical Literature 1986 Seminar Papers,* edited by Kent Harold Richards, 17-26. Atlanta: Scholars, 1986. "Householder."

Flesher, Paul Virgil McCracken. *Oxen, Women, or Citizens? Slaves in the System of the Mishnah.* BJS 143. Atlanta: Scholars, 1988. *Slaves.*

Flusser, David. "Do You Prefer New Wine?" *Immanuel* 9 (1979) 26-31. "New Wine."

Foakes Jackson, F. J., and Kirsopp Lake. "The Zealots." In *The Acts of the Apostles,* edited by F. J. Foakes Jackson and Kirsopp Lake, vol. 1, *Prolegomena I: The Jewish, Gentile, and Christian Backgrounds,* 421-25. BC 1. London: Macmillan, 1920.

Foerster, Werner. "δαίμων, δαιμόνιον." In *TDNT,* 2:1-20.

———. "εὐάρεστος, εὐαρεστέω." In *TDNT,* 1:456-57.

———. "σῴζω and σωτηρία in the Greek World." In *TDNT,* 7:966-69. "σῴζω and σωτηρία."

Fohrer, Georg, et al. "υἱός, υἱοθεσία." In *TDNT,* 8:334-99. "υἱός."

Fohrer, Georg, and Werner Foester. "σωτήρ." In *TDNT,* 7:1003-21.

Ford, J. Massyngbaerde. "Bookshelf on Prostitution." *BTB* 23 (1993) 128-34. "Prostitution."

———. *My Enemy Is My Guest: Jesus and Violence in Luke.* Maryknoll, NY: Orbis, 1984. *My Enemy Is My Guest.*

———. "Zealotism and the Lukan Infancy Narratives." *NovT* 18 (1976) 280-92. "Zealotism."

Forestell, James T. "Old Testament Background of the Magnificat." *MS* 12 (1961) 205-44. "Magnificat."

Fornara, Charles William. *The Nature of History in Ancient Greece and Rome.* ESCK. Berkeley: University of California, 1983. *Nature of History.*

Fowl, Stephen, and L. Gregory Jones. *Reading in Communion: Scripture and Ethics in Christian Life.* Grand Rapids: Wm. B. Eerdmans, 1991. *Reading in Communion.*

Freed, E. D. "The Parable of the Judge and the Widow (Luke 18.1-8)." *NTS* 33 (1987) 38-60. "Parable of the Judge."

Freyne, Sean. *Galilee, Jesus and the Gospels: Literary Approaches and Historical Investigations.* Philadelphia: Fortress, 1988. *Galilee.*

Frid, Bo. "A Brief Note on πλήν in Roman Times." *SEÅ* 51-52 (1986-87) 65-71. "Brief Note."

Fridrichsen, Anton. "Exegetisches zum Neuen Testament." *SO* 13 (1934) 38-46. "Exegetisches."

Friedrich, Gerhard. "εὐαγγελίζομαι κτλ." In *TDNT,* 2:707-37.

Fuchs, Albert. "βάτος." In *EDNT,* 1:209.

Fuks, Alexander. *Social Conflict in Ancient Greece.* Jerusalem: Magnes; Leiden: Brill, 1984. *Social Conflict.*

Fuller, Reginald H. "A Note on Luke 1:28 and 38." In *The New Testament Age: Essays in Honor of Bo Reicke,* 2 vols., edited by William C. Weinrich, 1:201-6. Macon, GA: Mercer University, 1984. "Luke 1:28."

Funk, Robert W. *The Poetics of Biblical Narrative.* FF:LF. Sonoma, CA: Polebridge, 1988. *Poetics.*

Furnish, Victor Paul. *The Love Commandment in the New Testament.* Nashville: Abingdon, 1972. *Love Commandment.*

Fusco, Vittorio. " 'Point of View' and 'Implicit Reader' in Two Eschatological Texts (Lk 19,11-28; Acts 1,6-8)." In *The Four Gospels 1992: Festschrift Frans Neirynck,* edited by F. Van Segbroeck, C. M. Tuckett, G. Van Belle, and J. Verheyden, vol. 2, 1677-96. BETL 100. Leuven: Leuven University, 1992. "Point of View."

———. "Problems of Struction in Luke's Eschatological Discourse (Luke 21:7-36)." In *Luke and Acts,* edited by Gerald O'Collins and Gilberto Marconi, 72-92. New York/Mahwah: Paulist, 1991. "Luke's Eschatological Discourse."

Gagnon, Robert A. J. "Statistical Analysis and the Case of the Double Delegation in Luke 7:3-7a." *CBQ* 55 (1993) 709-31. "Statistical Analysis."

Gamble, Harry Y. *Books and Readers in the Early Church: A History of Early Christian Texts.* New Haven: Yale University, 1995. *Books and Readers.*

Garnsey, Peter, and Richard Saller. *The Roman Empire: Economy, Society and Culture.* Berkeley: University of California, 1987. *Roman Empire.*

Garrett, Susan B. *The Demise of the Devil: Magic and the Demonic in Luke's Writings.* Minneapolis: Fortress, 1989. *Demise of the Devil.*

———. "Exodus from Bondage: Luke 9:31 and Acts 12:1-24." *CBQ* 52 (1990) 656-80. "Exodus from Bondage."

———. " 'Lest the Light in You Be Darkness': Luke 11:33-36 and the Question of Commitment." *JBL* 110 (1991) 93-105. "Luke 11:33-36."

———. "The Meaning of Jesus' Death in Luke." *WW* 12 (1992) 11-16. "Jesus' Death."

Garrison, Roman. *Redemptive Almsgiving in Early Christianity.* JSNT 77. Sheffield: Sheffield Academic, 1993. *Redemptive Almsgiving.*

Gasque, W. Ward. *A History of the Interpretation of the Acts of the Apostles.* 2d ed. Peabody, MA: Hendrickson, 1989. *History of the Interpretation.*

Gebara, Ivone, and Maria Clara Bingemer. *Mary, Mother of God, Mother of the Poor.* LT 7. Maryknoll, NY: Orbis, 1989. *Mary.*

Geddert, Timothy J. "Peace." In *DJG,* 604-5.

Geertz, Clifford. *Local Knowledge: Further Essays in Interpretive Anthropology.* New York: Basic, 1983. *Local Knowledge.*

Geiger, Ruthild. *Die lukanischen Endzeitreden: Studien zur Eschatologie des Lukas-Evangeliums.* EH 23: Theologie 16. Frankfurt am Main: Peter Lang, 1973. *Die lukanischen Endzeitreden.*

Gellner, Ernest. "Patrons and Clients." In *Patrons and Clients in Mediterranean Societies,* edited by Ernest Gellner and John Waterbury, 1-6. London: Duckworth, 1977. "Patrons."

Genette, Gérard. *Narrative Discourse: An Essay in Method.* Ithaca, NY: Cornell University, 1980. *Narrative Discourse.*

—————. *Narrative Discourse Revisited.* Ithaca, NY: Cornell University, 1988.

Geninasca, Jacques. "To Fish/To Preach: Narrative and Metaphor (Luke 5:1-11)." In *Signs and Parables: Semiotics and Gospel Texts,* edited by The Entrevernes Group, 185-222. Pittsburgh: Pickwick, 1978. "To Fish/To Preach."

George, Augustin. "Le Parallèle entre Jean-Baptiste et Jésus en Lc 1–2." In *Mélanges Bibliques en Homage au R. P. Béda Rigaux,* edited by Albert Descamps and R. P. André de Halleux, 141-71. Gembloux: J. Duculot, 1970. "Parallèle."

Gerhardsson, Birger. *The Testing of God's Son (Matt 4:1-11 & par): An Analysis of an Early Christian Midrash.* ConBNT 2. Lund: Gleerup, 1966. *Testing of God's Son.*

Gibbs, James M. "Luke 24:13-33 and Acts 8:26-39: The Emmaus Incident and the Eunuch's Baptism as Parallel Stories." *BTF* 7 (1975) 17-30. "Luke 24:13-33 and Acts 8:26-39."

Giblin, Charles H. *The Destruction of Jerusalem according to Luke's Gospel.* AnBib 107. Rome: Pontifical Biblical Institute, 1985. *Destruction of Jerusalem.*

—————. "Reflections on the Sign of the Manger." *CBQ* 29 (1967) 87-101. "Sign of the Manger."

—————. " 'The Things of God' in the Question concerning Tribute to Caesar (Luke 20:25; Mk 12:7; Mt 22:21)." *CBQ* 33 (1971) 510-27. "Things of God."

Giesen, Heinz. "μισέω." In *EDNT,* 2:431-32.

—————. "ὑπόκρισις, ὑποκρίνομαι." In *EDNT,* 3:403.

Giles, Kevin. "Ascension." In *DJG,* 46-50.

Gill, David. "Observations on the Lukan Travel Narrative and Some Related Passages." *HTR* 63 (1970) 199-221. "Lukan Travel Narrative."

Gillman, John. *Possessions and the Life of Faith: A Reading of Luke-Acts.* ZSNT. Collegeville, Minnesota: Liturgical, 1991. *Possessions.*

Gilsenan, Michael. "Against Patron-Client Relations." In *Patrons and Clients in Mediterranean Societies,* edited by Ernest Gellner and John Waterbury, 167-83. London: Duckworth, 1977. "Patron-Client Relations."

Glendenning, F. J. "The Devil and the Temptations of Our Lord according to St Luke." *Theology* 52 (1949) 102-5. "Devil."

Gnanavaram, M. " 'Dalit Theology' and the Parable of the Good Samaritan." *JSNT* 50 (1993) 59-83. "Dalit Theology."

Gnilka, Joachim. "Der Hymnus des Zacharias." *BZ* 6 (1962) 215-38. "Hymnus."

Gnuse, Robert. *You Shall Not Steal: Community and Property in the Biblical Tradition.* Maryknoll, NY: Orbis, 1985. *Community and Property.*

Gold, Barbara K. *Literary Patronage in Greece and Rome.* Chapel Hill: University of North Carolina, 1987. *Literary Patronage.*

Goldingay, John. *Models for Scripture.* Grand Rapids: Wm. B. Eerdmans; Carlisle: Paternoster, 1994.

Good, Byron J. *Medicine, Rationality, and Experience: An Anthropological Perspective.* Cambridge: Cambridge University, 1994. *Medicine.*

Good, R. S. "Jesus, Protagonist of the Old, in Luke 5:33-39." *NovT* 25 (1983) 19-36. "Jesus."

Gooding, D. W. "Demythologizing Old and New, and Luke's Description of the Ascension: A Layman's Appraisal." *IBS* 2 (1980) 95-119. "Demythologizing Old and New."

———. "Demythologizing the Ascension — A Reply." *IBS* 3 (1981) 46-54. "Demythologizing the Ascension."

Gordon, Barry. *The Economic Problem in Biblical and Patristic Thought.* VGSup 9. Leiden: Brill, 1989. *Economic Problem.*

Gowler, David B. "Characterization in Luke: A Socio-Narratological Approach." *BTB* 19 (1989) 54-62. "Characterization."

———. "Hospitality and Characterization in Luke 11:37-54: A Socio-Narratological Approach." *Semeia* 64 (1993) 213-51. "Hospitality and Characterization."

———. *Host, Guest, Enemy and Friend: Portraits of the Pharisees in Luke and Acts.* ESEC 2. New York: Peter Lang, 1991. *Portraits of the Pharisees.*

Grant, Frederick C. *Roman Hellenism and the New Testament.* Edinburgh: Oliver and Boyd, 1962. *Roman Hellenism.*

Grassi, Joseph M. "Emmaus Revisited (Luke 24:13-35 and Acts 8:26-40)." *CBQ* 26 (1964) 463-67. "Emmaus Revisited."

Graubard, Baruch. "The *Kaddish* Prayer." In *The Lord's Prayer and Jewish Liturgy,* edited by Jakob J. Petuchowski and Michael Brocke, 59-72. New York: Seabury, 1978. *"Kaddish."*

Grayston, Kenneth. "The Decline of Temptation — And the Lord's Prayer." *SJT* 46 (1993) 279-95. "Decline of Temptation."

Green, Joel B. "Burial of Jesus." In *DJG,* 88-92. "Burial."

———. "Caring as Gift and Goal: Biblical and Theological Reflections." In

The Crisis of Care: Affirming and Restoring Caring Practices in the Helping Professions, edited by Susan S. Phillips and Patricia Benner, 149-67. HCPE. Washington, D.C.: Georgetown University, 1994. "Caring as Gift and Goal."

―――. "Crucifixion." In *DPL,* 197-99.

―――. "The Death of Jesus, God's Servant." In *Reimaging the Death of the Lukan Jesus,* edited by Dennis D. Sylva, 1-28, 170-73. AMTBBB 73. Frankfurt am Main: Anton Hain, 1990. "God's Servant."

―――. "Death of Jesus." In *DJG,* 146-63.

―――. *The Death of Jesus: Tradition and Interpretation in the Passion Narrative.* WUNT 2:33. Tübingen: J. C. B. Mohr (Paul Siebeck), 1988. *Death of Jesus.*

―――. "The Demise of the Temple as Culture Center in Luke-Acts: An Exploration of the Rending of the Temple Veil (Luke 23:44-49)." *RB* 101 (1994) 495-515. "Demise of the Temple."

―――. "Discourse Analysis." In *Hearing the New Testament: Strategies for Interpretation,* edited by Joel B. Green, 175-96. Grand Rapids: Wm. B. Eerdmans, 1995.

―――. "Good News to Whom? Jesus and the 'Poor' in the Gospel of Luke." In *Jesus of Nazareth: Lord and Christ. Essays on the Historical Jesus and New Testament Christology,* edited by Joel B. Green and Max Turner, 59-74. Grand Rapids: Wm. B. Eerdmans, 1994. "Good News."

―――. "Internal Repetition in Luke-Acts: Contemporary Narratology and Lukan Historiography." In *History, Literature, and Society in the Book of Acts,"* edited by Ben Witherington III, 283-99. Cambridge: Cambridge University, 1995. "Internal Repetition."

―――. "Jesus and a Daughter of Abraham (Luke 13:10-17): Test Case for a Lukan Perspective on the Miracles of Jesus." *CBQ* 51 (1989) 643-54. "Daughter of Abraham."

―――. "Jesus on the Mount of Olives (Luke 22.39-46): Tradition and Theology." *JSNT* 26 (1986) 29-48. "Mount of Olives."

―――. "Kingdom of God." In *NDCEPT,* 529-32.

―――. " 'The Message of Salvation' in Luke-Acts." *Ex Auditu* 5 (1989) 21-34. "Message of Salvation."

―――. "Preparation for Passover (Luke 22:7-13): A Question of Redactional Technique." *NovT* 29 (1987) 305-19. "Preparation for Passover."

―――. "The Problem of a Beginning: Israel's Scriptures in Luke 1–2." *BBR* 4 (1994) 61-85. "Beginning."

―――. " 'Proclaiming Repentance and Forgiveness of Sins to All Nations': A Biblical Perspective on the Church's Mission." In *The World Is My Parish: Methodist Perspectives on the Mission of the Church,* edited by Alan G. Padgett, 13-43. SHM. Lewiston, NY: Edwin Mellen, 1992. "Proclaiming Repentance."

———. " 'Salvation to the End of the Earth' (Acts 13:47): God as Savior in the Acts of the Apostles." In *The Book of Acts and Its Theology,* edited by I. Howard Marshall and David Peterson. Grand Rapids: Wm. B. Eerdmans, forthcoming. "Salvation to the End of the Earth."

———. "The Social Status of Mary in Luke 1,5-2,52: A Plea for Methodological Integration," *Bib* 73 (1992) 457-72. "Social Status."

———. *The Theology of the Gospel of Luke.* NTT. Cambridge: Cambridge University, 1995. *Gospel of Luke.*

Green, Joel B., and Richard B. Hays. "The Use of the Old Testament by New Testament Writers." In *Hearing the New Testament: Strategies for Interpretation,* edited by Joel B. Green, 222-38. Grand Rapids: Wm. B. Eerdmans, 1995. "Use of the Old Testament."

Greenblatt, Stephen. "Culture." In *Critical Terms for Literary Study,* edited by Frank Lentricchia and Thomas McLaughlin, 225-32. Chicago: University of Chicago, 1987.

Grimm, W. "θαμβέω, θάμβος." In *EDNT,* 2:128-29.

Grogan, Geoffrey W. "The Light and the Stone: A Christological Study in Luke and Isaiah." In *Christ the Lord: Studies in Christology Presented to Donald Guthrie,* edited by Harold H. Rowdon, 151-67. Leicester: Inter-Varsity, 1982. "Light and the Stone."

Grundmann, Walter. "ταπεινός κτλ." In *TDNT,* 9:1-26.

Gryglewicz, Feliks. "Die Herkunft der Hymnen des Kindheitsevangeliums des Lucas." *NTS* 21 (1974-75) 265-73. "Herkunft der Hymnen."

Guelich, Robert. "The Gospel Genre." In *Das Evangelium und die Evangelien. Vorträge vom Tübinger Symposium 1982,* edited by Peter Stuhlmacher, 183-219. WUNT 28. Tübingen: J. C. B. Mohr (Paul Siebeck), 1983. "Gospel Genre."

———. *The Sermon on the Mount: A Foundation for Understanding.* Waco, TX: Word, 1982. *Sermon on the Mount.*

Haenchen, Ernst. " 'We' in Acts and the Itinerary." *JTC* 1 (1965) 65-99. "We in Acts."

Hahn, Robert A. *Sickness and Healing: An Anthropological Perspective.* New Haven/London: Yale University, 1995. *Sickness and Healing.*

Hall, Robert G. *Revealed Histories: Techniques for Ancient Jewish and Christian Historiography.* JSPSup 6. Sheffield: JSOT, 1991. *Revealed Histories.*

Hamel, Gladas. *Poverty and Charity in Roman Palestine, First Three Centuries C.E.* UCP:NES 23. Berkeley: University of California, 1990. *Poverty and Charity.*

Hamm, Dennis. "The Freeing of the Bent Woman and the Restoration of

Israel: Luke 13:10-17 as Narrative Theology." *JSNT* 31 (1987) 23-44. "Freeing of the Bent Woman."

———. "Luke 19:8 Once Again: Does Zacchaeus Defend or Resolve?" *JBL* 107 (1988) 431-37. "Luke 19:8."

———. "Sight to the Blind: Vision as Metaphor in Luke." *Bib* 67 (1986) 457-77. "Sight to the Blind."

———. "What the Samaritan Leper Sees: The Narrative Christology of Luke 17:11-19." *CBQ* 56 (1994) 273-87. "Samaritan Leper."

Hands, Arthur R. *Charities and Social Aid in Greece and Rome.* Ithaca, NY: Cornell University, 1968. *Charities and Social Aid.*

Hanson, Paul D. *The People Called: The Growth of Community in the Bible.* San Francisco: Harper & Row, 1986. *People Called.*

Harrington, Daniel J. "Sabbath Tensions: Matthew 12:1-14 and Other New Testament Texts." In *The Sabbath in Jewish and Christian Traditions,* edited by Tamara C. Eskenazi et al., 45-56. "Sabbath Tensions."

Harris, Murray J. " 'The Dead Are Raised to Life': Miracles of Revivification in the Gospels." In *The Miracles of Jesus,* edited by David Wenham and Craig Blomberg, 295-326. GP 6. Sheffield: JSOT, 1986. "Miracles of Revivification."

Harrison, Roland K. "παραλυτικός." In *NIDNTT,* 3:999-1000.

Harvey, A. E. *Jesus and the Constraints of History.* Philadelphia: Westminster, 1982. *Constraints of History.*

———. *Strenuous Commands: The Ethic of Jesus.* Philadelphia: Trinity; London: SCM, 1990. *Strenuous Commands.*

———. " 'The Workman Is Worthy of His Hire': Fortunes of a Proverb in the Early Church." *NovT* 24 (1982) 209-21. "Worthy of His Hire."

Hart, H. St-J. "The Coin of 'Render unto Caesar . . .' (A Note on Some Aspects of Mark 12:13-17; Matt. 22:15-22; Luke 20:20-26)." In *Jesus and the Politics of His Day,* edited by Ernst Bammel and C. F. D. Moule, 241-48. "Coin."

Hasel, Gerhard F. "Sabbath." In *ABD,* 5:849-56.

Haslam, J. A. G. "The Centurion at Capernaum: Luke 7:1-10." *ExpT* 96 (1984-85) 109-10. "Centurion."

Hasler, Victor. "βρυγμός, βρύχω." In *EDNT,* 1:227-28.

Hatch, William H. P. "The Meaning of Acts 1:4." *JBL* 30 (1911) 123-28. "Acts 1:4."

Hauck, F. "μαμωνᾶς." In *TDNT,* 4:388-90.

Haudebert, Pierre. "La Samarie en *Luc-Actes:* Lc. 9,51-56 — Ac 8,4-8." *Impacts* (1, 1994) 25-34. "Samarie."

Hause, H. "λαγχάνω." In *TDNT,* 4:1-2.

Hay, David M. *Glory at the Right Hand: Psalm 110 in Early Christianity.* SBLMS 18. Nashville: Abingdon, 1973. *Glory at the Right Hand.*

Heard, Warren J. "Revolutionary Movements." In *DJG,* 688-98.

Hedrick, Charles W. *Parables as Poetic Fictions: The Creative Voice of Jesus.* Peabody, MA: Hendrickson, 1994. *Parables.*

Heil, John Paul. "Reader-Response and the Irony of Jesus before the Sanhedrin in Luke 22:66-71." *CBQ* 51 (1989) 271-84. "Luke 22:66-71."

Heiligenthal, Roman. "ἐργάζομαι κτλ." In *EDNT,* 2:48-49.

Hemer, Colin J. "ἐπιούσιος." *JSNT* 22 (1984) 81-94.

―――. "Luke the Historian." *BJRL* 60 (1977) 28-51.

―――. *The Book of Acts in the Setting of Hellenistic History.* Edited by Conrad H. Gempf. WUNT 49. Tübingen: J. C. B. Mohr (Paul Siebeck), 1989. *Acts.*

Hendrickx, Herman. *The Resurrection Narratives of the Synoptic Gospels.* London: Geoffrey Chapman, 1984. *Resurrection Narratives.*

Hengel, Martin. *Acts and the History of Earliest Christianity.* Philadelphia: Fortress, 1979. *Acts.*

―――. *The Atonement: The Origins of the Doctrine in the New Testament.* Philadelphia: Fortress, 1981. *Atonement.*

―――. *Between Jesus and Paul: Studies in the Earliest History of Christianity.* Philadelphia: Fortress, 1983. *Between Jesus and Paul.*

―――. *The Charismatic Leader and His Followers.* SNTW. Edinburgh: T. & T. Clark, 1981. *Charismatic Leader.*

―――. *Crucifixion in the Ancient World and the Folly of the Message of the Cross.* Philadelphia: Fortress, 1977. *Crucifixion.*

―――. *The "Hellenization" of Judaea in the First Century after Christ.* Philadelphia: Trinity; London: SCM, 1989. *Hellenization.*

―――. *Jews, Greeks, and Barbarians: Aspects of the Hellenization of Judaism in the Pre-Christian Period.* Philadelphia: Fortress, 1980. *Jews, Greeks, and Barbarians.*

―――. "Maria Magdalena und die Frauen als Zeugen." In *Abraham unser Vater: Juden und Christen im Gespräch über die Bibel: Festschrift für Otto Michel zum 60. Geburtstag,* edited by Otto Betz, Martin Hengel, and Peter Schmidt, 243-56. AGSU 5. Leiden: Brill, 1963. "Maria Magdalena."

―――. *Property and Riches in the Early Church.* Philadelphia: Fortress, 1974. *Property and Riches.*

―――. *The Zealots: Investigations into the Jewish Freedom Movement in the Period from Herod I until 70 A.D.* Edinburgh: T. & T. Clark, 1989. *Zealots.*

Herrenbrück, Fritz. *Jesus und die Zöllner: Historische und neutestamentlich-exegetische Untersuchungen.* WUNT 2:41. Tübingen: J. C. B. Mohr (Paul Siebeck), 1990. *Jesus und die Zöllner.*

Herzog II, William R. *Parables as Subversive Speech: Jesus as Pedagogue of the Oppressed.* Louisville, KY: Westminster/John Knox, 1994. *Parables.*

Hess, Adolf Johann. "γογγύζω." In *EDNT,* 1:256-57.

Hiers, Richard H. "Day of Judgment." In *ABD,* 2:79-82.

———. "Day of the Lord." In *ABD,* 2:82-83.

Higgins, A. J. B. *The Lord's Supper in the New Testament.* SBT 6. London: SCM, 1952. *Lord's Supper.*

———. "The Preface to Luke and the Kerygma in Acts." In *Apostolic History and the Gospel: Biblical and Historical Essays Presented to F. F. Bruce on His 60th Birthday,* edited by W. Ward Gasque and Ralph P. Martin, 78-91. Exeter: Paternoster, 1970. "Preface to Luke."

Hill, David. "The Rejection of Jesus of Nazareth (Luke iv 16-30)." *NovT* 13 (1971) 161-80. "Rejection."

Hock, Ronald F. "Lazarus and Micyllus: Greco-Roman Backgrounds to Luke 16:19-31." *JBL* 106 (1987) 447-63. "Lazarus and Micyllus."

Hofius, Otfried. "βλασφημία κτλ." In *EDNT,* 1:219-21.

———. *Jesu Tischgemeinschaft mit den Sündern.* Stuttgart: Calwer, 1967. *Jesu Tischgemeinschaft.*

Hollander, John. *The Figure of Echo: A Mode of Allusion in Milton and After.* Berkeley: University of California, 1981. *Figure of Echo.*

Holleran, J. Warren. *The Synoptic Gethsemane: A Critical Study.* AnGreg 191. Rome: Università Gregoriana, 1973. *Synoptic Gethsemane.*

Holtz, Traugott. *Untersuchungen über die alttestamentlichen Zitate bei Lukas.* TU 104. Berlin: Akademie, 1968. *Untersuchungen.*

Holzberg, Niklas. *The Ancient Novel: An Introduction.* London: Routledge, 1995. *Ancient Novel.*

Horsley, G. H. R. *New Documents Illustrating Early Christianity: A Review of the Greek Inscriptions and Papyri Published in 1976.* Macquarie University, The Ancient History Documentary Research Centre, 1981. *New Documents.*

Horsley, Richard A. *The Liberation of Christmas: The Infancy Narratives in Social Context.* New York: Crossroad, 1989. *Liberation of Christmas.*

Houtman, Cornelis. *De Hemel in het Oude Testament: Een Onderzoek naar de Voorstellingen van het Oude Israël omtrent de Kosmos.* Franeker: T. Wever, 1974. *Hemel.*

Hubbard, Benjamin J. "Commissioning Stories in Luke-Acts: A Study of Their Antecedents, Form and Content." *Semeia* 8 (1977) 103-26. "Commissioning Stories."

Huffard, Everett W. "The Parable of the Friend at Midnight: God's Honor or Man's Persistence?" *ResQ* 21 (1978) 154-60. "Friend at Midnight."

Hurst, Lincoln D., and Joel B. Green. "Priest, Priesthood." In *DJG,* 633-36.

Hurtado, Larry W. "Gospel (Genre)." In *DJG,* 276-82.

Ilan, Tal. *Jewish Women in Greco-Roman Palestine.* Peabody, MA: Hendrickson, 1996. *Jewish Women.*

"An Indonesian Example: The Miraculous Catch (Luke 5:1-11)." In *Voices from the Margin: Interpreting the Bible in the Third World,* edited by R. S. Sugirtharajah, 420-22. Maryknoll, NY: Orbis, 1991. "Indonesian Example."

Ireland, Dennis J. "A History of Recent Interpretation of the Parable of the Unjust Steward (Luke 16:1-13)." *WTJ* 51 (1989) 293-318. "Recent Interpretation."

Iser, Wolfgang. *The Fictive and the Imaginary: Charting Literary Anthropology.* Baltimore: Johns Hopkins University, 1993. *Fictive and the Imaginary.*

―――. *The Implied Reader: Patterns of Communication in Prose Fiction from Bunyan to Beckett.* Baltimore: Johns Hopkins University, 1974. *Implied Reader.*

Jeremias, Joachim. "ἄνθρωποι εὐδοκίας (Lc 2.14)." *ZNW* 28 (1929) 3-20.

―――. *The Eucharistic Words of Jesus.* Philadelphia: Fortress, 1966. *Eucharistic Words.*

―――. *Jerusalem in the Time of Jesus: An Investigation into Economic and Social Conditions during the New Testament Period.* Philadelphia: Fortress, 1969. *Jerusalem.*

―――. *Jesus' Promise to the Nations.* SBT 24. London: SCM, 1958. *Jesus' Promise.*

―――. "κεφαλὴ γωνίας." In *TNDT,* 1:792-93.

―――. "λίθος." In *TDNT,* 4:268-80.

―――. *The Parables of Jesus.* 3d ed. London: SCM, 1972. *Parables.*

―――. *The Prayers of Jesus.* Philadelphia: Fortress, 1967. *Prayers.*

―――. *Die Sprache des Lukasevangeliums: Redaktion und Tradition im Nicht-Markusstoff des dritten Evangeliums.* KKNT Sonderband. Göttingen: Vandenhoeck & Ruprecht, 1980. *Sprache des Lukasevangeliums.*

Jervell, Jacob. "The Center of Scripture in Luke." In *The Unknown Paul: Essays on Luke-Acts and Early Christian History,* 122-37. Minneapolis: Augsburg, 1984. "Center of Scripture."

―――. "The Daughters of Abraham: Women in Acts." In *The Unknown Paul: Essays on Luke-Acts and Early Christian History,* 146-57, 186-90. Minneapolis: Augsburg, 1984. "Daughters of Abraham."

―――. "The Twelve on Israel's Thrones: Luke's Understanding of the Apostolate." In *Luke and the People of God: A New Look at Luke-Acts,* 75-112. Minneapolis: Augsburg, 1972. "The Twelve."

Johnson, Alan F. "Assurance for Man: The Fallacy of Translating *Anaideia* by 'Persistence' in Luke 11:5-8." *JETS* 22 (1979) 123-31. "Assurance."

Johnson, Allen W., and Timothy Earle. *The Evolution of Human Societies: From Foraging Group to Agrarian State.* Stanford, CA: Stanford University, 1987. *Evolution of Human Societies.*

Johnson, Luke Timothy. *Decision Making in the Church: A Biblical Model.* Philadelphia: Fortress, 1983. *Decision Making.*

———. "The Lukan Kingship Parable (Lk. 19:11-27)." *NovT* 24 (1982) 139-59. "Lukan Kingship Parable."

———. *Sharing Possessions: Mandate and Symbol of Faith.* OBT. Philadelphia: Fortress, 1981. *Sharing Possessions.*

Johnson, Marshall D. *The Purpose of the Biblical Genealogies: With Special Reference to the Setting of the Genealogies of Jesus.* SNTSMS 8. Cambridge: Cambridge University, 1969. *Biblical Genealogies.*

Jones, Douglas. "Ἀνάμνησις in the LXX and the Interpretation of 1 Cor XI.25." *JTS* n.s. 6 (1955) 183-91. "Ἀνάμνησις."

———. "The Background and Character of the Lukan Psalms." *JTS* n.s. 19 (1968) 19-50. "Lukan Psalms."

Jones-Haldeman, Madalyn. "Implications from Selected Literary Devices for a New Testament Theology of Grace and Forgiveness." *JPC* 11 (1992) 136-46. "Grace and Forgiveness."

Josephus. *Josephus, with an English Translation.* 9 vols. LCL. Cambridge, MA: Harvard University, 1926-65.

Judge, E. A. *The Social Pattern of the Christian Groups in the First Century: Some Prolegomena to the Study of New Testament Ideas of Social Obligation.* London: Tyndale, 1960. *Social Pattern.*

Juel, Donald. *Messianic Exegesis: Christological Interpretation of the Old Testament in Early Christianity.* Philadelphia: Fortress, 1988. *Christological Exegesis.*

Just Jr., Arthur A. *The Ongoing Feast: Table Fellowship and Eschatology at Emmaus.* Pueblo. Collegeville, MN: Liturgical, 1993. *Ongoing Feast.*

Kariamadam, Paul. "The Composition and Meaning of the Lucan Travel Narrative (Lk. 9,51–19,46)." *Bible Bhashyam* 13 (1987) 179-98. "Composition and Meaning."

———. "Discipleship in the Lukan Journey Narrative." *Jeevadhara* 56 (1980) 111-30. "Discipleship."

———. "India and Luke's Theology of the Way." *Bible Bhashyam* 11 (1985) 47-60. "Luke's Theology."

———. *The Zacchaeus Story (Lk. 19,1-10): A Redaction-Critical Investigation.* PIP 42. Kerala, India: Assisi, 1985. *Zacchaeus Story.*

Karris, Robert J. *Luke: Artist and Theologian. Luke's Passion Account as Literature.* TI. New York: Paulist, 1985. *Luke: Artist and Theologian.*

———. "Luke 23:47 and the Lucan View of Jesus' Death." *JBL* 105 (1986) 65-74. "Luke 23:47."

————. "Luke 24:13-35." *Int* 41 (1987) 57-61.

Kaut, Thomas. *Befreier und befreites Volk: Traditions- und redaktions-geschichtliche Untersuchung zu Magnifikat und Benediktus im Kontext der vorlukanishen Kindheitsgeschichte.* AMTBBB 77. Frankfurt am Main: Anton Hain, 1990. *Befreier und befreites Volk.*

Kavunkal, Jacob. "Jubilee the Framework of Evangelization." *Vidyajyoti* 52 (1988) 181-90. "Jubilee."

Kazmierski, Carl R. "Evangelist and Leper: A Socio-Cultural Study of Mark 1.40-45." *NTS* 38 (1992) 37-50. "Evangelist and Leper."

Keck, Leander E. "The Spirit and the Dove." *NTS* 17 (1970-71) 41-67. "Spirit."

Kee, Howard Clark. *Medicine, Miracle and Magic in New Testament Times.* SNTSMS 55. Cambridge: Cambridge University, 1986. *Medicine, Miracle and Magic.*

————. *Miracle in the Early Christian World: A Study in Sociohistorical Method.* New Haven: Yale University, 1983. *Miracle.*

————. *Who Are the People of God? Early Christian Models of Community.* New Haven/London: Yale University, 1995. *People of God.*

Kennedy, George. *The Art of Rhetoric in the Roman World (300 B.C.–A.D. 300).* Princeton, NJ: Princeton University, 1972. *Art of Rhetoric.*

————. *New Testament Interpretation through Rhetorical Criticism.* Chapel Hill: University of North Carolina, 1984. *New Testament Interpretation.*

Kenney, E. J. "Books and Readers in the Roman World." In *CHCL,* 2:3-32. "Books and Readers."

Kenyon, Frederick G. *Books and Readers in Ancient Greece and Rome.* Oxford: Clarendon, 1932. *Books and Readers.*

Kerr, A. J. " 'No room in the kataluma'." *ExpT* 103 (1991-92) 15-16. "No room."

Kilgallen, John J. "John the Baptist, the Sinful Woman, and the Pharisee." *JBL* 104 (1985) 675-79. "John the Baptist."

————. "Luke 2,41-50: Foreshadowing of Jesus, Teacher." *Bib* 66 (1985) 553-59. "Luke 2,41-50."

————. "Provocation in Luke 4, 23-24." *Bib* 70 (1989) 511-16. "Provocation."

————. "The Return of the Unclean Spirit (Luke 11,24-26)." *Bib* 74 (1993) 45-59. "Return of the Unclean Spirit."

————. "What Kind of Servants Are We? (Luke 17,10)." *Bib* 63 (1982) 549-51. "Servants."

Kilpatrick, G. D. *The Eucharist in Bible and Liturgy.* Cambridge: Cambridge University, 1983. *Eucharist.*

————. "ΛΑΟΙ at Luke II.31 and Acts IV.25, 27." *JTS* n.s. 16 (1965) 127. "ΛΑΟΙ."

————. "Luke 2,4-5 and Leviticus 25,10." *ZNW* 80 (1989) 264-65. "Luke 2,4-5."

Kilpatrick, Ross S. "The Greek Syntax of Luke 2.14." *NTS* 34 (1988) 472-75. "Luke 2.14."

Kimball, Charles A. "Jesus' Exposition of Scripture in Luke 20:9-19: An Inquiry in Light of Jewish Hermeneutics." *BBR* 3 (1993) 77-92. "Luke 20:9-19."

————. *Jesus' Exposition of the Old Testament in Luke's Gospel.* JSNTSup 94. Sheffield: Sheffield Academic, 1994. *Jesus' Exposition.*

Kingsbury, Jack Dean. *Conflict in Luke: Jesus, Authorities, Disciples.* Minneapolis: Fortress, 1991. *Conflict in Luke.*

Kinman, Brent Rogers. " 'The stones will cry out' (Luke 19,40) — Joy or Judgment?" *Bib* 75 (1994) 232-35. "Joy or Judgment."

————. "Lucan Eschatology and the Missing Fig Tree." *JBL* 113 (1994) 669-78. "Lucan Eschatology."

Kirchschläger, Walter. *Jesu exorzistisches Wirken aus der Sicht des Lukas: Ein Beitrag zur lukanischen Redaktion.* ÖBS 3. Klosterneuburg: Österreichisches Katholisches, 1981. *Jesu exorzistisches Wirken.*

Kittel, Gerhard. "δόξα in the LXX and Hellenistic Apocrypha." In *TDNT,* 2:242-45.

Klassen, William. " 'A Child of Peace' (Luke 10.6) in First Century Context." *NTS* 27 (1980-81) 488-506. "Child of Peace."

Klein, Günter. "Lukas 1,1-4 als theologisches Programm." In *Zeit und Geschichte: Dankesgabe an Rudolf Bultmann zum 80. Geburtstag,* edited by Erich Dinkler, 193-216. Tübingen: J. C. B. Mohr (Paul Siebeck), 1964. "Lukas 1,1-4."

Kleinman, Arthur. *Patients and Healers in the Context of Culture: An Exploration of the Borderland between Anthropology, Medicine, and Psychiatry.* CSHSMC 3. Berkeley: University of California, 1980. *Patients and Healers.*

Klijn, A. F. J. "2 (Syriac Apocalypse of) Baruch." In *OTP,* 1:615-52.

Klinghardt, Matthias. *Gesetz und Volk Gottes: Das lukanische Verständnis des Gesetzes nach Herkunft, Funktion und seinem Ort in der Geschichte des Urchristentums.* WUNT 2:32. Tübingen: J. C. B. Mohr (Paul Siebeck), 1988. *Gesetz.*

Kloppenborg, John S. "The Dishonoured Master (Luke 16:1-8a)." *Bib* 70 (1989) 474-95. "Dishonoured Master."

————. *"Exitus clari viri:* The Death of Jesus in Luke." *TJT* 8 (1993) 106-20. "Death of Jesus."

Knipe, David M. "The Temple in Image and Reality." In *Temple in Society,* edited by Michael V. Fox, 105-38. Winona Lake: Eisenbrauns, 1988. "Temple."

Kodell, Jerome. "Luke and the Children: The Beginning and End of the Great Interpolation (Luke 9:46-56; 18:9-23)." *CBQ* 49 (1987) 415-30. "Luke and the Children."

———. "Luke's Gospel in a Nutshell (Lk 4:16-30)." *BTB* 13 (1983) 16-18. "Nutshell."

Koenig, John. *New Testament Hospitality: Partnership with Strangers as Promise and Mission.* OBT. Philadelphia: Fortress, 1985. *New Testament Hospitality.*

Koester, Helmut. *Ancient Christian Gospels: Their History and Development.* Philadelphia: Trinity; London: SCM, 1990. *Ancient Christian Gospels.*

———. "συνέχω." In *TDNT,* 7:877-85.

Koet, B. J. *Five Studies on Interpretation of Scripture in Luke-Acts.* SNTA 14. Leuven: Leuven University, 1989. *Five Studies.*

Korn, Manfred. *Die Geschichte Jesu in veränderter Zeit: Studien zur bleibenden Bedeutung Jesu im lukanischen Doppelwerk.* WUNT 2:51. Tübingen: J. C. B. Mohr, 1993. *Geschichte Jesu.*

Krämer, Helmut. "μυστήριον." In *EDNT,* 2:446-49.

Krieger, Murray. *A Window to Criticism.* Princeton, NJ: Princeton University, 1964.

Kruse, Heinz. "Das Reich Satans." *Bib* 58 (1977) 29-61. "Reich Satans."

Kurz, William S. "Luke 22:14-38 and Greco-Roman and Biblical Farewell Addresses." *JBL* 104 (1985) 251-68. "Luke 22:14-38."

———. *Reading Luke-Acts: Dynamics of Biblical Narrative.* Louisville, KY: Westminster/John Knox, 1993. *Reading Luke-Acts.*

Kürzinger, J. "Lk 1,3: . . . ἀκριβῶς καθεξῆς σοι γράψαι." *BZ* 18 (1974) 249-55. "Lk 1,3."

Kvalbein, Hans. "Jesus and the Poor: Two Texts and a Tentative Conclusion." *Themelios* 12 (1987) 80-87. "Jesus and the Poor."

LaHurd, Carol. "Rediscovering the Lost Women in Luke 15." *BTB* 24 (1994) 66-76. "Rediscovering the Lost Women."

Lake, Kirsopp, and Henry J. Cadbury. *The Acts of the Apostles,* edited by F. J. Foakes Jackson and Kirsopp Lake, Vol. 4: *English Translation and Commentary.* BC 1. London: Macmillan, 1933; reprint ed., Grand Rapids: Baker, 1933. *English Translation.*

Lambrecht, Jan. *The Sermon on the Mount: Proclamation and Exhortation.* GNS 14. Wilmington: Michael Glazier, 1985. *Sermon on the Mount.*

Lampe, G. W. H. "The Two Swords (Luke 22:35-38)." In *Jesus and the Politics of His Day,* edited by Ernst Bammel and C. F. D. Moule, 335-51. Cambridge: Cambridge University, 1984. "Two Swords."

Landry, David T. "Narrative Logic in the Annunciation to Mary (Luke 1:26-38)." *JBL* 114 (1995) 65-79. "Narrative Logic."

Lang, Bernhard. "Grußverbot oder Besuchsverbot? Eine sozialgeschichtliche

Deutung von Lukas 10,4b." *BZ* 26 (1982) 75-79. "Grußverbot oder Besuchsverbot?"

Larkin, William J. "The Old Testament Background of Luke xxii.42-44." *NTS* 25 (1978-79) 250-54. "Old Testament Background."

Lauer, Simon. "*Abhinu Malkenu:* Our Father, Our King!" In *The Lord's Prayer and Jewish Liturgy,* edited by Jakob J. Petuchowski and Michael Brocke, 73-80. New York: Seabury, 1978. *"Abhinu Malkenu."*

Laurentin, René. *Struktur und Theologie der lukanischen Kindheitsgeschichte.* Stuttgart: Katholisches Bibelwerk, 1967. *Struktur und Theologie.*

――――. *The Truth of Christmas: Beyond the Myths. The Gospels of the Infancy of Christ.* SS. Petersham, MA: St. Bede's, 1986. *Truth of Christmas.*

Lebourlier, Jean. "*Entos hymōn:* Le sens 'au milieu de vous' est-il possible?" *Bib* 73 (1992) 259-62. *"Entos hymōn."*

Legrand, L. "The Angel Gabriel and Politics: Messianism and Christology." *ITS* 26 (1989) 1-21. "Gabriel and Politics."

――――. "The Christmas Story in Lk 2:1-7." *ITS* 19 (1982) 289-317. "Christmas."

――――. "Christ the Fellow Traveller: The Emmaus Story in Lk 24:13-35." *ITS* 19 (1982) 33-44. "Christ the Fellow Traveller."

Leivestad, Ragnar. "ἰάομαι κτλ." In *EDNT,* 2:169-70.

――――. "μιμνῄσκομαι." In *EDNT,* 2:430-31.

Lenski, Gerhard E. *Power and Privilege: A Theory of Social Stratification.* 2d ed. Chapel Hill/London: University of North Carolina, 1984. *Power and Privilege.*

Leroy, Herbert. "ἀφίημι, ἄφεσις." In *EDNT,* 1:181-83.

Levenson, Jon D. *The Death and Resurrection of the Beloved Son: The Transformation in Judaism and Christianity.* New Haven: Yale University, 1993. *Beloved Son.*

Levinson, Stephen C. *Pragmatics.* CTL. Cambridge: Cambridge University, 1983.

Lewis, Theodore J. "Beelzebul." In *ABD,* 1:638-40.

Lindars, Barnabas. *Jesus Son of Man: A Fresh Examination of the Son of Man Sayings in the Gospels in the Light of Recent Research.* London: SPCK, 1983. *Jesus Son of Man.*

Link, Hans-Georg. "εὐλογία." In *NIDNTT,* 1:206-15.

Linnemann, Eta. *Parables of Jesus: Introduction and Exposition.* London: SPCK, 1966. *Parables.*

Linton, Olof. "The Parable of the Children's Game: Baptist and Son of Man (Matt xi,16-19 = Luke vii,31-35). A Synoptic Text-Critical, Structural, and Exegetical Investigation." *NTS* 22 (1975-76) 159-79. "Parable of the Children's Game."

Loewe, Raphael. *The Position of Women in Judaism.* London: S.P.C.K., 1966. *Women in Judaism.*

Loewe, William P. "Towards an Interpretation of Lk 19:1-10." *CBQ* 36 (1974) 321-31. "Lk 19:1-10."

Lohfink, Gerhard. *Die Himmelfahrt Jesu: Untersuchungen zu den Himmelfahrts- und Erhöhungstexten bei Lukas.* SANT 26. München: Kösel, 1971. *Himmelfahrt Jesu.*

Lohfink, Norbert F. *Option for the Poor: The Basic Principle of Liberation Theology in the Light of the Bible.* Berkeley, CA: Bibal, 1987. *Option for the Poor.*

Lohse, Eduard. *Die Geschichte des Leidens und Sterbens Jesu Christi.* Gütersloh: Gerd Mohn, 1979. *Geschichte des Leidens und Sterbens.*

———. "Lukas als Theologe der Heilsgeschichte." In *Die Einheit des Neuen Testaments,* 145-64. Göttingen: Vandenhoeck & Ruprecht, 1973. "Lukas als Theologe."

———. "χείρ κτλ." In *TDNT,* 9:424-37.

Lucian. *Lucian, with an English Translation.* LCL. Cambridge, MA: Harvard University, 1959.

Lüdemann, Gerd. "Acts of the Apostles as a Historical Source." In *The Social World of Formative Christianity and Judaism: Essays in Tribute to Howard Clark Kee,* edited by Jacob Neusner et al., 109-25. Philadelphia: Fortress, 1988. "Acts of the Apostles."

———. *Early Christianity according to the Traditions in Acts: A Commentary.* Philadelphia: Fortress, 1989. *Early Christianity.*

Luke, K. "Luke 2:14 in Some Ancient Versions." *ITS* 24 (1987) 185-201. "Luke 2:14."

Lull, David J. "The Servant-Benefactor as a Model of Greatness (Luke 22:24-30)." *NovT* 28 (1986) 289-305. "Servant-Benefactor."

Luz, Ulrich. "βασιλεία." In *EDNT,* 1:201-5.

———. *Matthew 1–7: A Commentary.* Minneapolis: Augsburg, 1989. *Matthew.*

Lyonnet, Père Stanislas. "Χαῖρε, κεχαριτωμένη." *Bib* 20 (1939) 131-41.

McArthur, Harvey K., and Robert M. Johnston. *They Also Taught in Parables: Rabbinic Parables from the First Centuries of the Christian Era.* Grand Rapids: Zondervan, 1990. *Parables.*

McCane, Byron R. " 'Let the Dead Bury Their Own Dead': Secondary Burial and Matt 8:21-22." *HTR* 83 (1990) 31-43. "Secondary Burial."

McClendon Jr., James W. *Systematic Theology.* Vol. 1: *Ethics.* Nashville: Abingdon, 1986. *Ethics.*

McHugh, John. *The Mother of Jesus in the New Testament.* London: Darton, Longman & Todd, 1975. *Mother of Jesus.*

McKay, Heather A. *Sabbath and Synagogue: The Question of Sabbath Wor-*

ship in Ancient Judaism. RGRW 122. Leiden: Brill, 1994. *Sabbath and Synagogue.*

McKelvey, R. J. *The New Temple: The Church in the New Testament.* London: Oxford University, 1968. *New Temple.*

McKnight, Scot. *A Light among the Nations: Jewish Missionary Activity in the Second Temple Period.* Minneapolis: Fortress, 1991. *Light among the Nations.*

McVann, Mark. "Rituals of Status Transformation in Luke-Acts: The Case of Jesus the Prophet." In *The Social World of Luke-Acts: Models for Interpretation,* edited by Jerome H. Neyrey, 333-60. Peabody, MA: Hendrickson, 1991. "Status Transformation."

Mack, Burton L., and Vernon K. Robbins. *Patterns of Persuasion in the Gospels.* FF:LF. Sonoma, CA: Polebridge, 1989. *Patterns of Persuasion.*

Maddox, Robert. *The Purpose of Luke-Acts.* SNTW. Edinburgh: T. & T. Clark, 1982. *Purpose.*

Magaß, Walter. "Semiotik einer Tischordnung (Lk 14,7-14)." *LB* 25-26 (1973) 2-8. "Semiotik einer Tischordnung."

Maile, John F. "The Ascension in Luke-Acts." *TynB* 37 (1986) 29-59. "Ascension."

Malina, Bruce J. *Christian Origins and Cultural Anthropology: Practical Models for Biblical Interpretation.* Atlanta: John Knox, 1986. *Christian Origins.*

————. " 'Let Him Deny Himself' (Mark 8:34 & Par): A Social Psychological Model of Self-Denial." *BTB* 24 (1994) 106-19. "Let Him Deny Himself."

Malina, Bruce J., and Jerome H. Neyrey. "First-Century Personality: Dyadic, Not Individualistic." In *The Social World of Luke-Acts: Models for Interpretation,* edited by Jerome H. Neyrey, 67-96. Peabody, MA: Hendrickson, 1991. "First-Century Personality."

Malina, Bruce J., and Jerome H. Neyrey. "Honor and Shame in Luke-Acts: Pivotal Values of the Mediterranean World." In *The Social World of Luke-Acts: Models for Interpretation,* edited by Jerome H. Neyrey, 25-65. Peabody, MA: Hendrickson, 1991. "Honor and Shame."

Malina, Bruce J., and Richard L. Rohrbaugh. *Social-Science Commentary on the Synoptic Gospels.* Minneapolis: Fortress, 1992. *Commentary.*

Maloney, Linda M. *"All That God Had Done with Them": The Narration of the Works of God in the Early Christian Community as Described in the Acts of the Apostles.* AUS 7: TR 91. New York: Peter Lang, 1991. *Narration of the Works of God.*

Mánek, Jindt'ich. "Fishers of Men." *NovT* 2 (1957) 138-41.

Manson, T. W. *The Sayings of Jesus as Recorded in the Gospels according to St. Matthew and St. Luke Arranged with Introduction and Commentary.* London: SCM, 1949. *Sayings.*

Marcus, Joel. "The Old Testament and the Death of Jesus: The Role of Scripture in the Gospel Passion Narratives." In *The Death of Jesus in Early Christianity,* by John T. Carroll and Joel B. Green, 205-33. Peabody, MA: Hendrickson, 1995. "Role of Scripture."

Marshall, I. Howard. "The Interpretation of the Magnificat: Luke 1:46-55." In *Der Treue Gottes Trauen: Beiträge zum Werk des Lukas. Für Gerhard Schneider,* edited by Claus Bussmann and Walter Radl, 181-96. Freiburg: Herder, 1991. "Magnificat."

————. *Last Supper and Lord's Supper.* Grand Rapids: Wm. B. Eerdmans, 1980. *Last Supper.*

————. "Luke and His 'Gospel'." In *Das Evangelium und die Evangelien: Vorträge vom Tübinger Symposium 1982,* edited by Peter Stuhlmacher, 298-308. WUNT 28. Tübingen: J. C. B. Mohr (Paul Siebeck), 1983.

————. *Luke: Historian and Theologian.* Enlarged ed. CEP. Grand Rapids: Zondervan, 1989.

————. "The Meaning of the Verb 'to Baptize'." *EvQ* 45 (1973) 130-40. "Baptize."

————. "Tradition and Theology in Luke (Luke 8:5-15)." *TynB* 20 (1969) 56-75. "Luke 8:5-15."

Martin, Dale B. *The Corinthian Body.* New Haven: Yale University, 1995. *Corinthian Body.*

————. *Slavery as Salvation: The Metaphor of Slavery in Pauline Christianity.* New Haven, CN: Yale University, 1990. *Slavery as Salvation.*

Martin, Josef. *Symposion: Die Geschichte einer literarischen Form.* 2 vols. SGKA 17. Paderborn: F. Schöningh, 1931; reprint ed., New York: Johnson, 1968. *Symposion.*

Martin, Ralph P. "Salvation and Discipleship in Luke's Gospel." *Int* 30 (1976) 366-80. "Salvation and Discipleship."

Martin, Wallace. *Recent Theories of Narrative.* Ithaca, NY: Cornell University, 1986. *Recent Theories.*

Martin-Schard, Robert. "Isaac." In *ABD,* 3:462-70.

Martínez, Florentino García. *The Dead Sea Scrolls Translated: The Qumran Texts in English.* Leiden: Brill, 1994. *Dead Sea Scrolls.*

Mastronarde, Donald J. *Introduction to Attic Greek.* Berkeley: University of California, 1993. *Attic Greek.*

Matera, Frank J. "The Death of Jesus according to Luke: A Question of Sources." *CBQ* 47 (1985) 469-85. "Death of Jesus."

————. "Jesus' Journey to Jerusalem (Luke 9.51–19.46): A Conflict with Israel." *JSNT* 51 (1993) 57-77. "Jesus' Journey to Jerusalem."

————. "Luke 23:1-25: Jesus before Pilate, Herod, and Israel." In *L'Évangile de Luc — The Gospel of Luke,* edited by F. Neirynck, 535-51. Rev. ed. BETL 32. Leuven: Leuven University, 1989. "Jesus before Pilate."

————. "Luke 22,66-71: Jesus before the ΠΡΕΣΒΥΤΕΡΙΟΝ." In *L'Évangile de Luc — The Gospel of Luke,* edited by F. Neirynck, 517-33. Rev. ed. BETL 32. Leuven: Leuven University, 1989. "Jesus before the ΠΡΕΣ-ΒΥΤΕΡΙΟΝ."

————. *Passion Narratives and Gospel Theologies: Interpreting the Synoptics through Their Passion Stories.* TI. New York/Mahwah: Paulist, 1986. *Passion Narratives.*

————. "Responsibility for the Death of Jesus according to the Acts of the Apostles." *JSNT* 39 (1990) 77-93. "Death of Jesus."

Mattill Jr., A. J. *Luke and the Last Things: A Perspective for Understanding Lukan Thought.* Dillsboro, NC: Western North Carolina, 1979. *Last Things.*

Mauser, Ulrich W. *Christ in the Wilderness: The Wilderness Theme in the Second Gospel and Its Basis in the Biblical Tradition.* SBT 39. London: SCM, 1963. *Wilderness.*

Mazamisa, Llewellyn Welile. *Beatific Comradeship: An Exegetical-Hermeneutical Study on Lk 10:25-37.* Kampen: J. H. Kok, 1987. *Beatific Comradeship.*

Mead, A. H. "Old and New Wine (St. Luke 5:39)." *ExpT* 99 (1987-88) 234-35. "Old Wine."

Meeks, Wayne A. *The First Urban Christians: The Social World of the Apostle Paul.* New Haven: Yale University, 1983. *First Urban Christians.*

————. *The Origins of Christian Morality: The First Two Centuries.* New Haven: Yale University, 1993. *Origins of Christian Morality.*

Meier, John P. *A Marginal Jew: Rethinking the Historical Jesus.* Vol. 1: *The Roots of the Problem and the Person.* ABRL. New York: Doubleday, 1991. *Marginal Jew.*

Menken, M. J. J. "The Position of σπλαγχνίζεσθαι and σπλάγχνα in the Gospel of Luke." *NovT* 30 (1988) 107-14. "Position of σπλαγχνίζε-σθαι."

Menzies, Robert P. *The Development of Early Christian Pneumatology: With Special Reference to Luke-Acts.* JSNTSup 54. Sheffield: JSOT, 1991. *Early Christian Pneumatology.*

————. *Empowered for Witness: The Spirit in Luke-Acts.* JPTSup 6. Sheffield: Sheffield Academic, 1994. *Empowered for Witness.*

Merklein, Helmut. "πλούσιος κτλ." In *EDNT,* 3:114-17.

Merrill, Eugene H. "The Sign of Jonah." *JETS* 23 (1980) 23-30. "Sign of Jonah."

Metzger, Bruce M. *Manuscripts of the Greek Bible.* New York: Oxford University, 1981. *Manuscripts.*

————. *A Textual Commentary on the Greek New Testament.* London: UBS, 1971. *Textual Commentary.*

————. "Seventy or Seventy-two Disciples?" *NTS* 5 (1958-59) 299-306.

Meyer, Ben F. " 'But Mary Kept All These Things . . .' (Lk 2,19.21)." *CBQ* 26 (1964) 31-49. "Mary."

Meynet, Roland. " 'Celui à qui est remis peu, aime un peu' (Lc 7,36-50)." *Gregorianum* 75 (1994) 267-80. "Lc 7,36-50."

Michaelis, Wilhelm. "εἴσοδος, ἔξοδος, διέξοδος." In *TDNT,* 5:103-9.

Michel, Otto. "πατήρ." In *EDNT,* 3:53-57.

————. "τελώνης." In *TDNT,* 8:88-105.

Midrash Rabbah. 10 vols. Translated and edited by H. Freedman and Maurice Simon. Vol. 1: *Genesis I.* 2d ed. London: Soncino, 1951. *Midrash Rabbah.*

Miller, Marvin Henry. "The Character of Miracles in Luke-Acts." Th.D. diss., Graduate Theological Union, 1971. "Character of Miracles."

Miller, Merrill P. "The Function of Isa 61:1-2 in 11Q Melchizedek." *JBL* 88 (1969) 467-69. "Function of Isa 61:1-2."

Miller, Robert J. "Elijah, John, and Jesus in the Gospel of Luke." *NTS* 34 (1988) 611-22. "Elijah, John, and Jesus."

Minear, Paul S. "Luke's Use of the Birth Stories." In *Studies in Luke-Acts,* edited by Leander E. Keck and J. Louis Martyn, 111-30. Philadelphia: Fortress, 1966. "Birth Stories."

————. "A Note on Luke 22.36." *NovT* 7 (1964) 128-34. "Luke 22.36."

Moehring, Horst R. "The Census in Luke as an Apologetic Device." In *Studies in New Testament and Early Christian Literature: Essays in Honor of Allen P. Wikgren,* edited by David E. Aune, 144-60. NovTSup 33. Leiden: Brill, 1972. "Census in Luke."

Moessner, David P. *Lord of the Banquet: The Literary and Theological Significance of the Lukan Travel Narrative.* Minneapolis: Fortress, 1989. *Lord of the Banquet.*

————. "Luke 9:1-50: Luke's Preview of the Journey of the Prophet Like Moses of Deuteronomy." *JBL* 102 (1983) 575-605. "Luke 9:1-50."

Moo, Douglas J. "Law." In *DJG,* 450-61.

————. *The Old Testament in the Gospel Passion Narratives.* Sheffield: Almond, 1983. *Passion Narratives.*

Moore, Stephen D. *Literary Criticism and the Gospels: The Theoretical Challenge.* New Haven: Yale University, 1989. *Literary Criticism.*

Morel, Jean-Paul. "The Craftsman." In *The Romans,* edited by Andrea Giardina, 214-44. Chicago: University of Chicago, 1993. "Craftsman."

Morris, Royce L. B. "Why ΑΥΓΟΥΣΤΟΣ? A Note to Luke 2.1." *NTS* 38 (1992) 142-44. "Why ΑΥΓΟΥΣΤΟΣ?"

Morris, William G. *Joy in the New Testament.* Exeter: Paternoster, 1984. *Joy in the NT.*

Morton, A. Q., and G. H. C. Macgregor. *The Structure of Luke and Acts.* London: Hodder and Stoughton, 1964. *Structure.*

Moule, C. F. D. "The Ascension — Acts I.9." *ExpT* 68 (1956-57) 205-9. "Ascension."

————. *An Idiom Book of New Testament Greek.* 2d ed. Cambridge: Cambridge University, 1959. *Idiom Book.*

————. "An Unsolved Problem in the Temptation Clause in the Lord's Prayer." *RefTRev* 33 (1974) 65-75. "Unsolved Problem."

Moulton, James Hope. "New Testament Greek in the Light of Modern Discovery." In *The Language of the New Testament: Classic Essays,* edited by Stanley E. Porter, 60-97. JSNTSup 60. Sheffield: Sheffield Academic, 1991. "New Testament Greek."

Mowery, Robert L. "God the Father in Luke-Acts." In *New Views on Luke and Acts,* edited by Earl Richard, 124-32. Collegeville, MN: Liturgical, 1990. "God the Father."

Moxnes, Halvor. *The Economy of the Kingdom: Social Conflict and Economic Relations in Luke's Gospel.* OBT. Philadelphia: Fortress, 1988. *Economy of the Kingdom.*

————. "Meals and the New Community in Luke." *SEÅ* 51 (1986) 158-67. "Meals."

————. "Patron-Client Relations and the New Community in Luke-Acts." In *The Social World of Luke-Acts: Models for Interpretation,* edited by Jerome H. Neyrey, 241-68. Peabody, MA: Hendrickson, 1991. "Patron-Client Relations."

————. "Social Relations and Economic Interaction in Luke's Gospel." In *Luke-Acts: Scandinavian Perspectives,* edited by Petri Luomanen, 58-75. PFES 54. Göttingen: Vandenhoeck & Ruprecht, 1991. "Social Relations."

Muddiman, John. "Fast, Fasting." In *ABD,* 2:773-76.

Müller, Paul-Gerd. "ἀποκαθίστημι, ἀποκαθιστάνω." In *EDNT,* 1:129-30.

————. "βλέπω." In *EDNT,* 1:221-22.

Mullins, Terence Y. "New Testament Commission Forms, Especially in Luke-Acts." *JBL* 95 (1976) 603-14. "Commission Forms."

Murray, Dom Gregory. "The Sign of Jonah." *DRev* 107 (1989) 224-25. "Sign of Jonah."

Mussies, G. "The Sense of συλλογίζεσθαι at Luke xx 5." In *Miscellanea Neotestamentica,* edited by T. Baarda, A. F. J. Klijn, and W. C. van Unnik, 59-76. NovTSup 48. Leiden: Brill, 1978. "Sense of συλλογίζεσθαι."

Mussies, Gerard. "Variation in the Book of Acts." *FilNT* 8 (1991) 165-82. "Variation."

Mußner Franz. "Die Gemeinde des Lukasprologs." In *The New Testament*

Age: Essays in Honor of Bo Reicke, 2 vols., edited by William C. Weinrich, 2:373-92. Macon, GA: Mercer University, 1984. "Gemeinde."

―――. "Die Idee der Apokatastasis in der Apostelgeschichte." In *Lex Tua Veritas: Festschrift für Hubert Junker zur Vollendung des siebigsten Lebensjahres am 8. August 1961,* edited by Heinrich Groß and Franz Mußner, 293-306. Trier: Paulinus, 1961. "Idee der Apokatastasis."

―――. "Καθεξῆς im Lukasprolog." In *Jesus und Paulus: Festschrift für Werner George Kümmel zum 70. Geburtstag,* edited by E. Earle Ellis and Erich Gräßer, 253-55. Göttingen: Vandenhoeck & Ruprecht, 1975. "Καθεξῆς."

Navone, John. *Themes of St. Luke.* Rome: Gregorian University, n.d. *Themes.*

Neale, David A. *None but the Sinners: Religious Categories in the Gospel of Luke.* JSNTSup 58. Sheffield: JSOT, 1991. *None but the Sinners.*

Nebe, Gottfried. "Das ἔσται in Lk 11,36 — Ein neuer Deutungsvorschlag." *ZNW* 108-14. "ἔσται in Lk 11,36."

Neirynck, Frans. "John and the Synoptics: The Empty Tomb Stories." *NTS* 30 (1984) 161-87. "Empty Tomb Stories."

―――. "Once More Luke 24,12." *ETL* 70 (1994) 319-40. "Luke 24,12."

Nelson, Peter K. "The Flow of Thought in Luke 22:24-27." *JSNT* 43 (1991) 113-23. "Flow of Thought."

―――. *Leadership and Discipleship: A Study of Luke 22:24-30.* SBLDS 138. Atlanta: Scholars, 1994. *Leadership.*

―――. "Luke 22:29-30 and the Time Frame for Dining and Ruling." *TynB* 44 (1993) 351-61. "Luke 22:29-30."

―――. "The Unitary Character of Luke 22.24-30." *NTS* 40 (1994) 609-19. "Unitary Character."

Neusner, Jacob. "Two Pictures of the Pharisees: Philosophical Circle or Eating Club." *ATR* 64 (1982) 525-38. "Two Pictures."

Neyrey, Jerome H. "The Absence of Jesus' Emotions — The Lucan Redaction of Lk 22,39-46." *Bib* 61 (1980) 153-71. "Absence of Jesus' Emotions."

―――. "Ceremonies in Luke-Acts: The Case of Meals and Table Fellowship." In *The Social World of Luke-Acts: Models for Interpretation,* edited by Jerome H. Neyrey, 361-87. Peabody, MA: Hendrickson, 1991. "Ceremonies."

―――. *The Passion according to Luke: A Redaction Study of Luke's Soteriology.* TI. New York/Mahwah: Paulist, 1985. *Passion according to Luke.*

Neyrey, Jerome H., ed. *The Social World of Luke-Acts: Models for Interpretation.* Peabody, MA: Hendrickson, 1991. *Social World.*

Nickelsburg, George W. E. "Riches, the Rich, and God's Judgment in 1 Enoch

92–105 and the Gospel according to Luke." *NTS* 25 (1979) 324-44. "Riches, the Rich, and God's Judgment."

Nicol, W. "Tradition and Redaction in Luke 21." *Neot* 7 (1973) 61-71. "Luke 21."

Noël, Timothy. "The Parable of the Wedding Guest: A Narrative-Critical Interpretation." *PRS* 16 (1989) 17-27. "Parable of the Wedding Guest."

Nolland, John. "Classical Rabbinic Parallels to 'Physician, Heal Yourself' (Luke iv 23)." *NovT* 21 (1979) 193-209. "Classical Parallels."

———. "Impressed Unbelievers as Witnesses to Christ (Luke 4:22a)." *JBL* 98 (1979) 219-29. "Impressed Unbelievers."

———. "Luke's Use of ΧΑΡΙΣ," *NTS* 32 (1986) 614-20. "ΧΑΡΙΣ."

———. "Words of Grace (Luke 4,22)." *Bib* 65 (1984) 44-60. "Words of Grace."

Noorda, S. J. " 'Cure Yourself, Doctor!' (Luke 4,23): Classical Parallels to an Alleged Saying of Jesus." In *Logia: Les Paroles de Jésus — The Sayings of Jesus. Mémorial Joseph Coppens,* edited by Joël Delobel, 459-67. BETL 59. Leuven: Leuven University, 1982. "Classical Parallels."

Oakman, Douglas E. "The Countryside in Luke-Acts." In *The Social World of Luke-Acts: Models for Interpretation,* edited by Jerome H. Neyrey, 151-79. Peabody, MA: Hendrickson, 1991. "Countryside."

———. "Ruler's Houses, Thieves, and Usurpers: The Beelzebub Pericope." *Forum* 4 (1988) 109-23. "Ruler's Houses."

———. "Was Jesus a Peasant? Implications for Reading the Samaritan Story (Luke 10:30-35)." *BTB* 22 (1992) 117-25. "Samaritan Story."

O'Brien, P. T. "Prayer in Luke-Acts." *TynB* 24 (1973) 111-27.

Oepke, Albrecht. "ἰάομαι κτλ." In *TDNT,* 3:194-215.

O'Fearghail, Fearghus. *The Introduction to Luke-Acts: A Study of the Role of Luke 1,1–4,44 in the Composition of Luke's Two-Volume Work.* AnBib 126. Rome: Pontifical Biblical Institute, 1992. *Introduction.*

O'Hanlon. John. "The Story of Zacchaeus and the Lukan Ethic." *JSNT* 12 (1981) 2-26. "Story of Zacchaeus."

Oliver, H. H. "The Lucan Birth Stories and the Purpose of Luke-Acts." *NTS* 10 (1963-64) 202-26. "Birth Stories."

Olsthoorn, M. F. *The Jewish Background and the Synoptic Setting of Mt 6,25-33 and Lk 12,22-31.* SBF 10. Jerusalem: Franciscan, 1975. *Jewish Background.*

Osborne, Grant. *The Resurrection Narratives: A Redactional Study.* Grand Rapids: Baker, 1984. *Resurrection Narratives.*

O'Toole, Robert F. *Interpreting the Resurrection: Examining the Major Problems in the Stories of Jesus' Resurrection.* New York/Mahwah: Paulist, 1988. *Interpreting the Resurrection.*

———. "The Kingdom of God in Luke-Acts." In *The Kingdom of God in*

20th-Century Interpretation, edited by Wendell Willis, 147-62. Peabody, MA: Hendrickson, 1987. "Kingdom of God."

———. "The Literary Form of Luke 19:1-10." *JBL* 110 (1991) 107-16. "Literary Form."

———. "Luke's Message in Luke 9:1-50." *CBQ* 49 (1987) 74-89. "Luke's Message."

———. "Some Exegetical Reflections on Luke 13,10-17." *Bib* 73 (1992) 84-107. "Exegetical Reflections."

———. *The Unity of Luke's Theology: An Analysis of Luke-Acts.* GNS 9. Wilmington, DE: Michael Glazier, 1984. *Unity.*

Ott, Wilhelm. *Gebet und Heil: Die Bedeutung der Gebetsparänese in der lukanische Theologie.* SANT 12. München: Kösel, 1965. *Gebet und Heil.*

Owen-Ball, David T. "Rabbinic Rhetoric and the Tribute Passage (Mt. 22:15-22; Mk. 12:13-17; Lk. 20:20-26)." *NovT* 35 (1993) 1-14. "Rabbinic Rhetoric."

Page, Sydney H. T. *Powers of Evil: A Biblical Study of Satan and Demons.* Grand Rapids: Baker, 1995. *Powers of Evil.*

Palmer, Humphrey. "Just Married, Cannot Come." *NovT* 18 (1976) 241-57. "Just Married."

Pannenberg, Wolfhart. *Jesus — God and Man.* London: SCM, 1968. *Jesus.*

Parrott, Douglas M. "The Dishonest Steward (Luke 16.1-8a) and Luke's Special Parable Collection." *NTS* 37 (1991) 499-515. "Dishonest Steward."

Parsons, Mikeal C. "Christian Origins and Narrative Openings: The Sense of a Beginning in Acts 1–5." *RevExp* 87 (1990) 403-22. "Christian Origins."

———. *The Departure of Jesus in Luke-Acts: The Ascension Narratives in Context.* JSNTSup 21. Sheffield: JSOT, 1987. *Departure of Jesus.*

———. "Narrative Closure and Openness in the Plot of the Third Gospel: The Sense of an Ending in Luke 24:50-53." In *Society of Biblical Literature 1986 Seminar Papers,* edited by Kent Harold Richards, 201-23. Atlanta: Scholars, 1986. "Narrative Closure."

———. "The Unity of the Lukan Writings: Rethinking the *Opinio Communis.*" In *With Steadfast Purpose: Essays in Honor of Henry Jackson Flanders, Jr.,* edited by Raymond H. Keathley, 29-53. Waco, TX: Baylor University, 1990. "Unity of the Lukan Writings."

Parsons, Mikeal C., and Richard I. Pervo. *Rethinking the Unity of Luke and Acts.* Minneapolis: Fortress, 1993. *Rethinking the Unity.*

Paschal Jr., R. Wade. "Farewell Discourse." In *DJG,* 229-33.

Patsch, Hermann. *Abendmahl und historische Jesus.* CThM 1. Stuttgart: Calwer, 1972. *Abendmahl.*

Payne, Philip B. "The Order of Sowing and Ploughing in the Parable of the Sower." *NTS* 25 (1978-79) 123-29. "Order of Sowing and Ploughing."

Pervo, Richard I. "Must Luke and Acts Belong to the Same Genre?" In *Society of Biblical Literature 1989 Seminar Papers,* edited by David Lull, 309-16. Atlanta: Scholars, 1989. "Same Genre."

―――. *Profit with Delight: The Literary Genre of the Acts of the Apostles.* Philadelphia: Fortress, 1987. *Profit with Delight.*

Pesch, Rudolf. *Das Abendmahl und Jesus Todesverständnis.* QD 80. Freiburg: Herder, 1978. *Abendmahl.*

―――. *Die Apostelgeschichte.* 2 vols. EKKNT 5. Zürich: Benziger; Neukirchen-Vluyn: Neukirchener, 1986.

Petuchowski, Jakob J. "Jewish Prayer Texts of the Rabbinic Period." In *The Lord's Prayer and Jewish Liturgy,* edited by Jakob J. Petuchowski and Michael Brocke, 21-44. New York: Seabury, 1978. "Jewish Prayer Texts."

―――. "The Liturgy of the Synagogue." In *The Lord's Prayer and Jewish Liturgy,* edited by Jakob J. Petuchowski and Michael Brocke, 45-57. New York: Seabury, 1978. "Liturgy."

Petzer, J. H. "Luke 22:19b-20 and the Structure of the Passage." *NovT* 26 (1984) 249-52. "Luke 22:19b-20."

Philo, with an English Translation. 10 vols. LCL. Cambridge, MA: Harvard University, 1937-62.

Pilch, John J. "Sickness and Healing in Luke-Acts." In *The Social World of Luke-Acts: Models for Interpretation,* edited by Jerome H. Neyrey, 181-209. Peabody, MA: Hendrickson, 1991. "Sickness and Healing."

―――. "Understanding Biblical Healing: Selecting the Appropriate Model." *BTB* 18 (1988) 60-66. "Biblical Healing."

―――. "Understanding Healing in the Social World of Early Christianity." *BTB* 22 (1992) 26-33. "Understanding Healing."

Pilgrim, Walter E. *Good News to the Poor: Wealth and Poverty in Luke-Acts.* Minneapolis: Augsburg, 1981. *Good News.*

Piper, John. *'Love Your Enemies': Jesus' Love Command in the Synoptic Gospels and in the Early Christian Paraenesis. A History of the Tradition and Interpretation of Its Uses.* SNTSMS 38. Cambridge: Cambridge University, 1979. *Love Your Enemies.*

Pitt-Rivers, Julian. "The Law of Hospitality." In *The Fate of Shechem; or The Politics of Sex: Essays in the Anthropology of the Mediterranean,* 94-112. Cambridge: Cambridge University, 1977. "Law of Hospitality."

Pleins, J. David. "Poor, Poverty: Old Testament." In *ABD,* 5:402-14.

Plevnik, Joseph. " 'The Eleven and Those with Them' according to Luke." *CBQ* 40 (1978) 205-11. "The Eleven."

————. "The Eyewitnesses of the Risen Jesus in Luke 24." *CBQ* 49 (1987) 90-103. "Eyewitnesses."

Plymale, Stephen F. "The Lucan Lord's Prayer." *BibTod* 27 (1989) 176-82. "Lucan Lord's Prayer."

————. *The Prayer Texts of Luke-Acts.* AUS 7: TR 118. New York: Peter Lang, 1991. *Prayer Texts.*

Pobee, John S. *Persecution and Martyrdom in the Theology of Paul.* JSNTSup 6. Sheffield: JSOT, 1985.

Pokorný, Petr. "Strategies of Social Transformation in the Gospel of Luke." In *Gospel Origins and Christian Beginnings: In Honor of James M. Robinson,* edited by James E. Goehring et al., 106-18. ForFasc 1. Sonoma, CA: Polebridge, 1990. "Strategies of Social Transformation."

Popkes, Wiard. "ζύμη κτλ." In *EDNT,* 2:104-5.

Porton, Gary G. "Sadducees." In *ABD,* 5:892-95.

Powell, Mark Allan. "Narrative Criticism." In *Hearing the New Testament: Strategies for Interpretation,* edited by Joel B. Green, 239-55. Grand Rapids: Wm. B. Eerdmans, 1995.

————. *What Is Narrative Criticism?* GBS. Minneapolis: Fortress, 1990. *Narrative Criticism.*

Porter, Stanley E. "Mt 6:13 and Lk 11:4: 'Lead us not into temptation'." *ExpT* 101 (1989-90) 359-60. "Mt 6:13 and Lk 11:4."

Pred, Allan. *Making Histories and Constructing Human Geographies: The Local Transformation of Practice, Power Relations, and Consciousness.* Boulder: Westview, 1990. *Human Geographies.*

Price, S. R. F. *Rituals and Power: The Roman Imperial Cult in Asia Minor.* Cambridge: Cambridge University, 1984. *Rituals and Power.*

Priest, J. "A Note on the Messianic Banquet." In *The Messiah: Developments in Earliest Judaism and Christianity,* edited by James H. Charlesworth et al., 222-38. The First Princeton Symposium on Judaism and Christian Origins. Minneapolis: Fortress, 1992. "Messianic Banquet."

Prince, Gerald. *A Dictionary of Narratology.* Lincoln/London: University of Nebraska, 1987. *Narratology.*

————. *Narrative as Theme: Studies in French Fiction.* Lincoln/London: University of Nebraska, 1992. *Narrative as Theme.*

Procksch, O. and F. Büchsel. "λύω κτλ." In *TDNT,* 4:328-56.

Pusey, Kare. "Jewish Proselyte Baptism." *ExpT* 95 (1983-84) 141-45.

Quesnell, Quentin. "The Women at Luke's Supper." In *Political Issues in Luke-Acts,* edited by Richard J. Cassidy and Philip Scharper, 59-79. Maryknoll, NY: Orbis, 1983. "Women."

Radl, Walter. *Das Lukas-Evangelium.* ErFor 261. Darmstadt: Wissenschaftliche, 1988. *Lukas-Evangelium.*

Räisänen, Heikki. *Die Mutter Jesu im Neuen Testament.* STTAASF 158. Helsinki: Suomalainen Tiedeakatemia, 1969. *Mutter Jesu.*

Ramaroson, Leonard. "Le coeur du Troisième Évangile: Lc 15." *Bib* 60 (1979) 348-60. "Lc 15."

Ramsey, George W. "Plots, Gaps, Repetitions, and Ambiguity in Luke 15." *PRS* 17 (1990) 33-42. "Luke 15."

Rapske, Brian. *The Book of Acts and Paul in Roman Custody.* A1CS 3. Grand Rapids: Wm. B. Eerdmans; Carlisle: Paternoster, 1994. *Roman Custody.*

Ravens, D. A. S. "Luke 9.7-62 and the Prophetic Role of Jesus." *NTS* 36 (1990) 119-29. "Luke 9.7-62."

———. "The Setting of Luke's Account of the Anointing: Luke 7.2–8.3." *NTS* 34 (1988) 282-92. "Setting."

———. "Zacchaeus: The Final Part of a Lukan Triptych?" *JSNT* 41 (1991) 19-32. "Zacchaeus."

Rawson, Beryl. "Adult-Child Relationships in Roman Society." In *Marriage, Divorce, and Children in Ancient Rome,* edited by Beryl Rawson, 7-30. Oxford: Oxford University, 1991. "Adult-Child Relationships."

———, ed. *The Family in Ancient Rome: New Perspectives.* Ithaca, NY: Cornell University, 1986. *Family in Ancient Rome.*

———, ed. *Marriage, Divorce, and Children in Ancient Rome.* Oxford: Oxford University, 1991. *Marriage, Divorce, and Children.*

———. "The Roman Family." In *The Family in Ancient Rome: New Perspectives,* edited by Beryl Rawson, 1-57. Ithaca, NY: Cornell University, 1986. "Roman Family."

Reicke, Bo. "Jesus, Simeon, and Anna (Luke 2:21-40)." In *Saved by Hope: Essays in Honor of Richard C. Oudersluys,* edited by James I. Cook, 96-108. Grand Rapids: Wm. B. Eerdmans, 1978. "Jesus, Simeon, and Anna."

Reid, Barbara E. "Prayer and the Face of the Transfigured Jesus." In *The Lord's Prayer and Other Prayer Texts from the Greco-Roman Era,* edited by James H. Charlesworth, 39-53. Valley Forge, PA: Trinity, 1994. "Prayer."

———. *The Transfiguration: A Source- and Redaction-Critical Study of Luke 9:28-36.* CahRB 32. Paris: J. Gabalda, 1993. *Transfiguration.*

Rengstorf, Karl Heinrich. "ἑπτά κτλ." In *TDNT,* 2:627-35.

———. "Die στολαί der Schriftgelehrten. Eine Erläuterung zu Mark 12,38." In *Abraham unser Vater: Juden und Christen im Gespräch über die Bibel. Festschrift für Otto Michel zum 60. Geburtstag,* edited by Otto Betz, Martin Hengel, and Peter Schmidt, 383-404. AGSU 5. Leiden: Brill, 1963. "Die στολαί."

Rese, Martin. *Alttestamentliche Motive in der Christologie des Lukas.* SNT 1. Gütersloh: Gerd Mohn, 1959. *Alttestamentliche Motive.*

Resseguie, James L. "Automatization and Defamiliarization in Luke 7:36-50." *JLT* 5 (1991) 137-50. "Automatization and Defamiliarization."

———. "Interpretation of Luke's Central Section (Luke 9:51–19:44) since 1856." *StBTh* 5 (2, 1975) 3-36. "Luke's Central Section."

———. "Point of View in the Central Section of Luke (9:51–19:44)." *JETS* 25 (1982) 41-47. "Point of View."

Rice, George E. "Luke 4:31-44: Release for the Captives." *AUSS* 20 (1992) 23-28. "Luke 4:31-44."

———. "Luke's Thematic Use of the Call to Discipleship." *AUSS* 19 (1981) 51-58. "Call to Discipleship."

Riches, John K. *The World of Jesus: First-Century Judaism in Crisis.* Cambridge: Cambridge University, 1990. *World of Jesus.*

Riesenfeld, Harald. "τηρέω κτλ." In *TDNT,* 8:140-51.

Riesner, Rainer. "Archeology and Geography." In *DJG,* 33-46.

Rigato, Maria-Luisa. " ' "Remember" . . . Then They Remembered': Luke 24:6-8." In *Luke and Acts,* edited by Gerald O'Collins and Gilberto Marconi, 93-102. New York/Mahwah: Paulist, 1993. "Luke 24:6-8."

Ringe, Sharon H. *Jesus, Liberation, and the Biblical Jubilee.* OBT 19. Philadelphia: Fortress, 1985. *Biblical Jubilee.*

———. "Luke 9:28-36: The Beginning of an Exodus." *Semeia* 28 (1983) 83-99. "Luke 9:28-36."

Robbins, Vernon K. "Beelzebul Controversy in Mark and Luke: Rhetorical and Social Analysis." *Forum* 7 (1991) 261-77. "Beelzebul Controversy."

———. "Prefaces in Greco-Roman Biography and Luke-Acts." In *Society of Biblical Literature 1978 Seminar Papers,* edited by Paul J. Achtemeier, 2:193-207. Missoula, MT: Scholars, 1978. "Prefaces."

———. "The Social Location of the Implied Author of Luke-Acts." In *The Social World of Luke-Acts: Models for Interpretation,* edited by Jerome H. Neyrey, 305-22. Peabody, MA: Hendrickson, 1991. "Social Location."

———. "The Woman Who Touched Jesus' Garment: Socio-Rhetorical Analysis of the Synoptic Accounts." *NTS* 33 (1987) 502-15. "Woman Who Touched Jesus' Garment."

Robinson, B. P. "The Place of the Emmaus Story in Luke-Acts." *NTS* 30 (1984) 481-97. "Emmaus Story."

Robinson, Gnana. *The Origin and Development of the Old Testament Sabbath.* BBET 21. Frankfurt am Main: Peter Lang, 1988. *Old Testament Sabbath.*

Robinson Jr., William C. "On Preaching the Word of God (Luke 8:4-21)." In *Studies in Luke-Acts,* edited by Leander E. Keck and J. Louis Martyn, 131-38. Philadelphia: Fortress, 1966. "On Preaching."

Rohrbaugh, Richard L. "The Pre-industrial City in Luke-Acts: Urban Social Relations." In *The Social World of Luke-Acts: Models for Interpreta-*

tion, edited by Jerome H. Neyrey, 125-49. Peabody, MA: Hendrickson, 1991. "Pre-industrial City."

Rosica, Thomas M. "In Search of Jesus: The Emmaus Lesson." *Church* 8 (1992) 21-25. "In Search of Jesus."

———. "The Road to Emmaus and the Road to Gaza: Luke 24:13-35 and Acts 8:26-40." *Worship* 68 (1994) 117-31. "Road to Emmaus."

———. "Two Journeys of Faith." *BibTod* 31 (1993) 177-80.

Ross, J. M. "The Genuineness of Luke 24:12." *ExpT* 98 (1986-87) 107-8. "Luke 24:12."

———. "Which Zechariah?" *IBS* 9 (1987) 70-73.

Rousseau, François. "Les Structures du Benedictus (Luc 1.68-79)." *NTS* 32 (1986) 268-82. "Benedictus."

Royse, James R. "A Philonic Use of ΠΑΝΔΟΧΕΙΟΝ (Luke X 34)." *NovT* 23 (1981) 193-94. "ΠΑΝΔΟΧΕΙΟΝ."

Ruddick Jr., C. T. "Birth Narratives in Genesis and Luke." *NovT* 12 (1970) 343-48. "Birth Narratives."

Ruppert, Lothar. *Der leidende Gerechte und seine Feinde: Eine Wortfelduntersuchung.* Würzburg: Echter, 1973. *Der leidende Gerechte.*

———. *Jesus als der leidende Gerechte? Der Weg Jesu im Lichte eines alt- und zwischentestamentlichen Motivs.* SBS 59. Stuttgart: Katholisches, 1972. *Jesus als der leidende Gerechte?*

Safrai, Shmuel. "The Place of Women in First-Century Synagogues." *JerP* 40 (1993) 3-6. "Place of Women."

Sahlin, Harold. "Die Früchte der Umkehr: Die ethische Verkündigung Johannes der Täufers nach Lk 3:10-14." *ST* 1 (1948) 54-68. "Früchte der Umkehr."

Sahlins, Marshall. *How "Natives" Think: About Captain Cook, for Example.* Chicago: University of Chicago, 1995. *How "Natives" Think.*

———. *Stone Age Economics.* London/New York: Routledge, 1972. *Economics.*

Said, Edward W. *Beginnings: Intention and Method.* New York: Basic, 1975. *Beginnings.*

Saldarini, Anthony J. *Pharisees, Scribes and Sadducees in Palestinian Society: A Sociological Approach.* Wilmington, DE: Michael Glazier, 1988. *Pharisees, Scribes and Sadducees.*

Saller, Richard. "Corporal Punishment, Authority, and Obedience in the Roman Household." In *Marriage, Divorce, and Children in Ancient Rome,* edited by Beryl Rawson, 144-65. Oxford: Oxford University, 1991. "Corporal Punishment."

Salo, Kalvervo. *Luke's Treatment of the Law: A Redaction-Critical Investigation.* AASFDHL 57. Helsinki: Suomalainen Tiedeakatemia, 1991. *Luke's Treatment of the Law.*

Sand, Alexander. "καρδία." In *EDNT,* 2:249-51.

———. "πείθω." In *EDNT,* 3:63.

Sanders, E. P. *Jesus and Judaism.* London: SCM, 1985.

———. *Jewish Law from Jesus to the Mishnah: Five Studies.* London: SCM; Philadelphia: Trinity, 1990. *Jewish Law.*

———. *Judaism: Practice and Belief 63 BCE–66 CE.* Philadelphia: Trinity, 1992. *Judaism.*

———. *Paul and Palestinian Judaism: A Comparison of Patterns of Religion.* Philadelphia: Fortress, 1977. *Paul and Palestinian Judaism.*

———. "Testament of Abraham: A New Translation and Introduction." In *OTP,* 1:871-902. "Testament of Abraham."

Sanders, Jack T. *The Jews in Luke-Acts.* Philadelphia: Fortress, 1987. *Jews.*

———. "The Parable of the Pounds and Lucan Anti-Semitism." *TS* 42 (1981) 660-68. "Parable of the Pounds."

Sanders, James A. "The Ethics of Election in Luke's Great Banquet Parable." In *Luke and Scripture: The Function of Sacred Tradition in Luke-Acts,* by Craig A. Evans and James A. Sanders, 106-20. Minneapolis: Fortress, 1993. "Ethics of Election."

———. "A Hermeneutic Fabric: Psalm 118 in Luke's Entrance Narrative." In *Luke and Scripture: The Function of Sacred Tradition in Luke-Acts,* by Craig A. Evans and James A. Sanders, 140-53. Minneapolis: Fortress, 1993. "Luke's Entrance Narrative."

———. "Isaiah in Luke." *Int* 36 (1982) 144-55.

———. "Sins, Debts, and Jubilee Release." In *Luke and Scripture: The Function of Sacred Tradition in Luke-Acts,* by Craig A. Evans and James A. Sanders, 85-92. Minneapolis: Fortress, 1993. "Sins."

Schaeder, H. H. "Ναζαρηνός, Ναζωραῖος." In *TDNT,* 4:874-79.

Schlier, Heinrich. "βραχίων." In *TDNT,* 1:639-40.

Schlosser, J. "Les jours de Noé et de Lot: À propos de Luc xvii,26-30." *RB* 80 (1973) 13-36.

Schmahl, Günther. "Lk 2,41-52 und die Kindheitserzählung des Thomas 19,1-5: Ein Vergleich." *BibLeb* 15 (1974) 249-58. "Lk 2,41-52."

Schmeichel, Waldemar. "Christian Prophecy in Lukan Thought: Luke 4:16-30 as a Point of Departure." In *Society of Biblical Literature 1976 Seminar Papers,* ed. George MacRae, 293-304. Missoula, MT: Scholars, 1976. "Christian Prophecy."

Schmidt, Daryl. "Luke's 'Innocent' Jesus: A Scriptural Apologetic." In *Political Issues in Luke-Acts,* edited by Richard J. Cassidy and Philip J. Scharper, 111-21. Maryknoll, NY: Orbis, 1983. "Luke's Innocent Jesus."

Schmidt, Karl Ludwig. *Der Rahmen der Geschichte. Literarkritische Untersuchungen zur ältesten Jesusüberlieferung.* Berlin: Trowitzsch & Sohn, 1919. *Rahmen der Geschichte.*

Schmidt, Thomas E. *Hostility to Wealth in the Synoptic Gospels.* JSNTSup 15. Sheffield: JSOT, 1987. *Hostility to Wealth.*

―――. "Taxes." In *DJG,* 804-7.

Schneider, Gerhard. *Die Apostelgeschichte.* 2 vols. HTKNT 5. Freiburg: Herder, 1982.

―――. "Zur Bedeutung von καθεξῆς im lukanischen Doppelwerk." In *Lukas, Theologe der Heilsgeschichte: Aufsätze zum lukanische Doppelwerk,* 31-34. BBB 59. Bonn: Peter Hanstein, 1985. "Bedeutung."

―――. "Jesu geistgewirkte Empfängnis (Lk 1,34f). Zur Interpretation einer christologischen Aussage." In *Lukas, Theologe der Heilsgeschichte: Aufsätze zum lukanische Doppelwerk,* 86-97. BBB 59. Bonn: Peter Hanstein, 1985. "Jesu geistgewirkte Empfängnis."

―――. *Lukas, Theologe der Heilsgeschichte: Aufsätze zum lukanische Doppelwerk.* BBB 59. Bonn: Peter Hanstein, 1985. *Lukas.*

―――. "ὀπίσω." In *EDNT,* 2:523.

―――. "The Political Charge against Jesus (Luke 23:2)." In *Jesus and the Politics of His Day,* edited by Ernst Bammel and C. F. D. Moule, 403-14. Cambridge: Cambridge University, 1984. "Political Charge."

―――. " 'Stärke deine Brüder!' (Lk 22,32): Die Aufgabe des Petrus nach Lukas." In *Lukas, Theologe der Heilsgeschichte: Aufsätze zum lukanische Doppelwerk,* 146-52. BBB 59. Bonn: Peter Hanstein, 1985. "Stärke deine Brüder!"

―――. "Die Verhaftung Jesu: Traditionsgeschichte von Mk 14,43-52." *ZNW* 63 (1972) 188-209. "Verhaftung."

―――. *Verleugnung, Verspottung und Verhör Jesu nach Lukas 22,54-71: Studien zur lukanischen Darstellung der Passion.* SANT 22. München: Kösel, 1969. *Verleugnung.*

Schneider, Johannes. "ἡλικία." *TDNT,* 2:941-43.

Scholer, David M. "The Magnificat (Luke 1:46-55): Reflections on Its Hermeneutical History." In *Conflict and Context: Hermeneutics in the Americas,* edited by Mark Lau Branson and C. René Padilla, 210-19. Grand Rapids: Wm. B. Eerdmans, 1986. "Magnificat."

Schönweiss, Hans. "Prayer." In *NIDNTT,* 2:855-79.

Schottroff, Luise. *Let the Oppressed Go Free: Feminist Perspectives on the New Testament.* GBT. Louisville: Westminster/John Knox, 1993. *Feminist Perspectives.*

―――. *Lydia's Impatient Sisters: A Feminist Social History of Early Christianity.* Louisville: Westminster/John Knox, 1995. *Lydia's Impatient Sisters.*

―――. "Non-Violence and the Love of One's Enemies." In *Essays on the Love Commandment,* by Luise Schottroff et al., 9-39. Philadelphia: Fortress, 1978. "Non-Violence."

Schottroff, Luise, and Wolfgang Stegemann. *Jesus and the Hope of the Poor.* Maryknoll, NY: Orbis, 1986. *Jesus.*

Schrage, Wolfgang. "τυφλός κτλ." In *TDNT,* 8:270-94.

Schreck, Christopher J. "The Nazareth Pericope: Luke 4:16-30 in Recent Study." In *L'Évangile de Luc — The Gospel of Luke,* revised and enlarged edition of *L'Évangile de Luc: Problèmes littéraires et théologiques,* edited by F. Neirynck, 399-471. BETL 32. Leuven: Leuven University, 1989. "Nazareth Pericope."

Schrenk, Gottlob. "διαλογισμός." In *TDNT,* 2:96-98.

————. "ἐκλεκτός." In *TDNT,* 4:181-92.

Schubert, Paul. "The Structure and Significance of Luke 24." In *Neutestamentliche Studien für Rudolf Bultmann zu seinem siebzigsten Geburtstag,* edited by W. Eltester, 165-86. 2d ed. BZNW 21. Berlin: Walter de Gruyter, 1957. "Structure and Significance."

Schürer, Emil. *The History of the Jewish People in the Age of Jesus Christ (175 B.C.–A.D. 135).* Vol 2. Rev. ed. Edited by Geza Vermes, Fergus Millar, and Matthew Black. Edinburgh: T. & T. Clark, 1979. *Jewish People.*

Schürmann, Heinz. "Der Dienst des Petrus und Johannes (Lk 22,8)." In *Ursprung und Gestalt: Erörterungen und Besinnungen zum Neuen Testament,* 274-76. Düsseldorf: Patmos, 1970. "Dienst des Petrus und Johannes."

————. *Einer quellenkritischen Untersuchung des lukanischen Abendmahlsberichtes (Lk 22,7-38).* Part 1: *Der Paschamahlbericht (Lk 22,[7-14.]15-18).* NTAbh 9:5. Münster: Aschendorffsche, 1953. *Paschamahlbericht.*

Schüssler Fiorenza, Elisabeth. *But She Said: Feminist Practices of Biblical Interpretation.* Boston: Beacon, 1992. *But She Said.*

————. "Luke 2:41-52." *Int* 36 (1982) 399-403.

Schwank, Benedikt. "λεπτόν." In *EDNT,* 2:349-50.

Schwankl, Otto. *Die Sadduzäerfrage (Mk 12,18-27 parr): Eine exegetisch-theologische Studie zur Auferstehungserwartung.* BBB 66. Frankfurt am Main: Athenäum, 1987. *Sadduzäerfrage.*

Schwartz, Daniel R. *Studies in the Jewish Background of Christianity.* WUNT 60. Tübingen: J. C. B. Mohr (Paul Siebeck), 1992. *Jewish Background.*

Schweizer, Eduard. "Zum Aufbau von Lukas 1 und 2." In *Neues Testament und Christologie im Werden: Aufsätze,* 11-32. Göttingen: Vandenhoeck & Ruprecht, 1982. "Aufbau."

————. "πνεῦμα κτλ." In *TDNT,* 6:332-455.

Scott, James M. "Luke's Geographical Horizon." In *The Book of Acts in Its Graeco-Roman Setting,* edited by David W. J. Gill and Conrad Gempf, 483-544. A1CS 2. Grand Rapids: Wm. B. Eerdmans; Carlisle: Paternoster, 1994.

Scott, James S. "Peasant Moral Economy as a Subsistence Ethic." In *Peasants and Peasant Societies: Selected Readings,* edited by Teodor Shanin, 304-10. 2d ed. London: Blackwell, 1987. "Moral Economy."

Scott, M. Philip. "A Note on the Meaning and Translation of Luke 11:28." *ITQ* 41 (1974) 235-50. "Luke 11:28."

Seccombe, David Peter. "Luke and Isaiah." *NTS* 27 (1981) 252-59.

————. *Possessions and the Poor in Luke-Acts.* SNTU B6. Linz: Fuchs, 1983. *Possessions.*

Seesemann, Heinrich. "πεῖρα κτλ." In *TDNT,* 6:23-36.

Segre, Cesare, with Tomaso Kemeny. *Introduction to the Analysis of the Literary Text.* AS. Bloomington/Indianapolis: Indiana University, 1988. *Analysis of the Literary Text.*

Seim, Turid Karlsen. *The Double Message: Patterns of Gender in Luke and Acts.* Nashville: Abingdon, 1994. *Double Message.*

Seitz, Oscar J. F. " 'What Do These Stones Mean?' " *JBL* 79 (1960) 247-54. "Stones."

Senior, Donald. *The Passion of Jesus in the Gospel of Luke.* PS 3. Wilmington, DE: Michael Glazier, 1989. *Passion of Jesus.*

Senior, Donald, and Carroll Stuhlmueller. *The Biblical Foundations for Mission.* Maryknoll, NY: Orbis, 1983. *Biblical Foundations.*

Seybold, Klaus, and Ulrich B. Mueller. *Sickness and Healing.* BES. Nashville: Abingdon, 1981.

Seymour-Smith, Charlotte. *Macmillan Dictionary of Anthropology.* London: Macmillan, 1986. *Anthropology.*

Shanin, Teodor, ed. *Peasants and Peasant Societies: Selected Readings.* 2d ed. London: Basil Blackwell, 1987. *Peasant Societies.*

Sheeley, Steven M. *Narrative Asides in Luke-Acts.* JSNTSup 72. Sheffield: JSOT, 1992. *Narrative Asides.*

Sheffler, E. H. "The Social Ethics of the Lucan Baptist." *Neot* 24 (1990) 21-36. "Social Ethics."

Shelton, James B. *Mighty in Word and Deed: The Role of the Holy Spirit in Luke-Acts.* Peabody, MA: Hendrickson, 1991. *Mighty in Word.*

Shepherd Jr., William H. *The Narrative Function of the Holy Spirit as a Character in Luke-Acts.* SBLDS 147. Atlanta: Scholars, 1994. *Narrative Function.*

Sherwin-White, A. N. *Roman Society and Roman Law in the New Testament.* Oxford: Clarendon, 1963; reprint ed., Grand Rapids: Baker, 1978. *Roman Society.*

Sherwood, Stephen K. " 'Blest Is the Womb That Bore You' Lc 11,22-28." *EMar* 43 (1993) 257-62. "Blest Is the Womb."

Shirock, Robert J. "The Growth of the Kingdom in Light of Israel's Rejection of Jesus: Structure and Theology in Luke 13:1-35." *NovT* 35 (1993) 15-29. "Growth of the Kingdom."

————. "Whose Exorcists Are They? The Referents of οἱ υἱοὶ ὑμῶν at Matthew 12.27/Luke 11.19." *JSNT* 46 (1992) 41-51. "Whose Exorcists?"

Sieber, John H. "The Spirit as the 'Promise of My Father' in Luke 24:49." In *Sin, Salvation, and the Spirit*, edited by Daniel Durken, 271-78. Collegeville, MN: Liturgical 1979. "Promise of My Father."

Sim, David C. "The Woman Followers of Jesus: The Implications of Luke 8:1-3." *HeyJ* 30 (1989) 51-62. "Woman Followers."

Sloan Jr., Robert Bryan. *The Favorable Year of the Lord: A Study of Jubilary Theology in the Gospel of Luke.* Austin, TX: Schola, 1977. *Favorable Year.*

————. "Jubilee." In *DJG,* 396-97.

Smalley, Stephen S. "Spirit, Kingdom and Prayer." *NovT* 15 (1973) 59-71.

Smallwood, E. Mary. *The Jews under Roman Rule: From Pompey to Diocletian.* SJLA 20. Leiden: Brill, 1976. *Jews.*

Smith, Charles W. F. "Fishers of Men: Footnotes on a Gospel Figure." *HTR* 52 (1959) 187-203. "Fishers of Men."

Smith, Dennis E. "The Historical Jesus at Table." In *Society of Biblical Literature 1989 Seminar Papers,* edited by David J. Lull, 466-86. Atlanta: Scholars, 1989. "Historical Jesus."

————. "Narrative Beginnings in Ancient Literature and Theory." *Semeia* 52 (1991) 1-9. "Beginnings."

————. "Table Fellowship as a Literary Motif in the Gospel of Luke." *JBL* 106 (1987) 613-38. "Table Fellowship."

Smith, Mahlon H. "No Place for a Son of Man." *Forum* 4 (4, 1988) 83-107.

Smith, Pamela. "Beatitudes and Woes." *JSF* 15 (1, 1994) 35-45.

Smith, Robert H. "Caesar's Decree (Luke 2:1-2): Puzzle or Key?" *CurTM* 7 (1980) 343-51. "Caesar's Decree."

————. *Easter Gospels: The Resurrection of Jesus according to the Four Evangelists.* Minneapolis: Augsburg, 1983. *Easter Gospels.*

————. "Hypocrite." In *DJG,* 351-53.

————. "Sign of Jonah." In *DJG,* 754-56.

Soards, Marion L. " 'And the Lord Turned and Looked Straight at Peter': Understanding Luke 22,61." *Bib* 67 (1986) 518-19. "Luke 22,61."

————. "A Literary Analysis of the Origin and Purpose of Luke's Account of the Mockery of Jesus." *BZ* 31 (1987) 110-16. "Literary Analysis."

————. "The Silence of Jesus before Herod: An Interpretive Suggestion." *AusBR* 33 (1985) 41-45. "Silence of Jesus."

————. *The Speeches in Acts: Their Content, Context, and Concerns.* Louisville, KY: Westminster/John Knox, 1994. *Speeches in Acts.*

————. "Tradition, Composition, and Theology in Jesus' Speech to the 'Daughters of Jerusalem' (Luke 23,26-32)." *Bib* 68 (1987) 221-44. "Jesus' Speech."

————. "Tradition, Composition, and Theology in Luke's Account of Jesus before Herod." *Bib* 66 (1985) 344-64. "Jesus before Herod."

Sobosan, Jeffrey G. "Completion of Prophecy: Jesus in Lk 1:32-33." *BTB* 4 (1974) 317-23. "Completion of Prophecy."

Soja, Edward W. *Postmodern Geographies: The Reassertion of Space in Critical Social Theory.* London: Verso, 1989. *Postmodern Geographies.*

Squires, John T. *The Plan of God in Luke-Acts.* SNTSMS 76. Cambridge: Cambridge University, 1993. *Plan of God.*

Stählin, Gustav. "ἐξαιτέω." In *TDNT,* 1:194.

————. "κοπετός κτλ." In *TDNT,* 3:830-60.

————. "χήρα." In *TDNT,* 9:440-65.

Stanton, Graham N. "Jesus of Nazareth: A Magician and a False Prophet Who Deceived God's People?" In *Jesus of Nazareth: Lord and Christ. Essays on the Historical Jesus and New Testament Christology,* edited by Joel B. Green and Max Turner, 164-80. Grand Rapids: Wm. B. Eerdmans, 1994. "Jesus of Nazareth."

Steele, E. Springs. "Luke 11:37-54 — A Modified Hellenistic Symposium?" *JBL* 103 (1984) 379-94. "Luke 11:37-54."

Sterling, Gregory L. *Historiography and Self-Definition: Josephos, Luke-Acts and Apologetic Historiography.* NovTSup 64. Leiden: Brill, 1992. *Historiography.*

Stewart, Charles. *Demons and the Devil: Moral Imagination in Modern Greek Culture.* Princeton, NJ: Princeton University, 1991. *Demons and the Devil.*

Steyn, G. J. "Intertextual Similarities between Septuagintal Pretexts and Luke's Gospel." *Neot* 24 (1990) 229-46. "Intertextual Similarities."

Stock, Augustine. "Chiastic Awareness and Education in Antiquity." *BTB* 14 (1984) 23-27. "Chiastic Awareness."

Stock, Brian. *Listening for the Text: On the Uses of the Past.* PRCS. Baltimore/London: Johns Hopkins University, 1990. *Listening for the Text.*

Stock, Klemens. "Die Berufung Marias (Lk 1,26-38)." *Bib* 61 (1980) 457-91. "Berufung Marias."

Strauss, Mark L. *The Davidic Messiah in Luke-Acts: The Promise and Its Fulfillment in Lukan Christology.* JSNTSup 110. Sheffield: Sheffield Academic, 1995. *Davidic Messiah.*

Strobel, August. "Die Ausrufung des Jobeljahrs in der Nazarethpredigt Jesu: Zur apokalyptischen Tradition Lc 4:16-30." In *Jesus in Nazareth,* edited by Walther Eltester, 38-50. BZNW 40. Berlin: Walter de Gruyter, 1972. "Ausrufung des Jobeljahrs."

————. "Der Gruss an Maria (Lc 1:28): Eine philologische Betrachtung zu seinem Sinngehalt." *ZNW* 53 (1962) 86-110. "Gruss an Maria."

————. *Die Stunde der Wahrheit: Untersuchungen zum Strafverfahren gegen Jesu.* WUNT 21. Tübingen: J. C. B. Mohr (Paul Siebeck), 1980. *Stunde der Wahrheit.*

Stronstad, R. *The Charismatic Theology of St. Luke.* Peabody, MA: Hendrickson, 1984. *Charismatic Theology.*

Stubbs, Michael. *Discourse Analysis: The Sociolinguistic Analysis of Natural Language.* Chicago: University of Chicago, 1983. *Discourse Analysis.*

Süring, Margit Linnéa. *The Horn-Motif: In the Hebrew Bible and Related Ancient Near Eastern Literature and Iconography.* AUSDDS 4. Berrien Springs, MI: Andrews University, 1980. *Horn-Motif.*

Swartley, Willard M. "Politics or Peace *(Eirēnē)* in Luke's Gospel." In *Political Issues in Luke-Acts,* edited by Richard J. Cassidy and Philip J. Scharper, 18-37. Maryknoll, NY: Orbis, 1983. "Politics or Peace."

Sweetland, Dennis M. "Discipleship and Persecution: A Study of Luke 12,1-12." *Bib* 65 (1984) 61-79. "Discipleship and Persecution."

————. *Our Journey with Jesus: Discipleship according to Luke-Acts.* GNS 23. Collegeville, MN: Liturgical, 1990. *Our Journey.*

Sylva, Dennis D. "The Cryptic Clause, *en tois tou patros mou dei einai me* in Luke 2:49b." *ZNW* 78 (1987) 132-40. "Cryptic Clause."

————. "The Meaning and Function of Acts 7:46-50." *JBL* 106 (1987) 261-75. "Meaning and Function."

Sylva, Dennis D., ed. *Reimaging the Death of the Lukan Jesus.* AMTBBB 73. Frankfurt am Main: Anton Hain, 1990. *Reimaging the Death.*

Syme, Ronald. "The Titulus Tiburtinus." In *Akten des VI. Internationalen Kongresses für Griechische und Lateinische Epigraphik München 1972.* VBAG 17. München: C. H. Beck'sche, 1973. "Titulus."

Talbert, C. H. *Literary Patterns, Theological Themes, and the Genre of Luke-Acts.* SBLMS 20. Missoula, MT: Scholars, 1974. *Literary Patterns.*

————. "Martyrdom in Luke-Acts and the Lukan Social Ethic." In *Political Issues in Luke-Acts,* edited by Richard J. Cassidy and Philip J. Scharper, 99-110. Maryknoll, NY: Orbis, 1983. "Martyrdom."

————. "Prophecies of Future Greatness: The Contribution of Greco-Roman Biographies to an Understanding of Luke 1:5–4:15." In *The Divine Helmsman: Studies on God's Control of Human Events, Presented to Lou H. Silberman,* edited by James L. Crenshaw and Samuel Sandmel, 129-41. New York: Ktav, 1980. "Prophecies."

————. *What Is a Gospel? The Genre of the Canonical Gospels.* Philadelphia: Fortress, 1977. *What Is a Gospel?*

Talmon, Shemaryahu. "The 'Desert Motif' in the Bible and in Qumran Literature." In *Biblical Motifs: Origins and Transformations,* edited by Alexander Altmann, 31-63. Cambridge, MA: Harvard University, 1966. "Desert Motif."

Tannehill, Robert C. "Israel in Luke-Acts: A Tragic Story." *JBL* 104 (1985) 69-85. "Israel in Luke-Acts."

———. "The Mission of Jesus according to Luke iv.16-30." In *Jesus in Nazareth,* edited by Walther Eltester, 51-75. BZNW 40. Berlin: Walter de Gruyter, 1972. "Mission of Jesus."

———. *The Narrative Unity of Luke-Acts: A Literary Interpretation.* Vol. 1: *The Gospel according to Luke.* FF. Philadelphia: Fortress, 1986. *Narrative Unity.*

———. "Rejection by Jews and Turning to Gentiles: The Pattern of Paul's Mission in Acts." In *Luke-Acts and the Jewish People: Eight Critical Perspectives,* edited by Joseph B. Tyson, 83-101. Minneapolis: Augsburg, 1988. "Rejection by Jews."

———. "Should We Love Simon the Pharisee? Hermeneutical Reflections on the Pharisees in Luke." *CurTM* 21 (1994) 424-33. "Simon the Pharisee."

———. "The Story of Zacchaeus as Rhetoric: Luke 19:1-10." *Semeia* 64 (1993) 201-11. "Story of Zacchaeus."

———. *The Sword of His Mouth: Forceful and Imaginative Language in Synoptic Sayings.* SBLSS 1. Philadelphia: Fortress; Missoula, MT: Scholars, 1975. *Sword of His Mouth.*

———. "What Kind of King? What Kind of Kingdom? A Study of Luke." *WW* 12 (1992) 17-22. "Kingdom."

Tannen, Deborah. "What's in a Frame? Surface Evidence for Underlying Expectations." In *Framing in Discourse,* edited by Deborah Tannen, 14-56. New York/Oxford: Oxford University, 1993. "What's in a Frame?"

Taylor, Charles. *Sources of the Self: The Making of the Modern Identity.* Cambridge, MA: Harvard University, 1989. *Sources of the Self.*

Taylor, Vincent. *The Passion Narrative of St. Luke: A Critical and Historical Investigation.* SNTSMS 19. Cambridge: Cambridge University, 1972. *Passion Narrative.*

Thébert, Yvon. "The Slave." In *The Romans,* edited by Andrea Giardina, 138-74. Chicago/London: University of Chicago, 1993. "Slave."

Theissen, Gerd. *The First Followers of Jesus: A Sociological Analysis of the Earliest Christianity.* London: SCM, 1978. *First Followers.*

———. *The Miracle Stories of the Early Christian Tradition.* SNTW. Philadelphia: Fortress, 1983. *Miracle Stories.*

———. *The Open Door: Variations on Biblical Themes.* Minneapolis: Fortress, 1991. *Open Door.*

———. *The Shadow of the Galilean: The Quest of the Historical Jesus in Narrative Form.* Philadelphia: Fortress, 1987. *Shadow of the Galilean.*

———. *Social Reality and the Early Christians: Theology, Ethics, and the World of the New Testament.* Minneapolis: Fortress, 1992. *Social Reality.*

Theobald, M. "Die Anfänge der Kirche: Zur Struktur von Lk. 5.1–6.19." *NTS* 30 (1984) 91-108. "Anfänge."

Thibeaux, Evelyn R. " 'Known to Be a Sinner': The Narrative Rhetoric of Luke 7:36-50." *BTB* 23 (1993) 151-60. "Known to Be a Sinner."

Thiselton, Anthony. "Christology in Luke, Speech-Act Theory, and the Problem of Dualism in Christology after Kant." In *Jesus of Nazareth: Lord and Christ. Essays on the Historical Jesus and New Testament Christology,* edited by Joel B. Green and Max Turner, 453-72. Grand Rapids: Wm. B. Eerdmans; Carlisle: Paternoster, 1994. "Christology in Luke."

Thompson, G. H. P. "Called — Proved — Obedient: A Study in the Baptism and Temptation Narratives of Matthew and Luke." *JTS* n.s. 11 (1960) 1-12. "Called — Proved — Obedient."

Thurston, Bonnie Bowman. *The Widows: A Women's Ministry in the Early Church.* Minneapolis: Fortress, 1989. *Widows.*

Tiede, David L. "The Kings of the Gentiles and the Leader Who Serves: Luke 22:24-30." *WW* 12 (1992) 23-28. "Kings of the Gentiles."

———. "Luke 6:17-26." *Int* 40 (1986) 63-68.

———. *Prophecy and History in Luke-Acts.* Philadelphia: Fortress, 1980. *Prophecy and History.*

Toolan, Michael N. *Narrative: A Critical Linguistic Introduction.* Interface. London/New York: Routledge, 1988. *Narrative.*

Toynbee, J. M. C. *Death and Burial in the Roman World.* London: Thames and Hudson, 1971. *Death and Burial.*

Trible, Phyllis. *God and the Rhetoric of Sexuality.* OBT. Philadelphia: Fortress, 1978. *Rhetoric of Sexuality.*

Trites, Allison. *The New Testament Concept of Witness.* SNTSMS 31. Cambridge: Cambridge University, 1977. *Witness.*

———. "The Prayer Motif in Luke-Acts." In *Perspectives on Luke-Acts,* edited by Charles H. Talbert, 168-86. Edinburgh: T. & T. Clark, 1978. "Prayer Motif."

———. "The Transfiguration in the Theology of Luke: Some Redactional Links." In *The Glory of Christ in the New Testament: Studies in Christology in Memory of George Bradford Caird,* edited by L. D. Hurst and N. T. Wright, 71-81. Oxford: Clarendon, 1987. "Transfiguration."

Trompf, G. W. *The Idea of Historical Recurrence in Western Thought: From Antiquity to the Reformation.* Berkeley: University of California, 1979. *Idea of Historical Recurrence.*

Trudinger, L. Paul. " 'No Room in the Inn': A Note on Luke 2:7." *ExpT* 102 (1990-91) 172-73. "Luke 2:7."

Tuckett, Christopher M. "The Lukan Son of Man." In *Luke's Literary*

Achievement: Collected Essays, edited by C. M. Tuckett, 198-217. JSNTSup 116. Sheffield: Sheffield Academic, 1995. "Son of Man."

————. "Luke 4,16-30, Isaiah and Q." In *Logia: Les Paroles de Jésus — The Sayings of Jesus. Mémorial Joseph Coppens,* edited by Joël Delobel, 343-54. BETL 59. Leuven: Leuven University, 1982. "Luke 4,16-30."

Turner, Max. "Holy Spirit." In *DJG,* 341-51.

————. "Jesus and the Spirit in Lukan Perspective." *TynB* 32 (1981) 3-42. "Jesus and the Spirit."

————. "The Spirit and Power of Jesus' Miracles in the Lucan Conception." *NovT* 33 (1991) 124-52. "Spirit and Power."

————. "Spirit Endowment in Luke-Acts: Some Linguistic Considerations." *VE* 12 (1981) 45-63. "Spirit Endowment."

————. "The Spirit of Prophecy and the Power of Authoritative Preaching in Luke-Acts: A Question of Origins." *NTS* 38 (1992) 66-88. "Spirit of Prophecy."

Turner, Victor. *The Forest of Symbols: Aspects of Ndembu Ritual.* Ithaca, NY: Cornell University, 1967. *Symbols.*

————. *The Ritual Process: Structure and Anti-Structure.* Ithaca, NY: Cornell University, 1969. *Ritual Process.*

Twelftree, Graham H. "Blasphemy." In *DJG,* 75-77.

————. *Christ Triumphant: Exorcism Then and Now.* London: Hodder and Stoughton, 1985. *Christ Triumphant.*

————. "Demon, Devil, Satan." In *DJG,* 163-72. "Demon."

————. " 'ΕΙ ΔΕ . . . ΕΓΩ ΕΚΒΑΛΛΩ ΤΑ ΔΑΙΜΟΝΙΑ . . .'." In *The Miracles of Jesus,* edited by David Wenham and Craig Blomberg, 361-400. GP 6. Sheffield: JSOT, 1986.

————. *Jesus the Exorcist: A Contribution to the Study of the Historical Jesus.* WUNT 2:54. Tübingen: J. C. B. Mohr (Paul Siebeck), 1993. *Jesus the Exorcist.*

————. "Temptation of Jesus." In *DJG,* 821-27.

Tyson, Joseph B. "The Birth Narratives and the Beginning of Luke's Gospel." *Semeia* 52 (1991) 103-20. "Birth Narratives."

————. "Conflict as a Literary Theme in the Gospel of Luke." In *New Synoptic Studies: The Cambridge Gospel Conference and Beyond,* edited by William R. Farmer, 303-27. Macon, GA: Mercer University, 1983. "Conflict as a Literary Theme."

————. *The Death of Jesus in Luke-Acts.* Columbia, SC: University of South Carolina, 1986. *Death of Jesus.*

————. *Images of Judaism in Luke-Acts.* Columbia, SC: University of South Carolina, 1992. *Images of Judaism.*

Untergaßmair, Franz Georg. *Kreuzweg und Kreuzigung Jesu: Ein Beitrag zur lukanischen Redaktionsgeschichte und zur Frage nach der lukanischen "Kreuzestheologie."* PTS 10. Paderborn: Schöningh, 1980. *Kreuzweg und Kreuzigung Jesu.*

van Aarde, A. G. "Narrative Point of View: An Ideological Reading of Luke 12:35-48." *Neot* 22 (1988) 235-52. "Narrative Point of View."

van der Loos, H. *The Miracles of Jesus.* NovTSup 9. Leiden: Brill, 1965. *Miracles.*

van der Meulen, Harry E. Faber. "Zum jüdischen und hellenistischen Hintergrund von Lukas 1,31." In *Wort in der Zeit: Neutestamentlichen Studien. Festgabe für Karl Heinrich Rengstorf zum 75. Geburtstag,* edited by Wilfrid Haubeck and Michael Bachmann, 108-22. Leiden: Brill, 1980. "Lukas 1,31."

van der Toorn, Karel. "Mill, Millstone." In *ABD,* 4:831-32.

van Dijk, Teun A. *Text and Context: Explorations in the Semantics and Pragmatics of Discourse.* LLL. London: Routledge, 1977. *Text and Context.*

van Gennep, Arnold. *The Rites of Passage.* London: Routledge & Kegan Paul, 1960. *Rites of Passage.*

Vanhoozer, Kevin J. *Biblical Narrative in the Philosophy of Paul Ricoeur: A Study in Hermeneutics and Theology.* Cambridge: Cambridge University, 1990. *Biblical Narrative.*

————. "The Reader in New Testament Interpretation." In *Hearing the New Testament: Strategies for Interpretation,* edited by Joel B. Green, 301-28. Grand Rapids: Wm. B. Eerdmans, 1995. "The Reader."

Vanhoye, Albert. "Structure du Benedictus." *NTS* 12 (1965-66) 382-89.

van Staden, Piet. *Compassion — The Essence of Life: A Social-Scientific Study of the Religious Symbolic Universe Reflected in the Ideology/Theology of Luke.* HTSSup 4. Pretoria: University of Pretoria, 1991. *Compassion.*

————. "A Sociological Reading of Luke 12:35-48." *Neot* 22 (1988) 337-53. "Sociological Reading."

van Stempvoort, P. A. "The Interpretation of the Ascension in Luke and Acts." *NTS* 5 (1958-59) 30-42. "Interpretation of the Ascension."

van Tilburg, S. "An Interpretation from the Ideology of the Text." *Neot* 22 (1988) 205-15. "Interpretation."

van Unnik, W. C. "*Dominus Vobiscum:* The Background of a Liturgical Formula." In *New Testament Essays: Studies in Memory of Thomas Walter Manson (1893-1958),* edited by A. J. B. Higgins, 270-305. Manchester: Manchester University, 1959. *"Dominus Vobiscum."*

————. "Die Motivierung der Feindesliebe in Lukas VI.32-35." In *Sparsa Collecta: The Collected Writings of W. C. van Unnik,* 1:111-26. NovTSup 29. Leiden: Brill, 1973. "Motivierung."

————. "Once More St. Luke's Prologue." *Neot* 7 (1973) 7-26. "Luke's Prologue."

―――. "Die rechte Bedeutung des Wortes treffen, Lukas ii 19." In *Sparsa Collecta: The Collected Writings of W. C. van Unnik,* 1:72-91. NovT-Sup 29. Leiden: Brill, 1973. "Die rechte Bedeutung."

―――. "Remarks on the Purpose of Luke's Historical Writing." In *Sparsa Collecta: The Collected Writings of W. C. van Unnik,* 1:6-15. NovTSup 29. Leiden: Brill, 1973. "Purpose."

Venetz, H.-J. "Die Suche nach dem 'einen Notwendigen': Beobachtungen und Verdächtigungen und um die Marta-Maria-Perikope (Lk 10,38-42)." *Orientierung* 54 (1990) 185-89. "Suche nach dem 'einen Notwendigen'."

Vermes, Geza. *The Dead Sea Scrolls in English.* 3d ed. Sheffield: JSOT, 1987. *Dead Sea Scrolls.*

―――. *Jesus the Jew: A Historian's Reading of the Gospels.* Philadelphia: Fortress, 1973. *Jesus the Jew.*

Veyne, Paul. *Writing History: Essay on Epistemology.* Middletown, CN: Wesleyan University, 1984. *Writing History.*

Via, E. Jane. "According to Luke, Who Put Jesus to Death?" In *Political Issues in Luke-Acts,* edited by Richard J. Cassidy and Philip J. Scharper, 122-45. Maryknoll, NY: Orbis, 1983. "According to Luke."

Vine, Victor E. "Luke 14:15-24 and Anti-Semitism." *ExpT* 102 (1990-91) 262-63. "Luke 14:15-24."

Vogels, Walter. "A Semiotic Study of Luke 7:11-17." *ET* 14 (1983) 273-92. "Semiotic Study."

Völkel, Martin. "Der Anfang Jesu in Galiläa: Bemerkungen zum Gebrauch und zur Funktion Galiläas in den lukanischen Schriften." *ZNW* 64 (1973) 222-32. "Angang Jesu."

―――. "Exegetische Erwägungen zum Verständnis des Begriffs ΚΑΘΕΞΗΣ im lukanischen Prolog." *NTS* 20 (1973-74) 289-99. "Exegetische Erwägungen."

von Dobbeler, Stephanie. *Das Gericht und das Erbarmen Gottes: Die Botschaft Johannes des Täufers und ihre Rezeption bei den Johannesjüngern im Rahmen der Theologiegeschichte des Frühjudentums.* AMTBBB 70. Frankfurt-am-Main: Athenäum, 1988. *Gericht und das Erbarmen Gottes.*

Wainwright, Geoffrey. *Eucharist and Eschatology.* London: Epworth, 1971.

Walaskay, Paul W. *'And so we came to Rome': The Political Perspective of St. Luke.* SNTSMS 49. Cambridge: Cambridge University, 1983. *Political Perspective.*

Wall, Robert W. "The Acts of the Apostles in Canonical Context." In *The New Testament as Canon: A Reader in Canonical Criticism,* by Robert W. Wall and Eugene E. Lemcio, 110-28. JSNTSup 76. Sheffield: Sheffield Academic, 1992. "Canonical Context."

———. " 'The Finger of God': Deuteronomy 9.10 and Luke 11.20." *NTS* 33 (1987) 144-50. "Finger of God."

———. "Martha and Mary (Luke 10.38-42) in the Context of a Christian Deuteronomy." *JSNT* 35 (1989) 19-35. "Martha and Mary."

Wanke, Joachim. *Die Emmauserzählung: Eine redaktionsgeschichtliche Untersuchung zu Lk 24,13-35.* ETS 31. Leipzig: St. Benn, 1973. *Emmauserzählung.*

Waterbury, John. "An Attempt to Put Patrons and Clients in Their Place." In *Patrons and Clients in Mediterranean Societies,* edited by Ernest Gellner and John Waterbury, 329-42. London: Duckworth, 1977. "Patrons and Clients."

Watson, Duane F. "People, Crowd." In *DJG,* 605-9.

Watson, Nigel M. "Was Zacchaeus Really Reforming?" *ExpT* 77 (1965-66) 282-85.

Weatherly, Jon A. *Jewish Responsibility for the Death of Jesus in Luke-Acts.* JSNTSup 106. Sheffield: Sheffield Academic, 1994. *Jewish Responsibility.*

Webb, Robert L. "The Activity of John the Baptist's Expected Figure at the Threshing Floor (Matthew 3.12 = Luke 3.17)." *JSNT* 43 (1991) 103-11. "Threshing Floor."

———. *John the Baptizer and Prophet: A Socio-Historical Study.* JSNTSup 62. Sheffield: JSOT, 1991. *John the Baptizer.*

Weinert, Francis D. "Luke, the Temple and Jesus' Saying about Jerusalem's Abandoned House (Luke 13:34-35)." *CBQ* 44 (1982) 68-76. "Jerusalem's Abandoned House."

———. "The Meaning of the Temple in Luke-Acts." *BTB* 11 (1981) 85-89. "Meaning of the Temple."

———. "The Multiple Meanings of Luke 2:49 and Their Significance." *BTB* 13 (1983) 19-22. "Multiple Meanings."

———. "The Parable of the Throne Claimant (Luke 19:12, 14-15a, 27) Reconsidered." *CBQ* 39 (1977) 505-14. "Parable of the Throne Claimant."

Weinrich, William C., ed. *The New Testament Age: Essays in Honor of Bo Reicke.* 2 vols. Macon, GA: Mercer University, 1984.

Weiss, Harold. "The Sabbath in Matthew, Mark, and Luke." *Spectrum* 19 (1, 1988) 33-39. "Sabbath."

Wengst, Klaus. *Pax Romana and the Peace of Jesus Christ.* London: SCM, 1987. *Pax Romana.*

Wenham, Gordon J. "BᵉTÛLĀH 'A Girl of Marriageable Age'." *VT* 22 (1972) 326-48. "BᵉTÛLĀH."

Werlen, Benno. *Society, Action and Space: An Alternative Human Geography.* London/New York: Routledge, 1993. *Society, Action and Space.*

⇌ Westerholm, Stephen. *Jesus and Scribal Authority.* ConBNT 10. Lund: Gleerup, 1978. *Jesus.*

————. "Pharisees." In *DJG,* 609-14.

————. "Sabbath." In *DJG,* 716-19.

Wheeler, Sondra Ely. *Wealth as Peril and Obligation: The New Testament on Possessions.* Grand Rapids: Wm. B. Eerdmans, 1995. *Wealth.*

White, Hayden. *The Content of the Form: Narrative Discourse and Historical Representation.* Baltimore: Johns Hopkins University, 1987. *Content of the Form.*

White, Richard C. "Vindication for Zacchaeus?" *ExpT* 91 (1979-80) 21.

Whittaker, Molly. *Jews and Christians: Graeco-Roman Views.* CCWJCW 6. Cambridge: Cambridge University, 1984. *Jews and Christians.*

Wilckens, Ulrich. *Die Missionsreden der Apostelgeschichte: Form- und traditionsgeschichtliche Untersuchungen.* 3d ed. WMANT 5. Neurkirchen-Vluyn: Neukirchener, 1974. *Missionsreden.*

Wilcox, Max. *The Semitisms of Acts.* Oxford: Clarendon, 1965. *Semitisms.*

Wilkens, Wilhelm. "Die Auslassung von Mark. 6,45–8.26 bei Lukas im Licht der Komposition Luk. 9.1-50," *TZ* 32 (1976) 193-200. "Auslassung."

————. "Die theologische Struktur der Komposition des Lukasevangeliums." *TZ* 34 (1, 1978) 1-13. "Struktur."

————. "Die Versuchungsgeschichte Luk. 4,1-13 und die Komposition des Evangeliums." *TZ* 30 (1974) 262-72. "Versuchungsgeschichte."

Wilkinson, John. *Health and Healing: Studies in New Testament Principles and Practice.* Edinburgh: Handsel, 1990. *Health and Healing.*

Williamson, H. G. M. "Samaritans." In *DJG,* 724-28.

Wilson, Robert R. "The Old Testament Genealogies in Recent Research." *JBL* 94 (1975) 169-89. "OT Genealogies."

Wilson, Stephen G. "The Ascension: A Critique and an Interpretation." *ZNW* 59 (1968) 269-81. "Ascension."

————. *The Gentiles and the Gentile Mission in Luke-Acts.* SNTSMS 23. Cambridge: Cambridge University, 1973. *Gentiles.*

————. *Luke and the Law.* SNTSMS 50. Cambridge: Cambridge University, 1983.

Wink, Walter. *John the Baptist in the Gospel Tradition.* SNTSMS 7. Cambridge: Cambridge University, 1968. *John the Baptist.*

Winter, Bruce W. *Seek the Welfare of the City: Christians as Benefactors and Citizens.* FCCGRW. Grand Rapids: Wm. B. Eerdmans; Carlisle: Paternoster, 1994. *Seek the Welfare.*

Winter, Paul. "The Cultural Background of the Narrative in Luke I and II." *JQR* 45 (1954-55) 159-67, 230-42, 287. "Cultural Background."

————. *"Hoti-*recitativum in Lk. 1:25, 61; 2:23." *HTR* 48 (1955) 213-16. *"Hoti-*recitativum."

Wise, Michael O. "Nazarene." In *DJG,* 571-74.

Wiseman, T. P. "There went out a decree from Caesar Augustus." *NTS* 33 (1987) 479-80. "Decree."

Witherington III, Ben. "Birth of Jesus." In *DJG,* 69-70.

—. *Jesus the Sage: The Pilgrimage of Wisdom.* Minneapolis: Fortress, 1994. *Jesus the Sage.*

—. "On the Road with Mary Magdalene, Joanna, Susanna, and Other Disciples — Luke 8:1-3." *ZNW* 70 (1979) 243-48. "On the Road."

—. *Women in the Earliest Churches.* SNTSMS 59. Cambridge: Cambridge University, 1988.

—. *Women in the Ministry of Jesus: A Study of Jesus' Attitudes to Women and Their Roles as Reflected in His Earthly Life.* SNTSMS 51. Cambridge: Cambridge University, 1984. *Women in the Ministry of Jesus.*

Wolf, Eric R. *Peasants.* FMA. Englewood Cliffs, NJ: Prentice-Hall, 1966.

Wolter, Michael. " 'Riech Gottes' bei Lukas." *NTS* 41 (1995) 541-63. "Reich Gottes."

Wolters, Al. "*ANTHRŌPOI EUDOKIAS* (Luke 2:14) and *'nšy Rwn* (4Q*416*)." *JBL* 113 (1994) 291-92. "*ANTHRŌPOI EUDOKIAS.*"

Wright, N. T. *Christian Origins and the Question of God.* Vol. 1: *The New Testament and the People of God.* Minneapolis: Fortress, 1992. *People of God.*

Wuellner, Wilhelm H. *The Meaning of "Fishers of Men."* Philadelphia: Westminster, 1967. *Fishers of Men.*

—. "The Rhetorical Structure of Luke 12 in Its Wider Context." *Neot* 22 (1988) 283-310. "Rhetorical Structure."

Wuthnow, Robert. *Communities of Discourse: Ideology and Social Structure in the Reformation, the Enlightenment, and European Socialism.* Cambridge, MA: Harvard University, 1989. *Communities of Discourse.*

Yamauchi, Edwin M. "Synagogue." In *DJG,* 781-84.

Yoder, John Howard. *The Politics of Jesus.* Grand Rapids: Wm. B. Eerdmans, 1972. *Politics of Jesus.*

York, John O. *The Last Shall Be First: The Rhetoric of Reversal in Luke.* JSNTSup 46. Sheffield: Sheffield Academic, 1991. *The Last Shall Be First.*

Zeller, Dieter. "ἀφροσύνη, ἄφρων." In *EDNT,* 1:184-85.

Zillessen, Klaus. "Das Schiff des Petrus und die Gefährten vom andern Schiff (Zur Exegese von Luc 5:1-11)." *ZNW* 57 (1966) 137-39. "Schiff des Petrus."

Zobel, H.-J. "הוי." In *TDOT,* 3:359-64.

Zorilla, C. Hugo. "The Magnificat: Song of Justice." In *Conflict and Context: Hermeneutics in the Americas,* edited by Mark Lau Branson and

C. René Padilla, 220-37. Grand Rapids: Wm. B. Eerdmans, 1986. "Magnificat."

Zwiep, A. W. "The Text of the Ascension Narratives (Luke 24.50-3; Acts 1.1-2, 9-11)." *NTS* 42 (1996) 219-44. "Text."

INTRODUCTION

1. READING THE GOSPEL OF LUKE

The purpose of this first introductory section is to identify, explain, and, to a lesser degree, defend the interpretive approach of this commentary. It will become immediately clear that this study does not, in part because it cannot, examine the Gospel of Luke from all of the many methodological vantage points in the biblical studies marketplace today. Instead, it pursues a line of study to which I have referred elsewhere as "discourse analysis" — correlating culture-critical and narratological concerns.[1] This approach will support an extended examination not only of Luke's literary art but also his narrative theology (i.e., theology, ethics, and spirituality) in a way that allows him to address contemporary readers without our constructing his work anachronistically as the product of contemporary concerns.[2]

1.1. THE GOSPEL OF LUKE AS "NARRATIVE" (διήγησις)

According to the Lukan preface (1:1-4), the author himself categorizes his work as a "narrative" or "orderly account" (and not as a "Gospel," as the tradition has it). This immediately invites a mode of reading appropriate to "narrative" — especially one that pays due respect to "order."[3] Within the first-century world of books and readers, Luke's preface also raises the possi-

---

1. See esp. Green, "Discourse Analysis"; also *idem, Gospel of Luke,* ch. 1. For methodological orientation, see further the two-article entry on "Discourse" in *The Johns Hopkins Guide to Literary Theory and Criticism:* de Beaugrande, "Discourse Analysis"; and G. L. Dillon, "Discourse Theory."

2. Central to this project is the methodological influence of Wuthnow's discussion of "the problem of articulation" in *Communities of Discourse,* 1-22.

3. See esp. Genette, *Narrative Discourse; idem, Narrative Discourse Revisited.*

1

bility that his "narrative" (as opposed, say, to epic poetry) might be understood with greater precision regarding its literary form or genre. Broadly speaking, the narrative choices available in Roman antiquity were historiography and biography, which take as their respective focus events that happened and people who lived; and novel, which has no necessary historical referent.

As recent study has indicated,[4] decisions about genre are important at both the generative and interpretive stages of the communicative process. Writers and readers alike follow repeatable patterns of speech — in the writer's case sometimes to establish, sometimes to subvert, expectations about meaning and aim. Genre decisions highlight particular ways of visualizing reality, of bringing to the surface specific aspects of experience.

As interesting and consequential as greater precision in genre identification might be, though, in terms of our task of "reading the Gospel of Luke," this area has become problematized in recent years by the growing recognition that, *from the standpoint of our reading of narrative,* the line separating historical narrative and nonhistorical cannot be sustained. This is not because historical narrative makes no historical claims (or has no historical referent outside of the text), but because the narrative representation of history is always inherently "partial" — both in the sense of its selectivity and in the sense of its orientation to a hermeneutical vantage point.[5] Historiography — in its choice of events to foreground at all, and in its ordering of those events in terms of temporal and causal relations — inevitably provides more, and less, than "what actually happened."[6] Consequently, the crucial first task even for those who read historiography (or biography) is to grapple fully with its status as narrative text.

Concerns of this nature do not render the quest of the genre of Luke's narrative obsolete or irrelevant, but do relativize somewhat the implications of the identification of genre for our reading of the Lukan enterprise.

The Genre of the Gospel of Luke. Since the seminal work on the preface of Luke by Henry J. Cadbury,[7] and largely based on it, a broad consensus has emerged that Luke 1:1-4 belongs squarely within the literary tradition of ancient historiography.[8] In addition to the preface, Luke's work shares many

---

4. See the helpful summary in J. L. Bailey, "Genre Analysis," esp. 197-203.

5. Cf. Clifford, "Partial Truths," 6-7.

6. On the growing recognition of the relationship between novel and historiography at the interpretive level, see, e.g., W. Martin, *Recent Theories;* also de Certeau, *Writing of History;* and, more pointedly, Iser, *Fictive and the Imaginary.*

7. Esp. Cadbury, "Commentary"; also, *idem,* "Knowledge Claimed"; *idem,* " 'We' and 'I' Passages in Luke-Acts."

8. "His prefaces and dedications at once suggest classification with the contemporary Hellenistic historians" (Cadbury et al., "Greek and Jewish Traditions," 15).

other features of Greco-Roman historiography — for example, a genealogical record (3:23-28); the use of meal scenes as occasions for instruction; travel narratives; speeches; letters; and dramatic episodes, such as Jesus' rejection at Nazareth (4:16-30) and Paul's stormy voyage and shipwreck (Acts 27:1–28:14).[9] This and other data have led to the identification of Luke-Acts as historiography and, then, to further attempts to designate with varying levels of precision the sort of history-writing Luke-Acts most approximates. For example, Aune has sought to clarify further the location of Luke-Acts within the broad framework of ancient historiography by classifying it as a "general history" — that is, the narration of ". . . the important historical experiences of a single national group from their origin to the recent past."[10] In this case, Luke's "national consciousness" embraces the origins of the people of "the Way" (Acts 9:2; 19:9, 23; 22:4; 24:14, 22), a distinct sect within first-century Judaism. Callan has also attempted to qualify the nature of Luke-Acts as historiography by designating Luke's work as one of the first examples of a type of history, concerned "to present a true account of something," which began to be written in the first century B.C.E.[11] And so on.

In spite of this consensus and the momentum it has fed for discerning in what sense Luke might be called an "historian,"[12] the identification of Luke-Acts as historiography in general and of Luke 1:1-4 as typical of prefaces in Greco-Roman historiography in particular has rested on uneasy ground. For some, Luke has always seemed too motivated by his *theological* agenda to be regarded as an *historian.* This is hardly the objection it once seemed, since no ancient historian was without motive, be it theological, apologetic, pedagogical, or whatever. The modern dichotomy that pits history over against theology has grown out of problematic philosophical (and especially epistemo-logical) commitments and is rightly being abandoned.[13] More to the point are

9. Aune, *Literary Environment,* 120-31.

10. Aune, *Literary Environment,* 88; see 77-153.

11. Callan, "Preface"; in addition to Luke-Acts, Callan lists the following in this category: Sallust, *On the Conspiracy of Catiline;* Josephus, *Jewish War;* Tacitus, *Annals;* Arrian, *Anabasis of Alexander;* Dio Cassius, *Roman History;* Herodian, *History of the Empire.*

12. See, e.g., Barrett, *Luke the Historian;* Gasque, *History of the Interpretation;* Hengel, *Acts;* Marshall, *Luke: Historian and Theologian;* Hemer, "Luke the Historian"; *idem, Acts;* Lüdemann, "Acts of the Apostles."

13. "Startling though it may seem, the concept of history in the *objective* sense, that is, as the aggregate of past events — was unknown to antiquity" (Fornara, *Nature of History,* 91; cf. 91-141). See the important directions in historiography signaled, e.g., by Cook, *History/Writing;* de Certeau, *Writing of History;* Stock, *Listening for the Text;* Veyne, *Writing History;* White, *Content of the Form.*

Cadbury seems to imply that an identification of Luke-Acts with Greco-Roman historiography carries with it the corollary that Luke must therefore have been defending

the formal differences between Luke's preface and those of the Greek historiographers. Thus, Luke's preface in Greek seems much too brief, consisting of only one sentence, as compared with the more lengthy openings of Greek historians; the transition from Luke's preface to the narrative itself is surprisingly abrupt, both in terms of style and with regard to providing any introduction to the narratological beginning in 1:5; unlike others, Luke does not engage in explicit criticism of his predecessors; and Luke's opening offers no general moral reflections, common among Greek historians.

Such problems as these led Alexander to a complete reassessment of the literary map of Greek preface-writing, with the result that she has been able to provide for an analysis of Luke 1:1-4 a wider frame of comparative reference. From her analysis of the syntactical structure of Luke's preface and other examples of Greek preface-writing, she finds the closest analogues to Luke 1:1-4 in the "scientific tradition" — that is, technical and professional writing on medicine, mathematics, engineering, and the like.[14] Alexander proposes that Luke's narrative presentation of Jesus and the early Christian movement is "scientific" in the sense that it is concerned to pass on the tradition of accumulated teaching on this subject.

The affinities Alexander documents do not support very well the notion that Luke's Gospel is a "scientific" treatise; formal, grammatical features cannot mask the significant discontinuity one recognizes when moving from the substance of the scientific tradition to the narrative of the Third Gospel. Nor do the affinities between Luke and the scientific tradition simply negate the identification of Luke 1:1-4 and Luke-Acts with the tradition of Greco-Roman historiography. First, that Luke-Acts does not match in every instance the formal features of Greco-Roman historiography presents no immediate problem, for the genre itself was loosely defined. What is more, Luke has been influenced as well by OT and later Jewish historiography,[15] especially with respect to the use of historical sequences to shape a narrative theology.

---

the Christian movement to the Roman authorities ("Commentary," 490; cf. *idem, Making of Luke-Acts,* 303-16; and the exaggerated claims regarding Luke's favorable portrayal of Rome in Wengst, *Pax Romana,* 89-105). In the wake of the two studies by Cassidy *(Jesus, Politics, and Society* and *Society and Politics)* it is no longer possible to see Luke-Acts simply as an apology for the benign character of the Christian movement, or, for that matter, of the Roman government. But such a reading is hardly demanded by Luke 1:1-4 and, *contra* Alexander ("Luke's Preface," 50), its implausibility should not be taken as a mark against identifying Luke's preface with the historiographical tradition.

14. Alexander, *Preface; idem,* "Luke's Preface"; also *idem,* "Preface to Acts."

15. For example, the Former Prophets, 1-2 Chronicles, Ezra, Nehemiah, and, later, the Maccabean literature. See the nuanced discussion of the relationship between the Lukan speeches and those in Greco-Roman, OT/Septuagintal, and Hellenistic Jewish historiography in Soards, *Speeches in Acts,* 134-61.

It is not simply that the Jesus-tradition was already in biographical form, as Alexander suggests, for other ways of re-presenting the significance of Jesus were available to Luke and "traditional" by his time. Rather, Luke intends to write a narrative, and in so describing his work[16] he identifies his project as a long narrative account of many events, for which the chief prototypes were the early Greek histories of Herodotus and Thucydides.[17] Third, we have already outlined ways in which literary components of Luke-Acts — symposia, travel narratives, speeches, and the like — support a positive comparison of Luke's work with Greco-Roman historiography. Finally, some of the difficulty with identifying Luke 1:1-4 with prefaces in Greco-Roman historiography is overcome when it is recognized that (1) many of Luke's predecessors in Israelite and Jewish historiography did not reflect on their aims and procedures within the context of the writing itself, and (2) in an important sense, Luke's work has not one but two openings — 1:1-4 and 1:5–2:52. It is especially in 1:5–2:52 that Luke actually locates a suitable point to begin his work, a series of narrative events capable of intending the whole of what follows in Luke-Acts.[18]

Apart from Alexander's work, with respect to the classification of Luke-Acts as historiography, the primary dissenting voice has been raised by those who find the closest generic parallels in Greco-Roman biography.[19] Biography grew out of historiography and, like it, has an historical referent(s). Taken on its own, the Gospel of Luke is susceptible to a biographical classification; understood in relation to the Acts of the Apostles, this designation is less easy to sustain. More importantly, as we will attempt to show, the Third Gospel is primarily focused on God and the fulfillment of God's ancient purpose, so it can only in a secondary sense be classified as an account of the life of Jesus. Its identification as a biography is seriously undercut by the recognition of this primary narrative aim,[20] as well as by the inability of the

---

16. διήγησις — Luke 1:1.

17. Hermogenes *Progymnasmata* 2; cf. Lucian *De Hist. Conscrib.* §55: "For all the body of the history is simply a long narrative" (διήγησις μαχρά); Aristotle *Rhetoric* 1.1360A35; Quintilian *Inst. orat.* 2.4.2; van Unnik, "Luke's Prologue," 12-14.

18. Cf. Fitzmyer, *Luke the Theologian,* 29-30. On the problem of beginnings for historians, see Said, *Beginnings,* 50.

19. Recently, e.g., Talbert, *Literary Patterns; idem, What Is a Gospel?;* Robbins, "Prefaces."

20. In his study of *The Plan of God in Luke-Acts,* Squires notes that Luke's central devotion to the divine purpose aligns his narrative with historiography.

The analysis of verb subjects by Burridge *(What Are the Gospels?),* indicating Jesus as by far the primary actor in the Gospel of Luke, proves to be too blunt an instrument, since actants who expressly operate as empowered or commissioned by God are in fact acting on his behalf and serving his aim. Such an analysis does not account for the pronounced treatment given in Luke-Acts to such concepts as "divine necessity," "the

biographical genre to account for Luke-Acts taken as a whole. What is none-theless clear is that Luke, perhaps more than the other Evangelists, has been influenced by Greco-Roman literary forms, especially those related to the biographical genre, even if other formal features and the theocentric focus of his narrative preclude identification of Luke-Acts as "biography" or "bio-graphical succession narrative."[21] The fluidity of such genres as "biography" and even, to some degree, "historiography," suggests the ease with which generic forms might be manipulated in practice.[22]

Identification of Luke-Acts as ancient historiography adds to the ex-pectations we may bring to the narrative. Alongside those raised by Luke's professed intentions (Luke 1:1-4), we may anticipate a narrative in which recent history is given prominence, issues of both causation and teleology are accorded privilege, and determined research is placed in the service of per-suasive and engaging instruction.

Throughout this discussion of genre, we have begged an important question that must now be taken up directly. This is the now-debated issue of the nature of the unity between Luke and Acts.

1.2. THE UNITY OF LUKE-ACTS

The unity of Luke-Acts — two volumes, one story — easily escapes the mod-ern reader in large part due to the canonical placement of these two books in the NT. Although the Gospel and Acts may have been completed and made available to the wider public separately, clearly in the second century C.E. the Gospel of Luke came to be located with the other Gospels, so as to form the "fourfold Gospel."[23] Acts, on the other hand, presumably as a bridge from the story of Jesus to the ministry of Paul, was eventually located in its present position between the Gospels and the Letters. In its canonical location, then,

---

Scriptures," and "God's purpose." Further, Burridge's analysis assumes without argued basis that the Gospel of Luke and the Acts of the Apostles can and probably should be divorced for purposes of genre specification. Moreover, even the identification of the Third Gospel's interest in one character, Jesus, does not immediately disqualify its designation as historiography. With the rise of Alexander the Great and the later Roman Empire, historiography became susceptible to a concentration on individuals — cf. Fornara, *Nature of History,* 34-46.

21. See the remarks in Aune, *Literary Environment,* 78-79; Barr and Wentling, "Classical Biography." Holzberg (*Ancient Novel,* 22-23) notes the novel-like affinities between Acts and the ancient novel.

22. For critiques of the biographical identification of the Gospels, see Aune, "Genre of the Gospels"; Guelich, "Gospel Genre"; Dihle, "Evangelien"; Hurtado, "Gospel (Genre)."

23. See Bruce, "Canon," 95; Koester, *Ancient Christian Gospels,* 242-44.

Acts has served to provide a framework for understanding the Pauline tradition,[24] and Luke's first volume has come to be thought of first and foremost as a "Gospel." It is worth reflecting on the near certainty that, in Luke's day, no such literary form existed, however, so that we would be amiss to think either that Luke set out to write a "Gospel" or that his readership would have understood his work within such a category.[25] Luke refers to his predecessors as "narratives," not as "Gospels," and there is no a priori reason to imagine that Luke's purpose was to write a story of Jesus to which he might later append an account of the early church. Rather, the "narrative" he wished to relate developed naturally and purposefully from the story of Jesus' earthly ministry to that of the continuation of Jesus' mission through the early church.[26]

On account of the content of the prefaces in Luke 1:1-4 and of the secondary preface in Acts 1:1-2, some relationship between the Third Gospel and Acts has long been assumed, and most today would agree that these two books share a common author.[27] In addition, it is generally agreed that Acts forms some sort of sequel to the Gospel of Luke — a consensus that is well grounded in a series of data.[28] For example, Acts 1:1 not only refers to a "first book," but also denotes as its subject "all that Jesus began to do and to teach." This is a transparent summary of the Third Gospel, which characterizes the ministry of Jesus as consisting of words and deeds, held in tandem, leaving no room for reductionism on either side of the equation. With the term "began," this summary suggests a continuation of the mission of Jesus, an expectation that is not disappointed, for Jesus' followers "call on his name" (e.g., Acts 2:21; 9:21; 15:17; 18:15; 22:16) — a name that signifies the continuing presence of Jesus to bring wholeness of life (e.g., Acts 3:6, 16; 4:7, 10, 12, 17, 30; 8:12; 9:15, 34; 10:43; 16:18).

The division of Luke-Acts into two volumes, then, need not signify that one story had ended and a new one begun, or that volume two would

24. See further, Wall, "Canonical Context."

25. For the use of "Gospel" (εὐαγγέλιον) as a designation of a book, see Justin *Dial.* 10.2; 100.1; *1 Apol.* 66. Koester (*Ancient Christian Gospels,* 1-43) argues that εὐαγγέλιον was not used to describe a book until Marcion.

26. See Marshall, "Luke and His 'Gospel'," 291-94.

27. See Parsons and Pervo, *Rethinking the Unity,* 7-8. It is true that a debate continues regarding common authorship of the Gospel of Luke and the Acts of the Apostles, particularly on stylistic grounds — e.g., *con:* Argyle, "Greek of Luke"; *pro:* Beck (in response to Argyle), "Common Authorship." More recently, stylistic peculiarities have led Dawsey to query in what sense one can speak of the *narrative* unity of Luke-Acts ("Literary Unity").

28. This much is also admitted by Parsons and Pervo *(Rethinking the Unity),* who otherwise discount the generic, theological, and narrative unity of Luke and Acts. See also Pervo, "Same Genre"; Parsons, "Unity of the Lukan Writings"; *idem,* "Christian Origins."

now turn to a different subject matter.[29] Rather, as a matter of physical expediency ancient authors divided their lengthy works into "books," each of which fit on one papyrus roll.[30] The maximum length of a papyrus roll extended to some thirty-five feet,[31] and Luke's two volumes, the longest books in the NT, would have each required a full papyrus roll. In fact, in size the two are roughly equivalent — the Gospel with some 19,400 words, Acts with approximately 18,400 words — so that they would have required papyrus rolls of about the same length. Thus, the division between Luke and Acts conformed to the desire of contemporary writers to keep the size of their books symmetrical.[32] In other ways, too, the plan of Luke and Acts suggests a purposeful proportionality. Both narratives begin in Jerusalem; the Gospel ends and Acts begins with commission narratives associated with reports of Jesus' ascension; the time span covered by each volume is approximately thirty years; Luke's narration of Jesus' last days in Jerusalem (19:28–24:53) and of Paul's arrest, trials, and arrival in Rome (Acts 21:27–28:31) each occupy some 25 percent of their respective books; and in many other ways Luke has consciously developed parallels between Jesus in the Gospel of Luke and his disciples in the Acts of the Apostles.[33]

Can one push the notion of unity further, in order to embrace "narrative unity" for Luke-Acts? This question revolves around how one constructs the concept of "narrative." This itself is contested ground,[34] though central ingredients would include temporal sequence (involving, in Aristotle's terms, a beginning, a middle, and an end) and, thus, an aim. In narrative, events are given temporal and causal relationship, sometimes construed by narratologists as "narrative cycle." A simple narrative cycle might consist of the progression from "possibility" to "realization" to "result."[35] Narrative cycles may appear within narratives — such as the progression from promise to realization to result in Luke's account of the birth of John (1:5-25, 59-80), but are also constitutive of entire narratives.

29. See Alexander, "Preface to Acts," 78-79, 92-94.

30. On the preparation of paper and papyrus rolls from papyrus, see Pliny *Naturalis Historia* 13.21-27 §§68-89, conveniently summarized in Finegan, *NT Manuscripts*, §§5-6; also, Gamble, *Books and Readers*, 44-45.

31. Cf. Metzger, *Manuscripts*, 16; Kenney, "Books and Readers," 18; and esp. Gamble, *Books and Readers*, 45-47; Kenyon, *Books and Readers*, 51-52.

32. Morton and Macgregor, *Structure*, 12-17; cf. Diodorus Siculus 1.29.6; 1.41.10; Josephus *Against Apion* 1.35 §320.

33. See Green, "Internal Repetition"; Aune, *Literary Environment*, 119; O'Toole, *Unity*, ch. 3.

34. See the introductory comments in Toolan, *Narrative*, 5-9; also W. Martin, *Recent Theories*.

35. See the discussion of "narrative cycle" in Bal, *Narratology*, 19-23.

Can the whole of Luke-Acts be understood as the outworking of a single narrative cycle, serving a single narrative aim?[36]

Viewing Luke-Acts on the large canvas of narrative analysis, it is possible to see in its entirety a simple narrative cycle, painted in broad strokes.[37] In it we see the working out of God's purpose to bring salvation in all of its fullness to all people. This aim is *anticipated* by God's messengers in 1:5–2:52, then made *possible* by the birth and growth of John and Jesus in households oriented around the purpose of God. According to the Lukan birth narrative, however, the divine aim will not be reached without opposition. The realization of God's aim is made *probable* through the preparatory mission of John and the life, death, and exaltation of Jesus, with its concomitant commissioning and promised empowering of Jesus' followers to extend the message to all people (Luke 3–Acts 1). Jesus himself prepares the way for this universal mission, even if he does not engage much with non-Jews, by systematically dissolving the barriers that predetermine and have as their consequence division between ethnic groups, men and women, adults and children, rich and poor, righteous and sinner, and so on. In his ministry, even conflict is understood within the bounds of God's salvific purpose, Jesus' death as a divine necessity, his exaltation a vindication of his ministry and powerful act of God making possible the extension of salvation to Jew and Gentile alike. The subsequent story in Acts consists of a narration of the *realization* of God's purpose, particularly in Acts 2–15, as the Christian mission is directed by God to take the necessary steps to achieve an egalitarian community composed of Jews, Samaritans, and Gentiles. The *results* of this narrative aim (Acts 16–28) highlight more and more Jewish antagonism to the Christian movement, and the church appears more and more to be Gentile in makeup. This, too, is God's purpose, according to the narrator, speaking above all through his spokesperson Paul (and through Paul, the Scriptures), even if efforts among the Jewish people at interpreting Moses and the prophets as showing the Messiah is Jesus should continue.[38]

The Gospel of Luke and the Acts of the Apostles, then, narrate one

36. The phrasing of the question is deliberate. Because we cannot know the mind of the author, we cannot determine whether the author *intended* narrative unity. Instead, we can ask whether the content and form of Luke-Acts are consistent with (and support) its characterization as a narrative unity. Moreover, we can ask whether the Gospel of Luke seems to intend its continuation in the Acts of the Apostles — i.e., whether narrative needs are established in Luke that find their satisfaction only in Acts.

37. What follows is largely borrowed from Green, "Beginning," 62-63.

38. This is to suggest neither that either of the two volumes of Luke's work is without aims particular to it, nor that the final verse of Acts marks the absolute closure (or resolution) of all possibilities. After all, Paul has not yet gone to trial (as anticipated) and, more pointedly, Jesus has not yet returned (as promised).

continuous story,[39] and the phrase from Luke's preface that describes the content of his work, "the events that have been fulfilled among us," refers both to the story of Jesus and to the activity of the early church.[40]

The narrative unity of Luke-Acts has important implications for our reading of Luke's work. Most significantly, it requires that our understanding of Luke's purpose in writing and, thus, our understanding of the need(s) and audience he addressed account for *all the evidence,* both the Gospel and Acts.[41] Similarly, it is critical that we understand that incidents in the Gospel anticipate aspects of the story narrated only (finally) in Acts. Notably, in 2:25-35 Simeon realizes that in this child Jesus a salvation has come that will be experienced as "a light for revelation to the Gentiles" (2:32), but during his ministry as recorded in the Gospel of Luke Jesus actually interacts only rarely with non-Jews. One must wait for Acts to see how the Gentile mission is begun, legitimated, and takes firm shape at the behest of God and as guided and empowered by the Holy Spirit. The last chapter of the Gospel closes off significant aspects of the story's plot, but there is a more overarching intent at work, the redemptive purpose of God for all people. Seen against this purpose, the Gospel of Luke is incomplete in itself, for it opens up possibilities in the narrative cycle[42] that go unrealized in the Gospel but do materialize in the Acts of the Apostles.[43]

39. See already Augustine *De cons.* 4.8.

40. Haenchen has been followed by a few, more recent scholars in insisting that Luke's reference to "many" literary predecessors in 1:1 rules out the possibility that here Luke had Acts in view ("We in Acts," 95-96). Higgins sought to overcome this obstacle by arguing that 1:1-2 refers "to the gospel alone, and not at all to Acts," whereas "verse 3 refers to both the Lukan writings" ("Preface to Luke," 81-82). Aside from the reality that we simply do not know what sorts of traditional material were available to Luke for use in the writing of the Acts of the Apostles (recently, see Lüdemann, *Early Christianity*), J. Bauer has shown that, as a literary convention, πολλοί ("many") need not refer to a crowd of predecessors, but points instead to the certification of Luke's work through appeal to his association with the tradition ("ΠΟΛΛΟΙ").

41. Cf. Maddox, *Purpose,* 3-6.

42. This is not to imply that all possibilities opened up in narratives are necessarily actualized. However, inasmuch as the Gospel creates anticipations fulfilled in the Acts of the Apostles (and not before), we can speak of the Gospel's *needing* its companion volume, Acts, for completion of its story line.

43. Already implicit here is a fundamental critique of the view of Conzelmann *(Luke),* followed more recently by Fitzmyer (esp. 1:18-22; *idem, Luke the Theologian,* e.g., 59-63), that Luke has divided salvation history into three periods — the period of Israel (from creation to the imprisonment of John the Baptist), the period of Jesus (from his baptism to his ascension), and the period of the church under stress (from Jesus' ascension to his parousia). See the critical discussion in Bovon, *Luke the Theologian,* 27-28; R. J. Dillon, *Eyewitnesses,* esp. 272-74; Marshall, "Luke and His 'Gospel'," 298-303.

1.3. METHOD IN READING THE GOSPEL OF LUKE

As historiographical narrative, the Gospel of Luke consists of a series of event-accounts. The significance of each of these accounts is incomplete when viewed on its own. Each must be read with reference to its narrative location. Hence, the order of the narrative, Luke's staging of events in their narrative sequence, is a primary control on the determination of meaning. For our purpose, it will not do to treat each "event" or "pericope" in isolation, as popular Bible reading, lectionary preaching, and tradition-critical scholarship often do.[44] The interests of narratology — including "order," but also, for example, perspective, characterization, setting, theme, and the like — are immediately relevant to our reading of the Third Gospel.[45]

Ultimately, of course, the Third Gospel is not simply a narrative text, but a "cultural product." That is, as literary text, the Gospel of Luke is itself a representation of the values and contexts within which it was generated, so any attempt to dislodge the Gospel from its own world would render it in some ways incomprehensible.[46] At the same time, Luke's narrative gives expression to a vision of the world that cannot be equated with the first-century context insofar as this can be reconstructed via historical inquiry. Luke's world is one in which God intervenes through miraculous conceptions, angels regularly mediate between heaven and earth, and diabolic forces are active, for example. What is more, by representing historical events and movements in a narrative framework, Luke has provided them with an interpretation that must of necessity escape the historian concerned primarily with the scientific verification of particular events. This is because Luke has woven into the same, seamless fabric events and their interpretation as the fulfillment of the divine purpose. His narrative, then, this cultural product, the Third Gospel, gives expression to an eschatological vision currently manifesting itself in the world wherein God "has brought down the powerful from their thrones, and lifted up the lowly" (1:52). Indeed, it is not too much to say that the Lukan narrative is an invitation to embrace an alternative worldview and to live as if the reign of God had already revolutionized this age.

44. See Eco, *Limits*, 21: ". . . symbols are paradigmatically open to infinite meanings but syntagmatically, that is, textually, open only to the indefinite, but by no means infinite, interpretations allowed by the context . . . any act of interpretation is a dialectic between openness and form, initiative on the part of the interpreter and contextual pressure"; Brown and Yule, *Discourse Analysis*, 35-50, 33-134.

45. See the helpful summary in Powell, "Narrative Criticism"; *idem, Narrative Criticism*. For general introductions, see Bal, *Narratology;* Chatman, *Story and Discourse;* Toolan, *Narrative*.

46. Cf. Greenblatt, "Culture," esp. 226-27.

All language is embedded in culture,[47] and because Luke's narrative enterprise will have been set within a particular discourse situation, it behooves modern interpreters to engage as fully as possible in an exploration of the cultural presuppositions Luke shared with his contemporaries. Hence, when we speak of discerning Luke's "social setting" we mean more than "narrative world" as this phrase is used in narrative criticism. We mean more than the world available to us only through the narrative viewed as a closed system, but less than the world often represented to us by historical-critical inquiry. The former strips the Gospel of Luke of its cultural embeddedness, while the latter assumes too easily that the (real) social world wherein Luke's story is set can and should simply be read into Luke's narrative.[48] As we will see, Luke does not represent the "real world" so straightforwardly, but both seeks to provide an alternative view of that world[49] and chooses aspects of that world to emphasize while downplaying others.[50] The question is, What aspects of the social world of antiquity has Luke chosen to represent in his story — and how has he done so?

All of this means that narratology provides a necessary but incomplete approach to the Third Gospel. In order to grapple with this "cultural product," one also needs in one's methodological quiver an historical method deeply rooted in social-scientific or culture-critical sensitivities. This form of historicism will not be concerned fundamentally with "what really happened," as though such a "History with a capital H"[51] were available to us or even possible to construct. Instead, it is concerned with (1) how Luke has "ordered" (1:3) events in order to serve a particular teleology and (2) how Luke's model readers[52] will have heard and been shaped by the episodes of which he has given an account as well as by his narrative understood as a whole.

47. Cf. Stubbs, *Discourse Analysis,* 8; G. Brown and Yule, *Discourse Analysis,* 27-31; Cotterell and Turner, *Linguistics and Biblical Interpretation,* 68-72.

48. So, e.g., Horsley, *Liberation of Christmas;* Neyrey, ed., *Social World.*

49. For example, by redefining power or undermining a patriarchal ideology — cf. Anderson, "Mary's Difference."

50. For example, he has little to say about the politico-economic power of the temple, an historical certainty, but highlights its socio-religious power — cf. Green, "Demise of the Temple."

51. This phrase is from Veyne, *Writing History,* 26-27. Cf. Fornara, *Nature of History,* 198: "The Rankean view that it is the task of history simply to discover the facts — i.e., that history is the total aggregation of fact — was speedily seen to be assailable not only because of the 'subjective' manner in which we perceive 'the facts,' but because the retrieval and reproduction of the totality of true facts is self-evidently an unattainable ideal."

52. The phrase "model reader" is Eco's: "The author has thus to foresee a model of the possible reader (hereafter Model Reader) supposedly able to deal interpretively with the expressions in the same way as the author deals generatively with them" (*Role of the Reader,* 7).

Some Key Terms. The sort of analysis undertaken in this study thus brings to the fore for investigation the social and linguistic webs within which speech occurs and derives its significance.[53] These "webs" are of various kinds and can be outlined with reference to the relationship of a given text to its co-text, intertext, and context.

Co-text refers to the string of linguistic data within which a text is set, the relationship of, say, a sentence to a paragraph, a pericope in Luke's Gospel to the larger Lukan narrative, and so on. "Local" co-text refers to the immediately preceding material and is often of paramount importance in shaping how a text will be received. This is because of the limitations of memory; that is, what we have heard or read just prior to the present text has a proportionately greater determinative role in the construction of its meaning in its narrative location. On the other hand, the meaning of a text is rendered more secure when read against the horizons of the narrative as a whole. Indeed, co-text may refer more broadly to what comes after as well as before a given text. We expect promises made in a narrative text, for example, to find their fulfillment later in the narrative, even if we are not always clear *how* or *in what sense* those expectations might be realized. Hence, expectations (or "narrative needs") can be reshaped or even set aside by subsequent co-text.

Intertext refers to the location of a text within the larger linguistic frame of reference on which it consciously or unconsciously draws for meaning. We are particularly interested in how Luke's narrative draws and/or builds on the LXX.

How is it possible to know when the narrator has drawn on the OT? In many cases, Luke's use of the OT is explicit. Direct citations such as one finds in 3:3-6 are unambiguous. Less certain are those locations where Luke seems to have drawn on an OT "type-scene" — a form of repetition of earlier biblical narrative, wherein an episode is composed of a fixed sequence of motifs often associated with a recurrent theme. For example, type-scenes like "the announcement of birth" (see below, §2) reiterate a progression of events in a manner typical of what one finds in OT texts, while drawing on a common inventory of actions. Often even more elusive are those places where Luke's dependence on the OT occurs in the form of allusions or linguistic echoes.

Although our capacity to hear such intertextual reverberations as these is not always (and cannot always be) circumscribed by what we may or may not believe about the intent of the narrator, in our comments on Luke's use of the OT we are guided by some criteria. These would include especially the criteria of (1) "availability" and (2) "volume" — that is, (1) the presence in the presupposition pool shared by Luke and his audience of the text(s) from which his narrative is alleged to have drawn, and (2) the presence within the

---

53. Cf. Green, "Discourse Analysis," 183-86.

Lukan narrative of any of a wide array of evidence that Luke's vision has been drawn to a particular OT figure and/or text. For example, the criteria of "volume" for a number of intertextual observations might be satisfied with reference to Luke's amply attested interest in tying his narrative into the story of Abraham, in portraying Jesus in hues borrowed from the Moses-story, or in inscribing the story of Jesus into OT material concerning Elijah and Elisha. In such cases, evidence might take the form of linguistic similarities, common motifs, the actual naming of OT figures, parallel patterns, and the like.

Intertextuality of this sort is not as concerned with finding the one and only, definitive answer to how Luke has employed the OT in such-and-such a text as in seeing how Luke's narrative serves as a kind of "echo chamber" for the interplay of the ancient, sacred stories with Luke's own story. Hence, we have much less need to certify to the exclusion of other probable candidates the precise source of an allusion in the Lukan narrative (which in any case is not always possible) than to appreciate the many voices from Israel's past given a fresh hearing.

Context, finally, refers to the socio-historical realities of the Lukan text — both the world to which it gives witness (i.e., the world of Palestine in the first decades, C.E.) and the world in which the Third Gospel was written (i.e., the wider Greco-Roman world of the latter decades, C.E.). Concern with context is focused on such presuppositions as socio-cultural scripts assumed by the narrator, or provided by the narrator in order to broaden further the presupposition pools of his audience. As we have already noted, and as will become abundantly clear in what follows, Luke may draw on widely held cultural assumptions in order to affirm as well as to undermine them. In order to grapple with Luke's narrative theology, then, it is important to appreciate how he has gone about the task of engaging the cultural assumptions of his world by means of his narrative.

Narrative, History, and Historicity. Against the backdrop of the last two centuries of biblical studies, the approach to the Lukan narrative we have sketched may seem ahistorical to some, or at least impoverished with reference to historical concerns. After all, this commentary is not focused on the identification of Luke's sources, nor on how Luke might have transformed the traditions available to him in the process of generating his Gospel, nor on whether each episode he records approximates what actually happened. This is not because we reject the idea of sources as such. Luke himself declares his cognizance of other narratives (1:1-4), and his narrative is clearly susceptible to tradition-historical investigation of various kinds. Indeed, the identification of Luke's two volumes as "historiography" raises immediately issues of Luke's method of historical inquiry, his access to diverse traditions, and his concern with and practices of verification. And, of course, these issues must be understood in the case of Luke against the backdrop of the canons of historical inquiry and of the narrative representation of history in Greco-Roman antiquity.

Not unlike the subsequent writing of history, including that among our contemporaries, ancient historiography was marked by the paradox of two more or less competing interests — *veracity* (the attempt to depict events that actually happened) and *narrative* (the attempt to set events within a coherent, meaningful series, the presentation of which accords privilege to causation and teleology).[54] This is no less true of Luke in the first-century Roman world than it would have been, say, of the earlier, Greek historiographer Thucydides, whose commitment to impartiality served as the ideal for centuries. Our reading of the Third Gospel is concerned above all with the "narrative" side of this equation — that is, with the sequencing of events and the interpretive aim that weaves its way forward through the narrative, surfacing here and there while lurking beneath the story elsewhere.

Of course, in an important sense, it is true that every sentence in Luke-Acts carries with it a documentary as well as an interpretive force.[55] Major commentaries on the Gospel of Luke in recent decades have been occupied primarily with the former of these, with such diachronic questions as how Luke might have used the Gospel of Mark as well as other sources, whether written or oral, or how an individual account in Luke might represent an actual event in the life of Jesus. This commentary takes as its challenge the second interest — the presentation of these events within a coherent narrative, within a meaningful sequence. This is not only because of the ready availability of diachronic commentary on the Third Gospel, however. Our perspective is also guided by our belief that the major challenge facing Luke was not one of verifying *that* these events actually took place (as though Luke's first readers had drunk deeply, as we have, from the wells of ninteenth-century historicism). Similarly, while we remain reasonably confident that one of Luke's major sources was the Gospel of Mark, and that other written narrative materials were available to him, we do not imagine that his first readers had access to their own copies of the Second Gospel or that they could (or would have been interested to) compare the texts of Luke and Mark in ways consistent with modern redaction criticism. (Indeed, given the general illiteracy of and nature of "publishing" in the Roman Mediterranean, even our use of the terms "readers" and "copies" is already enmired in anachronism.)

It may be helpful to provide a single illustration of the claim that Luke's primary challenge was related to the significance of the story of Jesus and not

54. See Cook, *History/Writing*, 55-72.
55. For this concept in historiography, see Cook, *History/Writing*, 55.

to its verification. Consider the general portrait of Jesus the healer, so central to the Lukan conception. Reasons for regarding this portrait as generally accurate from an historical perspective are plentiful.

How does the tradition painting Jesus as healer fare under the scrutiny of the criterion of dissimilarity, for example? What about other healers in the wider world of first-century antiquity; what about healing within the Christian communities after Jesus? Within Jewish circles, we know of two potential candidates who are sometimes compared with Jesus, Honi the Circle-Drawer and Hanina ben Dosa. We also know of Apollonius of Tyana, a first-century Gentile miracle worker. Traditions surrounding these persons are important both for indicating that healers were not unknown (or simply dismissed as charlatans) in the world of Jesus, but also for demonstrating how Jesus was dissimilar from such potential analogues as these. According to the evidence we have, both Honi the Circle-Drawer and Hanina ben Dosa easily qualify as "holy men," but neither can be called a "miracle worker" with respect to his *characteristic* activity. What is more, these two persons were known for their calling on Yahweh to work in spectacular ways. Jesus, on the other hand, is distinguished by his *typical* behavior as a healer, and, more importantly, is portrayed in the Gospel tradition as one who exercised in a direct way the saving power of God. He did not ask God to intervene on behalf of those in need of a miracle but pronounced their healing directly, in speech-acts that assumed his possession of divine authority to do so. These speech-acts also distinguish the healing of Jesus from that of his disciples, at least as this is evidenced in the Acts of the Apostles. They do not assume direct access to divine power even when they are engaged in ministries of signs and wonders; indeed, they often recoil from the suggestion of others that they possess divine power (e.g., Acts 14:14-15) and instead pronounced healing "in the name of Jesus" (e.g., 3:6, 16). Unlike Apollonius, Jesus often emphasized the component of faith in his ministry of healing — so much so that, according to the Gospels, one of the characteristic assertions of Jesus was, "Your faith has made you well." Jesus, then, was both like and unlike other healers, and the portrait of Jesus as healer satisfies the criterion of dissimilarity.

A second criterion often used to determine the authenticity of the traditions about Jesus is concerned with multiple attestation. Without delving much into the technicalities of this discussion, it is immediately possible to see that the portrait of Jesus as healer satisfies this criterion as well. In the Gospel of Matthew alone, we find nineteen stories of the miraculous alongside four summary statements indicating healing as one of the distinctive properties of Jesus' activity. The Gospel of Mark records eighteen miracle stories and four summaries, while the Gospel of Luke has twenty stories and three summaries. When we take into account that these three Gospels occasionally report the same episode, the list of independent accounts is still impressive: six episodes of exorcism, seventeen accounts of healing (including three resuscitations), and eight so-called nature miracles. In addition, the Evangelists themselves allude to miracles that are not specifically recounted, Jesus makes statements concerning the significance of his healing ministry, and his opponents are reported as offering alternative interpretations of Jesus' healing activity. Not only do we have "multiple attestation" utilizing different Gospel sources, not only do we have attestation from different types of Gospel material (summaries, debates, and actual accounts, for example), but we also have testimony from Josephus and from the Jewish polemical tradition. Josephus devotes a lengthy paragraph to Jesus that is so positive in its assessment of him that it has long been regarded as a Christian interpolation into the original text. More recent scholarship, however, has been inclined to view Josephus as having documented some information about Jesus, to which Christians later added in order to make his messianic status completely unambiguous. According to the report that is almost certainly derived from Josephus, Jesus was regarded as a wise man and doer of "parabolic works" — that is, a miracle worker (*Ant.* 18.3.3 §§63-64). The early Christian theologian Origen represents his debate partner, Celsus, as believing that Jesus went to Egypt, there learning the secrets of the magicians; Jesus was then able to return to Palestine, where he conducted himself as a deceptive quack (*Con. Cel.* 1.38). Similarly, in his *Dialogue* (69.7), the Christian apologist Justin observed that some Jews taught that Jesus' healing miracles constituted a display of magic art; he was a magician and a deceiver. And in a talmudic text, the extraordinary powers Jesus exercised are attributed to demonic powers, so that Jesus is again labeled as a sorcerer (*b. Sanh.* 43a, 107b).

Finally, among the criteria that have been of particular importance in recent study of the historical Jesus is the criterion of Jesus' suffering and death. Here the fundamental question is, How can we account for the level of hostility toward Jesus that led eventually to a Roman execution? Does the tradition of Jesus as healer assist us on this score? Evidence to which we have already alluded is helpful in this respect, since polemical attempts to label Jesus as a sorcerer within the Jewish tradition signal the sort of problem Jesus presented the Jewish leadership in Jerusalem. In fact, according to Luke 23:1-5 Jesus was handed over to Pilate on charges of perverting the nation of Israel and attempting to lead the people astray. These charges are self-evident echoes of language in Deuteronomy 13, where Israel is warned concerning false prophets who, through their signs and wonders, would attempt to lead God's people astray. Apparently, this is a significant aspect of the case against Jesus: Through his miracle-working he opened himself to being labeled as a false prophet, for whom the prescribed penalty was death.

We have seen, then, that the Gospel portrait of Jesus as healer satisfies the criteria of dissimilarity and multiple attestation, and was in all probability intricately interwoven into the fabric of hostility toward him that led to his execution. Other criteria might have been explored, but by any typical scholarly reckoning this would be enough to establish the authenticity of the tradition as a whole, even if individual miracle episodes would then be examined one by one.[56] Nevertheless, the veracity of Jesus' healing ministry is neither for Luke, nor apparently for his contemporaries, the point at issue. Luke's Gospel contains within itself two indications of opposition to Luke's perspective on Jesus as healer — the one from those who regarded Jesus as an agent of Beelzebul, the other from those who found in Jesus' healing activity cause for branding him as a false prophet (11:14-15; 23:1-5; see the commentary on these texts below). As we have intimated, nonbiblical tradition similarly labels Jesus negatively as a magician or quack. What is pivotal about these *testimonia* for our purposes is this: *Each of these voices* assumes *that Jesus was indeed a healer, then proceeds with attempts* to interpret *that activity with reference to its source. Similarly, Luke* presupposes *the possibility of miraculous healing — for such is the nature of his historicism — and* assumes *that Jesus was a healer,[57] but provides his activity as a healer with* interpretive significance *by wrapping it in OT cloth and situating it centrally within the narrative of a Spirit-anointed ministry of bringing near the blessings of God's domain.* This interpretive significance does not adhere to the accounts of healing themselves, each taken on its own terms, but becomes visible, even compelling, by their location within the Lukan narrative as a whole. With only very rare exceptions (to be noted in the commentary below), Luke's compulsion is to provide meaning for the events he recounts, not to argue for or demonstrate their veracity.

For these reasons, the historical concerns of our reading of the Third Gospel do not (often) relate to veracity or verification. Instead, they are tied to (1) how the events Luke recounts in narrative sequence might have been "heard," or given significance, within the sociohistorical mores of Luke's world and (2) how Luke, within his own discourse situation and in his narrative representation of history, might have accorded significance to these events.

Nevertheless, at the turn of the twenty-first century, it is perhaps inevitable that the approach taken in this commentary will raise questions about the historical veracity of Luke's account and, perhaps more particularly, about our construal of its historicity. The impetus for such questions is not

---

56. This is not to say, however, that scholars today are in unanimous agreement that Jesus was in fact a healer. It is to say, rather, that, when standard criteria are applied to this material, the case for the general picture of Jesus as healer is strong indeed.

57. This assumption, set within Luke's attempt to extend the biblical story, cannot be dismissed as "uncritical"; as with biblical history more generally, divine activity is for Luke integral to the unfolding of events and cannot be segregated from it.

hard to find, though one must probably think in terms of several, overlapping motivations. Among these, two surface immediately. There is first the scandal and significance of the Christian belief in the incarnation, the basis of which finds testimony in the Gospel of Luke. God acts in history, redemptively and decisively, according to Luke, so it is more than a matter of curiosity whether "the events that have been fulfilled among us" (1:1) are "true" events. Second, there is our claim that the Gospel of Luke would have been shelved, so to speak, in Roman libraries, along with other representations of the genre of historiography. And, at least in modern thought, the writing of "history" raises questions of accuracy and truth. By way of responding to such concerns, we may outline three programmatic statements.

(1) The approach of this commentary does not purport to answer all of the sorts of questions to which a text like the Third Gospel is susceptible. Beholding the Gospel of Luke as a cultural product in the form of a narrative foregrounds certain methodological choices. Identifying it more as a window[58] into historical processes emanating from the historical Jesus and early Christian communities and finding their zenith in the redactional activity of the Third Evangelist has produced already a full stable of commentary that need not be duplicated here.[59]

(2) The approach adopted here necessarily blurs the distinction between the world *of* the text and the world *behind* the text, for it treats the text itself, this historical representation in the form of narrative discourse, as an object of historical interest.[60] What is more, it does so in part because we believe Luke has himself invited this form of inquiry and engagement. This is not to say that the author of the Third Gospel was uninterested in actual events in the life of Jesus, only that the Lukan narrative is not the product of such an interest, narrowly defined.[61] Thus, for example, one looks in vain for argumentation within the narrative to the effect that this event "actually happened in this way." Often enough, Luke does not even locate in his accounting possible witnesses capable of providing a dispassionate, corroborating voice in support of the historical veracity of key events (e.g., the annunciation to Mary, the testing of Jesus in the wilderness, Jesus' prayer on the Mount of Olives, et al.).[62] Luke's contribution does not consist in such critical chron-

58. Cf. Krieger, *A Window to Criticism,* 3-4.

59. Recently, e.g., Fitzmyer, Marshall, Nolland, C. F. Evans, Bock, Schürmann, and Bovon.

60. See B. Stock, *Listening for the Text.*

61. See the important discussion of biblical narrative and historicity in Goldingay, *Models for Scripture,* 21-82.

62. Fornara *(Nature of History)* notes that ancient historians are concerned with the memorable, not the credible (91-98); and that bare historical facts required both supplementation and deductive interconnection (134-37). By this he does not mean to say

icle-keeping. Instead, as we hope to show, Luke concerns himself, self-consciously, with interpretive persuasion — that is, not with validation of events but with their signification.[63]

(3) The foregoing comments do not diminish the authority of the Gospel of Luke as Christian Scripture, though they may surface questions about how the authority of Luke, as narrative, is to be construed. This, however, is not really a question for the Third Gospel as much as it is for all biblical narrative. Narrators within the Scriptures of Israel, no more than the Third Evangelist, make no claims for prophetic inspiration. In fact, apart from the preface where Luke writes "himself" into the Third Gospel (1:1-4), he, like other biblical narrators, is absent from the narrative itself.[64] Paradoxically, by telling the story thus, the narrator of Luke actually enhances his claim to know the mind of God — that is, to have a divine perspective on these unfolding events. The authority of the Gospel of Luke does not rest on its claim to historical veracity, therefore, but on its capacity to speak for God, to make transparent the significance of the events it narrates.[65] After all, history — as "bare facts" — may be a necessary ground for faith, but "facts" are hardly a sufficient ground, nor do they necessarily assist us in our articulation of the nature of faith.[66]

1.4. WHAT OF THE QUESTION OF AUTHORSHIP?

This commentary proceeds under the assumption that our ability or inability to identify the author of the Third Gospel is unimportant to its interpretation.

---

that the historian was uninterested in fidelity to the truth. He argues, rather, that ". . . the historian is obliged to approximate reality while at the same time presenting a cogent, ordered, self-explanatory account" (99). This includes accounts of "marvels 'worthy of relation' " uncovered by investigation that might not pass the sieves of the historical method favored in modern times.

63. Of course, the notion of "objectivity" belongs on a continuum, so that, with respect to its relation to the external world of which it purports to be a record, historiography is not to be confused with other narrative-based genres. Our emphasis here is on how the narrative representation of historical events becomes itself an object of examination — as we seek to examine (in this case) how Luke has drawn out and/or given significance to the events he recounts. As Fornara observes (*Nature of History,* 201), "major historical writing . . . [is], above all, intrinsically concerned with the *exposition* of memorable events" (emphasis added). See further, Fornara, *Nature of History,* 169-201.

64. That is, he is absent from the narrative of the Third Gospel. The "we-passages" in Acts witness Luke's adoption of a perspective from within the narrative (16:10-17; 20:5–21:17; 27–28). Cf. Kurz, *Reading Luke-Acts,* 39-131.

65. See Goldingay, *Models for Scripture,* 257, 294.

66. Cf. Pannenberg, *Jesus,* 246.

Although the most likely candidate for the authorship of Luke-Acts is Luke the physician and sometime companion of Paul,[67] the author himself has not included his name within the Gospel itself and the title, "according to Luke," was added by others only decades later. This suggests that the identity of the author is not critical to our reading of the Gospel; as a consequence, for example, in our reading of the Gospel of Luke we will look elsewhere than to Luke's probable vocation as a physician to account for his interest in accounts of healing. Because the Gospel is anonymous, and because we know almost nothing about the *Lukas* of whom Paul writes (Phlm 24; Col 4:14; cf. 2 Tim 4:11), information about the author is largely available to us only by way of reconstruction from hints within the narrative. But information thus gleaned more properly gives us access to the "implied author" or "narrator."[68] Insofar as past discussions of the Gospel have referred to "Luke" as the voice through which the story of Jesus' mission and message has been related, they have drawn attention to Luke in a role that closely approximates contemporary understanding of the "narrator." It is in this sense that Luke will be named throughout the commentary.

2. THE PURPOSE AND THEOLOGY OF THE GOSPEL OF LUKE

Following the publication of *The Theology of the Gospel of Luke* (1995),[69] it remains here only to sketch the mainstays of Luke's narrative theology. This sketch is in large part determined by the approach to the Gospel adopted here, since narratology draws attention to the question of narrative "theme," the idea of narrative "aim," and the possibility of alignment with ("helpers") and against ("opponents") that aim.

We have seen that the genre of Luke's writing suggests the Evangelist's concern with legitimation and apologetic. Moreover, our discussion of the narrative unity of Luke-Acts has highlighted the centrality of God's purpose to bring salvation to all. In the conflicted world of the first-century Mediterranean, not least within the larger Jewish world, it is not difficult to see how this understanding of God's purpose and its embodiment in the Christian movement would have been the source of controversy and uncertainty. Against this backdrop, we propose that the purpose of Luke-Acts would have been to

67. See Fitzmyer, *Luke the Theologian*, 1-26.
68. See further, below, on 1:1-4; also Robbins, "Social Location."
69. Joel B. Green, *The Theology of the Gospel of Luke*, NTT 3 (Cambridge: Cambridge University, 1995).

strengthen the Christian movement in the face of opposition by (1) ensuring them in their interpretation and experience of the redemptive purpose and faithfulness of God and by (2) calling them to continued faithfulness and witness in God's salvific project. The purpose of Luke-Acts, then, would be primarily ecclesiological — concerned with the practices that define and the criteria for legitimating the community of God's people, and centered on the invitation to participate in God's project.

Our understanding of the aim of Luke-Acts must also account for its primary theological emphases. Recent scholarship has repeatedly identified "salvation" as the primary theme of Luke-Acts, theme being understood as that which unifies other textual elements within the narrative.[70] In order to make sense of the theme of salvation and to show the degree to which it is integrated into the overall purpose of strengthening the church, we may outline some of Luke's key theological concerns.

To a degree not fully appreciated in many earlier studies of the Third Gospel, Luke's narrative is *theo*logical in substance and focus; that is, it is centered on God. This is not to say that God often appears as a character within the narrative. Manifestly, this is not the case. Rather, it is to assert that the design guiding the progression of the narrative, the purpose being served or combated, is God's. If salvation is the central theme of Luke, then it is not accidental that, in one of the earliest references to God in the Gospel, Mary addresses him as "God my Savior" (1:47). Especially in the central section of the Gospel concerned with the meandering journey from Galilee to Jerusalem, Jesus attempts to reconstruct the view of God held by his followers in order that they might recognize God as their Father, whose desire is to embrace them with his gracious beneficence (e.g., 11:1-13; 12:32).

The divine purpose or perspective sometimes surfaces directly in the narrative — for example, when God speaks to Jesus at his baptism (3:21-22). More typical, though, is the way the divine purpose is made available and interpreted with reference to the Scriptures, by means of heavenly messengers, through a constellation of terms expressive of God's design (e.g., "purpose," "it is necessary," "to determine," et al.); and through instances of divine choreography of events. Behind the realization of the divine plan is the Holy Spirit, the power that puts into effect the will of God.

Luke's emphasis on the divine purpose serves his ecclesiological and hermeneutical interests. As the Christian community struggles with its own identity, not least over against those who also read the Scriptures but who refuse faith in Christ, the coherence between God's ancient agenda and the ministry of Jesus becomes crucial. In fact, Jesus' struggle with the Jewish leadership and with Jewish institutions is essentially hermeneutical: Who

---

70. Following Prince, *Narrative as Theme,* 3-7.

understands God's purpose? Who interprets the Scriptures faithfully? Or, to put it more starkly, Whose interpretation has the divine imprimatur? Whose receives divine legitimation? For Luke, the answer is simple. The advent of Jesus is deeply rooted in the ancient covenant, and his mission is fully congruent with God's intent. This is shown above all by the scriptural pattern of his life and by the divine vindication pronounced over him in his resurrection and ascension.

God may control the agenda of the story, according to Luke, but the main character in Luke's first volume is Jesus. Compared with characters within the narrative, Luke's own audience is fortunate in its ability, from the very beginning, to perceive Jesus' identity and role in God's redemptive plan. Jesus is portrayed as a prophet, but as more than a prophet; he is the long-awaited Davidic Messiah, Son of God, who fulfills in his career the destiny of a regal prophet for whom death, though necessary, is hardly the last word. For Jesus' disciples, the struggle is not so much to discern *who* Jesus is, but *how he can fulfill his role.* Their own views of the world remain conventional throughout most of the Gospel; hence, almost to the end of the Gospel, they lack the capacity to correlate Jesus' exalted status as God's Messiah with the prospect and experience of his heinous suffering.

Early on, Jesus is identified as Savior (2:11), and this is the role he fulfills in numerous ways. Among the most visible are his miracles of healing and the expansive nature of his table fellowship. Both are highlighted by the Third Evangelist, for whom such practices embody the truth of the inbreaking kingdom of God. In Jesus' interactions with people at the table and in his ministry of healing, he communicates the presence of divine salvation for those whose position in society-at-large is generally on the margins. This is "good news to the poor" (4:18-19). Such behaviors are matched by words, of course, and Jesus' teaching occupies major sections within the Third Gospel, especially in the middle section of the Gospel devoted to his journey to Jerusalem. What is often striking about his instruction is its orientation not to "proper behavior" per se but toward a reconstructed vision of God and the sort of world order that might reflect this vision of God. To put it differently, Jesus, as Son of God, is God's representative, whose life is characterized by obedience to God and who interprets for others (if they will only listen!) God's nature and plan and the contours of appropriate response to God.

For Luke, then, the call to discipleship is fundamentally an invitation for persons to align themselves with Jesus, and thus with God. This means that, for membership among the people of God, the focus is removed from issues of inherited status and a premium is placed on persons whose behaviors manifest their unmitigated embrace of the gracious God. Genuine "children of Abraham" are those who embody in their lives the beneficence of God, and who express openhanded mercy to others, especially toward those in need.

23

Jesus thus calls on people to live as he lives, in contradistinction to the agonistic, competitive form of life marked by conventional notions of honor and status typical of the larger Roman world. Behaviors that grow out of service in the kingdom of God take a different turn: Love your enemies. Do good to those who hate you. Extend hospitality to those who cannot reciprocate. Give without expectation of return. Such practices are possible only for those whose dispositions, whose convictions and commitments, have been reshaped by transformative encounter with the goodness of God. Within the Third Gospel, the chief competitor for this focus stems from Money — not so much money itself, but the rule of Money, manifest in the drive for social praise and, so, in forms of life designed to keep those with power and privilege segregated from those of low status, the least, the lost, and the left-out.

Jesus' disciples are not entirely successful in embodying faithfulness of this nature and magnitude. This makes all the more striking Luke's witness of others, near-nobodies in the narrative, who manifest unexpected insight into God's purpose and respond to the message of Jesus in exemplary ways: a sinful woman from the city (7:36-50), a wealthy toll collector (19:1-10), a crucified criminal (23:39-43), to mention three. For their part, the disciples find that "following Jesus" is mostly about being "with" Jesus — learning from him, becoming socialized anew according to the new world order his ministry serves, propagates, and anticipates — all in preparation for their role as witnesses in the Acts of the Apostles.

If disciples struggle to embrace faithfulness as this is defined and modeled by Jesus, others contend for the opposite. Those hostile to Jesus calculate the divine agenda along quite different lines and see his ministry as a threat to their own positions of leadership and to the institutions that perpetuate the present order of things. In short, they see Jesus as opposing God himself (i.e., God as they understand God to be), and thus someone to be resisted at all costs. The devil himself opposes the divine aim and, from the Lukan perspective, the devil's aims are served both by diabolic forces that oppress people and by others, including the Jewish leadership in Jerusalem, who oppose God. The river of hostility grows wider and wider, finally to overflow its banks at Jesus' passion, resulting in his final rejection, crucifixion, and death. The motif of hostility pushes Luke's narrative along with heightened suspense, but is also employed in order to show in what ironic ways the purpose of God might come to realization, turning opposition against its own ends so as to fulfill the divine plan.

Throughout, the Lukan narrative focuses attention on a pervasive, coordinating theme: salvation. Salvation is neither ethereal nor merely future, but embraces life in the present, restoring the integrity of human life, revitalizing human communities, setting the cosmos in order, and commissioning the community of God's people to put God's grace into practice among

24

themselves and toward ever-widening circles of others. The Third Evangelist knows nothing of such dichotomies as those sometimes drawn between social and spiritual or individual and communal. Salvation embraces the totality of embodied life, including its social, economic, and political concerns. For Luke, the God of Israel is the Great Benefactor whose redemptive purpose is manifest in the career of Jesus, whose message is that this benefaction enables and inspires new ways for living in the world.

OUTLINE OF THE GOSPEL OF LUKE

The Gospel of
LUKE

1. THE PROLOGUE (1:1-4)

1 *Since many have undertaken to set down an orderly account of the events that have been fulfilled among us, 2 just as they were handed down to us by those who from the beginning were eyewitnesses and servants of the word, 3 I too decided, after investigating everything carefully from the very first, to write an orderly account for you, most excellent Theophilus, 4 so that you may know the truth concerning the things about which you have been informed.*[1]

Much more so in antiquity than today, first sentences are the primary point-of-entry for literary productions. The first column of writing, even the first sentence, performed much the same purpose as the modern book jacket précis, table of contents, and title page. In the Greco-Roman world, a "book," available in the form of a rolled-up scroll,[2] did not allow for informal browsing for the purpose of divining its approach, genre, or subject matter. Hence, the opening sentence was crucial for putting those who either read it or heard it read on notice as to what could be expected in the work as a whole.[3]

Beginnings serve to usher readers from the world outside the text into the world of the text. According to the ancient rhetorician Quintilian, prefaces in oral speech should prepare the audience so that they will desire to listen to the speech as a whole, by rendering them well disposed, attentive, and ready for instruction.[4] Given the centrality of rhetorical training to classical

1. NRSV: "instructed."

2. The specifically Roman word for "book" (Greek: βιβλίον; cf. Luke 4:17, 20) was *uolumen,* "roll."

3. Cf. D. Earl, "Prologue-form," 856. On the importance of beginnings more generally, see Said, *Beginnings.*

4. Quintilian *Inst. orat.* 4.1.5. Although he wrote in the second half of the first century C.E., Quintilian's analysis of the function of the preface, or *exordium,* was traditional; cf. Aristotle *Rhetoric* 3.14.

education in general[5] and the reality that literary productions for wider audiences were more heard (through public reading) than read, it is not surprising that literary prefaces of all sorts followed the advice of such rhetors as Quintilian.[6] In *How to Write History* (second century C.E.), Lucian remarks that audiences will give their full attention to historians whose work is evidently "important, essential, personal, or useful." Like the orator, however, the historian should give the audience "what will interest and instruct them."[7] How is interest aroused and trust for the author engendered? In narratives, the narrator is typically concerned to communicate that his or her version of the story is "true."[8] For works like Luke's, this was accomplished with reference to firsthand knowledge of the subject matter — through intimacy with the tradition as well as research and/or personal experience.[9]

Openings also set a work within the larger context of other known literary productions, establishing a network of relationships with existing works, inviting comparisons of all kinds. As "the first step in the intentional production of meaning,"[10] a literary opening suggests continuity or discontinuity with predecessors, and so encourages the reader to approach what follows with a certain set of (sometimes nebulous) expectations.

Luke has inserted at the head of his narrative a Greek-style preface. In doing so, he has followed a well-trodden path, employing a literary convention already widespread in the Greco-Roman world. Prefaces of this sort were used by the authors of a wide variety of works — from the seriously literary to the technical and nonliterary — all of whom were influenced to varying degrees by the conventions of ancient rhetoric. These prefaces often shared common ingredients — (usually) the author's name; dedication and/or request; remarks regarding the subject matter, its importance and implications; (often diminutive) mention of predecessors; a claim to appropriate methodology; and the transition to the work itself.

Luke's prologue identifies Luke's work as a "narrative," and in these four verses we first encounter the *narrator.* In the latter half of the Acts of the Apostles, the narrator presents himself not outside the narrative, as in this

---

5. See Kennedy, *Art of Rhetoric,* 318-21; see also the comments on history and rhetoric in Aune, *Literary Environment,* 83-84.

6. That preface-writing in Greco-Roman historiography was influenced by rhetoric is not to say that it had its origins in rhetoric. In important ways, the preface-form was set by Herodotus and Thucydides already in the fifth century B.C.E. Cf. D. E. Smith, "Beginnings," 1-3.

7. Lucian *De Hist. Conscrib.* §53.

8. Cf. Chatman, *Story and Discourse,* 227-28.

9. Cf. Alexander, "Luke's Preface," 71; Callan, "Preface."

10. Said, *Beginnings,* 5.

instance, but as a character within the story;[11] this does not happen in the Gospel, however. A *narratee* is also identified, Theophilus (note: the narrator is not given a name, though we shall refer to him as Luke).[12] Although this narrative is directed toward Theophilus by Luke, the prologue-form itself indicates that it is being released for wider public dissemination (see below on v 3). With respect to the relationship established between narrator — narrative — narratee, three observations may be noted. First, Luke is making a claim for the trustworthiness of his book. This opening sentence is designed to impress, to underscore the believability of the narrative by its claims to offer rigorous standards of research, and thus to gain a favorable hearing.

Second, we gain a preliminary vision of the angle from which the narrative will be related. We are given little on which to base our identification of the narrative voice, but a few characterizations are possible. (1) That we are dealing with a *written* text at all is itself suggestive; even though we have no firm data on which to construct a precise judgment regarding illiteracy in the first-century Roman world, "in agrarian societies *limited literacy* was the rule. . . ."[13] This, together with the vocabulary and style of Luke 1:1-4, suggests a narrator of some means, educated, probably urban. (2) Recent work indicating the correlation of Luke 1:1-4 with the "scientific tradition" suggests that Luke's perspective is from the social location of those who traffic in technical or professional writing and who generally have an appreciation for the labors of those who work with their hands.[14] This is notable, since more "high-browed" writers in the Greco-Roman world often looked with disdain on the artisan class, and since recent investigations have underscored the presence of just such persons — free artisans and persons with small businesses — in early Christianity.[15] (3) It is not possible to

11. See Acts 16:10-17; 20:5-15; 21:1-18; 27:1–28:16. In the other Gospels, cf. Mark 13:14, where the narrator addresses the ideal reader in the second person; and John 1:14-16; 21:24, where the narrator speaks in the first person. On the "narrators" of Luke-Acts, cf. Kurz, *Reading Luke-Acts*.

12. Narrative critics typically make distinctions between implied author and narrator — e.g., Powell, *Narrative Criticism*, 25-27; Bal, *Narratology*, 119-20 — and Dawsey argues that the author identifies with Jesus over against the narrator in Luke *(Lukan Voice)*. Most narrative critics find no tension between the points of view of the implied author and narrator of Luke, however (Powell, *Narrative Criticism*, 26; on Dawsey's thesis, see Moore, *Literary Criticism*, 30-34; Darr, *Character Building*, 181-82n.18). Robbins refers to the narrator speaking in the Lukan prologue and we-passages in Acts as "the inscribed author" ("Social Location," 308-12). With respect to point of view, however, he posits no contrary relationship in Luke-Acts between implied author, narrator, and inscribed author; hence, this further distinction is not necessary for our purposes.

13. Lenski, *Power and Privilege*, 207-8.

14. Alexander, "Luke's Preface."

15. At least in the Pauline community — see Atkins, *Egalitarian Community;* Meeks, *First Urban Christians*, 51-73; Judge, *Social Pattern*, 49-61.

determine from the prologue how the narrator situates himself vis-à-vis Jesus and the Jesus-movement chronologically. Some have seen in these verses evidence that Luke is a "third generation" Christian — after the eyewitnesses and original compilers and narrators of the Jesus-story.[16] Luke only reports that his time in writing comes after some accounts have already been attempted, however, not that he does not belong to that generation of Christian writers — or, for that matter, that he himself had not observed some of the events he narrated. Indeed, as the narrator of Acts, he explicitly claims to have participated in the events he recounts in selected passages. The prologue does, however, communicate Luke's claim to being one of "us" — that is, a member of the larger community of persons whose lives were being shaped by the events he goes on to narrate. Luke writes as one of the "people of the Way," a "Christian."

Third, Luke himself raises the question of "truth" or "certainty," and suggests that a primary ingredient that will lead to certainty for Theophilus is the *order* of the narrative. Luke's purpose was apparently not to provide an historical foundation for the Christian message. Subsequent writers have struggled with the relationship between kerygma and history, but this does not seem to have been Luke's problem. For him, the narrative is not the basis of proclamation; rather, *narration is proclamation.*[17] For Luke, an "orderly account" is concerned above all with persuasion. He has "ordered" the events of his narrative so as to bring out their significance, to persuade Theophilus — who is not so much concerned with the issue, Did it happen? as with the queries, What happened? and What does it all mean? By providing a more complete accounting of Jesus in his significance, Luke hopes to encourage active faith.

With respect to structure and style, Luke 1:1-4 is periodic, with one complete sentence made up of five clauses organized into a balance unity:[18]

many have undertaken — I too decided
to set down an orderly account — to write an orderly account
the events that have been fulfilled among us — everything
from the beginning — from the very first
just as they were handed down to us — so that you may know.

Accordingly, one recognizes between vv 1-2 and vv 3-4 a balance of phrases that guide the interpretation of Luke's prologue.

16. Conzelmann, "Luke's Place," 305; Fitzmyer, 1:289.
17. See below, on 1:3; cf. Dillon, "Luke's Project," 208-9; *idem, Eyewitnesses,* 269-72.
18. See BDF §§458, 464. The use of the period is rare in the NT; cf. also Acts 15:24-26.

1 Luke sets forth the context for his writing (v 1a) and its content (v 1b). Although the first clause is causal,[19] it is not so much concerned with Luke's *motivation* for writing as its *justification*. Luke mentions other attempts at orderly accounts not to disparage them,[20] but to place his project in their company. Luke's purpose will have been to identify with and re-present previous narratological developments of the coming of redemption in Jesus. Luke is not simply a conservator of the tradition, but neither is he a novelist operating apart from a concern for the narrative tradition of interpreting Jesus' significance. He has his own contribution to make, and he will proceed in relation to that tradition of interpretation. He draws attention to other attempts at orderly narrative in order to certify the value of his subject matter and to open the way for a further work of similar compass.

Luke refers to the existence of these literary predecessors as if they

---

19. Ἐπειδήπερ ("since") is "purely causal" (MHT 3:318) and appears only here in the NT.

20. Many commentators find in Luke's prologue what Bovon (1:34) calls a "discreet and guarded critique" by Luke of his forerunners — this in order to justify Luke's decision to write yet another narrative. Luke's narrative, it is proposed, is to be more complete, more accurate, more oriented to the events in question, narrated in a better sequence, etc. See, e.g., Fitzmyer, 1:291-92; Klostermann, 2.

No nuance of failure resides in the verb ἐπιχειρέω ("to take in hand, to undertake") itself — cf. MM 250-51; Plummer, 2 (and most subsequent commentaries); *contra* Eusebius *Hist. Eccl.* 3.24.15, who regards earlier attempts as "rash"; Augustine *De cons.* 4.8, who suggests that "to attempt" implies "unable to complete" (cf. Bede, *Acts,* 4-5); Origen *Hom. in Luc.* 1, who found here an indictment against apocryphal Gospels, whose authors wrote at their own initiative and not as directed by the Holy Spirit. When used in the third person to describe the attempts of others to address a subject, however, this verb could be used in a pejorative way (e.g., Josephus *Life* 9 §40; 65 §338). Based on usage in Acts 9:29; 19:13 (neither of which is set within the context of literary intentions), Klein concludes that the verb casts a negative judgment on Luke's predecessors in Luke 1:1-4 ("Lukas 1,1-4," 195-96). Co-textual observations must be decisive, however, and Luke's deliberate inclusion of his own work alongside these previous attempts rules out a negative evaluation of them.

Goulder finds lurking behind this text an allusion to problems raised by discrepancies of order in the (for him) already existing Gospels of Matthew and Mark: "Luke is writing a reconciliation of Mark and Matthew to reassure Theophilus that the apparently dissonant Gospel tradition is trustworthy" (1:200). Not only does this interpretation place upon Luke's prologue with regard to Luke's predecessors both a specificity and negative tone it cannot bear, but it also posits a problematic reconstruction of concern over narrative order in the first century. Where is the evidence — until the second-century formulation of Tatian's *Diatessaron* — that discrepancies of order were troublesome? Moreover, given Luke's arrangement of such episodes as Jesus' sermon at Nazareth and the anointing of Jesus, in what sense can one speak of Luke as having ironed out the difficulties in order between Matthew and Mark? Quite the contrary, in his placement of these two scenes he seems to have created new problems.

were well known to his audience.[21] Unfortunately, their shared knowledge is not ours, and Luke gives us no hint as to whether his predecessors included one or more of our NT Gospels. Luke's use of the word "many" here follows a widespread practice both in oral and in written beginnings, where "many" is used for its rhetorical effect without necessarily implying "a great number."[22] Its value here is rhetorical: to vouch for the value of Luke's enterprise by its association with the tradition.[23]

Because Luke associates his own work so closely with these former attempts,[24] it is critical to understand what is meant by "an orderly account." Some have suggested that Luke is drawing on the rhetorical tradition, and is thus interested in a "longer narrative composed of a number of events," arranged "by the display of major developments and patterns."[25] Others have found Lucian's discussion of *How to Write History* decisive, concluding that "narrative" ". . . is a technical term for the well-ordered, polished product of the historian's work."[26] These suggestions are helpful, but we should also emphasize Luke's use of the cognate verb, "to narrate, to relate, to give an account,"[27] which he characteristically employs for the act of describing God's mighty deeds. For example, in Acts 9:27, Barnabas *narrates* to the Jerusalem disciples how Saul had seen the Lord on his journey to Damascus — and he does so (like Luke) in the third person. Here he tells of Saul's experience, and his narration is specifically persuasive in purpose and effect, with a primary emphasis on the Lord's doing, so that the disciples in Jerusalem are convinced of Saul's discipleship on the basis of Barnabas's report (cf. 9:28-29).[28] For Luke, "narrative" is proclamation.[29] Luke has in mind the use of history to preach, to set forth a persuasive interpretation of God's work in Jesus and the early church, and the medium of that proclamation is the narrative account whose "order" is crucial for our understanding of that interpretation.

21. ἐπειδήπερ refers to "a fact already well known" (BDF §456.3).

22. Cf. also, e.g., Acts 1:3; 24:2, 10; Heb 1:1; Sir 1:1; Dionysius *De orat.* 1.1; Demosthenes *Third Phil.* 110.

23. Cf. J. Bauer, "ΠΟΛΛΟΙ," 263-66.

24. Note the parallel between "to set down an orderly account" (v 1) and "to write an orderly account" (v 3).

25. Tannehill, *Narrative Unity,* 1:10.

26. Cf. van Unnik, "Luke's Prologue," 12-13; he refers especially to Lucian *De Hist. Conscrib.* §§47-48, 55. See also Bovon, 1:34.

27. διήγησις appears in the NT only in Luke 1:1; διηγέομαι appears five times in Luke-Acts, twice in Mark, and once in Hebrews.

28. This nuance may also be present in Luke 8:39, where "giving an account" is closely aligned with "preaching." Cf. also Luke 9:10; Acts 12:17; the verb διηγέομαι also appears in a citation of Isa 53:7 LXX in Acts 8:33.

29. See Du Plessis, "Luke's Prologue," 262-63; Dillon, "Luke's Project," 208-9.

What is the *content* of this narratological proclamation? Luke's emphasis on "events" directs our attention to historiographical rather than biographical interests — where the contributions of such persons as (even) Jesus, Peter, Stephen, and Paul are related within larger narrative sequences whose interest transcends their individual deeds. Luke's words, "that have been fulfilled among us,"[30] indicate his concern with how the events narrated in the Gospel and Acts are understood as divine affairs. This indicates, first, that these events are incomplete in themselves and must be understood in relation to a wider interpretive framework. Every writer whose focus is a narrative sequence must struggle with locating an appropriate beginning, a starting point sufficient to show how what follows grows out of narrated exigencies. In his opening phrase, Luke signals his understanding that the events he will narrate are related to God's purpose, evident in the OT and the history of God's people, as its culmination.[31] This same affirmation is continued throughout the Gospel and in the Acts of the Apostles, where Jesus' life, death, and resurrection and the shape and progress of the Christian mission are understood as manifestations of God's will.[32] One need not bring to bear on Luke's prologue the full weight of "prophetic fulfillment"[33] to see that Luke is nonetheless concerned to affirm that in these events God's purpose is realized.[34] But this is already to mention, secondly, that this modifier "have been fulfilled" suggests God as its unspoken subject. These are events by which God accomplishes his purpose.

Because of the framework within which these events are "fulfilled"

---

30. πληροφορέω appears only here in Luke and is a synonym for πληρόω, which he uses repeatedly with a variety of meanings — e.g., for scriptural fulfillment (4:21; 24:44; Acts 1:6; 3:18; 13:27), for the passing of time (Acts 9:23; 19:21; 24:21), for the process or result of filling (2:40; 3:5; Acts 2:2, 28), for the completion of a mission or work (Acts 12:25; 13:25; 14:26), and, as here, to describe an event that fulfills the divine purpose (1:20; 9:31; 21:24; 22:16). The alternative translation, "have been accomplished" (e.g., RSV), is too weak. Cf. the use of πίμπλημι in 1:23, 57; 2:6, 21, 22.

31. This interest becomes transparent in 1:5–2:52; cf. Green, "Beginning."

32. Cf., e.g., Acts 1:16; 3:18; 10:1–11:18; 13:27, 46-47; 15:6-9, 12-18, 28; passim.

33. That Luke is concerned in 1:1 with scriptural fulfillment is explicitly denied by, e.g., Cadbury, "Commentary," 495-96; C. F. Evans, 124.

34. Cf. Bovon, 1:35. A different approach is taken by Dillon, who distinguished between the events (in the past) and their "coming to fruition" — i.e., properly interpreted and received as "signs of messianic recognition" (*Eyewitnesses,* 270-72; "Luke's Prologue," 211-17). One need not take this approach in order to see that this "fulfillment" or "fruition" has ongoing implications (suggested by the perfect tense of this participle); cf. Klein, "Lukas 1,1-4," 196-99; Du Plessis, "Luke's Prologue," 263-64. In any case, the texts on which Dillon rests his case themselves indicate how the story of Jesus becomes clear only when understood in relation to "Moses and all the prophets" (24:27) or "the law of Moses, the prophets, and the psalms" (24:44; cf. 16:31).

— that is, the divine framework of God's purpose — those among whom these events are complete (the "among us" of v 1) cannot be restricted to the first generation of men and women who participated in Jesus' ministry and to whom he appeared after his resurrection. Luke's inclusion of himself in this "us" guarantees this, but even more significant is the tense of the verb, "have been fulfilled" — perfect, denoting the continuance of completed action. Luke has in mind the Christian community, with its organic unity across generations.[35]

2 For Luke, the basis of the tradition of God's work is not "the many" who had compiled narratives (v 1), but this new group — "eyewitnesses and servants of the word" — to whom he also had access. By observing that they handed on the tradition "to us," Luke again includes himself with the previously mentioned narrators and indicates that his own methodology extended beyond some sort of collation of already existent narrative reports. To describe this process of "handing on," Luke employs the technical term for the transmission of tradition,[36] but this need not refer to the service of authoritative dogmatic interests (cf. 1 Cor 15:3-5). "To pass on certain information either orally or by writing to save it from oblivion" is probably closer to the mark here.[37] This emphasis on the process of "handing down," together with the related information that these people were eyewitnesses and servants of the word *from the beginning,* constitutes the sort of appeal to tradition and to antiquity for which both the historiographical and scientific traditions were noted. One builds one's case in relation to past efforts, indicating one's respect for the tradition and validating one's message by appealing to its antiquity.[38]

Luke finds a parallel between his narratological forerunners and these eyewitnesses and ministers of the word. "Just as" the latter had passed on the tradition of these "fulfilled events," so the former had compiled narratives of those events, shaping them into a coherent unity.[39]

---

35. Cf. the similar perspective in McClendon, *Ethics,* 31-32. Goulder (1:201) helpfully draws attention to the parallel use of "us" in 1 Corinthians 10; Heb 11:40; cf. also Josephus *Ant.* 1.2 §5.

36. See Büchsel, "παραδίδωμι," 171-73; Acts 6:14.

37. van Unnik, "Luke's Prologue," 14; cf. Nolland, 1:8; Bovon, 1:36.

38. Hence, any search for an exact chronological referent for "from the beginning" — from the baptism of John? (cf. Acts 1:1, 21-22; 10:37-39); the births of John and Jesus? (cf. Laurentin, *Truth of Christmas,* 315-18; Du Plessis, "Luke's Prologue," 266; O'Fearghail, *Introduction,* 89-93) — is wide of the mark. This phrase, along with its parallel in v 3 ("from the very first"), is an imprecise carrier of a value-laden idea, affirming the age of the tradition.

39. This seems the best way to take this ambiguous use of καθώς; on its imprecision, see C. F. Evans, 125.

Two observations raise questions about Luke's use of "eyewitnesses" here. First, he prefers to designate people as "witnesses," and the term used here, "eyewitness," is found nowhere else in Luke-Acts.[40] Second, we typically associate the word "eyewitness" with a person who has personally observed an event, but this is not always the case in antiquity.[41] The concept of the eyewitness is important to historiography and actually describes the first step in the process of writing history. The historian may be fortunate enough actually to see the *events* themselves,[42] but this can scarcely be premeditated and is consequently the exception. Rather, the historian examined relevant *sites* of historical incidents, gaining firsthand experience of them. It appears that Luke has used the term "eyewitness" in his prologue in deference to the historiographical and scientific traditions, for which the term was so central, but meant by it both less and more than his identification with those traditions might suggest. He is not describing the first step in history-writing or in emphasizing his own firsthand observation of the data. On the contrary, by "eyewitnesses" he has in mind "witnesses" as that term is developed later — that is, people empowered by the Spirit who ". . . cannot keep from speaking about what [they] have seen and heard" (Acts 4:20). And for Luke, "seeing" is insufficient unless one's eyes are opened, as the Emmaus-story demonstrates (Luke 24:13-35).

"Eyewitnesses" and "ministers of the word" are parallel descriptions of the same group of people.[43] Luke's reference to "servants of the word" calls to mind the absolute use of "the word" in Acts, as well as its use in the phrases "word of God" and "word of the Lord."[44] "The word" is often "the

40. In fact, αὐτόπτης occurs only here in the Greek Bible. Μάρτυς is Luke's preferred term — see, e.g., Luke 24:48; Acts 1:8, 22; 2:32; 3:15; *5:32; 10:39,* 41; 13:31; 22:15, 20; *26:16.* Luke follows normal usage in employing μάρτυς in judicial settings also — Acts 6:13; 7:58.

41. See MM 93-94; van Unnik, "Luke's Prologue," 11-13, who cites relevant material but overlooks the distinction resident in his examples between "personally inspecting the site of an historic incident after the event" and "personally observing the event." The relevant data has been freshly surveyed in Alexander, "Luke-Acts," 101-4.

42. Cf. Josephus *Ag. Ap.* 1.10 §§53-55.

43. The use of the one definite article οἱ for both αὐτόπται and ὑπηρέται disallows attempts to distinguish these as different sets of persons. Dillon has argued that Luke's language denotes a process whereby original eyewitnesses "graduated" to become ministers of the word, and suggests the translation: ". . . who were eye-witnesses from the beginning and became servants of the word" ("Luke's Prologue," 214; see pp. 214-17; Marshall, 42; Nolland, 1:4, 7-8). This view rests on a problematic understanding of "eyewitnesses," however. Nolland points out that this two-stage interpretation makes sense of the implied stages in Acts 1:8, but there the disciples are to be "witnesses" (μάρτυρες), not graduates from being (only) eyewitnesses.

44. For the absolute use of "the word," cf. Acts 2:41; 4:4, 29; 6:4; 8:4, 21; 10:36,

Christian message, the good news" (e.g., Acts 10:36; 15:7), but this message is grounded in the coming of Jesus and his missionary activity (cf. 10:37-38) and embraces its consequences in the post-Easter mission and the community of Jesus' followers (e.g., 6:7; 12:24; 19:20). Acts 1:21-22 suggests that the people Luke has in mind are those who were disciples of Jesus already in Galilee and to whom he appeared following his resurrection, but the list of possible contenders quickly expands to include such persons as Barnabas and Paul and others of the early mission.[45]

3 Luke finally comes to his own decision to write an orderly account; outlining further his credentials and briefly characterizing his work, he names Theophilus as his narratee, the one to whom the work is aimed and dedicated.

The weight of Luke's description falls on the two adverbs "carefully" and "orderly." The first is usually taken with "to investigate" (as in the NRSV), thus indicating how or in what way Luke carried out his research. However, it could just as easily modify the main verb, "to write,"[46] and in any case provides a claim of "accuracy" for Luke's literary product. This is interesting in light of other contexts wherein Luke uses the term, especially in the story of Apollos in Acts 18:24-28.[47] Like Theophilus, Apollos had been informed (Luke 1:4; Acts 18:25), but he requires more accurate explication.

The second adverb, "orderly," is also of consequence, and is also illuminated by its appearance in Acts. Fundamentally, this term means "in sequence" or "one after the other," but it is still worth asking what sort of

---

44; 11:19; 13:26; 14:3, 12, 25; 15:7; 16:6; 17:11; 18:5; 20:7. For "the word of God," cf. Acts 4:31; 6:2, 7; 8:14; 11:1; 12:24; 13:5, 7, 46; 17:13; 18:11. For "word of the Lord," cf. Acts 8:4; 13:44, 48, 49; 15:35, 36; 16:32; 19:10, 20.

45. Trites (*Witness,* 128-53; esp. pp. 136-39) insists that the eyewitnesses of Luke 1:2 are ". . . plainly the apostles who have been with Jesus 'from the beginning' " (136; cf. Schürmann, 1:9; S. Brown, "Prologues," 103-4). In his view, they know the facts of Jesus' public ministry and can ". . . guarantee the major historic events in the life of Jesus of Nazareth." See, however, Acts 1:8; 2:32; 3:15; 5:32; 13:30-31; 22:15; 26:16 (ὑπηρέτην καὶ μάρτυρα). Clearly the apostles are not meant in an exclusive way. For Luke, Paul is a "minister and witness," but not an "apostle." The one place where Paul is named an "apostle" (along with Barnabas — Acts 14:14), the term is used in what is for Luke a nontechnical way to denote his being sent with good news. Trites's suggestion that the phrase "eyewitnesses and ministers of the word" corresponds to the concept of "witness" in Acts is more to the point.

46. Παρηκολουθηκότι ἄνωθεν πᾶσιν ἀκριβῶς καθεξῆς σοι γράψαι — "having followed everything from the beginning to write accurately and sequentially." Cadbury already noted the adverb's amphibolous position and wondered if it should go partly with both verbs ("Commentary," 504; cf. Kürzinger, "Lk 1,3," 254-55; van Unnik, "Luke's Prologue," 17).

47. In Acts 24:22, Felix is "rather well informed about the Way," but in 23:15, 20, the feigned need is for more accurate information about Paul's case.

42

sequence is meant.[48] Lucian counsels historians to arrange their material in order to give the story "beauty," enhanced "with the charms of expression, figure, and rhythm," and, by the arrangement of events, to "illuminate them as vividly as possible."[49] What is interesting about these instructions is their concern for the effect on the readers produced by the order or arrangement of events. Students of narrative have long recognized the power of signification resident in the order in which events are presented to a reader or auditor.[50] Helpful for our understanding of Lukan "order" is the parallel use of this word in Acts 11:4: "Then Peter began explaining everything to them in sequence. . . ." Although "orderly" is used by Luke elsewhere,[51] this text appears in a parallel context — namely, the narrating of events in which God has worked. This whole passage, the story of Peter's encounter with Cornelius and the subsequent report of this encounter to some in Jerusalem in 10:1–

48. Earlier commentaries often understood Luke to mean "chronological sequence" (e.g., Plummer, 5; Godet, 1:65), and in a general sense this is possible (Marshall, 43). Mußner ("Καθεξῆς"; *idem*, "Gemeinde," 386-89) argued that Luke intended the meaning "complete," in the sense of "neglecting nothing (lückenloss, ohne Ausnahme)," but this makes little sense of either the Gospel (cf. the Synoptic Tradition) or Acts (where the narrative sequence opens up many possibilities for further development, as with the story of the church in Antioch, only to leave them hanging). Völkel ("Exegetische Erwägungen") surveys the Lukan material and extrabiblical data and concludes, "καθεξῆς als Bezeichnung für die Modalität einer Darstellung bezieht sich somit nicht auf das Ereignis selbst, weder in der Form der chronologischen Korrektheit noch der der sachlichen Vollständigkeit, sondern auf das für das rechte Verständnis des Ereignisses Konstitutive. καθεξῆς ist somit nicht chronologisch, sondern sachlich strukturiert" (294). Völkel has been followed by a number of other scholars, some of whom have attempted to spell out with greater specificity the nature of that order — e.g., Schneider, "Bedeutung," who draws particular attention to the salvation-historical order of promise-fulfillment; and Fitzmyer, 1:299, who finds ". . . a veiled reference to the Period of Israel, the Period of Jesus, and the Period of the Early Church." The central question does not revolve around periodization, however, but around what Luke hopes to accomplish with his emphasis on "order." Cf. Dillon, "Luke's Project," 219-33 (whose emphasis on "logical" order is not very helpful, since in narrative studies "logic" refers to cause-effect sequence — e.g., a character cannot arrive in a given place before she has set out to go there — and this is certainly not descriptive of the order of Luke's story); Tannehill, *Narrative Unity*, 1:10-12.

49. Lucian *De Hist. Conscrib.* §§48, 50-51.

50. Ordering, in fact, is one of the primary means by which the reception of a story is conditioned, so that adherence to strict chronological sequence is the exception. Instead, a narrator may omit an element that belongs in a series only to recall it at some other point in the story. Other interruptions to the chronology of the story are possible — e.g., an event might enter the story prematurely, hints or announcements regarding the future might be given, events happening at the same time might be elaborated in parallel fashion, and so on. For the narratological significance of order, see esp. Genette, *Narrative Discourse;* also, e.g., Powell, *Narrative Criticism*, 36-38; Bal, *Narratology,* 37-43, 51-68.

51. Luke 8:1; Acts 3:24; 18:23.

11:18, is narrated twice. We hear it from *Luke's* point of view first, then from *Peter's,* with the result that we can observe how these events are "ordered" by two narrators.[52] A comparison of the two demonstrates that "orderly" cannot refer to "adherence to chronological sequence," nor simply "one after the other." Rather, Peter's "ordering" of the account is for the purpose of winning his audience over to his perspective on the events he recounts (cf. Acts 11:18). This notion of "persuasive order" fits well Luke's own agenda, too.

Who is Theophilus? Some have found in the narratee's given name a symbolic audience, for, etymologically, "Theophilus" means "dear to God" or "lover of God."[53] Though this helpfully points to the more general audience Luke apparently desired (see below),[54] such a symbolic rendering is highly unlikely: (1) Theophilus is a common name, found in the papyri and inscriptions as early as the third century B.C.E.;[55] (2) the appellation "most excellent" would then be pointless; and (3) a symbolic dedication of this sort would be unparalleled in Luke's literary culture. Having concluded this, there is no evidence by which to determine which "Theophilus" Luke had in mind. The title "most excellent," normally reserved for Roman political officials, may well be honorary,[56] though in either case we are dealing with a person of advanced status.

In this reference, Luke is apparently recognizing the role of Theophilus in providing inspiration or at least impetus for his writing, and especially that, through Theophilus's recommendation and circle of friends and influence, Luke's book will have gained a wider audience.[57] From the standpoint of our

52. Of course, when we speak of "Peter's ordering," we mean, "Luke's ordering of Peter's ordering," since, irrespective of source-critical concerns, Luke the narrator has final responsibility for the narrative shape.

53. Cf. Nolland, 1:10.

54. Cf. Bede, *Acts,* 9.

55. MM 288; Hemer, *Acts,* 221n.1.

56. As in, presumably, Josephus *Life* 76 §430; *Ag. Ap.* 1.1 §1. Cf., however, the proper use of the nomenclature in Acts 23:26; 24:3; 26:25.

57. Suggestions that Theophilus might have served as Luke's literary patron are often anachronistic, projecting the modern book-publishing industry back on to the first-century Roman world. In antiquity, "publishing" a work like Luke's had little, often nothing to do with the multiplication and distribution of copies of a book. "Publishing," rather, constituted an author's release of his or her control over a book's use and interpretation, the abandoning of a work to the public, the offer of blanket permission for anyone to copy a work (see E. J. Kenney, "Books and Readers," 4, 10-22; Easterling, "Books and Readers," 19-21). So in dedicating Luke-Acts to Theophilus and thus naming Theophilus as his literary patron, Luke was not seeking or acknowledging a monetary subvention for "publishing costs." Moreover, given his own probable social location, it is unlikely that Luke was recognizing Theophilus for supporting him materially as a writer. See Gold, *Literary*

understanding of Luke's prologue, this reality is most important for its expression of Luke's desire for a public readership beyond his narratee, Theophilus.[58] Consequently, what we can discern about Theophilus will provide us with some clues about Luke's purpose, but we should not assume that Theophilus is Luke's only desired audience or that Theophilus represents Luke's "community."[59]

4 The final clause of Luke's prologue defines the purpose of Luke's writing. Clearly, Theophilus has at least some familiarity with "the events that have been fulfilled among us," but he requires additional instruction in order to know their truth. Luke writes to persuade Theophilus to embrace their certainty.

"Certainty" or "truth," in the Greek text, appears in the emphatic position as the final word of this long and involved sentence. It has been easy to find in this concept Luke's affirmation of the historical veracity of his narrative.[60] Luke's terminology here suggests "the convincing nature of his presentation"[61] or "the certainty of these things."[62] So, while the Christian message is inseparably tied to the historical events related to its origins and progression, and Luke must therefore necessarily be concerned with "what happened,"[63] it is the question of interpretation that is vital for him. Luke wants Theophilus to be assured about what he has heard, that these events lead to "this" interpretation — that is, the interpretation Luke will present in his narrative.[64]

How much Theophilus already knows is unclear. Some regard him as a baptized Christian who has undergone formal instruction in the faith.[65] Others see him as a relative outsider to the Christian movement, someone who may have heard little more than rumors about Jesus and the early church.[66] The sort of formal catechetical process envisioned by the first option

---

Patronage. Gold makes the further interesting point that *literary* patronage departed from standard forms of patronage in Roman society in that it was not reciprocal — i.e., the writer did not become a "client" indebted to the benefactor. Because of the pointed critique of patronal relations in Luke, this is an important observation.

58. Thus, while we may draw no meaningful distinction between narrator and implied author in Luke-Acts, we can distinguish narratee and implied reader.

59. *Contra,* e.g., Creech, "Theophilus"; he assumes too readily that Theophilus represents Luke's implied reader, and on this basis attempts to identify what can be known of Theophilus. More helpful is Tyson, *Images of Judaism,* 19-41.

60. Cf. van Unnik, "Purpose"; Plummer, 5.

61. Cf. Xenophon *Mem.* 4.6 §15; C. Brown, "ἀσφάλεια," 663.

62. Cf. Acts 2:36; 25:26.

63. See the use of ἀσφαλής in Acts 21:34; 22:30 to signify "the facts" in a case.

64. Cf. Hall, *Revealed Histories,* 171-208; Darr, *Character Building,* esp. 53-55.

65. E.g., Schürmann, 1:15.

66. Cf. C. F. Evans, 136; van Unnik, "Luke's Prologue," 18.

is difficult to locate during the apostolic era,[67] nor does Luke use the term "to inform, to instruct" in this more technical way.[68] According to Acts 18:25, Apollos "had been instructed in the Way of the Lord," but still knows "only the baptism of John." It is only after he receives further explanation, we are told, that he was able to show "by the Scriptures that the Messiah is Jesus" (18:24-28). By analogy, we suspect that Theophilus has been informed about the mission of Jesus and the early Christian movement, and that he may even have attached himself to the community of Jesus' disciples, but key ingredients are lacking in his understanding.

67. Green, *Death of Jesus,* 176-82.
68. Cf. Acts 21:21, 24.

2. THE BIRTH AND CHILDHOOD OF JESUS (1:5–2:52)

Luke's prologue (1:1-4) is external to the narrative per se, so only with the introduction of Zechariah and Elizabeth in 1:5-7 do we enter the world of the Gospel story. Even if the Evangelist has to some degree anticipated this move with his reference to a narrative account of "the events that have been fulfilled among us" (1:1), the transition is nevertheless abrupt. Almost without warning we depart the cultural milieu wherein Greek preface-writing would have been fully at home, and enter the world of the struggles and faithfulness of a small town priest and his wife, a peasant girl, and two devout Jerusalemites — an environment permeated by the piety of Second Temple Judaism and hope for divine intervention and deliverance. The intersection of these two worlds is of critical importance for Luke, who will show through his orderly account how the unfolding events in this world of ancient Galilee and Judea are of universal significance.

The story of Jesus' birth and childhood is a celebration of God's love for Israel and, indeed, for all humanity. This love is manifest most brilliantly in the repeated declaration of the eschatological fulfillment of God's promise of redemption. One of the primary literary features of this section is its elegant intertwining of the stories of John and Jesus, presenting the two in parallel fashion. In its intricately woven fabric are the threads and patterns we will encounter throughout Luke-Acts.

§1 The Literary Structure of the Birth Narrative[1]

The parameters of this section of the Gospel are easily established. Luke 1:5, with its chronological ("the days of King Herod") and geographical ("Judea") indicators

1. In terms of form, Luke 1:5–2:52 is often positioned with Matthew 1–2 as examples of the "infancy narrative," and these two stories share a number of features; cf.

locate the events that open both the birth account and the Gospel as a whole. The similar but expanded notation in 3:1-2 is reminiscent of the beginnings of a number of prophetic books (cf., e.g., Hos 1:1; Amos 1:1; Mic 1:1), and so constitutes a fitting transition to the onset of John's prophetic ministry. Luke 3:1-2 also follows the summarizing conclusion of the narrative cycle related to Jesus' birth and childhood (2:52) and marks a fresh beginning, focused initially on John's ministry of preparation.

In a limited sense, Luke 1:5–2:52 is a self-contained unit within the Third Gospel, for it completes within itself the narrative processes concerning the births of John and Jesus anticipated in its opening stages. One may read in these verses three intertwined stories of promise moving to fulfillment and to praise response:[2]

Character	Promise	Evidence of Fulfillment	Praise Response
Zechariah	His wife would bear a son	John is born	Song of Zechariah
Mary	She would conceive a son	Unborn John bears witness to unborn Jesus and Elizabeth blesses Mary	Song of Mary
Simeon	He would see the Messiah	He sees Jesus	Song of Simeon

This analysis emphasizes the integral role of the three "songs" in the Lukan story,[3] but its basic framework can easily be expanded so that proper attention is paid to other aspects of the narrative in which possibilities are realized and their results narrated. Thus, for example, the episode that finds Jesus in the temple at age 12 fills out the concern with his identification as God's Son — predicted in 1:32, 35, symbolized in his conception, and now affirmed by the boy Jesus in his question, "Did you not know that I must be in *my Father's* house?" (2:49). In other words, the possibilities opened in the birth narrative, insofar as they are focused on the birth and identification of the two special children, are realized and their consequences affirmed, all within Luke's first two chapters.

Moreover, prior to 3:1, the information provided by the narrator is available only to the readers and, to varying degrees, to persons who will disappear from the

---

Fitzmyer, 1:305-9; R. E. Brown, *Birth,* 25-38. Luz (*Matthew,* 152-55) has shown the closer connection of Matt 1:18–2:23 to other "stories of the persecuted and royal child," however. More recent attempts to recover a characterization of Matthew 1–2 and Luke 1–2 within the category "legend of the birth of the hero" are critiqued in Horsley, *Liberation of Christmas,* 62-72.

2. Farris, *Hymns,* 100-102.

3. *Contra* R. E. Brown (*Birth,* 347), whose comments are representative: ". . . the canticles fit awkwardly into their present context. If they were omitted, one would never suspect their absence; in fact, the narrative would read more smoothly without them." Cf. Kaut, *Befreier und befreites Volk,* 86-97.

subsequent story. It is true that Mary will reappear briefly (8:19; Acts 1:14; cf. Luke 11:27), but not to inform other characters within the story of her special knowledge. Indeed, Mary serves much more to invite Luke's audience to join her in thoughtful reflection on the meaning of the narrated events. Consequently, in these two opening chapters Luke shares with his reader something of his omniscient point of view. The reader understands the identity of John and Jesus and the nature and basis of the people of God as it develops around Jesus in a way the characters of the story — including John (7:18-23) — must learn.

Of course, Luke 1:5–2:52 is intimately related in terms of narrative structure with what follows and must be read as such.[4] This is especially true for the section of Luke's Gospel from 3:1–4:13, The Preparation for the Ministry of Jesus,[5] for whereas 1:5–2:52 establishes the *possibility* of Jesus' mission as Son of God, 3:1–4:13 establishes its *probability* before that ministry actually commences with Luke 4:14. Luke 3:1–4:13 functions in this way by narrating the mission of John (as predicted — cf. 1:16-17, 76-77, 80; 3:3-6) and preparing for Jesus' mission through his baptism and the narratological exploration of the significance of the title "Son of God" (cf. 3:21-22, 38; 4:3, 9). But it is also true for the connection between this opening section of the Gospel and Luke-Acts as a whole. In fact, it is not too much to say that Luke 1–2 is incomplete in itself and utterly dependent on the narrative that follows. This interdependence can be illustrated in two ways.

First, Luke's birth narrative fosters a keen sense of anticipation and leads the reader to assume that those expectations will be fulfilled *in the narrative*. Some prophecies are fulfilled immediately — for example, Gabriel promises that Elizabeth will bear a son, and she does (1:13, 24, 57); "many will rejoice at his birth," and they do (1:14, 58); and so on. Other prophecies go unfulfilled in the story time of 1:5–2:52 — John's ministry of preparation, Jesus' royal service, a mission to the Gentiles, and so on — so that the reader reaches the end of Luke 2 with heightened expectations, ready to turn the page to see how these possibilities will be realized.

---

4. Conzelmann's decision to exclude Luke 1–2 from a consideration of Luke's theological enterprise (*Luke,* 172) has met with stiff resistance and need not be engaged here; cf., e.g., the early essays by Minear, "Birth Stories"; Oliver, "Birth Stories"; and more recently, Tyson, "Birth Narratives."

5. Talbert ("Prophecies," 129-30) regards 1:5–4:15 as a coherent unit anticipating Jesus' public destiny and rightly rejects the thesis that the Gospel originally began at 3:1. He argues that 1:5–4:15 contains three stories juxtaposing John and Jesus, but does not deal with the far-reaching distinction between the first two over against the third, nor with the narratological concerns we have raised. Similarly, Wilkens ("Struktur," 1-3) finds cycles of three throughout the Gospel, including three parallels between John and Jesus in the first section of the Gospel (1:5–4:44) — Announcement (1:5-56), Birth (1:57–2:52), and Debut (3:1–4:44) — but the last alleged parallel is less convincing; see the critique in Schweizer, "Aufbau," 13. The same may be said for O'Fearghail's recent argument for the unity of 1:5–4:44 (*Introduction,* esp. 9-38). His thesis depends in part on parallels similar to those identified by Wilkens and on conceptual parallels not unique to this section of Luke-Acts (e.g., the role of the Spirit); it is telling that he first insists on the unity of 1:5–2:52 and of 3:1–4:44.

Second, the nature of the actors introduced points to the dependence of Luke 1:5–2:52 on the subsequent narrative. From a narratological point of view the interpretive spotlight should shine brightest on the primary actor who follows an aim and who must marshall the necessary forces to achieve that aim.[6] Who is this primary actor? *Clearly, God is this actor.* Luke 1:5–2:52 introduces God, who is out to fulfill his redemptive purpose, while other characters are introduced as persons with whom and through whom God's aim will be advanced. Luke 1:5–2:52 cannot stand on its own since it only introduces what all of Luke-Acts will narrate — namely, the realization of God's purpose.

Within the story of Jesus' birth and childhood we find a number of markers that contribute to the dramatic effect of the story and move it along.[7] Some of these are chronological (1:5, 10, 23, 24 [2x], 25, 26, 36, 39, 56, 57, 59; 2:1, 6, 8, 11, 21, 22, 38, 41, 42, 43, 46). Others are geographical and geo-political in nature: Judea (1:5, 39, 65; 2:4), Galilee (1:26; 2:4, 39), the Roman Empire (2:1), and Syria (2:2). Still others are topographical: the hill country of Judea (1:39, 65); up to Bethlehem, the city of David (2:4), or Jerusalem (2:22, 42); and down . . . to Nazareth (2:51). Specificity of this nature is rare in the Gospels and is clearly of significance. These features and others contribute to the dramatic movement of the story and to the sense of perpetual motion within the story. They also provide a concrete representation of the world, indicating pointedly the time and space in which these remarkable events occurred. Some also have theological significance. Particularly as one reads through the ample list of time designations in this section of the Gospel, one senses that these events are not mere happenstance. They have been ordered and reflect a divine timetable.

The dominant feature on the literary landscape of Luke 1:5–2:52 is the point-by-point parallelism between John and Jesus. Most obvious is the juxtaposition of the annunciation stories (1:5-23, 26-38) and narratives of birth–circumcision–naming (1:57-66; 2:1-27, 34-39).[8] However, the parallels are much more extensive and, in fact, embrace this entire section of the Gospel:[9]

John		*Jesus*
1:5-7	(A) The Introduction of Parents	1:26-27
1:8-23	(B) The Annunciation	1:28-38
1:24-25	(C) The Mother's Response	1:39-56
1:57-58	(D) The Birth	2:1-20
1:59-66	(E) Circumcision and Naming	2:21-24
1:67-79	(F) Prophetic Response	2:25-39
1:80	(G) Growth of the Child	2:40-52[10]

6. See the discussion of actants in Ball, *Narratology,* 25-37.

7. See Kaut, *Befreier und befreites Volk,* 83-86; Laurentin, *Truth of Christmas,* 61-62.

8. See Dibelius, "Jungfrauensohn," 1-9; Laurentin, *Struktur und Theologie,* 27-39; R. E. Brown, *Birth,* 250-52.

9. See Green, *Gospel of Luke,* 51-55.

10. The parallel concerning Jesus is more complex, since into an *inclusio* marked by the dual summaries in 2:40, 52, Luke has inserted an illustrative story drawing out the nature of Jesus' maturation. Cf. the parallel narrative strategy in Acts 6:1a, 1b-6, 7.

The presence of such a pervasive parallelism is hardly accidental and indicates on the part of the narrator a conscious attempt to invite the reader to view these two narrative cycles together.

At a primary level these two stories are one, for they demonstrate how God will accomplish his salvific aim.[11] In this regard, the heavenly and prophetic voices have a signal role, giving expression to the divine purpose in the progress of the narrative and inviting reflection and response. The parallel accounts of promise–fulfillment–response tell one story, the story of God's intervention in human history to bring deliverance.

The similarities of these two story lines attract our attention first. Even without close analysis and charting these parallels, we are struck by the relationship between these four parents and their children. Their kinship extends beyond the ties between Mary and Elizabeth (1:36), for there is also a commonality concerning the centrality of their roles in the one purpose of God.[12] As the angel affirms, the births of John and Jesus constitute "good news" (1:19; 2:10).

Luke's parallelism, however, is not a juxtaposition of equals. Repeatedly, the balance is tipped in favor of Jesus, so that we are left in no doubt as to who is the preeminent of the two children. Structurally, this is represented by the simple fact that the story of Jesus receives almost twice as much space in Luke 1:5–2:52 as does the story of John. Moreover, for example, two prophetic responses attend Jesus' presentation in the temple compared to only one in the case of John's naming and circumcision, and when the two stories converge in 1:39-56, the weight of attention is given to Mary and her unborn child. Attention to content would highlight further the subordination of John — for example, Jesus will be "Son of the Most High," but John will be "prophet of the Most High" (1:32, 76).

This concern to put John in his place is not surprising in light of the evidence of Acts. In Acts 13:24-25; 18:25; 19:1-4 we discover the abiding influence of the Baptist movement in a surprisingly wide-reaching geographical sweep, including Asia Minor and Achaia — far from the center of John's activity in the region of the river Jordan. With the living presence of the Baptist circle, it was important to indicate its relation to the Jesus movement. Without disparaging the eschatological significance of John's ministry, then, Luke communicates in this imbalanced set of parallels the superiority of Jesus.

§2 God's Purpose, the Scriptures, and the "Beginning" of Luke-Acts[13]

Luke 1:1-4 may be the first point-of-entry into Luke-Acts, but, in terms of the Lukan *narrative* as such, the beginning of Luke-Acts is the account of Jesus' birth and childhood. On the one hand, this means it is here that we gain entry into the social world of Luke-Acts — its understanding of reality, its primary institutions, its social

11. This has been emphasized by Davis, "Literary Structure."
12. Cf. George, "Parallèle."
13. Cf. Green, "Beginning."

dynamics, and the like. To this question we will turn in §3, below. Here our focus initially will fall elsewhere, on the function of Luke 1:5–2:52 as a harbinger of the story to come. In doing so, however, we will see that the "beginning" of Luke's story is not the birth of Jesus after all.

Narrative beginnings open up possibilities, inviting their audience to a full hearing or reading to discover its outcome.[14] Luke accomplishes this not so much by holding back what will happen; angelic and prophetic voices repeatedly address this question. Rather, the reader is left to wonder *how* these far-reaching visions of redemption will come to fruition.[15]

Although Luke 1:5–2:52 initiates a narrative centered above all on God whose aim it is to bring salvation in all its fullness to all, the story of Jesus' birth and childhood does not really *introduce* this God or this aim, nor does it pretend to do so. The force of a narrative depends essentially on its capacity to show how an event is a product of discursive forces rather than a given report by discourse.[16] Historiography in particular orders events so as to postulate their end and/or beginning. For Luke, those discursive forces are God's promises and acts on behalf of Israel — promises and acts (1) that are themselves narrated in Israel's Scriptures, (2) to which Luke refers in his account by way of establishing narrative needs for development and resolution in Luke-Acts, and (3) that therefore constitute the pretext of Luke's narrative. Indeed, as Luke has already informed us in his prologue,[17] the events he will narrate are linked to the past history of God's salvific acts. Similarly, as Luke's employment of Israel's Scriptures in Luke 1:5–2:52 demonstrates, the proper "beginning" for his narrative is *there,* in the past, in God's redemptive purpose as set forth in the Scriptures. Luke is not introducing a *new* story, but continuing an old one, whose real "beginning" is the LXX. He roots the coming of Jesus and the universal Christian movement in God's purpose, continuous as one divine story. Hence, Luke does not at this juncture think of segmenting salvation history into "stages" nor even simply of a hermeneutical pattern of prophecy-fulfillment.[18] This is not to deny the important ways in which Luke 1:5–2:52 (or other portions of Luke-Acts) portray eschatological fulfillment[19] or to suggest that Luke does not regard the OT as essentially forward-looking.[20] Rather, it is to affirm that Luke self-consciously begins his narrative in the middle of the story, so to speak. The emphasis falls on salvation-historical unity: The God who has been working redemptively *still is,* now, and especially, in Jesus.

One example of the way in which Luke has wrapped this opening section of the Gospel in scriptural garb is his use of the Abrahamic material of Genesis 11–21 in the narration of the stories of John and Jesus. Luke's interest in Abraham is transparent at two points in the story, specifically in 1:55, 73. There, God's merciful activity on behalf of Israel is related directly to his faithfulness to Abraham. A close

14. See Aristotle *Poetics* 7.
15. Cf. Brawley, *Centering on God,* 58-60.
16. Culler, *Pursuit of Signs,* 175.
17. See above on 1:1.
18. *Pace* Bock, *Proclamation,* esp. 55-90.
19. See, e.g., Laurentin, *Struktur und Theologie,* 50-105; *idem, Truth of Christmas,* 43-68; Chance, *Jerusalem,* 48-56.
20. See, e.g., Jervell, "Center of Scripture."

reading of these two narratives side-by-side suggests a much more pervasive interest, as the following parallels indicate:[21]

Genesis	*Luke*
"Now Sarai was barren; she had no child" (11:30).	"But they had no children, because Elizabeth was barren" (1:7).
The Lord to Abram: "I will make of you a great nation, and I will . . . make your name great . . ." (12:2).	An angel of the Lord to Zechariah, concerning John: ". . . he will be great in the sight of the Lord" (1:15); Gabriel to Mary, concerning Jesus: "He will be great" (1:32).
The Lord to Abram: ". . . I will bless you . . ." (12:2); Melchizedek to Abram: "He blessed him and said, 'Blessed be Abram . . .' " (14:19).	Elizabeth, full of the Holy Spirit, to Mary: "Blessed are you among women, and blessed is the fruit of your womb. . . . And blessed is she who believed . . ." (1:41, 45). Simeon, on whom the Spirit rested, with respect to Jesus' parents: "Then Simeon blessed them . . ." (2:25, 34).
Promises to Abraham: 12:3; 15:5, 13-14, 18-21; 17:2, 4-8.	Promises to Abraham remembered by God (1:55, 73).
The Lord to Abram: "To your offspring I will give this land" (12:7); ". . . all the land that you see I will give to you and to your offspring forever" (13:14-17; cf. 17:7; 18:18; 22:17).	Mary, concerning God, who has helped Israel ". . . according to the promise he made . . . to Abraham and to his *offspring* forever" (1:55); Zechariah, concerning God, who has remembered ". . . the oath that he swore to our ancestor, Abraham, to *give* us . . ." (1:73).
Chronological and geo-political markers (14:1).	Chronological and geo-political markers (1:5).
Melchizedek to Abram: ". . . blessed be God Most High, who has delivered your enemies into your hand" (14:20; cf. 15:13-14; 22:17).	Gabriel to Mary: "[Jesus] will be called the Son of the Most High . . . and the power of the Most High will overshadow you . . ." (1:32, 35); Zechariah to John: "And you, child, will be called the prophet of the Most High" (1:76); Zechariah: God has granted ". . . that we, being rescued from the hands of our enemies, might serve . . ." (1:74).

21. Material appearing in italics departs from the NRSV in order to provide a more literal translation of the Greek text indicating further how these parallels extend even to words and phrases.

The Lord to Abram: "Do not be afraid, Abram . . ." — followed by words of God's gracious act on his behalf (15:1).

The angel of the Lord to Zechariah: "Do not be afraid, Zechariah . . ." — followed by words of God's gracious act on his behalf (1:13); Gabriel to Mary: "Do not be afraid, Mary . . ." — followed by words of God's gracious act on her behalf (1:30).

"And [Abram] believed the LORD; and the LORD reckoned it to him as righteousness" (15:6; cf. 18:19; 26:5).

"Both of them [Zechariah and Elizabeth] were righteous before God" (1:6).

"Now Sarai, Abram's wife, bore him no children" (16:1).

"But they had no children, because Elizabeth was barren" (1:7).

The angel of the Lord to Hagar: "Now you have conceived *in your womb* and shall bear a son; you shall call him Ishmael. . . . He shall be a wild ass of a man . . ." (16:11-12).

The angel to Mary: "And now, you will conceive in your womb and bear a son, and you will name him Jesus. He will be great . . ." (1:31-32).

"When Abram was ninety-nine years old, the LORD appeared to Abram . . ." (17:1).

"[Elizabeth and Zechariah] were getting on in years. . . . Then there appeared to him an angel of the Lord . . ." (1:7, 11).

God to Abram: "I am God Almighty; walk before me, and be blameless" (17:1).

"Both of them [Zechariah and Elizabeth] were righteous before God, *walking* blamelessly . . ." (1:6).

God promises to Abraham: "an everlasting covenant," "ancestor of a multitude of nations," "kings shall come from you" (17:4-8; cf. 17:16).

Zechariah, of God: "He has shown the mercy promised to our ancestors and has remembered his holy covenant, the oath that he swore to our ancestor Abraham . . ." (1:72-73); cf. "throne," "kingdom" (1:32-33); "our ancestor," "Abraham," "forever" (1:55).

"Throughout your generations every male among you shall be circumcised when he is eight days old . . ." (17:12); "And Abraham circumcised his son Isaac when he was eight days old . . ." (21:4)

Of John: "On the eighth day they came to circumcise the child . . ." (1:59); of Jesus: "After eight days had passed, it was time to circumcise the child . . ." (2:21).

God to Abraham: ". . . I will give you a son by [Sarah] . . ." (17:16); ". . . your wife Sarah shall bear you a son, and you shall name him Isaac" + future role of child (17:19).

The angel of the Lord to Zechariah: "Your wife Elizabeth will bear you a son, and you will name him John" + future role of child (1:13); Gabriel to Mary: "And now, you will conceive in your womb and bear a son, and you will name him Jesus" (1:31).

54

"And when he had finished talking with him, God went up from Abraham" (17:22).

"Then the angel departed from [Mary]" (1:38).

Abraham presents himself as a servant (Gen 18:3-5).

Mary presents herself as a servant (1:38, 48).

Abraham to God: "Can a child be born to a man who is a hundred years old? Can Sarah, who is ninety years old, bear a child?" (17:17); "Now Abraham and Sarah were old, advanced in age. . . . So Sarah laughed to herself, saying, 'After I have grown old, and my husband is old, shall I have pleasure?" (18:11-12).

Zechariah and Elizabeth ". . . were *advanced in age*" (1:7); Zechariah to God: "For I am an old man, and my wife is *advanced in age*" (1:18).

The Lord to Abraham: "Is anything *impossible with* God?" (18:14).

Gabriel to Mary: "For nothing will be impossible with God" (1:37).

Abraham a "prophet" (20:7).

Zechariah "prophesies" (1:67).

"Sarah conceived and bore Abraham a son . . ." (21:2).

"Elizabeth conceived . . . and she bore a son" (1:24, 57).

"Now Sarah said, 'God has brought laughter for me; everyone who hears will laugh with me' " (21:6).

Elizabeth observes that God has taken away her disgrace (1:25); "Her neighbors and relatives heard that the Lord had shown his great mercy to her, and they rejoiced with her" (1:58).

Of Isaac: "The child grew, and was weaned . . ." (21:8); of the son of Hagar: "God was with the boy, and he grew up; he lived in the wilderness . . ." (21:20).

Of John: "The child grew and became strong in spirit, and he was in the wilderness . . ." (1:80); of Jesus: "The child grew and became strong . . . and the favor of God was upon him" (2:40; cf. 2:52).

With respect to these points of contact between Genesis 11–21 and Luke 1:5–2:52, a number of observations may be made. (1) First, at key points, these narratives share a common repertoire of elements where they intersect with conventional forms found elsewhere in the biblical tradition. Luke has made use of an annunciation form or type-scene with these elements: Announcement of Birth, Name of Child, and Future of Child. Luke's use of this form raises expectations regarding the miraculous intervention of God and portends the heightened significance of the child to be born.[22] One may also speak of Luke's revision of a conventional commissioning form.[23] In

22. For parallels, see Gen 16:7-13; 17:1-21; 18:1-15; Judg 13:3-20; Matt 1:20-21; Luke 1:11-20, 26-37; 2:9-12. For the earlier identification of more elaborate forms, cf., e.g., R. E. Brown, *Birth,* 156; Fitzmyer, 1:318, 336, 396. More recently: Conrad, "Annunciation," 656-68; Alter, "Annunciation Type-Scene."

23. For parallels, cf. Exod 3:1–4:16; Judg 6:11-24; 1 Kgs 19:1-19a; Isaiah 6; Jer 1:4-12. See Mullins, "Commission Forms"; Hubbard, "Commissioning Stories."

this case, the interpretive focus would fall above all on the recipients of the message — Zechariah, Mary, and the shepherds — and so on their role in the realization of God's purpose. Even though the Lukan material lacks the commission-oriented language typical of commission scenes (e.g., Judg 6:14; Jer 1:7-10), as becomes apparent throughout Luke-Acts, Luke's point here seems to be that the miraculous, redemptive activity of God calls forth human response and partnership.

(2) Of course, not all of the suggested points of correspondence between the Abrahamic and Lukan stories are equally convincing. For some, however, there is a surprising linguistic overlap between the LXX and the Greek text of Luke, including material unrelated to the literary convention of the relating of a birth announcement or such stock themes as barrenness.[24] Moreover, Luke's clear interest in directing attention to the Abrahamic material is marked by his reference to "our ancestor" "Abraham" and concern with the "covenant" in Luke 1:55, 73.[25] Hence, even those parallels that are less certain begin to appear more promising precisely because of the otherwise amply attested concern of Luke with material from this portion of Genesis.

(3) This is not to say that Luke has created the framework or content of this account out of the Abrahamic material. Neither has he demonstrated a clearly delineated hermeneutical procedure for his use of Genesis 11–21. He can move easily from character to character in his employment of the Genesis story — thus, for example, Zechariah is like Abraham, but so is Mary; Zechariah is like Sarah, but so is Elizabeth; John is like Isaac and Ishmael; and so on. This demonstrates that Luke is making no straightforward typological argument here. Nor does he make use of "fulfillment language" to describe his use of Israel's Scriptures in Luke 1:5–2:52 — either with regard to the Abrahamic narrative or with the OT more generally.

Instead, what we have with the appearance of the Abrahamic material is evidence of Luke's own reading of and reflection on the story of Abraham, and

---

24. For example:

Luke 1:6: ἦσαν δὲ δίκαιοι ἀμφότεροι ἐναντίον τοῦ θεοῦ, πορευόμενοι ἐν πάσαις ταῖς ἐντολαῖς καὶ δικαιώμασιν τοῦ κυρίου ἄμεμπτοι.
Gen 17:1: καὶ ὤφθη κύριος . . . καὶ εἶπεν . . . ἐγώ εἰμι ὁ θεός σου· εὐαρέστει [i.e., "walk pleasingly" — cf. Foester, "εὐάρεστος"; as elsewhere in the LXX, the hithpael of הלך has been transformed from an action into a quality] ἐναντίον ἐμοῦ καὶ γίνου ἄμεμπτος. . . .
Luke 1:7: . . . καὶ ἀμφότεροι προβεβηκότες ἐν ταῖς ἡμέραις αὐτῶν ἦσαν.
Luke 1:18: . . . ἐγὼ γάρ εἰμι πρεσβύτης καὶ ἡ γυνή μου προβεβηκυῖα ἐν ταῖς ἡμέραις αὐτῆς.
Gen 18:11-12: Αβρααμ δὲ καὶ Σαρρα πρεσβύτεροι προβεβηκότες ἡμερῶν . . . ὁ δὲ κύριός μου πρεσβύτερος.

[Note that both narrators provide a report of their characters' advanced age, followed by a character who advances this theme in response to the divine promise of a son.]

Luke 1:37: ὅτι οὐκ ἀδυνατήσει παρὰ τοῦ θεοῦ πᾶν ῥῆμα.
Gen 18:14: μὴ ἀδυνατεῖ [MT: פלא] παρὰ τῷ θεῷ ῥῆμα.
25. See further Dahl, "Abraham."

reflection on the accounts of the births of John and Jesus in light of that narrative.[26] To the Abrahamic narrative Luke would have been drawn not only because of the similarities in context, but also by the central import of the covenant (reflected in Luke 1–2 by the use of the term "covenant" and the repeated covenantal language of mercy, remembrance, favor, promise, oath, et al.). He might also have been motivated by his interest in the universalistic embrace of God's purpose (cf. Gen 17:4; 22:17-18). In his writing, then, Luke has created a text that is itself an interplay of other texts — in this case to the story of Abraham, some doubtlessly intentional, others perhaps less so. In this way, Luke's account participates in a discourse situation in which the story of God's covenantal relationship with Abraham plays a noticeable role in establishing interpretive possibilities.

Importantly, what we have observed with reference to the points of contact between the Abrahamic story of Genesis 11–21 and Luke 1–2 has been developed along similar lines with reference to additional OT passages,[27] even if the significance of these observations has not always been explored adequately. Special attention has been devoted to the appearance of Daniel 7–10 and Genesis 27–43 throughout Luke 1:5–2:52; Zeph 3:14-17 in Luke 1:26-33; 2 Sam 7:12-16 in Luke 1:32-33; and Micah 4:7–5:5 in Luke 2:1-14, among others. In some instances, such as with the use of "great" to describe John and Jesus, evidence from this other OT material may overlap with what we have described as echoes from the Abrahamic story (cf. Gen 12:2; 2 Sam 7:9; Luke 1:15, 32), but this is not surprising. After all, we are not suggesting Luke's use of a closely governed hermeneutical technique whereby a particular scene is viewed in the light of a particular scriptural text. Instead, in the story of Jesus' birth and childhood large portions of the LXX have served as a kind of second language for Luke: Luke 1–2 has become a kind of echo chamber for the interplay of "the old stories" with Luke's own story.[28] Hence, we have much less need to certify to the exclusion of other probable candidates the precise source of an allusion in this Lukan material (which in any case is not always possible) than to appreciate the many voices from the past given a fresh hearing, and thus to reflect on the significance of their interplay in this new context.

(4) The echoes we have heard thus give subtle but sure indicators that the story of God's purpose has not drawn to a close but, quite the contrary, is manifestly still being written. Luke regards his opening chapters as though they were the continuation of the story rooted in the Abrahamic covenant. This is evident for the narrator in the divine machinations behind the extraordinary births of John and Jesus, workings which themselves constitute evidence that God has remembered his promise and that God is even now working graciously to bring to fruition his purpose. These echoes reverberate in the structure, themes, even language of Luke's narrative, drawing his account into the interpretive context of Abraham's story, affirming that the God who

26. Cf. J. A. Sanders, "Isaiah in Luke," 146: "What is remarkable about Luke's knowledge of his scripture was that apparently it came from his assiduous reading of it, or portions of it."

27. Cf., e.g., Laurentin, *Struktur und Theologie,* 74-105; *idem, Truth of Christmas,* 43-60; R. E. Brown, *Birth,* 268-75, 319-28, 420-24, 447-51; Ruddick, "Birth Narratives."

28. Cf. Hollander, *Figure of Echo.*

has mercifully initiated relationship and acted in surprising and mighty ways is acting in the same way, guided by the same purpose.

For Luke, then, the "beginning" can be located only in God's purpose, and his narrative beginning presupposes not only this divine aim, but also the articulation of that aim in the Scriptures and a concern for that aim on the part of his audience.[29]

§3 The Social Setting of Luke 1:5–2:52[30]

With a reading of the story of Jesus' birth and childhood, we gain entry into the social world of Luke-Acts — its understanding of reality, including the role of the supernatural, its primary institutions and their function, its social dynamics, and so on. Without anticipating overmuch the analysis that will follow, we can alert ourselves to some of the motifs that are prominent in the world of Luke's birth narrative. From the opening verse it is apparent that Luke is concerned with the *balance of power*.[31] The narrative opening, "in the days of King Herod of Judea" (1:5a), is more than a vague chronological marker,[32] but locates these events in a particular period of political tension. Herod came to power despite strong anti-Idumean feelings and resistance from the Jewish elders in Jerusalem. This, together with problematic economic and cultural affairs associated with his reign, must be factored into any reading of "the days of King Herod."

The same can be said of the census, mentioned repeatedly in Luke 2:1-7.[33] The prosperity and peace for which the Roman Empire is now known was produced through initial conquest and plunder, and maintained through subsequent taxation of a conquered people. The explicit naming of Caesar Augustus in 2:1 is also of interest, for this refers to Octavian, recognized in antiquity as "the divine savior who has brought peace to the world." That in this very context Jesus is presented as Savior, Lord, the one through whom peace comes to the world (2:11, 14), can hardly be accidental. Moreover, the angel who visits Zechariah and Mary, Gabriel (= "Divine

29. The question remains, Were Luke's first readers so proficient in locating Genesis-Luke parallels as our comments might suggest? In one sense, this question is unanswerable, since we have no record of how Luke's first readers actually read the Third Gospel. We may nonetheless infer that the narrator regarded his model readership as having such a capacity, not unlike what Paul seems to expect of his largely Gentile audience in, say, 1 Corinthians. Cf. Coleridge, *Birth,* 30.

30. On what follows, see Green, *Gospel of Luke,* ch. 1. See further, Neyrey, ed., *Social World;* Malina and Rohrbaugh, *Commentary,* 279-413; Horsley, *Liberation of Christmas.*

31. See further the sometimes extravagant claims on socio-political affairs in Luke 1–2 in Ford, "Zealotism"; *idem, My Enemy Is My Guest,* 1-36; Horsley, *Liberation of Christmas,* 23-52.

32. *Pace,* e.g., Schürmann, 1:29; R. E. Brown, *Birth,* 265.

33. *Contra* Grant (*Roman Hellenism,* 89), who expresses a widely held view when he suggests that Luke 2:1-7 is evidence that Luke shared the later view that divine purpose was behind the coming of Christ during the "peace" of Augustus.

Warrior"), is known elsewhere as one who destroys the wicked.[34] Mary's son, she is told, will have an everlasting kingdom, the throne of David (1:32-33). The Song of Mary portrays God's mighty acts of salvation as socio-political reversal, with the powerful brought down from their thrones and the lowly uplifted (1:52). The Song of Zechariah employs images of exodus while prophesying how ". . . we would be saved from our enemies" (1:71; cf. 1:73). Simeon and Anna, in their respective hopes for "the consolation of Israel" and "redemption of Jerusalem," must also have in mind the cessation of foreign occupancy and subjection, the renewal of Israel as a nation under Yahweh (and not under Caesar).

Recalling that *eschatological anticipation* in its myriad forms focused preeminently on the coming of God to rule in peace and justice highlights how Luke 1:5–2:52 must also be read against a socio-political backdrop. This is true inasmuch as the anticipated coming of God would bring an end to political dominance and social oppression. The appearance of Gabriel indicates already the eschatologically charged ethos in which the birth narrative is set, for he is known to us in part as an interpreter of end-time visions (Dan 8:16-26; 9:21-27). The association of John with the figure of Elijah, particularly against the backdrop of Mal 3:1-2; 4:5-6 (cf. Luke 1:16-17, 76), continues this motif, as does the regularity with which the Holy Spirit appears here. The litany of references to the Spirit brings to mind the old prophecies about the coming time of the Spirit (1:15, 35, 41, 67; 2:25, 26, 27; cf., e.g., Isa 44:3-5; Ezek 26:24-32; Joel 2:28-32). Differences of viewpoint about the sort of Messiah anticipated (and questions about how widespread in antiquity such expectation might have been) aside, the birth narrative repeatedly speaks of the coming of the Christ, and this advances even further the sense of eschatological anticipation in the narrative. Moreover, the eschatological visitation of God is noted in Luke 1:68; 2:38, signifying the appearance of divine help and deliverance. Finally, Mary, Zechariah, Simeon, and Anna each give expression to an expectation of God's end-time deliverance. In these ways, the birth narrative is potent with eschatological anticipation — an anticipation with clear ramifications for the cessation of Israel's subjection to its Herodian and Roman overlords.[35]

The social setting to which we are introduced in Luke 1:5–2:52 is one in which issues of *social status and social stratification* are paramount. This is not to say that Luke is especially concerned with economic class — for example, as a function of one's relative income or standard of living, or as related to one's relation-

34. Cf. *1 Enoch* 9:9-10; 54:6; 1QM 9:14-16; 15:14; Bede, *Homilies,* 1:20; Brueggemann, "Gabriel."

35. This is not to say that one finds evidence here to support Ford's view that Luke sets up a militaristic view of deliverance in the birth narrative only to reject it in Luke 3–24 *(My Enemy Is My Guest).* Luke 1:5–2:52 may set us up to expect socio-political deliverance (as one significant aspect of a larger vision of the coming of "peace on earth"), but we do not know yet *when* or *how* this will be accomplished. Moreover, her thesis requires that the narrator take sides against the voices of Gabriel, Zechariah, Mary, the angelic chorus, and Simeon. To the contrary, Zechariah and Simeon are presented as possessing exemplary character and speak as enabled by the Holy Spirit; Gabriel, who stands in God's presence (1:19), speaks on behalf of God; and Mary is characterized as God's servant. In no way are their words the utterances of unreliable characters.

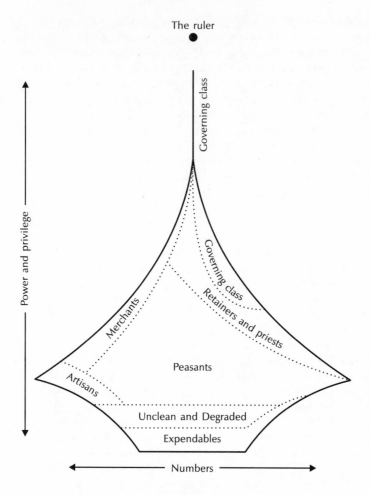

The ruler

Power and privilege

Governing class

Governing class

Retainers and priests

Merchants

Artisans

Peasants

Unclean and Degraded

Expendables

Numbers

FIGURE I.
A graphic representation of the relationship among classes in agrarian societies.

ship to the means of production (as in Marxism). Such matters of post-industrial society have little meaning in Greco-Roman antiquity.[36] Rather, Luke's social world was defined around power and privilege (see Figure 1 above),[37] and is measured by a complex of phenomena — religious purity, family heritage, land ownership (for nonpriests), vocation, ethnicity, gender, education, and age.

36. See Finley, *Ancient Economy,* 50-51; Green, "Good News."
37. Lenski, *Power and Privilege,* 284.

Introduced with titles appropriate to their status are *King* Herod and *Caesar* Augustus (1:5; 2:1) — the former of whom would have had direct control over the whole region in which these events are located, the latter indirect. At the opposite end of the social spectrum are the shepherds of 2:8-20, representative of the peasantry.

Luke spends more time presenting status markers for Zechariah (1:5-7, 9), Elizabeth (1:5-7, 25, 41, 58), and Joseph (1:27; 2:22-24). Simeon and Anna are similarly introduced (2:25, 36-37) and, in the context of turn-of-the-era temple piety, they are well presented. Especially consequential in the birth narrative and elsewhere in Luke-Acts is *status reversal,* together with Luke's concern to *redefine the basis by which status is determined.* The presentation of Elizabeth and Mary is important here. Though a "daughter of Aaron" married to a priest (admirable status — see Figure 1), Elizabeth was barren, thus unable to fulfill her role as a woman in society. As a result, she suffered disgrace among her people (low status honor). God intervenes, however, and so her honor within her community is restored. God has "lifted up the lowly" (1:52). Compared to that of the other parents in this narrative, Mary's introduction is striking.[38] It is as if she were an orphan: no family background is provided; she is betrothed to Joseph but as such has not yet entered into his house or inherited his status. Yet, she is favored by God (1:28, 30), though for no apparent reason other than God's gracious choice. Like Elizabeth, in this social world, Mary undergoes a startling transposition of status.

The characters at center stage in Luke 1:5–2:52 are for the most part exemplars of *the piety of Israel* in the period of Second Temple Judaism. As the character references given Zechariah and Elizabeth (1:5-7) and especially the presentation of Jesus in the temple (2:22-39; esp. v 39) underscore, Luke is concerned to show the importance of faithful obedience. This obedience is directed to the law, the validity of which is thus assumed in the birth narrative, even if this perspective will receive further development later in the Gospel. Obedience is also extended to the words of the angel, who speaks on God's behalf (cf. 1:13 → 1:59-63; 1:31 → 2:21), and the requirements of the Abrahamic covenant (1:59; 2:21). Moreover, portraits of Jewish piety appear in references to prayer, worship, fasting, and expectant waiting (1:10, 13, 25, 46-55, 69-79; 2:13, 14, 20, 25, 37, 38) — and, indeed, to the representation of life oriented around the Jerusalem temple (e.g., 1:8-10, 21-23; 2:22-51). In this world, we are breathing the air of first-century Palestinian Jewish piety.

This portrait has as its focal point *the centrality of the Jerusalem temple.* This is indicated above all by the way in which activity in the temple forms an *inclusio* around this section of the Gospel as a whole (1:5-23; 2:41-51) and the fact that approximately 40 percent of the story itself is set within the walls of the temple. Here, the temple's function as a "culture center" — the divinely legitimated, sacred point around which life is oriented and from which emanates the contours of the social dynamics with which life in this world is occupied[39] — has already begun to be clarified. Thus, the birth narrative shows that (1) the temple is God's house, his abode,

---

38. See Green, "Social Status."

39. See Geertz, *Local Knowledge,* 121-46. Douglas (*Institutions,* esp. ch. 4) notes how institutions derive their legitimacy from "the nature of the universe."

and thus (2) the nexus between God and humanity (3) segregating some space from others as more holy and some people (in this case, a priest) from others as having greater access to what is holy;[40] (4) the temple is the locus of holiness and purity, and so a place of sacrifices and cleansing, (5) where revelation can be given and received, (6) where issues related to the Law can be discussed, and (7) where eschatological fervor can be focused. For Luke, the power of the temple as a culture-defining institution is demarcated especially in social and religious terms, not politico-economic.

Other aspects of the social setting of the birth narratives (and the Gospel as a whole) will surface in more detailed analysis.

2.1. THE ANNOUNCEMENT OF JOHN'S BIRTH (1:5-25)

As we move into Luke's "orderly account" (1:1), the narrator orients us immediately to the time and place of this story: the geo-political arena of Herod's domain[1] — encompassing the regions of Galilee, Judea, Samaria, Western Idumea, and portions of Perea and Coele-Syria — during the period 37-4 B.C.E. This is the time marked by Luke's narrative opening, but the story into which he draws us predates the reign of Herod the Great by centuries. Through the proliferation of OT echoes Luke indicates the continuity of these events with Israel's past and, especially, with the purpose of God. This purpose, and Israel's hopes, are now coming to fruition on a stage dominated for Luke by faithful obedience on the one hand, and divine intervention on the other.

One part of this emphasis consists in the interwoven stories of Zechariah/Elizabeth and of faithful Israel: (1) Zechariah and Elizabeth have no children and she is barren (1:7, 18), a fate that parallels Israel's own need for divine assistance (1:5; cf. 2:25, 38). (2) When Gabriel announces that God has heard Zechariah's request (1:13) we may be surprised: We did not know that he had been praying for a son. In fact, the only prayers of which we had been made cognizant were those of "the whole assembly of the people" (1:10). Could these prayers, Zechariah's and the people's, be related? (3) God's promised intervention on behalf of Zechariah and Elizabeth in response to their need (1:13-14) turns out to be divine intervention on behalf of Israel, too, for John will have a role in restoring Israel to God (1:16-17, 76-79). God's favor toward Zechariah and Elizabeth anticipates and prefigures his gracious act on Israel's behalf. (4) Finally, Zechariah and Elizabeth respond

40. See Knipe, "Temple," 107-12.

1. Thus, "Judea" is used in a general sense for "the land of the Jews" — cf. 4:44; 6:17; 7:17; 23:5. Elsewhere, Luke can use "Judea" in a more specific way, for the southern area of Palestine — cf. (1:39), 65; 2:4; 3:1; 5:17.

differently to this "good news" (1:19) — Zechariah in unbelief (1:20), Elizabeth in acknowledgment of God's favor (1:25). How will Israel respond?

Though the spotlight seems to be on Zechariah in this section, it shines brightest on Elizabeth. Their introduction stresses their mutual righteousness and old age. In going on to mention Elizabeth's barrenness, the narrative raises a need (1:5-7) subsequently addressed by means of an angelic announcement (1:8-17), followed by individual responses from Zechariah (1:18-23) and Elizabeth (1:24-25). The dramatic crescendo turns the tables on Zechariah, chosen priest, in favor of Elizabeth. Hence, descriptions of her condition frame 1:5-25 — barren and disgraced at the outset, pregnant and restored to a position of honor at the close.

2.1.1. The Introduction of Zechariah and Elizabeth (1:5-7)

> 5 In the days of King Herod of Judea, there was a priest named Zechariah, who belonged to the priestly order of Abijah. His wife was a descendant of Aaron, and her name was Elizabeth. 6 Both of them were righteous before God, living blamelessly according to all the commandments and regulations of the Lord. 7 But they had no children, because Elizabeth was barren, and both were getting on in years.

Luke employs such techniques as repetition and association to introduce us to Zechariah and Elizabeth in as economic a way as possible.[2] His agenda seems not merely to provide background on this couple, but to win for them our sympathy. Verses 5-6 emphasize their socio-religious status, so that we anticipate that they will be on "the winning side of history" (cf. Deuteronomy 28). Verse 7 parallels v 6,[3] however, introducing tragedy into the story. Though the Lukan presentation is more economic in the way it juxtaposes righteousness and childlessness, it can be compared with the portrayal of Abraham and Sarah (esp. Gen 18:11) and Elkanah and Hannah (esp. 1 Sam 1:1-2). With this dissonance between blamelessness and lack of blessedness, a great need has been introduced into the narrative. The situation is impossible: Not only is Elizabeth barren, a condition that might conceivably be reversed, but both she and her husband are too old for childbearing. Still, comparison with these couples from Israel's past breathes into the narrative a wisp of hope. Had God not enabled the impossible in their lives?

---

2. On characterization in the Third Gospel, see Gowler, "Characterization"; Darr, *Character Building*.

3. Thus:

v 6a: ἦσαν δὲ δίκαιοι ἀμφότεροι. . . .

v 7c: καὶ ἀμφότεροι προβεβηκότες ἐν ταῖς ἡμέραις αὐτῶν ἦσαν.

5 Luke echoes language from the beginning of a number of prophetic books (cf. Isa 1:1; Jer 1:2-3; Hos 1:1; Amos 1:1; Mic 1:1; Zeph 1:1), suggesting the continuity of this account with the ongoing story of God's dealings with Israel. "The days of King Herod of Judea" mark the period of Israel's subjection to a Roman client-king. Regarded as an outsider, Herod encountered some opposition simply because he represented Rome to a people among whom many chafed under foreign domination. Herod exacerbated these feelings by his secular power base; his extravagant building programs, the funds for which were extracted from the Jewish people; his blatant control of the temple and high priesthood for his own political purposes; and his wide-ranging efforts at continued reform of Palestine along the lines of Hellenistic culture.[4] The setting of the events of Luke's birth narrative, then, is one of struggle during the process of the consolidation of the Jews under Roman rule at the hand of a king noted for his tyranny.[5] Into this context Luke introduces Zechariah and Elizabeth, a priestly couple.

The basis of the priesthood was genealogical, with "Levites" distinguished from priests (cf. Luke 10:31-32).[6] Because of their hereditary purity and vocation, their indispensable role in temple worship and sacrifice (cf. Exodus 28–29; Leviticus 8–10), and their positions of leadership in their local communities, members of the priesthood were honored among the Jews. They enjoyed the divine imprimatur, for priests were set apart by God, had unrivaled access to holy places and paraphernalia, pronounced blessing on God's behalf, and had roles of scriptural interpretation and instruction among the people.

Concern with priestly status and its maintenance is underscored by Luke. As a "priest" and member of the order of Abijah,[7] Zechariah himself is a descendant of Aaron, and he adds to this qualification his marriage to a daughter of Aaron. This is not due to castelike constraints; priests were allowed to marry Israelites (i.e., the daughters of nonpriests) with an unblemished ancestry. The primary issue was the genealogical preservation of the purity and dignity of the priesthood, for the male offspring inherited the priestly office from the father, provided the mother was of sufficient status. In the present case, priestly origins and purity, both measures of status, have clearly been kept inviolate.[8]

---

4. On Hellenization during this era, see Hengel, *Jews, Greeks, and Barbarians; idem, Hellenization.*

5. See Josephus *Ant.* 14.9.1 §268-17.8.4 §205; *J.W.* 1; Smallwood, *Jews,* 44-104.

6. That is, "Levites" were lesser priests, male members of the tribe of Levi — cf. Num 1:47-53; 8:5-26; while a "priest" was a Levite descended from Aaron — cf. Exod 28:1; 29:9; Numbers 18.

7. See 1 Chronicles 24; Nehemiah 12; Josephus, *Ant.* 7.14.7 §§363-67. On the service of priests by order, see below on 1:8-23.

8. On these issues, see Archer, *Her Price Is beyond Rubies,* 137-39; Schürer, *Jewish People,* 2:240-43; Sanders, *Judaism,* 170-82; Hurst and Green, "Priest, Priesthood."

6 Luke is fond of brief but weighty character references (cf., e.g., 2:25, 36-37; 23:50-51; Acts 10:1-2), and he uses this one to further his portrait of the exemplary character of Zechariah and Elizabeth. To their ancestral purity he now adds the conformity of their lives to the will of God. The parallelism of the two clauses — "both of them were

righteous	before God,
living blamelessly according to all the	
commandments and regulations	of the Lord"

— emphasizes their moral excellence through repetition. Moreover, it spells out the nature of their righteousness as a consequence of the ethical quality of their daily lives. The repetition of God/Lord indicates the standard against which their behavior has been measured as well as reveals before whom they have found approval.[9] Luke's phrase, "commandments and regulations," is reminiscent of similar expressions in the Pentateuch (e.g., Deut 4:40; Num 36:13), and, along with the reference to "walking"[10] blamelessly, recalls language used of Abraham (Gen 15:6; 17:1[!]; 18:19; 26:5[!]). Luke thus presents his readers with a positive view of the law as expressive of God's will.[11] And, given the linkage of obedience to God with the blessing of childbearing in passages like Deut 28:4, 11, we can hardly anticipate any news of childlessness — or any other tragedy for that matter. What is thus far transparent is (1) the honorable status of Zechariah and Elizabeth by any standard in first-century Judaism, and (2) the inability of the reader to lay the blame for any subsequently narrated misfortune at their feet.

7 Given the preceding affirmations, v 7 is startling.[12] The idea that God controls the womb is firmly embedded in Israel's Scriptures[13] — with the result that children signified God's blessing and were a source of honor in the community. On the other hand, childlessness was a sign of divine punishment and source of shame (see Luke 1:25, 38).[14] According to Deut

---

9. Cf. Origen *Hom. im Luc.* 2. On "righteousness" as conformity to God's will, cf. Gen 18:19; Lev 19:36; Deut 6:25; 1QS 1:5, 13; Luke 1:17; 2:25; 23:47, 50.

10. πορευόμενοι — "walking"; NRSV: "living." The image of living lives that conform to God's will as a journey is an important one for Luke, who develops it further in the central "journey" section of his Gospel and in the label he uses for the Jesus movement in Acts, "the Way."

11. See also the use of ἐντολή in 18:20; 23:56. Δικαίωμα is used only here in Luke-Acts, and 9 other times in the NT (Romans — 5x, Hebrews — 2x, Revelation — 2x).

12. On the use of καί to emphasize an unexpected element, see BAGD, 392.

13. Cf. Trible, *Rhetoric of Sexuality,* 34-38.

14. Cf. Gen 16:4; 29:32; 30:1, 22-23; 1 Sam 1:5-6; Pss 127:3-5; 128.

28:15, 18, failure to observe God's commandments would lead to the cursing of the womb, and it has always been easy to reverse this logic by insisting that the phenomenon of childlessness is a consequence of God's curse, itself a result of disobedience. But this cannot be the case here, for this interpretive option is expressly ruled out by vv 5-6.

Luke does not lead us to puzzle over this tension, however. Instead, he encourages us, first, to experience the pathos of this narrative opening, to recognize their pain and shame. Then, for those with ears to hear, Luke provides echoes of earlier stories in Israel's past so that we understand that contained within the framework of this tragedy are the seeds of its resolution. *The narration of barrenness itself becomes grounds for anticipating the gift of a child.*[15]

The answer to the problem of childlessness is not to be found in Zechariah. He, like Elizabeth, is too old for childbearing. By going on to mention Elizabeth's barrenness, Luke reminds us that God controls the womb. Zechariah cannot make Elizabeth pregnant; ultimately, her having a child (and having her honor restored) cannot depend on him. Her situation is impossible, hopeless, apart from miraculous intervention.

2.1.2. The Announcement of John's Birth (1:8-23)

> 8 *Once when he was serving as priest before God and his section was on duty,* 9 *he was chosen by lot, according to the custom of the priesthood, to enter the sanctuary of the Lord and offer incense.* 10 *Now at the time of the incense offering, the whole assembly of the people was praying outside.* 11 *Then there appeared to him an angel of the Lord, standing at the right side of the altar of incense.* 12 *When Zecha-*

---

15. Marshall (53) draws attention to the following midrash: "R. Levi said: Wherever 'she had not' is found, it means that eventually she did have. Thus: And Sarai was barren; she had no child: eventually she did have, as it is written, *And the Lord remembered Sarah* (Gen. xxi,i)" (*Gen. Rab.* 38:14 [on Gen 11:29-30]; ET in *Midrash Rabbah,* 1:312). Luke capitalizes on a well-known type-scene (see above, §2), drawing on the capacity of repetition to influence how a work is read. Readers, if they have followed the cue of the narrator that a well-known structure of events is about to be related, are led to expect a certain process and outcome. At times, of course, writers stretch such conventions, manipulating them to their own ends, so that readers familiar with the type-scene will be aware both of similarities with and departures from this convention. The annunciation type-scene contains a minimal number of common features, moving from (1) a recognition of a woman's barrenness to (2) an announcement of her impending conception to (3) the conception and birth of a child. In narrating vv 5-7, Luke seems deliberately to be echoing manifestations of this type-scene, especially in the Abrahamic material in Gen 11:30; 16:1; and 18:11; and the story of Hannah (1 Sam 1:1-2). But other reports of barrenness come to mind (Gen 25:21; 30:1; Judg 13:2), and in each of these cases, this diagnosis is followed by the birth of a child.

riah saw him, he was terrified; and fear overwhelmed him. 13 *But the angel said to him, "Do not be afraid, Zechariah, for your prayer has been heard. Your wife Elizabeth will bear you a son, and you will name him John.* 14 *You will have joy and gladness, and many will rejoice at his birth,* 15 *for he will be great in the sight of the Lord. He must never drink wine or strong drink; even before his birth he will be filled with the Holy Spirit.* 16 *He will turn many of the people of Israel to the Lord their God.* 17 *With the spirit and power of Elijah he will go before him, to turn the hearts of fathers*[16] *to their children, and the disobedient to the wisdom of the righteous, to make ready a people prepared for the Lord."* 18 *Zechariah said to the angel, "How will I know this is so? For I am an old man, and my wife is getting on in years."* 19 *The angel replied, "I am Gabriel. I stand in the presence of God, and I have been sent to speak to you and to bring you this good news.* 20 *But now, because you did not believe my words, which will be fulfilled in their time, you will become mute, unable to speak, until the day these things occur.*

21 *Meanwhile, the people were waiting for Zechariah, and wondered at his delay in the sanctuary.* 22 *When he did come out, he could not speak to them, and they realized that he had seen a vision in the sanctuary. He kept motioning to them and remained unable to speak.* 23 *When his time of service was ended, he went to his home.*

Having introduced Zechariah and Elizabeth and raised the issue of their childlessness, Luke proceeds to relate God's marvelous intervention on their behalf. In doing so, he turns the spotlight first on Zechariah (vv 8-23), then on Elizabeth (vv 24-25), contrasting the responses of husband (vv 18-23) and wife (vv 24-25). At the same time, that vv 8-23 constitute a single, unified narrative sequence is evident from its opening and finale: in v 8, the priest Zechariah (v 5) has come to the temple for his semiannual duties; and in v 23, the period of his service having expired, Zechariah returns home. What is more, vv 8-23 are presented chiastically, with the weight of emphasis falling, as we might expect, on the angelic message concerning John's birth and role in salvation history:

(A)   Service, Sanctuary, People (vv 8-10)
    (B)   Angel's Appearance and Zechariah's Response (vv 11-12)
        (C)   Announcement of "Good News" (vv 13-17; cf. v 19)
    (B′) Zechariah's Objection and Angel's Response (vv 18-20)
(A′) People, Sanctuary, Service (vv 21-23)

16. NRSV: "parents."

Verses 8-10, 21-22 raise questions for the modern reader about the customs and practices of the Jewish priesthood, especially vis-à-vis the incense offering, and it will be helpful to review these briefly.

§4 The Temple and the Incense Offering

Luke notes that Zechariah "belonged to the priestly order of Abijah" (v 5), and refers to Zechariah's "section" and "time of service" (vv 8, 23). This terminology reflects the division of the priesthood into twenty-four orders or courses, made necessary by the sheer quantity of priests. Each order would serve at the temple on a rotating basis during two separate weeks each year. This time of service extended from Sabbath to Sabbath. During normal periods — that is, apart from festival days with their increased temple traffic and extraordinary demands on its services — orders of priests were divided further. As a result, at any given time one would find only a subdivision on duty in the temple.[17]

The daily routine at the temple, alluded to in v 9, called for incense offerings before the morning and following the evening sacrifices (cf. Exod 30:7-8). Philo sees in this practice an expression of the special honor reserved for the altar of incense, "for it is not permitted to bring the victim of the whole burnt-offering outside until the incense has been offered inside at the first glimpse of day."[18] The honor attached to the incense offering is further suggested by its location, in the sanctuary or Holy Place, outranked in terms of relative holiness only by the Holy of Holies.[19] Like other daily priestly duties, those involved in the burning of incense were chosen by lot, with the exception that only those who had never before offered incense were eligible to participate in the casting of the lots for this special duty.[20] This again highlights the honor attending this task as well as the blessing supposed to be allotted to the priest thus chosen. The procedure for the offering of incense is described in the Mishnah,[21] wherein it is specified that five priests were required for this service — those who tended the candelabrum and prepared the altar in the Holy Place, the one chosen to offer incense, and his assistant.[22] Following the burning of the incense, those five priests participating in the offering would stand on the steps of the porch and bless the people, using the words of Num 6:24-26 as a benediction. Luke's account not only follows the outline of this practice but builds

---

17. See Schürer, *Jewish People*, 2:245-49; Sanders, *Judaism*, ch. 6.

18. Philo *Spec. Leg.* 1.51 §276; ET in *Philo*, 1:259-60.

19. See *m. Kelim* 1:6-9.

20. See *m. Tamid* 5:2; see also *m. Tamid* 3.

21. See *m. Tamid* 5-7; also Schürer, *Jewish People*, 2:302-7; Winter, "Cultural Background," 230-36.

22. The narrator has focused the spotlight so carefully on this exchange that details related to the offering itself (except that the dialogue took place in the Holy Place; cf. vv 9, 11) are lost from view. Josephus records a similar incident, this one involving Hyrcanus's reception of a divine revelation during the incense offering (*Ant.* 13.10.3 §§282-83).

on his earlier presentation of Zechariah's status by naming him as the one chosen (by God!)[23] for this blessed honor.

We encounter numerous echoes of the OT in these verses: (1) As we have seen, the *story of Abraham* is recalled in various ways.[24] (2) The phrase *"Fear not"* (1:13) often appears in tandem with promises and announcements related to offspring (e.g., Gen 15:1-6; 26:24; 35:17; 1 Sam 4:20; Jer 46:27-28). (3) John's future is outlined as though he were carrying on and fulfilling the role of *Elijah* (1:17; Mal 3:1; 4:5-6; Sir 48:10). (4) With the naming of Gabriel, but also with the inclusion of other details in this encounter, we are reminded of *Daniel 9–10*.[25] (5) In light of the citation of Isa 40:3-5 in 3:4-6 to describe John's ministry, we may be justified in finding echoes of *Isaiah 40* already in John's promised ministry of preparation (1:17; Isa 40:3) and in the characterization of Gabriel's announcement as "good news" (1:19; Isa 40:9). (6) Finally, v 15 cites *Num 6:3; Lev 10:9;* it also echoes *Judg 13:3-4,* where instructions concerning "wine or strong drink" follow on the heels of the promise of a son.

This list of scriptural echoes is by no means exhaustive, but already displays how the OT has served as a data bank for use in Luke 1:8-23 and demonstrates variety in the way the OT has been employed. Luke has constructed a narrative unit that is itself a complex network of echoes of other texts. This contributes to the ethos he is creating, locating his narrative in Israel's continuing history. It also evidences the continuity of this account with the one story of God's interaction with his people.

8-10   Zechariah is a priest (v 5), so we are not surprised to find him now in the temple "serving as priest before God." The theocentric focus of the story, the pervasiveness of scriptural echoes (especially as related to Abraham and Samuel), and the explicit reference to the presence of "the whole assembly of the people" (v 10) all provide hints that this episode will have repercussions far exceeding its direct relevance for this righteous couple.

23. See below on v 9.

24. See, e.g., the appearance of a divine messenger (1:11; Gen 17:1); the promise of a son with instructions given as to his name (1:13; Gen 17:16, 19); objections and questions given in response to the divine message (1:18; Gen 15:8; 17:17; 18:11-13); the report of conception (1:24; Gen 21:2; cf. 30:23); and the removal of shame (1:25; Gen 21:6; cf. 30:24). See above, §2.

25. For example, an encounter at the time of (evening?) sacrifice (1:9-10; Dan 9:20-21); the appearance of the angel to one person only (1:10; Dan 10:7); the reference to fear, followed by the admonition, "Do not fear . . ." (1:12-13; Dan 8:17; 10:8-9, 12, 19); the certification that these men have been heard (1:13; Dan 10:12); the reference to Gabriel, who stands in God's presence, now sent to "you" (1:19; Dan 7:16; 8:16; 9:21; 10:11); and, albeit for different reasons, both Zechariah and Daniel are unable to speak (1:20; Dan 10:15). See Winter, "Cultural Background," 236-37; Goulder, 1:211.

Background material related to the priestly customs mentioned here is discussed above (§4).

It was customary for the daily tasks of the priesthood to be allocated among the priests on duty according to the casting of lots. In wider Greek thought, the casting of lots was understood as a way of circumventing human will.[26] This usage is known in the OT, where the emphasis falls especially on ascertaining the divine will, and in Luke-Acts (Acts 1:17, 26). The selection of Zechariah to offer incense was no "arbitrary decision,"[27] nor is Luke merely asserting Zechariah's choice "according to the custom of the priesthood." He is affirming that in this custom God is at work, that God has chosen Zechariah for this signal honor and blessing.[28]

The honor reserved for Zechariah is symbolized in the spatial markers Luke employs: Zechariah goes *into* the sanctuary and the people remain *outside*. This language underscores the separation of people by status as measured above all by religious purity in Jewish antiquity. In this setting, purity (or cleanliness) was correlated with holiness, so that the closer one came to the presence of the divine, the more pure one had to be.[29] The "altar of incense" was located in the sanctuary itself, in the outer chamber or Holy Place. On the one side was a curtained doorway leading to the inner chamber or Holy of Holies. This was the locus of God's glory and could be entered on only one day each year, the Day of Atonement, and then only by the high priest.[30] The offering of incense, then, would bring Zechariah as close to the presence of God as any person other than the high priest might ever come. Many priests might never experience this honor, and it was forever out of the reach of nonpriests. Thus was the holiness-purity matrix epitomized in the architecture of the temple area.[31]

It is not that Zechariah and "the people" are characterized as opposites, however. Rather, on a continuum, he is more pure than they, with the consequence that he may offer incense *in* the sanctuary while they remain *out*side.

26. Cf. Hause, "λαγχάνω."

27. Godet, 1:74.

28. Thus, κατὰ τὸ ἔθος (cf. 2:42; 4:16 [εἰωθός]; 22:39) modifies τῆς ἱερατείας — cf. Plummer, 10.

29. See Douglas, *Purity and Danger*.

30. Luke employs a variety of terms to refer to the temple — e.g., ἱερόν, οἶκος, ἅγιος, τοῖς, and τόπος — but in the Gospel ναός is used consistently with reference to the "sanctuary" as distinct from the larger temple precinct (1:9, 21, 22; 23:45; cf. "shrine" in Acts 17:24; 19:24).

31. Jewish men might approach the sanctuary by entering the Court of Israelites, but were not able to climb the steps to the sanctuary itself; Jewish women were kept further away, being allowed only so far as the Court of Women; and Gentiles were held even further back, forbidden on pain of death from passing beyond the barricades separating the Court of Gentiles from the inner courts.

Zechariah is portrayed as having been selected by God for an honorable task, one that might even bring him divine blessing, while "the people" are portrayed as faithful Jews.[32]

Though apparently never legislated, the offering of prayer at the time of sacrifice is well attested.[33] In fact, Isa 56:7 represents the temple as a "house of prayer," and Luke shares this assessment (1:10; 18:9-14; 19:46; 24:53; Acts 3:1; 22:17). The presence of the praying crowd in v 10, together with the echo of Dan 9:21, may indicate that Luke has in mind "the time of the incense offering" *in the evening*.[34] More to the point is the initial appearance here of what will become for Luke a significant motif, prayer.[35] If analogy with other prayers at the time of sacrifice in the LXX are any indication, then we may assume that these prayers are on behalf of the nation of Israel. This assumption gains strength from the descriptions and words of pious Jews throughout the birth narrative, concerned as they are with divine intervention on behalf of Israel. Here, as elsewhere in Luke-Acts, prayer is a prelude to divine revelation; hearing, God speaks and acts.[36]

11-12   Luke continues to emphasize Zechariah's presence in the sanctuary by mentioning the angel's appearance "at the right side of the altar." The "right side" is the place of honor, and may suggest here the status of the angel as well as hinting that the message to be spoken will be propitious.[37] More than this, it keeps our attention fixed on what is happening in the Holy Place; we will return to the outside only in vv 21-22.

It is difficult to overemphasize the import of the setting in which this encounter takes place. This is holy space, the sanctuary serving as sacred space connecting and supporting heaven and earth. Hence, the temple is a place in which God speaks — as here, through an angel (1:18-23); in 2:25-32, through a Spirit-inspired prophet; and in Acts 22:17-21, in a vision.[38]

The motif of God's presence is furthered by Luke's introduction of an

32. As is frequent in the Third Gospel, "the people" represent Israel as the chosen people of God. Here they are the pious of Israel, present at the hour of sacrifice, engaged in prayer. For ὁ λαός, cf. 1:10, 17, 21, 68, 77; 2:32; 7:16; 20:1; 23:2, 13; 24:19.

33. See, e.g., Ezra 9:5-15; Dan 9:21; Jdt 9:1-14; Sir 50:12-21; cf. *Pss. Sol.* 6:4; Josephus *Ag. Ap.* 2.196; Dunn, "Prayer," 617.

34. Cf. Marshall, 54.

35. Cf. Smalley, "Spirit, Kingdom and Prayer"; O'Brien, "Prayer in Luke-Acts"; Trites, "Prayer Motif"; Navone, *Themes,* 118-31; Ott, *Gebet und Heil;* Plymale, *Prayer Texts;* Crump, *Jesus the Intercessor.*

36. Cf. 3:21-22; 9:28-36; 22:39-46; Acts 4:23-31; 10:3-5, 9-16, 30-32; 13:2; 22:17-21.

37. See Schürmann, 1:31; Kremer, 25.

38. See also Luke 2:36-38; Acts 2.

angel of the Lord, using phraseology familiar from the OT.[39] We will learn in v 19 that this angel is Gabriel, but in the interim we are left with "angel of the Lord," with its suggestive use in Israel's Scriptures. There the phrase occurs some sixty times, denoting an angel who comes to the aid of God's people (e.g., Exod 14:19; Judg 2:1) and who communicates divine revelation, including announcements of birth (Gen 16:11; Judg 13:3-5). This "angel of the Lord" is often presented in such a way as to be indistinguishable from the Lord himself (e.g., Gen 16:7-13; Exod 3:2-4; Judg 6:11-13).[40] Consequently, the appearance of the "angel of the Lord" takes on the character of an epiphany. His speech will be divine speech, and it is through this emissary that God's purpose, which we have seen *behind* Luke's narrative, will be brought to the *fore*.

Zechariah's fearful response is expected in this context, laden as it is with elements signifying a divine visitation. He has seen an angel *of the Lord* and, like persons in Greek, scriptural, and apocalyptic literature before him,[41] he is overcome with fear.

Visions and angelical visitations are a regular part of the birth narrative (1:11-20, 26-34; 2:8-20), but they also occur at strategic points in Luke-Acts.[42] As here, prayer to God and supernatural communication to people (via a vision, an angelical visitation, or through the voice of the Spirit) are often coupled (e.g., 1:10-11; 3:21-22; 9:28-31; 22:39-46; et al.). These data demonstrate how prayer is the context in which God's purpose is made known — and to what lengths God will go to initiate his purpose and certify that each step along the way bears his sanction.

13 The phrase "Do not be afraid" appears elsewhere in Luke-Acts usually by way of communicating the certainty of God's care.[43] Even when

---

39. We should not make too much of the lack of a definite article in the phrase ἄγγελος κυρίου. Comparable phrases (without ὁ) are found in the LXX — e.g., Gen 16:7; Exod 3:2; Judg 6:11, 12. Its absence in 1:11 is likely due to the successive clarification of this angel's identity as Gabriel (v 19).

40. In fact, the expression seems first to be a way of describing a personal manifestation of Yahweh, though in time this "angel of the Lord" might be distinguished from Yahweh (e.g., Zech 1:11-14).

41. Especially interesting are the similar occurrences in Dan 8:16-17, where, when Gabriel draws near, Daniel "became frightened and fell prostrate" (cf. 10:10-11); and *2 Enoch* 21:1-4, where the seer is overcome with fear, then comforted by Gabriel. Cf., e.g., Homer *Iliad* 20.130-31; Judg 6:22-23; 13:6; Dan 8:16-17; 10:10-11; *1 Enoch* 14:13-14, 24; *2 Enoch* 20:1; 21:2; Balz and Wanke, "φοβέω κτλ," 194, 206.

42. For example, at the Transfiguration (9:31), Mount of Olives (22:43-44), and Resurrection/Ascension (24; cf. Acts 1); and in Acts especially by way of directing the mission through obstacles and toward the Gentiles (e.g., 5:17-21; 7:56; 9:1-9 [cf. 22:17-21; 10; 16:9-10]).

43. Cf. 1:30; 5:10; 8:50; 12:4, 7, 12; Acts 18:9; 27:24.

the context is one of divine visitation, the ensuing message confirms that this encounter is for the purpose of providing comfort and good news, not judgment (2:10; Acts 18:9; 27:24). Similarly, here Zechariah's fear is waylaid because, according to the angel, this visitation is propitious: Zechariah's prayer has been heard; a son is promised. Hence, we hear in the angel's words a clear echo of Gen 15:1,[44] where the Lord's greeting was above all a promise to Abram that he had not been forgotten.

Thus, on the one hand, the angel's message is reminiscent of a divine remembrance motif in the Scriptures. Repeatedly, we are told, God remembers certain persons, turns to them in his mercy, and acts on their behalf.[45] Although the *language* of remembrance is absent from this immediate literary co-text (though cf. 1:54-55, 72), this *motif* is present.[46] This is most evident from a comparison of v 13 with such texts as Gen 30:22 (God remembered Rachel and allowed her to conceive) and 1 Sam 1:11, 19-20 (the Lord remembered Hannah, who had prayed for a son, and she conceived and bore a son).

On the other hand, the question remains, Whom has God remembered? That is, what prayer has been heard by God?[47] Does the angel refer to Zechariah's prayer for a son or for the deliverance of Israel? Three observations are telling. First, from Zechariah's point of view, the focus is apparently only on a son; references to Israel (cf. "many" in vv 14, 16) seem not to have entered his mind.[48] Second, we must remember that more than one perspective is present in this episode, and particularly that the narrator's aim is to present in these events the divine purpose. In this case, the prayers of the people in v 10 — related to the fate of the people of Israel — are interwoven with those of Zechariah. Thus far, Luke has related in explicit ways the *need* of Zechariah and Elizabeth (childlessness) and the *obstacle* to the resolution of their need (barrenness and age), but has only hinted at the *need* and *obstacle* facing Israel (vv 5, 10). Through divine intervention, both story lines — that of Zechariah/Elizabeth and of Israel — are brought together explicitly. By acting on behalf of Zechariah and Elizabeth ("you" — vv 13-14a), God is acting on behalf of Israel (vv 14b, 16-17). Third, because of the degree to which Luke's

---

44. Cf. Dan 10:12.

45. Cf. Gen 8:1; 19:29; 30:22; Exod 2:24; 6:5; 1 Sam 1:11, 19-20.

46. Note, too, that the etymological meaning of "Zechariah" (זכריה) is "Yahweh remembers."

47. Εἰσηκούσθη, then, is a divine passive. Δέησις, "prayer," is found in the Gospels only in Luke 1:13; 2:37; 5:33.

48. His objection to the divine message (v 18) suggests that he has only heard that portion of the speech addressed specifically to him and about him: "(you) do not be afraid . . . your prayer . . . your wife . . . you a son . . . you will name . . . you will have" (vv 13-14). He seems concerned exclusively with the angel's message as it pertains to the promise of a son (cf. "I know . . . I am . . . my wife" [v 18]).

story is interlaced with Abrahamic material we should be wary of either-or proposals to our original question. Through the divine intervention resulting in the miraculous birth of Isaac, (1) God will keep his covenant with Abraham, (2) Abraham and Sarah will have a son in their old age, and (3) all the nations will be blessed. "Your prayer has been heard" is a weighty affirmation of God's faithfulness to his covenant, his care for this faithful people, and his remembrance of the plight of Israel.

The naming of a child by God is known in the OT, and generally underscores the significance of that child in salvation history (cf. Gen 16:11; 17:19[!]; Isa 7:14). In the Jewish culture in which this narrative is set, names often have further significance derived from their etymological meaning. "John"[49] means "God is gracious," but only later will Luke show by his play on words that this etymology is of importance to him: the birth of a son is proof that "the Lord has shown great mercy" to Elizabeth (1:58), and his name is "God is gracious" (1:60).[50]

14-15[51] The angel's remarks escalate in their acknowledgment of the importance of John — first to Zechariah, then to "many," and finally "in the sight of the Lord." At this juncture the story of Zechariah's need and the story of Israel are shown to be only strands (albeit significant ones) of God's story. Verse 14b marks the transition in the angel's message from attention to Zechariah and Elizabeth to the wider panorama of John's mission in Israel. Seen in this way, v 15 functions in a parenthetical way, whereby the angel provides a description of John before defining his role in vv 16-17.

Just as the revelation Zechariah receives counters the condition of childlessness in v 7, so the stress on rejoicing[52] marks a mood shift from the distress of v 7. Joy becomes a dominant feature of the birth narratives (cf. 1:28, 44, 46, 58; 2:10). This is perhaps expected in stories of childbirth, but Luke's interest transcends the happiness attending childbirth in general. In his view, these are not ordinary births; they are of eschatological importance, marking the coming of salvation, and this calls for eschatological celebration.[53] Thus, John's birth will be an occasion for gladness particularly because

---

49. יוֹחָנָן.

50. In this way Luke displays here the same sort of interest in implicit echoes he has demonstrated elsewhere in his use of the OT. John's name is a reminder of God's graciousness to Elizabeth (cf. vv 25, 58), and only then describes his role in salvation history.

51. Verses 14-17 exhibit a series of well-crafted parallel clauses: 14a//14b, 14b//16, 15a//17a, 15cd//17b, 16//17c, 17c//17d. But these allow for no straightforward structural analysis.

52. Luke employs three related terms in v 14, all synonymous in this context, to emphasize John's birth as a joyful event: χαρά, χαίρω, and ἀγαλλίασις.

53. On joy as related to the advent of salvation, see 1:44; 2:10; 10:17; Acts 2:46; *Sib. Or.* 3:619-23, 767-95; Dibelius, "Jungfrauensohn," 61-62.

"he will be great in the sight of the Lord," a designation that underscores his divinely ordained status in redemptive history (cf. 7:28).

Complete abstinence from wine and other alcoholic beverages[54] is extraordinary in the biblical world, so the requirement that John embrace such ascetic behavior requires explanation. During their period of service in the temple, priests were to abstain from alcoholic beverages (Lev 10:8-9; Ezek 44:21). Abstinence was also integral to those who had taken a nazirite vow (Num 6:1-21). This suggests that refusal to drink wine and beer was associated with separation from normal life for a divine task, whether for a temporary, specified period (priests on duty, nazirites) or, as in the case of Samson, for life (Judg 13:7). That lifelong consecration to God is meant in John's case is suggested by later reports of his behavior (7:33). One may also point to the reminiscences of the Samuel story present here (see 1 Sam 1:11). More particularly, this angelic announcement echoes the material related to Samson, for there an angel announces the conception of a son and requires that his mother not "drink wine or strong drink" since "he shall be a nazirite to God from birth" (Judg 13:3-6); Samson would be instrumental in Israel's deliverance (13:6); and, later, Samson is empowered by the Spirit of the Lord (14:19). By analogy, then, John is set apart by God to God even before his conception.

A deliberate contrast is set between John's abstinence from wine and his being filled with the Spirit.[55] This is Luke's first mention of the Holy Spirit, who will play a dominant role in the events of the birth story while underscoring the intrusion of the divine purpose in human affairs and adding to the heightened sense of eschatological fulfillment in the narrative (1:35, 41, 67; 2:25, 26, 27). Luke's phrase, "filled with the Holy Spirit," occurs repeatedly in Luke-Acts (cf. 1:41, 67; Acts 2:4; 4:8, 31; 9:17; 13:9), where it can refer to the continuous state of being empowered and directed by the Spirit or to a special dispensation of the Spirit for a particular task or role. Here the former is in view, as is clear from the qualification, "even before his birth."[56] Why is it necessary for John to be Spirit-empowered before birth? This emphasizes that John's will be a ministry authorized by the Spirit, but it also anticipates — and, indeed, makes possible — the prophetic role of John even as an unborn child in vv 39-45.[57]

54. This is the meaning of the stereotypical phrase οἶνον καὶ σίκερα, the latter word borrowed from the Akkadian šikaru (via the Aramaic שׁכרא), referring to alcoholic drinks such as beer (BAGD 750). Cf., e.g., Lev 10:9; Num 6:3; Deut 29:6; Judg 13:4, 7, 14; 1 Sam 1:15; Prov 20:1; et al.

55. Cf. Eph 5:18.

56. Of itself, ἐκ κοιλίας might mean "before birth" or "at/from birth" — cf. Judg 13:3-5; 16:17; Isa 44:2; Pss 22:10; Isa 48:8. In this case, larger co-textual considerations (see below) and the presence of ἔτι vouch for the NRSV rendering.

57. Cf. Darr, *Character Building*, 62-63. Shelton (*Mighty in Word*) emphasizes the role of the Spirit in "inspired witness," and this is clearly the case with John.

16-17 Luke outlines in a compact way John's role in God's redemptive program. Through the structure of the angelic message and the use of scriptural allusions, Luke accents John's task as a prophet effecting repentance on the part of God's people. Verse 16 thus summarizes John's mission, with v 17 set in parallel to illustrate further the nature of that mission:

> *He will turn* many of the people of Israel to the Lord their God
> . . . he will go before him,
>> *to turn* the hearts of fathers to their children, and
>> [*to turn*] the disobedient to the wisdom of the righteous,
>> to make ready a people prepared for the Lord.

Thus, even though John is also presented as precursor and preparer, these roles are subordinate to his primary mission of calling Israel to repentance. This emphasis will be continued in Luke's narration of John's ministry in 3:13-14. The inclusion of the qualifier "many" in v 16 provides a proleptic sign that the response to John's "good news" (3:18) — and so to God's salvific initiative — will not be universally positive.[58]

Gabriel's sketch of John's vocation is fundamentally theocentric. John will turn Israel to its *Lord*. John will go before *him* — that is, *the Lord*. And so the people will be prepared for the advent of *the Lord*. This is a reminder that this is *God's* story. At this juncture, the solution to the priestly couple's childlessness has been caught up into the larger need of Israel for the reign of its God.

One aspect of John's ministry will be "to turn the hearts of *fathers* to their children." This clause is a little surprising given subsequent teaching in Luke subordinating family ties to the demands of discipleship (12:53; cf. 9:59; 14:26). At the same time, this clause is borrowed from Mal 4:6, and is one of the ways in which Luke fills out his portrait of John's mission by drawing on material related to eschatological Elijah (cf. Sir 48:10). By this means Luke also stresses the orientation of John's ministry around calling people to repentance in their daily lives.

Three factors suggest that Luke is doing more than simply using Elijah material to portray the mission of John, however, and that Luke in fact sees the need for the hearts *of fathers* to be turned to their children. First, at a structural level, v 17 places "fathers" in the company of the "disobedient," and "children" in the company of the "righteous." Interestingly, this positive emphasis on children will continue in the Gospel (e.g., 9:46-48; 18:15-17).

---

58. It is possible that Luke's πολλοί reflects a Hebrew (רבים) or Aramaic (סגיאין) usage, in which case it should be taken in an inclusive sense — i.e., "all." Cf., however, the actual response to John's mission as reported in 7:29-30.

"Fathers" (in the sense of "ancestors"), on the other hand, are sometimes presented as having rejected God's purpose (6:23, 26; 11:47-48). Second, fathers in Roman antiquity were known as more strict than mothers, with reports of sexual abuse of slave- and freeborn children, excessively cruel disciplinary measures, and imperial intervention against severe fathers easily documented. With the onset of the Empire this gruesome picture began to be mollified, and Luke's emphasis would support this trend.[59] Third, we discover other material in Luke in which "the hearts of *fathers*" have been turned to their children. God himself is presented as the Father who cares for his children and acts redemptively on their behalf (e.g., 6:36; 11:2, 13; 12:30, 32), and human fathers can be characterized along similar lines (e.g., 8:51; 9:42; 11:11; 15:11-32). In this first example of the character of John's mission, therefore, a problematic expression of authority is called into question and the call to repentance is aimed at specific practices (cf. 3:10-14).

The second illustration of John's mission focuses on the conversion of "the disobedient to the wisdom of the righteous."[60] This phraseology is uncommon in Luke-Acts,[61] but may echo Mal 3:18, where "the righteous" and "the wicked" are juxtaposed; and Mal 2:6, where a priest "turned many from iniquity." (Recall that, as the son of a priestly couple, John inherits the priestly vocation.) This way of putting repentance is most at home in the wisdom tradition, where "understanding" or "wisdom" signifies the fulfillment of the law (e.g., Prov 1:2-3; 10:23-24; Wis 3:10-19; Sir 19:20-24). As the parallelism with v 16 clarifies, "the disobedient" are the people of Israel. This usage is known in the OT, too (cf. Isa 30:9; Jer 5:23).

The multiplicity of allusions to Malachi (especially 2:6-7; 3:1, 18; 4:5-6) in vv 16-17 work together with the explicit reference to John's being anointed "with the spirit and power of Elijah" to identify the promised son as a prophet of no mean significance.[62] Elisha, too, had received the spirit of

---

59. It is our perception that, in Luke's discourse situation, *this* picture of fatherhood leads us to reject as anachronistic the NRSV's rendering of πατέρων as "of parents." In addition, inasmuch as Luke is not *quoting* the LXX (Mal 3:23) there is no obvious reason why he could not have employed the generic οἱ γονεῖς had he intended "parents" — as he has done in 2:27, 41, 43; 8:56; 18:29; 21:16. Cf. Rawson, "Adult-Child Relationships"; *idem,* "Roman Family"; Eyben, "Fathers and Sons"; Saller, "Corporal Punishment"; J. K. Evans, *War, Women and Children,* 166-209; Dixon, *Roman Mother,* 13-40.

60. That is, "so that they have the thought" of the righteous — BDF §218; cf. MHT 3:257.

61. Ἀπειθής appears only here in Luke, and once in Acts (26:19); this is the only appearance of φρόνησις in the Lukan corpus.

62. See Wink, *John the Baptist,* 42-43. Wink wants to disassociate John from Elijah on the basis of 1:17, but cf. 7:27. On the development of the Elijah motif in the Third Gospel, see the nuanced discussion in R. J. Miller, "Elijah, John, and Jesus."

Elijah (2 Kgs 2:9-15), and on this basis we might have anticipated John to be a miracle-working prophet. Luke himself is interested in the conjunction of Spirit and power in miraculous deeds (e.g., Acts 10:38), but he also understands the work of the Spirit as the basis of prophetic speech and boldness in proclaiming the word of God (e.g., 4:14-15; Acts 2; 4:31).[63] With these echoes of Malachi our text is engulfed in end-time anticipation. Adding to this sense are those Jewish texts outlining a relation between Israel's repentance and the advent of the eschaton.[64]

John's purpose, then, is to go before the Lord readying a people prepared for the Lord's coming. He accomplishes this by effecting repentance. No notion of a Messiah is yet in view in the narrative, even if the atmosphere is thick with eschatological anticipation. For now, the promise revolves around the direct intervention of the Lord God himself, whose coming would inaugurate the long-awaited dominion of God, shalom, peace with justice (cf. Isaiah 40).[65] The announcement of John's birth has thus provided the occasion for an even more astounding proclamation. The period of waiting is drawing to a close. God is on the move. Final preparations are necessary, and John will have the central, prophetic role in proclaiming the looming advent of the Lord.

18-20 The incredulity of the angel's message is lost neither on the reader nor on Zechariah. The rationale for their childlessness has already been given (v 7); their case is closed; Zechariah only repeats what the narrator has already communicated. Verses 18-20, then, address this obstacle head-on, stressing repeatedly the reliability of the message.

The veracity of the message is asserted most prominently by certifying the credibility of the messenger. This previously anonymous angel now provides his name, and with it his credentials. He is Gabriel, known to us from Daniel 8–9 as trusted by God to reveal divine mysteries. The angel identifies himself as one who stands in the presence of God — in the image of the heavenly throne room, a leading angel or archangel, God's personal servant.[66] What is more, he has been sent by God to deliver this message. Gabriel's words, however dubious, must be accepted, for he speaks with God's own voice.

Moreover, scriptural echoes certify the reliability of his message. We hear in Zechariah's question the voice of Abraham, "O Lord GOD, how am I to know. . . ?" (Gen 15:8), and in his explanation the objections of Abraham

63. Cf. M. Turner, "Spirit and Power"; *idem,* "Spirit of Prophecy."

64. See, e.g., *T. Dan* 6:4; *T. Jud.* 23:5; *T. Sim.* 6:2-7; *As. Mos.* 1:18; Allison, *End of the Ages,* 155-57.

65. Cf. von Dobbeler, *Gericht und das Erbarmen Gottes,* 162-63, 165-66.

66. Cf. *1 Enoch* 9:1; 20:1-7; 40:1-10; *T. Levi* 3:5-8; *Jub.* 2:18; 1QH 6:13; Davidson, "Angels," 9; Winter, "Cultural Background," 236-37.

and Sarah on the grounds of their advanced age (Gen 17:17; 18:12). In these ways, Zechariah's restatement of the barrier to their childbearing brings onto the stage that paradigmatic story of God's gracious intervention and reminds us that, with the Lord, nothing is "too wonderful" (Gen 18:14). A further echo can be heard in Gabriel's choice of the term "good news." As is generally the case in Luke-Acts,[67] the verbal form "to proclaim good news" is used here. This is not a reference to "the gospel" as "the Christian message,"[68] but a usage rooted in Isaiah 40–66 (especially 40:9; 52:7; 61:1). By it, Luke draws attention to and announces the in-breaking kingdom of God and the phenomena through which God's dominion comes to be realized in history. Gabriel's message is thus shown to be grounded in the divine promise of coming eschatological redemption.

Still further, Gabriel's announcement of John's birth is affirmed as an expression of the divine purpose by the language of fulfillment. In asserting that his words "will be fulfilled in their time," Gabriel employs a term, "to fulfill," repeatedly used in Luke-Acts for the realization of God's will — sometimes revealed in the Scriptures, sometimes (as here) made known in some other way (cf. 4:21; 9:31; 21:24; 22:16; 24:44; Acts 1:16; 3:18; 13:27). Subsequently, he uses a term for "time" that can signify "the divinely appointed time."[69] His final reference to the occurrence of "these things" further highlights the certainty of his promise.

Against this backdrop, Zechariah's silence must be seen above all as a "sign" — that is, as the proof he requested. On the face of it, the giving of a sign is not extraordinary in the biblical tradition; we may recall the signs given Abraham (Gen 15:7-16), Moses (Exod 4:1-17), Gideon (Judg 6:36-40), Hezekiah (2 Kgs 20:1-11), and Ahaz (Isa 7:10-17). As in those instances, so here this sign is given as a guarantee of God's promise. The sign given Zechariah is more than certification; it is also punishment for his unbelief, as Gabriel's words make clear. In Luke, God may of his own initiative give a sign (1:36; 2:12), but requests for signs are consistently interpreted negatively (11:16, 29-30; 23:8). Even this can be used to advance God's purpose, for Zechariah's silence will contribute in a key way to the later account of the naming of the child.[70] In the interim, Zechariah's silence

---

67. Εὐαγγελίζομαι appears 23x in Luke-Acts — see, e.g., 2:10; 3:18; 4:18; 7:22; 8:1; et al.; εὐαγγέλιον occurs only in Acts 15:7; 20:24.

68. As in Paul (e.g., Rom 1:16) and sometimes in Mark (e.g., 8:35).

69. Luke 1:20: τὸν καιρόν; NRSV: "the day." See 12:56; 18:30; 19:44: "the time of your visitation from God"; 21:8, 24; Acts 1:7; 3:20; 7:20.

70. Cf. Acts 13:4-12, where Paul curses "a Jewish false prophet" with blindness for "a while," with the result that the proconsul was astonished and believed. That the narrator invites a comparison of these two episodes is suggested by the parallels in structure and vocabulary between them.

serves to guard the news of God's unfolding purpose until the appointed time.[71]

21-23 Luke has focused our attention narrowly on the events inside the temple sanctuary, but now provides a transition back into the outside world — the temple area (vv 10, 21) and, indeed, Judea (vv 5, 23; cf. v 39). Verses 21-23 are thus set in parallel with vv 8-10, providing evidence of Luke's dramatic staging. Verse 21 is retrospective, refocusing our vision on "the people" who had been "praying outside," reminding us again of the significance of Zechariah's vision for all Israel. Verse 23 closes this episode, redirects our interest to Zechariah's home, and so prepares us for Elizabeth's response in vv 24-25.

On the customs related to priestly service to which the narrative alludes, see §4.

These verses function further to certify the trustworthiness of Gabriel's words. The "rhetorical redundancy"[72] of his pronouncement — mentioning first Zechariah's being "mute," then his being "unable to speak" — is repeated in the narration of its effect: "he could not speak . . . and remained unable to speak." Emphatic for the reader is the certainty of this portion of Gabriel's words, serving as proof that he is a supernatural and powerful messenger. If the pronouncement of the "sign" is thus immediately realized (and affirmed by witnesses — v 22), can we not assume the reliability of the angel's promise of a son who will go before the Lord?

The people not only witness Zechariah's muteness, evident to them in his inability to pronounce the priestly benediction, but also recognize the cause of his incapacity. According to Dan 10:15-17, a visionary experience might result in an inability to speak (cf. Acts 9:7; 2 Cor 12:2-4), and other divine-human encounters evidence how such an experience might disrupt normal physical faculties (John 18:6; Acts 9:8-9; 22:11; Rev 1:17).[73]

2.1.3. Elizabeth's Response to God's Favor (1:24-25)

24 *After those days his wife Elizabeth conceived, and for five months she remained in seclusion. She said,* 25 *"This is what the Lord has done for me when he looked favorably on me and took away the disgrace I have endured among my people."*

---

71. This nuance is suggested not only by the shape of the story, which allows Zechariah his voice at the time designated by the angel, but also by the echoes of the Danielic material (cf. Dan 10:15; 12:4, 9).

72. Bovon, 1:59.

73. Luke's language, ὁράω + ὀπτασία, is used elsewhere for a visionary experience — 24:23; Acts 2:17 (Joel 3:1 LXX); 26:16-19; cf. Acts 7:2, 30, 35; 9:17; Dan 9:23; 10:1, 7, 8, 16 Θ.

Verses 24-25 serve as the climax of this portion of the birth narrative, reminding us of Elizabeth's need juxtaposed with her exemplary righteousness (vv 5-7). Her open-handed acceptance of God's intervention on her behalf contrasts sharply with her husband's hesitation and unbelief (v 18). Hardly for the last time in Luke-Acts, a woman is put forward as a recipient of God's favor and as a model of faithfulness to God's purpose. That these two responses are thus placed side by side focuses the question for Israel in the narrative: How will "the people" respond to the divine initiative to redeem God's people, to remove their shame in the face of the nations? It also poses the question for the reader: Will we believe, acknowledging the gracious hand of God?

The narrative of Elizabeth's conception is reminiscent of 1 Sam 1:19-20, and her response echoes the words of Sarah (Gen 21:6) and, especially, Rachel: "God has taken away my reproach" (Gen 30:22-23). The formative story, wherein God intervenes to create a faithful people, continues.

The report of Elizabeth's conception is related to the annunciation to Zechariah by the expression "after those days." Just as the words of the angel regarding Zechariah's silence had been realized (vv 20, 22), so Gabriel's promise that Elizabeth would conceive has now come to fruition (vv 13, 24). Gabriel is a reliable spokesperson (vv 18-20), and thus far his predictions have come true; in this way we are assured that the rest will also take place just as he described.

Elizabeth's five months of seclusion remain a mystery. The marking of months in vv 24, 26, 36, 56 is a literary device, laying bare a divine timetable for these goings-on. One might appeal to this by way of explaining the *length* of her privacy, but not the *fact* of her seclusion. Jewish literature relates how young girls — that is, those yet to enter the bridal chamber — would be confined to the house, and otherwise discusses the importance of circumspection for women in the public sphere. But no mention appears to have been made of the need for or practice of seclusion during early pregnancy.[74] Confinement to the home would have been a manifestation of modesty thought appropriate to females, and it may be that this is as much as we can make of Luke's reference. On the other hand, if v 25 is regarded as a rationale for Elizabeth's seclusion,[75] a further explanation is possible. In this case, Elizabeth would remain in her home so as not to continue to suffer public disgrace as a barren women; after five months her pregnancy — and with it God's favor toward her — would be apparent to all.[76]

---

74. See Archer, *Her Price Is beyond Rubies,* 101-22, 239-50.

75. That is, if ὅτι has the nuance of "because" and does not (only) introduce direct discourse — see Vg *(quia);* Winter, "*Hoti*-recitativum."

76. See Godet, 1:85.

Elizabeth's response in v 25 anticipates the more developed response of Mary in vv 46-55 and highlights her understanding that God controls the womb. Set in apposition are God's favor and the people's disfavor, her experiences of grace from God and disgrace among the people. Introduced in this report is the motif of the celebration of God's grace that will pervade the entire birth narrative.

2.2. THE ANNOUNCEMENT OF JESUS' BIRTH (1:26-38)

26 *In the sixth month the angel Gabriel was sent from*[1] *God to a town in Galilee called Nazareth,* 27 *to a virgin betrothed*[2] *to a man whose name was Joseph, of the house of David. The virgin's name was Mary.* 28 *And he came to her and said, "Rejoice,*[3] *favored one! The Lord is with you."* 29 *But she was much perplexed by his words and pondered what sort of greeting this might be.* 30 *The angel said to her, "Do not be afraid, Mary, for you have found favor with God.* 31 *And now, you will conceive in your womb and bear a son, and you will name him Jesus.* 32 *He will be great, and will be called the Son of the Most High, and the Lord God will give to him the throne of his ancestor David.* 33 *He will reign over the house of Jacob forever, and of his kingdom there will be no end."* 34 *Mary said to the angel, "How can this be, since I am a virgin?"* 35 *The angel said to her, "The Holy Spirit will come upon you, and the power of the Most High will overshadow you; therefore, the child to be born will be holy; he will be called Son of God.* 36 *And now, your relative Elizabeth in her old age has also conceived a son; and this is the sixth month for her who was said to be barren.* 37 *For no word from God will be impossible."*[4] 38 *Then Mary said, "Here am I, the servant of the Lord; let it be with me according to your word." Then the angel departed from her.*

This second scene of annunciation is closely aligned with the first (1:8-23); in fact, they are so interwoven that we know before we are explicitly told in vv 39-45, 67-79 that these two mothers and their sons belong to one story. First, the opening reference to "the sixth month" (v 26; cf. vv 24, 36, 56) ties the report of Elizabeth's conception and response to this account. Second, the appearance of the angel recalls Zechariah's encounter in the temple (vv 11,

1. NRSV: "by."
2. NRSV: "engaged."
3. NRSV: "Greetings."
4. NRSV: "For nothing will be impossible with God."

19, 26). First from Daniel, more recently from the annunciation to Zechariah, we know Gabriel as an eschatological messenger; what will he say now? Luke uses Gabriel to stage this episode: he comes to the virgin (vv 26-27), delivers his message and receives her response (vv 28-38a), then departs (v 38b). With Gabriel's departure, Mary will serve as the central figure holding together the scenes of the birth narrative.

Third, both in *language* and *form,* vv 5-23 and vv 26-38 are set in parallel.[5] They share the following progression of elements: (1) Introduction of Parents; (2) Specification of Obstacles to Childbearing; (3) Encounter with an Angel, Gabriel; (4) Response to the Angel; (5) "Do Not Be Afraid," with Address by Name; (6) Promise of a Son; (7) Objection; (8) Giving of a Sign; and (9) Departure of Gabriel. Although both scenes are examples of an annunciation type-scene found elsewhere in the Bible,[6] these two are more like each other than either is like the other representatives of this form. This similarity can be extended with reference to comparable language:[7]

Luke 1:11-20	*Luke 1:28-38*
"he was *troubled*" (v 12)	"she was much *troubled* (v 28)[8]
"the angel said to him" (v 13)	"the angel said to her" (v 30)
"Do not be afraid" (v 13)	"Do not be afraid" (v 30)
"will bear you a son" (v 13)	"you will . . . bear a son" (v 31)
"and you will name him" (v 13)	"and you will name him" (v 31)
"he will be great" (v 15)	"he will be great" (v 32)
"said to the angel" (v 18)	"said to the angel" (v 34)
"*and replying,* the angel	"*and replying,* the angel
said to him" (v 19)	said to her" (v 35)[9]
"Gabriel . . . God . . . sent" (v 19)	"Gabriel . . . sent . . . God" (v 26)
"*and* now" (v 20)	"and now" (v 36)[10]

The one account recalls and interprets the other. These events take their significance in part from their shared form and language, demonstrating that these scenes and especially these sons function together within the one purpose

---

5. Cf. Kaut, *Befreier und befreites Volk,* 116-18; Nolland, 1:40.

6. See above, §2.

7. The NRSV text has been altered (indicated by italics) to show parallels in a more literal rendering.

8. Verse 12: ἐταράχθη; v 29: διεταράχθη.

9. Verse 19: καὶ ἀποκριθεὶς ὁ ἄγγελος εἶπεν αὐτῷ; v 35: καὶ ἀποκριθεὶς ὁ ἄγγελος εἶπεν αὐτῇ.

10. Verse 20: καὶ ἰδού; v 36: καὶ ἰδού.

of God. *Behind both chains of events thus set in motion, stands God, present via his messenger and the unveiling of his aim.*

The points of contrast between these two scenes are equally telling. First, Elizabeth has a need — she is childless, disgraced; but Mary has no apparent need. Similarly, the redundancy in the explanation of Elizabeth's childlessness (vv 7a, 7b, 18) signals how her *need* has led to the recognition of the *obstacle* that must be overcome prior to its *resolution*. But the triple assertion of Mary's virginity (vv 27a, 27b, 34) is not presented as an obstacle to the resolution of any need on her part. Because divergences from the expected in a type scene are often clues to the significance of a narrated account, these departures call for interpretive reflection. Fundamentally, they make explicit what was already implicit in the narrative — namely, the real needs here are not those of Mary or even of Zechariah and Elizabeth. Israel is estranged from God, under alien rule, oppressed. God's covenant with his people has not been realized fully. Hence, God is intervening in human history to bring forth an everlasting kingdom. In doing so, he solicits and embraces the partnership of Zechariah and Elizabeth, and Mary — themselves Israelites and representative in their own ways of the people of Israel.

Third, the descriptions of the promised sons are in some ways comparable, but Jesus obviously outdistances John in his significance. To note only one illustration of this contrast, while "even before his birth [John] will be filled with the Holy Spirit," Jesus' conception results from the activity of the Spirit (vv 15, 35). Both are important in the realization of God's redemptive will, but Jesus is primary.

Fourth, Zechariah's encounter with Gabriel takes place at the center of the Jewish world, the Holy Place, only a veiled doorway from the presence of God's glory. But Gabriel travels to Mary, far away from the temple mount in Jerusalem, to Nazareth in Galilee — insignificant, despised, unclean.[11] Finally, the devout, divinely chosen priest Zechariah responds to Gabriel's words with hesitation rooted in unbelief. Mary, on the other hand, though she is only a young girl, embraces God's plan, proclaiming herself as God's servant. These points of dissimilarity bespeak something profound about the focus of God's redemptive initiative in the Third Gospel, and portend the joy with which "the little people" will receive divine favor.

The significance of this pericope is also grounded in scriptural echoes other than those related to such formal considerations.[12] Especially transparent are the points of contact with the Davidic material. First, Joseph — who has scarcely any role in Luke 1–2 and is only mentioned otherwise in 3:23 —

11. Cf. Isa 9:1; 1 Macc 5:15; Matt 4:13-16; Luke 22:59; John 1:46; 7:41; Acts 2:7.

12. See above, §2.

84

receives more of an introduction than Mary, the primary character in the birth narrative. Why? Luke is interested in his royal ancestry. He is "of the house of David" (v 27), and this prepares for the identification of his (albeit adopted) son as a Davidide. Second, Jesus' acclamation as Son of God (vv 32, 35) must be read at least against the backdrop of the use of this expression to designate the Davidic king in the OT.[13] Even more obvious are the unmistakable reminiscences of the divine promise to David of an everlasting dynasty found in 2 Sam 7:11b-16 in vv 32b-33.

26-27 The annunciation to Mary is closely related to the former scenes by temporal and chronological markers, and by the reappearance of Gabriel. The "sixth month" recalls v 24, alerting us that Elizabeth has only now come out of seclusion. This prepares for the sharing of the news of her pregnancy in v 36 and her subsequent reception of her guest (vv 39-45). The geographical focus has shifted north, from Jerusalem and the Judean hills, to Nazareth in Galilee.[14] The narrative has departed the socio-religious culture center, the temple. Gabriel holds these scenes together as God's spokesperson.

Mary's status as a virgin is accented by its dual affirmation in v 27, and this has reminded many interpreters of the prophetic word of Isa 7:14.[15] The conjunction of so many points of correspondence between the Gabriel-Mary encounter and Isa 7:10-17 cannot help but produce an echo effect, though it would be going too far to suggest that Luke wants to narrate the *fulfillment* of Isa 7:10-17. Rather, these reverberations establish an interpretive link emphasizing how God is again intervening in history to bring his purpose to fruition.

Moreover, mention of Mary's status as a "virgin" prepares for the

---

13. Cf. 2 Sam 7:14; 1 Chr 17:13; 22:10; 28:6; Pss 2:7; 89:26-27.

14. Luke refers to Nazareth as a "city" (πόλις; NRSV: "town") in spite of its small size, where we might have expected κώμη ("village"); cf., e.g., 5:17; 9:6. As Oakman observes, however, this may not be evidence of Luke's ignorance of Palestinian geography: The Evangelist ". . . may have in mind a distinction between *polis* and *kōmē* that we are as yet unaware of — he may, for instance, use *polis* at times in the technical sense of 'town,' where a population settlement serves as an agricultural market center or tax collection point or simply as a granary for the surrounding fields" ("Countryside," 170).

15. Although he denies any link with the Isaianic passage, Fitzmyer (1:336) lists seven possible Lukan parallels to Isa 7:10-17, centering on the use of the term "virgin": "house of David" (1:27; Isa 7:13), "the Lord" (1:28; Isa 7:10), "virgin" (1:27; Isa 7:14 LXX), "will conceive" (1:31; Isa 7:14 LXX), "will . . . bear a son" (1:31; Isa 7:14), "you will name him" (1:31; Isa 7:14), and "over the house" (1:33; Isa 7:17). To his list we may add Gabriel's words of greeting, "The Lord is with you," as a possible echo of the name of the promised son in Isa 7:14: "Immanuel" or "God is with us." Fitzmyer insists that Luke's language is actually closer to Deut 22:23 and observes that the parallels just mentioned are hardly limited to the Isaianic co-text in the OT. Indeed, both the Lukan and Isaianic passages are related to the annunciation type-scene, and this alone would help to explain a number of these parallels. Bock (*Proclamation*, 61-62) allows that Isa 7:14 may have been in Luke's mind.

ensuing note regarding her relationship to Joseph as his betrothed and for Mary's objection to the angelic announcement (v 34). That "virgin" specifies Mary as a young girl of marriageable age[16] (i.e., approximately 12-13) *and* as a virgin in the more narrow, sexual sense is demonstrated both by her self-assertion in v 34 and by attention to Jewish marriage regulations.[17]

"The stature of important persons in Luke-Acts is communicated by special note of their pedigree, both kin and clan, thus extending the honor and identity of the ancestors to the contemporary individual."[18] This observation throws into sharp relief Luke's initial characterization of Mary. Joseph is a son of David, but Mary has not yet joined his household and thus has no claim on his inherited status. Mary's family is not mentioned. Indeed, she is not introduced in any way that would recommend her to us as particularly noteworthy or deserving of divine favor.

28-30 The juxtaposition of images related to status honor in vv 26-27 is advanced even further. The angel's greeting and declaration of Mary's favored status (v 28) form an *inclusio* with his reassurance of divine favor (v 30) around Mary's perplexity (v 29). Nothing has prepared her (or the reader) for this visit from an archangel or for such exalted words denoting God's favor. It is no wonder that she is perplexed and silently questions the meaning of this encounter.[19]

Gabriel's opening words to Mary — "*Rejoice,* favored one!" — are related by alliteration in the Greek[20] and by their conjoining of two motifs interwoven throughout the Gospel: God acts graciously, people respond (appropriately) with joy and praise. Many translations read the initial word as a

16. See G. J. Wenham, "BᵉTÛLĀH."

17. According to contemporary Roman law, the minimum age of marriage for girls was 12 (for boys, 14), with the minimum age for betrothal set by Augustus at 10 (Rawson, "Roman Family," 21). Jewish practices were comparable, so that marriage for a female usually took place before she reached 12½ years of age. This was advantageous for her husband, who thus received the benefits of her service over a longer period of time, but also for the girl's father. Practically speaking, he was able more easily to guarantee his daughter's purity (i.e., virginity) if he could arrange for her to be married by the time she reached puberty.

A marriage was constituted by the drawing up of a deed, the exchange of money to the groom (i.e., the "bride price"), and sexual intercourse. Earlier practices apparently made no distinction between betrothal and marriage, but before the first century B.C.E. a time lapse of some twelve months had become common. Consequently, a deed of betrothal and the bride-price were exchanged at betrothal, after which bride and groom were legally joined and could be separated only by death or divorce. During this betrothal period, the daughter remained in her father's house and under his control. The marriage itself was marked by intercourse between the betrothed couple. See Archer, *Her Price Is beyond Rubies,* 151-71; Loewe, *Women in Judaism,* 22-23. "Betrothal" is thus quite distinct from "engagement" in the modern sense of the word.

18. Malina and Neyrey, "First-Century Personality," 86.

19. See Green, "Social Status."

20. Χαῖρε, κεχαριτωμένη.

common greeting rather than as an invitation to rejoice,[21] and this is possible.[22] However, apart from the use of the word in openings to letters intended for Greek audiences in Acts 15:23; 23:26, Luke uses the Semitic term "peace" as a formula for greeting.[23] This suggests that this greeting fills in further the picture of rejoicing that will pervade the Third Gospel (e.g., 1:14, 47, 58; 2:10).[24] Moreover, his greeting is reminiscent of Zeph 3:14-15; Zech 9:9; Joel 2:21, where the formula is found: rejoice! + address + reference to the divine action or attitude to which joy is the proper response. "Favored one," then, functions as a name for Mary,[25] designating her as the object of divine benefaction. This reality is accented and clarified by its repetition in v 30, then celebrated (with rejoicing! — v 47) by Mary in v 48. *God has given his favor to one who had no claim to worthy status, raised her up from a position of lowliness, and has chosen her to have a central role in salvation history.*[26]

This message is confirmed by the angel's declaratory promise, "The Lord is with you." This is much more than a greeting,[27] for this language is often used in the OT with reference to a person chosen by God for a special purpose in salvation history; in such contexts this phrase assures human agents of divine resources and protection.[28]

---

21. Cf., e.g., NRSV, REB, NIV, NCV.

22. See the use of χαῖρε as a formula of greeting in Matt 26:49; 27:29; 28:9; Mark 15:8; John 19:3.

23. That is, εἰρήνη — 10:5; 24:36. Cf. Lyonnet, "Χαῖρε, κεχαριτωμένη"; McHugh, *Mother of Jesus,* 37-47; K. Stock, "Berufung Marias," 468-71. On the objections set forth by Strobel ("Gruss an Maria"), see the rejoinder in McHugh, *Mother of Jesus,* 44-45. Fitzmyer (1:344-45) and others object to this reading apparently on the grounds of its association with the related argument that "rejoice" joins other allusions to Zech 3:14-17 to identify Mary as "Daughter of Zion." In spite of the fact that Luke seems little concerned with typological hermeneutics in his birth narrative (see above, §2), this connection is often made (e.g., Laurentin, *Struktur und Theologie,* 75-82); it is not a necessary inference; cf. Räisänen, *Mutter Jesu,* 86-92.

24. On the theme of joy in Luke, see W. G. Morris, *Joy in the NT,* 91-104.

25. Χαριτόω has the form of a factitive (cf. BDF §108.1), but this need not lead to the understanding proposed by de la Potterie — namely, that Gabriel refers to a trans-formation that had already been caused *within* Mary by divine grace ("Étude philologique"; *idem,* "Étude exégétique).

26. Cf. Fuller, "Luke 1:28."

27. K. Stock, "Berufung Marias," 466; McHugh, *Mother of Jesus,* 48-50; cf. van Unnik, *"Dominus Vobiscum,"* 288-89.

28. Cf., e.g., Gen 26:24; 28:15; Exod 3:12; Jer 1:8. Elsewhere, Luke uses this language with precisely this content in Acts 18:9-10. Also noteworthy is the appearance of this affirmation in the narrative of Gideon's call (Judg 6:11-18), for there it is used as a greeting (6:12; cf. 6:16) and the scene is narrated using a repertoire of elements also found in Luke: the agency of the angel of the Lord, the language of finding favor, the raising of an objection, and the question of a sign.

31-33 The logic of the angel's presentation is telling: Mary will conceive, bear, and name the child; God will give him the throne of David; as a consequence, the promised son will reign forever, etc. In other words, the partnership of human and divine is essential if Jesus is to accomplish his mission.

Gabriel's words to Mary echo language used elsewhere in birth announcements, especially Gen 16:11; Isa 7:14. This ties the current scene into the heart of God's story; the eschatological import of the annunciation rests on vv 32-33, not on a "fulfillment" of Isa 7:14. In popular etymology, "Jesus" means "Yahweh saves" (cf. Matt 1:21). As before with John's name (v 13), Luke appears more interested in the role of God in giving the name (and the obedience of parents to the command) than in its etymology.[29] On the other hand, there are subtle hints that Luke considers this meaning to be of significance (see "God my Savior" — 1:47; "Savior" — 2:11; also 1:71, 74, 77).

On one level, God's promise is to fulfill his commitment to David, spelled out in 2 Sam 7:11-16, then repeated and developed elsewhere in the Scriptures and in later Judaism.[30] The connection of vv 32-33 with the expectation of a restored Davidic monarchy is unmistakable. See, for example, the reference to David's throne, "his kingdom" (2 Sam 7:12, 13; cf. v 16), the perpetual character of this kingdom (2 Sam 7:13, 16), and the correlation of kingship and sonship (2 Sam 7:14). (See also the Davidic echoes in 1:68-79.) Following such hints as those in Isa 9:7 and Dan 7:14, Luke has in mind a single ruler reigning forever as opposed to the dynasty ("house") envisioned by Nathan's prophecy to David. This reflects the eschatological correlation of David's reign with the greater emphasis on the definitive, everlasting dominion of Yahweh.[31]

Gabriel's announcement thus creates a complex of expectations related to Jesus' mission to "reign over the house of Jacob forever." Luke's language contains nationalistic, socio-political reverberations. When this is matched with similar material in the birth narrative, it is difficult to imagine that the anticipated redemption will be anything but a nationalistic restoration of Israel. Other possibilities are not yet excluded, however, and it behooves the reader to continue to listen to the narrative; how will Luke resolve the narrative needs introduced with these strong chords of eschatological anticipation?[32]

29. Cf. van der Meulen, "Lukas 1,31."

30. Cf., e.g., Psalm 89; Jer 23:5-8; Ezek 37:21-23; Zech 3:8-10; 12:17–13:1; Hag 2:21-22; 4 Ezra 12:31-32; *Psalms of Solomon* 17–18; 1QM 11:1-18; 4QFlor 1:11-14; 4QTest 9-13.

31. Cf. Sobosan, "Completion of Prophecy"; Strauss, *Davidic Messiah*, 88-89. "Jacob" is synonymous with "Israel" here, as often in the OT (e.g., Exod 19:3; Isa 2:5-6; 8:17; 48:1).

32. See Brawley, *Centering on God*, 30, 81.

According to the angel's words, Jesus will be "Son of the Most High," a designation synonymous with "Son of God" (see the parallel — vv 32, 35).[33] What "Son of God" connotes in the context of this Lukan scene must be discussed in light of v 35. At this point, it is worth mentioning that Luke otherwise associates Jesus' kingship/messiahship and sonship (cf. 4:41; 22:29, 67-70; Acts 9:20-22).

34-37   Although Mary's role in the realization of God's salvific will is crucial, the initiative and powerful work of God are much more so. Ultimately, the purpose of Mary's question (v 34) — which leads to Gabriel's answer (v 35) and the giving of a sign (v 36) and word of reassurance (v 37) — is to emphasize that all of this is God's doing.

It is not immediately clear how the objections of Zechariah and Mary differ, even if it is certain that the angel can distinguish one from the other.[34] In both cases we subsequently learn what motivated these questions — in Zechariah's case, unbelief (v 20); in Mary's case, belief (v 45). One can also distinguish between Zechariah's request for a sign ("How will I know?") and Mary's request for an explanation ("How can this be?"). The reader has seen God's miraculous work with Zechariah and Elizabeth, and Mary has become the recipient of God's grace, so neither we nor she entertains any doubt *that* the angel's words can be realized. The only question is, How? With her query, Mary repeats for us information already available from the narrator (1:27). What her question does not account for fully, however, is the information that she was betrothed to Joseph. As such, and since Joseph is "of the house of David," it might have been evident how she would conceive and bear a son of David to whom God could give the throne. What is more natural than for a betrothed virgin to expect to conceive and bear a child in the near future?[35] On the one hand, her question plays a vital theological role, for it accents the fact that she is still a virgin. After Gabriel departs, "in those days" Mary travels to the home of her kinswoman where we discover that she has now become pregnant (v 42) — and that without a narrated encounter of any kind

33. "To be called" is an idiomatic expression for "to be"; here the unspecified agent of this "calling" is God (see the parallel in v 32c). "Most High" as a designation for God is found in 1:32, 35, 76; 2:14; 6:35; 8:28; 19:38; Acts 7:48; 16:17, and otherwise in the NT only four times. Its usage in Luke does not suggest that this expression was particularly Hellenistic, though its appearance in Acts on the mouths of the Hellenist Stephen and a Philippian slave girl might indicate its usefulness in the Roman world outside Palestine. In any case, Fitzmyer, has put forward Aramaic evidence from Qumran for the title "Son of the Most High God" as well as for other parallels to Luke 1:32, 35 ("Contribution of Qumran Aramaic," 391-94).

34. Cf. Coleridge, *Birth,* 64-65.

35. That is, following her marriage celebration; cf. Davis, "Literary Structure," 222.

with Joseph (or any other man). By contrast, Zechariah "went to his home" and "after those days his wife Elizabeth conceived" (vv 23-24). This contrast shows how, in this narratological way, Luke has affirmed the virginal conception of Jesus.[36] On the other hand, the point of her question is rhetorical, inviting further information from the angel.

The first two clauses of Gabriel's response parallel one another and prepare for the third:

> The Holy Spirit will come upon you, and
> the power of the Most High will overshadow you;
> consequently, the child to be born will be called holy,
>   the Son of God.[37]

These parallel affirmations do not suggest sexual activity,[38] but do connote divine agency. The Holy Spirit is identified with God's power in a way that anticipates Acts 1:8. The verb "to come upon"[39] also anticipates Acts 1:8, and, then, the Pentecost event. The text may call to mind Isa 32:15, which anticipates the Spirit's being poured out upon God's people as a mark of the age of peace. The second phrase has connections with the transfiguration scene in 9:34, and more broadly with scriptural accounts of manifestations of the glory of God (e.g., Exod 40:35; Num 9:18, 22).

The report of the consequence of this divine agency focuses on its christological repercussions. God's intervention will result in the special nature of the child. Here Gabriel's words recall his earlier announcement:

> (v 32ab): He will be great, and
>   will be called   the Son of the Most High
> (v 35d): [He] will be called holy, the Son of God.

Previously, "Son of God" was related directly to Jesus' role as king, a usage well known in the Scriptures (v 32; cf. 2 Sam 7:14; Ps 2:7). Other uses of the title were known, however, and together these point above all to divine sonship in the first-century Palestinian milieu as connoting the special relationship of a person with God and that person's obedience to and representation of God on earth.[40] While Luke's interest in Jesus' sonship builds on these conceptual-

---

36. See also Schottroff, *Feminist Perspectives,* 160-61; Landry, "Narrative Logic."

37. On the problematic syntax of this verse and for this translation, see Schürmann, 1:41, 54-55.

38. See Fitzmyer, "Virginal Conception," 56.

39. Ἐπέρχομαι.

40. See Harvey, *Constraints of History,* 154-73; cf. the survey in Dunn, *Christology in the Making,* 13-22.

izations, his understanding has clearly developed beyond them in two significant ways. First, he emphasizes the relation of the Spirit's activity and Jesus' sonship: Jesus is "Son of God" not as a consequence of his assuming the throne of David (as in Ps 2:7), but as a result of his conception, itself the result of the miraculous work of the Spirit. As Jesus prepares for and commences his public ministry, the relation of the work of the Spirit and his identity as God's Son will be further developed (3:21-22, 38; 4:1, 3, 9, 14, 18).[41] Second, though Luke is not working with Johannine or later trinitarian categories, he is nonetheless moving toward a more ontological (and not only functional) understanding of Jesus' sonship. Like John, Jesus is set apart (i.e., "holy") from birth to special service in God's redemptive purpose; unlike John — indeed, uniquely in salvation history — Jesus' sonship extends backward to the prevenient work of God in his creation as a human being.

Mary has not requested a sign but, as often in scenes of this kind, she is given one. She receives what is for her new information; Elizabeth has just come out of seclusion (vv 24, 26, 36), so Mary could not have known of her pregnancy. The repetition of this information also serves to emphasize again the trustworthiness of Gabriel's words and the heightened sense of the miraculous already penetrating this story.[42]

The description of Elizabeth as "your relative"[43] serves three functions. Most obviously, it is one more way in which the stories of John and Jesus are interwoven. Second, it serves as a bridge back to the story of Elizabeth, preparing for the encounter between Elizabeth and Mary (vv 39-56) and John's birth (v 57). Finally, it is a further indication of how carefully Luke has staged his characterization of Mary. Only at the end of this scene do we learn that she belongs to the family of Elizabeth and may thus share her ancestral heritage; the timing of this disclosure is significant, for the most memorable quality of Mary for Luke is her relation to God, a relationship God initiated.

Gabriel's final words may echo the comparable statement of the Lord to Sarah in Gen 18:14 (LXX): "Is anything impossible with God?"[44] In this case, Gabriel's analogy would work best with reference to Elizabeth, since both Sarah and Elizabeth are old and barren. However, the purpose behind reporting Elizabeth's pregnancy to Mary was to provide her with a sign that

---

41. Cf. Schneider, "Jesu geistgewirkte Empfängnis," 88.

42. See Bede, *Homilies*, 1:25-26.

43. Συγγενίς appears only here in the NT and connotes nothing more specific than "kinswoman."

44. Gen 18:14: μὴ ἀδυνατεῖ παρὰ τῷ θεῷ; Luke 1:37: ὅτι οὐκ ἀδυνατήσει παρὰ τοῦ θεοῦ πᾶν ῥῆμα. The parallel would be stronger if one were to follow the alternative reading in ℵ² A C Θ Ψ et al., which substitute τῷ θεῷ for τοῦ θεοῦ (read in ℵ* B L W Ξ et al.), but the variant probably reflects assimilation to the LXX.

Gabriel's words in her case were trustworthy. Thus, this final affirmation of the infinite possibilities with God would be extended to Mary's case as well. This latter emphasis is highlighted all the more by Gabriel's denial of the impotency of any word of God; this point is taken up immediately by Mary ("Let it be with me according to your word," v 38), then underscored by Elizabeth ("And blessed is she who believed . . . what was spoken to her by the Lord," v 45). In this way, Luke's concern with the efficacy of divine power is intimately related to his further concern to present Mary as one whose response to the word of God is exemplary.

38 Mary's response to the divine announcement contrasts sharply with that of Zechariah, with the result that she, surprisingly in scenes of this type, has the last word. She unreservedly embraces the purpose of God, without regard to its cost to her personally. Her response is exemplary, demonstrating how all Israel ought to respond to God's favor.

In describing herself as the Lord's servant (cf. 1:48), she acknowledges her submission to God's purpose, but also her role in assisting that purpose.[45] Moreover, she claims a place in God's household, so to speak; indeed, in this socio-historical context, her words relativize and actually place in jeopardy her status in Joseph's household. For her, partnership in the purpose of God transcends the claims of family.[46] In antiquity, the status of a slave was determined by the status of the householder.[47] In his characterization of Mary as "slave of the Lord," Luke has begun to undercut the competitive maneuvering for positions of status prevalent in the first-century Mediterranean world. Mary, who seemed to measure low in any ranking — age, family heritage, gender, and so on — turns out to be the one favored by God, the one who finds her status and identity in her obedience to God and participation in his salvific will.

2.3. MARY'S VISIT TO ELIZABETH (1:39-56)

The scene of Mary's visit to Elizabeth is Luke's most obvious affirmation of the way in the two stories of these women are intertwined within the singular story of God's redemption. Luke has woven together these stories with repeated references to Gabriel, a shared repertoire of narrative elements and

---

45. For the use of δοῦλος for a person who has been commissioned and endowed for a special role in the divine plan, see also Acts 4:29; 16:17.

46. For this theme, cf. 8:19-21; 9:57-62; 12:51-53; 14:25-26; 18:28-30.

47. That is, the status of the head of the family was extended to all who shared with him a relationship of kinship. See D. B. Martin, *Slavery as Salvation,* 1-49; Flesher, *Slaves,* 90-94.

scriptural allusions, chronological notices marking the passing of time during Elizabeth's pregnancy, anticipations of the eschatological coming of God, the identification of Elizabeth as Mary's relative, and the ways in which the divine hand lies behind their pregnancies.

Formal considerations also reveal their interrelatedness. Following the annunciation to Zechariah are accounts of the realization of the sign Gabriel promised (v 22) and the reaction of Elizabeth to God's intervention on her behalf (v 25). Likewise, having narrated the annunciation to Mary, Luke now reports the consummation of the sign promised her (vv 39-45) as well as her response to the goodness of God (vv 46-55). The staging of the narrative from *promise* to *evidence of fulfillment* to *response of praise* is thus completed in Mary's case, even if, because of his unbelief, Zechariah's response is delayed (vv 69-79). This final narrative imbalance is purposeful. It, together with the relative length of Mary's response when compared with Elizabeth's (vv 25, 46-55) and the fact that Elizabeth blesses Mary (and not vice versa), indicates the superior importance allotted Jesus in the narrative as a whole.

The functions of the current scene in the Lukan narrative are several. This complexity derives from the plurality of narrative threads being developed at once by the Evangelist. On the one hand, Gabriel has promised that Mary will conceive; the realization of that promise is not reported directly (cf. v 24), but assumed in the responses to Mary's conception by Elizabeth and Mary. Luke has thus carried us from the narrative *possibility* to an (implicit) *event* to its *results*. On the other hand, Gabriel anticipates the birth and names the future role of a son — a *possibility* made *probable* by the narration of the fulfillment of the sign also promised to Mary. Along with the preceding account of Elizabeth's divinely assisted pregnancy, this leads us to anticipate the *event* of Jesus' birth and *responses* to it, along with his future, messianic role. Hence, even as the current scene completes one narrative thread, it keeps us looking forward to the completion of another. Indeed, the current scene opens up new *possibilities* as it develops further the nature of Jesus' perpetual reign with its suggestive identification of Mary's unborn child as "my Lord" (v 43) and celebration of God's revolutionary activity (vv 46-55).

As in previous scenes,[1] Luke stages this narrative unit with a travel motif: Mary journeys to the home of Zechariah (vv 39-40), then returns to her own home (v 56). This provides Luke with a way to portray these women together, on the same stage, then to leave Elizabeth on that stage for the next scene (vv 57-58).

---

1. See vv 8-9, 23 and vv 26, 38.

2.3.1. Mary and Elizabeth Exchange Greetings (1:39-45)

> 39 *In those days Mary set out and went with haste to a Judean town in the hill country,* 40 *where she entered the house of Zechariah and greeted Elizabeth.* 41 *When Elizabeth heard Mary's greeting, the child leaped in her womb. And Elizabeth was filled with the Holy Spirit* 42 *and exclaimed with a loud cry, "Blessed are you among women, and blessed is the fruit of your womb.* 43 *And why has this happened to me, that the mother of my Lord comes to me?* 44 *For as soon as I heard the sound of your greeting, the child in my womb leaped for joy.* 45 *And blessed is she who believed that there would be a fulfillment of what was spoken to her by the Lord."*

The exchange of greetings represented by Luke is both highly stylized and full of significance. Exodus 18:7 narrates a representative greeting: "Moses went out to meet his father-in-law; he bowed down and kissed him; each asked after the other's welfare, and they went into the tent." This text is interesting both for its illustration of the content of the greeting and for the nonchalant way it embodies issues of status honor. Moses is the host, yet comes out to initiate the greeting, showing appropriate respect to his elder and guest. Similar concerns are at work in the present pericope.[2]

Luke places great emphasis on Mary's greeting, mentioning it three times (vv 40, 41, 44). Since we are not privy to its contents, its primary significance seems to be on the response of Elizabeth's unborn child to it, mentioned twice (vv 41, 44). Unlike Moses, who goes out to welcome his father-in-law and extend first greetings, Elizabeth first receives greetings from Mary. This is proper, for Elizabeth is clearly the superior, by normal canons at least. She is a daughter of Aaron, the wife of a priest, the elder of these two women. What is more, had she not received divine affirmation in the blessing of a child? What is surprising, then, is Elizabeth's greeting to Mary. Prompted by the child in her womb, filled with the Holy Spirit, she places herself in the servant's role, bestowing honor on her guest whom she now recognizes as "the mother of my Lord," "blessed . . . among women." Suddenly the tables have turned, and we have from Elizabeth a second testimony to the favored status of Mary first proclaimed by Gabriel (1:28, 30).

39-40 The opening of this scene ("about that time") ties it directly back into Mary's encounter with Gabriel. As a young girl, Mary would not normally have left her home without accompaniment — either to browse in her own hometown or (especially!) to travel some seventy miles to the hill

2. Cf. Luke 7:36-50; 20:46.

country around Jerusalem.[3] Until she entered the bridal chamber, a girl lived in seclusion in her home.[4] Moreover, Mary's journey is apparently unmotivated. She does not go in obedience to the angel, who gave her no such instructions. Nor does Luke include a report of Mary's conception (though it is assumed in what follows). This lack of detail and reflection highlights the orientation of this narrative segment on her action, accented further by her "haste." And this prepares for the sharp contrast with the following material, wherein Luke introduces two pauses in the narrative to allow for concentrated reflection on the meaning of these events. Moreover, it allows for a closer parallel with the previous scene related to John's conception, juxtaposing as tightly as possible the promise of a sign and the sign itself.

This trip may also be theologically motivated, for Luke employs a word that will come to play a key theological role in his narrative — "journey,"[5] which can connote a "going" related to the fulfillment of the divine purpose (cf. 9:51). If so, Luke thus describes Mary's journey as consequential in redemption history, relating her journey to her primary identification as servant of the Lord (1:38) and to the narrative need to identify Gabriel's "sign."

41-44 Both from the hand of the narrator and the mouth of Elizabeth we have evidence of the remarkable character of this encounter. In fact, the report of Mary's greeting + the child leaping in Elizabeth's womb, repeated in vv 41, 44, forms an *inclusio* around Elizabeth's opening greeting and query. This draws our attention to Elizabeth's words and underscores the supramundane quality of this encounter by creating a pause in the narrative action.

John, we have been told, would be filled with the Holy Spirit even before birth and anticipate the coming of the Lord (1:15-17). Here is the purpose of his prenatal experience of the Spirit, embodied in his joyful leaping: Even from the womb he prophesies, implicitly transferring the designation of "Lord" to Mary's unborn baby, recognizing in this baby the eschatological coming of God. The association of "joy," already related to the advent of divine redemption in 1:14 (and cf. 1:47), with "leaping" encourages this reading of John's act.[6] The Spirit that fills him prompts his recognition and certifies for us the trustworthiness of his prophetic action concerning Jesus. The same can be said of Elizabeth's being filled with the Holy Spirit at this

---

3. For ἡ ὀρεινή as a designation for the district around Jerusalem, see Pliny *Nat. Hist.* 5.14; Josephus *J.W.* 4.8.2 §451. Cf. Luke 1:65. Most priests, and especially those of the aristocracy, dwelled in Jerusalem, but that priests lived outside Jerusalem is noted in Nehemiah 11; 1 Macc 2:1.

4. See Archer, *Her Price Is beyond Rubies,* 101-22, 239-50.

5. Πορεύομαι.

6. On the association of "leaping" with the experience of God's salvation see Mal 4:2; Fitzer, "σκιρτάω."

instant. The Spirit enables her to discern the significance of her baby's move-ments in her womb and to give voice to her child's recognition of Mary and her unborn baby. Her speech is inspired speech,[7] she speaks on God's behalf, and thus she agrees with Gabriel's earlier assessment of Mary's favored status.

Elizabeth's first words are reminiscent of the greeting and praise given to a superior in recognition of her or his advanced status and of the fact that God had blessed this person.[8] Her language in this instance differs from that in v 45;[9] here she acknowledges the superiority of her young relative, a status position due to Mary's prior reception of God's beneficence. Employing language reminiscent of Judg 5:24 and Jdt 13:18, Elizabeth keeps Mary's motherhood in primary focus. After all, it is in her role as mother that she will contribute to the salvation of her people. Mary is the mother of "my Lord" — a designation by which Elizabeth articulates her own submission to this unborn baby and which anticipates the identification of Jesus as "Lord" on the basis of his exaltation (cf. Ps 110:1; Acts 2:34-36). As a rule, the lesser greets the greater, the servant travels to the master. What is Elizabeth to make of this reversal of societal convention?[10] First, the superiority of Jesus over John is thus again highlighted. Second, however, the *nature* and *exercise* of the superior status of Jesus is anticipated. With his coming, social conventions will be turned on their head; the greater will serve the lesser (cf. 1:51-53; 22:25-27).

45 Elizabeth's second pronouncement of blessing employs the term known to us especially from the Beatitudes: "blessed" — spoken over those who are judged to possess what is necessary for a joyful life and especially over those who are the recipients of God's gift of redemption. While the basis of the former "blessing" was Mary's motherhood and, thus, signal role in the realiza-tion of God's purpose, here she is declared fortunate because of her faith.[11] The contrast with Zechariah could scarcely be more stark: he did not believe but she did; and in any case, it is affirmed, what had been spoken would come to pass. Elizabeth speaks to Mary of what had been spoken "by the Lord," thus emphasizing the fact that Gabriel had delivered God's own message. The result of this wording is to underscore first Mary's response of faith and, second, the certainty surrounding the fulfillment of the divine purpose.

7. This is certain from the connection of her experience of the Spirit in v 41, which leads to her speech in vv 42-45, and by the dramatic "exclaimed with a loud cry."

8. Link, "εὐλογία," 213.

9. Verse 42: εὐλογέω; v 45: μακάριος. Cf. R. E. Brown, *Birth*, 333.

10. Cf. Origen *Hom. in Luc.* 7; Davis, "Literary Structure," 221.

11. That ὅτι should be rendered "that" in this instance and not "because" is suggested by Acts 27:25. This translation also furthers the close (antithetical) parallel Luke has drawn between Zechariah and Mary: he did not believe, yet, the angel affirms, these things will still be fulfilled (v 20).

It is notable that Elizabeth's first blessing is in the second person ("Blessed are you . . ."), while the second blessing is in the third ("Blessed is she . . ."). Thus are others invited to respond, like Mary, with faith.[12]

2.3.2. Mary's Response to God's Favor (1:46-55)

46 *And Mary*[13] *said,*
"My soul magnifies the Lord,
47   *and my spirit rejoices in God my Savior,*
48 *for he has looked with favor on the lowliness of his servant.*
   Surely, from now on all generations will call me blessed;
49 *for the Mighty One has done great things for me,*
   and holy is his name.
50 *His mercy is for those who fear him*
   from generation to generation.
51 *He has shown strength with his arm;*
   he has scattered the proud in the thoughts of their hearts.
52 *He has brought down the powerful from their thrones,*
   and lifted up the lowly;
53 *he has filled the hungry with good things,*
   and sent the rich away empty.
54 *He has helped his servant Israel,*
   in remembrance of his mercy,
55 *according to the promise he made to our ancestors,*
   to Abraham and to his descendants forever."

The repetition of the unborn prophet's response to Mary's greeting in vv 41, 44 created a brief delay in the movement of the narrative. This contrasted pointedly with the report of Mary's journey — which encompassed some seventy miles of terrain in three brief prepositional phrases; and with the "haste" with which she had undertaken that journey. This temporary postponement of the action works like a magnet to draw our attention to the

12. Cf. Räisänen, *Mutter Jesu,* 110: "Das erstere Wort gilt nur für Maria persönlich. Das letztere kann aus seinem Zusammenhang gelöst werden, wodurch es Allgemeingültigkeit erhält und die grundsätzliche Einstellung des *Christen* zum Wort Gottes zum Ausdruck bringt. Maria gilt hier als Vorbild des Christen."

13. The *Magnificat* is attributed to "Elizabeth" by it[a,b,l]* Irenaius[lat] Origen[lat.mss] Niceta, and the question of attribution has been much debated from the turn of the twentieth century — see the older review by Benko, "Magnificat," 263-71. On both external and internal grounds it is now widely held that the original reading in Luke was "Mary"; cf., e.g., R. E. Brown, *Birth,* 334-36; Farris, *Hymns,* 108-13; Laurentin, *Truth of Christmas,* 3-11; Bemile, *Magnificat,* 5-19.

inspired words of Elizabeth spoken over Mary and her child. With only the briefest return to story time, Luke now introduces a pause of much greater proportion and significance. Mary's vocalized response, often referred to as Mary's Song or the *Magnificat,* actually brings the movement of the story to a complete halt. This is a reminder that Luke is not interested merely in *events* — past, present, and future — but especially in their *meaning.* The purpose of this narratological "time out," then, is hermeneutical — that is, to ensure that we understand the significance of the angel's annunciation to Mary, her conception, and the blessing pronounced by her relative. Not surprisingly, that meaning is rooted in the covenantal purpose of God.

§5 The Structure and Role of Mary's Song

By means of this pause Luke is able to provide his readers with a foretaste of the salvific themes he will develop throughout Luke-Acts, while at the same time rooting that salvation squarely in God's past dealings with his people.[14] Unfortunately, the role of Mary's Song as a narrative pause has led numerous interpreters to overlook the many ways it is embedded in its literary co-text:[15] (1) the use of "Lord" + "God" — 1:16, 32, 46-47;[16] (2) Mary "magnifies the Lord," the Lord "magnifies his mercy" — 1:46, 58;[17] (3) Mary rejoices — cf. 1:14, 28, 44, 48; (4) Mary identifies God as "my Savior," anticipating the concern with "salvation" elsewhere in the birth narrative — 1:31, 47, 69, 77; 2:11; (5) As with Elizabeth, so with Mary, God "has looked favorably on me" — 1:25, 48; (6) Luke has repeatedly characterized Mary as a person of low social status[18] and now she speaks of her "lowliness" — 1:26-38, 48; (7) Mary identifies herself as "servant" — 1:38, 48; (8) "all generations will call [Mary] blessed" just as Elizabeth has done — 1:45, 48; (9) Note other common words: Mighty One/power/impossible — 1:35, 37, 49;[19] great — 1:15, 32, 49; holy — 1:35, 49; and semantic domains: "looked favorably," "favored one," "favor," "looked with favor," "mercy," "mercy" — 1:25, 28, 30, 48, 50, 54; and (10) "the fruit of your womb" corresponds to "Abraham and his *seed*" — 1:42, 55.[20]

In these and other ways, Mary's Song pulls together threads from the surrounding narrative, casting them within the framework of a celebration of God's

---

14. Cf. Bemile, *Magnificat,* 134-236.

15. So, e.g., C. F. Evans, 171; Nolland, 1:63. For the positive connection of this pericope to its co-text in Luke 1–2, see above, §2; Farris, *Hymns,* 99-102; Kaut, *Befreier und befreites Volk,* 286-93.

16. "Lord" appears in vv 9, 11, 15, 16, 17, 25, 28, 32, 38, (43), 45, 46; "God" in vv 6, 8, 16, 19, 26, 30, 32, 35, 37, 47.

17. Both verses employ a form of μεγαλύνω.

18. See Green, "Social Status."

19. That is δύναμις, ἀδυνατέω, δυνατός.

20. σπέρμα; NRSV: "descendants." See Bemile, *Magnificat,* 40.

redemptive coming. Moreover, the Song brings to expression themes that are integral to the Lukan narrative as a whole.

Our understanding of Mary's Song is to some degree dependent on and is certainly enhanced by an appreciation of its structure. Several aspects of the Song's design merit attention. First, it shares with declarative psalms of praise the form: word of praise + reasons for praise (cf., e.g., Psalms 8, 33, 47, 100, 135, 136).

Second, again like the poetry of the Jewish milieu, Mary's Song is marked by extensive parallelism:

> (v 46b) my soul magnifies the Lord
> (v 47)   my spirit rejoices in God my Savior
>
> (v 48a) for he has looked with favor on the lowliness of his servant
> (v 49a) for the Mighty One has done great things for me
>
> (v 51a) he has shown great strength with his arm
> (v 51b) he has scattered the proud
>
> (v 52a) he has brought down the powerful from their thrones
> (v 52b) [he has] lifted up the lowly
>
> (v 53a) he has filled the hungry with good things
> (v 53b) [he has] sent the rich away empty
>
> (v 55a) according to the promise he made to our ancestors
> (v 55b) to Abraham and to his descendants

The fourth and fifth are set in a chiastic relationship to express even more dramatically the transposition they declare:

Parallelism of this nature has an important interpretive role, not least in poetic discourse. By juxtaposing related but not identical lines, the design expands the possible meaning of both lines, building the metaphorical field from which the audience will draw in order to hear and appropriate the Song.

A third aspect of the structure of Mary's Song is heard in its employment of verbs. Note that this Song describes dramatic acts of grace and power, places those active verbs repeatedly in the anterior position, presents this action in the aorist tense, and consistently locates God as the subject of these verbs. The effect of this presentation of divine activity is to underscore the decisive work of God, dramatically in operation, and unmistakably in control of human affairs, as the advent of God's peaceful, just kingdom is realized. That these verbs are *aorist* may remind us of God's prior activity on behalf of Israel, but, in the context of Luke's narrative, has a more profound meaning.[21] What has happened that could possibly justify this celebration of such far-reaching, divine, decisive activity? The only possible answer in this narrative co-text is also the impetus for John's leaping in the womb and Elizabeth's profound words of greeting to Mary. Mary's Song is a response to the miraculous event confirmed by Elizabeth's words — namely, the supernatural conception of a son who would be called "Son of the Most High," whose kingship would never end, who even in the womb might be addressed as "my Lord." Mary's Song proclaims that this act of conception has set in motion the decisive, eschatological work of God.

At the same time, that these verbs sponsor images of God's salvific work that are so concrete and this-worldly, and that they are set within a larger narrative world of foreign occupation and religio-political oppression, requires that we not relegate Mary's vision of redemption to some distant future or spiritualize it as though it were not concerned with the social realities of daily existence.[22] The decisive event, the advent of God's kingdom grounded in the miraculous conception of Jesus, has already occurred. Hence, already in Mary's exaltation is the vision of her Song coming to fruition. And the transposition she announces, summed up in the move from lowliness/humiliation to exaltation, is characteristic of Jesus' ministry. In fact, it is the very fabric of Luke's whole narrative.[23] Luke is very concerned with the coming of salvation *today*, in the present (cf., e.g., 4:21; 23:43), even if the consummation of God's work remains future. Hence, the revolution embodied in Mary's Song is a vision for the present.

This has caused some interpreters to locate in this hymn a call to revolution, to initiate and engage in revolutionary activity that, they perceive, will lead to a here-and-now incarnation of Mary's vision.[24] On this, two observations must be held in tension. First, as we have observed, the subject of these verbs of powerful action is in every case *God*. Mary's Song is not a revolutionary call to human action but a celebration of God's action. Indeed, God's dramatic work is *against* those who would take power into their own hands, according to this Song (v 52). On the other hand, the story of God's redemption is not God's story only. Through his gracious initiative, God seeks out other actors, partners like Mary and Anna, who will share in God's work. Mary's Song cannot be defined as a clarion call to revolutionary activity, then, but it does solicit from its audience outside the narrative, from us, a similar choice.

Finally, we turn to the structure of the Song as a whole, which begins by

---

21. The debate regarding the nuance intended by these aorists has often revolved around tradition-historical concerns. Thus, e.g., if Mary was in fact the originator of the Song, then these aorists are prophetic, but the view that the hymn was composed by Jewish Christians in the post-resurrection period might lead to the conclusion that they should be read as a reference to the salvific work of Christ in the past. See the discussion in R. E. Brown, "Gospel Infancy Research," 667-68; Farris, *Hymns*, 114-16. The point of our concern, however, is how they must be understood in their current literary co-text.

22. Cf. Scholer, "Magnificat"; Zorilla, "Magnificat"; Boff, *Maternal Face,* 196-201.

23. Green, "God's Servant"; cf. Grundmann, "ταπεινός," 20.

24. See, e.g., R. M. Brown, *Unexpected News,* 81. For a different view, see Bemile, *Magnificat,* 237-53; Marshall, "Magnificat."

focusing on Mary and ends by focusing on Israel, thus moving from the personal to the corporate. This progression divides the Song roughly in half, with vv 46-50 taken up with God's graciousness to Mary and vv 51-55 concerned with his mercy to Israel. Verses 50, 54-55 each function as a conclusion to their respective sections, emphasizing the breadth of God's covenantal mercy. On the other hand, to suggest a "division" in the movement of the psalm is probably to overstate the case, for these two portions of Mary's Song are stitched together by repeated terms and images:

Mary		*Israel*
v 48	"his servant"	v 54
vv 48, 50	object of favor/mercy	v 54
v 48	"lowly"	v 52
v 50	perpetuity of mercy	v 55

In addition, both sections emphasize God's "doing" (vv 49, 51)[25] and a contrast is developed around the use of the term "mighty/powerful"[26] in vv 49 and 51. The effect of this parallelism is twofold. First, it demonstrates how the narrative, very much concentrated on individual Jews — Zechariah, Elizabeth, Mary — thus far, actually concerns the whole nation of Israel. The portrayal of the realization of God's aim is expanded to embrace all Israel, perhaps even all humanity.[27] Second, it shows the relationship of God's favor to Mary and his larger salvific purpose: It is *by means of* his looking "with favor on the lowliness of his servant" Mary that "he has helped his servant Israel." It is through her that God has chosen to fulfill his covenantal promise. And his having "done great things for" Mary is already a manifestation of the socio-political revolution so graphically proclaimed in vv 52-53.

The relation of Mary's Song to its scriptural precedents has long been observed.[28] Of particular interest are other hymns of praise sung in response to God's gracious and powerful intervention on behalf of his people — including those of Moses (Exod 15:1-18), Miriam (Exod 15:19-21), Deborah (Judg 5:1-31), Asaph (1 Chr 16:8-36), Judith (Jdt 16:1-17), and especially Hannah (1 Sam 2:1-10). These echoes are significant for the way they so clearly extend the activity of God celebrated by Mary far back into the past, making transparent the Lukan notion that what he is now narrating is continuous with that story. Luke thus shows his debt to and respect for the tradition that has provided the impetus, framework, and imagery for this Song. As others have recognized, Mary's Song is a virtual collage of biblical texts. This

25. Both use the aorist form of ποιέω.

26. Verse 49: δυνατός; v 52: δυνάστης.

27. That is, v 50 is susceptible of being read in this universalistic way, as might the reference to Abraham in v 55.

28. See, e.g., Plummer, 30-31; R. E. Brown, *Birth,* 358-60; Bemile, *Magnificat,* 79-133; Forestell, "Magnificat," 205-25.

not only emphasizes its beauty, but also shows how the past can be reemployed to give meaning to the present.

Two motifs are held in balance throughout Mary's Song. The first is the portrait of God as the divine warrior who accomplishes deliverance.[29] God is the "Mighty One" who accomplishes "great things," who shows "strength" and scatters the proud, bringing down the powerful from their thrones and sending the rich away empty. This is the God who engages battle on behalf of his people (cf. Ps 24:7-10; Isa 42:13; Zeph 3:17). At the same time, God is the merciful God of the covenant. He looks with favor and lifts up the lowly, extends mercy to "those who fear him," fills the hungry, and helps Israel. He acts "in remembrance of his mercy," remembering his promise to Israel of old. These two images of God are complementary, and coalesce in the theme of transposition: As divine warrior, God acts dynamically against the proud and powerful; as the merciful God of the covenant, God's dynamic acts are for the sake of those who fear him, the object of his promise, Israel. This is not to say that God's overruling human rulers is God's last word for them. Quite the contrary, God's triumph over those who oppose him is itself a redemptive act, placing his opponents in a position whereby they might elect to join God's project. "God flings the proud of heart to the earth, in the hope that they will be . . . delivered from their ridiculous vaunting and flaunting, to become free and obedient children of God and brothers and sisters to others."[30] Mary's Song voices themes that will reappear throughout Luke-Acts.

46-50 Although hardly detached from vv 51-55, these verses are held together more closely by their more narrow interest in the divine benefits attending Mary personally. At the same time, it is noteworthy that even this more personal focus gives way to a corporate nuance in the motifs of "lowliness" and "servant" in v 48 and in the conclusion of v 50. Verses 46-47 give expression to Mary's praise. "Soul" and "spirit" are roughly equivalent ways of speaking in the first person singular, pointing to the depths of Mary's being (cf. Ps 77:2-3; Isa 26:9; Wis 15:11). Mary speaks of the Lord God as "my Savior," using language familiar from Hab 3:18 (cf. Ps 24:5; Isa 12:2; Zeph 3:17). *How* she perceives God fulfilling this role and, thus, *why* she praises him thus are outlined in the ensuing verses. The use of the verb "rejoice," in this particular setting where "joy" and "gladness" are related to the eschatological coming of God (vv 14, 28, 44), already provides strong hints, however.[31]

---

29. See Horsley, *Liberation*, 107, 111-14; Ford, *My Enemy Is My Guest*, 20-23; Gebara and Bingemer, *Mary*, 72-73.

30. Boff, *Maternal Face*, 199.

31. The shift in tense from present (μεγαλύνει) to aorist (ἠγαλλίασεν) has been variously explained, the latter being designated a timeless aorist (cf. BDF §333.2), an ingressive aorist (BDF §331), or a feature of Hebrew poetry carried into the Greek text

Verse 48 provides the first basis for Mary's praise: God has looked with favor on the lowliness of his servant. This line has clear connections with vv 49-50 in that God's might is contrasted with her lowliness, a contrast that works to her benefit; and v 50, since this looking with favor is one manifestation of God's mercy. "Lowliness" is sometimes used in Israel's Scriptures with reference to the humiliation of barrenness (e.g., Gen 16:11; 29:32; 1 Sam 1:11). This is not the case here.[32] The term might also be used with reference to the oppressed people of God.[33] This places Mary's affirmation of God's saving act squarely in the context of the lowliness experienced by Israel under foreign domination in its past and at the time of Mary's Song in Luke's narrative world (1:5). From such domination God has acted to deliver Israel (vv 52-53). Mary's low estate, then, can and should be taken as representative of her people's. Nevertheless, Mary's "lowliness" is not only metaphorical and representative. The term Luke uses[34] belongs to the semantic domain of "the poor" in Luke-Acts, a domain associated with low status honor.[35] This clearly was the case in Luke's characterization of Mary. Indeed, her favorable status — asserted by Gabriel, confirmed by Elizabeth, and now embraced by Mary herself — is a consequence solely of God's surprising grace. This leads her to sing her praise of "God my Savior."

This will also lead to the recognition by others of her divinely appointed status. Elizabeth's earlier affirmation (1:42-45) is to be prototypical, to be repeated by others — for the decisive era of salvation has dawned,[36] and Mary's role in the advent of the Savior is pivotal.

A second reason behind Mary's praise is joined in v 49. Mary now substitutes for the image of the Savior who brings deliverance to the lowly a second metaphor for God: the Divine Warrior who does battle with the enemies of his people (cf. Deut 10:17-18; Ps 24:8; Isa 10:20-27; Zeph 3:17). Again, while Mary continues to speak in the first person ("for me"), her celebration of God's mighty acts is already expanding to embrace God's acts on behalf of "the lowly," "the hungry," "Israel" (vv 52-54). Not surprisingly, then, the conclusion to this first portrait of Mary's Song expands the frame of reference explicitly to include generations of persons who honor God. Indeed, to speak of God's "mercy" is immediately to conjure up images of the corporate people of God, for this "mercy" is nothing less than God's gracious initiative that is

---

from a Hebrew source (most recently, Buth, "Magnificat"). The parallelism between vv 46b and 47 requires a translation like that of the NRSV.

32. *Contra,* e.g., Boff, *Maternal Face,* 196.

33. See, e.g., Deut 26:7; 1 Sam 9:16; 2 Kgs 14:26; Ps 136:23; 1 Macc 3:51; 3 Macc 2:12.

34. ταπείνωσις.

35. See §3.

36. For this interpretation of ἀπὸ τοῦ νῦν, see 5:10; 12:32; 22:18, 69; Acts 18:6.

the presupposition for his creating humanity as his covenant partner and for his continued relationship with humanity in spite of the repeated opposition of men and women to his purpose. This Song outlines a selection of forms that opposition has taken — oppression of people, pride, claims of power, wealth — and it is against such opposing forces that God has, in Mary's image, come to do war. But he has done so not out of obligation but out of his mercy.

51-55 The corporate implications of God's activity now come into full view — as if the camera, previously focused more narrowly on Mary, has suddenly been pulled back to reveal the company of all Israel of which she is a part. Similarly, there are small hints that Israel is itself part of the larger company of all humanity who is the object of God's mercy.[37]

Even if vv 51-55 are closely associated with the first half of Mary's Song, it has its own heading (v 51), examples of God's work (vv 52-53), and summary (vv 54-55). As a heading, v 51 functions first to broaden the scope of the locus of the divine activity. No longer directed at Mary in particular, the divine machinations appear against socio-religious, politico-economic forces working in opposition to God's purpose.[38] What is more, it continues the use of past tense (aorist) verbs, making clear that what God has done for Mary — her election and miraculous conception — signifies a fundamental shift in history. So decisive a moment is this that Mary's Song speaks of God's showing "strength with his arm." This expression has been used in the OT for the work of God in creation and the preservation of his people, but especially with regard to the Exodus (cf. Acts 13:17) and in anticipation of the age of salvation.[39]

By way of annunciating the shape of God's powerful acts, Mary's Song places in apposition three phrases: scatters the proud, brings down the powerful, and sends the rich away empty. This coupling of the proud, powerful, and rich anticipates a major theme of the Lukan narrative. The opponents of Jesus, and therefore of God's purpose, are portrayed as persons who grasp for social respect and positions of honor, who exclude the less fortunate and socially unacceptable from their circles of kinship, who enjoy the power that accom-

37. Cf. v 50 — the unspecified "those who fear him"; the description of Israel as God's "servant" in v 54, recalling Israel's special place *among* the nations as God's presence *to* the nations; and v 55 — with the mention of Abraham, whose descendants would be innumerable.

38. Attempts to find in v 51 a *moral* revolution, v 52 a *political* revolution, and v 53 a *social* revolution (Dupont, "Magnificat") are tempting but anachronistic, for such distinct categories would have been unknown in antiquity. Indeed, the effect of the structural parallelism of these poetic lines is to remind us how interrelated these realities were and are.

39. See Exod 6:1, 6; 15:16; Deut 3:24; 7:19; 33:27; Pss 78:10; 88:10; 97:1; Isa 26:11; 40:10; 51:9-10; 52:10; 65:12; et al.; Schlier, "βραχίων."

panies their privileged status.[40] Over against such persons, Mary's Song places the "lowly" and "hungry." Set in this co-text, these people are not simply the unfortunate, those for whom life in general has not been kind. The powerful and privileged oppose God and in doing so oppress other people. Similarly, God's powerful opposition to the proud, powerful, and rich is at the same time gracious activity on behalf of the lowly and hungry.

Mary's Song formulates a triadic relationship: The Mighty One is contrasted with the lowly, for it is as the Mighty One that God can act on behalf of the lowly; the powerful are contrasted with the lowly, with the former group oppressing (whether through malicious intent or seemingly benign neglect) the latter; and the Mighty One takes the side of the lowly. This is not to obliterate the powerful so that the lowly can achieve the positions of honor and privilege to which they previously had no access. Rather, God is at work in individual lives (like Mary) and in the social order as a whole in order to subvert the very structure of society that supports and perpetuates such distinctions.[41]

Finally, God's project of transposition is rooted deeply in God's covenantal relationship with his people. All of these operative words in vv 54-55 — servant, remember, mercy, promise, ancestors, and Abraham — point backward to God's history with Israel, to their election, to their covenantal relationship. In fact, these terms, and especially "mercy," point even further back, to the nature of God himself. The God Mary praises is the covenant-making God, the God who acts out of his own self-giving nature to embrace men and women in relationship. God remembers . . . and acts.

2.3.3. Mary's Extended Stay (1:56)

> 56 *And Mary remained with her about three months and then returned to her home.*

This section of the birth narrative began with a reference to Mary's departure to Zechariah's house (vv 39-40), where the ensuing interchange was located. Now, at the close of this section, Mary departs to her own house. This is an indication of how carefully Luke has staged his narrative, as well as a reminder that Mary is only betrothed, not married, and thus goes to *her* home and not

---

40. See Green, "Good News"; Moxnes, *Economy of the Kingdom.*

41. See Bede, *Homilies,* 1:30: "Now because the human race had perished at the touch of the plague of pride, it was proper that the time of salvation should first begin with the putting forward of the medicine of humility by which it might be healed." In proclaiming the reversal motif, Mary's Song echoes a long-standing affirmation of God's work; cf., e.g., 1 Sam 2:7-8; Job 5:8-11; Isa 2:11; 5:15-16; Sir 10:14.

Joseph's. Why would Mary extend her stay up to the moment of Elizabeth's delivery (6 months [v 36] + 3 months [v 56]), then depart? The answer may lie in Luke's predilection to clear the stage of all but the primary actor(s) prior to narrating a new scene.[42] Mary, Elizabeth's "relative" (1:36), may have been among the "neighbors and relatives" who shared in the birth, circumcision, and naming of John (1:57-66). With the focus now on Elizabeth and her child, however, Mary disappears from view temporarily.

2.4. THE BIRTH OF JOHN (1:57-80)

With v 57, Luke picks up the narrative cycle from v 25. Up to this point, the repeated pattern of promise + event/fulfillment + response has focused on *conception* and supernatural *signs,* building our anticipation of John's promised *birth.* This expectancy is grounded in the trustworthiness of the angel thus far, and on the fact that Luke has now reported the passing of nine months since Elizabeth's conception (vv 24, 26, 36, 56). The narrative seems to demand the first words of v 57: "Now the time came. . . ."

The account of John's birth follows the pattern: birth + response + circumcision + naming + response. Represented in the structure and content of this sketch are the fulfillment of Gabriel's words and Zechariah's obedience to the angel. In addition, one locates here, particularly in Zechariah's Song, broad echoes of Abrahamic material[1] as well as other Scriptures.

Verse 66 focuses the central issue: "What then will this child become?" Verses 57-65 lead up to and raise this question, and vv 67-80 begin the process of answering it, locating John in the story of God's redemption. At the close of this section, however, John is growing and has not yet appeared publicly to Israel. As attention turns again from John to Jesus, the question remains: What will he become? In this way, Luke teases his audience, raises curiosity, and promises a return to the story of John.

2.4.1. A Son Is Born (1:57-58)

57 *Now the time came for Elizabeth to give birth, and she bore a son.* 58 *Her neighbors and relatives heard that the Lord had shown his great mercy to her, and they rejoiced with her.*

---

42. Cf. 3:20-21. There, John is imprisoned (v 20), then Jesus is baptized (v 21). The opening clause of 3:21 ("when all the people were baptized") guarantees that Jesus was in fact baptized by John, even though the sequence otherwise suggests that John had already been imprisoned.

1. See above, §2.

The account of John's birth is so closely tied to the announcement to Zechariah that his absence now is noticeable. As a result of his disbelief, he has been moved offstage to reappear only when his obedience to the angel will be manifest (vv 63-64). Until then, Elizabeth stands in the limelight.

Zechariah had been told that his wife would bear a son, and so she does (vv 13, 57). Interestingly, Luke uses precisely the same language for the promise of a *son* and its fulfillment,[2] but in the intervening material we hear only of Elizabeth's "child."[3] In other words, Luke has carefully allowed Gabriel's words to be realized piece-by-piece. Elizabeth will conceive, and she does, but we must wait for the child's birth to certify that the child is indeed a *son.* This adds to the suspense of the narrative, just as it accents the precise fulfillment of Gabriel's words.

The archangel had also promised rejoicing at John's birth (v 14), and so there is. We may evaluate the rejoicing in v 58 in two ways. First, even though the full significance of John's role is unknown to Elizabeth's relatives and neighbors (cf. vv 63, 65-66), the hand of God is nevertheless apparent. They can see as easily as we the echoes of the Genesis material in Elizabeth's conception in her old age, and thus identify the extraordinary place of John in salvation history. Verse 14 is, at least in part, fulfilled in v 58.[4] Second, since honor is a socially determined attribute, we can appreciate how the rejoicing of v 58 relates to the removal of Elizabeth's disgrace, noted in v 25. She may have had other claims to status because of her family heritage, but she lacked the divine sanction signified by the blessing of a child. Now God had intervened so as to restore her to a place of honor in the community.

As with Mary's Song, then, we see how God's intervention on behalf of the individual has corporate implications. God vindicates Elizabeth and, coincidentally, provides a prophet of the coming of the Lord. This message is represented further in the wordplay between vv 49-50 and 58. In the former verses Mary speaks of the mercy and *magnif*icent things characterizing the Mighty One. In the latter, Luke reports that "the Lord had *magnified* his mercy to her."[5]

2.4.2. The Circumcision and Naming of the Child (1:59-66)

59 *On the eighth day they came to circumcise the child, and they were going to name him Zechariah after his father.* 60 *But his mother said, "No; he is to be called John."* 61 *They said to her, "None of your*

---

2. γεννήσει υἱόν; ἐγέννησεν υἱόν.

3. βρέφος.

4. Note the parallel language: v 14: χαρήσονται; v 58: συνέχαιρον.

5. Verses 49-50: μεγάλα + τὸ ἔλεος αὐτοῦ; v 58: ἐμεγάλυνεν + τὸ ἔλεος αὐτοῦ.

relatives has this name. 62 *They began motioning to his father to find out what name he wanted to give him.* 63 *He asked for a writing tablet and wrote, "His name is John." And all of them were amazed.* 64 *Immediately his mouth was opened and his tongue freed, and he began to speak, praising God.* 65 *Fear came over all their neighbors, and all these things were talked about throughout the entire hill country of Judea.* 66 *All who heard them pondered them and said, "What then will this child become?" For, indeed, the hand of the Lord was with him.*

Luke's initial characterization of Zechariah and Elizabeth concerned their righteousness. After Zechariah's brief expression of unbelief (1:18-20), they return now to their exemplary form. They obey the constraints of the covenant (circumcision on the eighth day) as well as the command of Gabriel regarding the naming of their child. Submission to God of this sort may be normal for them (1:5-6), but the mood of this account is anything but nonchalant. Repeatedly, this scene is bathed in the light of the miraculous — recognized already in the Lord's expression of mercy to Elizabeth (1:58), now evident in the processes by which the child is named (1:59-63) and Zechariah regains his voice (1:64). The people's reactions, amazement and fear (1:63, 65), are characteristic responses to the miraculous in Luke-Acts. These events also lead to pondering, "What then will this child become?" (1:66ab). And in an uncommon move,[6] the narrator addresses the reader in a brief aside in v 66c: "For, indeed, the hand of the Lord was with him." This attempt at "heightening the significance of events"[7] underscores the sense that God is at work behind and in these seemingly ordinary practices — the circumcision and naming of a Jewish baby — and suggests to us that we should join the people of the Judean hill country in pondering the future role of this baby.

59-61 Circumcision, commanded by God as the sign of faithfulness to the covenant made between him and Abraham (Gen 17:9-14), was formalized in the Mosaic law (Lev 12:3). As people who live blamelessly before the Lord (1:6), Zechariah and Elizabeth circumcise their son on the eighth day. "They," presumably the "neighbors and relatives" of 1:58 (cf. 1:65), are present as witnesses to this act of covenant faithfulness and will have an active role in the naming of the child (cf. Ruth 4:17). As readers of the Lukan narrative, we know that John has before him a signal role as prophet of the coming of the Lord. That he is thus embraced within the Abrahamic covenant underscores again that God is bringing redemption to Israel *from within Israel.*

The simplicity with which we expect the narration of such routine

---

6. Sheeley observes Luke's reserve in the use of narrative asides *(Narrative Asides).*
7. Booth, *Rhetoric of Fiction,* 196-97.

activity to proceed is interrupted by a struggle between Elizabeth and her neighbors and friends, between apparent societal norms[8] and obedience to the angel's words. Perhaps following the tradition in Genesis of naming children according to their significance (cf., e.g., Gen 25:26; 30:6, 8, 13, 18, 20, 24), Elizabeth opposes her neighbors and relatives, insisting that the child will be called "John" (= "Yahweh has shown favor" — cf. 1:25, 58). On the face of it, nothing unusual resides in the mother's having the leading role in the naming of her child.[9] And Luke does not tell us *how* Elizabeth knew that "John" was the name designated by Gabriel (by revelation to her? by means of a communique from her husband?) — or, indeed, *whether* Elizabeth had this information. In fact, the marvel of the narrative is that this collusion between Elizabeth and Zechariah is unmotivated and unexpected. What we have before us to this juncture is the command of Gabriel to Zechariah, raising the narrative *possibility* of the child's being named "John," followed by Elizabeth's independent witness to this name, raising that possibility to a *probability*. The opposition of the relatives and neighbors presents itself as an obstacle to Zechariah's obedience and raises the suspense of the narrative.

62-64   The opposition of the neighbors and relatives to the realization of the angel's words (1:13) is motivated by ignorance; they received no angelic message. The Lord's aim is known to Zechariah, but he had not demonstrated his readiness to respond with faith (1:13-20). How will he respond now? His answer to the crowd has the form of a fiat: "His name *is* John." He is obedient to the angel, and thus to God.

The way the people put their question to Zechariah reminds us of the condition in which the narrative left him — "mute, unable to speak" (1:20). Muteness and deafness were interrelated in antiquity, so that these people communicate with Zechariah via hand motions. This recalls Zechariah's affliction, but also reveals that Zechariah has not heard his wife's choice of a

---

8. That is, societal norms in Luke's narrative world, narrowly defined. With regard to its representation of the Palestinian world in which it is otherwise steeped, Luke's account raises two questions. First, we would not expect the naming of the child to take place at circumcision, for naming followed immediately after the birth (cf. Gen 4:1, 25; 25:25-26; et al. — though cf. R. E. Brown's comment: ". . . the ideas of circumcision and naming were kept proximate (Gen 17:5 and 10; 21:3 and 4)" [*Birth*, 369; cf. Malina and Rohrbaugh, *Commentary*, 293]). Second, no cultural bias seems to have existed for naming a son after his father. A few instances are recorded (Tob 1:1, 9; Josephus *J. W.* 5.13.2 §534; *Ant.* 14.1.3; §10; 20.9.1 §197), and the naming of a son after his grandfather is also known (1 Macc 2:1-2; *Jub.* 11:15; Josephus *Life* 1.1 §5). Was Luke guided by Hellenistic practice? In any case, the narratological effect is to stress *obedience* to the covenant/law and *fulfillment* of Gabriel's words.

9. "A woman giving the name is not uncommon in the OT. Out of forty-six cases, the mother gives the name twenty-eight times, and the father eighteen times . . ." (Laurentin, *Truth of Christmas*, 472n.2). Cf., e.g., Gen 4:25; 19:37; 29:32-35; 38:3-5; et al.

name for their son. That he agrees with her, then, is itself cause for amazement; the people see behind this concordance divine machinations and respond accordingly.[10]

Zechariah's response has a second result: "Immediately his mouth was opened. . . ." This, too, is evidence of the miraculous, with the first word, "immediately," especially important. On the one hand, this adverb appears repeatedly in Luke-Acts to indicate the presence and untroubled efficacy of divine power (4:39; 5:25; 8:44, 47, 55; 13:13; 18:43; Acts 3:7; 16:26). On the other, it demonstrates the precise fulfillment of Gabriel's words: ". . . you will become mute . . . until the moment[11] these things occur."

65-66 "Fear," too, is a characteristic reaction to the miraculous in Luke-Acts (e.g., 1:12; 5:26; Acts 19:17), and this is the response now of "all their neighbors." John has not yet appeared publicly to Israel, but the widespread effect of his ministry is already anticipated by that public (see 3:3, 21).[12] At this point, in the region as a whole, the primary response seems to be puzzlement. That something extraordinary is at work is transparent, but what does it all mean? More pointedly, what will this child's future role be? "Pondering" is associated with Mary elsewhere in the birth narrative (2:19, 51), but is otherwise characteristic of those seeking to understand the significance of the ministries of John (3:15) and Jesus (5:22).

With v 66c, Luke speaks to the reader directly, in an aside designed to draw the reader more fully into the narrative. Luke, not the people of Judea,[13] affirms what the narrative has already made abundantly clear — namely, God is actively present in these events.[14] By asserting for the reader in this summary way the significance of the events surrounding the birth of John, Luke invites the reader to join in this pondering, highlighting Luke's desire to lead his audience into a proper *interpretation* of these events. It also prepares for Zechariah's Song, already anticipated in the remark about his "praising God" (1:64).

2.4.3. The Prophecy of Zechariah (1:67-79)

67 *Then his father Zechariah was filled with the Holy Spirit and spoke this prophecy:*
68 *"Blessed be the Lord God of Israel,*
   for he has looked favorably on his people and redeemed them.

---

10. On amazement as a characteristic response to the supernatural in Luke-Acts, see, e.g., 8:25; 9:43; 11:14.

11. Greek: καιρός; NRSV: "day."

12. See Coleridge, *Birth*, 112-13.

13. *Pace* Schürmann, 1:83n.21; cf. D it syr^s, which omit ἦν, thus reading the final clause of v 66c as though it were a continuation of the query in v 66b.

14. For this expression, see Acts 11:21; cf. 1 Chr 4:10; Isa 31:3; 66:14.

69 *He has raised up a mighty savior for us*
    in the house of his servant David,
70 *as he spoke through the mouth of his holy prophets from of old,*
71   *that we would be saved from our enemies and from the hand of*
    all who hate us.
72 *Thus he has shown the mercy promised to our ancestors,*
    and has remembered his holy covenant,
73 *the oath that he swore to our ancestor Abraham,*
    to grant us 74 *that we, being rescued from the hands of our*
    enemies,
    might serve him without fear, 75 *in holiness and righteousness*
    before him all our days.
76 *And you, child, will be called the prophet of the Most High;*
    for you will go before the Lord to prepare his ways,
77 *to give knowledge of salvation to his people*
    by the forgiveness of their sins.
78 *By the tender mercy of our God,*
    the dawn from on high will break upon[15] *us,*
79 *to give light to those who sit in darkness and in the shadow of*
    death,
    to guide our feet into the way of peace."

The angel's words having been fulfilled (1:20), Zechariah regains his voice (1:64), and the result is his response to the birth of his son. A strict parallelism would have located this response — called Zechariah's Song or the *Benedictus* — more intimately with Zechariah's angelic vision, say, after 1:20 or 1:24. Then, Zechariah's and Mary's Songs would have functioned as parallel reactions to the divine promise of a son whose role in the realization of God's plan would be key. Zechariah hesitated in his response to Gabriel, however, and his consequent silence forbade any response until this moment. Mary's Song is matched with Elizabeth's response (1:25), therefore, and Zechariah's Song will find its parallel in the multiple responses to Jesus' birth by angels, shepherds, and prophets (2:8-40).

Zechariah's Song recapitulates major emphases of the birth narrative as a whole. (1) It stresses the import of John as forerunner to and preparer for the coming of the Lord (cf. 1:16-17, 76) and as prophet (1:15-17, 76). (2) It subordinates John to Jesus, especially in its reference to John as "prophet of the Most High" (1:76; cf. 1:32: "Son of the Most High"). (3) It weaves the stories of John and Jesus into the one tapestry of God's purpose. (4) As

---

15. Ἐπεσκέψατο ("has broken upon") is read by ℵ² A C D R Ξ Ψ et al., but this reading results from assimilation to v 68: ἐπεσκέψατο.

with the other hymns in the Lukan birth narrative, Zechariah's Song completes a three-part pattern, in this case: promise of a son → birth of a son → praise response. (5) It highlights key motifs that pervade Luke 1–2 — for example, the covenant-making God, the continuity with Abraham and fulfillment of eschatological expectations associated with David, the socio-political context in which the narrative is set and from which God will deliver his people, and the decisive coming of the epoch of salvation.

As a narrative pause,[16] 1:67-79 brings the movement of the narrative to a halt in order to promote reflection on the events just described. Through a narrative aside in v 66, Luke invited the reader to join the people within the Gospel who ponder what to make of the extraordinary phenomena accompanying the arrival of this baby. "What then will this child become?" Zechariah's Song draws time to a halt in order to answer this question. The Song reaches backward in time — to the words of the prophets (1:70), to the ancestors (1:72), to Abraham (1:73), and, indeed, to the character and purpose of God himself. This attempt to root current events in Israel's past depends only in part on explicit references to Abraham or the prophets, however. It is also firmly grounded in the interplay of scriptural echoes present in practically every clause of the Song.[17] What John will become can be appreciated only against the backdrop of what God has been doing, and how God is even now bringing his aim to its consummation in part through his human agent John.[18]

§6 The Structure and Role of Zechariah's Song

Zechariah's Song displays few of the formal structural elements of the Song of Mary,[19] but two features are obvious. First, within the Song words and motifs are repeated and associated with new contexts so as to accent and develop their meaning. A few examples can be given. God is blessed because "he has *visited* his people" according

---

16. See above on 1:46-55.

17. Cf. Plummer, 39; Gnilka, "Hymnus," 221-37; Jones, "Lukan Psalms," 28-40.

18. A similar perspective is present in the speeches in Acts, which typically set current events (especially the rejection and exaltation of Jesus) within the broad stream of redemptive history. Clearly, a proper interpretation of "the events that have been fulfilled among us" (1:1) views their significance within the embrace of God's purpose throughout the history of his dealings with his people. On this function of the speeches in Acts, see Hall, *Revealed Histories,* 183-205. On points of contact between the *Benedictus* and the speeches in Acts, see Gryglewicz, "Herkunft der Hymnen"; Benoit, "L'enfance de Jean-Baptiste," 189.

19. See, however, the creative attempts to find chiasms and other significant structural parallelism in the *Benedictus* in Vanhoye, "Structure du Benedictus"; Auffret, "Lc 1,68-79"; Rousseau, "Benedictus."

to 1:68, and in 1:78 "the dawn from on high will *visit* us."[20] The purpose of that gracious visitation is developed — first by employing Exodus typology (vv 68, 71 [cf. Ps 106:10], 74), then by using metaphors of light and darkness. But the subject of this visiting seems to have shifted — from God to the "dawn" that comes "by the tender mercy of our God." These similarities and differences beckon for explanation.

One can also point to the repetition of the language of salvation in vv 69 and 77 — the first building on Davidic images and set within a vision of socio-political deliverance, the second associated with John and understood as the forgiveness of sins. "Mercy" and "tender mercy" occupy strategic positions in vv 72 and 78; the "prophets from of old" are matched with "the prophet of the Most High" (vv 70, 76); "his ways" in v 76 is related to "the way of peace" in v 79; and, in the Greek text, one recognizes a wordplay on the characterization of both David and John as servant/son (vv 69, 76).[21] This complex network does not lead easily to a delineation of the Song's macrostructure, but it does underscore how rich an interplay of symbols provides signification for the events Zechariah interprets.

Some of the thematic puzzles raised by this repetition of words and semantic relatives are solved with reference to a second structural element. Zechariah's Song divides itself into two parts — the first a "Benediction," initiated with the clause "Blessed be the Lord God of Israel" (v 68); the second a "Prophecy," marked by the change to second-person address in v 76. The Song as a whole is a declarative psalm of praise, and is cast as Spirit-inspired prophecy (v 67).[22] Hence, the Song as a whole is proclamation, but the material of the proclamation shifts in a subtle but decisive way from v 75 to v 76. Part one (vv 68-75) celebrates the (past tense) visitation of God to bring deliverance. It employs Exodus typology and describes the agent of salvation in Davidic terms. Its fundamental metaphor concerns deliverance from enemies, and it roots this salvific action on God's part in God's mercy, manifest in his past dealings with his people. The purpose of deliverance is also cast in terms borrowed from the Exodus: "that we . . . might serve him." Part one focuses *what* God has done, emphasizing *that* God has acted to achieve deliverance.

Part two (vv 76-79) concerns not so much *what* God has done or will accomplish, though this emphasis and its basis in God's mercy is not absent, but rather *how* God has begun to bring to fruition his redemptive purpose. Verses 76-77 draw out the work of John on this stage of salvific drama, whereas vv 78-79 (anticipating Simeon's Song in 2:29-32) borrow a metaphor from one strand of messianic expectation — "the dawn from on high" — to point ahead to the advent of God's agent of salvation. Reading backward from Simeon's Song, we know that Zechariah has already anticipated the significance of the coming of Mary's son, Jesus. Zechariah can thus speak in the past tense of God's visitation, a reference to the divine intervention resulting in the childbearing of Elizabeth and Mary. But he must speak in the

---

20. Both verses employ a form of ἐπισκέπτομαι, used "of God's gracious visitation in bringing salvation" (BAGD 298); NRSV: "looked favorably"; "will break upon."

21. Verse 69: παιδὸς αὐτοῦ; NRSV: "his servant"; v 76: παιδίον; NRSV: "child." Παῖς can refer to a child or slave.

22. This point has been emphasized by Carter, "Zechariah," 242-44.

future tense of John's public, prophetic ministry, and of Jesus' arrival — both yet to be realized. In this portion of the Song, salvation is understood as reconciliation with God, borrowing language related to the new covenant with its promise of forgiveness (Jer 31:31-34) and the Isaianic vision of revelatory light (e.g., Isa 42:6; 49:6; 60:1, 19). Here the purpose of this gracious visitation appears to be one of transformed lives, the embracing of righteous behavior.

Zechariah's Song seems to portray two conflicting images of salvation, the one social and political, the other spiritual. It may be that the narrative is opening up possibilities in order to show how they are disappointed, or that a political kingdom is thus promised to Israel in order to show how Israel's rejection of its king disallowed the fulfillment of that promise.[23] However, it must not be overlooked that Zechariah has spoken under the inspiration of the Spirit, and this gives us no basis for regarding him or his message as in any way unreliable.[24]

The degree to which we posit a disjunction between these two apparently alternative conceptualizations of salvation depends in large part on how we evaluate the needs represented by the Song. Painting the picture of first-century Palestine with images of a grossly oppressive militaristic, economic, and political foreign presence will lead us to read in Zechariah's Song the expression of deep-seated revolutionary hopes held by a people thrust violently to the margins of society.[25] A much less desperate portrayal, one that emphasizes the need both to recognize the difficulties of alien domination and to place those within the wider perspective of common (especially peasant) life in antiquity,[26] orients "deliverance" less along militaristic-revolutionary lines and more in terms of socio-religious power. This whole problem is further exacerbated by three other factors. First, the Jewish people of Roman Palestine responded to their life-circumstances in a number of ways, so that "deliverance" could have been defined in a variety of ways. Second, the language of Zechariah's Song (e.g., "enemies," "all who hate us") is highly stylized, and it is not immediately clear how literally such terms are to be construed. Third, in Luke's own discourse situation, presumably a different set of issues would have surfaced through this language of salvation. In the larger Greco-Roman world of Luke, "enemies" might have appeared in faces other than those of the Roman soldier or toll collector; cosmic and rapidly evolving cultural forces threatened life in other ways. Perhaps most important to the present issue is the ease with which Zechariah's Song brings together these seemingly dis-

---

23. See Tannehill, "Israel in Luke-Acts"; *idem, Narrative Unity,* 1:32-38; cf. *idem,* "Rejection by Jews."

24. *Contra* Tannehill, *Narrative Unity,* 1:35n.46.

25. See, e.g., Ford, *My Enemy Is My Guest,* chs. 1-2; Horsley, *Liberation,* 114-19.

26. Cf. Sanders, *Judaism,* e.g., 146-69; Schmidt, "Taxes."

parate conceptions of salvation — and he does so in a way fully congruent with important strands of soteriology in Second Temple Judaism, where forgiveness of sins and restoration as a people were both woven into the tapestry of divine redemption.[27] For Luke, the reconciliation of God's people and deliverance from enemies are both part of one divine movement. For him, visions of salvation cannot be categorized as social or religious or political, for the epoch of peace is characterized by all of these.

67   In terms of story time, vv 67-79 belong at the close of v 64, where they fill out the content of Zechariah's praise.[28] Luke, however, is interested in an "orderly account" (1:3) governed not by chronological but by interpretive or persuasive interests.[29]

In Israel's past as well as in the early church of Acts, the filling of the Holy Spirit was often for the purpose of prophecy,[30] so that the prophet would be recognized as providing God's perspective on events. Under the direction of the Spirit, Zechariah communicates from the divine point of view the significance of the extraordinary events narrated thus far.[31] Because he is "filled with the Holy Spirit," Zechariah's words command attention and engender faith in his message. His repeated use of the first person plural pronoun — "for *us,*" "that *we,*" "to *our,*" et al. — also invites his audience (the neighbors — v 63) and Luke's (readers and hearers of his narrative) to adopt his interpretation.

68-71   Zechariah's Song begins with praise, then turns to enumerate the reasons for glorifying God. To express praise, Zechariah uses common psalmic language, even though this form of blessing is ordinarily located at the close of the psalm (e.g., Pss 41:13; 72:18-19). Two reasons for extolling God are set in parallel: he has graciously visited his people and he has raised up a Davidic savior. (The same apposition appears in 7:16.) We are thus encouraged to read these two affirmations as in some way interpreting the one divine act. How has God looked with favor on his people? By raising up a savior.[32]

---

27. See Strauss, *Davidic Messiah,* 35-74; Green, "Salvation to the End of the Earth," forthcoming.

28. Note the verbal continuity: v 64: καὶ ἐλάλει εὐλογῶν τὸν θεόν; v 68: εὐλογητὸς κύριος ὁ θεός.

29. See above on 1:3.

30. Cf., e.g., Num 11:26-27; 2 Sam 23:2; Hos 9:7; *Jub.* 25:14; 31:12; Josephus *Ant.* 4.5 §119; Acts 2:17-18; 11:27-28; 13:1-2(?).

31. Hence, from Luke's perspective, it is not a question of what Zechariah could or could not have possibly known. Endowed with the Spirit he now shares, however temporarily, in the all-knowing perspective of the narrator and of God.

32. Interestingly, Acts 15:13-18 evidences a similar juxtaposition, for there God's gracious visitation is set within the context of the rebuilding of the "dwelling of David" (cf. "house of David" — Luke 1:69); here it is on the Gentiles that God has looked with favor.

With "God" as subject, the verb "to look with favor"[33] refers to the visitation of God in judgment (e.g., Exod 32:34) or grace (e.g., Gen 21:1; Exod 4:31; Ruth 1:6). In Zechariah's Song, a gracious visitation is clearly in view, for this verb is interpreted immediately by its relation to "redemption" and then by the salvific emphases of the Song as a whole. Of course, redemption *for* "his people" requires deliverance *from* their enemies (vv 71, 74), so that grace and judgment may appear hand in hand. Given the wide-ranging echoes of Abrahamic material in Luke 1–2, and the semantically-related ways of describing God's "looking with favor" in reference to Elizabeth and Mary (1:25, 48), we may hear reverberations from Gen 21:1. There God looked favorably on Sarah, with the result that she conceived. This echo helps explain the past tense verbs in this portion of the Song: In the extraordinary events surrounding the conceptions and births of John and Jesus, God has acted powerfully and irreversibly to bring salvation. God's "visitation" might also hint that the work of God envisioned by Zechariah builds on memories of Exodus (cf. Exod 4:31; Pss 80:14; 106:4).

The appearance of the term "redemption"[34] determines the required sense of "to visit," but also sets Zechariah's vision of salvation squarely in the context of the Exodus. In that paradigmatic act of deliverance, God redeemed his people and created among them a new community, and in scriptural references to this act of deliverance the term Zechariah uses is paramount.[35] Verse 71, with its negative description of salvation as rescue from "our" enemies and those who hate "us,"[36] also borrows from the arsenal of scriptural metaphors derived from the Exodus. In particular, language employed here is reminiscent of Psalm 106, a celebration of Exodus.

Images of Exodus are not the only ones put to use here. With the use of "redemption" a further echo may be discerned, this time to the scriptural material associated with the Jubilee (cf. Lev 25:29, 48; Isa 63:4; cf. Luke 4:16-30). This segment of the Song also builds on Davidic imagery, correlating God's gracious visitation with his raising up "a horn of salvation" or "a mighty savior." "Horn" commonly appears in the ancient Near East as a symbol of strength.[37] Its usage here is similar to that in Ps 89:17, where a horn is raised, or, better, Ps 132:17, where a horn sprouts up from David.[38] Gabriel had promised that this role would be assigned to Jesus (of the house of David — 1:27, 32), and this Song reiterates this promise. To these two

---

33. ἐπισκέπτομαι, "to visit."

34. That is, λύτρωσις; cf. Procksch and Büchsel, "λύω," 331-35.

35. Exod 6:6; Deut 7:8; 9:26; 13:6; 15:15; 21:8; 24:18; 2 Sam 7:23; et al.

36. On the equivalence of these two characterizations of Israel's opponents, see Pss 18:18; 56:10.

37. See Süring, *Horn-Motif.*

38. Cf. also 1 Sam 2:1, 10; 2 Sam 22:3; Sir 47:7, 11; 1 Macc 2:48.

motifs — Jubilee and Davidic dynasty — might be added others,[39] but the point is already clear. Zechariah's Song draws together myriad images to show the profundity of the definitive salvific act now unfolding.

72-75   Though loosely connected, these phrases are clear enough in function. First, with its references to showing mercy and remembering the covenant, v 72 continues to enumerate why the praise of God is appropriate. Subsequent lines review the history of God's redemptive project, bringing onto the stage "our" ancestors, Abraham, and, again, the Exodus. Events related to Zechariah, Elizabeth, Mary, and their sons are inexplicable apart from God's story, grounded in God's aim, manifest in Israel's history as narrated in the Scriptures.

The mention of God's mercy, appearing near the middle of this first major segment of the Song (vv 68-75), is pivotal. Here we find the fundamental basis for God's behavior in any time, and it is surely significant that Jesus will later identify mercy as the primary motivation behind God's activity and as the basis for ethical behavior for the community of disciples (6:36). This mercy is active: literally, God has "done mercy."[40] Similarly, remembering is more than a cognitive exercise: remembering, God acts. Current events are for Zechariah a continuation of past divine performance.

If God's covenantal faithfulness is behind these events, where will they lead? Again, appeal is made to Exodus material. First, the verb "to rescue"[41] refers to an action sometimes rooted, as here, in divine mercy (e.g., Neh 9:8; Ps 33:18-19; cf. Judg 8:34; Isa 51:10). To this Exodus material can be added the description of those from whom "we" are rescued; thus, v 74a recalls v 71, itself an allusion to Ps 106:10, all reverberating with Exodus themes. Finally, reference may be made to the purpose of this divine rescue: to create a people freed to ". . . serve him without fear, in holiness and righteousness." This is precisely the purpose of the Exodus: "Let my people go, so that they may worship me . . ." (Exod 7:16; cf. Josh 24:14). "To serve" or "to worship"[42] is used to clarify the nature of the redeemed people, a community whose practices were to be formed in their worship of the Lord God. Thus, the freedom to worship without fear refers to much more than spiritual or cultic practices.[43] Worship or service embraces the whole way of communal life of those who have been delivered.

76-79   A shift in person and tense marks the second major segment

---

39. Note, e.g., that God "raises up" a deliverer in Judg 3:9, 15; and a servant in Isa 52:13 (cf. Acts 3:13).

40. ποιῆσαι ἔλεος.

41. ῥύομαι; see, e.g., Neh 9:8; Ps 33:18-19; cf. Judg 8:34; Isa 51:10.

42. λατρεύω.

43. *Contra* Farris, *Hymns,* 138.

of the Song. Having briefly surveyed the history of God's interaction with Israel, up to and including the epoch-making consummation of God's purpose now undertaken, Zechariah takes up his more immediate task. He addresses John directly — "and you, child" — first in order to proclaim John's prophetic role, then to relate John to the coming of God's agent of salvation.

The prophetic description of John is related to the angelic announcement in 1:15-17. Like it, the present passage speaks of John in his role as precursor, though here the allusion to Isa 40:3 is more obvious; this characterization is of manifest importance for the narrator, who repeats it in 3:3-4; 7:26.

The relationship between John and Jesus is the focus of Zechariah's description of John as one who goes "before the Lord to prepare his ways." Before, in 1:17, "Lord" could only be understood as Yahweh. But the subsequent narrative has embodied a subtle shift in this identification, with the result that *God's* visitation is now understood to take the form of the coming of *Jesus* — of whom the title "Lord" is appropriate (1:43; cf. 2:11). We know, then, that John will go before the Lord Jesus to prepare his way. However, this is an identification that is unknown to the characters in Luke 3–23; although "Lord" in its transcendent sense appears in the Gospel as a title for Jesus, it occurs thus only in the words of the narrator, who thus gives us his own assessment of Jesus' identity and reveals his own status as a believer.[44] Only in light of his exaltation is Jesus more widely acknowledged as "Lord" (e.g., 24:34; Acts 2:36).

It is interesting that the locus of John's ministry is again set among the people of Israel (1:16, 77), but "repentance" has been replaced by the experience[45] of salvation that comes through forgiveness. John's public ministry will demonstrate the intimacy with which these concepts are related (3:3, 7-14). In different ways, both point to the reconciliation of a people with God, and this Zechariah designates as "salvation." With this we are clearly in the thought world of the OT.[46]

Psalm 130:7-8 roots redemption and freedom from iniquities in the Lord's "steadfast love," just as this segment of Zechariah's Song revolves around "tender mercy." This phrase occurs in the exact middle of vv 76-79,[47]

44. See 7:19; 10:1, 39, 41; 11:39; 12:42; 17:5, 6; 18:6; 19:8a; 22:61; 24:3 (some mss.). Cf. Dawsey, "Characterization," 145-46; Dawsey notes that Luke thus positions himself on the side of the believing community but makes no distinction between κύριος in its transcendent sense and (at least potentially here) honorific sense.

45. This is the sense of "knowing."

46. Cf. Ps 130:7-8, which correlates redemption and forgiveness; Jones, "Lukan Psalms," 36-37.

47. See Menken, "Position of σπλαγχνίζεσθαι," 112. Menken finds that of the 53 words in this part of the Song, 26 appear before σπλάγχνα and 26 appear after.

suggesting again that what God does in bringing salvation springs fundamentally from his compassion.

The manifestation of God's mercy according to the Song is the coming of the Messiah. This way of understanding "the dawn from on high" recognizes a complex interplay of scriptural metaphors. "Dawn" might simply represent the coming of salvation, using the metaphor of light/star (e.g., Isa 60:1; Mal 4:2). A handful of texts translate this term as "Branch,"[48] however, and refer to an heir to the throne of David (Jer 23:5; Zech 3:8; 6:12). As *Tg. Onq.* Num 24:17 and even more clearly Rev 22:16 indicate, the messianic connotations of "Branch" could be and were carried over to the metaphor of illumination.[49] Consequently, "dawn" in 1:79 might be rendered as "Dawn"; that is, Zechariah prophesies God's sending a messianic figure. This understanding is supported further by the increasing emphasis in Luke 1 on an agent of salvation who is a Davidide (1:32, 35, 69).

As "Dawn," God's agent of redemption will give light and guide "our feet." "Light" occurs in Exod 13:21; Pss 27:1; 36:9; et al. as a metaphor of God's presence. Other texts develop the metaphor of salvation as enlightenment, some with reference to the eschaton (Ps 107:9-10; Isa 2:5; 9:2; 42:7; 60:1-3; Mic 7:8; Bar 5:9). The conceptualization of salvation as illumination makes only its first appearance in Luke-Acts at this juncture, and others will follow.[50] Many have found at the close of Zechariah's Song a hint of the universal embrace of God's redemptive visit and the advent of the Dawn from on high — an interpretation encouraged by the use of the light-darkness imagery in Isaiah (e.g., 42:7) and the mention of the covenant with Abraham with its universalistic repercussions, and by the grounding of God's project in God's boundless mercy. To this interpretation may be added the cosmic dimension of salvation, developed in the ensuing narrative but present in embryonic form here. Accordingly, "darkness" and "the shadow of death" represent an arena of existence ruled by cosmic forces in opposition to God — a domain into which the light of God's redemptive presence is made to shine by the advent of God's agent, the Dawn. This realm of darkness, then, is contrasted with the "way of peace," a cipher for lives marked by shalom, peace and justice, within the community of God's reign.

The Song presents a mélange of images — divine visitation, Exodus, Jubilee, New Covenant, illumination — not to specify with precision what

48. "Branch" is a rendering of the Hebrew צמח; the LXX reads (as in Luke 1:79) ἀνατολή. See the discussion in Gnilka, "Hymnus," 227-32.

49. Cf. Strauss, *Davidic Messiah*, 103-8.

50. Jesus' ministry, with its universalistic reach, is developed along these lines, e.g., in Simeon's Song (2:29-32). Moreover, salvation (i.e., the consequence of Paul's mission) is characterized as turning from darkness to light and from the authority of Satan to God (Acts 26:17-18).

form God's purpose will take but rather to project its magnitude, its immeasurability, its irreducible quality. What God is doing extends the reach of what God has done; it exceeds what had been hoped. And the result will be a new community in which God's peace and justice are incarnated.

2.4.4. The Growth of the Child (1:80)

> 80 *The child grew and became strong in the Spirit,*[51] *and he was in the wilderness until the day he appeared publicly to Israel.*

This summary statement completes the narrative about John in the Lukan birth narrative at the same time that it anticipates a return to that narrative later in the Gospel. He is maturing, but he has not yet appeared publicly to take up his prophetic role. Luke envisages these years of growth as the time during which the Spirit with which John was filled at conception (see 1:15, 17) fashions his life before God and prepares him for his prophetic ministry. In every other way the words of Gabriel have come to pass, so we cannot but believe that Luke will go on to report how John "went before the Lord."

With this summary statement Luke clears John from the stage, and with him the characters through whom John has been introduced. This prepares for a return to the story of Jesus.

Luke's summary is reminiscent of Gen 20:21; Judg 13:24-25, where similar summaries of childhood and youth are given. It also anticipates the similar, but more developed report of Jesus' maturation in 2:40-52, and the summary reports of the growth of the "word of God" in the Acts of the Apostles. We are left with the impression that all is going according to plan.

The reference to "the wilderness" may reflect the continuing association of John with the words of Isa 40:3. John is "in the wilderness" awaiting his public appearance as "the voice of one crying out in the wilderness" (3:4 [Isa 40:3]). The discernment of such echoes is supported by the presence of others from Isaiah 40 in 1:17, 18, 76.[52]

2.5. THE BIRTH OF JESUS (2:1-20)

Although interwoven with material related to John, the narrative cycle leading up to this climactic point in the birth narrative is clear. From a reliable source, God's own personal servant, Gabriel, Mary has received the promise of a son. The narrative *possibility* thus raised is strengthened by the fulfillment of the

---

51. NRSV: "in spirit."
52. Though 1:80 locates John ἐν ταῖς ἐρήμοις, whereas 3:4 reads ἐν ταῖς ἐρήμῳ.

sign given Mary — that is, that Elizabeth had conceived in her old age. Thus far, Gabriel has proven to be credible, so we assume that his birth announcement to Mary will also be fulfilled. Moreover, the interpretation of the role of Mary's son in the Songs of Mary and Zechariah underscores the *probability* that the angel's words will come to fruition. Hence, even though Luke initiates the account of Jesus' birth with a new chronological reference (2:1-2; cf. 1:5), this episode is bound securely to earlier material. From *possibility* and *probability,* we move now to *event* and *response.*

With *event* and *response,* however, we also encounter new possibilities — or, in this case, reaffirmation and clarification of possibilities already introduced. We are thus reminded that Luke 1–2 as a unit is incomplete in itself; it prepares for and, in important ways, requires the rest of Luke-Acts. Jesus is born, as promised, and even identified with exalted titles (2:11), but his public ministry as "Savior" or "Messiah" or "Lord" has not yet begun. Nor is it yet so clear what those titles might mean or how the roles to which they refer might be realized. Although "glorifying and praising God" are appropriate responses to the God at work in these events (2:20; cf. 2:10, 14), reflection or "pondering" is also called for (2:19). What does it all mean? is still a valid question.

§7 The Birth of Jesus in Literary and Social Perspective

Numerous parallels bind the stories of John and Jesus together at this point — for example, "the time came . . . give birth . . . son" (1:57; 2:6-7); and responses of joy (1:58; 2:10, 20), amazement (1:63; 2:18), and pondering (1:66; 2:19). The public nature of those responses also suggests a crucial point of contrast. The "neighbors and relatives" who rejoice over John's birth are overshadowed by the more universal and cosmic responses to Jesus' birth by angels and shepherds. The difference in relative length allotted to these two accounts is similarly telling. The births are bound together into one narrative, but the birth of Jesus is the more consequential.

This account is related to prior material by its attention to the religio-political repercussions of Jesus' birth, too. Anticipated implicitly (1:5) and explicitly (1:46-55, 68-79), this emphasis now comes to the fore. The registration of "all the world" asserts Augustus's sovereignty over that world. Yet the birth of Jesus, God's Son (1:35), is made known not to the Emperor or even to the Syrian governor, Quirinius, but to peasant shepherds. With the birth of Jesus, the powerful are already being brought down, while the lowly are lifted up (cf. 1:52).

The references to Emperor Augustus and the census in 2:1-2 are often taken as devices setting Jesus' birth within a chronological framework or on the stage of world history.[1] Thus, the efforts of the Emperor might be viewed as unwittingly

---

1. See, e.g., R. E. Brown, *Birth,* 414-15 (who notes the relation of Jesus' accolades to those given Augustus, but does not exploit them); Marshall, 97-98; Davis, "Literary Structure," 218.

serving the divine plan in having the Messiah born in Bethlehem (cf. Mic 5:2). Luke might even be understood as providing evidence for a positive attitude toward imperial rule within the Christian movement[2] or for the celebration of the rule of Augustus — who made one empire out of many nations and so created a suitable arena for the advent of God's Messiah.[3] Such a reading overlooks a number of key factors.

The Songs of Mary and Zechariah have already painted the advent of God's deliverance in political hues. This of itself provides a prima facie bias for reading the introduction of the governor of Syria and ruler of the Empire as more than background information. Moreover, in spite of Roman reticence vis-à-vis the imperial cult, under Augustus the reorganization of imperial religion aided the reunification of the Roman world. Even if he did not support his own veneration as (a) god during his lifetime, he reasserted the divinity of his adopted father, Julius Caesar, and allowed himself to be called "Son of God," paving the way for deification upon his death. Even the name he received from the Senate in 27 B.C.E., "Augustus," the name of Octavius repeated here by Luke, was of religious significance and suggested divine qualities. Augustus permitted the worship of powers operating through him — for example, peace, victory, liberty, and security — and, especially in the Empire's eastern reaches, distinctions between divine powers working through the emperor and emperor-as-divine were often obscured. Prominence was given those divinities that legitimized the reign of Augustus.[4] "The imperial cult, like the cults of the traditional gods, created a relationship of power between subject and ruler."[5] Augustus received such titles as "Savior" and was revered as the one who had brought peace to "all the world."[6] Hence, in the Lukan narrative, qualities for which Augustus was extolled are now attributed directly to Yahweh and to God's Son, Jesus; and qualities previously attributed to the Emperor are now called into question. Thus, for example, that God effects peace on earth presupposes that the "peace of Rome" is seriously deficient.

The census itself is also of significance, for it was a penetrating symbol of Roman overlordship. It is not without import that Luke devotes more space to the census, which he mentions four times in 2:1-7, than to the actual event of Jesus' birth. A census, which amounted to a listing of persons (presumably both males and females who had come of age)[7] and property, was conducted from time to time for purposes of taxation and military service. It has also been suggested that a census such as that envisioned by the Lukan account might have had the purpose of securing from the

2. See Bede, *Homilies,* 1:52-53; R. H. Smith, "Caesar's Decree"; Moehring, "Census in Luke."

3. For example, Origen *Con. Cel.* 2.30.

4. Fishwick, *Imperial Cult,* 1:1, 87.

5. Price, *Rituals and Power,* 248.

6. Braund *(Augustus)* provides English translations of numerous inscriptions describing Augustus as son of a deity (§§2, 6, 10, 11, 13 et passim), progenitor of his country and/or the world (§§19-21, 28, 44 et al.), bringer of peace and savior of the world (§§10, 36, 38, 44, 66, 123 et al.), and even referring to him as divine (§§75, 94). See also Fishwick, *Imperial Cult;* Price, *Rituals and Power.*

7. That is, women of at least 12 years of age, men of 14; cf. Ulpian 50:15:3.

populace oaths of allegiance to the Roman leadership.[8] In any case, the primary problem with the census is not its economic repercussions, for the tribute excised on the basis of the census probably amounted to only a denarius per head. Rather, many would have found in the census a disturbing reminder of the alien rule of Rome, and in the ensuing demand of tribute a sign of loyalty to the emperor that compromised fidelity to Yahweh.

Still further, the angel of the Lord characterizes the birth of Jesus as "good news" (2:10-11), working at the intersection of two traditions. On the one hand, we hear in the background the Isaianic vision of the coming of the Lord to bring salvation and establish his dominion of peace (Isaiah 40–66).[9] On the other hand, within the Greco-Roman world,[10] "good news" might be correlated with deliverance and used within the context of the imperial cult — for example, in oral announcements of the birth of the emperor. As the Gospel continues, the meaning of "good news" for Luke will be qualified more and more (cf. esp. 4:16-30; 7:21-22). At this early juncture, however, this usage sets Jesus in religio-political opposition to the emperor.[11]

In addition to the religio-political ramifications of Jesus' birth, a second motif spans the two sections of Luke's account of the birth of Jesus (vv 7, 12, 16). The humble origins of the Savior have often been discussed in this context,[12] and rightly so given Luke's interest in issues of Jesus' identification with humanity (e.g., 3:21, 38; 9:58) and the raising up of the lowly. In this case, the function of the "sign" is to help to interpret what God is doing. Along with the titles given Jesus in 2:11, the emphasis on the condition of the child develops Jesus' royal identity (cf. Wis 7:4) and his role as agent of God's redeeming presence among his people (cf. Isa 1:13).[13]

8. So Barnett, "ἀπογραφή."

9. See, e.g., Isa 40:9 — ὁ εὐαγγελιζόμενος (2x); 52:7 — εὐαγγελιζομένου + εἰρήνης; εὐαγγελιζόμενος + σωτηρίαν.

10. See Friedrich, "εὐαγγελίζομαι," 710-12, 721-25.

11. Cf. also Legrand, "Christmas," 290-92.

12. See, e.g., Bede, *Luc.* 1: "It should be carefully noted that the sign given of the saviour's birth is not a child enfolded in Tyrian purple, but one wrapped round with rough pieces of cloth; he is not to be found in an ornate golden bed, but in a manger" (ET in McHugh, *Mother of Jesus,* 89).

13. See further, below, on 2:7, 12, 16; and Giblin, "Sign of the Manger." C. F. Evans (200) describes as "far-fetched" the notion that we are to find scriptural allusions in these phenomena, believing that this requires too much biblical literacy on the part of these shepherds or of Luke's readers. Luke's audience, however, may be expected to hear such echoes (see above, §2). A very different approach is taken by Derrett, "Further Light," 17-18; *idem,* "Manger at Bethlehem," 43-47; *idem,* "Manger." In his view, the manger at Bethlehem finds its counterpart in the tomb at Jerusalem (birth — rebirth), and the manger conceals references to the Fall of Adam, the birth of Moses, and the immunity of the Holy Spirit from ritual impurity. But major aspects of this imaginative ("the product of a lively imagination" [Marshall, 106]) proposal depend on relatively late material of questionable relevance and on the location of Mary, Joseph, and Jesus in a cave — an assumption for which there is no support in Luke; cf., however, Justin *Dial.* 78; *Prot. Jas.* 18.

From a retrospective reading of the Third Gospel, one can also find in the manger scene an allusion to Jesus' death:

2:7: "wrapped him   in bands of cloth, and laid him in a manger"
23:53: "wrapped [Jesus' body] in a linen cloth,   and laid it   in a . . . tomb."[14]

Interestingly, later Christian iconography recognized and capitalized on this connection, giving the birthplace of Jesus the semblance of a sepulchre. That Luke's narrative is susceptible to such a reading is suggested both by these conceptual parallels and by the anticipatory reference to tragedy in 2:34-35.

2.5.1. The Birth in Bethlehem (2:1-7)

1 *In those days a decree went out from Emperor Augustus that all the world should be registered.* 2 *This was the first registration and was taken while Quirinius was governor of Syria.* 3 *All went to their own towns to be registered.* 4 *Joseph also went from the town of Nazareth in Galilee to Judea, to the city of David called Bethlehem, because he was descended from the house and family of David.* 5 *He went to be registered with Mary, to whom he was betrothed[15] and who was expecting a child.* 6 *While they were there, the time came for her to deliver her child.* 7 *And she gave birth to her firstborn son and wrapped him in bands of cloth, and laid him in a manger, because there was no place for them in the guest room.*[16]

Luke closes the story of John only temporarily in order to pick up the parallel narrative regarding Mary and her expected child, left on hold at 1:56. In doing so, he paints two settings in which to locate the birth of Jesus — the world of Emperor Augustus and the world of divine purpose. Against this backdrop Luke narrates the fulfillment of the angel's announcement of the birth of a son to Mary (1:31-35).

The census is mentioned repeatedly by Luke (vv 1, 2, 3, 5) and is therefore of obvious significance. Unfortunately, the details to which Luke alludes are problematical from an historical point of view.[17] From a narrato-

---

14. See Derrett, "Manger at Bethlehem," 43-44.

15. NRSV: "engaged"; for this rendering, see above on 1:27. Γυναικὶ αὐτοῦ ("his wife") is read by aur b c sy^s, and C^3 Θ Ψ 053 et al. have μεμνηστευμένη αὐτῷ γυναικί ("betrothed to be his wife"). "His wife" makes better sense in the present context (Why else would Mary need to accompany Joseph?), making "betrothed" the more difficult reading since it is also the best attested (א B C D L W Ξ et al.), it is the preferred reading.

16. NRSV: "inn."

17. See Nolland, 1:99-102; Marshall, 99-104; R. E. Brown, *Birth*, 547-56; Small-

logical point of view, it is significant that one reference to the census (2:2) appears in a narrative aside. This evidence suggests the narrator's desire to locate these events in a context familiar to the reader (cf. Acts 5:37). Whatever historians are able to make of Luke's reference here, Luke's ideal audience would likely have grasped the associations Luke draws between the birth of Jesus and this major event under Quirinius without being familiar enough with the issues of historical chronology to quarrel with the narrator.[18]

How, then, do the references to Augustus, Quirinius, and the census function? First, in contrast to the earlier chronological reference in 1:5, with its focus on Judean history, this one concerns "the world." This innovation implies that, whereas John's ministry was to be focused on Israel (cf. 1:16), the reach of Jesus' ministry would be universal. Second, issues of power and status immediately occupy center stage, for both Augustus and Quirinius are introduced with reference to their positions as wealthy sovereigns. Joseph, along with the rest of the world ("all" — v 3), is portrayed as their subordinate. Finally, the census locates the birth of Jesus in Bethlehem, this in fulfillment of Mic 5:2.[19]

From its opening reference to the emperor in 2:1, this pericope focuses its lens ever more narrowly — from "the world," to the region governed by Quirinius, to Bethlehem and Joseph, to the newborn child.

1-3 Luke's account has a somber beginning. This is evident, first, from the opening words — "in those days" — which suggest the narration of events of eschatological import (cf. 4:2; 5:35; 9:36; Acts 2:18).[20] Chronological and political references to the Roman emperor further this solemn tone.

Born Gaius Octavian as the grandnephew and later adopted son and designated heir of Julius Caesar, Augustus was recognized as sole leader of the Roman world in 27 B.C.E. Having restored Roman rule, now in the form of the Empire, he was accorded honor due one who seemed more a god than a human. See, for example, the Myrian inscription: "Divine Augustus Caesar, son of a god, imperator of land and sea, the benefactor and savior of the whole

---

wood, *Jews,* 568-71; G. D. Kilpatrick, "Luke 2,4-5"; Brindle, "Census"; Wiseman, "Decree"; Barnett, "ἀπογραφή."

18. See Sheeley, *Narrative Asides,* 103; *idem,* "Narrative Asides." Noting two striking events in Palestinian history — the death of Herod in 4 B.C.E. and the annexation of Judea in 6 C.E. — Syme ("Titulus," 600) observes, "Either might serve for approximate dating in a society not given to exact documentation."

19. Others have found in the census a messianic fulfillment of Ps 87:6: "The Lord records, as he registers the peoples, 'This one was born there' " — cf. Origen's *Quinta* Ps 87:6 ("In the census of the peoples, this one will be born there" [Ps 86:6]) and the targum on ("This king has been reared there") Ps 87:6; Eusebius *Psalms* 87. This interpretation is discussed in R. E. Brown, *Birth,* 417-8; and dismissed by Bock, *Proclamation,* 76.

20. Schürmann, 1:65n.162.

world. . . ."[21] Indeed, the name "Augustus" itself identified him as possessing divine characteristics, if not actually divine.[22] The census, too, signals an unwelcome, alien intrusion into the affairs of the Jewish people, a reminder of the allegiance required of Israel as a conquered people.

Twice, Luke emphasizes the universality of the census, referring to "all the world"[23] (2:1, 3). This accent is narrowed with the regionalized reference to Syria in 2:2, which itself prepares for the more localized focus in 2:4-7 on Joseph and the newborn child. This progression draws the birth of Jesus onto a universal stage and underscores the redemptive significance of that birth for the whole world.[24]

The business of census-taking grew out of attempts to regularize the collection of taxes, especially the poll or head tax in the Roman provinces. In other locales it might also be the precursor to military conscription, but, since the Jewish people were exempt from military service, this would not have been the case in Palestine. Little is known about the practices involved in census-taking, so it is difficult to know if the procedure outlined in 2:3 ("all went to their own towns") reflects historical conventions in the East[25] or accommodation to Jewish concerns with ancestral heritage or some other phenomenon. In any case, within the framework of the narrative, this peculiarity prepares for its corollary in the ensuing journey of Joseph to Bethlehem.

4-5 From the universal, we now move to the particular. To this point, it would appear that Augustus is sovereign over the whole world; he issues a decree and the whole populace travels here and there in order to participate in the Empire's tax burden. Now, however, we learn not only how the census is related to the unfolding of the angel's words, but also that a still higher purpose is at work than that of the emperor.

Like the others, Joseph travels to his "own town" — a phrase clarified in the hendiadys of 2:4 (house and family) to mean "ancestral town" or "place of origin." This is the first time in the Lukan account of Jesus' birth that Joseph *does* anything, though even here he is introduced to us primarily in his relationship to Mary and in his inherited status as a Davidide (cf. 1:27).

---

21. Braund, *Augustus,* §66.

22. One might have expected the Greek form Σεβαστός, "venerable" or "revered"; as *narrator,* Luke may have avoided the Greek term, choosing instead the less obvious Latinism (Αὐγοῦστος), so as to avoid the possibility of thus affirming the sacred connotation of the ruler's name (cf. R. L. B. Morris, "Why ΑΥΓΟΥΣΤΟΣ?").

23. πᾶσαν τὴν οἰκουμένην. Οἰκουμένη can be used in a hyperbolic way to connote the Roman Empire (BAGD 561), as here and in Acts 24:5.

24. Cf. Origen *Luc.* 11; Bede *Luc.* 1.

25. Cf. London Papyrus 904:20-21, which calls for registration by household in Egypt (dated in 104 C.E.).

Both the description of his journey as a *"going up"*[26] and the designation of his destination as "the city of David" invite the reader to speculate that he is traveling to Jerusalem.[27] Luke upsets such expectations by identifying Joseph's destination and identifying the city of David as Bethlehem. In this narrative aside, Luke intrudes briefly to render explicit that Joseph is fulfilling the Scriptures and, thus, fulfilling God's own purpose.

The divine purpose at work here has already been made transparent. In his announcement of Jesus' birth, Gabriel had noted that Jesus would be given the throne of his ancestor David (1:32, 35), and these sentiments were echoed in Zechariah's Song (1:69, 78). Moreover, Luke had introduced Joseph as "of the house of David" (1:27). The present passage indicates how the program introduced by the angel, itself an echo of the divine purpose expressed in 2 Sam 7:12-16, is fulfilled. Like David, Jesus hails from Bethlehem (cf. 1 Sam 16; 17:12-16, 58); born in Bethlehem, he is of the house of David. One also hears in the background of Luke's account an echo of Mic 5:2:

> But you, O Bethlehem of Ephrathah,
>> who are one of the little clans of Judah,
> from you shall come forth for me
>> one who is to rule in Israel. . . .

In 1:32-33, Gabriel notes that Jesus will rule over Israel forever, and now Luke informs his audience that a descendant of David has come to the city of David. Without a doubt, this repertoire of elements has been drawn in part from Mic 5:2, with the result that Luke again underscores how the story of Jesus is nothing less than the continuation of God's story of redemptive interaction with his people, that the unfolding narrative of Jesus' appearance is the expression of his salvific purpose.

As often in biblical narrative, then, we find here a conjunction of intentions. On one level, Joseph's journey is the consequence of the almighty decree of Augustus. On another, even the universal rule of Augustus is conceived as subordinate to another purpose, the aim of God. One may call this ironic, as if Rome is made unwittingly to serve a still greater Sovereign. But it is also prophetic, for it reveals the provisional nature of even Roman rule.

That Mary accompanies Joseph is likely a consequence of their cohabitation.[28] Even though Luke describes her only as betrothed to Joseph, this

---

26. ἀναβαίνω; NRSV: "went . . . to."

27. The trip to Jerusalem is an ascension, and Luke's term is used with regard to the journey to Jerusalem and the temple; cf., e.g., Pss 22:3; 122:1-5; Isa 2:2-3; 7:1; Luke 2:42; 18:31; 19:28. Moreover, Jerusalem is known in the Scriptures as the "city of David" (e.g., 2 Sam 5:7, 9).

28. It may be that she was required to register, too, but this is uncertain.

may be due simply to their marriage not having yet been consummated owing to her advanced pregnancy. In this case, the description of Mary serves primarily as a reminder of key elements of the narrative thus far: She is pregnant, but not via natural means; and we are awaiting the birth of the promised son.

6-7 With simplicity and economy of language, Luke records the "fulfillment of the days"[29] — no doubt a double entente designed to signify the realization of Gabriel's announcement (1:31) and the conclusion of the gestation period (cf. 1:57; Gen 25:24). The events are progressing according to the divine plan. The present account departs from its analogues, however, in specifying that this is Mary's "firstborn," a detail of some significance in its narrative co-text. First, this supports Mary's claim of virginity at the time of her conception (1:34) and vouches for the fact that this son is the fulfillment of the angel's announcement. Second, it designates Jesus as the possessor of the right of inheritance given the firstborn in Exod 13:2; Num 3:12-13; 18:15-16; Deut 21:15-17. What might Jesus inherit? Luke has consistently portrayed Joseph as possessing one quality of interest — namely, his birthright. He is of the house of David, and it is this that he will pass on to Jesus. Finally, in a manner typical of Luke, this seemingly trivial element introduces into the narrative at an early point a factor that will have a more developed role a bit later. In this case, "firstborn son" in 2:7 prepares for Mary's fulfillment of the law in 2:23.

Luke's account is curious for its attention to the care given the child upon its birth. The "bands of cloth" and "manger" mentioned here come in for development in 2:12, 16, so we will delay any additional discussion of them until 2:12.

Also peculiar is Luke's reference to the cause for laying the newborn child in a manger: "because there was no place for them in the guest room." The narrator apparently pictures Joseph and Mary arriving in Bethlehem and staying for some time before the delivery of Mary's baby (cf. 2:6: "while they were there"), not their inability to locate lodging on the night of their arrival resulting in the birth of the child in a stable. The term Luke employs here for *"guest room"* is often translated in English as "inn."[30] However, the same term appears in 22:11 with the meaning "guest room," and the verbal form[31] occurs in 9:12 and 19:7 with the sense of "find lodging" or "be a guest." Moreover, in 10:34, where a commercial inn is clearly demanded by the text, Luke draws on different vocabulary.[32] It is doubtful whether a com-

---

29. ἐπλήσθησαν αἱ ἡμέραι; NRSV: "the time came."
30. κατάλυμα; so the NRSV.
31. καταλύω.
32. πανδοχεῖον; cf. πανδοχεύς ("innkeeper") in 10:35.

mercial inn actually existed in Bethlehem, which stood on no major roads. It may be that Luke has in mind a "khan or caravansary where large groups of travelers found shelter under one roof,"[33] but this does not help our understanding of Mary's placing the child in a manger. That "guest room" is the more plausible meaning here is urged by the realization that in peasant homes in the ancient Near East family and animals slept in one enclosed space, with the animals located on a lower level. Mary and Joseph, then, would have been the guests of family or friends, but their home would have been so overcrowded that the baby was placed in a feeding trough.[34]

2.5.2. The Angelic Message and the Shepherds (2:8-20)

8 *In that region there were shepherds living in the fields, keeping watch over their flock by night.* 9 *Then an angel of the Lord stood before them, and the glory of the Lord shone around them, and they were terrified.* 10 *But the angel said to them, "Do not be afraid; for see — I am bringing you good news of great joy for all the people:* 11 *to you is born this day in the city of David a Savior, who is the Messiah, the Lord.* 12 *This will be a sign for you: you will find a child wrapped in bands of cloth and lying in a manger."* 13 *And suddenly there was with the angel a multitude of the heavenly host, praising God and saying,*

14 *"Glory to God in the highest heaven,*
   and on earth peace among those whom he favors!"[35]

15 *When the angels had left them and gone into heaven, the shepherds said to one another, "Let us go now to Bethlehem and see this thing that has taken place, which the Lord has made known to us."* 16 *So they went with haste and found Mary and Joseph, and the child lying in the manger.* 17 *When they saw this, they made known what had been told them about this child;* 18 *and all who heard it were amazed at what the shepherds told them.* 19 *But Mary treasured all these words and pondered them in her heart.* 20 *The shepherds returned, glorifying and praising God for all they had heard and seen, as it had been told them.*

---

33. Trudinger, "Luke 2:7"; R. E. Brown, *Birth,* 400 (who prefers the ambiguous translation "lodging").

34. Bailey, "Manger." Cf. Byrne, "Inn"; Witherington, "Birth of Jesus," 69-70; Kerr, "No Room"; Legrand, "Christmas," 308-9.

35. ℵ² B² L Θ Ξ Ψ et al. read the nominative form, εὐδοκία — thus, "goodwill toward people." Metzger (*Textual Commentary,* 133) regards the use of the genitive as the more difficult reading, presumably because it incorporates a Semitic idiom that seems odd in Greek. The genitive also has far better support in the manuscript tradition.

This pericope is framed by references to the shepherds (2:8, 20). Though their introduction may seem abrupt, they have been anticipated in implicit ways by the continued mention of David (shepherd-cum-king — 1 Kings 16:11-13; cf. 1:27, 32, 69; 2:4 [2x])[36] and of the lowly (1:52). This account is also tied to the preceding material by geographical ("in that region" — 2:8) and temporal ("this day"[37] — 2:11) markers.

The purpose of this section is to provide interpretive responses to the birth of the promised son. In this it parallels the responses to John's birth and related extraordinary phenomena in 1:58-79. And it anticipates subsequent material in the Gospel, where we find that Luke regularly includes in his narration of the miraculous (e.g., 13:10-17) and the serendipitous (e.g., 15:1-32) the element of response.[38] Although contemplation of the significance of God's machinations is necessary (2:19), enough is apparent already to produce responses of joy and praise. Having "heard and seen" just "as it had been told them," the shepherds glorify God. Luke's audience has been told by the narrator even more than the shepherds have heard; moreover, thus far everything has happened "as it had been told"; how will they/we respond?

The pivotal function of the shepherds invites investigation of their larger role, and in order to understand this, one must look to their status in society.[39] Shepherds in an agrarian society may have small landholdings, but these would be inadequate to meet the demands of their own families, the needs of their own agricultural pursuits, and the burden of taxation. As a result, they might hire themselves out to work for wages. They were, then, peasants, located toward the bottom of the scale of power and privilege.[40] That they

---

36. This is not to suggest any messianic link in the mention of shepherds in the region of Bethlehem. R. E. Brown (*Birth*, 421-24) proposes that מגדל-עדר ("tower of the flock"), from Gen 35:21; Mic 4:8, which may link the tower with the region of Bethlehem, together with the tradition found in *Tg. Ps.-J.* Gen 35:21 that the King Messiah would be revealed from the tower of the flock, lies in the background of the introduction of the shepherds here; cf. Laurentin, *Struktur und Theologie*, 99-102. But in all of the texts in question the connection to Bethlehem is at best tenuous. See further Fitzmyer, 1:396; Bock, *Proclamation*, 76-77.

37. That is, "today"; σήμερον.

38. See Green, "Daughter of Abraham," 644.

39. See above, Figure One, p. 60. Earlier commentators drew attention to the shepherds as members of a despised trade, ritually unclean — e.g., Godet, 1:130; Jeremias, *Jerusalem*, 303-12 — but this is doubtful. The positive image (both literal and metaphorical) of sheep and shepherd in Israel's Scriptures as well as Philo's affirming mention of the Jewish people as graziers, stock-breeders, and shepherds (*Spec. Leg.* 1.133, 136) imperil any negative evaluation of shepherds as a group on purity grounds during the era in question. Moreover, it is hard to imagine that a vocation on which the Jewish cult and Jerusalem temple were so heavily dependent — requiring, e.g., some 30,000 lambs for Passover (cf. Sanders, *Judaism*, 136) — would be labeled unclean by those very institutions.

40. See Lenski, *Power and Privilege*, 266-78.

are here cast in this dress is unmistakable, for the same contrast introduced in Mary's Song — the enthroned versus the lowly (1:52) — is represented here: Augustus the Emperor and Quirinius on one hand (2:1-2), the shepherds on the other.[41] As the recipients of a divine visitation, the shepherds are highly esteemed in the world of the birth narrative. This is not an esteem shared by the rulers of 2:1-2; their power is relativized and they receive no news of this divine intervention. Good news comes to peasants, not rulers; the lowly are lifted up.[42]

The other primary characters of this account are the angels. The "angel of the Lord" (2:9) is probably a reference to the personal servant of God already known to us, Gabriel (1:11, 19, 26), but here he is joined by "a multitude of the heavenly host" (2:13). Given the respect assigned earlier to the Jerusalem temple and particularly to its sanctuary as the *axis mundi* — the meeting place between the heavenly and the earthly, the divine and the human — this appearance of the divine glory is remarkable. God's glory, normally associated with the temple, is now manifest on a farm! At the birth of his son, God has compromised (in a proleptic way) the socio-religious importance of the temple as the culture center of the world of Israel. Luke thus puts us on notice that the new world coming is of a radically different shape than the former one, that questions of holiness and purity must be asked and addressed in different ways, and that status and issues of values must be reexamined afresh.

The angels add their voices to those already raised on God's behalf, interpreting the event of Jesus' birth from a heavenly perspective. In doing so, they continue to point ever more boldly in the direction of the universal implications of Jesus' coming.[43] Inklings of the specific embracing of Jew *and Gentile* have been present already (e.g., 1:55, 73, 78-79), and this motif was pushed to the fore in the reference to the worldwide census in 2:1-3. Now, according to the divine messengers, good news is "for all the people" (2:10), peace has come "on earth" (2:14).

---

41. Note also the general opposition between the peasant stratum of a society and the urban elite — cf. Wolf, *Peasants;* Shanin, ed., *Peasant Societies;* Seymour-Smith, *Anthropology,* 133, 219-21.

42. See the simplicity of the shepherds in Giorgine's *The Adoration of the Shepherds (ca.* 1508), especially when compared to the wealth of the shepherds and their gifts in other Renaissance art.

43. That a universalism is already at work here is denied by many scholars, who see the focus still more narrowly on Jesus as the Jewish Messiah (e.g., Tannehill, *Narrative Unity,* 1:38 — who nevertheless notes that "this birth is not just a family affair") and on the recipients of good news as the Jewish people (e.g., S. G. Wilson, *Gentiles,* 34-35; Nolland, 1:106-7). Cf., however, Petzke, 52: "Die verkündigte große Freude ist wahrscheinlich nicht nur auf das Volk Israel bezogen, wenn der universale Zug der Einleitung berücksichtigt wird"; and below.

8-12 Luke's introduction of the shepherds and the angelic message share a number of elements we recognized earlier as constitutive of the form of the birth announcement:[44] the Appearance of an Angel (2:9a), Reaction of Fear (2:9b), Announcement of Birth (2:10-11), and Sign (2:12). This overlap encourages our reading of this announcement in light of those found earlier in Luke, and this surfaces significant modifications. First, unlike the others, which are promissory and oriented to the future birth of a son, this annunciation concerns what has already happened, this very day.[45] Luke is fond of using the word "today" to emphasize *the present* as the time of eschatological fulfillment, *now* as the time of God's gracious deliverance (4:21; 5:26; 19:9; 23:43).

Second, the announcement of birth is directed to shepherds rather than to parents, and thus to "outsiders" in a double sense — that is, to persons who are outside the circle of Jesus' family of origin and are persons of low regard. This portends the considerable ramifications of this birth, which cannot be conceived as a family affair, and may also anticipate the redefinition of "family" in Jesus' ministry.[46]

Third, the shepherds do not learn the child's name from the angel (cf. 1:13, 31); this is not surprising, since he will receive his name from his parents (2:21). However, this does draw our attention to the way in which Jesus is identified — namely, as "Savior," "Messiah," and "Lord." His importance is acclaimed in exalted ways even as his role in God's plan is specified and interpreted.

Of course, by the time these "names" are given Jesus in 2:11, the process of interpreting Jesus' birth in this pericope is well underway. In fact, it is fair to say that in 2:11, the angel *tells* what the narrator has already begun to *show* in 2:9-10. Most interesting is the juxtaposition in 2:8-9 of the darkness of the *night* and the brilliance of the luminous glory of the Lord that *shone*. This is the language of epiphany,[47] the visible manifestation of the power of God certifying the presence of God himself in the coming of this child.[48] But it is also reminiscent of the last lines of Zechariah's Song: "the dawn from on high will . . . give light to those who sit in darkness. . . ." With the birth of Mary's child, the forecast of 1:78-79 has been realized, the new epoch ushered in. In light of our earlier messianic understanding of those words

---

44. See above, §2.

45. ἐτέχθη ὑμῖν σήμερον.

46. See Luke 8:19-21; 9:57-62; 12:51-53; 14:26.

47. Cf. the use of ἐφίστημι in 2:9; Acts 12:7; 13:11. Περιλάμπω appears only here and Acts 26:13 in the NT.

48. See Burge, "Glory," 269; Kittel, "δόξα in the LXX and Hellenistic Apocrypha," 244.

from Zechariah's Song, 2:8-9 launches the identification of Jesus as Messiah upon his birth.[49]

Another hermeneutical connection is made between 2:9 and 2:10, where the shepherds are told to trade their "great fear" for "great joy."[50] Responses of fear to the divine presence are expected (cf. 1:12), but Luke's choice of terms[51] emphasizes that this is especially the occasion for responses appropriate to the advent of God's dominion (cf. 1:14, 28, 47, 58).

"Great joy" is in order because of "good news." Here, as well as in the titles to come in 2:11, we encounter a complex conceptual development in Luke's narrative. Well-known images are seized, exploited, and undergo rebirth in this narrative co-text. Luke straddles the cultural fence. On the one side is the Hellenistic use of "good news" in contexts of victorious battle and the imperial cult. Thus, when Paullus Fabius Maximus, proconsul of Asia, proposed beginning the new year on Augustus's birthday, he observed:

> (It is hard to tell) whether the birthday of the most divine Caesar is a matter of greater pleasure or benefit. We could justly hold it to be equivalent to the beginning of all things . . . ; and he has given a different aspect to the whole world, which blindly would have embraced its own destruction if Caesar had not been born for the common benefit of all.[52]

In their decision to honor Augustus in this way, the provincial assembly explained:

> Whereas the providence which divinely ordered our lives created with zeal and munificence the most perfect good for our lives by producing Augustus and filling him with cirture [sic] for the benefaction of mankind, sending us and those after us a saviour who put an end to war and established all things; and whereas Caesar [sc. Augustus] when he appeared exceeded the hopes of all who had anticipated good tidings : . . ; and whereas the birthday of the god marked for the world the beginning of good tidings through his coming. . . .[53]

Universalistic references in these records such as "for the world" parallel Luke's "for all the people," which should also be understood in a universalistic

---

49. This imagery is taken even further by *Prot. Jas.* 19:2, where the "great light" appears at the birth itself and in the birthplace — an image represented faithfully in Christian iconography of the Nativity.

50. φόβον μέγαν (NRSV: "terrified") + χαρὰν μεγάλην.

51. In addition to "great" fear, note the cognate accusative (BDF §153): ἐφοβήθησαν φόβον μέγαν: "they feared with great fear."

52. ET in Price, *Rituals and Power,* 55.

53. ET in Price, *Rituals and Power,* 54; citing *OGIS* 2:458.

way.[54] The point is that another ruler has been born, one whose dominion is both universal and everlasting (1:33); and, appearing as it does in such close proximity to 2:1, this "good news" must be seen as countering the exalted claims made by and on behalf of Augustus. On the other hand, Luke's notion of "good news" borrows from Isaiah 40–66. There, the herald defines the "good news" as the coming of God (40:9), the salvific reign of God in peace and justice (52:7) on behalf of the outcast (61:1-2). Luke, then, has drawn on language embedded in the culture of Roman religion and legitimation of power and in the culture of Jewish trust in divine intervention and rule. He exploits the socio-politico-religious depth of that language in both cultures, then transforms that language by vesting it in a message about a newborn baby in a manger, spoken to peasant-shepherds.

The same may be said of "Savior," "Messiah," and "Lord" (2:11). First, these titles are all set within the interpretive context of Isa 9:1-7[55] and the prior material in Luke 1 pertaining to the throne of David. In drawing on Isaianic images, Luke shows the importance of this child in exalted, salvation-historical terms, grounding his interpretation of Jesus firmly in Israel's hopes for divine deliverance. This thematic is only emphasized all the more by the angelic reference to "the city of David" (2:11), itself reminiscent of the multitude of ways in which the anticipation of a Davidide has already entered the narrative (1:27, 32, 35, 69, 78-79; 2:4). Whatever else the titles of 2:11 might portend, they at least encapsulate the vision of salvation as transposition, deliverance, and reconciliation already resident in the narrative.

Like "good news," "Savior" would have been familiar along different streams of cultural background, Roman and Jewish.[56] Augustus himself was known as Savior, as were others — gods, rulers, physicians, and so on.[57] In

---

54. Πᾶς ὁ λαός elsewhere in the Third Gospel refers to "those present" and might be understood as "whoever hears/sees" — 3:21; 7:29; 8:47; 9:12-13; 18:43; 19:48; 20:6, 45; 21:38; 24:19. Wilson (*Gentiles*, 34-35) leaves open the possibility that the phrase here refers to "the new people of God, both Jews and Gentiles," but regards it as unlikely. His judgment, however, is influenced overmuch by the use of the singular λαός elsewhere in Luke-Acts to refer to Israel (though cf. Acts 15:14; 18:10) and does not take seriously enough wider co-textual issues in this narrative section and Luke's use of the phrase πᾶς ὁ λαός. Cf 2:31-32, where πάντων τῶν λαῶν clearly refers to Gentiles and Jews — and which Wilson (*Gentiles*, 36-38) regards as universalistic in scope.

55. See the following echoes: the eschatological work of God will embrace "Galilee of the Gentiles" (Isa 9:1; cf. Luke 2:1, 4, 10, 14); "darkness"/"light has shined" (Isa 9:2; cf. Luke 1:78-79; 2:8-9); eschatological joy (Isa 9:3; cf. Luke 2:10, 20); deliverance from the oppressor (Isa 9:3; cf. Luke 1:51-53, 69-75; 2:1-2, 10, 11); a child born "for us," "a son given to us" (Isa 9:6a; cf. Luke 2:7, 11); "authority rests upon his shoulders" + titles (Isa 9:6; cf. Luke 2:11); peace, throne of David, kingdom (Isa 9:7; cf. Luke 1:32-33; 2:11, 14).

56. Cf. Bovon, 125-26.

57. See Fohrer and Foester, "σωτήρ," 1004-12; MM 621.

the LXX, "Savior" is used especially of God, who helps or delivers his people (e.g., 1 Sam 10:19; Isa 45:15, 21; Wis 4:30; 1 Macc 4:30; Sir 51:1), and this is its referent in Luke 1:47. In 2:11 this role has been transferred to Jesus, and subsequently in Luke-Acts "Savior" is a designation of Jesus (Acts 5:31; 13:23). Jesus' birth calls into question both the emperor's status as Savior and the "peace of Augustus" that gave rise to that acclaimed status.

"Lord," too, could be used of the Roman emperor and was used of Augustus;[58] this usage grows out of the more general use of the term in the larger Greco-Roman world to designate one's benefactor or patron. In addition, we have already followed the development of the application of "Lord" from its use with respect to Yahweh (1:11, 17) to its employment with reference to Jesus (1:43, 76). By this we understand that the salvific activity anticipated of Yahweh is being realized in the coming of Jesus. The particular meaning of "Lord" is further conditioned by its close association with "Messiah," with the result that we are to understand them as complementary concepts (cf. 2:26; Acts 2:36). Together, they underscore the exalted status Jesus has in God's purpose and within the community of God's people.[59] The varieties of possible guises in which an agent of salvation might have been anticipated in Judaism at the turn of the era notwithstanding, the meaning of "Messiah" in this context is clearly to be understood along the lines of a Davidic deliverer.

The wealth of these acclamations stands in contrast to the poverty of the sign, a baby in a manger, wrapped in bands of cloth.[60] What sort of sign is this? The sign to the shepherds does not take the form of an extraordinary demonstration of divine power — as was the case with Zechariah's muteness and Elizabeth's conception. Although these three accounts are similar in structure, then, this does not mean that this last sign will function in a way familiar to us from the first two. A different approach is recommended by the appearance of the formula of sign-giving used by Luke but witnessed already in the Scriptures (cf., e.g., Exod 3:12; 1 Sam 2:34; 10:1; Isa 37:30). In these cases, the sign helps to bring out the meaning of the message.[61] In 2:7, 12, 16, this is accomplished by drawing out the significance, via scriptural echoes, of this oxymoron: the Savior–Messiah–Lord wrapped in strips of cloth lying in a feeding trough, "for no king has had a different beginning of existence" than to be "nursed with care in swaddling clothes" (Wis 7:4-5).[62] Moreover, with the coming of the Savior,

---

58. See, e.g., *BGU* 1197:1:15; P.Oxy. 1143.

59. The only analogue in Jewish literature is *Pss. Sol.* 17:32, where χριστὸς κύριος designates a Davidide who reigns over Israel.

60. Laurentin, *Truth of Christmas,* 184.

61. Giblin, "Sign of the Manger," 90-95.

62. Luke 2:12: ἐσπαργανωμένον; Wis 7:4: ἐν σπαργάνοις.

God's people are returned to their sustenance in God, a message that grows out of the echo of Isa 1:3:

> The ox knows its owner,
>> and the donkey its master's manger;[63]
> but Israel does not know me,
>> my people do not understand me.[64]

Because of God's prevenient activity in the birth of his son, Israel may again find its way to God.[65] Thus, the "sign" has a christological function, adding interpretive detail to the "names" given the child in 2:11. Even more important, though, is the *theological* role of the sign, laying bare God's gracious act to embrace anew, through this child, his people.

13-14 The theocentric focus of this encounter and its message comes to the fore in the sudden appearance of "a multitude of the heavenly host, praising God." Here and throughout the Gospel of Luke, responses to the miraculous take the form of praising *God*.[66] In this instance, the reaction is by the heavenly host, a reference to God's royal entourage.[67] Through their behavior, they demonstrate the appropriate response to God's gracious intervention to bring a Savior; indeed, note that the "glory" of the angelic choir in 2:13-14 is repeated by the shepherds in 2:20.

Their words can be set in parallel —

> "Glory to God in the highest heaven;
> on earth peace among those whom he favors!" —

with the following elements set in apposition: glory//peace, in the highest heaven//on earth, and to God//among those whom he favors.[68] It may be that the

63. LXX: φάτνη (as in Luke 2:7, 12, 16); NRSV: "crib."

64. LXX adds με.

65. The connection between the "sign" in Luke 2:12 and this Isaianic text is long-standing in Christian iconography, which regularly locates oxen and donkeys at the scene of the nativity in spite of their absence in Matthew and Luke's birth accounts. Cf. *Gospel of Pseudo-Matthew* 14.

66. Though cf. 17:15-16, where praising God is set in apposition with thanking Jesus.

67. Cf. 1 Kgs 22:19; Neh 9:6; Dan 7:10; 1QH 3:22.

68. This last phrase, ἐν ἀνθρώποις εὐδοκίας, has proven difficult largely (as with the rest of 2:14) because of the lack of syntactical data. The recent attempt by R. S. Kilpatrick ("Luke 2.14") to reckon with this problem led him to rank a translation like that represented in the NRSV (i.e., "among people of God's good pleasure") as "doubtful." However, Kilpatrick was working only with the criterion of syntax, while also assuming that 2:14 should represent good Greek idiom. As the discussion has indicated, the Greek is cryptic to a fault, with the most likely analogues located in texts of Semitic origin. See

best way to make sense of the relationship between these two lines is to interpret them as indicatives: "There is glory . . ." and "there is peace. . . ."[69] Because of the similarity between this hymn and the Song of Zechariah (especially 1:68, 79), and the larger co-textual emphasis on response to God's initiative, however, it may be better to see line one as an invitation to join in glorifying God because the divine activity resulting in the birth of his son has brought peace.[70] Two theological affirmations resident in the angelic chorus deserve comment. First, "on earth peace" meshes with the hope for shalom, peace with justice, universal healing, found in the Scriptures. Moreover, it is explicitly related to the dominion of God and the coming of salvation as "good news" in a text like Isa 52:7. And this is reminiscent of the collage of images gathered in angelic and prophetic voices that together describe the coming of Jesus (e.g., 1:33, 69-75; 2:10-11). The Isaianic hope of universal healing lies behind the interpretation of Jesus' significance here. This means, secondly, that the expression "those whom he favors" cannot be limited to its application to Israel only. Rather, shalom for Israel is tied up with shalom for the cosmos. Hence, although "whom he favors" is an affirmation of gracious election on God's part, that graciousness extends to humanity. It should not be read in an exclusive sense — that is, not peace *only* to a select group whom he favors — but in an inclusive way: In the birth of this child, God's mercy has fallen on the world.[71]

15-20   Luke records in each case of angelic visitation the immediate response of the recipient. Zechariah expresses unbelief (1:18, 20). Mary embraces God's aim, proclaims herself his servant, and journeys to her kinswoman's home (1:38-40). How will the shepherds respond? Like Zechariah? Mary? In fact, their response to the "good news" is delayed; first, like Mary, they follow through on the "sign" given them by an angel of the Lord. In narrating the conversation between the shepherds (2:15), Luke leaves two gaps in the account — gaps, however, that by now are easily filled in by the attentive reader. First, the angel speaks of the "city of David," but the shepherds discuss a trip to Bethlehem. As we have seen, this is not a natural equation, but it is one for which we have been prepared (2:4). Second, the shepherds attribute to "the Lord" what was spoken to them by "an angel of the Lord" (2:9-10, 15). This equation, too, has precedent in the Lukan narrative, for in her greeting to Mary, Elizabeth makes the same identification (1:26, 45). In this way, we gain another witness authenticating the message of the angel in 2:10-11; this was the Lord himself speaking through his personal servant.

Fitzmyer, "Peace upon Earth"; and the summary in Fitzmyer, 1:411-12; Wolters, *"ANTHRŌPOI EUDOKIAS"* (with reference to 4Q416).

69. See Jeremias, "ἄνθρωποι εὐδοκίας (Lc 2.14)," 19.
70. Cf. Luke, "Luke 2:14."
71. Cf. P. R. Berger, "Lk 2:14."

After getting Mary to Bethlehem (2:4-5), Joseph fades again into the background. His only role in Luke's account is to certify Jesus' status as son of David, born in Bethlehem. Consequently, now the shepherds behave as did Mary, going "with haste" (1:39; 2:16). And when they arrive at their destination, they find "Mary and Joseph" — this in a culture where whose name is listed first is of social significance.

Importantly, they also find, "as it had been told them" (2:20), "the child lying in a manger." In this way, the angel's message has been authenticated and the significance of the child confirmed.[72]

Only now is the anticipated response forthcoming, but the particular nature of the shepherds' reaction leads to other responses. Thus: the shepherds testified — 2:17; all who heard were amazed — 2:18; Mary treasured and pondered these words — 2:19; and the shepherds returned, glorifying and praising God — 2:20. That is, the shepherds become, together with Anna (2:38), the first evangelists of Luke-Acts. As such, they serve an important function in the narrative. It cannot be overlooked that the *content* of their report is not given, only *that* they made known what had been told them.[73] Why? Because we already know what they have been told. The narrator has already done for us what the shepherds do for the recipients of the shepherds' report. How will we respond?

Amazement is an expected response to a display of the supernatural (1:21, 63-66; cf. 2:33). It will continue to be so in the ensuing narrative (4:22; 8:25; 9:43; 11:14; 24:12, 41). Although not characterized as necessarily negative in tone, "amazement" is not tantamount to faith and is no guarantee that a correct understanding of the extraordinary has or will be reached. This is the response of the undifferentiated crowds in 2:18, but not of Mary. For her, more reflection is needed in order to appreciate fully the meaning of this concurrence of events, and her pondering is with a view to hitting on the right meaning of these things. Even in the presence of these exalted and direct affirmations of the identity of the newborn child, then, contemplation of what God is doing in and through these events continues.

2.6. THE PRESENTATION OF JESUS IN THE TEMPLE (2:21-39)

The events following the arrival of a firstborn son (2:7) are narrated in a way that combines the ordinary and expected (e.g., circumcision, naming, presentation) with the extraordinary (prophetic responses of Simeon and Anna). Even the mundane provides arenas in which the divine purpose may be realized.

72. See above on 2:12.
73. Kremer, 38.

This narrative section, focused on the recognition and affirmation of Jesus as God's agent of redemption by eminently reliable persons, is framed by demonstrations of Mary and Joseph's obedience to God (2:21, 22, 23-24, 39) and by reports of the journey of the family "up to Jerusalem" and back to "their own town of Nazareth" (2:22, 39). This concern with keeping the law is of obvious importance, repeated as it is throughout the account. Here, the law functions in concert with the Holy Spirit (2:25, 26, 27).[1] Behind both, law and Spirit, stands the design of Yahweh, who has choreographed this encounter.

Throughout, the narrative spotlight remains on Jesus. Even Mary's purification becomes Jesus' presentation (2:22-24), and the time devoted to providing character references for Simeon (2:25-27) and Anna (2:36-37) underscores the veracity of their claims about Jesus. Similarly, Simeon turns to address Mary directly (2:34-35), but his words to her concern Jesus. The child does nothing, but all words and deeds are oriented around him.

Then again, the spotlight shines on Jesus only in a qualified sense, for Jesus is repeatedly characterized in relation to God. He is presented to the Lord (2:22), and identified as "the Lord's Messiah" (2:26) and God's salvation (2:30). Moreover, the sight of the child is enough to cause both Simeon and Anna to praise God (2:28, 38). This narrative remains thoroughly theocentric.

As elsewhere in the birth narrative, so here one recognizes a parallelism between the stories of John and Jesus.[2] There are similarities, but also an important distinction: Thus far, John has been presented in light of his *future* significance (e.g., 1:66), but Jesus attracts responses regarding what is already the case (2:29; cf. 1:46-55; 2:10-11). With the conception, birth, and now presentation of Jesus, salvation has already come.

To whom salvation has come is key to this narrative section. With Jesus' parents, Simeon, and Anna, obedience and piety are measured in familiar, Jewish terms, and the hopes of Simeon and Anna focus on the consolation of Israel. But Simeon expressly anticipates a division within Israel — surely a significant qualification of nationalistic hopes. And he prophesies that the Gentiles will in some way be encompassed in divine redemption. This is not in itself surprising; through the OT one can hear an oft-repeated chorus: the Gentiles will come to Israel, acknowledging that the God of Israel is the true God. The temple itself would serve as the locus of this gathering.[3] Already

---

1. *Contra* Laurentin, *Truth of Christmas.* Nor should we follow Witherington (*Women in the Earliest Churches,* 140), who proposes that in his comparison of Simeon and Anna Luke allows "the OT prophetic order satisfied to see the Messiah" to pass away in favor of "the NT proselytizing plan that goes forth proclaiming the new thing God is doing."

2. See above, §1.

3. See *Pss. Sol.* 17:34-35; Jeremias, *Jesus' Promise,* 57-62; McKnight, *Light among the Nations,* 47-48.

in the promise to Abraham (e.g., Gen 17:4; cf. 1:55, 73),[4] and in the Isaianic vision expressly echoed in 2:29-32,[5] the fates of those within and outside Israel are related. What is problematic is the proleptic announcement of division: How can God's "salvation" be opposed by God's own people?

2.6.1. The Circumcision and Presentation of Jesus (2:21-24)

21 *After eight days had passed, it was time to circumcise the child; and he was called Jesus, the name given by the angel before he was conceived in the womb.*

22 *When the time came for their purification according to the law of Moses, they brought him up to Jerusalem to present him to the Lord* 23 *(as it is written in the law of the Lord, "Every firstborn male shall be designated as holy to the Lord"),* 24 *and they offered a sacrifice according to what is stated in the law of the Lord, "a pair of turtledoves or two young pigeons."*

Luke presents these actions — circumcision, naming, purification, presentation, consecration — as the normal flow of events following the birth of a firstborn son in a Jewish family. This is remarkable, since from a strictly historical point of view this passage bristles with difficulties. Why wait until the *eighth* day to name the child? Why speak of *their* purification, when the purity law applied only to Mary? Why relate *presentation* (2:22b) to a scriptural text concerned with *consecration* and *redemption?* Indeed, why mention *presentation* at all? Attempts to unravel these historical tangles aside,[6] Luke's focus remains clear. He presents Jesus' family as obedient to the Lord, unquestionably pious. Thus: (1) they circumcise Jesus on the eighth day (Gen 17:9-14; Lev 12:3; *m. Šabb.* 18:3); (2) they give the child the name mandated by Gabriel (1:31); and they act according to the law with regard to (3) purity following childbirth (Leviticus 12), (4) bringing Jesus to Jerusalem (Exod 13:2, 12, 15) and (5) offering the sacrifice for Mary's purification (Lev 12:8). In effect, Luke highlights not *what* they do but *why* they do it, and the *results* of their actions: (1) Their piety is disclosed in the narrative equivalent of 1:6;[7] and (2) the child is called Jesus (1:31 → 2:21) and designated "holy" (1:35 → 2:23). Hence, these "normal" occurrences are laden with narrative purpose,

---

4. See also the expansive use of the Abrahamic material documented above, §2.

5. Cf. Isa 40:5; 42:6; 46:13; 49:6; 52:9-10.

6. See, e.g., Bo Reicke, "Jesus, Simeon, and Anna," 97-100; Bock, *Proclamation,* 83-84.

7. In the case of Zechariah and Elizabeth, Luke *tells* of their righteousness; with regard to Mary and Joseph, he *shows*.

redirecting attention to the plan of God, revealing again that Mary and Joseph are willing supporters of God's aim, and certifying that Jesus will operate from within God's purpose.

Gabriel had instructed that the boy should be called "Jesus," that he would be holy, and that he would be called "Son of God" (1:31, 35). Luke accents the first by noting explicitly the angel's words at the annunciation to Mary. He accents the second in his reference to the law in 2:23. This is not a direct quotation of any scriptural passage, but it draws together Exod 13:2, 12, 15 — *to which Luke has added:* "shall be designated as holy." In this way he shows not only the fulfillment of the angel's words, but also how obedience to the angel and to the law has brought about that fulfillment.[8]

The material in 2:22-24 is tied to 2:21 (and 2:6) by parallel temporal phrases marking the fulfillment of time.[9] Verse 22a and 2:24 form an *inclusio* around this subsection, suggesting that the real purpose for the trip to Jerusalem is related to Jesus' being presented to the Lord (2:22b-23). Here Luke portrays Mary as faithful to the law, and his family as not wealthy.

Concerns with purity are focused on actions that blur, confuse, or contradict perceived boundaries, such as those between one group of animal and another, the threshold leading from one stage of life to another, or the emission of bodily fluids.[10] Childbirth constitutes a primary transformation of status and issues of purity related to it are regulated by the law, which is especially concerned with the matter of postpartum discharges (Leviticus 12). Following the birth of a son, the mother was impure for one week after which she was bathed as a means of purification. Following this, she remained at a secondary level of impurity for thirty-three days, during which time she could touch nothing holy. She then presented an offering — if she were poor, two turtledoves or two pigeons (Lev 12:8; cf. 12:6).

Again, though, the weight of emphasis does not fall on Mary as much as on Jesus. No necessary connection exists between the presentation of Jesus as conceived by 2:22b and the related reference to Exodus 13 (cf. Exod 34:19-20; Num 18:15-16; Neh 10:35-36). The latter is concerned with the redemption of firstborn sons from priestly service. By way of supporting the priesthood, firstborn sons were "redeemed" from priestly service by the

---

8. On the issue of waiting until the time of circumcision to name the child, see above on 1:59-61.

9. Thus:

2:6:	ἐκεῖ ἐπλήσθησαν αἱ ἡμέραι		τοῦ τεκτεῖν	αὐτήν
2:21:	καὶ ὅτε ἐπλήσθησαν	ἡμέραι ὀκτὼ	τοῦ περιτεμεῖν	αὐτόν
2:22:	καὶ ὅτε ἐπλήσθησαν αἱ ἡμέραι		τοῦ καθαρισμοῦ	αὐτῶν

10. See Douglas, *Purity and Danger,* 114-28; *idem, Implicit Meanings,* 9-26, 27-46, 47-59, 60-72, 261-73.

payment of five shekels. Such payment is not mentioned here, presumably in order to accentuate through economy of language what is mentioned — that is, Jesus' presentation to the Lord. In this, Luke's narrative seems to have been guided by continued reverberations from the story of Samuel, who ". . . is given to the Lord" (esp. 1 Sam 1:11, 21-28).

2.6.2. *The Manifestation of Jesus to Simeon (2:25-35)*

> 25 *Now there was a man in Jerusalem whose name was Simeon; this man was righteous and devout, looking forward to the consolation of Israel, and the Holy Spirit rested on him.* 26 *It had been revealed to him by the Holy Spirit that he would not see death before he had seen the Lord's Messiah.* 27 *Guided by the Spirit,*[11] *Simeon came into the temple; and when the parents brought in the child Jesus, to do for him what was customary under the law,* 28 *Simeon took him in his arms and praised God, saying,*
>
> 29 *"Master, now you are dismissing your servant in peace,*
> *according to your word;*
> 30 *for my eyes have seen your salvation,*
> 31 *which you have prepared in the presence of all peoples,*
> 32 *a light for revelation to the Gentiles*
> *and for glory to your people Israel."*
>
> 33 *And the child's father*[12] *and mother were amazed at what was being said about him.* 34 *Then Simeon blessed them and said to his mother Mary, "This child is destined for the falling and rising of many in Israel, and to be a sign that will be opposed* 35 *so that the inner thoughts of many will be revealed — and a sword will pierce your own soul too."*

Following the birth, circumcision, and naming of John, his significance was outlined in Zechariah's Song (1:68-79) — that Spirit-enabled, prophetic utterance (1:67) of a righteous man associated with the temple (1:5-6). In the same way, following the birth, circumcision, and naming of Jesus, his significance is outlined, both in Simeon's Song (1:29-32) and in the forward-looking message to Mary in 1:34-35. Moreover, as with Zechariah, so with Simeon,

---

11. ἐν τῷ πνεύματι; NRSV margin: "In the Spirit."
12. A number of witnesses (A Θ Ψ et al.) read Ἰωσήφ rather than ὁ πατὴρ αὐτοῦ (i.e., "Joseph" rather than "his father"), an apparent concession to belief in the virginal conception (cf. 3:23). The addition of αὐτοῦ following ἡ μήτηρ (thus, "his mother") was likely motivated by stylistic concerns, in balance with ὁ πατὴρ αὐτοῦ in ℵ L, or by an attempt to specify Mary as Jesus' parent as opposed to Joseph in those texts that read Ἰωσήφ (A Θ Ψ 053 et al.).

we have to do with a righteous man associated with the temple who acts under the inspiration of the Holy Spirit (2:25-27).

These parallels are obvious, as is the further resemblance between Simeon and Anna, evident already in their introductions:

"Now there was a man in Jerusalem whose name was Simeon . . ." (2:25)

"There was also Anna, a prophet . . ." (2:36).[13]

In similar ways, Luke establishes the credibility of these two witnesses to the child: Note their exemplary piety (2:25-27; 2:36-37), their anticipation of redemption (2:25; 2:38), and their responses of praise to God (2:28, 38). Luke has thus portrayed Simeon and Anna as male-female counterparts, who represent the best of expectant Israel and testify to the central place Jesus already occupies in God's redemptive plan.

This pericope shares a more far-reaching, structural similarity with the Lukan hymns. Like those of Mary (1:46-55) and Zechariah (1:68-79), it is the finale in a narrative cycle leading from *promise* to *fulfillment* to *response* of praise.[14] Indeed, the pattern of conceptual repetition here operates on three levels:

(1) Simeon looks forward to the consolation of Israel (v 25)
     Simeon is informed that he will see the Lord's Messiah (v 26)
     Simeon sees God's instrument of salvation (v 30)
(2) Simeon would not see death before seeing the Messiah (v 26)
     Simeon is now ready to die (v 29)
(3) it had been revealed to him by the Holy Spirit (v 26)
     it has happened according to the word of the Lord (v 29)

These parallels demonstrate not only how literally the promise-fulfillment cycle is represented by Luke, but also how closely tied to its context Simeon's Song is. Moreover, this juxtaposition of phrases indicates how Luke can use a variety of images to refer to what are fundamentally the same phenomena — compare, for example, the apparent equivalence between "consolation of Israel" and the advent of "the Lord's Messiah," and between what is revealed by the Holy Spirit and the word of the Lord.

With regard to the larger narrative cycle oriented around the promise of a son to Mary, the present pericope functions as a continuation of the responses to that birth. Like those reported in 2:8-20, these responses are interpretive in character, confirming earlier expectations regarding the position

13. This word order follows more closely the Greek; NRSV: "a prophet, Anna."
14. Farris, *Hymns,* 101.

of this child in God's purpose, unveiling additional information about his role, and introducing further prospects for narrative development. In particular, Simeon's prophetic utterances surface Luke's emphasis on the universality of the effects of Jesus' mission. Simeon also introduces in the clearest way thus far the motif of conflict that will pervade the Lukan narrative. Not all will take the side of God's salvific purpose; some, in fact, will oppose Jesus, God's salvific instrument.

One hears in this narrative subsection a symphony of echoes to earlier material — some to the OT, others to earlier material in the Third Gospel. This passage borrows heavily from the Isaianic vision of the advent of God's consolation and the mission of the Servant in Isaiah 40–66.[15] The echoes from within Luke 1–2, being more proximate, are the more resonant:

- exemplary piety — 1:5-6; 2:22-24; 2:25-27
- presence and inspiration of the Holy Spirit — 1:15, 35, 41, 67; 2:25-27
- hope for deliverance — 1:51-53, 68-75 et passim; 2:25
- joy, exultation, praise — 1:14, 28, 44, 47, 68; 2:10, 28-29
- Lord/Master and slave — 1:38, 47-48; 2:29
- peace — 1:79; 2:14, 29
- Savior, salvation, instrument of salvation — 1:47, 69, 71, 77; 2:11, 30
- advance preparation — 1:17, 76; 2:31
- universalism — 1:55, 73; 2:1-14, 31-32
- dawning, light — 1:78-79; 2:9, 32
- sifting of Israel — 1:16, (20); 2:34-35
- social transposition — 1:51-53; 2:34

These points of similarity indicate how Luke has been building up a portrait of Jesus' mission and his role in God's purpose.[16] Careful attention to these elements, their repetition, and the points at which they are introduced also suggests that Luke's depiction of the nature of Jesus' mission and its consequences is not static but growing, being molded continually by the narrative. The most obvious emphases now coming to the fore are the universalistic reach of God's salvation in Jesus and the opposition his mission will engender.

This may be why the focal point of the characterization of Simeon in this narrative is his believability. In multiple ways — a character reference (from the unimpeachable narrator) supporting his piety, his status as an agent of the Holy Spirit, his physical location in the Jerusalem temple, and his capacity to borrow heavily from Isaiah to express his praise to God — Simeon is presented as a reliable witness.

15. Cf. Grogan, "Light and the Stone."
16. See Tannehill, *Narrative Unity,* 1:42-43.

25-26 Luke is fond of presenting compact "character references" (cf. 1:5-6).[17] This places Simeon in the company of those who act in unexpected or extraordinary ways, or whose testimony is required for a momentous turn in the narrative. That Simeon serves in this role is underscored by Luke's introduction of Simeon as "devout."[18] Simeon's revelatory message may appear to compromise the status of Israel as God's people, but his is a message of one who is working from within the historic purpose of Israel's God.

What is more, he is working from within the hopes of Israel for deliverance from its oppressors. This locates Simeon in the company of a member of the Jewish council (Joseph — 23:50-51); far from being a relative outsider, Simeon personifies faithful and expectant Israel. "Looking forward"[19] is used by Luke in contexts of eschatological anticipation here as well as in Luke 2:38; 12:36; 23:51; Acts 24:15, but "consolation" is used in the sense of the restoration of Israel under the reign of God only here in Luke-Acts.[20] Undoubtedly, then, this usage rests on the Isaianic context that is otherwise resoundingly echoed in Simeon's Song.[21] This anticipation is theocentric, emphasizing God's intervention to deliver Israel from its enemies and so to usher in the epoch of peace under the peaceful, just dominion of God.

Finally, Simeon is portrayed as one on whom the Holy Spirit rested, thus adding to Luke's presentation of Simeon's prophetic stature. There is, first, the unmistakable parallelism between Zechariah (who prophesies) and Anna (a prophet). Second, there are historical analogues for Simeon, persons related geographically to the temple, whose aim is one of prognosticating with the help of the Scriptures the coming messianic age.[22] Third, like the prophets (cf. Jer 23:18), Simeon shares in the counsel of God, having received by way of revelation news of the imminence of the Messiah's appearance.[23] The identification is now furthered by Luke's attempt to portray Simeon in prophetic terms borrowed from Isaiah: "The Spirit of the Lord is upon me" (66:1).[24]

---

17. Further, e.g., Anna (2:36-37), Joseph (23:50-51), Stephen (Acts 6:3, 5, 8); Cornelius (Acts 10:1-2, 22); Barnabas (4:36-37; 11:24), and Ananias (22:12).

18. εὐλαβής, used in the NT only in Luke-Acts; cf. Acts 2:5; 8:2; 22:12.

19. προσδέχομαι.

20. Elsewhere, παράκλησις has the sense of comfort or encouragement — 6:24; Acts 4:36; 9:31; 13:15; 15:31.

21. See Isa 40:1-2; 49:13; 51:3; 57:18; 61:2; 66:13; cf. 2 Apoc. Bar. 44:17.

22. See Josephus, J.W. 1.3.5 §§78-80; Reicke, "Jesus, Simeon, and Anna," 101-2.

23. Χρηματίζω can be used with regard to oracular speech (cf. BAGD 885) and is used here and in Acts 10:22 with regard to divine revelation.

24. Luke 2:25: ἐπ᾽ αὐτόν; Isa 61:1 LXX: ἐπ᾽ ἐμέ. Luke's construction is anarthrous, as in 1:15, 35, 41, 67.

The images used in Simeon's introduction mark a development from the more general Isaianic hope of divine deliverance to a more nuanced messianism. The "consolation of Israel" of which Isaiah spoke was promised by God and related to his own, personal intervention in world affairs. For Simeon, who speaks for God, the coming of the "consolation of Israel" is construed as the appearance of the Lord's Messiah. It is still *God's* aim reaching its consummation, but that purpose is being realized in the coming of God's Son, the "Lord's Messiah."[25]

27-33 God, active by means of the guidance of the Holy Spirit, has Simeon come to the temple at just the right time and place. God, active by means of "what was customary under the law," requires Jesus' parents to bring their son to the temple at this time also. The result of this choreography is this rendezvous. This appointment is not the result of divine coercion, however. Although God is operative through the law and the Spirit to achieve this end, this encounter is dependent on the obedience of these human actors, who by their actions are helpers or supporters of the divine purpose. Their status as helpers contrasts sharply with those about whom Simeon will cryptically speak in 2:34-35a.

The location of this encounter is not without significance: the temple is the locus of God's presence,[26] the meeting place between the divine and the human. Here it is presented as an important site of divine revelation (cf. 1:11-20; 2:36-38; Acts 22:17-21). This portrayal is ironic, for here and in Acts 22:17-21 this location helps to legitimate the universal reach of the gospel: precisely in the center of the world of Israel, the Jerusalem temple, God discloses that salvation for Israel includes salvation for the Gentiles.

At the center of this pericope stands Simeon's response to his encounter with Jesus. This "song" is framed by other responses — praise from Simeon (2:28-29), wherein Simeon seems to join the angelic chorus in praise of God (2:13), and the amazement of the child's father and mother (2:33). Amazement is neither negative nor necessarily positive (cf. 2:18). It is an expected reaction to the miraculous, but does not promise correct understanding or faith in the present or future. That such a response is credited to Mary and Joseph — especially Mary, who has been portrayed so positively — should encourage us to pause for reflection. What Simeon has asserted in his prayerlike hymn is so extraordinary that even Mary and Joseph are amazed. Apparently this portion of the narrative has opened up possibilities requiring further development and clarification.

The Song itself is presented in three couplets, opening with an implicit

---

25. On "Lord's Messiah," cf. Luke 2:11; 1 Sam 1:14; Pss 2:2; 18:50; *Pss. Sol.* 17:32; 18:5, 7.

26. See above on 1:8-10.

word of praise (2:29) and proceeding to an explication of the motive for praise (2:30-32).[27] The Song borrows heavily from the vision of salvation resident in Isaiah 40–66 LXX, especially 40:5; 42:6; 46:13; 49:6; 52:10; 56:1; 60:1.[28] These echoes function at a number of levels: (1) they root Simeon's message firmly in the purpose of God, manifest in the Scriptures; (2) they root Simeon's message more particularly in the Isaianic vision of divine restoration and healing; (3) they emphasize the universalistic reach of God's redemption; and (4) they point to the image of the Isaianic Servant of Yahweh as a fundamental scriptural metaphor for interpreting the mission of Jesus as a whole.[29]

In the Greek text, the word "now" has been placed in the emphatic position: *"Now* you are *releasing* your servant, *Master."* This emphasizes once again the importance for Luke that salvation has already dawned on humanity with the coming of Jesus (cf. 1:48; 2:11). Also in an emphatic position, at the end of this opening phrase, is the unusual address for God, "Master."[30] This term, emphasizing submission to God, appears only here and in Acts 4:24 ("Sovereign Lord") in Luke-Acts. In both co-texts God as "Master" is set in apposition to particular humans as "servants" — here, Simeon; there, David (4:25), Jesus (4:27), and the Jerusalem church (4:29). This underscores that God is the one whose primary aim drives the narrative from creation to redemption, that God will overcome the efforts of those who oppose his purpose, and that the persons named above are those who act in submission to God and through whom God's purpose is realized (cf. 1:38).

These images are conjoined here with that of "release" or "dismissal," with the result that we hear a dual message. On the one hand, "to dismiss" can be a euphemism for "to let die."[31] Cast as it is in proximity to God's promise that Simeon "would not see death before he had seen the Lord's Messiah" (2:26), a vow God has kept (2:29b), this is a viable reading here.[32] On the other hand, "to dismiss" can be used in the sense of "to discharge," as from faithful vigil or service.[33] This also describes Simeon, particularly insofar as we picture him as a prophetic figure, serving God while awaiting the peaceful era of God's dominion. With the arrival of God's "salvation" (2:30), his task is complete.

---

27. Farris, *Hymns,* 145.

28. See Jones, "Lukan Psalms," 40-43; Bock, *Proclamation,* 85-87; Plymale, *Prayer Texts,* 37-46.

29. Note, however, that in doing so they do not grapple with or in any way embrace the atoning significance of the Servant's death in Isaiah 53. See Green, "God's Servant," 18-25.

30. δεσπότης.

31. See BAGD 96.

32. Cf. K. Berger, "Canticum Simeonis."

33. See MM 66-67.

God's "salvation," introduced in 2:30, might be rendered "*instrument of* salvation."[34] In the NT this term appears only in 2:30; 3:6; Acts 28:28; Eph 6:17. In Luke 3:6 and Acts 28:28, it is used in contexts that emphasize the universalism of God's salvation, which "all flesh shall see," including the Gentiles. And in each case of its appearance in Luke-Acts the Isaianic background of this terminology is evident.[35] Simeon identifies Jesus as this agent of salvation, practically equating the arrival of Jesus, the Lord's Messiah, with the advent of the new era of divine consolation. In 2:30, 32, "salvation" is set in apposition with "light"[36] (cf. Isa 51:4-5), and in 2:31-32 salvation for "all peoples" is clarified as "revelation to the Gentiles" (cf. Isa 49:6; 49:9) and "glory to your people Israel" (cf. Isa 46:13; 60:1, 19). This complex patterning leaves us in no doubt that the salvation that God has brought is universal in its reach.[37]

Some have doubted whether the phrase "a light for revelation to the Gentiles" implies that the Gentiles are included in God's salvation, since "open disclosure" need not imply inclusion in salvation.[38] However, the metaphor of "light" is already familiar to us from Zechariah's Song (1:78-79; cf. 2:8-9), where its salvific purpose is manifest: Through God's agent of salvation, people do not merely see evidence of the advent of God's dominion, they are engulfed in it; they are, as it were, led from the dominion of darkness into the light.[39]

34. σωτήριον.

35. Cf. Isa 40:5; 51:5, 6, 8; 56:1; 59:17; 60:6, 18; 61:10; 62:1; 63:1.

36. *Contra,* e.g., Nolland, 1:120. The use of δόξαν (accusative case) urges the recognition of a structural parallel, with the εἰς of 2:32a doing double duty for both clauses. That Luke could have in mind the need for enlightenment for Israel is manifest from, e.g., 1:78-79; Acts 26:23.

37. Some have objected to this conclusion, arguing that "peoples" in 2:31 finds its closest analogue in the Lukan corpus in Acts 4:25, 27, where the referent is plainly "Israel" (so G. D. Kilpatrick, "ΛΑΟΙ"). According to this reading, the Gentiles would behold but not necessarily participate in the announced epoch of consolation. However, the immediate co-text must be given decisive sway here, and on this score three points are of note. First, the narrator has gradually been building a case for the open introduction of the universalism we have found here. Second, the pattern of Simeon's Song juxtaposes in a programmatic way "all peoples" on the one hand, "Gentiles" and "your people Israel" on the other. Third, if Simeon only affirms that salvation has been offered Israel, it is difficult to ascertain why Mary and Joseph would react with astonishment; apart from a universalistic message having been made explicit in Simeon's Song, we are otherwise well within the thought world of Mary's Song.

38. In Brawley's view (*Centering on God,* e.g., 55), it is only in hindsight that we understand the significance of Simeon's words as an indication that the Gentiles are included in God's salvation.

39. This imagery is repeated in Acts — first in 13:47 of the salvation of the Gentiles; then in 26:22-23, where it is affirmed that the Messiah ". . . would proclaim light both to our people [i.e., the Jews] and to the Gentiles." See Wilson, *Gentiles,* 36-38.

34-35 Simeon's blessing of Joseph and Mary is reminiscent of the similar episode in the story of Samuel (1 Sam 2:20-21). Set within this narrative co-text, it must refer to the divine fortune they share in their role as parents of him who already occupies so central a role in God's salvific aim.

From blessing, Simeon turns momentously to address Mary. Now we discover that the "salvation" and "light" of 2:30, 32 are metaphors not only of consolation but also of eschatological crisis. In fact, "light" has this double meaning in the Scriptures.[40] As in Mary's Song, God's mighty work exalts some, humbles others (1:52-53; cf. Isa 40:3). The vocabulary is absent, but the well-known image of God as the stone that causes God's own people to stumble is echoed in Simeon's words (cf. Isa 8:14-15; 28:13, 16). Simeon emphasizes the identification of Jesus himself as this point of crisis, the one destined within God's own purpose to reveal the secret thoughts of those who oppose the divine aim (cf. Luke 12:1-2).[41] "Not all within Israel are poor and godly. The role of the King will be to effect a judgement. The reversal already begun will include a surprising reversal within the leadership of Israel."[42] Thus we gain sight of an ominous cloud, the first explicit manifestation of the reality that God's purpose will not be universally supported, and the first candid portent that the narrative to follow will be a story of conflict.

In 2:35b, Simeon moves from the general to the specific, showing that the division that will strike Israel will affect Mary too. The metaphor he employs is particularly difficult. In this co-text, it is related to Jesus' role as "a sign that will be opposed."[43] The image of the sword, then, relates to Jesus' mission of segregating those within Israel who embrace God's salvific will from those who do not. In fulfilling this divine role, he will be opposed, just as God's aim is opposed; indeed, the opposition will be such that it will reach as far as the experience of Mary. Does this refer to her distress at seeing her son thus opposed (cf. Ps 37:15; Zech 12:10)? Does it refer to the subordination of family ties to obedience to God's purpose (taking the sword as a symbol of discriminating judgment, as in Ezek 14:17; *Sib. Or.* 3:316; cf. Luke 8:21; 11:27-28)? In fact, the closer we come to the culmination of the narrative cycle introduced by the promise of a baby to Mary, the more such passages as these perform two related purposes. In narrating these responses, Luke brings to closure earlier narrative processes but also introduces new puzzles, making certain that the climax of the birth narrative actually carries us over

40. Of salvation: e.g., Exod 10:23; Job 12:22; Pss 4:6; 36:9; Isa 2:5; 9:2; 60:1. Of judgment: e.g., Job 28:11; Ps 37:6; Isa 10:17; 51:4. Cf. Wilson, *Gentiles,* 37-38.

41. That "thoughts" must be understood in this negative way, cf. Ps 56:5; Isa 59:7; Luke 5:22; 6:8; Schrenk, "διαλογισμός," 97.

42. Davis, "Literary Structure," 224.

43. In the Greek text, "and a sword will pierce your own soul too" follows directly after "a sign that will be opposed."

into the story of Jesus' mission in subsequent chapters. In other words, we have received from Simeon an unmistakable anticipation of coming conflict surrounding the mission of Jesus and are aware that this opposition will arise from within God's own people. What shape will this take? What will its meaning be? Luke leaves open these questions, encouraging us to be open to the development of these narrative possibilities, to join Mary and the others in mulling over these matters in order to understand them within the Lukan narrative of the consummation of God's purpose.

2.6.3. The Manifestation of Jesus to Anna (2:36-39)

36 *There was also a prophet, Anna the daughter of Phanuel, of the tribe of Asher. She was of a great age, having lived with her husband seven years after her marriage,* 37 *then as a widow to the age of eighty-four. She never left the temple but worshiped there with fasting and prayer night and day.* 38 *At that moment she came, and began to praise God and to speak about the child to all who were looking for the redemption of Jerusalem.*

39 *When they had finished everything required by the law of the Lord, they returned to Galilee, to their own town of Nazareth.*

As a counterpart to Simeon, Luke introduces Anna. Both are prophetic figures (cf. Acts 2:17-18), aged, pious, related to the temple, and among those who await eschatological salvation. And both recognize in Jesus the advent of God's redemptive intervention in the world, with the result that they praise God. In this way, Anna's testimony is added to that of the angels (2:10-14) and Simeon (2:28-35), who respond to the appearance of this wondrous child by praising God and interpreting the significance of Jesus' coming. Focusing as they all do on *God* and on eschatological hope, however, they bear witness to Luke's interest in a narrative aim that transcends the birth and manifestation of Jesus. Luke is concerned preeminently with the redemptive purposes of God, grounded ultimately in God's own designs, expressed in the Scriptures, anticipated by the faithful of Israel, now coming to fruition in the arrival of Jesus. In the present scene, Luke actually devotes more time to emphasizing Anna's reliability than to her reaction, a further attempt to render unimpeachable her testimony concerning Jesus.

36-37 Like Simeon before her, Anna is introduced with a number of coordinated clauses marking her credentials as a faithful Jew. As a prophet, she is by implication endowed with the Spirit (cf. 1:67; 2:25-27). She also retains the ancestral heritage of her family, and it is first with regard to these relationships that she is known to us. Though Phanuel is otherwise unfamiliar, and the mention of Asher (one of the northern tribes) bears no apparent

150

significance, these references locate Anna squarely within her heritage as an Israelite.

What is more, she is of great age, itself a symbol of respectful status in her world, but all the more so inasmuch as she has achieved her advanced age as a widow. It may be that, *contra* the NRSV rendering, we are to imagine that Anna has reached the age of 105 (married at age 14 + 7 years of marriage + 84 years as a widow);[44] in this case, her portrayal would overlap even more pointedly with that of Judith, that pious hero of Israel (Jdt 16:23).[45] Even if Anna is only 84, however, the effect is the same, for she exemplifies the ascetic ideal of marrying once and devoting oneself only to God in widow-hood.[46] Moreover, her similarity to Judith remains, for Judith is presented as a woman whose long widowhood was valued as an emblem of her piety, who was "God-fearing and [served] the God of heaven night and day," and whose piety found expression in fasting and prayer (Jdt 8:1-8; 11:17; 16:21-25).

Verse 37b holds in parallel two clauses: "she never left the temple" and "but worshiped there with fasting and prayer night and day." The latter spells out the importance of the former, and both make their point — the extraordinary devotion of Anna (like Judith) to the God of the temple — by hyperbole. Her continual presence in the temple emphasizes again the impor-tant and positive role this architectural space plays in these early chapters; that it is here that she would gain sight of God's redemption is no surprise.[47]

Fasting is of special significance precisely because it is a deliberate departure from cultural norms, not least in the world of Luke-Acts where meals are of such exaggerated social significance in their own right.[48] Fasting constitutes a form of protest, an assertion that all is not well. As was the case with Judith (Jdt 8:1-8; cf. 2 Sam 1:12), Anna's fasting may have been moti-vated by her loss — that is, as a sign of mourning. More likely in this es-chatologically charged narrative environment, Anna's abstinence is an expres-sion of her hope, a form of prayer entreating God to set things right.

38   We discern in this passage the divine hand orchestrating human movements. Herod's temple was a massive structure; how could it be that she arrived in the right place at just the right moment apart from divine direction?

---

44. In this case, ἕως would be rendered "as long as (eighty-four years)," rather than (as is the case with the NRSV) "until the age of (eighty-four)."

45. J. K. Elliott ("Anna's Age") sets forth a virtual phalanx of reasons to support a reading of Anna's age as 105. However interesting such a view might prove, it cannot overcome the obvious difficulties that Luke neither clarifies at what age Anna was married (hence, 14 must be assumed) nor mentions a total age of 105.

46. Cf. 1 Cor 7:8-9, 39-40; 1 Tim 5:3-16. See Tertullian *On Fasting* 8; *On Single-ness* 8; Origen *Hom. in Luc.* 17; Thurston, *Widows,* 23-25; Ilan, *Jewish Women,* 149.

47. See above on 1:8-10; 2:27.

48. On fasting, see Malina, *Christian Origins,* 185-204.

Given the insight particular to the prophetic vocation (cf. 7:39), even had Anna not heard Simeon's identification of Jesus she was nevertheless able to recognize the child's significance. She perceives in him the answer to her prayers, her hopes, and those of others for the redemption of Jerusalem. Like the shepherds before her (2:17-18, 20), she responds to God's gracious and salvific act by praising God and relaying what she had discovered to others.

This phrase, "redemption of Jerusalem," marks the signal importance of Jerusalem as the culture center of Israel.[49] The language itself echoes Ps 130:5-8; Isa 52:8-10, and in the present narrative parallels "consolation of Israel" (2:25; cf. 1:68). Clearly, to redeem Jerusalem is to redeem Israel, the former expression a synecdoche for the latter.

39 Luke 2:39 forms an *inclusio* with 2:21-24 and thus serves as the conclusion of this lengthy section devoted to the presentation of Jesus in the temple. One may hear here an echo of 1 Sam 2:20, but the primary reverberations are more local. Thus, 2:21-24 had accented the commitment of Jesus' parents to obeying the law of Moses/the Lord (a commitment repeated in 2:27), and now Luke informs us that "they had finished everything required by the law of the Lord." Their obedience is not portrayed as in any way inspired by "legalism"; indeed, Luke seems at pains to indicate that the law is an expression of the Lord's purpose. Hence, this closing remark reminds us that Jesus will be reared in a home headed by parents who stand on the side of God's purpose.

2.7. THE GROWTH OF JESUS, SON OF GOD (2:40-52)

40 *The child grew and became strong, filled with wisdom; and the favor of God was upon him.*

41 *Now every year his parents went to Jerusalem for the festival of the Passover.* 42 *And when he was twelve years old, they went up as usual for the festival.* 43 *When the festival was ended and they started to return, the boy Jesus stayed behind in Jerusalem, but his parents did not know it.* 44 *Assuming that he was in the group of travelers, they went a day's journey. Then they started to look for him among their relatives and friends.* 45 *When they did not find him, they returned to Jerusalem to search for him.* 46 *After three days they found him in the temple, sitting among the teachers, listening to them and asking them questions.* 47 *And all who heard him were amazed at his understanding and his answers.* 48 *When his parents saw him they were astonished; and his mother said to him, "Child, why have you treated us like this?*

49. See above, §4.

Look, your father and I have been searching for you in great anxiety."
49 *He said to them," Why were you searching for me? Did you not
know that I must be in my Father's house?" 50 But they did not understand what he said to them. 51 Then he went down with them and came
to Nazareth, and was obedient to them. His mother treasured all these
things in her heart.*

52 *And Jesus increased in wisdom and in years, and in divine and
human favor.*

We now come to the close of Luke's narrative of Jesus' birth. Although
episodic in character and considered by many to be only loosely (if at all)
tied to its narrative co-text, its location here is not at all artificial. First, it is
tied to Gabriel's announcement to Mary that her child would be called Jesus,
holy, and Son of God (1:31-32, 35). Up to this point, the child has been named
Jesus (2:21) and designated as holy (2:23), but only in this passage does he
appear as God's son (2:48-49). Second, with the report of Mary's response in
2:51b, and with the larger emphasis on the identity of Jesus' father in this
pericope, we are reminded of the continuing emphasis in Luke 1–2 on interpreting correctly the significance of these events and characters in God's story
of redemption. We leave this major subsection of the Lukan Gospel (1:5–2:52)
with many questions waiting to be answered, and Mary's reaction (2:51b)
encourages further contemplation on our part too. Finally, and most importantly, 2:40-52 is bound to its larger co-text by the John-Jesus parallelism so
pervasive in 1:5–2:52.[1] Specifically, these verses find their parallel in 1:80.
Both provide summary statements of the growth of their respective subjects.
Both raise the prospect of the public appearance of their subjects: John's public
ministry to Israel is forecast for the future, while Jesus' is proleptically present
in the temple scene.[2] This disparity points to the imbalance of the John-Jesus
parallelism, in favor of Jesus, and this is emphasized even more by differences
of structure. In contrast to the one-verse summary devoted to John, Jesus
receives two such summary statements, an illustrative story, and a notation
about his mother's treasuring all these things in her heart. Clearly, greater
interpretive attention is called for in Jesus' case, with the parental ignorance
of 2:50 and the treasuring of 2:51b serving together as an invitation to further
reflection and, especially, to continue reading the narrative.

The two summary statements (2:40, 52) form an *inclusio* around the
account of Jesus' visit to the temple. Both summaries note Jesus' particular
relation to God (characterized as one of "favor"), and both mention the boy's
"wisdom." Importantly, these two matters serve as focal points in the illustra-

1. See further above, §1.
2. See Sylva, "Cryptic Clause"; Kilgallen, "Luke 2,41-50."

tive account, for at issue here is Jesus' remarkable understanding (2:47) and the implications of his particular relation to God (2:48-49).[3]

Luke 2:40-52, then, and particularly 2:51b-52, bring to closure the narrative cycle initiated by the promise of a child to Mary. The child has been born, his coming repeatedly interpreted and celebrated. Now we see him grappling with his divine vocation, albeit provisionally, and we are informed of God's continued favor on behalf of the child as he matures. With this news, we are prepared for the anticipated return to the story of John (cf. 1:80), who will pave the way for the public ministry of Jesus (1:76-77).

40 Luke is fond of summary statements that allow both for the passage of time in the story with minimal representation and commentary, and for brief valuative comments on his part. His chief concern is Jesus as an adult, but as with contemporary Jewish and Greco-Roman literature, he relates that the child already possessed the qualities that will make him extraordinary in later life. Of special interest is Jesus' wisdom and a certification of God's valuative point of view vis-à-vis the child. Both qualities will come to the fore in the following story, which may be understood as an illustration of these features.

This brief report has precedent in Israel's Scriptures — for example, Gen 21:8, 20; Judg 13:24; 1 Sam 2:21, 26. Echoing these earlier, sacred texts, Luke's statement draws on their capacity to communicate the progression of the story under God's care and within his purpose. Luke's summary also echoes the similar report concerning John in 1:80 and anticipates the summaries of the growth of the Christian movement in Acts.[4] The effect is the same, to tell of the advancement of God's aim toward its consummation.

41-51a We have heard repeated testimony validating the exemplary piety of Joseph and Mary (cf. 2:21-24, 27, 39), certifying that Jesus would be reared in a household that sided with the purpose of God. This story, designed to illustrate the growth of the child Jesus in wisdom and divine favor, elaborates this theme in a serendipitous way. First, as we would expect of a pious Jewish family, pilgrimages to Jerusalem to celebrate Passover were annual (2:41) and customary (2:42).[5] Did Jesus attend with his parents each year? Luke does not say so explicitly, but neither does he document explicitly in 2:43a that Jesus went with his parents at age 12; we must await the news of his remaining behind in Jerusalem in 2:43b before we can conclude with

---

3. In terms of structure, see the analogue in Acts 6:1-7. Thus, Acts 6:1a, 7 provide summary statements related to the growth of the early Christian movement, and 6:1b-6 relate an example of a problem raised by that growth and how it was resolved to the strengthening of the Christian community.

4. Cf., e.g., Acts 2:41, 47; 4:4; 5:14; 6:1, 7; 9:31; 11:21-24; 15:5; Laurentin, *Truth of Christmas,* 473n.7.

5. κατ' ἔτος, κατὰ τὸ ἔθος; NRSV: "every year," "as usual." For this requirement, see Deut 16:1-8.

certainty even on this occasion that he attended with his parents.[6] It is likely, then, that Jesus' presence with his parents year after year as they celebrated the Passover is assumed in the narrative. This accentuates the place of Jesus in his family and the family of Jesus as a household that serves God.

But Luke introduces a surprising countermeasure as well. Jesus is being raised in a pious environment, but his commitment to God's purpose transcends that piety and that environment. In this case at least, acting on behalf of God's aim places Jesus' behavior against parental expectations.

Within 2:41-51a one recognizes immediately a competition for focal attention. With regard to location and pure mathematical count, the center of the story is 2:46: Jesus is in the temple amazing the teachers with his scriptural acumen. Jesus and his family go up to the temple in Jerusalem at the outset, they depart from this location in the end, and it is there that Mary and Joseph find Jesus. Moreover, according to de Jonge, this pericope contains 170 words, so that the central phrase is "among the teachers."[7] This movement draws our attention to Jesus' status as a person already known from an early age for his wisdom. This might recommend Jesus as a messianic figure endowed with divine wisdom[8] and certify Jesus' heroic character in a way appreciated by the Greco-Roman world.[9] The presentation of Jesus on equal footing with the Jewish teachers[10] furthers this motif.

---

6. That he was twelve years old does not seem to introduce any new requirement that he attend now (as opposed to before); legislation related to his becoming a "child of the law" (*bar mitzvah*) cannot be dated to this early period with certainty, nor would it necessarily have applied to a boy of 12 (see H. J. de Jonge, "Sonship," 317-19). What is more, the rabbinic schools of the Shammaites and Hillelites both held that children of a considerably younger age would have been required to attend Passover (*Ḥag.* 1:1), and the scriptural basis for the celebration of Passover envisions a family affair with explicit pedagogical value for the young (Exod 12:26-27). Whether Mary and/or Jesus were *required* to go is beside the point for Luke, whose interest at this early juncture in the account is to provide yet one more indication of the piety of Jesus' family. Sanders (*Judaism,* 129-31, 137) not only finds evidence that families did attend (e.g., the existence of the Court of Women at the temple; Josephus *Ant.* 11.109; Exod 12:26-27), but also remarks, "Social reality was more important than Pharisaic debates about who attended the festivals. They were times for feasting and rejoicing, and men brought their families" (131).

7. That is, μέσῳ in v 46 is the 85th word, so that ". . . the phrase ἐν μέσῳ τῶν διδασκάλων . . . forms the mathematical centre of the pericope" (H. J. de Jonge, "Sonship," 338n.5). Less compelling is de Jonge's attempt (338-39) to see in this story a chiastic structure revolving around 2:46b-47. This passage hardly presents a "textbook case of 'concentric symmetry,' " for the parallels between vv 43//49-50 and 44-46a//48 are artificial; further, it does not account for the dramatic movement of the account.

8. Cf. Isa 11:2-4; *Pss. Sol.* 17:37; *1 Enoch* 49:2-3. See Turner, "Holy Spirit," 344.

9. Cf. Josephus *Life* 9; H. J. de Jonge, "Sonship," 340-42.

10. Nothing in this text serves to portray Jesus as a *pupil* — *contra* most commentators (e.g., C. F. Evans, 225; Fitzmyer, 1:442. See Sylva, "Cryptic Clause," 36-37n.15).

On the other hand, vying for center stage is the reply of Jesus to his mother in 2:49. This is the scene's dramatic nucleus.[11] Several observations support this judgment, the most prominent being that this is the first time Jesus has spoken in the Gospel of Luke. In addition, the movement of the story is not simply to Jerusalem and back to Nazareth; rather, one recognizes in these geographical markers a subtle deixic shift.[12] As the scene opens, Mary and Joseph are the subjects of the action, but as it unfolds Jesus takes on an active role — for the first time in the Gospel. As the scene closes, *he* went to Nazareth, *accompanied by them; he* has become the subject of the verbs. This active role requires explanation, for it distances him from his parents, and this is the function of Jesus' words in 2:49. Finally, the pericope contrasts two sorts of piety, not in order to negate the one but to underscore the preeminence of the other. It is a good thing to keep the Passover, but the sort of pious environment to which Jesus has become accustomed at home serves and must serve the more fundamental purpose of God. Not even familial claims take precedent over aligning oneself uncompromisingly on the side of God's purpose.[13]

Jesus' words, then, are pivotal, and contain within them both an affirmation of his particular relation to God and his commitment to God's purpose. The first is emphasized by the dramatic development of the story, wherein Luke repeatedly refers to Jesus' *parents,* Mary refers to Jesus as *child* and speaks of Jesus' *father,* and Jesus counters by naming the God of the temple as his *Father.* That is, Luke has staged this interchange so as to pinpoint as the primary issue, Who is Jesus' father? To whom does he owe primary allegiance?[14] Jesus' aligning himself first with God's aim comes to the fore especially through his use of the expression "it is necessary"[15] — employed regularly throughout Luke-Acts as an indicator of salvation-historical necessity.[16]

This dramatic unfolding in the narrative has important repercussions for our understanding of the problematic phrase in 2:49b, translated variously as "in my Father's house" (so the NRSV), "about my Father's business," or "with those belonging to my Father."[17] The emphasis on *place* (where Jesus

---

11. Cf. Schmahl, "Lk 2,41-52."

12. Cf. C. F. Evans, 51.

13. Cf., e.g., 8:19-21; 14:26-27; Davis, "Literary Structure," 225-26; Schüssler Fiorenza, "Luke 2:41-52," 401-2.

14. Note that Mary's statement, ἰδοὺ ὁ πατήρ σου κἀγώ, places "your father" in the initial position, not as a requirement of courteous style but as a point of emphasis. See H. J. de Jonge, "Sonship," 330.

15. δεῖ; NRSV: "must."

16. See in the Gospel: 4:43; 9:22; 13:14, 16, 33; 15:32; 17:25; 19:5; 21:9; 22:7, 37; 24:7, 26, 44. Cf. Cosgrove, "Divine Δεῖ"; Green, *Gospel of Luke,* ch. 2.

17. ἐν τοῖς τοῦ πατρός μου. See the survey in Sylva, "Cryptic Clause," 133-34. Weinert ("Multiple Meanings") rightly draws back from too narrow a specification of the

was; where they found him; why would anyone look elsewhere?) encourages a rendering that is spatial: "in my Father's house." However, the issue is not simply a matter of location. Recalling that the notion of "household" in the Greco-Roman milieu was not only a designation of place but also of authority, we may gain a more helpful view of what this scene portends. Jesus is in the temple, the locus of God's presence, but he is there under divine compulsion engaged in teaching. The point is that he must align himself with God's purpose, even if this appears to compromise his relationship with his parents.

As this scene draws to a close, the public ministry of Jesus remains future; the occasion of his remarkable interchange in the temple provides us with a foreshadowing of what is to come, but for the present he will return with his parents to Nazareth. He returns under different circumstances than before. Now he is an active agent in the story, set on working within the contours of God's aim irrespective of the consequences.

51b-52   Where will this radical identification with God's salvific program lead? This is not yet clear, and it is not surprising that Luke records the inability of Mary and Joseph to understand. Mary "treasured all these things in her heart" — a phrase reminiscent of similar responses to the extraordinary in 1:29, 66; 2:19. As in those settings,[18] so here the reader is invited to respond in kind, to put aside hasty conclusions, and to maintain an openness to the course the narrative will take as it develops these themes further. Hence, 2:51b plays an ambiguous role in the narrative. It grows out of the immediately preceding account and registers Mary's attempt to grapple with its significance. But it also serves with 2:52 as the conclusion of the Lukan birth narrative as a whole.

Verse 52, then, which is comparable to 2:40 and the earlier 1:80, summarizes the passing of the years prior to Jesus' baptism (3:21-22) by reporting that Jesus' life continued along a similar course to that briefly exposed in the temple scene (2:41-51a). As the years[19] pass, the wisdom exemplified in the temple scene — manifest in Jesus' understanding of the Scriptures and discernment of God's purpose — also increased. This emphasis on Jesus' wisdom, noted in v 40 as well as here, may be rooted in the Isaianic notion of a coming Davidic ruler endowed with wisdom.[20] And, as Jesus was

---

meaning of this phrase, but his recommending reading, ". . . in my Father's [company]," is obtuse.

18. See above on 1:66; 2:19.

19. Ἡλικία is sometimes rendered as "stature," but such a reading is very rare in Hellenistic literature and absent from the papyri (MM 279); of the exceptions noted in BAGD 345 (cf. also J. Schneider, "ἡλικία"), only in Lucian *Verae Historiae* 1.40 do we find an unambiguous use of the term in a context that demands a reference to physical size.

20. See Isa 11:1-3; 4QpIsaᵃ fr. 8-10.iii.11-12; *Pss. Sol.* 17:37. So Strauss, *Davidic Messiah*, 122-23.

met with favorable responses among the teachers in 2:47, so he continues to be evaluated positively and esteemed by people. Finally, to the perspectives of angels, shepherds, Simeon, Anna, and many others in Luke 2, Luke adds God's own point of view concerning Jesus. He enjoys divine favor.

Luke's birth narrative reaches its finale on a positive note, but even this cannot mask the brooding questions that remain. On the one hand are questions related to God's purpose. What shape will this redemption take? How will it be accomplished? On the other are questions of human intentions and response. What relation has God's salvation to the sifting of Israel, raised to the fore in Simeon's words to Mary? How is it that God's own people will oppose God's instrument of salvation? What are the repercussions of Jesus' careless alignment with God's design?

3. THE PREPARATION FOR THE MINISTRY OF JESUS (3:1–4:13)

Critical to our understanding of the role of this narrative section in Luke's larger project is the solemn declaration of 3:2b: ". . . the word of God came to John son of Zechariah in the wilderness." This is a narrative flashback to the intertwined accounts of the births of John and Jesus in 1:5–2:52 and presents the first in a series of ways in which the appearances of John and Jesus here are deeply rooted in that earlier material. We left John as a maturing boy in the wilderness, awaiting his public appearance to Israel (1:80). He is still in the wilderness but now at the threshold of his public ministry. He is the "son of Zechariah," a reminder of the awe-inspiring intervention of God leading to the birth of a son to Zechariah and Elizabeth, too old to have children. The mention of Zechariah also ushers back into view the promises to Zechariah from Gabriel and Zechariah's own celebration of God's eschatological visitation, both underscoring John's role in the restoration of Israel (1:14-17, 68-79). Luke has thus chosen an economic way to lay the groundwork for his depiction of the adult John: he is the one foretold, the divine gift whose birth has already brought honor to his disgraced mother, and the prophet of the Most High.

The narrator intricately integrates the accounts of birth and ministry preparation. Perhaps of greatest significance at the thematic level are the prospective identities of John and Jesus. John was to be "prophet of the Most High" (1:76), a role he now fulfills; and Jesus was to be designated "Son of God" (1:35) — an identity affirmed by God (3:21-22), confirmed by Jesus' heritage (3:38), allowed but perversely interpreted by the devil (4:3, 9), and embraced as a mission by Jesus (4:1-13). Other themes are equally transparent, including:

- John's relation to Zechariah (1:5-80; 3:2);
- the wilderness (1:80; 3:2, 4);

- the programmatic use of Isaiah 40 (1:17, 19, 76; 3:4-6, 18);
- the accent on the universalistic reach of God's aim (1:55, 73; 2:1-2, 10, 14, 31-32; 3:1, 6);
- the role of John as one who prepares the way (1:14-17, 76-77; 3:4-6);
- prayer (1:10, 13; 3:21);
- the activity of the Holy Spirit (1:15, 35, 41, 67; 2:25-27; 3:16, 22, 41);
- repentance and forgiveness of sins (1:16-17, 76-77; 3:3, 8-14); and
- conflict (2:34-35; 3:1-2, 7-14, 19-20; 4:1-13).

Luke 3:1-2, with its prominent chronological and geo-political markers, may signal a new beginning in the narrative, but it does not initiate a new story. The consummation of eschatological redemption has already commenced with the divine interventions of 1:5–2:52.[1]

Luke's phrase in 3:2, "the word of God came," is also reminiscent of Luke's theocentrism. This phrase marks the source of inspiration behind John's work but also puts us on notice that Luke's prior emphasis on God as the story's primary actor will be carried forward and enlarged. Other evidences of this cardinal element materialize in this section — for example, the citation of *Scripture* by the narrator (3:4-6) who thus presents God's own perspective on John's ministry, by Jesus (4:4, 8, 12) who is engaged in a process of discerning the way of God, and by the devil (4:10-11) who tries to garner the authoritative voice of God for his own agenda of frustrating God's purpose; the activity of the *Holy Spirit,* God's empowering and guiding agent (3:16, 22; 4:1); the *voice of God,* heard by Jesus and Luke's audience, breaking into the narrative in a way that echoes his voice to Israel in the past (3:22); the *genealogy* of Jesus (3:23-28), showing Jesus' relation to Israel's past, recalling significant aspects of the story of God's interaction with his people, and testifying to the relation of Jesus to God as his Son; and above all the account of *Jesus' test in the wilderness* (4:1-13), pitting the aim of God and the design of the devil against each other.

Thus we are reminded that, though the narrative spotlight turns first on John then on Jesus, this is not their story. God is the primary actor around whose purpose the narrative develops. In 1:5–2:52 Luke has anticipated the roles of John and Jesus in God's plan. Will they indeed embrace God's aim and serve his design? This is the central question Luke must now address.

Luke 1:5–2:52 may present the *possibility* of Jesus' mission as Son of God but 3:1–4:13 establishes its *probability* — both by exhibiting how John prepared the way (as anticipated — cf. 1:16-17, 76-77) and by narrating Jesus' status transformation prior to his taking up his public ministry from 4:4

1. See above, §§2-3.

onward.[2] The importance of this narrative of transition is accentuated by the reality that participation in God's purpose even by God's own people is not guaranteed. God may be the primary actor and his aim may be central to the unfolding of events, but the realization of God's objective of necessity depends on the response of other actors. And there are powers at work to prevent the consummation of God's purpose[3] — hostile forces such as Roman and Jewish leaders (3:1-2, 19-20), a Jewish audience (3:7-9), and the devil himself (4:1-13).

Luke 3:1–4:13, therefore, assures us that Jesus will take up his divine mission and adds to our belief that God's aim will in fact be realized. Thus, he narrates: (1) the completion of the narrative cycle concerning John demonstrating that promises from divine spokespersons are reliable; (2) that Jesus has been empowered for his mission by the Holy Spirit and has divine sanction; (3) that Jesus is appropriately credentialed to serve God's eschatological purpose on behalf of Israel; (4) that Jesus has discerned correctly the nature of his mission from God, in contradistinction to the counterfeit offered him by the devil; and (5) that Jesus has determined to embrace God's purpose and submit to God as his Son in spite of opposition.

3.1 THE MINISTRY OF JOHN (3:1-20)

The introduction and conclusion of this narrative section are clear, and this is a fine example of Luke's concern with dramatic staging. He moves John onto center stage for his prophetic mission, then removes him so as to center exclusively on Jesus. At the same time, 3:1-20 is closely tied to previous material regarding John in Luke 1. From Luke 1 to Luke 3 a narrative thread runs from *possibility* to *realization* and *response/results*. John's public ministry of preparing the way for Jesus had been promised, and by means of the empowering of the Holy Spirit even before his birth he had been prepared for this service; here the narrative cycle is completed by the narration of his ministry and its results. The outcome of John's ministry takes two forms: (1) he attracts hostility leading to his imprisonment; and (2) he paves the way for Jesus' ministry by provoking a crisis and directing popular hopes to the coming of a future deliverer. Significantly, in spite of his own experience of opposition and even his removal from the public sphere, the divine aim to

---

2. Cf. V. Turner, *Forest of Symbols; idem, Ritual Process.* Although he has allowed the demands of his model of status transformation to overrule the details of Luke's narrative, McVann has helpfully interpreted Luke 3:1–4:30 as the narrative of Jesus' transformation from a private person to a public teacher ("Status Transformation").

3. See above on 1:78-79; 2:9, 34-35.

which he committed his service continues. In this way, these verses concerning John are themselves suggestive of the pattern of Jesus' experience (and, later, the experience of the church in Acts) — public ministry, attraction of opposing forces and imprisonment, but the continuation of God's purpose. Thus Luke 3:1-20 is a discrete unit in the Gospel, but it is tightly woven into the fabric of the narrative.

With regard to Luke's staging of this account, the relation of 3:19-20 and 3:21-22 is of particular import, for it appears that he has removed John from the scene prematurely.[1] That is, it is evident from the language of 3:21 that Jesus was baptized, like the others, by John, but by the time of the narration of his baptism, John is unavailable. Thus Luke has departed the normal order of events so as to turn the spotlight narrowly on one character, one event. The separation of Jesus' baptism from the others is dramatically motivated, allowing Jesus alone to occupy the center of our attention from his baptism onward.[2]

Hence, these verses provide no basis for distinguishing the ministries of John and Jesus as belonging to two separate periods in salvation history.[3] The intertwining of their accounts of birth according to the one salvific aim of God has already prepared us for Luke's presentation of their ministries as a continuous series of events. Thus, for example, the message of repentance and forgiveness of sins is identified with John (3:3), but also with Jesus (e.g., 4:18; 5:27-32; 7:36-50) and the mission of the Christian movement (e.g.,

---

1. Cf. the staging in, e.g., 1:23, 38; 2:20, 39.

2. Anachronies of this sort are not uncharacteristic of Luke. We have already encountered two examples of this phenomenon — 1:56-58 and, probably, 1:64-79. In the first, Mary appears to leave her relative Elizabeth just before delivery (1:56), but the presence of "neighbors and relatives" rejoicing with Elizabeth in 1:58 suggests Mary's continued presence too, and so Luke's attempt simply to direct attention again (as in 1:24-25) solely to God's graciousness to Elizabeth. In the second, *that* Zechariah praised God is reported in 1:64, but the *content* of his praise is given, finally, in 1:68-79; this departure from story time allows Luke to report the responses of others so that Zechariah's inspired words serve as an answer to their pondering the future significance of the child.

3. Conzelmann (*Luke*, e.g., 22-27) posited such a distinction, insisting that John belonged to the first period, the epoch of Israel, and he has been followed by numerous scholars, including Dunn (*Baptism*, 8-10, 25-32), who, however, saw clearly (*contra* Conzelmann) that John's ministry, like Jesus', was one of "good news." Others have modified Conzelmann — e.g., Fitzmyer (*Luke the Theologian*, 102-10) and Ernst (*Johannes der Täufer*, 81-112) see John as a transitional figure from the first to the second epoch, while Wink (*John the Baptist*, 46-57) and Webb (*John the Baptizer*, 64-65, 70) regard him as belonging to the second epoch but his ministry still distinct from that of Jesus — but in various ways continued to segregate John from Jesus and to embrace Conzelmann's notion of Luke's having segmented salvation history into three parts. For what follows, cf. Brawley (*Centering on God*, 174) and Tannehill (*Narrative Unity*, 1:48-53), who reject any such segregation.

24:47; Acts 2:38). Moreover, in his recitation of salvation history in Acts 13:16-25, Paul confers on John a prominent place as one who ". . . proclaimed a baptism of repentance to all the people of Israel" and anticipated the deliverer (13:24-25). In 3:18, Luke summarizes John's message as "good news," in the same way that Jesus' message is characterized subsequently (e.g., 4:18, 43; 7:22; 8:1). Other points of contact might be added, but none is of greater consequence than our recognition that Luke is concerned fundamentally with God's aim throughout Luke-Acts, and that, in their own ways, John and Jesus are characterized as serving the one purpose of God.

§8 The Prophetic Ministry of John in Luke 3:1-20

Luke 3:1-20 raises questions of another sort, however — namely, the nature of John and his baptism, and the relationship between his baptism "with water" and the anticipated baptism "with the Holy Spirit and fire." First, John is portrayed by Luke as a prophet concerned with social renewal and transformation. His prophetic vocation had been anticipated both implicitly (1:16-17) and explicitly (1:76). The introduction of his prophetic ministry is reminiscent of the accounts of the prophets of Israel's past — for example, with regard to chronological and geo-political markers (cf. 3:1-2a; Isa 1:1; Jer 1:2-3; Hos 1:1) and the declaration, "the word of God came" (cf. 3:2; Isa 38:4; Jer 1:2; 13:3; Jonah 1:1). John's ministry is associated with the *wilderness* and the *Jordan River,* settings the mention of which echo exodus and conquest themes rooted in the deliverance and the formation of Israel as a covenant people. Such echoes would have reverberated all the more audibly against the sounding board of prophetic figures roughly contemporary with John. For example, Josephus speaks of a number of renewal prophets, such as those during the rule of Felix (52-60 C.E.) who led the masses ". . . out into the wilderness so that God would show them signs of deliverance" (*J.W.* 2.13.4 §259).[4] Also adding to the portrayal of John as a renewal prophet is Luke's interpretation of John's appearance with the citation of Isa 40:3-5, suggesting that the promised eschatological deliverance of God's people was imminent. Finally, the arrest of John in 3:19-20 identifies John with the rest of the prophets whose fate was open hostility and death.[5]

John is thus situated squarely in the midst of social turmoil with profound economic, political, and religious implications. Indeed, the prophetic movements with which he shares affinity were themselves concerned with the quest for deliverance from oppression. This does not imply that political domination by Rome through its representatives or the restructuring of economic society under Roman rule had resulted

---

4. My translation. On the conjunction of the themes of wilderness, the Jordan, and prophetic figures during our period, cf. Josh 1:2; Isa 40:3; Josephus *J.W.* 2.13.5 §§261-63; 6.5.2 §§285-86; *Ant.* 20.5.1 §§97-98; 208.10 §188; Allison, "Mountain and Wilderness," 565; Heard, "Revolutionary Movements," 689-93; Barnett, "Jewish Sign Prophets"; Webb, *John the Baptizer,* 307-48.

5. Cf. Neh 9:26. See also Luke 7:26.

in an experience of life that might be classified as oppressive in absolute terms. Peasant culture — that is, the culture of the nameless crowds most affected by renewal prophets — need not experience absolute poverty before determining that something has gone awry and participating in movements calling for change. In the moral economy of the peasant, perceived deprivation is tantamount to real deprivation, and such perceptions are fueled by relative changes during the lifetime of the peasant.[6] The appeal of prophetic movements such as John's grows out of the widespread sense of injustice and oppression among common folk. It is no mere coincidence that Luke's record of John's ministry indicates that John received a vastly different response from "all the people" than from "Herod the ruler," and that the examples of behavior growing out of repentance are concerned with social justice (3:10-14). John's ministry defies neat categorization, for its religious and covenantal roots of necessity blossomed in socio-politico-economic justice.

At the center of this ministry stood the baptism of John, and it is worth inquiring how this act might have been understood in the world Luke portrays. Numerous studies have been devoted to unveiling the Jewish precedents to John's baptism, with the result that both similarities and dissimilarities have been noted.[7] Of particular import is the linkage of baptism with the use of water to cleanse a person in Jewish thought. This phenomenon is related to the use of water in scriptural texts concerned with cleanness and uncleanness (e.g., Leviticus 14–15), and with the correlation of washing and ethical comportment found in a text like Isa 1:16-17. Conceptually, John's baptism is more at home in later Jewish literature in which physical and metaphorical cleansing are combined.[8] Also of interest is the use of immersion at Qumran as a rite of initiation.[9] On the other hand, it is remarkable that John administered baptism, in contrast to Jewish analogues wherein one dipped or bathed oneself.

According to Luke, John's baptism was intimately tied up with repentance and must give rise to behaviors that demonstrate repentance. Moreover, John's call to a repentance-baptism is related co-textually to his radical questioning of an ethnic basis for membership in the people of God. The effect of these observations is to suggest that John's primary interest is in calling people out of normal social existence in order to align themselves fundamentally with God's eschatological, redemptive purpose. Through submitting to repentance-baptism, in which their roles were passive, they signified their surrender to God's aim, distanced themselves from past ways of life oriented away from God's purpose, and professed their (re)new(ed) allegiance to his will. By coming out into the wilderness to meet John they symbolized their separation from ordinary life, through baptism they embraced a conversion of loyalties and were themselves embraced into the community of God's people, and in returning

6. See, e.g., Scott, "Moral Economy."

7. See, most recently, Webb, *John the Baptizer,* 95-216; also Dockery, "Baptism," 55-58 (56-57).

8. Cf., e.g., Zech 13:1; *Jub.* 1:22-25; *Sib. Or.* 4.162-70; 1QS 3:6-9.

9. For example, 1QS 5:7-15. The possible connection of John's baptism with Jewish proselyte baptism is debated — cf. the opposing views of Pusey, "Jewish Proselyte Baptism"; McKnight, *Light among the Nations,* 82-85.

to their everyday lives they accepted the vocation to reflect behaviors apropos true children of Abraham.[10]

From this description it is evident that John's baptism is not presented by Luke as an alternative to the baptism "with the Holy Spirit and fire." Although the two are contrasted (3:16; cf. Acts 19:1-7), clearly the one anticipates and prepares for the other, as in the imagery of Ezek 36:25-26:

> I will sprinkle clean water upon you, and you shall be clean from all your uncleanness, and from all your idols I will cleanse you. A new heart I will give you, and a new spirit I will put within you. . . .

John's baptism forces a distinction between the community of authentic children of Abraham and those outside the community, while Jesus' baptism gathers up scriptural images of eschatological blessing and destruction (cf., e.g., Isa 4:4; 11:15; 30:27-28; 32:11-20; 44:3; Mal 3:2-4; 4:1). Here, then, is another testimony to John's role as the one who prepares the way for Jesus by provoking a crisis within Israel.

Luke's presentation of John's public career (1) introduces John by placing him in socio-political and salvation-historical context (3:1-6), (2) illustrates the content of his message (3:7-18), and (3) concludes by reporting how opposition to John led to his imprisonment (3:19-20). Thus, Luke draws to its finale the narrative cycle related to John by demonstrating that what was anticipated concerning him by angelic and Spirit-inspired voices (Luke 1) has been realized. Eschatological judgment, with its promise of blessing and woe, and of division, has already begun; the stage is set for the public ministry of God's agent of salvation, Jesus, the Son of God.

3.1.1. John, Prophet of the Most High (3:1-6)

> 1 *In the fifteenth year of the reign of Emperor Tiberius, when Pontius Pilate was governor of Judea, and Herod was ruler*[11] *of Galilee, and his brother Philip ruler of the region of Iturea and Trachonitis, and Lysanias ruler of Abilene,* 2 *during the high priesthood of Annas and Caiaphas, the word of God came to John son of Zechariah in the wilderness.* 3 *He went into all the region around the Jordan, proclaiming a baptism of repentance for the forgiveness of sins,* 4 *as it is written in the book of the words of the prophet Isaiah,*
> *"The voice of one crying out in the wilderness:*

10. In this sense, then, the presentation of John's baptism is reminiscent of the initiation ritual as outlined by van Gennep, *Rites of Passage;* having passed through this rite, people then participated in a form of ritual kinship marked by a transformed network of social relations and by group-sanctioned behaviors.

11. NRSV margin: "tetrarch"; likewise for Philip and Lysanias.

> 'Prepare the way of the Lord,
>   make his paths straight.
> 5 Every valley shall be filled,
>   and every mountain and hill shall be made low,
>   and the crooked shall be made straight,
>   and the rough ways made smooth;
> 6 and all flesh shall see the salvation of God.' "

John takes up the role prophesied of him (1:76; cf. 1:16-17). In other ways, too, 3:1-6 is tied back into the material of Luke 1 — for example, analogous geo-political markers (1:5; 3:1-2), the motifs of conversion and forgiveness (1:16-17, 77; 3:3), the wilderness setting (1:80; 3:2, 4), the identification of John as Zechariah's son, and so on. These apparent redundancies serve a vital function in the Lukan narrative and are in no way artificial.[12] The strict concentration on Jesus' birth and childhood in Luke 2 has created a lengthy hiatus in the account concerned with John, set aside after 1:80. These points of contact, then, provide a bridge from earlier narrative. Although 3:1-2 obviously signal the beginning of John's public ministry, this public appearance is itself the realization of promises and probabilities narrated earlier.

This narrative section also opens up new possibilities for development. Of special interest are the relation of this fresh work of God to the political figures introduced in 3:1-2 and the nature of John's ministry, characterized so economically in 3:3. Most importantly, though, 3:1-6 locates John in the anticipated public arena and on the stage of salvation history. Verses 1-2 present John in a manner reminiscent of prophetic texts from Israel's Scriptures and of passages from Hellenistic historiography. These echoes certify his identity as a prophet whose significance can hardly be relegated to a corner of the world. Verses 4-6 link John's mission with the eschatological consolation of God. Verses 1-2, 4-6 thus frame and focus attention on the summary characterization of John's mission in 3:3,[13] while that mission is at the same time interpreted in socio-political and redemptive-historical terms.

On the one hand, the universal scope of the coming salvation is suggested by the list of civic and religio-political leaders in 3:1-2;[14] seen in this way, this list forms an *inclusio* with "all flesh" of 3:6. But this characteristically Lukan emphasis must not be allowed to overshadow the apparent tensions resident in these introductory verses. For example, what are we to make of the deliberate apposition of institutional religion, embodied in Annas and Caiaphas, with the anointing of a prophet with the word of God? What

---

12. *Contra*, e.g., Fitzmyer, 1:450, 459.
13. See A. Stock, "Chiastic Awareness," 23.
14. Cf. Origen *Hom. in Luc.* 21.

significance should we find in the fact that the word of God has come to Zechariah "in the wilderness" — a locale both pregnant with revolutionary meaning from Israel's past and distant from the direct influence of the urban, power elite? Clearly, John's "wilderness" is not outside the public eye and these observations portend a coming collision between him and those who possess power and privilege in his world. That is, already at this juncture Luke portrays John as an agent of renewal, questioning the status quo and raising hopes for divine deliverance.[15] This, it is clear, is God's doing, for John bears the word of God and his ministry is firmly grounded in "the book of the words of the prophet Isaiah."

1-2   The centerpiece of this lengthy sentence appears in its final clause, wherein the main verb is found: "the word of God came to John. . . ." Together with earlier anticipations of John's prophetic ministry (1:16-17, 76), this affirmation and the geo-political markers of 3:1-2a all conspire to identify John as a prophet in the OT tradition. The sentence as a whole is reminiscent of numerous prophetic texts — including those that also situate the prophet in an historical context with reference to national leaders, those that declare the coming of the divine word to the messenger, and, as in Luke 3:1-2, those combining both of these elements. Similar lists of contemporary authorities are found in ancient historiography, and this will have had some significance for Luke's audience.[16] However, the extent to which Luke has already shown his concern to read the story of God's redemptive work in John and Jesus against the backdrop of the Scriptures encourages in particular our hearing of scriptural echoes here.

This is not to imply that Luke's sole interest in the lineup of rulers he provides in 3:1-2a is to paint John in prophetic garb. Nor is Luke's primary purpose to provide data for a precise dating of the beginning of John's prophetic work. After all, the conjunction of the imperial and more local reigns he enumerates does not specify the chronology of John's ministry except in a general sense. Even the seemingly definite benchmark he does provide — "in the fifteenth year of Emperor Tiberius" — proves ambiguous (at least to modern readers) due to the uncertainty surrounding the reckoning of Tiberius's first year of rule.[17] Presumably, the onset of John's ministry should be fixed to the period 28-29 C.E., but concern with *chronological* specificity is for Luke clearly eclipsed by his interest in portraying the *socio-historical* climate within which John ministered. Otherwise, it would be difficult to explain why he

15. Cf. Brueggemann, "Luke 3:1-4," 405-8.
16. National leaders: Isa 1:1; Amos 1:1; prophets: Joel 1:1; Jonah 1:1; both elements: Jer 1:1-4; Ezek 1:1-3; Hos 1:1; Mic 1:1; Zeph 1:1; Hag 1:1; Zech 1:1; ancient historiographers: Thucydides 2.2; Polybius 1.3; Josephus *Ant.* 18.4.6 §106.
17. See Meier, *Marginal Jew,* 1:383-86.

continues his list beyond Tiberius to mention Pilate, Herod, Philip, Lysanias, Annas, and Caiaphas.

What is the importance of these figures and their domains to the Lukan narrative? For some — that is, Pilate, Herod, Annas, and Caiaphas — this is the first mention of persons who will play important roles elsewhere in the narrative. Among these, the most important to the immediate co-text is Herod, who places John in prison (3:19-20). Pilate, Annas, and Caiaphas will have similar roles of opposition to God's purpose in subsequent accounts (cf. 22:54; 23:1-25; Acts 4:5-6, 27). The others — that is, Tiberius, Philip, and Lysanias — are absent from Luke-Acts apart from this brief passage, so it is less clear why they deserve mention at all. Luke 3:1-2a may be read within the interpretive matrix of earlier material, such as the critique of "the powerful" and "the rich" in Mary's Song (1:52-53); having read the preceding narrative, we now have a bias against rulers who enter the narrative. And this inclination is generally supported by the juxtaposition of these rulers with John and by their wider reputations in the Roman world.[18]

The reign of Tiberius may be best remembered for numerous trials for treason and sedition and his deportment of Jews from Rome. In Luke's discourse situation, he is likely to have been infamous for his last years as emperor; following personal tragedy, his mental health declined so that those final years have been characterized as a period of pure terror. Pilate, prefect of the Roman province of Judea from 26-36/37 C.E., is known from Jewish sources as "inflexible, a blend of self-will and relentlessness," whose administration was marked by briberies, insults, robberies, outrages, wanton injuries, frequent executions without trial, and endless savage ferocity.[19] Unlike his predecessors, Pilate apparently held in low esteem Jewish religious sensibilities; for example, he introduced tokens of emperor worship into Jerusalem and took money from the temple treasury.[20] Perhaps of equal or greater importance, Pilate will have been known to Luke's audience, as he was to the Latin historiographer Tacitus,[21] as the Roman provincial ruler under whom Jesus was executed. Hence, his introduction at this juncture cannot have served merely to provide "a Roman and Palestinian ambience,"[22] but itself adds to the growing sense of tension in the narrative.

Herod Antipas, tetrarch[23] of Galilee and Perea (4 B.C.E.–39 C.E.), over-

18. For more detail, see Green, "Discourse Analysis," 187-92.

19. Philo *Leg. Gai.* 37 §§301-2.

20. See Josephus *J.W.* 2.9.2-4 §§169-77; *Ant.* 18.2.2 §35; 18.3.1-2 §§55-62; 18.4.1-2 §§85-89; Philo *Leg. Gai.* 38 §§299-305; Luke 13:1; Smallwood, *Jews,* 160-74.

21. Tacitus *Ann.* 15.44.4.

22. *Pace* Fitzmyer, 1:453.

23. τετραρχέω — literally, to rule a fourth part of a region, eventually used of a ruler whose rank and authority were lower than a king (BAGD 814).

stepped Jewish sensibilities by constructing his new capital city, Tiberias, on a graveyard (i.e., on unclean ground), and placing images in public places.[24] His loyalty to Rome and concomitant concerns of a political nature led to his unpopular imprisonment and later execution of John the Baptist[25] — an action likely reserved in the memory of Luke's audience already, and in any case noted in the immediate co-text (3:19-20). According to Luke, he also had a role in the execution of Jesus (cf. 23:6-12; Acts 4:27). Philip reigned from 4 B.C.E. to 34 C.E. in a largely Gentile area situated in the northeastern section of the former kingdom of Herod the Great. Because of his locale and the makeup of his realm, he was able to take Hellenization much farther than his contemporaries to the south. Almost nothing is known of Lysanias, who reigned over Abilene, located to the north of the Sea of Galilee, from *ca.* 28 C.E. to *ca.* 29-37.[26] Clearly these two could not have been added to the list because of a Lukan concern with geographical inclusiveness. Otherwise, we would have expected Herod's rule of Perea to be mentioned, along with, for example, the situation in Syria. It may be that they are mentioned because they help to extend the more local geographical references to include the Gentile world of the Empire in a more pointed way.

A further problem arises in 3:2a with the mention of "the high priest-hood [singular] of Annas and Caiaphas [plural]." Annas was high priest from 6-15 C.E.; following him in this office were his five sons, his son-in-law Joseph Caiaphas (18-36/37 C.E.), and, perhaps, a grandson.[27] Hence, even though Caiaphas would have been the high priest during the period in question, the continuing presence of Annas throughout this period must have been ominous. His near-dynastic control of the office would have signified his overpowering influence, and this would explain Luke's usage here. This would also suggest that the real point of interest at this juncture is not on the office per se, but on the power resident in these individuals who controlled the temple and its machinations (cf. Acts 4:6). As the head of the temple and its cult, Caiaphas and Annas would have exercised virtually unrivaled power and privilege among the Jewish people.

Luke's synchronism in 3:1-2a provides, therefore, more than an historical setting for or local color to the narrative. Rather, they bespeak a particular, tension-filled, top-heavy, socio-historical milieu.

The wilderness is reminiscent of the formative event in Israel's life as a nation, the exodus, and biblical and extrabiblical tradition came to associate

24. Josephus *Ant.* 18.2.3 §§36-38; *Life* §§65-66.
25. See Josephus *Ant.* 18.5.2 §§116-19.
26. Smallwood, *Jews,* 190n.35.
27. Josephus *Ant.* 18.2.1-2 §§26-34; 18.2.2 §35; 18.4.3 §95; 18.5.3 §123; 19.6.4 §§313-16; 20.9.1 §197-98; 20.9.7 §223.

the wilderness with a new exodus.[28] This tradition encourages an association of John's prophetic ministry with eschatological deliverance and portrays the powerful of 3:1-2a as those from whom God's people would be delivered (cf. 1:68-79).

3   Having received his call and empowerment as a prophet, John now begins his public ministry (cf. 1:16-17, 76-77, 80). "He went" does not signify his departure from the wilderness, but rather connotes his traffic in the vicinity of the Jordan (necessary for his baptismal ministry) with people who came out to him (cf. 3:7). He remains apart from the world's urban centers in a location related symbolically to the experiences of exodus and conquest.

Verse 3b provides a summary description of his ministry as one of proclamation. The term itself appears a few times in the LXX with a sense similar to what one finds here — namely, the announcement of imminent, eschatological judgment.[29] In Luke-Acts it has no particularly messianic or eschatological sense, though it is used regularly to summarize the mission of God's messengers, often with the kingdom of God or the significance of Jesus as its content.[30] Interestingly, in Acts 10:37 John's mission is again characterized as one of proclaiming, and this assists Luke's overall identification of John as the Isaianic herald of redemption (Isa 40:1-9; Luke 3:4-6). Luke, however, in no way distinguishes John's mission as qualitatively distinct from that of the Christian movement, as though John's were somehow provisional or belonged to a different age in salvation history. Indeed, the fundamental elements of John's ministry — proclaim + repentance + forgiveness of sins — are paralleled in the ministry to which Jesus' followers are commissioned in 24:47.

We have already discussed the nature of John's baptism,[31] and so here we need only draw attention to three critical issues. First, John's baptism is necessarily qualified as a "repentance-baptism," so that his proclamation and baptism are inseparably connected.[32] He thus follows biblical precedent in insisting on the correlation of cleansing and moral rectitude. Second, his emphasis on repentance signals his understanding that the status quo of his socio-historical environment has been found wanting. As such, his message constitutes a prophetic appeal for people to turn their backs on previous loyalties and align themselves fundamentally with God's purpose. Third, by definition the forgiveness of sins has a profound communal dimension; as sin

28. Cf., e.g., Isa 35:1-2; 40:3-5; Ezek 20:33-44; Hos 2:14-23; Mic 7:15; CD 8.12-16; 1QS 9.20; Mauser, *Wilderness*, 44-58; cf. Talmon, "Desert Motif."

29. κηρύσσω; cf. Isa 61:1; Joel 2:1; Zeph 3:14-15; Zech 9:9.

30. Cf. 4:18-19, 44; 8:1; 9:2; 24:47; Acts 8:5; 9:20; 10:42; 19:13; 20:25; 28:31.

31. See above, §8.

32. See Sahlin, "Früchte der Umkehr."

is the means by which persons exclude themselves from community with and the community of God's people, so forgiveness marks their restoration to the community. These points will surface in greater detail in 3:7-18, where this mission summary is illustrated with the words of John.

4-6 First, however, Luke introduces into the narrative a pause during which he can provide a direct scriptural voice as an unimpeachable witness to John's significance in God's redemptive design. John is set within a particular socio-political context (3:1-2a), but he can only be understood rightly and fully with reference to his role as the Isaianic herald. In citing Isa 40:3-5, Luke is not so concerned with presenting John as the "fulfillment" of this passage as he is in locating John and the sequence of events of which John is a part within this redemptive-historical context. In doing so, he does not extract Isa 40:3-5 from its Isaianic co-text.[33] As is generally the case in the construction of intertextual discourse,[34] Luke's text both absorbs and transforms the earlier text. Luke exploits the concerns of Isaiah 40 with the advent of God and decisive consolation of Israel; John's is the proclaiming voice, and he is the herald of good news (cf. Isa 40:3, 9; Luke 3:3, 4, 18). Set now within the co-text of Luke's Gospel, Isaiah's words will be read in fresh ways, but precisely because these are Isaiah's words (explicitly referenced, 3:4a), Luke's narrated events are interpreted by the Isaianic vision of eschatological salvation.

The citation of Isa 40:3-5 at this juncture is far from abrupt and is an event for which Luke has obviously prepared. As a result it picks up key terms of the narrative and both interprets and is interpreted by its co-text. (1) Note the importance of the "wilderness" due to its associations with the new exodus (cf. 1:80; 3:2, 4). (2) John, we have been told, will prepare the way of the Lord (1:17, 76; 3:4; cf. 2:31). By this point in the narrative, the original proposal that John's ministry would prepare for the coming of Yahweh (1:17) has undergone a crucial shift. By "Lord" we now understand "Jesus," as in 1:43, 76; 2:11. This interpretation of divine redemption along christological lines is further advanced by Luke's amendment of the Isaianic text he cites — from "make straight the paths of our God" to "make his paths straight."[35] "His" now refers to the coming one — Jesus, the Lord. (3) According to 1:16-17 and 3:3, "preparation" has taken the explicit form of turning to God and embracing his purpose — or, in this co-text, undergoing repentance-baptism and living transformed lives (3:3, 7-14). (4) Closely related is the importance of "the way," mentioned in 1:76, 79; 3:4-5,[36] but

33. Among those who attribute an atomistic hermeneutic to Luke here, see C. F. Evans, 237.

34. See Culler, *Pursuit of Signs,* 107, 118.

35. LXX: εὐθείας ποιεῖτε τὰς τρίβους τοῦ θεοῦ ἡμῶν.

36. Note that ὁδός in 3:5 (i.e., ὁδὸς λεῖος — *"smooth path";* NRSV: "smooth") is a Lukan innovation vis-à-vis the LXX, which reads πεδίον, "level place."

later used in an absolute sense to designate the church in Acts 9:2; 19:9, 23; 22:4; 24:14, 22.[37] Luke's subsequent use of the term seems to be rooted here in the designation of a people who align themselves with and serve God's salvific aim. (5) The metaphorical language related to the straightening of the path in 3:5 must be understood in two ways. First, it echoes earlier language of transposition in 1:52-53; 2:34. Second, it reminds us that John's purpose is to prepare a people ready to receive the Lord, having themselves undergone repentance (i.e., "made straight . . . and smooth"). (6) Luke's citation of Isa 40:3-5 also employs language from the vocabulary of salvation (see already 1:47, 69, 71, 77; 2:11; 3:6) and, therefore, which must be interpreted in the holistic ways we have heretofore encountered.[38] (7) Finally, the scope of God's salvation is again identified in a universal way (cf. 1:55, 73; 2:14, 31-32; 3:6). John's ministry may be more narrowly directed to Israel (cf. 1:16; 3:3), but it is part of God's larger project of bringing redemption to all humanity.

3.1.2. John Proclaims the Good News (3:7-18)

7 *John said to the crowds that came out to be baptized by him, "You brood of vipers! Who warned you to flee from the wrath to come?* 8 *Bear fruits worthy of repentance. Do not begin to say to yourselves, 'We have Abraham as our father';[39] for I tell you, God is able from these stones to raise up children to Abraham. 9 Even now the ax is lying at the root of the trees; every tree therefore that does not bear good fruit is cut down and thrown into the fire."*

10 *And the crowds asked him, "What then should we do?"* 11 *In reply he said to them, "Whoever has two shirts[40] must share with anyone who has none; and whoever has food must do likewise."* 12 *Even toll[41] collectors came to be baptized, and they asked him, "Teacher, what should we do?"* 13 *He said to them, "Collect no more than the amount prescribed for you."* 14 *Soldiers also asked him, "And we, what should we do?" He said to them, "Do not extort money from anyone by threats or false accusation, and be satisfied with your wages."*

15 *As the people were filled with expectation, and all were questioning in their hearts concerning John, whether he might be the Messiah,* 16 *John answered all of them by saying, "I baptize you with water; but*

37. Cf. 1QS 9:17-18; 10:21.
38. See above, especially on 1:46-55, 68-79.
39. NRSV: "ancestor."
40. NRSV: "coats."
41. NRSV: "tax."

one who is more powerful than I is coming; I am not worthy to untie the thong of his sandals. He will baptize you with the Holy Spirit and fire. 17 His winnowing shovel[42] *is in his hand, to clear his threshing floor and to gather the wheat into his granary; but the chaff he will burn with unquenchable fire."*

18 *So, with many other exhortations, he proclaimed the good news to the people.*

Luke portrays the baptism of John as integrally related to his proclamation and in fact spends far more time revealing the content of John's message than describing the act of baptism itself. This accentuates John's role as the Isaianic herald of good news (Isa 40:1-9) and provides extensive interpretation of the ritual act of baptism. Here the emphasis does not fall on any particular mode of baptism as a purveyor of symbolic meaning.[43] Rather, baptism is seen as an initiatory rite of passage as people (1) come away from their normal lives to participate in John's ministry through baptism, (2) undergo a repentance-baptism signifying their (re)new(ed) allegiance to God's purpose, and (3) return to their normal lives having accepted the challenge to reflect in their lives ways of living appropriate to true children of Abraham. John's proclamation ensures that his baptism is understood as an assault on the status quo, that to participate in his baptism is to embrace behaviors rooted in a radical realignment with God's purpose. In this way, 3:7-18 should be understood as following on from the brief summary of John's ministry in 3:3, providing substance to that outline.

Contra attempts to find in 3:7-18 three separate teaching segments, we must understand how closely connected these paragraphs are. It is true that Luke's repeated designation of John's audience draws attention to the division of this narrative unit: "the crowds" — 3:7, 10; "the people" — 3:15, 18. But this should not detract from the ways these subsections are related. On the one hand, we may discern here a linear progression: The concern with "fruits worthy of repentance" in 3:7-9 gives rise to dialogue spelling out the nature of those "fruits" in 3:10-14, and the provocation of crisis in John's call to repentance and questioning of long-held understandings of the covenant gives rise to the exchange concerning the Messiah and eschatological judgment in 3:15-17.[44] On the other hand, one may detect a chiasmus in these verses:

---

42. NRSV: "fork."

43. Marshall ("Baptize") shows the difficulty in seeing John's baptism as an immersion; he concludes, "What John meant was . . . 'I have cleansed/purified you with water, but He will cleanse/purify you with the Holy Spirit' " — a purifying associated with the ideas of washing and pouring (139).

44. Cf. Sheffler, "Social Ethics," 30.

A 3:7-9: Impending Judgment and the Need for Readiness
  B 3:10-14: Instruction on Readiness
A′ 3:15-17: Impending Judgment and the Need for Readiness
C 3:18: Summary

This structural development is crucial in providing a covenantal and eschatological context in which to interpret the ethical material of 3:10-14. Luke 3:7-9 and 3:15-17 also maintain a central interest in the agricultural metaphor of fruitbearing as it is related to judgment. Moreover, while the subject of judgment in 3:7-9 is God, the Messiah has this function in 3:15-18.

John's ethical instruction in 3:10-14 has been labeled as more at home in the ethical programs of Greco-Roman philosophy, and as compromising and bourgeois.[45] These judgments ignore a number of factors. First, instruction of this nature is clearly at home within the Scriptures and Judaism (e.g., Job 3:17, 20; Isa 58:7; Ezek 18:7; Tob 1:17; 4:16).[46] Moreover, John's preaching is related to that of Jesus in 6:32-34 as well as to the sort of aphoristic counsel typical of the wisdom tradition.

John's ethical message contains within it a social critique the profundity of which is appreciated only when it is recognized that it not only points the finger of judgment at large-scale injustice but in fact reaches into the realities of day-to-day existence. Life at the local level and one's own normal network of relationships are touched by this ethical vision, with the result that "repentance" must be understood within and related to even the most mundane.

Also of pronounced import is the context provided for 3:10-14 by the surrounding material. John is only *like* the prophets and *like* the wisdom tradition. At the same time that he appears to be parroting their counsel, he violates their presuppositions. He insists that behavior of this sort is not only, for example, "activity arising out of the covenant," but, indeed, that one's relationship to the covenant *at all* is determined by engaging in behavior that brings the aim of God to expression within the human community. The eschatologically charged context in which this ethical instruction is uttered raises the stakes profoundly, insisting that membership in the covenant is and must be marked by its fecundity. This is the only basis on which judgment will be passed.

Within the narrative, the combination of new exodus themes and the emphasis on eschatological crisis gives rise naturally to the question whether John might be the Messiah. John's answer not only continues Luke's procedure

---

45. Cf. Riches, *World of Jesus,* 63-64, 74-77; Bammel, "Baptist," 105.

46. Indeed, John's words on ethical comportment constitute the only material we have in the NT that would help us understand Josephus's commendation of John as ". . . a good man [who] exhorted the Jews to lead righteous lives, to practise justice towards their fellows and piety towards God . . ." (*Ant.* 18.5.2 §117). See further Sahlin, "Früchte der Umkehr"; Ernst, *Johannes der Täufer,* 94.

of subordinating John to Jesus, but also points out how loosely "the people" refer to the Messiah. That is, the title "Messiah" appears on their lips with no developed meaning, apart from some apparent relation to God's final act of judgment. John's negative reply begins the process of shaping the meaning of the title for the crowds — who do not share our knowledge from 1:5–2:52 but who will carry John's description into the narrative of Jesus' public ministry.

7-9 These verses are related to the preceding introduction of John by a "therefore" left untranslated by the NRSV,[47] but it is important that we recognize this as a dramatic identification of John's baptism as a repentance-baptism. Isaiah had castigated God's people for their meaningless participation in cultic sacrifices and religious assembly (Isa 1:10-17); like Isaiah, John rails against misuse of such meaningful rituals, asserting that participation of this kind offered no prophylactic against judgment. Instead, the significance of the ritual act of baptism as a resounding rejection of old ways of living and a ready acceptance of God's will must be recognized with sufficient serious-ness so as to blossom in behavior sanctioned by God. For John, the urgency of the moment ("even now[48] the ax is lying at the root" — 3:9) allows for no leisure in this matter; people must act "at once"[49] to manifest their re-alignment of loyalties around God's purpose in concrete ways.

By labeling the crowds as a "brood of vipers," John underscores their hopeless position apart from the way of repentance he presents to them. Indeed, his choice of words seems deliberately to contrast with their supposed self-identification. They are the offspring[50] of poisonous snakes, not children of Abraham. As elsewhere, to be born of something or someone is to share its character by nature.[51] For John, the crowds may claim to be children of Abraham but their behavior deviates radically from that of Abraham; their actions suggest the influence of the viper. The relation between the snake and the devil is suggestive (cf. Rev 12:9 et al.), particularly since Luke has already begun to portray the fundamental conflict in his narrative as between two forces, light (related to God and Jesus — cf. 1:78-79; 2:8-9) and darkness (to be identified with Satan). Even without this identification explicitly developed, however, the qualities associated with vipers — poisonous, hostile to life, evil — are enough to give rise to John's question, "Who warned you to flee from the wrath to come?" Clearly, the crowds are destined for "the wrath to come" — a cipher for judgment on the day of the Lord.[52]

---

47. οὖν.

48. Luke employs both δὲ καί for added emphasis, and ἤδη to score this point.

49. So Plummer (89) understands the force of the aorist imperative, ποιήσατε, in 3:8.

50. γέννημα — "fruit," "what is born"; NRSV: "brood."

51. Cf. Isa 57:4; John 8:39, 44.

52. Cf. Zeph 1:14-15; 2:1-2; Mal 3:2-3, 19; *Jub.* 15:34; 36:10; 1 Thess 1:10.

Verse 8a and 8b are more closely connected than the NRSV might imply, joined in the Greek text by "and,"[53] suggesting that they present two alternative responses. John advises the one and rules out the other in a way that undercuts one of the critical and most pervasive pillars of first-century Judaism — namely, Israel's self-understanding as God's people. E. P. Sanders has developed this identity in terms of "covenantal nomism":

> the view that one's place in God's plan is established on the basis of the covenant and that the covenant requires as the proper response of man [sic] his obedience to its commandments, while providing a means of atonement for transgressions.[54]

Such an understanding is repudiated by John, who insists that children of Abraham are not identified by birth into the covenant community but through response to God's gracious initiative.[55] The crowds are like the wilderness to which they have come to hear John — empty, unproductive, lifeless — and so they must become fruitful, producing in their lives behaviors that demonstrate their relation to God (cf. Acts 26:20).

John produces two warnings to the crowd, both of which follow hard upon his declaration that their privileged status is now insecure. First, he reminds them that they can be replaced, by stones! John draws on a number of pertinent images — Abraham, the father[56] of many nations; the ability of God to give Abraham a child (Gen 18:14); the portrayal of "stones" as inanimate, used as a metaphor for lifeless gods and humans (cf. Acts 17:29); the election and shaping of a nation, God's people, in the exodus and crossing of the Jordan, together with the stones used to memorialize this event;[57] the fact that God's promises to Abraham have been coming to realization in the Lukan narrative (1:55, 73) as God has again shown his ability to raise up children (cf. 1:37); and the echo of Isa 51:1b-2:

> Look to the rock from which you were hewn,
>   and to the quarry from which you were dug.
> Look to Abraham your father
>   and to Sarah who bore you;
> for he was but one when I called him,
>   but I blessed him and made him many.

---

53. καί.

54. E. P. Sanders, *Paul and Palestinian Judaism*, 75.

55. See Bovon, 1:172; Allison, "Jesus and the Covenant," 59-60.

56. That is, progenitor and not merely "ancestor," as in the NRSV of Luke 3:8. Cf., e.g., Gen 12:1-2; *Ps. Sol.* 18:3.

57. Cf. Joshua 4; Seitz, "Stones."

John communicates God's capacity, even intent, to make a new people, to arouse life from the lifeless — including persons in these crowds who have come out to John. Perhaps, too, in this reference to children from lifeless stones, we should find a promise to the Gentiles.[58] Hence, while the situation facing this "brood of vipers" is severe, it is not without hope, for God can do the impossible and bring forth life from the lifeless. "Children to Abraham," however, will be those who embrace God's purpose and act accordingly (cf. 16:24-31).

A second warning follows — namely, the prospect of judgment. John employs two disturbingly graphic images to convey the immediacy of his message. First, unfruitful trees will be cut down — a metaphor of judgment also found in Isa 10:33-34; Wis 4:3-5; Sir 6:3, and used later by Jesus (13:6-9). "Even now" underscores the necessity of response in the present, for divine judgment is imminent. Following as it does so closely the use of God as subject in 3:8, the undeclared subject of "to cut down" in 3:9 is presumably divine as well. However, it is already clear, especially from Simeon's words (2:34-35), that the division or judgment with which John is concerned is focused on the coming of Jesus. Co-textual concerns also clarify "good fruit" as "fruits worthy of repentance" — noted in 3:8, illustrated in 3:10-14. The second metaphor on which John draws is that of fire, an image that is also known to us from the OT. Of particular interest is Mal 4:1, where the day of the Lord is likened to a burning oven, in which "all the arrogant and all evildoers" will be burned up so that "neither root nor branch" remains; and Isa 66:24, echoed more strongly in 3:18, where those who have rebelled against God will be judged with an unquenchable fire. In each case, those judged are regarded as opponents of God's purpose and for this reason are cut off, burned up in the fires of judgment. By linking these images to the present as John does and by insisting that those who have truly aligned themselves with God's purpose manifest appropriate behaviors, John accentuates the necessity of readiness *now.* He provokes a crisis, raising the concern among his audience regarding the nature of those behaviors, those fruits.

10-11   The question of the crowds, "What then should we do?" is repeated by tax collectors in 3:12, soldiers in 3:14, a lawyer in 10:25, a ruler in 18:18, a Jerusalem audience in Acts 2:37, a jailer in Acts 16:30, and a zealous Jew in Acts 22:10. Apart from the one exception of 18:18, in each case the question is provoked by instruction, preaching, or a miraculous event in the immediate co-text. This query underscores the relation of 3:10-11 to the preceding material, but it also demonstrates in an explicit way that the redemptive visitation of God demands response.

58. So Jeremias, "λίθος," 271.

What behavior is appropriate to those who claim to have repented? The question and its answer are oriented around a general audience, as if to suggest that sharing with those who lack the basic necessities of life is expected of all. Of course, that John can speak of the possibility of having extra clothing and food is evidence that he recognizes in these crowds people beyond the subsistence level.[59]

In a sense, John's response is nothing more than what one finds already in the Scriptures.[60] Indeed, in Luke's perspective, care for the hungry and naked is nothing more than obeying Moses and the prophets (cf. 16:19-31). Moreover, as in the Scriptures, the behaviors for which John calls are not themselves the basis for membership in God's covenant people; rather, they are manifestations of that relationship. To put it differently, these are the natural outgrowth of lives reoriented around the God who is himself merciful (cf. 6:36). At the same time that John appears to be working very much from within the framework of scriptural tradition, and especially the aphoristic tradition of the wisdom literature, his message is distinguished by its eschatological edge. For him, the present is much more than the needed occasion to recover the covenantal instruction of the past. The present is rushing toward its crisis, when the opportunity for taking up the lifestyles of authentic children of Abraham will have passed.

12-13 From the crowds in general (3:10-11), the spotlight focuses more narrowly on toll collectors who had come to be baptized. This brief scene serves as an amplification of the first, both because it represents an exemplification and concretization of the "fruits of repentance" as articulated to the crowds and because it highlights the positive response to John's preaching of a particularly offensive subgroup within John's audience. John's reply to these toll collectors presupposes a widely documented judgment of such people in antiquity as dishonest persons who exploit the system of taxation for their own financial gain.[61]

---

59. The NRSV translates χιτών as "coat," but it more generally refers to the garment worn next to the skin. It is used elsewhere by Luke in 6:29; 9:3; Acts 9:39. Βρῶμα is a generic word for "food" and appears elsewhere in Luke-Acts only in 9:13. Basic necessities appear to be in view.

60. Isaiah had insisted that participation in ritual acts like the sacrificial cult or fasting would be worthless apart from seeking justice, sharing bread with the hungry, covering the naked, and the like (Isa 1:10-20; 58:6-7). Ezekiel remarks that the characteristic behavior of the righteous includes giving bread to the hungry and clothing the naked (18:5-9), and Tobit refers to these same behaviors as the loving acts of the pious (1:16-17; 4:16).

61. Cf. Michel, "τελώνης," 99-103. On Roman taxation and collection more generally, cf. Badian, *Publicans;* Smallwood, *Jews,* e.g., 150-53; Donahue, "Tax Collectors"; Herrenbrück, *Jesus und die Zöllner,* chs. 4, 6.

The system of taxation operative in Palestine and assumed by Luke was open to abuses of this sort. By this time, the *publicani* of the Roman republic had disappeared from the scene in Palestine and the two forms of taxes were collected by two different enterprises. Direct taxes (the land tax and head tax) were collected by Jewish councils. Collection of indirect taxes (tolls, customs, duties) was handled by private entrepreneurs who bid for this task.[62] It is with those hired to collect these tolls and customs that we are concerned here. The highest bidder won the contract to collect tolls, advanced to the state the amount bid, then set up a machinery for recouping his investment and subsequent costs, and making a profit. In spite of senatorial and imperial concern to minimize abuse, the points at which the value of goods was assessed and the percentage of tariff to be collected was determined remained open to fraudulent behavior. For other reasons, too, toll collectors would have shared an unenviable status in Greco-Roman society,[63] but it is their reputation for involvement in a kind of institutionalized scheme of extortion or robbery that is in view in this context.

Hence Luke writes, "Even Roman toll collectors came,"[64] drawing attention to the response even of this despised element of the Greco-Roman world. Surprisingly, John's reply stops well short of demanding that they find new work. Instead, he challenges them to work out the substance of repentance within the day-to-day activities of their duties as toll collectors. As toll collectors, they work under the authority of those who hired them and have instructions regarding how much to collect;[65] their responsibility is to reflect God's justice by not exceeding that amount.[66] His message here is not that of ascetic idealism, just as his instruction to the crowds in 3:10-11 did not call for communitarianism, an ideal known otherwise in the Greco-Roman world.[67] This leaves open the possibility of a surprisingly positive characterization of toll collectors in the Lukan narrative, a possibility Luke will repeatedly exploit in his attempt to portray salvation as status transposition.[68] Even toll collectors

62. This explains our preference for the translation "toll" rather than "tax" collector (*pace* the NRSV).

63. See below on 5:27-32.

64. Δὲ καί is intensive.

65. Luke elsewhere uses διατάσσω for activity performed under the authority of another — cf. 8:55; 17:9-10; Acts 18:2; 23:31; Donahue, "Tax Collectors," 58.

66. John does not take the more revolutionary stance of insisting that toll collectors leave their jobs or that the whole system be overthrown, but rather insists that such collection reflect a commitment to justice. How radical a stance John is perceived to have thus taken within Luke's narrative is dependent of the view one takes of the tax burden in that world. Unfortunately, Luke himself provides us with very little basis for a judgment of this kind; his concern is much more with toll collectors as persons of despised status than as representatives of an economic or political, systemic evil.

67. Cf., e.g., Plato *Rep.* 5.46.2c; Aristotle *Nic. Ethics* 9.8.1168b; Cicero *De officiis* 1.16.51; Philo *Quod omn.* §§75-86.

68. Cf. Neale, *None but the Sinners,* 164.

receive repentance-baptism and align themselves with God's purpose (cf. 7:29-30).

14 Alongside toll collectors, soldiers are introduced as an amplification and unexpected concretization of John's ethical instruction.[69] Assuming that "the region around the Jordan" refers to Perea, these soldiers could have been Jews in the military service of Herod.[70] Nothing in the narrative co-text demands such a reading, however, and the possibility that Gentiles are thus responding to John cannot be dismissed. (In any case, John behaves toward Jews as though they were Gentiles — 3:7-8.) As in the previous cases, the question provoked by John's preaching concerns the nature of one's response: What would it mean to bear fruits worthy of repentance? John's reply borrows language appropriate to those involved in military occupations[71] and calls for the cessation of characteristic behaviors by which soldiers manipulate the local populace to their own advantage.

15-16 John's provocation of eschatological crisis (3:7-9) elicits two forms of questions from his audience. First, they inquire how they might ready themselves for impending judgment (3:10-14). Now, they query whether he is the Messiah. Recognizing in John's mission the first hints of eschatological consolation (Isaiah 40; cf. Luke 3:4-6), they wonder if he is God's agent of salvation. For them, the meaning of "Messiah" is manifestly fluid at this point; hope is present but ill defined. They do not know if John and the anticipated messianic figure fit the same profile, and this allows John to begin the process of outlining what to expect of the Messiah. At the same time, he is able to identify his own relationship to the coming one. According to the narrator, John's answer is to *all* the people; everyone receives the invitation to accept his baptism and receive the baptism "with the Holy Spirit and fire."

John addressed the people by characterizing the Messiah in comparison with himself. As a result, the step parallelism of 1:5–2:52[72] is carried over from the birth narrative into the larger narrative of Luke-Acts and explicitly foregrounded in John's self-awareness. (1) The Messiah is superior to John in terms of status. John does not count himself worthy even to serve as the Messiah's slave by removing the thong of his sandals.[73] (2) John characterizes himself as the messenger or prophet who prepares the way for the coming one, using language that echoes Mal 3:1; 4:5, thus embracing the role anticipated for him in 1:17, 76; 3:4-6. (3) John designates the Messiah as "more

---

69. The use of καὶ ἡμεῖς seems to suggest this relationship with 3:12-13.

70. Cf. Josephus *Ant.* 18.5.1 §113.

71. On διασείω, cf. 3 Macc 7:21; MM 153; on συκοφαντέω, MM 596.

72. See above, §2.

73. In rabbinical discussions, this act was related to slave-master relations — cf. *b. Sanh.* 62b; *b. Qidd.* 22b; *b. Pesaḥ.* 4a; et al.

powerful" than himself — a comparison that apparently resides in his superior status and above all in his mode of baptism. The character of John's baptism has been articulated in 3:3-14 as repentance-baptism, a cleansing by which one's life is oriented anew around the service of God, especially in the context of interpersonal relations and care for the poor, and in daily occupation. What is the Messiah's baptism?

The conjunction of the Holy Spirit and fire in this baptism is puzzling[74] within the context of Luke-Acts. The Holy Spirit has been present repeatedly in 1:5–2:52, where such roles as empowering and guiding were paramount; for Luke thus far the Holy Spirit has been a manifestation of eschatological blessing and an empowering presence critical to God's redemptive mission. Baptism "with the Holy Spirit," then, must surely be related to these themes, even if other connections of the Spirit with cleansing and purging are also in view. Fire, too, can have this meaning, and it may be that the figure John anticipates will administer a single baptism of refinement and empowerment.[75]

According to this reading, 3:16 might be read in parallel with its repetition and realization in Acts:

Luke 3:16: "He will baptize you with the Holy Spirit and fire."
Acts 1:5: ". . . you will be baptized with the Holy Spirit. . . ."
Acts 11:16: ". . . you will be baptized with the Holy Spirit."

Clearly, Luke saw the full actualization of John's promise in the outpouring of the Spirit at Pentecost and subsequently in the Christian mission (see the reference to "divided tongues, as of fire," in Acts 2:3). This also encourages a reading of the phrases in Acts as elliptical — that is, as the reduction of the definition of Jesus' baptism ("with the Holy Spirit and fire") to the first term ("with the Holy Spirit") for purposes of emphasis.[76]

Another reading is possible, however, which views the coming one as administering, as it were, two baptisms — one with the Holy Spirit, one with fire.[77] This reading is supported by Jesus' announcement in 12:49 — "I came

---

74. See the discussion and opposing conclusions in Dunn, "Spirit-and-Fire Baptism"; Webb, *John the Baptizer,* 289-95.

75. On the theme of blessing, cf. Isa 32:15; 44:3; Ezek 18:31; Joel 2:28-30; 1QS 4:20-21; on cleansing, cf. Isa 4:4; 1QS 3:7-9; 4:20-22; on fire, cf. Dan 7:10; Mal 3:2-4; 1QH 3:20-26; 4 Ezra 13:10-11. Cf. Dunn, "Spirit-and-Fire Baptism."

76. On this form of ellipsis, see Dupriez, *Literary Devices,* 151-52.

77. Cf. most recently Webb, *Jesus the Baptizer,* 289-95 (similarly, *idem,* "Threshing Floor"). This is a much stronger option than most recent commentators have assumed, not least in light of the twofold judgment of 3:17. Nolland's objection (1:152), that the language of 3:16 requires a single baptism, too easily turns Luke's verb ("he will baptize") into a noun ("baptism") and places too much weight on the appearance of a single

to bring fire to the earth, and how I wish it were already kindled!" — in a co-text that correlates "fire" with "division" (12:49-53), and by the familiar use of fire as a metaphor or instrument of judgment (cf. 3:9, 17; 9:54; 17:29). In this case, even though the mission of John was already the occasion for division between those who embrace God's purpose and those who do not, and even though the mission of Jesus and his followers will continue to serve thus, the realization of this aspect of John's promise lies outside the narrative and points to the final judgment.

In any case, it is important to realize that John presents his baptismal activity as an anticipation of the Messiah's; his baptism forces a decision for or against repentance, and this prepares for the Messiah's work (cf. Ezek 36:25-26).

17 Although the image described here is generally taken to be that of winnowing — that is, tossing harvested grain into the air by way of allowing the wind to separate the wheat from the chaff — the language John uses actually presumes that the process of winnowing has already been completed. Consequently, all that remains is to clear the threshing floor, and this is what John pictures.[78] This means that John's ministry of preparation is itself the winnowing, for his call to repentance set within his message of eschatological judgment required of people that they align themselves with or over against God's justice. As a consequence, the role of the Messiah is portrayed as pronouncing or enacting judgment on the people on the basis of their response to John.

Narrative meaning develops as the narrative itself evolves, and this is nowhere more true than here. John establishes an expectation for immediate judgment that is not actualized with the appearance of the coming one. This is not a loose thread left hanging by the narrator, for he picks it up again in 7:18-20 — where John wonders if in fact Jesus is the anticipated one (if so, where is the anticipated judgment?); and in 12:49, where Jesus himself wishes for the commencement of judgment. As before, the question is less *what* will happen, and much more *when* and *how*. Our understanding of the mission and messiahship of Jesus is still being shaped.[79]

---

preposition ("with," ἐν) — as Webb has shown (*Jesus the Baptizer,* 290-91). Fitzmyer (1:473) argues that such a reading ignores the common object, "you" (ὑμᾶς), which requires a single baptism. Why this should be so is unclear, for the narrative section in which 3:16 is found is concerned quite pervasively with the division of "the crowds," "the people," "all," "you," according to their responses to the call to repent.

78. See the discussion in Webb, *John the Baptizer,* 295-300 (likewise, *idem,* "Threshing Floor"; based on Dalman, *Arbeit und Sitte in Palästina,* vol. 3).

79. That the process of dividing Israel continues beyond John's activity into the mission of Jesus and his disciples is a further factor that tells against theses positing a salvation-historical wedge between John and Jesus.

18 The content of John's message to which we have been exposed is portrayed as a summary of the sort of thing John regularly communicated (cf. Acts 2:40). His preaching comes under the heading of "good news," a description undoubtedly recommended to Luke by his presentation of John as the Isaianic herald of good news (cf. Isa 40:3, 9; 52:7; Luke 1:19; 3:3-6). This guarantees John's place in God's redemptive activity, but it also again signifies that John's mission marks the onset of the advent of the Lord to bring his peaceful kingdom.

3.1.3. The Imprisonment of John (3:19-20)

> 19 *But Herod the ruler,*[80] *who had been rebuked by him because of Herodias, his brother's wife, and because of all the evil things that Herod had done,* 20 *added to them all by shutting up John in prison.*

The mention of Herod and his identification as "ruler," following on from Luke's summary of John's message,[81] is abrupt. Since "the word of God came" to him in 3:2, John has been the focus of attention and primary actor. Herod now appears in an antagonistic role, and this recalls the litany of rulers in 3:1-2a and serves to place them in a negative light (cf. 1:52). Luke's concern is to move John off the stage before introducing Jesus in 3:21; in doing so he raises again the theme of opposition.

Luke is vague about the reasons behind John's rebuke of Herod. Perhaps he assumes on the part of his readers a common knowledge of Herod's breach of Jewish law by marrying his brother's wife;[82] otherwise, his phrasing leaves the imagination to conjure up notions of an illicit relationship. Likewise, he is uninformative regarding the nature of the evil things of which John found Herod guilty. Luke is manifestly impervious about such details, preferring instead to depict Herod as possessing a history of evil deeds. In this narrative co-text, we can be certain that these had to do with infractions related to justice and practical holiness — that is, the sorts of behaviors against which John regularly spoke.[83] Herod lives in opposition to God, so it is only to be expected that he will oppose God's spokesperson, John. If this is the lot of those who identify fundamentally with God's redemptive aim and carry out his mission, what will happen to the one for whom John's ministry was a preparation?

---

80. NRSV margin: "tetrarch."

81. Note the μὲν . . . δέ clause, 3:18-19.

82. On this act of Herod, cf. Josephus *Ant.* 18.5.1 §§109-10; Mark 6:17-18. For the law forbidding such a union, see Lev 18:16; 20:21.

83. *Contra* Marshall (149), we should read no contrast between John's exhorting the people (3:18) and rebuking Herod (3:19); cf. 3:7-9, which Luke regards as characteristic speech for John.

3.2. THE INTRODUCTION OF JESUS, SON OF GOD (3:21–4:13)

Luke has now completed his account of John's preparatory activity and has carefully removed John from the public eye. Though the people have been readied for Jesus' arrival by John, Jesus' public appearance is delayed. First, Jesus himself must be readied. His preparation for undertaking his divine mission is the subject of this narrative unit. Here Luke demonstrates Jesus' reception of his divine vocation; his empowerment by the Holy Spirit; his status as a representative of David, Abraham, and, indeed, all humanity; and his uncompromising solidarity with God's purpose. He narrates the crucial stage of transition from the anticipation of Jesus' salvific mission in the service of God's aim to its actualization in his public ministry. That characters within the story will embrace faithful obedience to God is not a given; we may recall the presence of hostile forces at work to frustrate God's purpose. Jesus has been empowered by the Spirit and has heard the heavenly voice, but he must nevertheless discern God's will and align himself with it if he is to take up his divine vocation.

Central to Jesus' preparation is his identity as Son of God (3:22, 38; 4:3, 9) and experience of the Spirit (3:22; 4:1, 9). These two are inextricably linked (see 1:35), with the latter foundational to the former: The Spirit both certifies and makes sonship possible. Luke draws on a number of associations to interpret in what sense Jesus is God's Son. The most immediate is the contrast between the designation of Jesus as Son of God and the description of would-be children of Abraham as the offspring of vipers (3:7-8). "Progeny" exhibit the qualities of their "parents," and this accentuates Luke's characterization of Jesus as one whose behavior reflects that of God. In fact, in the world of ancient Israel the concept of sonship was correlated with the son's active obedience to his father and his representative service on his father's behalf.[1] In the OT, this notion of faithful agency on God's behalf could take on royal trappings, so it is noteworthy that the heavenly voice in 3:22 echoes the voice of God in Ps 2:7. The title could also be used of Israel as a people, so as to lay before them the vocation of covenantal relationship and obedience.[2] Luke also appears to employ the title in 3:38 by way of drawing out the representative character of Jesus for all humanity.

Jesus is Son of God in consequence of his extraordinary conception. It is, however, one thing to be thus designated, another to embrace this identity and the vocation it entails. Gabriel identified Jesus thus in his announcement to Mary, and in a remarkable prolepsis Jesus himself recognizes his status as God's Son and the repercussions of this identification in terms of ultimate

---

1. See Harvey, *Constraints of History,* 159-62.
2. See Luke 1:32, 35. On the sonship of the monarch (cf. 2 Sam 7:14; Pss 2:7; 89:26-27) and of Israel (cf., Exod 4:22; Jer 3:19; Hos 11:1), see Fohrer, "υἱός," 349-53).

allegiance and service (1:32-35; 2:41-51). In 3:21–4:13, the transition Luke narrates for Jesus is not so much that of status *reversal* as of status *actualization,* whereby the adult (cf. 3:23) Jesus receives his commission, explores its meaning in the wilderness and especially in the vulnerability of hostile testing, and so is readied to perform in ways that serve God's gracious aim. It is as God's agent, empowered by the divine Spirit and obedient to God's purpose as exhibited in the Scriptures, that Jesus emerges from his preparations ready to take up his divinely ordained ministry in obedience to God.

3.2.1. The Anointing of Jesus (3:21-22)

> 21 *Now when all the people were baptized, and when Jesus also had been baptized and was praying, the heaven was opened,* 22 *and the Holy Spirit descended upon him in bodily form like a dove. And a voice came from heaven, "You are my Son, the beloved;*[3] *with you I am well pleased."*

Luke is less interested in Jesus' baptism as such, and more concerned with his endowment with the Spirit and God's affirmation of his sonship. Thus, this complex sentence centers on three infinitive clauses set in parallel: "the heaven was opened," "the Holy Spirit descended," and "a voice came."[4] In fact, these actions are reported to have occurred not during Jesus' baptism, but afterward, while he was praying. The initial dependent clauses lead into the focal point of this pericope by stressing Jesus' solidarity with those who had responded positively to John's message; by participating in the ritual act of baptism, we may recall, they (he) communicated their (his) fundamental orientation around God's purpose.

This scene is set in the world of apocalyptic, with its emphasis on the unveiling of divine mystery. The opening of heaven is familiar from apocalyptic literature, as is the heavenly voice.[5] Of particular interest is Ezekiel 2, where the divine voice is accompanied by an empowering spirit, and the message is one of prophetic commissioning. While the *topos* of prayer is not particularly apocalyptic, in Luke-Acts prayer is often mentioned in the context of revelation and commission or empowerment (1:19-20; 2:37-38; Acts 4:23-31; 9:10-19; 10; 13:1-3; 22:7-21).[6]

---

3. Some mss. add "today I have begotten you" (D it), probably under the influence of Ps 2:7.

4. ἀνεῳχθῆναι, καταβῆναι, γενέσθαι.

5. Opening of heaven: e.g., Ezek 1:1; *2 Apoc. Bar.* 22:1; *T. Lev.* 18:6-7; Rev 4:1; 19:11; heavenly voice: e.g., Ezek 1:25, 28-2:1; Rev 4:1; 10:4.

6. See Crump, *Jesus the Intercessor.*

These apocalyptic elements direct our attention to one of the two central foci of this scene — namely, the divine pronouncement of Jesus' status. Of course, we (Luke's audience) are already aware of Jesus' son- and messiahship (1:32-35, 41; 2:11). Now, however, Jesus' identity in relation to God and God's redemptive project is proclaimed by God himself. Heaven itself has opened, providing us with direct insight into God's own view of things. That the voice of God agrees with those earlier voices (i.e., of Gabriel, Elizabeth, and the angelic host) accents their credibility. It also underscores the bi-polarity of possible responses to Jesus. One can join Elizabeth, the angels, the narrator, and others who affirm Jesus' exalted status and/or identity as God's Son, or one can reject this evaluation and so pit oneself over against God.

Significantly, God's words in 3:22 echo the OT, and this confirms their capacity to speak on his behalf too. One hears first Ps 2:7. The verbal resemblance is minor,[7] but God's voice resonates with the earlier words of God's personal servant Gabriel in 1:32-35, where the connection was made between "Son of God" and the Davidic throne. What is more, for Luke the occasion of Jesus' baptism is manifestly his anointing for divine service. This is the interpretation given by Jesus in 4:18-19 and repeated by Peter in Acts 10:37-38. This confluence teases out from Psalm 2 another key description of the Davidic king: the Lord's anointed one. As a result, the heavenly voice draws on the psalm, with its important picture of the anointed, Davidic monarch who is God's earthly representative, employing those associations along with the hope it spawned, to aid the signifying process at work in the Lukan scene. Equally consequential are the ways in which that psalmic message is transformed in its Lukan application, where "Son of God" can no longer be understood in an adoptionistic sense and where anointing with oil has been superseded by endowment with the Spirit.[8]

Thus, Jesus' baptism as traditionally understood has been cast by the narrator as Jesus' anointing by the Spirit. This is a pivotal experience for Jesus that (1) sets in motion the sequence of events to follow and, by implication, sets the course of his entire mission (cf. 4:1, 14, 18-19); (2) is expounded as the event that determines his understanding of his divine mission and empowers him to perform accordingly (4:18-19; Acts 10:37-38); and (3) anticipates the analogous empowering of Jesus' followers in Acts (e.g., Acts 1:8;

---

7. LXX: υἱός μου εἶ σύ; Luke 3:22: σὺ εἶ ὁ υἱός μου.

8. Fitzmyer (1:485; cf. *Luke the Theologian,* 105) denies that Luke has intended an allusion to Ps 2:7 here or that he has interpreted the baptism scene as messianic (though he allows for the messianic interpretation of Jesus' baptism by Peter in Acts 10). His view is overly determined by his conclusion that "Son of God" would not have been equated with "Messiah" in pre-Christian times (though cf. 4QFlor 1:10-14; 1QSa 2:11-12; 4Q246) and not determined enough by the interpretive bias already given Luke's audience by (especially) 1:32-35; 2:11; 3:15-16.

2). No symbolic equation of Spirit and dove has been found in literature earlier than or contemporaneous with the Gospels,[9] and it may be that this simile is intended to evoke the symbolism of the dove as a herald or bearer of good tidings; this would advance the portrait of Jesus' empowerment to proclaim good news.[10] Luke's "in bodily form" emphasizes the materiality of this apocalyptic scene in a characteristic way (cf. 22:43-44; 23:44-45; 24:50-53; Acts 1:9-11; 2:1-4).

The second text foregrounded by the heavenly voice in 3:22 is Isa 42:1,[11] a passage that also intimately links the object of divine pleasure with the anointing of the Spirit for divine mission. Our hearing an echo of Isa 42:1 also picks up on earlier intertextual connections with the Isaianic Servant in the Gospel — for example, Isa 42:6; 49:6 in 2:32.[12] Finally, we may hear echoes of Gen 22:2, not only because of linguistic parallels, but also because of the importance of the story of Abraham for Luke thus far.[13] This would help to link further the realization of the divine promise to Abraham with the commission of Jesus.

The purpose of the divine voice in 3:22 is above all that of providing an unimpeachable sanction of Jesus with regard to his identity and mission. Working in concert with the endowment of the Holy Spirit, this divine affirmation presents in its most acute form Jesus' role as God's agent of redemption. This accentuates Jesus' role as God's representative, the one through whom God's aim will be further presented and worked out in the story, but it also demonstrates at least in a provisional way the nature of Jesus' mission by calling attention to the boundaries of his exercise of power.[14] His mission and status are spelled out in relation to God and with reference to his purpose as expressed in the Scriptures, as God's Servant and Son who fulfills his mission of redemption and establishes peace with justice in ways that flow out of his uncompromising obedience to God. It is this notion of the boundaries determined by obedience to God's purpose that the devil will test in 4:1-13.

9. See the survey in Keck, "Spirit."

10. See Gen 8:11; *b. Giṭ.* 45a; *b. Sanh.* 95a; M. Turner, "Jesus and the Spirit," 11-13.

11. The verbal association in this case would be closer to the MT and certain Greek translations (cf. Theod. and Aq.: εὐδόκησα) than the LXX (προσεδέξατο); cf. Matt 12:18.

12. Others have suggested echoes of Exod 4:22-23; Isa 41:8; 44:2; but these are less easy to establish with reference to the local co-text in Luke 3. Cf. the discussion in Bock, *Proclamation,* 99-105.

13. Verse 22: σὺ εἶ ὁ υἱός μου ὁ ἀγαπητός; Gen 22:2: λαβὲ τὸν υἱόν σου τὸν ἀγαπητόν, ὃν ἠγάπησας; cf. Gen 22:12, 16. For the importance of Abraham material to Luke's depiction of Jesus, see above, §2.

14. Cf. Seymour-Smith, *Anthropology,* 166: Legitimacy not only justifies one's position but also sets boundaries by its moral and normative qualities on the exercise of power.

3.2.2. The Genealogy of Jesus (3:23-38)

> 23 *Jesus was about thirty years old when he began his work. He was the son (as was thought) of Joseph son of Heli,* 24 *son of Matthat, son of Levi, son of Melchi, son of Jannai, son of Joseph,* 25 *son of Mattathias, son of Amos, son of Nahum, son of Esli, son of Naggai,* 26 *son of Maath, son of Mattathias, son of Semein, son of Josech, son of Joda,* 27 *son of Joanan, son of Rhesa, son of Zerubbabel, son of Shealtiel, son of Neri,* 28 *son of Melchi, son of Addi, son of Cosam, son of Elmadam, son of Er,* 29 *son of Joshua, son of Eliezer, son of Jorim, son of Matthat, son of Levi,* 30 *son of Simeon, son of Judah, son of Joseph, son of Jonam, son of Eliakim,* 31 *son of Melea, son of Menna, son of Mattatha, son of Nathan, son of David,* 32 *son of Jesse, son of Obed, son of Boaz, son of Sala, son of Nahshon,* 33 *son of Amminadab, son of Admin, son of Arni, son of Hezron, son of Perez, son of Judah,* 34 *son of Jacob, son of Isaac, son of Abraham, son of Terah, son of Nahor,* 35 *son of Serug, son of Reu, son of Peleg, son of Eber, son of Shelah,* 36 *son of Cainan, son of Arphaxad, son of Shem, son of Noah, son of Lamech,* 37 *son of Methuselah, son of Enoch, son of Jared, son of Mahalaleel, son of Cainan,* 38 *son of Enos, son of Seth, son of Adam, son of God.*

Having narrated the divine affirmation and empowerment of Jesus as Son of God (3:21-22), Luke interrupts the progression of the story in order to provide information directly to his audience. Following this pause, he will resume the story at the point where he left it, stitching together the two scenes with references to the Jordan (4:1; implied in 3:22), the Holy Spirit (3:22; 4:1), and to Jesus' identity as God's Son (3:22; 4:3). In the interim, he provides further legitimation of Jesus as Son of God in the form of a genealogy.

First, however, he mentions that Jesus was "about thirty years old," thus indicating in a circuitous way that Jesus had attained the age of public service.[15] The genealogy itself finds a natural niche here at the outset of Jesus' public ministry.

In lineage- or descent-based status systems like that into which Jesus was born, genealogies served the crucial function of determining membership in a given kinship group. (Luke has already registered his sensitivity to such questions [1:5, 27, 55, 69, 73; 2:4; 3:8].) Genealogies serve as indicators of (inherited) status; as such, it is commonly recognized that they might be subject to "genealogical amnesia" (where insignificant or problematic ancestors are suppressed) and idealism (where lists are adjusted to fulfill new social

---

15. Cf. Gen 41:46; Num 4:3, 23; 2 Sam 5:4; Dionysius *Rom. Ant.* 4.6.

requirements). As a literary form, genealogies are concerned as much with theological and apologetic issues as with historical; in them resides remarkable social power.[16]

How does this genealogy function in this context? First, it is noteworthy that Jesus, not John, receives a genealogy in the narrative (though cf. 1:5-6). This indicates again the superiority of Jesus.[17] Second, the genealogy of Jesus is carefully framed — with references both to "son of God" in 3:22, 38 and to Jesus' solidarity with humanity in 3:21, 38. Even though with 3:23 Luke changes the mode of his narration, from "showing" to "telling,"[18] these two framing themes guarantee how closely 3:23-38 is integrated into its narrative co-text. Moreover, these concepts help interpret the importance of this genealogy. The concatenation, or chain of causes, represented by the repetition of "son of,"[19] is rare in biblical genealogies (though cf. 1 Chr 3:10-24; 6:16-30), but serves an important function. It not only links together these members of Jesus' family line, but especially provides for a kind of crescendo culminating in the acknowledgment of God as the originator of Jesus' ancestral line. Jesus is thus rooted securely in the past of God's covenantal interaction with God's people, and his ancestral credentials as God's redemptive agent are asserted.[20] The reference to Adam as son of God presents the divine origin of the human race and indicates Jesus' solidarity with all humanity. But this is not all.[21]

At the outset, Luke provides a deliberate aside to his audience: Jesus "was the son (as was thought) of Joseph" (3:23). This comment serves as a kind of heading for the genealogy as a whole. Other appearances of the verb "to think" or "to assume" in Luke-Acts show that Luke has in mind an assumption, wrongly made, that leads to persons acting as if it were true.[22] This suggests that, while characters within the story will view Jesus as an ordinary human, the son of Joseph, Luke's auditors should share with the narrator a different (and correct) view. Jesus is only the apparent son of Joseph;

---

16. See Douglas, *Institutions,* chs. 6-7; M. D. Johnson, *Biblical Genealogies;* R. R. Wilson, "OT Genealogies"; Abel, "Genealogies"; Malina and Neyrey, "Honor and Shame," 28.

17. See above, §1.

18. See Booth, *Rhetoric of Fiction,* 3-20.

19. The Greek text does not repeat υἱός after 3:23, preferring instead the genitive of relationship.

20. How well-rooted is Jesus in God's covenantal promise is indicated in the examination of the basis of Luke's genealogy by Bauckham, *Jude,* 315-73.

21. Cf. Acts 17:28-31; Philo *Virt.* 204-5. Some scholars have developed elaborate schemes related to the numerical structure of Jesus' genealogy, but these seem to play no role for the narrator.

22. νομίζω — see 2:44; Acts 7:25; 8:20; 14:19; 16:27; 21:29; cf., however, 16:13.

in fact, his identity as Son of God need not be traced back through Joseph to Adam at all, but rests on his miraculous conception. Thus, the genealogy provides Jesus with the legitimation needed in the world in which he will carry out his mission. As those possessing an insider's vantage point, however, Luke's readers are aware of a more direct means by which to ascertain his exalted status.

3.2.3. The Testing of Jesus (4:1-13)

1 *Jesus, full of the Holy Spirit, returned from the Jordan and was led by the Spirit in the wilderness,* 2 *where for forty days he was tempted by the devil. He ate nothing at all during those days, and when they were over, he was famished.* 3 *The devil said to him, "If you are the Son of God, command this stone to become a loaf of bread."* 4 *Jesus answered him, "It is written, 'One does not live by bread alone.'"*

5 *Then the devil led him up and showed him in an instant all the kingdoms of the world.* 6 *And the devil said to him, "To you I will give their glory and all this authority; for it has been given over to me, and I give it to anyone I please.* 7 *If you, then, will worship me, it will all be yours."* 8 *Jesus answered him, "It is written,*

'Worship the Lord your God,
    and serve only him.'"

9 *Then the devil took him to Jerusalem, and placed him on the pinnacle of the temple, saying to him, "If you are the Son of God, throw yourself down from here,* 10 *for it is written,*

'He will command his angels concerning you,
    to protect you,'

11 *and*

'On their hands they will bear you up,
    so that you will not dash your foot against a stone.'"

12 *Jesus answered him, "It is said, 'Do not put the Lord your God to the test.'"* 13 *When the devil had finished every test, he departed from him until an opportune time.*

Luke's account of the testing of Jesus is a discrete unit within the narrative as a whole. Following the narrative pause represented by 3:23-38, with 4:1 the narrative action commences once again. And 4:1-13 is set off from 4:14 by its geography (the undesignated wilderness versus Galilee); by parallel actions of "returning";[23] and especially by the active presence of the devil, who appears unannounced in 4:2 and withdraws from the narrative stage in

23. Luke 4:1, 14:

190

4:13. In this characteristic way, Luke stages this account so as to foreground the critical interaction between Jesus and the devil.[24] This is not to deny how tightly interconnected this scene is with its narrative co-text. Luke 4:1-13 presents a number of key elements linking it, some almost subliminally, to surrounding material, helping to ensure its interpretation as a bridge scene moving Jesus from his endowment with the Spirit to his public ministry. The most obvious such *topoi* include references to the cosmic and visionary (3:21-22; 4:5), the location in the wilderness in the vicinity of the Jordan (3:2-3, 4, 21; 4:1, 14), the Holy Spirit (3:22; 4:1, 1, 14, 16), Jesus' sonship (3:22, 38; 4:3, 9, 41), the concern with the meaning of Jesus' mission (passim), and Jesus' encounter with hostile forces (4:2-13, 22-30, 33-36). Interestingly, Jesus appears in a much more active role, in some ways reminiscent of his behavior in 2:43-51, than has otherwise been the case since his reintroduction in 3:21. He was baptized, the Spirit descended upon him, he was the assumed son of Joseph — these all portray him in a passive mode; now, he becomes the deixic center, the one around whom the narrative and its actants are oriented, the one preparing to take the initiative (4:14-15) for which he has been equipped.

There is one immensely consequential proviso with respect to this reading of Jesus' active role, however. This is Luke's narratological declaration that Jesus is not acting on his own. Empowered by the Spirit, Jesus is full of the Spirit, and inspired by the Spirit. His central, active role is therefore fundamentally as God's agent, and it is this special relationship and its implications that lie at the root of Jesus' identity in Luke-Acts. Not surprisingly, then, it is this that will be tested in the encounter between Jesus and the devil.

As an episode of transition, 4:1-13 is concerned with finalizing the establishment of Jesus' performative competence prior to his actual assumption of public ministry in the service of God's salvific aim. Luke 3:21-38 was in its own way integral to the demonstration of his competence, indicating his possession of the requisite credentials, power, and authority to set forth on his mission. But these are not enough. They must be matched with Jesus' positive response to God's purpose. Hence, here Jesus will signal his alignment with God's will in a way that surpasses the evidence already provided by his display of submission to God at his baptism. In the OT and in subsequent Jewish tradition, fidelity to God was proven in the midst of testing — whether by the direct action of God himself, through difficult circumstances, or by the direct activity of the devil.[25] In the present scene, the testing conducted by

---

24. Cf. the similar strategy in 1:23, 38, 56; 2:20, 38, 39, 51; 3:19-20.

25. For example, Gen 3:1-19; 22:1-19; Exod 15:25-26; Job; *2 Apoc. Bar.* 79:2; CD 1:15; 1QS 3:24; 5:4-5. See Heinrich Seesemann, "πεῖρα," 25-27; Tweltree, "Temptation of Jesus," 821. Cf. Gerhardsson, *Testing of God's Son,* 27-28, 31-35.

the devil seeks specifically to controvert Jesus' role as Son of God either by disallowing the constraints of that relationship or by rejecting it outright.

Clearly, 4:1-13 pulls together in a profound and programmatic way the various threads of opposition and hostility we have discerned in the story to this point. Such images as "darkness and . . . the shadow of death" (1:79) and the predicted and experienced hostility of 2:34 and 3:19-20, as well as other, less visible evidences of opposition are exposed as manifestations of the evil that would thwart the advent of God's salvation. Behind those efforts stands the devil, who now steps out from behind the curtain for a direct confrontation with the one through whom God would manifest his redemptive will. Behind Jesus, on the other hand, stands the Holy Spirit, so that, through its dramatis personae, 4:1-13 presents a clash of cosmic proportions. This account thus exhibits the basic antithesis between the divine and the diabolic that will continue throughout Luke-Acts.[26]

In addition to the more immediate Lukan co-text, the narrator provides a further and formative interpretive context — namely, the testing of Israel in the wilderness.[27] Indeed, Luke seems deliberately to have drawn together a repertoire of elements from scriptural narration of and reflection on Israel's wilderness wanderings. Particular attention may be drawn to the following:

- divine leading in the wilderness (Deut 8:2; cf. Luke 4:1);
- "forty" (Exod 16:35; Num 14:34; Deut 8:2, 4; cf. Luke 4:2);
- Israel as God's son (e.g., Exod 4:22-23; cf. Luke 4:3, 9);
- the testing of Jesus is analogous to that experienced by Israel and the scriptural texts he cites derive from those events in which Israel was tested by God (Deuteronomy 6-8); and
- though Jesus was full of the Spirit and followed the Spirit's guidance, Israel "rebelled and grieved his holy spirit" (Isa 63:10).

We may note especially the far-reaching similarity between the nature of their testing and his. According to Deuteronomy, (1) Israel was allowed to hunger in order to learn that one does not live by bread alone (8:3); (2) Israel was instructed to worship the one and only God, and not to follow after any other god (6:4-15); and (3) Israel was commanded not to put the Lord God to the test (6:16). In each case, however, Israel failed in their obedience to God (e.g.,

---

26. See Brawley, *Centering on God,* 75-76; Garrett, *Demise of the Devil,* 38-43; Fitzmyer, *Luke the Theologian,* 157. On the devil in Luke, in addition to Garrett, *Demise of the Devil,* see the excursus in Bovon, 1:196-97.

27. A number of Lukan commentators have seen an Adam typology at work here as well, with reminiscences of Gen 3:1-19 found in Luke 4:1-13; cf., e.g., Godet, 1:207-8; Plummer, 109; et al. Cf., however, Fitzmyer, 1:512.

Exod 17:1-7; Deut 9:6-29; cf. Acts 7:35, 39-43). The deployment of these scriptural texts in the production of this new text opens the door to a particularly fertile discursive play; we hear a virtual choir of voices telling this story and giving it significance. The similarities are sufficient in scope and quantity to show that the narrator has drawn attention deliberately to Jesus in his representative role as Israel, God's son. But no sooner are the resemblances sensed than remarkable discontinuities assert themselves. Unlike Israel, Jesus proved his fidelity in the wilderness and so is ". . . presented as the true Son of God, in whom the destiny of Israel was recapitulated and the divine purpose accomplished in that he renders to God the obedience and trust that Israel failed to give."[28] *Now* Jesus is ready to engage in his public ministry in the service of God's redemptive program.

1-4 Luke 4:1 takes up the development of narrative action following the pause in 3:23-28. We discern no rupture in story time as Luke relocates our attention back to Jesus' reception of the Spirit at the Jordan. Luke 4:1-2 sets the stage for the scene of testing as a whole, especially by (1) juxtaposing the supernatural agents influencing Jesus, the Holy Spirit, and the devil, and (2) placing Jesus in the wilderness,[29] separating him from normal communal life for the purpose of testing.[30] This charged setting is further interpreted along these lines by the reference to "forty," a figure associated with Israel's wilderness experience (cf. Ps 95:10; Acts 7:36), and by Jesus' abstinence from food. Jesus is not known in the Third Gospel for his habit of fasting (cf. 7:34!), though in general fasting is understood as a departure from the norm and may be a corollary of spiritual struggle.[31] (See the parallel in Acts 13:1-2, where fasting and discernment for mission are intertwined.)

These ingredients of "setting" are in fact integral to the first test. Jesus' fasting has resulted in his near starvation, and this foregrounds an immediate need, the provision of food. This, together with the language of the devil's suggestion (note that "bread" is in the singular)[32] tells against interpretations that find in this temptation an attempt to incite Jesus to gain acclaim as a kind of welfare king who provides food for the hungry masses. The tension resident

28. C. F. Evans, 256. Cf. G. H. P. Thompson, "Called — Proved — Obedient"; G. J. Steyn, "Intertextual Similarities."

29. The ambiguity of the NRSV — 4:11: "returned from the Jordan . . . in the wilderness" — is potentially confusing. After all, Jesus seems not to have "returned" at all, and, inasmuch as he was with John, he was already in the wilderness (3:2-4). Ὑπο- στρέφω, however, can mean "to turn away" (BAGD 847), and the sense here must be, "Jesus, full of the Holy Spirit, *withdrew* from the Jordan and was led *around* by the Spirit in [not "into"] the wilderness."

30. See Deut 8:2-3; Gerhardsson, *Testing of God's Son,* 40.

31. See above on 2:36-37.

32. Cf. W. Wilkens, "Versuchungsgeschichte," 263.

in the narrative is elsewhere: Will Jesus follow the leading of the Spirit and manifest unwavering trust in God to supply his needs; or will he relieve his hunger by exercising his power apart from God? The devil does not deny *that* Jesus is God's Son, but *exploits* this status by urging Jesus to use his power in his own way to serve his own ends; he thus *reinterprets* "Son of God" to mean the opposite of faithful obedience and agency on God's behalf. Jesus' reply, borrowed from Deut 8:3, does not minimize his need for food; in fact, he thus identifies with the starving people of God in their hunger while at the same time he affirms his trust in divine provision (cf. Deut 28:1-14; Pss 33:18-19; 34:10; Wis 16:26).

5-8 We move immediately from the mundane of daily bread to a visionary spectacle. Jesus is allowed a glimpse of all the kingdoms of the world "in an instant" from an undisclosed but elevated vantage point. At the outset it is worth noting two sources of irony present in Luke's description of this setting. First, we have been led to believe that "all the world"[33] was under the charge of the Roman emperor (2:1; 3:1). Now, however, in a way clearly parallel to the scenario painted in Revelation 13, we discover that the world of humanity[34] is actually ruled by the devil.[35] Luke elsewhere gives us no reason to doubt that the world of both Jews and Gentiles is characterized by the darkness of satanic rule.[36] The perspective he thus outlines is fully at home with the language of reversal and portrayal of hostility characteristic of Luke 1–3, even if it goes beyond them in identifying the activity of those human and systemic agents that oppose God's plan and God's people as manifestations of diabolic rule.

Second, co-textual considerations have kept Psalm 2 at the fore of our developing understanding of Jesus as Son of God, so it is worth contemplating the significance of Ps 2:8:

> Ask of me, and I will make the nations your heritage,
> and the ends of the earth your possession.

God's purpose is to grant Jesus an everlasting kingdom — a promise made in 1:32-33, now recalled by this faint echo of Ps 2:8 and indeed by the devil's own offer. The devil proposes to displace God as Jesus' benefactor. The devil will give him what is due, but in the process extract a great price — that is, Jesus' allegiance. In effect, this is an invitation for Jesus to deny his identity as God's Son, substituting in its place an analogous relationship to the devil.

---

33. Luke 2:1: πᾶσαν τὴν οἰκουμένην; Luke 4:5: πάσας τὰς βασιλείας τῆς οἰκουμένης.

34. That is, οἰκουμένη, not κόσμος.

35. Note that the devil's statement, "for it has been given over to me" (4:6), forbids our proposing for Luke any sort of ultimate dualism; cf. Kruse, "Reich Satans," 50-56.

36. See above on 1:78-79.

Resident in the devil's own words, though, is a recognition that these two possibilities are not really parallel after all, since the devil is not co-equal with God. Whatever rule the devil exercises is that allowed him by God; he can only delegate to Jesus what has already been delegated to him.[37] What Jesus is offered, then, is a shabby substitute for the divine sonship that is his by birth. Jesus' reply, again borrowed from the pages of Deuteronomy (see above), is a rejection of the devil's pretensions to absolute sovereignty and a reaffirmation of his uncompromising fidelity to God.

9-12   The final test is located in Jerusalem, this undoubtedly in symbolic anticipation of the definitive test to face Jesus in his passion (cf. 22:3, 28, 31, 39-46, 53).[38] The temple setting (the locus of God's presence and refuge from danger) is appropriate to the devil's choice of psalms, since Psalm 91 is addressed to "you who live in the shelter of the Most High" (Ps 91:1).[39] It has become clear that Jesus' ears are attuned to the voice of God in Scripture, so the devil adopts a different strategy, purporting now to speak with God's own voice. It is easy enough to dismiss the devil's efforts: Since the devil is an unreliable character, even his use of the OT is duplicitous.[40] One must not overlook the hermeneutical quandary which lies at the root of the different stances taken by the devil and Jesus, however. Both quote Scripture; why prefer one reading over the other?[41]

Fundamentally, the issue here is akin to that in the first test. Jesus is radically committed to one aim, God's eschatological agenda; the devil has an alternative aim, a competing agenda. He wants to recruit Jesus to participate in a test of the divine promises of Psalm 91. In doing so, the devil overlooks the critical reality that the psalm is addressed to those who through their fidelity to God reside in God's presence; even in the psalm faithful obedience to God is the controlling need. Moreover, the devil fails to recognize an even deeper mystery, known already to the believing community of which Luke is a part, that divine rescue may come *through* suffering and death and not only *before* (and *from*) them.[42] Jesus, then, does not deny the validity of God's

37. See further Garrett, *Demise of the Devil,* 38-43 (who explores further the possibilities offered by the commonality of 4:5-7 and Rev 13:7-8); Kruse, "Reich Satans," 44-59.

38. On the order of Luke's tests, cf. Fitzmyer, *Luke the Theologian,* 153; Twelftree, "Temptation of Jesus," 823.

39. See further Gerhardsson, *Testing of God's Son,* 54-59.

40. Brawley, *Centering on God,* 23; cf. McVann, "Status Transformation," 354-55.

41. See Green, *Gospel of Luke,* 26-28; and, more generally, Fowl and Jones, *Reading in Communion.*

42. In this case, the devil shares the viewpoint of those who mock Jesus in 23:35-36: "He saved others; let him save himself if he is the Messiah of God, his chosen one!" Cf. Wisdom 2, 4-5.

promises as quoted by the devil, but he does deny the suitability of their appropriation in this context. He recognizes the devil's strategy as an attempt to deflect him from his single-minded commitment to loyalty and obedience in God's service, and interprets the devil's invitation as an encouragement to question God's faithfulness. Israel had manifested its doubts by testing God, but Jesus refuses to do so (cf. Deut 6:16).

13 On occasion, the threefold performance of an action shows that it is complete, finished,[43] and this is clearly the case here. This means that the tests faced here encapsulate all the tests Jesus would meet during the course of his ministry. And tests would certainly continue — not merely where demonic forces or Satan himself is mentioned (e.g., 4:33-36; 22:3), but throughout his ministry as he encounters forces hostile to God's purpose. As we have learned, behind all such opposition stands the devil,[44] so that Jesus can characterize his whole ministry with the language of testing (22:28).[45]

The completion of this testing is evident in a second way too. By facing these tests and proving his fidelity, Jesus has demonstrated unequivocally his faithful obedience to God and thus his competence to engage in ministry publicly as God's Son. As in similar scenes in roughly contemporaneous Jewish texts, the devil's departure from Jesus signals the devil's concession of defeat and concomitant shameful withdrawal.[46]

---

43. Delling, "τρεῖς," 222; cf. 20:12; 23:22; Acts 10:16.

44. This is most obviously true in the case of Jesus' healing activity, for in almost every account the source of the ailment is traced back to Satan — cf., e.g., 13:10-17; Acts 10:38; Green, "Daughter of Abraham," 652-53; Busse, *Wunder*.

45. Luke 4:2: πειράζω; 22:28: πειρασμός. See Glendenning, "Devil."

46. See *T. Job* 27:2-6; *Hermas Mandate* 12.5.2; cf. Jas 4:7; Garrett, *Demise of the Devil*, 41-42.

4. THE MINISTRY OF JESUS IN GALILEE (4:14–9:50)

Building on the purpose of God to bring salvation, especially as that aim is exhibited in Israel's Scriptures, Luke first introduced his audience to a constellation of narrative anticipations centered on God's redemptive agent, his Son, Jesus (1:5–2:52). Possibilities thus raised were underscored in 3:1–4:13 — both as earlier prophecies concerning John were realized and as Jesus himself was empowered for his divine mission and proven unreservedly faithful to God. With 4:14, then, the Lukan narrative takes a momentous step forward as it initiates the long-awaited account of Jesus' public ministry. With 9:51, the journey to Jerusalem looms large as the context of Jesus' mission. From 4:14–9:50, though, the focus is on the mission of Jesus in Galilee; indeed, it is noteworthy that, later, Galilee will be acknowledged as the region from which Jesus' public ministry was launched (23:5; Acts 10:37; cf. 13:31).

The birth narrative documented *what* we might expect of God's gracious visitation, but it less forthcoming regarding *how* God's purpose would be achieved. Significantly, 4:14–9:50 articulates the pattern of ministry by which God's aim would be actualized — first by providing a more definitive understanding of the outworking of Jesus' sonship and empowerment by means of a publicly proclaimed missionary program (4:16-30), then by demonstrating that program in concrete missionary practice. Also of consequence is the calling and instruction of disciples, beginning in 5:1-11 and thereafter occupying a key role in the gathering of the people of God. *Hence, 4:14–9:50 demonstrates how Jesus, empowered by the Spirit, understood the nature of his vocation and engaged in its performance by means of an itinerant ministry balancing proclamation and miraculous activity and occasioning a division between supporters/disciples and opponents.*

§9 Luke 4:14–9:50 in Literary Perspective

With Luke 4:14, we enter the performance stage wherein we encounter the actualization of possibilities related earlier in Luke's narrative. Among these, Jesus' salvific activity and the opposition it engendered are chief. One obvious manifestation of opposition is cosmic evil of the sort previously encountered in the description of Jesus' testing (4:1-13), now apparent in the hostile presence of evil spirits (e.g., 4:33-36, 41; 8:26-39). More generally for Luke, though, diabolic forces are behind diseases of all sorts,[1] and Jesus' mission is in part to do battle with those forces through healings and exorcisms. On the other hand, opposition is the product of the division among human actors as they respond in different ways to Jesus. Both forms of opposition have been anticipated (e.g., 1:79; 2:34-35) and, indeed, are the experience of all of those who serve God's purpose — in Luke's narrative, first John, now Jesus, and later Jesus' followers (cf. already 9:5). In his Galilean ministry, Jesus encounters human opposition immediately in 4:16-30. Also of interest is the juxtaposition of those who oppose him with those who embrace or receive his message in Luke 5; here, as in 7:29-30, one can discern with no difficulty between good and ill — that is, between people who embrace God's purpose and serve God on the one hand, and those who reject his will and oppose its expression in Jesus' ministry on the other. At the same time, Jesus' followers, presumed servants of God's purpose, do not always understand that aim and in fact are sometimes portrayed more as opponents than helpers. Because for Luke-Acts a central concern is the continuation of God's redemptive work even after Jesus' execution, training in discipleship is foregrounded in this narrative section (e.g., 6:17-49; 8:9-18), and carried over into the next for even greater emphasis.

Mention of God's aim is a reminder that the Lukan narrative heretofore has been markedly theocentric. The present section does not depart from the radical alignment of the narrative toward God. This is represented in a variety of ways, initially by the programmatic report that Jesus returned to Galilee and carried on his teaching ministry "filled with the power of the Spirit" (4:14-15). Repeated in other ways in 4:18-19 and 5:17 (cf. Acts 2:22; 10:38), this characterization of Jesus serves as a kind of heading for what follows, underscoring that throughout his ministry Jesus is God's agent, serves his aim, acts on his behalf, and works by his power.[2] Similarly, along with Peter, supernatural voices recognize Jesus as "of God" (cf. 4:34, 41; 8:28; 9:20, 35). Jesus himself represents the shape of his mission with direct and indirect reference to the Scriptures (e.g., 4:18-19, 25-28), which exhibit God's purpose, and he grounds the itinerant quality of his ministry in divine necessity (4:43). A further testimony to the theocentrism of this lengthy narrative section is the typical response of the people to Jesus' miraculous activity. Miracles lead to doxology and faith in God (e.g., 5:25-26; 7:16).[3]

---

1. See Acts 10:38; Busse, *Wunder,* e.g., 79; Green, "Daughter of Abraham," 652-53; Kee, *Miracle,* 190-220.

2. Cf. M. Turner, "Spirit Endowment," 53; Chilton, "Announcement in Nazara," 151. *Contra* Schmeichel ("Christian Prophecy," 299-300), who has it that, to this point, Jesus is "controlled and motivated by the Spirit," but from henceforth is on his own, so to speak.

3. Thus, "God [in Luke] is the Most High who enters human history to show his mercy and to call for a response of praise and glory" (Donahue, "A Neglected Factor,"

Luke 4:14–9:50 exhibits no straightforward narrative structure. Instead, this narrative section is teeming with the complexities of interactive narrative cycles, actualizing narrative possibilities previously raised while at the same time opening up new possibilities for further development. For example, Luke 5:1-11 introduces the calling of disciples as a means of satisfying the primary objective of gathering God's people. In calling disciples, however, Jesus sanctions a further narrative need — namely, for disciples to be about the task of "catching people." Subsequently, the twelve are in fact commissioned to proclaim the kingdom of God and to heal (9:1-6) and in this way to manifest their growing competence for participating even more fully in the realization of God's redemptive purpose.

A handful of structural features appear regularly in 4:14–9:50. First, Jesus' activity is balanced between proclamation and miracle-working, both serving as manifestations of the good news, both designated as integral to Jesus' mission,[4] and both attracting response. Response, in fact, is a key theme in this section, both in terms of Luke's interest in Jesus' widening reputation and with respect to the division caused by Jesus' missionary activity. There is no way to predetermine how one will respond, nor do all of one group — say, Pharisees or Jesus' disciples — always respond in a "typical way." The only given is that response is forthcoming; and, as we are drawn into the narrative and identify with its characters, we also encounter the need for response to Jesus' mission and the divine purpose it manifests.

Jesus' activity is not entirely public in nature. He returns to the wilderness or engages in prayer or retreats from the public at regular intervals in this narrative section (e.g., 4:42; 5:16; 6:12). These reports are reminiscent of the testing of Jesus in the wilderness (4:1-13) and serve to remind us of Jesus' need continuously to discern God's purpose and orient himself around it — not least in the midst of competing claims (cf. 4:42-43), conflict (cf. 5:16; 6:12), and momentous decisions (cf. 6:12).

Throughout 4:14–9:50 Luke also makes use of narrative summaries (e.g., 4:14-15, 44; 5:15; 7:17; 8:1-3). These appear regularly not so much to compress into a brief compass an extended period in the story;[5] rather, these summaries are made necessary by the episodic character of Luke's account. They serve as précis, reorienting Luke's audience to the thread holding the various scenes together, reminding the reader what overarching aim is being served and what overall effect Jesus' ministry is producing.

---

568). On responses of faith and praise, cf. Achtemeier, "Lucan Perspective"; Tannehill, *Narrative Unity*, 1:86-87.

4. *Contra* Kilgallen, who thinks that Luke is concerned to counter an overemphasis on *deeds* by accentuating *words* ("Provocation"); see Green, "Daughter of Abraham," 645-46. A number of recent studies have argued that Luke distinguishes "power" (δύναμις) from the Spirit, relating the former to the miraculous and the latter to inspired speech (cf., e.g., Schweizer, "πνεῦμα," 404-15). For the view that the Spirit in Lukan conception is especially related to inspired speech, see Stronstad, *Charismatic Theology;* Menzies, *Early Christian Pneumatology; idem, Empowered for Witness;* Shelton, *Mighty in Word.* See, however, the critique of this view in M. Turner, "Spirit and Power."

5. See Bal, *Narratology,* 72-73.

§10 Luke 4:14–9:50 and the Region of Galilee

Geographically, 4:14–9:50 is centered in Galilee. This narrative section begins with a summary statement locating Jesus' ministry in Galilee, followed immediately by the account of Jesus' inaugural sermon in one of Galilee's towns, Nazareth. In 9:51, however, we are informed that Jesus "set his face to go to Jerusalem," some of his messengers immediately find themselves in Samaritan territory (9:52), and the remainder of Jesus' public ministry is narrated with him more or less en route to Jerusalem. For the present, Jesus' ministry is located almost solely in Galilee (4:14, 31); subsequently, different characters will refer back to these Galilean beginnings (e.g., 10:13-15; 22:59; 23:5-6). Galilean towns are mentioned — Capernaum (4:23, 31; 7:12; cf. 10:15), Nain (7:11), and Bethsaida (9:10; cf. 10:13) — or implied, as in the case of Tiberias, Herod's headquarters (8:1-3; 9:7-9). In 10:13-15, in a narrative reversion to an earlier ministry, Jesus also mentions his ministry in the Galilean town of Chorazin. The Sea of Gennesaret (Galilee) is mentioned in 5:1-2; 8:22-23, and at one point Jesus enters the region of the Gerasenes (8:26-39), adjacent to Galilee.

The one puzzle in this geographical picture is 4:44, where Luke summarizes Jesus' continued ministry with reference to "the synagogues of Judea."[6] As we noted earlier on 1:5, Luke can use "Judea" in this more inclusive way to signify "the land of the Jews" (cf. esp. 23:5). Here the ambiguity may reflect the fact that Luke portrays Jesus' Galilean ministry as attracting audiences from villages in Galilee and Judea, Jerusalem, and from the coast of Tyre and Sidon (5:17; 6:17). Consequently, even though Galilee is the locus of his ministry, the reach of Jesus' reputation and mission extends beyond the borders of Galilee.[7]

Galilee is more than a geographical location, and it is important to ask how this section of Luke's Gospel is located on the cultural map. Galilee (together with Jericho) was the heart of agricultural production in Palestine. Its fertile soil contributed to the growth of such crops as grapes (for wine), figs, olives, and wheat, as well as to pasturage, while the Sea of Galilee (lake of Gennesaret) served as the hub of an important fishing industry.[8] This was an agrarian society marked by many features of peasant culture, as reflected in this narrative segment. One encounters, for example, agriculture-related settings for Jesus' ministry (5:1-11; 6:1; 8:32) and parabolic teaching (8:5-8);[9] indeed, peasant life provides a metaphorical arsenal for his instruction — cf., for example, 5:37-38; 6:38, 41-44, 48-49; 7:32; 8:5-8, 18.

---

6. This incongruence is reflected in the manuscript tradition, where A D Θ Ψ et al. read τῆς Γαλιλαίας, and W (1424) read εἰς τὰς συναγωγὰς τῶν Ἰουδαίων. The reading followed by the NRSV, τῆς Ἰουδαίας (p75 ℵ B et al.), is clearly the more difficult.

7. Theobald ("Anfänge," 91-92) and Völkel ("Anfang Jesu") believe that the Galilean ministry of Jesus embraces only 4:14-44, and that with 5:1 his ministry is extended to all of Palestine or to the whole Jewish people (cf. Schürmann, 1:260; Nolland, 1:215-16). A review of the places Jesus is found in this section (see above) will not support this interpretation, however.

8. See Josephus, *J.W.* 3.3.1-2 §§35-43; 3.10.8 §§516-21. See Oakman, "Countryside"; Freyne, *Galilee*, 90-115.

9. Cf. Jeremias, *Parables*.

Peasant societies typically evidence a general (though not absolute) polarity between the city (locus of power, wealth, and privilege) and the village/countryside (rural populace of peasants). And some interpreters have read this distinction into Luke-Acts, suggesting, for example, that ". . . John and Jesus flourish in 'villages,' but experience conflict in 'cities.' "[10] Within Luke's Galilee, however, such a distinction has no place. In fact, a survey of Luke's language of the city, village, and country[11] reveals that Luke is relatively indiscriminate in his use of such categories and, in any case, that Galilean cities are not characterized as the habitats of the power elite who trouble Jesus. More to the point is that the city is for Jesus a fundamental focal point of his ministry. Thus, mission statements include direct reference to the need to evangelize cities (4:43; 9:5),[12] mission summaries locate Jesus' ministry in cities (8:1; cf. 8:39), and accounts of his missionary practice are set in cities (4:16,[13] 31; 5:12; 7:11, 12, 37) or among people from the city (8:4). Resistance can arise in the city (4:29, 31), but so can the city serve as a place of retreat (9:10). Similarly, villages can serve as the setting for ministry (8:1; 9:6) and as the home of those who come out to see Jesus (5:17; 8:4). The presence of the power elite in the Galilean ministry of Jesus is mostly indirect — as in the mention of a toll office (5:27), and in the allusion to Tiberias, Herod's home, in 7:18 (cf. 3:19-20); 9:7-9. When Jesus first encounters hostility from the power brokers of his people, it is significant that they have been joined by their colleagues from outside Galilee — that is, from Judea and (the city of) Jerusalem (5:17; cf. Acts 14:19). Later however, anonymous people, people not known as Pharisees and teachers of the law, arrive from the larger area including Jerusalem, but they seem only to want to participate in and do not oppose Jesus' ministry (6:17-19).

Under Luke's eye, then, Galilee does not typify the general polarity of urban and rural, and Jesus' ministry is directed especially to "cities" but also to villages. The power elite have almost no direct presence, and the opposition Jesus meets from Jewish leaders seems to be related to the arrival of those from outside the region. That Jerusalem is singled out in 5:17 is not only evidence of its geo-political and socio-religious importance in ancient Palestine, but also serves proleptically to identify the Jewish leaders from Jerusalem as the primary group hostile to Jesus. Jerusalem as a whole is not implicated, however, as 6:17 makes clear. These observations show Luke's capacity to use normal cultural expectations in parodic ways, transforming them to accentuate the relevance of Jesus' good news for both rural and urban environs.

In other ways Luke's narrative reflects more straightforwardly what would be expected in an agrarian culture, especially as this relates to economics.[14] First, peasant existence generally is characterized by the ever-present demands of one's family, the needs of one's ongoing agricultural operation, the demands for meeting the social

---

10. Oakman, "Countryside," 172.

11. That is, πόλις, κώμη, and ἀγρός.

12. Luke 9:5: Greek: πόλις; NRSV: "town."

13. Cf. 1:26, where Nazareth is a city (Greek: πόλις; NRSV: "town").

14. Cf. Shanin, ed., *Peasant Societies;* A. W. Johnson and Earle, *Evolution of Human Societies,* 271-301.

obligations of village life, and the requirements of external demands — in this case, the Jerusalem temple and Rome. Peasant life, then, rests uneasily on a narrow margin between subsistence and abject poverty, and it is against such a background that gleaning rights (6:1) and a feeding miracle (9:12-17) might gain special significance. Moreover, this underscores the unwelcome presence of toll collectors like Levi and his friends (5:27, 29).

Second, we may refer to systems of economic exchange within the peasant village, of which two sorts were operative. The first is generalized reciprocity — that is, a transaction characteristic of those who share close kinship ties, whereby the exchange is essentially one-sided, altruistic, the giving of a gift without explicit stipulations for any reciprocation in kind. The second is balanced reciprocity — the direct exchange of goods of approximately equal value within a relatively narrow period of time.[15] Concerns with reciprocity are present in Luke's account — for example, "the measure you give will be the measure you get back" (6:38c) — and, as we will see shortly, can be brought to the forefront in order to be dismissed or parodied. Here, it is important to observe the central role allotted kinship relations, evaluations of social distance and nearness, in peasant life. Characters in Luke's account show a marked concern for determining the boundaries of "our group" and stipulating the nature of appropriate interaction with those outside the group (e.g., 4:23-29; 9:49-50). Numerous factors can contribute to the definitions of acceptable limits in kinship-based cultures, including physical maladies that are marks of uncleanness or keep one from making the expected contribution to village subsistence. Jesus not only condemns the way this concern with boundaries is manifested, but he himself engages in practices such as extending forgiveness and healing that restore community status (e.g., 4:18-19, 39; 5:14; 7:15, 34, 36-50; 9:12-17).

Third, and closely related, Luke's narrative reflects the patronage system characteristic of the Mediterranean world — a system of relationships grounded in inequality between the two principals. "A patron has social, economic, and political resources that are needed by a client. In return, a client can give expressions of loyalty and honor that are useful for the patron."[16] A textbook illustration of patronage appears in 7:1-10: According to the elders (i.e., the clients), the centurion (i.e., the patron) deserves Jesus' help since he built the synagogue in Capernaum. Overall, however, Luke's accounts are less focused on individual patron-client relations and less friendly toward the institution of patronage. In fact, Luke's material is more concerned with the patronal system as such, a system by means of which those in need (clients) are controlled by those (patrons) to whom they are indebted. Of special interest, then, is Jesus' instruction to give without expectation of return — a message applicable to

---

15. This nomenclature is based on anthropological work among the Trobriands and is generalized for primitive societies by Sahlins, *Economics,* 185-230. Although requiring nuance in the social setting of Luke's world, this perspective helpfully underscores the relation of kinship distance to economic relations.

16. Moxnes, "Patron-Client Relations," 242. See further *idem, Economy of the Kingdom; idem,* "Social Relations"; J. Elliot, "Patronage"; Danker, *Benefactor;* Gellner, "Patrons"; Gilsenan, "Patron-Client Relations": Waterbury, "Patrons and Clients"; Seymour-Smith, *Anthropology,* 219.

patronal relations and to systems of balanced reciprocity — in 6:34-35, together with his portrayal of God as the Supreme Benefactor who gives freely (6:35b-36).[17] In these contexts it is imperative to remember that Jesus thus makes an economic statement grounded ultimately in his vision of a transformed system of social relations, itself grounded in his portrayal of God. People who follow Jesus are to give to each other as they would to those of their immediate kinship group. Distinctions based on social status as defined in the larger world are thus overturned as Jesus challenges people to accept the previously unacceptable as though they were family.

Interestingly, Luke reflects Galilean culture in his narrative, but he does so in creative and critical ways. His account is clearly rooted in those cultural norms, but in a parodic way. Through the shaping of the story he seems to cater to, then transform normal expectations. This is an outgrowth of his portrayal of the actualization of God's redemptive aim as status reversal.

4.1. JESUS PROCLAIMS THE GOOD NEWS IN JEWISH SYNAGOGUES (4:14-44)

Luke 4:14-44 is interwoven with previous material, but it also exhibits its own internal coherence. References to the Spirit in 4:14, 18 are interpretive throwbacks to Jesus' anointing (3:21-22)[1] and testing in the wilderness (4:1). With these tags, the narrator observes that the onset of Jesus' public ministry is the natural development of 3:21–4:13. Having been empowered and sanctioned as God's Son, Jesus now performs as God's Son. On the other hand, 4:14-15 and 4:42-44 form an *inclusio* around 4:16-41. In this way summaries of Jesus' missionary activity (with parallel references to proclamation, synagogues, and Jesus' reputation) receive concrete illustration in Jesus' public proclamation, exorcism, and healing in synagogues (4:16, 28, 33, 38) and a home (3:38).[2] The initial reference to the power of the Spirit (4:14) is echoed in 4:18, then applied to Jesus' teaching and exorcism in 4:32, 36. Jesus' paradigmatic reference to a ministry of providing "release" is exemplified immediately in accounts of exorcism and healing (4:31-41). And both 4:18-19 and 4:43 employ the Isaianic language of the herald to characterize Jesus' mission and message. In these ways and others these verses exhibit their connectedness as a narrative unit.[3]

These scenes are concerned especially with the origin and nature of Jesus' authority, an emphasis first sounded in an ironic way by the attempts

---

17. See also 4:18-19; 6:20-21; 7:41-42.
1. Cf. Finkel, "Sermon at Nazareth."
2. Luke earlier employed this literary device, summary + concrete illustration + summary, in 2:40-52.
3. Cf. Busse, *Nazareth-Manifest*, 47-54.

to identify Jesus' father: son of Joseph (4:22) or Son of God (4:41; cf. 1:35 → 4:34)? Jesus himself claims a special status in God's eschatological purpose (4:16-21), and, even though in the end it is rejected by his townspeople, it is sanctioned by the active presence of the Spirit (4:14) and recognized, however incompletely, by synagogue crowds (4:23, 32, 36) and by demons (4:34, 41).[4]

These scenes are also taken up with the consequences of Jesus' status, the ministry activity that grows out of his obedience to and empowerment from God. Taken together, they highlight four features of Jesus' ministry. First, his is a ministry empowered by the Spirit.[5] Second, Luke's central interest in Jesus' message, and the inseparability of teaching/preaching (4:15, 16-21, 31, 43-44) and the miraculous (4:16-21, 33-36, 38-41), is foregrounded here. Indeed, 4:18-19 establishes a narrative need for Jesus "to bring good news to the poor," and so these verses characterize the form and primary recipients of Jesus' ministry. Third, 4:43 establishes a second need — namely, for Jesus to carry out a ministry noted for its itinerant nature. Both needs are rooted in God's purpose — 4:18-19 by reference to the Scriptures, 4:43 by reference to divine necessity ("must"). Finally, Luke highlights the importance of response to Jesus' ministry — whether positive (4:15, 39, 42), negative (4:28), or, at least, a recognition that may lead to a faith-response (4:22, 32, 36).[6] Jesus, we may recall, has come to clear the threshing floor (3:17), to cause a division within Israel (2:34), for the manifestation of God's purpose in his ministry elicits responses both negative and positive.

4.1.1. Jesus Returns to Galilee (4:14-15)

> 14 *Then Jesus returned to Galilee in the power of the Spirit,[7] and a report about him spread through all the surrounding country.* 15 *He was teaching in their synagogues, being praised by everyone.[8]*

Luke introduces Jesus' public ministry by characterizing Jesus and orienting us to his style of ministry. The parallel with 4:1 — agency of the Spirit +

---

4. Cf. Malina and Neyrey, "Honor and Shame," 49, 58; McVann, "Status Transformation," 355-56.

5. If the subsequent narrative neglects to mention the continuing presence of the Spirit, this is surely because it is everywhere assumed. The nature of 4:14 as a heading and of 4:18-19 as a programmatic announcement accentuates the understanding of the narrator and of Jesus that his ministry would be undertaken in the power of the Spirit.

6. Cf. Nolland, "Impressed Unbelievers."

7. NRSV: "Jesus, filled with the power of the Spirit, returned to Galilee"; this seems an unnecessary harmonization with 4:1 (where πλήρης is read).

8. NRSV: "began to teach . . . and was praised." The imperfect (ἐδίδασκεν) highlights the function of this summary as a heading for what follows.

return[9] — is obvious and deliberate. Thereby Luke underscores Jesus' anointing and empowerment with the Spirit, but also draws attention to the intervening material in 4:1-13 wherein Jesus demonstrated his faithfulness to God, aligning himself with the impulse of God's Spirit. Jesus now returns from the wilderness to (the populated region of) Galilee, equipped for and committed to his divine mission as a charismatic (or pneumatic) figure. As such, he draws on power from the Spirit for his ministry.[10]

By way of identifying his ministry, Luke draws special attention to Jesus as teacher, though without specifying the content of his message. (This will be clarified in 4:16-21.) It is precisely in this role that Jesus often appears — cf. 4:31; 5:3, 17; 6:6; et al. — though it would be erroneous either to argue from this that for Luke teaching outweighs the miraculous in importance, or to suppose that for Luke the Spirit's empowerment is narrowly related to Jesus' ministry of proclamation. Luke carefully balances teaching and the miraculous; in fact, just as he draws attention here to teaching, so elsewhere he can accentuate healing and exorcisms (cf., e.g., 4:40-41; 6:17-19; Acts 2:22; 10:38). Moreover, as the material related to Jesus and the Spirit in the birth narrative, the account of Jesus' anointing, and the description of his testing make clear, the Spirit's activity with regard to Jesus is integral to his birth, identity, and mission as Son of God (e.g., 1:35; 3:21-22), and cannot be narrowly focused on his proclamation.[11]

Both 4:14b and v 15b emphasize the extension of Jesus' reputation from early on in his public career. The first such evidence of this is neutral; "a report . . . spread," but the nature of that report is lacking. The second is overwhelmingly positive and has its closest parallel in Luke's Gospel in 17:15-16, where praising God and thanking Jesus are set in parallel. Indeed, "praise" is elsewhere directed by humans only to God,[12] so here it may mean nothing more than that he enjoyed human favor at the onset of his mission

---

9. Thus:

    4:1: Ἰησοῦς . . . ὑπέστρεψεν . . . ἐν τῷ πνεύματι ἐν . . .

    4:14: ὑπέστρεψεν ὁ Ἰησοῦς ἐν τῇ δυνάμει τοῦ πνεύματος εἰς . . .

10. That is, Jesus operates in the sphere of the Spirit and his power is derived from the Spirit; cf. M. Turner, "Spirit of Prophecy," 72-76; Schürmann, 1:222; Nolland, 1:186.

11. That Jesus' ministry is oriented around "their synagogues" is unlikely to refer to "Jewish synagogues" as opposed to places for Christian gatherings in Luke's time (*contra* Petzke, 77). Such polemics would be out of character for Luke, who has already emphasized the Jewish orientation of the redemptive intervention of God, and who will continue to locate Jesus' and the Christian mission in Jewish synagogues in Luke-Acts. Instead, this shows how Jesus' anticipated mission *to Israel* is now coming to fruition.

12. See 2:20; 5:25-26; 7:16; 13:13; 17:15; 18:43; 23:47; Acts 4:21; 11:18; 13:48; 21:20. Δοξάζω is used in Acts 3:13 of the servant, Jesus, glorified by God.

(cf. 2:52). This contrasts sharply with the final response given him in the first episode of his public career (4:28-29).

4.1.2. Good News in Nazareth (4:16-30)

16 *When he came to Nazareth, where he had been brought up, he went as was his custom to the synagogue on the sabbath day and stood up to read.* 17 *The*[13] *scroll of the prophet Isaiah was given to him. He unrolled*[14] *the scroll and found the place where it was written:*

18 *"The Spirit of the Lord is upon me,*
   because he has anointed me.
To bring good news to the poor he has sent me:[15]
   to proclaim release to the captives
      and recovery of sight to the blind,
   to let the oppressed go free,
19 *to proclaim the year of the Lord's favor."*

20 *And he rolled up the scroll, gave it back to the attendant, and sat down. The eyes of all in the synagogue were fixed on him.* 21 *Then he began to say to them, "Today this scripture has been fulfilled in your hearing."* 22 *All spoke well of him and were amazed at the gracious words that came from his mouth. They said, "Is not this Joseph's son?"* 23 *He said to them, "Doubtless you will quote to me this proverb, 'Doctor, cure yourself!' And you will say, 'Do here also in your hometown the things that we have heard you did at Capernaum.'"* 24 *And he said, "Truly I tell you, no prophet is accepted in the prophet's hometown.* 25 *But the truth is, there were many widows in Israel in the time of Elijah, when the heaven was shut up three years and six months, and there was a severe famine over all the land;* 26 *yet Elijah was sent to none of them except to a widow at Zarephath in Sidon.* 27 *There were also many lepers in Israel in the time of the prophet Elisha, and none of them was cleansed except Naaman the Syrian."* 28 *When they heard this, all in the synagogue were filled with rage.* 29 *They got up,*

---

13. NRSV: ". . . he went to the synagogue on the sabbath day, as was his custom. He stood up to read, and the. . . ." This amendment shows that κατὰ τὸ εἰωθός relates also to "stood up to read" and not only to attending the synagogue.

14. Ἀναπτύσσω, "to unroll," is well suited to this context and is read by ℵ D Θ et al.; ἀνοίξας, "having opened," is strongly attested (A B L W Ξ et al.), but may have been introduced by scribes accustomed to codices rather than scrolls (cf. Metzger, *Textual Commentary*, 137).

15. NRSV: ". . . me to bring good news to the poor. He has sent me. . . ." Some mss. add "to heal the brokenhearted" after "he has sent me" (A Θ Ψ et al.), but why would this phrase from Isa 61:1 have been dropped?

*drove him out of the town, and led him to the brow of the hill on which
their town was built, so that they might hurl him off the cliff.* 30 *But he
passed through the midst of them and went on his way.*

Luke 4:16-30 is the dramatic account of Jesus' return to his hometown where,
on the Sabbath, he proclaimed a message of grace (4:22) and met with a
startlingly violent rejection by the people of Nazareth. Its central importance
for the narrative as a whole is signified by a number of factors.[16] (1) It stands
as a concrete representation of the ministry of Jesus summarized in 4:14-15.
(2) This is the first narrated episode of Jesus' public ministry. (3) Elsewhere
in the Third Gospel, Jesus conducts his ministry in the synagogues (see esp.
the summaries in 4:15, 44; also 4:31-37; 6:6; 13:10-17), but nowhere else
does Luke include a report of the content of his teaching. Hence, here we
have an exemplar of the sort of message Jesus proclaimed in synagogues
throughout his public ministry. (4) Luke has tied 4:16-30 together with the
preceding material, from 3:21 onward, by the common concern with the
activity of the Spirit and the consequent identification of Jesus and the nature
of his mission. The repeated interest in Jesus' sonship (3:21-22, 23-38; 4:1-13)
has foregrounded the question, As Son of God, what will Jesus do? In 4:18-19,
Jesus interprets his baptism as a Spirit anointing for his mission, then outlines
the content of his mission as God's Son. (5) Subsequent summaries of Jesus'
ministry refer back to this account (7:21-22; Acts 10:38). As Luke has shaped
his narrative, then, the ministry of Jesus in Nazareth at the outset of his public
ministry is of central importance to the Gospel as a whole, and thus also to
Luke-Acts. It defines to a significant extent the nature of Jesus' ministry,
establishing a critical narrative need for Jesus to perform in ways that grow
out of and reflect this missionary program.

What of the overall structure of 4:16-30? First, even if our knowledge
of the form of first-century synagogue services is sketchy,[17] it is nevertheless
clear that Luke's account narrowly limits our field of vision to one person,
Jesus, and, especially at the outset, to one action, the reading from the Isaiah
scroll. Though other characters are present — the attendant in 4:20 and the
congregation — he is the center of our attention and theirs (4:20c). Second,

16. On what follows, see Green, "Proclaiming Repentance," 24-32. Recent discussion of this pericope has been helpfully surveyed in Schreck, "Nazareth Pericope."

17. See, however, Acts 13:15. Yamauchi ("Synagogue," 782) is typical: "We know
that later synagogue services included such features as the recitation of the *Šᵉma'* . . . ,
prayer facing Jerusalem, the 'Amen' response from the congregation, the reading of
excerpts from the scrolls of the Torah . . . and of the Prophets, translation of the Scriptures
into Aramaic paraphrases, a sermon and a benediction. . . ." McKay *(Sabbath and Synagogue)* argues for more informal gatherings, not so much oriented toward worship, during
this period.

apart from the obvious *inclusio* of 4:16a, 30b ("he came . . . and went"), setting this passage off from its larger co-text, the most noticeable structural feature is the alternation between Jesus' address (4:16b-20a, 21, 23-28) and congregational response (4:20b, 22, 29).[18] This underscores the element of response while inviting reflection on the developing interchange as the account progresses.

With regard to the identity of the recipients of Jesus' ministry, Jew or Gentile, what does this sermon portend?[19] Luke himself has already provided an important interpretive guide, once one remembers how closely the Lukan narrative of Jesus' birth is tied narratologically and theologically to the larger Lukan enterprise. Not only is there thus far in the Lukan narrative no inherent, salvation-historical necessity for the extension of the good news to the Gentiles to be accompanied by (much less caused by) the rejection of the Jews, but also Luke posits no such compulsion in this narrative. The logic of Jesus' announcement does not rest on the negative response of the people of Nazareth. Quite the contrary, the initiative is his throughout; at every step in his address at Nazareth he asserts the universal embrace of God's salvific purpose. And in doing so, he portends the earlier emphasis of the birth narratives on the realization of God's purpose to form a people of all nations.

16a Verse 16a forms an *inclusio* with 4:30, with the result that our attention is immediately centered and remains throughout this passage on the goings-on in the synagogue in Jesus' hometown. Reference to Nazareth as the place of Jesus' rearing is reminiscent of 1:26 and especially 2:39-40, 51-52,

---

18. Cf. Busse, *Nazareth-Manifest*, 47; Koet, *Five Studies*, 27-29.

19. It is the potentially paradigmatic quality of that interchange that lies at the heart of recent discussion on this passage. Thus, a number of interpreters regard the rejection of Jesus by those of his hometown as in some sense prototypical, signifying in a proleptic way the rejection of Jesus by the Jews and the consequent Gentile mission (e.g., J. T. Sanders, *Jews,* 166-68; David Hill, "Rejection," 170; Tuckett, "Luke 4,16-30"). Others have questioned this interpretation, calling attention to the alleged primary role of this passage as one of identifying Jesus as a prophet who will be rejected (cf. Brawley, *Luke-Acts,* 6-27; Koet, *Five Studies,* 24-55; Schmeichel, "Christian Prophecy," 296-301) or urging the view that the program at work here is not one of rejection of one people in favor of another but of reconciliation of all peoples within God's gracious embrace (cf. Crockett, "Luke 4:25-27"; Kodell, "Nutshell"). In fact, how one treats this question is intertwined with how one treats a series of interpretive problems in this passage (cf. van Dijk, *Text and Context,* 19-42) — including the function of the Isaianic material in 4:18-19, the puzzling response of the people in 4:22, the role of the aphorisms Jesus cites in 4:23-24, and the purpose behind his use of the Elijah-Elisha material in 4:25-27. Moreover, how one treats this question is determined by how one discerns the relation of this passage to the Lukan narrative more holistically, both in terms of what precedes it and, eventually, teleologically, with reference to how it is interpreted by what follows it (cf. Toolan, *Narrative,* 12-46; Brawley, *Centering on God*).

but also prepares for the important interchange between Jesus and his townspeople about the recipients of God's favor and the fate Jesus will suffer in Nazareth (4:24).

Questions about its origins aside,[20] it is clear that the synagogue occupied a central place in Jewish religious observance by the first century. As this text exemplifies, on the Sabbath the synagogue was especially the locus for the reading and exposition of Scripture — a practice sanctioned with appeal to Mosaic commandment. What is more, synagogue architecture seems to have encouraged free exchange among those assembled and synagogue practice allowed anyone to speak who had something of significance to say; again, this is presumed in 4:16-30 (cf. Acts 13:15). Luke's presentation indicates not only that Jesus regularly demonstrated his piety by attendance of the synagogue on the Sabbath, but also that it was his habit to take the role of the one who read and expounded the Scriptures (cf. Acts 17:2). This phrase, "as was his custom," underscores the paradigmatic quality of this episode, both with regard to his Sabbath practices, and with regard to the content of his proclamation.

16b-20   On the one hand, these verses are set apart as presenting the first of three examples of the address-response cycle that characterizes this passage. On the other, a more formal structure distinguishes these verses.[21] Thus, vv 18-19 are framed by vv 16b-17 on the one end, and v 20 on the other, with the verbs related to Jesus' reading adding a sense of drama to the story and slowing down the action. This draws special attention to what is read. Hence:

> A   (vv 16b-17) he stood up (to read) . . . he was handed . . . he unrolled
> B   (vv 18-19) citation from Isaiah
> A'   (v 20) he rolled up . . . he handed . . . he sat down.

We find no parallel in "A'" to the phrase "to read" in "A." This creates expectation;[22] indeed, this element of the story is brought to the fore explicitly in the anticipation of the gathered people in 4:20b.

The primary point of focus, then, is the citation from Isaiah, which is itself a mix-text.[23] The bulk of 4:18-19 derives from Isa 61:1-2, but two departures from this passage are of particular interest. First, Isa 61:2b, "and

---

20. See Sanders, *Judaism,* 195-202; Yamauchi, "Synagogue."

21. Cf. Green, "Mission," 27-28; Koet, *Five Studies,* 27-28; Nolland, 1:191-92; Combrink, "Luke 4:16-30."

22. Koet, *Five Studies,* 28.

23. On the text form, see esp. Bock, *Proclamation,* 105-7; also Albertz, "Antritts-predigt," 182-84; Holtz, *Untersuchungen,* 39-41.

the day of vengeance of our God," has been omitted from Luke 4:19, probably to suppress what would have been taken as a negative aspect of the Isaianic message. Second, language from Isa 58:6, literally, "to send forth the oppressed in release," has been added at the end of Luke 4:18, thus to draw special attention to the word "release" as a characteristic activity of Jesus' ministry.[24] Consequently, three structural features are emphasized. First, the first three lines each end with "me," repeating the pronoun in the emphatic position. This underscores in the clearest possible way the inexorable relation of the Spirit's anointing and the statement of primary mission, "to proclaim good news to the poor." Second, and as a consequence, the three subsequent infinitive phrases appear in parallel and in a position subordinate to Jesus' statement of primary mission. Third, as we have observed, the notion of "release" is twice repeated. These features are highlighted in the following, more wooden translation:

> Spirit of the Lord is upon *me,*
>> For he has anointed *me;*
> To preach good news to the poor he has sent *me:*
>> To proclaim for the captives release,
>>> and to the blind sight;
>> To send forth the oppressed in release;
>> To proclaim the year of the Lord's favor.

Taking these structural observations seriously leads us to emphasize three theological features of this missionary program, particularly as they are developed elsewhere in Luke's narrative.[25]

Who are the poor?[26] Numerous attempts have been made to find here a

---

24. Luke's citation also omits the phrase "to bind up the brokenhearted" (Isa 61:1), but his reason for doing so is unclear.

25. Seccombe (*Possessions;* cf. *idem,* "Luke and Isaiah") insists that the hermeneutical key to Luke's presentation here is the interpretive history resident already within Isaiah and, to a lesser extent, the psalms. Thus, his argument that "poor" in 4:18 refers to "Israel," standing in need of salvation, is grounded in his observation that Luke has drawn on psalmic and especially Isaianic demarcations of the "poor" as "the nation Israel suffering and in great need" (39). Despite the helpfulness of this perspective, it does not wrestle adequately with what has happened to the hermeneutical history on which Seccombe's point is based once it is located within the Lukan narrative as primary intratext (cf. Albertz, "Antrittspredigt," 184-86). Thus, e.g., his early equation of "poor as Israel" does not grapple with the reality that already in the Lukan birth narrative Israel is presented as divided. More importantly, as Seccombe recognizes, his understanding of "poor" is developed primarily from the *Magnificat* and the Nazareth-sermon and does not account for the way in which "poor" is employed through the Gospel. In fact, in other co-texts, "poor" for Seccombe refers to the economically needy.

26. See Green, "Good News"; *idem, Gospel of Luke,* 79-94.

referent to the "spiritually poor" or, more recently, reflecting the concerns of a materialist-oriented interpretative method, to the economically poor. Both of these definitions of the "poor" are inadequately grounded in ancient Mediterranean culture and the social world of Luke-Acts. In that culture, one's status in a community was not so much a function of economic realities, but depended on a number of elements, including education, gender, family heritage, religious purity, vocation, economics, and so on. Thus, lack of subsistence might account for one's designation as "poor," but so might other disadvantaged conditions, and "poor" would serve as a cipher for those of low status, for those excluded according to normal canons of status honor in Mediterranean world. Hence, although "poor" is hardly devoid of economic significance, for Luke this wider meaning of diminished status honor is paramount.

It is thus evident that Jesus' mission is directed to the poor — defined not merely in subjective, spiritual or personal, economic terms, but in the holistic sense of those who are for any of a number of socio-religious reasons relegated to positions outside the boundaries of God's people. By directing his good news to these people, Jesus indicates his refusal to recognize those socially determined boundaries, asserting instead that even these "outsiders" are the objects of divine grace. Others may regard such people as beyond the pale of salvation, but God has opened a way for them to belong to God's family.

Jesus' words concerning "the blind" in 4:18 reflect a similar concern with literal and symbolic meaning. Recovery of sight is in the Lukan narrative clearly an issue of physical healing (cf. 18:35-43; Acts 9:18-19), but it is also presented as a metaphor for receiving revelation and experiencing salvation and inclusion in God's family (see already 1:78-79; 2:9, 29-32; 3:6).[27]

A further theological feature of Jesus' missionary program is highlighted by the repeated reference to "release," itself developed further in the Third Gospel in at least three ways. Elsewhere in Luke-Acts, "release" is often best translated as "forgiveness" — that is, "release from sins" or "forgiveness of sins"[28] — with the result that Jesus is presented as the Savior who grants forgiveness of sins.[29] Remembering that forgiveness implies res-

---

27. See Hamm, "Sight to the Blind"; Hamm's observations on the connection between healing and revealing are helpful, though his attempt to find the phrase "and recovering of sight to the blind" at the center of an elaborate chiasm embracing 4:16-20 is forced (especially with regard to the alleged parallels to 4:19 in 4:18).

28. Thus: ἄφεσις — Luke 1:77; 3:3; 24:47; Acts 2:38; 5:31; 10:43; 13:38; 26:18; ἀφίημι — Luke 5:20, 21, 23, 24; 7:47 (2x), 48, 49; 11:4 (2x); 12:10; 17:3, 4; 23:34; Acts 8:22. Cf. the use of χαρίζομαι in Luke 7:42, 43.

29. Cf. Leroy, "ἀφίημι," 182. Esler (*Community and Gospel,* 181-82) believes that "release" must be taken literally, so that the holding of thousands of Jewish slaves following the Roman conquest of 70 C.E. provides the *Sitz im Leben* for this mandate. But Luke does not develop this meaning anywhere in Luke-Acts.

toration to or entry into the community, this mission of "release" would have important spiritual and social ramifications (cf. 5:27-32; 7:36-50).

It is also clear that the "release" made available via Jesus' ministry is set in opposition to the binding power of Satan. Especially in Luke 13:10-17 and Acts 10:38 — but in fact with reference to almost all of Jesus' healing ministry — healing is not only physical but also signifies wholeness, freedom from both diabolic and social restrictions.[30]

The third major theological feature of Jesus' missionary program grows out of a further way of construing "release" in the Lukan narrative — namely, as "release from debts" (cf. 11:4). This draws our attention to Jubilee legislation (Leviticus 25)[31] — the freeing of slaves, the cancellation of debts, the fallowing of the land, and the returning of all land to its original distribution under Moses. The jubilary theme is most evident in 4:18-19 by the repeated use of "release" (cf., e.g., "the year of release" — Lev 25:10)[32] and the phrase, "the year of the Lord's favor," borrowed from Isa 61:2. It is now widely recognized that Isaiah 58 and 61 develop jubilary themes, describing the coming redemption from exile and captivity in the eschatological language of jubilary release. Other texts follow a similar interpretive maneuver, moving away from more literal applications of Jubilee legislation to the employment of jubilary themes to signify the eschatological deliverance of God (with its profound social implications).[33] This interpretive tradition encourages a reading of Luke 4:18-19 as the announcement of the eschatological epoch of salvation, the time of God's gracious visitation, with Jesus himself presented as its anointed herald.[34]

30. See Green, "Daughter of Abraham"; Busse, *Wunder.*

31. See already Godet, 1:234; more recently: Sloan, *Favorable Year; idem,* "Jubilee"; Ringe, *Biblical Jubilee;* Kavunkal, "Jubilee."

32. See further Koet, *Five Studies,* 31-35.

33. Cf. 11QMelchizedek (see Fitzmyer, "Melchizedek"; de Jonge and van der Woude, "11Q Melchizedek"; *Jub.* 1:21-25; *Psalms of Solomon* 11; Dan 9:24-27). It seems more prudent, then, to speak of 4:18-19 as encouraging our reading of Jesus' mission against the backdrop of the theme of the eschatological jubilee, but not our concluding that Luke thus develops or is controlled by a theology of Jubilee. Cf., e.g., Abraham, "Good News," 72-73. There is no need to posit Jesus' demand here for the immediate implementation of jubilary legislation (*pace* Yoder, *Politics of Jesus,* 34-40, 64-77). Nor need we follow Strobel in his suggestion that Jesus' announcement occurred in a Jubilee year ("Ausrufung des Jobeljahrs"); not only does the specific legislation of Leviticus 25 lack any key role in the subsequent Lukan narrative, but the obstacles related to the chronological data on which Strobel's thesis is based are formidable.

34. The debate over whether Jesus' anointing is that of a prophet or messiah (see Schreck, "Nazareth Pericope," 439-43) is of little consequence; in light of 1:32-35; 2:11; 3:21-22; 4:24-27, neither can be ruled out (cf. Strauss, *Davidic Messiah,* 219-50). More to the point is Jesus' claim to having been anointed by the Spirit with the consequence

Among related texts, 11QMelchizedek is of particular import for the way it weaves together jubilary and Sabbath motifs from Leviticus 25; Deut 15:2; Isa 52:7; 61:1-2; Pss 7:8-9; 82:1-2, all by way of setting release and restoration within the context of the end.[35] A comparison of Luke 4:16-30 with 11QMelchizedek is thus interesting for the way both underscore the inauguration of the epoch of salvation and spotlight a messianic figure whose role it is to mediate God's final deliverance — Jesus in Luke, Melchizedek in the Qumran text.[36] Of equal importance, however, is the way these texts differ in their description of the beneficiaries of that epoch. For the Qumranic text, the jubilary message is employed so as to certify how God will deliver God's people (defined as those of this community), while damning others (i.e., those outside the community). Within the Lukan co-text, however, God's favor is foregrounded, release is moved very much to the center, and any note of damnation (as Isa 61:2b might have represented) has been discarded. In the end, of course, this must be set within (1) the larger presentation of salvation as reversal (e.g., the Songs of Mary and Zechariah) and (2) the reality, illustrated so well in 4:16-30, that the universal availability of the good news of God's visitation does not necessarily have as its corollary its universal acceptance (cf. 2:34-35).

Our discussion of 4:18-19 has been from an insider's vantage point, dealing in part with how material from the birth narrative and later ministry of Jesus sheds light on the meaning of his inaugural address. We must be aware of the reality, though, that Jesus' audience *within* the narrative, the people of Nazareth who have congregated in the synagogue on this Sabbath, have no such background against which to understand what is happening. They have heard the Scriptures read, Scriptures that will have incorporated for them certain hopes of God's deliverance along lines not so distant from those voiced by people like Simeon and Mary in Luke 1-2; what will the exposition of the Scriptures bring?

21-22   With these verses we move to the second address-response cycle that marks the structure of this passage. Jesus' address constitutes the heart of his exposition of the Isaianic citation, which then will be developed in response to the reactions of his auditors (4:23-27). His first words must be taken in two senses, both grounded in the verb "to fulfill," but also interpreted by the keyword "today." "To fulfill" can be used in a variety of ways in Luke-Acts,[37] including "scriptural fulfillment" and the completion of a period of time. Inasmuch as "this scripture" (i.e., the one just read)

---

that he thus characterizes his ministry as one that will manifest the power and presence of the Spirit (cf. M. Turner, "Spirit Endowment," 47-49). On this language, cf. Isa 9:6-7; *Pss. Sol.* 17:22-25; CD 2:12; 6:1; 1QM 11:7 (9:7?).

35. M. P. Miller, "Function of Isa 61:1-2."

36. On the importance of the Melchizedek tradition for understanding Lukan soteriology more broadly, see Green, "God's Servant," 12-25.

37. See above on 1:1; similarly, Koet, *Five Studies,* 36-37.

is the object of the verb "to fulfill," it is transparent that Jesus has in mind at least the realization of the hopes contained in the Isaianic citation. The appearance of the word "today," so important elsewhere in Luke-Acts,[38] keeps us from missing the second nuance, particularly given its emphatic location at the beginning of the sentence. By this we understand that with the onset of Jesus' ministry the long-awaited epoch of salvation had been inaugurated. Given the repeated first person singular references in 4:18 ("me" — 3x), the "fulfillment" of which Jesus speaks must be rooted in his person: He is the one anointed by the Spirit, the herald of good news, the one who brings the new era.

This does not mean, however, that only with the announcement in Nazareth has a new era begun. The dawning of the new day in Luke's view is traced back already to the announcement of Jesus' birth. Indeed, Mary's Song had declared that, with the extraordinary conception of Jesus, God had worked mightily and graciously to remember his covenant and bring deliverance to his people. Thus, the eschatological significance of Jesus' appearance is already known to Mary and Elizabeth within the narrative, and to Luke's readers outside the narrative. Now Jesus makes this known more broadly, to the people of his own hometown. At the same time, he embraces his divine mission for himself.

Jesus' final words, "in your hearing,"[39] do more than signify the locale of this preaching, as if to say, "in your presence." By building on the traditional role of hearing in revelation and the symbol of the listening ear as a sign of openness to the divine message,[40] this phrase invites, even demands, response. Appropriately, then, the episode moves from address to reaction.

The formerly expectant crowds (v 20b) are impressed by Jesus, recognize in his message the active grace of God, and respond positively to it.[41] It is true

---

38. For σήμερον, see 2:11; 13:32-33; 19:5, 9; 23:43; Carroll, *End of History*.

39. Literally, "in your ears." Cf. Deut 5:1; 2 Sam 3:19.

40. Cf., e.g., Deut 6:4; Isa 6:9-10; Luke 6:27; 8:8; 9:44; Acts 7:51-60.

41. Verse 22 has proven difficult for interpreters, first, because of the range of meaning made possible by the verbs Luke employs in v 22a. Did the audience speak well of Jesus (cf. Acts 13:22; 14:3; 15:8; 22:5) or bear witness against him (cf. Matt 23:31; John 7:7; 18:23)? Did they marvel in admiration (cf. 7:9; 8:25; 9:43) or in opposition (cf. 11:38; John 7:15)? Second, what are we to make of λόγοις τῆς χάριτος; NRSV: "gracious words"? Does Jesus' audience respond to his "words about God's grace" (e.g., Godet, 1:236; Jeremias, *Jesus' Promise*, 44-45; Tannehill, "Mission of Jesus," 72), his "winsome words" (e.g., Eltester, "Israel," 138), or his "words endued with the power of God's grace" (e.g., Marshall, 186; Nolland, "Words of Grace"; *idem*, "ΧΑΡΙΣ")? Still further, the whole of the verse has been problematic because of the apparent incongruence between the audience's first (usually perceived as positive, as in the NRSV) and second (apparently negative) reaction.

A number of interpreters have sought a resolution of this conundrum by arguing that 4:22 narrates a consistently negative reaction against Jesus. Jesus' audience bears witness *against* his "words about God's grace," for they are angry that Jesus would have

that some interpreters have read the people's question, "Is not this Joseph's son?" in a negative way, but this reading fails to grapple sufficiently with the development of Jesus' identity by the narrator to this point.[42] Luke has already informed us that people assumed that Jesus was son of Joseph (3:23); Mary herself had acted on this presumption (2:48-49). In this way, Mary and now the congregation at Nazareth are caught in a case of situational irony,[43] for they respond to Jesus according to their own parochial understanding. It is easy to see from an orientation within the synagogue in this narrative, then, that their response is one of admiration. In fact, it may be that Jesus' auditors recognize in his gracious words good news for themselves. They would thus see themselves as the immediate beneficiaries of the Lord's favor, for they claim Jesus as the son of one of our own — indeed, as "one of us." Reading their response from within the narrative — that is, from the (albeit limited) vantage point of Jesus' audience within the narrative — we can understand that their response is positive, even expectant. But in being thus presented, Jesus' auditors in Nazareth fall casualty to a subtle joke between narrator and reader. *We* (Luke's readers outside the narrative) know that their understanding of Jesus is erroneous, for we know that Jesus is Son of God, not son of Joseph; he comes to fulfill the purpose of God, not to be restricted either by the demands of the devil (4:1-13) or, now, by those of his own townspeople.

23-29   This third stage of the interaction between Jesus and the people of Nazareth allows Jesus to develop more fully his self-presentation, and this attracts a startlingly negative response. The positive response to Jesus by his

---

spoken of the universalism of divine grace, suppressing any note of vengeance against the Gentiles (e.g., Godet, 1:235-36; Baarlink, "Gnadiges Jahr"; Beasley-Murray, *Kingdom of God*, 85-91). This position has met with widespread resistance primarily because it requires that the language of 4:22a be construed in a way that runs against Luke's usage elsewhere and because the language in this co-text provides no encouragement for a negative reading (see the survey in Schreck, "Nazareth Pericope," 429-36). More problematic, though, is the way this whole debate has been carried on under the assumption that an inconsistency between v 22a and v 22b needs somehow to be explained or overcome. As we will argue, it is unnecessary to read any change of tone between the two reported responses of the crowd, for both are positive. (That v 22b can be read positively, see also Fitzmyer, 1:535.)

42. Nolland (1:199) is typical in his decision to read 4:22b against its parallel in Mark 6:3, incorporating the negative meaning from the Markan co-text into the Lukan. Although Fitzmyer wants to read the question in a positive light, signifying "pleasant surprise or admiration" (1:535), he nevertheless refuses on tradition-critical grounds to see the question of identity against its development in Luke 1–2. Malina and Neyrey ("Honor and Shame," esp. 28, 53-54) interpret the people's response with the matrix of a challenge-riposte exchange, and so attribute to the audience more hostility than seems warranted within the larger narrative co-text.

43. Cf. Booth, *Rhetoric of Irony*, 61-67; *idem, Rhetoric of Fiction*, 300-308; Powell, *Narrative Criticism*, 30-32.

audience within the synagogue was based on a narrow, provincial understanding of his identity and mission. It is as though to this juncture they have filtered his message through their restrictive presumptions about him. As a consequence, he acts now to unveil further the nature and implications of his identity and mission; but "when they come to understand more fully the nature of Jesus' mission, he will not be acceptable to them."[44]

Structurally, these verses divide easily into the address-response cycle characteristic of 4:16-30. Jesus' address is itself divided into two parts — the first consisting of two aphorisms (4:23-24),[45] the second an appeal to the example of two biblical prophets (4:25-27). The second aphorism, which introduces into this passage the fate of the prophet, prepares for and leads into the allusions to Elijah and Elisha. With Jesus' speech we have a further elaboration of his self-identity, his claim to status as the agent of God's favor and as a prophetic figure; in this way he counters his earlier characterization at the hands of his townspeople as "son of Joseph."

"You will quote . . . you will say" in 4:23 indicates Jesus' inside knowledge of the thoughts of his audience — an omniscience that surfaces repeatedly in the Lukan narrative[46] and which is apparently characteristic of a Spirit-endowed prophet.[47] These phrases may refer to the future actions of the people at Nazareth, but more likely Jesus is simply drawing out the implications of the audience's reaction in the present.[48] This reading is supported by the relevance of the first aphorism to this narrative co-text. "Doctor, cure yourself!" was a well-known maxim in antiquity,[49] and appears to have been used rhetorically in a way that has direct bearing on our understanding of the interchange between Jesus and his audience in this scene. It could be employed in an argument to insist that one must not refuse to do to one's own relations the favors one does to others, or that one must not benefit others

44. Tannehill, *Narrative Unity,* 1:69.
45. Cf. 4:23: καὶ εἶπεν πρὸς αὐτούς; 24: εἶπεν δέ.
46. See, e.g., 5:21-22; 6:7-8; 7:36-50; 9:47; cf. 2:35.
47. See 7:39; cf. 22:64; Acts 13:9-10.
48. Cf. Hill, "Rejection," 168-69, 171; Nolland, 1:199. This view need not stand in formal contradiction to the fact that Luke only later narrates a Capernaum ministry (4:31); 4:14-15 has summarized Jesus' itinerant ministry in Galilee with the result that we understand 4:16-30 not so much as the first episode of Jesus' ministry as the first episode Luke relates in this more detailed way. That is, it stands first in the narrative in a paradigmatic sense. We may recall from our discussion of 1:3 that the order in which Luke is proceeding with the narrative is not "logical" or "chronological," but hermeneutical and persuasive. Hence, this reference to Capernaum may be an anachrony, or it may simply presuppose an earlier ministry in Capernaum that has not been related more explicitly than by the Galilean summary of 4:14-15.
49. See, most recently, Nolland, "Classical Parallels"; and Noorda, "Classical Parallels." 466-67.

while refusing the same benefits to one's own relations.[50] It is clear, then, that the following sentence — that is, the anticipated appeal to doing in Nazareth what was done in Capernaum — is only an interpretation of the first aphorism. In effect, Jesus addresses the parochial vision of his townspeople directly, countering their assumptions that, as Joseph's son, he will be especially for them a source of God's favor.

Why will Nazareth not be the (or a) beneficiary of Jesus' ministry? What we have seen heretofore suggests that their assumption that Jesus will act as "one of us" — that is, their inhibiting vision of who he is and what he is to accomplish — stands as a primary obstacle to their receiving through him God's favor. His is a ministry to all, and especially, according to 4:18-19, to those who have no claim to status or favor with God. A further explanation may be given by the second aphorism in 4:24, which highlights Jesus' claim to be a prophet and thus prepares for the eventual response his words will precipitate at Nazareth. This maxim grows out of the historical perception that the lot of all of the prophets is rejection and death (e.g., Neh 9:26) and here foreshadows the fate Jesus himself will meet.[51] Hence, Jesus will be unable to carry on his mission in his own hometown because his own people, far from embracing his identity and mission, resist him. Ironically, he who has been anointed to proclaim the year of the Lord's "favor" (4:19) himself does not receive the "favor"[52] of his own townspeople.

Does Jesus' rejection at the hands of his own townspeople negate his status, his divine mission and identity? The maxim related to the rejection of prophets and the subsequent reference to Elijah and Elisha point in the opposite direction. In the latter case, this is not because Jesus shows that even prophets like Elijah and Elisha were rejected (for this is missing from his brief rehearsal of one aspect of their ministry). To the contrary, these anecdotes demonstrate that the sort of mission for which he has been anointed has as its precedent the prophetic activity of Elijah and Elisha. Jesus' status as a prophet is certified, first, by the relation of his ministry to theirs and then by the fact that, like prophets of old, he is rejected.

The material from which 4:25-27 is largely drawn is 1 Kgs 17:8-24; 2 Kgs 5:1-19, though the episodes concerning Elijah and Elisha have been shaped in the Lukan context so as to stand parallel to one another:

---

50. Noorda, "Classical Parallels," 466-67 (with reference to Dio Chrysostom 49.13); cf. Plummer, 136 (with reference to Cornelius à Lapide).

51. Cf. Busse, *Nazareth-Manifest*, 50.

52. That is, δεκτός; NRSV: 4:19 — "favor"; 4:24 — "accepted." We thus adopt a passive reading of this term ("favorable," "acceptable," "welcome") rather than an active reading ("salvific," "of benefit"). The latter reading is adopted by, e.g., Bajard, "Péricope de Nazareth"; Koet, *Five Studies*, 43-44. Cf. Brawley, *Luke-Acts*, 14-15.

> But the truth is,
>> there were many widows in Israel
>>> in the time of Elijah . . .
>>>> yet Elijah was sent to none of them
>>>>> except to a widow at Zarephath in Sidon.
>> there were also many lepers in Israel,
>>> in the time of the prophet Elisha,
>>>> and none of them were cleansed
>>>>> except Naaman the Syrian.[53]

This parallelism underscores (1) the neediness of people in Israel, (2) the divine mandate under which Elijah ("was sent") and Elisha ("the prophet") worked, and (3) the exceptional character of the recipients of their ministries in these anecdotes. It is important to note that neither the Scriptures nor the current narrative presents these prophetic figures as programmatically oriented to the Gentiles; nor are they portrayed as having turned their backs on Israel.

In Jesus' address, the role of Elijah and Elisha as agents of healing to (and thus the exercise of God's grace among) outsiders is paramount.[54] Elijah is sent to a woman, a non-Jew, a widow — surely a person of low status. Elisha encounters a non-Jew, too, a Syrian whose disease, leprosy, served as a further marker of his socio-religious distance from the community of God's people (Leviticus 14). With these examples, Jesus underscores that "good news to the poor" embraces the widow, the unclean, the Gentile, those of the lowest status.

By now, the significance of Jesus' mission has become all too clear to his audience in Nazareth, who respond by seeking to stone him in their rage.[55] Their actions may have been motivated by scriptural legislation related to the stoning of persons making a false claim to divine legitimation as prophets (Deut 13:1-11). In any case, they are indicative of the people's rejection of Jesus' self-assertions regarding his identity. Moreover, taken with 4:30, the hostile reaction of the people at this beginning point of Jesus' public ministry prefigures his end: from increasing hostility to execution, then from extraor-

---

53. See Crockett, "Luke 4:25-27," 177.

54. For the various ways recent interpreters have attempted to make sense of the appeal to Elijah and Elisha in this co-text, see the summaries in Marshall, 188; Nolland, 1:200-201. That the primary concern is Luke's characterization of Jesus' identity and mission and not a proleptic announcement of the rejection of Israel and consequent mission to the Gentiles, see Brawley, *Luke-Acts,* 6-27; Koet, *Five Studies,* 44-52. Koet's view that the Elijah and Elisha material is employed in order to reveal the prophetic task to spur one's own people to repentance seems to build too much on subtleties of nuance at the intratextual level in 4:16-30.

55. Cf. Acts 7:54, 57-58.

dinary "escape" (here by "passing through" the crowds, later through resurrection) to ongoing mission.[56]

30 The nature of Jesus' escape from the violent mob bent on stoning him is not developed, though one may hear in the background reverberations of the divine promise misapplied by the devil in 4:10-11. This would heighten the sense that we have here a prefiguring of God's rescue of Jesus from the grave (e.g., Acts 2:24-32). Having passed through the crowds, Jesus "went on his way" — that is, the path of obedience to God's purpose in fulfillment of the mission for which he was anointed.[57] With this, the scene in Nazareth reaches its finale, but the public ministry of Jesus has only begun.

4.1.3. Good News in Capernaum (4:31-44)

31 *He went down to Capernaum, a city in Galilee, and was teaching them on the sabbath.* 32 *They were astounded at his teaching, because he spoke with authority.* 33 *In the synagogue there was a man who had the spirit of an unclean demon, and he cried out with a loud voice,* 34 *"Let us alone! What have you to do with us, Jesus of Nazareth? Have you come to destroy us? I know who you are, the Holy One of God."* 35 *But Jesus rebuked him, saying, "Be silent, and come out of him!" When the demon had thrown him down before them, he came out of him without having done him any harm.*[58] 36 *They were all amazed and kept saying to one another, "What kind of word*[59] *is this? For with authority and power he commands the unclean spirits, and out they come!"* 37 *And a report about him began to reach every place in the region.*

38 *After leaving the synagogue he entered Simon's house. Now Simon's mother-in-law was suffering from a high fever, and they asked him about her.* 39 *Then he stood over her and rebuked the fever, and it left her. Immediately she got up and began to serve them.*

40 *As the sun was setting, all those who had any who were sick with various kinds of diseases brought them to him; and he laid his hands on each of them and cured them.* 41 *Demons also came out of many, shouting, "You are the Son of God!" But he rebuked them and would not allow them to speak, because they knew that he was the Messiah.*

42 *At daybreak he departed and went into a deserted place. And the*

---

56. See Elias, "Furious Climax."
57. Cf. 4:42; 7:6, 11; 9:51-53, 56-57; 13:33; 17:11; 22:22, 39.
58. Cf. MHT 3:245; Moule, *Idiom Book,* 34.
59. λόγος; NRSV: "utterance."

crowds were looking for him; and when they reached him, they wanted to prevent him from leaving them. 43 *But he said to them, "I must proclaim the good news of the kingdom of God to the other cities also; for I was sent for this purpose."* 44 *So he continued proclaiming the message in the synagogues of Judea.*[60]

Luke 4:31-44 begins to flesh out the shape of Jesus' mission, programmatically outlined in 4:16-30.[61] Although often viewed as a series of autonomous episodes, these incidents are knit together closely by chronological (vv 31, 40, 42) and geographical (vv 31, 33, 38, 42) notations and by shared thematic concerns. This section is boundaried by Jesus' entry into Capernaum (v 31) and his departure to other synagogues and cities throughout the land of the Jews (vv 42-43). A number of motifs work together to underscore Luke's more general accent on clarifying the nature of Jesus' ministry and intimating further the range of responses he attracts.

(1) The beginning of this pericope raises questions about the relationship between Jesus' ministry in Capernaum and that in Nazareth. Note, thus, the parallels between vv 16, 31, 33 (teaching in the synagogue on the Sabbath) and vv 22, 32 (initial responses of wonder). However, v 23b, with its proleptic reference to the things done at Capernaum, suggests a more favorable hearing at Capernaum and, in fact, raises expectations for an effective ministry in this city. Is the scene at Capernaum a duplication of that set in Nazareth? Yes and no. Although receptive to his ministry among them and affirming of his status as one who works authoritatively, the people at Capernaum also make the mistake of their counterparts in Nazareth: Failing to understand who Jesus is and, therefore, the scale of his mission, they hope to limit his ministry to their own boundaries (4:42b).

(2) Nevertheless, Luke is able to show how the bare outline of Jesus' self-understanding as proclaimed in Nazareth (4:18-19, 25-27) begins to work itself out in Capernaum. As anticipated, his is a ministry to the marginalized of society — to the demonized, to the diseased, to women as well as men. Moreover, as projected, Jesus' ministry carefully balances word and deed, teaching and healing/exorcism. In fact, in this section both exorcism and teaching are described as "word . . . with authority."[62]

In Luke's presentation, healing is portrayed along similar lines as exorcism, with comparable language employed in both cases ("rebuke" + "come out/leave" — vv 35, 39, 41). This is not to interpret illness as nec-

---

60. On the text-critical problem of v 44, see above, p. 200, n. 6.

61. See Busse, *Wunder,* 58; Rice, "Luke 4:31-44."

62. Verse 32: ἐν ἐξουσίᾳ . . . ὁ λόγος; v 36: ὁ λόγος . . . ἐν ἐξουσίᾳ. Cf. Achtemeier, "Lucan Perspective," 550-59; Green, "Daughter of Abraham," 645-46.

essarily a consequence of demon possession. Rather, it is to recognize Luke's view that people who "have a demon" and those who suffer from illness are both oppressed by diabolic forces and both in need of "release." Hence, the heightened emphasis on "release" noted in Jesus' citation from Isaiah (Luke 4:18-19) is developed first in the Third Gospel in terms of *release from diabolic power*. It is worthy of note that the very thing the devil promised to give Jesus, "authority," has come to Jesus as a consequence of his resisting the devil and operating in the sphere of the Holy Spirit, with the result that he now exercises authority and power against the forces of evil (4:6, 14, 32, 36).

(3) We may follow throughout this section an interest in Jesus' identity. The townspeople are ignorant on this score, though they marvel at him and acclaim his authoritative status. Not knowing who he is, they fail to understand the nature of his mission (vv 42-44). Demons, on the other hand, recognize him as "Jesus of Nazareth," "the Holy One of God," "Son of God," and "Messiah." This awareness sets up the motif of conflict in this extended pericope, for their knowledge leads to resistance, not acceptance. It also contrasts sharply with human incomprehension: Although a demon remarks, "I know who you are . . ." (v 34), the people can only marvel at his works. Luke neither records any more full perception on their part, nor their responding to him in faith.

(4) The conflict between Jesus and the townspeople comes into focus in their discordant understandings of his mission (vv 42-44). Conflict between diabolic forces and Jesus is marked above all by the language Luke employs — Jesus is "in the Spirit" (4:1, 14), a man has "the spirit of an unclean demon"; Jesus is anointed with the Spirit of the Lord, the Holy Spirit (3:22; 4:1, 18), and is recognized as "the Holy One of God" (v 34), while the spirits at work here are "unclean," "demons" (vv 33, 41) — and by Luke's images of struggle, authority, and conquest (vv 34-35, 41). The mission of Jesus is set against demonic forces, for they are at variance with God's purpose for human wholeness.

(5) Finally, as we have repeatedly seen in the narrative thus far, Luke highlights the importance of response to God's work in Jesus by narrating a range of responses to Jesus' activity. In 4:31-44, the sequence of action-response is repeated four times: Jesus' teaching results in the astonishment of the people (vv 31-32), Jesus' exorcism leads to wonder and regionwide acclamation (vv 36-37), Jesus' healing Simon's mother-in-law is followed by her service (vv 38-39), and Jesus' ministry leads everyone to bring their needy to him and the crowds to attempt to prevent him from leaving them (vv 40-42). Perhaps it is too early to tell in the narrative what responses are advocated by the narrator, but the inevitability of response is again proposed.

31-32 The reference to Capernaum as a "city in Galilee" both speaks of its relative size and importance,[63] and recalls the summary of Jesus' itinerancy in the region of Galilee in 4:14-15. As the Nazareth-account was a programmatic instance of Jesus' activity in Galilee, so the narration of his Capernaum ministry illustrates and develops the nature of his ministry. The content of Jesus' teaching is not indicated, but the parallels between vv 15-16 and vv 31-32 imply that Jesus' message in Capernaum was analogous to that in Nazareth. Here, however, the reason for their astonishment is specifically related to their recognition that his word carried authority. No hint in the text points to a particular mode of argumentation; rather, Jesus' authority is grounded in the power of the Spirit (4:14).

33-35 Luke does not stop to puzzle over the presence of a demonized man in the synagogue,[64] but is more concerned with communicating the evil influence at work in this man. For this reason, he employs a clumsy phrase, combining "spirit," "unclean," and "demon." "Spirit," of course, has already been used with reference to the Holy Spirit, the Spirit of the Lord (e.g., 4:1, 14, 18), so additional adjectives are needed here to negate any possible confusion between the spirits at work in the narrative. "Demons," on the other hand, might refer to divinities in a more neutral or positive way in the Greco-Roman world, even if in Second Temple Judaism they were diabolical agents of ruin.[65] By using all three terms in this one instance, then, Luke can specify for his audience his own vocabulary for evil spirits.[66]

---

63. Recent excavations suggest some 1,500 residents in this town set on the imperial road from the Mediterranean Sea to Transjordan and Damascus. Note the references to a toll booth, a synagogue, and to the presence of a centurion in 5:27; 7:2, 5. That Jesus traveled "down to Capernaum" reflects that fact that Nazareth was situated at an altitude some 1,800 feet above Capernaum.

64. Just as the origins of the synagogue are shrouded in mystery, so their practices, particularly for the century in which Luke wrote, are difficult to ascertain and, in any case, would have been diverse (see Sanders, *Judaism*, 198-202; Schürer, *Jewish People*, 2:423-54; Cohen, *From the Maccabees*, 111-15). Their primary focus on *teaching* (as here, v 31) does not seem to have elicited a particular concern with purity as this was in evidence elsewhere, especially in the architecture and practices of the temple in Jerusalem. There is, e.g., no evidence that women were segregated from men (so Brooten, *Women Leaders*, 103-38; cf. Luke 13:10-17), and the record in Acts presumes no attempt to exclude Gentiles (e.g., Acts 13:16, 26); both such divisions were axiomatic for the temple.

65. For a more neutral use of δαιμόνιον, see Acts 17:18 (cf. δεισιδαιμονέστεροι in 17:22); Foerster, "δαίμων," 1-9. For a summary of contemporary Jewish usage, see Böcher, "δαιμόνιον," 271-72.

66. Subsequently, Luke can use, e.g., "demon" (4:41), "unclean spirit" (6:18), "evil spirit" (7:21), and "spirit" (9:39), but these expressions must be read in light of the lexicon Luke has here begun to establish.

At the prompting of the demon, the man may have shouted, "Ha!" —
a spontaneous interjection (NIV, TEV, NAB).[67] More probably, we should
follow the NRSV: "Let us alone!"[68] This reading is encouraged by the
appearance of the same verb in v 41. Hence, in spite of their demands, Jesus
would not let the spirits alone, and especially would not let them vocalize
their awareness of his identity (vv 35, 41). The demon intensifies its request
to be left alone by its hostile and defensive assertion of the lack of any common
ground between itself and its kind on the one hand, and Jesus on the other:
"What have you to do with us?"[69] The chasm between the work of the
demonic and that of Jesus is highlighted further by the appellation of Jesus
as the Holy One of God, a title that recalls Jesus' divine origins (1:35) and
identifies him as one in God's service.[70]

Who is the "us" to whom the demon refers? It is possible to find
here a dissolution of the boundaries between the demon and the man it is
controlling, with the demon assuming that to destroy it would necessitate
the destruction of the man as well. In light of the programmatic nature of
the story of testing (4:1-13), situating Jesus' ministry in the context of
struggle with the diabolic (cf. 22:28), it is evident that a more expansive
reading is called for here. That is, in attacking this one unclean spirit, the
Spirit-empowered Jesus has initiated a ministry of "release" constituting
an onslaught against all the forces of evil (cf., e.g., 3:16; 11:14-23; 13:16).
This view gains further support from the ongoing exorcistic activity of
Jesus' followers in the book of Acts,[71] and from the broader understanding,
shared by Luke, that the coming of the messianic age spelled the demise
of the rule of Satan.[72] "Have you come to destroy us?" the demon inquires
of Jesus. Yes!

67. That is, taking ἔα as a particle in Attic Greek serving as an interjective; cf. Job
15:16; 19:5; 25:6; GELS, 125; BAGD 211; Thayer, 162.

68. That is, taking ἔα as an imperative of ἐάω.

69. Cf. Judg 11:12; 2 Sam 16:10; 19:22; 1 Kgs 17:18; 2 Kgs 3:13; Twelftree, *Jesus
the Exorcist,* 63-64.

70. See Acts 3:14; 4:27, 30. The title is used of human agents in 2 Kgs 4:9; Ps
106:16; Jer 1:5; Sir 45:6, identifying them as persons in the service of God.

71. Twelftree (*Christ Triumphant,* 106) believes that one of the purposes of Luke's
portrayal of Jesus the exorcist in the Third Gospel is to provide a ministry pattern for the
early church.

72. See, e.g., Isa 24:21-22; John 12:31; Revelation 20; *Jub.* 23:29; 50:5; *As. Mos.*
10:1, 3; *1 Enoch* 55:4; 69:27-29; 1QM; 1QS 4:18-19; *T. Sim.* 6:6; *T. Lev.* 18:12-13; *T. Zeb.*
9:8-9; *T. Dan* 5:11; et al. Most or all of these references in *Testaments of the Twelve
Patriarchs* probably reflect Christian interpolations, but nevertheless help to support the
notion of the broad circulation of the nexus between eschatology and the demise of the
reign of the devil. See Twelftree, *Christ Triumphant,* 95-106; *idem, Jesus the Exorcist,*
217-24; Garrett, *Demise of the Devil,* 39-40.

Jesus' command of silence is, in part, a measure aimed at exerting control over the demon; Jesus' rebuke is in this case an assault against the spirit's original defensive posture. Indeed, not only had the spirit ordered Jesus to let them alone, but, through asserting knowledge of Jesus' name and origins, it had also attempted to gain control over Jesus.[73] Additionally, Jesus' command may be an attempt to avoid further acclamation by an agent of evil, lest Jesus thus be seen as working in league with an unclean spirit.[74] It is not that what the demon says is erroneous, but (1) that it is said by one whose awareness of Jesus' status as God's holy agent leads not to acceptance but to defensiveness, and (2) that within the Lukan narrative Jesus has only begun the process of identifying more fully the character of his mission. Phrases like "Holy One of God," "Son of God," and "Messiah" (vv 34, 41) can and should be understood with reference to Jesus' ministry to those oppressed by Satan, but there is more, including the suffering and exaltation of Jesus, that must be taken into account before an authentic acclamation will be possible.[75] The spirit's response, throwing the man down before them, may appear to be an act of violence, but Luke explicitly disallows such a reading by his conclusion, "without having done him any harm." The picture is rather of the complete acquiescence of the demon and his delivering the man over to Jesus. The demon's work is ended; the man is free of its influence and restored to his people.

36-37 The synagogal responses to Jesus' encounter with the demon parallel the response to his teaching. Both expressions of the good news, exorcism and teaching, are "words with authority," and both elicit responses of wonder and amazement. In Luke, these are at best neutral reactions; although "amazement" may suggest a reaction to a manifestation of divine power,[76] in Luke such reactions may or may not lead to faith. Just as the reference to the "power" with which Jesus rebukes the demons is reminiscent of Luke's report that Jesus returned from his testing in the wilderness "in the power of the Spirit" (4:14), so the escalation of his popularity throughout the region recalls the summary statement in 4:14-15. In the present text, however, these "village stories"[77] will have served to advance Jesus' authoritative status and to restore the formerly demonized man to his position in the community.

38-39 The move from synagogue to household may seem unwarranted, given the apparent success of Jesus' ministry in the synagogue. In fact, this change of venue is proleptic, establishing a pattern of things to come.

---

73. See *PGM* VIII.6-7; VIII.13.
74. See Theissen, *Miracle Stories,* 140-52.
75. Cf. Nolland, 1:214.
76. Cf. Grimm, "θαμβέω, θάμβος," 129.
77. Cf. Bailey, "Oral Tradition."

Jesus has already encountered open hostility in a synagogue (4:16-30), and it will be the site of further conflict as the narrative progresses (e.g., 6:6-11; 13:10-17); similarly, in Acts Paul and his companions repeatedly preach first in the synagogue only to be met with opposition (e.g., 13:14-52; 14:1-7). In Acts 18:7-8, only after Paul leaves the synagogue and enters a home is his message received with faith. That this is *Simon*'s house may strike the first-time reader as odd, since Simon does not fully enter the narrative until 5:1-11. This anachrony is not unusual for Luke, who regularly introduces characters briefly only to bring them more fully onto the stage later (e.g., Philip — Acts 6:5 → 8:5-40; Saul/Paul — 7:58 → 9:1-31), and whose interest in "order" (Luke 1:3) does not necessarily extend to chronological or logical order.

Simon's mother-in-law is apparently a widow without sons of her own (else why would she be living with Peter?). Although her "high" fever may reflect current medical terminology,[78] the severity of her illness, and thus the challenge of her healing, is more likely in view. Luke paints this scene very much as an exorcism, even if no mention is made of demons per se.[79] Jesus "bends over" the woman, signifying his authority over the fever, a practice paralleled in stories of exorcism.[80] As Jesus "rebuked" the demon in the previous story (vv 35-36), so he "rebukes" this fever; just as the demon "went out" of the man, so the fever "departs" this woman. Clearly, Jesus' ministry of "release" (4:18-19) has begun to take shape.[81]

Luke's record of the outcome of Jesus' healing activity stresses the immediacy and completeness of the cure,[82] but there is more to the woman's "service" than this. Jesus' ministry dealt with the fever, but it also restored this woman to her household. Her response is not one of "wonder," as was the case with the synagogue congregation, but is one of hospitality and gratitude.[83] As

---

78. Galen *Diff. feb.* 1.1; but see the discussion in Cadbury, "Medical Language."

79. Even if "fever is often regarded as a demon" (Theissen, *Miracle Stories,* 86), Luke does not seem to think along these lines. After all, it is not only here but throughout his narrative that "healing" is cast in terms of release from the oppression of the devil; cf. esp. Acts 10:38.

80. Twelftree ("Demon," 171) draws attention to *PGM* IV.745, 1229, 2735; see Derrett, "Getting on Top of a Demon."

81. ἐπιτιμάω + ἐξέρχομαι — v 35; ἐπιτάσσω + ἐξέρχομαι — v 36; ἐπιτιμάω + ἀφίημι (cf. vv 18-19!) — v 39.

82. So Plummer, 137.

83. Her "service" may reflect patterns of reciprocity (so Moxnes, "Meals," 162-63). More consistent with the Lukan narrative would be the view that this woman serves not as Jesus' debtor, but as benefactor for him and for his companions (see 8:1-3). Even though Luke uses what will become a heavily freighted term, διακονέω (see esp. 12:37; 22:26-27), it is doubtful that one should read much more into the woman's activity (though cf. Witherington, *Women in the Ministry of Jesus,* 67). See Seim, *Double Message,* 60-62.

will become evident as the narrative progresses, Luke regards this as an authentic, positive response to Jesus' salvific ministry (cf., e.g., 7:36-50; 8:1-3; Acts 16:33-34).

40-41 Only with the passing of the Sabbath ("as the sun was setting") do the people bring the sick to Jesus. He seems to have had no qualms about healing on the Sabbath (vv 31-39), though this will become an issue shortly (6:6-11). In any case, the popular response to Jesus recorded here seems to grow out of his success in healing earlier in the day; indeed, the large numbers of people we are meant to imagine ("all," "many") point to the immediate growth of Jesus' reputation as a healer with authority. One looks in vain for direct OT precedence for the laying on of hands as a component of the process of miraculous healing, though in one Qumran text, Abram recounts how he was asked to "pray for the king [of Egypt, afflicted by a disease caused by a chastising spirit], and lay my hands upon him so that he would live."[84] Might this practice, which is characteristic of Jesus and, according to Acts, of his followers, grow out of the extension of God's own hand to act in creation and redemption (i.e., his effective power, which is amply attested in the OT)? If so, then in reporting Jesus' laying on of hands, Luke is drawing attention to the power of God active in and through him.

As before, healing and exorcism are paired and, as before, demons are rebuked and silenced (see above on v 34), with the consequence that they come out of many persons. Before departing, though, demons shout that Jesus is the "Son of God," a title Luke immediate collates with a second, "Messiah." This is not unusual for Luke, who earlier clarifies Jesus' messiahship in terms borrowed from OT portrayals of the Davidic Son of God.[85] As of yet, though, this identification of Jesus is known only to Mary, whose presence in the narrative will not be noted again until Acts 1:14, and to angelic and diabolic figures. Slowly, Luke is developing his portrayal of Jesus as the regal prophet whose salvific activity fulfills the missionary program drafted in 4:18-19.

42-44 The wilderness has thus far served as a site for preparation and achieving vocational clarity (e.g., 1:80; 4:1-13), and this is its role here. Juxtaposed in Luke's account are Jesus' popular acclaim and his divine mission. Though the former is rooted in the mission of the Son of God, it has yet to lead to widespread faith in God; apart from the hospitality shown Jesus by Simon's mother-in-law, Jesus' teaching and healing have not yet given rise to persons ready to (re)orient their lives around the divine purpose. The crowds are still potential disciples, but for now they remain intent on securing the gracious activity of Jesus for themselves. They do not understand his mission

---

84. 1QapGen 20:21-22; see also 20:28-29; ET in Martínez, *Dead Sea Scrolls,* 233. See further Lohse, "χείρ," 428-29, 431-32.
85. Cf. 1:32-35; 2:10-11; 3:22; 4:3, 9; Strauss, *Davidic Messiah,* 218.

and, therefore, like the devil before them (4:1-13), function as a force set on waylaying Jesus from his vocation.

In Jesus' response congregate penetrating echoes of earlier material reflective of his call: his emphasis on divine necessity,[86] the language of bringing good news (4:18, 43), his itinerant ministry in the synagogues (4:14-15, 43-44),[87] and his awareness of having been sent by God to proclaim (4:18, 43-44).[88] As he regathers for continued ministry, he reaffirms the primary contours of his mission and his fundamental commitment to God's aim.

The fresh element introduced in Jesus' statement of mission is his reference to the "kingdom of God." No doubt this expression draws on the notion of the everlasting kingdom to which the angel had referred (1:33), just as it is set in opposition to the "kingdoms of the world" over which the devil exercises authority (4:5-6). Within its local co-text, "kingdom of God" is associated with the "good news" announced in 4:18-19 and the Spirit-anointed ministry of Jesus in 4:31-41 — that is, it connotes a new world order where the demonized, the sick, women, and others living on the margins of society (see above on 4:18-19) are embraced in the redemptive purpose of God. Already embodied here is a fundamental clash between the kingdoms over which the devil has authority and the authority and power of Jesus — the one intent on the bondage and segregation of persons, the other on release and human wholeness in community. Hence, "kingdom of God" refers both to God's saving activity and, as will become increasingly clear, to the community and practices that embody God's saving purpose.[89]

4.2. MISSION AND CONTROVERSY (5:1–6:11)

Jesus has just disclosed his intent to follow God's purpose by engaging in an itinerant ministry in the land of the Jews (4:43-44). Immediately following in this section are six episodes that illustrate in concrete interactions with Jewish

86. This motif is represented here by the term δεῖ ("it is necessary"), also witnessed in 2:49; references to the Scriptures in 4:4, 8, 12, 18-19, 25-27 also serve this purpose.

87. On the expression "synagogues of Judea," see above, §10.

88. Verse 18: εὐαγγελίζομαι + ἀποστέλλω (2x) + κηρύσσω; vv 43-44: εὐαγγελίζομαι + ἀποστέλλω + κηρύσσω.

89. See, e.g., Tannehill, "Kingdom"; Green, "Kingdom of God"; *idem, Gospel of Luke,* esp. 94-96, 118-21. We will follow the NRSV in translating βασιλεία as "kingdom" for the sake of convenience, not because "kingdom" has particular currency in contemporary vernacular (it does not). Attempts to avoid the gender-specific "kingdom" (esp. "reign") often fall prey to a disturbing reductionism that emphasizes the dynamic of God's rule without taking seriously its concrete embodiment in this world.

people the nature of this ministry.[1] Although this section begins with the call of the first disciples, disciples are either conspicuously absent (5:12-26; 6:6-11) or appear as little more than cardboard figures, undeveloped as characters (5:30–6:5). This is startling because Jesus explicitly calls these fishermen for the purpose of active service in his ministry ("from now on you will be catching people," v 10), thus establishing a narrative need that remains unfulfilled. In fact, the disciples have little role to play in the Third Gospel, a reality that, in retrospect, is easily explained: (1) the disciples will move into the foreground with the onset of Luke's second volume, Acts, where they will indeed be involved in "catching people"; (2) in the interim, their primary role is to learn, and this is a major focus of 6:12-49 and the central, journey section of Luke (9:51–19:27); and (3) here they are exemplars of appropriate response to Jesus and his message (5:11, 28).[2]

The calling of disciples in this section highlights two of Luke's larger concerns — on the one hand with the sort of people with whom Jesus will associate, on the other with the importance of response. Peter, a self-professed "sinner," responds positively to Jesus' beckoning, and in doing so prepares for the larger emphasis in this section on sin (and law-breaking), sinners, and forgiveness (5:8, 13-14, 20-24, 30-32; 6:2, 7, 9). Jesus' attention is directed to sinful and diseased persons; as we shall see, in social terms these two groups share the label of "outsider" and thus are the objects of God's grace. What is more, they respond to Jesus with openness, while the religious (i.e., religious "insiders") view Jesus with suspicion, even hostility (5:21, 30, 33; 6:2, 7, 11).

Hence, the theme of this section surfaces explicitly in Jesus' response to the Pharisees in 5:32: "I have come to call not the righteous but sinners to repentance." In Luke's hands, this becomes a statement not only about the people to whom Jesus' message is directed but also, and perhaps first, about the character of those who respond gladly, obediently, gratefully — and, in Luke's perspective, correctly — to the good news of the kingdom of God.[3]

---

1. Theobold ("Anfänge") argues that this section of Luke's Gospel runs from 5:1 to 6:19, primarily because (1) "during those days" (6:12) connects the material beginning with 6:12 to the preceding, and (2) the two pericopae, 5:1-11 and 6:12-19, stand in parallel. However, 6:12-16 is even more closely tied to 6:17-19 (contra Nolland, 1:219), and 6:12-17 to 6:20-49 (with Nolland, 1:219). As with 5:1-11, 8:1-3, and 9:1-17, so 6:12-16 should be read as a disciple-oriented pericope that begins a fresh section of the Lukan narrative of Jesus' Galilean ministry, with 6:12-16 read as a transitional pericope and as preparatory for Jesus' instruction of his disciples in the Sermon on the Plain (6:17-49). Moreover, given the relative absence or inactivity of the disciples, it is probably too early in the Lukan narrative for Theobold's description of this section of the Gospel as "The Beginning of the Church."

2. See Green, *Gospel of Luke*, 102-5. On the general theme of discipleship in Luke, see further R. P. Martin, "Salvation and Discipleship"; Fitzmyer, *Luke the Theologian*, 117-45; Sweetland, *Our Journey*.

3. On this theme, cf. Kee, *People of God*, 187-92.

§11 Faith and Possessions in Luke

The response of the disciples to Jesus' call in 5:11, "they left everything and followed him," draws attention to a key theme in the Lukan narrative, the place of possessions among those who follow Jesus. Its prominence notwithstanding, Luke's presentation on possessions is perplexing; as Johnson observes, "Although Luke consistently speaks about possessions, he does not speak about possessions consistently."[4] One finds, for example, examples of complete renunciation either practiced or demanded (e.g., 5:11; 14:33; 18:22). Yet, the giving of alms (and restitution) seems an appropriate response to the good news too (19:1-10). Elsewhere, followers of Jesus practice hospitality and benefaction on behalf of his movement (e.g., 4:38-39; 7:34; 8:1-3) — in the case of Levi, we are told, after he had "left everything" (5:28-29)! Jesus also affirms, though, that no one can serve God and Mammon (16:13) and that it is difficult for the wealthy to enter the kingdom (18:24).

What are we to make of this disparity? We may outline three important issues.[5] (1) Wealth presents itself as a temptation to prestige and security apart from God (e.g., 12:13-21; 16:14, 19-31; 18:18-23). Hence, although wealth itself is not evil, one can never remain passive or neutral toward it. Wealth masters if it is not mastered. (2) For Luke wealth cannot be abstracted from all aspects of faithful living before God, for it cannot be segregated from one's social relations more generally. To share with others, including and especially the poor, is to treat them as within one's circle of friends, family, and kin; conversely, to refuse to share with others is tantamount to treating them as outsiders. But it is toward people defined as outsiders that the good news is directed! (3) Wealth and the sharing of wealth are not and cannot be the basis of kinship or belonging and social status, according to the values of the kingdom in Luke. Gifts in the Mediterranean world were not regarded as "free," but brought with them obligations for reciprocal behavior,[6] yet Jesus counsels his followers to "lend, expecting nothing in return" (6:35; see 6:27-36), and advises them to ask God for forgiveness of sins even as they pardon the obligations of others (11:4).

Luke, then, calls for economic redistribution on behalf of those in need, and for the wealthy to give without using their wealth to gain status or to place others in their debt. Discipleship demands that one no longer be a slave to wealth or cling to possessions as though they were one's source of security or social position, and that one give precedence to the family of God and especially to those in need.

---

4. L. T. Johnson, *Sharing Possessions,* 13.

5. See further the helpful, recent discussions in Balch, "Rich and Poor"; Gillman, *Possessions;* Green, "Good News" (with extensive bibliography, 60-61n.7); *idem, Gospel of Luke,* 112-17; Moxnes, *Economy of the Kingdom; idem,* "Social Relations"; and the survey in Donahue, "Two Decades."

6. See above, §10. Derrida *(Given Time;* similarly, Bourdieu, *Language and Symbolic Power)* argues that the giving of gifts of anthropological necessity renders the gift into an obligation awaiting fulfillment — an observation that underscores not only the radicality of Luke's message but also its ongoing relevance for cultural critique in the contemporary world (cf. Green, *Gospel of Luke,* 140-44, 147-50).

4.2.1. The Calling of the First Disciples (5:1-11)

> 5:1 *Once while Jesus was standing beside the lake of Gennesaret, and the crowd was pressing in on him to hear the word of God,* 2 *he saw two boats there at the shore of the lake; the fishermen had gone out of them and were washing their nets.* 3 *He got into one of the boats, the one belonging to Simon, and asked him to put out a little way from the shore. Then he sat down and taught the crowds from the boat.* 4 *When he had finished speaking, he said to Simon, "Put out into the deep water and let down your nets for a catch."* 5 *Simon answered, "Master, we have worked all night long but have caught nothing. Yet if you say so, I will let down the nets."* 6 *When they had done this, they caught so many fish that their nets were beginning to break.* 7 *So they signaled their partners in the other boat to come and help them. And they came and filled both boats, so that they began to sink.* 8 *But when Simon Peter saw it, he fell down at Jesus' knees, saying, "Go away from me, Lord, for I am a sinful man!"* 9 *For he and all who were with him were amazed at*[7] *the catch of fish that they had taken;* 10 *and so also were James and John, sons of Zebedee, who were partners with Simon. Then Jesus said to Simon, "Do not be afraid; from now on you will be catching people."* 11 *When they had brought their boats to shore, they left everything and followed him.*

Within his overall narrative strategy, the initial purpose of this episode is to secure for Luke's audience the nature of appropriate response to the ministry of Jesus. Simon's obedience and declaration of his sinfulness, and especially the final note that Simon, James, and John "left everything and followed" contrast both with the earlier "amazement" of the crowds and with the questions and opposition characteristic of the Pharisees and teachers of the law in the later episodes of this chapter. His further statement, "Go away from me, Lord," contrasts even more sharply with attempts by people at Nazareth and Capernaum, as it were, to keep Jesus to themselves.

Beyond this, this episode establishes a narrative need, unfulfilled in this pericope, for Jesus' followers to participate actively in his ministry. Still further, we see here a parallel emphasis to that less directly witnessed in the portrayal of John's ministry (3:1-20) — namely, the gathering of those who have chosen to embrace and serve God's redemptive purpose.

The account begins with a wide-angle view: the press of the crowd leading to Jesus' teaching in a natural amphitheater from a boat on the lake. Quickly, however, events on the boat are foregrounded and the crowd disap-

---

7. For the use of ἐπί + dative to denote cause (also in 5:5), see MHT 3:272.

pears completely from view. The important interaction here is between Jesus and Peter, who represents the others who respond positively to Jesus. Jesus speaks to Peter about what he and his companions should do (the verbs in v 4 are second person plural), and they do as he asks; though Jesus speaks to Peter in v 10b (where the verbs are singular), these companions respond to Jesus in the same way as does Peter (vv 10a, 11). Later, especially Peter, but also James and John, will be prominent among the disciples.[8]

That Simon and his partners are fishermen provides the raw material for the pun in Jesus' commission, "you will be catching people" (vv 4, 9, 10b). Does their vocation indicate something of their status in Palestinian society?[9] Although in general fishermen might be peasants with artisan-type skills (see figure 1), the fishermen in this scene command their own boats and depend on a cooperative business partnership rather than on hired day-laborers. There is nothing in the vocation of fishing per se that would suggest that Peter and his partners are despised or that would otherwise lead to Peter's self-declaration, "I am a sinner" (v 8).

That Peter declares himself a sinner is nonetheless important for the development of Luke's narrative. Jesus' commission to Peter, a sinner, lays the groundwork for Jesus' ministry of forgiveness and the growing reputation of Jesus as "friend of sinners" (7:34). Jesus' ministry of "release" (4:18-19) is thus seen also to entail the release from the power and stigma of (or forgiveness of) sin.[10]

1-3 These verses, prepared for earlier in Luke's narrative, set the stage for the coming encounter between Jesus and Peter. Instead of "Sea of Galilee," Luke writes "lake of Gennesaret," named for the fertile region on its northwest border.[11] Jesus, then, has not traveled far from Capernaum in his itinerancy (4:43-44); moreover, although Luke leads us to anticipate that Jesus will work in synagogues (4:44), his ministry has already broken out into other, more everyday venues (4:38-41), like this one.[12] Luke's opening phrase, "once," suggests that the Evangelist is gathering together "typical" episodes in that ministry. Jesus' growing reputation (4:37) has resulted in this crowd. That it is "pressing in on him" suggests the need for a boat as a platform from which to teach, and the presence of "two boats" prepares for the narration of the massive catch (v 7). Simon is already familiar to us (4:38-39).

---

8. For example, 9:18-20, 28-36; 22:8, 31-34; Acts 1:15; 2:14; 3:1; et al.

9. See the discussion in Wuellner, *Fishers of Men,* 36, 45-61; cf. Freyne, *Galilee,* 94, 154; Theissen, *Social Reality,* 65-66.

10. See Neale, *None but the Sinners,* esp. 108-10; Rice, "Call to Discipleship."

11. Josephus notes that the native inhabitants call the lake "Gennesar" (*J.W.* 3.10.1 §463); see also *J.W.* 3.10.7-8 §§506-21; 1 Macc 11:67. For λίμνη, see 8:22, 23, 33.

12. "Indonesian Example," 420.

This is the first occurrence of the phrase "word of God" (cf. 1:2; 3:2[13]), used in Acts especially for the message about Jesus but also occasionally for Jesus' own message.[14] Its present usage must be understood in relation to "the good news of the kingdom" in 4:43; against an OT backdrop,[15] it marks Jesus' ministry as prophetic. As we might anticipate given the careful balancing of word and deed in Jesus' ministry, and as the parabolic nature of this pericope evidences, teaching the word of God embraces miraculous activity and may be understood as "catching people." As before (4:20), Jesus sits to teach.

Bivin identifies the nets being used as "trammel nets" — made of linen, visible to fish during the day and so used at night, requiring two to four men to deploy, and needing washing each morning[16] — thus matching the details of this realistic account precisely. This identification also underscores the miraculous nature of the catch: Normally during the day, fish would see and avoid the net.

4-7 From the crowds, the narrative focus narrows to Peter, where it will remain until v 11; Peter's partners are present only in the background. Jesus' instructions to Peter seem absurd. Not only has a night's work by people who fish by profession produced nothing, but the nets used are for night fishing only. Peter's response, then, echoes that of Mary in 1:34, 38 — incredulity leading to service. Having witnessed Jesus' power (4:34, 38) and teaching (4:32; 5:3b), is Peter more willing to follow his directions? This view is bolstered by Peter's address to Jesus as "master," a term connoting his transfer of authority over the boat to Jesus,[17] and by his reference to the authoritative "word" of Jesus.[18]

The magnitude of the catch, and thus of the miracle, is heightened by the details of Luke's narration. In spite of a night of unproductive work, when the nets were let down once(!) so many fish were caught that the nets were about to break, two boats were required, and even they were about to sink.

Numerous attempts have been made to find symbolic, allegorical, and mythological meaning in this episode, with reference to the size of the catch, the boat(s), and so on.[19] Impetus for such views tends to originate from outside

---

13. In Lukan usage, however, ῥῆμα τοῦ θεοῦ (3:2) can be a synonym of λόγος τοῦ θεοῦ (5:1).

14. See Luke 8:11, 21; 11:28; Acts 4:31; 6:2, 7; 8:14; 11:1; 12:24(?); 13:5, 7, 44, 46, 48; 16:32; 17:13; 18:11.

15. For example, 1 Sam 9:27; 2 Sam 16:23; 1 Kgs 12:22; 1 Chr 17:3.

16. Bivin, "Miraculous Catch." Cf. Josephus *J.W.* 2.21.8 §635.

17. ἐπιστάτα (cf. 8:24, 45; 9:33, 49; 17:13; MM 245) may replace ῥαββί in Luke (Marshall, 203), but it has more breadth than "teacher." Cf. Abogunrin, "Three Variant Accounts," 591; Danker, 116.

18. ἐπὶ δὲ τῷ ῥήματί σου; NRSV: "Yet if you say so. . . ."

19. See, e.g., Derrett, "Jesus' Fishermen," 121-25; Mánek, "Fishers of Men"; Zillessen, "Schiff des Petrus."

the text. We are on more solid ground when we refer to the parabolic interpretation of the miracle drawing on clues from within the pericope.[20] Most
transparent is the nexus between catching fish and proclaiming the word:
success in fishing, under Jesus' authority, is a prophetic symbol for the mission
in which Peter and the others will participate, while Jesus himself, in his word
and miraculous deed, is himself engaged in "catching."

Also of importance is Luke's use of a type scene familiar to readers
of the LXX. The broader "commission story" is perhaps more familiar,[21] but
a greater kinship is evident with the form as it is revised in Isa 6:1-10 (cf.
Rev 1:10-19), where commission is the final element:

Luke 5:1-11		*Isa 6:1-10*
vv 4-7 (9-10a)	epiphany	vv 1-4
v 8	reaction	v 5
v 10b	reassurance	v 7
v 10b	commission	vv 8-10

The miracle of the catch is theophanic for Luke, though his audience may not
recognize this until the connection with Isaiah is solidified in Peter's reaction
in v 8.

8-11 The miraculous regularly leads to faith in Luke;[22] although
Peter's response is not explicitly one of faith, he does respond in trust and
discipleship. To assume within the narrative that Peter recognizes that Jesus
is God is to employ alien categories, but this does not mean that we must be
content with an interpretation of "Lord" as "polite address."[23] Instead, the
type scene on which Luke has drawn (see above) encourages the view that
Peter recognizes in Jesus the agency of God. As a consequence, Peter, aware
of the profound status of this teacher-prophet, responds by falling at Jesus'
knees in humility[24] and referring to himself as a sinner. Unlike the crowds at
Capernaum (4:42), Peter does not attempt to use Jesus' power for his own
ongoing benefit, but asserts his lack of claim on Jesus (cf. 7:6-7).

This is the first use of the term "sinner" in Luke, and it is tempting to read
any number of definitions external to the narrative into this usage — for example,
as a reference to Peter as superstitious, a person of the land who does not respect

---

20. See, e.g., Geninasca, "To Fish/To Preach," e.g., 196; Tannehill, *Narrative
Unity,* 204; Sabourin, 148.

21. See above, §1; Talbert (60-61) reads this pericope against the backdrop of the
commission form.

22. See, e.g., 5:25-26; 7:16; 13:13; 17:15, 18.

23. Cf. Dietrich, *Petrusbild,* 46-47; Abogunrin, "Three Variant Accounts," 592.

24. Cf. 22:41; Acts 7:60; 9:40; 20:36; 21:5. For parallels, see BAGD, 718.

the law, one who practices a despised trade, a wicked person, even a criminal.[25] But this is the problem: there are too many possibilities and too few bases, in this co-text, for determining which is a probable reading. At this juncture, perhaps it is enough to say that Peter recognizes the vast difference between Jesus and himself and so recoils in "the terror experienced in the presence of the revelation of the Holy One (cf. Exod 3:5-6; Isa 6:1ff.)."[26] This interpretation leaves room for the development of a more definitive understanding of "sinner" (which Luke will use to indicate people who either recognize themselves in need of divine redemption or who are ostracized by others and so stand in the greatest need of gracious intervention), while at the same time highlighting Jesus' identity as one who crosses boundaries to bring good news to the unworthy.

In spite of the narrow focus on Peter throughout this encounter, we now gain a slightly larger picture, and realize that James and John have mirrored in their actions and responses those of their partner, Peter. In v 7, Luke uses the more technical term for a "business partner," but in v 10 he employs a more general description, "those who share with Simon."[27] This alteration may be deliberate, a way of hinting that these business partners are about to undergo a change of relationship wherein they will share much more (cf. Acts 2:42-47; 3:6).

Nevertheless, Jesus continues to address Simon, as before, though given the way vv 10a, 11 frame v 10b, it is difficult to imagine that only Simon is commissioned to "catch people."[28] The verb "to catch," or, more literally, "to capture alive" or "to spare life," builds on the vocabulary of the miraculous "catch" (vv 4, 9), but has a prehistory in the OT and in Greek literature, where it belongs to the vocabulary of war and hunting. The nuance in this co-text may not be far from the usage in Josh 2:13 (cf. Herodotus 5.77), where life is spared and there is hope of liberation. The immediate co-text must be determinative, however, so that we hear loudest not the history of prior uses but the etymological pun ("to catch [with a net]" + "alive").[29]

25. Neale (*None but the Sinners,* 69-75) surveys recent attempts to identify the referent of "sinners" historically. Derrett ("Jesus's Fishermen," 123) seems to think Peter is guilty of "fishers' superstition."

26. Grimm, "θαμβέω, θάμβος," 129; cf. Schürmann, 1:270.

27. V 7: μέτοχος (on which see MM 406; Wuellner, *Fishers of Men,* 23-24; G. H. R. Horsley, *New Documents,* §40); v 10: κοινωνός, which can be used for a fishing cooperative (cf. MM 351; Schürmann, 1:270), but is capable of much wider nuances.

28. *Contra* Fitzmyer, 1:569; C. W. F. Smith, "Fishers of Men," 197.

29. The metaphorical use of the language of fishing is well attested (e.g., Mark 1:17; Amos 4:2; Hab 1:14-15; Jer 16:16; 1QH 5:7-8; Wuellner, *Fishers of Men,* 64-231), and some (e.g., C. W. F. Smith, "Fishers of Men," 189-90) have objected to the distasteful possibilities of this metaphor used for missionary activity; after all, fish, having been caught, die, and are eaten. This objection is based on a confusion of virtual and actual properties of a metaphor; cf. the discussion in Eco, *Semiotics,* 87-129.

Disciples will no longer catch dead fish in order to sell them in the market-place, but will catch people, giving them liberty.[30]

Jesus' phrase "from now on" (cf. 1:48; 2:52; 22:18, 69; Acts 18:6) emphasizes the disciples' break with the past, a motif advanced even further by v 11. Having returned to shore, they leave the boats (and marvelous catch!) — indeed, they leave everything, a notation with obvious economic and vo-cational but also with deep-seated social ramifications. Leaving all that has been of value, they will now find their fundamental sense of belonging and being in relationship to Jesus, the community being built around him, and the redemptive purpose he serves.[31]

4.2.2. The Cleansing of a Leper (5:12-16)

12 *Once, when he was in one of the cities, there was a man covered with leprosy. When he saw Jesus, he bowed with his face to the ground and begged him, "Lord, if you choose, you can make me clean."* 13 *Then Jesus stretched out his hand, touched him, and said, "I do choose. Be made clean." Immediately the leprosy left him.* 14 *And he ordered him to tell no one. "Go," he said, "and show yourself to the priest, and, as Moses commanded, make an offering for your cleansing, for a testimony to them."* 15 *More than ever the word about Jesus spread abroad. Many crowds would gather to hear him and to be cured of their diseases,* 16 *and he would withdraw to deserted places and pray.*[32]

Begun in 4:31-37, now taken up in earnest, is a narrative strategy that highlights through the placement of one episode after another the new situation (4:21) marked by the onset of Jesus' ministry. One reads through this section (4.2) with a sense of déjà vu, as details are repeated and as different characters are the recipients of the same sort of ministry, with each episode leading to release and acceptance.

The linguistic and conceptual echoes of this pericope with preceding material are obvious — for example: "once" (5:1, 12), "one of the cities" (4:43; 5:12), bowed (5:8, 12), "Lord" (5:8, 12), stretched out his hand/touched (4:40; 5:13), a disease or demon "departs" (4:35, 39, 41; 5:13), growing

30. See *TLNT,* 2:161-63; Wuellner, *Fishers of Men,* 237-38; Num 31:15, 18; Josh 6:25.

31. For the use of ἀκολουθέω to denote "discipleship," see further 5:28; 14:33; 18:22, 28; 21:4. "Following Jesus" also calls to mind the Lukan emphasis on discipleship as a journey and as "the way" — see above, on 3:4-6.

32. The NRSV sets up a series of unnecessary adversatives: "*But* [δέ] now more than ever the word about Jesus spread abroad; many crowds would gather to hear him and to be cured of their diseases. (16) *But* [δέ] he would withdraw to deserted places and pray."

reputation (4:14-15, 37; 5:15), combination of word and deed (4:40; 5:15), and wilderness (4:42; 5:16). Significantly, by focusing so adamantly on the cleansing of a leper, this scene advances the relationship established between Jesus and the prophet Elisha in 4:27. In these and other ways, this pericope is rooted in its co-text, (1) demonstrating that Jesus' mission is proceeding as promised and (2) giving to Luke's audience a clear sense of some of the key characteristics of Jesus' mission as these motifs are asserted and repeated.

12-14 An unnamed man is said to be "covered with" ("full of") leprosy,[33] no doubt in order to heighten the problem with which Jesus must contend (cf. 4:38). Leprosy as portrayed by Luke was almost certainly unrelated to the disease so identified in modern times,[34] and in any case cannot be adequately understood in biomedical terms. Whatever physical symptoms might be identified, "leprosy" was foremost a social disease in the sense that those so labelled were regarded as impure and separated from others (Leviticus 13).[35] Since lepers were not welcome within the boundaries of a city, how is it that Jesus encounters this leper "in one of the cities"? Jesus has maintained that his work would be "to the other cities" (4:43), so this location is expected in terms of the larger scheme of Jesus' mission, even if it is surprising in this instance. No doubt, apart from Pharisaic scrutiny and with the temple far away in Jerusalem, legal requirements of this sort would have been relaxed on a local scale.[36]

---

33. πλήρης λέπρας.

34. On the biomedical identification of "leprosy," see van der Loos, *Miracles,* 465-68; Avalos, *Illness and Health Care,* 311-15.

35. See 2 Chr 26:16-21; Josephus *Ag. Ap.* 1.31 §§281-82; Luke 17:12. On the social ramifications of "leprosy," see Seybold and Mueller, *Sickness and Healing,* 139; Douglas, *Risk and Blame,* 94-100; Pilch, "Biblical Healing," 62-65. As in contemporary medical discourse and practice generally, so in discussions of medicine with reference to biblical accounts, biomedicine has enjoyed an almost unquestioned hegemony. This has led to a preoccupation in exegetical discussion with the diseased as individuated physiological entities in need of being "controlled" or "fixed." On the need for anthropological perspectives in medical discourse and practice, see the earlier benchmark, Kleinman, *Patients and Healers;* and now Good, *Medicine;* Hahn, *Sickness and Healing.* In his attempt to mine the field of medical anthropology for biblical study, Pilch ("Biblical Healing"; cf. *idem,* "Understanding Healing"; *idem,* "Sickness and Healing"; similarly, Malina and Rohrbaugh, *Commentary,* 315-16) drives a wedge between biomedicine and what he calls "the cultural or hermeneutical model," and thus finds no room for physiological "cures" of diseases in his quest for psychosociological resolution of "illness realities." Such a perspective helpfully redresses the balance by giving needed emphasis to the restoration of people to social intercourse, but does not do justice to the complexities of the Lukan text, which repeatedly highlights physiological indications and their resolution, as well as psychosocial, pneumatic, and cosmic aspects of the cause, experience, and healing of illnesses.

36. Cf. Kazmierski, "Evangelist and Leper," 43-44.

The leper's initial response to Jesus is familiar (cf. 5:8). His bowing to the ground,[37] his begging, his assertion that Jesus is able to help him even if he is not willing, and his use of the term "Lord" with reference to Jesus — these details underscore the authority and superior status of Jesus and the deference, humility, and dependence of the leper.

Not so clear is the nature of his request. The emphasis clearly falls on cleanliness, repeated in vv 12, 13, and 14, but is Jesus being asked to pronounce the leper clean, or actually to cure him of his disease? The parallel with 2 Kgs 5:3 (cf. Luke 4:27) is suggestive, for there Naaman is advised to seek a prophet so that he can be cured; as a Syrian, he is not in need of Israelite "cleansing." In addition, the leper asserts that Jesus is able to cleanse him, but this would not be strictly true if he were asking to be pronounced clean by Jesus; according to the levitical code this task was reserved for priests. Moreover, Luke announces not that the leper was made clean, but that the leprosy "left him" (cf. 4:35, 41) — suggesting, as in previous scenes, that this man was released from a condition whose basis was diabolic.[38] Hence, it seems clear that this man seeks (and receives) healing from Jesus. And in relating this account as he does, Luke continues his pattern of rooting diseases of all kinds (usually indirectly) in diabolic activity, allowing the cleansing of this man to be interpreted along the lines of the "release" announced in 4:18-19.

Leviticus 13–14 outlines when one is to be regarded and how one is to be treated as leprous, then documents how lepers are to be declared clean (not made clean; priests inspect and interpret, but are not given a biomedical-therapeutic role) and readmitted into society. In his interaction with the leper, Jesus' actions express an ambiguity vis-à-vis the law (i.e., "Moses").[39] On the one hand, he is in violation of the law. Luke describes Jesus' action as deliberate ("stretched out his hand" + "touched"), human contact that violated the law (since uncleanness was communicable)[40] but also communicated acceptance and reentry into the community. Jesus is presented as one who is

---

37. See 2 Sam 9:6; 14:4, 22, 33; Reid, "Prayer," 44.

38. 5:13: ἀπῆλθεν ἀπ' αὐτοῦ; 4:35: ἐξῆλθεν ἀπ' αὐτοῦ; 4:41: ἐξήρχετο . . . ἀπὸ πολλῶν. See Busse, *Wunder,* 112. BAGD (84, 274) asserts that ἀπέρχομαι is used figuratively of the departure of diseases, while ἐξέρχομαι can be used of the departure of spirits. However, (1) ἀπό encroaches on ἐκ (MHT 3:251, 259; Moule, *Idiom Book,* 71-72), (2) 4:35; 4:41; 8:35 all use both prepositions for the departure of demons, and (3) in 8:31 ἀπέρχομαι is used of the departure of demons. The above-noted phrases function as potential synonyms.

39. Cf. Klinghardt, *Gesetz,* 121-22.

40. Leviticus 13 does not explicitly forbid touching a leper, but demands separation of lepers from others. See, though, Josephus (*Ag. Ap.* 1.31 §§281): Anyone who touches a leper is regarded as unclean; Lev 13:45-46.

both able and willing to cross conventional boundaries in order to bring good news. On the other hand, his practices are in harmony with Moses,[41] for he sends the man to the priest for the legislated inspection and offering (see Lev 14:1-32). In fact, Jesus requires the man to say nothing until he has complied with the law and, thus, has been officially reintroduced into social discourse.[42]

15-16 Luke's summary statement holds together two related phenomena: the growth of Jesus' reputation and his ongoing practice of retreating for prayer. In spite of the narrow focus in vv 12-14 on the miraculous, this summary statement again holds in tandem word and deed (cf. 4:40; 5:1). In 4:42-44, Jesus' rise in popularity threatened to sidetrack him from his mission, a threat that was thwarted through prayer; here, though, the crowds make no attempt to reserve his power for themselves (cf. 4:42). Luke speaks rather of Jesus' habit of withdrawing for prayer, during which he would be strengthened for divine service.[43]

4.2.3. Power to Heal, Authority to Forgive (5:17-26)

17 *One day, while he was teaching, Pharisees and teachers of the law were sitting near by (they had come from every village of Galilee and Judea and from Jerusalem); and the power of the Lord was with him to heal.* 18 *Just then some men came, carrying a paralyzed man on a bed. They were trying to bring him in and lay him before Jesus;* 19 *but finding no way to bring him in because of the crowd, they went up on the roof and let him down with his bed through the tiles into the middle of the crowd in front of Jesus.* 20 *When he saw their faith, he said, "Friend, your sins are forgiven you."* 21 *Then the scribes and the Pharisees began to question, "Who is this who is speaking blasphemies? Who can forgive sins but God alone?"* 22 *When Jesus perceived their questionings, he answered them, "Why do you raise such questions in your hearts?* 23 *Which is easier, to say, 'Your sins are forgiven you,' or to say, 'Stand up and walk'?* 24 *But so that you may know that the Son of Man has authority on earth to forgive sins" — he said to the one who was paralyzed — "I say to you, stand up and take your bed and go to your home."* 25 *Immediately he stood up before them, took what he had been lying on, and went to his home, glorifying God.* 26 *Amazement seized all of them, and they glorified God and were filled with awe, saying, "We have seen incredible[44] things today."*

---

41. See Fitzmyer, *Luke the Theologian,* 180; Busse, *Wunder,* 114.
42. Cf. Wilkinson, *Health and Healing,* 51.
43. So Crump, *Jesus the Intercessor,* 143-44.
44. NRSV: "strange."

Jesus' prayer in 5:16 was related to his strengthening for divine service, recalling his anointing (3:21-22; 4:18-19); hence, now he is portrayed as empowered by the Lord for healing, authorized to forgive sins. These two, healing and forgiveness, are interwoven by means of a renewed emphasis on conflict. Note how paralysis is the focus at the beginning and end of this encounter (vv 18-19, 24b-25), whereas forgiveness of sins is the focus of the center of the account (vv 20-24a); we are to understand that the need, paralysis, is addressed through the announcement of forgiveness. The healing of the paralytic comes in spite of two obstacles — first, the crowd, which separates him from Jesus; second, the Pharisees and scribes, who interrupt his encounter with Jesus (v 21), generating the interlude between his reception of forgiveness and his returning to his home. From Jesus' point of view, healing paralysis and forgiving sins have the same therapeutic end in this case, but the Pharisees and scribes intrude into the healing encounter, opposing Jesus' claim to release people from sin. As a result, Jesus' final pronouncement of healing is directed both to his opposition and to the paralytic, providing verification and restoration at the same time (v 24). Jesus' power to heal and authority to forgive sins are manifest in the paralytic's return to his home, walking and carrying his bed, and confirmed by the responses of the people (vv 25-26).

Although Luke's narrative manifests here an episodic quality, with no apparent chronological or geographical connectives from one incident to the next, we may nonetheless discern development from one pericope to the next. Luke uses each episode to further his characterization of Jesus' mission, each one building on prior material and preparing for the next. The motif of sin was introduced in 5:8, where it was collocated with the notion of separation; these will be foregrounded even more fully in 5:27-32. Here Luke interweaves two needs, paralysis and sin (and separation), so as to establish further the range of Jesus' competence to bring release and restoration. As in the previous account, Jesus' newly commissioned disciples remain off-stage.

17-19   Luke opens this scene by drawing attention to a paralytic on a quest for healing and the competing possibility of conflict. The diagnostic term Luke employs is found among medical writers, though elsewhere he uses the more popular term for "crippled." The lame were banned from the priesthood in Israel and, at Qumran, were excluded from full participation in the community.[45] Alienation seems to have been their fate in Luke's world too, a condition Jesus seeks to overturn (14:13, 21). It is not surprising, then, that

45. See Harrison, "παραλυτικός." Here Luke uses the perfect passive participle of παραλύω (5:18, 24; also Acts 8:7; 9:33). Elsewhere Luke denotes "crippled" or "lame" with χωλός (7:22; 14:13, 21; Acts 3:2; 8:7; 14:8). On the exclusion of the "crippled," cf. Lev 21:18-24; 1QM 7:4-6; 1QSa 2:5-7.

the crowd is thus portrayed as a barrier to his restoration, or that this scene culminates in Jesus' returning this man to his household.

A more ominous note is struck by the presence of the Pharisees and teachers of the law. This is their first appearance in the Third Gospel. They are portrayed fundamentally as persons concerned with faithful observance of the law. That Jesus' attitude toward the law was ambiguous in the preceding scene is important then, as is the deliberate tension in the opening clause of v 17: Jesus is *teaching* in the presence of some *teachers* of the law (scribes, v 21). Will their instruction overlap or compete? What is more, the Pharisees and scribes are sitting, a posture we have learned to associate with teaching (4:20; 5:3), but which might also suggest authority and judgment. In fact, Luke has structured this and the ensuing pericopae (5:17–6:11) as consecutive confrontations between Jesus and the Pharisees and scribes. Luke's parenthetical note (v 17) draws attention to the organized and official character of the delegation that seems to represent not only every Jewish village but also the city of Jerusalem itself.[46] Given their introduction, we are not surprised in v 21 to learn of the animosity of these Pharisees and teachers toward Jesus' ministry.

As we have come to expect, Jesus' ministry is characterized by word and deed, "teaching" and "healing" (v 17). That the phrase "power of the Lord" is synonymous with "Spirit of the Lord" is clear from Lukan usage elsewhere.[47] In a brief flashback, Luke reminds his audience both that Jesus' mission is carried out in the power of the Spirit and that this power, though now rarely mentioned in the narrative, is ongoing (cf. 3:21-22; 4:14-15, 18-19). Additionally, Luke thus insists that the work of Jesus in this scene is an outgrowth of his anointing for mission, and, so, that the healing of this paralytic is a ministry of "release."

20-24 This is the first use of the noun "faith" in the Gospel. Elsewhere in Luke it can serve as a precursor to redemptive activity and signifies "the basic positive response to the visitation of God";[48] it is used in this way here. Interestingly, Jesus responds not specifically to the paralytic's faith, but to "their faith" — an apparent reference both to his faith and to the faith of those who share and enable his quest for healing by going to extraordinary means to overcome the obstacle embodied in the crowd (vv 18-19).

Central to this segment of the episode is Jesus' pronouncement of

---

46. Brawley, *Luke-Acts,* 85, 100.

47. See 1:17, 35; 4:14; 24:49; Acts 1:8; 10:38. Against those who see a separation in Lukan usage between "power" and "Spirit" (e.g., Tuckett, "Luke 4,16-30," 347; Menzies, *Early Christian Pneumatology*), see M. Turner, "Spirit and Power"; Shelton, *Mighty in Word,* 75-77. Cf. Shepherd, *Narrative Function,* 137.

48. Johnson, 93; cf. Green, *Gospel of Luke,* 106-7. The verbal form (πιστεύω) has been used in 1:20, 45. Cf. 7:9, 47-50; 8:48; 17:19; 18:42.

forgiveness, which becomes the focus of controversy and is mentioned four times (vv 20, 21, 23, 24a). In many traditional, non-Western societies, the domain of biological medicine is not differentiated from that of religion, politics, and broader social life, with the result that healing may include or require the resolution of spiritual and social disorder. Hence, we should not be surprised that Jesus refers to the man's new psychosocial state and spiritual condition rather than to his physiological presentation, nor should we imagine that forgiveness was in some way (only) preparatory to the cure that would come. Rather, Jesus' address to the crippled, "Friend,"[49] and pronouncement of forgiveness *is the healing moment.*[50] This reality is rendered ambiguous by the interruption of the Pharisees and scribes (momentarily drawing attention away from the healing of the paralytic to the competence of the healer) but disambiguated in v 24 (where power to heal and authority to forgive are set in parallel). As promised in his inaugural address, Jesus offers this poor man "release."[51]

Jesus' pronouncement of forgiveness is cast in the perfect passive ("your sins have been forgiven you"), first denoting that the man's sins had been forgiven *by God,* then asserting that Jesus is authorized by God to announce forgiveness on God's behalf. Luke's audience may recall that, as Son of God, Jesus is God's agent. These scribes and Pharisees share no such awareness, however, and so conclude that Jesus' action has encroached on divine prerogative.[52] As a consequence, the issue of Jesus' competence moves

49. Literally, "Man" (ἄνθρωπε), though the equivalent of "friend."

50. See Hahn, *Sickness and Healing,* 4. Cf. 4QPrNab ar 1-3:1-4, where a Jewish exorcist forgave the sin of a man suffering "a malignant inflammation" (ET in Martínez, *Dead Sea Scrolls,* 289); Vermes, *Jesus the Jew,* 67-69.

51. See Ringe, *Biblical Jubilee,* 71-72; J. A. Sanders, "Sins," 88-90. M. Turner ("Spirit and Power," 147-48) argues that "forgiveness of sins" for Luke is not rooted in the Nazareth pericope since in 4:18-19 "release" is not collocated with "sins"; moreover, he argues, Luke does not view sin as an oppressive power from which one needs to be released. But (1) the problem of Lukan usage must be situated more fully within the context of the biblical usage (and in literature influenced by biblical usage), since ἀφίημι/ἄφεσις never otherwise occurs in the religious sense (Leroy, "ἀφίημι, ἄφεσις," 181); (2) "debt" could be used in Second Temple Judaism with reference to "sin" (cf. 4QMess ar 2:17; Fitzmyer, 1:223-24); (3) the present pericope does develop the sense of sin as an oppressive power manifest in the physiological condition of paralysis and the sociological condition of separateness; (4) this usage prepares for the subsequent development of "release" especially as "release from/forgiveness of sins" elsewhere in Luke-Acts (cf. 23:34, where ἀφίημι refers to "forgiveness" even though the verb is not collocated with "sins"; and (5) Luke's version of the Lord's Prayer shows how closely these two, debt and sin, could be related, both requiring "release" (11:4). That this pericope is to be interpreted in relation to 4:16-30 is also suggested by the use of "today" (σήμερον) in 5:26.

52. Although in a handful of cases someone might extend forgiveness on God's behalf (e.g., Isa 40:1-11; 4QPrNab ar 1–3:1-4 [in the mouth of a Babylonian]), in Jewish tradition it is God who forgives sins.

to the center, with the healing of the paralytic temporarily out of focus. The question of the legitimacy of Jesus' actions is important, since it relates to Jesus' ministry with "sinners" in the next pericope and with outsiders throughout the narrative, and since, within Luke-Acts, Jesus is portrayed as the Savior who forgives sins (1:76-77; 2:11; Acts 5:31).

By way of response, first, Jesus' competence as a prophet is accentuated by the phrase "in your hearts" (v 22), recalling Simeon's prophecy that through this child "the inner thoughts of many will be revealed" (2:35; cf. 4:23; 7:39). The "questioning" of the scribes and Pharisees is emphatic, mentioned three times in close proximity, stressing their antagonistic role. Of course, especially since it appears early on in the narrative of Jesus' public ministry, an objection to the legitimacy of Jesus' ministry also serves the purpose of allowing the narrator to endorse further Jesus' status as divine agent.

Usually for Luke, "power" (v 17) is the inherent capacity to perform, while "authority" (v 24) is the attribution of the right to act. Both are related to the notion of Jesus' competence in Luke, and both are displayed in Jesus' rejoinder to the scribes and Pharisees. His authority to forgive sins is comprehensive: ongoing in duration,[53] embracing the (whole) earth. It is rooted fundamentally in his status as Son of Man — an assertion the significance of which is not immediately clear in this, Luke's first usage of the phrase. Neither here nor elsewhere does Luke use "Son of Man" to designate Jesus' identity, preferring for this purpose other terms such as Messiah, Son of God, and the like. Instead, here and elsewhere, "Son of Man" is a self-reference distinguishing Jesus in his singularity, drawing attention to his extraordinary, unique, qualities.[54] Thus begins the Lukan portrayal of Jesus as the Son of Man: the one who has divine legitimation yet experiences opposition from the Jewish leadership, especially as that leadership is associated with Jerusalem (v 17).

Verse 24 may be awkward grammatically,[55] but its significance is clear. Word (v 24a) and deed (24b) come together to bring to completion the healing of the crippled man and to legitimate Jesus' status as the one who can forgive sins (v 24c). Jesus' question (v 23), then, does not call his listeners to rank the relative difficulty of forgiving sins or of causing a paralytic to walk; rather, his query serves to draw an equation, at least in this case, between these two pronouncements.

25-26 The combination "stand up" + "take your bed" + "go to your home," used in Jesus' pronouncement to the paralytic (v 24d), is repeated with only insignificant variation. That the paralytic is able to respond "im-

---

53. ἀφιέναι, "to forgive," is the present active infinitive.
54. See Kingsbury, *Conflict in Luke*, 73-78; Bock, "Son of Man."
55. See Sheeley, *Narrative Asides*, 117.

mediately" to Jesus' words emphasizes what these actions already manifest — namely, the power of Jesus to heal and the authority of Jesus to forgive sins. Jesus has addressed the presenting need of this crippled man, returning him to his household network of relations and responsibilities, and, in doing so, has overcome the opposition of the scribes and Pharisees. The healed man is joined in praising God by the others present, certainly the crowd and presumably also the scribes and Pharisees. Although "praising God" need not for Luke yet signify "faith," it is a positive and appropriate response denoting the recognition that in Jesus' ministry God is at work. Those who witness Jesus' ministry on behalf of the paralytic respond as they might to a theophany, with wonder and fear and praise.[56] In their words, though much to their surprise,[57] their interpretation echoes Jesus' own perspective: *Today,* in Jesus' ministry, the deeds of God are visible (cf. 4:21; 19:9; 23:43)!

4.2.4. Table Practices/Table Talk (5:27-39)

27 *After this he went out and saw a toll[58] collector named Levi, sitting at the toll booth; and he said to him, "Follow me." 28 And he got up, left everything, and followed him. 29 Then Levi gave a great banquet for him in his house; and there was a large crowd of toll collectors and others sitting at the table with them.[59]*

30 *The Pharisees and their scribes were complaining to his disciples, saying, "Why do you eat and drink with toll collectors and sinners?" 31 Jesus answered, "Those who are well have no need of a physician, but those who are sick; 32 I have come to call not the righteous but sinners to repentance."*

33 *Then they said to him, "John's disciples, like the disciples of the*

---

56. Cf., e.g., 1:12, 65; 2:9. ἔκστασις appears only here in the Third Gospel, though see Acts 3:10. Verse 26 explicitly notes that "all" responded thus, leaving no room for the segregation of the scribes and Pharisees. With respect to this pericope, J. T. Sanders *(Jews),* whose purpose is to portray in as negative a light as possible the Jews in Luke-Acts, believes that Luke ". . . conceives of the Pharisaic 'mind set', so to speak, as being unable to grasp Jesus' *halakah*" (170). This is demonstrative of two errors that pervade his work: (1) he treats the Pharisees (and all things Jewish) as though they were a composite character, so that what is said of one is said of all (similarly, and wrongly, e.g., Kingsbury, *Conflict in Luke;* Darr, *Character Building,* 85-126; against which, see, e.g., Gowler, *Portraits of the Pharisees;* Green, *Gospel of Luke,* 68-75); and (2) his thesis has predetermined what will count for evidence. Hence, he fixates on Pharisaic "traditional rational categories" and their being "amazed" or "confused," so cannot see their praise or the theophanic aspects of Luke's narration.

57. Luke uses the term παράδοξος, "against all expectations"; cf. Wis 5:2; 16:17; 3 Macc 6:33.

58. Here and throughout vv 27-30, the NRSV reads "tax" rather than "toll."

59. The NRSV provides a paragraph break after v 28.

Pharisees, frequently fast and pray, but your disciples eat and drink.
34 Jesus said to them, "You cannot make wedding guests fast while the
bridegroom is with them, can you? 35 The days will come when the
bridegroom will be taken away from them, and then they will fast in
those days." 36 He also told them a parable: "No one tears a piece
from a new garment and sews it on an old garment; otherwise the new
will be torn, and the piece from the new will not match the old. 37 And
no one puts new wine into old wineskins; otherwise the new wine will
burst the skins and will be spilled, and the skins will be destroyed.
38 But new wine must be put into fresh wineskins. 39 And no one after
drinking old wine desires new wine, but says, 'The old is good.' "[60]

In this the first of several meal scenes in Luke, the narrator blends together
two deeply rooted traditions, table fellowship as it was practiced in the Second
Temple period, especially by the Pharisees, on the one hand, and the practice
and representation of the Greco-Roman symposium on the other. Jesus' *prac-*
tices at the table, manifest in this scene primarily in his choice of eating
companions but also in the depiction of this meal as a festive occasion, are
joined with his *teaching* at the table. Both communicate, via deed and word,
the nature of his ministry and the concomitant enlargement of the boundaries
of God's people. This expansion does not come by the rejection of one people
and the embracing of another, but through Jesus' dispensing with all varieties
of credentials for membership other than repentance. In this case, repentance
is embodied concretely in leaving everything and following Jesus (v 28) and
more generally in the call to openness on the part of the Pharisees regarding
how God's ancient purpose is coming to fruition.

The Greco-Roman symposium constituted the second course of a banquet, a drinking-
and-talking party. In its literary representation, the symposium often focused on philosophical discourse, and Philo, in his description of the symposia among the Therapeutae,
notes how discussion would center around some question arising in the Scriptures.[61]
Steele outlines two characteristic aspects of the Hellenistic symposium: (1) a common
cast of characters: the host, usually notable for wealth or wisdom; the chief guest, noted
for his wisdom; and others who participate to varying degrees in the discussion; and (2) a
common narrative structure, moving from: the identification of the guests, to an action
or event that determines the topic(s) of discussion, to the discourse itself.[62] That Luke's

60. Verse 39 is omitted by D it Mcion Ir Eus, apparently so as to deny a possible
affirmation of the authority of the OT.

61. Philo *Vita Cont.* 10 §§75-78. Cf. Sir 9:15-16.

62. Steele, "Luke 11:37-54," 380-81. See J. Martin, *Symposion.* For Luke's use
of the genre, in addition to Steele, see Delobel, "L'onction"; de Meeûs, "Composition";
Nelson, *Leadership,* 52-56; D. E. Smith, "Table Fellowship."

account is modelled along these lines is obvious.[63] Concerning proper etiquette for symposia, of particular interest for analysis of the present Lukan pericope is the importance of the "friend-making character of the meal" — i.e., the importance of engaging in table talk that nurtured friendship, not divisiveness.[64] In effect, Jesus is being cited for a breach of convention, when it is the Pharisees and their scribes whose behavior — raising an unseemly point of discussion — is out of bounds.

Given the connectives Luke employs in vv 33, 36, together with the points of contact with the literary structure of the symposium, we should treat vv 27-39 as a single scene that unfolds as follows: (1) vv 27-29 — Setting; (2) vv 30-32 — Table Talk concerning Table Companions; (3) vv 33-35 — Table Talk concerning Fasting; (4) vv 36-39: Jesus' Parabolic Reflections on the Controversy at the Table.

Both questions — the one concerning the appropriateness of eating with toll collectors and sinners and the other concerning fasting — are broadly concerned with the maintenance of clear boundaries between groups. Hence, the pericope as a whole is concerned with the motifs of conflict, forgiveness, and inclusion.[65] Luke has been preparing his audience for the foregrounding of these motifs in this pericope through previous episodes. Regarding conflict, see especially 2:34-35; 5:17-26; for observance of the law, sin, and forgiveness, see especially 4:18-19; 5:1-11, 12-16, 17-26 (as well as the following section, 6:1-11); for inclusion, see the entire shape of Jesus' public ministry as it has been developed from 4:14 onward.

In this pericope, unlike the previous two, the disciples of Jesus are again present, but they are only indirectly developed. We hear the views of others regarding the behavior of Jesus' followers but are told nothing directly by them or about them by the narrator. At this juncture they remain only stage props, so to speak.

27-29   This episode begins with a chronological and topographical marker both connecting this scene to and distinguishing it from the previous incident. These verses establish the setting and the topical impetus for the table talk to follow.

This is the sole appearance of Levi in the Gospel. His introduction as a toll collector[66] identifies him within the Gospel as a person given to dishonesty and abuse of authority (cf. 3:12-13), and in the wider Greco-Roman world as a person of low status. In spite of the possibility for some (but by no means most) entrepreneurs involved in the business of collecting tolls to

---

63. Levi's wealth is suggested by his ability to give a *great* banquet, with *a large crowd* of guests (v 29).

64. See D. E. Smith, "Table Fellowship," 621, 634-35.

65. Cf. Neale, *None but the Sinners*, 110.

66. On the system of taxes and tolls, see above on 3:12-13.

gain wealth, the Roman elite avoided this politically important and potentially lucrative activity because of the social stigma intrinsic to it. Though doubtlessly there were exceptions, toll collectors as a group were despised as snoops, corrupt, the social equivalent of pimps and informants.[67] Nonetheless, because toll collectors responded positively to John in 3:12-13 (cf. 7:29), and were not advised to seek alternative professions, we may be more prepared for a positive response on the part of Levi.

Jesus' call to Levi is simple, without elaboration as to the portfolio of a disciple. The starkness of Jesus' request is matched by Levi's response. He had been sitting, now he stands; he was a toll collector, now he leaves everything (cf. 5:11) and follows Jesus. That Levi goes on to give a "great banquet" in his own house raises questions about the significance of Luke's report that Levi left "everything." The apparent tension between these two reports is resolved when it is realized that, for Luke, the ownership and disposition of possessions were embedded in a larger network of social relations and personal commitments.[68] As will become clear, by saying that Levi has left everything, Luke observes that Levi has repented (note the parallelism between vv 27, 32), reorienting his life completely around God's purpose as manifest in Jesus' mission.

Levi's "great feast"[69] provides the setting for the ensuing discussion in three ways. First, in her anthropological analysis of meals, Douglas remarks, "If food is treated as a code, the messages it encodes will be found in the pattern of social relations being expressed. The message is about different degrees of hierarchy, inclusion and exclusion, boundaries and transactions across the boundaries. Like sex, the taking of food has a social component as well as a biological one."[70] The focus of this episode around the table of a toll collector portends its significance as an embodied discourse concerning the character of Jesus' mission. Second, Luke has already begun to cast this episode in a way that recalls the Hellenistic symposium, so that the banquet scene almost demands the discourse to come. Third, the presence of Jesus at the table with social outcasts begs for rationalization, given that shared meals symbolized shared lives — intimacy, kinship, unity — throughout the Mediterranean world.[71]

67. For the portrait of toll collectors in Roman times, see Herrenbrück, *Jesus und die Zöllner,* 60-72; Schottroff and Stegemann, *Jesus,* 7-13. See also Badian, *Publicans;* Donahue, "Toll Collectors"; Finley, *Ancient Economy,* e.g., 60.

68. See above, §11.

69. In the NT, only Luke uses δοχή, here and in 14:13. In the LXX it refers to a feast in Gen 21:8; 26:30; Esth 1:3; 5:4, 5; Dan 5:1.

70. Douglas, *Implicit Meanings,* 249. See also Sahlins, *Economics,* 215.

71. Cf. Bartchy, "Table Fellowship"; Douglas, *Implicit Meanings,* 249-75; Moxnes, "Meals," esp. 159-60; D. E. Smith, "Table Fellowship," 633; *idem,* "Historical Jesus," 470.

30-32   Jesus' *action* (eating with toll collectors and others, v 29) has as its sequelae two questions, the first in v 30, the second in v 33; here his action leads to *protest* (v 30) and *response* (vv 31-32). In contrast to the designation of Jesus' opponents in 5:17, 21, Luke identifies only Pharisees; although this is strictly accurate — since scribes constituted a group of literate, educated persons concerned with the law who may or may not be of Pharisaic persuasion — the explicit presence of scribes in this instance draws attention to an impending confrontation concerning legal matters. In addition, the potential identification of scribes as persons closely identified with the temple but not presently serving as priests[72] and certainly as persons of high status, of power and privilege,[73] raises the stakes on the confrontation that unfolds here. As before, the Pharisees are present to monitor legal observance. Two implicatures lie behind their complaint. First, Pharisees interpreted the holiness of the temple as extending to their own households, with the ritual purity required of priests serving in the temple extended to their tables. The food to be eaten must be ritually clean; those with whom one ate likewise.[74] Second, these Pharisees apparently regard Jesus and his disciples as righteous, at least in comparison with their tablemates. Consequently, Jesus and his companions should not be associating in so friendly a manner with these sinners.

These Pharisees manifest their concern with boundaries most prominently in the labels they use to describe Jesus' table intimates: toll collectors and sinners. Luke had simply referred to toll collectors and "others," so it is the Pharisees who introduced the term "sinner," using it as a label.[75] In the hands of the Pharisees, "sinner" demarcates those who associate with toll collectors as persons living outside faithfulness to God. By means of vituperative apposition, then, toll collectors are dismissed, along with sinners, as possible friends; from the Pharisaic perspective, they are outside the boundaries, beyond the margins. In Lukan parlance, though, toll collectors and sinners would be included among "the poor," those to whom Jesus has been sent to proclaim good news.[76]

Adopting other imagery more at home in Luke 5, Jesus portrays toll collectors and sinners as sick, and himself as a physician. Given the categories of illness and health developed in 5:12-26, this signifies the psychosocial displacement of Jesus' tablemates. Indeed, Jesus thus draws on traditional

72. Cf. Schwartz, *Jewish Background,* 89-101; E. P. Sanders, *Judaism,* 170-82.
73. Cf., e.g., 14:1-3; Sir 38:24-34; 39:1-11; Saldarini, *Pharisees, Scribes and Sadducees,* 241-76.
74. See Neusner, "Two Pictures."
75. Green, "Good News," 70-71; cf. Neale, *None but the Sinners,* 130-31. Failure to recognize the use of "sinner" as a label led Corley (*Private Women,* 131-32) to the inaccurate conclusion that Luke never has Jesus eating with sinners.
76. See above on 4:18-19.

conceptualizations of Yahweh as physician and of divine redemption as healing. Against this backdrop, "healing" is understood as restoration to relationship with Yahweh and his people — that is, as forgiveness.[77] In coming to them as physician, Jesus participates again in boundary-crossing and, in doing so, opens the way to spiritual and social restoration for these outcasts. What is more, Luke's narrative seems to echo Ezekiel 34, where Israel's leadership is indicted for their failure to strengthen the weak, heal the sick, and the like — an allegation that would now apply to these Pharisees and their scribes.[78] The parallelism between vv 27-28 and v 32, then, renders Jesus' call to Levi as a programmatic call to discipleship for sinners,[79] Levi's response to Jesus as a concrete embodiment of "repentance," and the banquet as a representation of the new community being formed around Jesus. Jesus thus uses the terms "sinner" and "righteous" in a parodic way, as if to say, "Those you thought were outside the boundaries of companionship are the very ones to whom I have been sent."

33-35 As before, Jesus' *action* (v 29) leads to *protest* (v 33) and *response* (vv 34-35). Those involved in the Jesus movement "eat and drink" (vv 29-30), while others "fast and pray" (cf. 7:33-34). Here, though it is not clear who raises the question. Luke simply reports, "Then they said to him. . . ."[80] Many assume that "they" refers to the Pharisees, but this would make the reference to "the disciples of the Pharisees" awkward.[81] In a symposium it is not at all unexpected that others will participate in discourse, and there is no reason not to imagine that the question of fasting is raised more generally at the table. Jesus' followers do not behave in the same way as those of the other renewal groups, that of John and that of the Pharisees; why not?

In an important sense, the question about fasting is similar to that regarding table fellowship, for both have to do with the maintenance of group boundaries through the prescription of acceptable practices. Pharisees[82] (as well as other Jews of this period) were noted for ascetic behavior, and Luke thinks of them as fasting twice weekly (18:12; cf. *Did.* 8:1). For his part, Jesus is not opposed to fasting per se (cf. 4:1-2), but does signal his rejection of fasting in the present. There are two reasons for this. First, the deliberate

77. See Oepke, "ἰάομαι κτλ," 203; Deut 30:3; Sir 28:3; et al.

78. So Neale, *None but the Sinners,* 131-33. Cf. Zech 11:6; Jer 6:14.

79. Note that καλέω might be used both "to call" to discipleship and "to invite" one to a dinner party.

80. οἱ δὲ εἶπαν πρὸς αὐτόν.

81. See R. S. Good, "Jesus," 20-23.

82. Luke's use of "disciples of the Pharisees" is likely motivated by the desire for comparison along similar lines with the group around John and that forming around Jesus. Strictly speaking, Pharisees would not have had "disciples," unless they were also rabbis. Cf. C. F. Evans, 311.

nonconsumption of food signifies a dissatisfaction with the present, in the OT typically in response to great loss or as an expression of hope.[83] The presence of the motif of hope in the current co-text is signaled by the reference to John's disciples, for John's ministry was oriented toward announcing the coming one (see 3:1-20). It is also marked by the saying about the bridegroom, which draws on an eschatological symbol for divine visitation.[84] Fasting that is eschatologically motivated would be anachronistic, out of time, Jesus declares. The thing for which hope is expressed in fasting is already present: "Today this scripture has been fulfilled in your hearing" (4:21; cf. 2:36-37). Sinners are being called to repentance: This is a time for feasting, not fasting! At the same time, in a veiled anticipation of his death, however, Jesus refers to the bridegroom's being "taken away." Then fasting will be appropriate — not only as an expression of mourning but also, as will become apparent, in anticipation of the eschaton.

Second, Jesus' attitude toward Pharisaical fasting is continuous with the prophetic criticism of fasting (and other acts of piety) when it was not accompanied by acts of justice and mercy (cf. 3:7-9).[85] Within the Lukan narrative, the Pharisaic practice of fasting seems concerned with boundary-making and, later, is explicitly related to claims of self-righteousness (18:11-12); in neither co-text is it related to the extension of divine care to outsiders. Nor, then, does it grow out of the sort of wholehearted embracing of God's purpose demonstrated by Levi (v 28).

36-39   After the give-and-take of table discourse, Jesus pronounces a parabolic commentary on the whole conversation, transparently casting the old and the new as fundamentally irreconcilable. If the motif of incompatibility is obvious, the nature of the particular analogy Jesus wants to draw is not so clear. According to many interpreters, Jesus pits his own, new way against the old way of the Pharisees and their scribes. In this case, one would read vv 36-38 as according privilege to what is new and fresh, v 39 as a troubling admission that for those accustomed to them, the old ways will always be more palatable, the new less inviting.[86] Another reading is possible, however, even preferable.

In fact, it would be difficult to imagine Luke insisting that what Jesus

83. See above on 2:36-37. Cf. 2 Sam 1:12; 7:6; 2 Sam 3:35; 12:16-23; Muddiman, "Fast, Fasting," 773-74. Fasting was also practiced so as to render one more receptive to divine revelation, as in Acts 13:2.

84. Cf. Isa 54:5-6; 62:4-5; Jer 2:2.

85. For example, Isa 58:3-9; Jer 14:12; Zech 7:5-6; cf. Joel 2:12-13.

86. Schneider, 1:141. As Johnson (100) puts it, "To drink the new wine offered at Jesus' banquet, to wear the new garment for his wedding feast, one must have a new heart, go through *metanoia,* a change of mind, such as that shown by tax-agents and sinners." Almost without exception, recent commentators on Luke adopt a similar position.

is doing in his ministry is "new."[87] The burden of the birth narrative, the genealogy, the temptation account, and the inaugural sermon in Nazareth (i.e., the greater part of Luke 1:5–4:13) is that Jesus is doing nothing more than bringing to fruition the ancient purpose of God. What is more, Luke, in adopting the genre of historiography, expresses a concern to root the Christian movement very much in Jewish antiquity.[88] Insofar as he rejected the OT, then, Marcion was right to excise v 39 from this pericope, for thus he seems to have read it as an affirmation of the old over against the new.[89]

Such an interpretation is grounded not only in Luke's tendencies to inscribe the story of Jesus very much into the ancient story of God's dealings with Israel. He portrays the old garment as in need of repair, while rejecting the ideas that new cloth might provide the needed solution or that the old cloth should simply be cast aside in favor of the new. Similarly, he does not assert that anything is wrong with old wineskins, but draws on everyday experience to insist that new wine cannot be placed in old wineskins. The new and the old are incompatible; someone interested in new wine should find new wineskins, but should not imagine that the old ones can be conscripted for the recent vintage. Finally, in v 39 Jesus, again drawing on life experience, asserts what was axiomatic in both Greek and Jewish circles — namely, old wine *is* good.[90] In effect, then, Jesus interprets his behaviors, which are questionable and innovative to some onlookers, as manifestations of God's ancient purpose coming to fruition, while the concerns of the Pharisees are rejected not only as innovative but also as quite inconsistent with God's program.

4.2.5. Concerning the Sabbath (6:1-11)

> 6:1 *One sabbath while Jesus was going through the grainfields, his disciples plucked some heads of grain, rubbed them in their hands, and ate them. 2 But some of the Pharisees said, "Why are you doing what is not lawful on the sabbath?" 3 Jesus answered, "Have you not*

87. The segregation of Jesus (and the early church) from the life of Israel is one of the calumnies arising from the deployment of Conzelmann's division of Luke's theology into three "ages" *(Luke)*. Salo *(Luke's Treatment of the Law,* 82-86), e.g., is committed to Conzelmann's view, yet realizes that Luke "wishes to see the validity of the old"; hence, he is left speaking of the "somewhat contradictory" nature of this text.

88. Cf., e.g., Esler, *Community and Gospel,* 216; Maddox, *Purpose;* Sterling, *Historiography.*

89. See Metzger, *Textual Commentary,* 138-39.

90. See, e.g., Flusser, "New Wine"; Mead, "Old Wine"; R. S. Good, "Jesus"; Talbert, 65. It is characteristic of Jesus in Luke to draw on conventional wisdom and common experience to make his point — e.g., 8:16; 11:11-13, 33; 16:1-9; 18:1-8.

read what David did when he and his companions were hungry? 4 *He entered the house of God and took and ate the bread of the Presence, which it is not lawful for any but the priests to eat, and gave some to his companions?"* 5 *Then he said to them, "The Son of Man is lord of the sabbath."*

6 *On another sabbath he entered the synagogue and taught, and there was a man there whose right hand was withered.* 7 *The scribes and the Pharisees watched him to see whether he would cure on the sabbath, so that they might find an accusation against him.* 8 *Even though he knew what they were thinking, he said to the man who had the withered hand, "Come and stand here." He got up and stood there.* 9 *Then Jesus said to them, "I ask you, is it lawful to do good or to do harm on the sabbath, to save life or to destroy it?"* 10 *After looking around at all of them, he said to him, "Stretch out your hand." He did so, and his hand was restored.* 11 *But they were filled with fury and discussed with one another what they might do to Jesus.*

Following Jesus' inaugural address in 4:16-30 is a series of pericopae that, at first glance, appear episodic and unrelated; on closer inspection, however, we see how these scenes, one after the other, yield a narrative strategy whereby Luke highlights the new situation marked by the onset of Jesus' ministry (see 4:21). Luke uses each incident to further his characterization of Jesus' mission, each building on prior material and preparing for the next. Thus, in 4:31-37 (an episode very much like that recorded in 6:6-11) Jesus heals on the Sabbath without encountering opposition. However, a report of his actions begins to spread (4:37), with the consequence that some scribes and Pharisees arrive on the scene in order to observe and question his activity (5:17-39). In the present pericope, the last of this subsection on "Mission and Controversy" (5:1–6:11), this gradual escalation culminates with the scribes and Pharisees contemplating a formal indictment against Jesus (6:7) and rejecting his claim to authority (6:5, 11).

With the opening words of v 6, "on another sabbath," the two incidents recorded in 6:1-11 are connected, both chronologically and topically, more closely than the previous episodes are related. The word "sabbath" appears six times (vv 1, 2, 5, 6, 7, 9), and the question of lawfulness is raised three (vv 2, 4, 9). Throughout, Jesus is opposed by "some of the Pharisees" or by "scribes and Pharisees," with the other characters, the disciples and the man with a withered hand, serving as little more than stage props, so to speak. The focus of this pericope, then, is Jesus' controversy with the Pharisees regarding what is lawful on the Sabbath — and, more importantly, Jesus' capacity to determine what constitutes acceptable Sabbath observance. Verses 1-4 elicit from Jesus his claim to authority (lordship) over the Sabbath (v 5), vv 6-10

251

illustrate his authority over the Sabbath, and v 11 documents the rejection of Jesus' claim to authority by the Pharisees and scribes.[91] Verse 11, then, concludes both accounts.

The point of this pericope is not to pit the alleged legalism of the Pharisees (and scribes) over against the libertinism of Jesus. As before, the Pharisees and scribes are present primarily in their role as monitors of legal observance, but more is at stake than accusations of "legalism" might suggest. Although one can locate references to Sabbath observance throughout Israel's history, Sabbath observance increased in its importance during the period of the Second Temple; along with circumcision and dietary restrictions, it "helped to nourish Jewish identity."[92] Indeed, in addition to evidence for the strict interpretation of the Sabbath from Jewish sources, one can also refer to non-Jewish comments on Jewish Sabbath observance, with both demarcating the keeping of the Sabbath as a characteristic marker of Jewish identity.[93] What is more, the role of Sabbath observance for the maintenance of group boundaries and as an emblem of group solidarity is evident in the two accounts of 6:1-11, for in both a particular interpretation of the Sabbath regulation against work is simply assumed, never argued. And a necessary implicature of both accounts of confrontation is that the legitimacy of this particular interpretation of the relatively vague OT law (Exod 20:8-11; 31:14-15; 35:2; Deut 5:12-15) had achieved the status of conventional wisdom.

For Jesus, though, the question remains, Who interprets Scripture (and, so, the Sabbath law) correctly? Or, to put it more starkly, Who knows and represents God's will? Not the Sabbath law per se, but this more fundamental question comes to the fore in Jesus' response to his rivals in vv 3 and 9. In both instances, Jesus' analysis is the same: Scribal specifications have missed the salvific purpose of God resident in the Sabbath,[94] but Jesus, in declaring the onset of the eschatological Jubilee (see above on 4:18-19), has made this day ("today," 4:21) the day for providing for humans. Jesus is less concerned with abrogating Sabbath law, and more concerned with bringing the grace of God to concrete expression in his own ministry, not least on the Sabbath;[95]

---

91. Cf. Schürmann, 306; Mack and Robbins, *Patterns of Persuasion,* 130-31; Darr, *Character Building,* 98-99.

92. Harrington, "Sabbath Tensions," 51.

93. Jewish sources include, e.g., *Jub.* 2:29-30; 50:6-13; CD 10:14–12:5; *m. Šabb.* 7:2; cf. the discussion in Schürer, *Jewish People,* 2:467-75; Sanders, *Judaism,* 208-11. For pagan reactions, cf. Whittaker, *Jews and Christians,* 63-73; Feldman, *Jew and Gentile,* 158-67. McKay (*Sabbath and Synagogue,* esp. chs. 2-4) has surveyed both Jewish and Greco-Roman sources, though her primary question is whether Jews gathered specifically for worship on the Sabbath.

94. Cf. Hasel, "Sabbath," 855; Robinson, *Old Testament Sabbath,* 347-50.

95. Cf. Green, "Daughter of Abraham," 650-51; Weiss, "Sabbath."

what is more, according to Luke, as lord of the Sabbath he has the authority to do just that!

1-2 The temporal location of this incident, on the Sabbath, is emphatic, establishing from the outset that the point at issue is not *what* the disciples are doing, but *when* they are doing it. What the disciples are doing would be regarded not as stealing, since Deut 23:25 allows for the plucking of another's grain, but as breaking the Sabbath. Even the Pharisaic interpretation of plucking on the Sabbath as an infraction is not a straightforward inference from OT Sabbath law, however. Exodus 34:21 obligates people to observe the Sabbath even during harvest, but the disciples are not "harvesting" (note the distinction between plucking and harvesting, "with a sickle," in Deut 23:25).[96] Only later did scribal tradition interpret "plucking" as a form of "harvesting," and in fact, according to this developing interpretation, the disciples were culpable not only for "reaping" but also for "threshing," "winnowing," and perhaps even "grinding."[97] Hence, in calling into question the legality of the disciples' actions, these Pharisees are working not so much with the Mosaic law itself, on its own terms, but with its ongoing elucidation. Given that they do not invite a discussion about the legitimacy of their interpretation, one may assume that they based their question on widely accepted norms; by not following these norms, the disciples of Jesus represented themselves as outsiders.

As before, Luke refers to "some of the Pharisees," refusing to treat Pharisees as though they all shared a standard response to Jesus.

3-5 The Pharisees address their question (v 2) to the disciples, yet Jesus answers them. Luke thus underscores the responsibility of the master for his followers, and Jesus' defense of his disciples.[98] It may be that Jesus' interpretive recitation of the Davidic story (1 Sam 21:1-6) is a reminder of Jesus' own status as a Davidide, and, so, that Luke is thus portraying Jesus as assuming the prestige of David (cf. 1:32). Such a view is little developed within the text, however. Even less obvious is any possibility of an argument from David's practice to the particular issue of transgressing Sabbath regulations.[99] More obvious is the analogy of the relaxation of legal observance in

96. *Contra,* e.g., Kingsbury, *Conflict in Luke,* 89; Westerholm, "Sabbath," 717. See Fitzmyer, *Luke the Theologian,* 183-84.

97. That is, by rubbing the grains in their hands, the disciples are engaged in "work" beyond mere "plucking." See *m. Šabb.* 7:2, which includes these four prohibitions among its list of 39 forbidden activities on the Sabbath. Cf. Philo *Vita Mos.* 2.4 §22: "it is not permitted . . . to pluck any fruit whatsoever."

98. Cf. Daube, "Responsibilities"; Mack and Robbins, *Patterns of Persuasion,* 130.

99. Cohn-Sherbok ("Jesus' Arguments") and others question whether Jesus' answer constitutes a valid halakhic argument; the importance of this observation depends on whether Jesus meant to engage in halakhic argument, which is doubtful — cf. Westerholm, *Jesus,* 97-99.

the face of human need — on the one hand the use of bread reserved for the priesthood (Lev 24:5-9), on the other the plucking of grain on the Sabbath.

The sense of Jesus' response to these Pharisees is determined in large part by his opening words, "Have you not read. . . ?" The use of this formula suggests that his interlocutors have read but not understood the real meaning of this story.[100] Whatever else one might say about Jesus' employment of the David-story, then, the essence of Jesus' reply is his claim that he, not these Pharisees, understands the significance of the Scriptures. Here, as elsewhere in Luke's Gospel, the authority of the Scriptures is upheld *insofar as they are interpreted by Jesus.* Accordingly, Jesus' point is that he, like David (a man after God's heart who carries out God's will — Acts 13:11) before him, appears to be breaking the law even while being obedient to God.[101]

Having been building the case for his interpretive authority, Jesus goes on explicitly to claim lordship over the Sabbath. Thus, he concludes by implication, the disciples have not violated the Sabbath, as they had been accused; rather, the Son of Man, who has authority over the Sabbath, has permitted them to pluck and eat on the Sabbath. This is not a rejection of the Sabbath or of Sabbath observance in general, but it does undercut the utility of Sabbath observance as a boundary-keeping mechanism (i.e., as a sign of faithfulness to God), and it designates Jesus as God's authorized agent to determine what was appropriate on the Sabbath.

In v 5, one hears distinct echoes of Jesus' similar claim in 5:24. In that context, Jesus' audience, including Pharisees, applauded Jesus' word and deed, affirming his status as Son of Man (5:25-26). Any response from Jesus' partners in discussion here is deferred until later; first, Luke will provide a remarkable illustration of Jesus' status as lord of the Sabbath. Will these Pharisees accept his claim?

6-7 Separated from its immediate co-text, this new scene has the appearance of a "typical" incident illustrating the nature of Jesus' mission. Teaching in the synagogue on the Sabbath is expected behavior for Jesus (cf. 4:14-15, 16, 31, 44), and we have come to anticipate the appearance of word (v 6) and deed (v 10) in tandem. Moreover, as usual the Pharisees and scribes are present to monitor legal observance. Innocuous appearances are shattered, however, when these verses are read within their narrative framework. That much more is at stake than a presentation of Jesus' presumed ordinary behavior is evident immediately from the lack of denouement in the previous scene taken together with the intimate relationship between that scene and the present one (see above). Moreover, so quickly following 6:1-5, a reference to Jesus' activity on the Sabbath invites uncertainty; what will the "lord of the sabbath"

---

100. Cf. 10:26; Kimball, *Jesus' Exposition,* 52n.19, 126-27.
101. See the helpful discussion in Nolland, 1:257.

do? In fact, this encounter illustrates more particularly Jesus' self-described status as "lord of the sabbath" (6:5), with Jesus deliberately engaging the scribes and Pharisees in a confrontation vis-à-vis his authority.

Earlier, the action of the disciples was the impetus for a dispute about what was lawful on the Sabbath. Now it is the presence of a man with a withered right hand. Even though the designation of the hand as the "right" (i.e., the more important) one intimates the tragic urgency of the man's condition, his is hardly a life-threatening condition. Hence, his treatment could wait for another day. According to scribal reckoning, then, his need did not supersede Sabbath law.[102] The scribes and Pharisees are present to observe legal compliance, but, as Luke presents it, they are no longer passive witnesses. Their "watching" Jesus takes the character of "spying"[103] with the intent of bringing formal charges against him.[104] These "regulators" thus function as barriers to the healing of this man, and in fulfilling this role they also represent the synagogue and Sabbath as entities segregating this needy man from divine help.

8-10 Following the sinister tone of v 7b, vv 8-9 only heighten the drama of this scene. First, though he knows their malevolent design, their "inner thoughts," Jesus nevertheless raises the issue of appropriate Sabbath conduct. Luke thus accentuates the motif of conflict by drawing on language used first to introduce that motif most explicitly, in Simeon's prophecy: because of Jesus, the "inner thoughts of many will be revealed" (2:35).[105] Second, the narrator reports that Jesus instructed the man to arise and stand in the middle of the audience, then Luke relates how he arose and stood in their midst. With this redundancy, Luke locates this needy man as the focus of attention, an object lesson for discerning the will of God (cf. 9:46).

Third, speaking to "them" — that is, to the scribes and Pharisees (v 7) — Jesus specifically raises the topic under scrutiny in 6:1-11: What is lawful on the Sabbath? He also raises that other, more weighty point of contention: Who decides what is lawful on the Sabbath? The form of Jesus' question narrows considerably the available options. In scribal deliberation, the first question had to do with whether it was proper to heal on the Sabbath as opposed to waiting for another day. Phrasing the question in this way, they were able to conclude that a non-life-threatening case could wait for the

---

102. Schürer (*Jewish People,* 2:474) observes that the basic rule that the saving of life takes precedence over the Sabbath was defined and universally accepted from the beginning of the Maccabean uprising; apart from actual risk of life, though, the intervention of a physician was not permitted. See *m. Yoma* 8:6; Westerholm, *Jesus,* 95.

103. παρατηρέω; cf. 20:20.

104. Balz ("κατηγορέω") refers to κατηγορέω as a juridical technical term in 22 of its 23 uses in the NT, including here. Cf. 23:2, 10, 14.

105. διαλογισμός is also used in 5:22; 9:46-47; 24:38.

passing of the Sabbath. This principle had become widely accepted, with further debate converging around (only) the discrimination of genuinely "at-risk" crises. The scribal way of articulating the options accorded privilege to Sabbath observance as an unimpeachable symbol of Jewish piety; on this reckoning, the issue was, When might Sabbath law be superseded? Jesus poses the options more starkly: to do good or to do harm, to save or to destroy — thus excluding any possibility of a benign interpretation of the scribal option to defer action.[106] Against these Pharisees and scribes, Jesus refuses to represent Sabbath observance as a litmus test for faithfulness to God. More fundamental for him is God's design to save — a purpose that is not incompatible with Sabbath observance but, in fact, is embodied in God's purpose for the Sabbath.

Luke employs two terms that deserve more attention.[107] The first is the verb "to save." In the wider Greco-Roman world of Luke's day, "salvation" had to do with "a general manifestation of generous concern for the well-being of others, with the denotation of rescue from perilous circumstances,"[108] including, but hardly limited to the healing of physical malady.[109] His usage here is consistent with Greco-Roman definitions, but is developed along broader lines too. Thus, for example, for Luke the one who saves/heals is God (1:47) and, on God's behalf, Jesus (2:11; cf. Acts 5:31). In announcing the healing of the crippled man, Luke uses a second, related term to describe the restoration of the man's hand, a term that, like the verb "to save," is used in the LXX of the restoration of Israel. We should not make the linguistic error of reading the redemption of all Israel into this one episode. Against the backdrop of the developing narrative, though, we can maintain that in this one scene, with reference to this one man with a crippled hand, we are to see an expression of Jesus' mediation of God's eschatological redemption. For Jesus, "today," including the Sabbath day, is the day when divine salvation is available to those who need it (see 4:21). What, then, is the nexus between Sabbath and healing in this instance? Jesus' ministry ". . . restores to the sabbath command its profound significance: *restoration* of human beings in their integrity as part of God's creation."[110]

The intentionality of Jesus' confrontation with these scribes and Pharisees is evidenced further in the deliberateness of his crowning act. He surveys the room, then instructs the man to stretch out his hand, to act as

---

106. Schürmann, 1:308.

107. σῴζω, "to save"; and ἀποκαθίστημι, "to restore."

108. Danker, *Benefactor*, 324 (with reference to σωτήρ and cognates).

109. See MM 620-22; Danker, *Benefactor;* Foerster, "σῴζω and σωτηρία," 966-69; *TLNT,* 3:344-49.

110. Müller, "ἀποκαθίστημι, ἀποκαθιστάνω," 129.

though it were well. The man obeys and is healed. In v 5 Jesus asserted his authority over the Sabbath; here he demonstrates it (similarly, 5:24).

11 Since v 5 we have waited to discover how Jesus' rivals would respond to him. We need wait no longer, for their response is an immediate and unequivocal rejection of his claim to authority over the Sabbath. Their "fury" is more than anger. This is rage born of incomprehension.[111] "At their wits' end,"[112] these scribes and Pharisees signal proleptically the nature of the opposition Jesus will meet in the narrative to come (cf. 19:48; 23:34).

4.3. JESUS INSTRUCTS HIS DISCIPLES (6:12-49)

Although Jesus has called a few persons to be his disciples, these new followers have had almost no role thus far within the narrative. The focus instead has been on Jesus, the shape of his ministry, and the division he is causing in Israel as he attracts diverse responses. Luke 6:12-49 further establishes the Lukan notion of discipleship, at least in these early stages, primarily as preparation.[1] Thus far, those whom Jesus has called have left all to follow him (5:1-11, 27-28), but their identity or purpose as disciples has remained undeveloped. This pattern is repeated again: Jesus names apostles, but gives them no explicit assignment; instead, he launches immediately into his ministry of gracious word and deed, speaking especially to his disciples in the hearing of "the people."

Luke 6:12-16 are transitional, and it is possible to regard this pericope as the close of the previous section rather than the opening of the present one. The close ties between this scene and the next are signaled in v 18 ("he came down with them"), however, and this return to a narrow emphasis on Jesus and his followers provides the setting for the extended discourse to come. More importantly, the connection between 6:12-16 and the rest of the chapter points to the important Lukan emphasis on prayer — in preparation not only for the choosing of the twelve apostles but also for the ministry of word and deed (cf. 6:18-19). The break following v 49 is easily discerned, marked as it is by Luke's phrase, "After Jesus had finished all his sayings . . ." (7:1).

We should also recognize the important topical shift with the onset of 6:12. The controversy developing throughout the previous section has ended and Jesus is now allowed to teach without interruption or contest. This does not mean that the motif of conflict has altogether evaporated: Luke proleptically identifies Judas Iscariot as a hostile figure in v 16, and in vv 22-23 Jesus

---

111. ἄνοια. Compare the use of θυμός in 4:28.
112. Marshall, 236.
1. Cf. Jervell, "The Twelve," 78; Green, *Gospel of Luke,* 103.

speaks of those who meet opposition "on account of the Son of Man." In the current absence of open animosity, however, Jesus can instruct his followers on the life of discipleship, including how best to respond in the face of opposition — namely, with joy (v 23) and love (v 27).

4.3.1. The Calling of the Twelve (6:12-16)

12 *Now during those days he went out to the mountain to pray; and he spent the night in prayer to God.* 13 *And when day came, he called his disciples and chose twelve of them, whom he also named apostles:* 14 *Simon, whom he named Peter, and his brother Andrew, and James, and John, and Philip, and Bartholomew,* 15 *and Matthew, and Thomas, and James son of Alphaeus, and Simon, who was called the Zealot,* 16 *and Judas son of James, and Judas Iscariot, who became a traitor.*

The naming of twelve disciples as apostles is prolegomenon to instruction in discipleship. Both — the choice of the twelve and the ministry to follow — grow out of Jesus' noctural prayer.

12-13 In spite of the Lukan view that all Jesus does is done as one anointed by the Holy Spirit (4:1, 14, 18), the Third Evangelist periodically reminds his audience that his fundamental interest is in demonstrating that, within this narrative, the purpose of God is coming to fruition. In his account of the selection of the twelve this is evident, first, in its topography; Jesus goes out to a mountain, a locale often associated in Jewish literature with theophanic episodes and divine revelation.[2] Second, in an unusual turn of phrase ("in prayer to God"),[3] combined with an emphatic description of Jesus' prayer,[4] Luke draws attention to the divine impetus for the selection of the twelve to serve as "apostles." Luke has not previously established a narrative need for the election of apostles, a reality that underscores its origination in the divine will, discerned in prayer. As Luke presents it, the *idea* of choosing itself, the election of *twelve* persons, and the choice of *these particular persons* from among the larger group of disciples — all three are divinely sanctioned.[5] Jesus thus acts as God's agent and in continuity with the divine will.

The segregation of twelve as apostles from the larger gathering of

---

2. See Allison Jr., "Mountain and Wilderness," 563.

3. Luke's phrase, προσευχῇ τοῦ θεοῦ, with the objective genitive, appears nowhere else in the NT (Plummer, 171).

4. Note both the dual mention of "prayer" and Luke's remark regarding its duration, "through the night."

5. Cf. Jervell, "The Twelve," 86-87; Schürmann, 1:313. For a similar emphasis, see Luke's description of the choosing of the apostles and the replacement of Judas in Acts 1:1-2, 15-26.

disciples serves little immediate, qualitative function. Jesus' teaching in 6:17-49, for example, is not restricted to this (or any other) group (cf. 7:1). Even the later sending of the twelve apostles as missionaries (9:1-10) does not mark their peculiar role in God's purpose, for it is paralleled in the subsequent sending of the seventy-two (10:1-16). That the apostles will come to play significant roles in Luke's two-volume work is clear (cf. Luke 22:29-30; Acts 1:21-22), but at present this is only implied in the name Jesus gives them: "apostles" — that is, authorized representatives.[6] When read against its local co-text — 5:1–6:11, with the theme of opposition that surfaces there — a second important note may be sounded here. With scribes and Pharisees responding to Jesus with misapprehension and anger, the choosing of the twelve signals a judgment on Israel's leadership for their lack of insight into God's redemptive plan and compassionate care for those in need. Hence, by inference, Jesus is establishing new leadership. The symbolic importance of the twelve as providing leadership for God's people is also evident from the relatively minor role played in the larger narrative of Luke-Acts by most of the persons named.

14-16 Of the apostles enumerated in vv 14-16, three are already known to us as disciples: Simon Peter, James, and John (5:1-11). To the names of Simon and four others, Luke has added a qualifying phrase. Luke 5:8 had given Simon's name as Simon Peter, but here we learn that it was from Jesus that Simon had received his new name, the name by which he will be known throughout most of Luke-Acts.[7] This change of name, first, emphasizes the new relationship between Jesus and Peter, and, second, suggests the deliberate, metaphorical association of Simon Peter and (a) "rock." In light of Jesus' teaching in 6:48, relating the hearing and doing of Jesus' words to building on a rock,[8] ". . . Jesus' name for Simon points toward his function and evaluates him as one who heeds Jesus' words."[9]

Andrew, previously unknown to us, is listed second as a consequence of his relationship to Peter. The second James and the first Judas are named in relationship to their fathers, presumably in order that they might be differ-

---

6. Although Luke will define ἀπόστολος more carefully (esp. Acts 1), he has not done so thus far. Hellenistic readers will be familiar with the basic sense, "envoy" (see MM 70; *TLNT,* 1:186-88), while those with a familiarity with the LXX's use of ἀποστέλλω will be aware of the more developed nuance of "the sending of a commissioned agent."

7. In Luke: 8:45, 51; 9:20, 28, 32, 33; 12:41; 18:28; 22:8, 34, 54, 55, 58, 60, 61; 24:12. "Simon" appears in Luke in 4:38; 5:3, 4, 5, 8, 10; 22:31; 24:34.

8. Πέτρος (Peter), used as a proper name, has the same sense as πέτρα (rock), found in 6:48.

9. Brawley, *Centering on God,* 142. Luke uses the verb ὀνομάζω, suggesting that this "naming" has something to say about Simon's character and person; cf. Dietrich, *Petrusbild,* 93-94.

entiated from other disciples bearing the same name. Likewise, "Simon . . . the Zealot" is so described, at least in part, in order to distinguish him from "Simon . . . named Peter." The narrator has no apparent interest in specifying in what sense Simon is "the Zealot."[10]

Luke was not content simply to mention Judas Iscariot either. He does not yet call him a "betrayer" (cf. 22:22), but opts instead for the more vague "traitor," denoting this apostle as one who would reject the purpose of God at work in Jesus and oppose his mission. In this introduction to Judas, then, we are given a proleptic view of Judas's role in the narrative, in the shape of a valuative comment that predisposes us to respond to Judas negatively.[11] That Judas is present at all in this elect group of the twelve should give us pause, however. Following the series of accounts in 5:1–6:11, we may already have begun to work out what we assume to be Luke's categories: Pharisees and scribes reject Jesus' ministry, but his disciples follow him without reservation and the crowds acclaim him. Reality, even reality as relatively simplified and as interpreted in the form of Luke's narrative, is not so rudimentary; as we have seen, not all Pharisees can be characterized negatively and, as we now learn, even a disciple, even one named an apostle in obedience to God's design, can oppose God's purpose. This brief depiction of Judas, then, appears as a warning to the reader and strikes again the note of suspense as it portends the opposition that will arise even from within the closest ranks of Jesus' followers.

4.3.2. The Status and Practices of Jesus' Community (6:17-49)

In debate with some of the Pharisees and scribes (5:17–6:11), Jesus has rejected what is for his interlocutors a divinely ordained understanding of the world and the practices it generates. Rejecting their view of the world, he undercuts the dispositions that orient the actions and inclinations that make up their daily lives.[12] Unfortunately for Jesus and his movement, the world-

---

10. ζηλωτής — also in Acts 1:13. In Acts Luke can characterize believers as ζηλωταὶ τοῦ νόμου (21:20: "zealous for the law") or τοῦ θεοῦ (22:3: "for God"). By analogy, Simon could have been (simply) "a zealous person" (so Foakes Jackson and Lake, "The Zealots," 425; Heard, "Revolutionary Movements," 696). Even if the traditional characterization of Simon as "the Zealot" indicates the existence of a group of persons known as "the Zealots" at the time of Jesus (so Hengel, *Zealots*, 69-70, 392), this would not necessarily imply that these belonged to the party identified by Josephus, which seems to have originated in the mid-60s C.E. Simon may have had nationalistic proclivities, but we will not learn this from Luke; and it is of interest that when they are present in Acts, revolutionary parties stand in contrast to the followers of Jesus (e.g., 5:34-39; 21:37-40).

11. προδότης; cf. Acts 7:52. See also Sheeley, *Narrative Asides,* 104.

12. This way of configuring Jesus' message is dependent on Bourdieu, *Language and Symbolic Power; idem, Logic of Practice.*

view of these Pharisees and scribes is widespread and has become institution-alized in patterns of expected behavior reinforced by social sanctions. Those who do not discriminate in their choices of table companions, those who do not fast, those who do not observe the Sabbath — such people are defined as outsiders, people of low regard in this system. Jesus now counteracts those negative sanctions by doing nothing less than redefining the world, positing as the foundation of this world the OT affirmation of the merciful Father (6:36)[13] and erecting on this foundation a new set of dispositions out of which will flourish new practices, perceptions, and attitudes. Having named new leadership for God's people (6:12-16), he now defines in positive terms both the new conditions of existence in his community and the general shape of the behaviors and appreciations that will come to seem natural for those who participate in this community.

This is not to say that Jesus works only to effect a transformation of worldview and group solidarity among those chosen to be apostles, or even among his larger circle of disciples. Even if his teaching in this section is directed to his disciples in particular (6:20), it is equally clear that he taught "in the hearing of the people" more generally (7:1). Here and elsewhere in Luke, "the people" are prospective followers; Jesus gives instructions on the way of discipleship that serve as an invitation and challenge to all.

The primary emphasis of this section is marked by the *inclusio* of vv 17-19 and vv 46-49. At the outset, Luke records how "a great crowd of his disciples and a great multitude of people" had "come to hear him and to be healed"; at the conclusion Jesus calls for people not only to come and hear, but also to act on his words. This emphasis is consonant with what was already implicit in the renaming of Simon as Peter (6:12-16), read as an evaluation of the apostle as one who heeds Jesus' words. Jesus' practices of healing, his table fellowship with toll collectors and sinners, and now the inclusive nature of this audience — these and other aspects of his ministry symbolize the wide reach of God's grace. All are welcome, but to stay, to be able to name Jesus as "Lord," Jesus' gracious invitation must be joined by obedience (cf. 6:45-46; 13:25-27).

4.3.2.1. A Crowd Gathers (6:17-19)

17 *He came down with them and stood on a level place, with a great crowd of his disciples and a great multitude of people from all Judea, Jerusalem, and the coast of Tyre and Sidon.* 18 *They had come to hear him and to be healed of their diseases; and those who were troubled with unclean spirits were cured.* 19 *And all in the crowd were trying to touch him, for power came out from him and healed all of them.*

13. Cf. Pokorný, "Strategies of Social Transformation."

In Jesus' descent from the mountain to speak to the people (6:20-49), some interpreters find a Moses-typology at work.[14] This is possible, especially in light of Exod 19:24; 24:3, where Moses and the elders are on Sinai while the people wait for the words of the Lord, to which they will respond, "All the words that the Lord has spoken we will do" (see Luke 6:46-49).[15]

More conspicuous within the Lukan narrative, though, is how these topographical notations ("he went out to the mountain . . . he came down" — vv 12, 17) build a bridge between Jesus' prayer and his ministry. The purpose for his retreat to the mountain was explicitly "to pray," and the outcome of his vigil is twofold: he discerns God's will regarding the selection of apostles and he is empowered for divine service. That is, in a way reminiscent of 3:21-22 and 5:16-17, Jesus' prayer in 6:12 solidifies his relationship to God and strengthens him for ministry. As before,[16] we are to understand the "power" that "came out from him" as the healing work of the Holy Spirit manifest in his ministry.

Luke envisions three groups: Jesus and those with him (i.e., apostles and the disciples from which the apostles were chosen, 6:13); a considerable crowd of disciples and people; and, within this latter group, "those who were troubled with unclean spirits."[17] The apostles and smaller band of disciples, from 6:13, have no apparent active role to play in the narrative; instead, they are "with" him — a key credential for serving as an apostolic witness in Acts (1:21), for now suggesting companionship with Jesus, identifying with and being shaped in relationship to his life and mission.[18] With respect to their function in the narrative, the Lukan distinction between "crowd of . . . disciples" and "multitude of people" is only nominal. They come from the same regions and with the same purpose: to hear and to be healed. Only with the passing of time, as his followers reflect more and more in their lives the values Jesus represents and teaches will such distinctions have practical utility.

The narrator seems deliberately to paint this scene in contrast to the episodes of conflict that brought the previous section (5:17–6:11) to a close. For example, most apparent about the crowd Jesus attracts is its size — emphasized by the repetition of "great" and "all" and use of the term "multitude" — this in spite of the rejection of Jesus' status and authority by those Pharisees and scribes who monitor faithful observance of the law. Second, the diversity of the multitude's geographical origins are equally reminiscent

---

14. E.g., Schürmann, 1:320; Marshall, 241; Danker, 136.

15. C. F. Evans, 322.

16. See above on 5:17.

17. See Kirchschläger, *Jesu exorzistisches Wirken,* 182-83.

18. For the motif of discipleship as "being with Jesus" see 7:11; 8:1, 22; 9:10; 22:11, 14, 28, 39; cf. 8:38; 22:33; Green, *Gospel of Luke,* 108-9.

of those in 5:17, with "Judea" now used for the whole of Palestine (as in 4:40) and Jerusalem singled out due to its socio-religious prominence.[19] The inclusion of Gentiles among the gathering masses may be suggested by this first reference to people from the coast of Tyre and Sidon, particularly in light of the earlier mention of the Sidonian widow in 4:26.[20] Third, the role of the Pharisees and scribes in 5:17–6:11 — to observe, monitor, and question Jesus, even to spy on him — diverges markedly from the aim of this crowd. They are not present to evaluate his ministry but to be its recipients.

In v 18, Luke holds together the twin motifs of word and deed in Jesus' ministry, even though the account of Jesus' words comes later, in vv 20-49. The interim focus is on healing or, more particularly, on curing those troubled with unclean spirits. "Troubled" is sometimes used in Hellenistic Greek for unrest caused by demons, but it also might simply connote "sick."[21] In Lukan perspective, no decision between these two options is necessary, since the diseases in view in this summary are those that result from unclean spirits.[22] This bespeaks Luke's wider view of health, embracing social, spiritual, and biomedical realities, but also reminds us that for Luke the foe of redemptive wholeness is the devil. That the diabolic is being overcome in Jesus' ministry is intimated by Luke's final comment: he healed them all.

4.3.2.2. Blessing and Woe (6:20-26)

20 *Then he looked up at his disciples and said:*
"Blessed are you who are poor, for yours is the kingdom of God.
21 *"Blessed are you who are hungry now, for you will be filled.*
"Blessed are you who weep now, for you will laugh.
22 *"Blessed are you when people hate you, and when they exclude you, revile you, and defame you on account of the Son of Man.* 23 *Rejoice in that day and leap for joy, for surely your reward is great in heaven; for that is what their ancestors did to the prophets.*
24 *"But woe to you who are rich, for you have received your consolation.*
25 *"Woe to you who are full now, for you will be hungry.*

19. See above, §3.
20. σιδῶνος (of Sidon) is used in 4:26.
21. BAGD 267; LSJ 572; GELS 154.
22. Bock (565), e.g., asserts that "Luke distinguishes between healing of disease and curing of demonic possession" in vv 17-18. However, the first clause reports why the crowd came ("to be healed of their disease"), whereas the second recounts the nature of the ministry they received, in which "those who were troubled with unclean spirits were cured"). The Evangelist uses both ἰάομαι (vv 18a, 19) and θεραπεύω (v 18b) in this summary, apparently for linguistic variety; there is no difference in meaning.

"Woe to you who are laughing now, for you will mourn and weep.
26 *"Woe to you when all speak well of you, for that is what their ancestors did to the false prophets."*

As Luke relates it, Jesus launches his discourse on the constitution of the new community with a series of beatitudes and woes embodying the topos of transposition. By "topos of transposition," we mean to draw attention to the presence throughout Luke but also in Jewish and Greco-Roman literature more widely of a stable configuration of motifs sketching the reversal of fortunes.[23] Its presence in Luke is marked by a number of texts in addition to this one — for example, the Song of Mary (1:46-55), Jesus' instructions on table fellowship (14:7-24), the story of the rich man and Lazarus (16:19-31), the story of the Pharisee and the toll collector (18:9-14), and, most importantly, the Lukan account of the exaltation of the crucified Jesus (Luke 22–24).[24] Outside of Luke, and with reference more narrowly to the respective predicaments of the rich and poor, a key motif in this pericope, one may refer to stories of the empowerment of the Roman poor and of the humbling of their proud opponent, Coriolanus,[25] and to such Jewish texts as *1 Enoch* 92–105.[26] In Luke's cultivation of a new symbolic world, then, he is planting and irrigating where others had already prepared the ground.

That Luke makes use of an available topos of reversal is not to say that his message grows out of or simply mimics those others. To the contrary, passages such as that found in *1 Enoch* forecast the coming vindication of the righteous poor as victory over one's foes, while the ongoing rearticulation of the Greco-Roman stories reviewed by Balch seems more expressive of the altruistic impulses of the Roman elite than of fundamental change in the world order.[27] Luke, however, portrays Jesus as redefining, both now and for the

23. York *(The Last Shall Be First)* refers to bipolar reversal as "a theme of Luke's Gospel," by which he means (citing Alter, *Art,* 95) "an idea which is part of the value-system of the narrative." Following Prince *(Narratology,* 97), we understand "theme" differently, to refer to the pragmatic "aboutness" of a text. This definition of "topos" is also borrowed from Prince, *Narrative as Theme,* 3-4.

24. See York, *The Last Shall Be First;* Green, "God's Servant."

25. Balch, "Rich and Poor."

26. See Nickelsburg, "Riches, the Rich, and God's Judgment."

27. One may grant Balch's ("Rich and Poor"; Balch is dependent on Fuks, *Social Conflict,* esp. 52-79, 172-89) insistence that Greco-Roman values that relate rich and poor and hold open the possibility of role reversal were more widespread than commonly thought without dismissing the fact that this is not the way the Roman world is portrayed by Luke. It may be that Luke is reinforcing values already known in the Roman tradition (see above, on 1:17), but in doing so he is also undercutting the patronal ethics of the Empire as well as such widely held and determinative values as honor and shame.

eschatological future, the way the world works; he is replacing common representations of the world with a new one.

The motif of reversal is most obviously apparent in the structure of this preamble to Jesus' address, in the bipolar opposition in what is affirmed and disaffirmed. In several instances, in fact, one recognizes an exact linguistic correspondence between the wording of the beatitudes and woes, leaving no doubt as to the care of the construction of this text. Less obvious, but no less important, are the echoes of the reversal segment of Mary's Song (1:46-55) heard in this preamble: "blessed" (1:45, 48; 6:20, 21a, 21b, 22); "hungry" versus "filled" (1:53; 6:21, 25); "rich" (1:53; 6:24). Similarly, the "good news to the poor" promised in Jesus' inaugural address (4:18-19) explicitly surfaces here (6:20). Images of salvation declared in Mary's Song to have already happened are again reaffirmed by Jesus as he articulates his understanding of reality in this new day.

This way of understanding the cluster of beatitudes in Luke 6 emphasizes their ascriptive (and not prescriptive) purpose: They define, as it were, "the way things are in the world." Although this is consistent with the location of these and other beatitudes throughout antiquity in wisdom teaching,[28] it also stands in tension with those sapiential associations since Jesus' claims clearly do not represent "conventional wisdom." Is not wealth a sign of God's blessing (Deuteronomy 28)? How then can the poor be declared fortunate and the wealthy be warned of God's curse? From this perspective, Luke has recounted "anti-beatitudes."[29] Four observations point toward a resolution of this tension. (1) Although beatitudes are wisdom-type ascriptions, the woes of vv 24-26 draw more on the prophetic tradition, where they were used to draw the attention of people to coming disaster stemming from divine judgment.[30] (2) The first and fourth beatitudes and corresponding woes occur in the present tense, but the middle two portray a future reversal of a present condition. (3) The implied agent of reversal in each case is God. (4) Jesus' teaching follows immediately on the heels of his controversial ministry to persons commonly regarded as socially unacceptable (5:1–6:11).

These observations have important consequences: (1) Jesus' vision of the new world is eschatological, but it is not relegated to the future. The end has already arrived, and the values he asserts in debate with his opponents and in instruction to his followers and the crowds reflect those of this new era. (2) Jesus' "wisdom teaching," based as it is on an unconventionalized understanding of the world, is designed to jolt his audience into new percep-

28. Cf. Guelich, *Sermon on the Mount*, 63-66; Dupont, "Béatitudes egytiennes"; *TLNT,* 3:432-41; P. Smith, "Beatitudes and Woes."
29. Cf. Betz, *Sermon on the Mount*, 33: "anti-macarism."
30. See Zobel, "הוֹי."

tions of God's redemptive aim. Because the old ways carry with them alleged divine sanction, Jesus is calling for a paradigm shift of colossal proportions. (3) As a cluster of ascriptions, these beatitudes and woes are words of hope and comfort to people like those who have already been the recipients of Jesus' ministry: lepers, sinners, the demonized, toll collectors, women, and so on. Unacceptable in the socially defined world in which they live, they are not only tolerated but embraced and restored in the new world Jesus proclaims and embodies. (4) One therefore finds in these verses no idealization of poverty, for example; instead, Jesus' characterizes the new world, the kingdom of God, as a place where poverty is absent.[31] (5) Moreover, the new world and the values it embodies will catch unawares those who measure their lives by the old order; their sense of well-being and self-assurance is grounded in false values.

20, 24 The question, To whom does Jesus address these beatitudes and woes? is as critical as it is disputed. Some find a distinction between the audience of vv 20-23 and that of vv 24-27, with blessings spoken to the disciples (v 20a) and woes to people in the larger crowd (v 17b).[32] Others want to distinguish "the poor" in general from "the poor = disciples," insisting that Jesus limits the beatitudes to the latter.[33] In reality, distinctions of this sort are difficult to make on the basis of this text. One cannot assume, for example, that the "disciples" to whom Jesus addresses these words have left all and thus become poor. Even if Luke customarily uses the term "disciple" to refer to the narrow circle of Jesus' followers, including Peter and others who have "left everything," he can use it to refer to the larger circle of followers (6:17; 19:37) — that is, to persons who will be called upon for such commitments (14:26-33) but who may not have done so yet. No markers in the text itself suggest that Jesus means by the "you" of v 20 anything different than he might by the "you" of v 24. Moreover, no distinction is drawn between the larger group of disciples and the gathered people with regard to geographical origins (v 17), purpose in coming (v 18), or how they receive Jesus' message.[34] Finally, often in rhetorical situations someone or some group can serve as the formal addressee even though in fact the speaker is addressing all present (cf. 12:1; 20:45).[35] Even if Jesus first lifts his eyes to the disciples, then, this preamble is directed to the whole crowd. In pro-

---

31. Pokorný, "Strategies of Social Transformation," 113; Harvey, *Strenuous Commands,* 138.

32. Cf., e.g., Tannehill, *Narrative Unity,* 1:207-8; Schottroff and Stegemann, *Jesus,* 72-73.

33. Cf., e.g., Stein, 204; Kvalbein, "Jesus and the Poor," 81.

34. Cf. Tiede, "Luke 6:17-26," 65-67.

35. Kennedy, *New Testament Interpretation,* 41; see also 65-66.

nouncing beatitudes and woes, Jesus is engaged in the practice of sifting, of causing division, just as had been prophesied concerning him (2:34; 3:17).

Crucial to this way of understanding Jesus' audience is how one construes the "poor" and "rich," and how one understands Jesus' purpose at this early point in his discourse. We have seen that "the poor" in Luke refers above all to those who have been marginalized in the larger world, whether on the basis of economic or other measures (see above on 4:18-19), those for whom only God can bring good news. "Wealthy" is interpreted along similar lines in this Gospel. Thus, for example, in 1:51-53 the proud and mighty are contrasted with the humble, the rich (who are well fed) with the hungry; in 12:16-21 and 16:19-31 the rich are those with significant resources at their disposal, yet who fail to consider the plight of others; and in 14:12 "rich neighbors" are catalogued with one's "inner circle" — friends, brothers, kin — persons with whom one enjoys relationships of equality and mutuality. Like "poor," then, "rich" is not simply a declaration of economic class; it is related fundamentally to issues of power and privilege, social location as an insider, and arrogant self-security apart from God.[36] "Poor" and "rich," then, are socially defined constructs — and Jesus is overturning the way these terms have been constructed in ordinary discourse. In effect, he insists, you who are poor are accustomed to living on the margins of society and you who are rich routinely find yourselves surrounded by friends as you use your resources to solidify your position in society, but the reality under which you have been operating has been overturned. By asserting that the kingdom of God belongs to the poor, then, Jesus is redefining the working assumptions, the values that determine daily existence.

21a, 25a This second pair of beatitude and contrasting woe is closely aligned with the first, inasmuch as the hungry and the poor stand in parallel in the OT (e.g., Ps 107:36, 41; Isa 32:6-7; 58:7, 10; cf. Luke 1:53). The eschatological promise of food (cf. Isa 49:10; 65:13) is often related to the messianic banquet (e.g., Isa 25:6-8; 49:10-13), a motif Luke will develop elsewhere (12:37; 13:29; 14:14-24). In both beatitude and woe, the antithesis is between present condition ("now") and eschatological reversal ("you will . . .").

21b, 25b As in the second pair, so in this one the reversal is exact, the only addition coming in v 25b with the supplementary term "mourn." "Laughing" appears nowhere else in the NT, and in the LXX it is usually ironic or flippant, even haughty or foolish[37] (as it is unveiled to be in v 25b). Perhaps drawing on Psalm 126,[38] Luke overturns this negative image, por-

36. Green, "Good News," 68; cf. Johnson, 108.
37. γελάω, though see γέλως in Jas 4:9. See Gen 17:7; 18:12-15; et al.; GELS, 87.
38. Schürmann, 1:331-32.

traying instead laughter and joy appropriate to divine restoration. Weeping and mourning are stock responses to rejection, ridicule, and loss.[39]

22-23, 26   Often regarded as qualitatively distinct from the other pairs of beatitudes and woes, this one, concerned with social acceptance and honor, is instead central to its co-text. The behavior of Jesus' disciples has been challenged on two accounts (eating and drinking, 5:33; plucking grain on the Sabbath, 6:1-2); even more has Jesus' authority as Son of Man been called into question (6:1-11; cf. 5:17-26). God's people, past (cf. 1:71) and future (21:17), may expect nothing less than hate and rejection, just as, according to widely held social norms, sinners, the diseased, and others are excluded from full social discourse (5:1–6:11). Because those social norms are not only pervasive but are also presumed to be rooted in God's will, within that symbolic world banishment would have been tantamount to divine malediction. Not so, Jesus says, and he is able to reject such an interpretation of marginalization and expulsion precisely because he has first rejected the view of the world on which it is based.

People of the old order speak well only of those who follow its routines and conform to its canons. Those whose behaviors are grounded in a contrary worldview can expect defamation. As Son of Man, Jesus has already begun the process of redefining how God's redemptive purpose is coming to fruition, and, in his unique role of wielding divine agency as Son of Man, he has attracted opposition. Those who recognize his authority and orient themselves around God's purpose as manifest in his ministry can also expect opposition. This is not because God has rejected them, but because their persecutors have rejected God's purpose. The day of one's opposition, then, is a time of joy,[40] not because rejection entitles one to a reward, as though Jesus had introduced a moral contract, but because persecution "on account of the Son of Man" authenticates one's identification with God's purpose. As testimony of the truth of his claim, Jesus draws on the record of the prophets — not because Jesus' followers will necessarily be prophets too, but because Israel's history had been one of opposition to those who represented God's will (cf. Neh 9:26; Ezek 2:1-7; Acts 7:52). False prophets, on the other hand, were celebrated because their message was consistent with popular inclinations (e.g., Jer 5:12-13; 6:13-15; Mic 2:11).

---

39. Cf., e.g., 2 Sam 19:1-2; Ps 35:11-14. Read in its co-text, with its emphasis on marginalization, rejection, and eschatological reversal, it is doubtful that the "weeping" of v 21b is a sign of reliance on God, as in, e.g., Psalm 126; Isa 25:8; 35:10; 65:17-25.

40. σκιρτάω ("to leap [for joy]") also appears in 1:41, 44, but nowhere else in the NT.

4.3.2.3. On Giving and Receiving (6:27-38)

27 *"But I say to you that listen, Love your enemies, do good to those who hate you,* 28 *bless those who curse you, pray for those who abuse you.* 29 *If anyone strikes you on the cheek, offer the other also; and from anyone who takes away your coat do not withhold even your shirt.* 30 *Give to everyone who begs from you; and if anyone takes away your goods, do not ask for them again.* 31 *Do to others as you would have them do to you.*

32 *"If you love those who love you, what credit is that to you? For even sinners love those who love them.* 33 *If you do good to those who do good to you, what credit is that to you? For even sinners do the same.* 34 *If you lend to those from whom you hope to receive, what credit is that to you? Even sinners lend to sinners, to receive as much again.* 35 *But love your enemies, do good, and lend, expecting nothing in return. Your reward will be great; and you will be children of the Most High,*[41] *for he is kind to the ungrateful and the wicked.* 36 *Be merciful, just as your Father is merciful.*

37 *"Do not judge, and you will not be judged; do not condemn, and you will not be condemned. Forgive, and you will be forgiven;* 38 *give, and it will be given to you. A good measure, pressed down, shaken together, running over, will be put into your lap; for the measure you give will be the measure you get back."*

A new beginning in Jesus' sermon is marked by his words, "But I say to you that listen. . . ." This should not blind us to the intimate relationship of this middle section of the address to what has preceded, however, for to do so would be to confuse the behaviors Jesus announces with an inventory of "absolute demands,"[42] as if he were primarily or fundamentally concerned with actions. To the contrary, vv 27-38 are integrated into the beatitudes and woes in two ways: (1) this section, and especially vv 35b-36, continues to define the new conditions of existence in Jesus' community; and (2) this portion of his sermon unveils the general perspectives and practices that will characterize those who participate in this community. Having undercut the conventional view of the world that oriented the actions and inclinations of daily existence, Jesus redefines the world, then begins to indicate what comportment and practices this new foundation and these new dispositions will generate and support.[43]

41. The NRSV reads: "Your reward will be great, and you will be children of the Most High; for he is kind to the ungrateful and the wicked."
42. *Pace* C. F. Evans, 333; and many others.
43. Cf. Green, "Caring as Gift and Goal," 157-60.

The structure of this segment of Jesus' sermon is relatively straight-forward. Verses 27-31 identify behaviors becoming those who have fully embraced Jesus' message, while vv 31-38 summarize those behaviors and develop their motivational bases. "Love your enemies" is the heading for all behavior, but this is amplified as "doing good" and as giving (true) gifts. These three actions are interwoven:

> Love your enemies: vv 27b, 32, 35a
> Do good: vv 27c-29, 33, 35a
> Give (true) gifts: vv 30, 34, 35a.

In the midst of these emphases is situated the so-called Golden Rule (v 31) — which, as a consequence, must be regarded as pivotal and interpreted fully within its carefully constructed co-text.

Verses 32-35 not only reiterate behaviors appropriate to Jesus' new community, but they do so in a way that differentiates this community from others. One corollary of Jesus' message, then, is the construction of a boundary, the delineation of behavior characteristic of those within the community. This is an important observation, since one of the distinguishing marks of his ethic is a worldview that advocates love of enemies. But as a practice, it would appear that love of enemies is designed to mitigate social tensions that, if habitual, would jeopardize the identity of any group. How can this community be distinguished by a practice that dissolves any such distinctions? How Jesus disentangles this morass is related to the constitution of the community as it is further outlined in vv 32-38; in essence, Jesus calls on his followers to form a community the boundaries of which are porous and whose primary emblematic behavior is its refusal to treat others (even, or especially, those who hate, exclude, revile, and defame you) as though they were enemies.

We may go on to notice the symmetry within vv 32-34 and vv 37-38. In these verses, Jesus refutes one form of reciprocity in favor of another.[44] He first rejects the balanced reciprocity and patronal ethic characteristic of life in the peasant village and in its external relations with the wider Roman world (vv 32-34). This was everyday life marked in part by the imbalance of social and economic relations typified in claims of honor and status and in the exertion of power over others. Jesus rejects the life of obligation and debt (see above on 4:18-19). In its place he first posits a generalized reciprocity, the sort of open-handed sharing characteristic within families, and urges that actions typical among kin and friends be the norm for interaction with all persons. But he also envisions a form of ideal benefaction: give to others without expectation of return, and God will give to you. One may speak at

44. See above, §10.

this juncture therefore of these two motivations for Jesus' message of love for one's enemies in Luke, boundary-redefinition and ideal benefaction.[45] To these a third should be added, for Luke unmistakably roots all expected behavior firmly in the character of God (v 36). That is, in redefining the world for his followers, potential and actual, Jesus posits as its foundation his image of God as merciful Father (6:36) — a base on which he can draft the character of his followers, character that will manifest itself in the demeanor and practices here described.

27a   "But I say to you that listen" marks a second stage in the sermon. Verse 18 had identified Jesus' audience as those eager to "to hear" him. This redundancy recalls the nature of those gathered around Jesus; it also serves as an invitation, for the verb "to hear" often has the sense "to hear and obey,"[46] an emphasis that will be made explicit in vv 46-49. The unfolding sermon further identifies Jesus' audience as persons of some means — that is, as persons with shirt and coat, with goods that might be stolen, as people capable of loaning to others. Even if some within the audience are destitute, and even if the assertion of the principle of generalized reciprocity is more important than the actual possibility of exercising patronage over another (see §10), Jesus' point is particularly germane to those who would understand it best — namely, those in a socio-economic position that renders them susceptible to theft and capable of lending.

This twofold characterization of Jesus' audience works simultaneously on (at least) two levels. First, of course, it identifies those within the narrative who have come out to be the recipients of Jesus' ministry of word and deed. For them, Jesus' address provides an important corrective: Jesus has repudiated the conventional wisdom and practices typified by those scribes and Pharisees who monitor legal observance in 5:17–6:11, and now he lays out for them an alternative vision of life in the world. In addition, this long teaching segment directly addresses Luke's own audience, with the "you" of v 27 serving double duty. Disciples *within* the narrative are not the only ones with questions about the consequent nature of Jesus' message; if he rejects that vision, what does he propose in its place? How will the message of release and favor work itself out concretely in the community of those who follow him? Jesus' sermon, then, serves an interpretive function for the narrative as it has developed thus far, casting in positive and constructive terms the world-

---

45. See further, below. Theissen (*Social Reality,* 116-32) uses the language of "motive," but attributes to Luke especially "reciprocity" and "eschatological reward," and only secondarily "differentiation" and "imitation of God." We have spoken of "differentiation" in terms of boundary-making, and of reciprocity and reward in terms of ideal benefaction.

46. ἀκούω; cf., e.g., 9:35; 16:29, 31.

view and concomitant practices Jesus' message portends. It is also challenging, summoning its audience(s) to adopt this alternative view of the world and so to measure its practices by its canons.

27b-30 The injunction to enemy-love flies in the face of the conventional wisdom by advocating the insensibility of failing to distinguish enemies from friends. Even if ancient sources counsel compassion for the enemy in need,[47] they provide only the most general context of moral attitude for Jesus' command. Jesus' words, "Love your enemies," lack any commonly held ethical base and can only be understood as an admonition to conduct inspired by God's own graciousness (vv 35d-36). This is not love for all humanity in general,[48] but more specifically for those who stand in opposition to Jesus' followers — those whom Luke has already noted in narration (5:27–6:11) and about whom Jesus has already spoken (vv 22-23). The centrality of the love-command is marked by its appearance as a heading, followed by references to particular actions that embody its content more concretely.[49] Love is expressed in doing good — that is, not by passivity in the face of opposition but in proactivity: doing good, blessing, praying, and offering the second cheek and the shirt along with the coat.

The category of "enemies" may include others, however, and not only those who deliberately oppose Jesus' followers. Because the beggar is habitually defined as outside the circles of companionship of all but other beggars, they would not be classed as "friends" but as "enemies," outsiders. Love is due them as well, as though they were comrades and kin, and in their case love is expressed in giving. The closer the perception of kinship, the more liberal the generosity; conversely, such self-interested gain as stealing is indicative of adversarial status.[50] Jesus does not deny the link between social distance and material exchange, but he radicalizes it by insisting that all persons should be treated as though they were close kin, whose actions, therefore, could not be regarded as stealing or begging. Jesus' mode of presentation certifies that his message is not simply one of prescriptive morality, as though he were telling people how they should or should not act. Rather, he is asking people to accept an inversion of the world order, to agree with him that the world order has been inverted, and to act accordingly.

31 The so-called Golden Rule has a distinguished pedigree in Hellenistic and Jewish literature long before the time of Jesus. Although Jesus is thus appealing to generally accepted standards of conduct, however, this

---

47. See Piper, *Love Your Enemies,* ch. 2.

48. See Schottroff, "Non-Violence."

49. On the centrality of the love-command for Luke more generally, see Furnish, *Love Commandment,* 84-90.

50. See Sahlins, *Stone Age Economics,* 196; cf. above, §10.

saying is nevertheless well integrated into its present context, especially by the repetition of the keyword "do" (vv 27, 31 [2x], 33 [3x], 35). In Hellenistic discussion of ethics, it was ordinarily contextualized within an ethic of consistency and reciprocity: act in such-and-such a way so that you will be treated analogously.[51] Within this immediate co-text, however, this can hardly be the meaning, for the possibility of calculation and just desserts seem to have been excluded from the outset. Others are to be treated lovingly, period, without thought to reciprocating behavior.

32-34 As in the factional social context of Jesus' world,[52] so here, "sinners" are those whose behaviors mark them as outsiders to the community. Unlike earlier uses of the term in the Third Gospel, here "sinners" are those whose lives are marked by the calculations of balanced reciprocity — that is, by a circle of exchange that turns gifts into debts that must be repaid. Pictured are essentially closed groups, whose members are free to give only to one another since integral to their gifts is the obligation of return in kind.

Picking up the triad noted earlier (vv 27, 30) of loving, doing good, and giving/lending,[53] Jesus clarifies the distinction between the practices he advocates and those symptomatic of the larger Mediterranean world.[54] The world governed by patronal ethics cannot exemplify the ethic of enemy-love. As Jesus' question, "What credit is that to you?" recognizes, according to the conventional model, that one's behaviors are scripted by prior liabilities.[55] But Jesus is promulgating the cessation of obligation, insisting that behaviors are not predetermined by what one owes to whom, nor by what one expects to receive from another.

35-36 Jesus summarizes the message of vv 27-34 by repeating the triad of love, doing good, and lending/giving, and by contending that all three must be exercised freely, without calculation, without expectation of return.[56] In doing so, he incorporates into one utterance the character of this new people and the practices it engenders; theirs will be a countercultural existence indeed, for their lives are based on an inverted understanding of their social world. What motives does Jesus offer for these new practices?

First, he vouches for the continuance of the notion of reciprocity, albeit

---

51. See Nolland, 1:298; also Marshall, 262; Theissen, *Social Reality,* 138.

52. See Dunn, "Pharisees, Sinners, and Jesus," 275-80.

53. δαν(ε)ίζω ("to lend") is borrowed from the language of ancient commerce; cf. MM, 136.

54. See van Unnik, "Motivierung"; Lambrecht, *Sermon on the Mount,* 227; Harvey, *Strenuous Commands,* 96, 103-4; Moxnes, *Economy of the Kingdom,* 133.

55. χάρις in this case denotes an effort to pay off a debt by returning benefit for benefit; cf. *TLNT,* 3:503-4.

56. ἀπελπίζω, in this co-text, refers to "giving up hope or despairing [of receiving]."

in a radicalized form. Those who act without expectation of return, even on behalf of their enemies, will be rewarded. Now, however, their reward does not consist of acts of gratitude from the recipients of their benefaction; rather, God rewards them (cf. 12:33; 14:14). In the ethics of the larger Lukan world, a patron solidifies his or her position in the community by "giving," by placing others in his or her debt, and receiving from them obliged acts of service and reverence. In this new economy, however, the patron gives without strings attached, yet is still repaid, now by a third party, God, the great benefactor, the protector and the benefactor of those in need.[57]

Does this mean that God has entered into a moral contract with those who follow Jesus? The reciprocity Jesus begins to develop is not about a pact with God. Note, for example, that reward is given to those who expected none. More importantly, the ethic Jesus unfolds has its basis in God's own character and is not essentially contractual.

Within Luke's world, the question of making a bargain with God would hardly have been in the foreground in discourse about the ethic outlined here. Of much greater significance would be the way Jesus has just subverted a key organizing factor of the Roman Empire — namely, patronal ethics. The Empire was an intrusive, suffocating web of obligation, with resources deployed so as to maintain social equilibrium, with the elite in every village, town, city, and region, and of the Empire as a whole given esteem due them in light of their role as benefactors. If God, and not the emperor, is identified as the Great Benefactor, the Patron, and if people are to act without regard to cycles of obligation, then the politics[58] of the Empire is sabotaged.

The second motive, less an incentive and more a ground for this new behavior, is now identified: the practices Jesus outlines are the marks of "children of the Most High." That is, Jesus declares that such behavior demonstrates that one is a child of God.[59] This declaration echoes John's message in 3:7-9: (1) To be the progeny of something or someone is to share its character by nature.[60] (2) Jesus defines the character of the Most High (cf. 1:32) in terms of kindness to "the ungrateful and the wicked." In doing so, he plays on the word earlier translated "credit," as if to say, ". . . he is kind even to those who do not return his benefaction with grateful worship."[61] This is the nature of the Great Benefactor: he gives even to those who, by

57. Moxnes, *Economy of the Kingdom,* 156.

58. By "politics" we mean the legitimation, distribution, and exercise of power.

59. According to the punctuation of the NRSV, the meaning would be that such behavior qualifies one or makes one to be a child of God. This is a possible reading, but is unlikely given Luke's amply attested interest in the demonstration of one's status as a "child/son" (here, υἱός, "son") through one's behavior. Cf. Marshall, 264.

60. See above on 3:7-18.

61. Verses 32-35: χάρις; v 35: ἀχάριστος.

their ingratitude and wickedness, portray themselves as his enemies. (3) Just as God is merciful — that is, just as God is active graciously and creatively to bring redemption — so should his children be merciful.[62] Hence, the critical value is not reciprocity but behavior rooted in the imitation of God. (4) As in 3:7-9, eschatological reward (and punishment) is a consequence of one's "parentage," revealed in one's behavior.

37-38 The economy asserted in v 35 is now fleshed out with reference to three parties — two explicit, one implicit. Jesus' followers are to behave in certain ways toward others, and God will behave in seemingly symmetrical ways toward Jesus' followers. The symmetry is only apparent, since v 38b borrows imagery from the marketplace to show the extravagant generosity of God, now compared to a merchant who is neither stingy nor fair to himself but excessively fills the measuring vessel. The practices Jesus outlines follow immediately and grow out of the practices of God (vv 35d-36). Just as the merciful God does not predetermine who will or will not be the recipients of his kindness, so Jesus' followers must refuse to "judge" — that is, to prejudge, to predetermine who might be the recipients of their graciousness. This is nothing but the command to love one's enemies restated negatively. In an important sense, Jesus' instructions are to refuse to act as those scribes and Pharisees had done in 5:27-32, as they calculated beforehand the status of those toll collectors and sinners and thereby excluded them from their circles of social interaction. By "forgive," Jesus means "release"[63] — that is, "release from obligations," or "give, without expectation of return"; again, and throughout these two verses, Jesus states negatively what has been asserted previously. The one difference is that the reciprocity denied in vv 32-35a has been restored, with one telling exception. Jesus' followers give freely, without dragging others and especially those in need into the quagmire of never-ending cycles of repayment and liability. And God will lavishly repay them.

4.3.2.4. The Measure of a Disciple (6:39-49)

39 *He also told them a parable: "Can a blind person guide a blind person? Will not both fall into a pit?* 40 *A disciple is not above the teacher, but everyone who is fully qualified will be like the teacher.* 41 *Why do you see the speck in your neighbor's eye, but do not notice*

---

62. The term used here, οἰκτίρμων, is rare, but it is a close semantic kin of ἔλεος, a keyword in the Songs of Mary and Zechariah (1:50, 54, 58, 72, 78; cf. 10:37). Luke may be echoing the targum on Lev 22:28 — "My people, children of Israel, since our Father is merciful in heaven, so should you be merciful on the earth" (*Tg. Ps.-J.* Lev 22:28).

63. ἀπολύω ("to release, to set free") is a semantic partner of ἀφίημι (see 4:18-19).

*the log in your own eye? 42 Or how can you say to your neighbor,
'Friend, let me take out the speck in your eye,' when you yourself do
not see the log in your own eye? You hypocrite, first take the log out
of your own eye, and then you will see clearly to take the speck out of
your neighbor's eye.*

*43 "No good tree bears bad fruit, nor again does a bad tree bear
good fruit; 44 for each tree is known by its own fruit. Figs are not
gathered from thorns, nor are grapes picked from a bramble bush.
45 The good person out of the good treasure of the heart produces
good, and the evil person out of evil treasure produces evil; for it is
out of the abundance of the heart that the mouth speaks.*

*46 "Why do you call me 'Lord, Lord,' and do not do what I tell you?
47 I will show you what someone is like who comes to me, hears my
words, and acts on them. 48 That one is like a man building a house,
who dug deeply and laid the foundation on rock; when a flood arose,
the river burst against that house but could not shake it, because it
had been well built. 49 But the one who hears and does not act is like
a man who built a house on the ground without a foundation. When
the river burst against it, immediately it fell, and great was the ruin
of that house."*

These apparently disparate sayings have puzzled commentators.[64] How do
they function within Jesus' address? Luke's opening words, "He also told
them a parable," is itself enigmatic, since what follows is a series of proverbial
sayings, similes, and a parabolic story. Despite nagging questions on the role
of some of its ingredients, the purpose of this segment of the sermon as a
whole is plain. With these words, Luke signals a change of direction within
Jesus' discourse and draws his speech to a close with a clarion call to add
obedience to the hearing of Jesus' message.

One senses a heightened interest in "doing" in this segment of the
sermon. The word "(to) do" appears five times (vv 43 [2x], 46, 47, 49), and
thus serves as a catchword rooting this pericope into the larger co-text of the
sermon. "Doing," together with the compound verb "doing good," had already come to the fore in earlier segments of the sermon;[65] in fact, taking
seriously the practical demands of the gospel is key throughout Luke-Acts.[66]
It is thus easy to discern here an emphasis on behavior, and one might be
tempted to conclude that Jesus is fundamentally concerned with actions. Such
a conclusion would be misguided, however, grounded as it would be in a

---

64. See Nolland, 1:306-8; Bock, 1:609-13.
65. ποιέω — 6:23, 26, 27, 31 (2x), 33 (2x); ἀγαθοποιέω — 6:33 (2x), 35.
66. Cf., e.g., 3:10-14; 8:21; 10:25, 27; 11:28; Acts 2:37.

superficial reading of the sermon. Even here, where "doing" is accorded such privilege, fundamental to Jesus' closing remarks is the contrast between two sorts of people whose hearts are revealed in their actions. The issue is one of *character* and *commitments* issuing forth in *action*.[67] The two, character and action, are inseparable for Jesus, and those who attempt to sunder them are guilty of hypocrisy (vv 41-42, 46).

According to the finale of the sermon, Jesus is concerned with the nature of a person, the heart, but such a concern does not lead to what today we might call psychological evaluation. In Luke's (pre-Freudian) world, a person's "inside" is accessible not through his or her psychology but through his or her social interactions. People, like trees, are known through what they produce.

Jesus employs a range of metaphors and proverbial sayings for distinguishing between these two kinds of people. Some are blind, hypocritical, produce evil fruit, hear without acting, and build without a foundation. Others produce good fruit, hear *and* act, and build on a foundation of rock. Luke peppers these concluding remarks with the evaluative language of good and evil to drive home this bipolar distinction.[68]

Clearly, then, the following Jesus seeks is a full-orbed one; his is a message that calls for total transformation, with a consistency of goodness between the inside and outside of a person. Even if the language of repentance is absent, the idea of change of heart and life, of a thorough reorientation around God's purpose, is very much present. This is communicated so forcefully and in such variegated ways that it is impossible not to imagine that Jesus' audience is being challenged to take additional steps in their response to him. They have been eager to come and to hear; now they are put on notice that these are not enough. But neither is acting enough, taken on its own; the practices for which Jesus is looking are generated out of the good treasure of the heart of a good person (v 45); they are not the consequence of the posturing of those who want to appear pious but have refused to commit themselves wholeheartedly to following in the way of Jesus. Even the multitude of the disciples who have gathered to hear Jesus are confronted with this challenge, just as Luke's own audience, outside the world of the narrative, stands in need of hearing and acting in ways faithful to what Jesus has spoken.

39-40 "Parable" can refer not only to parabolic stories, with a beginning, middle, and end, such as is recorded in vv 48-49, but also, as in these two verses, to proverbial instruction (cf. 4:23; 5:36). The case of the blind

---

67. Cf. 6:6-11 (esp. v 9), where Jesus confronts the scribes and Pharisees with two options for practice, each rooted in its own commitments and worldview.

68. Words for evil: πονηρός — 6:(22), 35, 45 (3x); σαπρός — 6:43 (2x). Words for good: ἀγαθός — 6:45 (3x); καλός — 6:38, 42 (2x).

leading the blind had achieved proverbial status in antiquity.[69] Underscored here, as often in Luke,[70] is the metaphorical use of the term "blind" to refer to those who lack faith or those who lack insight. The saying about the teacher-pupil relationship is also proverbial, and, when read together, these two verses underscore the necessity of seeking trustworthy, insightful guidance. In direct discourse, Jesus asks, in effect, Whom will you follow? In narrative form, Jesus' role as teacher has already been juxtaposed with teachers who fail to understand and who question his authority (see above on 5:17-22).

Luke also introduces a note of suspense, for, even though it is evident what teacher Jesus' addressees ought to follow, it is not certain which one they will follow. It is not clear that, having decided to hear Jesus, they will also act on his message. Nor is it clear whether, in the end, these disciples will become "fully qualified" — that is, whether they will complete their training.[71] Throughout this sermon, as in his earlier ministry of healing and instruction, Jesus has been renegotiating norms; will these gathered masses accept this reversal of values? Will they hear and internalize this unconventional worldview? How will they become like their teacher?[72]

If Jesus' words raise questions about would-be followers, they also introduce a plumb line by which to mark those in the narrative who are followers indeed. This is important because the point at which some join Jesus' circle of influence is not always evident; repeatedly we are introduced for the first time to persons who seem already to have begun to embody the values of Jesus' message and to manifest them in their practices. Complicating matters further, such persons — for example, a woman from the city (7:36-50), a wealthy toll collector (19:1-10), and a condemned bandit (23:40-43) — are judged according to widely held societal norms as persons living outside the will of God, as sinners. How can we recognize them otherwise? Jesus provides the measure: They are "like the teacher" and have refused the option of blindness. How is this manifest? Their actions and words (see 6:43-45) provide the evidence.

41-42 Jesus continues to traffic in well-known sayings, though again turning them to his own end within this narrative co-text.[73] Aristotle was neither the first nor the last to give voice to the common expectation that those

---

69. See the texts in Schrage, "τυφλός κτλ," esp. 275, 286, 292.

70. See above on 4:18-19.

71. καταρτίζω, used only here in Luke-Acts.

72. Cf. Brawley, *Centering on God,* 52.

73. That is, in line with discourse analysis more generally, we assume that a critical constraint on the meaning of this and other traditional materials in this section of the speech is the local co-text provided by the speech itself. Cf. G. Brown and Yule, *Discourse Analysis,* esp. 46-50; Eco, *Limits,* e.g., 8-22.

who reprove others ought not suffer from the same shortcoming.[74] This saying in its many forms illustrates the epidemic reticence to receive correction; or is it, rather, that "satisfactory rebukers are scarce"?[75] Earlier, Jesus had indicated that behavior becoming persons oriented around God's purpose excluded stereotyping, or prejudging so as to exclude others from the possibility of social intercourse (6:37); this is not at issue here, as the repeated reference to "friends" and "neighbor" (literally, "brother[s]") makes clear. Nor is the possibility of reproof ruled out of court, since Jesus allows that, in the right circumstances, one can remove a "speck" from a neighbor's eye (v 42b). Central to Jesus' admonition is his own rebuke of those who see the faults of others but not of themselves. He calls them "hypocrites." In general usage today, the negative connotations of this label are incontrovertible, but in Greco-Roman antiquity a more nuanced understanding is required. In parlance contemporary with Luke, a "hypocrite" might refer to someone whose behaviors were not determined by God (LXX) or someone who is playing a role, acting a part (Roman theater).[76] In this case, a decision between these two is difficult and probably unnecessary. Jesus indicts persons who attempt to substantiate their own piety through censuring the shortcomings of others as acting inconsistently. Their hearts and actions are inconsistent. While they themselves posture for public adulation, their behavior is not determined by God.

43-45   In many ways, but especially with reference to the equation of "doing" as "producing fruit," the present pericope is reminiscent of Luke's summary of John's message in 3:7-14. Both employ the symbols of agrarian culture, with "fruit" used metaphorically of human conduct (cf. Pss 1:3; 58:12; Isa 3:10), including speech (cf. Sir 27:6), which, then, divulges the central commitments and quality of human beings. Jesus thus speaks of one's "fruit" as his or her signature, exposing the heart.

Drawing on common sense — common, at least, among agriculturalists — Jesus argues for the irrepressible connection between dispositions and practices. The agronomical insight that grapes are not to be found on bramble bushes or good fruit produced from bad trees, for example, is carried over into the sphere of human character and conduct and interpersonal relations. Jesus could hardly have underscored with greater profundity the inexorable relation between human being and doing. If his audience agrees with him thus

74. Aristotle *Rhetoric* 1384b; see the parallels in Danker, 153-54; Derrett, "Christ and Reproof."

75. Derrett, "Christ and Reproof," 273.

76. See Job 34:30; 36:13; 2 Macc 6:21-25; 4 Macc 6:15-23; *Pss. Sol.* 4:5-6, 22; Batey, "Jesus and the Theatre," 564; R. H. Smith, "Hypocrite," 352; Giesen, "ὑπόκρισις, ὑποκρίνομαι."

far, though, then the trap is baited. Indeed, Jesus' final analogy, regarding the speech that emanates from the heart (and not only from the mouth), prepares his audience to grapple with the perplexity of v 46.

46 It is only one small step from the agronomical case studies in vv 43-45 to their application in v 46. If one assumes an essential consistency between the constitution of a plant and the nature of its yield, and if one allows the metaphorical application of that insight into the sphere of human affairs, then Jesus' question has achieved its forceful aim: How is it that humans can be so inconsistent when it comes to their dispositions vis-à-vis the ways of God? In this instance, "Lord" is a term of great respect; those who use it would thus be designating Jesus as their patron, the one to whom they owe allegiance. How can they *speak* of allegiance and not grant it?

Within this co-text, one's response to Jesus' query is not simply to begin doing what he says! The issue is one of lordship, commitment, the offer of allegiance and fidelity. Hence, the initial question is, On what basis might people refer to Jesus as lord? Within the structure of Jesus' message, the corresponding answer would be that they must embrace his topsy-turvy characterization of the world, be transformed in their dispositions, and engage in the loving of enemies, the doing of good, and lending without expectation of return — that is, in practices determined by the gracious character of God (vv 27-38).

At this juncture in the Third Gospel, only two characters within the narrative have referred to Jesus as lord, Peter and a leprous man (5:8, 12). Neither of these has entered into the narrative in such a way thus far as to merit Jesus' rebuke. Nor should we imagine that his scolding words are directed at the Pharisees and scribes he has encountered thus far, for they seem not to have acknowledged his claim to lordship (6:1-11). To whom are Jesus' words directed? Apparently we are to understand them as proleptic, spoken (like his words to the gathering in Nazareth, 4:23) in anticipation of those — whether internal or external to Luke's narrative world — whose affirmation of his lordship would be no more than nominal. They might be eager to be the recipients of his gracious ministry, but only those who also embrace and internalize his message to the point that it has begun to generate such practices as those outlined in his sermon might be genuine in addressing Jesus with the words, "Lord, Lord."

47-49 This closing subunit stands in parallel with the opening of Luke's account of Jesus' address. In 6:18, masses of "disciples" and "people" had come to hear and to be healed. In spite of their eagerness, and in spite of the identification of many as "disciples," however, Jesus' discourse has unveiled that his audience is made up especially of persons who might be described as followers only in a rather loose sense. Indeed, his sermon is a fulfillment of his role as the one who would "sift" or "divide" Israel (3:17; 2:34).

As the capstone of his closing remarks, Jesus provides an illustration of the importance of adding obedience to an eagerness to come and to hear his message.[77] Contrasted are two house builders, one who lays the foundation on rock, the other who lays no foundation. Assailed by a flooded river, the one, well built, stands strong, while the other suffers great ruin. The image has its parallel in v 35, where those whose practices reflect the values of the inbreaking age of salvation are promised a great reward. Such doing, rooted in Jesus' message, manifests the true nature of a person in a way that is relevant in the final judgment. Hearing without doing has its recompense too.

4.4. THE COMPASSIONATE MINISTRY OF JESUS (7:1-50)

Luke 7 constitutes a discreet section of the Gospel, bordered on each side by reports of Jesus' teaching (6:12-49; 8:1-18). Luke 7:1 both intimates the completion of Jesus' sermon and marks a geographical change for the events to follow. Luke 8:1 registers a chronological shift and marks Jesus' return to an itinerant ministry following his activity in Capernaum (cf. 4:42-44).[1]

What role does ch. 7 serve in the narrative? In 4:16-30, Jesus set forth his missionary program in the words of Isaiah, interpreting those words already in the form of their citation, and then in his ensuing exposition. Beginning with 4:31, Luke related a series of encounters whereby the contours of Jesus' ministry of "release" to the "poor" would be developed further. In 6:20-49, Luke defined in positive terms both the new conditions of existence in his community and the general shape of the behaviors and values that would come to seem natural for those who participate in this community. The message of Jesus' deeds and words now coalesce in Luke 7, which embodies in three exemplary stories (7:1-10, 11-17, 36-50) the character of the salvation made available in Jesus' mission. The quality of Jesus' ministry raises the question of his identity (7:18-19; cf. 7:18-35), a question Jesus answers with reference back to the quality of his ministry (7:21-22, in terms borrowed from Isa 61:1-2; cf. Luke 4:18-19). Compassion (7:13) and extension of friendship to sinners (7:34, 37) — such dispositions and behavior are apparently unexpected (cf. 7:21, 39).

---

77. ὑποδείκνυω and ὑπόδειγμα are used in Hellenistic ethical instruction to introduce an exemplary act with the value of a lesson (*TLNT,* 3:403-5). For rabbinic parallels to this parabolic story, see McArthur and Johnston, *Parables,* 184-85.

1. Luke 8:1-3 may be taken as a summary statement that brings this section to a close (cf. 4:42-44), recapitulating the emphasis in Luke 7 on the remarkable reach of the good news (see further Ravens, "Setting"). It clearly serves a transitional role. With its twofold focus on proclamation and discipleship, we have preferred to take it as an introduction to the next section (8:4-56).

Luke thus brings again to the surface the message Jesus first articulated in 4:16-30. One finds (1) Jesus exercising his prophetic ministry on behalf of a Gentile soldier, just as Elisha had done (4:27; 7:1-10); (2) Jesus exercising his prophetic ministry on behalf of a woman and her son, just as Elijah had done (4:25-26; 7:11-17); (3) Jesus performing in ways that closely parallel the missionary program provided by Isa 61:1-2; 58:6 (4:18-19; 7:22); and, in a way consonant with intervening episodes concerned with sinners, (4) Jesus articulating the "release" of 4:18-19 in a way that spells forgiveness for a sinful woman (7:36-50).

(5) Moreover, as in 4:16-30, so in Luke 7 one discerns a heightened interest in the response Jesus' ministry garners. As Luke's audience might anticipate on the basis of the preceding narrative of Jesus' ministry, reactions to Jesus are mixed: some respond with fear and glorify God, others question among themselves, another answers with gratitude and love, and so on (4:28-30; 7:16-17, 19, 41-49). Verses 29-30 put the options more starkly: people can either "acknowledge the justice of God" or "reject God's purpose for themselves."

More pronounced in this section of the Gospel than in earlier episodes is the ongoing negotiation of Jesus' identity by those who observe or who are the recipients of his ministry. The centurion recognizes Jesus as a benefactor (or savior, with healing power), and addresses him accordingly as "Lord" (7:6). John's disciples give him no appellation, for they are on a quest to determine his "name," so to speak (7:19-20). Jesus refers to himself as "Son of Man" (7:34), whereas Simon the Pharisee calls him "teacher" (7:40). The crowds recognize in Jesus' ministry a divine visitation and speak of him as "a great prophet" (7:16). Some apparently regard him as "friend of toll collectors and sinners" (7:34), an epithet on which the narrative itself will build (7:36-50). Clearly, with the narratological crystallization of the character of Jesus' mission, the complementary question of his own identity has begun to move to center stage.

4.4.1. The Healing of a Centurion's Slave (7:1-10)

7:1 *After Jesus had finished all his sayings in the hearing of the people, he entered Capernaum. 2 A centurion there had a slave whom he valued highly, and who was ill and close to death. 3 When he heard about Jesus, he sent some Jewish elders to him, asking him to come and heal his slave. 4 When they came to Jesus, they appealed to him earnestly, saying, "He is worthy of having you do this for him, 5 for he loves our people, and it is he who built our synagogue for us." 6 And Jesus went with them, but when he was not far from the house, the centurion sent friends to say to him, "Lord, do not trouble yourself, for I am not worthy to have you come under my roof;* 7 *therefore I did not presume to come to you. But only speak the word, and let my servant be healed.* 8 *For I also am a man set under authority, with soldiers under me; and I say to one, 'Go,' and he goes, and to another, 'Come,' and he comes, and to my slave, 'Do this,' and the slave does it."* 9 *When Jesus heard this he was amazed at him, and turning to the crowd that followed him, he said, "I tell you, not even in Israel have I found such faith."* 10 *When those who had been sent returned to the house, they found the slave in good health.*

Following the demarcation of the completion of Jesus' sermon (7:1), this pericope is effectively boundaried by the inverted parallelism of vv 2-3, 10:

A   A centurion's slave is terminally ill (v 2)
   B   The centurion sends a delegation (v 3)
   B′ The delegations return to the centurion's house (v 10a)
A′ The slave is in good health (v 10b)

As in earlier episodes, in spite of the presence of a crowd of Jesus' disciples (v 9), so narrowly focused on Jesus is the narrative lens that he seems to enter Capernaum alone (v 1).

The principal issue of this account was raised within Jesus' sermon: If love is to be extended even to enemies, are there any functional perimeters for the reach of Jesus' gracious ministry? Sharply put, will the active presence of the good news extend even to the Gentile world?[2] How far will Jesus go in "doing good"?[3] The centrality of this question explains the double dele-

---

2. The problem of a mission to the Gentiles is an obvious concern for the narrative, even if the question of a wider Jewish missionary presence among Gentiles in the Second Temple Period remains contested (cf., e.g., Senior and Stuhlmueller, *Biblical Foundations;* McKnight, *Light among the Nations;* Feldman, *Jew and Gentile*). McKnight makes a helpful distinction between active missionary presence on the one hand and integration into larger society on the other, with the latter consonant with an openness to a Gentile presence, e.g., in the synagogues, without a necessary inference in favor of the identification of Second Temple Judaism as a proselytizing religion.

3. *Contra* Gagnon ("Statistical Analysis," 730; also, *idem,* "Luke's Motives"), who asserts that Luke's concern is to absolve Christ of ". . . blame for religious fraternization with uncircumcised Gentiles," it is rather Luke's point to show Jesus' willingness to bring salvation (διασῴζω) to this Gentile's slave. Gagnon's analysis falters because it is grounded in a redaction criticism that is practiced on pericopae in relative isolation from narrative development. To suggest as he does that Jesus must be convinced by the Jewish elders of the centurion's extraordinary worthiness ("Luke's Motives," 130) is contrary to the force of Jesus' message as articulated in Luke 4–6, and with the more general rejection of conventionally defined status operative since Luke 1. Additionally, on this point Gagnon

gation from the centurion. As a Gentile, he (believes he) has no access to Jesus, so he sends members of the local sanhedrin on his behalf. Jesus' immediate willingness to assist him generates a crisis. If Jesus enters his home, the centurion must extend hospitality to him, but this would grossly overstep Jewish sensibilities; hence, a second delegation is sent to intercept Jesus before he reaches the centurion's home. Jesus' failure to draw insider-outsider lines, even when faced with possible Gentile defilement (as well as the potential of corpse impurity — cf. v 2), is manifest, first, in his intention to enter the centurion's home (v 6) and, second, in his praise of the centurion as an example worthy of emulation (v 9). The prophecy of Simeon (2:29-32) seems at the point of consummation.[4]

Our understanding is assisted by the account of Naaman in 2 Kings 5, an account to which the Evangelist has already alluded with reference to Jesus' ministry in Luke 4:27. Because Luke has already directed our attention to the story of Naaman, the following echoes are all the more vibrant:[5]

Luke 7	*2 Kings 5*
The centurion: a well-respected Gentile officer (vv 2, 4-5).	Naaman: a well-respected Gentile officer (v 1).
Intercession of Jewish elders in the healing (vv 3-5).	Intercession of a Jewish girl in the healing (vv 2-3).
The centurion does not meet Jesus (vv 6-9).	Naaman does not meet Elisha (vv 5-10).
The healing takes place at a distance (v 10).	The healing takes place at a distance (v 14).

A second key element of this account surfaces in the interactions between Jesus and the centurion's emissaries. This is the importance of patronal ethics in the Roman Empire and, at first blush, this pericope presents itself as a textbook example.[6] The repeated language of honor (vv 2, 4, 6-7) and even the mention of the centurion, Caesar's representative in Capernaum

---

evidences no sensitivity to issues of perspective; although, in the end, Luke is responsible for the words of the Jewish elders, this does not mean that these persons reflect the narrator's (or Jesus') point of view (see further below).

4. This is remarkable since Jesus is not known in the Third Gospel for his interaction with Gentiles. This is left to the narrative of Acts, though Jesus' preparation for and anticipation of this mission is key to Luke's soteriology.

5. See Derrett, "Law," 162, 174; Ravens, "Setting," 287. Less helpful is Brodie's suggestion that Luke has drawn on 1 Kgs 17:1-16 ("Not Q but Elijah").

6. See above, §10; Moxnes, "Patron-Client Relations."

(vv 1-2), supports the presence of a social relationship of patronage that would simply be taken for granted. Thus, the centurion has placed the Jewish council (and, indeed, the Jewish populace in this town) in his debt by building the synagogue; that obligation is serviced by the laudatory tone the Jewish elders use when speaking of their benefactor and, it is hoped, by Jesus' assistance in healing the centurion's slave. Jesus, it would appear, operates within this system of gift and obligation by acquiescing to their request.

If this is an accurate representation of this scene, however, this would be a very strange way to demonstrate the embodiment of Jesus' message in daily living. After all, he has just undermined the whole system of patronal ethics by abolishing the distinctions and inequities on which that system is based. In reality, the immediately preceding sermon must be regarded as more indicative of Jesus' motivation for helping the centurion than his alleged participation in a social norm he has just censured (6:20-38). What is more, in declaring his lack of patronal control over Jesus, the centurion first contradicts the Jewish elders' assessment of the social networks of this situation, then provides an alternative rationale for Jesus' help — namely, his recognition of Jesus' authority together with his faith in Jesus' capacity and willingness to exercise that authority in his case. In effect, this episode presents these Jewish elders as captive to a world system that has been nullified by the dawning of salvation, this centurion as possessing remarkable insight into the character of Jesus' mission, and Jesus as behaving graciously toward outsiders (an enemy! — cf. 1:71) in a way fully congruous with his earlier, spoken word.

1 Luke emphasizes that Jesus' extended sermon was heard by everyone, in spite of the more narrow audience suggested by 6:20 (cf. 6:17-18). Drawing his account of Jesus' teaching to a close, Luke relocates Jesus in Capernaum and narrows the spotlight dramatically so that it illuminates only his movements. Later Luke will widen the frame of this account, revealing that a crowd of disciples had accompanied Jesus (v 9). Capernaum has already been the locus of powerful ministry (cf. 4:23, 31-41), so Luke's topographical note may raise expectations for more such demonstrations.

2-5 The centurion is characterized from three perspectives: common knowledge, Luke the narrator, and the Jewish elders. As a centurion, he was a commander of approximately 100 men, a Gentile, and a Roman citizen.[7] Within the Lukan narrative his identification as a officer in the military would locate him, at least provisionally, in the good company of those soldiers who had responded positively to the good news (Luke 3:10-14) and as one, like Naaman (see above), who might receive divine help.

---

7. Cf. Acts 10:28; 11:1-3; Josephus *J.W.* 18.3.5 §84; Broughton, "Roman Army"; Walaskay, *Political Perspective,* 32-34.

He is known further in relationship to his slave, terminally ill,[8] whom he held in high regard. His desire to see his slave returned to health need not imply an extraordinary humanitarian concern on his part, since care for sick slaves was advised in Roman antiquity as a way to prolong their usefulness.[9] At the same time, such care was not universally practiced,[10] and Luke's language suggests that the centurion not only regarded the slave as useful, but actually esteemed him.[11] There is no socio-historical reason to doubt that, as an urban slave in the home of a wealthy master (cf v 5b), this dying man might have enjoyed friendship with the centurion,[12] even if this characterization also serves Luke's wider concern with the raising up of the lowly. Finally, Luke notes that the centurion, having heard of Jesus, regards him as a savior (for healers were often regarded as "saviors" in Roman antiquity) to whom he had no immediate access. As a Gentile, he did not presume to contact Jesus directly, but did so only through those Jews with whom he had a previous bureaucratic association, the Jewish elders — that is, the local Jewish council or sanhedrin.

These Jewish elders portray him as a broker and benefactor of the people.[13] As Rome's representative in an outpost like Capernaum,[14] the centurion would have found himself in the role of intermediary between the local population and the demands of the Empire. It would not be unusual for such a person to adopt the religion of the local population, nor would it be unusual for him to have underwritten the building of the synagogue as a calculated maneuver to win favor among the local Jewish leadership. In any case, this is how the Jewish elders present him to Jesus. In this manner they discharge something of their ongoing obligation to acknowledge and advertise their benefactor's generosity and eminence.[15]

---

8. τελευτάω.

9. Cf. Xenophon *Memorabilia* 2.10.1; Columella 12.3.6.

10. Cf. Dio Cassius 60 (61).29.7; Suetonius *Claudius* 25.2.

11. ἔντιμος; cf. Luke 14:8, where the term is also used to signify honor. These are the only two occurrences of the word in Luke-Acts.

12. See the nuanced discussion of Thébert, "Slave," esp. 142-44.

13. Derrett ("Law," 175) claims that he is also presented as a God-fearer; this is possible, though Walaskay (*Political Perspective*, 32) notes that Luke uses terms for "God-fearer" (φοβούμενος τὸν θεόν or σεβόμενος τὸν θεόν) or "proselyte" when this identification is intended. On brokers, see F. G. Bailey, "Peasant View"; on benefactors and clients, see above, §10.

14. Phraseological Latinisms are rare in the NT and are usually found in connection with Roman authorities (BDF §5[3b]); Luke's Latinism, ἄξιός ἐστιν ᾧ παρέξῃ τοῦτο (7:4), is consonant with the overall portrayal of the centurion as a Roman.

15. Garnsey and Saller, *Roman Empire,* 149. The Jewish leaders use stylized language: he is *worthy* (ἄξιος — cf. 15:19, 21; and the use of the cognate ἀξιόω in 7:6) and *loves* our people (as in 23:2; Acts 24:17, where representatives of the Empire are in view, ἔθνος is used for "the people of Israel").

In the development of this account, it is critical to recognize, then, the basis on which these elders appeal to Jesus for assistance. They do not employ the language of kinship or need, nor do they frame their request with any language that one might regard as harmonious with the new dispositions and behaviors Jesus has outlined in the preceding chapter (esp. 6:27-38). Instead, they assume and propagate the insider-outsider categories of honor and obligation prevalent throughout the Empire. Their words betray their captivity to a world system whose basis and practices run counter to the mercy of God. Even though they apparently seek the welfare of the centurion's household, within Luke's narrative world their motives are suspect. Their comportment is not that of God's children (6:35-36).

6-8 Given the duplicity of these elders of the people, we may be surprised that Jesus goes with them. Given that the centurion is a Gentile, we may be doubly surprised that Jesus seems intent on going to his home to heal his slave. Jesus, however, has outlined a new worldview in which such distinctions are not determinative for social interaction and certainly not for manifestations of saving power.

Consistent with his earlier deference to Jewish sensibilities, the centurion communicates with Jesus a second time through emissaries. Did the first envoy misrepresent the centurion? That is, did he presume that they would approach Jesus on the basis of a prior relationship of debt? One can do little more than speculate,[16] of course, but it is worthy of note that he now clarifies that he neither has any claim nor presumes to tender any claim on Jesus' assistance.[17] What is more, he does so via persons more likely to represent him faithfully to Jesus, his friends; indeed, the mention of friends recasts this episode along fresh lines that emphasize (at least as a Roman ideal) mutuality and commonality, not the duress of perpetual debt.[18] The centurion repeatedly denies what the Jewish elders have asserted as he emphasizes his lack of worth,[19] he insists that Jesus not defile himself by entering his home,[20] and

---

16. But in the manifest discontinuity between the words of the two envoys the narrative is rendered susceptible to — indeed, it invites — such speculation; on textual gaps to be filled in by the reader, see Iser, *Implied Reader,* passim.

17. Luke, who appreciates linguistic variety, apparently uses ἀποστέλλω (v 3) and πέμπω (vv 6, 10) as synonyms; that this second envoy speaks in the first person leaves no room to suppose that they represent the centurion in a less binding way than the first.

18. This is not to suggest that friendship existed sans favors and exchange of favors, only that friends were thought to exist on equal footing, with material favors less orchestrated. See Garnsey and Saller, *Roman Empire,* 154-56.

19. Thus, σκύλλω (v 6, in the passive, "[do not] trouble"), ἱκανός (v 6; cf. 3:16), and ἀξιόω (v 7; cf. Acts 15:38).

20. On the problem of hospitality between Jew and Gentile, see Acts 10:28; 11:3; and the secular and Jewish literature surveyed in Feldman, *Jew and Gentile,* 167-70; Esler, *Community and Gospel,* 78-86.

he provides a rationale for urging Jesus to assist him without his casting further doubt on his faithfulness as a Jew.

The centurion, then, is present as a model of deference, but his discourse focuses even more centrally on his understanding and recognition of authority. As one "under commission,"[21] he gives directives, knowing that they will be carried out; similarly, he can trust that Jesus' authoritative word (cf. 4:32, 36), even if spoken at a distance, will achieve its intended results. This centurion seems to know more than he ought! Luke's readers know that Jesus has been commissioned by God and that the power of the Spirit is operative in his ministry; the centurion seems to act on the basis of similar awareness. In this way, he sets himself apart not only from the Jewish council in Capernaum, but also from those Jewish observers within the narrative thus far who fail to recognize or acknowledge the authority of Jesus (cf. 5:21; 6:2).

9-10 As though the camera has been pulled back, we now have a wide-angle view of this encounter, with the presence of the crowd accompanying Jesus acknowledged for the first time (cf. v 1). That Luke has in mind a large mass of disciples is suggested by his designation of the crowd as "followers."[22] The addition of the crowd accents the dramatic quality of the proclamation to follow; similarly, Luke generally speaks of Jesus' "turning" to speak in order to add emphasis to Jesus' statement.[23]

The centurion had "heard about Jesus" and acted accordingly (v 3); Jesus, now having heard the words of the centurion through his messengers, responds with amazement and with an astounding proclamation. He makes explicit what the account has already made implicit — namely, the disjunction between this Gentile and Israel. Unlike Israel, he recognizes Jesus' authority and trusts that Jesus will exercise it on his behalf, even though, as a Gentile, even as one who had acted on behalf of Israel, he does not deserve such treatment. Perhaps Jesus is more subtle, but the force of his proclamation is reminiscent of the words of John negating the special status of Israel (3:7-9). Are not the people of Israel the people of faith? Not in comparison to this Gentile centurion.

Jesus' proclamation presents this Gentile as exemplary. The return of the two envoys to find the terminally ill slave in good health validates the centurion's insight. Jesus does have the authority to heal, even from a distance, and even when that distance is measured as much in religio-cultural terms as in meters or yards. As in earlier episodes, faith and the healing power of Jesus overcome socio-religious barriers (cf. 5:12-14, 18-25).

---

21. See Haslam, "Centurion."
22. That is, he uses the verb ἀκολουθέω, on which see 5:11. Cf. 6:17.
23. στρέφω — cf. 7:44; 9:55; 10:23; 14:25; (22:61?); 23:28.

4.4.2. The Raising of a Widow's Son (7:11-17)

11 *Soon afterwards he went to a town called Nain, and his disciples and a large crowd went with him.* 12 *As he approached the gate of the town, a man who had died was being carried out. He was his mother's only son, and she was a widow; and with her was a large crowd from the town.* 13 *When the Lord saw her, he had compassion for her and said to her, "Do not weep."* 14 *Then he came forward and touched the bier, and the bearers stood still. And he said, "Young man, I say to you, rise!"* 15 *The dead man sat up and began to speak, and Jesus gave him to his mother.* 16 *Fear seized all of them; and they glorified God, saying, "A great prophet has risen among us!" and "God has looked favorably on his people!"* 17 *This word about him spread throughout Judea and all the surrounding country.*

Temporal and geographical changes mark the beginning of this pericope, but these are not so significant that they mask the obvious relationship between the account of the healing of the centurion's slave (7:1-10) and the current episode. The crowd that followed Jesus (7:9) is now differentiated, with some designated more specifically as "disciples." Luke's portrayal of the character of Jesus' ministry is further developed via the intertextual relationship between these two pericopae, the Nazareth sermon (4:16-30) and the stories of Elijah and Elisha. The relation between these opening pericopae in Luke 7 is further cemented by Luke's presentation of these two episodes, following normal Lukan practice, as a male-female pair — first highlighting Jesus' ministry to a centurion (male) and his household, then his compassion for a widow. The particular focus of this scene on the raising of the dead prepares dramatically for the summary of Jesus' powerful activity of communicating good news to the poor in 7:22.

The male-female parallelism is heightened by the almost incidental way in which the healing of the previous pericope and the raising of the dead son in this one are narrated. In 7:1-10 the nature of the centurion's request is far more developed than is the healing itself, while the woman, and not her dead son, is located at the deictic center of this account.[24] Surprisingly in a social context in which females are typically identified in relation to males, this dead man is presented as "his mother's only son." Following this, the focus of attention is on her: *she* was a widow, the crowd was with *her;* Jesus saw *her,* had compassion on *her,* spoke to *her,* and, finally, gave the dead man brought back to life to *her.* She who is husbandless and sonless and in mourning, she who epitomizes the "poor" to whom Jesus has come to bring

---

24. Cf. Busse, *Wunder,* 171, 173; Seim, *Double Message,* 40.

good news,[25] is the real recipient of Jesus' compassionate ministry. In fact, it is not too much to say that "healing" in this instance, although it entails the miraculous raising of this young man from the dead, should be interpreted as the restoration of this woman within her community.

The interpretation of this pericope is fundamentally guided by Luke's location of the woman at the center of this story. The significance of this account is also amplified by the resounding echoes of scriptural material concerning Elijah in 1 Kgs 17:8-24,[26] to which we have already been pointed in 4:25-26 (and, to a lesser degree, concerning Elisha in 2 Kgs 4:18-37). The most impressive of these echoes is the identification of the dead man as the only son of a widow, the meeting of the prophet and the widow at the gate of the city, and the return of the resuscitated son to his mother.

As is typical in intertextuality, so in this instance the interplay between the Elijah-account and the present pericope registers both similarities and variation, and at the heart of such parody are important indicators of how the figure of Elijah is now used. On the one hand, the close resemblance of these parallel accounts, underscored already by Jesus' having drawn attention to this relationship in 4:25-26, helps to identify Jesus as a prophet of God (see v 16). It also indicates what the Lukan narrative has already made transparent — namely, the extension of the good news to the socially marginalized. On the other hand, Luke's narration emphasizes Jesus' compassion in a way not evidenced in 1 Kings 17; what is more, whereas Elijah pleads with God on behalf of the woman and her dead son, then expends physical energy in the process of prayer for restoration, Jesus speaks directly to the corpse. At his word, the young man is brought back to life. Jesus is thus shown to be more than a prophet; indeed, the narrator refers to him as "Lord" in v 13, and in his authoritative word through which the young man is brought back to life Jesus the Lord fulfills the role performed by the Lord God in 1 Kgs 17:21-22. More than a prophet, Jesus is the compassionate Benefactor of the poor.

11-12 Luke establishes the scene by identifying its location, the audience for the encounter to come, and the state of the woman who will occupy center stage in this episode. Nain is a Galilean town located some six miles to the southeast of Nazareth;[27] Luke refers to it as a city, though he goes on to present a village-like atmosphere, with community mourning of the widow's loss.

Not least in contrast with the previous episode, where Jesus initially

25. See above on 4:18-19.
26. See esp. Brodie, "Luke 7.11-17"; C. A. Evans, "Elijah/Elisha Narratives," 79-81; Steyn, "Intertextual Similarities," 240-41; Harris, "Miracles of Revivification," 299-300.
27. For discussion, see Riesner, "Archeology and Geography," 37.

appeared to travel alone, this scene is remarkable for the sheer number of witnesses gathered: a large crowd following Jesus, a large crowd with the widow, and the disciples of Jesus. As in previous scenes, the disciples' presence is not an active one. They are (simply) "with" Jesus, a role later identified as one of the key credentials for apostolic office (Acts 1:21). This companionship with Jesus will be developed further as the narrative progresses, signifying their identification with Jesus and their being shaped within the context of association with his life and mission.[28]

Most telling in Luke's account is his portrayal of this woman's catastrophic state. She is a widow who has lived since her husband's death in relation to her only son, himself a young man.[29] With his passing, she is relegated to a status of "dire vulnerability"[30] — without a visible means of support and, certainly, deprived of her access to the larger community and any vestiges of social status within the village.

Little is known of Jewish funerary customs in the first century, though the warm climate in Palestine necessitated a speedy burial. Following death the eyes of the deceased were closed, the mouth bound up, and the corpse washed and anointed; the deceased were buried either in their own clothes or wrapped in cloth prepared for this purpose, carried on a bier (as in this case) or, perhaps, in a coffin, and entombed in sand or salt.[31]

13-15 Verse 13 constitutes the dramatic turning point and the christological high point of this episode. Luke's identification of Jesus as Lord, his remark concerning Jesus' affective response to the woman, and his record of Jesus' first words to the woman, "Do not weep," all point to an understanding of this account that does not accord privilege to Jesus as someone capable of powerful acts. Indeed, Jesus' miraculous power has been amply demonstrated thus far in the narrative, and tales of his powerful deeds have been broadcast throughout the region. Luke's focus lies elsewhere. Especially by locating the remark, "He had compassion for her," at the midpoint of this account,[32] Luke identifies Jesus as the compassionate benefactor of this widow. That is, this is less an account of healing and more a disclosure of the character of Jesus' mission and, therefore, of the nature of God's redemptive intervention.

Jesus performs three acts. First, he tells the widow not to weep, a

28. See 7:11; 8:1, 22, 38; 9:10; 22:11, 14, 28, 33, 39; Green, *Gospel of Luke,* 108.

29. 7:14: νεανίσκος.

30. Malina and Rohrbaugh, *Commentary,* 320; cf. Seim, *Double Message,* 230; Ilan, *Jewish Women,* 147-51.

31. See Mark 15:46; John 10:40; *Gos. Pet.* 6.24; *m. Sanh.* 13:5; Green, "Burial," 89.

32. Menken, "Position of σπλαγχνίζεσθαι," 108-11; for a similar perspective, see Vogels, "Semiotic Study."

transparent reminder to Luke's audience that the good news of salvation will turn weeping into laughter (6:21). Second, he touches the funeral bier or wooden plank on which the body is being carried. This is not an act of healing, but seems designed only to stop the procession; nevertheless, simply by touching the bier Jesus has again crossed the boundaries of ritual purity (cf. 5:12-14).[33] Finally, Jesus speaks, not in prayer to God (as Elijah had done), but directly to the corpse, commanding it to be revived. This is the act of healing, and with this speech-act Jesus evidences striking dimensions of his apparent authorization, status, and institutional role in the salvific purpose of God.[34] Even if the exact nature of this identification is not yet available to the crowds, who respond to Jesus as a prophet (7:16), the narrator makes this more apparent for his audience by explicitly identifying Jesus as "Lord." The twofold response of the corpse,[35] sitting up and speaking, signals his revivification (cf. Acts 9:40).

That Luke's central concern is with the widow is evidenced by the *inclusio* formed in vv 13-15. At the beginning of this encounter, Jesus saw, had compassion for, and spoke to her; at its close, he returns her restored son to his mother. The young man's resuscitation is a concrete parable of his mother's, for with his life returned to him her life is again made whole.

16-17 The purpose of the crowds, first introduced in vv 11-12, now becomes clear. They are present to witness, to interpret, and to report this miracle of restoration. Responses of fear are expected in epiphanic scenes (cf., e.g., 1:12, 65; 5:26), and the crowds manifestly view what they have seen as divine activity. Thus, they glorify God (cf. 5:25-26; 13:13) and affirm that God has "looked favorably on his people" (cf. 1:68, 78). With divine deliverance at hand, people respond with praise to God, reminding us that Luke's narrative is fundamentally theocentric in its emphasis.

This is not to say that Luke's interest is not also christological. Gabriel had prophesied that Jesus would be called "great" (1:32), and now the masses proclaim him "a great prophet." In doing so, they use language that is reminiscent of God's promise of a prophet-like-Moses whom God would "raise up" (Deut 18:15-18). Jesus had already identified his baptism as the anointing of a regal prophet (4:18-19), his fate as that of the prophets (4:24), and the character of his ministry as continuous with that of Elijah and Elisha (4:25-27).

---

33. See Godet, 1:341. On corpse impurity, see Num 19:10b-22; E. P. Sanders, *Judaism,* 217-19; *idem, Jewish Law,* passim. Sanders notes that, although corpse impurity was not a bad thing (in this case it kept one from entering the temple until the proper time period had elapsed and washings performed), purity was so highly valued in practice that corpse impurity was to be avoided if possible whether or not one had plans to enter the temple.

34. Cf. Thiselton, "Christology in Luke," 471.

35. ὁ νεκρός.

Not without good reason, then, do the crowds, enlightened by what they have seen and heard, thus recognize him as a great prophet. Even if this epithet is incomplete for Luke, it is correct as far as it goes. As in previous scenes, the consequence of Jesus' miraculous deeds is the ensuing broadcast of news about him (e.g., 4:37; 5:15). In this case, however, "this word about him" undoubtedly includes not only reports of his miraculous activity but also its significance in the form of news of a great prophet in whose ministry God's salvation was being made available.

4.4.3. Jesus and John (7:18-35)

18 *The disciples of John reported all these things to him. So John summoned two of his disciples* 19 *and sent them to the Lord to ask, "Are you the one who is to come, or are we to wait for another?"* 20 *When the men had come to him, they said, "John the Baptist has sent us to you to ask, 'Are you the one who is to come, or are we to wait for another?' "* 21 *Jesus had just then cured many people of diseases, plagues, and evil spirits, and had given sight to many who were blind.* 22 *And he answered them, "Go and tell John what you have seen and heard: the blind receive their sight, the lame walk, the lepers are cleansed, the deaf hear, the dead are raised, the poor have good news brought to them.* 23 *And blessed is anyone who takes no offense at me."*

24 *When John's messengers had gone, Jesus began to speak to the crowds about John: "What did you go out into the wilderness to look at? A reed shaken by the wind?* 25 *What then did you go out to see? Someone dressed in soft robes? Look, those who put on fine clothing and live in luxury are in royal palaces.* 26 *What then did you go out to see? A prophet? Yes, I tell you, and more than a prophet.* 27 *This is the one about whom it is written,*

'See, I am sending my messenger ahead of you,
*   who will prepare your way before you.'*

28 *I tell you, among those born of women no one is greater than John; yet the least in the kingdom of God is greater than he."* 29 *(And all the people who heard this, including the toll collectors,*[36] *justified God, having been baptized*[37] *with John's baptism.* 30 *But by refusing to be baptized by him, the Pharisees and the lawyers rejected God's purpose for themselves.)*

31 *"To what then will I compare the people of this generation, and*

36. NRSV: "tax collectors."
37. NRSV: "acknowledged the justice of God, because they had been baptized. . . ."

*what are they like? 32 They are like children sitting in the marketplace
and calling to one another,*

*'We played the flute for you, and you did not dance;
we wailed, and you did not weep.'*

*33 For John the Baptist has come eating no bread and drinking no
wine, and you say, 'He has a demon'; 34 the Son of Man has come
eating and drinking, and you say, 'Look, a glutton and a drunkard, a
friend of toll collectors[38] and sinners!' 35 Nevertheless, wisdom is
vindicated by all her children."*

No temporal or chronological markers isolate this lengthy section from the
preceding narrative. On the contrary, Luke's reference to "all these things"
ties this pericope directly into the antecedent material, so that the question
and issues arising in 7:18-35 are firmly grounded in the portrayal of the
character of Jesus' ministry above all in 7:1-17. As in those paired episodes,
so here the narration revolves around the nature of Jesus' ministry, his identity,
and the responses he engenders.

Though mentioned indirectly in 5:33, John has been offstage since his
arrest in 3:19-20. In that earlier material, and indeed in the intertwined accounts of the births of John and Jesus in 1:5–2:52, the importance of John's
prophetic identity and activity was cultivated primarily to show how John's
primary role in God's salvific purpose was to prepare for the coming of the
Lord. Here again, John's incomparable significance is traced to his role as
precursor.

In an important sense, then, this section presents us with an interpretive
recapitulation of Jesus' identity as God's agent of salvation. In performing
this function, it credits Jesus' inaugural sermon with a paradigmatic role
(7:18-23; cf. Acts 10:38), draws together numerous threads of the earlier
Lukan narrative, portrays the mission of John and Jesus over against the
conventional wisdom that has as its sequel the historic stubbornness of many
of God's people, foregrounds the import of the response necessitated by that
mission, and prepares for the climax of this larger section of Luke's Gospel,
Luke 7, in the subsequent account of Jesus' encounter with a Pharisee and a
sinful woman (7:36-50).

The structure of this large section is easily discerned by the coming
and going of the disciples of John, and by topical shifts. In addition, each unit
(other than the parenthetical remark of the narrator in vv 29-30) closes with
a "punch line" poignantly expressing its conclusion.[39]

18-23 The organization of this unit is largely determined by the

38. NRSV: "tax collectors."
39. I. J. Du Plessis, "Contextual Aid," 120.

movement of John's disciples, who report to John, are summoned by John, are sent by John, come to Jesus, and are sent by Jesus. Their departure (v 24) marks the onset of the next unit in this larger section. John has been absent since his arrest (3:19-20), though his disciples are mentioned in 5:33; disciples of John will reenter the Lukan narrative in Acts 19. Here, mention of his followers helps Luke's readers to recall the two prongs of John's instruction (3:1-18) — his teaching in the area of divine election and social ethics, which will come under the spotlight in 7:29-35; and his anticipation of a coming one more powerful than he, identified in 3:15-17 with the Messiah.

The importance of John's question is emphasized indirectly for Luke's audience by the long line of negative responses Jesus' activity has attracted already in the narrative. How could God's agent of salvation encounter such opposition from God's people? In Luke's staging of this particular scene, the significance of John's query is underscored by its precise repetition in vv 19 and 20. The foundation of John's question in his own expectations, earlier recounted, is assured by the parallel use of the verb of expecting[40] in 3:15; 7:19, 20, and by analogous language referring to "the coming one" (3:16; 7:19, 20; cf. 4:34; 5:32). Apparently, John's interest lies on the fault line between his eschatological expectations and the realities of Jesus' performance.

John's immediate concern with the identity of Jesus derives from the report he has received concerning "all these things." The intimate association of 7:18-23 with 7:1-17 provides a frame for understanding what has been reported to John. One should thus think immediately of Jesus' beneficence on behalf of a Gentile military officer and his compassion for a widow.[41] Even were one to expand the field of vision to include the whole of Jesus' ministry as thus far narrated, however, it would still differ substantially and strikingly from the quality of John's own (see the harsh images of judgment in 3:9) and from John's expectations of the coming one who would bring judgment (3:17). Is Jesus the expected one, the Messiah?[42] For John (and, no doubt, for others),

40. προσδοκάω.

41. This is not only because of the attempt to find a referent for "all these things" in its local co-text (cf. Brown and Yule, *Discourse Analysis*, 59), but also because of memory limitations: as reading or listening progresses, comprehension of past utterances become more and more summary; hence, immediately preceding material is often of paramount importance in shaping any text's reception — cf. Segre, *Analysis of the Literary Text*, 163.

42. Fitzmyer (1:664; *Luke the Theologian*, 97-98) thinks that John is looking forward to the coming of an Elijah-figure, a fiery reformer, not a Messiah. In Luke's presentation of Jesus, however, only one constellation of the available virtual properties concerning Elijah is actualized — namely, his being sent to bring restoration to a widow who has lost her only son (cf. 4:25-26; 7:11-17). Moreover, 3:15-17 had already collocated the notion of a "coming one" with messianic expectation, an association that is strongly sanctioned in 19:38. *Contra* Fitzmyer, then, the issue in this Lukan unit is messiahship.

the nature of Jesus' activity seems to disqualify any claim he might have to this status. As Luke's account goes on to demonstrate, however, this is due to misperceptions about messiahship, about how God's eschatological visitation would be realized. After all, Jesus is engaged in the work of "sifting" John had described in anticipation (3:17-18), even though this sifting of Israel had apparently proceeded along unanticipated lines. In Jesus' reply to John, then, one finds that a potential disconfirmation of Jesus' messiahship has been transformed into a redefinition of the messianic role and, accordingly, a confirmation of Jesus' identity as Messiah.[43]

The Third Evangelist employs the phrase "in that hour," or analogous phrases, at signal moments in the narrative (v 21).[44] This is surely a propitious moment, for the fundamental question of Jesus' identity has been raised by John — that is, by a person who has himself been recognized within the narrative as one miraculously conceived and divinely endowed for prophetic ministry and who had proclaimed the good news and been imprisoned on account of his message of repentance. John's voice has been established as the voice of a friend of God's purpose; if he has questions about the expression of God's purpose in Jesus' activity, they are surely worth contemplating. Following is a characteristically Lukan summary statement of the powerful activity of Jesus, healer-exorcist (e.g., 4:40-41; 6:18-19). Its purpose is to provide testimony in support of the delineation of his mission, elaborated in language of eschatological salvation borrowed from Isaiah, in v 22.

Of these, only the giving of sight to the blind is unprecedented in Jesus' healing practices thus far. Although Luke will provide an account of Jesus healing the blind in 18:35-43, the presence of this motif in the current co-text has significance beyond its application to the physically blind. First, Luke notes that Jesus "gave" sight, using an unexpected verb associated with benefaction.[45] This, combined with the narrator's identification of Jesus as "Lord" in v 19, underscores for Luke's reader that Jesus' identity is secure even if someone as credentialed within the narrative as John has questions. As 7:1-17 had shown, Jesus is the beneficent Lord who gives graciously especially to those on the margins of society. Second, "blindness" has a metaphorical sense that is not far from the surface here, even though we may presume that physical healing is primarily in view.[46] Jesus' ensuing instruc-

---

43. Brawley, *Centering on God,* 127; cf. Tannehill, *Narrative Unity,* 1:80; Bock, 1:664-65.

44. NRSV: "just then." See 2:38; 10:21; 12:12; 13:31; 20:19; 22:53; 24:33.

45. χαρίζομαι; cf. 7:41-43; BAGD 876.

46. This is suggested by the collocation of "sight to the blind" with "diseases, plagues, and evil spirits." On the metaphorical sense of "sight to the blind" in Luke, see above on 4:18-19; also Hamm, "Sight to the Blind"; Culpepper, "Seeing the Kingdom of God."

tions to John's disciples to tell John what they have seen and heard suggests his designation of these persons as witnesses who will enlighten John regarding this transformation of the connotations of messiahship.

Drawing on Isa 29:18-19; 35:5-6; 42:18; 43:8; 61:1, Jesus' description of his ministry is in form a symphony of Isaianic echoes and in substance a "festival of salvation."[47] Jesus' inventory of salvific activity is not meant to limit but to amplify and concretize the nature of his mission, and to suggest the expansive scope of salvation. Because of its proximity, having already been cited by Jesus in 4:18-19, Isa 61:1 will likely be heard as the source of the clearest echoes. The obvious overlap of Jesus' inaugural sermon and his answer to John provides a powerful sanction for the integrity of his mission: He is doing what the Spirit of the Lord had anointed him to do.

Is it only circumstance that locates the phrase "the blind receive their sight," immediately following Jesus' instructions to John's disciples to report on what they had "seen and heard"? Luke may thus have marked the enlightening of these disciples of the Baptist so as to equip them to bear witness to John concerning himself and the nature of his divinely appointed ministry (cf. 24:31). Of equal importance is Jesus' mention of good news to the poor, located in the final, emphatic position in this register of salvific activity. Collocated with these other persons who stand in need of divine intervention and appearing at the conclusion of the list, "the poor" interprets and is amplified by these other designations of those who stand on the margins of respectable society yet are the unexpected recipients of salvation. As in 4:18-19, "the poor" include but are not limited to those who are without material resources; the centurion of 7:1-10, for example, is wealthy enough to underwrite the building of a synagogue in Capernaum, yet is a religious outsider who becomes a recipient of divine benefaction.[48]

This unit reaches its finale in the beatitude of v 23. Although the terminology used here is not common in Luke,[49] that Jesus' ministry is the stuff of scandal is attested regularly. Simeon had predicted that he would be "the rise and fall" of many (2:34), and throughout the narrative Jesus' ministry is portrayed as a source of offense leading, finally, to his execution (cf. 4:48-49; 20:18; 22–23).[50] In light of this, Jesus pronounces a blessing on any who are willing to undergo a conversion in their views of God's purpose, the inbreaking eschatological salvation, and, so, of Jesus' mission.

24-28   The departure of John's disciples does not designate the end of interest in the Baptist. Accordingly, we are led to think that the issues raised

---

47. Schürmann, 1:410-11.
48. See above on 4:18-19; also Green, "Good News," esp. 66-69.
49. σκανδαλίζομαι appears in Luke-Acts only here and in 17:2.
50. See Carroll and Green, *Death of Jesus*, 61-81; Tyson, *Death of Jesus*.

by John are not limited to someone whose knowledge of Jesus' ministry is secondhand. They are more global and merit airing in the presence of the multitudes who apparently have witnessed Jesus' healing activity and this exchange (7:11-12). The Lukan presentation of John in 3:1-18 is again on display, as we are reminded of the masses that went out to hear John and to participate in his ministry. What was the purpose of this movement out into the wilderness? On this, Luke's earlier account was transparent, with John portrayed as a prophet, proclaiming the word of the Lord in the wilderness. The present rehearsal of information about John does nothing to diminish that earlier presentation. Jesus' question to the crowds, "What did you go out to see?" appears three times. The first two serve a narrow, rhetorical aim. Surely no one would go out to see reeds bending in the wind; would such a com- monplace, something so trivial attract an audience?[51] Surely no one journeyed into the wilderness to see someone of high status, with the clothes of the wealthy (cf. 16:19); who would go into the desert to see what could only be seen in royal palaces?[52] The only reasonable choice remaining is that people went into the wilderness to see a prophet. In this way, the options Jesus allows lead inexorably to only one possible conclusion — and it is no coincidence that this estimation of John's status is fully consonant with Luke's earlier presentation in 3:1-9.

Jesus goes beyond what might have been available to John's audiences in 3:1-9, however. He asks people to view John's ministry through a wide- angle lens, including data available to Luke's audience (but not to John's within the narrative) in the birth narrative and in Luke's citation of Isa 40:3-5 in 3:4-6. This does not mean that Jesus simply repeats what was already proclaimed by the angel Gabriel (1:16-17), by Zechariah (1:76), or by the Third Evangelist (3:4-6). However, by interweaving Mal 3:1 (cf. Mal 4:5) and Exod 23:20, he clearly embraces the perspective of these divine spokesper- sons. John is the end-time prophet foretold in the Scriptures, the Elijah figure who would forerun the coming of the Lord.[53] The primary deviation between Mal 3:1 and its reappearance in this Lukan co-text is the amendment from the first-person singular pronoun ("before me") in Malachi to the second- person ("before you") in Luke. In this divergence, Luke follows Exod 23:20,

51. It is possible to read Jesus' question along more allegorical lines, as though some might think that John were weak, spineless, easily blown about. Nothing in the Lukan narrative — either in the voice of the narrator or from his opponents or followers — supports this reading, however.

52. Some interpreters find here a deliberate contrast with John's lack of luxurious attire, but the Third Evangelist never provides a description of John's wardrobe, whether austere or elegant.

53. That is, if 1:17, 76 communicated the association of John and Elijah, 7:26-27 makes this identification; see R. J. Miller, "Elijah, John, and Jesus," 618.

with the result that Jesus has begun speaking with greater existential urgency to those who make up his audience in this scene.[54] John, he says, was God's agent to prepare *you*. It is in this way that Jesus shows how John is "more than a prophet." In showing this, though, he has also accentuated the importance of positive response to the message of the good news. This prepares for the Lukan parenthetical aside in vv 29-30.

This unit reaches its finale in v 28 with Jesus' closing assessment of the significance of John in God's purpose. As the prophetic precursor, John was "more than a prophet"; in fact, his status was greater than any human being (cf. 1:15). That to which John's ministry pointed and for which it prepared has broken into the world, however, so that conventional ways of measuring honor and status have been inverted. The "little ones" who have been the focus of Jesus' activity (i.e., the blind, lame, leprous, deaf, dead, poor — 7:22) have been "raised up" (1:52b). The language of the kingdom of God speaks to this new reality, just as Jesus' articulation of John's place in the kingdom urges all, including people like those who follow John, to put away conventional patterns and expectations concerning God's purpose in favor of the perspective on God's design being advanced and served by Jesus.

29-30   Luke interrupts his narration,[55] breaking into the account in order to provide unimpeachable categories for interpreting the relationship between responses to John (and, by extension, to Jesus, since John also proclaims the good news [3:18] and his ministry prepares for that of Jesus)

---

54. Luke's version also reads "your way" instead of "the way." A number of scholars conclude that in v 22 the citation should be read as though God were speaking to Jesus — namely, God is sending his messenger . . . before Jesus (e.g., Godet, 1:350; Fitzmyer, 1:674; Nolland, 1:337). This, however, would make the final amendment to the text in Malachi not only superfluous but confusing; the use of Malachi's "before me" would have been much easier to understand. Moreover, with the progression of Luke's account toward the concentration on appropriate response in vv 29-30, a direct address to "the people" at this juncture makes good sense of this mixed citation. Bock (1:674) also notes the parallel thus established between the Baptist's ministry in 1:17: to prepare a people. Nolland (following Fitzmyer) seems to claim that the influence from Exod 23:20 cannot be determinative of meaning since Mal 3:1 is "the controlling citation"; it is not clear, however, from where the category of "controlling citation" derives, what it means, or how it ought to be applied. The narrator offers no such restriction of our reading of this text by explicitly attributing it to Malachi. As with the phenomenon of intertextuality more broadly, so here the use of pre-texts introduces important resonances and inscribes this Lukan text into the authority of these older, already sacred ones. The employment of other texts in a new one does not require \of the new text (and might even forbid) a slavish agreement with the sense of the old (see Green and Hays, "Use of the Old Testament"). Parody is always possible. In any case, the primary constraint on meaning is not the use of traditional sources but the present co-text.

55. On the possibility that vv 29-30 represent Jesus' continued discourse rather than a narrative aside, see the discussion in Bock, 1:676-77.

and one's relationship to God and the divine purpose. In effect, this is Luke's commentary on 3:1-18, and especially on the people's responses to John's call to embrace the will of God as embodied in John's repentance-baptism and as articulated in his social ethic. The Third Evangelist could have provided this information in ch. 3, perhaps in order to legitimate John further as God's messenger in light of his imprisonment by Herod. Instead, he has held back his evaluation, placing it here, both to add his voice to that of Jesus as they together endorse John's importance in the divine plan and to guide our interaction with the rest of the Lukan narrative by providing firm canons for determining who "justifies God" and who "rejects God's purpose for themselves."[56]

The character of this narrative aside and its location in the Lukan narrative portend its significance for our understanding of the larger issue of Luke's narrative purpose.

The division of Israel that John had begun (see above on 3:16-17), according to Luke, can be represented by the acceptance or refusal of baptism. John's baptism serves in this co-text, then, as a metonymy for the whole of John's message, an interpretation that is corroborated by the inclusion of the phrase "even toll collectors" in v 22. This phrase, we may recall, first appeared in 3:12, where toll collectors joined the crowds and were joined by soldiers in requesting more specific clarification of the content of the "repentance" they were called upon by John to practice. John instructed them on how they might live faithfully as Abraham's children, bearing fruits "worthy of repentance" (3:8). Refusal to be baptized by John, then, is tantamount to a refusal to repent — that is, to orient one's heart and life around God's purpose. From John's perspective, persons who were unrepentant, who did not show by their lives that they had aligned themselves with God's salvific aim, were not children of Abraham but the offspring of poisonous snakes (3:7). The refusal to be baptized was a refusal of God's aim.[57]

The seriousness of this allegation becomes evident when the centrality of the motif of "God's purpose" for Luke-Acts is realized.[58] Indeed, Luke-Acts is nothing less than the self-conscious narration of God's purpose coming to fruition. By means of this motif, the Lukan enterprise is fundamentally inscribed in the ancient and ongoing story of God's engagement with his

---

56. Sheeley (*Narrative Asides,* 114-15, 167) speaks of Luke's delay of this narrative aside for rhetorical effect.

57. See Darr, *Character Building,* 100-101.

58. The term itself, βουλή (for the *divine* purpose), appears in 7:30; Acts 2:23; 4:28; (5:38-39); 13:36; 20:27. On the motif of the divine purpose in Luke, see Green, *Gospel of Luke,* 22-49; and, more broadly, Squires, *Plan of God.*

people. It is true that other aims are at work in the narrative (e.g., 23:51), but this only underscores the possibility of what Luke here intimates — namely, the possibility of resisting, even rejecting the plan of God. And it interprets resistance to God's purpose as manifest in God's agents, like John, as defiance of God's overarching salvific plan. The presence of contrasting aims within the narrative brings to the foreground for people within the narrative and for Luke's audience the invitation to align themselves with God's aim and to serve his project. Luke's overt commentary in these two verses, then, serves to encourage Luke's audience to join those who "justify God" and to distance themselves from those who reject God's purpose.[59]

What, then, does it mean to have "justified God"? The difficulty presented by this phrase, and the reason it is often interpreted in a paraphrastic way as "acknowledged the justice of God" (NRSV), is that it has seemed presumptuous to imagine that God needs to be vindicated.[60] Within the framework of Luke's discourse situation, however, it is not strictly true to say that God requires no vindication. After all, within the contentious, pluralistic environment of first-century Judaism, of which the Christian movement was a part, other ways to articulate the purpose of God and to measure faithfulness to God's design were available. An enunciation of that purpose that accorded privilege to the messiahship of an executed criminal and followed the progress of the divine purpose from Israel to the life and ministry of that victim of crucifixion to the inclusion of Gentile believers as full participants — that is, the Lukan enunciation of that plan — would have been, for many, something other than the most obvious reading of the ways of God. By embracing John's ministry, people, including toll collectors, acted in a way consistent with his rejection of privileged election and his affirmation of the necessity of repentance that involved the heart and material life. That is, their response to the good news, including the fruit of their repentant lives, is understood and presented by the Third Evangelist as a legitimation of the ways of God within the narrative. Given this perspective on God's salvific project, their positive response to God would be understood as "a verdict of approval on God's plan of salvation."[61]

Are the categories set forth by Luke absolute? That is, must we understand that the Pharisees and the lawyers (i.e., scribes) who rejected God's purpose for themselves when they rejected John's baptism are models of all

59. So Gowler, *Portraits of the Pharisees,* 216.

60. See Nolland, 1:342. Luke writes, ἐδικαίωσαν τὸν θεόν. The NRSV introduces a further problem by suggesting that the people acknowledge God's justice as a consequence of their having been baptized; no notion of causation is present. Instead, we are to understand that their vindication of God was exemplified in their having been baptized.

61. Fitzmyer, 1:676; cf. Johnson, 123.

Pharisees and scribes? This is a common reading,[62] but certainly not a necessary or even a judicious one. Because this issue is developed more directly in the next episode (7:36-50), a more substantive discussion must be delayed until then. In the interim it is worth noting that (1), according to this reading, "the people" of v 29 would also serve as representative of the crowds, who then must respond positively to God's purpose; but this is manifestly not the case (esp. in Acts); and (2) even if our experience of a linear text like Luke's Gospel means that our subsequent judgments about Pharisees will be colored by this scathing indictment, this does not mean that the Evangelist cannot revise his presentation and our appreciation of the Pharisees as a whole, of some Pharisees (e.g., see below on 13:31), or of individual Pharisees (e.g., Saul/Paul) in the developing narrative.

31-35 The degree to which Luke's parenthetical aside in vv 29-30 is integrated into the logic of Jesus' address to the crowds is indicated by the use of a resultative "then" (or "therefore")[63] at the beginning of v 31 and by the parallelism of vv 29-30 and vv 31-35. At first glance, it appears that Jesus is drawing out the implications of Luke's commentary on the polarity of responses to John's message of repentance-baptism: Since the Pharisees and scribes rejected God's purpose for themselves, to what shall I compare those of this generation? The conclusions Jesus reaches in vv 31-35 actually follow from his comments about John (and, less directly, about himself) in vv 24-28, however. Given John's importance and, more particularly, given the reality that John's ministry was directed at preparing the people for the coming of the Lord (see above), how might we think of the people of this generation? At the same time, it is interesting that Jesus' message in vv 31-35 follows from Luke's intrusion into the narrative in vv 29-30 just as easily as it follows from Jesus' earlier comments in vv 24-28; this is one of many indications within the Third Gospel that the narrator and Jesus share the same evaluative point of view.

Who are "the people of this generation"? Against the horizon of the Exodus story, to which Jesus' words have already alluded (v 27), we may hear important reminiscences of the frustrating portrayal of the people of God as stubborn, stiff-necked, rebellious.[64] What are they like, in Jesus' view? The relevance of the popular rhyme of v 32[65] is determined by two co-textual considerations. First, the fundamental comparison Jesus draws is between

---

62. E.g., Neale (*None but the Sinners,* 136-37): "For Luke's story the Pharisees' failure to respond to John confirms their status as the ideological enemies of God and his purposes. Luke's religious categories are absolute . . ." (136).

63. οὖν.

64. See, e.g., Exod 32:9; 33:3, 5; Deut 10:16; Acts 7:51-53; cf. Ezekiel 2; Bovon, 1:378.

65. Cf. Herodotus 1.141; Aesop *Fables* 27.

"people of this generation" and "children sitting in the marketplace."[66] Second, Jesus reports that both John and himself (as Son of Man) have been condemned for their failure to behave in expected ways (v 33). Accordingly, the people of this generation call out the games, but John and Jesus refuse to play them; this leads to the rejection of John and Jesus as being demonized and as a glutton and a drunkard, respectively.

In fact, as part of his divine appointment, John is known in the Gospel of Luke for his ascetic practices (cf. 1:15; 5:33). Similarly, as part of his divine commission, Jesus is known in the Gospel of Luke for his attendance at feasts and for his extending kinship to toll collectors and sinners (e.g., 5:27-32). This is the irony of the criticism both John and Jesus have received: They are rejected for behaviors that are actually symptomatic of their faithfulness to the work for which God set them apart. What is more, they are rejected for not following the conventions determined and propagated by religious people who claim that those conventions are divinely sanctioned.

Again, then, we come face-to-face with the presence of two, competing views of God's purpose and of the contours of faithfulness to that purpose. Because they fail to conform to the socio-religious "games" (or script) determined by "this generation," John and Jesus are branded as deviants, beyond the boundaries of acceptable social discourse, people not to be taken seriously.[67] The existence of two such widely divergent appraisals of the ministries of John and Jesus points to the inherent ambiguity of their ministry practices. By those who are aligned with the world system that supports and is supported by "this generation," they will be interpreted one way. Within that system Jesus has no claim to holiness, but as a companion of sinners and toll collectors he has distinguished himself as one of their company, and John is relegated to the status of a demoniac. But for those who visualize the world through the lens of allegiance to God and God's purpose, the characteristic practices of John and Jesus are understood along

---

66. Some have seen the point of comparison differently: (1) the children of the marketplace fail to agree on a game to play, so that play is paralyzed by selfishness (e.g., Neale, *None but the Sinners,* 138); or (2) John and Jesus are the children of the marketplace, one adopting one style of ministry, the other another style, with the people and/or their leaders refusing either form of play (e.g., Schürmann, 1:423-24; Fitzmyer, 1:678-79). On the view adopted here, see, e.g., Jeremias, *Parables,* 160-62; Linton, "Parable of the Children's Game"; Carson, "Matthew 11:19b/Luke 7:35," 138-41. The rejection of the reading adopted here as "allegorical" manifests a modern sensitivity to allegorical detail not shared by (at least) Luke.

67. That is, the identification and labeling of deviance are mechanisms of social control whereby dominant social norms and those who follow them are legitimated and maintained. See Seymour-Smith, *Anthropology,* 76-77. Douglas (*Risk and Blame,* 83-101) discusses the use of witchcraft accusations as techniques of rejection and social control.

vastly different lines. Now they are regarded as manifestations of the divine purpose at work in the world.

This, in fact, is the very point with which Jesus concludes this larger section in v 35.[68] The sense of this aphorism is shaped in this co-text by its relation to the preceding material, wherein we may observe an inverted parallelism:[69]

> v 29 All the people . . . justified God.
>> v 30 the Pharisees and scribes reject God's purpose for themselves.
>> vv 31-34 the people of this generation reject John and Jesus.
> v 35 Wisdom is justified[70] by all her children.

Verses 29 and 35, in fact, are set in chiastic relationship:

> All the people who heard this . . . justified God.
>
> Wisdom is justified by all her children.

The structure of this passage urges the following identifications: (1) *"Wisdom" with God.* Wisdom is thus personified,[71] but is granted no status independent of God. It is simply a way of speaking of God and, by extension, of the purpose of God (cf. vv 29-30). (2) *Wisdom's children as those who align themselves with God's purpose.* This purpose is manifest in the mission of John, but 7:18-23 has demonstrated that John himself did not fully grasp the nature of God's salvific will. Hence, Jesus is presented as the one who ultimately discloses the divine aim. Wisdom's children are those who, like John and Jesus, align themselves with God's purpose as this is revealed in the person and work of Jesus. As servants of God's purpose, John and Jesus are also identified as "wisdom's children," rather than socio-religious deviants. (3) *"Pharisees and lawyers" as "people of this generation" — that is, as those who stubbornly reject and/or oppose God's purpose and, so also, God's agents of good news.* The highly stylized presentation of this parallelism may suggest that, at least in this co-text, the phrase "Pharisees and lawyers"

---

68. Hence, the καί in v 35, translated in the NRSV as "nevertheless," may be a logical adversative, but it signals v 35 as the dramatic conclusion of Jesus' discourse (Carson, "Matthew 11:19b/Luke 7:35," 142).

69. Many (e.g., I. J. Du Plessis, "Contextual Aid," 124) refer to this structure as a chiasm, but vv 30, 31-34 are not presented chiastically.

70. δικαιόω; NRSV: "vindicated."

71. Cf., already in the OT, Prov 8:1–9:6; more broadly, Dunn, *Christology in the Making,* 168-76.

now functions figuratively, as a label, appropriate for any who oppose God's purpose, whether or not they are actual members of the sect of the Pharisees or are legal experts by profession.

4.4.4. Jesus, a Pharisee, and a Woman (7:36-50)

36 *One of the Pharisees asked Jesus to eat with him, and he went into the Pharisee's house and took his place at the table.* 37 *And a woman, known in the city as a sinner,[72] having learned that he was eating in the Pharisee's house, brought an alabaster jar of ointment.* 38 *She stood behind him at his feet, weeping, and began to bathe his feet with her tears and to dry them with her hair. Then she continued kissing his feet and anointing them with the ointment.* 39 *Now when the Pharisee who had invited him saw it, he said to himself, "If this man were a prophet, he would have known who and what kind of woman this is who is touching him — that she is a sinner."* 40 *Jesus spoke up and said to him, "Simon, I have something to say to you." "Teacher,"* *he replied, "Speak."* 41 *"A certain creditor had two debtors; one owed five hundred denarii, and the other fifty.* 42 *When they could not pay, he canceled the debts for both of them. Now which of them will love him more?"* 43 *Simon answered, "I suppose the one for whom he canceled the greater debt." And Jesus said to him, "You have judged rightly."* 44 *Then turning toward the woman, he said to Simon, "Do you see this woman? I entered your house; you gave me no water for my feet, but she has bathed my feet with her tears and dried them with her hair.* 45 *You gave me no kiss, but from the time I came in she has not stopped kissing my feet.* 46 *You did not anoint my head with oil, but she has anointed my feet with ointment.* 47 *Therefore, I tell you, her sins, which were many, have been forgiven; hence she has shown great love. But the one to whom little is forgiven, loves little."* 48 *Then he said to her, "Your sins are forgiven."* 49 *But those who were at the table with him began to say among themselves, "Who is this who even forgives sins?"* 50 *And he said to the woman, "Your faith has saved you; go in peace."*

No temporal markers separate Luke's account of Jesus' encounter with Simon the Pharisee and the sinful woman from the immediately preceding discourse. Nor are there any major shifts in scene; even though Jesus goes into the home of the Pharisee (v 36), they are still in the town of Nain.[73] Topically, moreover,

---

72. NRSV: "a woman in the city, who was a sinner."
73. Luke uses πόλις in vv 11 and 37.

this new episode continues the emphases of Jesus' discourse on a number of levels. In fact, this scene serves as a concrete example of the irony of the popular indictment against Jesus as one who eats and drinks and is a friend of sinners, voiced in v 34. It demonstrates that such practices are indeed characteristic of Jesus while at the same time showing that they are an outgrowth and material manifestation of the ministry of salvation.

This pericope is related to preceding material in other ways too. Significantly, it continues the now-familiar topos of polarization around Jesus, with opinions about him diverging markedly (cf., e.g., vv 29-30). Like the Gentile centurion (7:1-10), so this woman exercises remarkable insight into the nature of Jesus' mission, not least when compared with those who exercise leadership in the community. And the characterization of salvation as forgiveness of sins, developed in earlier scenes (5:1-11, 17-26, 29-32), is promoted here.

When compared with previous scenes depicting Jesus' ministry, this one shows Luke developing more dramatically the depth of its major characters. The woman may not be given a name, and at a crucial point she may appear as little more than an object lesson, yet she is depicted more fully than many other persons we have encountered. She has a past that is undeveloped but is nonetheless important to the narrative, acts of her own volition, takes risks, and so on. Simon is known first and foremost as a Pharisee, but even he is developed as an individual with table companions, internal thoughts, the capacity to make judgments, and he has a future that lies beyond the narrative but is nonetheless important to the message of the narrative. Luke's depiction of the character of Jesus is advanced in this scene in large part in the interaction of competing perspectives concerning him. The woman has an obvious if undefined relationship to Jesus and brings certain expectations concerning him to this scene. The Pharisee's relationship to Jesus is less explicit but still evident; he also has implied expectations of Jesus.

The immediate setting for what transpires at Simon's house is a banquet to which Jesus has been invited. Within the narrative world of Luke, this setting raises possibilities and concerns along two related lines.[74] First, Luke has often cast his meal scenes in the form of Greco-Roman *symposia,* wherein conversation, perhaps even lively debate, follows the meal itself. Within the topos of the *symposium* a certain decorum was expected; hence, for example, apropos 7:36-50, philosophical conflict might be expected in the "talking party" following the meal, even to the extent that the chief guest would best his host, but this would (and should) not involve a breach of the basic rules of hospitality.[75]

---

74. See above on 5:27-32.

75. Hence, *contra* Carroll ("Luke's Portrayal," 610-11), the conflict between Jesus and Simon should not be interpreted as integral to Luke's presentation of this scene as a *symposium.*

Second, the meal-setting raises issues of ritual purity, all the more since this meal is hosted by a Pharisee. The woman who enters Simon's house, whose sinful state is evident to all, comes into this scene like an alien, communicable disease; given Pharisaical views of holiness, the propriety of Simon's response to the spectacle transpiring before him would be assumed.

In recent years, numerous scholars have read this account as "an exposé of the 'typical' Pharisaic attitude" in Luke designed to illustrate the alleged global view of the Pharisees (and experts in the law) advanced in 7:30.[76] For them, Simon is a stereotype of the Lukan Pharisee, and the Pharisees a caricature of those who reject God's purpose. We have already outlined two observations militating against this view (see above on vv 29-30) — namely, (1) by analogy, this reading of vv 29-30 would require that "the people" throughout Luke-Acts respond positively, but this is not consistently the case; and (2) a narrative reading of Luke-Acts leaves open the possibility that the Evangelist will revise the characterization of the Pharisees, either as a group or otherwise.[77]

Other factors disallow the interpretation of Simon as a stereotypical Pharisee who, because he is a Pharisee, is thereby understood within the narrative as someone who opposes the will of God. Thus, (3) the Third Gospel's presentation of the Pharisees is more variegated than is usually thought. They are consistently portrayed negatively when they appear in the company of scribes (a.k.a. legal experts, lawyers, teachers of the law), as in 7:30, but from an historical viewpoint this is not surprising. "Scribes" have been identified as off-duty priests,[78] and Luke lays the blame for the death of Jesus above all at the feet of priests and others of the Jerusalem leadership associated with the temple (and not the Pharisees).[79] Outside the company of scribes, however, Luke's portrait of the Pharisees is capable of more nuance.[80] (4) That Simon invites Jesus to a banquet suggests that he has not yet formed a negative opinion of Jesus.[81] (5) By referring to Jesus as a prophet, Simon

76. Neale, *None but the Sinners*, 140-42. See also, e.g., Darr, *Character Building*, 101-3; Carroll, "Luke's Portrayal," 609-11; J. T. Sanders, *Jews*, 176-78; et al.

77. For Darr *(Character Building)*, this is essentially a problem of method. He argues that Luke "builds" characters progressively without accounting sufficiently for the possibility of deconstruction or retrospective modification of earlier character-building material.

78. That is, priests who were not serving in the temple; see Schwartz, *Jewish Background*, 89-101; E. P. Sanders, *Judaism*, 170-82.

79. See 9:22, 47; 20:1, 19; 22:2, 4, 50, 52, 54, 66; 23:4, 10, 13; 24:20. Cf. Matera, "Death of Jesus."

80. Cf. Green, *Gospel of Luke*, 72-75.

81. On this and the following points, see Tannehill, "Simon the Pharisee," 431-32; Cotterell and Turner, *Linguistics*, 272-74.

indicates his openness to regarding him at least as positively as had the crowds and the disciples of Jesus (7:16). (6) Jesus addresses Simon directly as an individual, calling him by name. (7) Jesus attempts to teach Simon, apparently in the hope that he can be persuaded not to condemn but actually to accept this woman known as a sinner. (8) Finally, as Luke tells it, the narrative of this episode is completed before the story has ended; we do not know how Simon responded. This form of narration may well be an attempt to invite the reader who identifies with Simon's concern with boundaries to respond with the expansive love characterizing Jesus' actions.[82]

In fact, this account is open-ended at the beginning and the end. The woman's actions assume some encounter with Jesus prior to the onset of this scene, and the narrative anticipates some form of response on the part of Simon to Jesus' remarks to him concerning the woman (vv 44-47).[83]

36-38 The episode begins by framing the story in contrasts. Three times in these opening verses, Jesus' host is mentioned as a Pharisee, known to us from earlier episodes as monitors of legal observance who distance themselves from sinners. Yet, following the introduction of the Pharisee and Jesus, the spotlight falls on a sinful woman. Already the normal polarization of Pharisee and sinner has been undermined, since this sinner has entered the Pharisee's home. What is more, Jesus has entered this home in order to participate in a formal banquet.[84] This means, on the one hand, that the Pharisee has sufficient trust in Jesus' ritual purity to share a meal with him, and, on the other, that the woman's presence has introduced a powerful contagion, ritual impurity, into these goings-on.

Nevertheless, as the scene opens it is still possible to imagine that all is proceeding as it should, and the curtness of Luke's narration — a Pharisee asked, Jesus went, Jesus reclined at the table — continues the charade of the normal by masking what will become obvious by the end of the account. This is the glaring neglect of deeply ingrained laws of hospitality, operative when receiving a guest of any stature and certainly an honored guest (like Jesus) who can be regarded as a prophet and addressed as "teacher" (vv 39, 40). One may find a hint of the deliberate omission of any mention of Simon's lack of attention to his guest in the repeated identification of the Pharisee as Jesus' host in vv 36 and 39, apart from any narration of his actually acting as a host, but this is easily passed over.

The scene is carefully staged, with the result that, as it progresses, the

---

82. Cf. Meynet, "Lc 7,36-50."

83. Cf. Derrett, *New Resolutions,* 124; Gowler, *Portraits of the Pharisees,* 222.

84. He is described as "reclining at the table" (κατακλίνω), a detail that marks this event as a banquet (cf. Jeremias, *Eucharistic Words,* 48-49); v 49 notes the presence of the other guests.

narrative "imaginatively deforms" conventional assumptions.[85] The woman arrives, apparently before or simultaneously with Jesus,[86] and Luke narrates her outrageous behavior as though it were expected and acceptable. Everything about this woman, though, is wrong; she does not belong here and the actions she performs are inappropriate in any setting for someone like Jesus.

She is a sinner in the city — that is, a woman known in the city as a sinner. Undoubtedly, this characterization marks her as a prostitute by vocation,[87] a whore by social status, contagious in her impurity, and probably one who fraternizes with Gentiles for economic purposes.[88] What is she doing in this house? Some interpreters have found her presence unobjectionable, noting that the doors of homes in a Palestinian village would be open with anyone welcome to come in,[89] but this seems highly problematic in light of the issues of holiness and purity attached to Pharisaic meal practices. On the contrary, she is present as an intruder, at least from one perspective. From another, she is present because she is known as a sinner, and Jesus is known as a friend of sinners (v 34).

Our understanding of her position vis-à-vis Jesus and his ministry is shaped further by our understanding of her social status. It was and is easy enough to dismiss such a person as immoral as well as unclean and deviant, without grappling with the social realities faced by a woman, perhaps a freedwoman, forced into the marketplace by her lack of attachment or identification with a man, who prostitutes herself in order to live according to one of the very few options available to her; or a woman or girl sold into prostitution by her parents on account of economic misfortune.[90] In short, this unnamed woman belongs to a category of persons who qualify as "the poor," for whom Jesus has been anointed to bring good news (4:18-19; 7:22). This is true even if she has been successful enough in her occupation to possess "an alabaster jar of ointment" (v 37).

Her actions are accentuated by the narrator, who allows each to stand out individually and who notes that each was performed continuously.[91] She is behind Jesus because of the placement of people around the U-shaped table;

85. Resseguie, "Automatization and Defamiliarization," 139.

86. See v 45: "from the time I came in"; cf. K. E. Bailey, *Through Peasant Eyes,* 7.

87. See Corley, *Private Women,* 92, 124; Schottroff, *Feminist Perspectives,* 150.

88. See Seim, *Double Message,* 90-91; Witherington, *Women in the Ministry of Jesus,* 54-55.

89. So Bailey, *Through Peasant Eyes,* 4-5; cf. Witherington, *Women in the Ministry of Jesus,* 55.

90. See Corley, *Private Women,* 52, 124; Schottroff, *Feminist Perspectives,* 151-52; Ford, "Prostitution."

91. That is, Luke uses a paratactical construction, employing καί repeatedly, and casts the verbs in the imperfect.

reclining on his left side, his legs would have stretched out behind the person to his right, giving her ready access to his feet. Within her cultural context — especially with women readily viewed as temptresses and/or sex objects, and all the more given her apparent reputation as a prostitute — her actions on the whole would have been regarded (at least by men) as erotic. Letting her hair down in this setting would have been on a par with appearing topless in public, for example. She would have appeared to be fondling Jesus' feet, like a prostitute or a slave girl accustomed to providing sexual favors.[92] It is no wonder that Simon entertains serious reservations about Jesus' status as a holy man. Even if her actions will receive a different interpretation with the narrative, within her Palestinian world they were obviously susceptible to this reading.

We are given no unambiguous guidelines for understanding the cause of her tears. Do they identify her as a recipient of eschatological blessing (cf. 6:21b)? Are they symbolic of her (new?) reliance on God (cf. Psalm 126; Isa 25:8; 35:10; 65:17-25)? Are they tears of remorse or repentance? What we do know is that actions are rooted in the disposition of the heart, that actions divulge one's fundamental allegiances (cf. 3:10-14; 6:43-49). What do these actions disclose about this woman? Luke's account provides two, mutually exclusive interpretations.

39 Up to this point in the account, Jesus' host is known only as "the Pharisee." After reading v 30, it would be difficult for us to be very sanguine about any Pharisee, apart from the fact that Jesus did accept his invitation and, in doing so, had opened the possibility of friendship with his host. Optimism of this sort is not immediately supported, however, since within the Lukan account those who engage in soliloquy have been persons lacking insight into Jesus' divine commission or even opponents of God's purpose (cf. 2:35; 5:21-22; 6:8). This is the case here, too.

Having interpreted the woman's actions at the table in a way consistent with her reputation in the town — that is, as shamelessly erotic — this Pharisee labels her a sinner. His response is automatic, his conclusion regarding Jesus legitimate given the assumptions under which he is operating. Since the godly do not associate with the wicked, Jesus, who allows this shameless behavior, must not be a prophet. In Simon's view, Jesus neither practices prophetic insight into the character of this woman nor, by allowing her ministrations, behaves in a way consistent with those set apart for divine service. Accordingly, Simon is the victim of an irony being played out between Luke and his audience, for we share with Luke the knowledge that Jesus is God's

92. See the perhaps less offensive but nevertheless symbolic actions in Ruth 3:4, 7. Cf. further Epictetus 4.1.17; *b. Sanh.* 45a; *b. Soṭa* 8a; Corley, *Private Women,* 124-25; Derrett, *New Resolutions,* 126-27; Witherington, *Women in the Ministry of Jesus,* 56.

redemptive agent and that his divinely ordained ministry entails a manner of association with "the sick" and with "sinners" that others regard as inappropriate (cf. 5:31-32). In fact, in contradistinction to Simon's analysis, Jesus' status as a prophet is manifest in this pericope in his ability to overhear Simon's interior monologue (see v 40) and in his recognition of Simon as a sinner.[93]

This scene, then, plays on the potential polysemy of the woman's actions. Her behavior is open to divergent interpretations that can only be disambiguated within a larger system of meaning or a worldview.[94] This Pharisee represents accepted social conventions in the larger Palestinian world; as we will see, Jesus has a different vantage point from which to make sense of this encounter.

40-43   Although the Pharisee has spoken only to himself (v 39), Jesus "answers"[95] him. Jesus thus proves himself to be a prophet, the divine vocation just denied him by the Pharisee. Now the Pharisee calls him "teacher," a title of respect within the Lukan narrative (cf. 6:40). When used with reference to Jesus it is normally found on the lips of those who are outside the circle of Jesus' followers but who are open to learning or want to receive something from him.[96] Jesus, on the other hand, initiates personal dialogue with this Pharisee, refusing to count his host merely as a member of a particular Jewish sect within Second Temple Judaism. He has had enough of labels (see vv 34, 39), so he addresses the Pharisee by his name, Simon.

Jesus' parable is hardly innocent. Indeed, the connection between "canceling debts" and "forgiving sins" has been cultivated since Jesus' inaugural proclamation of "release" in 4:18-19. In this case, Jesus presents a creditor who has become a gracious benefactor, canceling the debts of his clients. Relationships of debt and obligation were rooted in the patronal ethics that pervaded Roman antiquity. As a relatively wealthy man,[97] this Pharisee would have had firsthand knowledge of such relationships; indeed, his hosting a dinner would place his guests in his debt, ensuring reciprocal invitations or other forms of repayment at an undetermined, future date. The cancellation of debts would denude relationships of their inherent dimensions of status

---

93. Cf. Darr, *Character Building,* 102.

94. See Resseguie, "Automatization and Defamiliarization," 143; Thibeaux, "Known to Be a Sinner," esp. 154.

95. ἀποκριθείς; NRSV: "spoke up."

96. See 8:49; 9:38; 10:25; 11:45; 12:13; 18:18; 19:39; 20:28, 39; 21:7; 22:11. In 20:21, Jesus is addressed as "teacher" by persons who have approached him dishonestly.

97. His relative wealth is suggested by his ability to host a formal banquet with a number of guests. This does not mean that Pharisees as a group were wealthy or enjoyed high status, though Luke does refer to them as "lovers of money" (16:14). As we will see, the sense of that text is not far from this one, since both have to do with the Pharisaic concern to enjoy advanced status and positions of power and privilege.

discrimination and duress; if widely practiced, the cancellation of debts would radically undermine the "rules" governing interpersonal interaction.

With his parable, Jesus has begun to call such conventions into question, but he does not push the point to its logical extreme. By asking, "Who will love him more?" he continues to work within the patronal system enough to allow Simon to follow his point and render a judgment. The clay has already begun to crumble, however, as Jesus summons Simon to reconsider the meaning of this woman's actions — not the repayment of a debt, as though she were a slave girl or prostitute, but an expression of love that flows from the freedom of having all debts canceled. At the same time, he invites Simon to reconsider the basis of his own interactions with others, and thus the possibility not only of forgiving debts but also of having debts forgiven (cf. 11:4).

44-47 The importance of this discourse within this larger pericope is communicated by Jesus' dramatic "turning" before he speaks.[98] That he turns to the woman while speaking to Simon momentarily reduces her from the role of central actor to that of object lesson. This is important for the rhetoric of the narrative, however, for in this way Jesus hopes to persuade Simon to adopt Jesus' own view of matters concerning this woman. He wants to transform Simon's view of the world and so to have Simon reconsider his premature judgment regarding this woman. Jesus' opening query, "Do you see this woman?" is an invitation to enlightenment, the consequence of which would be acceptance of both her (i.e., no longer viewing her as a "sinner" but as one who loves extravagantly) and of new behaviors modeled on those of this woman.

What we might have regarded as an abruptness of narrative style in v 36 is now disclosed as a deliberate omission of Simon's dishonorable behavior; Luke has held back this information in order to present it here, juxtaposed with his rehearsal of the woman's action, for rhetorical effect. Though he was the host (vv 36, 39), Simon did not fulfill his role as host, at least with respect to Jesus. Hence, he who has so carefully followed social conventions in his condemnation of the woman as a sinner has himself failed to follow related conventions. Simon implicates himself in a serious breach of the laws of hospitality whereby he has challenged the honor of his guest, Jesus. With regard to duties of the host, certain behavior would have been axiomatic: He must honor his guest, not insulting or showing any hostility toward his guest; he must protect the honor of his guest from challenge by others at his table; and he must attend to his guests, granting them all due deference. Failure to do so would be to denigrate the guest.[99] What is fascinating about Simon's behavior in this scene is that he does seem concerned

---

98. See above on 7:9.
99. See Pitt-Watson, "Law of Hospitality," 110.

with Jesus' status when it is called into question by the unseemly actions of the woman from the city, yet does not even begin to show him the requisite honor when welcoming Jesus into his home. Moreover, when the other table guests question Jesus' status (v 49), Simon is not said to have intervened in any way. In effect, this woman fulfills the role expected of Simon, and thus shames Simon as a host who did not honor his guest.[100]

We should not think, however, that the woman's actions simply substituted for Simon's. Instead, her ministrations on Jesus' behalf are notable for their lavishness. Jesus outlines what was proper: the provision of water for his feet, a kiss of greeting (on the cheek or hand), the anointing of his head with (olive) oil.[101] The woman's actions are not only honorable by comparison, but extravagant. She does not provide water for his feet, but instead washes them herself, with tears; she has no towel but uses her own hair to dry them. She does not kiss his cheek or hand, but his feet. She does not anoint his head, but his feet, and that not with household olive oil but with costly perfume. All of her actions are performed on Jesus' feet, that unseemly, unclean part of the body,[102] thus accentuating all the more the extraordinary and humble nature of her attendance to his needs.

What conclusion is to be drawn from her behavior? We have already seen one interpretation: her actions are erotic and out of place, indicative of and consonant with her reputation as a prostitute. Jesus offers another: because she has been forgiven much, she loves much. That is, her behavior gives expression to her forgiveness.[103] In this way, Jesus draws out the immediate relevance of the parable of vv 41-42, using Simon's own response to the parable (v 43) to interpret the woman's actions.

When had she been forgiven? As in narratives more generally, so here we are confronted with a gap in the story line,[104] and we must assume some prior encounter the effect of which was her forgiveness. This is hardly unusual for Luke, who occasionally introduces persons into the narrative who have already begun the journey of discipleship in some sense though we are never told when or how.[105] What we are told is that she had already been forgiven.

---

100. Cf. Seim, *Double Message,* 94; Gowler, *Portraits of the Pharisees,* 223-25.

101. On these culture-specific acts of greeting, see K. E. Bailey, *Through Peasant Eyes,* 8-10, 16-17.

102. Cf. 3:16; Ps 110:1; 1 Cor 12:14, 23; Bailey, *Through Peasant Eyes,* 5.

103. Thus, the ὅτι of v 47, translated in the NRSV as "hence," is resultative: she has received forgiveness and she responds with expressions of love.

104. Some interpreters (e.g., Kilgallen, "John the Baptist," 676-77) regard this viewpoint as problematic, since it depends on reading into the narrative a previous encounter between Jesus and the sinful woman. But gaps of this nature are characteristic of literary texts. See, e.g., Iser, *Implied Reader.*

105. See, e.g., 7:1-10; 8:43-48; 19:1-10; 23:40-43; Green, *Gospel of Luke,* 105.

Jesus' affirmation of her forgiveness is told in the third person, still addressed to Simon. Simon is not aware of her new status; he still regards her as a sinner with whom a man of God ought not to associate. Jesus' affirmation is thus for Simon's sake, in order that he might realize her condition and embrace her in the community of God's people.

48-50 Having endorsed the divine action resulting in this woman's forgiveness (v 47), Jesus now turns to address the woman directly. As a consequence, we might be tempted to think that *she* needs this assurance of her forgiveness. The presence of v 49 encourages another reading. Verses 48 and 50 are set in parallel, with Jesus, using different words, proclaiming to the woman her salvation. Verse 49 demonstrates why Jesus needed to repeat himself. His words were unnecessary as far as she as an individual was concerned; she has already been forgiven and has acted in accordance with her new-found freedom. Others, however, are unaware of her new state and, like Simon, will continue to regard her as "a woman known in the city as a sinner." She does not need forgiveness from God, but she does need recognition of her new life and forgiveness among God's people.

It is not clear how Simon's guests will respond to the woman, though v 49 gives us little hope that they will embrace and extend friendship to her. Speaking to themselves (cf. 2:35; 5:21-22; 6:8; 7:39), they raise questions about Jesus' authority to speak on God's behalf and, more specifically, to forgive sins (cf. 5:21). As we have seen, this is an affront to his honor, and this establishes a striking contrast between Luke's portrayal of the alleged sinful woman and his brief characterization of Simon's table companions. Had they known who Jesus was, they would have accepted his authority — as the centurion had done (7:1-10), and as this woman had done. Moreover, had they come seeking forgiveness, they too would have had their debts canceled (vv 41-42) and been able to respond lovingly rather than in sectarian judgment.

That Jesus' fundamental concern in these verses is with this woman's restoration to the community of God's people (and not with her individualistic experience of forgiveness or assurance of divine acceptance) is suggested, first, by the fact that she is presented as already behaving in ways that grow out of her new life. In addition, Jesus addresses her with words usually reserved for the conclusion of miracles of healing: "your faith has made you whole" (8:48; 18:42; 17:19); and he sends her away "in peace." Such language cannot be limited to "spiritual" well-being or even, in other co-texts, to "physical" vitality, but speaks of a restoration to wholeness, including (even if not limited to) restoration to the full social intercourse from which she has been excluded.

Luke closes the curtains on this scene before the action is completed. It is one thing to have Jesus proclaim her forgiveness in order that her renewed status might be recognized by the community; it is quite another for that community actually to accept his pronouncement and to extend kinship to her. How will they respond? Will they adopt the view of the world that Jesus displays in his interactions in this episode? Will they learn to view God as one who cancels debts and invites others to do the same so that all might behave toward one another with love unfettered by the constraints of past behaviors and reputation and by interminable contracts of reciprocity? Will they recognize Jesus as God's authorized agent to pronounce forgiveness and to bring restoration? How will they respond? How will Simon respond? And how will Luke's readers respond?

4.5. PROCLAIMING THE GOOD NEWS OF THE KINGDOM OF GOD (8:1-56)

Following the further identification of the compassionate nature of Jesus' ministry and the confirmation of his identity in Luke 7, ch. 8 propels the narrative forward with its twin focus on Jesus' proclamation of the good news and on the consequence of one's response to the good news. Luke 8:1-3 serves as a heading for this section, introducing three tightly intertwined motifs:

(1) *The salvific agency of Jesus.* Others are with him, but Jesus is the primary actor throughout Luke 8. His teaching and power are on display as he disseminates the word of God. Though the names by which he is called — Master (v 24) and Son of the Most High God (v 28) — are not without their significance, even more important are the faith of people (cf. vv 12, 13, 25-48, 50) and their recognition of his redemptive authority (signified by falling down before him/at his feet — cf. vv 28, 35, 41, 47).

(2) *The active presence of diabolic agents and influence.* The aim of God, manifest in Jesus' ministry, is not the only one at work in this narrative. Evil spirits/demons, diseases, diabolic testing, even the agency of the devil himself — these are the various guises through which the presence of evil is evident (cf. vv 2, 11, 13, 24, 26-39, 40-56). The objective of diabolic activity is to keep people from authentic faith and, thus, from the experience of salvation.

(3) *The gathering of followers and the consequent importance of authentic response to Jesus.* Although Jesus had been about the business of calling and appointing followers in chs. 5–6, their presence in the narrative has been little felt. Their proximity to the ministry of Jesus had been heightened in chapter 7, but it is in ch. 8 that they are not only "with Jesus," but also begin to engage Jesus in conversation, call on him for assistance, and begin to enjoy a privileged role as witnesses to his healing ministry. The crescendo of interest in the disciples leads into ch. 9, at which point they will actively participate in his ministry and struggle with the implications of his

activity with respect to his identity. And this prepares for the slow, meandering journey to Jerusalem, beginning in 9:51, during which the emphasis will be on the training of disciples.

The Third Evangelist provides no textual indicators for a topical shift in the material of 8:4-21, with the consequence that we are invited to explore in which ways these three apparently incongruous sets of instructions cohere.[1] In fact, the text provides no break between vv 15-16, nor does v 19 introduce any necessary token of topical shift. As we will see, the three paragraphs contained in 8:4-21 develop the need for authentic hearing of the word of God (cf. esp. vv 11, 18a, 21b).

Similarly, the episodes narrated in 8:22-56 continue a common emphasis. The two scenes recounted in vv 40-56 are correlated by means of the literary device of intercalation, and so are to be interpreted together. But these two episodes are themselves associated with the accounts of the stilling of the storm and the Gerasene demoniac by means of a carefully outlined itinerary: they went across the lake (v 22), they arrived on the other side of the lake (vv 26-27), he (they) returned (vv 37, 40). The episodes of healing and exorcism (vv 26-56) are related further by their common interest in submission to Jesus (vv 28, 35, 41, 47) and in the question of who will be given access to reports of Jesus' salvific activity (vv 39, 47b, 56a).

Throughout ch. 8, a premium is placed on authentic response to Jesus in the face of recognizing and receiving the gracious benefaction he brings.

4.5.1. Good News of the Kingdom of God (8:1-3)

> 8:1 *Soon afterwards he went on through cities and villages, proclaiming and bringing the good news of the kingdom of God. The twelve were with him, 2 as well as some women who had been cured of evil spirits and infirmities: Mary, called Magdalene, from whom seven demons had gone out, 3 and Joanna, the wife of Herod's steward Chuza, and Susanna, and many others, who provided for them out of their resources.*

The summary is a useful literary device for linking scenes, for presenting what is typical, and for providing background information. The present pericope

---

1. Of course, one of the primary axioms of discourse analysis — namely, "the natural effort of hearers and readers alike is to attribute relevance and coherence to the text they encounter until they are forced not to" (Brown and Yule, *Discourse Analysis,* 66) — has typically been voided by the efforts of form criticism. Redaction criticism, building its analysis largely on the foundation of form criticism's identification of textual units, typically subdivides this larger section into modest components without examining their co-textual relations.

fulfills all three of these functions. In doing so, it gathers up previous emphases — especially from Jesus' missionary agenda in 4:18-19, Luke's summary of his divine commission in 4:43-44, and the reiteration and confirmation of the nature of his mission in 7:18-35. Included among these emphases are the following: bringing good news, proclaiming, the kingdom of God, the message of "release," and Jesus' itinerancy.[2] By reviewing these emphases, the narrator both sums up the previous section of the Gospel (ch. 7) and provides an interpretive heading for what is to come. Luke 8:1-3 thus serves an important transitional role at this point in the Gospel.

As a summary, this text also introduces more blatantly what has only begun to be apparent in the narrative — namely, the ongoing presence of traveling companions "with" Jesus. Being "with Jesus" connotes "discipleship"[3] — an implication immediately born out by the identification of Jesus' companions as "the twelve" and as women who (as we will see below) embody the meaning of discipleship for Luke. The presence of Jesus' followers in this précis in no way implies that they participate actively in "proclaiming and bringing the good news of the kingdom of God." Rather, Luke's summary identifies the twelve and these women as companions and witnesses of Jesus' ministry (cf. 23:49; Acts 1:21); they are being prepared for involvement in mission (cf. 9:1-6; 10:1-11), but they are not yet active agents of God's mission at this stage of the narrative.[4]

This is the first mention of "the twelve" since their having been chosen in 6:12-16. There they were identified as a group within the larger company of disciples; in ch. 8 they will observe Jesus' ministry, but they will not appear as especially enlightened (vv 45, 51).

Luke identifies a second group within the larger mass of those who followed Jesus, distinguished by their significant, ongoing role as Jesus'

2. εὐαγγελίζομαι — 4:18, 43; 8:1; κηρύσσω — 4:18, 44; 8:1; βασιλεία τοῦ θεοῦ — 4:43; 8:1; "release," anticipated in 4:18, realized in exorcism and healing in 8:2-3 (on the relationship between healing and exorcism in Lukan thought and, thus, the significance of identifying "healing" as a liberating aspect of Jesus' ministry, see above on 4:31-33; cf., more generally, Busse, *Wunder;* Green, "Daughter of Abraham"; Seim, *Double Message,* 41-42); itinerancy — 4:43-44; 8:1; cf. 5:12.

3. See above on 7:11-12; also S. Brown, *Apostasy and Perseverance,* 83.

4. *Contra,* e.g., Quesnell ("Women," 68), who asserts that both the twelve and the women were at this stage involved as active agents in Jesus' mission. The word order of the Greek text, well represented in the NRSV, identifies Jesus as the one evangelizing and proclaiming, the others as his companions during this segment of his itinerant ministry. Quesnell's suggestion that "Jesus, the Twelve and the woman are three subjects of the verb *diōdeuen* (singular, to agree with the nearest subject)" overlooks the grammatically more likely possibility that Luke has simply omitted the verb "to be" to describe the twelve and the women as having been with Jesus. Quesnell seems not to appreciate that being "with him/Jesus" constitutes an important Lukan theme (cf. Green, *Gospel of Luke,* 108).

followers. These are "some women who had been cured of evil spirits and diseases . . . who provided for them out of their resources." Even had they never been included in ministries of proclamation and healing, and it would be hard to exclude them from the mission of the seventy-two (10:1-11), in the larger Greco-Roman world even this degree of identification and partici-pation by women with a traveling teacher would have been extraordinary.[5] Their presence in apparently significant numbers in Jesus' entourage ("many others," v 3) is likely due to the reach of Jesus' ministry to include (and the effectiveness of the good news among) single women — for example, widows (7:11-17) and prostitutes (7:36-50). The identification of Mary as "Mag-dalene" and the mention of Susanna, both without any reference to husbands or even to elder sons, supports this reading.[6] Given the reality that persons who were ill or demonized also experienced different measures of social ostracism, the experience of healing among some of these women may have been accompanied not by a return to their own communities and families, to the extent that these might have existed for them, but by incorporation into this new community being formed around Jesus. Possibly, the sort of rearticu-lation of family allegiances characteristic of Jesus' message later in the Gospel[7] may lie behind the experience of others of these women as they established their new identities as followers of Jesus.

In any case, the recounting of the presence of women in a wandering company — and especially the narration of their presence as *typical* of Jesus' mission — would have triggered questions about their status and role. Luke portrays them as recipients of Jesus' gracious ministry[8] but also as benefactors of that ministry.[9] This is important since, as with the woman's behavior in 7:37-38, so here the presence of these women in this band of travelers is suspect;[10] at the very least their behavior is shameless and quite likely would

5. Cf. Witherington, "On the Road," 245.

6. Cf. Sim, "Woman Followers," 53-55; Seim, *Double Message,* 33-34.

7. Cf. 8:19-21; 9:57-62; 12:51-53; 14:25-35; 18:18-30.

8. As usual, Luke draws no sharp distinction between "diseases" and the influence of "evil spirits"; in Jesus' ministry both are conditions from which one might be "cured."

9. The rabbinic analogues often noted in this context (cf. Witherington, "On the Road," 244-45n.9) are irrelevant because (1) often (always?) the gift from a woman to a rabbi or rabbis is directed by her husband, a detail completely missing from the Lukan report, and, unlike these parallels in rabbinic writings, the Lukan summary has it that (2) the women are first recipients of the gracious ministry of the teacher; consequently, (3) they are included in his band of followers; and (4) as we will see, these women do not function within the patron-client system as "patrons" of Jesus' company.

10. See Corley, *Private Women,* 24-79; she shows how Greco-Roman legislation and conventions sought to limit the public movements of "honorable" women. Corley misses Luke's point, however, when she insists that Luke has turned these women disciples into "respectable Greco-Roman patronesses" (119); Luke is not a slave to the patronal

have been regarded as illicitly sexual. After our having read 7:36-50, however, our views are constrained in other directions; that is, we may well be pre-disposed to see their actions as manifestations of gratitude and generosity rather than as having pushed beyond the boundaries of honor and morality. In light of Jesus' dialogue with Simon the Pharisee in 7:40-47, our reading might be constrained further, so as to disallow the possibility that the bene-faction of these women is the repayment of a debt owed to Jesus (or to Jesus and the twelve). In Jesus' ministry debts are canceled. His mission is to release persons from evil in all of its guises, including the evil of the never-ending cycle of gifts leading to obligations. His graciousness toward these women is not repaid by their benefactions; rather, his graciousness is mirrored in theirs.

Luke strikes two chords that will be heard again and again in the Third Gospel — those of service (NRSV: "provided") and of appropriate disposi-tion of resources.[11] "To serve" usually has the connotation of "waiting on tables" in Luke-Acts, though this practice comes to serve as a metaphor for leadership;[12] the verb and noun forms of service are also expanded along different lines, to include the notion of "support" or "provision."[13] In this case, women are said to serve/provide "out of their resources." Generally, this again suggests that the women around Jesus were single, not because married women had no resources but because single women would have been in an easier position to dispose of their resources as they saw fit.[14]

---

ethics of the empire and his rhetoric is often directed (as it is here) to showing how people might give "without expectation of return" (6:35) — i.e., in a way that undermines the patron-client system that pervaded the Mediterranean world.

11. Luke uses the present participle of ὑπάρχω to designate possessions.

12. Luke 4:39; 10:40; 12:37; 17:8; 22:26-27; Acts 6:2.

13. See BAGD 184; GELNT §§35.38, 57.119 (with reference to Acts 6:1); cf. Acts 11:29. These semantic developments do not introduce a *new* meaning for this lexeme, however, but only exploit the possibilities already resident in the disposition to assist or care for others — *contra* Sim ("Woman Followers," 56-57), who insists that διακονέω cannot mean "service." Sim argues thus apparently because he wants to distance himself (and/or Luke) from the view that liberation for women does nothing to address their traditional roles of hospitality and service. In arguing along these lines, Sim tries to counter the reading of Witherington ("On the Road," 246-48), that in the Christian movement these traditional roles simply have been extended from the physical family to include the family of faith; and the even more problematic position represented, e.g., by Hengel ("Maria Magdalena," 247-48), who visualizes women doing little more than "waiting on tables" in the early church. Luke 8:1-3, however, cannot be made to support any of these three positions, and it is best to major on what is clear from the text — namely, the identification of these women as "with" Jesus (in the same way that the twelve were "with" him, for neither group within the larger company of disciples is regarded as actively engaged in preaching or healing) and as exemplars (more so than are the twelve at this point in the narrative) of Jesus' message. Cf. the nuanced discussion in Seim, *Double Message,* 72-76.

14. Cf. Sim, "Woman Followers," 54-55.

This does not leave the women to provide for the ministries of Jesus and the twelve, as though Luke is operating at this juncture with a firmly established view of the unassailable authority of the twelve[15] or of a divinely legitimated division of labor in the mission of those who follow Jesus. Indeed, the twelve have not yet demonstrated faithfulness or evidenced competence (see below on 8:4-21), nor have they been granted any authority; like these women, the twelve are (only) *with* Jesus. More importantly, these women are thus characterized as (1) persons who mirror the graciousness of Jesus' own benefaction, (2) persons who, like Jesus, "serve" others (cf. 22:24-27), and (3) exemplars of Jesus' message on faith and wealth (see above, §11), whose lives anticipate Luke's portrait of the early Christian community among whom "no one claimed private ownership of any possessions, but everything they owned was held in common" (Acts 4:32).[16] In its current co-text, 8:1-3 thus parades these women (and not the twelve) as persons who both hear *and act* on the word of God (8:21; cf. 6:46-49).

Luke singles out three women of particular prominence among the several women in Jesus' following: Mary, Joanna, and Susanna. Mary is further distinguished (from the other Mary, Jesus' mother, present earlier in the narrative) as a former resident of the city of Magdala (modern Migdal; northeast of Tiberias about three miles). She is mentioned first undoubtedly because of her importance in the resurrection account (24:10). The mention of seven demons underscores the magnitude of her prior demonization (cf. 11:24-26).[17]

Joanna is introduced in an expected way with reference to her husband, Chuza, who is himself further identified as a steward in Herod's household; following this introduction, Joanna is mentioned with a simple reference to her name (24:10). What is the relevance of her husband's position? Some have found in this reference evidence that those who supported Jesus' ministry were persons of wealth. This may be, but if it were so, it only raises further puzzles: Has she left her husband to join the wandering teacher? Permanently? Temporarily? If so, does she have continued access to wealth?[18] There is a

---

15. *Contra* Corley, *Private Women*, 115-17.

16. Luke 8:3: ἐκ τῶν ὑπαρχόντων αὐταῖς; Acts 4:32: τῶν ὑπαρχόντων αὐτῷ. According to Jeremias (*Sprache des Lukasevangeliums*, 178), Luke is the only NT writer to write τὰ ὑπάρχοντά τινι — i.e., the substantive participle with the dative of the person (Luke 8:3; 12:15; Acts 4:32).

17. Luke neither characterizes Mary as having been previously a particularly immoral person nor gives any reason to suggest that she is to be identified with the "sinful woman" of 7:36-50.

18. This tension was apparently felt by Theissen, who pictures Joanna living with her husband Chuza in a "modern house in Graeco-Roman style"; in his "narrative exegesis," she is not a member of Jesus' traveling company but a secret supporter of Jesus (*Shadow of the Galilean*, 119-26).

further complicating factor. Although as Chuza's wife Joanna would have shared in the social status of her husband, and as a steward in Herod's household his status she would have been lofty indeed, status is always a relative commodity. In 7:1-10, for example, a wealthy Roman centurion recognizes that his advanced status furnishes him with no privileges before Jesus the Jewish teacher. As the Roman centurion functioned as a broker within Capernaum, so Herod served as a broker for the Roman Empire throughout Galilee. How will his loyalties to Rome have affected his standing among Galilean villagers and peasants? Within the narrative itself, Herod has been presented in a negative light, as have rulers in general.[19] Joanna does not necessarily possess enviable status, then, nor is her presence among those who follow Jesus easily construed as a potential source of their legitimation. Instead, Joanna's status is mixed, among her own people dubious. Just as many factors were capable of leaving one in a socially marginalized state in Palestinian antiquity, so Joanna fits in with others who find unequivocal kinship in the community being formed around Jesus.[20]

Finally, Luke mentions Susanna, but he does not characterize her in any way that distinguishes her from the "many others" except for the prominence given her by her being named.

Luke 8:1-3 thus bears witness to the consolidation of a group of followers around Jesus. In the following pericope (8:4-21) Luke will begin to define the nature or makeup of that group more fully.

4.5.2. On the Need for Authentic Hearing (8:4-21)

4 When a great crowd gathered and people from town after town came to him, he said in a parable: 5 "A sower went out to sow his seed; and as he sowed, some fell beside the path[21] and was trampled on, and the birds of the air ate it up. 6 Some fell on the rock; and as it grew up, it withered for lack of moisture. 7 Some fell among thorns, and the thorns grew with it and choked it. 8 Some fell into good soil, and when it grew, it produced a hundredfold." As he said this, he called out, "Let anyone with ears to hear listen!"

9 Then his disciples asked him what this parable meant. 10 He said, "To you it has been given to know the secrets of the kingdom of God; but to others I speak in parables, so that
'looking they may not perceive,
and listening they may not understand.'

---

19. See on 3:1, 19-20; also the negative portrayal of "rulers" in 1:46-55.
20. Seim, *Double Message*, 35-36, 39.
21. NRSV: "on the path."

11 *"Now the parable is this: The seed is the word of God.* 12 *The ones on the path are those who have heard; then the devil comes and takes away the word from their hearts, so that they may not believe and be saved.* 13 *The ones on the rock are those who, when they hear the word, receive it with joy. But these have no root; they believe only for a while and in a time of testing fall away.* 14 *As for what fell among the thorns, these are the ones who hear; but as they go on their way, they are choked by the cares and riches and pleasures of life, and their fruit does not mature.*15 *But as for that in the good soil, these are the ones who, when they hear the word, hold it fast in an honest and good heart, and bear fruit with patient endurance.*

16 *"No one after lighting a lamp hides it under a jar, or puts it under a bed, but puts it on a lampstand, so that those who enter may see the light.* 17 *For nothing is hidden that will not be disclosed, nor is anything secret that will not become known and come to light.* 18 *Then pay attention to how you listen; for to those who have, more will be given; and from those who do not have, even what they seem to have will be taken away."*

19 *Then his mother and his brothers came to him, but they could not reach him because of the crowd.* 20 *And he was told, "Your mother and your brothers are standing outside, wanting to see you."* 21 *But he said to them, "My mother and my brothers are those who hear the word of God and do it."*

Luke's accounts of the calling of disciples and choosing of apostles in chs. 5–6 have been surprisingly nondescript. Similarly lacking in detail is his characterization of the large numbers who follow Jesus or the group of those who travel with him from town to town. Exceptions to this generalization are concerned with the disposition of some toward possessions; thus Peter, James, and John "left everything" (5:11), as did Levi (5:28), and women disciples are portrayed in 8:2-3 as exhibiting practices that depict them as embodying the graciousness evident in Jesus' own ministry. In the Sermon on the Plain, Jesus had outlined the character or disposition of those who would participate in the community of God's people, together with the behaviors that would grow out of that disposition (6:20-49). That Sermon concluded with a pronounced emphasis on obedience to the word of the Lord (6:46-49). With a renewed and more pointed emphasis on the presence of a company of disciples joining him in his itinerancy, Jesus now returns to that theme in order to underscore the nature of the gathering community as a people who listen "correctly."

That genuine "hearing" is the principal theme of this narrative section is evident from the melody that weaves its way through the sometimes disparate material:

"Let anyone with ears to hear listen!" (v 8);
"so that . . . listening they may not understand" (v 10);
"those who hear" (in various forms, vv 12, 13, 14, 15);
"pay attention to how you listen" (v 18); and
"those who hear the word of God" (v 21).

Throughout this section, Jesus' point is not only to counsel "hearing" but also to specify the nature of "appropriate" (and "inappropriate") hearing. For this purpose, a number of qualifiers are used, especially: hear + "believe" (vv 12-13), hear + "choked" (v 14), hear + produce fruit (vv 14-15), hear + hold fast . . . with patience (v 15), and hear plus do (v 21). In all of these cases, hearing is associated with response, accentuating the necessity of acting on the basis of and consistent with what is "heard." Given the nature of the parable of vv 4-8, particularly as it is interpreted in vv 12-15, failure to respond is not an option; to generalize, having heard the word, one may produce fruit or fail to produce fruit. Those who produce fruit are thus identified as those who hear correctly; they are included in the family of Jesus and they are the ones who are being saved (vv 12, 21).

Importantly, Jesus' message is not proclaimed in an esoteric way at all. He tells the parable of the seed to a large crowd (v 4), which obviously includes his disciples (v 9). Even when addressing a question raised by his disciples, though, he is not said to have spoken to them privately. Indeed, at the end of Jesus' parabolic teaching the crowds are still present (v 19b). As is typical in the Third Gospel, then, Jesus' message is broadcast widely; teaching directed to the crowds is also for the disciples, and teaching for the disciples is also for the crowds. All are potential followers, and those who have begun to follow him continue in their need for instruction and formation.

4-8 In the midst of his itinerant ministry through the cities and villages of Galilee (v 1), Jesus now attracts an audience of great magnitude (cf. 6:17-19). Its enormity is emphasized by Luke's use of two coordinated clauses, "a large crowd was gathering" and "people from city after city were coming to him."[22] Luke signals in this way the breadth of Jesus' reputation and the reach of his ministry throughout Galilee. The disciples are not explicitly mentioned in this opening, but their presence is assumed from vv 1-2 and 9. Luke identifies Jesus' address as parabolic,[23] not that he told his audience "a parable." This implies that Luke is about to narrate an event in which the story Jesus tells is itself enacted. Hence, Jesus is represented not so much as teaching the people as interpreting what happens when he broadcasts the

22. In light of Luke's fondness for constructions with the genitive absolute (cf. MHT 4:59), this seems to be the best way to understand his construction here.
23. That is, διὰ παραβολῆς functions adverbially.

"good news of the kingdom of God" (v 1).[24] Like an ancient historian (of either the biblical or the Hellenistic tradition, or both), the Third Evangelist utilizes this address to disclose the meaning of the mixed responses Jesus has attracted within the Lukan narrative.[25] Why do/will some embrace the good news and others reject it? According to the perspective provided by Jesus' story, this question is less about who "hears" the word (for it is available to all), and more about the quality of one's hearing.

On the one hand, the tale Jesus narrates seems quite ordinary as it provides the beginning, middle, and end of the yearly cycle experienced by farmers. A farmer sows, the seed and fledgling crop encounter the normal array of hindrances to growth and maturity, and he harvests his crop. No mention is made of plowing the field, either before or after broadcasting the seed,[26] but this seems not to be an important factor in the story. That the farmer seems to take care not to sow the seed on the path,[27] and that the threat from birds is apparently from wild (and not domestic) fowl,[28] suggests that the farmer has avoided whatever hazards he could.[29] Those remaining — the trampling of the seed lying alongside the path, and so on — are unavoidable threats to the crop that help to paint this story in graphic realism. Finally, the quantity of the harvest is significant, but not beyond reason.[30]

If Jesus' story is thoroughly commonplace, how might it have been heard by this large audience, whose lives and livelihood were rooted in agriculture? Clearly, Jesus expects this story to have meaning; note his closing words, "Let anyone with ears to hear listen!" At the same time, the subsequent request for interpretation by the disciples (v 9) implies that the relevance of

24. Cf. Johnson, 134; Nolland, 1:373.

25. For this function of historical narrative, cf. Hall, *Revealed Histories;* Goldingay, *Models for Scripture,* part one.

26. Apparently, first-century Palestine was the home for various practices concerning the process of planting; cf. Payne, "Order of Sowing and Ploughing."

27. *Contra* the NRSV, Luke writes παρὰ τὴν ὁδόν.

28. Cf. Luke's "birds of the air."

29. Hence, it seems problematic to regard this farmer's sowing as striking on account of its extravagance. He does not, e.g., sow on the path. It is difficult to know what we are to make of his sowing on "the rock" (πέτρα, rather than, say, on "rocky soil"); there are no textual indicators that would suggest an allegorical or metaphorical identification of the rock. Does the narrator have in mind an area of a field with an unusually shallow topsoil, incapable of supporting growth? Is Luke simply too much of an urbanite to realize what interpretive problem has thus been introduced into the story?

30. Hedrick (*Parables,* 172-73) cites classical authors who outline similar hazards as those mentioned by Jesus as well as the anticipation of comparable harvests. On the latter, cf. Pliny *Nat. Hist.* 18.40.141, 162; Jeremias, *Parables,* 150.

Jesus' story was not immediately self-evident, at least to them. Three clues suggest the direction an interpretation might go. First, Luke has already begun the process of interpreting Jesus' story by his introduction of Jesus' speech as "parabolic." This description does not introduce the word "parable" as a technical term but insinuates, paradoxically, (1) that Jesus is using the obvious to shed light on the obscure and (2) that the form of his communication has its own enigmatic quality. His teaching has relevance, but it requires reflection, "hearing," a process Jesus will assist when he exegetes the story, beginning in v 11.

Second, the cadence characterizing the sowing phase of Jesus' story ("some fell, some fell, some fell . . .") draws attention to the prepositions used in each case: some fell *beside,* some fell *onto,* some fell *in the midst of,* some fell *into.*[31] Not least given the absence of any mention of plowing following the sowing of seed, only in the last case is it obvious that the seed has actually found its way into the soil so that it can produce a good stand and, eventually, a substantial crop.

Third, Jesus introduces into this story a set of categories that, although realistic in their representation of farming practices, are nonetheless overstated. For example, though seed planted on *any* soil is susceptible to the pillage of "birds of the air," in Jesus' story only the soil along the path gives up its seed in this way. Similarly, thorns grow on good soil as well as bad, yet "good soil" is distinguished from those conditions wherein thorns grow and keep the crop from maturing. In other words, the fundamental characteristic that distinguishes the "good soil" from other soil conditions is not the presence of hazards (since threats to crop production are universally present), but the production of a crop that reaches harvest.[32]

These clues, taken together with Luke's presentation of Jesus' address as a speech-event in which the broadcasting of the seed is actually taking place in his sermon, portend an emphasis on fecundity, a metaphor borrowed from the world of Galilean agricultural realities and applied to those who listen to Jesus' message.

9-10 The disciples' question indicates that, for them, Jesus' parabolic speech is enigmatic speech. Jesus' reply distinguishes between two groups, one that receives insight into "the secrets" of the kingdom, the other only

31. παρά, ἐπί, ἐν μέσῳ, εἰς; cf. Godet, 1:369.
32. See Hedrick, *Parables,* 173-74. One may go even further to point out that Jesus' point seems not to rest on the quality of the soil *qua* soil — i.e., he does not distinguish between soil types on the basis of inherent qualities such as those researched by soil scientists today. By analogy, then, he does not distinguish some people (or some group of people) as inherently receptive, others as inherently unreceptive. The word is broadcast widely (cf. 6:35), with people distinguished from one another only in retrospect, with reference to their obedience or lack thereof.

parabolic speech.[33] This is the only appearance of the lexeme "secret" in Luke-Acts, but the concept of God's (hidden but now disclosed) purpose is central to Luke's narrative.[34] Some are enabled to understand; others, whose worldview has not been reshaped by their orientation to God's purpose, can only puzzle over his message. In this way, Luke signals one of the leitmotifs of his narrative theology: the importance of interpretation, without which one cannot understand what they have hear (or read).[35]

In spite of such distinctions, the lack of a rigid barrier segregating the disciples and the larger crowd in Luke is conspicuous. It is true that the disciples request an explanation of the story of the sower, and it is true that Jesus addresses them ("to you," v 10) with his answer, so it might seem that we are confronted with insider-outsider categories. However, Luke records no change of scene, no separation of Jesus and the disciples from the others, and the presence of the crowds is assumed throughout (vv 4, 19). Hence, the narrative at this juncture allows no hint of private instruction. Jesus' answer is directed to the disciples, but it is given in the presence of the multitudes who had gathered.[36]

What, then, are we to make of the distinction between "you" and "others" (v 10)? The absence of a firm barrier does not denote the absence of any difference between disciples and others; rather, it insinuates the degree to which the boundaries between followers of Jesus and the crowds are porous. Thus, the allusion to Isa 6:9-10 in v 10 provides a scriptural rationale for the reality that some see and hear but do not perceive and understand, but it does not signal an insurmountable partition between those who respond in these ways. Although the devil may come and take away the word so that some might not believe and be saved (v 12), this is not God's doing or the outworking of his predetermination. Nor, given the practice of the sower in vv 4-8, should the failure of some to perceive and understand lead one to conclude that continued proclamation would be useless or that candidates for hearing the good news ought to be more carefully sifted. "Good soil," after all, is recognized as good only when its fruitfulness has become evident.

<hr />

33. Cf. C. A. Evans, *Isaiah 6.9-10*, 115-18. The use of δέδοται (perfect passive) designates God as the subject of this "giving." Luke's ellipsis — "but to others . . . in parables" — is completed in the NRSV with "I speak," through presumably the longer form would be "to others the secrets of the kingdom of God have been given in parables." Thus, the first group would be given the secrets that they might know God's purpose, but the others, having not responded to Jesus' message in faith (see below), would be unable to disambiguate those mysteries.

34. μυστήριον is used in the LXX in this way — cf. Dan 2:18-19, 27-30, 47; Wis 2:22; 6:22. See further Krämer, "μυστήριον," 447; Fitzmyer, 1:708. On the motif of the purpose of God in Luke-Acts, cf. Squires, *Plan of God;* Green, *Gospel of Luke,* ch. 2.

35. See above on 1:4; cf. 24:45; Acts 8:26-40, esp. vv 30-31, 35.

36. Similarly, see above on 6:20a; cf. 12:1; 16:1.

By the repetition of the language of the kingdom (vv 1, 10), Luke indicates the role of Jesus' story in interpreting Jesus' ministry. These remarks, understood within this wider co-text in which the necessity of authentic hearing is foregrounded, provide us with the categories and grounds for understanding the mixed responses Jesus has already begun to engender and which will increasingly characterize his ministry in the next chapters. What is more, inasmuch as Luke's literary achievement is to provide a narrative presentation of the realization of God's purpose in the ministry of Jesus, we must reckon with how the parable of vv 5-8 is enacted and reenacted with reference to Luke's audience(s) too.

11-15   Although Jesus continues to speak to the disciples, he does so within the context of the larger crowd that has gathered about him (see above). Having provided a vantage point from which to understand his ministry and the diverse responses to it (vv 9-10), he now turns to address more directly the question of meaning the disciples had raised. In doing so, he first situates his story in a network of interpretation, identifying the "seed" of the farming story with the "word of God" in the story of the realization of God's purpose in his ministry.[37] In identifying the seed as the word of God, he also grounds the meaning of his ministry in the ancient story of Israel. Yahweh was active in creation and redemption by means of his word, and the prophets were bearers of the word of God/Yahweh. In associating Jesus' ministry so intimately with the word of God (cf. 5:1), the narrative presents Jesus as the one who discloses and brings to fruition the divine purpose, in the face of which response is not only possible but mandatory. "To declare God's word is not merely to convey information but to implement a decision; the recipients of the word are permitted to overhear the declaration so that they may align themselves with it by trust or repentance."[38] In addition to these three stories is a fourth, the Lukan narration of John's ministry, echoes from which resound in Jesus' interpretation of the tale of the sower; these echoes serve only to accentuate Jesus' identification with the purpose of God and the necessity of

37. Like many redaction critics, concerned with a text's *Sitz im Leben* in the conditions and experience of the church of the author's day, W. C. Robinson ("On Preaching") identifies "word of God" with the church's preaching. Consequently, Jesus' parable becomes a way to rationalize the rejection of the church's message by outsiders. From a narrative point of view, such an identification is impossible, except insofar as the narrative goes on, in Acts (cf. also Luke 1:1-4), to portray Jesus' followers as servants and proclaimers of the word. Even then, however, the narrative role of the text is less to provide an apology for the rejection of the word by others and, as we shall see, more to encourage those who follow Jesus to hear *and* persevere in obedience to the word.

38. Goldingay, *Models for Scripture,* 210, with reference to the prophetic "word of Yahweh" in the OT.

a response that is manifest in behaviors that grow out of the alignment of one's heart with the redemptive plan of God (3:7-14).

Having drawn these stories into this interpretive complex, Jesus concentrates on the three possible outcomes of broadcasting the word of God: (1) no growth, (2) some growth but no fruit, (3) growth and bearing fruit. Growth, in turn, is linked to the twin attributes of faith and faithfulness.[39] In the first instance, faith is prevented by the intervention of the devil. In retrospect, one may find here a veiled anticipation of the agency of Satan, manifest in the activity of the Jewish leadership in Jerusalem, whose rejection of Jesus and his message leads to Jesus' execution.[40] In any case, Jesus' interpretation of the story of the sower, and thus of his own story, highlights the ongoing presence of an aim (or aims) that opposes the purpose of God. This explains why some might oppose the mission of Jesus. Jesus' words also prohibit any interpretation that might suggest that God had kept some from salvation; to the contrary, the message has been broadcast widely, but God has not decreed how it will be apprehended. Everyone may "hear" the word, but not all will believe and be saved (cf. 7:50).

Verses 13-14 outline different paths to the same outcome: initial but temporary growth. Why is this outcome emphasized by the provision of two illustrations? The potential of initial growth identifies those who have heard the word of God as disciples who go on to face threats in the form of trials and/or possessions. The "trials" of v 13 concern persecution or testing related to one's fidelity to God's purpose,[41] whereas the cares, riches, and pleasures refer to the drive for security apart from God and from the needs of one's neighbor.[42] Luke's characterization of the women who followed Jesus (vv 2-3) indicates that they have not fallen prey to this latter threat to the life of discipleship. The importance of one's comportment vis-à-vis opposition and possessions in the life of discipleship was developed earlier in the Sermon on the Plain (cf. 6:22-23, 27-35), and it will provide the foci for much of Jesus' teaching during the journey from Galilee to Jerusalem (9:51–19:27).

Not surprisingly, the "good soil" is identified by Jesus as those who, having heard, respond with faith and faithfulness. The motif of faith has already been poignantly underscored in vv 12-13, so it is not repeated here. Instead, Jesus' description focuses on the contrast between those who believe "only for a while" but "whose fruit does not mature" on the one hand, and, on the other, those "hold the word fast" and "bear fruit with patient en-

39. See Marshall, "Luke 8:8-15," 74.
40. See 22:3, 28, 31, 40, 46, 53; Acts 26:18; Chance, *Jerusalem,* 120; Green, "Demise of the Temple," 505.
41. See above on 4:1-13; also 22:40, 46; Acts 20:19.
42. Cf. 12:22-34; 16; see further above, §11.

durance." In doing so, he pinpoints the need for consistency of heart (or character)[43] and outward obedience (see 3:7-14).

"Authentic" hearing is thus presented as hearing that leads to faith, and faith that leads to behaviors consistent with the word of God. One cannot escape the fact that Jesus focuses so heavily on the possibility of short-term faith, however. This is a reminder that most who have determined to follow Jesus, including the apostles whom he has chosen, are still in the "possibility" or "probability" stage of the narrative. In some cases their lives may no longer be determined by their possessions (e.g., 5:11, 28), but within the narrative even these followers have yet to be tested. They have yet to demonstrate their competence as disciples. Jesus' parable leaves open the possibility that some will fall away, just as it furnishes the canons by which discipleship, or authentic hearing, can be measured.

16-18   Although the metaphor field changes abruptly, Luke registers no shift in topic. The central concern of Jesus' interpretation of the tale of the sower has been "how one hears." Having established the norms of hearing by which to determine authentic discipleship in vv 11-15, Jesus continues along the same lines by insisting that authentic (and inauthentic) hearing, although grounded in one's heart, is manifest in one's behaviors. The truism of v 16, with its list of bizarre attempts to conceal what is obviously meant to provide illumination, is just that, a saying with which everyone would agree. In the same way, Jesus argues, how one has heard the word of God cannot be hidden but eventually will manifest itself — either in practices appropriate to God's people (and outlined in the Sermon on the Plain) or in failure to do so.

Verse 17, with its language of what is hidden and disclosed, leaves open the possibility of another, complementary reading of these verses. When it is recalled that Jesus' audience throughout this discourse has consisted of both disciples and a larger mass of people, then Jesus' words might be taken as a reminder that his teaching is not esoteric but accessible to all. Nor is the sense of his message hidden. Understanding is available to any who choose to hear.

Both interpretations lead directly into the punchline of v 18b, wherein Jesus admonishes his listeners to attend to how they listen. In the first instance, Jesus' meaning would be, "How you listen will become evident to all, so listen well!" In the second, he would be saying, "The word is available to you, if only you will attend to it!" After all, as he has declared, some hearing leads to incomprehension, others only to short-term faith. Because neither yields any fruit, hearing of these varieties only appears to be genuine.[44] Even

---

43. Johnson, 133.

44. Luke thus uses the term δοκέω to speak of faith that is not authentic, but only seems to be genuine.

if the word of God is broadcast widely, then, it is perceived only by those who hear and believe, and whose enduring faith produces the fruit of obedience. What of those who refuse to believe, who only seem to have really heard the word? From them the devil will snatch the word, with the result that they neither believe nor are saved.[45]

19-21 The message of this unit of the Gospel culminates here, as Jesus articulates the basis of kinship with him. In his narration, Luke brings together threads from previous material. These include the need to clarify the nature of the company that has begun to coalesce around Jesus (vv 1-3), the presence of a large crowd (vv 4, 20), and the return to the cadence established in Jesus' interpretation of the tale of the sower: those who hear + outline of response (vv 12-15, 21).

Luke does not present members of Jesus' family in any way that would mark them as "outsiders" to his mission;[46] their distance from him seems unavoidable in light of the magnitude of the gathered crowds and their own late arrival on the scene. On the other hand, neither does Luke at this point present his mother and brothers as exemplary disciples,[47] though he will count them within the group of Jesus' followers after Jesus' ascension (Acts 1:14). Jesus neither rejects nor praises his physical family; rather, he uses their arrival as a catalyst to redefine in the hearing of his disciples and the crowds the basis of kinship. Kinship in the people of God is no longer grounded in physical descent, he contends, but is based on hearing and doing the word of God (cf. 3:8). More particularly, given the identification of the word of God with his own ministry (see above; also 5:1), the basis for kinship is now understood as sustaining a positive response to his message — that is, hearing and doing it (cf. 6:46-49).

4.5.3. Responding to the Power of Jesus: From Fear to Faith (8:22-56)

Although chronologically connected to Jesus' discourse in vv 4-21 only loosely, this new series of episodes continues to underscore the premium he has placed on one's response to the word of God promulgated in Jesus'

45. Note that both vv 12 and 18 use a form of αἴρω; the analogy of v 12 suggests that the implicit subject of the passive form in v 18 is the devil.

46. *Contra,* e.g., Schneider, 1:188; and even more problematic the view of Conzelmann (*Luke,* 58) that they, like Herod in 9:9b, have come to see Jesus perform miracles.

47. For this view, see Fitzmyer, 1:222-25; his emphasis on Luke's presentation of Jesus' physical family as model disciples does not keep him from seeing that Luke's primary emphasis falls elsewhere, on the "voluntary attachment involving the acceptance of God's word, which he preaches, as the norm of one's life" (1:723). *Contra* Fitzmyer's emphasis on the exemplary character of Jesus' physical family, see Bauckham, *Jude,* 51; Tannehill, *Narrative Unity,* 1:212-13.

mission. As Luke has ordered these scenes (cf. 1:1-4), Jesus first speaks parabolically to emphasize the need for hearing with a faith that perseveres (vv 4-21). This will now be followed by narrative exemplars of Jesus' parabolic speech. The word of God is being proclaimed in deeds of power, and people do respond differently — with fear and amazement, with fear and rejection, with the desire to join Jesus' band of disciples and obedience, with faith, and with astonishment.

The Third Evangelist presents these four miracle stories as a trilogy, with the latter two closely bound both by shared details at numerous levels and through intercalation (8:40-56). The first two are also constructed so as to shed light on each other, even if each also stands on its own terms. Thus, (1) they open with references to traveling to the other side of the Galilean lake (vv 22, 26); (2) both devote dramatic detail to the description of the calamity Jesus must face and conquer (vv 23-24a, 27, 29b-30, 32-33);[48] (3) in each Jesus issues commands to chaotic forces (vv 24b, 25c, 29a); (4) in both, Luke narrates the serenity that results from Jesus' intervention (v 24c, 35); and (5) in both, Luke records responses of fear (vv 25b, 35c, 37b).

These parallels hold the two episodes in interpretive juxtaposition, so that we may hear the one in light of the other. As a consequence, we may leave our reading of the boat trip across the lake with questions about the disciples. They have been given the secrets of the kingdom (v 10), but they seem to respond to this glimpse of Jesus' power no better than those in the region of the Gerasenes who have just encountered him for the first time. Will the fear of the disciples lead them, as it does these other persons, to rebuff Jesus? Why does the demoniac who has been rescued by Jesus recognize the word of God in Jesus in a way that seems not yet to be comprehended by those who are already "with" him, these disciples who are also rescued by him? The resemblance of these stories has a further ramification; it also suggests that we see the catastrophe overtaking the boat as it crosses the lake as an exhibition of diabolic power. This would undergird the view that the episode of Jesus stilling the storm is primarily cast as "a time of testing" for those who are already disciples (cf. v 13).

Where will Jesus find faith expressing itself?

4.5.3.1. Jesus Stills the Storm (8:22-25)

22 *One day he got into a boat with his disciples, and he said to them, "Let us go across to the other side of the lake." So they put out,* 23 *and while they were sailing he fell asleep. A windstorm swept down on the lake, and the boat was filling with water, and they were in danger.*

48. Cf. Sheeley, *Narrative Asides,* 101.

24 *They went to him and woke him up, shouting, "Master, Master, we are perishing!" And he woke up and rebuked the wind and the raging waves; they ceased, and there was a calm.* 25 *He said to them, "Where is your faith?" They were afraid and amazed, and said to one another, "Who then is this, that he commands even the winds and the water, and they obey him?"*

Luke indicated the itinerant nature of Jesus' ministry at the beginning of this larger unit (v 1). Without showing any necessary temporal relationship to the speech-event of vv 4-21 — indeed, without providing any additional motivation for this trip — Luke narrates the journey across the lake in a boat. This is Lake Gennesaret, mentioned earlier in 5:1, known outside of Luke's Gospel as the Sea of Galilee.[49] Previously, the sea was the setting for the display of Jesus' authoritative teaching and power (5:1-11). It will have a similar function here. Within that earlier episode, Peter had named Jesus as "Master," as the disciples do here; Jesus' power was on display in the miraculous catch of fish, as it is here in the calming of the storm; and Peter and his companions responded in fear and amazement, as they do here. If it were not for the co-text of the present scene, these points of correlation might be dismissed as unremarkable. Following the pointed emphasis on the insight given Jesus' followers and on the necessity of appropriate response in the previous section, however, these parallels divulge how little these first disciples seem to have grown in their faith since first joining Jesus in his ministry. This impression is born out by further details in the story.

Who is present on the boat? Because Luke provides no explicit evidence to the contrary, we might imagine the crew and passenger list to include the twelve and Jesus' women followers, as in vv 1-3; this seems unlikely, however. Although Luke's "boat"[50] might be used to designate a larger, seafaring ship, it is also used with reference to the smaller fishing vessels found on the Lake. The latter is in mind in 5:2, and we might be hard-pressed to imagine that Jesus, the twelve, Mary, Joanna, Susanna, and "many" other women (v 3) made their way onto a boat of this capacity. Moreover, Luke does not tend to be very specific in his use of the term "disciples," so that sometimes it is a synonym for "the twelve," at other times it refers to a larger group of followers, and at still other times to a much larger and less well-defined group. The twelve are probably in view here.

Luke's description of the near catastrophe in which the disciples find themselves is as dramatic in detail as it is realistic (v 23).[51] Even the disciples,

---

49. Luke uses λίμνη only in 5:1-2; 8:22-23, 33. See further above, on 5:1-2.

50. πλοῖον; cf. BAGD 673.

51. Cf. Plummer, 226.

some of whom were fishermen, declare, "We are perishing," and the magnitude of the storm is further emphasized by its being twice mentioned — first in v 23, when the disciples recognize their peril, then in v 24, when Jesus rebukes "the wind and raging waves." A further sign of the immediacy of real danger and the gravity of the scene Luke has painted becomes explicit as Jesus takes charge of the scene. He "rebukes" the wind and waves and is said by the disciples to have "commanded" the winds and water. That is, he confronts these apparently natural forces as though they were demonic powers (cf. 4:35-36). Not surprisingly, the OT sometimes portrays the powers of nature as demonic; what is of equal interest is that it also depicts Yahweh as Lord of the sea and his power over the sea as mastery of a monstrous, evil power.[52] Hence, as Jesus rebukes the storm he is acting as God acts, manifesting his authority over the powers of evil.[53]

As they wake Jesus, the disciples refer to him as "Master," employing a title that grants him the status of the authoritative leader of the group, but hardly suggests that they understand him fully.[54] Their lack of perception of either his power or purpose is further highlighted by Jesus' question to them, "Where is your faith?" Importantly, he does not describe them as faithless, but he clearly wonders why their faith had not shown itself in these circumstances. Against the norms developed in the Jesus' explanation of the tale of the sower, the disciples are portrayed as people who have heard the word but whose faith has not yet proven itself in testing (v 13).

In fact, Jesus is more than "master," in the sense of "the person in charge of this boat or of this group." This is evident in his response to the crisis of the storm. Luke's audience might have compared Jesus' actions with those alleged of Greco-Roman gods or heads of state revered as gods, who claimed or were thought to exhibit similar mastery over the sea.[55] Alterna-

52. Cf. Pss 65:7; 69:2-3, 15-16; 74:13-14; 89:9; 104:4-9; 106:9; 107:23-30.
53. This reading is supported not only by the vocabulary of Jesus' confrontation with the storm (which is identical to what we find in earlier stories of exorcism, 4:35-36: ἐπιτιμάω, ἐπιτάσσω), but also by the aforementioned linguistic and thematic parallels with the subsequent account of the curing of the demoniac (8:26-39). van der Loos (*Miracles,* 644-48) recognizes the cosmic conflict at work here, but he is cautious about the idea of seeing "many devils" at work in the storm. Our point, though, is not to suggest that demons were active in an explicit way in this episode, but to suggest that Luke sees those aims that are set against the divine purpose and that test the agents of God as diabolic. Jesus' stilling the storm is not an exorcism, in the same way this his cleansing a leper is not an exorcism; in both calming the storm and cleansing a leper, though, the redemptive work of God has drawn near to overcome evil in all its forms. Cf. Busse, *Wunder,* 200-203; Kirchschläger, *Jesu exorzistisches Wirken,* 88-89.
54. ἐπιστάτης is used in the NT only in the Gospel of Luke, in 5:5; 8:24 (2x), 45; 9:33, 49; 17:13.
55. See the materials gathered in Theissen, *Miracle Stories,* 99-103; cf. Nolland, 1:399.

tively, as we have noted, the OT tradition of Yahweh as sovereign of the sea was readily accessible to them. Jesus' companions in the boat react as they would to a theophany, with fear;[56] but their amazement,[57] followed by their uncertainty about Jesus' identity, indicates that they do not yet fathom what they have seen. They have had their first test (v 13) and have not performed well.[58]

4.5.3.2. Jesus Cures the Gerasene Demoniac (8:26-39)

26 *Then they arrived at the country of the Gerasenes, which is opposite Galilee.* 27 *As he stepped out on land, a man of the city who had demons met him. For a long time he had worn no clothes, and he did not live in a house but in the tombs.* 28 *When he saw Jesus, he fell down before him and shouted at the top of his voice, "What have you to do with me, Jesus, Son of the Most High God? I beg you, do not torment me"* — 29 *for Jesus had commanded the unclean spirit to come out of the man. (For many times it had seized him; he was kept under guard and bound with chains and shackles, but he would break the bonds and be driven by the demon into the wilds.)* 30 *Jesus then asked him, "What is your name?" He said, "Legion"; for many demons had entered him.* 31 *They begged him not to order them to go back into the abyss.*

32 *Now there on the hillside a large herd of swine was feeding; and the demons begged Jesus to let them enter these. So he gave them permission.* 33 *Then the demons came out of the man and entered the swine, and the herd rushed down the steep bank into the lake and was drowned.*

34 *When the swineherds saw what had happened, they ran off and told it in the city and in the country.* 35 *Then people came out to see what had happened, and when they came to Jesus, they found the man from whom the demons had gone sitting at the feet of Jesus, clothed and in his right mind. And they were afraid.* 36 *Those who had seen it told them how the one who had been possessed by demons had been healed.* 37 *Then all the people of the surrounding country of the Gerasenes asked Jesus to leave them; for they were seized with great fear. So he got into the boat and returned.* 38 *The man from whom the demons had gone begged that he might be with him; but Jesus sent him away,*

56. Cf. 1:13, 30, 50; 2:9-10; 5:10; et al.
57. Cf. 1:21, 63; 2:18, 33; et al.
58. Compare the confidence in the salvific power of God to rescue Paul and his companions at sea in Acts 27:13-44.

saying, 39 *"Return to your home, and declare how much God has done for you." So he went away, proclaiming throughout the city how much Jesus had done for him.*

The encounter of Jesus with the Gerasene demoniac is stitched into its narrative co-text by conscientious references to the boat excursion begun in v 22. Jesus had intended to cross the lake with his disciples; having done so, they now find themselves "opposite Galilee," stepping "out on land." The end of this section will have them making the return voyage. Although this narrative unit is part of the sequence of scenes held together by these references to a journey, then, its position at the midpoint of this sequence and its identification of the goal of Jesus' intended trip (v 22) portend its particular importance in this chain of episodes.

What is its significance? The first observation of consequence is the phrase repeated so often and in such variegated yet similar ways that it seems to constitute the melody of this pericope. This is the description of "a man . . . who had demons" and later, "the man from whom the demons had gone" (vv 27, 35; also vv 29, 33, 36, 38). The one who shares center stage with Jesus has no name in the narrative; his foremost characteristic is his bondage to and release from demonic power (cf. 4:18-19). If these variations on a theme help us to identify the melody, then the countermelody is recognized in the assorted clues that this is the first time Jesus has crossed over into predominantly Gentile territory. In this sense, the expression "opposite Galilee" is more than a geographical designation, even if it is significant at this level for the way it signals Jesus' crossing of the geographical boundaries characteristic of this section of the Third Gospel.[59] Gentiles have come to him, to be sure (6:17; cf. 7:1-10), but this is Jesus' first foray into Gentile country and, as will become clear, it is also his last.[60] That Jesus is now on Gentile ground is signaled in many ways, only the most obvious of which is geographical. One can also point to the heightened emphasis on things unclean — the demon is an "unclean spirit" (v 29), the man lives among the tombs (v 27), and there are swine and swineherds in the area that are clearly important to the local economy (vv 32-35). Moreover, the first words from the demoniac employ a title for God that Josephus regards as appropriate to the larger Gentile world of the Romans.[61]

At a fundamental level, then, this text concerns the crossing of bound-

59. That is, the Galilean section, 4:14–9:50; cf. §10.
60. Cf. Freyne, *Galilee,* 92-93.
61. That is, "the Most High God" appears in an imperial decree credited to Caesar Augustus in Josephus *Ant.* 16.6.2 §163. On the use of this title in this co-text, see further below.

aries in Jesus' mission, and more particularly the offer of salvation in the Gentile world. Within the larger narrative setting of this account, this emphasis is striking, for Luke thus portrays how the lessons of the story of the sower (8:4-21) are appropriate to the Gentile world too. Here is a man, first full of demons, then saved,[62] who responds as a disciple and becomes the first person to be commissioned by Jesus for missionary activity grounded in his own. This may not seem surprising in a Gospel that has documented the purpose of God to bring salvation in all of its fullness to all people. It ought to be remembered, though, that the divine purpose will not be achieved within the confines of the Third Gospel; instead, this narrative purpose reaches into Luke's second volume, Acts, for realization. It is worth noting, too, that Jesus' success in the region "opposite Galilee" is mixed; the former demoniac's proclamation of the divine activity evident through Jesus, God's agent, must be counterbalanced by the overwhelming rejection of Jesus by the people of the city. Seized with great fear, they ask him to leave their country. This scene is thus proleptic in its anticipation of both the power of the gospel and the opposition it will attract in the Gentile world.[63]

Luke's concern with order and knack for dramatic staging are both evident in his narration of this scene. Verses 26-30 may seem garbled in their presentation; in fact, they move back and forth in story time in order to underscore the immediacy of the confrontation between Jesus and the demoniac. Of equal importance for the rhetoric of the account is the careful, point-for-point correspondence between Luke's summary of the man's prior condition and his outline of his condition following the encounter:

a man had many demons (v 27) // the demons had gone from the man (v 35)
he had worn no clothes (v 27) // he was clothed (v 35)
he did not live in a house but in the tombs (v 27) // return to your home (v 39)
he fell down before him and shouted (v 28) // he was sitting at the feet of Jesus (v 35)
the demon seized him and he was out of control (v 29) // he was in his right mind (v 35)

As we attempt to come to terms with the ministry of Jesus on behalf of this man, we should add to these parallels that this man is almost surely a Gentile, and that, at the end of his encounter with Jesus, he begs to join the travelling band of Jesus' disciples (v 38). Clearly, when Luke reports that the man "had been healed" (v 36), he uses this word in its most profound and wholistic sense.

26-30 The itinerant ministry of Jesus, focusing on the communication of good news (8:1-3), reaches a new level in this scene. Jesus has temporarily

62. Verse 36: σῴζω; NRSV: "healed."
63. See, e.g., Acts 16:16-40.

left the region of Galilee, entering instead a region whose culture was more deeply rooted in Hellenism.[64] Jesus is among Gentiles, he is sharing a site with a herd of pigs, and Luke portrays him in an encounter with a man whose habitat was among tombs — a source of impurity for the Jewish people.[65] His earlier travels had led him into significant encounters with persons beyond the boundaries of what was considered appropriate on ritual or other behavioral grounds, but in this case Jesus has outdone even his own problematic behavior.[66]

Luke has staged Jesus' entry into the country of the Gerasenes[67] in order to highlight both the immediacy and challenge of Jesus' confrontation with the demoniac. In order to achieve his aim, the Third Evangelist employs three narrative devices: the studied rearrangement of the events constitutive of this account, the use of narrative asides, and the application of graphic detail, employing culture-specific indications of social deviance in his portrayal of the man's condition.

First, he transposes the order of events as they would actually have happened in the "real world":

Real Time	*Narrative Time*
(1) For a long time this man had been demonized and many times he had been controlled by demons.	(2) Jesus arrived.
	(1a) For a long time this man had been demonized.
(2) Jesus arrived.	(4) The demoniac fell down before Jesus and shouted.
(3) Jesus commanded the unclean spirit to come out of the man.	(3) Jesus commanded the unclean spirit to come out of the man.
(4) The demoniac fell down before Jesus and shouted.	(1b) Many times this man had been controlled by demons.
(5) Jesus asked him, "What is your name?"	(5) Jesus asked him, "What is your name?"

64. Browning, *Jerash.*

65. On corpse impurity, see above at 7:13-15.

66. In this instance, he has transgressed the perimeters of acceptable behavior to such an extent that no scribes or Pharisees are even present to monitor his behavior.

67. Not without good reason does Bovon (1:428, 434) opt for the reading, "in die Gegend der Gergesener," since Gergesa (Kursi) is located on the shore of the lake, whereas Gerasa (Jerash) is located some thirty-three miles to the southeast of the lake. The other choice in the manuscript tradition is Gadara, located five to six miles southeast of the lake, which at least possessed lands extending to the lake (Josephus *Life* 9 §42). The strongest manuscript evidence favors Γερασηνῶν (as in the NRSV), however; this is also by far the most difficult reading. Irrespective of how one settles this issue, for the Third Evangelist the chief concern is that Jesus has crossed over into Gentile territory, "opposite Galilee."

Such manipulation of the relation between the order of events in which they might actually have occurred and in which they are recounted is not unusual, but is integral to the narrator's craft (cf. 1:3).[68] In storytelling of all kinds, information may be delayed or brought forward in order to direct how a story is heard and interpreted.

In the real world, this man has a long-standing condition, with numerous instances of acting out on account of the demonic control exercised on him. Luke holds back this information, however, choosing instead to introduce this scene by focusing first on Jesus' arrival. He then allows one narrative flashback in order to explain the nature of this man from the city (v 27b). This allows him immediately to raise audience curiosity about this man. He is "of the city"? Why is he not there? The answer is also immediate: he has demons. In fact, his adverse condition is so advanced that he had crossed the boundaries of human decency. He had lost any claim to status; naked and living in the tombs, he was scarcely even human.[69]

A second flashback appears in v 29b, in the form of a narrative aside, wherein the narrator speaks directly to his audience. In this instance, the low esteem in which this man was held in the city is developed further. Uncontrollable, out of his mind, he was chained and guarded as a societal menace, like a wild animal. The strength of the evil forces at work inside of him is further underscored by Luke's observation that attempts at containment had been unsuccessful. The destructive power of the demonic on this man could hardly be portrayed more strikingly. Completely displaced from his community, living among the tombs, he might as well be dead. Moreover, the repetition of the words "demon," demons," and "unclean spirit" portend the development of this scene as an encounter of cosmic proportions. At the same time, having just seen Jesus display mastery over the monstrous forces of nature (8:22-25), we are equally convinced of Jesus' power and ability to save.

The order of events is manipulated again in vv 28-29, so that we read of the man's response to Jesus before we discover that Jesus had addressed the demon. The demoniac's actions, now under diabolic control, signal the tension of the moment of encounter. Falling before Jesus is a sign of reverence, even submission,[70] but the demoniac's loud shout suggests a defensive posture, even resistance.[71] The demoniac uses a question to issue a defensive directive: Let me alone![72] Within the Lukan narrative, the demon correctly

68. Cf. Genette, *Narrative Discourse*.

69. Cf. Hamel, *Poverty and Charity*, 73-75.

70. See 7:38, 44-46; 8:41; 10:39; 17:16; Acts 4:35; 10:25; 22:3; cf. Josh 10:24; 1 Sam 25:24, 41; 2 Sam 22:39; Pss 8:7; 17:10; 46:4; et al.

71. Cf. Theissen, *Miracle Stories*, 53-54.

72. The demoniac's words are reminiscent of the demonic behest in 4:34 (see above).

identifies Jesus as God's Son, just as the devil had done (4:1-13); and, in particular, as "Son of the Most High God" — preparing for the words of the demon-inspired slave girl in Philippi, who refers to Paul and his companions as "slaves of the Most High God" (Acts 16:17). Such language is known within Palestinian Judaism as well as in wider Greco-Roman circles; it is even used by the angel Gabriel with reference to Jesus in 1:32, 35.[73] Within this co-text, however, a more combative sense is probably to be understood. This demon finds himself in the presence of one related to "the Most High God" — that is, one more powerful than he, and more powerful than the one he serves. This is underscored by Luke's anachrony; only now (v 29a) do we discover that Jesus had commanded the spirit to leave the man, and this information is given in order to explain why the demoniac addresses Jesus in this way and begs him not to torment him.[74] That is, the demon's address is motivated by his recognition of his own inferior position.

Because the possession of one's name was considered equivalent to having power over that person,[75] it is likely that we should see the continued discussion between the demoniac and Jesus as the progression of a power encounter of enormous proportions. Rather than immediately departing the man, this demon attempts to negotiate with Jesus and, indeed, to gain ascendancy over him. Jesus counters by demanding, and receiving, the name of the demon: Legion, from the Latin term *legio,* designating a military unit of some 5,600 men. The significance of this term in this co-text is signaled immediately by the narrator, who interprets the demon's reply to mean that the number of demons who had entered the man was "many."[76] With this, the confrontation between opposing powers has reached its zenith, with Jesus the victor. Not only does the compassion of Jesus expand to include the Gentiles, then, but so also does his power and authority.[77] All that remains is the resolution of

73. See above on 1:31-33. In addition, Twelftree (*Jesus the Exorcist,* 82) refers to *PGM* 4.1067-68; 5.46.

74. That is, v 29 begins with the resultative γάρ.

75. See Aune, "Magic in Early Christianity," 1546; Twelftree, *Jesus the Exorcist,* 84; Stewart, *Demons and the Devil,* 214-16, 255, 284n.5.

76. That the number of demons active in a person is significant is assumed in 8:2; 11:24-26. Λεγιών may also suggest the organization of the demonic world (so Annen, "λεγιών," 345). The derivation of the metaphorical use of this term in the Roman occupation is of interest, for this presumably indicates the fear and abhorrence directed at the Roman presence, but the Lukan narrative gives no clues in support of Theissen's view (*Miracle Stories,* 255; *idem, First Followers,* 101-2) that this episode marks a "transfer of aggression" in which the story symbolically satisfies the desire to drive the Romans into the sea like pigs. Although the Empire can be portrayed as a manifestation of diabolic power, constraints within this local co-text point in a different, less symbolic, interpretive direction. On related historical questions, see Twelftree, *Jesus the Exorcist,* 84-85.

77. Cf. Talbert, 97-98.

the tension between the obvious potency of this demonic presence and its recognition of Jesus' mastery in this setting.

31-33 That the demons recognize Jesus' superior authority is evident from their request, which presupposes that they realize that he is capable of relegating them to the abyss. Just as they had used their power to gain freedom from the shackles and chains of those who sought to control their host, the demoniac (v 29b), so they now seek to avoid the abyss, that prison reserved for the punishment of demons.[78] The presence of swine further marks this scene as occurring in Gentile territory,[79] but this is almost incidental to their purpose in the narrative. Instead, they are introduced by way of the concession requested by the demons.[80] Jesus allows the transfer of the demons into the swine with the result that they, like the demoniac before him, are "driven" (v 29) into self-destruction. They are driven to their death, whereas, through their influence in his life, the demoniac had been relegated to an existence among the dead.

34-37 The presence of swineherds at the scene guaranteed testimony regarding the crazed behavior and demise of the pigs. Their return to the city (from whence the man hailed, v 27) provides for the additional witnesses of what Jesus had done for this man. Hence, the repeated phrase "what had happened" must be taken to mean both the drowning of the pigs and the healing of the former demoniac. Luke's narration is emphatic on this last point: this is the man who had been but no longer was demonized (see the repetition in vv 35-36). The descriptive phrases used to clarify what these people saw are culture-specific ways of indicating the reversal he had experienced. He had been uncontrollable, but now he is sitting at Jesus' feet; he had been naked, but now he is clothed; he had behaved as a demented man, but now he is in his right mind. His position vis-à-vis Jesus portrays his placid comportment in direct contrast to the behavior formerly characteristic of him. It also indicates his submission to Jesus and status as a disciple. Luke presents the former demoniac as a learner, sitting at the feet of his teacher.[81] His former condition of nakedness had symbolized his lack of status, his alienation from other humans; similarly, his clothes now signal his acceptance. His former comportment as a maniac has been replaced by self-discipline and meritorious dignity.[82] All of this is included in the description of

78. See *1 Enoch* 10:4-6; 18:11-16; *Jub.* 5:6-10; Rev 9:1; 20:1-3. Cf. *PGM* 4.1227-64 (though it reflects Christian influence — cf. Garrett, *Demise of the Devil,* 151n.22), wherein the demon is relegated to "the black chaos in perdition."

79. Cf. Lev 11:7; Deut 14:8; Luke 15:5.

80. Theissen (*Miracle Stories,* 75) notes how the tension between demonic resistance and capitulation can be mediated in exorcism accounts by the plea for a concession — in this case, to enter the pigs.

81. Cf. 10:39; Acts 22:3; Schürer, *Jewish People,* 2:334.

82. σωφρονέω refers to being reasonable or of sound mind, a condition that was extolled among the Hellenistic virtues; cf. *TLNT,* 3:359-65.

the change that has come over the former demoniac, and these qualities assist us in our attempt to understand the full extent of what it means for him to have been saved.

According to Luke, the response of those who have gathered from the surrounding country is to the transformation they witness in the former demoniac. Fear in the face of evidence of divine activity is expected in the Gospel,[83] but the fear of these people is not portrayed as a positive response. They have gathered from city and country (v 34), and now all from the region share in a common verdict. In fear they reject Jesus. Is this for economic reasons, as will be the case in the parallel in Acts (e.g., Acts 16:16, 19)?[84] In this co-text, Luke speaks of no motivation other than fear, and this fear seems to have nothing to do with the loss of the pigs. The offer of good news rebuffed, Jesus departs. Unlike the disciples in the boat (8:22-25), in spite of the unambiguous evidence of divine intervention before them in the form of their transformed acquaintance, these people seem not to have any faith at all.

38-39   Why does Luke record conversation between Jesus and the man after Jesus has already departed? Luke's dramatic technique is familiar to us from his account of Jesus' baptism (3:18-22). There as here he is able to clear the stage of all distractions by introducing a minor anachrony into the narrative. The camera lens is focused narrowly on the concluding dialogue between Jesus and the former demoniac. Asking to be "with him," he is requesting the same relationship with Jesus enjoyed by the twelve and the women who make up Jesus' company (8:1-3). Surprisingly, his request is denied — surprising, that is, both because others rescued from demons have been included (8:2) and because of the nature of the unprecedented task Jesus sets before this man.

Luke's introduction of this man had marked him as displaced, alienated from home and city (v 27). Now Jesus returns him to his home and gives him an assignment within his city. His healing, then, is not only physical and cerebral, but religious and psychosocial and vocational. He is restored to his community and given a commission. In speaking of his assignment, Luke employs two parallel phrases:

> return   + tell the story of how much God   has done for you
> he went + proclaiming   how much Jesus had done for him

Jesus thus gives the former demoniac the very task that Luke has exercised in the writing of Luke-Acts — namely, the "narration"[85] of God's mighty

---

83. See, e.g., 5:8, 26; 8:47.
84. So, e.g., Talbert, 98-99.
85. In 1:1-4, Luke uses the term διήγησις; here he uses the verbal form, διηγέομαι.

acts. What is more, the juxtaposition of these parallel clauses identifies this "narration" as proclamation,[86] the very task Jesus has been fulfilling throughout his public ministry in Luke (cf. 4:18; 8:1). Still further, it is pivotal to the narrative that this man hears in the directive to speak of *God's* activity a charge to speak of *Jesus'* activity. Unlike the disciples who are overcome with fear in the boat in the previous episode (8:22-25), this man, this Gentile — whose existence only moments before was determined by numerous demons and subhuman by almost any measure — recognizes Jesus as the one through whom God's salvific purpose is being enacted.

In other words, (1) the former demoniac is to have a share in the ministry of Jesus, and (2) telling the story of God's mighty acts on his behalf is to be the content of his proclamation. A more transparent anticipation of the ministry of Jesus' followers in Acts could hardly be found at this early stage in the Lukan narrative.[87]

4.5.3.3. Jesus Heals a Sick Woman and Raises a Dead Girl (8:40-56)

40 *Now when Jesus returned, the crowd welcomed him, for they were all waiting for him.* 41 *Just then there came a man named Jairus, a leader of the synagogue. He fell at Jesus' feet and begged him to come to his house,* 42 *for he had an only daughter, about twelve years old, who was dying.*

As he went, the crowds pressed in on him. 43 *Now there was a woman who had been suffering from hemorrhages for twelve years; and though she had spent all she had on physicians,*[88] *no one could cure her.* 44 *She came up behind him and touched the fringe of his clothes, and immediately her hemorrhage stopped.* 45 *Then Jesus asked, "Who touched me?" When all denied it, Peter said, "Master, the crowds surround you and press in on you."* 46 *But Jesus said, "Someone touched me; for I noticed that power had gone out from me."* 47 *When the woman saw that she could not remain hidden, she came trembling; and falling down before him, she declared in the presence of all the people why*

---

86. κηρύσσω.

87. For this emphasis in Acts, cf. Maloney, *Narration of the Works of God.*

88. The phrase ἰατροῖς προσαναλώσασα ὅλον τὸν βίον is included in brackets in NA[26], denoting its questionable status in the Lukan text. Discussion of this textual problem has led to no definitive conclusion, since the manuscript evidence favors omission but internal evidence favors inclusion (see the summary in Metzger, *Textual Commentary*, 145). However, its presence only heightens a motif already present in the text — namely, the hopeless situation in which this woman has found herself.

she had touched him, and how she had been immediately healed. 48 *He said to her, "Daughter, your faith has made you well; go in peace."*

49 *While he was still speaking, someone came from the leader's house to say, "Your daughter is dead; do not trouble the teacher any longer." 50 When Jesus heard this, he replied, "Do not fear. Only believe, and she will be saved." 51 When he came to the house, he did not allow anyone to enter with him, except Peter, John, and James, and the child's father and mother. 52 They were all weeping and wailing for her; but he said, "Do not weep; for she is not dead but sleeping." 53 And they laughed at him, knowing that she was dead. 54 But he took her by the hand and called out, "Child, get up!" 55 Her spirit returned, and she got up at once. Then he directed them to give her something to eat. 56 Her parents were astounded; but he ordered them to tell no one what had happened.*

This is the third in a trilogy of scenes in which the narrator has presented Jesus as a miracle-worker. All three are presented in order to illustrate the emphasis of the story of the sower on appropriate response to the promulgation of the word of God. Coming last, this one is the climactic in the series; here Luke exemplifies in the most explicit form thus far the nature of "saving faith." In doing so, he contrasts faith with fear (cf. 8:25, 35, 37), and faith that does not evidence itself in the midst of testing (as in 8:25) with faith that does.

The most obvious and important structural feature of this unit is the intercalation of the two episodes: The narrative of the healing of the woman suffering from a hemorrhage (8:42b-48) has been embedded into the narrative of the raising of Jairus's daughter (8:40-42a, 49-56). The relationship between these two episodes transcends concerns of structure. They are also tied together by numerous commonalities at the linguistic and topical levels — for example, falling before Jesus (vv 41, 47), daughter (vv 42, 48, 49), twelve years (vv 42, 43), desperate circumstances (vv 42, 43, 49), the fact and immediacy of healing (vv 44, 47, 55), touching (vv 44, 45, 46, 47, 53), impurity (flow of blood — v 43, corpse — vv 53, 54), fear (vv 45, 47, 50), and the inseparable connection between faith and salvation (vv 48, 50).

Through the technique of intercalation, the Evangelist presents the simultaneous unfolding of these two narrative events. Moreover, the interruption of the one story of healing by the other heightens the drama of the first. The little girl is dying; does she not need immediate attention? In fact, during the time lapse necessitated by Jesus' encounter with the sick woman the condition of Jairus's daughter completely deteriorates. Consequently, in the eyes of everyone except Jesus, by the time they have reached her home the possibility of successful intervention has already passed. The thematic and linguistic parallels enumerated above suggest that the appearance of these episodes in this form is not only for dramatic effect; these textual connections also urge that these accounts be interpreted together. Taken together, they document the sort of faith for which Jesus has been looking. Moreover, the completion of the one incident prepares for the finale of the other. After the abundance of healing power available in the case of the woman with a hemorrhage, might we not anticipate Jesus' ability to raise a dead girl to life?[89]

Expectations of this nature are even more firmly grounded in earlier segments of the Lukan narrative. This is because Luke's account of the raising of this man's daughter has several points of contact with the account of the raising of the widow's son in 7:11-17. For example, at the most basic level both are stories of resuscitation, both involve an only child (7:12; 8:42) who is therefore all the more valued, both contain echoes of the analogous Elijah-account (1 Kgs 17:8-24), and Jesus' words, "Do not weep," are replicated (7:13; 8:52). As such, both are understood as evidence of Jesus' messiahship and the extension of good news to the poor (7:22).

A further element characteristic of this narrative unit is the presence of the crowds, who are as ubiquitous as their role is ambiguous. When they first appear they are portrayed positively, awaiting Jesus' return and welcoming his arrival (v 40). Soon, however, they are described in a way reminiscent of the thorns of the story of the sower, as unwanted foliage growing up alongside sprouting seedlings that will eventually choke the desired vegetation. In the final scene (vv 51-54) unspecified bystanders laugh at Jesus, disbelieving his claims regarding the child, failing to recognize his authority to make such statements (and to make his words effective). The crowds are not portrayed as particularly malicious, nor are they presented as persons of faith, as persons whose faith is manifest in the harvest of perception and obedience. Against this backdrop, the woman with a hemorrhage is revealed as a person with faith that survives the test, and with faith that has human wholeness as its consequence. Similarly, even in the face of those who mock Jesus' claims, Jairus and his wife are able to put aside their fear and to embrace faith in Jesus' capacity to bring restoration.

40-42a In terms of setting and dramatis personae the contrast between this scene and the previous one (8:26-39) could scarcely be more blatant. From Gentile country, Jesus has returned to the land of the Jews. Rebuffed by people from the city and country, he returns to be welcomed by an expectant crowd. He had been in a situation that epitomized ritual impurity — interacting with a demoniac who made the tombs his abode, in close proximity to a herd of pigs, with no hint of any observance of the Mosaic law or the monitoring

89. Cf. Robbins, "Woman Who Touched Jesus' Garment," 502; Theissen, *Miracle Stories,* 184.

of the observance of others; now he is confronted with the need of a leader of the synagogue, one whose role it was to maintain the reading of the law and the teaching of the commandments.[90]

The juxtaposition of these two scenes is rich with interpretive possibilities. This is especially true given the generally negative portrayal of (1) rulers[91] and (2) those whose role it has been to monitor legal observance thus far in the Third Gospel.[92] This — together with the overwhelmingly positive response Jesus has just received from a Gentile, the Gerasene demoniac — might lead Luke's audience to imagine that the communication of the good news was no longer intended for such persons as Jairus (i.e., a ruler concerned with scriptural exposition and observance). The Song of Mary (1:46-55) had made it clear, though, that the eschatological transposition constituting the entry of salvation into the world does not include the humble in order to exclude the proud. Rather, the high and mighty would be brought down and the poor raised up in order that all might be enabled to respond with open arms to the redemptive activity of God. Crucial to Luke's narration, then, is that Jairus, though he is a "ruler," makes neither claim to advanced status nor demands upon Jesus; instead, he comes in humility with a plea for help. Nor does he intervene in Jesus' encounter with the sick woman, though she exudes ritual impurity. The Gentile centurion had expressed his lack of worth through emissaries (7:6-8); Jairus declares his humility and submission by falling at Jesus' feet.[93]

Luke is fond of male-female pairs, and this scene presents two important possibilities: the centurion's need was for his male slave (7:1-10), the widow's need related to her only child, a son (7:11-17), while Jairus was concerned for his only child, a daughter. At twelve years of age, she was at the point of puberty, near the age of betrothal and preparation for marriage,[94] and she was dying.[95] These details serve both dramatic and structural aims — namely, (1) to underscore Jairus's heightened concern and to nurture the pathos of this scene, and (2) to tie this healing episode to the next.

In light of developments in the narrative as a whole, we should not

---

90. Brooten, *Women Leaders,* 28; Yamauchi, "Synagogue," 782. See 13:14, which suggests that the synagogue ruler was responsible for the maintenance of faithful observance. Luke apparently regards ἄρχων τῆς συναγωγῆς and ἀρχισυνάγωγος as synonymous, even though there is some evidence to suggest that their roles ought historically to be distinguished (Brooten, *Women Leaders,* 15-30).

91. See esp. 1:52.

92. See esp. 6:1-11.

93. On the significance of this form of paralinguistic communication, see above on 8:26-30.

94. On these and related issues, see above on 1:27.

95. The sense of the imperfect, ἀπέθνῃσκεν, is ingressive.

regard the architectural details of this narrative opening as lacking significance. Since the onset of his public ministry, Jesus has generally met with opposition within the space delimited by the synagogue and from those, especially scribes, whose interpretive agenda are embodied in the teaching practices of the synagogue. More and more, then, Jesus will be found in homes rather than in synagogues, a condition that will be recapitulated in the mission of the early church according to Acts.

42b-44 No words pass between Jairus and Jesus in direct discourse, with the result that Jesus' response seems all the more immediate. The apparently short journey[96] to Jairus' home is not without incident, however. On the one hand, he must contend with the crowds, whose presence suddenly takes on a less positive or even benign look. They are "pressing in on him"; in the words of Jesus' tale of the sower, they threaten "to choke" him. That vv 14 and 42 are the only two places where this term, "to choke," is used in the Lukan corpus,[97] and that this account is calculated as a vignette illustrating Jesus' earlier tale, make it altogether conceivable that we should read the smothering action of the crowd as integral to the setting Luke is working to establish. According to Jesus' teaching in vv 4-21, faith on its own is not enough, for it must prove itself in testing. In these verses Luke will portray such a test — not of Jesus but, as will become clear, of the faith of the woman who comes to Jesus on a quest for healing.

On the other hand, there is the woman herself, whose behavior redirects Jesus' attention away from the needs of Jairus and his daughter. The woman whom Luke introduces provides the Evangelist with yet another opportunity to define "the poor" to whom the good news is brought (4:18-19; 7:22; 8:1). The simple fact that she is a woman in Palestinian society already marks her as one of relatively low status. In addition to this, she was sick, and her sickness, while apparently not physically debilitating,[98] was socially devastating. Her hemorrhaging rendered her ritually unclean,[99] so that she lived in a perpetual state of impurity. Although her physical condition was not contagious, her ritual condition was, with the consequence that she had lived in isolation from her community these twelve years. Her unenviable life situation is only underscored dramatically by this use of the word "twelve," indicating that she has suffered during the whole of the life of Jairus's daughter (v 42). Her prospects for renewed social intercourse had dropped to nil with her lack of help from the physicians. Whether her doctors had been the celebrated

96. This is implied by v 51.

97. συμπνίγω. The parallel in 8:45 uses the synonym ἀποθλίβω — its only appearance in the NT.

98. After all, she has suffered with this problem, presumably uterine bleeding, for twelve years.

99. See Lev 15:19-31; 11QTemple 48:14-17; *m. Niddah.*

physicians whose exorbitant fees made them accessible only to the elite or the quacks that exploited members of a naive and needy public,[100] the outcome is the same. To her otherwise sorry condition is now added a further factor: her material impoverishment.[101]

Her degraded status vis-à-vis the larger crowd could hardly be more pronounced; the same, of course, could be said of her need, which has been depicted as indeed grave. Just as the Gerasene demoniac had dwelled among the dead (v 27), so this woman exists outside the boundaries of the socially alive in her community. The press of the crowds guarantees that she will infect others with her impurity, and her aim to touch Jesus is a premeditated act that will pass her uncleanness on to him. What is it that motivates her to risk the rebuff of the crowds, of the synagogue ruler (who, we may presume, is walking with Jesus back to his home), and of Jesus on account of her social impropriety? This is the story of her resolution to cross the borders of legitimate behavior to gain access to divine power.[102]

The effect of touching Jesus' garment is immediate. Her bleeding stops, and so she experiences a reversal of her malady. As we shall see, however, though her physical problem may be cured, she is not yet healed.[103]

45-46   The significance of the woman's action is highlighted by the fourfold appearance of the verb "to touch" in vv 44-47. Its first importance is its ambiguity. Why did this unclean, disgraceful woman presume to touch one to whom even a synagogue ruler had bowed (v 41)? Even when interpreted in the most obvious (and negative) way available within the narrative, the damage she has done is not irreversible; the law contained a remedy: rites of purification for Jesus, a reprimand for the woman.[104] But Jesus does not adopt

---

100. Kee (*Medicine, Miracle and Magic,* 64) notes this distinction between the two classes of physicians available to the two groups of patients.

101. In addition, given her condition it is difficult to imagine that this woman is married. In this case, it is possible that we are to imagine that she had inherited money on which to live, money that is now in the hands of her unsuccessful physicians. This would have placed her in an ultimate state of risk. At the same time, it is always worth reflecting on the degree to which purity laws might have been relaxed as one distanced oneself from proximity to the temple and its cult. The realities of this woman's actual social situation in this (unnamed) village is impossible to reconstruct with certainty.

102. This analysis borrows from the insights of Theissen, *Miracle Stories,* 43-45, 74-80.

103. *Contra* numerous interpreters (e.g., Bock, 1:795). Working at both explicit and implicit levels of this account is an understanding of human wholeness that cannot be equated with biomedical definitions of wellness (see esp. Hahn, *Sickness and Healing*). As we have suggested, this woman's debilitating problem is not physical but religious and social. Until the latter is resolved, she will not be "well."

104. See Brawley, *Centering on God,* 184-85.

this reading; instead, he recognizes that her touch instigated a transfer of "power."

It is at this juncture that the real test of this woman begins, for Jesus calls upon her to acknowledge her actions to the whole crowd. In fact, at this point Luke's account is largely concerned with the movement of this woman from seclusion — the isolation first of ritual impurity and now of denial — to public proclamation. The crowds are pressing in, ready to choke faith as it sprouts (cf. vv 13-14); will she give in to her fear or respond in faith (cf. v 25)? At this juncture, the narrative is emphatic: All (including this woman) denied having touched Jesus.

One thing remains clear. In spite of what the disciples have seen, through Peter's response to Jesus we gather that they are not yet any closer to enlightenment. This is signaled by the nature of Peter's question, based on a lack of understanding. It is also indicated by the title with which he addresses Jesus, "Master." With this epithet Peter acknowledges Jesus' leadership, but little else regarding his identity or purpose.[105]

Jesus' reply to Peter concerns his "power." His usage here is reminiscent of Luke's characterization of Jesus in 5:17-19 and 6:19 as one in whom and through whose ministry the Spirit (or power) of God was manifest. Therefore, although his words may suggest the presence of magical power,[106] we must instead read this expression within the larger scheme provided by Luke's portrait of Jesus as bearer of the Spirit of God.[107]

47-48 Indeed, in his statement, "I noticed that power had gone out from me," Jesus presents two unspoken premises concerning himself — namely, that he is the bearer of divine power and that he is able to discern when it is conveyed to others. Perceiving the significance of Jesus' self-disclosure, the woman recognizes that hiding is useless.[108]

Why does she hide in the first place; and why, when she realizes that hiding is futile, does she let herself be known in "trembling"? It is important to remember that her touching Jesus was irregular and thus open to interpretation. How would the stifling crowds respond? How would the synagogue ruler? How would Jesus? Crossing the boundaries from the nonhuman world of socio-religious quarantine into the human world, and extending beyond the human world so as to access divine power is, on the one hand, a violation of the biblical purity code. On the other, it is an act of faith, or so it is interpreted by Jesus. In order for that faith to express itself fully, however, it must traverse

---

105. On ἐπιστάτης, see above at 5:5; 8:24.

106. Cf. Acts 5:12-16; 19:11.

107. See M. Turner, "Spirit and Power."

108. So Theissen, *Miracle Stories*, 135; also Robbins, "Woman Who Touched Jesus' Garment," 512.

the perimeters of the holiness code and overcome the stranglehold of the crowds, the disgrace of social banishment. In actuality, given her social position, her hiding and trembling are expected behaviors. So is her falling down before Jesus, a token of her humility (see above).

What is unprecedented and unanticipated is her touching Jesus in the first place, and now, even more so, her public announcement. Luke spares her no potential embarrassment. Her proclamation is before *all* of the people. Note, too, the content of her declaration. She is concerned with *why* she touched him; that is, she is presented as a hermeneut and not simply as one who chronicles what had happened. She also declares the immediacy of her cure.

Only now, in response to her public testimony, does Jesus commend the woman and pronounce that she is whole. Her cure was realized in the privacy and anonymity afforded by the crowds, yet (as we have observed) her real problem was a public one. Hence, he has her make a public declaration of her actions and her understanding of what she had done. Then, he confirms her story and verifies her healing, ruling out all possible interpretations of her unconventional behavior except one — namely, his view that it was an expression of her faith. Jesus' actions are calculated to signal, first, that her faith, tested by the boundaries of ritual purity legitimated by community sanctions, is genuine. Its authenticity is manifest in her willingness to cross the barriers of acceptable behavior in order to obtain salvation.[109] Second, he signals that he is not content to leave her cured according to biomedical definitions only.[110] He embraces her in the family of God by referring to her as "daughter," thus extending kinship to her and restoring her to the larger community — not on the basis of her ancestry (cf. 3:7-9), but as a consequence of her active faith. Now she is not the only one who knows what God has done for her; so do the crowds gathered around Jesus. Because he has pronounced her whole, they are to receive her as one restored to her community.

49-50 Luke returns to the episode with which he had opened this narrative unit, with the initial clause, "while he was still speaking," serving as the seam at the intersection of these two stories of healing. Because of the heightened drama of the encounter between Jesus and the hemorrhaging woman, Jesus' original destination must be brought again into the foreground. This is accomplished by the introduction of a messenger from the house of the leader of the synagogue. In the opening of this scene, Jairus's daughter had been described as "dying"; the delay caused by the exchange with the woman en route to Jairus's house prevents Jesus from arriving in time to heal the daughter. Her situation is beyond hope.

---

109. In this sense, her behavior is analogous to that exhibited in 5:18-20; 7:36-50.
110. Note that only in v 48 does the word σῴζω appear; in v 47 ἰάομαι is used. Of the two, σῴζω has the more expansive range of meaning; cf. *TLNT,* 3:344-57.

"Teacher," the title by which Jesus is known to the messenger, is generally a term of respect used by those outside the circle of Jesus' disciples.[111] In this co-text, combined with the instruction that Jesus need not "trouble" himself,[112] it marks the lack of perception as to Jesus' true identity and the redemptive power that characterizes his ministry.

Jesus' response to the message encapsulates the whole of the larger section constituting ch. 8 of the Gospel. Fear must give way to a faith that encompasses a proper recognition of Jesus' identity and concomitant trust in his ability to provide salvation.[113]

51-56 Thus far, even the disciples of Jesus have been slow to perceive who he is, but they were not the first to have questions. John the Baptist had wondered whether Jesus was the Messiah and, in support of this identification, Jesus performs miracles in keeping with the Isaianic vision of eschatological salvation, brings good news to the poor, and raises the dead. By these means, it is hoped, people will gain insight into the nature of Jesus' person and work (7:18-22). With the disciples as primary witnesses, Jesus has been about the same activities since 8:22, culminating in this episode in which he will raise a young girl from the dead. This explains why he takes only the child's parents and representatives of the twelve with him into the room — in order to assist their perception of him, in preparation for Jesus' question in 9:20, "Who do you say that I am?"[114]

Luke's narration is potentially confusing at this juncture. If Jesus takes only these five persons into the house with him, to whom does Jesus address his words, "Do not weep?" Who is weeping and wailing? Who laughs? This confusion is resolved when it is realized that the narrator has again reorganized his account for dramatic effect, ordering the events outside of chronological time so as to focus separately on two distinct discourses. One is concerned with Jesus' response to the crowds gathered to mourn the passing of the daughter of Jairus and his wife. As he had promised in the Sermon on the Plain, those who weep will have cause for laughing (6:21). In the present case, however, laughter is not grounded in the celebration of salvation Jesus had anticipated; instead, it is the laughter of those who mock Jesus' words. In interpreting the girl's condition as "sleep" rather than "death," he has made an authoritative claim they are unwilling to accept. Of course, in an important sense, the crowds speak the truth; the girl's death has already been reported to Jairus (and thus to Luke's audience), and is known by all who

---

111. See above on 7:40-43.

112. The messengers from the centurion use σκύλλω as well in 7:6, but there the content of their message takes a very different turn.

113. Green, *Gospel of Luke,* 106-7.

114. Cf. Nolland, 1:421.

have gathered. Capitalizing on the wordplay available to him in the use of the term "sleep" as a euphemism for "death,"[115] Jesus asserts that her condition is more temporary than the crowds might think. Rejecting his declaration, they also refuse to recognize him as one who might exercise the divine power of giving life.

The other discourse is centered on the girl and her parents, with the three disciples invited only as witnesses. First, Jesus crosses the boundary between life and death, between purity and impurity,[116] by taking the girl by her hand and commanding her to arise. The effect is immediate.[117] He directed them to give her something to eat both to provide material evidence of her resuscitation and to signify her restoration to kinship, symbolized in the sharing of food.[118] They, in turn, respond with "astonishment," a typical reaction to the wonderful activity of God.[119]

The growth of the crowds gathered to hear Jesus (cf. 8:4) has not been accompanied by maturation in the general perception of Jesus; indeed, the crowds seem actually to have served as a potential impediment to the communication of good news in these two episodes. Hence, Jesus directs the child's parents to be silent regarding her restoration to life. A mission of proclamation and healing is in the offing (9:1-2); what is not needed at present, though, is an increase in the number of persons attracted to Jesus on the basis of miraculous events such as these.

4.6. JESUS' IDENTITY AND THE NATURE OF DISCIPLESHIP (9:1-50)

The break between chs. 8 and 9 is not abrupt. In fact, the groundwork for the twin focus of 9:1-50, christology and discipleship, is laid in ch. 8, with its concerns with perceptiveness and active faith. This new section is distinguished from the previous one primarily by the explicitness of its portrayal of the disciples and by its heightened, even candid concern with Jesus' identity. Already in ch. 8, the presence of the disciples *with* Jesus had become more emphatic than at any other time since their being called in chs. 5–6. Now, however, they are active agents involved in the mission of Jesus, and they begin to be developed less as companions and more as characters in their own

---

115. καθεύδω can be used literally of sleep or figuratively for death (and figuratively for either physical or spiritual death); cf. BAGD 388.

116. On corpse impurity, see above on 7:14.

117. Luke thinks of death as the departure of one's spirit (i.e., "life"; cf. 23:46; Acts 7:59), so her resuscitation would dictate the return of it. Cf. 1 Kgs 17:21.

118. Cf. 24:30, 41-43; Acts 10:41.

119. ἐξίστημι; cf. Acts 2:7, 12; 8:13; 9:21; 10:45; 12:16.

right within the larger narrative of Luke-Acts. The end of this new section is clearly marked, with Jesus departing from his divine mission in the region of Galilee (cf. 4:14-15; §10) in order to begin the meandering journey to Jerusalem (see 9:51, 53). Consequently, 9:1-50 should be regarded as a transitional unit, bringing the Galilean segment of Jesus' ministry to a close and setting the stage for the next major stage of his mission.[1] With the closing of the Galilean section, the central issues of Jesus' identity and mission and the character of discipleship are on display in a way that renders necessary the more concentrated periods of discipleship instruction and formation that will characterize the journey.

As will become immediately transparent, the two grand motifs of this unit, christology and discipleship, are closely intertwined. This is because, as Luke presents them, these two are mutually interpretive. That is, one cannot embody authentic discipleship unless one perceives faithfully the nature of Jesus' person and work; yet, one cannot adequately comprehend Jesus' person and work apart from genuine discipleship. This raises the stakes on the key issue raised in ch. 8 — namely, the import of an appropriate reception of the word of God, manifest in the fecundity of obedience grounded in a vital and active faith in Jesus. At the same time it shows that the maturation of christological perception and authentic discipleship is a process. The tale of the sower, spoken parabolically by Jesus in 8:4-8, thus introduces an apt metaphor: growth leading to harvest.

§12 Christology and Discipleship in Luke 9:1-50

(1) Who Is Jesus? Concern with Jesus' identity or status is firmly rooted in the birth narrative (Luke 1:5–2:52) and in Luke's narrative of the preparation for Jesus' public ministry (3:1–4:13). That differences of viewpoint would be the order of the day was signaled in a variety of ways, not least in the juxtaposition of the divine point of view with the assumed opinion of the people: Is he "Son of God" or "son of Joseph" (3:22-23)? With the onset of the Galilean ministry questions about Jesus' identity appear with regularity — see, for example, 4:22, 36; 5:21; 7:16, 19-20, 39, 49; 8:25. In ch. 9, however, the issue of Jesus' identity breaks onto the stage in an unprecedented, if not unanticipated, way. Thus, the textual units comprising 9:1-50 revolve around the central questions of Herod ("Who is this about whom I hear such things?" [v 9]) and Jesus ("Who do the crowds/you say that I am?" [vv 18, 20]).

The issue of Jesus' status is explored in both implicit and explicit ways. Implicitly, one might wonder, Who is this who is able to mediate divine power so that others might exercise it (v 1)? Who is this who can provide for the multitudes (vv 12-17)? Moreover, portions of Luke's narration seem deliberately to recall the

1. Cf. O'Toole, "Luke's Message," 75.

prophetic tradition and, so, to identify Jesus in his prophetic role. For example, the accounts of the miraculous feeding, the transfiguration, and the disciples' faithlessness recall the feeding of Israel with manna in the wilderness, the experience of Moses on Sinai, and Israel's subsequent unfaithfulness in the creation of the golden calf.[2] More explicit echoes of the Moses-story also appear in vv 31 (where the topic of conversation is Jesus' "exodus") and 35 (with its portrayal of Jesus as the prophet like Moses; cf. Deut 18:15-18).

The importance of Jesus' portrayal as a prophet like Moses in Deuteronomy who recapitulates and consummates the career of Moses, and who thus leads the disciples on a journey, cannot be denied.[3] And its importance is underscored all the more by the pervasiveness of echoes of Moses and the prophetic tradition in Luke 9:1-50. This is not the whole story, however; indeed, for Luke it is a perspective in need of significant modification.[4]

Within the narrative itself — that is, in the interchange between various characters within the narrative — 9:1-50 puts forward a number of views related to Jesus' identity. Because these originate from different characters, we realize that the status of Jesus is contested and that differences of vantage point will yield different resolutions. Herod has access to popular answers concerning Jesus, and these are repeated by the disciples as they report on who the crowds regard Jesus to be: John, Elijah, or one of the ancient prophets (vv 7-8, 19). Jesus was anointed as a prophet (4:18-19), spoke of his fate as a prophet (4:24; cf. 13:33), associated his ministry with that of Elijah and Elisha (4:25-27), and was acclaimed as "a great prophet" (7:16). There is some substance to these reports, then, but Luke's audience knows that this identification is inadequate. John was presented as "prophet of the Most High" (1:76), but Jesus was presented as even greater than John (1:5–2:52). For his part, Herod is not convinced by these popular attributions, but he has no alternative to propose in their stead. He remains perplexed regarding Jesus' status.

Jesus' disciples, through the voice of Peter, seem to know that the opinions of the crowds are deficient. Hence, they declare Jesus to be "the Messiah of God" (v 20). When compared with the earlier words of God's messengers (2:11; also 2:26; cf. 4:41), this acclamation is shown to be correct, as far as it goes. That is, just because Peter identifies Jesus correctly does not mean that he has genuinely perceived who Jesus is — as becomes clear in v 33, where Peter refers again to Jesus as "Master." John does the same in v 49. This is the epithet the disciples have used previously in contexts wherein they acknowledge their subordinate role vis-à-vis Jesus but fail to comprehend his purpose or mission.[5]

Jesus himself uses the phrase "Son of Man" as a form of self-identification (vv 22, 26). In doing so, however, it cannot be said that he has provided a titular

2. Ravens, "Luke 9.7-62," 121.

3. See Moessner, "Luke 9:1-50"; *idem, Lord of the Banquet,* esp. 45-79. The centrality of the Lukan characterization of Jesus as a New Moses as this is developed by such scholars as Moessner is downplayed by Fitzmyer, "Composition," 146-47; O'Toole, "Luke's Message," e.g., 79n.5.

4. See Strauss, *Davidic Messiah,* 261-305.

5. ἐπιστάτης — cf. 5:5; 8:24, 45.

accounting of himself; the use of this expression does not by itself tell us much of anything about who Jesus is. Indeed, "Son of Man" appears less as a title and more as a technical term in Luke's Gospel.[6] Although it refers directly to Jesus, its meaning as a self-designation is thoroughly ambiguous apart from those descriptive phrases with which it is affiliated in specific co-texts. Here, it is developed in terms of rejection and death followed by vindication. It is probably not too much to say that Peter and the others fail in their understanding of Jesus because they are unwilling or unable to collocate their understanding of Jesus' messiahship with the possibility of his embodiment of his own message of the experience of reversal awaiting those who are hated, excluded, reviled, and defamed (6:22-23). Their constant reference to him as "Master" (i.e., *not* as "Benefactor-Lord," but as "overseer" or "chief" or even "boss") suggests that they have not made the connection between his words and deeds on the one hand and, on the other, his character and divine commission.

The matter of Jesus' status is taken up finally by God, whose presence in the narrative is marked by the overshadowing cloud of v 34. In a way reminiscent of the Lukan baptismal scene (3:22), God declares, "This is my Son, my Chosen; listen to him!" (v 35). With this, a constellation of images appears: Jesus is the Son of God, the Davidic Messiah; God's Chosen One, the Servant of Yahweh, whose suffering and vindication would serve the divine purpose; and the prophet like Moses, the leader of God's people. From this perspective, the unimpeachable perspective of God, Jesus is not simply a prophet or even the prophet like Moses. Rather, he is the Messiah, the Son of God. As such he stands in the prophetic tradition, identifying above all with Moses (and Elijah), and inaugurating the hoped-for redemption foretold and described in the language of the new exodus, by the prophets and especially by Isaiah.

Within this narrative section, prayer has a special role to play in the disclosure of Jesus' identity.[7] Significantly, it was as Jesus was praying that he was transfigured (vv 28-29), and this is the setting in which his status as God's Son is disclosed. Similarly, the question of Jesus' identity arises earlier in the unit "when Jesus was praying," and it is in this setting that Jesus' status as the Messiah of God is first articulated by one of Jesus' followers (vv 18-20).

(2) What Is Discipleship?[8] The importance of the disciples in this section is signaled immediately by the structure of the unit and by the sheer number of times they are named and appear as active agents. Thus, this unit begins and ends with instructions to the disciples (vv 1-6, 43b-50); the presence of the disciples is explicitly noted in vv 1, 10, 12, 14, 18, 40, and 43; and specific disciples are named in vv 20, 28, 32, 33, and 49. The fluidity of the term "disciples" for Luke is marked here; clearly, this unit is focused narrowly on the twelve apostles (vv 1, 10, 12, 28, 32, 33, 49), to whom the narrator can also refer with the broader term "disciples." Even though the twelve come in for special development, then, we are reminded that they are representative of a larger group who will also be involved in the instruction and formation this narrative unit anticipates.

6. See Kingsbury, *Conflict in Luke,* 73-78.
7. On this motif in Luke, see Crump, *Jesus the Intercessor.*
8. Cf. O'Toole, "Luke's Message"; Wilckens, "Auslassung," 193-94, 199-200; Green, *Gospel of Luke,* 103-4.

To data emphasizing the increased presence of the disciples we may add the nature of the roles in which they now appear. For the first time in the Lukan narrative, they share actively in Jesus' ministry (vv 1-6, 12, 40). Indeed, the portfolio of Jesus' disciples begins now to unfold in a way that adds content and vitality to their previous status as his companions. (a) They are empowered and sent out to engage in a mission the focus of which obviously reflects his own (vv 1-6). (b) They are instructed regarding personal comportment and social relations — particularly with respect to issues of kinship and status. Thus, they are to deny themselves, engage in daily crossbearing, welcome children, and so on (vv 23, 46-50). (c) Above all, the assignment given them is "to listen" to Jesus (vv 35, 44).

Luke's record of their initial successes notwithstanding (v 6) and in spite of their heightened role in the narrative, the disciples are presented as persons who continue to lack perception into Jesus' status and mission. Rather than depending on Jesus' benefaction, they assume that the crowds must dissipate to find food, or that they must buy food for the crowds, in spite of Jesus' earlier instructions regarding food and money (vv 3, 13). Peter and his companions fail to grasp the significance of Jesus' transfiguration (vv 32-33), the disciples' inability to exorcise a demon leads to Jesus' reproof of them as "faithless and perverse" (vv 40-41), they are unable to understand Jesus' teaching concerning his destiny (vv 44-45), they argue with one another over status (v 46), and one of their number seems preoccupied with boundary-keeping (v 49). These tokens of the blindness of the disciples have the rhetorical effect of grounding the lengthy journey, with its concentration on discipleship formation, in narrative necessity.

4.6.1. The Mission of the Twelve (9:1-17)

9:1 *Then Jesus called the twelve together and gave them power and authority over all demons and to cure diseases, 2 and he sent them out to proclaim the kingdom of God and to heal. 3 He said to them, "Take nothing for your journey, no staff, nor bag, nor bread, nor money — not even an extra tunic. 4 Whatever house you enter, stay there, and leave from there. 5 Wherever they do not welcome you, as you are leaving that town shake the dust off your feet as a testimony against them." 6 They departed and went through the villages, bringing the good news and curing diseases everywhere.*

7 Now Herod the ruler[9] heard about all that had taken place, and he was perplexed, because it was said by some that John had been raised from the dead, 8 by some that Elijah had appeared, and by others that one of the ancient prophets had arisen. 9 Herod said, "John I beheaded; but who is this about whom I hear such things?" And he tried to see him.

10 On their return the apostles told Jesus all they had done. He took

---

9. NRSV margin: "tetrarch"; cf. on 3:1.

them with him and withdrew privately to a city called Bethsaida.
11 *When the crowds found out about it, they followed him; and he*
welcomed them, and spoke to them about the kingdom of God, and
healed those who needed to be cured.

12 *The day was drawing to a close, and the twelve came to him and*
said, "Send the crowd away, so that they may go into the surrounding
villages and countryside, to lodge and get provisions; for we are here
in a deserted place." 13 But he said to them, "You give them something
to eat." They said, "We have no more than five loaves and two fish —
unless we are to go and buy food for all these people." 14 For there
were about five thousand men. And he said to his disciples, "Make
them sit down in groups of about fifty each." 15 They did so and made
them all sit down. 16 And taking the five loaves and the two fish, he
looked up to heaven, and blessed and broke them, and gave them to
the disciples to set before the crowd. 17 And all ate and were filled.
What was left over was gathered up, twelve baskets of broken pieces.

With the opening of ch. 9, the narrative revolves more narrowly around the relationship of Jesus and the twelve. Like 9:1, 8:1 had also mentioned the twelve as a discreet group, recalling the selection of twelve apostles from among the larger group of disciples in 6:12-16. It is significant that, though in some ways segregated within this larger group, the twelve have fulfilled no unique function within the ministry of Jesus thus far. Along with many others they have been Jesus' companions. Luke refers to them as "disciples" in v 14, reminding us of their affinity with the larger group of Jesus' followers, but his more focused concern with the twelve is marked by the appearance of more restrictive language ("twelve," "apostles") in vv 1, 10, and 12. The symbolic significance of the twelve as providing fresh leadership for God's people, noted in 6:12-16 (see above), is cultivated here; it will be actualized more fully in Acts.

Two narrative devices facilitate the reading of this unit of the Gospel. First, Luke has embedded the report of Herod's perplexity regarding Jesus' status (vv 7-9) within the account of the mission of the twelve (vv 1-6, 10). This intercalation provides an immediate co-textual constraint on how we are to understand the nature of what Herod has heard (v 7). He is concerned above all with the work of Jesus' emissaries.[10] Moreover, the shocking information

---

10. This actually makes good sense from a socio-historical vantage point. Even had Herod heard of the work of Jesus, the Galilean focus of one person's activity might have appeared relatively localized and nonthreatening to a Roman ruler. Luke narrates the dissemination of Jesus' message (in word and deed) by means of those acting on his behalf, however, and this is an altogether different matter that might merit closer scrutiny.

that Herod had beheaded John[11] raises the prospect of similar opposition, perhaps even a similar fate, for those whose activity is continuous with John's. In this co-text, via this narrative intercalation, then, the prospect of official hostility to Jesus and his apostles raises its head.

Second, v 10 serves to join together two episodes concerning Jesus and the twelve, with the one proceeding directly into the other. These two incidents are consequently juxtaposed and become mutually interpretive. One effect of this narrative strategy is to provide immediate legitimation for the ministry of the apostles, since theirs is described in the same way as Jesus' (vv 1-2, 6, 11). If the twelve are thus confirmed, they are also disconfirmed by this juxtaposition. In the first scene they are instructed to take nothing, not even bread and money — that is, they are instructed to put their faith into action in the crucible of missionary activity; in the second, however, their responses reveal a lack of faith regarding such basic provisions as food (vv 3, 12-13).

The design of Luke's narrative thus foregrounds the twin issues of the perception (or imperception) of the disciples and the identity of Jesus.

1-6   Jesus' parabolic tale of the sower (8:5-8) has been paradigmatic for the interpretation of people's response to Jesus as the bearer of God's word. In particular, Jesus has spoken of the disciples as persons who have some faith but who need to express that faith more fully in the midst of testing. The miracles of 8:22-56 were each performed in the presence of all or some of the twelve, providing them with fresh opportunities to grapple with Jesus' power and authoritative status. How will they respond? Will their perception be enriched? Will their faith manifest itself in perception and obedience?

Following a string of scenes wherein Jesus has been powerfully active to save, Jesus now involves the twelve more thoroughly in his ministry, thus placing them in the realm of the divine mission wherein their faith might bloom. Luke provides a series of three actions on the part of Jesus: he calls, empowers, and sends the twelve. Since the twelve have already been chosen in order to serve as emissaries (6:13), the weight of emphasis clearly falls on their being given power and authority, then commissioned for service. In 5:10, Jesus had said of Peter and his companions that they would be "catching people" — that is, participating fully in Jesus' ministry of bringing liberty to people.[12] Despite such potentially exhilarating prospects, until this point in the narrative Peter and the rest have been surprisingly passive, joining "with" but hardly working alongside Jesus.

11. To this juncture in the narrative, Luke has narrated only that Herod had imprisoned John (3:20); as recently in narrative time as 7:18-19 John was still (alive) in prison, communicating with the larger world via his disciples.

12. On the meaning of "catching people," and on the extension of that job description to Peter and his companions, see above on 5:8-11.

That a fundamental shift in the comportment of the apostles is marked in this text is evident from the straightforward parallels associating the apostles' work with Jesus' own. Thus, Jesus gives them power and authority, a combination descriptive of Jesus' own credentials in 4:36.[13] These terms had been used to describe Jesus' capacity to work on behalf of God to proclaim and bring salvation and to indicate that he exercises divine strength and prerogatives as one who is sanctioned by God himself. The same power and authority are now extended to the apostles, who will exercise them as participants in Jesus' ministry, in a way that points forward to the apostolic mission in Acts (cf. Acts 1:8). In particular, they are empowered with respect to ministries of exorcism and healing, a characterization reminiscent of Jesus' own salvific activity of release (cf. 4:18-19; 7:21-22). That the apostles are subsequently said to have been sent "to heal" and that they went "curing diseases" suggest, again, that Luke sees no firm distinction between exorcisms and healing, since both constitute liberation from diabolic bondage.[14] Indeed, their proclamation of the "kingdom of God" calls into question the ongoing potency of any other kingdom, particularly over the kingdom of the devil that works to enslave persons. The kingdom Jesus preached in word and deed, and so the kingdom communicated by his ambassadors, is the inbreaking presence of the reign and realm of God's saving activity to effect liberty in all its forms.[15]

In addition, when they are commissioned, they are sent to proclaim the kingdom of God and to heal — a combination already familiar to readers of Jesus' ministry in 4:18, 40-44; 6:17-18; 8:1-2. The shape of Jesus' ministry has been one that held in tandem both word and deed, and this is the form of their missionary activity as well. The subsequent report of their activity in v 6 combines additional descriptions of the nature of Jesus' mission; like him, they engage in an itinerant ministry (cf. 4:43; 8:1) in which they bring the good news (cf. 4:18-19, 43; 7:21-22; 8:1-2). Although Luke does not use the verb "to send" as a technical term throughout his work, in this co-text it clearly demarcates the twelve as Jesus' emissaries whose ministry is grounded in and an extension of his own.[16] Even if they will come into their own as active agents of divine salvation only following their commission in Luke 24–Acts 1, already the twelve are described as persons involved in the two

13. Cf. 4:32; 5:17, 24; 6:19; 7:8; 8:46.

14. Cf. Busse, *Wunder;* Green, "Daughter of Abraham."

15. See above on 4:42-44. On the kingdom of God in Luke, see further Carroll, *End of History,* 80-87.

16. They have already received the title of ἀπόστολος; the use of the verb ἀποστέλλω connotes "sending with a commission," and this nuance is supported by the parallels we have outlined. See also Hengel, *Charismatic Leader,* 74-75; Tannehill, *Narrative Unity,* 1:215.

primary foci of Jesus' missionary activity — proclaiming the good news of the kingdom and healing those who are sick and demonized.[17]

Within the narrative as a whole, then, this scene (and its parallel in 10:1-11) has a crucial role to play. The narrative need driving the Lukan story forward is God's own purpose to bring salvation in all of its fullness to all persons. Early on in the narrative, Jesus was presented as the one through whom redemption would come. Yet, as early as 5:1-11, with the calling of the first disciples to join in his ministry, it became obvious that others would be called upon to serve the divine aim. The potential contribution of these helpers has remained undeveloped; only vestiges of their nascent competence have been evident, manifest in their exemplary commitments to Jesus as demonstrated in their "leaving all" to follow him. At last, if only in a proleptic way, the twelve enter the performance stage of the narrative, at which time they begin actively to further the salvific will of God against all forms of bondage.

According to Luke, Jesus prepares the twelve for service with three sets of instructions. First, they are to "take nothing," a directive that Jesus will suspend in 22:35-36. Comparison of these two texts suggests that a key assumption behind these current instructions is Jesus' expectation that his followers will enjoy the same welcome as they travel through the villages of Galilee that he has enjoyed. During this phase of their apprenticeship, then, they are to depend on village hospitality. Already in vv 7-9, however, with their mention of Herod, we gain a premonition that the anticipated measure of popular reception and goodwill may be short-lived. Within its local co-text, these instructions regarding what to carry on the journey also underscore the importance of faith on the journey of vital discipleship. The twelve are not even to take an extra change of clothes, so to speak, trusting that God will provide not only the extra tunic if one is needed but also daily bread (cf. 11:3). A more pronounced statement against the possibility of having a lively faith "choked by the cares and riches and pleasures of life" (8:14) is difficult to imagine.

Second, having been welcomed into a home, the itinerant apostle is to remain there until the time of departure from the village. In light of the apparent concern with a faith undistracted by material goods in v 2, and in light of the known practices of some in the first century who abused the conventions of village hospitality to their own advantage,[18] this is likely a prophylactic admonition against moving from house to house in a village for the sake of better accommodations. Not only would this practice call into

---

17. Cf. Just, *Ongoing Feast,* e.g., 16-17.
18. On the concern in the early church with those who "make traffic of Christ," cf. 2 Cor 2:17; *Didache* 11–13.

serious question one's narrow focus on faithfulness to one's commission, not only would this indicate concerns counter to a faith in the ability of the gracious Lord to provide, it would also constitute a serious breach of conventions governing the social role of the guest that would bring the mission unnecessarily into disrepute.

Finally, in spite of his earlier instructions portending the positive reception the apostles might expect, Jesus warns them of the possibility of rejection, which he himself had experienced (e.g., 4:28-30), by advising them on how to respond in the case of the refusal of hospitality. "Dusting of the feet" was an act connected to ridding oneself of defilement, such as when one had traversed Gentile lands.[19] Ordinarily an action related to self-purification, here it is specifically interpreted as a performative testimony against the village — designed not, then, to render the traveler clean (again), but to declare the village "unclean." That is, Jesus' instructions, albeit in a subtle way, circumvent ordinary rules of purity by turning them on their head. Jesus performed no such act of self-purification upon his return from the land of the Gentiles and the domain of the unclean in 8:40, for he had found responsive faith even in the midst of impurity and rejection (8:26-39). No longer working narrowly with an ethnic definition of Israel as the people of God, he now declares that those who refuse the salvific visitation of God — present not only in his ministry but also in the extension of his ministry via these twelve envoys — are to be regarded as though they were outside the people of God.[20] As in Jesus' ministry so with the apostles', to receive the kingdom of God was to receive its heralds.

7-9 Into the story of the sending of the twelve Luke has inserted a brief report concerning Herod. This intrusion serves immediately to cast a dark cloud across the hopeful mission of the twelve, since Herod appears in the narrative "almost as a bad omen."[21] As a figure whose general reputation may presumably have been known to Luke's audience, Herod first appears in a narrative introduction set in opposition to the word of God at work through John (3:1-6); only verses later he is distinguished for his imprisonment of John (3:19-20). More widespread in the Gospel is a negative assessment of those in the narrative, like Herod, who make their appearance in their roles as rulers (e.g., 1:52-53). Subsequently, he will reappear in connection with the plot against Jesus and in connection with Jesus' death (13:31-33; 23:7-11;

---

19. Cf. Caird, "Uncomfortable Words," 41; Cadbury, "Dust and Garments," 269-71.

20. According to Acts 13:51, Paul and Barnabas actually followed these instructions upon their departure from Antioch in Pisidia. Cf. Schneider, *Apostelgeschichte,* 2:147-48.

21. Moxnes, *Economy of the Kingdom,* 59. Luke prepared for this reintroduction of Herod by mentioning him indirectly in 8:3.

Acts 4:27). Against this narrative sweep, it is difficult to regard his intrusion into the present scene as anything but menacing, portending the possibility that the apostles will share fully not only in Jesus' ministry but also in his fate. That his chief quality in this report is his "perplexity" only intensifies his presentation as one who opposes God and those agents who serve the divine purpose, for he is thus aligned with those who hear but do not perceive the word of God (cf. 8:4-21).[22]

What is it that Herod had heard about? As his jurisdiction was Galilee (3:1), it is not unthinkable that "all that had taken place" is a reference to the sum of the Galilean ministry Luke has narrated since 4:14. The placement of this report here suggests a more narrow referent, however, with the extension of the ministry of Jesus through the twelve providing the more immediate cause of concern. This more focused reference makes sense of the narrative, since the aggregate work of so many emissaries would raise the attention of the regional authority in a way that the work of one might not. It would also serve to identify the work of the twelve more closely with that of Jesus; like his, their message would thus be presented as the word of God which might be heard and perceived in diverse ways.

Herod's question, "Who is this about whom I hear such things?" presents the defining issue for this longer section; indeed, it is paradigmatic for the whole of the Lukan narrative, since crowds of all sorts align themselves with and against the purpose of God by their perception of Jesus and their willingness to identify themselves with him. Within this terse report, however, only popular opinion regarding Jesus' status is indicated. In the view of the crowds who have Herod's ear, Jesus' status is firmly rooted in the prophetic tradition, though there are differences of viewpoint even here. Apparently Herod believes he has refuted the possibility that Jesus is the resuscitated John by observing that he had beheaded John. For the narratee, this is new information, since when we had last heard of John he remained in prison (7:18-23). Why has the news of John's demise only now surfaced? In this way, Luke underscores what is already clear from the prophetic tradition — namely, the fate that awaits all of the prophets: rejection and death.[23] The Third Evangelist has himself ruled out the possibility of identifying Jesus with Elijah; though the ministry of Jesus is kin to that of Elijah in some ways, Luke thinks more along the lines of John as the Elijah-figure.[24] Such counterevidence should not be taken as a denial of Jesus' prophetic status, however. Clearly, the crowds have acclaimed him as a prophet (7:16), and many narrative details serve further to depict Jesus in prophetic garb (see above, §11). Hence, Jesus may

---

22. διαπορέω; cf. Crump, *Jesus the Intercessor,* 29.
23. Cf. Neh 9:26; Jer 2:30; Aune, *Prophecy,* 157-59.
24. Cf., e.g., 1:16-17; R. J. Miller, "Elijah, John, and Jesus."

be a prophet whom God has "raised up";[25] at least, the identification of Jesus within the prophetic tradition is plausible. Of course, whether this is all that can be said of him is another matter altogether, and, in any case, Herod seems less than satisfied with any of the answers provided him by popular speculation.

Herod's question, Who is this? is pivotal for the unfolding of Luke's narrative. Similarly, his quest to see Jesus anticipates his ongoing role in the narrative,[26] just as his bewildered reaction presages the hostile nature of that role.

10-11 Following the brief report concerning Herod's perplexity over the ministry of the twelve, the narrative returns to the apostles. Verse 6 had served as a summary, describing in a short space the passing of enough story time to allow for an itinerant ministry significant enough to attract the attention of the regional sovereign. Without providing any details or descriptions of typical encounters in their ministry, Luke simply notes that they return to Jesus and narrate what had taken place. Given Luke's use of this term elsewhere,[27] we may assume that the content of their account was focused on the great things God had done in the context of their missionary activity.

At one level, Jesus' attempt at privacy with his disciples appears as a foil to the gathering of the crowds. As he had expected that they would receive hospitality from others on the journey (v 3), so now he extends welcome and engages in a ministry of healing and of proclamation about the kingdom. This summary of his ministry is indistinguishable from the ministry in which the twelve had participated (vv 1-2, 6) — a reality that serves at least initially to blur even further any possible lines of distinction between their activity on God's behalf and his own.

Presumably, the presence of the crowds must also be regarded as unexpected and, therefore, intrusive.[28] When Jesus "withdraws," it is normally for the purpose of getting away from the crowds in order to pray; moreover, as we have seen, such prayer is regularly related to the nature of his divine commission and empowerment for ministry.[29] If a period of prayer was intended by Jesus, it has had to be postponed until v 18 by the crowds,

---

25. The NRSV may be understood to suggest that some thought Jesus was one of the ancient prophets who had been resurrected (ἀνέστη). This is possible, but it is more likely that this third theory is related to the popular viewpoint expressed in 7:16: God has raised up (ἠγέρθη) a prophet (like Moses). See Deut 18:15: προφήτην ἐκ τῶν ἀδελφῶν σου ὡς ἐμὲ ἀναστήσει σοι κύριος ὁ θεός σου . . . ; Acts 3:22.

26. Cf. 23:8: "When Herod saw Jesus, he was very glad, for he had been wanting to see him for a long time. . . ."

27. διηγέομαι — cf. 1:1-4; 8:39; Acts 9:27; 12:17.

28. Cf. Crump, *Jesus the Intercessor,* 26-27.

29. See above on 4:42-44; cf. 5:16; 6:12; 9:28-29; 22:39-46.

whose presence, then, would both delay Jesus' prayer and dialogue with his apostles concerning his status, and present, though their material needs, a test for the disciples (cf. 8:13-14). Having participated successfully as his fellow workers in ministry, do they understood fully who he is? Has their faith matured?

In fact, the failure of the twelve in the account of the miraculous feeding followed immediately by their exceptional perception into Jesus' identity (vv 18-20) raises forcefully the issue of how their understanding was mediated. What has happened to assist the disciples? One can point immediately to two things — first, the object lesson provided by the miraculous feeding (esp. v 17) and, second (and more importantly), the efficacious, revelatory character of Jesus' prayer (v 18).

12-14a Only when viewed against the backdrop of Jesus' prior instructions to the twelve does their request to him seem odd. Their location in the rural environs of Bethsaida[30] places them in close proximity to the possibility of food and lodging; why not take advantage of it? Jesus, however, had earlier instructed his disciples to take no bread on the journey (v 3); thus they were counseled to carry on the divine mission while trusting in divine benefaction and resources. Had they not trusted and been successful earlier? If one reaches further back into the Lukan narrative, one remembers Jesus' instructions on Simon's boat that had led to a miraculous catch of fish (5:1-11). If he was able to provide then, why not now? Even further back in the memory is Elisha's instructions to feed a hundred people with five barley loaves and fresh ears of grain (2 Kgs 4:42-44), the potential relevance of which is underscored by Luke's earlier use of Elisha-material to portray Jesus (e.g., 4:27). In light of their present location in the "wilderness,"[31] memories of God's provision of manna in the wilderness (Exodus 16; Numbers 11) might also be activated. In light of these narrative realities, could the twelve not continue to trust now, even if these fresh circumstances presented obstacles more severe than those they had yet faced? Against such a backdrop, the extraordinary nature of their request to send the crowd away is seen in their lack of any vocalized expectation that Jesus might be able to provide for their needs.

The disappointment of the apostles' initial behavior is further exacerbated by their response to Jesus' directive to them. Their resources are few, they respond, unless they are to buy food for the multitudes. But Jesus had already instructed them to take nothing on the journey — no food, as we have

---

30. Is this how we are to understand Luke's reference to Bethsaida (v 10) as "a deserted place"? This would not be the first time in the Lukan narrative that a city has been presented as the hub of a larger, rural area (cf. 8:26, 34).

31. ἔρημος; the NRSV's reading, "a deserted place," is technically correct, but misses the verbal resonances with the Exodus story.

seen, but also no money (v 3); how is it, then, that he might expect them to buy food? Indeed, if they carry no money, how is it that they inquire whether he wants them to purchase food? Have they money? Or have they sunk into sarcasm in light of Jesus' latest incredulous directive?

Luke thus appears to narrate this episode as a setback in the formation of Jesus' followers. The presence of the crowds and their needs is unveiled as a test to their faith, a test in the face of which they flounder. If the disciples' faith is not adequate on this occasion, this is surely due to the enormity of the problem with which they are confronted. The narrator seems to underscore this in a narrative aside at the beginning of v 14a: "For there were about five thousand men."[32] Against the meager resources represented by five loaves and two fish, the need is great indeed. The stage is thus set for a manifestation of miraculous beneficence of immense proportions.[33]

14b-17 The heightened role of the twelve signaled in v 1 continues in spite of the expression of their lack of faith in this incident. They participate actively in the provision of food for this huge crowd, first by organizing them for distribution and then by setting the food before the crowd. Although the vocabulary of "service at the table"[34] is missing, the conceptual field is clearly present, with the result that the vocation of the apostle is further developed as one of welcoming and providing for those in need.[35] (That the apostles are nonetheless oblivious to the significance of the assignment Jesus has given them in this miracle story is evident from vv 46-48.)

The actions accompanying Jesus' handling of the food are neither magical nor in some other way striking. They do not in any way forecast the miraculous benefaction about to occur. Nor are they related uniquely to the distribution of food at the Last Supper (22:19-20) or the later celebration of the Lord's Supper in the church. Taking, blessing, breaking, giving — these actions are those expected at any meal among pious Jews, in preparation for the eating of the food itself.[36] Other particulars of this text and its resonances

---

32. Does the narrative exclude women in this scene? Although the NRSV translation is possible, ἄνδρες is not used consistently within Luke-Acts for "men." It may be that we should read "people" here, though the accent of the narrative would remain on enormous need contrasted with paltry resources.

33. Cf. Sheeley, *Narrative Asides,* 101-2.

34. That is, διακονέω; Luke instead uses the term παρατίθημι, "to set [food] before [someone]." As a term for the extension of hospitality, it also appears in 10:8; 11:6; Acts 16:34.

35. Cf. 12:42-48, where the disciples are implored to be good stewards who distribute food to the servants under their care.

36. Just (*Ongoing Feast,* 159-60) is typical of those who see in the account of the miraculous feeding a prefigurement of the Last Supper. But this is neither a necessary reading, since Jesus' actions are in no way remarkable or in any way unique to the Last Supper scene,

are of greater importance in pointing to its meaning for Luke than these commonplace gestures.

First, in light of the aforementioned question concerning his identity, Jesus' involvement in a miraculous feeding ties him into the prophetic tradition (2 Kgs 4:42-44) and helps to portray him against the background of the story of Exodus (Exod 16:4-36). Second, the close association of Jesus' communication of the kingdom of God and healing with the miraculous feeding of the multitudes intimates that the latter is itself an expression of the saving activity of God.[37] In fact, Mary had predicted that the hungry would be filled (1:53), and Jesus had interpreted the meaning of salvation, in part, as the filling of the hungry (6:21). In lifting his eyes to heaven, Jesus had recognized God as the source of this meal — that is, as the gracious Benefactor of these needy people. Jesus himself is presented, then, as the one through whom God's benefaction is present. In light of this, it is surely of significance that no repayment is demanded from those who have received: the mercy of God is extended to all without reference to predetermined boundaries and without incipient demands for reciprocity (cf. 6:32-36).

Third, once the boundary-setting and boundary-maintaining function of meals is recalled,[38] the failure of Jesus and his disciples either to observe this role or otherwise to encourage the crowds to observe practices affiliated with it is startling. Here are thousands of people, an undifferentiated mass of people, some undoubtedly unclean, others clean, some more faithful regarding the law, others less so. The food itself — is it clean? Has it been properly prepared? Have tithes been paid on it? Where is the water for washing in preparation for the table? Such concerns are so lacking from this scene that we might miss the extraordinary character of this meal, extraordinary precisely because these concerns are so completely absent.[39] No attempt has been made by Jesus and the twelve, this representation of the renewal of Israel, to preserve the social boundaries that characterize first-century Jewish life. Again, Luke's narration underscores the degree to which God's benefaction is without limits.

---

nor is it particularly suitable to the narrative of Luke-Acts, which is surprisingly uninterested in what ecclesiastical tradition would come to refer to as the Eucharist or the Lord's Supper (cf. Green, *Death of Jesus,* 209-13; cf. Dunn, *Jesus and the Spirit,* 184-85; *m. Ber.* 6:1). This is not to deny the obvious and significant relationship between the account of the miraculous feeding and two other meals in the Third Gospel that employ similar language — the Last Supper (22:19-20) and the Emmaus meal (24:30); rather, it is to insist that those who thus read back into the miraculous feeding eucharistic overtones or a presaging of the Eucharist have begged the question of the significance of these meals *for Luke.*

37. Cf. Moxnes, "Meals," 159, 165-66. Cf. the eschatological promises of God's provision for his people in Isa 25:6; 65:13-14.

38. See above on 5:27-32.

39. See Moxnes, "Meals," 160-61, 166; Neyrey, "Ceremonies," 380.

Finally, Luke observes not only that all ate and were filled, but also that twelve baskets of leftovers were collected. This underscores immediately the magnitude of the miracle, together with the superabundance of God's good gifts (cf. 6:38). That there were *twelve* baskets full, within a narrative co-text wherein the presence of twelve apostles has been so emphatic (vv 1, 10, 12), insinuates further that the message of divine provision embodied in the miraculous feeding of the multitudes is intended for the twelve. The outstanding question, then, is whether they will "hear" this message. Will their hearing be one of genuine perception that manifests itself in the fruit of faith and faithfulness (cf. 8:4-21)?

4.6.2. Peter's Confession and the Nature of Discipleship (9:18-27)

18 *Once when Jesus was praying alone, with only the disciples near him, he asked them, "Who do the crowds say that I am?"* 19 *They answered, "John the Baptist; but others, Elijah; and still others, that one of the ancient prophets has arisen."* 20 *He said to them, "But who do you say that I am?" Peter answered, "The Messiah of God."*

21 *He sternly ordered and commanded them not to tell anyone,* 22 *saying, "The Son of Man must undergo great suffering, and be rejected by the elders, chief priests, and scribes, and be killed, and on the third day be raised."*

23 *Then he said to them all, "If any want to become my followers, let them deny themselves and take up their cross daily and follow me.* 24 *For those who want to save their life will lose it, and those who lose their life for my sake will save it.* 25 *What does it profit them if they gain the whole world, but lose or forfeit themselves?* 26 *Those who are ashamed of me and of my words, of them the Son of Man will be ashamed when he comes in his glory and the glory of the Father and of the holy angels.* 27 *But truly I tell you, there are some standing here who will not taste death before they see the kingdom of God."*

Luke's presentation of the inseparability of christology and discipleship reaches its acme in the tightly woven sequence of this narrative unit. In the moments following Jesus' acclamation by Peter as the Messiah of God, Jesus moves immediately from his clarification of the nature of his messiahship to his interpretation of the nature of discipleship. This topical connection is further highlighted by Jesus' observation that one's comportment vis-à-vis the Messiah/Son of Man in the present age determines one's status before the Messiah/Son of Man in the age to come.

In vv 1-17, the focus on Jesus' followers had narrowed so as to include only the twelve apostles; immediately following the present narrative unit, only particular followers, all belonging to the smaller circle of the twelve (vv 28, 32, 33, 49), are named. As a result, "disciples" should be taken as a reference to the twelve (as in v 14), but then, by extension, to the twelve as representative of the larger group of those who follow (and will follow) Jesus. This representational function is underscored not only by the more general need for disciples in all times and places to come to terms with Jesus' identity. Rather, Luke signals this broader reference in v 23 with his observation that Jesus addressed "them all" and with Jesus' opening words, "If anyone. . . ." By means of these narrative devices Jesus' question and invitation are pushed beyond the narrative to encourage among Luke's readers and auditors firsthand involvement in this discourse.

Peter's confession is a world away from the fear and astonishment of the disciples that earlier led them to wonder about Jesus' identity (8:22-25). Similarly, the deficiencies in the disciples' understanding of Jesus noted in the account of the feeding miracle (9:12-17) hardly prepare us for the clarity of this acclamation of Jesus' status. How does one explain the development in the disciples' understanding from 8:25 to 9:20? Was their witnessing of and participation in the feeding miracle sufficient to generate the enlightenment Peter manifests on behalf of Jesus' followers? This is often claimed. In fact, however, Luke records no response on the part of the disciples to the feeding miracle, and the current scene, in which Jesus is acclaimed by Peter as the Messiah, is not woven into the feeding account by any temporal, geographical, or explicitly causal connectives. Hence, even if causality is implicit in the narrative sequence,[40] the Evangelist provides no particular reason to think that the feeding miracle is more significant as an immediate cause of the enlightenment of the disciples than are the other miraculous events recounted in 8:22-56. Luke simply does not ground Peter's enlightened perspective in his observation of Jesus' powerful deeds.[41] Indeed, as repeated reference to the popular views of the crowds proves (9:7-9, 18-19), even though miraculous acts may put forward the necessary evidence, these are insufficient in and of themselves to lead to a correct interpretation of Jesus' status. What is needed is a lens through which to grapple with the meaning of these phenomena, and this is what Luke provides in his staging of this

---

40. Cf. Prince, *Narratology,* 11-12; Chatman, *Story and Discourse,* 45-48.

41. Cf. Strauss, *Davidic Messiah,* 252; Brawley, *Centering on God,* 27. *Contra* Fitzmyer, 1:763-64; Nolland, 1:434-35. Tannehill (*Narrative Unity,* 1:218-19) thinks that it was especially the eschatological associations of the feeding miracle that led Peter to recognize Jesus as the Messiah. The lack of clear causal connections between these two narrative units (just noted) and, more particularly, the absence of any explicit development of the eschatological significance of this meal tell against this conclusion. Given even these data, the question remains, How did Peter and the others come to this particular interpretation of Jesus' status?

account. He associates Peter's confession with Jesus' praying, as if to declare that access to Jesus' identity is supernaturally mediated.[42]

This does not mean that Peter and the others understand fully the nature of Jesus and his mission, only that they have moved beyond their former incomprehension, and certainly beyond the helpful but inadequate perspectives of the crowds. Following this appraisal of his status, Jesus goes on to nuance it further with reference to suffering and vindication, and to draw out the immediate implications of his status for the character presumed of those who would follow in his footsteps. In this way, (1) the miraculous deeds of Jesus that have characterized his Galilean ministry are fully integrated into his message of social transformation and transposition, (2) a fresh narrative need is established that focuses on the divine necessity of Jesus' execution and resurrection, and (3) a foundation is laid for the presentation of the nature of discipleship that will increasingly occupy center stage during the meandering journey of Jesus and his band of followers to Jerusalem in the Gospel's central section (9:51–19:27). Luke has thus begun to draw together the narrative threads of his portrayal of Jesus' ministry in Galilee at the same time that he establishes narrative needs that will occupy the narrator and propel the subsequent narrative forward.

18-20 The quality of Luke's narration shifts in a subtle way with the introduction of this pericope. From 8:22 to 9:17 he has used temporal and geographical markers to indicate the association of each pericope with the next. Now, however, his presentation takes on a more episodic look,[43] with the dialogue between Jesus and his followers only loosely connected to the preceding account of the feeding miracle. The report of Peter's confession is therefore more closely related to the material that follows — the transfiguration scene, the exorcism account, the passion prediction, and the argument concerning the relative greatness of the disciples (9:28-50) — than to the material that precedes it. As a consequence, this scene is determined above all by the picture of Jesus' praying apart from the crowds, with only his disciples present.[44]

The portrait of Jesus at prayer has already been thematized by the narrator, so that the mere mention of his praying is enough to draw onto the stage important interpretive associations. In particular, Luke has shown that it is in prayer that Jesus solidifies his relationship with God and receives guidance and empowerment from God.[45] Prayer as the setting for divine

---

42. Cf. Kingsbury, *Conflict in Luke,* 50; Crump, *Jesus the Intercessor,* 33-34.

43. Cf. 5:1, 12, 17.

44. Previously, when Jesus retreated for prayer, he did so alone (4:42; 5:16; 6:12); with the heightened presence of his disciples characteristic of ch. 9, they now withdraw with him (cf. 9:10).

45. See 3:21-22; 5:16; 6:12-20; Green, *Gospel of Luke,* 59-60. For the prayer motif in Luke-Acts, see the bibliography at 1:8-10.

disclosure is developed even further in this co-text, since prayer is antecedent to (1) Jesus' questions concerning his identity and (2) Peter's declaration of Jesus' messiahship.[46] The nature of Jesus' person and work is ambiguous; the work of disambiguation requires divine disclosure.

Jesus' first question and the answers he receives are reminiscent of the earlier report about Herod's concern over Jesus' identity in 9:7-9 (see above). This suggests the thematic nature of Herod's question,[47] but also prepares for the conspicuous and important contrast between vv 7-9 and 18-20: Herod is aware of public opinion, rejects it, but remains perplexed, unseeing, while the disciples are aware of public opinion, reject it, and go on to respond (accurately!) to the question of Jesus' status.

As we noted, Herod's continuing perplexity suggests his unhappiness with the options presented him; Luke regards them as inadequate representations of Jesus' status too (see above on vv 7-9). For Luke, although it is appropriate to grant Jesus the status of a prophet, such a characterization ultimately falls short. Jesus is more than a prophet.[48]

Jesus' second question, introduced with the adversative "but," indicates his own displeasure with popular hypotheses regarding his status that have been circulating. Indeed, he rejects those answers and calls upon all of his disciples ("you" is plural) to tender an alternative evaluation. As a result, for the first time within the narrative of Jesus' public ministry, a human being recognizes Jesus as God's Messiah. That is, though Luke's readers are aware of Jesus' identity as Messiah, this is privileged knowledge shared heretofore only by supernatural characters.[49] Thus, the prior usage of messianic language in the Gospel provides additional confirmation that, as the spokesperson of the disciples, Peter was able to come to this conclusion only as a consequence of the efficaciousness of Jesus' prayer of revelation.

What does it mean to refer to Jesus as the Messiah of God? Given that Peter does not go on to interpret his confession, his understanding of its nature is not at all clear. Luke's readers know (1) that Gabriel had identified Jesus as the Messiah in religio-political terms as the one who would exercise rule in an everlasting kingdom, (2) that Jesus has been anointed by the Spirit of the Lord (i.e., he is the Anointed or Messianic Prophet) in order to carry out the eschatological work of salvation, (3) that the unfolding of Jesus' anointed ministry had raised questions in John's mind about whether Jesus was the anticipated Messi-

---

46. Cf. Crump, *Jesus the Intercessor,* 22-25. See also 9:28-29; 10:21-24; 23:34, 46; 24:30-31.

47. Cf. Reid, "Prayer," 48; *idem, Transfiguration,* 96-97; Strauss, *Davidic Messiah,* 250-51.

48. See above, §12; Kingsbury, *Conflict in Luke,* 50-52.

49. Angels — 1:31-35; 2:11; God — 2:36; demons — 4:41. In 3:15, the people ask whether John is the Messiah.

ah, and (4) that Jesus had begun the work of interpreting the title not by denying its political implications but by redefining the nature of the politics that are grounded in and grow out of the message of the inbreaking kingdom of God. Jesus is the Messiah whose status encompasses but surpasses that of a prophet.

Does Peter (and do the other disciples) understand all of this when he acclaims Jesus as "The Messiah of God"?[50] Luke does not say; what Luke does maintain, however, is that Peter (and the others) could have known all of this and still not understood fully the nature of Jesus' person and work. This is because Jesus' divine commission continues to unfold. Having summoned this level of comprehension from his followers, Jesus now goes further to disclose even more concerning his role in the divine purpose.

21-22 In 4:40-41, Jesus had rebuked the demons and refused to allow them to speak "because they knew he was the Messiah." Superficially, Jesus' response here is similar. This correspondence does not mark the disciples as diabolic, however, because Jesus' warning to them is differently motivated than was his earlier directive to the unclean spirits. Nevertheless, the disciples' knowledge is thus designated as inappropriate, perhaps even dangerous, but this is due to the partiality of their information. Luke has coordinated the clauses of vv 21-22 so that v 22 provides the basis for v 21. The disciples must maintain silence *because the Son of Man must suffer and be vindicated.* This means, first, that Jesus' requisite suffering and vindication have not yet been integrated into their messianic conception,[51] and, second, that the time for proclaiming openly the messiahship of Jesus will come following the events Jesus has predicted. Jesus, then, uses this Son of Man–saying to adapt messianic belief to reflect more completely the whole purpose of God, and, in doing so, to introduce explicit narrative needs regarding his execution and resurrection, and to presage the proclamation of the "suffering Messiah" (e.g., Acts 3:17-18; 17:3) in the apostolic ministry of Acts.

---

50. From a narratological point of view, Dietrich (*Petrusbild,* 96-103) attributes too much to the expression "Christ of God": "das Petrusbekenntnis bildet bei Lukas die christologische Zäsur [including reference to Jesus' death and resurrection] im Leben Jesu" (103). Up to this point in the narrative, we simply have no firm basis for imagining that the Messiah, in order to be true to his divine mandate, must suffer.

51. The point is not, as many have argued, that the disciples have a "political" view of the Messiah and Jesus has an "unpolitical" or "apolitical" view that they must come to adopt. Luke's presentation of messiahship (and so of Jesus' ministry) *is* political — cf. Tannehill, "Kingdom"; Tiede, "Kings of the Gentiles." There is more support for the supposition that the disciples have nationalistic tendencies, but this does not surface until Acts 1:6-8; even then, Jesus does not reject their concern with Israel but refocuses their interests on the missionary task at hand.

"Son of Man" is used by Jesus in a self-referential but nontitular way in order to add nuance to the narrative presentation of his mission (see above, §12). Here this phrase is related to Jesus' status as one who serves the purpose of God (signified by the use of the favorite Lukan term, "it is necessary"),[52] and who does so by taking the path of suffering that leads to divine vindication.[53]

Those responsible for his suffering are not the Jews in general but the elders, chief priests, and scribes — that is, the Jewish leadership in Jerusalem in particular, those who constitute the sanhedrin.[54] This is the first appearance of the Jerusalem "elders" in the Third Gospel; they will reappear, typically alongside the chief priests, as agents of Jesus' denunciation and execution.[55] This is also the first appearance of the "chief priests" in the Lukan narrative; these priests were centered in Jerusalem and members of the temple elite; they appear in the narrative consistently as a group in opposition to Jesus.[56] Scribes (a.k.a. "lawyers" and "teachers of the law") from Jerusalem have appeared on the scene before (5:17); they, too, are cast in a negative light as those who test, accuse, take offense at, or otherwise oppose Jesus.[57] When appearing as a kind of triumvirate in the Lukan narrative, these groups are invariably joined in their hostility toward Jesus.[58]

23 From a description of his own fate, Jesus moves directly to the comparable life of the disciple (cf. 6:40). As dreadful as his destiny as Son of Man might be, those who choose to follow him may expect nothing other than the opposition that will become his trademark by the end of the narrative.

---

52. δεῖ; cf. above on 2:41-51a.

53. That is, ἐγερθῆναι is a divine passive, signifying that, whereas Jesus' suffering, rejection, and execution are at the hand of the Jewish council in Jerusalem, his resurrection is God's doing. Cf. the similar presentation of this reversal motif in the speeches in Acts (e.g., 2:23-24; 3:14-15).

54. Cf. 22:66; 24:20; Josephus *Ag. Ap.* 2.21 §§184-87; Schürer, *Jewish People,* 2:212-13. For the responsibility of the Jewish leadership in Jerusalem for Jesus' death, see Carroll and Green, *Death of Jesus,* 194-99; Weatherly, *Jewish Responsibility.*

55. Assuming the equivalence of the expressions "the elders," "the first/leading ones," and "the leaders," cf. 19:47 (οἱ πρῶτοι τοῦ λαοῦ); 20:1; 22:52, 66 (probably a reference to the sanhedrin as a whole); 23:13 (οἱ ἄρχοντες); 24:20 (οἱ ἄρχοντες).

56. 19:47; 20:1, 19; 22:2, 4, 52, 66; 23:4-5, 10, 13; 24:20; cf. Hurst and Green, "Priest, Priesthood," 635-36.

57. Lawyer(s): 7:30; 10:25; 11:45-46, 52; 14:3. Teachers of the law: 5:17. Scribe(s): 5:21, 30; 6:7; 11:53; 15:2; 19:47; 20:1, 19, 46; 22:2, 66; 23:10. Interestingly, though Luke can waver in his representation of the Pharisees, when appearing in the company of the scribes in the Gospel of Luke, they are always represented as hostile to Jesus (5:17, 21, 30; 6:7; 7:30; 11:53; 14:3; 15:2). That scribes are not always presented in a negative light, cf. 20:39; Acts 5:34; 23:9.

58. In addition to 9:22, see 19:47; 20:1, (19); (22:2); (22:52); (22:66); (23:10). Cf. Acts 4:5; 6:12.

This is not because Jesus is a masochist who embraces suffering, but because he is unreservedly committed to the purpose of God — a purpose that resists, and is resisted by, the habits and patterns and powers of the larger world. As the Son of Man fulfills God's design, he will encounter hostility and experience great suffering; can those who follow him along the path of God's purpose expect less (cf. Acts 14:12)? Jesus' message to his disciples portends a lifetime of discipleship as cross-bearing, not for the sake of suffering but because this is how God's salvation will permeate the world: undermining the enslaving power of coercion and the onerous burden of reciprocal obligation through daily refusal to engage in the world system. For Luke, then, the theology of the cross is rooted not so much in a theory of the atonement, but in a narrative portrayal of the life of faithful discipleship as the way of the cross.[59]

Jesus' summons to discipleship is not limited to the twelve, but is given "to them all." Within this narrative co-text, Jesus is speaking to the apostles (see above), but Luke's introduction signals the universal reach of his invitation.[60] Jesus' saying is expressed as a conditional sentence with the protasis (or *if*-clause: "If any wish to come after me") asserting what Jesus is taking for granted. His expression "come after me" connotes "discipleship."[61] The apodosis, or *then*-clause, outlines the content of this "coming after" Jesus. Hence, while Jesus' saying assumes that those to whom this saying is directed do in fact desire to come after him, his summons to discipleship does not contain within itself any judgment concerning the probability that they will in fact do so. This is a grammatical reminder of what has already become clear in the Lukan narrative — namely, hearing the word and even responding with faith do not necessarily indicate that one will continue in faithfulness. Note, for example, Luke's introduction of the twelve, one of whom "became a traitor" (6:12-16); note, too, the possibility that faith will grow, then wilt or be choked out (8:4-15).

Accordingly, discipleship entails radical self-denial, daily crossbearing, and accompanying Jesus. Because of the degree to which individuals in Roman antiquity were embedded in networks of kinship, the call to denial cannot be understood along strictly individualistic terms.[62] Rather, to deny oneself was

---

59. See Green, "Salvation to the End of the Earth," forthcoming; Barrett, "Theologia Crucis."

60. Cf. Caba, "Lukan Parenesis," 51; Tannehill, *Narrative Unity,* 1:222.

61. ὀπίσω μου ἔρχεσθαι; cf. 14:27; 21:8; Acts 5:37; 20:30; Schneider, "ὀπίσω."

62. See Malina, "Let Him Deny Himself." In this and other contributions to a social-psychological reading of the NT materials Malina describes the worlds of Greco-Roman antiquity and the contemporary West as polar opposites. At an elevated level of abstraction, this is possible, perhaps sometimes even desirable. However, there is a compelling sense in which self-denial in the midst of contemporary, Western, autonomous individualism would have meaning only with reference to a defining community, since the

to set aside the relationships, the extended family of origin and inner circle of friends, by which one made up one's identity. By "radical" self-denial, then, is meant openness to constructing a wholly new identity not based on ethnic origins (cf. 3:7-9) or relationships of mutual obligation (e.g., 6:27-38), but in the new community that is centered on God and resolutely faithful to Jesus' message. Taking up the cross in its Roman context would have referred literally to the victim's carrying the crossbeam of the cross from the site of sentencing to the place of crucifixion.[63] Within Luke's narrative, however, this act has been transformed into a metaphor by the addition of the phrase "day by day," signifying that one is to live on a daily basis as though one had been sentenced to death by crucifixion. In this sense dead to the world that opposes God's purpose, disciples are free to live according to the values of the kingdom of God proclaimed in Jesus' ministry. It may be of interest, too, that persons who had been legally condemned to death forfeited their estates and were denied burial.[64] In the wider Roman world, then, Jesus' metaphor would have spoken to Luke's heightened concerns with the peril of possessions and the pursuit of honorable status.[65] Disciples, then, are called upon to identify with Jesus in his suffering even if they are not necessarily to be sentenced to death on account of their witness for him.[66]

These first two actions, self-denial and crossbearing, appear in the aorist tense, conveying an action that is instantaneous and contains conceptually its completion. The effect of this verb tense is somewhat mitigated in the second clause by the use of the term "daily." These first two actions nonetheless stand in contrast with the third, in which the prospective disciple is called to follow, and to keep on following Jesus.[67] Along with "follow," a sense already present in the *if*-clause, one may think in terms of Jesus calling persons to "accompany" him on the road, a sense that is fully consonant with Luke's portrait of the characteristic activity of Jesus' disciples.[68] The present

---

individual "rights" (by which we today often give expression to self-identity in public discourse) we assert are typically actualized in relation to others. More generally, as C. Taylor has noted, we construct our notions of "self" always in relation to "webs of interlocution" (*Sources of the Self,* 36).

63. For descriptions of the practice of crucifixion, see Hengel, *Crucifixion,* 22-32.

64. See Tacitus *Ann.* 6.29.

65. In the Greco-Roman world, not to be buried was to be dishonored in an ultimate way. Note the contrast between the descriptions of the rich man and Lazarus — the wealthy man is buried, but Lazarus is not (16:22). Cf. Toynbee, *Death and Burial.*

66. In the course of the Lukan narrative some are executed on account of their witness — cf. Acts 6:8–8:1; 12:1-2.

67. That is, ἀκολουθέω is in its present imperative form, denoting continuous action in the present.

68. Cf. Caba, "Lukan Parenesis," 52; Luke 5:11, 28. On the Lukan portrait of the disciples "with Jesus," see above on 8:1-3.

tense of the verb "to follow," the present tense of the verb "to come," and the utilization of the modifier "daily" — these components of Jesus' call to discipleship stress the importance of persistence in the life of discipleship. We may be reminded of Jesus' parabolic proclamation of the tale of the sower, with its contrast between those seeds that fall on shallow soil or among weeds and those that grow to maturity and come to be known for their fecundity.

The importance of Jesus' call to discipleship extends beyond its presence in this co-text. Luke's observation that Jesus addressed his summons to "them all" points to a much wider audience than the twelve. The emphasis on perseverance in one's discipleship points to the ongoing character of the journey, one that begins with momentous decisions but is not content only with good beginnings. Jesus, we might think, is putting forward emphases that will occupy the disciples in the days ahead. In retrospect, the degree to which this logion and the further explanations of discipleship in vv 24-26 serve as introduction to the travel narrative, and, thus, to Luke's understanding of discipleship, will become even more transparent. This is because the content of Jesus' "recruiting speech"[69] is repeated during the journey (see 12:8-9; 14:27; 17:33).

24-27 Verses 24-27 are designed to draw out the meaning of the summons to discipleship in v 23,[70] and they do so by focusing on the disposition of one's life, symbolized first in socio-economic terms, then in the language of honor and shame. The key word, "life,"[71] refers to the totality of human life, which, paradoxically, is saved only when it is lost. This is, first, a reference to the denial of self (within one's social relations); forsaking previous forms of constructing the self gives rise to this new life, life in the new community of God's people. Second, Jesus makes clear that he is not calling people into a form of masochism, as though "losing" one's life was its own reward. Would-be disciples are to lose their life for the sake of Jesus. The pledging of life for the sake of another, for friends, or even for "the truth" already had a history in Second Temple Judaism and in Greco-Roman myth,[72] so Jesus is working with categories that would have been both recognizable and recognizably meritorious. What Jesus is asking is that people give up their lives — their relationships, their conceptions of the world, and the practices that flow from these — in order to follow him in his unreserved commitment to the salvific purpose of God. One cannot cling to this life and also serve the redemptive plan of God (see, then, the irony of 23:35, 39).

---

69. So Derrett, *New Resolutions*, 71-84.

70. Note the use of γάρ at the beginning of vv 24 and 25.

71. ψυχήν — used twice and referred to twice again through the corresponding pronoun (αὐτήν).

72. Cf. Hengel, *Atonement*, 4-18; Derrett, *New Resolutions*, 74.

Verse 25 is tied to v 24 by the common use of the verb "to lose," but the images with which Jesus is now working are financial. "To profit" and "to forfeit"[73] — these words stem from the world of commerce, and so constrain what Jesus means by "the whole world": He is concerned with possessions, whose potential for strangling faith he has already mentioned (8:14). Jesus thus uses the language of business dealings — at one level to highlight again the threat of possessions, and at another, more direct level as a symbol of the disposition of the self.

The importance of how one responds to Jesus' summons to discipleship is established in the vision Jesus presents in vv 26-27. The vision of reality Jesus has been communicating and seeking to establish is topsy-turvy according to the standards of the world-at-large, with the result that those who adopt it can expect ostracism, conflict, and social dishonor. The alternative would be to rebuff Jesus and his message so as not to suffer shame before one's peers. Although such a decision may be understandable for those who have not yet adopted Jesus' vision of the world, it is nevertheless the case that how one responds to Jesus now will determine one's position vis-à-vis Jesus in the future. He and his way may be rejected by "the elders, chief priests, and scribes" (v 22) now, but Jesus will be vindicated, and his vision of reality will be shown to be right. Those who are ashamed of him now will be shamed then.

The notion of vindication is found in the threefold reference to "glory" — the glory of the Son of Man, the glory of the Father, and the glory of the holy angels.[74] The glory of the Lord — that is, the visible manifestation of the power of God signifying God's presence[75] — was evident earlier in the narrative (2:9, 14; cf. 19:38). The Son of Man, we now learn, will come in a way reminiscent of the "human being coming with the clouds of heaven" of whom Daniel speaks (Dan 7:13), marking the end of the age (cf. Luke 24:26). No particular role is yet attributed to the Son of Man upon his coming;[76] all that is clear at this point (but this is very clear) is that — against all appearances, in spite of his ignominious demise and galling message (as these will

---

73. ζημιόω — cf. MM 273; κερδαίνω — MM 341. See *TLNT,* 2:159: "in the language of business and *diatribe, zēmia-zēmioō* are normally opposed to gain and profit, *kerdō-kerdainō.*" ζημιόω is often interpreted in relation to ἀπόλλυμι in v 25b; however, ἀπόλλυμι appears primarily to indicate how v 25 builds on and explains v 24; the sense of ζημιόω is thus established by its pairing with κερδαίνω. Cf. 17:31-33.

74. The Greek text uses the term δόξα only once, followed by three genitive clauses; hence, the NRSV is potentially misleading in its use of "glory" with reference to the Son of Man and the Father, but not with reference to the holy angels.

75. See above on 2:9.

76. However, the idea of the role of Son of Man as "judge" is probably implicit in the phrase "the Son of Man will be ashamed"; cf. Tuckett, "Son of Man," 209.

appear to those who do not share Jesus' understanding of reality) — it will become manifest that Jesus had in fact served God's purpose. Those who refuse to identify with him in the present, then, will have no share in his glory in the future.

Specific mention of "his glory" (i.e., the glory of the Son of Man) in v 26 prepares for and explains the saying in v 27. If Jesus' coming in glory signals the end of the age, this is only another way of saying that the kingdom of God has been consummated. When will "some" see this? In the immediately adjacent scene, three disciples "see" Jesus in his glory, the glory of the Son of Man (vv 26, 32). That is, those who witness the transfiguration of Jesus (vv 28-36) witness thereby, albeit in a proleptic way, the kingdom of God.[77]

4.6.3. The Transfiguration of Jesus (9:28-36)

28 *Now about eight days after these sayings Jesus took with him Peter and John and James, and went up on the mountain to pray.* 29 *And while he was praying, the appearance of his face changed, and his clothes became dazzling white.* 30 *Look! Two men, Moses and Elijah, were talking to him.*[78] 31 *They appeared in glory and were speaking of his departure, which he was about to accomplish at Jerusalem.* 32 *Now Peter and his companions were weighed down with sleep; but since they had stayed awake, they saw his glory and the two men who stood with him.* 33 *Just as they were leaving him, Peter said to Jesus, "Master, it is good for us to be here; let us make three dwellings, one for you, one for Moses, and one for Elijah" — not knowing what he said.* 34 *While he was saying this, a cloud came and overshadowed them; and they were terrified as they entered the cloud.* 35 *Then from the cloud came a voice that said, "This is my Son, my Chosen; listen to him!"* 36 *When the voice had spoken, Jesus was found alone. And they kept silent and in those days told no one any of the things they had seen.*

The question of Jesus' identity — raised explicitly in the Lukan report concerning Herod's perplexity (vv 7-9) and again by Jesus (vv 18, 20) — has not been fully resolved. In spite of the penetrating acclamation of Peter regarding Jesus' messiahship, followed by Jesus' interpretation of the nature of that messiahship in terms of the suffering and vindicated Son of Man (vv 18-27), more remains to be said about Jesus' status. This is true in large part because, as this narrative unit illustrates, Jesus' followers still do not understand ade-

---

77. See Trites, "Transfiguration," 77.
78. NRSV: "Suddenly they saw two men, Moses and Elijah, talking to him."

quately the one they are following. Nor do they comprehend what his status implies about their discipleship. The disjunction between the two scenes of confession and transfiguration is most conspicuous on this point — the profound difference between them on how Jesus is understood by his followers. Is he the Messiah of God or (only) the overseer (master) of the apostolic band (vv 20, 33; see above, §12)? Separated from Luke's account of Peter's confession by some eight days (v 28), these two pericopae are nonetheless bound together by a common concern with how the apostles construe Jesus' identity and by common emphases on the role of prayer in divine disclosure (vv 18, 28-29) and on "glory" (vv 26, 31-32); additionally, the opening phrase of v 28 ties this scene to the account of Peter's confession by drawing attention to the words of Jesus spoken in reply to Peter. In short, in the transfiguration scene Jesus and his words, even when they are unconventional or seem bizarre, receive divine sanction.[79]

Luke's transfiguration scene places a premium on the motif of sight. The "appearance" of Jesus' face changed, Luke's audience is invited (along with the apostles) "to behold" Moses and Elijah on the mountain with Jesus, these two OT figures "appeared" in glory, and the apostles "saw" Jesus' glory. Clearly, however, this "seeing" is not enough, for Peter and those with him are able to witness all of this yet still seriously distort the meaning of these phenomena. From "seeing," then, the narrative turns to "hearing" (vv 35-36a), after which, we are informed, the apostles told no one what they had "seen." Luke thus works in this scene with an understanding that is common in biblical narration — namely, "unaided human intellect cannot grasp history's significance. One who reckons to understand the past implies a claim to God-given insight into the matter."[80] The divine word illuminates; hence we may follow the narrative from the "seeing but not perceiving" of vv 28-34 to the "seeing and (beginning the process of) perceiving" in v 36.[81] The whole scene is thus cast as a moment of revelation.

This understanding of the transfiguration scene is aided by a virtual choir of intertextual voices whose presence is so forceful that they threaten to drown out the narrator's own voice. (1) Luke's model readers may well recognize his use of what have become stock expressions or conventional patterns borrowed from and based on the OT story of the Exodus (esp. Exodus 24–34) — for example, the presence of companions, the setting on a mountain, the explicit mention of Moses, Jesus' change of countenance, reference to

79. Cf. Brawley, *Centering on God,* 50.
80. Goldingay, *Models for Scripture,* 294; cf. Hall, *Revealed Histories.*
81. Incredulously, even following this divine disclosure, the apostles as a whole, including these three, will continue to demonstrate their lack of genuine perception (e.g., vv 41, 46, 49).

tents (or tabernacles), the cloud, the motif of fear, the clear allusion to Deut 18:15 ("Listen to him"), and the Lukan summary of Jesus' conversation with Moses and Elijah as having to do with his "exodus" (NRSV: "departure"). (See Acts 3:22-23; 7:37.) Because of the overwhelming presence of Exodus motifs,[82] the meaning of the terms and phrases used in this scene overflows the boundaries of a strictly denotative interpretation.[83] Although these (and other) echoes of the Exodus story are widely recognized, less appreciated has been the degree to which Luke's interpretive agenda has not been constrained by the story of Exodus but draws even more heavily on anticipations of the New Exodus in the prophets and especially in Isaiah.[84]

What is the significance of these echoes? It is worth noting at the outset that, like other Hellenistic historiographers, Luke has reflected in his writing a general perception of history as the arena in which certain types of situations and characters reappear. For Luke, if not for historiographers in general, this was due to his notion that historical events are divinely guided.[85] This means that the Evangelist will have seen in the mission of Jesus a virtual, divinely ordained, reenactment of the exodus from bondage. This assertion needs to be nuanced in a number of ways.

First, occasions of intertextuality are important both for the similarities they represent between old and new uses of an interpretive frame like "the Exodus," and for the differences accentuated all the more because of those similarities.[86] Hence, it will not do simply to draw an equation between Jesus and Moses or between Jesus' journey and that of Moses and Israel, and so on. Nor will it do to read the Lukan narrative against the background of the Pentateuch as though the Exodus story had not been interpreted and reinterpreted — in eschatological, mythological, and other ways — in the interim.[87] Addi-

---

82. Of course, taken individually, most of these motifs and expressions can be found in other co-texts unrelated to the Exodus. It is their presence in aggregate that points to their derivation from the story or interpretation of the Exodus.

83. On stylistic overcoding of this nature, see Eco, *Role of the Reader,* 19-22. The presence of echoes of the Exodus story in this scene is widely acknowledged; for details, see, e.g., Schürmann, 1:553-67; Ringe, "Luke 9:28-36"; Strauss, *Davidic Messiah,* 268-72. Moessner (*Lord of the Banquet,* 60-69) develops similar parallels with reference to the portrait of Moses in Deuteronomy. The attempt to downplay such echoes by Reid (*Transfiguration,* 99-143) is due largely to her apparent view that to allow for Mosaic echoes would disallow other interpretive possibilities.

84. See Garrett, "Exodus from Bondage"; *idem,* "Jesus' Death," 11-12; Strauss, *Davidic Messiah,* 285-305. Garrett and Strauss apparently arrive at this conclusion independently, but they develop the significance of this interpretive background along different lines. Both indicate the presence of related interpretation in Second Temple Judaism.

85. Trompf, *Idea of Historical Recurrence,* 129, 315.

86. Cf. Tannen, "What's in a Frame?"

87. Cf., e.g., Isa 51:9-11; Jeremiah 23; *Pss. Sol.* 11:2-5; 1QM 11:7c-10a; et al.

tionally, uses of pretexts like the Exodus story within the Lukan narrative help to augment and/or regulate meaning, but those pretexts are themselves given fresh meaning within their new co-texts. Read within Luke-Acts, these echoes are shaped definitively by the mission statement of Jesus in 4:18-19 as it has been developed within the narrative thus far. Consequently, the transfiguration scene calls upon this choir of voices especially to stress the image of Jesus as liberator from bondage, his ministry as one of release from captivity in all its guises. How is this release accomplished? Clearly, release has already been available in Jesus' itinerant ministry in Galilee and in the extension of that ministry in the missionary activity of the twelve. Luke's account of the transfiguration does nothing to discount the effectiveness of Jesus' powerful ministry of liberation heretofore, but does go on to intimate the redemptive power of his upcoming journey through death to exaltation.

(2) The voices of Exodus are not the only ones to be discerned in this text. Also present are echoes from within the Lukan narrative itself. Thus, by way of such motifs as the recognition of Jesus as God's Son, the presence of a heavenly voice, prayer, Jesus' glory, drowsy disciples, the importance of "sight," the clouds, the presence of "two men," and so on, one may recognize in the transfiguration account echoes of earlier and later scenes in the Gospel and Acts: the baptism of Jesus, his temptation in the wilderness, the confession of Peter, his agony in the garden, the resurrection, the ascension, and the anticipation of his parousia.[88] These internal reverberations are important for what they emphasize about this scene — namely, the way it (a) summarizes critical issues related to Jesus' status in relation to God, (b) proleptically alerts representative apostles to the full significance of his heavenly status, and (c) supplies the apostles (and Luke's audience) with an interpretive framework for making sense of the ensuing narrative, including the fulfillment of Jesus' predicted suffering and death. As Jesus promised (v 27), these apostles have now seen, if only for a moment, the consummation of the kingdom, for they have seen the Son, the Chosen One, Jesus, in his glory.

28-29 The opening both separates temporally and associates thematically the transfiguration scene and the previous account of Peter's confession. Luke thus underscores the importance of Jesus' words and indicates that the scene now unfolding somehow builds on Jesus' teaching about his destiny and the shape of discipleship.

Peter, John, and James were segregated from the others in 8:51 (cf. Acts 1:13), too; in the future Peter and John will be paired as servants and

---

88. These connections are also widely noted. See, e.g., Caird, "Transfiguration," 292; Trites, "Transfiguration," 75-78; Ringe, "Luke 9:28-36," 86-87; Reid, *Transfiguration*, 95-96.

leaders.[89] Following notations of time and dramatis personae, Luke furthers his setting of the scene with reference to their ascent of an unnamed mountain, a location often associated with theophanic episodes and divine revelation.[90] With Luke's emphatic reference to Jesus at prayer, the backdrop is complete. The importance of this last note is difficult to overstate. Not only is prayer mentioned twice, but this reference follows hard on the heels of the parallel reference in v 18, where prayer is represented as the setting for divine disclosure. In fact, through the use of the participial form, Luke has it that *while Jesus was praying* he was transfigured (cf. 3:21-22).

The nature of this revelatory scene is found initially in the report of Jesus' "change of face" and "dazzling" clothes, then explicitly in v 32, where the effect of his transformation is that his followers are able to behold "his glory." In OT and Jewish tradition, one's countenance is a mirror of one's heart and a manifestation of one's relationship to God.[91] Throughout Luke-Acts, clothes are a signifier of status, dazzling clothes denoting heavenly glory.[92] Luke's point, then, is not that Jesus experienced an internal adjustment of some sort that led to his transformed appearance, but that his inner being was made transparent to those who accompanied him. In other words, the change Luke describes is a disclosure of Jesus' status — not to Jesus, who already exercised authority on God's behalf and, in any case, seems unconcerned about such issues; not to Luke's audience, who already knows that Jesus is God's Son by way of his miraculous conception (1:31-35); but to Jesus' followers. That is, as in the previous episode, the revelation is primarily for the benefit of those who accompany Jesus, not for Jesus himself.[93] The transfiguration scene, then, is primarily about legitimation, as Jesus' glory, the glory that will be manifest upon his exaltation, is proleptically unveiled.[94]

---

89. See 22:8; Acts 3:1, 3, 4, 11; et al. See Schürmann, "Dienst des Petrus und Johannes"; Green, "Preparation for Passover," 313.

90. See 6:12; 22:39; Allison Jr., "Mountain and Wilderness," 563.

91. See, e.g., Acts 6:15; Exod 34:29-30; 1 Sam 1:9-18; Ps 34:5-6; Dan 10:6; Sir 13:25; 2 Esdr 7:97; *1 Enoch* 18:4; Reid, "Prayer," 44-47; *idem, Transfiguration,* 107-12.

92. See 24:4; Acts 1:10; cf. Trites, "Transfiguration," 80; Reid, *Transfiguration,* 112-14. On clothes as markers of status, see 7:25; 8:26-35; 16:19; 23:11; Acts 10:30; Hamel, *Poverty and Charity,* 73-93.

93. In the view of some, Luke understands that Jesus, in communion with God in this scene, comes to the realization that it would be through his death that his mission would be accomplished (e.g., Reid, "Prayer," 47; Conzelmann, *Luke,* 57-58). Conzelmann is himself aware of the problem this view creates: Why does Jesus need to have disclosed to him on the mountain what he has already disclosed to his disciples (v 22)?

94. Interestingly, the appearance of "two men" in "dazzling/white clothing" in 24:4-6; Acts 1:10-11 serves a similar hermeneutical purpose, though the instructions these angelic figures give also register key differences. In ch. 24, the women are reminded by the heavenly messengers of the past so that they might interpret correctly the present. In

30-31 Luke's narration foregrounds the role of Jesus' followers as eyewitnesses, the nature of Jesus' mission, and the naming of Jesus' destination.[95] Luke has already employed words and phrases that privilege the sense of sight: "appearance" and "dazzling white"; to these he now adds "Look!" and "they appeared," and to these will be added the further affirmation, "they saw" (v 32). This emphasis on seeing illuminates the transfiguration scene from the vantage point of the apostles, with Luke's focus set on the significance of this event for them. At the same time, Luke invites his audience to share their viewpoint through the use of "Look!"[96]

The appearance of Moses and Elijah with Jesus certifies, first, that the crowds are wrong when they speculate that Jesus is Elijah (vv 8, 19). Although Luke uses Elijah-material to assist his portrayal of Jesus, he never identifies Jesus as Elijah. Instead, he casts John the Baptist more in this role and, in doing so, takes advantage of the anticipated, eschatological role of Elijah in preparation for the day of the Lord.[97] When he does associate Elijah with Jesus, it is to cast Jesus as one who, like Elijah, engages in a prophetic ministry in which the power of God is active on behalf of those not normally regarded as the elect — that is, Gentiles, Samaritans, and the poor.[98] Moses is also portrayed along dual lines — first in his identification with the law of God (e.g., 2:22), but more pervasively as the great prophet of God (see above, §12). Luke tells concerning them what he has just shown concerning Jesus — namely, that they are present "in glory," sharing in the status of those who belong to the heavenly court. That Jesus is engaged in conversation with these two figures of such high status makes it difficult to imagine that Luke wants to censure them or what they represent (e.g., "the law and the prophets"), but rather implies a basic continuity between their work on God's behalf and his own. In an initial sense, the presence of these persons from Israel's past serves to interpret and to legitimate the shape Jesus' mission is taking.

Luke often portrays people in conversation regarding Jesus' identity or mission,[99] and this is true in the present case. Unlike so many others in the

---

Acts, those present are given a promise of the parousia (regarding in the future) in order to sanction their carrying on of Jesus' mission in the present. In the scene of transfiguration, the apostles are given a glimpse of Jesus' future glory in order to provide an unimpeachable endorsement of the grounding of his mission and message in the divine purpose.

95. Cf. Acts 1:10-11.

96. Although sometimes untranslatable (BAGD, 370-71), this particle (ἰδού) functions here to draw Luke's audience even further into the narrative so that they might grasp the significance of these goings-on from a perspective alongside the disciples.

97. See above on 1:17.

98. See above on 4:25-26; Evans, "Elijah/Elisha Narratives." See the survey of views in Reid, *Transfiguration,* 116-25; Bock, 1:868-69.

99. Cf. 3:15; 6:11; 8:25; et al.

Third Gospel, their conversation is not cast negatively, as though they lack understanding or oppose what they do understand, but is summarized as having been concerned with Jesus' "exodus." What is this? The term itself is used in the LXX and Hellenistic Jewish literature with reference to the exodus from bondage in Egypt,[100] though it can also be used with reference to one's "departure" as one's "death."[101] Given the profusion of echoes of the story of exodus in this co-text, it seems almost certain that the former sense is the more appropriate one here.[102] Given the opening reference in this narrative unit to Jesus' words (v 28), which functions almost as a thematic heading, it is likewise difficult not to imagine that Jesus' own articulation of the divine purpose is related in a substantive way to this conversation about his "exodus." The point of their discussion, then, would be the nature of Jesus' journey through rejection and death to his exaltation. That this would be fulfilled in Jerusalem adds fresh information, establishing a new narrative need for Jesus to travel to the city (cf. 9:51, 53). Because Jerusalem has already been established as the locus of the priesthood and the scribes (cf. 1:9-11; 2:46; 5:17) — who would be joined by the elders in rejecting Jesus (v 22) — this news also adds to the tension of the narrative as the Galilean section draws to a close. Jesus will fulfill the divine purpose in Jerusalem, but it is in Jerusalem that he will be rejected.

Such heightened tension does not altogether eclipse more hopeful motifs in this text, however. First, the association of Jesus with Moses and Elijah on the mountain is itself an auspicious portrait of the continuation and consummation of God's ancient, eschatological purpose. Moreover, the encasement of Jesus' mission in the language of exodus reminds us that, whatever shape it takes, that mission is grounded in the purpose of God to bring liberation from bondage. Through the journey Jesus is undertaking, release from the constraints of demonization, from the darkness of satanic intent, and from the diverse expressions of diabolic power, whether in disease or in social marginalization or in the patronal ethics of the Roman world, will be effected. Finally, if Jerusalem is the place where Jesus' opposition will overtake him and bring him to his death, it is also the location where he will be vindicated through resurrection (v 22). The change of appearance he experiences on the mountain, after all, is an anticipatory vision of his coming in glory (cf. vv 26-27).

32-35 Luke structures this scene so as to present two distinctive

---

100. ἔξοδος — cf., e.g., Exod 19:1; Num 33:38; Ps 104:38; Michaelis, "εἴσοδος, ἔξοδος, διέχοδος," 104-5.

101. For example, Wis 3:2; 7:6; 2 Pet 1:15.

102. See also the Exodus imagery earlier in the narrative — e.g., in 1:68-79; 4:1-13. Garrett, "Exodus from Bondage," 657; Strauss, *Davidic Messiah,* 263, 303-4.

viewpoints regarding this event, the apostles' and God's. The apostles are characterized as weighed down with sleep, barely awake,[103] but aware of the scene unfolding before them; acting again as their representative, Peter sees the moment slipping away but tries to preserve it by constructing dwellings or tents for Jesus, Moses, and Elijah. Peter's response may be reminiscent of the Feast of Tabernacles (booths, tents),[104] a celebration in remembrance of God's provision during the journey in the wilderness and in anticipation of eschatological deliverance; this would not be out of character in the larger Lukan co-text, with the feeding of the multitudes only recently recounted (vv 12-17) and with eschatological sensitivities heightened in the current scene. Speaking directly to his audience, Luke, however, censures Peter's remarks: he did not know what he was saying. This negative evaluation of Peter is corroborated (1) by the disciples' drowsiness, unmotivated in the narrative, and is, therefore, likely a figurative allusion to their spiritual dullness;[105] and (2) by the appellation with which he addresses Jesus, "master," a term of respect, but one that signifies a lack of understanding of Jesus' person and mission (see above, §12). Moreover, as will become more and more evident, the narrative of Luke-Acts situates itself against all attempts, including this one, to station the glory of God in one place.[106]

It is not surprising, then, that Peter's outburst is interrupted. The way he is interrupted may be surprising, however, since, throughout the Lukan narrative thus far, God has been content largely to operate, as it were, behind the scenes, via the Scriptures, angelic messengers, and Spirit-endowed spokespersons, and above all through Jesus. God's presence is marked by the emphatic reference (three times!) to the cloud (a symbol for the divine presence),[107] by its overshadowing presence,[108] and by the voice from the cloud.[109] Who "enters" the cloud? Moses and Elijah were about to depart

---

103. Many translations read that the three apostles were asleep and had to be awakened. The NRSV legitimately renders διαγρηγορέω as "to remain awake," though it can also be rendered "to awaken fully." Either way, the overall sense is not significantly affected (Marshall, 385), though we have maintained the NRSV reading because it coheres best with the important distinction between "seeing" (vv 29-33, 36) and "hearing" (vv 34-35) otherwise attested in this pericope.

104. Cf. Num 29:12-34; Lev 23:34-36, 39-43; Deut 16:13-17; Zech 14:16-21; 11QTemple 27:10–29:2.

105. Not only might "sleep" potentially have this sense (BAGD 843), but eschatological discourse frequently admonishes persons to "stay awake." See 12:37; 21:36; Acts 20:21(?); Matt 25:13; Mark 13:33, 34, 35, 37; 1 Cor 16:13; Eph 6:13; Col 4:2; 1 Thess 5:6; 1 Pet 5:8; Rev 3:2, 3; 16:15.

106. Cf. Acts 7:44-50; Green, "Demise of the Temple"; Johnson, 153, 155.

107. Cf. Exod 13:21-22; 33:9-11; 34:5; 1 Kgs 8:10-11; et al.

108. See above on 1:35.

109. See Exod 19:16; Deut 5:22.

and, in any case, Jesus, Elijah, and Moses are each portrayed as already sharing in some way in the divine glory; hence, it makes little sense to picture the cloud as encompassing them. More likely, the divine presence envelops the apostles (cf. Exod 24:15-18), bringing them into the radiance of divine power and glory. They respond, as is typical in theophanies, with fear.[110] Divine disclosure in this scene then takes the form of the spoken word. With this, the narrative has moved from an emphasis on seeing (which is no longer possible, given the overshadowing cloud) to hearing.

The word of God identifies Jesus in three ways — as the Son of God (cf. 1:31-35; 3:21–4:13), as the Isaianic Servant of Yahweh (cf. Isa 42:1; Luke 23:35), and as the prophet like Moses (cf. Acts 3:22-23). (On these divine affirmations, see above, §12.) The importance of this divine intrusion into the narrative lies in the fact that Jesus' apostles have not heretofore been privy to information of this kind.[111] In fact, even when God declares Jesus to be "my Son" in the baptismal scene in 3:21-22, God is said to have spoken directly to Jesus: "You are my Son." This stands in contrast to the present scene, where God speaks not to Jesus but to these representative followers, underscoring for them Jesus' status. From an unimpeachable source, Jesus has been identified for them; as a consequence of this divine confirmation, they should regard his words, including his teaching on his destiny and the concomitant nature of discipleship (vv 21-27), as reliable.

36 The importance of "hearing" at this point in the episode is underscored by the backward reference to it. Apparently, with the divine message delivered, the cloud of the divine presence has lifted as well. Able to see again, the apostles are now able to observe that Moses and Elijah, earlier reported as "leaving" (v 33), have departed, leaving Jesus by himself. Though his work is built on and shaped by theirs, their interpreting and legitimating presence is no longer needed. God himself has unveiled and sanctioned Jesus' status and mission. The journey that must be fulfilled is his. The voice the apostles are to heed is his. Indeed, as Luke will make clear, even these OT figures are now to be interpreted by Jesus, for his role as divine spokesperson has been endorsed by God himself. That is, it is not so much that the time of the law and prophets has passed as it is that Jesus has been designated as their authorized interpreter.

Luke's final statement of summary reaches far into the future, casting a blanket of silence over the whole period covered by the narrative of the Gospel. What motivates this silence? As the ensuing narrative will clarify, though their eyes and ears have begun to be opened, so that they will begin

---

110. See above on 1:12.

111. At least, they have not heard it from a reliable source. Luke 4:34, 41; 8:28 record the recognition of Jesus as God's Son by demoniacs.

to comprehend with the help of the divine voice what they have seen, it is only following the resurrection that they are able to grasp the significance of this event and, indeed, of the rest of the story of Jesus.

4.6.4. The Misunderstanding of the Disciples (9:37-50)

37 *On the next day, when they had come down from the mountain, a great crowd met him.* 38 *Just then a man from the crowd shouted, "Teacher, I beg you to look at my son; he is my only child.* 39 *Suddenly a spirit seizes him, and all at once he shrieks. It convulses him until he foams at the mouth; it mauls him and will scarcely leave him.* 40 *I begged your disciples to cast it out, but they could not."* 41 *Jesus answered, "You faithless and perverse generation, how much longer must I be with you and bear with you? Bring your son here."* 42 *While he was coming, the demon dashed him to the ground in convulsions. But Jesus rebuked the unclean spirit, healed the boy, and gave him back to his father.* 43 *And all were astounded at the greatness of God.*

While everyone was amazed at all that he was doing, he said to his disciples, 44 *"Let these words sink into your ears: The Son of Man is going to be delivered[112] into human hands."* 45 *But they did not understand this saying; its meaning was concealed from them, so that they could not perceive it. And they were afraid to ask him about this saying.*

46 *An argument arose among them as to which one of them was the greatest.* 47 *But Jesus, aware of their inner thoughts, took a little child and put it by his side,* 48 *and said to them, "Whoever welcomes this child in my name welcomes me, and whoever welcomes me welcomes the one who sent me; for the least among all of you is the greatest."*

49 *John answered, "Master, we saw someone casting out demons in your name, and we tried to stop him, because he does not follow with us."* 50 *But Jesus said to him, "Do not stop him; for whoever is not against you is for you."*

Although comprising four discreet subunits at the close of the Galilean section of Jesus' ministry, these verses are nevertheless tightly bound together topically and in terms of structure and setting. Indeed, after initially linking this material to the previous scene of the transfiguration, Luke provides no topo-

---

112. NRSV: "betrayed." παραδίδωμι is employed in the NT passion materials as a reference to Jesus' being "handed over" to death, but the subject of this "handing over" is variously named — God, Jesus himself, Pilate, the Jewish council in Jerusalem, and so on. The NRSV assumes that the subject is "Judas" (cf. 6:16), but this decision is not rooted in the present co-text. Jesus' passion announcement is much more vague.

graphical or temporal shifts. On the contrary, he ties his record of Jesus' sayings to his disciples (vv 43b-45) into the exorcism account (vv 37-43a) by means of the genitive absolute construction in v 43b ("While everyone was amazed . . .");[113] he formulates the disciples' argument over greatness (vv 46-49) in relation to their reluctance to query Jesus about his suffering (v 45);[114] and John's concern with the exorcism practices of an outsider (vv 49-50) is cast as an "answer" to Jesus' teaching about relative greatness (vv 47-48). In addition to these structural connections, one may refer to numerous catchwords and concepts that hold these subunits together — for example, the shift from "son" (vv 38, 41) to "child" (vv 42, 48),[115] amazement (vv 43a, 43b), and especially the focus on the disciples (vv 40, 43, 45, 46-50).

Thematically, although it is not without christological import,[116] this larger unit focuses above all on the disciples, and especially on their failure. After the christological high point of the transfiguration scene, the deficiencies they exhibit in the current scene are positively disastrous. Previously, they were indicted for failing to exhibit their faith while responding in fear (8:22-25); now, however, they not only display fear but are actually ruled by Jesus to be "faithless" (vv 45, 41). They fail to exorcise a demon (v 40), fail to understand Jesus' message about his passion (v 45), spar over relative status (v 46), and attempt to exercise control over one whose ministry succeeds where theirs had not (v 49).

Do all fail? Could it be that the three who witnessed Jesus' transformation on the mountain escape this scathing characterization? It is true that they were not present when the (nine) disciples failed in their attempt to help the demoniac (v 40), but even they (who have heard the heavenly voice and received an analeptic view of Jesus' glory) do not understand Jesus' passion saying, and it is they who forbade the ministry of another because he did not belong to the inner circle of Jesus' followers. All are indicted in this portrait of the bankruptcy of faith and perceptiveness.

Wherein lies the problem? In this one narrative unit, Luke brings together central components of the ministry of Jesus as this has come to expression in the Galilean segment of the Gospel (see above, §9): the ministry of release displayed here in terms of healing and exorcism, the nature of Jesus' divine commission and the wide reach of God's graciousness that extends even to those of low status, the link between christology and discipleship, and

---

113. πάντων δὲ θαυμαζόντων . . .

114. With the adversative δέ, Luke contrasts the disciples' willingness to discuss Jesus' suffering with their interest in determining relative rank within the circle of disciples (Johnson, 159).

115. That is, the shift from υἱός to παῖς.

116. Cf. Aichinger, "Epileptiker-Perikope," 142.

so on. All of these point in the same direction, emphasizing that *the exercise of redemptive power and authority is not related to normal canons of honor and status and kinship.* The ministry of "release," in this case from demonization, is not a matter of magical ability or correct procedure, and the reception of "power and authority over all demons and to cure diseases" (9:1) does not substitute for the need to embody in one's life the message of Jesus. *Faith-full and faithful comportment is necessary if one is to engage effectively in the divine mission.* It is here that the disciples' failure is most evident, as Jesus' stinging words (v 41) make clear and as their own behavior corroborates (vv 43a-50).

The profundity of this failure establishes the narrative need for the long journey that commences with 9:51 — a journey whose central focus will fall on the formation of perceptive, faithful disciples.[117]

37-40   Although v 37 begins a fresh narrative unit, its relation to the transfiguration scene is marked emphatically by dual chronological and topographical markers. That episode may have been concluded, but it has some obvious connection to the present one. Only as this scene unfolds will it become clear how the transfiguration scene places its stamp on this one. Only as this scene unfolds will it become clear how important it is that Jesus' followers learn to integrate into their understanding of the one divine purpose these seemingly disparate elements: dishonor, rejection, and even death on the one hand, the exercise of divine authority, elevated status before God, and service in the salvific mission on the other.

The crowds, almost a permanent fixture on the Lukan landscape, have been backstage since the feeding miracle of vv 12-17. They are brought into view again, but only temporarily, as Luke turns the spotlight on one needy man from within the crowd. Later they will be brought back into focus (v 43), with the consequence that they are presented as witnesses of Jesus' ministry who respond with astonishment at God's majesty.

First, however, the narrator provides a detailed assessment of this man's problem. Verse 39 seems to spare nothing of his son's repulsive behavior. The list of symptoms elicits pathos from the reader, but also accentuates this as a particularly difficult case.[118] The stakes are raised when

---

117. On different, tradition-critical grounds, Kodell ("Luke and the Children") comes to a similar conclusion; for him, the unifying theme of the central section is that a disciple of Jesus is known by a lowliness characterized by availability for God's action and dependence on God. See further below, on 9:51–19:48.

118. Many regard these symptoms as arising from one of the neurological disorders identified as epilepsy — see the discussions in van der Loos, *Miracles,* 401-5; Page, *Powers of Evil,* 160-61. In the hands of many modern interpreters, however, such a diagnosis transforms this illness account into a report susceptible in an unmediated way to the categories of Western biomedicine (even Bock [1:884] wants to distinguish a biomedical

the man mentions that his demonized boy is his only child — a reality that reminds us of earlier accounts (esp. 7:12; cf. 8:42) and suggests this family's precarious situation in their community. If their son is not restored to health, who will maintain the family line?[119] The challenge of this case is emphasized even further when the man notes the failure of the disciples to cast out the demon. We are reminded that the disciples had been given the capacity to do the very thing they have now proved themselves to be incapable of doing; indeed, they were given power and authority over *all* demons (9:1). Why not this one? In spite of their status as emissaries of the Messiah of God (v 20), in this instance they are no better than the physicians who failed to help the hemorrhaging woman (8:43). In the face of such obstacles, the man's approach to Jesus is remarkable. He cries out for help[120] and begs for assistance; his faith apparently persists in spite of his son's condition and the failure of the disciples.[121]

The form of the man's request foregrounds an immediate comparison between Jesus and the disciples. He had begged the disciples; now he begs Jesus. How will he fare this time (cf. 9:1-2, 6, 11)?

41-43a Jesus' answer focuses first on the failure of the disciples to exorcise the spirit.[122] Had they not been given power and authority over "all demons" (9:1)? If so, then their inability to appropriate that authority is due to their faithlessness. Jesus, in fact, finds in their behavior a parallel to the children of God in the Exodus story — "a crooked and perverse generation"

---

diagnosis from the effect of a demon: "the demon is exploiting a physical ailment and making it worse"), rather than accounting for (1) the report of how this malady is experienced (too easily dismissed as "primitive") — i.e., as a manifestation of a spirit that needs to be cast out — and (2) the report of its resolution: the demon was rebuked and the boy was restored to health, not incidentally including his being restored to his family. Against the imperialism resident in the reductionistic use of the biomedical paradigm, see, e.g., Hahn, *Sickness and Healing;* Good, *Medicine.* The latter, e.g., challenges "the empiricist program of studying culturally relative beliefs about natural disease objects . . . on two grounds — for its essentialist conception of disease and for a superficial analysis of how illness is cognized and comes to be known as a dimension of human experience and understanding" (171).

119. Cf. Malina and Rohrbaugh, *Commentary,* 344.

120. βοάω. This term is used in Luke-Acts for the cry of the needy and powerless (18:7, 38) and of those who desire a person in authority to intervene on their behalf (18:7, 38; Acts 17:6; 25:24).

121. Cf. Theissen, *Miracle Stories,* 177.

122. It is possible to read Jesus' words as an indictment against "the crowd," in addition to or instead of against the disciples. However, Luke casts Jesus' words as a response to the man's plea for help, and the only thing that is visibly objectionable about his petition is the report that the disciples were unsuccessful in their attempt to deal with his demonized son.

in contrast to a "faithful God" (Deut 32:4-5).[123] In the Lukan text, Jesus seems deliberately to have shaped his indictment of the disciples — first, drawing on OT language used to depict the state of God's people on the Exodus journey so as to interpret the condition of his disciples as they begin the journey ("exodus," v 31) to Jerusalem; and second by using the particular language of "faithlessness," attested already in the Deuteronomic co-text and much more suitable to Lukan concerns (cf. 8:11-15). The incorrigibleness of the disciples is exacerbated by the inconsistency, even deterioration, of their faith — present but not manifest in the boat scene of 8:22-25, on display in their ministry activity in 9:6 but again hidden in the episode of the feeding miracle of 9:12-17, and now altogether absent. Jesus is already anticipating his execution (9:22, 44), after which his followers will share responsibility in the divine mission, and they are in a deplorable state of readiness.

Jesus' answer focuses second on the man's request for divine intervention. He had described the boy's symptoms (v 39), emphasizing the severity of his case, and, as though in reaction to the presence of Jesus, its seriousness is evidenced as the demon took control of the boy again (cf. 8:28). Jesus manifests his authority over the demonic by commanding the spirit.[124] By this point in the narrative, the outline is a familiar one,[125] so familiar that it need not be repeated in detail here; rather, we are to understand that the word of Jesus is sufficient to cause the unclean spirit to depart from the boy. This is encapsulated in the report that the boy was healed and returned to his father. This report also indicates the degree to which Luke refuses to draw a sharp line between diseases and demonic tyranny,[126] and evidences the social construction of the concept of "healing" so as to include the dissipation of spiritual and physical indications, the departure of their diabolic cause, and the restoration of kinship relations.[127]

Luke rounds out this scene with reference to the reaction of "all" — that is, the crowd, present at the beginning (v 37) but since only in the background, and the disciples. They recognize in Jesus' authoritative ministry an exhibition of the majesty of God, a response that is reminiscent of the image of Jesus wrapped in the glory of God in the immediately adjacent scene of transfiguration (v 29).

123. Luke writes, γενεὰ ἄπιστος καὶ διεστραμμένη. In Deut 32:4, God is said to be "faithful" (θεὸς πιστός), while his "degenerate children" are said to be "a crooked and perverse generation" (γενεὰ σκολιὰ καὶ διεστραμμένη); cf. Acts 2:40 ("crooked [σκολιός] generation"); 13:8, 10.

124. ἐπιτιμάω.

125. Cf., e.g., 4:33-36, 41; 6:18; 8:26-33; Kirchschläger, *Jesu exorzistisches Wirken*.

126. Cf. Luke 13:10-17; Acts 10:38; Green, "Daughter of Abraham."

127. See the parallel in 7:15; cf., e.g., 4:39; 5:14, 26; 8:39, 47-48.

43b-45 From the exuberant responses of the crowds, Jesus turns to his disciples to discuss his approaching demise. It is not coincidental that these two realities concerning his person and ministry — his exalted status and his impending dishonor — are set side by side. Rather, there is a studied transition from one to the other, so that Jesus' words of doom to his disciples are spoken "while everyone was amazed" (see above). Moreover, the parallel between v 43a and v 43b underscores the exhibition of God's majesty in Jesus' activity through the apposition of the parallel phrases "the greatness of God" and "all that [Jesus] was doing." Together, then, vv 43-44 again demonstrate the necessity of the integration in the disciples' conceptualization of Jesus' messianic identity of his elevated status vis-à-vis the divine purpose and his rejection at the hands of human beings.

But it is this integration, or collocation of terms, that the disciples do not grasp. Although they, like the others, are able to grasp Jesus' noble status as God's redemptive agent (v 43), they do not understand his "words" about suffering. Consequently, their faith is characterized as immature and in danger of being nullified.[128] The disciples' lack of perception is emphatic. It is accentuated, first, by Jesus' apparent need to urge the disciples to internalize his words, to hear and to perceive (cf. 8:10). Following this, Luke outlines their failure to hear in four phrases: they lacked understanding, its meaning was concealed, they lacked perception, and they declined to discuss this subject further on account of their fear (cf. 8:25). Could it be that God had concealed the meaning of Jesus' words?[129] Although their failure to comprehend may serve the divine purpose, it is doubtful that imperception can be attributed to divine intent: (1) the disciples are those to whom the secrets of the kingdom are revealed (8:10) and (2), in the current co-text, Jesus' initial injunction assumes that they should be able to understand.[130]

That they cannot comprehend is rooted in their failure thus far to embrace fully the new view of the world that is the content of Jesus' procla-

---

128. See 8:11-15. Jesus' refers to his message as τοὺς λόγους τούτους, echoing the identification of the sower's seed as ὁ λογός, and thus establishing the interpretation of the tale of the sower as the matrix within which to measure the disciples' disappointing response. In vv 45-46, Luke refers to Jesus' ῥῆμα, his "message," but this shift seems to be motivated by nothing more than the desire for linguistic variation.

129. παρακαλύπτω, which appears in the NT only here, is in the perfect passive participle form. Hence, it is susceptible to being read as a "divine passive" — i.e., they were kept from understanding by God.

130. Cf. Kingsbury, *Conflict in Luke,* 120; Tannehill, *Narrative Unity,* 1:227. Noting the complexity of issues of agency and responsibility in the analogous Exodus accounts of the hardening of the heart of Pharaoh, Tiede notes, "Similarly, Luke's composition defies mere literary, psychological, moral, or even purely theological resolutions of the problem of historical causation, although, finally, theocentric convictions dominate" (*Prophecy and History,* 84).

mation, a world in which conventional perspectives on honor and shame and on the meaning of suffering in relation to God's purpose are subverted. Because they have not adopted this view of the world, they cannot really understand Jesus' identity and mission. Not understanding Jesus, they cannot understand the nature of their own discipleship — as becomes abundantly clear in vv 46-50.

46-48   The fear of v 45 is not the awe or astonishment expected in a theophanic scene, but constitutes at least skepticism (cf. 24:38) and more probably, in this co-text, a denial of faith. The debilitating presence of such fear recasts the disciples not as helpers of the divine mission, but as opponents. This adversarial role is furthered now by Luke's dual reference to the disciples' considerations, their inner thoughts, using language normally, though not exclusively, associated with Jesus' opponents.[131] The content of their deliberations betrays them even further. Even though persons in any gathering in Greco-Roman antiquity would naturally be concerned with questions of relative status (and behavior appropriate to one's place with regard to the station of others), Jesus' message has been oriented against such maneuvering and positioning. As he reveals their inner thoughts (cf. 2:35), he displays their marked failure to embody in their relations with one another the central tenets of his message.

Rather than dismissing them in frustration, though, he provides them with an object lesson of profound significance. Taking a child, perhaps even the child he had just restored to health,[132] he places the child in a position of honor at his side, then makes a pronouncement that undermines everything that the Roman world would have taken for granted regarding questions of status and social relations. "To welcome" people would be to extend to them the honor of hospitality, to regard them as guests (cf. 7:44-46), but one would only welcome a social equal or one whose honor was above one's own. Children, whose place of social residence was defined at the bottom of the ladder of esteem, might be called upon to perform acts of hospitality (e.g., washing the feet of a guest), but normally they would not themselves be the recipients of honorable behavior.[133] Jesus thus turns the social pyramid upside down, undermining the very conventions that led the disciples to deliberate

131. διαλογισμός (cf. διαλογίζομαι) — see 2:35; 5:21-22; 6:8; 20:14.

132. The shift from υἱός (vv 38, 41) to παῖς (vv 42, 47-48) and the lack of any geographical or temporal shift from that earlier episode to this one are suggestive.

133. Children were the weakest, most vulnerable among the population. They had little implicit value as human beings, a reality that is related to the high likelihood that they would not survive into adulthood. Even if women procured their place in the household by bearing children, especially sons, children themselves were of the lowest status. See, e.g., Rawson, ed., *Family in Ancient Rome; idem,* ed., *Marriage, Divorce, and Children; idem,* "Roman Family"; Garnsey and Saller, *Roman Empire,* 136-41.

over relative greatness within the company of disciples and, indeed, that had led the disciples away from any proper understanding of Jesus' status.

While the disciples are aware of Jesus' greatness (as one who shares in divine glory and through whom the majesty of God is evident [vv 29, 43a]), their categories do not allow for his predictions of shameful rejection. Jesus' counterproposal is relentless, for he calls upon his followers to welcome those of the lowest status, the poor (see above on 4:18-19), even this child, "in my name" (see above on v 24); that is, to act in this way is to perform in a way consistent with Jesus' own commitments and commission. Albeit in a round-about way, he goes so far as to assert that this topsy-turvy social ethic is grounded in the divine purpose. To honor children is to honor Jesus, and to honor Jesus is to honor the one who sent him — that is, God himself (cf. 4:18, 43; 10:16). In proclaiming this message of social transformation and trans-position, then, Jesus is only faithfully representing the ways of God.[134]

49-50 The level of incomprehension of these disciples is exemplified by one of their number, John. He had witnessed Jesus' transfiguration and received from God instructions to attend to Jesus' words (vv 28-35). Neverthe-less, his words of concern not only contradict Jesus' message, but are actually cast as a *response* to Jesus. Jesus had effectively negated conventional issues of status, yet John and his companions had operated within those conventions in order to deny this "outsider" permission to work in Jesus' name. That is, they had engaged in boundary-making on the basis of conventional notions of perceived honor. He did not belong to the community around Jesus, so his behavior was disallowed.

The irony is that this unnamed exorcist had been working in the name of Jesus — just as Jesus' disciples had been instructed to do (v 48; cf. v 24) — and he had been successful in the very arena of salvific activity in which the disciples had just been found wanting (v 40). Whatever neat categories that had seemed to have been operative within the Lukan narrative are thus thrown into disarray. The disciples are given access to the secrets of the kingdom so that they might perceive (8:10), and power and authority so that they might exorcise demons (9:1), yet they are unable to do either. This unnamed exorcist, though his primary identity is not with Jesus' inner circle,[135] is nonetheless represented as having faith that wells up in the fruitfulness of

---

134. ἀποστέλλω is thus used with the more technical nuance of "representative."

135. That is, he does not "follow" as "we" do. What is the status of the exorcist with regard to the mission of Jesus? Luke does not say, though the presence of the phrase "in your name," combined with his success (cf. Acts 19:13-16!), implies that he is among the wider circle of Jesus' followers. This is also suggested by the proverbial expression with which Jesus concludes his reply to John, wherein Jesus counsels John and the others (ὑμῶν) not to recognize or act on boundaries that have not been constructed by the prior hostility of others.

effective ministry. What is more, as Luke's audience will discover shortly, apart from the twelve there are many who are sent to carry on the work of the kingdom (10:1-11).

The failure of the disciples is represented at its most basic level in this: Jesus had implored the disciples to honor those of no status at all, but they have refused partnership with one who did not share the status they assumed for themselves.[136]

136. Thus, κωλύω is present as the antonym of δέχομαι. Koenig, *New Testament Hospitality,* 31. Cf. Num 11:24-30.

5. ON THE WAY TO JERUSALEM (9:51–19:48)[1]

With 9:51, Luke begins a fresh section of the Gospel, sometimes referred to as the Travel Narrative. If the Galilean section of the Gospel (4:14–9:50) was primarily oriented around establishing the nature of Jesus' messianic mission, the narrative needs that come to the fore in the central section of the Third Gospel are somewhat different. The Galilean section had at times an episodic look, as Luke peppered his account of Jesus' itinerant ministry in the region of Galilee with comparable scenes so as to underscore through redundancy the portrait of Jesus' ministry as one of "release." Luke's narrative of Jesus' journey to Jerusalem has a similar look, though for different reasons. No longer is Luke concerned especially to develop Jesus' identity or to demonstrate the nature of his mission in interpretive relation to Isa 61:1-2; 58:6 (cf. Luke 4:18-19; 7:21-22). Luke's concerns lie elsewhere, as he foregrounds five interrelated narrative needs in his recounting of Jesus' journey to Jerusalem.

(1) First, within this lengthy central section of the Gospel, the Evangelist develops further the overall theme of Luke-Acts — namely, *the coming of salvation in all of its fullness to all people*. This narrative need was signaled in a variety of ways in the account of Jesus' birth, not least in the Songs of Mary (1:46-55) and Simeon (2:29-32), firmly established in the privilege accorded to "the poor" in Jesus' inauguration speech in 4:16-30, then developed with reference to the leprous, the diseased and demonized, women, toll collectors, and others whose existence was on the margins of society in Luke's world. Hence, the journey narrative does not surface a new need regarding the universal embrace of God's salvific aim. It does carry it forward, however,

---

1. The compositional and thematic problems of the central section of Luke's Gospel have occasioned a great deal of scholarly attention. See the surveys of research in, e.g., Resseguie, "Luke's Central Section"; Egelkraut, *Jesus' Mission,* 30-59; Blomberg, "Luke's Central Section," 217-44; Baum, *Lukas als Historiker,* 1-35.

both in Jesus' deeds (e.g., the healing of the bent-over woman and the cleansing of a Samaritan leper — 13:10-17; 17:11-19) and words (e.g., his teaching regarding "the poor, the crippled, the lame, and the blind" and children — 14:13; 18:15-17). Indeed, it is within this section of the Third Gospel that Jesus' mission is encapsulated so memorably as seeking and saving the lost (19:10).

This lengthy section of the Gospel, then, is, like the rest of the Lukan narrative, soteriological in focus,[2] and Jesus' demolition of barriers — separating women and men, children and those of high status, Samaritans and Jews, and so on — presages the achievement of a mission extending salvation even to the Gentiles (cf. 2:32; 3:6).[3]

(2) A second narrative need is also firmly rooted in the birth narrative and developed in the Galilean section of the Gospel. This is *the expectation that Mary's son would be the cause of division in Israel* (2:34). Already on the basis of his ministry to outcasts, wherein Jesus claims unusual authority, even to the point of breaking bread with sinners and practicing redemptive activity on the Sabbath, Jesus had attracted hostility from among the Jewish leadership (e.g., 6:1-11). Toward the end of the Galilean section, however, the motif of conflict was accentuated dramatically when Jesus predicted that he would be "rejected by the elders, chief priests, and scribes, and be killed" (9:22; cf. 9:44). The identification of this particular triumvirate assumes that Jesus will meet his ultimate opposition in Jerusalem, and it is to Jerusalem that he is traveling. One would expect, then, that the narrative of Jesus' journey would be punctuated by reminders of the fate awaiting him in Jerusalem and by a crescendo in the hostility between Jesus and his adversaries that would provide the narrative rationale for such a pronounced level of animosity. On neither score are we disappointed.

Worthy of reflection in this respect is Luke's interest in delineating the composition of the audience witnessing Jesus' ministry at any given time. On the surface, we might gain the impression that Luke takes great care to show that some teaching is for Jesus' disciples, some for the crowds, some for the Pharisees, and so on. This is true only superficially, however.[4] For example, even when the addressees are explicitly named as the disciples in 16:1, we learn that the Pharisees have been eavesdropping (16:14); indeed, Peter exclaims at one point, "Lord, are you telling this parable for us or for everyone?" (12:41). Throughout the journey, Jesus gives instructions regarding disciple-

---

2. This is emphasized by Kariamadam, "Discipleship"; *idem,* "Composition and Meaning." On the theme of "salvation" in Luke-Acts, see Green, *Gospel of Luke; idem,* "Salvation to the End of the Earth," forthcoming.

3. Cf. Gill, "Lukan Travel Narrative."

4. *Contra* Johnson, 164-65; Kingsbury, *Conflict in Luke,* 56, 124.

ship that serve his concern for the formation of faithful followers but which also provoke and invite others who are, then, prospective followers.

Even so, Luke documents sometimes harsh confrontations between Jesus and his antagonists, so much so that, by the end of the journey, Luke's audience should have a clear view of how the rejection of Jesus by the Jewish leadership came about.[5] What is more, hostility toward Jesus is not limited to the Jewish leadership or to those whose role in Luke thus far has been to inspect his faithfulness regarding the Mosaic law, but extends, however subtly, to the crowds as well. The Galilean section of the Gospel has already prepared us for the chief point of contention between Jesus and his rivals — namely, their quite distinctive points of view regarding the character of the divine purpose and its present consummation. Within the journey narrative, this controversy will spill over into the unnamed crowds as well: Though they constitute for Jesus a pool of potential disciples, they are equally capable of embodying the cause of or being swayed by the opposition (e.g., 12:13, 54-59; 19:7, 39).

(3) Closely related is the developing portrait of Jesus as one who, in order to fulfill God's purpose, must suffer rejection and be killed. This motif surfaced at the end of the Galilean segment of the Third Gospel (9:22, 44), and will come into sharp focus again in the Gospel's central section through Jesus' predictions (12:49-50; 13:31-33; 17:25; 18:31-34). Because the journey narrative is punctuated with these reminders of what awaits Jesus in Jerusalem, the journey itself is cast in the dark hues of the passion. It becomes difficult, then, to read of the demands of discipleship or of the hostility Jesus encounters without reference to the significance attached to them by their location on the journey toward death. Even if it remains true that subsequent exaltation by God is also prophesied, death looms large. The journey thus has a christological edge, but even this emphasis has a pedagogical side, for it urges Jesus' followers to come to terms with the nexus of rejection and divine mission. As Paul and Barnabas would come to proclaim, "It is through many persecutions that we must enter the kingdom of God" (Acts 14:22).[6]

(4) A further narrative need served by the Jerusalem journey has only recently surfaced in the obduracy of the disciples. Called to share in his ministry, by the end of the Galilean section of the Gospel they have shown themselves to be surprisingly obtuse regarding the nature of Jesus' divine

5. Egelkraut *(Jesus' Mission)* sees this conflict as the primary theme of the journey narrative, though his way of putting the issue needs significant nuancing. He concludes that the travel narrative is Luke's way of showing how the rejection of Israel came about, neglecting the fact that, in Luke-Acts, Israel is divided vis-à-vis Jesus. On the motif of conflict in the travel account, see also Matera, "Jesus' Journey to Jerusalem"; Resseguie, "Point of View"; Dawsey, "Jesus' Pilgrimage," 219-20.

6. Cf. Korn, *Geschichte Jesu,* 93-99.

mission and, thus, the character of their own discipleship. Their failure, especially when combined with the foreshadowing of Jesus' impending departure,
moves into the foreground the need for intensive training in discipleship. The
travel notices interspersed throughout the narrative,[7] together with the overwhelmingly didactic content of the travel narrative,[8] point to the Lukan concern with the formation of disciples on the journey. Clearly, a major purpose
of the Jerusalem journey narrative is to prepare for the time following Jesus'
departure.[9]

It must be admitted, though, that judged on these terms the journey is
not successful. Although there are important evidences of enlightenment and
faithfulness that should not be overlooked (esp. 10:1-24), by the end of the
journey Jesus' followers are — perhaps surprisingly, certainly disappointingly
— unchanged. At the close of the Galilean section of the Gospel, Luke observes of the disciples, who have just witnessed Jesus' passion prediction,
"But they did not understand this saying; its meaning was concealed from
them, so that they could not perceive it" (9:45) — words that seem frustratingly similar to Luke's observation at the close of the Jerusalem journey, again
following a passion prediction: "But they understood nothing about all these
things; in fact, what he said was hidden from them, and they did not grasp
what was said" (18:34). Two points are of consequence. First, one learns as
the narrative unravels that enlightenment is possibly only in light of the
resurrection of the crucified one (ch. 24). By this means, Luke, writing some
decades following the resurrection of Jesus, can in his own discourse situation
communicate the expectation that his audience will be engaged in "enlightened," authentic discipleship. Second, it is worth remembering that discipleship as Luke has presented it requires a reconstruction of the self within a
new web of relationships, a transfer of allegiances, and the embodiment of
new dispositions and sensibilities. Such a "conversion" (a term not yet introduced in Jesus' ministry, though see 10:13) requires resocialization in the new
community being formed around Jesus. Jesus' direct involvement in this
process will not be completed until his ascension (cf. Acts 1:1-11).

(5) Although other narrative needs may be served by the Lukan account
of the journey to Jerusalem, the final one that will occupy our attention here
is one that has emerged only recently in the narrative but whose pedigree in
the Third Gospel is more pervasive. This concerns *Jesus' "exodus,"* about

---

7. Cf. Gill, "Lukan Travel Narrative"; Resseguie, "Luke's Central Section," 32.
8. Only 9:51-56; 11:14-16; 13:10-13; 14:1-6; 17:11-19; 18:35-43 contain material
other than sayings, and the disciples appear more often in this section than elsewhere in
the Gospel, often receiving instruction; cf. Green, *Gospel of Luke,* 104-5.
9. This is a major emphasis of Baum's examination of the travel narrative *(Lukas
als Historiker).*

which Jesus conversed with Moses and Elijah in the transfiguration scene (9:31). We have already noted that there are significant reasons why too direct a reading of the Lukan narrative against the backdrop of Israel's "Exodus" is problematic,[10] but this is not surprising and should not detract from our hearing important echoes of the Exodus material in the Lukan account. Cases of intertextuality, we may recall, not only borrow from but also parody — that is, signal differences in the midst of similarities — earlier material in order to give fresh meaning to current narration. In this case, Luke has built up a series of reminiscences, some linguistic and others conceptual, of Exodus material (see above, §12), but he has done so in a way that mimics the Deuteronomic portrayal of the Exodus journey as a series of speeches delivered by Moses to the people of God.[11] These speeches call for faithfulness to the covenant or, in Lukan terms, for a people whose kinship with Jesus is marked by their hearing and doing the word of God (8:21).

This way of construing the narrative of the Jerusalem journey locates the emphasis less on the idea of a travelogue, from Galilee to Jerusalem, and more on the *motif* of journeying and its *destination,* Jerusalem. This is consistent with the Lukan material in three ways. (a) First, the Lukan data signal clearly the onset of the journey, but thereafter provide very little by way of structuring a discernible journey itinerary. Indeed, what Luke does provide by way of travel notices[12] are generally nondescriptive and may seem convoluted.[13] (b) Throughout the Gospel Luke emphasizes the notion of "the way" — not only in its central section, but, for example, early on in the description of John's role as one who prepares the way of the Lord so that Jesus might "guide our feet in the way of peace,"[14] and at its end as the two disciples are instructed by Jesus on their way from Jerusalem.[15] It is not coincidental that the movement propagated by Jesus' followers is called in Acts "the Way."[16] (c) Even if the route by which Jesus arrives is not so important for Luke, it

10. See above, §12; also Dawsey ("Jesus' Pilgrimage," 218-24), whose focus is less on the identification of Jesus and Moses and more on the important disjunctions between the travel narrative in Luke and the Exodus journey. Dawsey's attempt to overcome the difficulty that Luke really presents nothing comparable to "the Promised Land" (cf. Egelkraut, *Jesus' Mission,* 57) is both unconvincing and unnecessary.

11. So Dawsey, "Jesus' Pilgrimage," 228.

12. 9:51, 53, 56, 57; 10:1, 38; 13:22, 33; 14:25; 17:11; 18:31, 35-36; 19:1, 11, 28, 29, 37, 41, 45.

13. For example, long after Jesus moves from Galilee into Samaria (9:51-56), Jesus is said to be journeying "through the region between Samaria and Galilee" (17:11). Cf. K. L. Schmidt, *Rahmen der Geschichte,* 246-54, 269.

14. 1:76, 79; cf. 3:4-5; Isa 40:3-4; 59:8.

15. 24:13-35; cf. Just, *Ongoing Feast,* 58. See also Kariamadam, "Luke's Theology," 47-52; *idem,* "Discipleship."

16. Acts 9:2; 19:9, 23; 22:4; 24:14, 22.

is important that he arrives in Jerusalem, for this is the place where Jesus will fulfill God's purpose for him (9:31, 51, 53). It is in Jerusalem, the centerpiece of the Jewish world, with its holy place and holy people, that God's aim must finally become manifest and be achieved, and from Jerusalem that the universal mission must have its beginning.[17] In short, the "journey" in which Luke is interested is not about narrative structure or travel itinerary; rather, it concerns the fulfillment of God's redemptive purpose together with the thematization of the formation of a people who will hear and obey the word of God.

Beyond this what can be said about the structure of the travel narrative? The closing of the Galilean section of the Third Gospel and the commencement of the journey narrative is marked definitively in 9:51-56 with the fourfold use of the word "to journey" and the repeated references to Jesus' determination to go to Jerusalem. Less easy is the resolution of the end of this section. On almost any reckoning, however, 19:28-48 serves a transitional function, with the question of whether this account of Jesus' final entry into Jerusalem[18] belongs most appropriately to the journey section or to the Jerusalem section still much discussed. Although we have chosen to mark the end of the journey at that point where Jesus has actually entered Jerusalem,[19] this is not critical to the interpretation of the narrative.[20]

17. See Acts 1:8. On the identification and significance of Jerusalem as a "culture center," see §3.

18. See Luke's careful plotting of these final steps: Jesus is "near" (19:11), "going up to" (19:41), "approaching" (19:45), and finally "enter[s]" (19:47) Jerusalem.

19. That is, with 19:45-48. Luke 19:47-48 might be taken as a summary heading for the following section on Jesus' teaching in the temple (20:1–21:38), in which case one might regard 19:47 as forming an *inclusio* with 19:37: "Every day he was teaching in the temple."

20. Numerous attempts have been made to find in the travel narrative sometimes elaborate chiasms (see the survey in Blomberg, "Luke's Central Section"; more recently, e.g., Kariamadam, "Composition and Meaning"; Farrell, "Structure and Theology"). As interesting as these may be, it is difficult to find them ultimately persuasive precisely because of the length of Luke's central section, and thus the improbability that Luke's audience (especially his auditors!) would be able to balance in their short-term memories so complex a structure over such a lengthy span of narrative time. The chief obstacle for theories regarding the structure of the journey section is its narrative presentation of material with such a small number of elements of story — i.e., the presence of so few markers normally governing narrative discourse by which to ascertain how the narrator has manipulated the elements of the story at the level of its presentation as discourse (cf. Brown and Yule, *Discourse Analysis,* 96; Prince, *Narratology,* 93; Segre, *Analysis of the Literary Text,* 34). This does not negate the importance of structure, however; because one's perception of meaning is cumulative, at the very least the order in which Luke has located these scenes remains important to his audience (cf. Chatman, *Story and Discourse,* 31-35).

5.1. DISCIPLESHIP: HEARING AND DOING THE WORD (9:51–10:42)

The primary emphasis on the formation of a people who embody the word of God — key to the final episodes of the Galilean ministry (cf. 8:4-21) — is not discarded but heightened with the onset of the journey narrative. With the departure for Jerusalem (9:51-62) Luke makes it clear that "following" Jesus is related to joining him in the journey and in the proclamation of the kingdom of God. This portfolio is immediately unveiled further by the sending of the seventy-two for the purpose of preparing the way for Jesus and engaging in a style of ministry that signifies the advent of the kingdom of God. This leads to the high point in the experience of the disciples in the Gospel, for they are not only successful in their ministry, but are also the recipients of rare insight into Jesus' person and mission. It is not too much to say that the knowledge previously shared by Peter, James, and John in the transfiguration scene (9:28-36) has now been made available to this larger group of Jesus' followers. Although the form of presentation shifts with the question of the lawyer in 10:25, the message is the same: those who will share life in the kingdom are those whose lives are determined by Jesus' message. Throughout this narrative section Luke correlates soteriological terminology — "kingdom of God" (9:60, 62; 10:9, 11), "peace" (10:5, 6), "names . . . written in heaven" (10:20), revelation (10:21-24), "eternal life" (10:25, 28) — but the conditions for sharing in this salvation remain constant. As Jesus puts it to the legal scholar, "Go and do likewise" (10:37).

Wrapped up in this presentation of salvation is one of the more noticeable leitmotifs of this section, the import of "welcoming" Jesus and his message. On this matter Luke presents good and bad examples. The folk of a Samaritan village do not receive him, nor do representative Galilean villages. This is counterbalanced in an interesting way by the hospitality and care shown by a Samaritan traveler (10:33-36). Jesus prepares his missionaries for both eventualities. Finally, though welcomed into a home by Martha, the form of receptiveness he commends is that of her sister, Mary. Clearly, what Jesus seeks is not (only) conventional hospitality but a welcome that embraces fully the message of peace.

What may be surprising about Luke's presentation is the degree to which he has begun in this narrative section to push the boundaries of Israel in his attempt to portray discipleship as embodying the word of God. It is not only that Jesus and his entourage unexpectedly travel into Samaritan territory or that a Samaritan is chosen over a priest and Levite as an exemplar of faithfulness to the Jewish(!) law. It is also the symbolic significance of the sending of the seventy-two, a number representing a concern with the peoples of the world. Still further, it is the privilege accorded to the Gentile cities Tyre and Sidon, at the expense of their Galilean counterparts, at the coming of the kingdom of God. At issue is how one responds to the divine message, with the possibility of restricting the communication of that message to a subgroup of the whole of humanity simply never considered.

One of the more serious and potentially fruitful narrative gaps in this section is Luke's failure to indicate how potential disciples (9:57-62) and a Jewish lawyer (10:25-37) finally respond to Jesus' articulation of the demands of discipleship. Do they embrace his message gladly and join him in the journey? Do they turn away in sadness? These and other responses are possible, but in the end Luke has left to the reader the responsibility to provide them. No doubt this is an invitation from the narrator to his audience; how will they/we respond to Jesus?

5.1.1. Departure for Jerusalem (9:51-62)

> 51 When the days drew near for him to be taken up, he set his face to go to Jerusalem. 52 And he sent messengers ahead of him. On their way they entered a village of the Samaritans to make ready for him; 53 but they did not receive him, because his face was set toward Jerusalem. 54 When his disciples James and John saw it, they said, "Lord, do you want us to command fire to come down from heaven and consume them?" 55 But he turned and rebuked them. 56 Then they went on to another village.
>
> 57 As they were going along the road, someone said to him, "I will follow you wherever you go." 58 And Jesus said to him, "Foxes have holes, and birds of the air have nests; but the Son of Man has nowhere to lay his head." 59 To another he said, "Follow me." But he said, "Lord, first let me go and bury my father." 60 But Jesus said to him, "Let the dead bury their own dead; but as for you, go and proclaim the kingdom of God." 61 Another said, "I will follow you, Lord; but let me first say farewell to those at my home." 62 Jesus said to him, "No one who puts a hand to the plow and looks back is fit for the kingdom of God."

The line demarcating the onset of a new section of the narrative is clearly drawn, with Jesus moving with premeditation out of Galilee (4:14–9:50) toward Jerusalem. This does not mean that the nature of his mission, or the responses it attracts, will be so easily distinguished from the Galilean narrative, however. This brief narrative unit introduces the journey to Jerusalem while recapitulating important emphases of Jesus' message thus far and anticipating their further development in the narrative to follow.[1] At center stage appear

---

1. Cf. Sweetland, *Our Journey,* 33-35; Tiede, *Prophecy and History,* 55.

in tandem the importance of an orientation to God's purpose — on the part of Jesus and of those who would follow him — that relativizes all other commitments and considerations, and the hostility that such an orientation toward God will engender.

Most striking about this unit are the redundancies that appear and reappear in such a short pericope. (1) Sometimes hidden by attempts to provide a smooth translation are the numerous references to the journey: "to go," "while going," "his face was going," "they went," "as they were going," "along the road," "wherever you go," "let me go," and "go";[2] and (2) references to Jesus' face: "he set his face," "he sent messengers before his face," and "his face was going."[3] Luke thus establishes Jesus' resolve to embark on a journey whose destination is Jerusalem (vv 51, 53), a destination firmly rooted in the divine purpose (cf. 9:31). Also emphasized through redundancy is (3) the presence and role of disciples on this journey. Jesus' disciples first appear as those who share both John's role as Jesus' precursor (v 52) and John's misunderstanding of Jesus' ministry, as though it were preoccupied with judgment (v 54). Then, in three vignettes presented in staccato fashion, the stringent demands of discipleship and the rigor of the way of discipleship are set forth.[4]

A further common thread running through these verses is the motif of rejection and being rejected. The refusal of the Samaritan village to receive Jesus and his company prepares for the aphorism in v 58 regarding the homelessness of the Son of Man. Similarly, would-be disciples are warned of impending rejection at the same time that they are told to discard their former allegiances. Not far below the surface of this text are other texts, echoes of the OT stories of Elijah and Elisha[5] and of such Lukan texts as the rejection of Jesus at Nazareth (4:16-30). Taken together, these motifs and reverberations all serve the one theme of this narrative unit — namely, the single-minded orientation that Jesus has, and that his followers must come to share, as he begins the divinely ordained journey to Jerusalem.

51 Luke's ponderous opening successfully demarcates a major shift in narrative focus. Now that the days of Jesus' assumption were reaching their fulfillment,[6] the time for itinerating in Galilee (4:14-15) has passed. On purely

---

2. A form of πορεύομαι appears in vv 51, 52, 53, 56, and 57; a form of ἀπέρχομαι appears in vv 57, 59, and 60. ὁδός appears in v 57.

3. 9:51, 52, 53.

4. Language related to discipleship in this co-text appears throughout this section: ἀποστέλλω (v 52), ἄγγελος (v 52), μαθητής (v 54), ἀκολουθέω (vv 57, 59, 61).

5. See esp. 1 Kgs 19:19-21; 2 Kgs 1:9-16. Cf. Brodie, "Departure for Jerusalem."

6. ἐν τῷ + infinitive is a typical Lukan construction reflecting LXX influence (MHT 3:144-45). With the present participle, the expression suggests contemporaneity. On the strength of the analogy in 17:26, Goulder (2:460) proposes, "the days of (sc. leading up to) his taking up." Cf. Moule, *Idiom Book*, 76.

lexical grounds, this reference to Jesus' "assumption" could be taken as an allusion to his death, but the Elijah-typology manifest in vv 51-56 indicates that his "ascension" is in view (cf. 2 Kgs 2:10-11; Sir 48:9; 1 Macc 2:58).[7] Such a narrow focus on the ascension of Jesus is unprecedented in the Third Gospel;[8] here again, though, the connection to the Elijah-material is of interest, since it is at Elijah's ascension that "the spirit of Elijah" is passed on to Elisha (2 Kgs 2:9-15). Similarly, it is just before his ascension that Jesus promises the outpouring of the Spirit on his followers, and shortly thereafter that they are filled with the Spirit (Acts 1:8-11; 2:1-4). Thus, in a way appropriate to its co-text in ch. 9 (see §12), this narrative shift brings together the christologically significant event of Jesus' ascension and the profound importance of preparing the disciples for their Spirit-empowered mission following Jesus' ascension. The necessity of the journey to Jerusalem is rooted in both of these causal factors. These factors, however, are rooted even more deeply in the divine purpose. This reading is encouraged by Luke's use of a verb of fulfillment to mark the approaching time of Jesus' ascension (cf. 9:31),[9] then secured by Luke's observation that Jesus "set his face." This last phrase, connoting the austerity of Jesus' resolve, evokes analogous formulations of prophetic vocation.[10]

7. This is the only appearance of ἀνάλημψις in the NT. On the basis of collateral evidence in the Hellenistic world, van Stempvoort ("Interpretation of the Ascension") argued that Luke's reference was to Jesus' death — both here and in Acts 1:2 (where the cognate verb ἀναλαμβάνω is found). Parsons (*Departure of Jesus,* 130-33) agrees with van Stempvoort, though modifying his position so as to include a reference to "Jesus' entire journey back to God" in both Luke 9:51 and Acts 1:2. In light of the Elijah-typology (cf. Davies, "Prefigurement"; *idem, He Ascended,* 186), a narrow interpretation of ἀνάλημψις as "death" is unlikely. Acts 1:11, 22 employ ἀναλαμβάνω in co-texts that require the sense "to ascend [into heaven]." Cf. Korn, *Geschichte Jesu,* 95-96.

8. In light of the use of the plural τὰς ἡμέρας ("days"), most scholars conclude that such a restricted interpretation is implausible, with the result that "assumption" is made to embrace the whole of "Jesus' pathway through death to exaltation at the right hand of God" (Nolland, 2:535; cf. Schneider, 1:229). However, Baum (*Lukas als Historiker,* 356-57) has noted that αἱ ἡμέραι is used in analogous LXX expressions (e.g., Gen 47:29; Deut 31:14; 1 Sam 2:1) where the notion of "process" is not in view, but where a single event — whose exact date has not yet been determined — is intended.

9. συμπλήρόω (NRSV: "drew near"), instead of, e.g., ἤγγισαν. Cf. Acts 2:1. Luke often uses verbs of fulfillment in temporal clauses so as to mark the progression of events according to the ancient purpose of God (see on 1:1).

10. See, e.g., Isa 50:7; Jer 3:12; 21:10; Ezek 21:2; et al. In this particular co-text (cf. vv 54-55!), and in the absence of any preposition denoting that Jesus set his face "against" something or someone (e.g., ἐπί, as in his examples), C. A. Evans's suggestion that the narrator is thinking not only of Jesus' determination but also his vocation of judgment seems unlikely ("He Set His Face"; *idem,* "Luke 9,51 Once Again").

The most immediate cue for understanding the designation of "Jerusalem" as the final destination of the impending journey is found in 9:31, where Luke summarizes the conversation between Jesus, Moses, and Elijah as having to do with the exodus Jesus was about to fulfill in Jerusalem. In light of the adjacent prediction of Jesus' death at the hands of Jewish leaders associated with Jerusalem and the temple, Jesus' "exodus" or departure clearly includes his path through suffering and death, even if it also includes his being raised from the dead by God. Hence, this resolve on Jesus' part to go to Jerusalem comes in spite of the fate that awaits him there — or perhaps one might better say, *because of* the fate that awaits him there, since it is through his execution and vindication that he will fulfill God's salvific purpose. This reference to Jerusalem, repeated in v 53, centers attention on the consummation of the divine will even while it recognizes the central role Jerusalem plays as the "culture center" of the Jewish world. By "culture center" we mean the sacred space that establishes the order of the world and provides the center point around which human life is oriented (see §3). Jesus' activities in the Gospel thus far have been positioned against the world order established by and emanating from Jerusalem, but because they have been centered in the region of Galilee, far from the "center of the world," their radical character has not been widely felt. If Jesus takes this same message to Jerusalem, announcing a new worldview that undermines the world established in and by the temple, what will happen? This is the sort of question raised by Jesus' resolve to journey to Jerusalem.[11] Therefore, the way in which Luke thus signals this major shift in the narrative serves important and intertwined narratological, theological, and dramatic interests.

52-53 Just as John had made ready for the public ministry of Jesus, so now Jesus' disciples perform this function. The parallels are strong: (1) the rare description of disciples (and of John himself) as "messengers" (7:24, 27);[12] (2) being sent before his face (1:17, 76; 7:27), (3) to prepare or make ready for him (1:17, 76; 3:4; 7:27); and (4) the misconstrual of Jesus' mission as one of bringing the fire of judgment (3:9, 17; 7:19-20).[13] This marks the disciples as full participants in the divine mission, as John was, even if they, like John, remain unenlightened concerning important aspects of the nature of that mission.

This is the first of several references to the Samaritans in Luke-Acts, and it accesses common knowledge of the traditional animosity characterizing

11. Compare the resolve of Paul, e.g., in Acts 19:21-22; 20:22-24; 21:10-14.

12. ἄγγελος is used of humans in Luke-Acts only in 7:24, 27; 9:52.

13. The first three of these parallels are noted by Tannehill, *Narrative Unity*, 1:229-30.

Jew-Samaritan relations. Any discussion of the origins of the Samaritans is problematized by the issues of partial and competing sources.[14] What is evident is that the Samaritans were a religious group focused on Mount Gerizim and inhabiting parts of the central hill country bordered by Galilee in the north and Judea in the south; like the Jews more generally, Samaritans also gathered in communities in the Diaspora. Though they are best known for their outright rejection of the Jerusalem-centered salvation history (since this set them apart most radically from other forms of Judaism), they also had competing views of Scripture, of messianic expectation, and, most importantly, of what constitutes authentic faith before God. According to Josephus, such differences were sometimes manifested in acts of violence.[15] Luke's narrative presupposes an awareness of the Samaritans' status as foreigners (from a perspective within Judaism) who are not as peripheral to conventional understandings of God's purpose as Gentiles would be, but who are nonetheless not expected to exemplify the graciousness of God.[16]

Against this background, perhaps the most notable feature of Luke's account is that Jesus and his entourage did not altogether bypass the region of the Samaritans by taking the circuitous but preferred route of Galileans making pilgrimage to Jerusalem through Transjordan. Instead, they actually journeyed into Samaritan territory. The rejection of Jesus by the Samaritans — that is, by a people who had repudiated the centrality of Jerusalem — may be due simply to the identity his destination, Jerusalem. The parallelism between vv 51 and 53, however, suggests another, or at least an additional, nuance. That Jesus is rejected precisely on the terms in which his prophetic resolution had first been expressed is reminiscent of Jesus' rejection by the people of Nazareth (4:16-30).[17] Like them, these Samaritan villagers rebuff Jesus because they cannot accept his understanding and embodiment of the divine purpose.

54-56 Earlier, Jesus had instructed his disciples regarding the appropriate response when faced with inhospitality (9:5). Skirting that directive, they instead act as persons intoxicated with their own sense of power (cf. 9:46-50). They thus indicate their misunderstanding of Jesus' mission and their misappropriation of his authority (1) by replicating John's error in thinking that messianic authority would be incarnated in a mission of judgment,[18] (2) by thus assuming that their own exercise of power would

14. See Crown, ed., *Samaritans;* and the summary in Williamson, "Samaritans," 725-27.

15. See Josephus *Ant.* 18.2.2 §§29-30; 20.6.1-3 §§118-36. Cf. *Jubilees* 30.

16. In the Gospel, see 10:33-35; 17:11-19. Cf. Maddox, *Purpose,* 169; Ford, *My Enemy Is My Guest,* 78-95; Haudebert, "Samarie."

17. See Tiede, *Prophecy and History,* 61.

18. See 3:17. On the use of "fire" for "judgment," see 12:49-53; 17:29.

include the capacity to command fire and dole out judgment, and, thus, (3) by making too easy an equation between Elijah and Jesus. It is true that Elijah had called down fire from heaven to consume representatives of Ahaziah, king of Samaria, for his failure to acknowledge the God of Israel (2 Kgs 1:1-16), and that Luke has used Elijah-material to portray Jesus (most recently in v 51!); but Jesus is not Elijah (cf. 9:19-20, 33-36). The affinity between the Elijah-story and the Samaritan rejection of Jesus may have been obvious to the disciples, so that their proposed action against the Samaritans would seem to have had scriptural sanction. But Luke's presentation of Jesus uses Elijah both as type and antitype. In this case, Jesus' refusal to act according to the script provided by the ancient presentation of Elijah signals a serendipitous extension of clemency and mercy that will be matched both by the exemplary behavior of other Samaritans in the journey narrative (10:25-37; 17:11-19) and, in Acts, by the proclamation and reception of the message of the kingdom of God in Samaria (Acts 1:8; 8:5-26).[19]

The inadequacy of the disciples at this juncture is underscored by their explicit identification as James and John. These two were among the trio who accompanied Jesus in the scene of transfiguration, and who thus heard Jesus and his message legitimated in the most profound way possible, by God himself (9:28-36). Had they in fact "listened to him," would they not have remembered his words regarding the divine necessity of his rejection? Unable to collocate "power and authority" with "rejection," they continue to act brashly and wrongly. Their proposal places them in an adverse position vis-à-vis the divine will, and Jesus rebukes them accordingly, as if they were representatives of a diabolic mission.[20]

With this episode, Luke marks again the need for the journey, a central emphasis of which is the formation of a people who will hear and obey the word of God. With the need again underscored, then, v 56 notes that the journey is rejoined.

57-58 As will often be the case in the travel narrative, Luke correlates a travel notice with material on discipleship. Expected notations about the journey — for example, current location and direction of travel — are characteristically missing; what is important is that they are "on the road," for it is on the journey that instruction leading to the formation of faithful disciples will be provided.

This and the following encounters paint a stark, demanding picture of

19. Cf. C. A. Evans, "Elijah/Elisha Narratives," 78-79.
20. ἐπιτιμάω is not always used with reference to the rebuke of demonic powers, but it often is — cf., e.g., 4:35, 39, 41; 8:24; 9:42; et al. On the significance of Jesus "turning" to address his disciples, see above, on 7:9-10.

discipleship. Here, an unnamed person volunteers herself for discipleship in an exemplary fashion.[21] Jesus' reply takes the form of an aphorism,[22] embracing at once two characteristic features of the journey. First, as vv 52-53 have just indicated, the lot of the Son of Man is one of rejection. As a traveler, he is dependent on the hospitality of others; without it, he is homeless. Second, Jesus' wisdom saying is reminiscent of earlier material on the Third Gospel related to possessions — specifically on the necessity of not allowing possessions or "the cares of life" to imperil the growth of genuine faith (e.g., 8:14; see §11). Although Jesus typically employs "Son of Man" as a self-referent designed to intimate what is unique about his person, as a reply to this would-be disciple Jesus' words disclose as well the fate of those who would journey with him (cf. 6:40; 9:22-23).

What is the response of this would-be disciple? That none is provided, and that Luke notes only that "someone" asserted her willingness to follow Jesus, gives this scene a certain timeless quality. In this it is reminiscent of Jesus' address to his followers about the requirements of discipleship in 9:23-27; in both cases Jesus' words are addressed to all who would follow him, both in the narrative and outside of it. Those who would be his disciples then and now must reckon with how identifying with Jesus might place them outside the boundaries of what is acceptable to a world not oriented toward the aim of God.

59-62 The next two vignettes appear in parallel form: invitation/petition to follow + proposal to delay discipleship until something is accomplished ("first") + reference to "the kingdom of God" included in the rejection of the proposed delay. Again, the analogy provided by Elijah and Elisha is instructive, for Elijah allowed Elisha to return to his home to bid his parents farewell before "he set out and followed Elijah" (1 Kgs 19:19-21). By way of contrast, Jesus allows for no delay. Why is this? On the one hand, it is notable that burying one's father and bidding father and mother farewell fall within the realm of assumed behavior for those who would honor their parents, as the Mosaic law required.[23] Similarly, one should recall the obligatory obedience to one's living father expected in the

---

21. That is, she uses the verb associated with discipleship, ἀκολουθέω (see, e.g., 5:1-11); and she asserts her willingness to join the journey. Luke does not specify whether this would-be disciple is male or female (in Luke-Acts, αὐτῷ does not necessarily designate a man).

22. Cf. M. H. Smith, "No Place for a Son of Man."

23. Deut 5:16. This is not to say that the OT law concerned itself with the burial of one's father (or other relatives). It does not, though one can find evidence for the burial of one's parents as a moral corollary of the command to honor one's father and mother — cf. Gen 23:3-4; Tob 4:3-4; 6:14-15; 14:11-13; Salo, *Luke's Treatment of the Law,* 101-2.

Roman world, even among his adult sons.[24] On the other, the presence of dual references to the kingdom of God announces the reorganization of former allegiances, with the result that one may be called upon, as in this case, to engage in behavior deemed deviant by normal conventions.[25] But this is the nature of the kingdom of God in Luke, which makes its presence known through a reordering of the character of human interaction. The ministry of the kingdom (v 60) and fitness for the kingdom (v 62) presume a redefinition of kinship relations centered on hearing and doing the word of God (8:19-21; cf. 14:26).

Consequently, the response of each of Jesus' unnamed partners in conversation sounds a note of irony. Both refer to Jesus as "Lord," recognizing him as a person whose beckoning was to be taken with seriousness. Through their attempts to delay obedience, however, they expose the hollowness of their affirmation (cf. 6:46).

How can the dead bury their own dead? This is normally taken metaphorically: "Let the spiritually dead bury the physically dead."[26] This reading would make good on the change of life for which Jesus calls, particularly with regard to the reconstruction of one's dispositions and behaviors (see on 6:20-49) and of one's self-identity (see on 9:23). Contemporary Jewish funerary customs make possible another reading.[27] The practice of primary burial (in which the corpse is placed in a sealed tomb) followed by secondary burial (following a twelve-month period of decomposition the bones were collected and reburied in an ossuary or "bone box") is well attested, with the additional twelve months between burial and reburial providing for the completion of the work of mourning. According to this reckoning, Jesus' proverbial saying would refer to the physically dead in both instances: "Let those already dead

---

24. This is especially relevant for the question of taking leave of one's parents. K. E. Bailey (*Through Peasant Eyes*, 26-27) argues that the burial request is tantamount to an expression of a son's duty to serve his father until his father is respectfully buried.

25. Hengel (*Charismatic Leader*, 8-14) concludes his investigation of the sharpness of Jesus' directive on the burial of one's father thus: "There is hardly one logion of Jesus which more sharply runs counter to law, piety and custom than does Mt 8.22 = Lk 9.60a . . ." (14). Cf. E. P. Sanders, *Jesus and Judaism*, 252-55; Esler, *Community and Gospel*, 117-18 — though it is not clear why one must see in Jesus' statement in Luke an abrogation of the Mosaic law, since, at least strictly speaking, the law made no such demands.

26. So, e.g., Marshall, 411; Fitzmyer, 1:836. See Hengel, *Charismatic Leader*, 7-8.

27. That a further reading may be called for is suggested by the use of the reflexive pronoun, ἑαυτῶν, which makes the second group of dead persons a subset of the first — a reality that is hard to understand on the usual interpretation. For a summary of contemporary funerary practices, see Green, "Burial," 89; on this alternative reading, see McCane, "Secondary Burial."

in the family tomb rebury their own dead." In either case, Jesus' disrespect for such a venerable practice rooted in OT law is matched only by the authority he manifests by asserting the priority of the claims of discipleship in the kingdom of God.

In this way, Luke brings to a close his introduction to the journey narrative by asserting through the repetition of rigorous demands the nature of commitment required of those who would follow Jesus on the journey. They must match the depth of his resolution to serve the purpose of God, even when it leads to rejection and execution. Apart from conviction measured in these terms, the lessons of discipleship cannot be fully absorbed.

5.1.2. The Mission of the Seventy-two (10:1-20)

10:1 *After this the Lord appointed seventy-two*[28] *others and sent them on ahead of him in pairs to every town and place where he himself intended to go.* 2 *He said to them, "The harvest is plentiful, but the laborers are few; therefore ask the Lord of the harvest to send out laborers into his harvest.* 3 *Go!*[29] *See, I am sending you out like lambs into the midst of wolves.* 4 *Carry no purse, no bag, no sandals; and greet no one on the road.* 5 *Whatever house you enter, first say, 'Peace to this house!'* 6 *And if a child of peace*[30] *is there, your peace will rest on that person; but if not, it will return to you.* 7 *Remain in the same house, eating and drinking whatever they provide, for the laborer deserves to be paid. Do not move about from house to house.* 8 *Whenever you enter a town and its people welcome you, eat what is set before you;* 9 *cure the sick who are there, and say to them, 'The kingdom of God has come near to you.'* 10 *But whenever you enter a town and they do not welcome you, go out into its streets and say,* 11 *'Even the dust of your town that clings to our feet, we wipe off in protest against you. Yet know this: the kingdom of God has come near.'* 12 *I tell you, on that day it will be more tolerable for Sodom than for that town.*

13 *"Woe to you, Chorazin! Woe to you, Bethsaida! For if the deeds of power done in you had been done in Tyre and Sidon, they would have repented long ago, sitting in sackcloth and ashes.* 14 *But at the judgment it will be more tolerable for Tyre and Sidon than for you.*

---

28. NRSV: "seventy." Though the manuscript evidence favors the reading with "seventy-two," NA[27] prints δύο in brackets (see, though, the extended discussion in Metzger, "Seventy or Seventy-two Disciples?"). In light of the widespread use of "seventy" in the biblical tradition, it is much easier to imagine that δύο was omitted than that it was added. See the discussion by Kurt Aland in Metzger, *Textual Commentary,* 151.

29. NRSV: "Go on your way"; Greek: ὑπάγετε.

30. NRSV: "anyone . . . who shares in peace"; Greek: υἱὸς εἰρήνης.

15 And you, Capernaum, will you be exalted to heaven? No, you will be brought down to Hades.

16 "Whoever listens to you listens to me, and whoever rejects you rejects me, and whoever rejects me rejects the one who sent me."

17 The seventy-two[31] returned with joy, saying, "Lord, in your name even the demons submit to us!" 18 He said to them, "I watched Satan fall from heaven like a flash of lightning. 19 See, I have given you authority to tread on snakes and scorpions, and over all the power of the enemy; and nothing will hurt you. 20 Nevertheless, do not rejoice at this, that the spirits submit to you, but rejoice that your names are written in heaven."

Luke's account of the mission of the seventy-two is closely related temporally and thematically to his sketch of the onset of the journey to Jerusalem. This is not incidental. In an important sense, the missionary instructions the seventy-two receive are determined by the exigencies of the journey. Because of its relative proximity in the narrative, Luke's report of the sending of an advance party in 9:51-56 guides our reading of the current scene. Similarly, in 9:1-6 Luke had established a frame for the missionary work of Jesus' followers, so that it is difficult not to read this second episode of sending in light of the first. In fact, there are important hints that the narrative supports this reading strategy. For example, we are told explicitly that the twelve were given power and authority over demons (9:1); Luke mentions no such equipping on the part of the seventy-two, yet we learn in retrospect not only that the seventy-two had been involved in a ministry of exorcism, but that they had done so on the basis of authority from Jesus (10:17-20). Following 9:1-6, then, we are encouraged, first, to believe that Jesus' "sending" incorporates somehow the provision of the competence necessary to achieve the missionary end for which persons are sent. Second, that Jesus' instructions to "cure the sick" (10:9) can be fulfilled in ministries of exorcism (10:17) is a reminder of the link between disease and diabolic oppression in Lukan thought.[32] Third, and most significant, apart from revisions introduced explicitly, we come to assume that the instructions provided earlier are presumed in successive accounts of sending, even though Luke's audience is spared the redundancy this entails. This presumption will find support in the actual missionary activity reported both in this pericope (which follows the forms of ministry proposed in 9:1-6) and more fully in the book of Acts.

Luke provides no geographical setting for the mission of the seventy-two, and there is no reason to expect that Jesus' envoys participate at this

31. See above on v 1.
32. See esp. 13:10-17; Acts 10:38.

juncture in a mission to the Gentiles.[33] Nevertheless, in other ways Luke uses this scene to prepare for and anticipate a mission that is in the process of expanding beyond the land of the Jews. This is suggested by the number of important parallels between the sending of the seventy-two and the mission "to the end of the earth" as it is portrayed in Acts — for example, the thread that runs from the mission of John to the mission of the seventy-two to the mission of Jesus' followers in Acts, as well as the parallels between the forms of ministry ("in the name of Jesus") and anticipated reception of the seventy-two and their counterparts in Acts.[34] In indirect and figurative ways, too, this narrative unit points to the wider mission. The appointment of the seventy-two portends in a symbolic way a concern for all the peoples of the world. Moreover, the rejection of Jesus and his message among Galilean towns, set against the claim that a mission oriented toward Gentile settings would certainly have produced repentance, raises the prospect of opportunities for response to the good news outside the land of the Jews.

Overall, though, the significance of Luke's narration of the mission of the seventy-two lies elsewhere. The mission itself is not reported; rather, the focus lies more narrowly on Jesus' instructions and, within these, especially on the motif of the division that will result from the presence of the kingdom of God (cf. 2:34). Peace will be pronounced; will it reside with "children of peace" (vv 5-6)? The kingdom of God will be proclaimed; will it be experienced as human restoration or as judgment (vv 8-11)? This idea is pushed even further in this unit, where it becomes evident that the propagation of the message is not only about human responses but has also to do with Satan and his minions. Through the clever juxtaposition of images in vv 13-20, Luke communicates that to reject Jesus' messengers is to reject Jesus and his message, to reject Jesus is to reject God, to reject God is to align oneself with Satan, and to align oneself with Satan is to place oneself in a position to be cast down in judgment. The theme of this narrative unit, then, concerns *the experience of the mission as the arena of conflict and eschatological engagement with diabolic forces.* Importantly, this clash is not without its limits. The ultimate triumph of God's purpose is presaged by Jesus' vision of the downfall of Satan, as well as by his identification — by the narrator, by himself, and by the seventy-two — as "Lord." Indeed, as Jesus interprets the mission of

33. Attempts to read this mission as directed toward, e.g., Perea, "the Gentiles," Galilee, or even Samaria falter due to the lack of any geographical marker in this narrative unit (or of any geographical connection to 9:51-56) and, more generally, on the deficit of geographical progression in the journey narrative as a whole (i.e., until 19:1). That Jesus is continually portrayed as "going toward Jerusalem" is a metaphorical reference more than it is a claim by which to work out a travel itinerary; see above on 9:51–19:48.

34. See the discussion in Korn, *Geschichte Jesu,* 112-26; Tannehill, *Narrative Unity,* 1:232-37.

the seventy-two (first in vv 17-20, but also in vv 21-24), its eschatological significance moves into the forefront.

1-2 Jesus' concern with recruiting disciples to serve the kingdom of God through single-minded devotion and proclamation was registered emphatically at the close of ch. 9 (vv 60, 62). It follows easily from this that he would involve others, in addition to the twelve (9:1), in the mission. At the outset, the seventy-two are portrayed in ways reminiscent of the "messengers" of 9:51-52, who were themselves reminiscent of John the Baptist.[35] Like their predecessors, they are "sent"[36] "before his face,"[37] marking them, like John, as full participants in the divine mission.

The number "twelve" was meaningful in the choosing of apostles,[38] so we are predisposed to regard the number seventy-two as significant too. According to Genesis 10 in the LXX, the number of the world's nations is seventy-two. Seventy-two is also reckoned in *3 Enoch* 17:8; 18:2-3; 30:2 as the number of princes and languages in the world. And according to legend, seventy-two elders were commissioned to translate the law from Hebrew to Greek, a project undertaken in order to win renown throughout the whole world for the Jews and their God (*Epistle of Aristeas* 35–51). Accordingly, the appointment of the seventy-two can be understood as prefiguring the universal mission in Acts.[39]

In 9:1-2, the twelve had been sent to preach and to heal, while in 9:51-52 some messengers had been commissioned to prepare for his arrival along the way to Jerusalem. These two functions are combined in the sending of the seventy-two, who will both prepare the way for Jesus and work as laborers in the harvest. (1) Explicit mention of this former role, going ahead to the places Jesus intended to go, reminds us also of the distinction between

35. Luke uses the verb ἀναδείκνυμι of the appointment of the seventy-two. Should we read a linguistic echo of his characterization of John's ministry (ἀνάδειξις, 1:80)? In favor of this is the fact that the verb appears in the NT only in 10:1; Acts 1:24; the noun in the NT only in 1:80. However, the meaning in the current co-text is "to assign," while in the other two instances the notion is one of "appearance."

36. ἀποστέλλω — 7:20, 27; 9:2, 52; 10:1.

37. πρὸ προσώπου — 1:17, 76; 7:27; 9:52; 10:1.

38. See above on 6:12-16.

39. Cf. the table of nations in Acts 2:9-11, on which see J. M. Scott, "Luke's Geographical Horizon," 524-43. See Korn, *Geschichte Jesu,* 117. Alternatively, if the Lukan narrative originally referred to the mission of the "seventy" (see the note on the translation, above), the significance is not dramatically altered; in the MT of Genesis 10, there are reckoned to be seventy nations in the world (cf. Rengstorf, "ἑπτά," 634-35; Marshall, 415). Alternatively, one might see in the background of the sending of the seventy an allusion to Moses' appointment of seventy assistants (Numbers 11) — an allusion that would further the echoes of Moses and the exodus tradition in the Lukan narrative (cf. Garrett, *Demise of the Devil,* 47-48).

the mission of the twelve and this one. This difference is marked by the journey to Jerusalem, already marked by rejection (9:53). This change of circumstances, with the hostility that comes with it, gives rise to the sending of these others "in pairs."[40] (2) The latter employs images from agrarian realities everywhere. When the fruit has ripened, only weeks, sometimes only days, are allowed to bring in the crop, with the result that laborers are added to the normal workforce.[41] With regard to both aspects of the portfolio shared by the seventy-two, then, an anxious, urgent note is sounded.

3-4 Jesus' instructions to the seventy-two are economic in Luke's rendering. This is due in part to our memory of the instructions in 9:1-3, which are brought forward into the present co-text by verbal resemblances. Their brevity is also due to Luke's concern to spotlight instead the nature and consequences of the changing circumstances in which these followers will be operating. Since 9:21-26, Jesus' passion, and the solidarity of his followers with his suffering, has begun to loom over the narrative; indeed, as a result of his commitment to the divine purpose, he has already been refused hospitality in a Samaritan village (see above on 9:53). Earlier, the offer of welcome was the rule, but this can no longer be assumed. The heightened vulnerability of the disciples in this new situation is underscored by their comparison with lambs among wolves. The urgency of their circumstances necessitates their traveling light and with single-minded dedication to their task (cf. 2 Kgs 4:28).[42]

5-7 "Peace" as metonymic for "salvation" is well attested in the Third Gospel,[43] where the Greco-Roman notion of "peace" as the absence of war, social discord, and sedition has been shaped by the expanded presentation of peace, shalom, in the OT as communal well-being: euphoria, security, plenty, and the like.[44] The Israelite greeting, whether in correspondence or in

---

40. It is noteworthy that, in the context of the passion, Jesus will again revise his missionary instructions. Because of heightened hostility, they may no longer anticipate the normal extension of hospitality (22:35-38).

41. ἐργάτης, "one who does something for wages" (cf. 10:7), is used for farm laborers in, e.g., Philo *Agr.* 1 §5; Josephus *J.W.* 9.10 §557.

42. Lang ("Grußverbot oder Besuchsverbot?") theorizes that Jesus' meaning is that those who regard themselves on a missionary journey ought not take this as an opportunity to visit extended family or friends. This is a possible extension of the sense of ἀσπάζομαι (cf. Acts 18:22; 21:7), and follows well on Jesus' insistence on total dedication (cf. Luke 9:57-62).

43. See 1:79; 2:14, 29; 7:50; 8:48; 19:38, 42; 24:36.

44. See *TLNT,* 1:424-27. Often, too sharp a wedge is drawn between Hebrew and Roman notions of "peace" (as in, e.g., Geddert, "Peace," 604). This is based on too narrow an understanding of the cessation of war, without proper regard for the assumed religious basis for the cessation of war or for the promise of postwar circumstances for the perpetuation of socio-political consonance.

conversation, was a wish for peace. At least this much is meant by the greeting Jesus' followers are instructed to convey upon entering a household. Verse 6 suggests that more is at stake, however. Peace is portrayed not merely as something one might wish for another, but as an entity that can be transmitted and possessed or returned. Inasmuch as peace is the gift of Yahweh (e.g., Num 6:26; Isa 26:12; 45:7; Luke 2:14), the nature of Jesus' directive is to identify these sent ones as persons capable of extending the peace that is God's to others. "Child of peace" — that is, one whose life is characterized by peace — then, is capable of more than one nuance.[45] It can refer to one who has already begun to embody the wholeness these delegates of Jesus' mission will communicate,[46] or it can refer to those who are predisposed to welcome these messengers together with their message. Importantly, one does not predetermine to whom God's wholeness is transmitted; the division that results from the communication of peace is without human premeditation, but arises through its acceptance or rejection.

On Jesus' instructions to remain in one house, see above on 9:4. In addition to what is found there in the directions to the twelve is the present emphasis on the wages of the laborer. Though the saying is proverbial,[47] in its current co-text it was anticipated by Jesus' description of the mission as a harvest involving workers-for-hire (v 2). The term used in both instances generally describes one who works for wages;[48] in the case of the mission, pay is specified as the reception of hospitality. In the juxtaposition of these two forms of instructions in v 7, Jesus places his emissaries in a place of tension between dependence on and the abuse of hospitality.

8-11 Again, the picture Jesus paints through his instructions is a familiar one. The welcome people extend to the messengers is commensurate with the welcome they extend to the message. (1) If Jesus' agents are received, they are to accept hospitality, comport themselves as exemplary guests (cf. v 7), and proclaim the coming of salvation in deed and word. In this way they identify themselves intimately with Jesus' own ministry of healing and proclaiming the kingdom (esp. 9:11; also, e.g., 4:43; 8:1-3). In this case, the expression "curing the sick" is synecdochic for the ministry of restoration that is characteristic of the good news in Luke — including, for example, the

---

45. See Klassen, "Child of Peace," 496-97. On the expression "son/child of . . . ," see above on 3:7-9.

46. That is, here and elsewhere in the Gospel of Luke one must allow for the possibility that, through means unknown to the reader, there are those who already embody an openness to divine restoration (e.g., 2:25, 38) that is exhibited in dispositions and practices consistent with Jesus' message. Cf., e.g., 7:1-10; Green, *Gospel of Luke,* 105-6.

47. Harvey ("Worthy of His Hire," 211) draws attention to *Pseudo-Phocylides* 19; Euripides *Rhesus* 191; Lev 19:13; Deut 24:14-15; Mal 3:5 LXX; Sir 34:22; Tob 4:15.

48. ἐργάτης; see above on v 2; also Heiligenthal, "ἐργάζομαι," 49.

vanquishing of demonic forces (explicitly noted in the report of v 17). Even if the kingdom has not yet appeared in its fullness,[49] the clear focus in this text (as in Luke-Acts taken as a whole) is on the presence of God's saving activity in the mission of Jesus and through those he recruits. In v 9, as a consequence of their welcoming Jesus' emissaries, the townspeople experience the kingdom as restoration to health. (2) The kingdom is no less present for those who refuse Jesus' agents (v 10), but for them the message of divine visitation is transmuted into one of judgment. Inhospitality, after all, could be a form of negative sanction in the context of disputes over appropriate faith and behavior;[50] refusal to accept the envoys designated by Jesus was a demonstration of the spurning of the good news of the kingdom propagated in Jesus' ministry. On the meaning of wiping the dust from one's feet in vv 10c-11a, see above on 9:5. In the directive to the seventy-two, this action takes on more the form of a prophetic action of judgment,[51] with the heightened drama of symbolic action accompanied by words of warning.

The pattern of vv 8-9 is paralleled in vv 10-11:

entry into a town → manner of reception and its consequences + kingdom saying.

This underscores what was already made clear in v 7, though using different soteriological language. Earlier, the conveyance of peace was the constant, with variety introduced at the point of openness and reception. In the same way, the kingdom of God is presently at work to transform the world of these townspeople, but it remains to be seen how they will experience the actualization of God's project: as restoration to wholeness or as judgment? The mission of the seventy-two, and especially the question of how they and their message are received, thus serves the larger Lukan themes of the division and reversal that accompany the inauguration of salvation.[52]

12-16   The prospect of inhospitality raised in vv 10-11 leads directly into the interlude of vv 12-16. Though specific towns are mentioned, the point of Jesus' invective is more general: "that town [which rejects you]" (v 12), "whoever rejects you" (v 16). Jesus' references to "that day" (v 12) and "the judgment" are both shorthand for the more common expression "the day of

---

49. See Marshall, *Luke: Historian and Theologian,* 132-34. Although the precise temporal sense of ἤγγικεν is still debated, it seems clear that the term itself, devoid of co-textual considerations, embraces both imminence and arrival. See the summary in Beasley-Murray, *Jesus and the Kingdom,* 72-73. Mattill (*Last Things,* 70-79), mostly on linguistic grounds, argues for the rendering, "The kingdom of God is fast approaching!" (76, 79); cf. Maddox, *Purpose,* 123-24.

50. Cf. 3 John 9-10; Meeks, *Origins of Christian Morality,* 105-6.

51. Cf. Isa 20:2-4. A prophetic act of warning is recounted in Acts 21:10-11.

52. See Carroll, *End of History,* 86-88.

the Lord" — that is, the time of Yahweh's judgment. During the Second Temple Period, "the day" was generally associated with the end of the age.[53] Even if the kingdom of God "has come near" (vv 9, 11), then, for the Lukan narrative the consummation of God's purpose, including the final judgment and deliverance, remains future. This is an important nuance in light of the expectation of John that the Messiah would bring judgment (leading to John's doubts about the identification of Jesus as the Messiah — 3:15-17; 7:18-23) and in light of the act of judgment proposed by Jesus' disciples when Jesus and his entourage were denied hospitality in a Samaritan village (9:52-55). The working out of God's plan through Jesus does not signify the absence of judgment in that plan; it does, however, raise important questions about *when* and *by whom* judgment will be exercised.[54] It is on these latter points that the knowledge of John the Baptist and of Jesus' disciples has proven deficient.

The sin of Sodom was proverbial in the OT and other Jewish texts (Gen 19:1-23; see Isa 3:9; Ezek 16:48). Some interpretive texts note the general sexual immorality associated with the Sodomites (e.g., *Jub.* 16:5-6; 20:5; Jude 7), and Philo explicitly speaks of the sin of Sodom as homosexual practice.[55] However, Jewish interpretation of Genesis 19 focused above all on the violation of hospitality at Sodom.[56] The association of the Sodomites with inhospitality is also in view in the current co-text: They are symbolic of any town that refuses welcome to Jesus' agents, and are thus guilty of refusing hospitality to God's emissaries. Because the kingdom of God has drawn near, however, those towns that follow the example of Sodom in its inhospitality toward the envoys of the kingdom will be judged even more strictly.

In a surprising move, Jesus goes on to compare such a town with Chorazin,[57] Bethsaida (cf. 9:10), and Capernaum — Galilean towns that had been the recipients of the redemptive activity of Jesus and his followers, and that would be judged harshly. This is surprising because we have heard nothing of their general lack of hospitality heretofore. Rather, with the close of the Galilean segment of Jesus' ministry, Jesus provides a retrospective summary in which these towns are indicted for their overall failure to respond genuinely to the message of salvation. Consequently, we are informed analeptically that

53. Cf. Hiers, "Day of Judgment," 79; *idem,* "Day of the Lord," 82.

54. Cf. Luke 17:20, 24; Acts 17:30-31.

55. Philo *Abr.* 26 §§133-36; cf. *Vita Mos.* 2.10 §58.

56. According to Josephus, e.g., God resolved to chastise the Sodomites because of their insolence and impiety, manifest in their hatred of foreigners and unwillingness to have dealings with others (*Ant.* 1.11.1 §§194-95). See Ezek 16:48; Wis 19:13-15.

57. Chorazin appears nowhere else in the Third Gospel, but is located by archaeologists in the hills above Capernaum and the north shore of the Lake of Gennesaret. This is consistent with Luke's earlier portrayal of Jesus' ministry as an itinerary in the region of Galilee (e.g., 4:14-15, 43).

the ambivalence of the crowds that will also characterize the Jerusalem journey was already typical of Jesus' itinerary in Galilee.[58] Luke had recorded initial responses of wonderment, even praise, but, apparently, genuine faith (hearing and doing the word) had not emerged. As a consequence, Jesus borrows language from the ancient prophetic oracles to characterize these Galilean towns (and their fates) as though they were the enemies of the people of God.[59]

Indeed, although Isaiah had railed against the wickedness of Tyre and Sidon (Isaiah 23),[60] Jesus asserts that these Gentile urban centers would have welcomed the message (through repentance) in a way that the Jewish people had not. "Deeds of power," then, refer synecdochically to the various manifestations of the kingdom in the ministry of Jesus and, by extension, of his followers (cf. vv 9, 11, 17). This is the first use of the term "repent" in the public ministry of Jesus (though cf. 3:1-14), and its presence is marked all the more through the image of "sitting in sackcloth and ashes" — a traditional symbol for repentance (e.g., Jonah 3:6). The concept of "repentance" has made its appearance on multiple occasions, however — for example, in "leaving everything to follow Jesus" (5:11, 28) or in the summons to reconstruct one's identity in light of the absolute claims of the kingdom (9:23-26, 57-62). Repentance has to do with redirecting one's life toward the one purpose of God and, thus, is key to one's response to the good news in Luke-Acts.[61]

Why does Jesus speak so harshly of those towns that refuse to extend welcome to the seventy-two? Verse 16 presents the available choices along bipolar lines: one either "listens" or "rejects." Jesus thus employs the wider notion of "listening" as "hearing and obeying." Then, through the rhetorical device of concatenation, with "to reject" repeated from one clause to the next, he equates the rejection of his messengers with the rejection of himself and, indeed, of God.[62] Jesus' reference to "whoever" universalizes this axiom, pointing forward to the mission in Acts and beyond.[63]

17-20 Remarkably, in spite of the attention Luke gives to Jesus' instructions to the seventy-two, he provides no account of the mission itself. Again, the narrator maintains a more narrow focus on Jesus, allowing Acts to serve as testimony of the success and conflict characteristic of the mission

58. Cf. Egelkraut, *Jesus' Mission,* 149-50.

59. See esp. Isa 14:11, 13-15.

60. Cf. Ezek 26:15-21; 28.

61. The language of repentance is more pervasive in Acts (e.g., 2:38; 3:19; 5:31). See further Green, *Gospel of Luke,* 107-8.

62. This point is made both through the linkage provided by the repetition of "to reject," and through the use of ἀποστέλλω in its sense of "authorized sending."

63. See further Korn, *Geschichte Jesu,* 125-26.

of those commissioned by Jesus. What is provided is a modest report in which the seventy-two rejoice at their power over demons, a retrospective summary that occasions additional commentary on the part of Jesus.

Verses 17-20 are bound together by the *inclusio* of vv 17 and 20, with their repetition of "joy" and the clause "the demons submit to us/you"; and by the dual emphasis on names. That Jesus' reuses the language of the seventy-two marks his speech as a mild corrective to theirs. It is a mild one, though, since overall they are portrayed positively in this scene. Their reference to him as "Lord" (cf. vv 1, 2) marks their recognition of his royal and messianic dignity and beneficence, and this is in no way vitiated in this scene. (Indeed, it seems to be validated in vv 21-24.) They describe themselves as operating "in his name," which again signifies their genuine identification with him,[64] and their description as persons whose names are "written in heaven" only accentuates this overall picture.[65]

Heretofore, Luke has referred to "the devil" rather than to "Satan" — the latter a loanword from the Aramaic: God's supernatural adversary, the chief of those diabolic forces opposed to God's purpose.[66] Jesus had just used Isaianic imagery to describe the descent of Capernaum (v 15; Isa 14:1-27); the same is now used with reference to Satan, whose claim to glory and allegiance (cf. 4:5-7; cf. Isa 14:13) is antecedent to, even mandates, his fall.[67] The deployment of the Isaianic imagery is important for Luke, who thus correlates the positions of Capernaum and of Satan over against God. In v 16b, Jesus had observed that rejecting his emissaries was tantamount to rejecting God; in light of the parallel drawn by the dual use of Isaiah 14, a further equation can be drawn by way of interpolation: To reject God is to align oneself with Satan, and to align oneself with Satan is to place oneself in the position of being cast down in judgment.

The question is, When did/will Satan fall? Some find in Jesus' assertion

---

64. See above on 9:49; cf. 9:24. Engagement in mission "in the name of Jesus" by the seventy-two prefigures the activity of the church in Acts; there, Christians heal (3:6, 16; 4:10, 30; 19:13), preach (4:12; 5:28, 40), and are baptized (8:16; 10:48; 19:5) in the name of Jesus; suffer for his name (5:41; 9:16; 21:13); and "call upon the name" of Jesus (9:14, 21; 22:16).

65. Crump ("Scribal-Intercessor," 59-63) refers to a number of biblical and extra-canonical texts wherein the tradition of the divine inscription of the names of the righteous in the heavenly books is developed — e.g., Exod 32:32-33; Pss 69:29; 139:16; Dan 7:10; 12:1; Phil 4:3; Heb 12:23; Rev 3:5; 13:8; 17:8; 20:12, 15; 21:27. Crump (58-59) wrongly associates the fall of Satan with the writing of the names of the seventy-two in the heavenly books, however; not only is his structural analysis of vv 17-20 overdrawn, but he also fails to grapple adequately with the overall portrayal of these disciples as those who "hear and act" in conformity with the message (and "name") of Jesus.

66. שָׂטָן — cf. 11QApPs[a] 4:12; 4Q504 1–2:iv:12(?); Sir 21:27; T. Dan 3:6; 5:6; 6:1.

67. See the discussion in Garrett, *Demise of the Devil*, 50.

a reference to a primordial event[68] or an event in the life of Jesus himself,[69] but neither of these options makes sense of the actual, ongoing exercise of satanic influence in the Lukan narrative. Indeed, in the Lukan presentation the death of Jesus itself is a manifestation of the power of darkness (22:53; 23:44). Nor is it likely that the fall of Satan is occasioned by Jesus' resurrection and ascension — again, since Satan remains proactive in the narrative of Acts (e.g., Acts 13:4-12; 26:18).[70] Certainly the success of the ministry of exorcism by the seventy-two does not presuppose the downfall of Satan;[71] rather, their mission presupposes only what Jesus claims (analeptically) — namely, that he had given them authority over all satanic forces. Luke portrays Jesus as having a prophetic vision,[72] then, whose content was the future (and ultimate) downfall of Satan, presumably scheduled for the time of the judgment to which he alludes in vv 12 and 14. Such a view is consonant with some Second Temple Jewish texts,[73] but Jesus' view in this Lukan co-text pushes beyond the content of those. The decisive fall of Satan is anticipated in the future, but it is already becoming manifest through the mission of Jesus and, by extension, through the ministry of his envoys.

In 1:68-79 (esp. 1:71, 74), speaking on behalf of God, Zechariah had characterized salvation as deliverance from the hands of our enemies. Because Luke-Acts does not document Israel's rescue from Rome, Zechariah's words have puzzled some readers of Luke. Here, however, a key interpretive move is introduced. This is the explicit identification of Satan as the real "enemy"[74] that is to be overcome. Rome is not the adversary, only one of its partners, joined by many others; in the current scene Satan's minions are referred to as "snakes and scorpions"[75] and, more generally, by all that would "harm"

---

68. See, e.g., Gen 6:1-4; Isa 14:12; Jude 6. Of course, Luke places no emphasis on the preexistence of Jesus.

69. The scene of temptation is the usual candidate — cf., most recently, Page, *Powers of Evil*, 110.

70. *Contra* Garrett, *Demise of the Devil*, 51-53. If *T. Sol.* 20:12-17 could be taken as an analogy (as argued by Crump, "Scribal-Intercessor," 54-55), then it would allow for a reading of the fall of Satan at, e.g., Jesus' temptation or ascension. In this text, demons fall as a consequence of their weakness, but are nonetheless capable of going back and forth from heaven to earth. This text does not refer to Satan (by this or any other of his manifold names), however, nor does it depict the ultimate defeat of evil.

71. *Contra* Crump, "Scribal-Intercessor," 57-58.

72. ἐθεώρουν is used in Daniel 7 to introduce an apocalyptic vision. *Contra*, e.g., Plymale (*Prayer Texts*, 48), who sees in the past tense of this verb necessary and sufficient cause to insist that (1) Jesus had an earlier vision of Satan's fall, and, thus, (2) that the activity of God — not Jesus nor his disciples — was responsible for Satan's action.

73. See *T. Lev.* 18:12; *T. Sim.* 6:6; *T. Zeb.* 9:8; cf. *T. Sol.* 20:17.

74. ἐχθρός; cf. Acts 13:10.

75. Cf. Page, *Powers of Evil*, 111.

these messengers — that is, reject the good news manifest in Jesus', and their, redemptive activity. When it is recognized that Luke identifies "the enemy" as the cosmic power of evil resident and active behind all forms of opposition to God and God's people, it is plain that Zechariah's hope has not been dashed but clarified and, indeed, radicalized.[76]

5.1.3. The Blessedness of the Disciples (10:21-24)

21 *At that same hour Jesus rejoiced in the Holy Spirit and said, "I thank you, Father, Lord of heaven and earth, because you have hidden these things from the wise and the intelligent and have revealed them to infants; yes, Father, for such was your gracious will.* 22 *All things have been handed over to me by my Father; and no one knows who the Son is except the Father, or who the Father is except the Son and anyone to whom the Son chooses to reveal him."*

23 *Then turning to the disciples, Jesus said to them privately, "Blessed are the eyes that see what you see!* 24 *For I tell you that many prophets and kings desired to see what you see, but did not see it, and to hear what you hear, but did not hear it."*

Rather than making a clear break between vv 20 and 21, Luke signals the important connection of this section to the previous account concerning the sending and return of the seventy-two. Their separation for the sake of comment is primarily for convenience. In an important sense, vv 17-20 had already taken up the matter continued here — namely, the interpretation of the mission of the seventy-two. As such, it has an important function at the outset of the Lukan journey narrative, just as it also presages the mission of the church in Acts.

The links from vv 17-20 to vv 21-24 are temporal, semantic, and theological. (1) "At that same hour" allows for no chronological disjunction between the words of Jesus to the seventy-two in the prior section and the onset of Jesus' prayer in the present. (2) Verses 17-24 are bound together by language from the semantic field Louw and Nida designate by the terms "Happy, Glad, Joyful":[77] "the seventy-two returned with joy," "do not rejoice at this," "rejoice that your names are written," "Jesus rejoiced in the Holy Spirit," "blessed are the eyes." Even if different lexemes are used to signal it,[78] eschatological jubilation pervades Luke's interpretation of the mission of

---

76. This form of salvation — from the power of darkness, of Satan — is also prominent in Acts; see, e.g., 5:16; 13:4-12; 16:16-18; 19:8-20; 26:17-18; Garrett, *Demise of the Devil.* See Green, "Salvation to the End of the Earth," forthcoming.

77. GELNT 1:302-4.

78. That is, χαρά (v 17), χαίρω (v 20 [2x]), ἀγαλλιάω (v 21), μακάριος (v 23).

the seventy-two. (3) The apposition of Jesus' words to the seventy-two regarding Satan and his rejoicing in the Spirit and words concerning revelation continue the contrast marked early on in the Gospel between the activity of Satan and the empowerment of the Spirit.[79]

Taken on its own terms this brief unit is fundamentally about the filial relationship of Father and Son, God and Jesus, and the disclosure of this relationship and its eschatological significance to the seventy-two.[80] This is important, for it brings into the cognizance of Jesus' followers the divine disclosure previously known to Luke's audience on account of the words of Gabriel to Mary (1:32-35) and to the three apostles, Peter, John, and James (9:35), but otherwise hidden. The import of this disclosure is related not only to its content but also to the identity of its recipients: "infants," rather than "the wise and the intelligent" — continuing the Lukan pattern of reversal (cf. 1:51-53; 2:34). Its relevance is further underscored by the teaching of Jesus in ch. 11, to the effect that Jesus' followers are to think of God and address God as their Father too (11:2, 13).

This unit cannot be read simply on its own terms, however, for its purpose is integrated into the larger narrative of the sending of the seventy-two. Read within this co-text, Jesus' prayer and words to his envoys become a means by which Luke interprets the significance of their being sent out and their mission "in his name." What is revealed to them, then, is a major Lukan concern — namely, that (1) the dominion of God is historically present in the redemptive activity of Jesus and (2), thus, also in the activity of Jesus' emissaries who act (and may, like him, encounter rejection) "in his name." With these verses, then, we reach a christological peak in the Gospel of Luke as well as a high point in the characterization of Jesus' disciples. We would be hard pressed to imagine how the prominence within God's redemptive plan of the church's mission in Acts could be anchored more firmly than it is here, in the ministry of Jesus.

21-22 Luke carefully ties this unit into his account of the return of the seventy-two, especially by his opening clause, "At that same hour." We are thus made aware of the relationship of the mission of Jesus' envoys (vv 1-20) and this pericope at the interpretive level. The significance of this section is signaled immediately by the explicit mention of Jesus' acting "in the Holy Spirit." This is not a new characterization of Jesus, but a lengthy period of narrative time has passed since we have been reminded that Jesus operates as

---

79. See esp. 4:1-19; Brawley, *Centering on God,* 82, 192; Shepherd, *Narrative Function,* 138. More generally, cf. Kingsbury, *Conflict in Luke,* 11-14; Green, *Gospel of Luke,* 22-49; Garrett, *Demise of the Devil,* 58 ("The struggle between Jesus [or the Holy Spirit] and Satan lies at the very heart of Luke's story").

80. This has been emphasized recently by Crump, *Jesus the Intercessor,* 56-60.

one anointed by the Spirit. Luke had established the anointing of Jesus by the Spirit as a major means by which to make sense of Jesus' mission (cf. 3:21-22; 4:1-19) and has now chosen to signal this motif again, here at the outset of the journey narrative.

In the Lukan narrative, the Holy Spirit is often portrayed as inspiring prayer/praise and speech, and this is the Spirit's role in this instance.[81] The form of Jesus' prayer is well known in Jewish literature: introductory formula of thanksgiving + reason.[82] The basis for thanksgiving is twofold:[83] God has concealed "these things" from some and revealed them to others. Both actions, according to Jesus, concern the same content and both are manifestations of the gracious will of God.[84] This double action draws immediate attention to the reversal motif pervasive in the soteriology of Luke-Acts, here displayed in the contrast between the elders of the community, regarded with high status on account of their wisdom, and infants, who have no status at all.[85] Jesus' prayer is thus reminiscent of the Song of Mary (1:51-53), his own teaching regarding those who honor the least in society (see above on 9:46-48), and the general portrayal of his ministry as bringing good news to "the poor" (see above on 4:18-19). If Jesus' words embody the message of reversal, however, they also entail a demand for people to dispense with customary concerns with status and conventional measures of wisdom, and to comport themselves as infants ready to operate not on the basis of their own prowess or potency but in the name of Jesus.[86]

At the forefront of Jesus' prayer is his identification of God as "Father" (5 times!), "Lord of heaven and earth," and the concomitant identification of himself as Son (3 times!). This identification accesses the wider Hellenistic-Jewish understanding of the father-son relationship as involving both the son's general education and the transmission of privileged information.[87] The filial relationship Jesus accentuates, then, identifies him as the one able to give the

81. Cf. Menzies, *Empowered for Witness,* 158; Shelton, *Mighty in Word,* 91.

82. "I thank you that . . ." (with ἐξομολογέομαι) is reminiscent of such psalms of thanksgiving as Pss 86:12-13; 118:21; *Pss. Sol.* 16:5; 1QH 2:20, 31; 3:19; et al.

83. Against interpretations that attempt to lessen the impression that Jesus thanks God for *concealing* as well as disclosing his revelation, see Crump, *Jesus the Intercessor,* 51-53.

84. εὐδοκία can lexicalize the concept of "decree" or "will," and, in this co-text, should be read in parallel with the "choosing" (βούλομαι) Jesus exercises according to v 22.

85. The degree to which Jesus' prayer embodies a subversion of conventional wisdom is suggested by the contrast with 2 Esdr 12:35-38, wherein "the secret of the Most High" is to be taught to "the wise among your people, whose hearts you know are able to comprehend and keep these secrets." Cf. 1 Cor 1:18-31.

86. See Brawley, *Centering on God,* 192.

87. Harvey, *Constraints of History,* 160.

definitive revelation of God's character and purpose. This relationship is not first the *content* of Jesus' revelation to the seventy-two; rather, it is foremost the precondition of that revelation. That is, the possibility of disclosure is raised by Jesus' sonship. Jesus' prayer goes on, then, to emphasize the sovereignty of God, the universality of God's dominion, and the authority of the Son as the one capable of revealing God.[88] Also disclosed in Jesus' prayer is the Father's "gracious will" to upset conventional wisdom through his redemptive plan to bring salvation to "the poor."

Can more be said about the content ("these things," v 21) of the divine disclosure? Yes, but in order to do so, vv 23-24 need also to be in view.

23-24   Jesus turns to his disciples and addresses them privately, not so much to transmit to them esoteric instruction but in recognition of their privileged status (cf. 8:9). From whence does their privileged status derive? Prophets, faithful spokespersons of God who anticipated the coming of salvation, did not see what the disciples have seen; what, then, gives these disciples such importance? Kings, people of great status according to normal canons, desired to see also, but did not; what, then, gives these disciples such significance? One thing is clear from these contrasting images: Their privileged status is not a consequence of any inherent qualification on their part. Jesus' words continue to build on the appositions already manifest in this narrative unit:

	hidden/do not see		*disclosed/see*
v 21	wise and intelligent	versus	infants
v 22			whoever the Son wishes
vv 23-24	prophets and kings	versus	"you [disciples]"

It is to those in the last column of persons that disclosure comes; they are the ones who can "see." Why? First, because this is the topsy-turvy way God works; second, because these followers of Jesus have acted in the mission as persons under his authority in the service of God's aim. By means of the mixture of words for sight and sound, Jesus identifies them as people who really see and really hear (cf. 8:10-11, 18), whose enlightenment is demonstrated in their obedience to the word of God.

What is it that they have been enabled to see? What has been lacking in their understanding thus far is the wherewithal for integrating the exercise of power and authority, the motif of glory, with the experience of suffering and rejection. In Jesus' instructions to the seventy-two, he stresses the possibility of rejection, placing side-by-side his guidelines for behavior in cases of

88. See Mowery, "God the Father," 127; Brawley, *Centering on God,* 116.

welcome and of inhospitality. Irrespective of outcome, he emphasizes, the message is the same. The kingdom of God has drawn near regardless of whether it is received or rejected. This is because, for Luke, the kingdom of God is historically present in the ministry of Jesus; wherever he is active, the kingdom is being manifested.[89] The blessed state of the disciples[90] resides in their recognition that the kingdom is being manifested, irrespective of how it is received, not only when Jesus is present but also when his envoys act in his name, under his authority and in harmony with the purpose of God. Jesus thus interprets the work of the seventy-two in an eschatological way, thus enabling them to see in Jesus' mission, in which they now participate, the revelation of God's salvific will coming to expression. Luke's readers may well be reminded of Simeon, whose eyes beheld God's salvation in its universal proportions, and whose vision of God's redemptive purpose was not diminished by the knowledge that the coming of salvation would engender conflict and anguish (2:29-35).

5.1.4. The Parable of the Compassionate Samaritan (10:25-37)

25 *Just then a lawyer stood up to test Jesus. "Teacher," he said, "what must I do to inherit eternal life?"* 26 *He said to him, "What is written in the law? How do you read it?"*[91] 27 *He answered, "You shall love the Lord your God with all your heart, and with all your soul, and with all your strength, and with all your mind; and your neighbor as yourself."* 28 *And he said to him, "You have given the right answer; do this, and you will live."*

29 *But wanting to justify himself, he asked Jesus, "And who is my neighbor?"* 30 *Jesus replied, "A man was going down from Jerusalem to Jericho, and fell into the hands of robbers, who stripped him, beat him, and went away, leaving him half dead.* 31 *Now by chance a priest was going down that road; and when he saw him, he passed by on the other side.* 32 *So likewise a Levite, when he came to the place and saw him, passed by on the other side.* 33 *But a Samaritan while traveling came near him; and when he saw him, he was moved with compassion.*[92] 34 *He went to him and bandaged his wounds, having poured oil and wine on them. Then he put him on his own animal, brought him to an inn, and took care of him.* 35 *The next day he took out two*

---

89. See Korn, *Geschichte Jesu*, 99-104, 122-24; Wolter, "Reich Gottes"; Luz, "βασιλεία," 204.

90. On μακάριος, see above, 1:45; 6:20-22; 7:23.

91. NRSV: "What do you read there?"

92. NRSV: "pity."

denarii, gave them to the innkeeper, and said, 'Take care of him; and
when I come back, I will repay you whatever more you spend.' 36 *Which*
of these three, do you think, was a neighbor to the man who fell into
the hands of the robbers?" 37 *He said, "The one who showed him*
mercy." Jesus said to him, "Go and do likewise."

The high point in the narrative portrayal of Jesus' relationship with his disciples, reached in vv 20-24, is abruptly interrupted by a lawyer. Luke records
no shift in scene, so he pictures the lawyer breaking in on what had become
a private conversation between Jesus and the seventy-two (v 23). That the
lawyer is present at all raises questions about the boundaries between the
disciples and others outside the circle of Jesus' followers both here and
elsewhere in the journey narrative.[93]

To label the lawyer's question as abrupt is not to say it is out of place,
however, or that it moves the narrative in a fresh direction. Jesus has been
about the task of presenting faithfulness to God as hearing and doing God's
word. This motif is served well, even advanced, by his dialogue with this
man.[94] Jesus has just affirmed the genuine insight of the seventy-two, manifest
in their faithful service in the mission. Will he find similar faithfulness in his
encounter with the legal expert?

That the practice of God's word is the central issue in this narrative
unit is obvious from the repetition and placement of the verb "to do." The
lawyer inquires, "What must I *do?*"; following their exchange, Jesus responds, *"Do* this" (vv 25, 28). In this way the first segment of this unit (vv
25-28) is bound together with references to *praxis*. The question of the
identity of one's neighbor leads into a further exploration of appropriate
behavior, however, with the conclusion drawn by the lawyer himself. The
one who was a neighbor, he acknowledges, is "the one who *did* mercy";[95]
Jesus responds, *"Do* likewise" (v 37). Jesus' closing words, then, do not
summarize the parable of the compassionate Samaritan (as though the purpose of the parable were to present a moral obligation to act in such-and-such
a way). Rather, they return to the original question of the lawyer: "What
must I do to inherit eternal life?" The parable thus serves a hermeneutical
function. It interprets the summation of the law provided by the legal expert.[96] Although it is too easy to pit "obedience to the law" over against

93. See above on 9:51–19:48.
94. This is true all the more when the coherence of this narrative unit with
Deuteronomy 6–7 is recognized — cf. Wall, "Martha and Mary," 21-24; C. A. Evans,
"Luke 16:1-18," 138-39.
95. ὁ ποιήσας τὸ ἔλεος; NRSV: "the one who showed mercy." A form of ποιέω
appears in vv 25, 28, and 37 (2x).
96. Cf. Bailey, *Through Peasant Eyes*, 41; Hedrick, *Parables*, 94-95.

"discussing the law"[97] — since the parable itself must be read as Jesus' attempt to clarify the law (Lev 19:18) by means of narrative exegesis[98] — it is nonetheless true that, for Luke, hearing is authenticated in doing (cf. 6:46-49; 8:21).

The particular focus of the kind of praxis leading to eternal life articulated in this narrative unit is underscored by three elements — two internal to this unit, the other external. First, located at the midpoint of Luke's account is the response of the Samaritan to the condition of the one assaulted on the road: "he was moved with compassion." Luke's presentation of the Samaritan's comportment thus replicates that of God in his covenant faithfulness (1:78) and of Jesus in the face of a widow's loss of her only son (7:13). Employing comparable language, the lawyer recognizes the "mercy" characterizing the Samaritan's behavior (v 37). This is an important reminder of the message of the Sermon on the Plain (6:17-49), that practices are manifestations of one's character and dispositions; in the language of the current passage, love of neighbor flows out of radical love of God. Second, the parable itself is framed with questions concerning the identification of "neighbor" (vv 29, 36). Whereas Jesus' teaching in the Sermon on the Plain had eliminated the lines that might be drawn between one's "friends" and one's "enemies," this legal expert hopes to reintroduce this distinction. He does so by inquiring, "Who is my neighbor?" — not so much to determine to whom he must show love, but so as to calculate the identity of those to whom he need not show love. By the end of the story, Jesus has transformed the focus of the original question; in fact, Jesus' apparent attempt to answer the lawyer's question turns out to be a negation of that question's premise. Neighbor love knows no boundaries. Third, the geography of the parable (on the road from Jerusalem), and the identification of two of its characters as temple personnel and a third as a Samaritan, provide reminders of the geography of Jesus' mission.[99] Jesus has already attempted to involve himself with a Samaritan village (9:51-56), and he is now on the way to the center of the Jewish world, Jerusalem, which, with its temple, had come to perpetuate and determine the boundaries of

97. For example, Salo, *Luke's Treatment of the Law,* 108-9: "Thus Luke wishes to concentrate on the practical application of the law leading to eternal life, not on a philosophical discussion of legal issues." Similarly, Wilson, *Luke and the Law,* 14-15.

98. "Narrative exegesis" is an exposition of a text that takes the form of a story rather than of a prose-oriented argument or presentation — cf. Banks, "Narrative Exegesis," 570 (though Banks's discussion does not deal with the presence of this form of explication already in the Gospels).

99. This, of course, reminds us that geographical markers are not neutral or objective, but are social products that reflect and configure ways of understanding the world (cf. *m. Kelim* 1:6-9; Pred, *Human Geographies;* Soja, *Postmodern Geographies;* Werlen, *Society, Action and Space*).

acceptable social intercourse. In his Galilean ministry, Jesus had worked to exterminate those boundaries that predetermine human interaction; what was begun there will continue to characterize his message on the way to Jerusalem. His portrayal of a Samaritan as one who embodies the law, and whose comportment models the covenant faithfulness of God — and whose doing so stands in sharp contradistinction to the practices of temple personnel on the road — serves this wider motif as it obliterates the construction of human existence sanctioned by the religious establishment in Jerusalem. Although Luke does not document the response of the lawyer, he nevertheless shows the degree to which his encounter with Jesus, if taken seriously, would destabilize the world of this lawyer and challenge him to embrace the new world propagated through Jesus' ministry.[100]

The structure of this narrative unit is straightforward, with its two parts presented in parallel:

	Part 1	Part 2
Identification of the Lawyer's Motive	v 25	v 29
The Lawyer's Question	v 25	v 29
Jesus' Answer and Counterquestion	v 26	vv 30-36
The Lawyer's (Appropriate) Reply	v 27	v 37a
Jesus' Final Word, in the Imperative	v 28	v 37b

25-28 Luke's presentation of an unnamed lawyer is mixed. On the one hand, he stands before Jesus, a sign of esteem, and addresses Jesus respectfully as "teacher." On the other hand, his identification as a "lawyer" accesses earlier information provided by the narrator: (1) Legal experts have been present to monitor Jesus' faithfulness to the law. (2) Legal experts are among those identified as persons responsible for Jesus' pending rejection and suffering.[101] When it is recalled that priests functioned as experts on the law when not performing their priestly duties at the temple,[102] this adds to the drama of the unfolding encounter — not least since the ensuing parable will have as one of its primary characters a priest returning from duty at the temple (v 31). That is, within the socio-historical context imagined by the narrative, the identification of this lawyer and the temple staff of the parable may be more immediate than normally thought. Moreover, Luke explicitly portrays

100. See Mazamisa, *Beatific Comradeship,* 106; Crossan, "Parable and Example," 75-76. This point is registered in a more focused way, with reference to the ethics of election, in J. A. Sanders, "Ethics of Election," 113; C. A. Evans, "Luke 16:1-18," 138.

101. See above on 5:17-19; 9:22. Luke uses "lawyers," "teachers of the law," and "scribes" interchangeably (cf. on 9:22).

102. See Schwartz, *Jewish Background,* 89-101; E. P. Sanders, *Judaism,* 170-82.

the lawyer as intent on "challenging" Jesus.[103] On the other hand, the content of the lawyer's question employs another of the range of terms Luke uses to depict salvation, "life" — in particular, "eternal life," a phrase that first appears in Dan 12:2 and is then developed in apocalyptic Judaism to refer to the life of the coming epoch.[104] The question itself is admissible and will provide the platform for Luke to expound on the behavior appropriate to an orientation to the resurrection. Yet, the encounter as a whole is formulated along antagonistic lines.

Jesus, challenged with respect to his status as a teacher, maintains common ground with this expert on the law while at the same time redirecting the challenge with a counterquestion. Inquiring into the content of the law, Jesus assumes and endorses its ongoing normativity. What is at stake for him is not the law per se, but its construal. Hence, he inquires into the nature of his antagonist's legal interpretation.[105] Just as the lawyer's question had derived from the axiomatic connection between obedience to the law and inheritance/life resident in Deut 6:16-25,[106] so his answer reflects the Shema (Deut 6:5) — a passage that was fundamental to Jewish life and worship in the home, the synagogue, and the temple.[107] To the Shema the lawyer attaches, inexorably, the law of neighbor-love found in Lev 19:18. In its co-text in Leviticus, love of neighbor is a disposition of the heart expressed in tangible behaviors — related, for example, to a neighbor's honor and possessions. Jesus concurs with the lawyer's answer, and rightly so, given the impressive degree to which it meshes with Jesus' own message. Indeed, the lawyer has stated more succinctly than Luke has recorded of Jesus the need for a comprehensive love of God,[108] encompassing uncompromising allegiance and conformity to his purpose, from which springs love for others. Of course, it is one thing to interpret the law correctly, another to internalize and perform it. Returning to the lawyer's original question concerning behavior appropriate to eternal life, then, Jesus counsels not only this representation of the law but also its practice.

103. ἐκπειράζω — cf. 4:12.

104. See Bultmann, "Concept of Life," 856-57. This question is repeated in 18:18.

105 For the use of ἀναγινώσκω in Lukan co-texts where the issue of interpretation is at stake, see 6:3; Acts 8:28-35 (vv 28, 30, 32); 13:27; 15:21.

106. Wall, "Martha and Mary," 21-22; see also *Psalms of Solomon* 14.

107. See the discussion in E. P. Sanders, *Judaism,* 195-96; Schürer, *Jewish People,* 454-55.

108. Although no clear line can be drawn between these four aspects of the human, each is capable of nuance — e.g., "heart" (the seat of one's emotions), "soul" (one's vitality)," "strength" (one's drive and energy), and "mind" (one's understanding and dispositions); the primary purpose of this fourfold inventory is to stress the totality of one's love for God. On the text-form of Luke's citation vis-à-vis the LXX, cf. Kimball, *Jesus' Exposition,* 123-25.

29   If the level of concordance between Jesus and the lawyer has masked those original indications marking this as at least a potentially antagonistic exchange, Luke's second reference to the lawyer's motives provides a pointed reminder. Refusing the standard of God's purpose, this legal expert is bent on self-justification — that is, the assertion of his status based on the wrongheaded but widely held canons of his day, and the use of his knowledge and position to invoke for himself the respect of others.[109] His question grants the importance of Lev 19:18 as a summary of the law,[110] but also exploits its ambiguity — at least, the ambiguity that came to be attached to it in Second Temple Judaism. In its co-text in Leviticus 19, love for the neighbor is love for fellow Israelites, though love for the other is extended to "resident aliens" who embrace the covenant with Yahweh (Lev 19:33-34). As a consequence of Hellenistic imperialism and Roman occupation, it could not be generally assumed in the first century of the Common Era that those dwelling among the people of Israel qualified as "neighbors." Different attitudes toward these foreign intrusions developed into a fractured social context in which boundaries distinguished not only between Jew and Gentile but also between Jewish factions.[111] How far should love reach?

30-32   Like other contemporary Jewish teachers, Jesus employs a parable in order to expound a scriptural text — in this case, Lev 19:18.[112] The details of the parable are true-to-life[113] and therefore may be elucidated in light of the socio-historical context in which the parable is set.

The choice of opening, "a certain man," constitutes a powerful rhetorical move on Jesus' part. In light of the debate surrounding the reach of love, grounded in how one reads Leviticus 19, the impossibility of classifying this person as either friend or foe immediately subverts any interest in questions of this nature. Stripped of his clothes and left half-dead, the man's anonymity throughout the story is insured;[114] he is simply a human being, a neighbor, in need.

---

109. See 7:29-30! Also, 18:9; 20:46-47.

110. On the popularity of Lev 19:18 in this role, see E. P. Sanders, *Judaism,* 257-60.

111. See Jeremias, *Parables,* 202-3; he notes, e.g., the division between love for the children of light and hate for others in 1QS 1:9-10.

112. McArthur and Johnston (*Parables,* 112-13) note that the majority of extant rabbinic parables function exegetically, to explain a scriptural text, incident, or narrative.

113. This is helpfully emphasized by Hedrick, *Parables,* 93-116.

114. See Champion, "Parable," 32; Bailey, *Through Peasant Eyes,* 42-43; Hedrick, *Parables,* 103 — though they do not make the connection to Leviticus 19. This is not to say that Jesus' auditor might not identify the wounded man in some way, for this is a narrative gap that can be filled easily enough by one's imagination; rather, it is to recognize that neither Jesus nor Luke provides any support for one reading of his nationality or religious commitments over another.

Jerusalem is located about 2,500 feet above sea level, Jericho in the Jordan rift valley about 800 feet below sea level. That the man is traveling *down* thus adds to the realism of the story. Realistic, too, is the picture of violence on the road, since travel in general — and especially travel on this particular road — was replete with danger.[115] The narrative itself commences with a man traveling down the road, a narrative beginning full of possibilities abruptly cut short by the violent acts of these bandits. That he fell into the hands of robbers, though, becomes a prominent feature of the narrative, mentioned twice (vv 30, 36). New options for plot development are thus introduced, especially: If this unknown man is treated so by robbers, how will he be treated by others?[116]

An answer is quickly provided by a priest and Levite,[117] whose actions establish a cadence: they came → saw → passed by on the other side (vv 31-32). Why do they not assist the wounded man? No particular motivation is given. It is true that some have found here a concern with defilement: A man who is half-dead (v 30) may appear to be dead, with the result that these holy men might have feared the contraction of corpse impurity.[118] This is doubtful, however, since (1) that they are journeying away from Jerusalem is a probable indication of the completion of their temple duties;[119] and (2) even priests had an obligation to bury a neglected corpse.[120] In fact, given the concern with motives characteristic of the interchange between the legal expert and Jesus (vv 25, 29), it is remarkable and probably significant that no inside information regarding the incentive(s) of the priest and Levite is provided. The stark reality is simply that they do nothing for this wounded man.

The importance of their identification as a priest and Levite, respectively, probably lies not in the possibility that they would have a heightened concern with corpse impurity. Nor is Jesus' immediate concern simply that these persons are Jewish. Rather, the combination of their identification with the temple in the proximity of Jerusalem by Jesus, who is himself on the road to Jerusalem, raises much larger issues of a socio-cultural variety. Priests and Levites shared high status in the community of God's people on account of ascription — that is, not because they trained or were chosen to be priests but because they were born into priestly families.[121] They participated in and were legitimated by the world

---

115. Cf., e.g., Josephus *J.W.* 2.12.2 §§228-30; Strabo *Geography* 16.2.41; Bailey, *Through Peasant Eyes*, 41-42.

116. So Champion, "Parable," 31.

117. On the difference between these temple functionaries, see above on 1:5.

118. E.g., Bailey, *Through Peasant Eyes*, 44-46.

119. On the schedule of priestly duties, see §4.

120. See Hedrick, *Parables*, 106, 115; Salo, *Luke's Treatment of the Law*, 110.

121. See Lev 21:16-24, and the helpful discussion in Eilberg-Schwartz, *Savage in Judaism*, 195-216. On the status issues resident in vv 31-33, see also Gnanavaram, "Dalit Theology," 77-80. Cf. Sanders, "Ethics of Election," 113.

of the temple, with its circumspect boundaries between clean and unclean, including clean and unclean people. They epitomize a worldview of tribal consciousness,[122] concerned with relative status and us-them catalogueing. Within their world, their association with the temple commends them as persons of exemplary piety whose actions would be regarded as self-evidently righteous. They are accustomed to being evaluated on the basis of their ancestry, not on the basis of their performance (cf. 3:7-9). Accordingly, their failure to assist the anonymous man would have been laudable in the eyes of many.[123]

33-35   Against the picture thus established, the introduction of this traveler is shocking. First, he is a Samaritan, whose status as a socio-religious outcast (see above on 9:52) would seem to disqualify his presence in a story thus far concerned with activity in the vicinity of Jerusalem and with temple staff. Second, unlike the prior two characters, he is not portrayed as a holy man at all, but rather as a traveling merchant.[124] Third, his actions initially follow, then depart from that of his predecessors. They came → saw → passed by on the other side (vv 31-32); he came → saw → was moved with compassion → went to the wounded man + cared for him. As a result, what distinguishes this traveler from the other two is not fundamentally that they are Jews and he is a Samaritan, nor is it that they had high status as religious functionaries and he does not. What individualizes him is his compassion, leading to action, in the face of their inaction. Having established this point of distinction, his status in comparison with theirs becomes shockingly relevant, for it throws into sharp relief the virtue of his response. For the same reason, his actions condemn their failure to act. Unlike them, he has compassion, and this is the turning point not only of his encounter with the wounded man but, indeed, of this entire narrative unit (vv 25-37).[125] The Samaritan, then, participates in the compassion and covenantal faithfulness of God, who sees and responds with salvific care.[126] The parable of the compassionate Samaritan thus undermines the determination of status in the community of God's people on the basis of ascription, substituting in its place a concern with performance, the granting of status on the basis of one's actions.

---

122. Champion, "Parable," 32-33.

123. Cf. Sir 12:1-7: "If you do good, know to whom you do it. . . . Give to the one who is good, but do not help the sinner."

124. This is suggested by his possession of an animal (presumably a donkey), money, oil, and wine — all on the road. Given the Samaritan denial of the religious significance of Jerusalem, his status as a merchant is also suggested simply by his presence on the road from Jerusalem (Why else would he be there?).

125. Menken ("Position of σπλαγχνίζεσθαι," 111) observes that ἐσπλαγχνίσθη, in the NA[26] of 10:25-37, is preceded by 68 words and followed by 67, making it the center of this unit.

126. See 1:76-78; 7:13; 15:20; Donahue, *Gospel in Parable,* 132.

The care the Samaritan offers is not a model of moral obligation but of exaggerated action grounded in compassion that risks much more than could ever be required or expected.[127] He stops on the Jericho road to assist someone he does not know in spite of the self-evident peril of doing so; he gives of his own goods and money,[128] freely, making no arrangements for reciprocation (cf. 6:32-36); in order to obtain care for this stranger, he enters an inn, itself a place of potential danger; and he even enters into an open-ended monetary relationship with the innkeeper, a relationship in which the chance of extortion is high.[129]

36-37 Having completed his exposition-parable, Jesus, as before, counters the question of the legal expert with a question of his own. Interestingly, however, his counterquestion proposes a focal shift. Rather than asking again, Who is my neighbor? Jesus inquires, Who acted as a neighbor? The lawyer's question would have focused on whether the wounded man possessed neighborly status, but the parable has failed to provide the grounds necessary for conjecture on this matter. It is a nonissue. Rephrased, Jesus' question presupposes the identification of "anyone" as a neighbor, then presses the point that such an identification opens wide the door of loving action.[130]

By leaving aside the identity of the wounded man and by portraying the Samaritan traveler as one who performs the law (and so as one whose actions are consistent with an orientation to eternal life), Jesus has nullified the worldview that gives rise to such questions as, Who is my neighbor? The purity-holiness matrix has been capsized. And, not surprisingly in the Third Gospel, neighborly love has been concretized in care for one who is, in this parable, self-evidently a social outcast ("the poor" — cf. on 4:18-19), and in the uncalculated disposition of one's possessions.

The lawyer seems to agree with Jesus; at least, he follows the point of the parable, noting (1) the quality ("compassion," "mercy") of the Samaritan that set him apart from the priest and Levite, and (2) the action of the Samaritan over against the inaction of the others. How does he respond to Jesus' directive to "do" likewise? What we do know is that the lawyer has received the answer for which he originally sought; indeed, with his own mouth he has articulated the response. What we know also is that Jesus' exegesis of neighborly love subverts the world system shared by this lawyer and by society-at-large. Beyond this, though, Luke's description of the encounter between Jesus and this expert on the law is open-ended. He has heard the word; will he do it?

---

127. Cf. Coote, "What Is a Person Worth?" 208; Champion, "Parable," 32-33.

128. Two denarii would be equal to two days' wages (cf. Matt 20:9-13).

129. The negative image of inns in antiquity is noted by Oakman, "Samaritan Story," 122-23; Royse, "ΠΑΝΔΟΧΕΙΟΝ."

130. Cf. 6:27!

5.1.5. How to Welcome Jesus (10:38-42)

38 *Now as they went on their way, he entered a certain village, where a woman named Martha welcomed him into her home.*[131] 39 *She had a sister named Mary, who sat at the Lord's feet and listened to his word.*[132] 40 *But Martha was distracted by her many tasks; so she came to him and asked, "Lord, do you not care that my sister has left me to do all the work by myself? Tell her then to help me." 41 But the Lord answered her, "Martha, Martha, you are worried and distracted by many things; 42 there is need of only one thing.*[133] *Mary has chosen the better part, which will not be taken away from her."*

Although long interpreted as establishing the priority of the contemplative life over against the active one,[134] the interests of this brief narrative unit lie elsewhere. Luke's narration is manifestly concerned with the motif of hospitality. This is apparent already in the opening sentence, with the use of language that ties this episode to the preceding scenes of journeying and receiving welcome (and rejection). Within its local co-text (esp. vv 1-37), Jesus' encounter with Martha and Mary clarifies the nature of the welcome he seeks not only for himself but also for his messengers — that is, for all who participate in the drawing near of God's dominion.

The Evangelist sketches an immediate and important comparison between this and the preceding episode — that is, between the encounters framed by vv 25-37 and vv 38-42. By means of this juxtaposition, Luke illuminates

131. Even though "into her home" is not found in N[26.27], having been omitted in p[45.75] B et al., variant forms of the phrase are found in a number of important mss. Brutscheck (*Die Maria-Marta-Erzählung,* 18-19) argues on internal grounds that the phrase is original. Even if, as seems probable, variant forms were introduced to draw out the meaning of ὑποδέξατο αὐτόν (cf. Metzger, *Textual Commentary,* 153), this phrase is already implicit in the Lukan use of "to welcome" (or "to extend hospitality").

132. NRSV: "what he was saying."

133. This reading, supported by p[45.75] A C* W Θ Ξ Ψ et al., is probably original, but the starkness of ἑνός has given rise to several alternative readings — especially (1) substituting ὀλίγων for ἑνός ("but of a few things there is need"), and (2) conflating these two readings ("but of a few things there is need, or of one"). Cf. Schürmann, 2:159-60; Fitzmyer, 2:894. Fee ("One Thing Is Needful?") argues for the originality of the reading that includes both "few things" and "one thing," but this is improbable on internal grounds (cf. Godet, 2:45: " '*There needs but little* [for the body], *or even but one thing* [for the soul].' There is subtlety in this reading; too much perhaps"). Corley (*Private Women,* 138-40) follows Fee because she believes that it supports her reading of the Lukan text as an attempt to highlight the "quiet, submissive role" of Mary over against the active role of Martha, but this interpretation is problematic on other grounds (see below).

134. For a critical review of the interpretation of this text, see Schüssler Fiorenza, *But She Said,* 58-68.

his overarching concern with genuine "hearing" of the word of God (cf. 8:4-21).[135] The lawyer "heard," but, thus far, his hearing had not generated action. The Samaritan of Jesus' parable, having compassion, had "done mercy" on behalf of the injured man; that is, he is portrayed as one who hears and acts. Now, Mary is depicted as one who has begun the journey of discipleship by acknowledging through her posture her submissiveness to Jesus and by "listening" to his word. Martha's "doing," on the other hand, is censured, rooted as it is in her anxiety as a host rather than in dispositions transformed by an encounter with the word.

To put it differently, although "service" is perfectly acceptable against the moral landscape of her first-century world, the manner of Martha's practices exposes them as ill adapted to the sort of hospitality for which Jesus seeks. As high a value as Luke puts on service (by which he often denotes leadership, cf. 22:24-27), service grounded in and brandishing moral intuitions other than those formed through hearing the word is unacceptable. The welcome Jesus seeks is not epitomized in distracted, worrisome domestic performance, but in attending to this guest whose very presence is a disclosure of the divine plan.[136]

The pivotal importance of Jesus' authority in this scene is signaled in his fourfold identification as "Lord" — explicitly by the narrator (vv 39, 41) and Martha (v 40), implicitly by the posture Mary assumes (v 39). Even for Luke, who regularly introduces this title in his narration, this is extraordinary, and this portends the revolutionary character of the message of this scene. Of course, at one level, Jesus is thus identified as the authoritative teacher within the narrative, as well as the character within the encounter who comes to function as if he were the host in this household. More importantly, however, is the way Luke affirms and reaffirms in this account Jesus' authoritative status in order to legitimate in no uncertain terms the substance and implications of the message that follows. Culturally, the problem presented by this pericope is not the portrait of a woman serving (for this is expected), but of a woman assuming (and not only assuming, but even preferring) the role of disciple. To defend this transposition, the word of the Lord is required! "Indeed, the defence is made with such emphasis that the implicit challenge of the narrative about Martha and Mary is to choose with Mary and to enter a relationship with Jesus in which one listens to his word rather than being concerned about the table."[137]

38 Luke initiates this episode with reference to the journey motif,

---

135. See esp. Donahue, *Gospel in Parable,* 136-38. A parallel conclusion is reached by Wall ("Martha and Mary"), though along different lines.

136. Cf. Seim, *Double Message,* 98-116; Johnson, 175-76.

137. Seim, *Double Message,* 106.

not in order to signal a new beginning in the narrative, but to tie this scene formally to the preceding concern with extending or refusing hospitality to those on the road.[138] Luke uses a virtual technical term for hospitality to describe Martha's reception of Jesus into her home,[139] and otherwise presents her as a patron: prosperous, independent, ready to host this traveler.[140] Interestingly, though "they" (i.e., Jesus and his followers) are traveling together, the spotlight of this encounter so narrowly falls on "him" (i.e., Jesus) that, for dramatic effect, Jesus' traveling companions fall temporarily out of view.

39-40   Luke draws an important contrast between Mary and Martha. "Mary" is a common name; this woman is recognized simply as Martha's sister and need not be identified with any other Mary within the Lukan narrative. She is positioned "at the Lord's feet," signifying her submissiveness,[141] particularly her status as a disciple (cf. Acts 22:3). The latter nuance is commended by her activity at his feet: she "listened to his word." For the Third Gospel, to listen to the word is to have joined the road of discipleship (e.g., 6:47; 8:11, 21; 11:28) — in spite of the reality that, in this period, Jewish women were normally cast in the role of domestic performance in order to support the instruction of men rather than as persons who were themselves engaged in study.[142]

---

138. Cf. 9:53; 10:5-16.

139. ὑποδέχομαι — cf. 19:6; Acts 17:7; Jas 2:25. Earlier (9:53; 10:8, 10), δέχομαι was used.

140. See also 4:38-39; Acts 9:36-37, 39; 12:12; 16:14-15, 40. Cf. 8:1-3.

141. Cf. 7:38, 44-46; 8:35, 41; 17:16; Acts 4:35, 37; 5:2; 7:58; 10:25; 22:3.

142. This possibility has already been explicitly raised in 8:1-3, 19-21. Women were taught certain requirements of the law, of course, for they were responsible for those aspects of legal observance that impinged on females. As a rule, though, such guidance was confined to the mother-daughter relationship. See the discussion in Seim, *Double Message*, 102-3; Witherington, *Women in the Ministry of Jesus*, 101. Schüssler Fiorenza (*But She Said*, 59) rejects this view as anti-Jewish, but it is hard to understand why. In order to make this point we do not and need not deny that some women were learned, or even that some rabbis (like Jesus) did not extend their instruction to include women; rather, we mean only to affirm that women, as a rule, were excluded from such relationships.

Schüssler Fiorenza's reading of this text (and her larger reconstructive project) unfortunately requires a level of egalitarianism in the earliest Christian communities and their settings in favor of which there is (almost?) no evidence and against which there is plenty. One cannot help but wonder whose definition of "egalitarianism" Schüssler Fiorenza must use (cf. Seim [*Double Message*, 105], who notes that Schüssler Fiorenza's "problem with the conflict seems to be primarily that Martha, who has her sympathy, loses out"; and LaHurd's ["Rediscovering the Lost Women," 70-72] observation that criticisms of Luke on women are generally rooted in *Western* cultural assumptions about what constitutes status and power for men and women). As Sahlins

Though v 38 suggested nothing negative about the nature of Martha's welcome, it is with respect to her hospitality that she is contrasted with Mary. Here and in v 41, she is characterized as one who serves, normally a positive quality in Luke, but whose service is marked by distractions and worry that conflict with the growth and expression of authentic faith (see 8:14; 12:22, 26).[143] Indeed, Martha's address to Jesus takes an unexpected, perhaps unconscious turn; while she engages in the irony of self-betrayal,[144] her attempt to win Jesus' support in a struggle against her sister ends in self-indictment.

---

has written in the context of a parallel discussion concerned with history and cultural difference,

> Each people knows their own kind of happiness: the culture that is the legacy of their ancestral tradition, transmitted in the distinctive concepts of their language, and adapted to their specific life conditions. It is by means of this tradition, endowed also with the morality of the community and the emotions of the family, that experience is organized, since people do not simply discover the work, they are taught it. (*How "Natives" Think,* 12)

It will not do, then, to engage in an adventitious historicism that assumes that our predispositions, commitments, and ontologies must fully and in every case have been theirs, nor need we allow room for a primitivism that posits in the earliest Jesus movement a paradisal state that must now be recovered. In order to engage related theological issues both historically and with an eye to the constructive task within our own socio-cultural exigencies, the more pressing question is, Given the largely patriarchal world in which Luke's narrative is set, how, within this narrative, does the good news articulate with *and* over against larger cultural moors? Hence, a profitable line of questions might begin with the methodological issue raised by Wuthnow (with reference to the Reformation, but equally relevant to the apostolic church): Why have the social conditions that shaped its ideology not shaped it more? What are the ways in which the convictions embedded in the Lukan narrative seem to have been shaped by and yet also seem to have succeeded in transcending their socio-historical contexts? (*Communities of Discourse,* 5).

143. Hence, *pace* Schüssler Fiorenza (*But She Said,* ch. 2; followed by Corley, *Private Women,* 136-42), the contrast is not between "service" (namely, women's active leadership in the community) and "listening" (namely, the passive role of women in the community), but between "hearing the word" (namely, discipleship) and "anxious" behavior (namely, the antithesis of discipleship). For the primary emphasis of Luke's account, which has to do with the nature of authentic hospitality, the fact that the two contrasting characters are women is not the most crucial point. See Brutscheck, *Maria-Marta-Erzählung,* 47; Donahue, *Gospel in Parable,* 138-39; Seim, *Double Message,* 104-5. Their identification as women becomes critical when it is realized that Jesus has thus refused to allow social forces to reduce Mary to a domestic role *in favor of her identification as a disciple* (cf. Schottroff, *Feminist Perspectives,* 116-17). *Contra* Schüssler Fiorenza's proposal, see further the excursus in Donahue, *Gospel in Parable,* 138-39.

144. On which see Dupriez, *Literary Devices,* 243. Nelson (*Leadership and Discipleship,* 67) observes how often in the Third Gospel scenes at the table function to disclose both the identity of Jesus and the hearts of those with him at the table — cf., e.g., 7:36-50; 10:38-42; 11:37-54; 14:7-24; 22:21-23).

The nature of hospitality for which Jesus seeks is realized in attending to one's guest, yet Martha's speech is centered on "me"-talk (3 times).[145] Though she refers to Jesus as "Lord," she is concerned to engage his assistance in her plans, not to learn from him his.

41-42 Jesus is "Lord," according to the narrator, and this disallows attempts to tie him into the stratagems of others. Instead, his status as Lord identifies him as the one whose design transcends self-oriented or conventionally correct plans and whose message takes precedence over the same. Thus, over against the attempt of Martha to assert the priority of her enterprise over that of her sister, Jesus provides his own two-sided valuation of the scene before him. Martha is engaged in anxious, agitated practices,[146] behavior that contrasts sharply with the comportment of a disciple characteristic of Mary. Martha is concerned with many things, Mary with only one. Hence, Martha's behavior is negatively assessed, Mary's positively. What is this "one thing," this "better part" Mary has chosen?[147] Within this narrative co-text, the infinite range of possibilities is narrowed considerably: She is fixed on the guest, Jesus, and his word; she heeds the one whose presence is commensurate with the coming of the kingdom of God.[148] With Jesus' presence the world is being reconstituted, with the result that (1) Mary (and, with her, those of low status accustomed to living on the margins of society) *need* no longer be defined by socially determined roles; and, more importantly in this co-text, (2) Mary and Martha (and, with them, all) *must* understand and act on the priority of attending to the guest before them, extending to Jesus and his messengers the sort of welcome in which the authentic hearing of discipleship is integral.[149]

5.2. THE FATHERHOOD OF GOD (11:1-13)

This narrative section is related to the foregoing in two fundamental ways. (1) Most recently, Mary had exemplified in her demeanor the nature of the

---

145. Cf. Brutscheck, *Maria-Marta-Erzählung,* 42-43.

146. For μεριμνάω, see 8:14 (in contrast to an authentic reception of the word); 12:22-31 (in contrast to "seeking the kingdom"); 21:34-36. θορυβάζω is found in the NT only in v 41, but its cognates are used with reference to the agitation of crowds in Acts 17:5; 20:1; 21:34; 24:18.

147. Moule (*Idiom Book,* 97-98) notes the use in NT Greek of the positive (in this case, ἀγαθή) for the comparative.

148. Cf. Venetz, "Suche nach dem 'einen Notwendigen' "; Seim, *Double Message,* 106-7; Schottroff, *Feminist Perspectives,* 116.

149. This reading assumes the parabolic significance of this scene in Martha's home; cf. Donahue, *Gospel in Parable,* 134-35.

life of the disciple focused on learning from the Lord (10:38-42). On account of this orientation, all other expectations are relegated to secondary positions. The Lukan account of Jesus' interaction with Martha and Mary, then, prepares for Jesus' teaching on the fatherhood of God by focusing on one's disposition toward authentic hearing in the presence of the inbreaking kingdom. (2) Earlier, in a scene characterized as this one is by the relative seclusion of Jesus with his disciples, Jesus referred to God as his Father five times, both in prayer and instruction (10:21-22). In that co-text, he spoke of himself as the Son who was uniquely able to reveal the Father to those whom he chose. *This is precisely what he does in the current scene.* Note how the beginning and end of this section refer to God as the Father of the disciples (vv 2, 13 — in contrast to human fathers, v 11), with the section as a whole fashioned to show Jesus teaching his followers about God's generosity and faithfulness. Because of God's faithfulness, Jesus insists, life apart from the anxiety and agitation experienced by Martha (10:38-42) is possible; in the face of the goodness of the Father, disciples may respond with trust and fidelity.[1]

Within his own discourse situation, Luke has important reasons to qualify in what sense God is "Father." John's ministry, it may be recalled, included the conversion of "fathers" vis-à-vis their children (1:16-17), and, given Greco-Roman realities, not without cause. Dionysius, for example, was full of admiration for the Roman system wherein a father had virtually unlimited authority over his children (and their children) as long as he lived. Gaius reports, "There are hardly any people who wield as much power over their sons as we do" (1.557).[2] Would a newborn child be reared in the family? Sold? Exposed? Killed? Would the children be scourged? Pawned? Allowed or refused marriage or divorce? The resolution of such issues and many others concerned with the well-being of even adult children was a father's prerogative. Even if, with the onset of the Empire, this portrait of the Roman father was in the process of metamorphosis away from such a troubling picture,[3] it was not enough simply to refer to God as "Father." The question was (and is) no less pressing, In what sense is God thus to be understood? Hence, God is presented by Luke as the Father who cares for his children and acts redemptively on their behalf.

---

1. Cf. Green *Gospel of Luke,* 111-12. Other logia portraying God as the Father of the disciples in Luke include 6:36; 12:30, 32; cf. 15:11-32; Mowery, "God the Father," 128-30.

2. See Eyben, "Fathers and Sons," 114-15.

3. For related discussion and bibliography, see above on 1:17.

5.2.1. The Disciples' Prayer (11:1-4)

> 11:1 *He was praying in a certain place, and after he had finished, one of his disciples said to him, "Lord, teach us to pray, as John taught his disciples."* 2 *He said to them, "When you pray, say:*
> '*Father, hallowed be your name.*
>   *Your kingdom come.*
> 3   *Give us each day our daily bread.*
> 4   *And forgive us our sins,*
>   *for we ourselves forgive everyone indebted to us.*
>   *And do not bring us into testing.'* "[4]

The brevity of this episode of teaching on prayer is deceptive, for within this narrative unit are amassed numerous motifs important to the Lukan message:[5] the centrality of prayer to Jesus' life, the position of the disciple in the Gospel as a learner, the prospective importance of prayer in the life of the church in Acts, as well as numerous theological motifs — for example, the theocentricity of Lukan thought, the anticipation in the present of the future consummation of God's work, the historic and eschatological provision of God for his people, forgiveness and the release of debts, and behavior in the face of testing. The prayer itself has affinities to Jewish tradition, especially to the *Qaddish* and the Eighteen Benedictions.[6] The former begins in a manner analogous to Jesus' model prayer:

> Exalted and hallowed be his great name
>   in the world which he created according to his will.
> May he establish his kingdom
>   in your lifetime and in your days,
>   and in the lifetime of the household of Israel,
>   speedily and at a near time.

The latter, constituting the chief prayer of Judaism,[7] contains such parallel phrases as the following: "You are holy and your name is holy . . ." (3) and "Forgive us, our Father, for we have sinned . . ." (6), as well as the petition, "reign over us . . ." (11).[8] Within its Lukan co-text, the prayer Jesus teaches

---

4. NRSV: "to the time of trial."

5. Cf. Trites, "Prayer Motif," 179; Plymale, "Lucan Lord's Prayer," 178. For bibliography on the motif of prayer in Luke-Acts, see above on 1:8-10.

6. See, e.g., Petuchowski, "Jewish Prayer Texts"; *idem,* "Liturgy"; Graubard *"Kaddish";* Lauer, *"Abhinu Malkenu."* Cf. the summary in Dunn, "Prayer," 617.

7. Cf. Schuerer, *Jewish People,* 2:455-63.

8. Cf. also the references to the throne of David and the coming of salvation (14, 15).

his disciples is integral to the socialization of the disciples in this new community who are taught to name God as Father. The habit of prayer along the lines counseled by Jesus would serve as an ongoing catalyst for community formation. Within the practice of such prayer, a premium would be placed on the infusion of a worldview centered on the gracious God, on dependence on God, and on the imitation of God, all understood against an eschatological horizon in which the coming of God in his sovereignty figures prominently.

1-2a Luke gives this opening scene two important foci. The first is the connection between Jesus' habit of praying and the corresponding habit of his disciples.[9] The second is the position of the disciples as genuine learners (on the model of Mary in 10:39) who address him as "Lord" and who request his instruction.

The portrayal of Jesus as a person of prayer, imprinted indelibly in the minds of Luke's audience,[10] has not gone unnoticed by the disciples. In this instance, his own pattern of prayer catalyzes their request for instruction in prayer.[11] Luke draws attention to a second impetus for their entreaty too. This is the need of the disciples for practices serving to differentiate them as followers of Jesus, according to the example of John and his band of disciples. That John's followers were known for certain practices is evident within the Lukan narrative (e.g., 5:33; cf. 7:33); these served as boundary markers distinguishing John's disciples from other sects within first-century Judaism. On the strength of this analogy, Luke depicts the act of praying Jesus' model prayer (vv 2-4) as a habit whose repetition could never be dismissed as an exercise in rote learning or ineffectual recitation.[12] Jesus' followers pray in this way because this is a distinctive practice of Jesus' followers. Such practices nurture dispositions appropriate to the community of Jesus' followers; through its repetition the message of this prayer would engrave itself into the life of the community.

2b The disciples' capacity to recognize and address God in prayer as "Father" is rooted, most immediately, in revelation, for Jesus had recently asserted that knowledge of the Father was unavailable apart from the Son's disclosure of the same (10:22). That he chooses to unveil who the Father is to these disciples signals their having been chosen to receive this insight. In

---

9. See the threefold repetition of προσεύχομαι in vv 1-2a.

10. See the accounts of prayer in 3:21-22; (4:42); 6:12; 9:18, 28; 10:21-22; as well as the important summary in which Jesus' withdrawal to pray is presented as characteristic activity in 5:16; cf. Barton, *Spirituality,* 90.

11. The parenetic function of prayer in the Third Gospel has been emphasized by Ott, *Gebet und Heil.* Cf. also Trites, "Prayer Motif," 176-77; O'Brien, "Prayer in Luke-Acts," 120.

12. ὅταν + present subjunctive usually denotes an iterative action (MHT 3:112) — in this case, "whenever [you pray]."

this way, Jesus invites these disciples, who have already begun to look to God in trust and obedience,[13] to regard God as Father and themselves as God's children. Beyond this, even though God is only rarely addressed in Jewish prayer as "Father,"[14] the identification of God as Father is grounded in the OT and subsequent Jewish literature, and especially in the election of Israel, in the covenant, and in eschatological promise: "Is not [the LORD] your father, who created you, who made you and established you?" (Deut 32:6); "You, O LORD, are our father; our redeemer from of old is your name" (Isa 63:16).[15] Fatherhood in these cases (and in the prayer Jesus teaches the disciples) is not concerned with identifying God as progenitor (cf. 1:26-38), but with adoption and relationship — and with a reconstruction of one's relationships within a "family" or household whose head is God the Father.[16] Because of the notion that authentic children represent in their character the nature of their father, the father-child relationship could be restricted so as to apply to particular groups of the righteous or even to righteous individuals[17] — a usage already familiar in the Lukan narrative (cf. 3:7-9). Though often carrying connotations of authority (and, thus, of the response of obedience), in this case "father" actualizes other properties of this metaphor as well — for example, love, nurture, mercy, and delight.[18]

Following the opening address, the first clause of the model prayer is distantly related to the command to honor the name of God (Exod 20:7; Deut 5:11). These and many other biblical texts assume that one's name is more than a label, but actually communicates something essential or substantive about the nature of its bearer; the name is related to the essence of a person. More distinct are the reverberations of Ezek 36:16-32 in the prayer of Jesus. There God asserts that he will bring eschatological vindication and restoration for the sake of his name: "I shall sanctify my great name . . . and the nations shall know that I am the LORD, says the Lord GOD, when through you I display my holiness before

---

13. Plymale ("Lucan Lord's Prayer," 180; cf. Dunn, *Jesus and the Spirit*, 24) notes that the prayer as a whole assumes such a relationship with God.

14. Cf., e.g., Sir 23:1, 4; 51:10; 3 Macc 6:3, 8; 4QapocrJoseph[a] 1:16 (summoning God, Joseph shouts, "My father and my God, do not abandon me to the Gentiles" [ET in Martínez, *Dead Sea Scrolls,* 225]).

15. Cf., e.g., Deut 14:1; 2 Sam 7:14; Ps 2:7; Jer 31:9; Hos 11:1-4; *Jub.* 1:24-25.

16. This might entail the rejection of one's family of origin and radically revised notions of household relations — cf., e.g., 8:19-21; 12:49-54; Acts 4:32–5:11.

17. Cf. 1QH 9:35-36; Wis 2:13-20.

18. Cf. 6:36; Hos 11:1-4; Ps 103:13; Prov 3:12; Jer 31:20; Tobit 13 (esp. v 4); Jeremias, *Prayers,* 11-29; Deissler, "Spirit of the Lord's Prayer," 5-6; Michel, "πατήρ," 54. That *Abba* (Aramaic, אבא) underlies the Greek πατήρ is virtually certain (cf. Rom 8:15; Gal 4:6), as is Jeremias's contention that this form of address is without exact parallel in contemporary Palestinian Judaism (*Prayers,* 16-29; cf. Dunn, *Jesus and the Spirit,* 21-26); this seems not to have been important to the Third Evangelist, however.

their eyes" (v 23). This perspective from Ezekiel is important not only for establishing the eschatological edge of the opening of this prayer of Jesus, but also for the way it summons those who pray this prayer to behave. Why must God sanctify his name? Because it has been profaned by God's own people (cf. Lev 22:32; Isa 52:5-6; Ezek 36:20-21). God's eschatological work to reestablish the holiness of his name, then, invokes shame on the part of his people and invites them to embrace practices that honor him.[19]

The second petition, "Your kingdom come," maintains a similar, two-edged focus. It is God's kingdom that will come; only God can overturn the powers at work in the world and establish his universal reign, so the faithful do well to join persons like Simeon and Anna in their hopeful anticipation of the decisive, divine intervention (2:25, 38). At the same time, with the coming of Jesus the kingdom is already being made present, necessitating lives oriented toward serving the divine project and restorative practices that participate in and further the reach of the new order being established by God (cf. 9:2, 11, 27, 60, 62; 10:9, 11).

3-4 Having established (1) a theocentric worldview (2) that is eschatological in focus and (3) that calls for human partnership in the divine purpose, the prayer Jesus teaches his followers turns more fully to the nature of life before God and within the community of God's people. This does not mean that the eschatological horizon is no longer in view. Instead, it is precisely in view of the nature of the eschatological undertaking of God that faithful life in the present can and must take the form outlined in vv 3-4.

First, disciples are to depend on God for daily sustenance.[20] Such dependence was highlighted in the missionary instructions to the twelve and seventy-two in 9:1-6; 10:1-11; and God's faithfulness to provide was illustrated in the feeding of the thousands in 9:12-27. The term rendered in the NRSV as "daily" has occasioned a great deal of debate,[21] but in light of the evidence of Acts, the meaning of Luke's phrase is most probably, "the bread pertaining to the coming day." This may connote nothing more than "the bread needed for the rest of today" or, like the divine promise of manna for Israel in the wilderness (cf. Exod 16:9-21), "enough bread for today and the promise of sufficient bread for tomorrow as well."[22] The latter would under-

19. Cf. Cullmann, *Prayer,* 44-45.
20. ἄρτος can refer more narrowly to "bread," but it has wider possibilities as well, including "food" in general.
21. See the bibliography in Nolland, 2:609.
22. The lexicographical data are critically surveyed by Hemer, "ἐπιούσιος." He argues that ἐπιούσιος is tied closely to ἐπιοῦσα (i.e., to the expression ἡ ἐπιοῦσα [ἡμέρα]; cf. Acts 7:26; 16:11; 20:15; 21:18; 23:11), then notes that "the coming (day)" can refer to "tomorrow," but that it is sometimes used to refer to "the day ahead" in a way that contrasts with "tomorrow."

score the disciples' freedom, in light of God's care, from the torment of tomorrow's worries.[23] It may mean even more than this, however, not least given the Lukan tendency to read into the present the blessings of eschatological salvation; in this case, "bread for the coming day" would refer to the bread of the kingdom (cf. 14:15), and disciples would be instructed by Jesus to entreat God to make available now the blessings of the eschaton.[24] However polysemic Luke's phrase may thus seem, this does not detract from what is most clear about this petition — namely, its concern with the reliance of Jesus' followers on God's provision for the basics of daily life.

Because of the centrality of "release" in Jesus' missionary program (see above on 4:18-19); and because the Lukan narrative has elaborated the meaning of "release" to include liberation from demonic subjugation, deliverance from diseases of all kinds, freedom from liabilities defined by the ethics of patronage, forgiveness of sins, and so on (see chs. 4–8), we should not be surprised to discover the central role of forgiveness of sins and of debts in Jesus' model prayer. Forgiveness of sins, in fact, is a pervasive motif in the Lukan narrative,[25] and its correlation to the reciprocity of creditors and debtors was noted already in 7:40-47.

Critical to our understanding of forgiveness in this co-text is, first, that we not capsize too quickly the distinction between "sins" and "debts" in its two members, and, second, that we not treat the forgiveness entailed in the second member as a necessary condition for the forgiveness of the first. (1) A form of enslavement was built into the fabric of the Greco-Roman world, a pervasive ethic whereby favors done for others constituted a relationship characterized by a cycle of repayment and debt; this system condoned the widespread exercise of coercive power by some persons over others.[26] The prayer Jesus teaches his followers embodies the urgency of giving without expectation of return — that is, of ripping the fabric of the patronage system by treating others as (fictive) kin rather than as greater or lesser than oneself (cf. 6:27-38). (2) The "for" of v 4b does not introduce a relationship of *quid pro quo* between divine and human forgiveness,[27] as though God's forgiveness

---

23. So Theissen, *Open Door,* 65.

24. See Wainwright, *Eucharist and Eschatology,* 30-34. To oppose this reading of "bread" as signifying "spiritual food" over against a rendering of "bread" as "physical food" is to miss the point entirely. This petition is concerned with dependence on God for the fundamentals of life, period.

25. In the Third Gospel, cf. 1:77; 3:3; 5:20-21, 23-24; 7:47-49; 12:10; 17:3-4; 23:34; 24:47.

26. See the discussion of economic relations and social solidarity above, §10.

27. Cf. Sir 28:2: "Forgive your neighbor . . . and then your sins will be pardoned when you pray." καὶ γάρ can and generally does designate a causal relationship as in the NRSV, "forgive . . . , for we ourselves forgive." It is worth exploring, though, the possi-

were dependent on human activity (cf. 6:35; 23:34!).[28] Instead, Jesus grounds the disciples' *request* for divine forgiveness in their own practices of extending forgiveness. As in previous texts (esp. 6:36), Jesus spins human behavior from the cloth of divine behavior; the embodiment of forgiveness in the practices of Jesus' followers is a manifestation and imitation of God's own character.

The difficulty of the final petition is a consequence of the ambiguity of the term for "testing" in Jewish literature.[29] Within the Lukan narrative, OT testimony regarding God's provision of tests "to prove" (and cultivate) the faithfulness of his people may be in view,[30] but in Luke's narrative the presence of testing is consistently viewed negatively as a detriment to faith (esp. 8:13; 22:40, 46). For those on the journey with Jesus, opposition is already a matter of course (see above on 9:51–19:48); hence, Jesus advises his disciples to ask God for the favor of being excused from further testing. In this way, they recognize and acknowledge their lack of what might pass as heroic faith and their need for divine care.

---

bilities resident here if καὶ γάρ were translated without reference to cause — e.g., "yes, even" or "in fact" — as attested in Attic Greek.

28. Marshall, 461.

29. See the summary of early interpretations in C. F. Evans, 483-84; more recently, cf., e.g., Moule, "Unsolved Problem"; Porter, "Mt 6:13 and Lk 11:4" — both of whom struggle with the difficulties of this clause but are inconclusive as to the resolution of its meaning.

Does πειρασμός refer to "the time of testing" (apparently as in the NRSV), the great tribulation of apocalypticism? The absence of an article or other modifier seems to exclude this view. See, however, the notion of eschatological testing in 22:40, 46. Does it refer to "temptation," normally associated with diabolic initiative against persons? πειρασμός/ πειράζω can have this connotation in Luke (e.g., 4:1-13), and in 22:40, 46, "trial" is defined in part by a co-text in which diabolic activity is conspicuous. But the subject of the testing in the current co-text is God. It is possible to associate "temptation" with God in an indirect way by observing that God allows the satanic testing of the faithful (e.g., Job). Alternatively, others have argued on syntactical grounds that this petition can be rendered, "Cause us not to succumb to temptation" or "Do not cause us to enter into temptation by the devil" (see the extended discussion in Cullmann, *Prayer*, 58-66; he prefers the latter over the former). These may represent possible readings, but their dependence on a peculiarity of Semitic usage (i.e., the attribution of a causative force to the verb) in order to achieve this sense, when the Third Evangelist writes in Greek and presumes on the part of his model readership a knowledge of Greek (and not of a Semitic language), is troubling. That is, this exegetical maneuver may be illuminating for study of the historical Jesus or of Aramaic-speaking Christian communities, but is suspect as a reading of the Lukan narrative.

30. See, e.g., Gen 22:1; Exod 15:25; 16:4; 20:20; Num 14:22; Deut 8:2; 13:3; Ps 26:2-3; Jdt 8:25-26; Sir 2:1; 44:20; Wis 3:5-6, *Jub.* 19:8-9; et al.; *TLNT*, 3:82-84. Some have urged that the testing of this final petition refers to God's being tested by the faithful. Most recently, Grayston ("Decline of Temptation") contends that ". . . disciples are to ask God not to lead them into a situation where they either experience *peirasmos* or engage in *peirasmos*" (293) — in effect, a request that "God not press too hard" (294).

5.2.2. Encouragement to Pray (11:5-13)

> 5 And he said to them, "Which of you[31] has a friend, and you go to
> him at midnight and say to him, 'Friend, lend me three loaves of bread;
> 6 for a friend of mine has arrived, and I have nothing to set before
> him,' 7 and he[32] answers from within, 'Do not bother me; the door has
> already been locked, and my children are with me in bed; I cannot get
> up and give you anything'? 8 I tell you, even if[33] he will not get up
> and give him anything because he is his friend, in order to avoid
> dishonor[34] he will get up and give him whatever he needs.[35] 9 "So I
> say to you, Ask, and it will be given you; search, and you will find;
> knock, and the door will be opened for you. 10 For everyone who asks
> receives, and everyone who searches finds, and for everyone who
> knocks, the door will be opened.
>
> 11 Which father among you whose child asks for a fish will[36] give
> a snake instead of a fish? 12 Or if the child asks for an egg, will give
> a scorpion? 13 If you then, who are evil, know how to give good gifts
> to your children, how much more will the heavenly Father give the
> Holy Spirit to those who ask him!"

The request of the disciples in v 1 had been, "Lord, teach us to pray. . . ."
Following Luke's presentation of Jesus' model prayer (vv 2-4), vv 5-13 carry
on his response to the disciples with no break whatsoever. This instruction,
then, should be viewed as a continuation of Jesus' attempt to teach his followers how to pray. The unit divides easily into two sections (vv 5-10, 11-13),
each with a similar structure: parabolic material (vv 5-8, 11-12) → ramifications (vv 9-10, 13).

The question of "how" to pray is ambiguous, as it might provide an
opening for a kind of "technology of prayer": "Pray like this, in this manner,
on this timetable, using these steps." Verses 5-8 have often been read in
precisely this way: How should one pray? "With persistence!"[37] Luke's

---

31. NRSV: "Suppose one of you. . . ."

32. NRSV: ". . . before him. And he. . . ."

33. NRSV: "though."

34. NRSV: "at least because of his persistence."

35. The NRSV introduces a paragraph break at v 9 and not at v 11.

36. NRSV: "Is there anyone among you who, if your child asks for a fish, will. . . ."

37. See, e.g., NRSV; Bede, *Homilies*, 2:124-25; more recently, Fitzmyer, 2:910-11;
Donahue, *Gospel in Parable*, 186-87; et al. This interpretation has inexplicably persisted
in spite of the complete absence of the concept of "persistence" in the actions of the
would-be host or in the asking (etc.) counseled in vv 9-10; and in spite of the lack of
first-century lexical support for the rendering of ἀναίδεια as "persistence" (cf. MM 33;
LSJ 105; A. F. Johnson, "Assurance," 125-27). Although Jeremias (*Parables,* 158) does

position is somewhat different. He is not so much concerned with the technology of prayer as he is with the shaping of prayer in relation to an accurate recognition of the one to whom prayer is offered. That is, Luke shaped this narrative unit not with an eye to the "how-to" of pray, but with a central emphasis on the worldview leading to and informing prayer. Hence, although vv 5-13 are tied to vv 2-4 linguistically — through repeated references to "bread" (vv 3, 5) and the transformation of the verb "to ask" into a virtual equivalent of the verb "to pray"[38] — these links do not identify the primary theme of this narrative section. Much more pivotal is the way in which Jesus continues in vv 5-13 what he had begun in vv 2-4 — namely, the identification of God as the Father whose graciousness is realized in his provision of what is needed, and indeed far beyond what might be expected, to those who join him in relationship.[39] Because the disciples have to do with such a God, they are liberated to ask, to search, and to knock (vv 9-10), knowing that God will not answer their prayers with harmful gifts but with good (vv 11-13).

5-8 Luke introduces no break between vv 1-4 and v 5, other than to signal that Jesus' instruction on prayer would continue. His parable thus serves to illustrate and develop the teaching on prayer comprising vv 2-4. As Luke does occasionally, so here he relates a story whose primary focus is simply to register what everyone already knows about the way the world works. The interpretive strategy, then, is not immediately to wonder who the friend, traveler, or householder might represent, but simply to hear the story. Of course, the range of conceivable meanings of Jesus' story is restrained by its appearance in this co-text, boundaried by Luke's concern to portray the character of God as it impinges on community habits of prayer.

The opening of Jesus' story, "Which of you . . . ," typically introduces a hypothetical question ("Can you imagine . . . ?") for which the anticipated

---

not regard vv 5-8 as concerned with "persistence," he asserts that vv 9-13 turn Jesus' point into "an exhortation to unwearied prayer"; although Fitzmyer only allows the possibility that vv 5-8 can be read in another way, and even offers a literal rendering of "because of his persistence" as "because of his shamelessness indeed" (2:912), he follows Jeremias without argument in his view that Luke is concerned with "persistence in human prayer to God." This view is often based on the assumption that vv 5-8 and the parable in 18:1-8 make a parallel point about the need for persistence. As we will see, neither the present text nor 18:1-8 is concerned with persistence; rather, both have to do with issues of honor and shame in the community of the one being petitioned.

38. αἰτέω — vv 9, 10, 11, 12, and 13; προσεύχομαι — vv 1 (2x) and 2; cf. Crump, *Jesus the Intercessor*, 134.

39. That relationship is assumed, not that Jesus is directing this instruction to the disciples (v 1), who are able to refer to God as Father (v 2; cf. v 13), and that the parabolic material of vv 5-8, 11-13 revolves around what is expected in relationships defined by friendship and family relations.

answer is immediate and self-evident.[40] Jesus invites his disciples to envision a scene that encompasses all of vv 5-7: Can you imagine a friend who refuses to assist you in your undertaking to provide hospitality at the arrival of an unexpected friend?[41] The answer to this question is, of course, No! In order for us to arrive at this decision, though, we must understand some of the realities presumed in the implausible scene Jesus paints. On the mundane level, we should note that bread is baked and consumed daily, so that the dearth registered in v 6 is not extraordinary; that the request is for three loaves of bread has no symbolic value but is the appropriate number of loaves for an evening meal; and that the house Jesus depicts is presumably a one-room peasant home in which the whole family makes their bed on a floor mat. On a related, less mundane note is the probability that the scene includes (again, at the level of presupposition) a small peasant village in which houses are located in close proximity to one another, where the disturbance of sleep in the one home could not remain an isolated event but would be known by others immediately and by all shortly, and that the requirements for hospitality in the one home would naturally spill over into the village as a whole.[42]

Also of importance in the scene Jesus envisages, but operative at the level of preunderstanding, would be the social scripts signaled by the fourfold use of the term "friend" (vv 5 [2x], 6, 8) and by concerns of hospitality. "Friend" is not a well-worn term in the Scriptures of Israel, but was the subject of extensive reflection among Greco-Roman philosophers. Even a cursory perusal of this literature shows that friendship and issues of material exchange belonged to the same grammar, with friends categorized with reference to their resources: superior friends, equal friends, lesser friends, and so on.[43] Discussions of ideal (or equal) friendship foreground the practice of holding "all things in common" and shun the self-interest otherwise associated

---

40. Cf. 12:25; 14:5; Jeremias, *Parables,* 103, 158; Derrett, "Friend at Midnight," 33, 35. This form of introduction renders ambiguous the subject of πορεύσεται: Does "one of you" go as the would-be host; or does the would-be host come to "one of you"? The former reading is supported by the Lukan co-text, in which the "you" refers to the disciples who are being instructed regarding prayer (i.e., who come with requests); while the latter — adopted by, e.g., Jeremias, *Parables,* 158; Fitzmyer, 2:909, 911 — introduces an awkward change of subject (as Fitzmyer acknowledges) and is more difficult to understand in this co-text.

41. So Jeremias, *Parables,* 158; K. E. Bailey, *Poet and Peasant,* 119-33. Admittedly, this makes for a lengthy and inelegant sentence. Catchpole ("Friend at Midnight," 411) regards v 8 as the actual response of the householder, but this is based on his decision that the householder must be presented as wicked.

42. These and related matters are discussed in more detail in Herzog, *Parables,* 199-207.

43. Cf. Pliny *Ep.* 7.3.2; 2.6.2; Seneca *Ep.* 94.14; Garnsey and Saller, *Roman Empire,* 149, 154-56.

with economic exchange, but even ideal friendship assumed economic exchange, even if it was not formally codified or ritualized. Along a related line of thought, to share friendship was to share honor — again, with the ideal expressed in a denial of status disjunctions among friends. Hence, solely on the basis of friendship, one would simply assume, the householder is expected to assist the would-be host. In addition, the conventions of hospitality involve not only the person surprised by his traveling friend but also the whole village in the need to provide a respectable meal. The need of the would-be host thus becomes the need of the village. For these reasons, the hypothetical reply of the householder, a claim of inconvenience that presumes the possession of extra bread that could be shared, is laughable in its absurdity (cf. Prov 3:27-28).[44]

The punch line of Jesus' story comes in v 8, where he both admits that the scene he has envisaged is preposterous and outlines why the householder will arise from his sleep and assist his friend. Jesus' commentary on the positive response that would certainly be forthcoming from the householder raises two possible motivations. The "even if . . . certainly" construction[45] underscores that, generally, the demands of friendship are sufficient to secure the help needed. Even in those cases where friendship is insufficient, however, the outcome will be the same on account of the threat of dishonor if assistance is not granted.[46] Interestingly, this reading of Jesus' story picks up on two

44. See the discussion in Huffard, "Friend at Midnight," 157-60; Derrett, "Friend at Midnight," 33-35.

45. The particle γέ is sometimes left untranslated, but it usually intensifies the lexeme to which it is joined. The construction εἰ καί . . . γέ could be translated, "even though [although] . . . at least," as in the NRSV, but "even if . . . certainly" is also possible and actually makes better sense of the cultural phenomena discussed above.

46. The meaning of ἀναίδεια has been much debated, even when it is admitted (see above, the introduction to this unit) that "persistence" is not a viable option. ἀναίδεια is an abstract noun formed from the negation of αἰδώς (via αἰδός, "shame, self-respect, what causes shame or scandal"). Bailey (*Poet and Peasant,* 131-32) derives the meaning "avoidance of shame" by positing a mistranslation of an original Aramaic logion; Bailey does not address the question of how Luke's Greek readers would have handled this innovation. Long ago, Fridrichsen ("Exegetisches," 40-43) accepted "shamelessness" as a negative quality, but argued that the concern of the householder is to avoid the shamelessness that will be attributed to him if he does not help the would-be host. This view is adopted by Nolland (2:626; against the objections of Bailey, *Poet and Peasant,* 130; and Fitzmyer, 2:912) and here. Many interpreters now agree that the householder will act in order to maintain his honor (and not be judged as shameless) in the village — cf., e.g., Huffard, "Friend at Midnight," 156-57; A. F. Johnson, "Assurance," 129-31; Malina and Rohrbaugh, *Commentary,* 351. Derrett ("Friend at Midnight"; followed by Blomberg, *Parables,* 276) argues that it is the would-be host, the petitioner who acts in a shameless way, thus proving his claim to friendship with the householder. According to this reading, the emphasis would fall on the confidence with which the disciple may approach God in

themes present in the preceding model prayer (vv 2-4) — namely, (1) the grounding of prayer in the relationship one has with God the Father (note that in Greco-Roman antiquity, "father" is a synonym for "lord of the house") and (2) the notion that God engages in eschatological redemption in order that he might restore honor to his name (see above on v 2).

9-10   "So I" places these verses in a consequential relationship to Jesus' story in vv 5-8.[47] Using language from everyday life, he teaches that, because God will arise and act on behalf of those in need, they ought to bring their requests to him. What is remarkable about this instruction is its universality: "everyone" is encouraged to recognize God's fidelity and the expansiveness of his goodness and to respond with a confidence expressed in venturing forth in relationship to God with one's entreaties. As vv 11-13 go on to demonstrate, Jesus' instructions do not give the petitioner carte blanche; already, the emphasis has fallen on what one needs (vv 2-4, 8) and, in what follows, Jesus will go even further to show that God's liberality extends even to the identification and provision for genuine need previously unrecognized or unexpressed by the petitioner.

11-13   Jesus continues his teaching on prayer by returning to the realm of daily life, this time within the household. As in vv 5-7 (see above), he again poses hypothetical questions for which the anticipated answer would be immediate and self-evident. Thus, in vv 11-12 he observes, simply, that children who request food from their parents will not be given malevolent alternatives.[48] Comparing human fathers with the heavenly Father,[49] arguing from lesser to greater, Jesus maintains that God, whose goodness far exceeds even that of those human fathers who would never answer their children's requests

---

prayer — clearly a complementary point to the one we are making. The recent position of Herzog (*Parables,* 212-14) — that ἀναίδεια refers to "attitudes that challenge socially constructed boundaries or behaviors and that break those established boundaries" (213) and that, in this case, the shameless behavior is realized in the extension of hospitality to a virtual stranger — runs aground on the identification of the guest as a "friend" as well as on the conventions of hospitality. The "moral economy of the peasant," which Herzog discusses, measures "subsistence" in terms of the requirements for daily living for the peasant family, preparation for next year's crop, the claims of the state (and temple), *and for the fulfillment of social obligations* (see above, §10).

47. κἀγώ.

48. Some scholars have seen the denial of a more injurious point in Jesus' words, suggesting that a serpent has the profile of a fish and a scorpion, and, rolled up, might pass as an egg (e.g., Ott, *Gebet und Heil,* 104-6; Bailey, *Poet and Peasant,* 136-37; Stein, 328). Although such similarities in appearance might explain the pairing of these objects, the additional nuance of deception is not necessary.

49. The text is uncertain, but the meaning is not greatly affected. Whether it is "the heavenly Father [will] give the Holy Spirit" or "the Father [will] give the Holy Spirit from heaven," human fathers are distinguished from God as Father. The latter reading goes further, however, to highlight the heavenly origin of God's gifts.

with malice,[50] can likewise be counted on never to give harmful gifts. Pushing the comparison even further, the superiority of the fatherhood of God is realized in the superiority of his gift. Human parents give "good gifts," while God gives what he has determined to be the best gift, the Holy Spirit. That is, to those whose confidence in God is manifest in prayer, even if their supplications included no request for the Spirit,[51] God grants the Spirit. By this indirect route, we come to perceive that the fatherhood of God is realized in a graciousness and faithfulness that includes his determination and communication of what is best for those who come to him in prayer.

Before departing this short teaching session on prayer we should observe that Jesus' final statement has established a new narrative need — namely, the Father is to give the Holy Spirit to his children. What form this might take is not yet evident, nor will it become apparent by the close of the Third Gospel; instead, this is a promise that carries Luke's audience forward into his second volume (cf. 24:49; Acts 1:8; 2:1-4).[52] What should be clear to Luke's audience, however, is how this promise further binds the fortunes of Jesus' disciples into his own. Just as Jesus had introduced to his followers language for God consistent with his own ("Father" — e.g., 10:21-22; 11:2, 13), so he now anticipates that they will be given the Spirit in some fashion analogous to his own Spirit-anointing (cf. 3:21-22; 4:18-19).

5.3. JESUS' BEHAVIOR QUESTIONED (11:14-54)

The move from Jesus' teaching his disciples to the present narrative unit, populated by nameless crowds and the Pharisees and experts on the law, is abrupt; so also is the topical shift, from instruction on prayer centered on the character of God as Father to escalating hostility and attempts at censure. The break between vv 13 and 14 is thus easy to recognize. Following v 54, Jesus will again turn more directly to his disciples, this time to draw out the implications for his followers of the inimical situation Luke summarizes in vv 53-54.

The intervening material encompasses two scenes that, on the face of it, are quite different. One locates Jesus out in the open, among the crowds (vv 14-36); the other is in a house, among Pharisees and legal experts (vv 37-52). In the first, a characteristic activity of Jesus, exorcism, provides the impetus for a deleterious characterization of Jesus, leading to an address centered on the rhetoric of reproof or censure. The second also situates Jesus

---

50. πονηρός, then, should not be overinterpreted; in this co-text it refers to nothing more than the characteristic sinfulness of human beings in comparison with God (cf. 5:8).

51. Note that αἰτέω has no direct object.

52. Cf., e.g., Sieber, "Promise of My Father."

in a familiar setting, at a meal, where Jesus' behavior marks him as a deviant; this again leads to a discourse whose primary aim is censure. Verse 37a ("While he was speaking, a Pharisee invited him to dine with him") ensures that these two scenes are read together though, while v 53 ("When he went outside") marks the finale of the second episode.

Direct notations that Jesus and his followers are on a journey (beginning in 9:51) are conspicuously absent from this unit. Faint echoes do appear when it is recalled that the goal of the journey is Jerusalem, where Jesus will meet his death at the hands of the leaders of the people (9:21-22, 44). Against the backdrop of the general acclamation following Jesus in the Galilean section of his ministry, how are we to understand the animosity Jesus' mission must have engendered if the predictions of his impending death are to be realized? The beginning of the journey had already occasioned hostility (9:52-53; cf. 10:10-16), but here opposition to Jesus' ministry surfaces dramatically. What is more, it comes not only from Pharisees and legal experts (whose hostility has been reported earlier — e.g., 6:1-11), but also from some from within the crowds themselves. Heretofore, the crowds had been cast as generally positive, sometimes neutral, and with only traces (forebodings?) of discord. Now, however, some among the crowds graphically align themselves over against Jesus.

In the heart of this narrative of surging animosity, Luke sounds clearly the theme of this larger unit. *Hostility provides the horizon against which is underscored the urgency of a decision regarding Jesus.* Jesus' words to the unnamed woman in v 28 — "Blessed rather are those who hear the word of God and obey it!" — are only the most obvious in this respect, for the necessity of faithfulness vis-à-vis Jesus is prevalent in this material (cf. vv 23-26, 28, 31-32, 35-36). The language of fidelity and fecundity may be absent from the table scene (vv 37-54), but the same note is sounded. In the presence of the Pharisees and legal experts, Jesus outlines the shape of faithful response that gets to the root of the Pharisaic concern with purity and to the heart of his own message concerning possessions and care for the poor (v 41; cf. above, 4:18-19); since he has already reaffirmed that kinship within the people of God is assessed not on ancestral grounds but on the basis of faithful performance (v 41; cf. 3:7-14), his words to the Pharisees and legal experts are all the more provocative.

5.3.1. Jesus Responds to the Crowds (11:14-36)

The first of the two scenes of this narrative unit (vv 14-54) begins innocently enough, given Luke's extensive portrait of Jesus as exorcist.[1] In comparison

---

1. See above on 4:18-19. Cf., e.g., 4:31-37, 40-41; 8:1-3; et al. More broadly, Kirchschläger, *Jesu exorzistisches Wirken;* Garrett, *Demise of the Devil;* and the relevant sections in Twelftree, *Jesus the Exorcist;* Page, *Powers of Evil.*

with previous scenes, however, this one goes awry in the unanticipated move from "amazement" on the part of the crowds to their divided, skeptical responses (vv 15-16). This exorcism thus identifies Jesus as engaging in characteristic activity but at the same time functions as the occasion for controversy with the crowds. Both of these narrative roles are important, not least in light of the fact that this pericope follows immediately on the heels of Jesus' characterization of God and concomitant invitation for persons to recognize God's fidelity and respond in confident faith. In their response to Jesus' ministry of "release" (see above on 4:18-19), people from the crowds do nothing less than dispute the divine origins of Jesus' benefaction and, thus, attempt to refute that his ministry is a representation of God's graciousness. In this they will soon be joined by the Pharisees and legal experts (vv 37-54).

The three responses of those in the crowds — amazement, attribution of Jesus' work to Beelzebul, and demand for a sign — provide the framework for Jesus' subsequent response. He will take up each in turn, dealing first with the charge that he is in league with Beelzebul (vv 17-26), then with a woman whose exuberance is misdirected (vv 27-28), and finally with the demand for a sign (vv 29-36). Throughout, Jesus engages in invective rhetoric,[2] attempting (1) to dislodge the charge leveled at him as well as the need for sign-seeking and (2) to secure an alternative response to his ministry, one that recognizes its divine origins and leads to enlightenment and faithfulness.

5.3.1.1. Diverse Opinions (11:14-16)

14 *Now he was casting out a demon that was mute; when the demon had gone out, the one who had been mute spoke, and the crowds were amazed.* 15 *But some of them said, "He casts out demons by Beelzebul, the ruler of the demons."* 16 *Others, to test him, kept demanding from him a sign from heaven.*

Luke opens this scene with a now-familiar frame: Jesus practicing a ministry of "release,"[3] in this case from demonic activity manifest in a biomedical disorder; the close relationship of physical malady and diabolic activity in the Lukan narrative;[4] the presentation of "healing" as a return to social discourse;[5]

---

2. That is, the negative form of epideictic rhetoric — cf. Kennedy, *New Testament Interpretation,* 19-20, 73-77; Robbins, "Beelzebul Controversy," 261-62.

3. See above on 4:18-19.

4. Cf. esp. 13:10-17; Acts 10:38.

5. This is signified in this instance by the ability of the previously mute person to talk. Interpreters of Luke must step outside the biomedical paradigm for understanding such illness episodes as the one summarized here (cf., e.g., Hahn, *Sickness and Healing*); otherwise, the intertwining of social, cosmic/spiritual, and physiological

and a reaction of wonder on the part of the crowds. As he goes on to describe in more detail the nature of the responses of the crowds, however, Luke breaks out of the commonplace, underscoring his point through disorientation. We are accustomed to seeing the crowds portrayed in positive terms, at least as potential followers of Jesus. Now, however, with the onset of the journey to Jerusalem (9:51–19:48), the division within Israel presaged by Simeon (2:34-35) and John (3:17) begins to come to fruition. The vagueness of the response of "wonder"[6] is never so striking as it is here.

The repetition of the word "demon" (4x) and the care the Evangelist allots to documenting the success of Jesus' intervention on behalf of this mute person suggest that Luke's brief report of exorcism serves a function other than setting up the controversies introduced in vv 15-16, though it certainly does this too. At stake is the nature of Jesus' ministry — not just in the present scene but as this has been worked out from 4:18-19 onward. Because of the centrality of the act of exorcism to Jesus' ministry of "release,"[7] questions regarding the identity, role, and authority of Jesus are all foregrounded in this scene.[8] Two challenges are expressed, both concerned with Jesus' identity (cf. Deut 13:1-3): Is he a false prophet? Is his ministry authenticated by God? Interestingly, the *fact* of Jesus' exorcism is not under scrutiny, only the *source* of Jesus' authority (Beelzebul?) and the possibility of his receiving indisputable sanction from God (sign-seeking, "from heaven"). Such questions are reminiscent of the devil's testing of Jesus in the wilderness (4:1-13), when he attempted to recruit Jesus to serve his aims and, failing this, tried to involve Jesus in abuses of his power.[9]

The attribution to Beelzebul of Jesus' authority to exorcise demons is a slanderous remark designed to exercise a form of social control on Jesus. Attempting to locate Jesus in a place of subjugation to Satan,[10] some in the crowds venture to paint Jesus as nothing more than a magician,[11] a false

---

realities will be missed. κωφός can refer to either muteness or deafness; in light of Luke's description of the outcome of Jesus' intervention ("he spoke"), the former is in view here.

6. θαυμάζω is at best an equivocal response — cf., e.g., 1:21, 63; 4:22; 8:25; 9:43.

7. See above on 4:18-19; 10:17-20; Acts 10:38; cf. Garrett, *Demise of the Devil.*

8. See Thiselton, "Christology in Luke," 461.

9. The association of these two episodes is encouraged by the common use of πειράζω (4:2; 11:16), the only two appearances of the verb in the Third Gospel. Plummer (301) thinks that 11:16 marks the renewal of the devil's third temptation (4:9-12).

10. Beelzebub is another name for Satan (cf. the apposition of "Satan" and "Beelzebul" in v 18 — *contra* Böcher, "Βεελζεβούλ"). For the discussion on the origins of this name, see the survey in Lewis, "Beelzebul."

11. That is, one who invokes the aid of one spirit(s) against another spirit.

prophet, a deviant not to be taken seriously (cf. 7:33).[12] Incidental to the charge against Jesus but significant within the worldview assumed by the Lukan narrative is the recognition of Satan as the "ruler of the demons." This image presupposes that demons serve an aim other than their own, that they are deployed by their lord in the service of his purpose and as instruments of his dominion (cf. 4:5-6). This portrait has immediate relevance for the unfolding discourse, since it implies that an offensive against demonic activity is also an offensive against Satan.

5.3.1.2. The Kingdom of God Has Drawn Near (11:17-26)

17 *But he knew what they were thinking and said to them, "Every kingdom divided against itself becomes a desert, households collapsing against each other.*[13] 18 *If Satan also is divided against himself, how will his kingdom stand? — for you say that I cast out the demons by Beelzebul.* 19 *Now if I cast out the demons by Beelzebul, by whom do your exorcists cast them out? Therefore they will be your judges.* 20 *But if it is by the finger of God that I cast out the demons, then the kingdom of God has come to you.* 21 *When a strong man, fully armed, guards his castle, his property is safe.* 22 *But when one stronger than he attacks him and overpowers him, he takes away his armor in which he trusted and divides his plunder.*[14]

23 *"Whoever is not with me is against me, and whoever does not gather with me scatters.* 24 *When the unclean spirit has gone out of a person, it wanders through waterless regions looking for a resting place, but not finding any, it says, 'I will return to my house from which I came.'* 25 *When it comes, it finds it swept and put in order.* 26 *Then it goes and brings seven other spirits more evil than itself, and they enter and live there; and the last state of that person is worse than the first."*

These verses constitute a unified, continuous discourse in response to the accusation brought against Jesus in v 15 and repeated in v 18b — namely,

---

12. For the relevance of the charge of "magician" in this context, see the discussion of the connection between the diabolic and magic in Stanton, "Jesus of Nazareth," 171-75; Kee, *Medicine, Miracle, and Magic,* ch. 4; Garrett, *Demise of the Devil,* ch. 1. On the social control attempted by thus labeling Jesus, see, e.g., Douglas, *Risk and Blame,* 83-101; Seymour-Smith, *Anthropology,* 76-77.

13. NRSV: "and house falls on house."

14. The NRSV provides a paragraph break after v 23, not after v 22. Godet (2:67) likewise notes that vv 24-26 serve to illustrate the declaration of v 23, though he reads vv 24-26 differently than we do.

that his practice of exorcism was grounded in the authority of Beelzebul. By means of this slanderous accusation, some of Jesus' nameless opponents in the crowds had sought to marginalize his effectiveness and influence. Jesus' reply takes three essential forms, all of which are designed to solicit a response on the part of his audience. First, he defends his ministry against what he argues is an absurd label. Reason will show, he seems to say, that he cannot be a magician, a witch, who overpowers evil spirits by manipulating the spirits. Second, he provides an alternative interpretation of his exorcisms. They are manifestations of a stronger power than that wielded by Beelzebul; they bring to expression the sovereignty of God. Third, he extends an invitation of sorts, asserting the urgency of responding positively and completely to his message.

Pervasive throughout this discourse is the image of competing kingdoms (see the language of "kingdom," "household," "castle," "house," the presentation of Satan as commander of the demonic forces, and the language of the battlefield and plunder of the enemy). Jesus thus positions the work of exorcism within the larger matrix of the struggle between the dominion of Satan and the dominion of God.[15] The inability of Jesus' detractors to recognize this exposes this episode as concerned with a fundamental clash of perception. Distorting the nature of Jesus' identity and mission, these antagonists similarly misconstrue the coming of God in his mission. Jesus not only calls them to a new way of seeing, one shaped fundamentally by the vibrant presence of God's power, but also challenges them to responses of robust faithfulness.

17-18   Verses 14-16 serve as a heading to this larger narrative unit (vv 14-54), setting the stage for the escalation of conflict surrounding Jesus' ministry. Luke now marks a return to v 15, made explicit by the backflash in v 18b, where the charge against Jesus had been his collusion with Beelzebul. As before, Jesus discerns the inner thoughts of his opponents — indeed, Jesus' role is, in part, to make public those who oppose the salvific coming of God.[16] In vv 17-22, Jesus presents a series of counterarguments, the first of which is an error in the logic of his interlocutors (vv 17-18). Jesus' reply presupposes: (1) that the names Beelzebul and Satan refer to the same entity, (2) the propriety of referring to Satan as the head of a kingdom, (3) the marshaling of demons under the command of Satan and in the service of his aim, and, thus, (4) the unity of Satan's dominion.[17] To imagine that Jesus was one of Satan's

---

15. Cf. Theissen, *Miracle Stories,* 90-91.

16. See 2:35; 5:22; 6:8; 7:39-40; 9:47.

17. The characterization of Beelzebul as "ruler of the demons" (v 15) belongs to the same semantic field of imperial rule as "kingdom" and "household" in vv 17-18. On this use of "household," see the discussion in Oakman, "Ruler's Houses," 114-17. More generally, cf. Shirock, "Whose Exorcists?" 41; Page, *Powers of Evil,* 102-3, 108.

deputies and that he was casting other satanic agents from people, then, would be to pit Satan against himself. Why would Satan himself endorse a civil war in his own domain?

19 Jesus' second argument assails his opponents for a further lapse in logic. If his practices of exorcism are open to such slanderous scrutiny, why not those of other Jewish exorcists? Jesus thus admits (and in no way censures) the analogous activity of other exorcists among his people;[18] indeed, given that the only two alternatives within this pericope (and within Luke-Acts) are that they have derived their power from God or from Satan, his point must be that their ability (like his) stems from God. His claim that these Jewish exorcists will serve as judges in this matter is susceptible to at least two different readings. On the one hand, Jesus' words may simply be tantamount to saying, "Why do you not ask them regarding the source of their power? They will tell you that they are empowered by God!" Alternatively, given their identification with God's purpose, evident in their drawing on divine power and opposition to the work of Satan, these exorcists may be expected by Jesus to participate in the eschatological condemnation of these who attribute divine activity to diabolic purpose. According to this latter scenario, these Jewish exorcists would appear alongside the queen of Sheba and the people of Nineveh, who will judge those who refuse to recognize in Jesus' mission the power of God (vv 31-32).

20 There is no necessary or logical connection between v 20 and the

18. For Jewish exorcists, see, e.g., Josephus *Ant.* 8.2.5 §§45-49; *PGM* 4.3019ff.; cf. Twelftree, "ΕΙ ΔΕ . . . ΕΓΩ ΕΚΒΑΛΛΩ ΤΑ ΔΑΙΜΟΝΙΑ . . . ," 383. This has caused no little grief among scholars. Wanting to assert that Jesus was unique, they have sought to interpret this assertion in some way so as to denigrate others' ministries of exorcism as, e.g., not as successful, not as authoritative, etc. (cf., e.g., Harvey, *Constraints of History,* 109; Caragounis, "Son of Man," 230-31); support for this interpretive maneuver is absent from the Lukan text, however. Others have insisted that Jesus' argument is simply *ad hominem* and should not be pressed: Jesus' adversaries were simply demonstrating the inconsistency in their own beliefs (recently, e.g., Page, *Powers of Evil,* 104-5). The problem with such arguments is helpfully observed by Shirock, "Whose Exorcists?" 41-46. Shirock's own view — that "your exorcists" (NRSV) is actually a reference to Jesus' disciples — is unpersuasive as a reading of the Lukan narrative. His attempt to deny that "your exorcists" refers to the exorcists of the Pharisees overlooks the fact that Luke specifically has not introduced the Pharisees; Jesus' interlocutors are simply people from the crowd (some of whom may be and apparently are Pharisees [v 27], but for the referent of "your" we must nevertheless cast much more widely). Moreover, his discomfort with the service of these exorcists as "judges" is unnecessary (see below). A verdict with regard to the current matter (i.e., the source of Jesus' and their authority for performing exorcisms) is all that is required of Luke's language. With regard to this whole debate, what remains unclear from the Lukan text (or even with regard to an analysis of a proposed *Sitz im Leben Jesu*) is why Jesus *must* be distanced from his contemporaries with respect to his practices of exorcism.

counterarguments comprising vv 17-19. Instead, Jesus simply asserts his interpretation over against theirs, which he has just undermined. The phrase "the finger of God" is used occasionally in Jewish literature, denoting the active power of God;[19] here it stands in close relationship to the Exodus story, where, against the backdrop of the plagues against Egypt, Pharaoh's magicians exclaim, "This is the finger of God!" (8:19).[20] In the same way, the exorcisms of Jesus are manifestations of God's liberating power, but this is to say nothing less than that his exorcisms must be understood as the kingdom of God at work, now (cf. 10:9, 11). This is a statement, then, about the advancing kingdom (11:2), but it is also a legitimation of Jesus, designating him as one through whom God's power is at work; in this roundabout way, the testimony requested in v 16 ("a sign from heaven") has actually been provided in the act of exorcism itself (v 14).[21]

The use of the term "kingdom" in this co-text itself indicates the function of exorcisms according to Jesus. They are an important means by which the kingdom of Satan (vv 17-18) is surmounted. Similarly, in the LXX the verb "cast out" has militaristic roots and is used for the expulsion of the enemy in order that God's purpose might be realized.[22] Jesus leaves no doubt, then, regarding his own understanding of his practices of exorcism. In the same breath, though, he includes the work of other exorcists; working against Satan (v 19), they also render present the kingdom of God.[23]

21-22 In order to drive home this interpretation of his ministry of exorcism (and, only incidentally, to distance himself further from the slanderous association of his activity with Beelzebul in v 15), Jesus continues his response with a lesson from common knowledge about the world — not least in the Roman world where the household mansions of local and regional Roman administrators would have invoked images of a retinue of armed soldiers signifying the institutionalization of foreign power and of a distribution system whereby material goods were siphoned off from the people. Such a strong man, occupying his "castle," can only be defeated by one who is yet stronger, but the whole Roman system worked to ensure the perpetual, relative

19. See Exod 8:19; 31:18; Deut 9:10; Ps 8:3.

20. One may hear, with Wall ("Finger of God"), the additional reverberation of Deut 9:10 (the law was written on two stone tablets by the finger of God), but the relationship of the Deuteronomic co-text to the present one seems much more elusive.

21. See Schürmann, 2:238-39.

22. So Twelftree, *Jesus the Exorcist,* 110.

23. Herein we come face to face with the binary opposition of Luke's narrative theology. There is only one narrative aim driving the story of redemption forward. This is God's purpose. Either one embraces this purpose and serves it or one opposes it. To oppose God is to align oneself with Satan, and to oppose Satan is to align oneself with God. See further Green, *Gospel of Luke,* ch. 2; and above on 10:17-20.

weakness of its conquered peoples. Who is more powerful than Rome? Jesus' story is this well rooted in the life of ancient Palestine, and for this reason it may well have articulated with the wider Lukan concern to present Jesus as Savior and Lord in a more powerful sense than even the Roman emperor (see above on 2:1-20).

In its current co-text, though, our reading of this short story is guided more directly by the overarching concern with Jesus as exorcist. This means that the point of Jesus' story is not concerned with Rome even if its impact depends on such a vivid picture in the wider mural in which Rome dominated. Nor is the point of Jesus' parable a message about the defeat of Satan — which is not currently in view and, in any case, has not yet occurred (cf., e.g., 4:13; 22:3). At issue is Jesus' practices of exorcism. The strong man — that is, Satan, represented by one of his demonic agents — guards his mansion and property — that is, the person demonized;[24] Jesus, operating with divine power, is the one who is stronger still; he attacks not the castle but the strong man, with the result that his conquest frees the castle and returns the property to the human being who had suffered under diabolic rule.[25] The militaristic imagery is strong, expanding the portrait of the clash of kingdoms in Jesus' ministry. This imagery also allows for the added portrayal of the stronger man, Jesus, as the benefactor whose offensive maneuvers bring about human liberation.

23-26 It is not enough for Jesus merely to deflect the misrepresentation of his ministry as diabolic in origin (v 15) nor even to assert and explain the true significance of his practices of exorcism. Because his ministry is the focal point of the eschatological clash between God's salvific project and satanic opposition (vv 20-22), it is imperative, even urgent, that people align themselves for battle. This message is communicated, first, in the form of a two-part axiom, with both parts oriented toward the same point but employing different metaphors. In a co-text marked by conflict and invective rhetoric, Jesus' audience is first charged to declare their loyalties in the battle (cf. Josh 5:13).[26] If the initial image is militaristic, the second is agricultural, pointing to the gathering of God's people.[27] What is remarkable is that the side on which one chooses to engage the struggle is fundamentally determined by how one responds to Jesus; suddenly, Jesus' concern to legitimate himself with reference to common wisdom and his similarity to other exorcists is overridden by this assertion of his distinctiveness.

Verses 24-26 make much the same point, though in a less direct way.

24. Cf. "my house," a reference to a human being, in v 24.

25. On this view, cf. Garrett, *Demise of the Devil*, 45; Twelftree, *Jesus the Exorcist*, 111-12; *idem*, "EI ΔE . . . ΕΓΩ ΕΚΒΑΛΛΩ ΤΑ ΔAIMONIA . . . ," 390.

26. The co-text of the analogous saying in 9:50 is quite different.

27. Cf. 3:17; also the image of gathering (and scattering) the flock of Israel in Isa 11:12; 40:11; Ezek 5:12; 34:13, 21; Zech 11:16; Tob 3:4.

Jesus' words read like "an extract from a text book on demonology"[28] — that is, as though he were going over what would have been standard ideas about the behavior of unclean spirits.[29] This would presumably have included, for example, such notions as the following: demons are capable of independent existence apart from a host; having been cast out of a person,[30] spirits range over desert regions;[31] they prefer to indwell human beings; and humans are capable of being possessed by multiple spirits.[32] Why does he rehearse these apparently common views? First, Jesus thus develops a striking contrast between the work of the exorcist through whose activity the kingdom of God is rendered present and that of the world of evil spirits; the one leads to a life[33] that is clean and in order, the other to destruction.[34] Second, this comparison renders all the more pressing the need not only to enjoy the benefits of Jesus' ministry (as the crowds have thus far been doing),[35] but positively to respond in ongoing faithfulness (cf. 8:11-15).

28. C. F. Evans, 494; cf. Page, *Powers of Evil,* 172. Some (e.g., Godet, 2:67-69; Marshall, 479) have argued that in vv 24-26 Jesus is characterizing the ineffectual ministries of exorcism of other Jewish exorcists (as in v 19). But there is no hint of any censure of those exorcists in v 19, nor does Jesus specify who is responsible for the exorcism of the unclean spirit in v 24.

29. On the association of "unclean spirits" and "demons," see above on 4:33.

30. Nolland (2:645-46) believes that the spirit leaves of its own accord: "As the spirit was free to leave, so the spirit is free to return . . . ," but the linguistic evidence on which he bases this reading is fallacious. He insists that Luke uses the language of "departure" rather than "expulsion"; however, ἐξέρχομαι is used to describe the departure of demons who have been commanded to depart by Jesus the exorcist in, e.g., 4:35; 8:2.

31. Of the texts often adduced as supporting this representation of the proclivities of demons, only Isa 34:14-15 LXX; 4 Macc 18:8 appear to be somewhat relevant; Bar 4:35 refers to a desolate locale, which seems to be the point of "waterless regions." Cf. Str-B 4.1.516.

32. See 8:2, 30.

33. The spirit refers to "my house" — i.e., its domicile, a human being. This metaphorical use of οἶκος was anticipated in the parabolic use of "castle" (αὐλή, "courtyard" or, by synecdoche, "house" or "mansion") in v 21.

34. Kilgallen ("Return of the Unclean Spirit") argues that the function of vv 24-26 is to continue Jesus' defense by contrasting the nature of Jesus' ministry with the work of the demonic. The contrast he notes is helpful. In our view, however, Jesus' defensive strategy included only the material in vv 17-19; with vv 20-26 he has moved on to a positive reinterpretation of his practices of exorcism, situating them within the context of the struggle of two kingdoms, in light of which appropriate response is now urgent.

35. Cf. 13:26-27; 17:11-19.

5.3.1.3. The Blessedness of Obedience (11:27-28)

27 *While he was saying this, a woman in the crowd raised her voice and said to him, "Blessed is the womb that bore you and the breasts that nursed you!"* 28 *But he said, "Blessed rather are those who hear the word of God and obey it!"*

In the course of his response to a protest concerning the source of the power by which he exorcises demons, Jesus had made what must have seemed rather extravagant claims concerning his role in God's redemptive purpose. His defensive reasoning had sought to establish the illogic of any suggestion that he had been working in league with Satan and to verify that behind his ministry activity stood God. He went even further to insist that his ministry of "release" (see above on 4:18-19) renders present the sovereignty of God over against the rule of Satan as well as to position his ministry at the frontline of the clash of these two kingdoms. Hence, he observed, one's posture vis-à-vis the divine project is a function of how one responds to Jesus. This constitutes a considerable claim to status before God that does not go unnoticed by at least this one woman in the crowd. From "amazement" (v 14), her response swells to one of exuberance, leading to her pronouncement of blessing.[36]

Her declaration likely already enjoyed proverbial status,[37] and is reminiscent of material in the Lukan birth narrative. Of special importance is Elizabeth's announcement of Mary's blessedness on account of her being pregnant with "the Lord" in 1:42. This earlier parallel is consequential precisely because it comes from the Spirit-inspired Elizabeth (1:41); this indicates that the words of the woman in the crowd are not altogether wrong even if they are in need of significant modification. This latter need is signaled linguistically by Jesus' response, "Blessed rather . . . ,"[38] as well as by the progression of thought within the narrative about what constitutes a state of divine blessedness shared among God's people.[39] Hence, even though the woman's reaction is more fitting than the others Luke records (vv 14-16), it is still inadequate.

36. For earlier statements of blessedness in Luke, see 1:45; 6:20-22; 7:23; 10:23.

37. Cf., e.g., Gen 30:13; 2 *Apoc. Bar.* 54:10; Petronius *Satyricon* 94.1; Ovid *Metamorphoses* 4.32-24 (the latter two are cited in Danker, 234-35).

38. μενοῦν in the initial position of a sentence is rare. Among the translation options (surveyed in Moule, *Idiom Book*, 162-64) is the one that fits this co-text best, "much more" or "yes, but" (cf. BDF §450[4]; MHT 2:337-38; Fitzmyer, *Luke the Theologian*, 77). M. P. Scott ("Luke 11:28") argues that Jesus did not contradict the woman but only adds to her statement of Mary's blessedness, but he reckons neither with the sense of μενοῦν nor with the larger question of the criteria of blessedness in Luke 1–11.

39. Cf. Brawley, *Centering on God*, 52-53.

Jesus' response to the woman, then, should be understood as corrective. The issue for him is not so much the status that attaches to his mother on account of the status of her son. Although the values represented in this way of thinking would represent well one of the primary means by which status would have been understood among and attributed to women in Palestinian antiquity, this is precisely the sort of common wisdom Luke had begun to subvert in his narration of Gabriel's announcement to Mary regarding Jesus' birth in 1:26-38.[40] Subsequent to this, Luke has undercut the notion of Israel's privileged position by placing a premium not on physical descent but on faithful performance (cf. 3:7-14) — that is, in a form more at home in the present co-text, on "hearing and doing the word" (cf. 8:4-21).[41]

With respect to the initial focus on Jesus' mother in this brief unit, it is important to note that Mary is a candidate for blessedness according to the criterion set forth by Jesus. Luke has portrayed her as one who hears and reflects on the divine word, who responds to it positively, even as one who proclaims it in prophetic fashion (1:26-38, 46-55; 2:19, 51); consequently, the Spirit-inspired Elizabeth also declares that Mary is blessed on account of her faith (1:45). This is important because of the ideology embodied in the proverbial declaration of Mary's blessedness on account of the status of her son. This pronouncement has the potential of restricting Mary's hope for divine fortune to her role as a mother — in the words of this woman, to the fecundity of her belly and breasts.[42] In the life-world represented in Jesus' message, restrictions of this nature have no place, not for Mary nor for anyone else. His beatitude disallows the establishment of such conventional boundaries to divine fortune, for his message works to construct a new world that subverts the values and practices of the existing world, in the same way that his practices of exorcism signal the defeat of the realm of Satan (vv 17-26). Even in this respect, though, Jesus' beatitude affords no special status for Mary, for it functions as an invitation to all, both in and outside the narrative, to hear and observe the word of God (cf. 8:19-21).

40. See above on 1:26-38; also Green, "Social Status."

41. Sherwood ("Blest Is the Womb") notes the importance of hearing and doing the word in Luke-Acts, over against the claims of physical relationship. Luke employs the term φυλάσσω here and in 18:21; Acts 7:53; 21:24 to register the idea of obedience ("keeping, observing") to God/the law.

42. This is observed by Schottroff, *Feminist Perspectives,* 115-16; Seim, *Double Message,* 114. Craig and Kristjansson ("Women Reading") employ a structuralist model to pit Jesus against female, male against female, in this brief pericope; they suggest that the woman's perspective is regarded as erroneous because she adopts a concern with maternal ancestry. Within the socio-historical context of Palestinian antiquity, however, the woman's statement would not have been censured for these reasons; what is more, Jesus' words indicate his complete lack of concern with a status constructed along (any) ancestral lines.

5.3.1.4. The Sign of Jonah (11:29-36)

29 *When the crowds were increasing, he began to say, "This genera-tion is an evil generation; it asks for a sign, but no sign will be given to it except the sign of Jonah. 30 For just as Jonah became a sign to the people of Nineveh, so the Son of Man will be to this generation. 31 The queen of the South will rise at the judgment with the people of this generation and condemn them, because she came from the ends of the earth to listen to the wisdom of Solomon, and see, something greater than Solomon is here! 32 The people of Nineveh will rise up at the judgment with this generation and condemn it, because they re-pented at the proclamation of Jonah, and see, something greater than Jonah is here!*

33 *"No one after lighting a lamp puts it in a cellar, but on the lampstand so that those who enter may see the light. 34 Your eye is the lamp of your body. If your eye is healthy, your whole body is full of light; but if it is not healthy, your body is full of darkness. 35 Therefore consider whether the light in you is not darkness. 36 If then your whole body is full of light, with no part of it in darkness, it will be as full of light as when a lamp gives you light with its rays."*

Luke has carefully staged Jesus' interaction with the crowds, now recounting Jesus' response to those who sought to test him by demanding a sign from heaven (vv 14-16). He has already dealt with those who slandered him by attributing his ability to exorcise demons to the agency of Beelzebul as well as responded to a woman who had spoken highly of Jesus and, so, of his mother. In the interim, between his casting a demon out of a man and the present, an even larger crowd had formed, giving Jesus an even larger platform from which to speak.

His message comes in two parts that, on the surface, appear to have nothing to do with each other. There is one highly significant linguistic connection between the two, however, though it is masked in most English translations. This is the characterization of "this generation" as "evil" in v 29 and of one's eye as "evil" (NRSV: "not healthy") in v 34.[43] This is a minimal connection, but it is enough to indicate that "this generation" is an "evil one" precisely because their eyes are "not healthy." Understood metaphorically and ethically, this means that the request for a sign itself betrays an inner disposition oriented away from the light, away from God's salvific project, and toward the realm of darkness whose head is Satan.[44]

43. Both verses use πονηρός.
44. For this combination of metaphors, see Acts 26:18; cf. Garrett, "Luke 11:33-36," 102, 105.

The contrast with Jesus' identification of "the blessed" as those who hear and obey the word of God (v 28) is striking. Indeed, the invective tone of the exchange between some from the crowds and Jesus in vv 15 → 17-26 and 16 → 29-36 highlights the importance of vv 27-28. The response for which Jesus seeks is clearly formulated best there.

29-30   References to the crowds and to sign-seeking are evidences of Luke's narrative artistry as he carries us back to vv 14 and 16, and reminds us of his more general negative valuation of seeking signs. For requesting a sign, Zechariah had been censured (1:18); otherwise in the Lukan narrative, such "testing" of Jesus (v 16) is associated with the devil (4:1-13). In the current co-text, Jesus has previously reasoned that his performance of an exorcism was already verification of his divine authority (see above on v 20). Hence, in light of what should already be self-evident, requests for proof that Jesus really does enjoy the backing of God are absurd, even evil.[45] This characterization is harmonious with Jesus' reference to "this generation," drawing on language previously employed (cf. 7:31; 9:41), the meaning of which is related to the portrayal of Israel as stubborn and rebellious.[46] In this case, the recalcitrance of the people is manifest in their sign-seeking.

Jesus refuses all signs apart from "the sign of Jonah" (v 29), an expression further developed in v 30 with the phrase, "Jonah became a sign to the people of Nineveh." How Jesus might serve an analogous role to this generation is dependent on how one understands "sign of Jonah." The views on this are multitudinous, probably due in large part to our general ignorance regarding its usage in antiquity.[47] Among the possible interpretations, two make good sense within the Lukan narrative.

(1) Just as Jonah became a sign to the people of Nineveh by means of his divine rescue, so Jesus will become a sign to this generation by means of his. This interpretation (a) makes sense of the future tense of the verb governing when Jesus will become a sign to his people, (b) is corroborated by the

45. On this understanding of the nature of the "sign" requested, see R. H. Smith, "Sign of Jonah," 755.

46. Cf. Exod 32:9; 33:3, 5; Deut 10:16; Acts 7:51-53.

47. For surveys of possibilities, see R. H. Smith, "Sign of Jonah," 755; Bayer, *Jesus' Predictions,* 133-42. Adam ("Sign of Jonah") borrows from reader-response theory to assert that we have a seemingly infinite number of possible interpretations of this expression because of the interpretive role and needs of particular communities who read this text. Although we do not want to diminish overmuch the important role of interpretive communities in the hermeneutical process (cf. Vanhoozer, "The Reader"), it is nevertheless clear that (1) the Third Evangelist has provided few clues as to how this expression makes sense in its present co-text (cf. Matt 12:40!), and that this contributes significantly to the relative polysemy of the text; and (2) what interpretive clues the narrator does provide render some views more probable than others as well as oppose other readings (cf. Eco, *Limits,* 21).

interest of the missionary sermons in Acts in presenting the divine vindication of Jesus in his exaltation, (c) meshes well with the pronounced note of hostility toward Jesus in the current co-text, and (d) builds on Jewish interpretation of the Jonah-story wherein the possibility is established that the Ninevites were cognizant of God's rescuing Jonah from the belly of a fish.[48] One might think (as Jesus does, v 20) that Jesus' ministry of exorcism is enough to authenticate the place of his ministry in God's plan (cf. Acts 2:22); failing this, according to his witnesses in Acts, Jesus' status and mission are vindicated at his exaltation.

(2) A second interpretation is also possible in this co-text: Just as Jonah proclaimed repentance to the people prior to their judgment, so does Jesus. This interpretation (a) capitalizes on the possibility of interpreting the future form of the verb "to be" (v 30b) not as a temporal but as a logical future referring to Jesus' present ministry,[49] and (b) is corroborated by the subsequent reference to the repentance of the Ninevites in response to the message of Jonah (v 32b).[50]

31-32 These two sentences are bound together closely by their parallel structure and comparable content. Jesus' reference to the queen of the South brings onto the interpretive stage the account of 1 Kgs 10:1-13; 2 Chr 9:1-12, an account with important points of contact with the larger Lukan co-text. The queen of Sheba came to test Solomon and found that he was indeed an agent of Yahweh, having been placed on the throne by him; having acknowledged his divine legitimacy, she enters into an alliance with him, signified by the mutual exchange of gifts. The comparison with the current audience that Jesus evokes is particularly apt, since their testing of Jesus has not led to a similar recognition even though he is greater than Solomon. Moreover, Jesus' audience is drawn from the people of Israel, while Solomon's was a foreigner. Her insight and response, compared to their lack of the same, will situate them on opposite sides at the judgment, when she will be vindicated and they will be condemned. The reference to Jonah and the Ninevites is the same, though in this instance Jesus reports not only that they listened to God's agent (as in v 31), but that they responded with repentance.

Jesus' message is reminiscent of his earlier discourse in 10:12-15, where he contrasted the responses of those within Israel with those outside.

---

48. On this last point, see the material discussed in Bayer, *Jesus' Predictions*, 133-38. See also, e.g., Merrill, "Sign of Jonah," 28-29.

49. See the discussion in, e.g., Lindars, *Jesus: Son of Man*, 41-42.

50. Cf., e.g., Edwards, *Sign of Jonah*, 93-95. One is tempted to add that the "sign" to which Jesus refers is the mission to the Gentiles (cf., e.g., Murray, "Sign of Jonah"), not least given the Gentile orientation of vv 31-32. It is not clear, however, how the analogy with Jonah would then work; the prophet went to the Gentiles, but was the mere fact of his going a sign to them?

This point is underscored in the current scene, first, by his description of the queen's coming "from the ends of the earth" — a geographical description that has profound socio-religious significance; she is thus labeled as a socio-religious outsider whose response identifies her nonetheless as an insider.[51] The people of Nineveh were likewise outsiders, though their response to the message of repentance resulted in their being extended God's favor. Both the queen of Sheba and the people of Nineveh, Jesus says, will participate in the resurrection and in eschatological judgment, where their status as the people of God will be manifested in their judgment of the recalcitrant of Israel.

33-36   This new paragraph seems to depart radically from Jesus' previous concern with sign-seeking. Actually, it is closely related to the foregoing, for it indicates the nefarious dispositions from which sign-seeking arises and, at the same time, urges those in the crowd to take care lest they stand condemned by such faithful persons as the queen of Sheba and the people of Nineveh.

Key to making sense out of this subunit are two considerations. (1) According to a physiology prevalent in Greco-Roman antiquity, the eyes do not function by allowing light to come in but by allowing the body's own light to go out. The eye is the conduit or source of the light that makes sight possible.[52] Jesus' assertion, "Your eye is the lamp of your body," thus expresses a commonly held view, identifying the eyes as sources of light insofar as they allow the body's light to go forth. Given this physiology, the pivotal issue is whether the eyes are sick or healthy — that is, whether the body is full of darkness or light. Jesus thus trades on a double entente in his description of one's eyes — the one medical, the other ethical[53] — with the one sense folding into the other. This allows for Jesus' point, the identification of a "sick

51. Cf. 8:19-21; 10:25-37. The phrase "ends of the earth" here uses the term πέρας — cf. Pss 2:8; 22:28; 46:10; 59:14; 65:6. This description harmonizes with the description of the queen's land as in "the South" — i.e., on the border of the known world. It also anticipates the appearance of a synonymous phrase in Acts 1:8: "end of the earth" (ἐσχάτου τῆς γῆς; cf. 13:47, citing Isa 49:6), signifying, in that co-text, "everywhere," "among all peoples," "across all boundaries" (Green, "Salvation to the End of the Earth," forthcoming). That geography is not a "naively given container," but rather a social production that both reflects and configures an understanding of the social world; cf. *m. Kelim* 1.6-9; Soja, *Postmodern Geographies,* 82, 25 et passim; Pred, *Human Geographies;* Werlen, *Society, Action and Space.*

52. Greek theories of vision, including the extramission theory of vision relevant to this passage, are discussed by Betz, "Greek Theories"; Allison ("Eye Is the Lamp") has gone on to demonstrate that the premodern notion of the human eye as a source or channel of light is also familiar in contemporary Jewish sources. On what follows, see Allison.

53. Both ἁπλοῦς and πονηρός are used in physiological and moral discourse — cf. Allison, "Eye Is the Lamp," 76-78.

eye" as an indication of inner darkness (e.g., selfishness, covetousness, and rebellion),[54] and a "healthy eye" as an evidence of inner light (e.g., generosity and sincerity).[55]

(2) The capacity of the categories of "good eye" and "bad eye" to address issues of ethical comportment, together with the language of light and darkness so prominent in this paragraph, opens up a further critical interpretive consideration. This has to do with the metaphorical use of the imagery of light and darkness throughout the Lukan narrative — already present, for example, in Zechariah's Song (1:78-79), but most explicit later in the narrative, in Acts 26:18. There, Paul's commission is cast in terms that relate "open eyes" to turning "from darkness to light and from the power of Satan to God." The arrangement of this language in that co-text intimately relates "darkness" with the power of Satan and "light" with the power of God. "The light in you," interpreted against this metaphorical horizon, speaks to the essential stance one has taken toward the kingdom.[56] At stake is whether one has embraced God's purpose and serves his aim or, alternatively, whether one is governed by the dominion of Satan. By raising such questions in this discourse, Jesus indicates that the sign-seeking that characterizes this generation is not at all a benign practice, for it is grounded in dispositions that are contrary to the salvific purpose of God.

Jesus' message is not a pronouncement of a fait accompli, however, for he urges his audience to consider the nature of their dispositions. Like Jesus' admonition in 8:18 ("Pay attention to how you listen"), v 35 is present as an existential challenge to self-evaluation, a warning to be filled with light rather than darkness. Clearly, those who test Jesus (v 16) — as well as those Pharisees and lawyers of the subsequent unit (vv 37-54), whose inner avarice and malevolence generate a neglect of justice and love of God — are condemned by their own actions as people full of darkness. The possibility of repentance is left open; what is not debatable for Jesus is the certainty that one's inner constitution is broadcast in one's behaviors.[57]

---

54. Cf. Deut 15:9; 28:54, 56; Prov 23:6; 28:22; Tob 4:7; et al.

55. Cf., e.g., Job 1:1; Prov 22:9; Sir 32:8; et al.

56. This is developed in a helpful way by Garrett, "Luke 11:33-36."

57. Can something more specific be said of v 36? The problem of this verse is a vexed one because of the ambiguity of its expression in Greek. Does it refer to the eschaton — i.e., those full of light will be made completely bright, like lightning? Does it refer to the present — i.e., those full of light will, like a lamp on a lampstand, dispense light all around them; or, those whose "whole body" is full of light do not require the alleged enlightenment that might follow from sign-seeking? Central to this discussion is the significance of the future tense of the verb "to be" — see the recent discussion in Nebe, "ἔσται in Lk 11,36," 108-10; he opts for a "voluntativ-imperativische" sense ("let it be") (110-14).

466

5.3.2. Jesus Responds to the Pharisees and Teachers (11:37-54)

37 *While he was speaking, a Pharisee invited him to dine with him;
so he went in and took his place at the table.* 38 *The Pharisee was
amazed to see that he did not first wash before dinner.* 39 *Then the Lord
said to him, "Now you Pharisees clean the outside of the cup and of
the dish, but inside you are full of greed and wickedness.* 40 *You fools!
Did not the one who made the outside make the inside also?* 41 *So give
for alms those things that are within; and see, everything will be clean
for you.*

42 *"But woe to you Pharisees! For you tithe mint and rue and herbs
of all kinds, and neglect justice and the love of God; it is these you
ought to have practiced, without neglecting the others.* 43 *Woe to you
Pharisees! For you love to have the seat of honor in the synagogues
and to be greeted with respect in the marketplaces.* 44 *Woe to you! For
you are like unmarked graves, and people walk over them without
realizing it."*

45 *One of the lawyers answered him, "Teacher, when you say these
things, you insult us too."* 46 *And he said, "Woe also to you lawyers!
For you load people with burdens hard to bear, and you yourselves do
not lift a finger to ease them.* 47 *Woe to you! For you build the tombs
of the prophets whom your ancestors killed.* 48 *So you are witnesses
and approve of the deeds of your ancestors; for they killed them, and
you build their tombs.* 49 *Therefore also the Wisdom of God said, 'I
will send them prophets and apostles, some of whom they will kill and
persecute,'* 50 *so that this generation may be charged with the blood
of all the prophets shed since the foundation of the world,* 51 *from the
blood of Abel to the blood of Zechariah, who perished between the
altar and the sanctuary. Yes, I tell you, it will be charged against this
generation.* 52 *Woe to you lawyers! For you have taken away the key
of knowledge; you did not enter yourselves, and you hindered those
who were entering."*

53 *When he went outside, the scribes and the Pharisees began to be
very hostile toward him and to cross-examine him about many things,*
54 *lying in wait for him, to catch him in something he might say.*

Even though Luke marks a direct connection between Jesus' responses to
those in the crowds who question his status as an agent of God (11:14-36)
and the current scene, the Evangelist also presents this section as a discrete
narrative unit. From his interaction with the masses in the open, Jesus now
engages Pharisees and legal experts at the table of a Pharisee. The parameters
of this narrative unit are carefully marked: "he went in . . . he went out" (vv
37, 53-54).

Sharing conversation over a meal is characteristic activity for Jesus in the Third Gospel.[58] This current scene is especially reminiscent of 7:36-50, for in both a Pharisee invites Jesus to a meal; Jesus accepts and takes his place at the table; and conflict ensues as Jesus' behavior crosses the line of what is acceptable when sharing a meal with a Pharisee and as Jesus responds to the unspoken censure of his host. Conflict seems to be a staple ingredient of table scenes in the Third Gospel thus far, even if the pitch of Jesus' disparaging remarks here reaches an unprecedented height. The offensiveness of Jesus' comments is set in even sharper relief when it is remembered that scrupulous conventions governed the behavior of guests and the sharing of another's table. Even given the possibility of reading this episode within the literary frame of a Greco-Roman symposium, where lively argumentation is expected, such vitriolic exchange departs from the ordinary.[59]

The theme of this unit draws together several important narrative elements. The first is the presence of Pharisees and legal experts;[60] when these two groups appear in tandem, they are consistently portrayed as negatively disposed toward Jesus. This note of antagonism is somewhat mitigated by the way Luke has staged this scene, delaying our awareness of the presence of legal experts at the table until after Jesus has already opened the door for the repentance of the Pharisees. Second, there is the meal scene itself, with its built-in standards for proper behavior for both host(s) and guest(s). With respect to such conventions, Jesus is clearly in the wrong, though Luke develops this scene in order to show that Jesus is justified in transgressing these conventions. If Jesus presents himself in a number of ways — some having to do with social protocols, others more weighty on account of their grounding in the law — as a deviant, he is nonetheless recognized as "Lord" by the Evangelist; through these and other means, paradoxically, Jesus' status is maintained, even enhanced, at the expense of the Pharisees and legal experts whom he joins at the table. Indeed, it is not too much to say that the status of the Pharisees and legal experts has been severely compromised by this denunciation of their claim to represent God's will.

Third, the table scene is pivotal for a further reason: Located in the home of a Pharisee, the meal setting foregrounds important issues of purity.

58. For the Lukan motif of table fellowship, see Bartchy, "Table Fellowship," 798-99; Bösen, *Jesusmahl;* Corley, *Private Women,* ch. 4; Esler, *Community and Gospel,* ch. 4; Green, *Gospel of Luke,* esp. 86-89; Hofius, *Jesu Tischgemeinschaft;* Karris, *Luke: Artist and Theologian;* Neyrey, "Ceremonies"; Moxnes, "Meals"; D. E. Smith, "Table Fellowship."

59. Steele ("Luke 11:37-54") regards this as a modified Hellenistic symposium. On symposia, see above at 5:27-39.

60. *Contra* Steele ("Luke 11:37-54"), Luke uses "scribes" and "lawyers" (as well as "teachers of the law") interchangeably — cf. above on 9:22; Klinghardt, *Gesetz,* 310.

Because purity is central to the Pharisaic worldview, and because purity is an institution[61] that, being socially constructed, is also rooted in the community's understanding of the divine, the obvious fact that Jesus and his interlocutors understand purity along radically different lines raises the level of hostility dramatically. After all, what is at stake is how one understands the very nature of God, as well as, then, how one construes the nature of faithful response to this God. Importantly for how we understand the nature of the Lukan enterprise as a whole, Jesus navigates these opposing views without negating the law per se; he censures certain ways of practicing the law, but not the law itself.[62] As is typical in Luke-Acts, then, this scene represents Jesus as the authorized hermeneut with respect to the law of God — in this case over against the parallel claims of the Pharisees and legal experts.[63]

These and other elements of this discourse help us to recognize that Luke presents this scene as an exemplar of the heightened hostility associated with the articulation of Jesus' message, which seeks to reconstruct the lifeworld of the people of God. Jesus' message is revolutionary precisely because it confronts and subverts as evil the worldview embodied in the practices of the Pharisees and legal experts. What is more, he does so at the very points where the adeptness and mastery of the Pharisees and legal experts, as Luke portrays them, are most evident: in the interpretation of the law and maintenance of purity. Moreover, he crosses swords with them at the table, where issues of honor and purity come to expression in everyday life most conspicuously. This, then, is the nexus at which Luke ties this episode directly to Jesus' immediately preceding discourse (vv 33-36). These Pharisees and legal experts are exposed as people whose "body light" is full of "darkness"; they are concerned with outward expressions of piety, but inside they are rapacious, full of avarice. Their eyesight is impaired by their invidious dispositions. Lacking a fundamental orientation to God's purpose, their behaviors are exposed as diabolic in their neglect of the poor and in their opposition to God's messengers.[64]

37-38   Through much of this section of the Gospel, the narrative has an episodic look, as though incidents were gathered together without particular

---

61. By "institution" we refer here to patterns of expected behavior that receive reinforcement via social sanctions; "institutions" may also refer to those organizational structures embodying and broadcasting those behaviors — cf. Bellah et al., *Good Society,* 10-11; Wuthnow, *Communities of Discourse,* 5-17.

62. Cf. Wilson, *Luke and the Law,* 19; Salo, *Luke's Treatment of the Law,* 120; Moxnes, *Economy of the Kingdom,* 124.

63. Cf. Green, *Gospel of Luke,* 68-75.

64. Cf. Garrett, "Luke 11:33-36," 105; Gowler, "Hospitality and Characterization," 227, 242; Moxnes, *Economy of the Kingdom,* 109-10.

attention to order and relationship.[65] Luke, however, does draw connections between events and, in this case, locates Jesus' invitation to dine with a Pharisee within the framework of his response to the crowds about sign-seeking. What this connection means is not immediately obvious, though it will soon be made manifest in the inside/outside contrast highlighted in vv 39-41. First, though, Luke sets the scene with reference to a Pharisee, a meal, and Jesus' failure to observe either the laws of hospitality or the laws of purity.

Thus far, Pharisees are known to us largely as persons who scrutinize Jesus' legal observance and who repeatedly find themselves at odds with his legal views and religious practices. The fact that a Pharisee would even invite Jesus to dinner suggests a certain openness to him, though we should also recognize that the extension of hospitality might itself serve as a test. The extension and acceptance of an invitation signaled the abeyance of hostility, a social contract whereby host and guest were to act with honor toward one another. This would require, for example, that Jesus prepare for the meal in the way prescribed by the Pharisees and that he withhold any negative (insulting) valuations of the host or his treatment in the home of the host; to perform otherwise would signal a breach in the implicit social contract. Unlike the parallel scene in 7:36-50, in this account no evidence is brought forward to suggest that Jesus has been snubbed. To the contrary, the cryptic form of Luke's narration — Jesus "went in and took his place at the table" — at first masks what the Pharisee cannot miss: Jesus snubbed his host by failing to wash before the meal. Even then the Pharisee maintains social propriety, for he does not call attention to his guest's behavior, in spite of its aberrant quality.

Handwashing before a meal in this case was not an issue of physical but of ritual cleanliness. As a behavior concerned with purity, it is not an OT requirement though it might be seen as a remote implicature of the law.[66] Its importance in this scene is not thereby blunted, however, because, in the setting Luke envisages, "the concern for clean hands is a symbol of concern for a strong overall system of purity."[67] Handwashing apparently served as a boundary-making and -keeping device (like fasting, 5:33); to overlook this practice was to mark oneself as an outsider in this community. In light of the laws of hospitality, failure to wash in this scene also constituted an insult to the host.

39-41 Jesus' deviant behavior might have led to his negative valuation, a possibility Luke circumvents by referring to Jesus as "Lord" and by

65. Cf. Shirock ("Growth of the Kingdom"), who remarks that many students of Luke see in the journey section only a collection of *miscellanea*.

66. Westerholm, *Jesus,* 73; E. P. Sanders, *Jewish Law,* 203-4, 228-31; Salo, *Luke's Treatment of the Law,* 120.

67. Gowler, *Hospitality and Characterization,* 227.

reasserting Jesus' capacity and mission, prophesied by Simeon, to make known the inner thoughts of others (2:35).[68] In a remarkable turn of events, then, the one whose behavior seems deviant is acknowledged to Luke's audience as Lord, and the Lord classifies those whose behaviors apparently have not transgressed the boundaries of socio-religious propriety as "fools." He thus brands them as lacking understanding — indeed, as persons whose rejection of God's order cultivates damaging behavior.[69] Clearly, Luke has staged this encounter as a clash of perspectives on the attitudes and behaviors sanctioned by God.

Jesus censures the Pharisees on four interrelated grounds, the first two of which are developed here, the others in vv 42-44. First, in spite of their characteristic concern with legal observance, they are rebuffed for their misguided views and practices. This is because their concern for ritual purity (exemplified in the cleanliness of vessels — cf. Lev 11:32-33; 15:12) overlooks the need for integrity between one's inner constitution and one's public behavior. Because both are made by God, neither should be overlooked. Yet, this is exactly what the Pharisees have done, majoring on such outward practices of purity as ritual washing before meals while neglecting the filth on the inside. Second, then, Jesus characterizes the Pharisees as persons governed by a desire to plunder, rapacity, and by moral corruption (cf. 16:14).[70] In spite of their intentions and public persona, they are implicated in Jesus' invective against "this evil generation" and in his description of those whose eyes are "evil" (11:29, 34).[71]

Jesus' interest in redefining purity is highlighted in v 41.[72] What behavior would represent the sort of purity sanctioned by God? Jesus directs attention toward a purity that overcomes socio-religious barriers, in direct contrast to one that separates people from one another and keeps them separated. This is a purity manifest in social relations — explicitly, on a behavior, almsgiving, that collapses the distance between the social elite and the needy. Almsgiving, then, does not correspond well to modern-day notions of charity; rather, for Luke, almsgiving was an expression of genuine social solidarity, of embracing those in need as if they were members of one's own kin-group. As is typical for the Third Evangelist, then, the disposition of one's possessions signifies the dispositions of one's heart, with both character

68. See also 5:22; 6:8; 7:39-40; 9:47; 11:17.

69. See Zeller, "ἀφροσύνη, ἄφρων."

70. "Greed" (NRSV) may be too weak a translation of ἁπαργή. See 18:11; Moxnes, *Economy of the Kingdom,* 111-12; Gowler, "Hospitality and Characterization," 231.

71. Verses 29, 34 employ the term πονηρός; v 39 uses the term πονηρία.

72. On the use of πλήν, not in an eliminative sense but with a balancing force, see Frid, "Brief Note."

and behavior expected to reflect the message of Jesus for "the poor" (see above on 4:16-30; §11).[73]

As Luke will soon document, shared meals with Jesus do not necessarily constitute a guarantee of salvation (13:26-27); nevertheless, they do signal the possibility of salvation. Hence, it is of ongoing interest that Luke's narration of the previous scene in which Jesus dines with a Pharisee (7:36-50) ends before the story ends; that is, we do not know how Simon the Pharisee responded to Jesus' message. Similarly, in this case, Jesus may use the meal setting to raise hard questions about Pharisaic concerns, but he also extends an invitation.[74] In counseling almsgiving — which by Lukan definition involves an inner transposition toward the values of the kingdom that is manifest in concrete, material practices — moreover, he opens the door for repentance on the part of the Pharisees.

42-44 Having registered the possibility of reformation in Pharisaic dispositions and practices, Jesus returns to his assault on Pharisaic interests. Continuing from vv 39-41, the third in the series of four charges is concerned with their neglect of God and neighbor. Though the language is different, conceptually he is very close to the interaction recorded in 10:25-37, where the conditions for "life" were outlined. The Pharisees have expanded the OT laws of tithing as a prophylactic against any possibility of eating impure food (i.e., produce that had not been properly tithed),[75] but this was not an expression of a comprehensive love for God and concrete expressions of love for the neighbor. Jesus' criticism is not thoroughgoing — that is, tithing (as an expression of obedience to the law) is not singled out as a bad thing. Nevertheless, Pharisaic concentration on this activity had led to a neglect of those habits of heart and life that would lead to eternal life.[76]

---

73. See esp. Moxnes, *Kingdom and Community*, 109, 113, 120, 122-23. In terms familiar from §10, Jesus calls for the practice of generalized reciprocity between persons who are not "equal" by conventional norms, nor who are blood kin, whereas the Pharisees are portrayed as persons involved in negative reciprocity (theft).

74. In arguing that meals between Jesus and the Pharisees in Luke do not give rise to a new alliance between them, Moxnes ("Meals," esp. 160-63) appropriately notes the function of the meal scene as a starting mechanism for a new group but moves toward closure of the story more quickly than the narrative will allow. The hospitality of Simon (7:36-50) may be found wanting, but Luke goes on to teach Simon and invite a change of perspective in him. How does Simon respond? We are not told. Similarly, in this scene Pharisees are castigated for being full of avarice and wickedness, but the report of Jesus' message in v 41 does not treat this condition as necessary or as immutable.

75. On the tithe, cf., e.g., Lev 27:30-33; Num 18:21; Tob 1:7-8; Luke 18:9-14; Salo, *Luke's Treatment of the Law*, 122-23; S. G. Wilson, *Luke and the Law*, 18-19. Luke's list of items tithed goes further than contemporary sources, but this does not affect the fundamental contrast embedded in the text. On the eating only of food on which a portion had been tithed, see Westerholm, "Pharisees," 611-12.

76. So Esler, *Community and Gospel*, 119.

The fourth charge brought against the Pharisees concerns their propensity to engage in behavior leading to self-aggrandizement. Just as the aforementioned lawyer had attempted to justify himself (10:29), so the Pharisees concern themselves with public recognition and enhancement of their honor. Their need for honor extends both to the public square, the marketplace, the center of social activity in a town, and to the center of religious instruction for the Jew (cf. 20:46). In a devastating play on words, Jesus remarks that Pharisees love to be the center of attention, but neglect the love of God. The far-reaching condemnation to which the Pharisees thus opened themselves is underscored three times by the pronouncement of woe — a verbal form portending the coming disaster that would befall them on account of divine judgment (see above on 6:24).

The irony of the Pharisaic position is illustrated with reference to corpse impurity — clearly an important issue in legal observance.[77] In striving to maintain purity, Jesus observes, the Pharisees have actually made themselves impure. What is more, rather than separating themselves from the impurity of others, Pharisees are now actually endangering the relative purity of those around them. A more comprehensive renunciation of the Pharisaic project is difficult to imagine.

45-46   The third woe pronounced on the Pharisees (v 44) actually appears without a definitive object, anticipating the introduction of additional persons whose characteristic activity identifies them as the recipients of Jesus' censure. An unnamed lawyer, or legal expert, acknowledges Jesus' extreme departure from social norms in castigating his host and other guests at the table. Hence, even though the lawyer himself maintains a level of civility, addressing Jesus as "Teacher," his answer to Jesus must nonetheless be viewed as an initial attempt to take up the challenge Jesus' remarks signify. Like the Pharisees, legal experts are already known to Luke's audience via the narrative. They often appear in tandem with the Pharisees as persons concerned with Jesus' observance of the law; in particular, as "teachers of the law" their message has consistently been set in opposition to that of Jesus.[78] Additionally, they have recently been named as persons who will become affiliated with the religious elite of Jerusalem in a successful plot to have Jesus executed (9:22). The present co-text actually brings these two aspects of the Lukan portrayal of the legal experts together; on the one hand, their association with the Pharisees as persons concerned with examining Jesus' legal observance implicates them in the woes Jesus pronounces over the Pharisees, while, on the other hand, Jesus' words of insult lead them toward a greater level of hostility that will evolve into a full-blown plot to put Jesus

77. See above on 7:13-15.
78. See esp. 6:1-11; 7:29-30.

to death (e.g., 22:1-2). Interestingly, by the time hostility reaches this level, the Pharisees will have dropped from view in the narrative.

As elsewhere in Luke-Acts, so in this statement of woe, the law is not presented as the culprit; rather, scribal elaboration of the law comes in for criticism. Through their attempts to ensure that people do not transgress the requirements of the law, they have embellished its specifications with an eye toward contemporary practices. Far from enabling faithfulness to God — far from enabling persons to present themselves as true children of Abraham, known for hearing and doing the word of God (e.g., 3:7-14; 8:4-21; 11:28) — scribal efforts have burdened God's people. The burden of the ensuing tradition of interpretation and legal obligation has not worked to assist the faithfulness of the Jewish people.[79]

47-48 The second woe is presented as an inverted parallelism:

> v 47b You build the tombs of the prophets
>> v 47c Your ancestors killed the prophets
>>> v 48a You are witnesses and approve of the deeds of
>>> your ancestors
>> v 48b Your ancestors killed the prophets
> v 48c You build the tombs of the prophets

This form of repetition (1) draws on the deeply rooted tradition concerning the fate of the prophets: sent to an obdurate people, their destiny is death;[80] and it (2) employs the symbol of tomb-building[81] to underscore the complicity of the present, "evil generation" in the historic spurning of God's messengers, whose deaths insulate their intended audience from the sting of their message. Indeed, it becomes clear in vv 49-51 that the message Jesus is constructing rests on a contrast between honoring those divine messengers who have been killed and listening to the word of God proclaimed by the living, present messengers of God. Jesus' message at the table thus recalls his message in the public arena, where he warns "this generation" that they will be judged (by faithful Gentiles!) for their refusal to hear and repent (vv 29-32). In an irony that is not lost on his audience (see vv 53-54), Jesus thus observes that these scribes and Pharisees, so concerned with legal observance, actually comport themselves as those who not only fail to hear and observe the word of God, but who also spurn the bearers of the divine word.

---

79. Cf. the analogous statement, though with reference to Gentile inclusion in the community of God's people, in Acts 15:10.

80. See Neh 9:26; Jer 2:30; Luke 4:24; 6:23; Acts 7:52; Aune, *Prophecy,* 157-59.

81. Jesus' message depends on tomb-building as a metaphor of veneration, not on evidence for a first-century interest in building tombs for dead prophets.

49-51   Having just declared the predisposition of the experts in the law to follow in the steps of their forebears, Jesus further characterizes "this generation" as persons who will act harmoniously with historic Israel; that is, they will follow the age-old pattern of silencing God's messengers. Their participation in the historic rejection of God's purpose will be exemplified in their rejection of his messengers. The comprehensiveness of the pattern of killing those who sided with God is marked by the time span implied in the references to Abel, whose death at the hands of his brother Cain is the first recorded in the Hebrew Scriptures (Gen 4:1-12), and to Zechariah, whose death is the last recorded in the Hebrew Scriptures (2 Chr 24:20-22).[82] "Apostles," then, should be understood first in a more general way as "envoys," though this would include "apostles" in the more restrictive sense; hence, within the larger Lukan co-text, Jesus is speaking of the resistance his followers will encounter (cf. 6:22-23; Acts) as well as of the destiny he himself will endure at the hands of the scribes and others of the Jerusalem leadership (cf. vv 53-54; 9:22).[83]

In developing the significance of vv 47-48 along these lines, Jesus appeals to "the Wisdom of God." In doing so, Jesus asserts his elevated status over these experts on the law as a person with direct access to God's own design (cf. 10:21-22), the divine Wisdom that communicates to persons and that sends messengers.[84]

52   This final woe against the scribes parallels Jesus' summation of his case against the Pharisees in v 44. That earlier pronouncement of woe had condemned the entire Pharisaic project for achieving an end diametrically opposed to that for which it had been intended. Similarly, Jesus insists, the portfolio of the expert in the law is to pull back the veil on the meaning and relevance of the law of God, but their efforts have had the opposite effect — both for themselves and for those for whom they were to serve as teachers.

---

82. This last reference assumes that the Zechariah Luke names is Zechariah son of Jehoiada, and on the order of the books in the MT (where 2 Chronicles appears last). Both assumptions are open to doubt, however. On the first, e.g., Ross ("Which Zechariah?") notes other possibilities — Zechariah, son of Barachiah (Matt 23:35); and Zechariah, son of Baris (Josephus *J.W.* 4.5.4 §§335-44) — but concludes that Luke's referent is actually unknown to us. On the second, the question of when the canonical order of the Hebrew Scriptures was set remains open.

83. It should be noted that these "others," within the Lukan perspective, ultimately do not include the Pharisees. Although Jesus is opposed by the Pharisees during the Galilean ministry and journey to Jerusalem, they have no role in his execution.

84. Cf., e.g., Prov 1:20-33; 8; Wis 7:27; 8:8; Marshall, 503; Nolland 2:667-68. Witherington (*Jesus the Sage,* 228) has recently seen at least an implicit identification of Jesus as pre-existent wisdom, but Luke does not otherwise develop a wisdom christology, nor does the Third Evangelist elsewhere work with any notion of Jesus' preexistence.

Jesus thus censures the Pharisees and scribes as persons lacking the necessary credentials — measured in terms of their orientation toward God's will and behaviors in light of God's will — to provide leadership for Israel. Not coincidentally, the thoroughgoing manner in which Jesus has called into question the interpretive competence of these persons serves also to legitimate his own position concerning the law, and to present him as the divinely sanctioned hermeneut of God's purpose.

53-54 It is no wonder, then, that these legal experts and Pharisees respond with increased animosity. Luke marks a basic change in their tactics vis-à-vis Jesus; in the past they had engaged in reactive opposition (though cf. 6:11), but from now on[85] their relations with Jesus will be characterized more by their proactive attempts to cast him in a negative light and to snare him (e.g., 14:1; 15:2).[86] Luke thus underscores the location of this encounter in the larger narrative of Jesus' journey to Jerusalem; resolved to fulfill God's plan, Jesus will encounter opposition along the way among those who do not share his basic orientation to God's purpose (cf. 9:51-56).

5.4. VIGILANCE IN THE FACE OF ESCHATOLOGICAL CRISIS (12:1–13:9)

This extensive narrative segment supports the overall complexion of the journey narrative comprising the center of Luke's Gospel as one concerned primarily with instruction. A fresh beginning is marked by Luke's notation regarding the heightened presence of the crowds (12:1; cf. 6:17; 11:29); only with 13:9 does the narrator observe a change of scene.[1] In fact, from 12:1 to 13:9 Luke records what is essentially one continuous discourse, with several topics woven together into a frame provided by the leitmotif of vigilance in the face of crisis.[2]

---

85. Luke marks this change with the verb ἄρχομαι — which, then, should not be read as an auxiliary in this instance.

86. ἐνεδρεύω and θηρεύω are terms borrowed from the hunt, as though Luke means to portray Jesus' opponents as tracking him.

1. *Contra* Shirock ("Growth of the Kingdom"), 13:1-9 is narratologically tied into the preceding material. As we will see, it is also conceptually related to 12:1-59. Shirock does not consider the presence of boundary markers that normally denote topical shifts in narrative, but instead emphasizes the conceptual parallels between 13:1-9 and 13:31-35 as part of a larger chiastic structure he discerns in 13:1-35. Sweetland ("Discipleship and Persecution," 65) notes that Luke uses the heightened presence of the crowds (12:1: μυριάς) to introduce a new section.

2. Tannehill (*Narrative Unity*, 1:240-43) agrees that this material constitutes "a single discourse, given at a single time and place," but sees no apparent connection between the three or four topics raised in this address. On the thematizing of this discourse, see Carroll, *End of History*, 53; Johnson, 196-97.

Toward the close of the previous section, Luke had registered a heightened sense of crisis, first by reporting Jesus' prediction, itself a representation of God's wisdom, regarding the hostile treatment expected of God's messengers. Following this, and closing out Jesus' dialogue with the Pharisees and scribes, Luke observes that these religious leaders had adopted a new policy concerning Jesus. No longer would they simply scrutinize his practices in light of the law; from now on they would actively stalk him. Given the note on which the previous section ended, it is not surprising to find Jesus instructing his disciples on behavior appropriate to times of persecution in 12:1-12. What is more, in the midst of this teaching, Jesus raises the connection between present-day persecution and the eschatological crisis (12:5); with this, the stage is set for the dialogue-and-discourse sequence to follow.

Jesus' teaching in this section is profoundly shaped by the eschatological worldview he presupposes and depicts throughout. To take three prominent examples, we may note, first, how the kingdom saying of 12:32 reflects backward, and negatively, on all attempts to find one's security in possessions. It has pleased God to give the kingdom to the disciples; hence, they are liberated from the peril of possessions and are enabled to reorder their lives in order to care for the needs of others. Similarly, Jesus' portrait of the comportment of the Son of Man in the eschaton as a table servant determines the nature of faithfulness in the present for Jesus' followers (12:37b). This portrait prohibits violence that accompanies conspicuous consumption (12:45) as well as those concerns with status that label as demeaning practices of servanthood such as those modeled by the Lord himself. Service and faithfulness to the task set before disciples — these are the responses sanctioned by the nature of Jesus' eschatological vision. Third, Luke records material wherein the urgency of response, leading to faith and fecundity (cf. 8:4-21), is underscored (12:56-57; 13:3, 9). Here, too, is a reminder that Jesus is "on the way" to Jerusalem, and it is on the road that people are challenged to orient themselves around the priorities of the kingdom of God (12:58: "on the way"; cf. v 31).

Throughout this narrative segment, then, Luke remains concerned (as he had been most explicitly in 11:1-13, and earlier in 6:17-49) with the resocialization of those who have joined (or who would join) the band of Jesus' followers. This reorientation of life, to which he sometimes refers as "repentance," involves a "theological transformation" — that is, a change in one's understanding of the nature of God and of God's eschatological purpose. This theological reformation has a relationship of mutual dependence with a further transformation, this one in the arena of social practices — especially vis-à-vis persecution, possessions, and issues of social relations and status.

Jesus' address appears to move back and forth from one audience to the next, first to the disciples, then to the crowds, then back again. The disciples are addressed specifically in 12:1, 4,[3] 22, and the crowds (or one from the crowds) are addressed specifically in 12:1, 13, 14, 16(?), 54; 13:1(?). Although these audience designations are not without importance, their significance should not be overdrawn. As in 6:20,[4] Jesus may address the disciples, but he does so in the hearing of the crowds as well, just as his teaching to the crowds is delivered in the presence of the disciples. In fact, the ambiguity that actually characterizes the question of Jesus' audience throughout this discourse surfaces explicitly in 12:41, where Peter wonders to whom Jesus has addressed his parabolic teaching. This is a reminder that the line between disciples and others is not always clearly defined, with Jesus giving instruction to his disciples that serves also to challenge and invite prospective followers.[5] This is all the more remarkable when it is recognized that Jesus does not assess the crowds in a positive way in this narrative segment. In fact, he refers to them as "hypocrites" (12:56), using the same epithet he has already used in his valuation of the Pharisees (12:1). That he admonishes the disciples to beware of the Pharisees' hypocrisy, though, reminds us that their position as those who embody his teaching is not yet secure; they are not yet so different from the crowds that they are incapable of earning the hypocrite emblem themselves.

5.4.1. Persecution and Identification with God's Purpose (12:1-12)

12:1 *Meanwhile, when the crowd gathered by the thousands, so that they trampled on one another, he began to speak first to his disciples, "Beware of the yeast of the Pharisees, that is, their hypocrisy. 2 Nothing is covered up that will not be uncovered, and nothing secret that will not become known. 3 Therefore whatever you have said in the dark will be heard in the light, and what you have whispered behind closed doors will be proclaimed from the housetops.*

4 "I tell you, my friends, do not fear those who kill the body, and after that can do nothing more. 5 But I will warn you whom to fear: fear him who, after he has killed, has authority to cast into hell. Yes, I tell you, fear him! 6 Are not five sparrows sold for two pennies? Yet not one of them is forgotten in God's sight. 7 But even the hairs of your head are all counted. Do not be afraid; you are of more value than many sparrows.

---

3. In 12:4, Jesus refers to the disciples as "friends." In its attempt to use inclusive language, the NRSV has unfortunately introduced where there is none a parallel reference to "friend" in v 14. See below.

4. See above.

5. Green, *Gospel of Luke,* 105.

8 *"And I tell you, everyone who acknowledges me before others, the Son of Man also will acknowledge before the angels of God; 9 but whoever denies me before others will be denied before the angels of God. 10 And everyone who speaks a word against the Son of Man will be forgiven; but whoever blasphemes against the Holy Spirit will not be forgiven. 11 When they bring you before the synagogues, the rulers, and the authorities, do not worry about how you are to defend yourselves or what you are to say; 12 for the Holy Spirit will teach you at that very hour what you ought to say."*

Although Jesus' departure from the Pharisee's home (11:53-54) and the gathering of "tens of thousands"[6] in crowds mark a new beginning in the Lukan journey narrative, the Evangelist also ties this new scene to the old. First, he uses a temporal indication, "meanwhile," to show the association of this new episode with the one just preceding.[7] Second, Jesus' characterization of the Pharisees as hypocrites provides an apt summary for the invective discourse unleashed against them and their table companions, legal experts, in the previous scene. Third, in the context of his table talk, Jesus had cited the wisdom of God, tying the fate of God's messengers in the present to that of the prophets of the past, thus anticipating persecution for himself and those who would follow him. Moreover, the narrator had drawn the previous scene to a close with reference to the new tactics of the Pharisees and legal experts concerning Jesus, again presaging an imminent rise in hostility. These proleptic remarks provide the immediate setting for Jesus to return to his disciples, as he does here, to prepare them for times of public defamation, even death. Jesus' message to his disciples in this section, in turn, provides a heading for his instruction on faithfulness throughout the larger section that runs to 13:9.

Jesus' instruction is permeated by his vision of God, who has ultimate oversight in the unfolding of earthly events. It is also shaped by his confidence in the reciprocal relationship between the behavior of disciples in the present, particularly in trying circumstances, and the status of disciples in the eschaton (cf. 9:26; 21:12-19). This is a reminder that, in spite of the Lukan emphasis on the presence of salvation now, in this world, there is also a future aspect of salvation yet to be unveiled.

1-3 The introduction to Jesus' extended discourse on vigilance in the face of eschatological crisis is reminiscent of the preparation for the Sermon on the Plain (6:17-20) insofar as Luke registers the presence of a huge crowd in the company of whom Jesus addresses his followers. Earlier, however, our

---

6. 12:1: μυριάς; cf. Acts 19:19; 21:20.
7. Cf. Plummer 317. ἐν οἷς (NRSV: "meanwhile") might be rendered "during which things" or "in the midst of which."

view of the crowds was perhaps more benign than it can be now, in light of its inclusion of persons who test Jesus or who attribute his activity to the devil (11:14-16); in addition, Luke presents its sheer size in an almost threatening way.[8] The resulting setting of this discourse only adds to the heightened sense of drama provided by the decision of the Pharisees and scribes in 11:53-54 to take a more proactive role in their opposition against Jesus. Nevertheless, in light of the explicit recognition of the crowds pressing in (12:1) and of the intruding question from a member of the crowd (12:13), it is hardly possible to regard Jesus' address to his disciples as private instruction. Instead, as is generally true in Luke, the formation of disciples is conducted in the presence of others who might then be moved to respond with faith and to join the band of Jesus' followers.

Notably, Jesus does not warn his followers that persecution is coming as much as he warns them regarding improper and proper responses to persecution. Persecution, then, appears as an inevitability. In particular, because of impending trials, disciples must guard against "the yeast of the Pharisees, that is, their hypocrisy."[9] As a result of the penetrating power of yeast (or leaven), references to it in figures of speech were familiar.[10] Such figures of speech might draw on the corrupting influence of yeast as well as its capacity to penetrate in a concealed fashion. Here, the properties of this metaphor are developed along all three lines, so that, for Luke, the Pharisaic mind-set is represented as a contaminant with potential to invade even the company of Jesus' followers. Pushing the metaphor further, Jesus also builds on the secretive nature of yeast, the work of which is concealed at first, apparent later (12:2-3).

What is this yeast? Jesus defines it as "hypocrisy," an unfortunate transliteration of a Greek lexeme, the meaning of which in Luke is closely aligned with its usage in the LXX; there it describes "a person whose conduct is not determined by God and is thus 'godless.' "[11] This understanding of Jesus' concern with the Pharisees ties in well with his earlier censure of them as persons whose concerns with legal observance were not rooted in the love of God or in a commitment to justice (11:42; cf. 10:25-37). Hence, Jesus'

---

8. The use of ἐπισυνάγω together with μυριάς suggests a continued swell in the size of the crowd since 11:29. Now the crowd is so large that people are trampling one another underfoot (καταπατέω).

9. προσέχω + ἀπό has the meaning of "watch out" in 20:46; in 17:3; 21:34, Luke uses the verb with a reflexive pronoun to achieve the same end. Here, he writes προσέχω + reflexive pronoun + ἀπό.

10. Cf. Matt 13:33; 1 Cor 5:6; Gal 5:9; Popkes, "ζύμη."

11. Giesen, "ὑπόκρισις, ὑποκρίνομαι"; see further Smith, "Hypocrite"; and the discussion of the semantic evolution of the term in *TLNT,* 3:406-13. Cf. Job 34:30; 36:13; 2 Macc 6:21-25; 4 Macc 6:15-23; *Pss. Sol.* 4:5-6, 22.

point is not that they are play-acting, but that Jesus regards them as misdirected in their fundamental understanding of God's purpose and, therefore, incapable of discerning the authentic meaning of the Scriptures and, therefore, unable to present anything other than the impression of piety. Important from a rhetorical point of view, Jesus does not regard the Pharisees as unique in their failure to live with integrity a life oriented around absolute love of God and neighbor. His followers, too, are susceptible; hence, he presents this warning lest they contract the same ingressive agent whose decay has already become evident among the Pharisees.

Such yeast must be avoided, Jesus warns, because nothing will remain hidden. His instruction on this matter is capable of at least three explanations, none of which excludes another in this co-text. First, as he has repeatedly insisted, Jesus may be reiterating simply that what is hidden, what is on the inside of a person, will be manifest (cf. 8:17; 11:33-36); the inner dispositions of people are evident in their outward behavior (cf. 6:43-45). Second, and more at home in this co-text, the true constitution of a disciple will come to light in the experience of persecution — and, as is becoming more and more clear, persecution is the lot of those who are faithful to God in the midst of an evil generation. Indeed, the depth of one's love and the source(s) of one's security become evident in times of opposition (see above on 6:22-23, 27-28). Third, Jesus' caution that all will be made manifest may be read as an eschatological warning: Conversation presumed to be secret now will become public then. In fact, as 12:8-10 will demonstrate, these last two options are probably intertwined: How one responds in the context of persecution now cannot be separated from one's fate at the eschaton.

Underlying all of these possibilities is a further one that surfaces repeatedly in the Third Gospel. This is the new reality that Jesus proclaims as having drawn near but which is nevertheless less than evident to most. Jesus' sometimes outrageous counsel — including his instruction not to fear those who can kill only the body, with its possibly masochist-seeming consequences — *is* outrageous unless one adopts, believes in, the ultimate perspective on God's redemptive project around which Jesus' mission and message are oriented. Not yet visible to those, for example, who attribute his ministry to the devil or continue to demand signs of divine legitimation (11:14-16), this reality will be made manifest; when this happens, those who have embraced its (hidden) wisdom and acted accordingly will be vindicated.

4-5 As he addresses his followers more directly, as "friends," the intensity of Jesus' message reaches a new level. Fear, in this case, is not awe in the face of divine splendor but the trepidation indigenous to situations of life imperilment. Although Luke provides no record of a conversation between Jesus and his followers about the fate of John the Baptist (cf. 9:9), Jesus has spoken of his own impending death and promised few alternatives for those desiring to become his followers (9:22-23). Moreover, although the presence of disciples was not mentioned in the previous scene (11:37-54), Luke's audience, if not also the band of disciples, is aware that the Wisdom of God has foreseen the persecution and execution of some of God's messengers, "prophets and apostles" (11:49). Fear in the face of death, then, is more specifically fear in the face of life-threatening persecution on account of one's identification with God's purpose as this is expounded by Jesus.

By insisting on the substitution of one fear for another — fear of those who can kill the body versus fear of him who has the authority to cast into hell — Jesus introduces a logic whose point is not immediately obvious. A first hint appears in Jesus' reference to his disciples as "friends." Luke has used the language of friendship before (7:6, 34; 11:5-8), but this is the only instance in which he records Jesus thus referring to his disciples. "All things are common to friends," according to the ancient ideal, and the commonality in view here apparently includes shared enemies, shared fate at the hands of those who spurn God's purpose for themselves, and shared knowledge.[12] As this has been developed thus far from the Lukan vantage point, shared insight doubtlessly has to do with the character of God as Father (cf. 10:21-22; 11:1-13). And this anticipates the continuation of Jesus' instruction in 12:6-7, where Jesus again clarifies the nature of God who oversees events in the world. In other words, Jesus asserts that, in hostile situations of life imperilment, God is the only one who should be feared, but the character of God is such that one need not fear him!

"Hell" is "Gehenna" — in the OT the Valley of Hinnom, site of the sacrifice of children, declared unclean under Josiah and converted into a trash heap, then associated with eschatological judgment in the prophets and subsequently. With time, then, Gehenna came to be associated with the fiery judgment of eschatological punishment.[13] With this phrase, then, Jesus has clearly introduced an eschatological horizon into his instruction on faithfulness in the midst of trials.

6-7 Key to Jesus' overall message according to Luke is his portrayal of God, so his return to this subject in his instruction on faithfulness in the context of persecution is not unexpected. What may be unsettling, however, is that Jesus does not present God as "savior" in the usual way — that is, as one who rescues his people *from* danger. Sparrows, though of little value in

---

12. Spicq notes this specific identification of a φίλος as a "confidant, one to whom a secret is entrusted" (*TLNT,* 3:448); cf. Sweetland, "Discipleship and Persecution," 68-69.

13. On the Valley of Hinnom, see Josh 15:8; 18:16; cf. 2 Kgs 23:10. On the sacrifice of children, see 2 Kgs 16:3; 21:6; and, more generally, Levenson, *Beloved Son,* 3-17. For the Valley under Josiah, see 2 Kgs 23:10. For its association with judgment, see Isa 31:19; 66:24; Jer 7:31-32; 19:6; Rev 14:7-13; *1 Enoch* 26:4; 27:1-3; 54:16; cf. 4 Ezra 7:36; *2 Apoc. Bar.* 59:10; 85:13.

the marketplace (a "penny" is a small coin whose value is measured as one-sixteenth of a denarius), are remembered by God; arguing from lesser to greater, Jesus can thus affirm that disciples are similarly not forgotten by God. Nevertheless, that none of them is forgotten by God does not keep sparrows from being sold in the marketplace and eaten, nor does God's knowledge of the number of hairs on "your head" portend a divine guarantee of one's safety.

It is true that elsewhere in the Lukan narrative reference to hair can be related to divine protection, but in those instances notions of care and security are stated explicitly (cf. 21:18; Acts 27:34).[14] This is not true in the present co-text. Here an alternative interpretive tradition is being accessed. This is the conceptualization of God as one who can count what humans cannot count and, so, whose knowledge surpasses that of humans and whose design, therefore, cannot be grasped fully by humans.[15] The point, then, is that sparrows can be bought and sold and that humans can suffer persecution, but not apart from God's attentiveness, not outside of God's care, not in a way that circumvents the redemptive plan of God. Jesus' words contrast the limited knowledge of human beings with the mysterious omniscience of God, in this co-text with reference to the significance of the experience of even life-threatening hostility among Jesus' followers.

Human ignorance might lead to hasty and unsuitable responses to persecution, but, according to the theodicy of this text, recognition of the mystery of God's incomparable wisdom makes evil endurable. It may also deter Jesus' followers from responding faithlessly in the ordeal of persecution.[16] God is not absent from or unaware of persecution; rather, as will become clear in the following verses, it is precisely in such circumstances that the Holy Spirit enables inspired witness. A God who has the authority to cast people into Gehenna ought to be feared over those who can only kill the body (12:4-5), but the God who has this authority is also the God whose redemptive will or care is not confuted by persecution.

8-10   If bearing authentic witness to Jesus in situations of persecution provides no warranty against danger, what does it portend? In 12:5, Jesus had brought into view the eschatological horizon against which life in the present must be understood if it is to be lived faithfully. The relationship between the present and the future of God's purpose is now further developed, with the result that Jesus highlights the importance of present response for one's future status vis-à-vis the Son of Man. The phrase "before others" accords privilege to public acknowledgment; in this co-text, public acknowledgment in the face

---

14. Cf., e.g., 1 Sam 14:45; 2 Sam 14:11; 1 Kgs 1:52.

15. Allison Jr., "Hairs of Your Head." Cf., e.g., Job 38:37; Sir 1:2; 4 Ezra 4:7; *1 Enoch* 93:14.

16. Allison Jr., "Hairs of Your Head," 335.

of hostility, especially in an official hearing of some sort (see 12:11), is certainly in view (cf. 9:26). With the phrase "before the angels of God" Jesus envisages a parallel, juridical scene, this time in the setting of the heavenly court.[17] Using a play on words to make his point, Jesus contends that acknowledging him "before humanity" is a prerequisite to being acknowledged by the "son of humanity."[18] A positive exemplar of Jesus' teaching is provided by Stephen (Acts 7:55-56).

The parallel in 12:8-9 is straightforward: public acknowledgment leads to heavenly acknowledgment and public denial leads to heavenly denial.[19] The relation of the two clauses of 12:10 is not so straightforward. As a general term, the verb "to blaspheme" refers to speaking ill or abusively of someone,[20] and clearly Jesus draws a sharp distinction between insulting himself (as Son of Man) and mocking the Holy Spirit. Based on the analogy of similar fates — eschatological rejection — engendered by the public denial of Jesus in 12:8-9, as well as on the strength of the adjacent material concerning the empowering presence of the Spirit in times of persecution in 12:11-12, we may be confident that, for Luke, blasphemy of the Holy Spirit refers to committing apostasy in the face of persecution.[21] Speaking ill of the Son of Man does not carry with it so dire a consequence, however — a fact that bodes well for the fate of such persons as those Pharisees who have snubbed Jesus and his message heretofore; the door has not yet been closed on them, for they remain possible candidates for forgiveness.[22]

11-12 Lest, in light of the frightful consequences of denying Jesus in the hour of persecution disciples become fearful and anxious, Jesus immediately waylays any such response with his promise that disciples will not face experiences of persecution defenseless. The Holy Spirit, otherwise known in part in the Lukan narrative for its role in empowering persons for inspired witness, is present in such instances in order to teach the persecuted what to

17. See *1 Enoch* 99:3.

18. ἔμπροσθεν τῶν ἀνθρώπων, καὶ ὁ υἱὸς τοῦ ἀνθρώπου. . . .

19. Note how Jesus foresees Peter's public denial, but intercedes on his behalf (22:31-34, 54-62).

20. See Bock, "Jesus' Blasphemy," 184-85; Twelftree, "Blasphemy," 75.

21. So, e.g., Brawley, *Centering on God,* 115; Shelton, *Mighty in Word,* 105; Menzies, *Empowered for Witness,* 165-66; Sweetland, "Discipleship and Persecution," 73; et al.

22. Some interpreters find a flat contradiction between 12:8-9 on the one hand and 12:10a on the other, but such readings are based on atomistic readings of the text that do not allow meaning to arise within particular narrative settings. One of the presumptions of discourse analysis, which examines meaning within discourse units (rather than seeking, e.g., word-for-word or even sentence-by-sentence "meaning") is that "the natural effort of hearers and readers alike is to attribute relevance and coherence to the text they encounter until they are forced not to" (Brown and Yule, *Discourse Analysis,* 66).

say. This, together with the inventory of antagonistic contexts wherein disciples will be called upon to provide witness, sets the stage for the witness of the faithful in the book of Acts (cf. Luke 21:12-15).[23]

5.4.2. Faithfulness concerning Possessions (12:13-34)

13 *Someone in the crowd said to him, "Teacher, tell my brother to divide the family inheritance with me." 14 But he said to him, "Man,[24] who set me to be a judge or arbitrator over you?" 15 And he said to them, "Take care! Be on your guard against all kinds of greed; for one's life does not consist in the abundance of possessions." 16 Then he told them a parable: "The land of a rich man produced abundantly. 17 And he thought to himself, 'What should I do, for I have no place to store my crops?' 18 Then he said, 'I will do this: I will pull down my barns and build larger ones, and there I will store all my grain and my goods. 19 And I will say to my soul, "Soul, you have ample goods laid up for many years; relax, eat, drink, be merry."' 20 But God said to him, 'You fool! This very night your life is being demanded of you. And the things you have prepared, whose will they be?' 21 So it is with those who store up treasures for themselves but are not rich toward God."*

22 *He said to his disciples, "Therefore I tell you, do not worry about your life, what you will eat, or about your body, what you will wear. 23 For life is more than food, and the body more than clothing. 24 Consider the ravens: they neither sow nor reap, they have neither storehouse nor barn, and yet God feeds them. Of how much more value are you than the birds! 25 And can any of you by worrying add a single hour to your span of life? 26 If then you are not able to do so small a thing as that, why do you worry about the rest? 27 Consider the lilies, how they grow: they neither toil nor spin; yet I tell you, even Solomon in all his glory was not clothed like one of these. 28 But if God so clothes the grass of the field, which is alive today and tomorrow is thrown into the oven, how much more will he clothe you — you of little faith! 29 And do not keep striving for what you are to eat and what you are to drink, and do not keep worrying. 30 For it is the nations of the*

---

23. See, e.g., Acts 4:1-22 (5-6); 5:12-42 (17); 6:8–8:2; et al. Cf. Shepherd Jr., *Narrative Function*, 145-46.

24. NRSV: "Friend." The NRSV has introduced the term "friend" in the interest of inclusive language also at 5:20 (for ἄνθρωπος) and 6:42 (for ἀδελφός), but in those instances the co-text is more supportive of this innovation. Here, ἄνθρωπε is used to introduce a reprimand.

world that strive after all these things, and your Father knows that you need them. 31 *Instead, strive for his kingdom, and these things will be given to you as well.*

32 *"Do not be afraid, little flock, for it is your Father's good pleasure to give you the kingdom.* 33 *Sell your possessions, and give alms. Make purses for yourselves that do not wear out, an unfailing treasure in heaven, where no thief comes near and no moth destroys.* 34 *For where your treasure is, there your heart will be also.*

Jesus has been instructing his disciples on the need for faithfulness in situations of persecution (12:1-12), but in Luke's narration this is abruptly interrupted by someone from the crowd who demands assistance from Jesus. Luke thus allows the intrusion of a fresh, apparently irrelevant topic into Jesus' address, as well as recalls for us the presence of a wider audience for that discourse. What has this man's inheritance to do with bearing authentic, Spirit-inspired witness to the Son of Man (12:8-12)? Almost immediately, Jesus patches over this seeming incongruity, returning to the wider theme of attentiveness in the face of eschatological crisis, though developing this theme now with reference to the motif of possessions. Hence, although the change of focus is abrupt, it is not as impertinent as might at first appear.

Nor should we make too much of the change of audience registered in 12:13. The presence of crowds in the midst of whom Jesus had begun to teach his disciples was noted in 12:1, and he will return almost immediately to disciple-oriented instruction in 12:22. This means that the topic of possessions is no less important for the disciples than for the crowds at large, and reminds us that Luke often portrays Jesus teaching one group in the hearing of another because of the general suitability of Jesus' message.[25] It is certainly arguable, moreover, that the "them" Jesus addresses in 12:15, 16 explicitly includes not only the crowds but also the disciples.

In fact, Jesus' words to the crowds are interwoven into his subsequent teaching to the disciples in a complex way. "Life," for example, appears first in 12:15, then reappears in 12:19, 20, 22, 23, and (25).[26] "Possessions" (12:15) are transformed into "goods" in 12:18, then reappear as "possessions" in 12:33. Different sorts of "treasures" are discussed, first in 12:21, then in

25. Speaking more broadly, Harvey (*Strenuous Commands*, 130) also observes that the lack of such clear distinctions in audience casts doubt on any suggestion that the instruction directed to the first disciples by Jesus would have lost its urgency for subsequent generations of disciples.

26. Luke uses three different terms, ζωή, ψυχή, and σῶμα ("body"), but in this co-text all refer generally to the human being as a holistic entity and qualitatively to the human being with respect to his or her relationship to God. The NRSV, but not the Greek text, has "life" in v 25.

12:33-34. "Barns" are mentioned in both sections, too (12:18, 24), and with the same purpose. And concern with eating and drinking surfaces first in 12:19, then again in vv 22-24, 29.

More pervasive and pivotal is the *theo*logy of Jesus' two-part discourse. In Jesus' parable to the crowds, God labels a rich landholder as a "fool" — that is, a person whose practices deny God; indeed, the principal deficiency of the wealthy farmer is his failure to account for God in his plans. In light of this, Jesus' instructions to his disciples are appropriately theocentric. Turning to them, he emphasizes the sort of practices that would emanate from a rebirth of their understanding of God's character and purpose.[27] If they could accept his portrait of the caring God who provides for them, as the Father whose pleasure is manifest in his provision of the kingdom, would this not be impetus enough for a radically reconstructed attitude toward and set of behaviors concerning "the abundance of possessions"? Could they not find their security in him rather than in them? And, given the proximity of the kingdom,[28] would not this fresh perspective on God's character and activity serve as an invitation for new practices now? As this narrative unit highlights, for Jesus, within this new economy, alertness and kingdom-seeking are accorded privilege over worry and fear.

How does Jesus argue his case? The opening demand concerning inheritance serves as a launching pad for a transition from the motif of authentic, public witness (12:1-12) to the motif of possessions (12:13-34), with the parable (12:16-21) doing double duty — first to foreground the issue of greed, second to surface the problem of anxiety related to one's long-term security. Following this, Jesus admonishes his disciples concerning the impropriety of worry, observing the inadequacy of the view of life on which it is based (12:23), its uselessness in light of God's care for the birds and the grass (12:24, 27-28), and its impotence as a strategy for prolonging life (12:25); and, finally, calling for an alternative vision of life distinguished *from* the worldview of "the nations of the world" *by* the orientation to the kingdom of God (12:29-31) it engenders. According to Jesus, kingdom-seeking will have as its effects (1) divine provision in this life (12:31), (2) freedom to engage in practices of disinvestiture and almsgiving (i.e., in behaviors that

27. In his discussion of Luke's contribution to the discussion on "the economic problem," Gordon (*Economic Problem*, 64-65) does not take with sufficient seriousness the profound degree to which Luke's discussion of economic practices explicitly presupposes a conversion in worldview. Such responses as radical disinvestment and almsgiving are not preconditions but (possible) consequences of discipleship. Wheeler (*Wealth*, 68) more helpfully observes that obedience to Jesus' instruction in these matters ". . . is not the *requirement* of faith; it is rather what *follows* from faith, the reasonable response of one who perceives in Jesus the advent of the kingdom. . . ." See above, §11.

28. See, e.g., 10:9, 11; 11:20; Olsthoorn, *Jewish Background*, 27; cf. Phil 4:5-6.

are antithetical to those of the Pharisees of 11:39-41 and the wealthy farmer of 12:16-19) signifying the reconstruction of the people of God wherein conventional economic and social distinctions are immaterial (12:33), and, therefore, (3) divine provision in the eschaton (12:33-34).

13-15 The stage is set for Jesus' discourse on possessions by a man in the crowd who intrudes into Jesus' tutelage of his disciples with an attempt to recruit Jesus' assistance. As abrupt as this interruption may seem, Luke had prepared for it with his reference to the presence of an enormous crowd (12:1), presumably assembled around the much smaller gathering of Jesus and his band of followers. Luke stitches this interchange into the wider co-text of the narrative in a second way. In 12:1, Jesus had warned his disciples to beware of the Pharisees. The need for alertness is repeated in 12:15,[29] this time without direct reference to the Pharisees, but with language that is nonetheless reminiscent of the Pharisaic mind-set as this is developed in 11:39. There, Jesus describes Pharisees as full of rapacity and wickedness; now he warns people against all forms of greed. (In the same way, in 12:33 he will counsel behaviors that contrast sharply with the Pharisaic practices noted in 11:39-41.) Jesus thus continues to portray the Pharisees as people of corrupt constitution, using them as a foil against which to articulate an authentic representation of God and God's purpose and to outline the nature of genuine faithfulness to God.

The man presents himself as one of two brothers, now unable to live in harmony together (cf. Ps 133:1). As a consequence he seeks his share of the family holdings. Presumably, the one who comes to Jesus is the younger of the two, who, because of his lesser position in the household, requires outside assistance in his attempt to achieve a settlement. The laws of inheritance are put forward in Num 27:1-11; 36:7-9; Deut 21:16-17; as these did not cover all imaginable situations a request such as this man's would not have been novel. He addresses Jesus as "teacher," acknowledging Jesus' authority to render a decision in his case, but his is less a request, more a directive. He knows already the ruling he expects and needs only for Jesus to place on it his imprimatur. Echoing language from Exod 2:14, Jesus refuses the role in which he has been cast, addressing instead the dispositions out of which he apparently perceives the man's dispute to have arisen.[30]

"Greed" can denote the hunger for advanced social standing as well as the insatiable desire for wealth, though in Luke's world these two images

29. In fact, it is highlighted by repetition, using first a verb of perception, ὁράω — a usage that anticipates Jesus' teaching in 12:54-56 (where seeing should have led to recognition and recognition to appropriate action); and then φυλάσσω, which, in the middle voice, has the sense "to be on guard against" (cf. Acts 21:25).

30. Such words as "presumably" and "apparently" dot this paragraph because Luke's narration is so terse; clearly, the exact nature of the man's dispute is not nearly so important for the narrator as is the teaching moment Jesus will derive from this interruption.

are intricately related. This is because, in his world, wealth is one of the several important units of exchange that could be translated into advanced status honor.[31] Greed was widely regarded as a form of depravity, both in Jewish literature and in the larger Greco-Roman world.[32] In the present case, the intertwining of community standing and wealth is obvious, since landholders (the rank this younger brother seeks to join in his request for Jesus' intervention) enjoyed advanced status both in the village economy presumed here and throughout the Empire.

Verse 15b presents difficult translation issues,[33] but this does not detract from the indisputable antithesis Jesus posits between "life" and "possessions." In fact, in light of the adjacent material in 12:4-12, with its emphasis on faithfulness in situations of life-threatening persecution, it is possible to see in this polarity a similar emphasis, this time on faithfulness with respect to life-threatening possessions. As in 10:25-37, then, "life" is a metaphor for salvation. Those who would enjoy it must beware of one of its chief adversaries — namely, possessions.[34]

16-21 In an important sense, the message of the parable of vv 16-20 is determined for Luke by its frame, vv 15 and 21. This means, first, that Jesus presents the situation of this wealthy farmer-landholder[35] as an illustration, among the many possibilities, of the greed for which one is to beware according to v 15. Second, it means that this farmer is cast as one who has fallen victim to the polarity between an existence oriented toward life and one oriented toward possessions (v 15) or between a life in pursuit of the pseudo-security resident in possessions (= "storing up treasures for themselves") and a life in pursuit of riches vis-à-vis God (v 21). From the Lukan perspective,

---

31. See Green, "Good News," 64-65.

32. Greed is "the metropolis of all evil deeds" (Diodorus Siculus), the root of evil (Thucydides 3.82.8), "a baneful passion" (Philo *Spec. Leg.* 4.5); etc. See Schottroff and Stegemann, *Jesus,* 96; *TLNT,* 3:117-19.

33. The translation offered by Schmidt (*Hostility to Wealth,* 146; following Derrett, "Rich Fool") is similarly obscure: "(it is) not while one has abundance (that) life is his — (it does not) come from his [*sic*] possessions."

34. Luke uses a participial form of ὑπάρχω to designate "possessions" — i.e., "what one has" (8:3; 11:21; 12:33, 44; 14:33; 16:1, 14; 19:8). Typically, they are presented as an alternative landmark according to which one might define one's life, and thus as a peril to eternal life; against this backdrop, Jesus urges freedom from "possessions," an act or series of acts that might take any number of forms (see above, §11), but is best represented for Luke in a form of divestiture in which those in need are embraced as one's "friends" or "kin."

35. Moxnes (*Economy of the Kingdom,* 56-58) notes that the inhabitants of the villages represented in the Lukan parables appear on a continuum running from the landed wealthy (cf., e.g., 14:16-24; 16:19-31), to the wealthy landowner who also takes part in working the land (as in this parable; cf. also 15:11-32), to peasants, and so on.

then, the wealthy farmer has failed to comport himself properly with respect to his possessions, for he has not entrusted his life to God and, as a consequence, has not acted faithfully with respect to his possessions.

On one level, the scenario depicted in Jesus' parable presents no departures at all from what might be expected.[36] Due to a bumper crop, the farmer has insufficient storage room for his harvest. Rather than building additional barns and thus taking up land that might otherwise be used for agricultural production in subsequent years, he elects to tear down his current storage facilities in order to make room for larger ones. He thus makes it clear that he does not plan to contribute to the current year's saturation of the market with his surplus, but will hold his harvest back in order to achieve a higher price when the market is not glutted.[37] It would appear, then, that Jesus portrays this wealthy farmer as having a good head for agribusiness.

What is wrong with this picture? First, as we have intimated, the framing of this parable by the Evangelist will not allow a positive interpretation of this wealthy farmer; in this co-text, he is explicitly represented as an exemplar of greed. Second, Luke's audience has already learned to attach negative connotations to the adjective "rich" (cf. 1:52-53; 6:24). The extent of this man's wealth is suggested not only by Luke's initial characterization of him as "rich," and not only by his capacity to undertake a building program without the benefit of the sale of this year's produce, but also by his need to build bigger barns both for his grain and for the rest of his "goods" (v 18). Given the subsistence economy of the peasant population surrounding him,[38] this need for increased personal storage space not directly related to his agricultural activity must have seemed odd in the extreme, if not utterly monstrous. Third, Jesus portrays the farmer as engaging in self-talk. Although this might seem perfectly natural in this setting, persons engaged in soliloquy are consistently portrayed negatively by Luke (cf. 2:35; 5:21-22; 6:8; 9:46-47). In this instance, given the high level of interconnectedness characteristic of the village economy, it is worth asking why this farmer lays out a course of action in isolation from others whose well-being is affected by this decision.[39] Ad-

36. See the helpful discussion of Hedrick, *Parables,* 142-63. Hedrick has little patience for Luke's interpretation of the parable, but he fails to recognize how alike his reading is to Luke's.

37. Incidentally, this course of action requires him to rebuild larger storage facilities, rather than make-do with additional, temporary facilities since (1) he does not entertain the possibility of discontinuing his farming activity in the ensuing years and thus will continue to need as much arable land as possible, and (2) he will require the additional capacity in order to store future produce along with the yield of this bumper year.

38. See above, §10.

39. Cf. Donahue, *Gospel in Parable,* 178; Bailey, *Through Peasant Eyes,* 64-65; Moxnes, *Economy of the Kingdom,* 88-89.

ditionally, the content of the farmer's self-talk echoes similarly self-damning language in Jewish literature.[40]

Fourth, and closely related, what is "good business practice" for this wealthy farmer-landholder has detrimental consequences for the peasants and tenants who are his neighbors and who far outnumber him in the village economy.[41] Not least because of his evidently vast landholdings and the magnitude of his surplus yield, his decision to hold back his produce will reflect harmfully on the regional economy.[42] It will, at the same time, secure his economic power and position of status in the village as others are made more and more dependent on him. Fifth, in fact, the prudence we might attribute to this farmer-businessman is mitigated by the tardiness of his awareness of the problem he faces. Why did he not recognize the extent of his yield and take suitable action long before the time of harvest? Within the wider Lukan co-text, where Jesus castigates his audience for their failure to interpret correctly the signs before them (11:14-32; 12:54-56), the farmer's failure to read the signs is incriminating.

Underlying all of the above considerations is one final observation. This farmer has sought to secure himself and his future without reference to God. This is the force of the label given him by God, "fool," used in the LXX to signify a person who rebels against God or whose practices deny God[43] — a usage that coheres with the representation of "greed" (v 15) as a form of idolatry.[44] He did not consider that his life was on loan from God.[45] Failing to account for the will of God in his stratagems, he likewise failed to account for the peril to life constituted by an abundance of possessions (v 15) and for the responsibility that attends the possession of wealth. He thus appears as one of several exemplars of the wealthy over whom "woe" is pronounced in the Gospel of Luke (cf. 6:24). Such persons are not simply those with possessions, but more particularly those whose dispositions are not toward the needs of those around them, whose possessions have become a source of security apart from God, and, thus, whose possessions deny them any claim to life.[46] The worthlessness of the farmer's machinations is well represented in God's parting words: These possessions, whose will they be now?

22-23 Until he was interrupted by a man from the crowd in v 13,

---

40. See esp. Sir 11:18-19; cf. also Tob 7:9-11.

41. See above, Figure 1, p. 60.

42. See Schottroff and Stegemann, *Jesus,* 97.

43. See, e.g., Prov 14:1; Jer 4:22.

44. See 2 Macc 4:50; *T. Jud.* 19:1; Col 3:5.

45. ἀπαιτέω/ἀπαίτησις can refer to the collection of a loan — cf. Jeremias, *Parables,* 165; Bailey, *Through Peasant Eyes,* 67.

46. Against earlier claims that in this parable Luke speculates on the nature of an individualized eschatology, see Carroll, *End of History,* 62-64.

Jesus had been instructing his disciples and, following the parable of the rich fool, he returns to his disciples. This does not mean they were absent in the intervening period; surely they are to be included in the "them" of vv 15 and 16. Nor does this mean that the crowds have dissipated. Although they drop from explicit view as the focus narrows again on Jesus and his disciples, the crowds remain present as the secondary audience of Jesus' discourse. What is more, the issue of "greed" that surfaced in the exchange between Jesus and the man from the crowd remains on the table as Jesus turns to address his disciples. They, too, require guidance in the area of possessions.

In fact, Jesus' opening words, "on account of this" (NRSV: "therefore"), indicate that his disciple-oriented teaching is intimately related to his dialogue with the man from the crowd. His further instruction is cast, first, as an attempt to draw out the implications of his earlier assertion that "life does not consist in the abundance of possessions." References to "life" and "eating" (vv 19, 22-23) indicate Jesus' intention to exegete the parable for his disciples. "Life" and "body" should not be regarded as separate entities, but are mentioned to draw attention to the totality of a person and to what is needed for the fundamental sustenance of human life. Regarding these things, Jesus remarks, people ought not to worry; after all, it is for such things that disciples have already been taught to pray with the expectation that the character of God as Father is such that he will provide for them (11:1-13). As will become clear in the remainder of this narrative unit (12:22-34), "worry" (and later, "fear" [v 32]) derives from a view of God at odds with the *theo*logy embodied in the message of Jesus.[47]

From this new assertion, Jesus turns to a series of arguments in its support, the first of which comes in v 23. Here Jesus simply asserts that such anxiety is based on a confusion; distress concerning food and clothing betrays an inappropriately minimalist view of human life, which consists of much more than these (cf. 4:4). The probing character of Jesus' message rests in our recognition of the village setting of this discourse on possessions (vv 16-20). Is not concern with subsistence precisely what occupies the peasant family?[48] What meaning might Jesus' message have in such an environment? The "more" to which Jesus refers is not yet clear, though it begins to surface in the immediately ensuing verses.

24-26 Jesus' second argument is comprised of an illustration drawn from the observable world. Ravens neither produce nor preserve their food, yet God provides for them. Arguing from lesser to greater, then, Jesus can assert as superfluous the anxiety of those who through their agitation seek to secure their livelihood. The force of this stage of Jesus' argument is heightened

47. See 10:41; 12:11. Cf. 8:14.
48. See above, §10.

by his choice of examples. A raven is a bird of prey, a "rapacious unclean bird";[49] if God feeds even such as these, how much more human beings? In this and the following illustration (vv 27-28), Jesus attempts to engage his audience in reading the signs of God's gracious presence all around them. If they are able to do so, their views of God will be reshaped and the character of their lives reformed.

Jesus observes, thirdly, the impotence of anxiety as a stratagem for securing the future. Disquiet associated with material security did not guarantee years of luxury for the wealthy farmer-landowner of vv 16-20, nor is it capable of adding even a single hour to the length of one's life.[50] In fact, according to Sir 30:24, anxiety has the opposite effect, bringing on "premature old age." On pragmatic grounds, then, anxious concern must be rejected as a worthwhile practice.

27-28 In v 22 Jesus had spoken of what one will both eat and wear. Having addressed the former concern with his reference to ravens, he returns to his second argument to address the latter. As before, he points to reality in the observable world, this time to lilies and the grass of the field, with the hope that his audience will discern there the gracious hand of God. Jesus first argues from the greater to the lesser, insisting that even the splendor of Solomon, as great as it was, did not match the splendor of the flowers to which Jesus points in the midst of his address. This is remarkable, given the legendary glory of Solomon's court;[51] could this comparison provide an implicit criticism of Solomon, whose resplendence was marred, according to the viewpoint for which Jesus is arguing, by Solomon's vainglorious attempts to achieve international security and eminence? In any case, Jesus' argument turns again on the lesser-greater comparison, drawing attention to the brief existence of field grasses[52] used in the fuel supply in order to assert God's incomparable care for human beings.

Jesus' parting reference to people of "little faith" is highly significant in this context. First, he thus casts the disciples as persons who are not (at this point[!] — cf. 8:25; 9:45) consumed with worry or fear. Second, and of greater rhetorical importance in this co-text, Jesus' entire message here is based on the possibility that some will see with the eyes of faith what is otherwise hidden from view. Jesus can apparently locate evidences of God's generosity and care in the world all around him and can therefore counsel this alternative approach to life in this world. But what is so obvious to him is obscure apart from faith in this God and, as is clear in the Lukan narrative as

49. Olsthoorn, *Jewish Background,* 35.
50. On ἡλικία, see above on 2:52.
51. Cf. 1 Kings 10; 2 Chronicles 9.
52. Cf., e.g., Pss 37:1-2; 90 (esp. vv 5-6); Isa 37:26-27; 40:6-8.

a whole, faith in the presence of God's restorative activity in the mission of Jesus. That his followers have "little faith" is a hopeful sign that they will be able to attend to his message and, then, that they will orient their lives in what must, apart from faith, seem a reckless direction.

29-31 Jesus reaches the climax of his argument by juxtaposing as distinct alternatives the life of sustenance-seeking and arrogant worry on the one hand, and, on the other, the life of kingdom-seeking. The appropriateness of "striving" (NRSV) — in the sense of setting one's heart and life on the pursuit of something, but not in the sense of anxious struggle — is determined by the object of the quest. The quest for security, represented in metonymic references to searching for things to eat and drink (cf. vv 19, 22), is regarded as characteristic activity of persons who have no awareness of God as Father. Such people likewise engage in arrogant behavior, acting as though they can be self-sufficient, or, perhaps, characterized by anxious behavior.[53]

The pivotal point in Jesus' instruction is *theo*logical. The practices he condemns are rooted in an erroneous perception of the character of God. Those who know God as Father (cf. 11:1-13) will know God as the one capable of and committed to providing for his people. Knowing this, they are liberated from the consuming concerns of self-security. Thus liberated, they are able to orient their lives completely around the propagation in word and deed of God's restorative project.[54] This is the kingdom, the coming of which overturns those worldly systems and values at odds with God's purpose.

32-34 If vv 29-31 constitute the climax of Jesus' argument, these

---

53. It is not clear how we are to understand Luke's use of the verb μετεωρίζομαι, used only here in the NT. The NRSV follows the majority in rendering it with the verb "to worry" (cf., e.g., *TLNT*, 2:483-85 ["Thus we can with complete certainty translate Luke 12:29 'do not be anxious' " (485)]; Balz, "μετεωρίζομαι"). This meaning is rarely attested, though, and it is worth inquiring into the possibility that the more widespread sense of "to be arrogant" or "to make high demands" (cf. Ps 130:1; 2 Macc 7:34) is possible in this co-text. Although certainty seems beyond our reach on this point, insofar as Jesus illustrates "all kinds of greed" with a story about a man whose pursuit of self-security is intertwined with his position as a landholder of high status and insofar as Jesus is concerned to undercut the human pursuit of autonomy that manifests itself in anxiety and independence from God, this more common sense is appropriate here. The notion of making arrogant demands is also supported by Jesus' reference to "the nations of the world," whose presence in Palestine in the first century is felt most through the residence of Roman political appointees and their military and through the redistribution of land from the hands of small farmers (peasants) to those of large landholders who live in urban centers.

54. This way of construing the phrase "strive for the kingdom" assumes that in this phrase Jesus' previous instructions regarding the disciples' comportment with regard to the kingdom are recapitulated. Previously, they have been told to render the kingdom present through their participation in his ministry and to pray for the kingdom (cf. 9:1-6; 10:1-11; 11:2).

verses comprise its denouement. Here we encounter both the foundation and the resolution of his message on faithfulness regarding possessions. Fear, in this instance, refers to the anxiety and misgivings associated with the uncertainty of life, modeled so well by the wealthy farmer-landholder in Jesus' parable (vv 16-20). Jesus' disciples, referred to in language that recalls God's care for his people as a shepherd for the flock,[55] need experience no such dread. This is because God's pleasure (or will)[56] is manifest in his gift of the kingdom. It is likely that we are to understand the kingdom as having already been given[57] — undoubtedly, then, a reference to the ministry of Jesus among them.[58]

In spite of their seeming diminutive presence ("little flock"), the disciples are nonetheless the recipients of God's dominion. This makes possible lifestyles that are not consumed with anxiety and fear but, instead, have as their perpetual objective the service of the kingdom. The nature of this kingdom-service is spelled out clearly in this co-text, demonstrating that the kingdom of God is not only a gift but also an obligation. Rather then being occupied with the buildup of treasures with an eye to self-security in this life (v 21), disciples need to be concerned with ensuring that they possess treasures in heaven. Therefore, seeking the kingdom (v 31) is tantamount to setting one's heart on the kingdom (v 34), and the consequence of this orientation of life is a heavenly treasure that is neither subject to the exigencies of earthly existence nor endangered by the unexpected intervention of God.

At work in this instruction is a subtle but significant shift in the forms of reciprocity familiar throughout the Roman world. Normally, one with treasures to share does so in order to place others in her debt; gifts are given in order to secure or even advance one's position in the community. Inherent to the giving of "gifts" in this economy is the obligation of repayment. The material sharing Jesus counsels has a different complexion. Disinvestment and almsgiving grounded in a thoroughgoing commitment to the kingdom of God are to be practiced in recognition that God is the Supreme Benefactor

55. Cf., e.g., Ezekiel 34.

56. Cf. 2:14; 3:22; 10:21.

57. This, however, is not clear from the syntax of the clause. Luke uses an aorist indicative (εὐδόκησεν), thus suggesting, at least, that God's decision to grant this benefaction is complete. The significance of the aorist infinitive (δοῦναι) — typically associated with occurrences that are self-complete, instantaneous, or unique — in this clause is not so clear, and 22:29 may suggest that the conferral of the kingdom should be timed much later in the course of (or following) Jesus' ministry. But there is no essential contradiction between saying that the disciples are recipients of the kingdom as they join with, share, and identify with Jesus' ministry and that, as a consequence of their standing with Jesus in his "trials," they become the authorized successors of the kingdom.

58. Cf., e.g., 11:20; Acts 8:12; 28:31; Wolter, "Reich Gottes."

who provides both for the giver and for the recipient. Such giving has the effect not of placing persons in debt, but rather of embracing the needy as members of one's own inner circle. In the economy intrinsic to the kingdom, those who give without exacting reciprocation, for example, in the form of loyalty or service, are actually repaid by God. Such giving, then, is translated into solidarity with the needy on earth and into heavenly treasure (see 6:35).[59]

5.4.3. Faithfulness within the Household of God (12:35-48)

35 *"Be dressed for action and have your lamps lit;* 36 *be like those who are waiting for their master to return from the wedding banquet, so that they may open the door for him as soon as he comes and knocks.* 37 *Blessed are those slaves whom the master finds alert when he comes; truly I tell you, he will fasten his belt and have them sit down to eat, and he will come and serve them.* 38 *If he comes during the middle of the night, or near dawn, and finds them so, blessed are those slaves.*

39 *"But know this: if the owner of the house had known at what hour the thief was coming, he would not have let his house be broken into.* 40 *You also must be ready, for the Son of Man is coming at an unexpected hour."*

41 *Peter said, "Lord, are you telling this parable for us or for everyone?"* 42 *And the Lord said, "Who then is the faithful and prudent manager whom his master will put in charge of his slaves, to give them their allowance of food at the proper time?* 43 *Blessed is that slave whom his master will find at work when he arrives.* 44 *Truly I tell you, he will put that one in charge of all his possessions.* 45 *But if that slave says to himself, 'My master is delayed in coming,' and if he begins to beat the other slaves, men and women, and to eat and drink and get drunk,* 46 *the master of that slave will come on a day when he does not expect him and at an hour that he does not know, and will cut him in pieces, and put him with the unfaithful.* 47 *That slave who knew what*

---

59. See Green, *Gospel of Luke,* 115-16. On almsgiving, see above on 11:41; also Moxnes, *Economy of the Kingdom,* 113-23; more generally, Garrison, *Redemptive Almsgiving.* Garrison's work is concerned with the rationale for the "doctrine of redemptive almsgiving" in the postapostolic church, so the relevance of his study for understanding Lukan economics is minimal. If taken seriously in Lukan scholarship, however, the direction of his work would be troubling, since he analyzes the *act* of almsgiving without reference to a larger understanding of the social economy in which such an act might have found meaning and, indeed, without reference more generally to an understanding of the practical character of social life. His readers may be alerted to his reductionistic tendencies when, in his introduction, Garrison writes, "Redemptive almsgiving as a doctrine functions for the theological benefit of the rich but for the material benefit of the poor" (10).

his master wanted, but did not prepare himself or do what was wanted, will receive a severe beating. 48 But the one who did not know and did what deserved a beating will receive a light beating. From everyone to whom much has been given, much will be required; and from the one to whom much has been entrusted, even more will be demanded.

Without pausing, Jesus continues the discourse begun in v 22, apparently, then, addressing his disciples. His opening words (v 35), cast in the imperative and calling for readiness, however, recall the analogous directive in v 15, addressed to both disciples and crowds. As though he were using a telephoto lens, Luke has centered our attention on the disciples, but the presence of many others continues to be felt. This contributes to the ambiguity Luke's readers may experience as they attempt to discern the nature of Jesus' audience at this juncture, and to which Peter gives voice in v 41: "Lord, are you telling this parable for us or for everyone?"[60] The importance of this narrative strategy on Luke's part is derived from the fact that the prohibition of an easy identification of Jesus' audience also keeps those in Luke's audience from potentially dismissing his message as irrelevant to them. Irrespective of which characters within the story readers have come to identify with, the collapsing of all characters into a single, "universal audience" raises the prospect of the significance of Jesus' teaching for everyone.

A narratological reading of this segment of Jesus' discourse also brings to the foreground the important reminder that in v 35 Jesus has not simply moved on from one topic to another. A narratological focus presses the question of thematic unity for the discourse as a whole. In fact, Jesus has not moved abruptly from a discourse on "possessions" to a discourse on "watchfulness." Not only this section but the whole of this address, beginning in v 1, has an eschatological timber, with such tones surfacing explicitly in vv 5 (Gehenna), 9 ("acknowledged before the angels of God"), and 33-34 (heavenly treasure). Throughout, Jesus has expounded on the *theme* of "vigilance in the face of eschatological crisis," including as *motifs* vigilance with respect to persecution (vv 1-12), possessions (vv 13-35), and, now, more generally, faithfulness within the household of God.[61] What is more, Jesus' words to his disciples — "Do not be afraid . . . for it is your Father's good pleasure to give you the kingdom" (v 32) — already applied to questions of security and material goods, are equally relevant to his present instruction on fidelity with respect to what "has been given" (v 48b).

---

60. See Botha, "Wandering Viewpoint," 260, 262; Wuellner, "Rhetorical Structure," 297-98.

61. This understanding of the relationship between "theme" and "motif" is borrowed from Prince, *Narrative as Theme,* 3-7.

The entirety of this section is set within the metaphorical field of the Roman household *(domus)* or family *(familia),* with particular emphasis on master/lord-slave relations. The move back and forth between direct and more parabolic instruction complicates how the function of these metaphors may be perceived, however. In particular, the problem of distinguishing between a metaphor's virtual properties and those properties actualized within this co-text is a pressing one.[62] For example, although the portrait of the returning master who serves his faithful servants does not depend on an identification of the "master/lord" with Jesus, (1) it does nonetheless articulate with the topsy-turvy world Jesus has otherwise addressed in his message, (2) this identification will be made by Jesus later in the narrative (22:26-27), and (3) in the current co-text Jesus is identified as "Lord" by both Peter (v 41) and the narrator (v 42). Again, the importance of constant vigilance does not require that one identify Jesus with the "thief" of v 39;[63] the point of the observation contained in v 39 competently serves to add a note of urgency to the admonition to readiness regarding the unexpected coming of the Son of Man without appeal to this form of allegory. A third example of the problem of determining the reach of Jesus' metaphorical arsenal lies in the importance he allots to the role of "steward" ("manager") in v 42; the identification of a person serving in this capacity suits its local co-text well, but it may take on added meaning when contrasted with the wealthy landowner/farmer of Jesus' earlier parable, who failed to recognize his role as a custodian of God's good gifts (v 20; see above). Though such ambiguity opens the door to a number of possible readings of this segment of Jesus' discourse, the basic issues with which Jesus is concerned remain clearly defined.

The examples on which Jesus draws throughout this portion of his address[64] are predominantly rooted in the lord/slave relationship, the presence of which was felt throughout the Empire. Both were viewed as members of a single household or family, that basic social unit through which

---

62. On these interpretive challenges, see, e.g., Eco, *Role of the Reader,* 18; *idem, Semiotics,* 123-24 (and, more broadly, 87-129).

63. Though such an identification is apparently assumed by van Staden, "Sociological Reading," e.g., 346.

64. van Aarde ("Narrative Point of View," 240-42) unnecessarily and inappropriately collapses all of these examples into one story: (1) The householder appoints slaves in his household, (2) he gives each of them orders, (3) he goes to a wedding and (4) is delayed, (5) some slaves stop working while others remain faithful, (6) the owner returns and serves the faithful, and so on. But the narrator has given us no reason, other than his drawing from the same metaphorical well throughout, to imagine that all of this material should be read as comprising episodes of a single story. Indeed, this view would require that we treat vv 39-41 as an unsightly intrusion into Jesus' narrative representation of this underlying "story" — a reality that speaks against this view.

wealth and status were transmitted, which in practice included the slave staff.[65] Though not deriving from any particular ethnic group or social class, slaves were of relatively low status within the household, with no distinction made between their work and their person; indeed, the head of the household (i.e., the "lord" or "master") and his slaves occupied opposite ends of the status continuum within the household. The number of slaves in a household and the degree to which they were assigned specialized roles were proportional to the honor associated with the household.[66] These cultural realities help to set the stage for our reading of Jesus' teaching, especially in vv 37, 42, and 44.

In presenting his picture of faithful response, Jesus borrows from standard images of the household in Roman times, but also redefines household relations. His most surprising — and no doubt to some, outlandish — innovation is his implicit request that, in order to identify oneself among the faithful in the household of God, one should identify oneself with the slaves of his example; this innovation embraces even the authority figure, the master/lord, whose actions upon his return are themselves servile. By serving those who are slaves, the returning lord esteems the humble, overturning socio-religious and socio-political norms, just as Mary's Song had foretold (1:52b).[67]

As a whole, this section of Jesus' speech presents the certainty but unpredictability of an awaited event as a motivation for constant alertness and fidelity. This awaited event is the eschatological coming of the Son of Man.[68] Luke's presentation leaves room for a delay in the return of the Lord, but his dominant emphasis falls elsewhere — first, on the *certainty* of his coming and, second, on the *uncertainty* of its timing.[69] This dual focus leads directly into the primary emphasis of this passage, not on living a life of abandonment

65. See Garnsey and Saller, *Roman Empire,* 126-28.

66. Thébert, "Slave," 139, 142-43.

67. This transformation of images is helpfully reviewed in van Tilborg, "Interpretation."

68. Tannehill (*Narrative Unity,* 1:249), following the seminal study of Dupont ("Individuelle Eschatologie"), acknowledges that the Lord's return is in view in this text, but argues that its meaning in the Lukan narrative is oriented toward the eschatology for the individual at each person's death. Evidence for Luke's interest in what happens at one's death is easy to find (e.g., 23:39-43; Acts 7:55-60), but this must not detract from Luke's ongoing and essential interest in the end-time intervention of God. This latter interest in a eschaton that embraces not only the individual but also the cosmos serves for Luke to underscore the need for present fidelity. As Carroll (*End of History,* 60-71) observes, ". . . the theory of 'individual eschatology' places the accent in the wrong place" (71).

69. On the motif of the uncertain timing of an awaited event, see esp. vv 35, *36,* 37, 38, *39, 40,* 43, *46,* and *47;* cf. Carroll, *End of History,* 53-55; Mattill, *Last Things,* 87. *Contra,* e.g., Conzelmann, *Luke,* 108, 232.

in light of the eschaton,[70] but on the present need and opportunity for alertness and fidelity. Structurally, this means that Jesus moves back and forth from an emphasis on the need for preparation/alertness (vv 35-38, 42-44) to an emphasis on the unpredictability of the master's return (vv 39-40, 45-48a). Within this outline, Peter's question in v 41 ensures that Luke's readers see themselves as implicated in Jesus' warnings, and v 48b generalizes the basis on which present fidelity and end-time judgment are correlated. Apart from such structural considerations, this segment of Jesus' discourse employs a wide range of images to present in positive and negative terms the sought-after comportment of the disciple: dressed for action, lamps lit, waiting expectantly, alert, ready, the unexpected hour, the faithful and prudent manager (rather than the unfaithful), working (rather than eating and drinking and getting drunk), being prepared, and knowing and doing (rather than knowing and not doing or not knowing).

35-38 Verse 35 functions as a kind of heading both for this subunit and for the larger segment of Jesus' address that spans vv 35-48. Here the motif of alertness is sounded through the use of two metaphors for readiness. The first — literally, "let your loins be girded" — borrows language from instruction to Israel regarding the Passover (Exod 12:11); they were to eat with "loins girded" — that is, with their long robes belted up in order to free the feet for action. This echo, together with common knowledge that the Passover meal was prepared sans any trace of leaven (e.g., Exod 12:8), suggests a further connection with Jesus' opening remarks in v 1. There he instructed his disciples to watch out for the "leaven of the Pharisees." As we have seen,[71] this "leaven" is manifest in the Pharisees' fundamental misunderstanding of God's purpose, their incapacity to discern the authentic meaning of the Scriptures and, therefore, their inability to present anything other than the impression of piety. Continuing to use the Pharisees as a foil against which to sketch the nature of genuine faithfulness to God, Luke now adds that the Pharisaic mind-set that must be avoided is represented in a lack of vigilance and preparedness for the redemptive coming of God.[72] The second metaphor is also one of readiness, but draws more deeply

---

70. *Contra* Mattill, *Last Things*, 87-88. Mattill thinks that, for Luke, Jesus teaches the imminence of the Lord's return and that this temporal nearness lies behind Jesus' counsel to live carefree with regard to what to eat and what to wear (vv 22-34). As we have indicated above, however, Jesus does not advise carefree living in light of the parousia, but faithfulness with regard to possessions in light of the provision of God.

71. See above on 12:1-3.

72. It is true that the expression "gird your loins" is used elsewhere to refer to a state of readiness — e.g., 2 Kgs 4:29; 9:1. What is intriguing here are the intertextual possibilities raised by these two reminiscences (absence of leaven and having loins girded) of the community's preparation for Passover. Botha ("Wandering Viewpoint," 258-59) notes this connection, but takes it in a different direction, suggesting that Luke has

on the imagery of light and darkness manifest in the Lukan narrative more pervasively.[73] Accordingly, disciples are to identify with "the dawn from on high . . . [who] will give light to those who sit in darkness" (1:78-79), ready for service in the conquest of darkness, the power of Satan (Acts 26:18). The sort of alertness Jesus counsels is not understood best as a set of activities but rather as a state of mind and heart. Disciples are to be the kind of people who are always on the alert.[74]

Having used two metaphors to communicate the necessity of readiness, Jesus continues by weaving together a short example story and pronouncements of blessing for those who maintain perpetual alertness. Jesus' story centers on a banquet scene that draws together three important elements from the wider Lukan perspective on meals. First, and most obvious in this co-text, the master provides a meal for the faithful, just as Jesus had promised in his portrait of the kingdom in vv 22-31. Whatever else the meal setting might serve, it is most obviously a place for eating[75] — no small matter in the context of the proclamation of good news for the marginalized (see above on 4:18-19) and in light of the perspective on life sanctioned by Jesus in vv 13-34. Second, working within the lines of an important stream of end-time thinking in Judaism as well as in Luke-Acts, Jesus situates his concern for vigilance within the eschatological framework of anticipation of the heavenly banquet.[76]

Third, as is the case elsewhere in Luke-Acts, so here the table provides the setting for Jesus' self-revelation.[77] In this case, a scene that otherwise reflects household norms — slaves awaiting the arrival of their lord — actually subverts the basis of the slave system. The master undergoes a status reversal, so that he engages in slavish activity on behalf of slaves. This means that the vigilant no longer have the status of slaves, though Jesus does not push so far as to portray them now as masters. Instead, he seems to posit in the place of common household conventions governed by a hyperconcern with status consciousness the household of God, characterized by blindness with

---

introduced an irony: "the Pharisees are the ones who are supposed to be very particular about preparedness, but now Jesus warns his audience against them." In the end, though, Botha agrees with the basic position adopted here: "beware of the Pharisee's leaven (be prepared) and again: gird your loins (be prepared)" (259).

73. See above on 11:33-36.

74. For the first metaphor, Luke uses the present imperative of εἰμί + the perfect passive participle of περιζώννυμι (see Marshall, 535). For the second, the present passive participle of καίω is used. Verse 36a ("be like those who are waiting . . .") also employs a present participle (of προσδέχομαι).

75. Cf. Moxnes, "Meals," 164-65; Nelson, *Leadership*, 68-69.

76. In Luke-Acts, see, e.g., 6:21; 13:29; 14:15; more broadly, e.g., Isa 25:6-8; 55:1-2; 65:13-14; Rev 19:9. See the brief survey in Nelson, *Leadership*, 56-59.

77. Cf., e.g., 5:31-32; 7:47-50; 9:10-17; 19:10; and esp. 22:19-20; 24:30-31.

respect to issues of status and the roles that attend them. Here, mutual service is the order of the day.[78] On the one hand, this surprising end to the story might be understood as nothing more (or less) than an embodiment of the message of Jesus as this has been proclaimed since the onset of his public ministry.[79] In addition, Jesus' parable can be read in a self-referential way, in which he presents himself as the lord who serves the faithful; in fact, this is exactly how Jesus speaks of himself to his disciples at their last meal together (22:24-27).[80] Either way, it is important to realize that Jesus' message goes beyond any attempt to establish the parameters of a new social order. Instead, Jesus provides for his audience a vision of the eschaton, of a household reality wherein hierarchies of status are nullified; with this vision he both declares the nature of the reward awaiting the faithful and alerts his audience to the nature of fidelity in the interim *and in the eschaton.*[81]

Jesus' story, and especially his reference to the watches of the night in v 38, opens the door to the possibility of delay in the master's return. More critical in Luke's view, though, is constancy during the duration of his absence. Hence, he records a redundancy in Jesus' pronouncement of the blessedness that accompanies alertness (vv 37, 38).[82]

39-40 Though the image of the household remains, the focus has changed. Now it is not the master[83] whose arrival one must anticipate, but the thief.[84] The focus similarly changes, though only slightly, to emphasize more one's inability to foresee the arrival of an event. No allegorical connections need be made in order to understand how Jesus appropriates the brief parable of v 39.[85] The coming of a thief is unpredictable; so is the coming of the Son of Man, whose arrival marks the eschatological denouement.

78. Cf. J. H. Elliott, "Temple Versus Household," 228.

79. On salvation as "status reversal" in Luke, see Green, *Gospel of Luke,* esp. 94-97; cf. York, *The Last Shall Be First.*

80. On the Jewish background of this motif, see Derrett, *New Resolutions,* 31.

81. See J. G. du Plessis, "Implicature," 316-17; Wuellner, "Rhetorical Structure," 301-2.

82. On Lukan beatitudes, see above on 6:20-26. Here, one may hear in the background of Jesus' pronouncements the blessings that follow obedience to Yahweh (cf. Deut 28:3-6; so Derrett, *New Resolutions,* 30).

83. οἰκοδεσπότης might refer to the manager of the household (cf. οἰκονόμος, v 42), but it is apparently used by Luke to denote the owner of the house (cf. 13:25; 14:21; 22:11); in either case, the person in view is whoever is responsible for the security of the house.

84. For this image in early Christian reflection on Jesus' return, see 1 Thess 5:2, 4; 2 Pet 3:10; Rev 3:3; 16:15.

85. Hence, e.g., the destructive aspects of burglary are not developed in this co-text. See above, the introduction to this segment of the discourse, where we called attention to the need to consider carefully how far the metaphorical language used in this discourse may be pushed.

41   Peter's question appears as an interruption in Jesus' address, but it serves a vital function. Central to the protocols that govern conversation is the "cooperative principle": people engaged in discourse, it is expected, will say something suitable at that point in the development of the discourse.[86] One may assume, then, that Peter's question serves a deliberate narrative function for Luke, drawing attention in an explicit way to an ambiguity in the identification of Jesus' audience at this point. It is apparent that Jesus has been addressing his disciples (vv 1, 4, 22) in the midst of the crowds (vv 1, 13); in typically Lukan fashion, such classifications have become blurred. Peter seems to want to work with a distinction between "us" (i.e., the disciples) and "everyone," but the narrator will allow no such contrast.[87]

Perhaps Peter will be as frustrated as the reader may be with Jesus' answer in vv 42-48, for no direct answer is forthcoming. Instead, Peter's question (1) draws attention to the universal relevance of Jesus' message regarding alertness — equally applicable to Pharisees and scribes, the masses, and the disciples; (2) heightens, however, the responsibility of the disciples as people to whom the divine will has been disclosed (see 10:21-24, and cf. the ensuing development of the motif of "knowing" in vv 47-48); and, thus, (3) at least potentially captures the reader in the web of self-reflection: Is this instruction for *us?*

This does not mean that Peter is portrayed as recoiling from Jesus' instruction. Indeed, he refers to Jesus as "Lord," signifying his recognition and acknowledgment of Jesus' status. In using this appellation, Peter also marks his recognition of Jesus as the "lord" (NRSV: "master") who returns to find alert servants and serves them.

42-48   The narrator echoes Peter's designation of Jesus as Lord in a purposeful redundancy, indicating that Jesus does indeed have this status. More importantly in this co-text, Luke thus signals that Peter has correctly intuited the viability of an identification of Jesus the Son of Man as the master/lord whose coming would be unpredictable but certain and whose future, pending return called for present vigilance.[88]

---

86. Fasold, *Sociolinguistics,* 129-33.

87. From a narratological point of view, efforts to find in Peter's question a Lukan emphasis on the applicability of Jesus' teaching more precisely to leaders of the (later) Christian community (e.g., Fleddermann, "Householder," 20; Koenig, *New Testament Hospitality,* 101; Tannehill, *Narrative Unity,* 1:250) falter on their lack of attention to how v 41 functions *within* its narrative setting and, more specifically, on Luke's portrayal of Jesus' audience for this discourse. See Carroll, *End of History,* 53, 55-58; Botha, "Wandering Viewpoint," 262-63; J. G. du Plessis, "Implicature," 319.

88. The NRSV translates κύριος as "master" in vv 35, 37, 42b, 43, 45, 46, and 47; as "Lord" in vv 41 and 42. The NRSV thus takes advantage of the semantic range of κύριος, but masks the potential link between Jesus' identification as Lord by Peter and the narrator on the one hand and as the delayed-but-returning lord in the parabolic material.

By way of addressing Peter's question, Jesus presents a further parable, again drawn from household conventions. In Roman antiquity, a steward might possibly be a free person or a slave; Jesus' story assumes the latter (see vv 43, 45-47). The prominence of slaves in this socially and economically important role is related to the juridical status of slaves. They were susceptible (in ways a free person was not) to all forms of interrogation, even torture, by the master, who was able to take justice into his own hands.[89] Within the socio-historical context of the Lukan narrative, then, the portrait of rewards and punishments presented in vv 46-48 carries the weight of realism. Managers were given a variety of responsibilities; the two that are immediately relevant in this co-text are the supervision of the master's household (including, e.g., management of the master's slave staff) and the administration of his business affairs. The larger, more estimable the estate, the greater the degree of differentiation of responsibilities and specialization of roles within the slave staff. As one who manages the affairs of another, the steward was chosen for precisely the characteristics Jesus enumerates, faithfulness and prudence (v 42), as well as such other qualities as zeal, competence, and industriousness.[90]

Against this background, it is immediately obvious that Jesus does not subvert the slave system as he had done in v 37. He instead uses it intact for illustrative purposes. Given Luke's usual predilection for bipolarity with regard to one's response to God (light or dark, blind or seeing, embracing or rejecting God's purpose, etc.), the elaboration of this parable is surprising in that it provides for three possible narrative resolutions. Narratives are characterized by their possessing beginnings, middles, and ends. In this case, all three begin in the same way. Each is predicated on the installation of a manager whose charge[91] is the daily provision of food for the slave staff of the household. This means that he is given a role of authority over the other slaves, but also that his charge is to provide for their daily needs. All three also presume the departure of the master from the household as well as the lack of any hint regarding the timing of his return. The tension of the narrative derives from the juxtaposition of these two facts at its beginning. How will the manager perform in the (possibly protracted) absence of the lord of the house? That is, what are the middle and end of the narrative thus begun?

The first possible narration resolves this tension by assuming fidelity in its middle and reward as its outcome. Hence, it is introduced by a pro-

---

89. Thébert, "Slave," 157.

90. See *TLNT,* 2:568-69.

91. θεραπεία is sometimes used in the LXX with reference to service — e.g., Gen 45:16; Esth 2:2; cf. GELS 1:204.

nouncement of blessing reminiscent of the beatitudes in vv 37 and 38. Vigilance in his charge over the slave staff is rewarded by even greater responsibility and, thus, standing in the community: he is made the agent of the master with respect to the disposition of his possessions. Given the immediate proximity of this outcome to Jesus' earlier remarks concerning possessions (vv 13-34), this cannot but mean that, again, he is charged with the weight of fidelity both to his master, who in fact owns everything that the steward manages, but also to those in need around them That is, to have charge of possessions in the Third Gospel is to have charge of their disposition on behalf of those in need.[92]

What is the nature of his fidelity? What does it mean to be found "at work"? This is not elaborated by Jesus, though its characterization is available to us in broad outline both in the lord's description of stewardship (v 42) and in the more detailed exposition of infidelity in v 45. In light of the emphases that begin to emerge, it seems hardly accidental that the whole of stewardship is represented by the metonym of providing food, for the divine provision of food was at issue in the preceding discourse segment. Fidelity must be measured, then, in the steward's embodiment of the beneficence of his master, in the steward's care for others on behalf of his lord (cf. 10:25-37).

The second plot takes a bad turn almost immediately. Throughout the narrative, self-talk (literally, "saying in [his] heart") is negatively construed, a practice characteristic of those who oppose the divine purpose.[93] In typical fashion, then, engaging in soliloquy, this steward finds in his lord's delayed return an opportunity for violence toward those under his charge and, with respect to his own desires, an opportunity for excess. Luke's audience may hear in the background Jesus castigating the Pharisees for their greed (11:39) or the words of the fool concerned to use his wealth and power to provision for himself a life of food, drink, and leisure (12:19) — the very qualities and concerns Jesus censures in vv 22-34.

The "middle" of this second narrative, then, does not resolve as much as it enhances the tension in the narrative. How will infidelity be punished? Verses 46-47 paint a horrifying picture. "Cutting in two" is known as a severe punishment.[94] Though in the present co-text its meaning is not likely to be taken in such a literal, physical way, this does not detract from its repulsiveness. The fate of the "cut" one is spelled out in terms of having a portion with the unfaithful (v 46), possibly in anticipation of the fate of Judas, who had a "portion in this ministry" but "turned aside" from it and so was cut

92. With regard to the disposition of possessions, see above, §11; also on 12:33.
93. See esp. 12:17-19; also 2:35; 5:21-22; 6:7-8; 7:39, 49; 9:46-47.
94. For example, 3 Apoc. Bar. 16:3: "dismember them with a sword."

off[95] from the twelve (Acts 1:17, 25). But if Jesus thus presages the fate of Judas, his words also concern those in Luke-Acts who reject God's salvation and turn aside from their heritage and divine charge as God's people.[96] Such persons are aware of the master's will but their knowledge is not translated into performance (v 47); they are like the legal expert of 10:25-37 — able to summarize the law of God accurately, but not actively involved in practices that grow out of their understanding.

The third "telling" of this narrative presumes but does not elaborate on infidelity. It also plays on the familiar distinction made between sins done knowingly and those committed in ignorance.[97] Because in this case the steward acted in ignorance, his punishment is less severe.[98]

These three "plots" and their outcomes underscore the constant presence of an authority figure who judges on the basis of fidelity in his absence. Even though the second narrative introduces the idea of "delay" (v 45), the importance of this motif is mitigated by our awareness that the steward cannot know if his lord has actually been detained since he is uninformed regarding the timing of his arrival (v 46). Again, then, the overall emphasis falls on the unpredictability and certainty of the return and, thus, on the importance of faithful behavior for the duration of one's stewardship.

These three possible resolutions of the one narrative beginning also highlight a concern for proportionality that surfaces explicitly in the axiom of v 48b. In this light, the fundamental question concerns the identification of what has been "given" or "entrusted" by God.[99] Three answers, none of which excludes the other, are possible in this co-text. (1) Most immediately, what is given must refer to knowledge of the master's will (vv 47a, 48a). This places a special onus on the disciples, for Luke has presented them as the recipients of enviable knowledge (10:21-24). (2) Equally clear in this co-text, what has been entrusted is the stewardship (v 42), with its demands for fidelity to one's lord and, thus, to those over whom care has been placed. In the world of Luke's Gospel, this places a special onus on the scribes (e.g., 11:45-52)

---

95. In light of the distinction between sins committed knowingly and those arising from ignorance, made in vv 47-48a, Lev 15:27-31 is of relevance. Persons guilty of knowing yet transgressing the will of God are to be "cut off" (LXX: ἐκτρίβω; "driven off") from the people of God.

96. Cf. the related remarks in Brawley, *Centering on God,* 180-81.

97. See, e.g., Num 15:27-31.

98. In fact, ignorance will play an important role in the missionary sermons in Acts; those who acted in ignorance in their rejection of Jesus may yet hear and receive the good news — cf. Luke 23:34; Acts 3:17; 13:27. More generally, cf. Acts 14:16; 17:30; 26:9.

99. That is, we take these verbs as divine passives.

and, in the subsequent narrative, first on the priests and elders of the people (e.g., 20:9-19), but also, in Acts, on the leaders of the Christian sect (cf. Acts 10:28). (3) Finally, Jesus' words in v 32 should not be forgotten. There, Jesus grounds his counsel against fear in his observation that the Father's good pleasure has been realized in his gift of the kingdom of God. In this sense, v 32 is programmatic in a sense that transcends its immediate application to the issue of possessions, for the kingdom speaks to all of life, present and future.

Is Jesus speaking to the disciples or to everyone (v 41)? Yes! And if the picture of accountability that ensues appears threatening, even gruesome, this is no grounds for fear. God has granted the kingdom to those willing to orient their hearts and lives around it. As a consequence, they are liberated and equipped for vigilance and fidelity.

5.4.4. Recognizing the Coming Crisis (12:49-59)

49 *"I came to bring fire to the earth, and how I wish it were already kindled!* 50 *I have a baptism with which to be baptized, and how it consumes me*[100] *until it is completed!* 51 *Do you think that I have come to bring peace to the earth? No, I tell you, but rather division!* 52 *From now on five in one household will be divided, three against two and two against three;* 53 *they will be divided:*

father against son
  and son against father,
mother against daughter
  and daughter against mother,
mother-in-law against her daughter-in-law
  and daughter-in-law against mother-in-law."

54 *He also said to the crowds, "When you see a cloud rising in the west, you immediately say, 'It is going to rain'; and so it happens.* 55 *And when you see the south wind blowing, you say, 'There will be scorching heat'; and it happens.* 56 *You hypocrites! You know how to interpret the appearance of earth and sky, but why do you not know how to interpret the present time?* 57 *"And why do you not judge for yourselves what is right?* 58 *Thus, when you go with your accuser before a magistrate, on the way make an effort to settle the case, or you may be dragged before the judge, and the judge hand you over to the officer, and the officer throw you in prison.* 59 *I tell you, you will never get out until you have paid the very last penny."*

---

100. NRSV: "what stress I am under."

Luke provides no markers to signal a shift in audience or topic with the onset of this segment of Jesus' lengthy discourse. Assuming coherence,[101] then, we should inquire into how this material advances the overarching theme of vigilance in the face of eschatological crisis. This is not a difficult task. The immediately preceding discourse section had drawn to a close with a primary focus on the basis of future judgment in present watchfulness and fidelity. From those images of future judgment, Jesus now turns to the reality of judgment already at work in his ministry. The division accompanying his mission is itself both integral to his purpose for coming (vv 49-53) and a portent of eschatological judgment (vv 54-59). Interestingly, the two subunits of the present discourse segment, together with their paired faces of judgment, are made to overlay each other by the metaphorical play between images of fire and blazing heat (vv 49, 55) and between images of immersion and cloudburst (vv 50, 54), set in inverse parallelism.

Wider connections can be discerned too. In particular, Jesus' teaching here is reminiscent of the sign-seeking of the crowds in 11:14-16, 29-36. Just as he did with the crowds in that earlier encounter, so here he argues that the necessary signs are already present, if only people would open their eyes to them.

Luke's notation in v 54, "He also said to the crowds," may be taken as a shift in audience. As will be recalled, however, for those wanting precision in the identity of those to whom Jesus is speaking the evidence is by now in shambles (see above on vv 35-48). Throughout this entire discourse Jesus has been surrounded by the band of his followers and by enormous crowds (see v 1), with the consequence that no easy distinction could be made between what instruction was peculiar to which group. In vv 41-48, however, distinctions are more thoroughly blurred as Jesus seems to lump everyone into a single, universal audience, as if to declare that his parabolic material is suitable for all. In the absence of any markers identifying more precisely in v 49 the nature of his audience, we must assume, then, that these words are intended for everyone too. Thus, v 54 does not so much introduce a new audience as (1) provide an explicit reminder of the presence of the larger cast of listeners and (2) pinpoint the crowds as persons for whom the material of vv 54-59 is particularly apt. As we shall see, however, even with regard to this material the distinction between crowds and disciples cannot be drawn precisely.

49-53 The preceding images of severity (vv 46-48) may seem surprising, coming as they do from one who earlier characterized his ministry as "good news to the poor" (4:18; 7:22). Jesus dismisses any notions of

---

101. One of the axioms of discourse theory is that hearers and readers attribute coherence and relevance to the text until they are forced not to — see Brown and Yule, *Discourse Analysis*, 66.

incompatibility, however, insisting instead that it was to inaugurate judgment that he had come. In order to establish this motif, he refers both to metaphors and a sign of destruction. The first is the metaphor of fire, in this co-text clearly the fire of judgment, portended in such passages as 3:9, 17; 9:54.[102] The image Jesus uses may recall the apparently quite different evaluation of his purpose in 2:14, where the angelic host announced not the casting of fire but the inauguration of peace "on the earth."[103] How these two images are to be correlated is an issue that Jesus seems to anticipate and will take up momentarily. The metaphor of "baptism" may also portend calamity and judgment;[104] this reading is rendered plausible especially in light of the parallel reference to a cloudburst in v 54, since sudden rain in the desert areas of Palestine could lead to perilous flash flooding.

For testimony that judgment has already begun, Jesus turns to the motif of division, highlighting its importance through repetition of the term.[105] Borrowing language from Mic 7:6, Jesus applies this image of the division of loyalties within families to the context of his ministry.[106] As his present discourse, begun in 12:1, has already made clear, a decision to adopt his canons of faithfulness to God would require a deeply rooted and pervasive transformation of how one understands God and how one understands the transformation of the world purposed by this God. This would involve Jesus' disciples in dispositions and forms of behavior that could only be regarded as deviant within their kin groups. Earlier Jesus had been concerned to prepare his disciples for the persecution before the authorities that would result from identification with his mission (vv 1-12); now he maintains that his ministry has as one of its consequences the deconstruction of conventional family bonds.[107]

This message potentially serves an important apologetic function in community definition. Within a culture wherein kinship ties played so crucial a socio-religious role, a message such as this one might well be suspect. How could a ministry the effects of which include the dissolution of family ties be sanctioned by God? Jesus posits just such divisions not only as a legitimate consequence of his mission but as confirmation that he is carrying out a divine charge.

Paralleling the notion of judgment in these verses is the significance of Jesus' remarks as a purposeful mission statement. This is evident, first,

---

102. See the discussion above, on 3:17. Cf. 17:29.
103. 12:49: πῦρ βαλεῖν ἐπὶ τὴν γῆν; 2:14: ἐπὶ γῆς εἰρήνη.
104. See 2 Sam 22:5; Pss 42:7; 69:1-2; Isa 43:2; 1QH 3:13-18. Cf. Marshall, 547.
105. διαμερίζω is used three times, once each in vv 51-53.
106. See *Jub.* 23:16, 19; Black, "Not Peace," 288.
107. Cf. 8:19-21; 9:57-62; 14:25-35; 18:28-30.

simply from his use of the phrase, "I came to. . . ."[108] The whole of v 50 —
with its three elements: baptism + being consumed + completion — should
be understood along these lines as well. That is, Jesus' reference to "baptism"
might serve less as a metaphor for judgment and more as a reference to this
event in his own life, since Luke presents Jesus' baptism, in part, as an episode
of commissioning.[109] It would be this divine mandate that consumes Jesus or
drives him forward.[110] Again, the choice of the verb, "to complete,"[111] conveys the idea that Jesus is concerned in this co-text to stress the divine nature
of his charge. Judgment, from this perspective, is not a surprising consequence
of his ministry and is not a contradiction of his mission; rather, it is integral
to it. He had come as God's representative to bring division, so the dissolution
of family bonds (which, in the Lukan narrative, has as its consequence the
formation of a new kinship group around Jesus) should be taken as confirmation that he is God's agent and that he is bringing to fruition the purpose
of God. Jesus' phrase "from now on" further locates the significance of the
division Jesus describes within the interpretive framework of his mission; it
is from this statement of his divine charge that division within families will
take its meaning.[112]

How can this be? Jesus' question, "Do you think I have come to bring
peace?" underscores Jesus' awareness that the presence of division and judgment will, for many, stand in stark contrast to what might have been expected
of the divine intervention. Indeed, it seems to stand in tension with the Lukan
representation of Jesus' own mission.[113] After all, the birth narratives had
moved into the foreground the hope for peace (1:79; 2:14), Jesus himself had
pronounced peace in the course of his redemptive activity (7:50; 8:48), and
he had taught his followers to do the same (10:5-6); moreover, later in the
narrative Peter will represent the content of the gospel as "peace" (Acts
10:36). How can this expression of Jesus' mission — judgment expressed
already in family division — be harmonized with the gospel of peace? Hints

---

108. See 4:43; 5:32; 19:10; cf. 4:18-19.

109. See above on 3:21-22.

110. συνέχω is used only 12 times in the NT, 9 of which are in Luke-Acts. Given
its relatively few appearances, it is surprising the degree to which the polysemy of the verb
is represented in Luke-Acts (see the discussion in *TLNT*, 3:337-41). Most translations of
v 50, including that found in the NRSV, take the verb as a metaphorical reference to Jesus'
duress, but the closest analogue to its usage in this co-text appears in Acts 18:5: Paul is
thoroughly engrossed in the proclamation of the word. With respect to v 50, Koester
("συνέχω," 884) suggests, "How I am totally governed by this."

111. τελέω.

112. For the phrase ἀπὸ τοῦ νῦν, a Lukan favorite, see 1:48; 5:10; 22:18, 69; Acts
18:6.

113. This point is made well by Tannehill, *Narrative Unity*, 1:251-52.

have already been given in the narrative. Thus, for example, Jesus' communication of peace to the sinful woman from the city is accompanied by disapproval from his table companions (7:36-50). As Luke has continually shown,[114] and as Jesus has endeavored to teach his followers, the realization of God's purpose will engender opposition from those who serve a contrary aim. Both Simeon and John had prophesied Jesus' role as one who would divide Israel (2:34-35; 3:17); major streams of Second Temple Jewish speculation held that the coming of the age of salvation would be accompanied by great distress;[115] and Jesus himself had emphasized the centrality of suffering and death in the consummation of God's purpose (cf. 9:21-22).

54-56 Explicit mention of the crowds recalls their presence throughout this discourse, but in this case it may also serve to recall for us Jesus' characterization of the crowds as sign-seekers (cf. 11:14-16, 29). In that earlier co-text he had castigated the crowds for their inability to recognize the signs already in front of them, and the purpose of his present words to them is not much different. The climatological phenomena he describes are indigenous to Palestine, where the west wind would bring moisture inland from the Mediterranean (cf. 1 Kgs 18:44-45) and the south wind would bring the heat from the Negev desert, "a furnace blast of desert air (common in late spring) that can raise the temperature thirty degrees in an hour."[116] Jesus castigates his audience for being able to read these signs, but unable to interpret the present time.

Key to his message is the label he gives the crowds, "hypocrites." The usage of this term here corroborates our earlier view that, in the world of Luke, "hypocrite" does not refer to someone who simply plays a role (see above on vv 1-3). Jesus plainly regards the crowds not as deceivers or phonies but as people who "do not know."[117] His question, then, is not why they say one thing and do another, but why they have joined the Pharisees (see v 1) in living lives that are not determined by God. Misdirected in their fundamental understanding of God's purpose, they are incapable of discerning the authentic meaning of the signs staring them in the face. What signs are these? Others have been noted previously (cf. 7:21-22; 11:20, 29-32); here, the sign requiring interpretation is the reality of family division — itself a manifestation of Jesus'

---

114. See Green, *Gospel of Luke,* 22-49; Kingsbury, *Conflict in Luke;* Tyson, "Conflict as a Literary Theme"; *idem, Death of Jesus,* esp. 49-62.

115. See the helpful survey in Allison, *End of the Ages,* 5-25.

116. Malina and Rohrbaugh, *Commentary,* 362.

117. Batey ("Jesus and the Theatre") assumes that "the Greek word ὑποκριτής denotes a stage actor" (563). He observes that the LXX does not use the lexeme in this way, but asserts that the septuagintal meaning "godless" is not important in the Synoptics (572n.3). He does not show how "stage actor" would make sense in this or any other Lukan co-text, however.

divine mission and a portent of coming judgment. "The present time" is thus to be read in apposition to Jesus' earlier phrase "from now on" (v 52).

It is worth mentioning that, though Jesus has specifically turned his attention to the crowds at this point, the disciples are not completely out of view. It is the crowds whose actions have evoked the appellation "hypocrites," but this does not insinuate that the disciples are immune from this contagion. Jesus had begun this discourse by admonishing the disciples to beware of the contaminant known as hypocrisy (v 1); the crowds heard this warning too, but have nonetheless been caught up in it. How the disciples will fare remains to be seen.

57-59 If the people were capable of interpreting the present time, where would this lead them? Jesus makes the transition from the analogies of vv 54-56 to this brief parable by substituting for the word "to interpret" the term "to judge," thus preparing for the presence of the "judge" in v 58. If they were able to judge for themselves the nature of Jesus' ministry, not least with respect to the judgment already present on account of his propagation of the divine purpose, they would act now in order to avoid eschatological judgment. In more conventional terms within the Lukan narrative, they would repent, orienting their hearts and lives around the redemptive aim of God.

Jesus' parable has a Roman provenance (note the presence of a court rather than an appeal to a respected teacher [cf. v 13]) and borrows from the debt system. In this case, rather than being indentured until the debt was paid off through slave-labor, the debtor is thrown into prison until the liability could be cleared, for example, through the sale of property. The severity of this course of action, and hence the urgency to act now, is accented by Jesus' reference to "the very last penny" — the coin with the lowest value in ancient Palestine.[118]

5.4.5. *Warning concerning Repentance and Fecundity (13:1-9)*

> 13:1 *At that very time there were some present who told him about the Galileans whose blood Pilate had mingled with their sacrifices.* 2 *He asked them, "Do you think that because these Galileans suffered in this way they were worse sinners than all other Galileans?* 3 *No, I tell you; but unless you repent, you will all perish as they did.* 4 *Or those eighteen who were killed when the tower of Siloam fell on them — do you think that they were worse offenders than all the others living in Jerusalem?* 5 *No, I tell you; but unless you repent, you will all perish just as they did."*

---

118. λεπτόν. A day's wage is usually considered to be one denarius (cf. Matt 20:1-16); 128 lepta ("pennies") would equal a denarius.

6 Then he told this parable: "A man had a fig tree planted in his vineyard; and he came looking for fruit on it and found none. 7 So he said to the gardener, 'See here! For three years I have come looking for fruit on this fig tree, and still I find none. Cut it down! Why should it be wasting the soil?' 8 He replied, 'Sir, let it alone for one more year, until I dig around it and put manure on it. 9 If it bears fruit next year, well and good; but if not, you can cut it down.' "

Although a report concerning Pilate's maltreatment of some Galileans may seem to alter the direction of Jesus' sermon, Luke ties this last interchange between Jesus and the crowds to the lengthy dialogue-and-discourse unit that had begun in 12:1. In fact, this last segment serves the larger oration as its climax; having heard Jesus address a number of topics relevant to the general theme of vigilance in the face of eschatological crisis, the people of Jesus' audience are now called upon to change their hearts and lives so that they might live fruitful lives and escape judgment.

It is possible to read the report of the demise of this group of Galileans as an attempt to test Jesus, to ascertain in a public way whether he has pro-Roman or pro-revolutionary sympathies.[119] Such an interpretation is not easy to support in this co-text, however, unless one could identify the "some who were present" (v 1) with the scribes and Pharisees who had earlier determined "to catch him in something he might say" (11:53-54) — an identification for which Luke provides no immediate support. It is easier to imagine that mention of these Galileans is a rhetorical device on the part of some, designed to shift Jesus' attention toward people whose appalling deaths obviously (obviously, i.e., according to widely held conventions that drew a direct line from iniquity to judgment) marked them as deserving the sort of judgment of which Jesus had been speaking (cf. 12:47-59). Jesus will not allow such comparisons, either of Galileans or of Jerusalemites. Instead, he insists, people who are able to interpret the present (12:56), with its signs of present and future judgment (12:49-59), would respond with repentance with the consequence that their lives would be characterized not by sterility but by fecundity. Jesus pushes his message even further, insisting that his auditors had thus far escaped a fate like that of these Galileans or of those Jerusalemites not because of their relative sinlessness or goodness but because of God's temporary clemency.

1-5   The narrator ties this report of disaster directly into Jesus' discourse with the temporal marker, "At that very time." This allows for no break in Jesus' address. Instead, as with the earlier intrusion of the man seeking Jesus' intervention in a family affair (12:13), so in this instance Jesus uses

119. See Bailey, *Through Peasant Eyes,* 74-80.

the interruption as a beachhead from which to launch further admonitions concerning the judgment of God.

The scenario presented to Jesus is of Pilate's execution of Jewish pilgrims from Galilee, cut down while in the act of offering sacrifices.[120] Otherwise unattested, the event thus reported is nonetheless consistent with what is more generally known of Pilate according to Jewish sources.[121] The form of Jesus' reply (vv 2-3) is repeated in vv 4b-5, and both are similar to his query in 12:51. On the analogy of 12:51, then, Jesus' reply here is cast as a correction to a misunderstanding alleged on the part of his audience.

Behind this report Jesus reads an attempt at self-justification rooted in the common notion that disaster befalls those who deserve it.[122] Jesus is right to presage judgment, his interlocutors will allow, but judgment is reserved for those whose sin sets them apart from "us." It is true that Deuteronomy 28–30 (to name only one example) insists that judgment will overtake those whose lives are characterized by disobedience, but this is not the same thing as arguing that disasters come only to those who are disobedient. In fact, Jesus' reply does not deny sin its consequences, nor that sin leads to judgment; instead, he rejects the theory that those who encounter calamity have necessarily been marked by God as more deserving of judgment than those who do not. The progression of his argument, then, is that judgment will overtake people, whether Galilean or Jerusalemite or of some other origin, unless they repent. The universality of judgment, apart from repentance, is emphasized by the fourfold use of "all" in vv 2, 3, 4, and 5.

As well suited as this message is to its co-text, it is still worth asking why the reference to "Galileans" is explicitly repeated three times in a co-text where the representative Roman authority, Pilate (cf. 3:1), and disaster in Jerusalem are both in view. Jesus is himself a Galilean, after all, and he is presently on pilgrimage to Jerusalem. As an undercurrent, we must recognize in this interaction between Jesus and the crowds the portrait of Jerusalem as an ominous place. Jesus himself had foretold his demise at the hands of the leadership in Jerusalem (9:21-22) — the very city toward which he and his followers are now heading.[123] Upon his execution under Pilate, no doubt it will be tempting to dismiss Jesus as one deserving of God's judgment; as he has noted beforehand, however, disaster and God's judgment are not synony-

120. See the discussion in Derrett, *New Resolutions,* 102. The sacrifice of the Passover lamb is the only sacrifice in which nonpriests generally participated fully.

121. See, e.g., Josephus *J.W.* 2.9.4 §§175-77; *Ant.* 18.3.2 §60-62; cf. Smallwood, *Jews,* 160-74.

122. Jesus' terminology is reminiscent of 11:4, where he had juxtaposed "sin" and "indebtedness"; here he uses "sinner" (ἁμαρτωλός) and "the one liable [for sin]" (ὀφειλέτης).

123. Cf. Freyne, *Galilee,* 92, 110; Cassidy, *Jesus, Politics, and Society,* 41.

514

mous and, in particular, those who encounter tragedy are not necessarily those whose wickedness had qualified them for it.

6-9 For those eager to regard others as more deserving of God's judgment than themselves, Jesus continues by insisting that the unrepentant have escaped judgment not because of their relative sanctity but because of God's mercy. In fact, comparison of Jesus' parable of the unfruitful tree with its parallel in the Syriac version of *Ahiqar* (8:35) shows what a novelty the motif of clemency would have been. Nothing else about Jesus' parable seems out of the ordinary. The presence of a fig tree in a vineyard is not unknown,[124] and there is no hint in the parable that the owner of the vineyard expected fruit from the tree out of season or before it was sufficiently mature to produce fruit. The details of the parable, then, are oriented toward highlighting the sterility of the tree and point dramatically to the lenience allotted the tree in order to give it additional nutrients and time for fruit-bearing. Not incidentally, the parable also holds for the possibility of fruit-bearing in spite of a history of sterility — or, in human terms, the possibility of change leading to faith expressed in obedience to God's purpose. If it announces a warning of judgment, then, it also dramatizes hope.

The importance of fruit-bearing has been emphasized repeatedly in the Third Gospel. Especially significant is its development in the message of John (3:7-9), where repentance manifests itself in behavior ("fruit") appropriate to repentance, and where those trees that do not bear good fruit are "cut down," just as is anticipated here.[125] In the Sermon on the Plain Jesus similarly notes the import of bearing good fruit (6:43-45), but this element is especially well developed in his parabolic teaching on sowing (8:4-15). There, "authentic hearing" of the word of God is demonstrated in "bearing fruit."[126]

Hence, this accent on fruit-bearing goes hand-in-hand with the emphasis on repentance in vv 3 and 5; both signify expected responses from Jesus' audience to the manifestation of God's purpose in his mission. The two parts of this final portion of Jesus' discourse are coordinated in a further way. The execution of the Galileans was presumably unforeseen, certainly disastrous; similarly, the tower of Siloam fell on those eighteen persons without warning.

---

124. See Pliny *Nat. Hist.* 17.35; Mic 4:4; Zech 3:10.

125. The linguistic parallels between these two texts are important — esp. ποιέω + καρπός + ἐκκόπτω.

126. Does the narrator hope that his audience will hear Isa 5:1-7 in the background of this parable? If so, an identification of Israel with the vineyard is likely, with the further identification of the fig tree as Israel's barren leadership also conceivable. The parable is effective as a foundation for the call to respond with repentance without reading it in this way. In fact, inasmuch as Jesus' audience remains "the crowds," a more general call to orienting one's heart and life around God's purpose is the most obvious way to hear this text.

In the same way, the parable of the fig tree ends on a note of clemency counterbalanced by the ongoing threat of imminent judgment. God may have acted in mercy in holding back destruction for the moment, but this stay of judgment is temporary. Grounded thus is Jesus' final note of urgency: Now is the time to repent and to live fruitful lives.

5.5. WHO WILL PARTICIPATE IN THE KINGDOM? (13:10–17:10)

Luke's method throughout this extended section is subtle but deliberate. He continues to indicate Jesus' fundamental involvement in the formation of disciples, but in most cases this interest is carried out in an indirect fashion. The disciples, after all, appear explicitly only rarely in this section (16:1; 17:1, 5), and Jesus' primary interaction is with Pharisees. The heightened presence of Pharisees — and, to a much lesser degree, the presence of a synagogue leader, crowds, and scribes — pushes forward the motif of conflict within which programmatic questions and assertions can be foregrounded. These include

"Lord, will only a few be saved?" (13:23);
"Blessed is anyone who will eat bread in the kingdom of God!" (14:15);

and a host of others that continue the Lukan emphasis on division by making more and more central the issue of what qualifies a person for fellowship in the community of God's people (see also, e.g., 14:24, 25-27; 16:9, 27-31). Questions of boundary-making and community definition are very much at home at meals, so it is of particular interest that much of Jesus' instruction throughout this narrative section is set within or centers around occasions for table fellowship, celebration with a shared meal, and the extension of hospitality.

As his readers will have come to expect, Luke outlines qualifications for participation in the kingdom (1) without allowing any dichotomy between one's dispositions and behaviors and (2) by demonstrating how novel Jesus' message must seem. This latter point is highlighted by such topsy-turvy sayings as "those who are last will be first, and those who are first will be last" (13:30) and "all who exalt themselves will be humbled, and those who humble themselves will be exalted" (14:11; cf. 14:24), as well as by Jesus' presentation of characters within parables who, according to conventional wisdom, should attract respect and yet, within those parables, are casualties of a reversal of values and fortune (see the "elder son" of 15:25-32 and the wealthy man of 16:19-31). The former emphasis is found in Jesus' ongoing interest in addressing issues of one's fundamental commitments and inclinations alongside the perceptions and practices they generate.[1]

If Jesus is concerned with the formation of disciples on his journey from Galilee to Jerusalem,[2] why are the disciples not more present in this narrative section? Several responses are possible. First, it is important to remember that Jesus continues to invite followers and, as this narrative segment demonstrates, those followers might include Pharisees. In spite of testimony to the conflict between Jesus and the Pharisees (cf. 14:1; 15:1-2; 16:14), some Pharisees show their care for Jesus by warning him of an attempt on his life (13:31), and Jesus indicates his hope for the Pharisees by continuing to share his message with them (esp. chs. 14–16). Perhaps of greatest importance, Jesus' parables in 15:3-32 and 16:19-31 are open-ended; we do not know whether the elder brother (read: the Pharisees and scribes, 15:1-2) will join in the celebration that follows the finding of the lost, nor whether the five brothers who survive the one wealthy man will actually hear Moses and the prophets (15:27-31). Clearly, the door of discipleship remains open, even to Pharisees. Second, throughout this section Luke continues to make use of a narrative technique that draws particular attention to the presence of various characters for dramatic effect without necessarily excluding others. When Jesus teaches the disciples in 16:1-13, we discover that the Pharisees have been listening as well (16:14). When Jesus replies to the Pharisees in 16:15-31, are we to assume that the disciples are no longer present? The fact that in 17:1 Jesus returns to the disciples suggests a negative response to this question. Throughout much of this section, Jesus is drafting the character of discipleship by showing what it is not as much as by asserting what it is — using, then, a rhetorical strategy much at home in such a conflicted setting. Third, if we may imagine that the disciples are present within this narrative section largely as eavesdroppers, we should also account for the capacity of Luke's audience to engage with and internalize the message of Jesus throughout this section. The formation of disciples happens in front of the text too, not only within it, and Luke's depiction of Jesus in contentious discussion with those who are critical of him serves well to present Jesus' message along lines that are consequently more sharply honed.

At the same time, no quarter is given for those who might adopt an attitude of superiority vis-à-vis the Pharisees or the scribes or the synagogue ruler (or anyone else) because of a greater sense of one's perceived obedience to Jesus' message. Fidelity is no basis for demanding greater honor or elevated status (17:7-10); after all, fidelity is manifest, in part, in a lack of concern for issues of honor and status (cf. 14:1-24).

1. See above on 6:17-49.
2. For reminders of the journey motif, cf. 13:22, 31-35.

5.5.1. The Unsettling Presence of the Kingdom (13:10-21)

10 *Now he was teaching in one of the synagogues on the sabbath.*
11 *And just then there appeared a woman with a spirit that had crippled
her for eighteen years. She was bent over and was quite unable to stand
up straight.* 12 *When Jesus saw her, he called her over and said, "Woman,
you are set free from your ailment."* 13 *When he laid his hands on her,
immediately she stood up straight and began praising God.* 14 *But the
leader of the synagogue, indignant because Jesus had cured on the
sabbath, kept saying to the crowd, "There are six days on which work
ought to be done; come on those days and be cured, and not on the
sabbath day."* 15 *But the Lord answered him and said, "You hypocrites!
Does not each of you on the sabbath untie his ox or his donkey from the
manger, and lead it away to give it water?* 16 *And ought not this woman,
a daughter of Abraham whom Satan bound for eighteen long years, be
set free from this bondage on the sabbath day?"* 17 *When he said this, all
his opponents were put to shame; and the entire crowd was rejoicing at
all the wonderful things that he was doing.*

18 *He said therefore, "What is the kingdom of God like? And to
what should I compare it?* 19 *It is like a mustard seed that someone
took and sowed in the garden; it grew and became a tree, and the birds
of the air made nests in its branches."* 20 *And again he said, "To what
should I compare the kingdom of God?* 21 *It is like yeast that a woman
took and mixed in with three measures of flour until all of it was
leavened."*

The association of Luke's account of Jesus healing the bent-over woman and
Jesus' parabolic teaching on the kingdom is marked by the conjunction,
"therefore," in v 18. This insinuates that the parables follow the healing
account in order to spell out its consequences or, better, in order to legitimate
Jesus' action in the synagogue as kingdom activity. The topographical shift
in v 22 indicates that these kingdom parables relate to Jesus' ministry in the
synagogue.

With this episode, Luke marks the first change of setting since 11:53
and, so, the close of Jesus' address on vigilance in the face of eschatological
crisis (12:1–13:9). As it turns out, this setting — temporally on the Sabbath
(noted five times!), spatially in a synagogue (noted twice) — becomes crucial
to the significance of this pericope. Reentry into the synagogue is surprising;
Jesus has not been associated with Jewish synagogues since the onset of the
journey to Jerusalem in 9:51, nor will we find him again in a synagogue.
Moreover, in 12:11 (cf. 21:12) he had identified the synagogue as a place of
prospective persecution for his followers. Why does Jesus move back into the
synagogue? What response will he receive?

Within the Lukan narrative, this return to the architectural space of a synagogue evokes the Galilean ministry of Jesus (e.g., 4:14-15, 43-44) and especially Jesus' inaugural address at the Nazareth synagogue (4:16-30). As will become clear, such reminiscences as these are actually supported by Luke's account, which brings to the fore not only the linguistic combination of synagogue + Sabbath + Jesus' teaching, but also the highly significant portrayal of Jesus' ministry as one of "release."[3] What Luke records here is nothing other than ". . . a marked fulfillment of the programme of the ministry as announced in the synagogue at Nazareth (iv.18)."[4]

Just as 4:18-19 (4:16-30) sets the agenda for the Galilean ministry of Jesus and, indeed, for the whole of Luke-Acts, so in a more restricted sense 13:10-21 is programmatic for the narrative section that encompasses 13:10–17:10. This way of construing the importance of this episode within its larger co-text is dependent on our recognizing in Luke's scene a single, integrated account whose focal point is not the controversy between the ruler of the synagogue and Jesus (i.e., vv 14-16) but Jesus' encounter with this woman and his ensuing interpretation of her liberation as a necessary manifestation of the divine will, an outworking of the presence of the kingdom, on this day, the Sabbath.[5] That is, the intrusion of the indignant synagogue ruler into Jesus' encounter with the woman bent over (v 14) provides Jesus the opportunity to interpret that healing as a fulfillment of God's purpose and, thus, of Jesus' mission (vv 15-21).

In at least three additional ways, this episode signals key emphases that will be developed in the narrative section that follows. First, it is

---

3. See the language of binding and loosing in vv 12 (ἀπολέλυσαι), 15-16 (λύει, ἔδησεν, λυθῆναι ἀπὸ τοῦ δεσμοῦ). Büchsel ("δέω [λύω]," 60n.3) notes that δέω + λύω are commonly used with regard to the power exercised over someone by a sorcerer, god, or spirit.

4. Plummer, 343; cf. Green, "Daughter of Abraham"; Tannehill, *Narrative Unity,* 1:65, 83.

5. For arguments to this effect, see Green, "Daughter of Abraham," 644-49; cf. Theissen, *Miracle Stories,* 114. Against Green, O'Toole (Exegetical Reflections") denies the literary integrity of this pericope, identifying it as "a controversy dialogue occasioned by a healing" (89). O'Toole seems not to realize that this formal identification contradicts his otherwise very helpful insistence that Luke presents this episode as an actualization of the kingdom of God of great profundity for the Third Evangelist (a point also made by Kee, *Miracle,* 204). His analysis thus plays into the argument he had hoped to counter — namely, the insistence of Schüssler Fiorenza (*But She Said,* 196-217) that Luke has allowed an account of the healing of a woman to be eclipsed by a male-centered conflict over who possesses the religious authority to interpret "a male-centered sacred text" (208). Schüssler Fiorenza (253n.36) works with a form-critical valuation of the episode that is kin to O'Toole's, stating that I concede in my essay that one can distinguish two "forms" of the story — a concession for which my essay explicitly does not allow.

significant that Luke presents this bent-over woman without reference to any credentials she might possess, as though in some sense she *deserved* having Jesus single her out for redemptive intervention. Quite the contrary, this woman is painted in lowly dress indeed, rendering all the more significant Jesus' recognition of her as "daughter of Abraham." This portends the extremely negative valuation Jesus will place on concerns rooted in the honor-shame system of Luke's world. Closely related, Luke thus contrasts the sometimes apparently paltry and obscure activity of the kingdom with the ostentation of public religion represented by this synagogue ruler in this synagogue on this Sabbath.[6] Second, Luke introduces Jesus as "Lord," then presents him as one with authority to interpret God's salvific purpose. Directly or indirectly, both synagogue ruler and Jesus appeal to the Scriptures, but Jesus is represented as the divinely sanctioned hermeneut. There are, then, christological implications in this account on which the subsequent narrative will continue to build as Jesus finds himself in an ongoing exchange especially with Pharisees. Third, given the character of these other motifs, it is not surprising that this scene presages the continued hostility the achievement of Jesus' mission will attract.

10-11 Luke sets the scene in two ways. First, he describes Jesus as teaching in a synagogue on the Sabbath. The importance of the scenario Luke pictures is highlighted by the fact that this is the first mention of Jesus in the synagogue since the onset of the journey to Jerusalem in 9:51. Thus, even though the content of his teaching is not given, the frame is familiar to us from the Galilean ministry of Jesus. There, when teaching in a synagogue on

---

6. Schüssler Fiorenza (*But She Said,* 210) argues against a perspective such as this one, referring to such an interpretation as anti-Jewish. In the current environment of theological study in the West, she thus holds the moral high ground for her own position, but she can do so only by introducing into the discussion a debilitating anachronism. After all, within the Lukan world, Jesus is presented very much as a Jew (and the Christian movement is represented as existing within the broad boundaries of Judaism). What is more, if he takes a critical stance vis-à-vis the Jewish interpretation of the Sabbath represented in this pericope, he would hardly be the first prophetic figure to raise his voice, from within Israel, against Israel. If this is "anti-Judaism," then all efforts at reform from within Judaism, recounted already within the OT itself and continuing to the present day, must likewise be labeled. In a different but relevant context, Sahlins (*How Natives Think,* 119) speaks of the paradox of defending another culture's ". . . mode of existence by endowing it with the highest cultural values of Western societies." Of course, Schüssler Fiorenza might rather draw attention to how Luke and/or his community might thus be using Jesus and/or the Jesus-tradition to slander Jewish interpretation and/or institutions that have become their enemies. Such a view would not be novel (see esp. J. T. Sanders, *Jews*), but it is not consistent with a reading of Luke-Acts *as narrative,* nor, in our reading, does it represent a defensible interpretation of all the evidence of Luke-Acts — see the brief but programmatic remarks in Green, *Gospel of Luke,* 68-75.

the Sabbath, Jesus proclaimed "good news to the poor," "the good news of the kingdom of God" (see above on 4:18-19, 43-44).[7] Recalling that well-established script, we may assume that Luke has chosen at this fresh point of departure in the narrative to remind us of the central concerns of Jesus' ministry and, thus, to present Jesus engaged in the characteristic activity by means of which he fulfills his divine mission.

The scene is further established by the presence of an unhealthy woman in the synagogue.[8] From a biomedical perspective,[9] this bent-over woman is thought by some to have protracted *spondylitis ankylopoietica,* though *hysteria* has also been suggested. Luke, however, is not really interested in a biomedical diagnosis. He attributes her condition, instead, to a "spirit." In doing so, he uses language that might be taken more generally as "a condition of weakness,"[10] but in light of Jesus' remarks in vv 12 and 16 it is more appropriate to regard Luke's description of her crippled state as grounded in satanic bondage. This does not necessarily mean that Luke regards her as demon-possessed, but it does underscore his more general perspective on the insep-arability of physical malady and diabolic influence and, thus, on the insepa-rability of healing and liberation.[11] From this ethnomedical perspective, then, this woman's illness has a physiological expression but is rooted in a cosmo-logical disorder.[12] Because Luke has presented Jesus as the divine agent of salvation in whose ministry the kingdom of God is made present and in whose ministry the domain of Satan is rolled back, Luke's depiction of this woman's illness prepares us for a redemptive encounter of startling proportions. First, though, a further aspect of this woman's illness is worth mentioning. Crippled

7. With regard to synagogue practices and Jesus' credentials for teaching in the synagogue, see above on 4:16-30.

8. Earlier discussion often assumed that this woman was out of place — either because she did not belong in the synagogue at all (see Schweizer, 222) or because she should be out of sight in the "gallery for women" (e.g., Wilkinson, *Health and Healing,* 70). Data concerning the segregation of women in the synagogue are much too late to be taken seriously with respect to practices in the first century, however, and a phalanx of (largely circumstantial) evidence contests such a view — cf. Safrai, "Place of Women"; Brooten, *Women Leaders,* esp. 103-41.

9. See the summary of suggested diagnoses in Wilkinson, *Health and Healing,* 71-75.

10. πνεῦμα . . . ἀσθενείας. Note that Jesus proclaims that she is "set free" (ἀπολέλυσαι) from her "illness" (τῆς ἀσθενείας) in v 12; this language urges the view that this woman is in some sense demonized and needs liberation.

11. See Acts 10:38; cf., e.g., Hamm, "Freeing of the Bent Woman," 32-33; Page, *Powers of Evil,* 119; and, more generally, Busse, *Wunder,* 79.

12. From this perspective, then, most of Luke's accounts of "illness" could more accurately be termed "disorder accounts." See the helpful discussion in Hahn, *Sickness and Healing,* e.g., 27-28.

for eighteen years,[13] she may well have come to regard as ordinary experience the social ostracism meted out to her in the village where she lived. In fact, the verb Luke uses to describe her symptom, "bent over," portrays her physical appearance and serves as a metaphor for her ignominious social position.[14] From this point of view, the otherwise unremarkable words, "there appeared a woman . . . Jesus saw her" (vv 11-12), become significant indeed, for they portend the materialization of a person otherwise socially invisible.

12-13 Luke's account of healing, or liberation, is cast in language that parallels each point of his account of illness: she is set free from her illness,[15] released from diabolic activity at the root of her illness, and is now able to do what she could not do before — namely, stand up straight. As in previous scenes of healing, the act of touching and the pronouncement of healing appear in tandem (5:13; 8:54; cf. 4:40). The language of Jesus' pronouncement acknowledges the cause of her ailment as an agent of subjugation, something from which she needed to be released. This is harmonious with Luke's overall characterization of Jesus' ministry as "healing all who were under the power of the devil" (Acts 10:48), and more particularly comports well with Jesus' portrayal of his divine mission as one of setting people free (see above on 4:18-19). That he does so through God's power is evident both from the nature of his pronouncement — "you are set free [by God]" — and by her reaction of praise, in recognition that in Jesus' ministry God is at work (see 5:26). Her other (i.e., her first) response, standing up straight, testifies to the effectiveness of Jesus' ministry on her behalf.[16]

Also of importance is the deixis of this episode. Luke positions Jesus at the center of attention, not only for Luke's audience but also and more importantly, by naming Jesus as the teacher, for the people gathered in the synagogue. When Jesus sees her, he does not go to her but calls her to him, thus inviting her to join him in front of those gathered and so to join him at

---

13. The appearance of the number "eighteen" in vv 4 and 11 certainly invites speculation. Does this repetition suggest that the woman's condition was no more a consequence of her greater sinfulness than those who suffered tragedy in Jerusalem? Or is "eighteen" simply a convenient, conventional number (see Derrett, "Two Lucan Miracles," 274, 284n.14; Nolland, 2:724). Luke's decision to report this detail highlights the gravity of her decision and the significance of her being healed.

14. συγκύπτω is used to designate a position of humility in Sir 12:11.

15. The NRSV renders ἀσθενεία in v 11 as "crippled," but in v 12 as "ailment."

16. Some interpreters see her standing up straight as having a further, symbolic importance. Noting that people are to "straighten up" in anticipation of redemption (21:28: ἀνακύπτω), and in view of other eschatological allusions he finds in 13:10-17, Hamm ("Freeing of the Bent Woman," 33; cf. O'Toole, "Exegetical Reflections," 100) thinks that this woman is being empowered to assume "the eschatological posture." Such echoes seem too weak to be heard (or for one to expect them to be heard) by many, however.

the focal point of this scene. Locating this woman of such low status thus is not unrelated to the healing moment, but is directly relevant as a symbolization of her restoration within her community.

14 The role of the synagogue ruler was to maintain the reading and faithful teaching of the law;[17] here, the leader fulfills this role in a way that is reminiscent of the scribes and Pharisees who appear earlier in the Lukan narrative in order to monitor Jesus' behavior and ensure proper legal observance.[18] Jesus' infraction is highlighted by its repetition — mentioned first by the narrator as the cause of the leader's indignation, then in an indirect indictment of Jesus by the leader of the synagogue himself. Interestingly, the leader takes his case directly to the people, addressing them, not Jesus, with his concern. In this way he publicly challenges Jesus' authority as a teacher and reasserts himself as the authorized interpreter of Scripture.

Sabbath observance increased in importance during the period of the Second Temple as a central means by which to nourish Jewish identity.[19] The role of Sabbath observance for the maintenance of Jewish identity and as an emblem of group solidarity is evident here, since the synagogue ruler does not so much argue for a particular interpretation of Deut 5:13 (cf. Exod 20:9) as assert what, he believes, everyone of genuine faith will affirm. That is, his pronouncement contains within it the implicature that the legitimacy of his interpretation is a given. He does not even cite the relevant texts, but grounds his view in what "ought to be done" — that is, in the divine will.[20] In the present case, although perhaps no one will deny the tragedy of this woman's disorder, hers is hardly a life-threatening condition; after all, she has been thus crippled for eighteen years. Her treatment could thus wait until tomorrow, so, according to scribal reckoning, her need did not supersede Sabbath law.[21]

15-16 Jesus' authority is reestablished immediately, at least for Luke's audience, by the narrator's reference to Jesus as "Lord." Jesus' status as authoritative teacher had been rejected by the ruler of the synagogue, who based his case on the self-evident will of God; but now Jesus will counter what seemed self-evident, and, for Luke's audience, he will do so in his capacity as the divinely sanctioned hermeneut.

In one sense, Jesus begins with the question of legal interpretation.

---

17. See above on 8:41.

18. Cf. 5:17-26.

19. See above on 6:1-11.

20. In Lukan parlance, this is evident from the use of δεῖ, often used in the Lukan narrative as shorthand for what is necessary according to the divine purpose. More broadly, Douglas (*Institutions*) notes how institutions "endow themselves with rightness and send their mutual corroboration cascading through all levels of our information system" (92) and "secure the social edifice by sacralizing the principles of justice" (112).

21. See above on 6:6-7.

Because the ruler of the synagogue had alluded to Deut 5:13, Jesus returns to that deuteronomic co-text in order to remind his debate partner that the prohibition to work extends not only to human beings but also to oxen and donkeys (Deut 5:14). If this is so, why then are people allowed to untie their animals, and why are these animals allowed to walk to the trough for water? (It is not because the need is life-threatening!)

In a deeper sense, though, Jesus seems content to engage the argument just as the synagogue ruler had left it, with reference to the divine will. What "ought"[22] to take place, he insists, is this: This woman ought to be set free from satanic bondage on the Sabbath. How does he reach such an ostentatious conclusion? Most obviously, he sets up a series of parallels, arguing from the lesser to the greater:

> If an animal, how much more a daughter of Abraham?
>
> If one whom you have bound for a few hours, how much more one whom Satan has bound for eighteen years?
>
> If you can loose the bonds of an animal on the Sabbath as well as the other six days of the week, how much more is it necessary for God to loose this woman's bond on the Sabbath?

From this exegesis of the deuteronomic law and contemporary practices based on it, Jesus is able to expose the ruler of the synagogue and those who think as he does[23] as "hypocrites" — that is, as persons who do not understand God's purpose, who therefore are unable to discern accurately the meaning of the Scriptures, and, therefore, whose piety is a sham.[24]

More significantly, Jesus roots his presentation of God's purpose in the character of his mission. We have already drawn attention to how this scene is tied into Jesus' announcement of his mission in 4:16-30. Now it becomes significant that Jesus declared to his audience at Nazareth that the prophecy of Isaiah was coming to fulfillment "today," in their hearing, on the Sabbath.[25] The synagogue leader's view led him to function as a barrier to the healing of this

---

22. Again, using δεῖ.

23. That is, the "you" in the exclamation, "You hypocrites!" is not a general reference to the audience in the synagogue. Jesus has "opponents," including the synagogue ruler, in this crowd, but not everyone present sides against Jesus — see v 17.

24. See above on 12:1. See also Derrett, "Two Lucan Miracles," 283.

25. M. D. Carroll ("Isaías 58:6 en Lucas 4:18") argues that the purpose of the citation of Isa 58:6 in 4:19 was to emphasize the celebration of Sabbath: "On a sabbath day, Jesus takes a passage that refers to the sabbath in order to describe what he will do and announce in his ministry" as Lord of the Sabbath (73; trans. D. W. Gabbard). Although Carroll's thesis is overdrawn, both in its caricature of ancient Judaism and in its denial of the Jubilee associations of the Isaianic material, his is nevertheless a helpful perspective.

woman, and, thus, to represent the synagogue and Sabbath as entities segregating this needy woman from divine help. Jesus' view led him to regard today, this day, even a Sabbath day, as the right time for the redemptive purpose of God to be realized. In the end, then, the fundamental issue at work in this scene is the divine legitimation of the character of Jesus' mission — liberation and restoration for such poor persons as this woman of lowly status, through which activity he renders present the dominion of God in the present.[26]

This reading is bolstered by Jesus' own interpretation of what he has accomplished for this woman. He regards his act of healing as an act of liberation from satanic bondage, as direct engagement in cosmic conflict, through which God's eschatological purpose comes to fruition (see 11:20). If this breaks the boundaries of the practices of Judaism, this does not mean that the Scriptures are thereby nullified. Jesus had already associated his work with that of Elijah and Elisha in order to show how God's grace was extended in surprising ways and to surprising people (4:25-28). What is more, Jesus' act on behalf of this woman was nothing more than the consummation of God's covenantal promise and the extension of God's covenantal mercy to Abraham (cf. 1:52-53, 73-75).[27] She is "a daughter of Abraham," an appellation that might signal heroic faithfulness in some other literature,[28] but with a profoundly different significance in the Lukan narrative.[29] She is thus presented as one of those persons denoted by others as having no place among the people of God, normally excluded from social intercourse and certainly not highly regarded for their fidelity, and yet raised up by God as children of Abraham[30] in the sense of becoming the recipients of the mercy reserved for Abraham by God. In the present case, indeed, the contrast between how she is presented and what she receives could hardly be more stark. She is bent over in a shameful position, demonized; this is a daughter of Abraham? Hers was no position of honor, but through Jesus' gracious ministry she is fully restored as a member of the community.[31] She and other children of Abraham

---

26. Cf. Kee, *Miracle,* 203; S. G. Wilson, *Luke and the Law,* 36-39.

27. Cf. Dahl, "Abraham." On "the exaltation of debased women" in Jewish (including NT) narrative, see Schottroff, *Lydia's Impatient Sisters,* 177-203.

28. Jervell ("Daughters of Abraham," 148) thought that the expression was unknown in contemporary literature, but Seim (*Double Message,* 44-47) and O'Toole ("Exegetical Reflections," 96-97) draw attention to important analogues especially in 4 Macc 14:20; 15:28; 17:6; 18:20. The importance of these parallels in 4 Maccabees lies in the contrast thus established between the portrait of heroic martyrdom that gives rise to the title "daughter of Abraham" there and its appearance here without reference to any possible qualifications on the part of the bent-over woman.

29. See the parallel expressions in 1:54-55; 3:7-9; 16:22-31; 19:1-10.

30. See 3:8!

31. Cf. 8:48.

in the Lukan narrative evidence how God's promise to Abraham is fulfilled through the activity of Jesus and how the recipients of liberation through Jesus' ministry are thus confirmed as Abraham's children.[32]

17   Just as the ruler of the synagogue had questioned Jesus' authority among the synagogue public, so Luke narrates their response to what they have seen and heard. He had attempted to shame Jesus but, in the end, he and those with him who oppose Jesus are shamed as the crowd sides with Jesus. This also means that they side with the narrator, attributing to Jesus the status of authoritative teacher and recognizing in the "wonderful things he was doing" the gracious hand of God (cf. Exod 34:10; Isa 45:16). In 12:56, the faceless crowds were castigated as "hypocrites" for their incapacity to interpret the signs of the consummation of God's eschatological purpose among them; Luke presents those gathered at this synagogue along vastly different lines, siding against hypocrites as they delight in Jesus' ministry (cf. 9:43).

18-21   Verse 17 is more than serviceable as an ending to the scene in the synagogue (vv 10-17), but the "therefore" at the beginning of v 18 demands that we read vv 18-21 in relation to the healing account. This is true whether or not we imagine that vv 18-21 are spoken by Jesus in the synagogue in the immediate aftermath of the restoration of the bent-over woman. Why does Jesus turn immediately to his double attempt to characterize the kingdom? One hint is found already in the nature of the comparisons he draws. Jesus does not scour palatial grounds or otherwise turn to the experiences of the elite; he does not reach for images normally associated with royalty and kingdom-making in order to depict the nature of God's dominion; instead, he draws on first-century Palestinian village life. His message about the startling work of God is thus grounded in a dissonance of images. In the healing account, some are caught off-balance by the nature of Jesus' restorative activity: out of place, out of time, and directed at the wrong sort of person. Jesus' commentary on this healing episode comes in the form of parables that also set conflicting images — royal rule and peasant existence — side by side. In this way, Jesus seeks to legitimate his work in the synagogue as kingdom activity.

The first parable (v 19) focuses on the contrast between the mustard seed and the tree into which it grows. One typically thinks of a shrub rather than a mustard "tree," so that Jesus seems deliberately to emphasize the notion of astonishing extravagance in his analogy. This idea is furthered by the detail that birds nest in the branches of this tree — a possible allusion to several OT texts emphasizing the bounty of God's favor and the universal reach of God's empire.[33] Why is this point not made with reference, say, to the mighty cedar

---

32. Seim, *Double Message,* 51.

33. See Ps 104:12; Ezek 17:22-24; 31; Dan 4:10-12, 20-27; cf. Donahue, *Gospel in Parable,* 37.

of Lebanon (cf., e.g., Ezek 17:23)? No doubt, this is grounded in the dissonance of Jesus' message: God's kingdom is established through means other than the coercive power and intrigue usually associated with the establishment of a new order, and his dominion purposefully seeks out persons who do not represent the socially powerful and privileged.

When it is remembered that Jesus' audience is being asked, at least temporarily, to identify with the characters in his parables in order to hear their message, his second kingdom-parable (v 21) is remarkable indeed. He asks people — male or female, privileged or peasant, it does not matter — to enter the domain of a first-century woman and household cook in order to gain perspective on the domain of God. In view is the invasive character of leaven, the work of which is hidden but pervasive. In this case, confidence is expressed in the ability of a typically small portion of yeast to invade even "three measures of flour" — that is, enough to feed as many as 150 people,[34] an enormous yield for a peasant household. Set in relation to the healing episode of vv 10-17, this parable declares that satanic domination is being repealed and the kingdom of God is made present even in such seemingly inconsequential acts as the restoration of an ill woman who lived on the margins of society.

5.5.2. Who Will Be Saved? (13:22-30)

> 22 *Jesus went through one town and village after another, teaching as he made his way to Jerusalem.* 23 *Someone asked him, "Lord, are only a few people being saved?"*[35] *He said to them,* 24 *"Strive to enter through the narrow door; for many, I tell you, will try to enter and will not be able.* 25 *When once the owner of the house has got up and shut the door, and you begin to stand outside and to knock at the door, saying, 'Lord, open to us,' then in reply he will say to you, 'I do not know you, where you are from.'*[36] 26 *Then you will begin to say, 'We ate and drank with you, and you taught in our streets.'* 27 *But he will say, 'I do not know you, where you are from; go away from me, all you evildoers!'* 28 *There will be weeping and gnashing of teeth when you see Abraham and Isaac and Jacob and all the prophets in the kingdom of God, and you yourselves thrown out.* 29 *Then people will come from east and west, from north and south, and will eat in the kingdom of God.* 30 *Indeed, those who are last will be first, and those who are first will be last."*[37]

---

34. Marshall, 561.

35. NRSV: "Lord, will only a few be saved?"

36. NRSV: "I do not know where you come from"; likewise in v 27.

37. NRSV: "Indeed, some are last who will be first, and some are first who will be last." "Some" is missing in the Greek text.

As the scene of stability suggested by a teaching assignment in a synagogue (13:10-17) dissolves, Luke reminds his audience that Jesus "has no place to lay his head" (9:58). Faced with opposition from the synagogue authority, he continues on his way to Jerusalem, his destination since 9:51.[38] On the way, a programmatic question is raised, "Are only a few people being saved?" This is programmatic not only for the current exchange, but for much of this larger section that runs from 13:10 to 17:10, because it gives voice to the issue of group definition so important to Second Temple Judaism in general and to those with whom Jesus will interact in this narrative section in particular.[39] On the one hand, Jesus' answer may seem ambiguous; after all, his first image, the narrow door (v 24), gives way to the door slammed shut (v 25), and, in the end, he acts as though there are infinite doors allowing entry to just about anyone (v 29)![40] His answer may seem ambiguous in another sense, too, insofar as it appears to avoid the question about how few people might be saved only to focus on the many who will be lost (v 24).[41]

On the other, Jesus' answer is quite intelligible when read against the horizons of the eschatological banquet scene in Isa 25:6-9, whose images and vocabulary are mirrored in the Lukan scene. Isaiah had described the end as a lavish banquet, a feast fit for royalty, yet prepared for *all* peoples; on that day it will be said by all the nations, including Gentiles, "Let us be glad and rejoice in our salvation" (v 9, LXX). Although Israel did not lose sight of Isaiah's vision of the eschatological banquet, the question of its participants did evolve in Second Temple Judaism, narrowing considerably in some instances. The targum, for example, maintains the notion of a meal for all peoples, but transforms it into an image of judgment against them[42] — a conclusion echoed in *1 Enoch* 62. Among the Dead Sea Scrolls (wherein testimony for the tradition of the messianic banquet is strong)[43] one finds evidence of the boundaries having been drawn even more tightly so as to exclude not only Gentiles but also blemished Jews.[44] Taking into account this trajectory of interpretation, the query, "Are only a few people being saved?" may well be understood with reference to who among the Jews are to be regarded as the saved remnant. Jesus' response signals a profound departure from the thought of many of his contemporaries at the same

---

38. See above on 9:51–19:48.

39. For discussions of how Jewish ideas of community evolved with the onset of the Hellenistic period, see, e.g., Hanson, *People Called,* 325-81; Sanders, "Ethics of Election"; Bailey, *Through Peasant Eyes,* 89-92.

40. Cf. Theissen, *Open Door,* 80.

41. So Godet, 2:124.

42. For the dating of the Targum of Isaiah in the latter part of the first century, see Chilton, *Galilean Rabbi,* 35-56.

43. Cf. Vermes, *Dead Sea Scrolls,* 6-7, 51; Priest, "Messianic Banquet," 228-29.

44. Cf. 1QSa 2:5-22.

time that it recalls the vision of Isaiah. Heredity, ancestral lineage as a Jew, does not figure into his reply; moreover, just as the kingdom parables of vv 18-21 had foreseen, so here his image of the kingdom banquet is marked by its explicit embrace of the Gentile world.

As Jesus has done throughout the section 12:1–13:9, so here he ties notions of judgment in the future to human behavior in the present. The original question about who are being saved (present tense) is related to an end-time vision of salvation. Some will attempt to enter through the door of the banquet hall when it is too late; now is the time for response.[45]

22-24 This is the first explicit notice of the journey to Jerusalem since it was joined in 9:51-62. It is devoid of topographical detail, with the consequence that we are reminded that Luke's interest in the journey is less about a travel itinerary and more about the motif of journeying and the identification of Jesus' destination. In this brief heading, Luke describes Jesus' characteristic activities as "making his way" and as "teaching," highlighting the orientation of Luke's journey narrative around soteriology, conflict, and the formation of disciples.[46] Mention of Jerusalem also prepares for Jesus' discourse in the next narrative section, 13:31-35.

Luke provides no hints concerning who addresses the soteriological question to Jesus. Rather, the "someone" and "them" of v 23 accent the continuing ambiguity in Luke's representation of Jesus' audience characteristic of much of the travel narrative thus far. Are they disciples? Pharisees? Crowds? Luke does not tell us, with the result that Jesus can be understood to address them all as a universal audience; apparently Jesus' message about "being saved" is needed by everyone, including disciples.

The question itself fits into a well-worn pattern in the Third Gospel: Someone raises a question that provides the stimulus for a discourse by Jesus.[47] It is a question also well rooted in Second Temple Judaism, where speculation regarding the sweep of salvation is not difficult to trace. See, for example, 4 Ezra 8:1: "The Most High made this world for the sake of many, but the world to come for the sake of only a few."[48] The way this question is framed in Luke's account is remarkable, however, for its concern with the present.[49] This is

---

45. See Plummer, 346: "Jesus does not say that there *are* many who *strive* in vain to enter, but that there *will* be many who *will seek* in vain to enter, *after the time of salvation is past.*"

46. See above on 9:51–19:48.

47. Cf. 9:57; 10:25; 11:15, 27, 45; 12:13, 41; 13:1; 17:37; 20:13; 24:5; Acts 1:6; Radl, *Lukas-Evangelium*, 45.

48. Cf., e.g., 4 Ezra 7:47; 8:3; 9:14-15.

49. *Pace* Marshall (654), who notices that σώζω appears in its present passive participial form but assumes that it must be read with "a future sense." Cf. the helpful discussion in Barrett, *Acts,* 1:231.

consistent with Luke's soteriology, in which the weight of emphasis is placed on the present. Likewise, it is consonant with Luke's soteriology on account of Luke's stress on the communal dimensions of the experience of salvation, inaugurated by a decision to reorient oneself around the purpose of God (repentance) and to join with the community of God's people being formed around Jesus. For Luke, life with God in the eschaton is directly related to identifying fully, personally, and in the present with the redemptive aim of God manifest in Jesus' mission.

Coming on the heels of the episode recounted in vv 10-21, this is an apt question. Jesus had contended that the kingdom is rendered present in the restoration of one, apparently insignificant, demonized woman, and that the kingdom is like a mustard seed and a bit of yeast. If this is so, does this mean that the reach of salvation is negligible?

Jesus' answer may not seem satisfying. Asked concerning how few are being saved, he remarks instead on how many will not be saved. More centrally, he turns a potentially speculative dialogue on soteriology into a pointed, existential challenge. The tenses are important: Strive now, for seeking to enter in the future is futile. This places the emphasis on "striving" in the present, using the athletic metaphor of "struggle," employed in Hellenism and Hellenistic Judaism with respect to the practice of virtue and obedience to the law of God.[50]

25-27 Jesus' brief parable underscores, first, the message of v 24: The opportunity for response will not always be available; do so now, before the door is shut. The puzzle of this parabolic material is that those outside the door seem genuinely to expect to be allowed in. On what basis do they stake their claim? In the first instance (v 25) no rationale is given, though in the second they claim some previous interaction with Jesus (v 26).

It is helpful to remember in this co-text how status is assigned to individuals in a social system, generally with weight being given either to "ascription" (the assignment of status on the basis of inherited traits or kinship ties) or to "performance" (the assignment of status on the basis of achievement of certain goals or behaving in certain ways).[51] In the first instance, those seeking entrance do so apparently on the sole basis of their ascribed status. Within the Lukan narrative, this would identity them as persons who claim Abraham as their father and so imagine that their status among the saved is unconditionally secure. This is a position that has been critiqued repeatedly throughout the Gospel thus far, beginning as early as the words of John in

---

50. See Dautzenberg, "ἀγών, ἀγωνίζομαι," 25. Luke uses different verbs in v 24a, ἀγωνίζομαι and ζητέω, but the contrast between the two actions, one successful and the other futile, does not seem to lie here. ζητέω is used with positive connotations in 11:9-13.

51. See the helpful summary in Eilberg-Schwartz, *Savage in Judaism*, 195-99.

3:8. We are not surprised to hear the words of the owner of the house,[52] then, who ironically claims not to know these people nor their origins.[53] That is, their claim to privileged status via family heritage is thwarted by his claim not to recognize them as members of this household!

Failing this, those seeking entrance claim association with Jesus, and at first their claim may seem justified. Has Luke not repeatedly depicted Jesus as extending the boundaries of salvation through his choice of table companions? Has Luke not placed a premium on hearing Jesus' teaching? Affirmative answers to these two questions are necessary but only in a superficial sense, for in the Lukan narrative Jesus is equally clear in interpreting table fellowship as the occasion for receptivity to him and his message, signified by repentance.[54] Likewise, *authentic* hearing of Jesus' message as the word of God entails hearing *and doing*.[55] Using the language of Ps 6:8,[56] Jesus' parable places a premium on a measure of status grounded not in ascription but in performance. Characterized as "doers of evil," these people come too late to seek entry, and their ties to Abraham and their previous association with Jesus count for nothing.

It is difficult not to see Jesus' parable as a metaphorical representation of his own ministry and, thus, of his future role in judgment as the parable's "owner of the house." This is most clear in v 26, where reference is made to people who ate and drank with "you" (read: "Jesus") and heard his teaching, yet who opposed his message. As in Wisdom's story of the righteous son of God who is opposed and shamefully killed, only to be vindicated and to serve as judge over those who had opposed him (Wisdom 2, 4-5), so, through the intertextual reference to Psalm 6, Jesus is represented as the one has suffered at the hands of those hostile toward him, and who will close the door and pronounce judgment on those who heard but opposed his message. Their reference to him as "Lord" (v 25) comes too late; opposing him in this life, they have shown themselves to be members of a household other than the one over which he is lord, so they are not counted among those who are being saved.[57]

---

52. οἰκοδεσπότης — cf. 12:39.

53. πόθεν, according to BAGD (680), should be read locally in 13:25, 27. Why this is so is not clear. Our interpretation takes the adverb as a reference to origin (cf. 20:7).

54. See esp. 5:32; cf. 14:24; 22:22. Moxnes ("Meals," 161-63) notes the function of meals as a potential for the construction of community, a potential that may go unfulfilled. See also Koenig, *New Testament Hospitality*, 114-19; Barth, *Das Mahl*, 148-49.

55. Cf. 8:11-15, 19-21.

56. Ps 6:9, LXX.

57. Jesus uses the term ἐγείρω in v 25 with reference to the householder's "arising" to shut the door. Elsewhere we find it in the sense of "to rise and act" (5:23, 24; 6:8), so it need not refer allegorically to the resurrection (*pace* Johnson, 216, 220), though it is tempting to read it in this way.

Similarly, the constant use of the second person "you" in vv 24-28 is of consequence. Jesus might have pitched his parabolic narrative in the third person, using "he" or "she" or "them." As Luke recounts it, though, Jesus' "you" immediately includes the one who raised the question in the first place (v 23), then also those of the larger crowd who are present (note "to them," v 23); soon, though, as Luke's readers, we are drawn into Jesus' parabolic teaching and hear firsthand his warning and reminder to act now lest we find the door slammed in our faces.

28-30 Although the parable is finished, Jesus' teaching continues along the same vein, denoting "the door" of the parable as the entry into the banquet hall of the kingdom of God, and supplanting further an ethic of election built on the privileging of ascription as the primary determinant of one's status within the eschatological people of God. Ironically, some who claim Abraham as father will be forbidden access to Abraham's table, not because they have miscalculated their family tree but because status among those being saved is not inherited.

In many cases in Luke-Acts, the kingdom of God is the saving dominion of God rendered present through the ministry of Jesus and his followers. Here, that saving dominion appears on a grand scale, has a transparently locative sense,[58] is projected into the future, and is represented as a great feast.[59] The last emphasis, envisioning the eschaton as an appropriation and celebration of divine blessing in the form of a feast, is well rooted in the literature of the OT and Second Temple Judaism.[60] Most resonant in its reverberations, though, is the Isaianic vision, with its capacity to embrace both the notion of the eschatological banquet and the universal embrace of God's salvation (esp. Isa 25:6-8). Luke's earlier emphasis on salvation to the Gentiles (2:30-32; cf. 12:18-21) appears again on the horizon, with the four winds representing the four corners of the earth, including the scattered remnant of faithful Israel wherever they may be found and,[61] with them, the faithful of the world (Isa 11:11-16; 43:5-6; 60).

In this respect, it is significant that, to the list of the great ancestors of Israel, Abraham, Isaac, and Jacob, are added "all the prophets." This echoes earlier material in Luke, material where the emphasis had fallen on the propen-

---

58. Such texts as these should warn us against too easily adopting the term "reign" (or "dynamic rule") as an English equivalent for βασιλεία.

59. For the kingdom of God in Luke-Acts, cf. O'Toole, "Kingdom of God"; Radl, *Lukas-Evangelium,* 131-33; Wolter, "Reich Gottes."

60. See, e.g., Isa 25:6-8; 55:1-2; 65:13-14; Zeph 1:7; 1QSa 2:15-22. In Luke, cf. 6:21; 12:37; 14:15. See the summary in Priest, "Messianic Banquet"; Nelson, *Leadership,* 58-59; Wainwright, *Eucharist and Eschatology,* 19-27.

61. As will become clear, those embraced in the kingdom feast will include even those Jews thought by many to be excluded from the family of God — cf. 14:21-23.

sity of some in Israel to oppose those who served God's purpose and spoke on his behalf — both in Israel's past and in its present (6:22-23; 11:49-51). In those earlier Lukan co-texts, woe is pronounced on those who persecute the prophets; such persons are promised mourning and weeping (6:22-26; 11:45-52). This, indeed, is their fate in the judgment: excluded from the joy of the eschatological feast, theirs is the lot of mourning, rage, despair.[62] Jesus thus insinuates how some from Israel might be excluded from the kingdom banquet. Opposing God's prophets, they oppose God's purpose; opposing God's purpose, they fail to comprehend who Jesus is and the nature of his divine mission (foretold by "all the prophets," 24:27; Acts 3:18, 24; 10:43); consequently, they do not reorient their hearts and lives around the word of God and, in this way, they demonstrate that they are not children of Abraham after all.

The language of "first" and "last" is particularly apt in this co-text, since, used thus, these words are borrowed from the vocabulary used to determine the relative status of persons within a social setting. Those of apparently high status — that is, within the Lukan narrative, those who accent their impeccable ancestry and conscientious attention to the laws of purity — should contemplate what counts for status before God. The presence of the kingdom nullifies conventional concerns for honor and introduces alternative canons for measuring status. Performance, understood as repentance, as hearing and doing the word, is the means by which one is counted among those who are being saved.

5.5.3. The Entwined Fates of Jesus and Jerusalem (13:31-35)

31 At that very hour some Pharisees came and said to him, "Get away from here, for Herod wants to kill you." 32 He said to them, "Go and tell that fox for me, 'Listen, I am casting out demons and performing cures today and tomorrow, and on the third day I finish my work. 33 Yet today, tomorrow, and the next day I must be on my way, because it is impossible for a prophet to be killed outside of Jerusalem.' 34 Jerusalem, Jerusalem, the city that kills the prophets and stones those who are sent to it! How often have I desired to gather your children together as a hen gathers her brood under her wings, and you were not willing! 35 See, your house is abandoned.[63] And I tell you, you will not see me until the time comes when you say, 'Blessed is the one who comes in the name of the Lord.' "

---

62. βρυγμός ("grinding of teeth"), according to Hasler ("βρυγμός, βρύχω") may refer to the enraged baring of teeth (cf. Acts 7:54; Job 16:9; Pss 34:16; 36:12; Lam 2:16) or to the despairing gnashing of teeth of the damned (cf. Ps 111:10, LXX; 1 Enoch 108:3-7).

63. NRSV: "left to you."

Central to the Lukan depiction of Jesus' mission is its grounding in the divine purpose; this perspective was signaled forcefully at the onset of the journey of Jesus and his followers to Jerusalem (9:51-53), and it is underscored again here. Here, though, Jerusalem comes into the limelight not only as Jesus' destination but also, more particularly, with reference to its significance for Jesus. As the divine agent of salvation, Jesus must take his message to the center of the Jewish world, Jerusalem. What can he expect by way of response in Jerusalem? The pattern for which Jerusalem is known is that of killing divine messengers. Will those of the city kill Jesus; or will they greet him with the words of the psalm, "Blessed is the one who comes in the name of the Lord"? Although it is possible to find in Jesus' prophetic words over Jerusalem a thread of hope, the motif of judgment is more prominent: As God's agent, Jesus must carry the divine message to Jerusalem, but Jerusalem kills those whom God sends; on account of this, Jerusalem itself is doomed.[64]

Luke has prepared for this scene, and stitched it into its local co-text, in two important ways. First, in v 22 he had provided an explicit reminder that Jesus was continuing on the journey to Jerusalem — a factor that comes into sharp focus in vv 31-35. Second, Jesus' reference to "all the prophets" who will join in the kingdom feast (v 28), especially when read in relation to his pronouncement over Jerusalem in the current scene, intimates why many within Israel will be excluded from the banquet. Opposing those whom God sends to them, they resist God's purpose and thus spurn the salvific message of Jesus, foretold by "all the prophets" (cf., e.g., 24:27). Indeed, Jesus' reply to the Pharisees (vv 31-33) and his declaration concerning Jerusalem (vv 34-35) are joined by the representation of Jerusalem as the city that kills the prophets (vv 33-34).

The two segments of Jesus' discourse are held together in a second way, by Luke's attempt to showcase the presence of competing desires or aims.[65] Herod *wants* to kill Jesus; Jesus has *wanted* to restore and shelter the people of Jerusalem; the people of Jerusalem have not *wanted* him to do so. These three statements each use a common verb, "to want," to express rival aims within this narrative unit.[66] A fourth occurrence of the concept of "purpose" or "desire" appears in v 33, where Jesus grounds his ongoing mission in the divine aim.[67] These four statements of desire dramatize the conflict at work throughout the Lukan narrative and are key to our appreciation of the role of this brief scene within the larger Gospel.

31-33 Luke ties this conversation into its local co-text by employing a temporal reference, "at that very hour," that urges his readers to see an

---

64. See Brawley, *Centering on God,* 50.
65. Cf. Tiede, *Prophecy and History,* 70-71.
66. θέλω — vv 31, 34 (2x).
67. δεῖ; see above on 2:41-51a.

interpretive link between vv 22-30 and the present pericope.[68] As in previous texts, impetus for Jesus' discourse is provided by what at first sight appears to be an intrusion into the narrative, a question or comment that seems to change the subject.[69] The previous scene — with its deliberate contrast between people who, through repentance, "strive to enter the narrow door," and those who do not identify with God's purpose and, so, are "evildoers" — brings into the foreground the notion of judgment. Identifying with or against the purpose of God, and doing so now, in the present, provides a suitable lead-in to the question of the purpose(s) being served by Herod, the Pharisees, Jesus, and especially Jerusalem.

The exchange between the Pharisees and Jesus revolves around two related questions: (1) Whose agenda is being served by Jesus' "journeying"? (2) Who will serve as Jesus' executioner? The Pharisees put forward one view of things, Jesus another.[70] In the first instance, the Pharisees advise Jesus "to depart" and "to travel" on account of the threat of Herod (v 31); Jesus replies that he will indeed "travel," but not to escape the menace of Herod's plans.[71] Given his characterization within the Lukan narrative thus far, we have every reason to imagine that the threat presented by Herod is a real one.[72] As tetrarch of Galilee,[73] Herod first put an end to John's prophetic ministry by having him imprisoned (3:19-20). Later, we learn, Herod is responsible for beheading John (9:9), and we hear nothing to mitigate Luke's sweeping characterization of Herod as a doer of evil things (3:20). Nevertheless, the peril represented by Herod's malevolence is not for Jesus a motivating factor. Instead, he refers to his intention to continue carrying out his ministry as before;[74] although he will be "on his way," just as the Pharisees had urged, his going is not for the purpose of escaping the hand of Herod. It is, rather, to bring to fruition the divine purpose for his mission.[75] In this co-text, the concern with daily activity

---

68. Cf. 10:21; 12:12; 20:19; 24:53.

69. See, e.g., 12:13; 13:1, 23. On the rules of conversation that bias readers to assume continuity and appropriateness, see above on 12:41.

70. This contrast is signified by the use of πλήν in v 33.

71. Verse 31: ἐξέρχομαι + πορεύομαι; v 33: πορεύομαι.

72. See Darr, *Character Building*, 127-46; Tyson, *Death of Jesus*, 133-35.

73. See above on 3:1-6.

74. In this case, then, exorcism and healing are metonymic for the whole of his divine mission. Cf. 4:18-19; 7:21-22. For related representations of his mission, see, e.g., 9:11; 10:17.

75. As he does generally, Luke employs the verb δεῖ in order to signify divine necessity — cf., e.g., 4:43; 9:22; Cosgrove, "Divine Δεῖ"; Green, *Gospel of Luke*, 28-37. Luke also uses the verb τελειόω to designate the fulfillment of his mission, but he does so in a way that does little to suggest its precise meaning here; several readings are possible — including, e.g., that Jesus will reach his goal, Jerusalem (cf. Tannehill, *Narrative Unity*, 1:154); or he will complete his mission (cf. 12:50; Acts 20:24).

— "today, tomorrow, etc." (vv 32-33) — underscores Jesus' design to continue on his current course without interruption, but also heightens the drama of the journey as he calls attention to an imprecise but limited period of time before he reaches the ominous destination of Jerusalem.[76]

It is within this co-text that the designation of Herod as a "fox" must be understood, particularly since "fox" has a range of virtual, metaphorical properties not all of which are actualized here. For example, we read in the Lukan narrative no hint that Herod is particularly cunning or crafty. More appropriate is the metaphorical presentation of Herod the fox as one who lacks the status or is impotent to carry out his threat. In this case, Herod's rank would be relativized by the recognition that Jesus, whose mission is rooted in divine necessity, thus serves one of greater status and power than Herod or the Rome he represents. Herod's threat is blunted because his design runs contrary to the divine will. A further foxlike trait is potentially actualized in Jesus' use of this metaphor — namely, the proclivity of fox for malicious destructiveness: "Upon hearing of Herod's threat," then, "Jesus pegs the Tetrarch as a varmint in the Lord's field, a murderer of God's agents, a would-be disrupter of the divine economy."[77]

The second contrast has to do with the death of Jesus. The Pharisees approach Jesus with information that would allow him to escape death. Jesus' death already looms over his ministry (9:22, 44), and he does not consider the option of eluding Herod, advised by the Pharisees. Instead, he develops the contrast between being killed by Herod and being killed in Jerusalem.[78] Elsewhere in the Lukan narrative the motif of the suffering of the prophets has already surfaced, drawing on a long-standing tradition regarding the destiny of the prophets to undergo persecution and martyrdom and applying that tradition to Jesus and, secondarily, to those who share in

---

76. On the expression σήμερον καὶ αὔριον καί . . . , see BAGD 749.

77. Darr, *Character Building,* 144. Darr (140-41) notes ancient linguistic evidence for all three of these views, as well as a fourth, intelligence. See also Buth, "Herod Antipas"; he opts for a metaphorical reference to Herod's impotence. Darr denies that the characterization of Herod as a fox (= one lacking the status, power, or courage to carry out his aim) is appropriate to this co-text by caricaturing this view of the ruler as though he were a "timid, hen-pecked person who agonizes over his actions and is easily swayed by the opinions of others" (144). He does not note, however, the deliberate contrast Jesus has just established between those who imagine that they are of high status but according to the divine reckoning are not (v 30), nor does he reckon with the contrast between Herod's will and the divine necessity that is central to this exchange.

78. This contrast anticipates the struggle with dual causation that will surface more clearly in the Lukan passion account and in reflection on the death of Jesus in Acts. Jesus' death is at the same time the act of those who oppose him and an event grounded in God's purpose and intended by Jesus himself (Carroll and Green, *Death of Jesus,* 68-69).

his mission.[79] The additional note about the impossibility of a prophet's being killed outside of Jerusalem, however, constitutes an innovation that can be explained only in light of the role Jerusalem plays in the narrative as a whole.[80] The City serves a crucial socio-religious function for the narrator, who depicts it as a "culture center" that embodies, legitimates, and propagates for the Jewish people its leading dispositions, ideas, practices, and institutions — that is, that performs a world-ordering function for the world Luke portrays.[81] Jerusalem, then, stands as a cipher for Israel as a whole; hence, not only must it be the ultimate destination of the prophet proclaiming a message of reform, but it is there, where the message of reform contrasts most sharply with accepted beliefs and practices, that resistance to the prophet will reach its acme.

What role is played by the Pharisees in this narrative subunit? Many interpreters see the Pharisees in a negative light, either because they regard the Pharisees as consistently having been portrayed negatively by Luke or because they think the Pharisees are here attempting to distract Jesus from the divine purpose, or both.[82] Such interpretations flounder on two grounds. First, in order to insist that, because they have been construed negatively in the past, the Pharisees must continue to be represented as Jesus' opponents is to overlook the reality that the narrator is capable of introducing new elements to our understanding of the Pharisees. Readers are constantly engaged in retrospective reevaluation as they are given new data in the process of reading. Moreover, Luke's mural of the Pharisees is neither finished nor painted with one color. He does not lump all Pharisees together in one composite group character, but, as here, he can speak not of "the Pharisees" but of "some Pharisees." In this case, faced with the option of siding with Herod over against Jesus, some Pharisees actually align themselves with Jesus. Furthermore, Jesus continues to share meals with the Pharisees and to instruct them, clearly signifying the possibility and hope that the Pharisees may join him in his solidarity with God's redemptive project (see ch. 14!). Second, a retrospective reading shows the close association of the Pharisees who warn Jesus of impending death in this text and those believers (including Luke as narrator) who urge Paul to avoid persecution by not going to Jerusalem (Acts 21:12-14). In neither case does Luke present the offer of guidance as a hostile act. For these reasons, it is inappropriate to attribute

79. See 4:24; 6:23; 11:47-52; cf. Acts 7:52. See also Neh 9:26; Jer 2:30; *Jub.* 1:12; Aune, *Prophecy,* 157-59; Brawley, *Centering on God,* 174-76.

80. Fitzmyer (2:1032) draws attention to the killing of prophets within Jerusalem (e.g., Jer 26:20-23; 38:4-6), but, as he goes on to admit, the tradition had it that prophets would meet a violent fate, not that they would necessarily do so in Jerusalem.

81. On "culture centers," see Geertz, *Local Knowledge,* 121-46; see above, §3.

82. Recently, see, e.g., Tiede, *Prophecy and History,* 71-72; Darr, *Character Building,* 105-6; Johnson, 217, 220-21.

malevolent incentives to the Pharisees, though, having come to this conclusion, we must face the further reality that Luke seems little concerned with their motives.[83] Clearly, like the disciples (e.g., 9:44-45), they do not understand the nature of Jesus' identity and mission, and so imagine that his best course of action is to avoid death. Their report of Herod's design provides Jesus with the opportunity to remind all who hear him that his divine mission actually involves the violent fate of a prophet.

34-35 Jesus' characterization of Jerusalem is not a flattering one, but it is congruous with his previously stated premise that Jerusalem is the site for the violent end of the prophets. To this he now adds that Jerusalem stones those sent to it — echoing the language of 11:49 concerning the sending of prophets and apostles who are persecuted and killed by obdurate Israel. Stoning is the most common form of execution found in the OT, used in such cases as those involving blasphemy (Lev 24:14, 16, 23) and apostasy (Lev 20:2; Deut 13:11). This OT background is important because the indictment against Jerusalem for stoning "those who are sent to it" thus identifies Jerusalem as attributing blasphemy or apostasy to the very ones whom God has sent. That is, the people are guilty of working with their own definitions of faithfulness, even when these definitions are contradicted by God's own agents. In this way they establish how far they are from understanding and embracing God's purpose.

How will Jerusalem respond to Jesus? Will its inhabitants receive him with pronouncements of blessing appropriate to "one who comes in the name of the Lord"? Or will they declare him to be a false prophet, an apostate, as they had God's earlier envoys? Jesus seems to hope for one response while expecting another. Citing Ps 118:26, his message takes the form of a conditional promise the form and content of which are well represented in Second Temple Judaism: If Israel will repent from its historic obduracy and receive "the one who comes in the name of the Lord" with blessing rather than animosity, then Israel will recognize and experience the coming of salvation.[84] (See the parallel use of "seeing" in the case of Simeon, who had awaited the consolation of Israel, 2:29-32.) Within the Gospel, Jesus has already been identified as "the one who comes" — in Lukan parlance, as the Messiah (3:15-16; 7:18, 22); will Israel so acknowledge him? In fact, when Jesus enters Jerusalem he is greeted as "the king" with the words of Ps 118:26. There, however, it is a large group of his disciples and not Jerusalem who receive him thus. This throws into sharp relief the reception Jesus will receive from the Jerusalemites: rejection and execution.[85]

83. See Gowler, *Portraits of the Pharisees,* 236-41.
84. See Allison, "Conditional Prophecy," 77-81.
85. See Tyson, *Images of Judaism,* 74-75; Carroll, *End of History,* 162-63. Some interpreters find in v 35 a reference to the parousia (e.g., Bock, *Proclamation,* 117-21;

As a consequence of its rejection of Jesus, Jerusalem will be judged. Drawing on language and images from Jer 12:1-7; 22:5, Jesus announces that, for its failure to conform to God's purpose for it, Jerusalem's "house" will be abandoned. What is this "house"? Luke can refer to the temple as a "house," but in those cases the reference is more specifically to *God's* house (not "Jerusalem's" house).[86] Hence, it is more appropriate here to think in terms of judgment falling on the "household" of Jerusalem — that is, on Jerusalem as the centerpoint of practices and institutions that (1) shape life throughout Palestine as Luke portrays it, and (2) are opposed to the will of God. Judgment, according to the image Jesus uses, would entail God's vacating Jerusalem, leaving it to its own devices. This is not because he wishes to do so.[87] Quite the contrary, again borrowing imagery from the OT,[88] Jesus so identifies with God's care for Jerusalem that he is able to affirm his long-standing yearning to gather together his people for shelter and in restoration.[89] Alas, this desire is not shared by the Jerusalemites.

5.5.4. Kingdom and Banquet (14:1-24)

Luke 14:1 marks a shift of scene that will remain constant until v 25 and which, then, helps to establish the unity of vv 1-24. Along with other narrative units within the Lukan travel section (9:51–19:48), wherein scenes shift by location and audience but with no discernible movement along the route to Jerusalem, this one has an episodic feel. The appearance of episodes tumbling one after the other in the Lukan account should not deter us from reflecting

---

C. A. Evans, "Prophecy and Polemic," 178-79; Strauss, *Davidic Messiah*, 315-17), as if Jesus anticipated that there would be a time, at the eschaton, when Jerusalem would respond with the words of Ps 118:26. This, however, does not reckon with the conditional nature of Jesus' promise, nor with the judgment pronounced on Jerusalem for its rejection of Jesus. What is more, it seems to demand that Luke foresees an end-time restoration of Jerusalem, an anticipation for which no corroborative evidence is forthcoming in Luke-Acts. We should note, though, that judgment on Jerusalem is not for Luke tantamount to judgment on the Jews as a whole (cf. Weatherly, *Jewish Responsibility*, 168-70).

86. Cf. 6:4; 11:51; 19:46. οἶκος is used with reference to one's ancestry (or a dynasty) in 1:27, 33, and 69, and to the people of Israel in Acts 2:36. See the discussion in Weinert, "Jerusalem's Abandoned House" (whose general claims regarding Luke's positive stance vis-à-vis the temple are exaggerated).

87. Cf. Brawley, *Luke-Acts*, 124; Tiede, *Prophecy and History*, 71-76.

88. Cf. Deut 32:11; Ps 91:4; Isa 31:5.

89. This reading builds on the use of ἐπισυνάγω in texts that speak of the hope of restoration (e.g., Pss 106:47; 147:2; Isa 27:12), takes "children" in the expression "your children" as a reference to the inhabitants of Jerusalem (cf. Jonah 2:23; Zech 9:13; Bar 4:19, 21, 25; 1 Macc 1:38), and builds on the expectation that salvation for Jerusalem was synecdoche for the salvation of Israel (see above on 2:38).

on the importance of the order of these episodes and their interconnections, however, for beneath the surface lie important questions of narrative substance. Remembering the importance of resocialization into the community of God's people for those whose allegiances and moral underpinnings have been transformed, this concatenation of scenes and accompanying repetition of motifs have a pivotal role to play within the journey narrative. They remind characters within the narrative as well as persons who read it of those ingredients that are constitutive of Jesus' message, even as growing evidence of hostility and of sharpness in Jesus' message contributes to the rising urgency of response. As will become evident, however episodic the present narrative unit may seem, it is rooted deeply in the prior narrative, which constitutes its necessary presupposition.

Although this unit invites further segmentation — with vv 1-6 centered on the healing of a man with dropsy, vv 7-14 taken up with meal protocols, and vv 15-24 concerned with banquet invitations — its sections comprise a unit marked by a common temporal, spatial, and occasional setting: on the Sabbath, in the home of a ruling Pharisee, over a meal. Additionally, the language of eating/dining and the vocabulary of invitation and summons weave together these subunits, and over the whole is draped the shadow of hostility.[90]

By threading together topics and patterned frames already established as important in the Third Gospel, this narrative unit brings the motif of conflict into the foreground while at the same time parading the possibility of appropriate response to the inbreaking of God's rule. *(1) The Meal.* In addition to their obvious importance in the provision of food,[91] meals serve pivotal social functions, the meaning of which is explored in this narrative section.[92] One may refer in particular to the practices of Pharisees, for whom meals functioned to establish "in-group" boundaries and embody socio-religious values pertaining to ceremonial purity. Such values were not unique to Pharisees, of course, but were shared by others, including the social elite, for whom the table was an expression of kin- or friendship and for whom dining served to give expression to concerns for honor and reciprocity. In addition to these more generic issues, one should also recognize how, in narrating this scene, Luke has drawn on the Greco-Roman tradition of the

90. For the language of eating, see vv 1, 7, 8, 12, 15, 16, and 24; for the language of summons (and refusal of invitation), see vv 7, 8, 9, 10, 12, 13, 16, 17, 18, 19, 20, 21, 23, and 24. On the unity of vv 1-24, see further Busse, *Wunder,* 304-5; Noël, "Parable of the Wedding Guest," 18-22; Braun, *Feasting and Social Rhetoric,* 14-20.

91. Such an obvious aspect of meals takes on heightened importance when those invited to eat include the hungry — cf. vv 13, 21, and 23.

92. On the symbolic importance of meals, see, e.g., Douglas, *Implicit Meanings,* 249-75; Bartchy, "Table Fellowship"; Moxnes, "Meals"; et al.

symposium.[93] As in other possible expressions of the symposia in Luke's presentation of Jesus, however, so in this one he seems to draw on the tradition in large part so as to show how Jesus' message and practices departed from accepted norms. Perhaps most prominently, though symposia were to advance ties of friendship, this scene is painted with the hues of conflict and Jesus protests against dining practices that were exclusionary and motivated by concerns for one's honor — that is, against the staples of the symposia.

Jesus' presence at the table for this scene recalls the thematizing of table fellowship throughout the Gospel thus far, relating the table to sharing, celebrating, inviting, suspending of boundaries, and so on.[94] In particular, the table in Luke is often the setting for the inclusion of the wrong people — "wrong," that is, as defined by conventional standards. See, for example, the inclusion of toll collectors and sinners in earlier material (5:29-32; 7:34, 36-50) and of the marginalized in the current scene (vv 1-6, 13, 21, 23). Meals can foster existing bonds of community, but in Luke they can also be used to establish new ones. When Jesus comes to dine at the home of a leading Pharisee in this scene, we might say that he uses this opportunity to lay out the conditions by which this gathering of socially elite scribes and Pharisees will be able to participate in the community of God's kingdom. Indeed, the opening of this scene, with its focus on the redemptive necessity of the healing on the Sabbath of a bloated man whose craving for more water is as self-destructive as it is unquenchable, subverts Pharisaic norms for religious purity and legal observance at the same time that it metaphorically and ironically opens up the possibility for Pharisees to be healed of an hypocrisy manifest in ravenous greed.

(2) *The Pharisees.* Luke depicts Jesus' host as a leading Pharisee, thus identifying him as one of those who, according to Mary's Song, would be "brought down" (1:52). According to dining conventions, this ruling Pharisee should invite only those whose presence would maintain or advance his own status in the community, with the result that we may expect this table to be occupied by others of roughly equivalent social status. The Pharisees and legal experts Jesus addresses (v 3c), then, would be among the social elite, a supposition fully consonant with the status-seeking behavior Jesus observes in v 7 and his expectation that their invitation lists would normally include the wealthy (v 12). This is important for at least two reasons. First, Luke's

---

93. See the brief summary of this tradition above, on 5:27-39. On its adaptation here, see Ernst, "Gastmahlgespräche," 57-63; and, more recently, Johnson, 225-26; Braun, *Feasting and Social Rhetoric,* 136-44.

94. Magaß, "Semiotik einer Tischordnung"; cf. Just, *Ongoing Feast;* Karris, *Luke: Artist and Theologian.*

characterization of Jesus' dining companions allows for the immediate relevance of Jesus' teaching in vv 7-14 and for their capacity to identify with characters within the parable of vv 15-24. Second, these considerations, together with the Lukan note that "they were watching him closely" (v 1), root this scene in its larger Lukan co-text, where Pharisees are notable for their rapacity and occupation with social esteem (11:42-44) and where Pharisees are joined by legal experts in stalking Jesus (11:53-54).

(3) Reversal. Throughout this scene, two expressions of the Lukan motif of reversal vie for prominence.[95] The first is the exaltation of the humble, predicted in Mary's Song (1:51-53), highlighted in Jesus' teaching as recently as 13:30, and in the foreground especially in vv 7-11. The second is the inclusion of the excluded, notably in vv 1-6 and 12-24. These are nothing less than interrelated ways of bringing into the limelight the Lukan theme of salvation, embodied in the Lukan message of "good news to the poor," and understood concretely in this scene as status transposition. What is of particular importance in this co-text is not only how Luke narrates the presentation of this theme, but also how in doing so he shows Jesus, first, in conflict with the Pharisees concerning this expression of God's purpose and, second, inviting the Pharisees (and others) to embrace this message and allow it to reshape their own practices, not least at the table.

Jesus transgresses Jewish and Greco-Roman dining conventions and reverses wider Mediterranean concerns with honor and shame because he is operating with his own, quite different set of "rules."[96] Their basis is not developed here, but presupposed from Luke's previous presentation of Jesus' message, including previous table scenes in the Third Gospel (cf. 5:27-39; 7:36-50; 11:37-54). Relative to his table companions in 14:1-24, Jesus has a distinctive view of the world, shaped fundamentally by his experience of the Spirit, his understanding of the merciful God, and his awareness of the presence of God's redemptive project, the kingdom of God, in his ministry. Within this immediate co-text, Jesus' version of dining etiquette, shaped fundamentally by these preunderstandings and dispositions, comes to expression as a warning and invitation to his companions at the table, Pharisees and scribes. Within its larger co-text in the Third Gospel, however, the reach of Jesus' message is more inclusive, calling for an embodiment of the kingdom of God in the social practices of Pharisees and legal experts, yes, but also in the

95. Cf. Karris, *Luke: Artist and Theologian,* 60-64; Noël, "Parable of the Wedding Guest," 22; Tannehill, *Narrative Unity,* 1:185; Just, *Ongoing Feast,* 171-80. More generally, York, *The Last Shall Be First.*

96. This is developed by van Staden (*Compassion,* esp. 152-240) in terms of Luke's advocation of compassion as a new, core value derived from the symbolic universe of his world.

behavior of his followers and the people as a whole. On account of Luke's thematizing of the table scene, it is impossible to read this narrative unit apart from the more general pattern of hospitality characteristic of all who respond with favor to the good news. Likewise, on account of the susceptibility of all — whether Pharisees or crowds or even disciples (12:1, 56; 13:15) — to misconstrue the divine purpose and so practice only a shoddy parody of true piety,[97] all are in need of Jesus' warning and invitation to practice hospitality to the least and the left-out.

5.5.4.1. Jesus Heals an Insatiable Thirst (14:1-6)

14:1 *On one occasion when Jesus was going to the house of a leader of the Pharisees to eat a meal on the sabbath, they were watching him closely.* 2 *Just then, in front of him, there was a man who had dropsy.* 3 *And Jesus asked the lawyers and Pharisees, "Is it lawful to cure people on the sabbath, or not?"* 4 *But they were silent. So, taking him, Jesus healed and released him.*[98] 5 *Then he said to them, "If one of you has a child or an ox that has fallen into a well, will you not immediately pull it out on a sabbath day?"* 6 *And they could not reply to this.*

Luke has repeatedly advised his readers that Jesus' custom was to observe the Sabbath (e.g., 4:16). In this setting, which introduces a larger dining scene nestled between episodes of traveling (13:22-25; 14:25-35), Luke continues this characterization, depicting Jesus enjoying Sabbath-day hospitality following the synagogue service.[99] In 13:32-33 Jesus had noted his need not only to continue on his way to Jerusalem but also to continue his ministry of healing and exorcism. Luke now narrates one of the rare episodes of healing in a section of his Gospel otherwise given over to Jesus' teaching (cf. 13:10-17; 17:11-19; 18:35-43).

This scene of healing has remarkable points of contact with the similar episode Luke narrates in 13:10-17[100] — including the following: (1) a healing on the Sabbath, along with (2) the question of what is appropriate on the Sabbath; (3) the explicit presence of a "ruler" — of the synagogue in the once case, of Pharisees in the other; (4) the use of the term "release"[101] to describe the act of healing; (5) the use of analogies from the treatment of

---

97. That is, in Lukan parlance, to be hypocritical.
98. NRSV: "Jesus took him and healed him, and sent him away."
99. Cf. Josephus *Life* 54 §279.
100. Cf. O'Toole, "Exegetical Reflections"; Derrett, "Two Lucan Miracles."
101. ἀπολύω.

domestic animals to show the propriety of Sabbath healing; and, in the use of those analogies, (6) the ad hoc symmetry between binding/loosing on the one hand (13:15 → 13:16), and rescue from drowning on the other (14:2 → 14:5).

The details of the scene Luke portrays raise important questions regarding its realism. First, given the nature of the gathering for this meal, how did Jesus come to be invited? After 11:53-54, we have little reason to anticipate that hospitality would be extended to Jesus by Pharisees and legal experts (though cf. 13:31). More to the point, given the obvious character of this party as an assembly of the social elite, Jesus (who "has nowhere to lay his head" [9:58]) seems out of place. As puzzling as Jesus' invitation to this Sabbath meal might be, more baffling is the appearance of the man with dropsy. His arrival imperils the ritual purity of the meal itself, just as this man, in his diseased state, threatens the honor of this gathering of the socially powerful and privileged. What is he doing here? Our engagement with these two queries must await a more thoroughgoing examination of the setting Luke establishes in vv 1-2 (see below).

In the interim, it is important to note how the literary-cultural scripts Luke has previously established surge onto the stage in these verses, providing a virtual deluge of interpretive nuance. The presupposition pools with which the Evangelist operates come in part from common information in the discourse situation he shares with his model readers, but are also built up through the definitions and relationships he has constructed earlier in the narrative.[102] In the current episode, largely at the level of presupposition he draws on such frames as table fellowship — especially table fellowship with Pharisees (cf. 5:27-39; 7:36-50; 11:37-54) — and healing on the Sabbath (cf. 4:31-37; 6:6-11; 13:10-17). With these interpretive scripts on the horizon, we are able immediately to grasp the importance of the current scene as an attempt on Jesus' part to challenge the social world of his table companions and to invite them to share in the redemption God has made available on the Sabbath. In order to do so, they must reorient their lives around the values and dispositions that surface in a healing act that brings near the new world order known in Luke's Gospel as the kingdom of God (cf. 13:18-19).

1-2 These verses, read together,[103] provide the setting for both the current scene (vv 1-6) and this larger narrative unit (vv 1-24). In staging this unit, Luke has drawn on a number of well-worn ingredients portending the character of the ensuing encounter as one of conflict and hostility. First, Jesus is at the home of a "leader" of the Pharisees. Jesus' host is not to be confused

---

102. Green, "Discourse Analysis," 185.

103. The NRSV treats these verses as two independent clauses, but v 2 should probably be read as the apodosis.

with those persons Luke will later designate, using similar terminology, as "leaders of the people."[104] Rather, he is one of several persons in the Lukan narrative who are characterized among the socially elite, the powerful for whom the good news generally involves loss of status.[105] Because his host is a person of noble status, we may assume that those who join him at the table are likewise persons of high status in the community. Meals, after all, were used to advertise and reinforce social hierarchy.[106] Second, his host is a Pharisee, rendering unlikely the presence of any other table companions other than Pharisees (cf. v 3a). The primary behavior for which Pharisees are noted in the Gospel is that of monitoring Jesus' legal observance, and this is their role here.[107] Third, this is a dining scene,[108] where the rules of hospitality are operative, where Pharisaic concerns for ritual purity at the table are critical, where matters related to what one eats and with whom one eats it are significant, and where issues of honor and status break out into the open.[109] Fourth, Luke accents the setting of this scene on the Sabbath (vv 1, 3, 5). Because of the importance of the Sabbath as an identity marker for Jewish faithfulness in the Second Temple period, this temporal marker is of immediate significance in this co-text. The question of appropriate Sabbath behavior was an important one, much debated but scrupulously enforced through socio-religious sanctions related to one's status in the community. Because Jesus has made a practice of healing on the Sabbath, much to the consternation of those who read the Mosaic law differently, and because Luke gives an unhealthy man a prominent position ("in front of him") in this scene, we may anticipate yet another healing on the Sabbath attended by questions of propriety and conflict (see esp. 6:6-11; 13:10-17).

Of course, conflict is not the only motif served by the elaborate setting Luke establishes in vv 1-2. There is also the motif of redemptive opportunity, represented most obviously by the possibility of again interpreting the Sabbath as a time for healing.[110] Less conspicuous, but no less present, is the occasion for divine restoration offered by Jesus to his table companions. The very act of eating with these legal experts and Pharisees conveys within it the potential

104. That is, the ἄρχοντες whom Luke holds responsible for Jesus' death (23:13, 35; 24:20; Acts 3:17; 4:5, 8; 13:27).

105. See the use of δυνάστης, ἄρχων, and nouns with ἀρχι- in 1:52; 3:2; 9:22; (11:15); 12:58; 13:14. Sometimes, these persons are further described as the wealthy (also a term of importance in designations of status), who likewise come in for judgment (cf., e.g., 1:52-53; 6:24-25; 16:19-31).

106. Cf. Hamel, *Poverty and Charity,* 55.

107. See also 6:7.

108. The language of "eating bread" (for dining) is also found in 6:4; 7:33; 14:15.

109. See above on 5:27-39.

110. See above on 4:18-19; 13:10-17.

for establishing redemptive community, as does the ensuing demonstration of Jesus' persistence in sharing his message with them (vv 3-24).

If Jesus joins an elite Pharisee for a meal as a sign of his hope that his host and table companions will hear his message and embrace it, the question remains why he was invited in the first place. Perhaps an answer should be read in v 1b: Jesus is present in order that he might be watched all the more closely. This explanation is immediately suspect, since it involves our attributing to these Pharisees a willingness to jeopardize their own legal practices and ceremonial cleanliness at the very point where these intersect most visibly, at the table. Given Pharisaic table norms, questions about the realism of Jesus' presence are more sensibly addressed by our recollection that (1) Jesus is a pilgrim journeying to Jerusalem and is thus a person for whom hospitality on the Sabbath might more commonly be forthcoming; (2) Jesus' custom has been not only to attend synagogue but also to teach (see above on 4:16-17), with the result that recognition of his status as a teacher might be presupposed in the scene Luke paints; and (3) Luke has not portrayed all Pharisees with a single hue, with the consequence that the level of animosity that surfaced in 11:53-54 cannot simply be regarded as characteristic of all Pharisees.

What is the dropsical man doing here? This question is pressing not only because the diseased were often catalogued with the indigent and marginalized,[111] but also because there is some evidence to suggest that dropsy was regarded as a punishment for sin.[112] Such persons clearly did not belong in the vicinity of a table whose cleanliness is determined by Pharisaic commitments, nor in the home of the socially elite. It is true that Lukan meal scenes with Jesus are notorious for their inclusion of the wrong people (e.g., 5:27-32; 15:31-32); as in those instances, so in this one, then, it is possible that Luke's point is to say no more than that Jesus is conducting himself, not least at the table, as though the transformation of the world had already occurred. In this case, one would have all the more reason to recognize the eschatological significance of the connections between "eating bread" in vv 1 and 15, and between the presence of the dropsical man in v 2 and the proposed presence of the marginalized in vv 13, 21, and 23. The healing of the man with dropsy, then, is an embodiment of "good news to the poor" (4:18-19).

Can more be said? From a biomedical point of view, "dropsy," an almost obsolete term for generalized edema, refers to bodily swelling due to an excess of fluid; not a disease itself, dropsy is an indication of malfunction in the body, especially congestive heart failure or kidney disease.[113] Already in antiquity, the

---

111. Cf. Hamel, *Poverty and Charity,* 55-56.

112. See the discussion in van der Loos, *Miracles,* 505; Derrett, "Two Lucan Miracles," 278; cf. Lev 13:2.

113. Clayman, ed., *Encyclopedia of Medicine,* 375.

paradoxical fate of the person with dropsy was proverbial: "nothing is as dry as a person with dropsy" — signifying the insatiable thirst of one whose body is already retaining too much fluid.[114] Also known in antiquity is the metaphorical use of "dropsy" as a label for money-lovers,[115] the greedy, the rapacious — that is, for persons who share the very condition for which the Pharisees are indicted in the Gospel of Luke (11:37-44; cf. 16:14).[116] The presence of the dropsical man, according to this reading, would constitute a vivid parable of Jesus' socially elite, Pharisaical table companions. Just as in front of Jesus stood a man who had dropsy, so, around the table, sat persons whose disorder was no less self-detrimental. As Jesus moves to heal the one, so with regard to the others is diagnosis pronounced and the prospect of health extended.

3-4   That others were present at the table of a leader of the Pharisees is evident from the mention of their actions in v 1. Now, however, we receive confirmation of what we could earlier only presume — namely, that this Pharisee is sharing his table with others of similar socio-religious commitments.[117] When appearing in the company of legal experts, the Pharisees have been portrayed consistently as adversaries of Jesus and of the plan of God (see 7:29-30).[118] Luke's inclusion of this information about additional table guests thus raises the tension level in an already conflict-laden scene.

Jesus' query is reminiscent of earlier discussions about appropriate behavior on the Sabbath (e.g., 6:2, 9; 13:14-16). For the reader, Jesus' capacity to determine what constitutes acceptable Sabbath observance has already been established (6:5), though it is worth remembering that the pivotal issue here is that the OT Sabbath law was nebulous enough to require (and invite) discussion concerning its observance. Jesus' question, then, is not designed to subvert the law itself, but to query conventional wisdom regarding its interpretation. According to common thinking, even if a man with dropsy might incite pity, his condition, since it was not immediately life-threatening, did not warrant the abrogation of the Sabbath command "to rest."[119] Why is the point of view of his interlocutors missing in this scene? Why do they remain silent? Two answers

---

114. See Braun, *Feasting and Social Rhetoric*, 30n.28.

115. Stobaeus *Florilegium* 3.10.45: "Diogenes compared money-lovers to dropsies: as dropsies, though filled with fluid crave drink, so money-lovers, though loaded with money, crave more of it, yet both to their demise" (cited in Braun, *Feasting and Social Rhetoric*, 34).

116. This connection has been made by Braun, *Feasting and Social Rhetoric*, 22-42. For reasons he does not disclose, however, Braun insists that this metaphorical use of dropsy is *the* (one and only) meaning it has for Luke in this pericope (e.g., 41).

117. The elevated social status of Jesus' table companions is collaborated by the socio-historical identification of scribes as persons of relatively advanced social position; cf. Saldarini, *Pharisees, Scribes and Sadducees,* 241-76.

118. See the data collected at 9:22.

119. See above on 6:6-11.

come to mind. First, Luke has already divulged their intent to "watch Jesus closely"; given the parallel in 6:7-9, this behavior and the silence that attended it must be read as purposeful and malicious, an expression of their attempt to catch Jesus in a misdeed (cf. 11:53-54). Second, at the same time, for the reader the position of Jesus' table companions is obvious enough, having been articulated most recently by the synagogue president in 13:14. In any case, Jesus' point is that scribal specifications have missed the salvific purpose of God resident in the Sabbath;[120] Jesus, in declaring the onset of the eschatological Jubilee (see above on 4:18-19), has made this day, even the Sabbath day ("today," 4:21), the day of divine benefaction for the needy.

Jesus actions vis-à-vis the man with dropsy appear in staccato, with an urgency that will be replicated in his description of rescue from a well in v 5 ("immediately"). As is typical of Luke, "healing" and "liberation" are set in parallel, indicating the coalescing of social, biomedical, and cosmic facets in Luke's conception of health.[121]

5-6 As in 13:15-16, Jesus follows up the act of healing with a rationale borrowed from the presumed practices of those who have had a child or ox fall into a well.[122] Moreover, as in 13:17, so here the scene ends with the failure of his opponents, in this case to catch him in a misdeed. No one could object to his reasoning.[123] This is important for three interrelated reasons: (1) the silence of his table companions marks this scene as a struggle regarding Jesus' relative position within a group of persons distinguished by lofty status; (2) it establishes Jesus as an authoritative teacher who is able to determine what constitutes acceptable Sabbath observance; and (3) this opens the door for his further instruction as an authoritative teacher in vv 7-24.

5.5.4.2. Recasting Meal Etiquette (14:7-14)

7 *When he noticed how the guests chose the places of honor, he told them a parable.* 8 *"When you are invited by someone to a wedding banquet, do not sit down at the place of honor, in case someone more*

---

120. Cf. Westerholm, *Jesus,* 100-102; Salo, *Luke's Treatment of the Law,* 133; Hasel, "Sabbath," 855; Robinson, *Old Testament Sabbath,* 347-50.

121. ἀπολύω is often translated "to dismiss" in this verse (so, e.g., the NRSV and most commentaries), ignoring the presence of this among other parallels with 13:10-17 (ἀπολύω, v 12). Given the pervasiveness of Luke's description of malady in psychosocial, biomedical, *and* cosmic terms, and the obvious relation of 14:1-6 to 13:10-17, the most natural translation of ἀπολύω in this co-text is with the nuance of "release" (from the illness). On Luke's more holistic understanding of health and healing, see the discussion and bibliography at 13:10-17.

122. For this debate, see *m. Šabb.* 18:3; CD 11:13-14. The Qumranic text evidences a position more stringent than the one Jesus presupposes.

123. For the motif of silence employed in this way, cf. 20:26; Acts 11:18.

distinguished than you has been invited by your host; 9 and the host who invited both of you may come and say to you, 'Give this person your place,' and then in disgrace you would start to take the lowest place. 10 But when you are invited, go and sit down at the lowest place, so that when your host comes, he may say to you, 'Friend, move up higher'; then you will be honored in the presence of all who sit at the table with you. 11 For all who exalt themselves will be humbled, and those who humble themselves will be exalted."

12 He said also to the one who had invited him, "When you give a luncheon or a dinner, do not invite your friends or your brothers or your relatives or rich neighbors, in case they may invite you in return, and you would be repaid. 13 But when you give a banquet, invite the poor, the crippled, the lame, and the blind. 14 And you will be blessed, because they cannot repay you, for you will be repaid at the resurrection of the righteous."

Having established his status as an authoritative teacher (vv 1-6), Jesus is in a position to address his table companions directly. His message takes its point of departure from the meal setting established in v 1, with vv 7 and 12 serving specifically to recall the setting. Although two topics are treated under the heading of "recasting table etiquette," they are best read together. First, they are bound together by the language of invitation that permeates these two paragraphs.[124] Second, they share a similar structure:

Verses 7-11	*Verses 12-14*
Jesus addresses his fellow guests	Jesus addresses his host
When you are invited to a meal . . .	When you host a meal with guests . . .
Do not . . . lest . . .	Do not . . . lest . . .
But when you are invited to a meal . . .	But when you host a meal with guests . . .
Then you will . . . because. . . .	Then you will . . . because. . . .[125]

124. καλέω — vv 7, 8 (2x), 9, 10 (2x), 12, and 13. φωνέω — v 12. ἀντικαλέω — v 13.

125. The NRSV has not in every case preserved the parallelism immediately obvious in the Greek text:

Verses 7-11	*Verses 12-14*
ἔλεγεν δὲ . . .	ἔλεγεν δὲ . . .
ὅταν . . .	ὅταν . . .
μὴ . . .	μὴ . . .
μήποτε . . .	μήποτε . . .
ἀλλ' ὅταν . . .	ἀλλ' ὅταν . . .
τότε ἔσται . . . δόξα . . . ὅτι. . . .	καὶ μακάριος ἔσῃ ὅτι. . . .

Cf. Noël, "Parable of the Wedding Guest," 20-21.

Because the sharing of food is a "delicate barometer" of social relations,[126] when Jesus subverts conventional mealtime practices related to seating arrangements and invitations, he is doing far more than offering sage counsel for his table companions. Rather, he is toppling the familiar world of the ancient Mediterranean, overturning its socially constructed reality and replacing it with what must have been regarded as a scandalous alternative.

Intimacy with two interrelated ingredients of the taken-for-granted world of Roman antiquity is assumed in this segment of Jesus' table talk.[127] First, this was a world in which social status and social stratification were vital considerations in the structuring of life, with one's status based on the social estimation of one's relative honor — that is, on the perception of those around a person regarding his prestige. For example, where one sat (was assigned or allowed to sit) at a meal vis-à-vis the host was a public advertisement of one's status;[128] as a consequence, the matter of seating arrangements was carefully attended and, in this agonistic society, one might presume to claim a more honorable seat with the hope that it (and the honor that went with it) might be granted. What is more, because meals were used to publicize and reinforce social hierarchy, invitations to meals were themselves carefully considered so as to allow to one's table only one's own inner circle, or only those persons whose presence at one's table would either enhance or at least preserve one's social position.

Second, central to the political stability of the Empire was the ethics of reciprocity, a gift-and-obligation system that tied every person, from the emperor in Rome to the child in the most distance province, into an intricate web of social relations. Apart from certain relations within the family unit and discussions of ideal friendship, gifts, by unwritten definition, were never "free," but were given and received with either explicit or implicit strings attached. Expectations of reciprocity were naturally extended to the table: To accept an invitation was to obligate oneself to extend a comparable one, a practice that circumscribed the list of those to whom one might extend an invitation. The powerful and privileged would not ordinarily think to invite the poor to their meals, for this would (1) possibly endanger the social status of the host; (2) be a wasted invitation, since the self-interests of the elite could never be served by an invitation that could not be reciprocated; and (3) ensue in embarrassment for the poor, who could not reciprocate and, therefore, would be required by social protocols to decline the invitation. As will become clear below, in recording Jesus' table talk, Luke exploits these cultural scripts in

---

126. So Sahlins, *Economics,* 215.

127. See above, §10.

128. Cf., e.g., Neyrey, "Ceremonies," 364; Gowler, *Portraits of the Pharisees,* 248-49; Moxnes, *Economy of the Kingdom,* 135.

order to undermine the taken-for-granted values and expectations of his discourse situation and, thus, to construct a new vision of life.

7 Luke's opening depiction of Jesus is almost comical. The Pharisees and scribes of this dinner party had been watching him closely (v 1), but now they are the ones being monitored; what is more, whereas in their attempts to unmask Jesus as one who transgresses the law they had been reduced to silence, he now exposes their impropriety. According to widespread cultural norms, seeking places of honor (literally, "the first seats") might be characterized as typical (if not universally sanctioned) behavior,[129] but within the Third Gospel such behavior is negatively assessed as consonant with a proclivity toward self-exaltation for which the Pharisees are becoming known (cf. 11:43).[130] Jesus' response takes the form of a "parable" — understood in this case as counsel regarding public posturing for recognition and status.[131]

8-11 Although Jesus refers to a "wedding banquet," he does not seem to understand his instruction as restricted to that distinctive social setting. In vv 12-13, he uses other language in a similarly nontechnical way.[132] The structure of his directive is straightforward. First, he appeals to the realities of an honor-shame culture in order to advise against taking the "first seats." Then he demarcates a more prudent strategy when entering a banquet room. Because honor is socially determined, if one's claim to honor fails to be reciprocated by one's audience, one is publicly humiliated. Better, Jesus says, to have your honor bestowed on you by another than to make a bid for honor that might not be granted. Luke envisions the impartation of honor in the form of a new, more lofty, seat assignment, but also in the use of the term "friend," signifying a relationship (again, not claimed by the guest but conferred by the host) of equality and mutuality with the host.

Thus far, it is tempting to imagine that Luke is working altogether within the social systems of Roman antiquity. Although he notes how Jesus advised against seeking honor, the reception of honor along ordinary, socially defined lines remains unquestioned. Seemingly, the only thing changed is the strategy by which one obtains one's objective. With v 11, however, Luke

---

129. Braun (*Feasting and Social Rhetoric*, 46) notes that, among ancient writers, Plutarch also devoted himself to censuring the practice of using one's position at the table as a measurement of social rank. Plutarch's comments serve to indicate, however, how normal concerns with rank and privilege at the table were.

130. See the similar depiction of the scribes in 20:46.

131. Luke can employ the term παραβολή in a variety of ways that do not always cohere with the idea of "parable" in English — cf., e.g., 4:23 and 5:36, where παραβολή denotes a proverbial saying.

132. γάμους, ἄριστον, δεῖπνον, and δοχήν appear to be used almost interchangeably for "a meal with guests."

narrates how Jesus moves from dispensing "good advice,"[133] whose central ideas are essentially shaped by his larger discourse situation, so as to disengage from that situation and, in fact, to recast the values of that social world in a significant way. On the one hand, his teaching has called into question the self-seeking agenda of his table companions, insisting that honor must be given, not pursued or taken. More fundamentally, however, he now goes on to hint at a life-world in which honor is measured and granted along unforeseen lines. "The humble," in the social world Luke addresses, usually denoted persons who are of low birth, base, and ignoble,[134] yet in the topsy-turvy world Jesus envisages, "the humble" are those most valued.

The aphorism of v 11, then, must first be read as an indication of what God values, of what is most highly valued in the kingdom of God, and of the basis on which judgment will be enacted. Evidence that, for Luke, these are the values being implemented by God is readily available, beginning already with the disgraced Elizabeth, who, in God's providence, is enabled to become pregnant in spite of her old age (1:7, 24-26); with Mary, whose encounter with God taught her to say, "God my Savior . . . has looked with favor on the lowliness of his servant" (1:47-48);[135] and more generally in Luke's construal of the divine purpose as manifest in "good news to the poor" (4:18-19). Second, for those whose dispositions have been transformed to reflect the divine economy, v 11 can be read as moral guidance, reflected in the behavior advised in vv 8-10; read in this way, Jesus' "parable" is not designed to provide one with a new strategy by which one might obtain the commendation of one's peers. Instead, it insists that the only commendation one needs comes from the God who is unimpressed with such social credentials as govern social relations in Luke's world — for example, family lineage, network of friends, and wealth.

12-14 Just as Jesus' fellow guests had occupied themselves in normal, honor-seeking pursuits upon arrival at the meal, so Jesus' host had followed ordinary conventions in putting together his invitation list. Because invitations served as currency in the marketplace of prestige and power, there is nothing extraordinary or particularly objectionable to the inclusion of one's social peers and family, persons from whom one could expect reciprocation. This is true, at least, for those willing to work within the established world system. Seen through Jesus' eyes, however, orthodox conventions have as their consequence the exclusion of the poor; after all, for the social elite the poor are

---

133. See the analogues in Prov 25:6-7; Sir 3:17-20.

134. See *TLNT*, 3:369; Spicq (3:370) goes on to note, however, that ταπεινός might refer to the virtue of "modesty." Cf. Johnson, 224; Braun, *Feasting and Social Rhetoric*, 50-52.

135. Green, "Social Status." See York, *The Last Shall Be First*, esp. 78-80.

unhelpful in the business of parading and advancing one's social position and, perhaps more importantly in the current co-text,[136] the poor could not reciprocate. The Pharisees are thus portrayed as persons who exploit hospitality for self-serving agenda, and whose patterns of hospitality both secure their positions of dominance in their communities and insulate them from the needy.[137]

Jesus' counterproposal, if conventionalized, would negate tendencies toward exclusionary social boundaries and the value of reciprocity. It is difficult to exaggerate the repercussions of such practices. First, they would deconstruct the categories of insider-outsider that come to expression in the two contrasting lists of invitees. In v 12, Jesus provides a catalogue of one's "inner circle," persons with whom one enjoys relationships of equality and mutuality — a list grounded in the commerce of power and privilege, and in social location as an insider. The list in v 13, on the other hand, is reminiscent of the inventories of certain Qumranic texts concerned with the identity of God's people and, more particularly, with who are excluded from the status of the elect.[138] Jesus' message overturns such preoccupations, presenting "the poor, the crippled, the lame, and the blind" — notable examples of those relegated to low status, marginalized according to normal canons of status honor in the Mediterranean world — as persons to be numbered among one's table intimates and, by analogy, among the people of God.

Second, such practices would sound the death knell for the ethics of patronage and, more generally, for the regulation of social affiliations according to the demands of reciprocity. The behaviors Jesus demands would collapse the distance between rich and poor, insider and outsider; reverting to anthropological models of economic exchange,[139] such relations would be characterized by "generalized reciprocity" — that is, by the giving of gifts, the extension of hospitality, without expectation of return (see above, 6:32-35). Persons previously treated as outsiders, strangers, would be embraced as members of one's extended kin group. Insofar as Jesus' host and table companions are comprised of the socially elite, his message to them would entail a form of unpremeditated generosity involving redistribution on behalf of "the poor."

Recognition of the structure of the beatitude, or pronouncement of blessing, of v 14a is critical. According to Jesus, the state of blessedness resides in the fact that one has given without expectation (or hope!) of return. It is true that, according to v 14b, blessedness will take the eschatological

---

136. Note the fourfold presence of the notion of reciprocation: ἀντικαλέω (v 12) and ἀνταποδίδωμι (vv 12, 14 [2x]).

137. Moxnes, *Economy of the Kingdom,* 131.

138. See above on 4:18-19.

139. See above, §10.

form of divine "repayment," but Jesus does not advise people to engage in guileless generosity *in order that* one might receive divine benefaction. Luke has already established that human generosity flows from an appreciation of the expansive mercy of God (6:36); to this he now adds that genuine, uncalculating generosity toward those of low status will not go unrewarded.

What form might this repayment take? Jesus' final words provide a clue. It is not coincidental that the "resurrection" is mentioned for the first time in the Lukan narrative in Jesus' discourse with the Pharisees, since the Pharisaic belief in the resurrection is otherwise important to Luke (cf. Acts 23:6; 24:15). It is of interest, though, that here the reference is to the resurrection *of the righteous only* (cf. "of both the righteous and the unrighteous" in Acts 24:15; see Dan 12:1-2), as if to intimate that "the righteous" are those whose worldview is transformed along the lines Jesus promulgates, who accept his notion of God as the Great Benefactor, and whose practices take the form of selfless generosity and redistribution on behalf of those who, for whatever reason, live at the margins of society.

5.5.4.3. A Wealthy Householder and His Invitation List (14:15-24)

15 *One of the dinner guests, on hearing this, said to him, "Blessed is anyone who will eat bread in the kingdom of God!"* 16 *Then Jesus said to him, "Someone gave a great dinner and invited many.* 17 *At the time for the dinner he sent his slave to say to those who had been invited, 'Come; for everything is ready now.'* 18 *But they all alike began to make excuses. The first said to him, 'I have bought a piece of land, and I must go out and see it; please accept my regrets.'* 19 *Another said, 'I have bought five yoke of oxen, and I am going to try them out; please accept my regrets.'* 20 *Another said, 'I have just been married, and therefore I cannot come.'* 21 *So the slave returned and reported this to his master. Then the owner of the house became angry and said to his slave, 'Go out at once into the streets and lanes of the town and bring in the poor, the crippled, the blind, and the lame.'* 22 *And the slave said, 'Sir, what you ordered has been done, and there is still room.'* 23 *Then the master said to the slave, 'Go out into the roads and lanes, and compel people to come in, so that my house may be filled.* 24 *For I tell you, none of those who were invited will taste my dinner.'"*

As Luke often has it, Jesus' instruction is again interrupted by someone whose anonymity allows the spotlight to remain on Jesus and whose intruding statement becomes for Jesus a launching pad for further instruction.[140] Thus far in

140. Cf., e.g., 11:27, 45; 12:13; 13:1, 23, 31.

this narrative unit, the practices of his fellow guests and host have provided the fodder for Jesus' message (vv 7, 12); now reference to one of their characteristic beliefs, concerning the eschatological banquet, plays this part. Luke 14:15-24 is carefully stitched into its co-text by references to a dinner guest and "eating bread,"[141] by the identification of the pronouncement of blessedness in v 15 as a response to Jesus' words about the resurrection of the righteous in v 14, and by the context-appropriate subject matter of Jesus' story in vv 16-24.

Our capacity to appreciate the force of Jesus' message is dependent in large part on our comprehension of important protocols related to dining in the Mediterranean world (see above on 5.4). These have especially to do with the use of invitations to grand meals for the purpose of promoting one's status in the community and more generally of meals to signal the lines of demarcation between social insiders and outcasts. That such conventions are being accessed is immediately transparent not only from the preparation for this story in vv 7-14, but also from the important markers of the host's advanced status in the description of the dinner as "great" (v 16) and the number of guests as "many" (v 16), the identification of the host as a "lord" and householder (vv 21, 22, 23), and the portrayal of the guests on the initial invitation list as persons of substance (vv 18-20). Jesus' story, then, combines the socially debilitating rejection of a well-placed host by his peers with a surprisingly unconventional list of invitees from among the destitute.[142] The result is the generation of an unorthodox social order that stands in glaring contrast to the system currently in place (and exhibited in vv 7, 12).

The significance of Jesus' banquet story in its immediate co-text is registered by the subtle but consequential shift from the third-person singular in v 16 ("Jesus said *to him*") to the second-person plural in v 24 ("For I tell *you* [all]"). Since Jesus and his conversation partner are at the table, it is not unusual that Jesus' reply would be directed to the one but intended for the hearing of all present. What is surprising is that, at the end of the story, the "master" refers to "you all" (plural) at the close of his directive to his slave (singular). Clearly, at this juncture the master addresses his table guests, but even more pointedly "he steps as it were on to the apron of the stage and addresses the audience."[143] This presses home the urgency of this story and raises the question of how it functions in this scene.

141. For "guests," cf. vv 1, 7, 15; "eating bread" is found in vv 1 and 15.

142. Jeremias (*Parables,* 178-80) draws attention to an analogous story of the rich toll collector Bar Ma'jan, who arranged a banquet for the elite of his city; with flimsy excuses, they decline his invitation, with the result that he invites beggars in their stead. Importantly, though, Luke's account provides no support for a comparison between the host and a socially dubious toll collection. See further Palmer, "Just Married," 250-52; Rohrbaugh, "Pre-industrial City," 142.

143. Linnemann, *Parables,* 90.

Interpreters have typically drawn attention to its importance in identifying those who will be on the guest list for the eschatological banquet.[144] Despite its near canonical status, this reading is not without its difficulties. Foremost is its unflattering portrait of God, who, according to this view, must be figuratively identified with the host of the great (read: end-time) banquet. Unraveled along these lines, the parable would have us imagine that, at some time, God had extended invitations in a way consistent with the socially elite of Luke's world. Such invitations would accordingly have included only the select — as though God's initial invitation list would have excluded "the poor, the crippled, the blind, and the lame," and so on, in favor of those with the wherewithal necessary, say, to be landowners (v 18b). According to this reading, the inclusion of "the poor" would be for God a kind of afterthought, an alternative course of action forced upon him by his need to have a full house (v 23) and by his having surprisingly been spurned by those first invited. But such a portrait is fundamentally at odds with Luke's *theology* (cf. 6:35-36),[145] with Luke's notion that the divine purpose being consummated in Jesus' mission is nothing other than the ancient promise to Abraham (e.g., 1:46-55), and with the Isaianic vision, already embracing both Jew and Gentile, on the horizon of the banquet scene Jesus imagines (Isa 25:6-10; see above, on 5.4). Nevertheless, Jesus' story has generally been read so as to suggest that the Jewish leadership (or even the Jewish people!) have refused their places at the table of salvation, with the result that their places are given to others, especially the marginalized and the Gentile.[146]

144. Recently, e.g., Bailey, *Through Peasant Eyes,* 88-113; Donahue, *Gospel in Parable,* 140-46; Blomberg, *Parables,* 233-37.

145. This does not mean that interpreters ought in principle to avoid finding allegory or allegorical elements in Jesus' parables, a point well argued in Blomberg, *Parables.* However, this is neither the first nor the last time in Luke that a straightforward, allegorical identification of an authority.figure with God is problematic — cf., e.g., 11:5-8; 16:1-9; 18:1-8.

146. In fact, in Luke's narration, Jesus' story provides no explicit means by which to disambiguate the Jewish or non-Jewish status of those invited in vv 16, 21, and 23. J. T. Sanders (*Jews,* 196) is nonetheless representative: "Taken alone, the parable in its Lucan form would seem to set up a three stage plan of salvation: to the proper Jews, to the outcasts . . . , and to Gentiles . . . , with the first group, of course, turning down the invitation. Either pattern — not the Jews but the Gentiles, or not the 'true' Jews but the periphery and then the Gentiles — would fit Luke's plan." Cf. Johnson (232), who finds here "a fairly transparent allegory of Luke's narrative as a whole"; Johnson, however, speaks of the rejection of the Jewish leadership, not of the Jews as such. (Anti-Jewish readings of Jesus' story are likewise rejected by Vine, "Luke 14:15-24.") Gowler (*Portraits of the Pharisees,* 246) argues that the invited guests who refuse to attend God's banquet are clearly the Pharisees, who oppose Jesus' ministry. For him, the parable serves in part as a warning for the Pharisees to change their attitude toward Jesus and no longer to refuse

An alternative reading would take v 14 — with its pronouncement of blessing for those who adopt the topsy-turvy forms of dining etiquette proposed by Jesus — as Jesus' challenge to his table associates, with the story Jesus now goes on to relate serving as an exemplar of a member of the socially elite who did undergo such a transformation.[147] In this case, the prestigious company with whom Jesus is dining would be lured into the story through their identification with the man who "gave a great dinner and invited many." The central question would thus be, Will Jesus' audience include the poor among their table intimates, without concern for reciprocation? Will they live according to an utterly transformed social order in which their practices as dinner hosts are oriented not toward the noble but toward the poor; not toward status maintenance or advancement, but toward the implementation of a social order privileging an uncalculating generosity toward the poor? (See above on vv 7-14.)

Of course, the question of who will be included or excluded from the end-time banquet is an important one, even if the primary focus falls on how to comport oneself in one's community. The initial statement of fortune in v 15, pronouncing blessing on those who will eat bread in the kingdom of God, builds on Jesus' identification of whose who "will be repaid at the resurrection of the righteous" in v 14. Who will be repaid at the resurrection? Who will eat bread in the kingdom? The answer to both questions is the same: those who, like the aristocratic host of Jesus' story (vv 16-24), take leave of deeply embedded social norms concerning status honor — norms that erect barricades between the rich and the poor and/or lead to power-ridden relationships of obligation — and embrace a new social order governed by the kingdom of God with its concern for the destitute and outcast (cf. 4:18-19; 7:22).

15 The beatitude spoken by an unnamed table guest may appear to introduce at best a side issue detracting from the flow of Jesus' instruction. In fact, it is closely bound up with both the scene Luke has painted and the locus of Jesus' message. Widespread sentiments among Jewish people are encapsulated in the representation of the eschaton as a feast;[148] moreover, at Qumran the normal cycle of meals anticipated the messianic banquet and in the Lukan narrative Jesus himself has repeatedly acted as though the kingdom were proleptically present in his meals.[149] Hence, it is not extraordinary that

---

their invitations. This ingenious reading helpfully accounts for the context of Jesus' teaching at the dinner table with Pharisees (and scribes), but falters on the logic of the story itself; if the Pharisees accept the invitation, the possibility of further invitations, for the poor and outcast, will never arise!

147. A similar reading is presented by Braun, *Feasting and Social Rhetoric,* 62-131.

148. For documentation, see above on 13:28-30.

149. For Qumran, see the helpful survey in Priest, "Messianic Banquet." In the Lukan narrative, see, e.g., 5:29-32.

we find in a meal the occasion for discourse on the kingdom banquet. Moreover, Jesus has himself just invited speculation of this sort by tying meal practices in the present to divine compensation in the eschaton (v 14); indeed, it is *this* statement of Jesus that provides the impetus for the pronouncement of blessing from the anonymous guest. The beatitude itself focuses attention on the identification of those "who will" participate in the end-time feast. Elsewhere, a beatitude pronounced by a bystander contains within it an erroneous perception of the nature of true piety (11:27-28). This may suggest a comparable flaw here, in which case the speaker would not be naively standing on neutral ground to proclaim a shared tenet of faith. Instead, he would be voicing his assumption, and that of his table companions, that he and they were among the blessed who would eat bread in the kingdom.

It is worth inquiring into the basis of such presumptuousness, and there is indirect evidence aplenty within the Lukan narrative to suggest that these Pharisees and scribes base their claim to "the resurrection of the righteous" on their lineage as children of Abraham and their noble status.[150] Jesus, however, has spoken of alternative credentials related to practices at the table. It is on account of faithful behavior growing out of a reorientation toward the purpose of God that one's invitation for the eschatological feast is confirmed.

16-17 By way of reply, Jesus relates a story, whether fictitious or actual we are not told, the beginning of which would appear to make common cause with his audience. After all, he is in the home of a ruler among Pharisees, gathered at the table with other socially elite Pharisees and scribes. They would easily see themselves in the mirror Jesus constructs, with references to the *great* dinner and the *many* invited serving to underscore the relative prestige of the host. At the same time, the size of the prepared feast necessitates the subsequent extraordinary attempts to "fill" the house (v 23b).

Jesus' story assumes the extension of double invitations, a practice rooted in pragmatic needs of more than one sort. First, preparation for the feast required a count of the number of invitations accepted. With the number of anticipated guests determined, the host is able to determine what animal(s) is to be killed and cooked.[151] Guests also needed time to prepare themselves. Also of consequence was the need for potential guests to ascertain who else was coming in order that they might determine the social propriety of their sharing a meal with others on the list. Again, the impor-

---

150. See, e.g., the discussion above, on 13:25-27.
151. Bailey (*Through Peasant Eyes,* 94): "He then decides on the killing/butchering of a chicken or two (for 2-4 guests), or a duck (for 5-8), or a kid (10-15 acceptances), or a sheep (if there are 15-35 people), or a calf (35-75)." Cf. Braun, *Feasting and Social Rhetoric,* 102.

tance of meals for publicizing and/or securing one's status in the community comes to the fore.[152]

From the standpoint of Jesus' story, it is important to realize that the feast-event is unfolding according to appropriate norms, all is proceeding as expected, and the final summons to the prepared meal is grounded in the assumption that all will come. We have been given no hint of the disastrous turn of events Jesus will now relate.

18-20   Social status is a product of peer approval; hence, it can be wrenched away just as it can be awarded. Typically in the world of Luke, those marginalized are the poor, the diseased, the impure, and so on. This is not always the case, however; as 19:1-10 will indicate, a wealthy ruler can be numbered among those rejected by the people of his own community.[153] Similarly, in this instance, the socially elite of the host's community close ranks against him and shame him publicly. Whatever one makes of their excuses, their refusal to join the great dinner is a social strategy the effect of which is the host's defamation.

Some interpreters have found legislation from Deut 20:5-7; 24:5 lurking in the background of the excuses put forward by these prospective guests. There, persons are excused from battle if they have built a house but not dedicated it, planted a vineyard but not enjoyed its fruit, or if they are engaged or newly married.[154] If such an allusion is present, it comes in the form of an irony, a joke at the expense of those who make such excuses.[155] In the deuteronomic co-text, people are excused from battle because of the threat of death and, thus, the possibility that they will not be able to enjoy their home, their vineyard, or their marriage. The proposed dinner is not life-threatening, however, so that an appeal to the deuteronomic analogy would accent the triviality of these excuses.

More pervasively rooted in the Lukan framework is the way these excuses identify the would-be guests as persons whose lives are wrongly embedded in their possessions and family relationships.[156] Although "many"

---

152. See Rohrbaugh, "Pre-industrial City," 141; Braun, *Feasting and Social Rhetoric,* 103.

153. Douglas (*Risk and Blame,* 85) observes that, although "techniques of rejection" are often taken "as ways of dealing with marginal categories," "sometimes the person to be rejected is not marginal at all: an unpopular leader, a young tyrant, an ageing monarch. It is necessary to realize that the same strategies of rejection may sometimes be used against the powerful."

154. Recently, cf., e.g., Donahue, *Gospel in Parable,* 141.

155. See Palmer, "Just Married," 241-44, 248-49.

156. Dominic ("Lucan Source," 281-86) identifies the problems as (1) preoccupation with possessions, (2) the exercise of authority, and (3) preoccupation with marriage. His second point is overly subtle, however, and misses the obvious reality that one who

were invited and "they all" made excuses (vv 16, 18), Jesus documents only three that must be deemed as representative. The first two clearly portray persons of wealth and property. Inasmuch as a farmer-landowner was unlikely to purchase a field without having carefully examined it, the first is apparently portrayed as an absentee landowner, a wealthy man of the city. Five yoke of oxen would be required to work a farm of well over a hundred acres, a substantial property in a socio-historical context wherein peasant families might farm three to six acres per adult.[157] Within its immediate co-text, the identification of these would-be guests as persons of wealth and probable status would not have been lost on Jesus' table companions, whose reactions might have ranged from the shock of hearing a host of means being snubbed by guests of substance, to the knowing nod as they recognized the behavior of the would-be guests as a calculated move to shame this man. Against the backdrop of the larger Lukan narrative, Luke's audience will recognize these would-be guests as persons who are preoccupied with possessions, marking them as persons who have not embraced the values and practices that flow from a fundamental commitment to the Father whose "good pleasure" is represented in the gift of the kingdom (12:32-34; cf. 14:33). The third excuse is closely related, since family, like possessions, must be subordinated to the demands of the kingdom (cf. 8:19-21; 9:59-62; 14:26).

21-23 Previously, the host was portrayed indirectly as a person of means; now this characterization is solidified with multiple references to him as "lord" (vv 21, 23) and as householder (v 21). Recognition of his position at least as a status equal of the wealthy people of the city portrayed in vv 18-19 is thus insured, and this (1) emphasizes the social vilification he had experienced at the hands of those who refused his invitation, and (2) accentuates the status disjunction between himself and his original guest list on the one hand, and the persons who comprise his second and third guest lists on

---

purchases five yoke of oxen must be wealthy. Moxnes (*Economy of the Kingdom,* 57) rightly notes that vv 18-19 describe people of property; cf. Gowler, *Portraits of the Pharisees,* 247; Rohrbaugh, "Pre-industrial City," 143; Bailey, *Through Peasant Eyes,* 95-98. Braun (*Feasting and Social Rhetoric,* 75-80) thinks that all three excuses are property-motivated. By making the third excuse a question of property, however, he (1) misconstrues marriage practices, assuming that in "taking over a woman" the man is "closing a deal," without realizing that the exchange of the "bride price" was related to betrothal, not the marriage itself; (2) adopts a view of women as "property" for which he provides no collaborative evidence in the Lukan narrative; and (3) neglects Luke's well-documented concern that "family ties" not take precedent over response to the word of God.

157. See the discussion in Wolf, *Peasants,* 19-35; Jeremias, *Parables,* 177; Rohrbaugh, "Pre-industrial City," 143. A small farm in Roman times would measure between 6 and 60 acres. On account of this one purchase, we may assume that this man is the owner of at least a medium-sized estate (cf. Hedrick, *Parables,* 154n.41).

the other. Indeed, the people invited to the feast in vv 21 and 23 come from the opposite extreme of the social spectrum than those first invited.

In the tug-of-war of an honor-shame society, anger and indignation are intrinsic to the game, for failure to receive an expected invitation or to accept an invitation is the negative currency of social fortune.[158] What is remarkable is that anger leads not to reprisal but to behavior that departs dramatically from the social system of reciprocity and status preservation that has thus far been characteristic of the socially elite in the larger narrative unit of vv 1-24. Indeed, this "lord" now seems to repudiate the need for approval from his peers; he certainly acts in a way that despises the social order in which he had previously demonstrated his deftness.

Thus, he engages in a second and third series of invitations, the third made necessary by the need to fill his sizeable banquet (v 16). It is sometimes thought that these new invitations are extended first to the marginalized among the Jewish population ("in the streets and lanes of the town") and then to the Gentiles (outside the town).[159] One looks in vain within the Lukan narrative or beyond for instances wherein these proximities (in or outside town) are used to distinguish Jews and Gentiles, however. Luke seems not to be interested in specifying the precise nature of the socio-religious divisions at work here, though the reverberations of the eschatological banquet scene from Isa 25:6-10 in this narrative unit preclude any attempt to suggest that Gentiles might not be included here (cf. 13:28-30).

Indeed, the point seems to be that, now working from a transformed understanding of social relations, this householder will include *anyone* among his table guests — that is, no one is too sullied, too wretched, to be counted as a friend at table. Thus, "the roads and lanes" of the city would be the location of the dwellings of those of low status, whether due to their despised occupation, their family heritage, their religious impurity, their poverty, or some other cause. With the proviso that the "blind" and "lame" are transposed in order, the second list of persons to be invited is a replica of the one Jesus provides in v 13. This identifies the master of Jesus' story as an exemplar of an elite who took Jesus' earlier counsel (vv 12-14) seriously and extended hospitality to those generally defined by their dishonorable status, their exclusion from circles of power and privilege. These belong to the category of people excluded from full membership in the people of God at Qumran. But these are the people for whom the coming of Jesus entails "good news."[160]

That such persons would not normally frequent the dinner parties of

---

158. See Braun, *Feasting and Social Rhetoric,* 114-15, esp. 115n.49.

159. Recently, e.g., Bailey, *Through Peasant Eyes,* 100-102; Blomberg, *Parables,* 234-35.

160. See the extended discussion above, on 4:18-19.

persons such as this master is equally evident from the language of invitation employed in v 21. They are not simply to be "invited," but must be "brought" or "led in" to his feast.[161] Similarly, those of the third invitation list must be compelled.[162] This is not merely because proper etiquette required them to decline an invitation. Rather, such persons knew (1) that they could not possibly reciprocate an invitation from a prestigious man capable of so sizeable a feast and (2) that they belonged to an altogether alien social world, across socio-religious barriers one simply did not cross. Indeed, the persons envisioned in the third invitation live outside the town, a probably reference not to peasants living in villages (note: "into the roads and lanes," not "into the outlying villages"), but to the utterly destitute and impure typically disallowed from living within the walls of the city.[163]

It is important to realize that the master/host, in extending hospitality to such persons, has not thereby become their benefactor. That is, there is no hint that his practices are based on the calculus of reciprocity and onerous obligation. Instead, by extending hospitality to such persons, he has stepped completely outside the patronal ethics of the Mediterranean world; in Jesus' earlier words, he has invited those who cannot repay him, from whom he has nothing to gain by way of enhanced prestige or monetary enhancement. He has participated in the creation of a new social order in which the boundaries that normally exclude people like himself from people like them are rendered inconsequential. He initiates a new community grounded in gracious and uncalculating hospitality.

24 The depth of the host's transformation is signaled in his parting words.[164] Those originally invited will have no part in the feast. This is not so much a statement of judgment against those who have shunned the host. After all, closing ranks against a peer is damaging but not irreparably so. This householder has raised the stakes considerably further by completely rejecting the very social order that gave power and significance to those who had heaped shame on him. Hence, it is difficult to imagine that they would want to share in the meal as it was now configured! If not as a pronouncement of judgment, how does this declaration function? First, it provides the host with an oppor-

161. Here Luke uses the term εἰσάγω rather than the more normal καλέω.

162. ἀναγκάζω.

163. See the helpful description provided by Braun, *Feasting and Social Rhetoric,* 86-94 (following Rohrbaugh, "Pre-industrial City," 144-45).

164. Exegetical discussion has revolved around whether v 24 belongs to the story (i.e., is spoken by the master) or is Jesus' comment on the story. The primary difficulty for the first view, which is otherwise the more natural, is the use of a second-person plural (v 24) in an address ostensibly to a slave (singular). This obstacle is surmounted if one recognizes that the plural "you" is a dramatic device whereby the master is allowed to speak to those outside his own story, as Linnemann (*Parables,* 90; cf. Nolland, 2:758) saw.

tunity for self-assessment: His transformation is without qualification. No longer will his social relations be governed by the old system. Second, the host, characterized throughout this story as a member of the elite, is thus allowed to address the elite of Jesus' own audience and, then, of Luke's audience as well. Presented as an exemplar of Jesus' message in vv 12-14, he now, as it were, addresses his peers with an implicit challenge that they embrace social identity with the poor and destitute, those incapable of participating in the social games of reciprocity and status augmentation.[165]

5.5.5. Conditions of Discipleship (14:25-35)

25 *Now large crowds were traveling with him; and he turned and said to them,* 26 *"Whoever comes to me and does not hate father and mother, wife and children, brothers and sisters, yes, and even life itself, cannot be my disciple.* 27 *Whoever does not carry the cross and follow me cannot be my disciple.* 28 *For which of you, intending to build a tower, does not first sit down and estimate the cost, to see whether he has enough to complete it?* 29 *Otherwise, when he has laid a foundation and is not able to finish, all who see it will begin to ridicule him,* 30 *saying, 'This fellow began to build and was not able to finish.'* 31 *Or what king, going out to wage war against another king, will not sit down first and consider whether he is able with ten thousand to oppose the one who comes against him with twenty thousand?* 32 *If he cannot, then, while the other is still far away, he sends a delegation and asks for the terms of peace.* 33 *So therefore, none of you can become my disciple if you do not bid farewell to all you have.*[166]

34 *"Salt is good; but if salt has lost its taste, how can its saltiness be restored?* 35 *It is fit neither for the soil nor for the manure pile; they throw it away. Let anyone with ears to hear listen!"*

With v 25 Luke marks a change of scene, first, by associating Jesus again with "large crowds" (cf. 11:29; 12:1, 54), then by an explicit return to the journey motif — this following his extended interaction with the Pharisees and legal experts in the table scene of vv 1-24. As will become immediately clear, this shift signals renewed possibilities for gathering disciples at the same time that it raises again the importance for Luke of the journey to Jerusalem as an opportunity for the formation of disciples.[167]

Notwithstanding such significant changes in audience and setting, there

---

165. Cf. Brawley, *Luke-Acts*, 103; York, *The Last Shall Be First*, 144.
166. NRSV: "give up all your possessions."
167. For this motif, see above, the introduction to 9:51–19:48.

are important topical connections between the current narrative unit and the preceding one.[168] Particularly in Jesus' story of the great banquet (vv 15-24), he had introduced the possibility that one's ties to possessions and family might disqualify one from enjoying the feast. As Jesus turns to address the crowds traveling with him, he lists allegiance to one's family network and the shackles that constitute one's possessions as impediments to authentic discipleship.[169] Albeit for a different audience, then, Jesus posits the necessity of a corresponding transformation of life in both instances. This conjunction of emphases reminds us that the new practices counseled by Jesus in vv 7-14 are not isolated behaviors but, from Luke's perspective, must flow out of a transformed disposition, reflecting new commitments, attitudes, and allegiances. That is, the conversion that characterizes genuine discipleship is itself generative, giving rise to new forms of behavior. For Luke's audience, Jesus' message here is not new; rather, in a summarizing, staccato format he presents teaching that is reminiscent of earlier material in, e.g., 8:4-21; 9:23-27, 57-62; 12:13-59.

25-27 The introduction to this new scene is significant in two ways. First, we are reminded immediately that Jesus is on a journey — begun in 9:51 and oriented toward Jerusalem. In Jerusalem Jesus anticipates encountering the hostility and violence appropriate to a prophet (cf., e.g., 9:22; 13:31-35), just as he expects to bring his mission to completion there (cf. 9:31, 51-53). Onto the narrative stage, then, a number of journey-related motifs clamber, including the orientation of the journey toward its goal in Jerusalem and its significance in the attraction and formation of disciples.[170] Second, Luke observes that Jesus is joined on the journey by "large crowds." Often in the Lukan account, crowds are presented as pools of neutral persons from whom Jesus might draw disciples, and this is clearly the case here.[171] In light of Jesus' message in 13:26-27, however, one should not immediately be overly sanguine about the realization of their potential as disciples; many, according to Jesus, will claim to have associated themselves with Jesus' teaching both at the table and on the road, but their fundamental allegiances will not have been altered. Such persons cannot be identified as disciples. Recognition of the paradigmatic role of 13:26-27 for appraising the outcomes of Jesus' interaction along the journey sets up the emphasis on the demands placed on would-be disciples in this narrative unit. Added emphasis for Jesus' teaching comes from the note that Jesus "turned" to address the crowds.[172]

168. In addition, the Pharisees and scribes will reappear as Jesus' primary interlocutors in 15:1-2, where their indictment against Jesus essentially counters his teaching in 14:1-24.

169. Cf. Tannehill, *Narrative Unity,* 1:157; Malina and Rohrbaugh, *Commentary,* 369.

170. See above, the introduction to 9:51–19:48.

171. See the summary in Watson, "People, Crowd," 608.

172. On this use of στρέφω in the Lukan narrative, see above on 7:9-10.

Verses 26 and 27 are presented in parallel fashion: whoever does not *x* cannot be my disciple; a further parallel, presented in the form of a summary, appears in v 33.[173] "Disciples" does not refer narrowly in this instance to a select group of Jesus' followers but, as the parallels to earlier teaching make clear (e.g., 8:19-21; 9:23-27), to all who, following him, identify with his mission.[174] Such persons are characterized, first, by their distancing themselves from the high cultural value placed on their family network, otherwise paramount in the world of Luke. That is, in this context, "hate" is not primarily an affective quality but a disavowal of primary allegiance to one's kin. In a way consistent with other teaching in Luke, then, Jesus underscores how discipleship relativizes one's normal and highly valued loyalties to normal family and other social ties.[175]

This emphasis on redirected loyalties is highlighted all the more in the current co-text by Luke's candid reminder that Jesus' instruction occurs in the context of the journey (to Jerusalem). Just as the Pharisees and legal experts in vv 1-24 regarded themselves as blessed with invitations to the kingdom banquet and so needed to be instructed regarding behavior consistent with the divine economy,[176] so these crowds need to recognize fully the repercussions of following Jesus.[177] Implicit in 9:23, now explicit, is the correlation between setting aside one's family allegiances and reforming the basis of one's self-identity. Again, then, "hating" one's self should not be taken as a reference to an affective self-abhorrence, but as a call to set aside the relationships, the extended family of origin and inner circle of friends, by which one has previously made up one's identity. As in 9:23, so here Jesus is calling for the reconstruction of one's identity, not along ancestral lines or on the basis of one's social status, but within the new community oriented toward God's purpose and characterized by faithfulness to the message of Jesus.

Again, as in 9:23, bearing the cross[178] is used as a metaphor of discipleship — indeed, as a requirement for one's identity as a disciple. Such

---

173. Note the repetition of the phrase, οὐ δύναται εἶναί μου μαθητής. Although this is not apparent in the NRSV, this phrase appears consistently in the posterior position of these conditional sentences.

174. That Luke has no more narrow, technical understanding of "disciples," see, e.g., 5:27-30; 6:1, 17; 8:2-3; 9:4-9; 10:1; 19:37. On earlier attempts to argue that the demands of these verses were for Jesus or for Luke relevant only to the inner circle of Jesus' followers, see Seccombe, *Possessions,* 101-5.

175. See 8:19-21; 9:57-62; 12:51-53; 18:28-30. Cf. Giesen, "μισέω," 431; Gillman, *Possessions,* 79; Sweetland, *Our Journey,* 142-44.

176. See above on v 15.

177. See Denney, "Hate," 41.

178. βαστάζω, "to carry along," appears in the present tense, continuing the emphasis in 9:23 on the ongoing quality of living a cruciform life.

persons would live as though they were condemned to death by crucifixion, oblivious to the pursuit of noble status, finding no interest in securing one's future via securing obligations from others or by stockpiling possessions, free to identify with Jesus in his dishonorable suffering.[179] Importantly, both statements concerning the conditions of discipleship are addressed to "whoever," a reminder that the invitation is an open one.

28-32 Jesus highlights the importance of considering the conditions he has placed on authentic discipleship with back-to-back parables. Assuming that his audience is capable of understanding the machinations of a landowner pondering the construction of some sort of fortification and of a king contemplating war, Jesus constructs these parables along parallel lines: a hypothetical, demanding enterprise + analysis of the adequacy of existing resources vis-à-vis the requisite resources for achieving a successful conclusion to the enterprise + outcome when available resources fall short. The presumption that Jesus' audience will be able to identify with one or another of these parables tells us little about its implied makeup. Although a landowner is in view in the first instance, the extent of his holdings is not indicated by the rather nebulous reference to building a "tower"; depending on his available capital, a watchtower in a vineyard, a tower for a city wall, or some more elaborate structure could equally tax his assets.[180] One need not be a "king" to appreciate the second parable,[181] and Luke elsewhere indicates the presence of military personnel among those who hear the good news.[182]

What outcomes are proposed if resources prove to be deficient? In both cases, the repercussions are tragic — the one resulting in mockery, the other in surrender; hence, a premium is placed on the inadequacy of one's resources.[183] By extrapolation, then, Jesus insists that such assets as one's network of kin, so important in Greco-Roman antiquity, are an insufficient foundation for assuring one's status before God. Dependence on the resources available to a person apart from "hating" family and "carrying the cross" cannot but lead to a tragic outcome. What is required is thoroughgoing fidelity to God's salvific aim, manifest in one's identity as a disciple of Jesus.

179. On the dishonor associated with crucifixion, see Carroll and Green, *Death of Jesus,* ch. 9; Hengel, *Crucifixion.*

180. πύργος is polysemous in this respect — cf. Luke 13:4; MM 561.

181. In fact, Luke's language changes at this point; "which of you" is used in v 28, not v 31.

182. Cf. 3:10-14; 7:1-10; Acts 10:1–11:18.

183. Schmidt (*Hostility to Wealth,* 150-51) helpfully observes, *contra* most commentators, that the interpretive crux does not lie in "counting the cost." The point is that, no matter what calculus one uses, no matter what resources one believes one can bring to bear, those assets will be insufficient to secure one's status before God. Alternative and decisive action is thus required for everyone.

33 With regard to laying out the conditions of discipleship, v 33 parallels vv 26 and 27; it does so, however, not by adding a third condition but by summarizing all other conditions.[184] Given the travel setting within which Jesus' assertion is set, Luke uses an appropriate image, "to bid farewell"; if one is truly to join Jesus on the journey, one must "bid farewell to all one has." This "leaving behind" is cast in the present tense, demarcating this condition not simply as a potential for which disciples must be constantly ready, but as a characteristic feature of the disciple.[185] As is generally the case in Luke, one's basic commitments are manifest or symbolized in the disposition of "all one has." Accordingly, the distinctive property of disciples is the abandonment with which they put aside all competing securities in order that they might refashion their lives and identity according to the norms of the kingdom of God.[186]

34-35 Although Jesus' saying on salt is not cast in the form of a parable, it is nevertheless parabolic in function. Drawing on common knowledge concerning the properties of salt, he underscores the tragic end of those who do not join the journey of discipleship having "bid farewell to all one has" (v 33). Unfortunately, our "common knowledge" regarding salt does not necessarily match that presumed by this text. Is Jesus making reference to the absurdity of salt's losing its saltiness? A second-century rabbinic saying, comparing the idea of salt's losing its savor with that of a mule bearing a foal, points in this direction.[187] Analyses sensitive to soil chemistry put forward the possibility that Jesus is referring to a property of Palestinian salt that allows for the leaching away of the actual salt content from salt crystals;[188] this would allow salt to "lose its taste." In either case, Jesus' point remains constant. Although salt is good, if it were to lose its saltiness it would be useless —

---

184. Hence, even if Luke can employ ὑπάρχουσιν with reference to "possessions" (e.g., 12:33), here it refers to "all one has"; cf. Green, *Gospel of Luke,* 114-17; Seccombe, *Possessions,* 114; Malina and Rohrbaugh, *Commentary,* 369.

185. For this thought in Luke, see, e.g., 5:11, 28; 6:24, 30; 8:3, 14; 11:21; 12:33. That Luke's interest is in one's openness to potential renunciation was advocated, e.g., by Plummer, 366. Schmidt (*Hostility to Wealth,* 152) rightly takes issue with this view, but his alternative is likewise in need of modification. He takes the present tense of ἀποτάσσομαι as an aoristic present, "a punctiliar act taking place at the moment of speaking" (BDF §320), thinking that discipleship requires an initial, decisive act of renunciation of one's possessions. The present stem, though, has the aspect of action not yet completed, or in progress, repeated, customary, or pertaining to general truth (Mastronarde, *Attic Greek,* 146). Luke's usage of the present indicative here, then, comports well with his overall portrait of discipleship as necessitating a particular and ongoing orientation with respect to "all one has."

186. With regard to the motif of possessions in Luke, see further above, §11.

187. *b. Bek.* 8b.

188. See the summary in Marshall, 596.

either for its taste or its agronomic applications. By analogy, those who attempt to journey with Jesus without a thoroughgoing commitment to God's purpose, an allegiance to God that relativizes all other relationships and social values, are not worthy of the designation of "disciple."

Jesus' parting words underscore the gravity of his teaching in this narrative unit. The injunction to listen is paralleled in 8:8, and it is likely that this connection is deliberate on the part of the narrator. In his parabolic teaching regarding the sowing of seeds Jesus had drawn attention both to the need for authentic hearing and to potential obstructions to hearing. Thus, for example, proper hearing might be undercut by "the cares and riches and pleasures of life"; proper hearing is the basis on which new family relationships are determined; and proper hearing leads to fecundity (8:4-21). The particulars of his teaching might be expressed in slightly different ways in the current co-text, but Jesus' message in the one narrative unit is fully congruous with his teaching in the other. With his salt metaphor, then, Jesus calls attention to the urgency of his instruction on the conditions of discipleship and bids his audience to respond.

5.5.6. *Rejoicing at the Finding of the Lost (15:1-32)*

Chapter 15 constitutes a discrete section of the Third Gospel, bound together by a common audience and setting, both provided in vv 1-2, with no narrative markers designating a change of scene until 16:1.[189] The three parables of Luke 15 — through common structure and subject matter, and repetition of key terms and phrases — present a cumulative response to the indictment of the Pharisees and legal experts in 15:2: "This fellow welcomes sinners and eats with them."[190] The first two parables are particularly close in structure, but all three share a common progression, moving from what a main character "has" to its loss, recovery and restoration, and the celebration that ensues.

At the same time, our identification of ch. 15 as a discreet section does not mean that it shares no points of contact with the surrounding narrative material. The setting for the previous chapter had been the table, and the

---

189. In 16:1, Luke notes that Jesus directs his discourse to his disciples. Austin's ("Hypocritical Son," 307-10) recognition of the points of structural contact between the material in 15:11-32 and 16:1-8 leads him wrongly to disregard the absence in the transition to the story of the Lost Son (15:11-32) of any sectional markers typical of narrative. As we will see, however, chs. 15 and 16 are related topically.

190. Jesus' words in v 3 come by way of response to the charges leveled against him. Luke signals new parables in vv 8 and 11, but does not otherwise signal a break in Jesus' discourse. See the related discussions in Bartolomé, "Comer en común"; Cloete and Smit, "Exegesis and Proclamation," 63; Neale, *None but the Sinners,* 156-57; Ramaroson, "Lc 15."

parabolic material in ch. 16 is likewise concerned with issues of hospitality and meals. Jesus' teaching in chs. 14 and 16 regarding the import of welcoming into one's homes those who live on the margins of society — "the poor, the crippled, the lame, and the blind" (14:13; cf. 14:21; 16:20) — underscores deeply the central question raised in 15:1-32. This is the question whether the Pharisees and legal experts will welcome such persons as toll collectors and sinners, joining in the heavenly rejoicing at the finding of the lost, celebrating their recovery at the banquet table.

The basic theme of this larger narrative unit moves between two related foci: (1) Jesus' defense of his ministry as an outworking of God's own purpose and (2) Jesus' implicit and open-ended invitation to his interlocutors to join him in reflecting in their practices God's own attitude toward sinners. Luke achieves this narrative aim through the accumulation of meaning from one parable to the next, all set in the context of and therefore understood in relation to the initial charge against Jesus in vv 1-2. We learn first, and especially from the first two parables, that in the divine economy the repentance of sinners (i.e., the restoration of the lost) is grounds for celebration. That is, these parables are especially *theo*logical, providing insight into God's own disposition vis-à-vis sinners.[191] The third parable relates the divine economy more directly to the setting of Jesus' remarks in vv 1-2, placing before the Pharisees and scribes an invitation to join in the celebration. They are invited, that is, not only to drop their concerns about Jesus but, indeed, to replicate his behavior in their own practices.[192] By implication, then, the positive response (i.e., repentance) of the toll collectors and sinners (i.e., the lost) as they gather around Jesus constitutes a restoration of the lost that calls for celebration (i.e., table fellowship). In welcoming such persons to the table Jesus is only giving expression to the expansive grace of God. As the chapter closes, the query remains open whether the Pharisees and legal experts will so align themselves with the divine economy and, thus, join the celebration at the table with the lost who have been restored.[193]

---

191. Cloete and Smit, "Exegesis and Proclamation," 64; Ramsey, "Luke 15," 41; cf. Donahue, *Gospel in Parable,* 150.

192. Cf. Gowler, *Portraits of the Pharisees,* 251; Bartolomé, "ΣΥΝΕΣΘΕΙΝ." *Contra* Neale (*None but the Sinners,* 158-62), who finds in vv 11-32 no invitation to the Pharisees and legal experts.

193. Cf. Cloete and Smit, "Exegesis and Proclamation," 64-65, 72; Ramaroson, "Lc 15"; Jones-Haldeman, "Grace and Forgiveness." *Contra* Darr (*Character Building,* 108-10), who has prematurely closed the door on the Pharisees (concerning which, see above on 7:36-50; more generally, Green, *Gospel of Luke,* 72-75), and thus will not allow for the open-ended quality of Jesus' parable. Note vv 28 and 31: The father goes out to plead with the elder son (i.e., the scribes and Pharisees) and announces, "All that is mine is yours."

5.5.6.1. Jesus' Troublesome Table Companions (15:1-2)

15:1 *Now all the toll collectors*[194] *and sinners were coming near to listen to him.* 2 *And the Pharisees and the scribes were grumbling and saying, "This fellow welcomes sinners and eats with them."*

The setting Luke provides for Jesus' parabolic discourse on rejoicing at the finding of the lost is both highly stylized and pregnant with significance drawn from earlier material in the Gospel. The cast of characters is itself of importance, especially given their appearance in 7:29-30, again on opposite sides of the response to Jesus' ministry. In fact, the present scene appears as a concrete illustration of the earlier characterization of toll collectors (and sinners)[195] as persons who "justified God," and the Pharisees and legal experts as those who "rejected God's purpose for themselves." The broad strokes of that earlier representation are matched in the present scene by Luke's note concerning "all" the toll collectors and sinners.

"Toll collectors," though generally notorious in Luke's world as a dishonest, despised element of society (see above on 3:12-13), have thus far in the Third Gospel been represented as persons responsive to the call to repent (cf 3:10-14; 5:27-32). Similarly, "sinners" — that is, persons whose primary attribute is that they cannot be included among the righteous and are therefore persons of low socio-religious status counted among the excluded, even damned — have been presented by the Third Evangelist as persons in need of forgiveness, as recipients of good news, and as those who comport themselves as willing to repent and are thus numbered among the people of God (cf. 5:29-32; 7:35, 36-50).[196] Against this backdrop, it is hardly coincidental that 15:1 follows hard on the heels of 14:35 — that is, that Jesus' admonition "to hear" his message is set in immediate proximity to the proactivity of the toll collectors and sinners to do just that! In this way, these outcasts present themselves as oriented toward discipleship.[197]

By way of contrast, even though Luke's portrayal of the Pharisees is capable of texture and nuance, when they appear in tandem with the scribes, Pharisees consistently have the role of Jesus' foes (e.g., 5:17–6:11; 7:29-30). They appear in the Lukan narrative often as monitors of Jesus' legal observance and, given the centrality of what one eats and with whom one eats to

---

194. NRSV: "tax collectors."

195. "Toll collectors" in 7:29 is synecdoche for "toll collectors and sinners," as in 7:34.

196. See Neale, *None but the Sinners,* 148-54.

197. On this understanding of "hearing," see esp. 6:27, 46-49; 7:29; 8:8-21; 9:35; 10:16, 24, 39; 11:28, 31; cf. also 5:1, 15; 6:17-18; Sweetland, *Our Journey,* 109-12.

the Pharisaic agenda,[198] their hostility toward Jesus is regularly occasioned by the status of his table intimates. Especially close to the present setting is the earlier table scene wherein the Pharisees and scribes also "complained" concerning Jesus, 5:29-32 (cf. 7:36-50 and esp. 19:1-10). This parallel urges that we find Jesus' presence with toll collectors and sinners at Levi's banquet as an illustration of what is for Luke typical of Jesus. It also associates the Pharisees and legal experts with those of the wilderness generation who complained against God's representatives, Moses and Aaron.[199]

Verse 2b summarizes the problem Jesus presents for the Pharisees and legal experts, according to Luke, for it is at the table that his (from their perspective) lack of sensitivity regarding accepted norms and his neglect of the law of God come into incontrovertible expression.[200] The importance of the table as an instrument for drawing and maintaining socio-religious boundaries, from the perspective of Jesus' adversaries, has been repeatedly ignored by Jesus. Indeed, in the present instance, not only is he blamed for eating with "sinners"[201] — that is, at their invitation, as in 5:29 — but apparently for extending hospitality to them as well.[202] Jesus thus behaves toward these outsiders, these unclean, contemptible persons of ignoble status, as though they were acceptable, as though they were his own kin. Understood against the backdrop of his instruction on invitations in 14:12-24, Jesus' behavior must be seen as an unequivocal rejection of the values and norms of his peer group, including those Pharisees and legal experts, some from among the social elite (cf. 7:36; 11:37; 14:1, 3), who had extended hospitality to him. His disregard for those norms has as its constructive consequence the generation of a new group whose very existence and characteristic openness raises an unflattering and, one might conjecture, threatening voice against conventional practices. As will become evident in what follows, though, this openness is not without its own boundaries; as in 5:29-32, the new group being generated around Jesus includes outsiders, to be sure, but outsiders whose

198. See the discussion above, at 5:27-39.

199. Here, διαγογγύζω (also 19:7); cf. γογγύζω in 5:30. Cf. 6:7; 11:53; 14:1. In the LXX, see esp. Exodus 15–17; Numbers 14–17; cf. 1 Cor 10:10; Hess, "γογγύζω," 256.

200. By implication, we may understand that the Pharisees and legal experts are essentially calling into question Jesus' status, asserting that he has stepped outside all legitimate prerogatives by sharing the table with social refuse. Similarly, Jesus' reply in vv 3-32 can be read as his attempt to ground the legitimacy of his behavior in the divine economy.

201. "Sinners" in v 2 is synecdoche for "toll collectors and sinners" in v 1.

202. προσδέχομαι, "to extend hospitality"; cf. the analogous use of δέχομαι in 9:53; 10:8, 10; 16:4, 9. That is, Jesus is understood to practice what he had earlier urged others to do — namely, extend hospitality to persons outside one's own social group (14:12-14).

status has been reversed in the economy of the gospel and ratified by their repentance.[203]

Hence, these opening verses serve, first, to establish the charge that Jesus will seek to answer in the parabolic material that follows and, second, to demarcate the legal experts and Pharisees as Jesus' primary audience for the ensuing discourse. The particular significance of this latter point is telling within Luke's own discourse situation, when the appropriate reach of table fellowship continued to be at issue; by this means, the Evangelist identifies with Jesus' opponents any persons among Luke's readers whose practices of table fellowship are similarly closed.[204]

5.5.6.2. Celebrating the Recovery of the Lost (15:3-10)

3 *So he told them this parable:* 4 *"Which one of you, having a hundred sheep and losing one of them, does not leave the ninety-nine in the wilderness and go after the one that is lost until he finds it? 5 When he has found it, he lays it on his shoulders and rejoices. 6 And when he comes home, he calls together his friends and neighbors, saying to them, 'Rejoice with me, for I have found my sheep that was lost.' 7 Just so, I tell you, there will be more joy in heaven over one sinner who repents than over ninety-nine righteous persons who need no repentance.*

8 *"Or what woman having ten silver coins, if she loses one of them, does not light a lamp, sweep the house, and search carefully until she finds it? 9 When she has found it, she calls together her friends and neighbors, saying, 'Rejoice with me, for I have found the coin that I had lost.' 10 Just so, I tell you, there is joy in the presence of the angels of God over one sinner who repents."*

The stage is set in vv 1-2 with Jesus having been indicted by the Pharisees and legal experts on account of his table practices with sinners and toll collectors. Jesus' riposte begins now, and continues through the end of Luke 15, taking first the form of two short parables intimately related by parallel structure and verbal repetition.[205] Thus, each parable (1) identifies the main character (vv 4, 8); (2) describes the loss and subsequent search (vv 4, 8); (3) narrates the recovery of what was lost (vv 5, 9); (4) relates the motif of rejoicing with friends and neighbors over the recovery (vv 5-6, 9); and (5) closes with Jesus' drawing a bridge from the parable's conclusion to the

203. Cf. Moxnes, "Meals," 162-63.
204. Cf. Acts 10:1–11:18; Esler, *Community and Gospel*, 71-109.
205. Cf. Donahue, *Gospel in Parable*, 147; Neale, *None but the Sinners*, 156.

heavenly rejoicing that accompanies the repentance of a sinner (vv 7, 10). In spite of such remarkable parallelism one may observe an escalation from one parable to the next. A shepherd suffers the loss of one sheep from a flock of one hundred, whereas the woman suffers the loss of one coin out of ten; this escalation will continue in the next parable (vv 11-32), with the loss of one of only two sons. The repetition of several key terms serves to bind these two parables together and to tie them into their co-text in ch. 15: "to lose/lost" (vv 4 [2x], 6, 8, 9; also in vv 17, 24, 32);[206] "sinner" (vv 1, 2, 7, 10);[207] "to rejoice/joy" (vv 5, 6, 7, 9, 10; also in v 32);[208] and "to call together" or "to invite" (vv 6, 9; cf. v 1).[209]

The form taken by the finale appended to each of these two parables is decisive for our understanding of how these parables function in their co-text. First, we find a symbolic identification of the lost sheep/coin with the sinner and, therefore, of the recovery of what was lost with the repentance of a sinner. Second, references to responses "in heaven" and "in the presence of the angels of God" make clear that these parables are fundamentally about God, that their aim is to lay bare the nature of the divine response to the recovery of the lost. Insofar as the good news is thus cast in terms that constitute a reversal of status and destiny, it is not insignificant that Jesus expects his auditors to follow his metaphorical representation of God first as a relatively wealthy shepherd, then as an impoverished widow.[210]

The motif of celebration comes so much to the fore that we may recognize the development in Jesus' parabolic reply of a well-defined contrast between the complaints and grumbling typical of the Pharisees and legal experts (vv 1-2) and the joy and festivity characteristic of God. The former see only that Jesus wrongly extends hospitality to socio-religious outcasts, while the latter indicates how Jesus' behavior signals the restoration of the lost through repentance.

3-6 Jesus' audience is made up of the Pharisees and legal experts, and he begins his response to their charge by inviting them to imagine themselves as shepherds.[211] Though difficult to represent in an English text, Jesus' parable

206. ἀπόλλυμι.
207. ἁμαρτωλός.
208. χαίρω (vv 5, 32), χαρά (vv 7, 10), συγχαίρω (vv 6, 9).
209. συγκαλέω appears in vv 6 and 9; used thus, it is a synonym for προσδέχομαι in v 1.
210. Luke often presents stories involving men and women in tandem (e.g., 1:6-7; 2:25-38; 4:25-27; et al.), though the present balance of the sexes is unusual since these parallel parables use male and female main figures to represent God.
211. Assuming that shepherds participated in a despised trade and were regarded as ritually unclean (cf. Jeremias, *Jerusalem,* 303-12), some interpreters (e.g., Donahue, *Gospel in Parable,* 148; K. E. Bailey, *Poet and Peasant,* 147) have argued that Jesus'

takes the form of a single, prolonged question, encompassing vv 3-6 — a question whose form anticipates an immediate, obvious, and negative reply.[212] The importance of this observation rests in its identification of the primary point to which Jesus' listeners are expected to assent. They are expected to agree not only that the shepherd would leave the ninety-nine in order to find the one, not only that he will rejoice as he carries it home on his shoulders, but also and especially that his homecoming with the lost-but-found sheep will provide the occasion for celebration with friends and neighbors. Although the motif of eating is not explicit, the action of inviting[213] friends and neighbors (cf. 14:12) over to share in one's joy may suggest a festive repast — tying this parable more securely into the content of the charge leveled against Jesus in vv 1-2 and preparing for the banquet motif in vv 23-24.

The parable itself leaves some questions unasked and, therefore, unanswered — for example, Where and in whose care are the ninety-nine left? Some details are easy enough to understand, however.[214] For example, the shepherd Jesus portrays is not a hired worker but the owner of the sheep, or, at least, a member of the family that owns them. If an average family has between five and fifteen animals, this one is cast as relatively wealthy, though the absence of any mention of a wage-earning shepherd to care for the sheep speaks against our pushing the question of his wealth too far. Because sheep are gregarious creatures, a sheep lost from its flock becomes quickly agitated and disoriented and must be carried back to the other sheep; for lengthy journeys this is most easily accomplished by placing the sheep on one's shoulders.

Why does Jesus ask his audience to identify with a shepherd? Clearly, he wants them to acknowledge for themselves the appropriateness of calling together a celebration in the event of the restoration of what was lost. On a further interpretive level, however, one may hear in Jesus' parable echoes of Ezekiel 34. There Yahweh commands the prophet to speak against the leaders of Israel, shepherds who had not cared for their charge, leaving Israel, Yahweh's sheep, to be scattered with no one to look for them. On account of the unfaithfulness of Israel's leaders, Ezekiel prophesies, Yahweh himself will

---

parable is ironic in tone: Jesus is accused of associating with the unclean, then asks his partners in debate to imagine themselves as members of an unclean profession. The positive image of sheep and shepherds in Israel's Scriptures, together with Philo's positive mention of the Jewish people as graziers, stock-breeders, and shepherds (*Spec. Leg.* 1.133, 136), casts doubt on a general, negative valuation of shepherds on grounds of impurity in first-century Palestine.

212. Cf. Jeremias, *Parables,* 133. On the form of the question, cf. 11:5-8; 12:25; 14:5; Jeremias, *Parables,* 103, 158; Derrett, "Friend at Midnight," 33, 35; Blomberg, *Parables,* 179.

213. συγκαλέω may carry the nuance of extending hospitality.

214. Cf. K. E. Bailey, *Poet and Peasant,* 148; Jeremias, *Parables,* 133-34.

seek out the sheep, rescue them, and care for them. By analogy, cast by Luke as leaders of the people, the legal experts and Pharisees who complain against Jesus' practices at the table find themselves under indictment for their failure to act in ways that befit faithful shepherds; similarly, through these intertextual echoes we may hear in Jesus' parable a commendation of Jesus, who acts in a way consistent with Yahweh's care for his sheep.[215]

7 Not strictly part of Jesus' parable, this appendage draws out the meaning of the parable by ensuring that it is read against the backdrop of the criticism of Jesus in vv 1-2. Divorced from its present narrative location, the parable might be read in a number of ways, but, set within its local co-text, it should be interpreted as a response to the Pharisees and scribes. Against such a horizon, Jesus' troublesome table fellowship is understood in association with the heavenly celebration that follows the repentance of a sinner.

Sharing a meal has the potential function of generating intimacy and creating group solidarity. In some meal-episodes, notably among toll collectors and sinners (e.g., 5:29-32), this end is successfully realized, while in others, notably among scribes and Pharisees, table fellowship terminates in protest and hostility (e.g., 7:36-50; 11:37-54). The fundamental difference between these two is not whether the good news is operative in one but not the other, but in how the various groups respond to Jesus' presence and message. As in the earlier meal-scene of 5:29-32, so here "sinners" and "the righteous" are presented in parodic ways — the former as repentant, the latter as unaware of their need for good news. Although not often mentioned in the Third Gospel, repentance is nevertheless a fundamental response to the good news.[216]

It is here that one might sense a tension between the parable and Jesus' appropriation of it in this scene. After all, the parable seems to focus especially on the efforts (seeking) of the shepherd while the inference drawn from it apparently centers on the action (repentance) of the sinner. This tension is only apparent, however, and easily mitigated by the realization that the emphasis of Jesus' reply does not in either case fall on *how* one is restored. In his reply Jesus does not assert but *simply assumes* that lost sheep are restored by the efforts of the shepherd and that sinners are restored via repentance.[217]

---

215. Can more be said? Is it possible to understand the parable not only *theo*logically but also christologically? If so, Jesus would be portrayed as fulfilling the role of Yahweh in caring for the lost sheep, then inviting others to share his joy in its recovery. In this case, the "friends and neighbors" invited to the celebration would include the Pharisees and scribes who have thus far preferred to keep their distance.

216. Cf. Green, *Gospel of Luke,* 107-8.

217. Cf. Chilton, "Jesus and the Repentance," 4 (of the historical Jesus, but equally apropos Luke): "Repentance, a turning back to what alone has value, is a necessary and inescapable aspect of entering the Kingdom; it is implicit within much of Jesus' discourse, and need not be named to be operative."

Rather, the accent of parable and appropriation is on the *consequence* of recovery, the necessity of celebration that follows restoration.[218]

8-9 Jesus' parable of the joy accompanying the recovery of a lost coin closely parallels in structure that concerning the retrieval of the lost sheep, and is tied to it also by the repetition of key words and phrases (see above). In this second parable, however, one may recognize in comparison with the first an escalation on two points. First, as important as one sheep is when compared with ninety-nine, the loss of one coin out of ten underscores even more the urgency involved in finding what is lost. The woman Jesus portrays is a village peasant, living in a house with no window (hence the need for a lamp), and so presumably living in an economy based on barter. Her coins, then, likely represent the family savings — not a great sum, totaling the equivalent of only (approximately) ten days' wages. The loss of even one coin would be a catastrophic incident. Second, Jesus devotes greater detail to his description of her efforts: she lights a lamp, sweeps the house, and searches carefully.

Although difficult to represent in the English text, all of vv 8-9 constitute a continuous question,[219] a grammatical move that locates the zenith of the story not so much in the finding as in the act of celebration that results. As in v 6, the motif of eating is not explicit, but the act of inviting friends and neighbors (in this case, female) over to share in her joy implies a festive repast — tying this parable more securely into the content of the charge levelled against Jesus in vv 1-2 and preparing for the banquet-motif in vv 23-24.

10 Functioning in the same way as its parallel in v 7, this addendum allows Jesus to draw out the relevance of the parable by drawing it back into the co-text provided by vv 1-2. In Jesus' appropriation of the parable, the emphasis again falls on the heavenly joy[220] that ensues from the repentance of a sinner, thus characterizing Jesus' table fellowship with toll collectors and sinners as an expression of the divine celebration accompanying the recovery of the lost. (On these motifs, see above on v 7.) Although Jesus' final remarks do not develop it, the enhanced portrayal of the woman's efforts as she attempts to locate what has been lost might also provoke reflection on the initiative taken by God in human recovery.

---

218. The importance of joy is recognized but not developed within this co-text in Jeremias, *Parables,* 135-36; Linnemann, *Parables,* 72-73. See, however, Donahue, *Gospel in Parable,* 151.

219. Cf. Jeremias, *Parables,* 134.

220. For the motif of heavenly joy, see also 2:13-15. For the identification of angels "of God" or as members of the divine court, cf. 9:26; 12:8-9; Acts 10:3; 27:23.

5.5.6.3. Responses at Finding a Lost Son (15:11-32)

11 Then Jesus said, "There was a man who had two sons. 12 The younger of them said to his father, 'Father, give me the share of the property that will belong to me.' So he divided his property between them. 13 A few days later the younger son gathered all he had and traveled to a distant country, and there he squandered his property in dissolute living. 14 When he had spent everything, a severe famine took place throughout that country, and he began to be in need. 15 So he went and hired himself out to one of the citizens of that country, who sent him to his fields to feed the pigs. 16 He would gladly have filled himself with the pods that the pigs were eating; and no one gave him anything. 17 But when he came to himself he said, 'How many of my father's hired hands have bread enough and to spare, but here I am dying of hunger! 18 I will get up and go to my father, and I will say to him, "Father, I have sinned against heaven and before you; 19 I am no longer worthy to be called your son; treat me like one of your hired hands."' 20 So he set off and went to his father. But while he was still far off, his father saw him and was filled with compassion; he ran and put his arms around him and kissed him. 21 Then the son said to him, 'Father, I have sinned against heaven and before you; I am no longer worthy to be called your son.' 22 But the father said to his slaves, 'Quickly, bring out a robe — the best one — and put it on him; put a ring on his finger and sandals on his feet. 23 And get the fatted calf and kill it, and let us eat and celebrate; 24 for this son of mine was dead and is alive again; he was lost and is found!' And they began to celebrate.

25 "Now his elder son was in the field; and when he came and approached the house, he heard music and dancing. 26 He called one of the slaves and asked what was going on. 27 He replied, 'Your brother has come, and your father has killed the fatted calf, because he has got him back safe and sound.' 28 Then he became angry and refused to go in. His father came out and began to plead with him. 29 But he answered his father, 'Listen! For all these years I have been working like a slave for you, and I have never disobeyed your command; yet you have never given me even a young goat so that I might celebrate with my friends. 30 But when this son of yours came back, who has devoured your property with prostitutes, you killed the fatted calf for him!' 31 Then the father said to him, 'Son, you are always with me, and all that is mine is yours. 32 But we had to celebrate and rejoice, because this brother of yours was dead and has come to life; he was lost and has been found.'"

From two brief parables about the celebration of the lost-and-found, Jesus turns to a more extended account of a lost-and-found son, the plot of which precedes along parallel, albeit more elaborate lines. The immediate co-text for this new parable is the whole of ch. 15, with this third parable, like the first two, cast as a reply to the indictment of the Pharisees and scribes in vv 1-2. To be sure, the stakes are significantly raised in this instance: The son lost is one of only two, compared with the one sheep of a hundred and one coin of ten in vv 3-10. This contributes to the intrinsic interest of the narrative as well as to its dramatic appeal.

Perhaps the most pressing question concerning the interpretation of Jesus' narrative is the identity of its central character. Whose parable is it?[221] The traditional answer, that it concerns a father with two sons,[222] has much to commend it. Most importantly, the parable begins by naming "a man (who had two sons)," and goes on to underscore his conciliatory responses to the insulting behavior of both sons. Three telling observations suggest that this is not the case, however.[223] First, the narrative has two primary segments, each allowing the same story to be recounted — fully by Jesus (vv 11-24), then in summary fashion by "one of the slaves" (vv 26-27). In the first, the emphasis falls on the younger son's "loss" and his father's celebrative response to his return, while in the latter the emphasis falls on the younger son's loss and his brother's indignant reaction to his return. Second, indeed, the turning point of both narrative segments comes in Jesus' description of an affective response to the return of the younger son: The father has "compassion" (v 20), while the elder son is "angry" (v 28). Although it is true that the consistency of the father's love toward both sons is crucial to the parable, with the younger son this love is expressed in acceptance and jubilation and in relationship to the latter it is expressed in an invitation for the elder son to practice reconciliation toward his brother (and, thus, join in the gala). Finally, the larger co-text of this well-crafted parable in ch. 15 highlights the critical motif of "celebration," the joyous repast at the recovery of what was lost (cf. vv 6, 9, 23-24, 27). In fact, the father in this third parable elevates such celebration to the level of divine necessity,[224] just as the previous parables had associated analogous expressions of joy to heavenly dispositions (vv 7, 10). Hence, as important as the father is to this parable, center stage belongs to the younger son — and especially to the contrasting patterns of response occasioned by his recovery.

The point at which this third parable advances significantly beyond

---

221. Donahue, *Gospel in Parable*, 152.
222. Recently, see Ramsey, "Luke 15," 41.
223. Cf. Funk, *Poetics*, 177-83.
224. See the use of δεῖ in v 32.

the framework of the earlier two is in its heightened attention to issues of kinship. As valuable as sheep and coins might be to a person, the loss and recovery of a son are of even greater importance. Critical to the development of this parable is how this loss and recovery are signified in familial terms. A younger son acknowledges his father as Father, but acts toward him in ways that are out of character according to normal canons of familial behavior. This leads eventually to his attempt to reconstrue their relationship as one of master/hired hand — a definition at odds with his father's persistence in regarding him in filial terms. Accepting his status as son, he is reconciled to his father and restored as a member of the family. The elder son, having never left home, nevertheless regards himself as a slave to his father and refuses to recognize his father's younger son as his own brother. Again, the father persists in acknowledging the elder as his son and in doing so invites him to embrace the lost-and-found one again as brother. Does he do so? Does the elder son recognize his status as a member of the family and rejoin the family that now includes his younger brother? The parable stops short of telling us.

Within its co-text, then, this parable serves in two ways. First, Jesus thus responds to those who question his choice of table companions (vv 1-2). As persons who respond positively to his message,[225] toll collectors and sinners are represented in the parable as those whose (re)turn to God constitutes a restoration that calls for celebration. In welcoming such persons to the table Jesus is only giving expression to the magnitude and consistency of the grace of God. Second, Jesus thus issues an invitation to the Pharisees and legal experts who have responded to such a celebration, like the elder brother, with indignation. Will they align themselves with the divine economy and, having done so, join the celebration at the table with the lost who have been restored?

It is worth recalling that a primary image of God in the Lukan travel narrative has been God as Father (e.g., 11:1-13; 12:22-34), a portrait continued in this parable. Against the interpretive horizons of the Roman world, wherein the characteristic attributes of the father as the paterfamilias are remembered especially in terms of authoritarianism and legal control, the picture Luke paints is remarkable for its counteremphasis on care and compassion.[226]

11-12 Breaking into Jesus' reply to the Pharisees and legal experts in a barely noticeable way, Luke signals a new phase in that discourse. The parable that begins to unfold here is thus intimately related to the preceding not only by parallel structure[227] but also by the lack of any evidence of topical, topographical, or audience shift. The stage is set by the introduction of the

225. See above on vv 1-2.
226. See further, above, on 1:17.
227. See above on 15:1-32.

579

three primary characters of this parable, a father and his two sons.[228] The elder son is immediately moved offstage, to reappear in v 25, while a transaction involving the younger son and father is recounted. Concern with inheritance surfaced in the Lukan narrative earlier, at 12:13; memory of that earlier account casts the younger son immediately in a disparaging light, in some ways consistent with the Middle Eastern caricature of "younger brothers" as lazy and irresponsible,[229] covetous and greedy. Upon his father's death, the younger son would be due part of the estate (though not as large as what would normally fall to the elder — cf. Num 27:8-11; 36:7-9; Deut 21:17), but the actual disposition of property prior to the father's death, while known in Second Temple Jewish literature (see Tob 8:21), is also frowned upon (see Sir 33:20-24). That such a disposition is undertaken at the initiation of the younger son (and not by the father) is strikingly presumptuous. Read on its own terms, his request is highly irregular; read as the first of a series of actions that lead to his characterization as "dead and lost" (vv 24, 32), his request clearly signifies his rejection of his family.[230]

Interestingly, Jesus observes that the estate is divided "between them"; that is, the elder son receives his portion as well, a detail that will come into play when the plot of the parable returns to the elder brother with v 25.

13-16 The division of an estate during the lifetime of the father is one thing; actually disposing of one's inheritance by turning it into transportable capital during his lifetime is quite another, and it is at this point that the younger son's shocking breach of familial ties surfaces dramatically. The parable outlines a series of acts that lead from one level of infamy to the next: the request for his inheritance in v 12 now gives way to his actual disposal of the same, his departure, and his squandering of his resources[231] while living as though he were a Gentile. "A distant country" already suggests the non-Jewish world, and this identification is helped along by the prominence of pigs, abhorrent to Jewish sensibilities,[232] in the story.

The deteriorating situation of the younger son is compounded by the onset of a famine. Had he possessed his initial, relative wealth he might have been able to ride out the ensuing period of depressed economy. Having spent all he had, however, he had little recourse but to locate himself in a situation

228. Some recent exegetes have wondered why no mention is made of the mother of these two sons — on which see the helpful, culturally sensitive remarks of LaHurd, "Rediscovering the Lost Women."

229. See LaHurd, "Rediscovering the Lost Women," 67.

230. See K. E. Bailey, *Poet and Peasant,* 161-69 (who seems to have overstated the case; cf. Jeremias, *Parables,* 129); LaHurd, "Rediscovering the Lost Women," 67.

231. διασκορπίζω, "to squander, to waste," appears in 15:13; 16:1; ἀσώτως, "dissolutely," appears only here in the NT.

232. Cf. 8:32; Lev 11:7; Deut. 14:8; 1 Macc 1:47; 2 Macc 6:18; 7:1.

wherein he has not only shamed his father (cf. Prov 28:7), but has plummeted from his status as the son of a large landowner to that of the "unclean and degraded" (see Figure 1, p. 60), for whom even the life of a day laborer would be preferable (see v 17). The general effects of a depressed economy in the midst of famine might be reason enough for Jesus' observation that "no one gave him anything." In addition to this, however, it is worth recalling that the practice of almsgiving was little observed among the Greeks and Romans. The remark of Plautus is telling: "He does the beggar a bad service who gives him meat and drink, for what he gives is lost, and the life of the poor is prolonged to their own misery."[233] Clearly, the younger son Jesus has portrayed has fallen victim to the ease with which persons experience downward mobility in an agrarian society; at this juncture he appears in dire straits indeed, with the transition to the ranks of the expendables (see Figure 1) — made up of especially of beggars and thieves, among whom mortality rates were very high (cf 16:19-22) — just around the corner.

17-20a In Jesus' narration, the phrase "he came to himself" marks a turning point in the younger son's story. This phrase does not on its own signify repentance. "Coming to one's senses" is more the idea,[234] though in this co-text — in which (1) the repentance of sinners is highlighted (vv 1-2, 7, 10) and (2) the younger son's internal monologue leads him finally to return home and to acknowledge his sin (vv 18, 21) — shades of repentance are clearly evident.[235] What he comes to recognize is his loss of status, the deteriorating social condition that has developed from the series of actions outlined in vv 12-14 by which he has shamed his father as he distanced himself further and further from his household. Now he realizes that even as a day laborer — a hireling whose subsistence is vulnerable to the full range of natural forces, the seasonal needs of the production of crops, and the whims of the estate manager[236] — his lot would be desirable when compared to his present condition. This recognition serves as a barometer of the depths to which the younger son has sunk.

---

233. Plautus *Trinummus* §339. On the general lack of Greco-Roman concern for assisting the needy, cf. Hamel, *Poverty and Charity,* 219-20; Hands, *Charities and Social Aid.*

234. εἰς ἑαυτὸν ἔρχεσθαι. The parallel in Acts 12:11 (ἐν ἑαυτῷ γενόμενος) might be rendered "came to his senses"; cf. *T. Jos.* 3:9, where Joseph "realized what was happening."

235. K. E. Bailey (*Poet and Peasant,* 173-80) and Ramsey ("Luke 15," 38-40) have seen in the younger son's interior monologue his shrewdness or the development of a self-serving conspiracy, but these interpretations do not take seriously enough the co-text in which this text is set.

236. μίσθιος refers to a day laborer, without the social, economic, and political security of household attachment (see the portrait in Matt 20:1-16); in terms of status, then, a day laborer would be far less secure than a slave.

The son's words "I will arise," the central verbal form of this chapter,[237] mark the onset of a new series of actions through which his lost status will be restored; in the metaphorical field of the parable, these words begin to signal his return to life from death (see vv 24, 32).[238] What is particularly noteworthy in the younger son's soliloquy is that, in spite of his recognition of his own sinful and shameful state and his own culpability, he assumes that his father will look on him with at least a modicum of favor and receive him as (albeit a) minor employee. The word "father" is repeated three times in this subsection — twice in his interior monologue, once in Jesus' narration of the son's return to his father. Co-textually, this confidence is easily understood, for we have been shown that recovery is associated with joy (vv 7, 10). Indeed, the use of "heaven" as a circumlocution for "God" together with the repetition of the verb "to sin" in v 18 may help us to recall the earlier response of "heaven" to repentant sinners (see esp. v 7). Within the larger Lukan narrative, "father" has again and again been correlated with compassion.[239]

20b-24 Although the younger son now places in motion his formulated plans, in Jesus' narration the son's initiative is quickly superseded by the proactivity of his father. Indeed, the confession for which the son had rehearsed (v 21) is now buried between dual demonstrations of acceptance and restoration — the compassion and embrace of the father (v 20) and the flurry of orders in preparation for the feast of homecoming (vv 22-24). His confession is thus qualified in two ways. First, although his acknowledgment of his sin and shame is important enough to be included in the story line,[240] it is the younger son's return, and not his confession, that makes reconciliation possible. Second, the phrasing of the confession — that is, as it is actually delivered versus its earlier rehearsal — has been cut short. Originally, acknowledgment of sin and shame led to the younger son's proposal for a new form of relationship with his father, that of a hireling. At the moment of his encounter with his father, though, before the younger son can frame his proposition, his father has already launched a full restoration to status in the family. The father's response, based solely on the return of his son, already undercuts his son's plans.[241]

As in Luke's account of the widow at Nain (7:11-17) and the parable of the Samaritan (10:25-37), so here compassion is central to the movement of the parable.[242] The father's compassion (promptly contrasted with the elder

237. Menken, "Position of σπλαγχνίζεσθαι," 107-8.

238. That is, within this co-text, ἀνίστημι suggests not only "the beginning of action," but also, metaphorically, "being raised from the dead."

239. See 6:36; 8:51; 9:42; 11:2, 11, 13; 12:30, 32; cf. 1:17.

240. Its repetition ensures that the younger son's *return* is to be understood as his *repentance*.

241. Cf. Donahue, *Gospel in Parable*, 155-56.

242. Cf. Menken, "Position of σπλαγχνίζεσθαι."

brother's anger, v 28) leads to symbolic acts of recovery. Indeed, his outlandish behaviors should be traced back to their source in this compassion. A
wealthy landowner running down the street of his village is itself extraordinary,[243] and this is coupled with the incredulity of what must be regarded as
a public embrace of the younger son — the very son whose own efforts had
been directed toward shaming his father.[244] The embrace, the kiss, and the
gifts of robe, ring, and sandals — these are all emblematic of the son's
honorable restoration to the family he had snubbed and abandoned.[245]

Within the co-text provided by the parable itself as well as the co-text in
which the parable is set, the father's instructions in vv 23-24 bear particular
significance. As in the parables of the lost sheep and lost coin, recovery gives
way to celebration (vv 5-6, 9).[246] Here, though, that celebration comes in the
guise of a full-blown banquet, with the table set with the best and most expensive
beef, enough for dozens, perhaps even scores, of guests.[247] It is as if the father
had declared, "Spare no effort! Spare no expense!" Why? Because the son who
had slandered his father, the son who had proposed to return as nothing more
than a day laborer in his father's fields, is nevertheless "this son of mine" (v 24).
The first metaphor the father uses speaks to the tragedy skirted — dead, now

---

243. See Jeremias, *Parables,* 130; K. E. Bailey, *Poet and Peasant,* 181.

244. The public nature of the son's restoration is only implicit in this parable, but
is suggested both by the father's running out to meet his son (an action that would demand
a public setting, given the layout of the Palestinian village) and by the slaughtering of a
calf for the ensuing celebration (the yield of which would have been far too much meat
for only one household — *pace* Jeremias, *Parables,* 130). On account of Jesus' staging of
these events, what becomes critical in the parable is not how "the public" responds to the
recovery of the lost but how the father responds. In an honor-shame society, this shifts the
focus dramatically away from public opinion with respect to the identity of "sinners" and
"the righteous," toward adopting God's own point-of-view (cf. 18:9-14; 19:1-10).

245. Compare the scene of reconciliation in Gen 33:4. It is usual to see such texts
as Gen 41:42; Esth 8:2; 1 Macc 6:15 in the background of the details related to clothing
and to conclude on this basis that the younger son is being invested with his father's
authority (cf., e.g., Jeremias, *Parables,* 130). This probably reads too much into the text,
however, since (1) the ring mentioned is nowhere identified as a "signet ring" (C. F. Evans,
594); (2) given his sorry living conditions (vv 15-16), he is probably in need of clothing
appropriate to his renewed status in the family (on clothing and social status, see Hamel,
Poverty and Charity, 73-92); (3) the younger son has an elder brother to whom it would
fall first to serve as their father's surrogate in business matters (note v 31: "all that is mine
is yours"); and (4) no more need be intended by these symbolic actions than that they
signify the restoration of the younger son's honor as a son. See Esth 6:6-11 for a similar,
and explicit, concern with honor (cf. Nolland, 2:785).

246. Thus, εὐφραίνω parallels χαίρω; cf. 15:32.

247. The adjective σιτευτός refers here to grain-fed beef. In *Through Peasant Eyes*
(94), K. E. Bailey notes that a slaughtered calf would provide enough meat for 35 to 75
persons; elsewhere he speaks of over a hundred at the table (*Poet and Peasant,* 187).

alive — recalling for Jesus' audience not only the gulf the younger son had dug between himself and his family by his initial actions (vv 12-13) but also the depth to which the younger son had subsequently fallen. In terms of his family relationships and identity, the younger son was dead, and he had come close to material death in the pig pens. The recovery of the lost calls for celebration!

25-32 The elder son has been offstage, his character undeveloped since his first having been mentioned in v 11. That he returns from the fields identifies his family further as a household of relative wealth — wealthy enough to have an estate of sufficient size to necessitate the presence of hirelings and slaves (vv 17, 26), but still requiring either the managerial oversight or, perhaps, manual work of the family.

His reappearance provides the opportunity for interpretive summaries of the activities of both father and younger son thus far in the narrative. The slave answers the elder son's request for information by a rehearsal of the father's point-of-view: the recovery of the younger son calls for a lavish gala. One can almost imagine the matter-of-fact tone in which this message is delivered, as though this form of restoration were natural, expected. Moments later, addressing his father, the elder son summarizes the younger son's behavior, intensifying the latter's failing by substituting for Jesus' earlier phrase, "he squandered his property in dissolute living" (v 13), his own interpretation, "[he] has devoured your property with prostitutes."[248] This revision is purposeful, serving to distance the elder son (honorable and responsible, at least according to his own testimony[!] — v 29a) from his brother (disgraceful, reckless).

In his narration, Jesus draws attention to the elder son's affective response to the return of his brother, just as he had noted the affective response of the father. Whereas the father responds in *compassion* (v 20), the elder son responds with *anger* (v 28). Herein lies the fundamental contrast in their comportment with regard to the younger son; from these divergent affective states derive contrasting behaviors. What follows in their exchange is an exercise in the construction of family relations.

In anger, the elder son refuses to join in the celebration, thus physically distancing himself from his family and his own role as elder son in a celebration of this magnitude.[249] His refusal to enter his own home is also a refusal to share

248. Cf. LaHurd, "Rediscovering the Lost Women," 67. In a sense, of course, the elder son is only stating what might otherwise have been taken for granted — namely, the association of prostitutes with celebrative meal settings in the Greco-Roman world (cf. Corley, *Private Women*, ch. 2). By making this explicit, though, the elder son underscores the slanderous behavior of his brother.

249. K. E. Bailey, *Poet and Peasant*, 194: "At such a banquet the older son has a special semi-official responsibility. He is expected to move among the guests, offering compliments, making sure everyone has enough to eat, ordering the servants around and, in general, becoming a sort of major-domo of the feast."

in the meal, a symbolic act of gargantuan proportions in a culture where kinship boundaries are secured through the sharing of food.[250] In his reply to the elder brother, the slave had referred to "your brother" and "your father," but the elder son's actions bespeak a different understanding of familial relations. When addressing his father, he does not name him as "Father" (cf. vv 12, 18, 21); similarly, the younger son is only "this son of yours."[251] Indeed, in spite of his protestations regarding his own commitments and obedience (v 29), the elder son demonstrates through his refusal to come into the feast that he has adopted a perspective quite different from his father's; he does not and will not support his father's resolution concerning the younger son.

Of course, in many ways, the elder son has social propriety on his side. The younger son had shamed his father and deserved to be shunned. Why is it that recklessness and shamelessness are rewarded with jubilation when responsibility and obedience have received no recognition? The degree to which the quest for recognition is wrongheaded will surface in 17:1-10. In the interim we discover, first, that, in spite of appearances, the elder son has apparently lived in alienation from his father.[252] Even now he acts outside cultural norms vis-à-vis his father — refusing to come in, failing to address him as Father, stressing his servitude to his father, and complaining (in the context of a party!) about the maltreatment he has received from his father.[253] More centrally to the parable, we discover that the father has recomputed what will be regarded as appropriate behavior, allowing himself to be shamed and even shaming himself for the sake of reconciliation with his son. Refusing to adopt his father's gracious calculus, the elder son actually caricatures himself with images borrowed from the earlier portrayal of his brother. Accepting his unworthiness to be counted as a son, the younger had opted for the status of a day laborer; having severed his relationship as a son, he hoped to reestablish it as a hireling. Ironically, the elder son comports himself now not as a son but as a slave.[254]

Just as the father had run out to meet his younger son, so, again dishonoring himself, he leaves the banquet over which he is host in order to plead with his elder son. Calling him "son" and conferring upon him the

---

250. See Douglas, *Implicit Meanings,* 249-75; Bartchy, "Table Fellowship"; Neyrey, "Ceremonies in Luke-Acts."

251. On the importance of address forms as signifiers of relationship, see Fasold, *Sociolinguistics,* 1-38.

252. Thus, e.g., breaching the kinship values operative in his world, he has wished for a celebration with his "friends" rather than with his father (and family).

253. See Gowler, *Portraits of the Pharisees,* 253, 255.

254. Not only does his discourse with his father include no familial language, but he even describes his obedience as slavish (δουλεύω, v 29). Cf. Donahue, *Gospel in Parable,* 157.

honor of an equal, he seeks restoration. In doing so, however, he advances a condition — namely, that the elder acknowledge the divine necessity of celebrating the recovery of the lost.[255] As the son of his father, the elder must embrace his father's gracious will. If he is really his father's son, he will act as he has acted and rejoice at the recovery of the lost (cf. vv 5-6, 10). Hence, the father's reference to his younger son as "this brother of yours" is presented as an invitation to restoration.

Set within its co-text in ch. 15, the narrative referents of this parable are easily identified. Indicted for his receptivity to those who have come near to hear his words, Jesus responds by asserting the divine necessity of joyous responses to the recovery of the lost. Like the father of this parable, he recognizes the import of receiving into table fellowship the lost who are recovered — whether a younger son whose sin and shame have sundered any conventional vestiges of relationship or those whose status as toll collectors and sinners makes of them unacceptable table companions. His declaration of the divine will serves as much more than an attempt at self-defense, however. Not least with the final act of this third parable, he asserts his table fellowship with sinners as an invitation to and potential indictment against those who grumble at his practices. Scribes and Pharisees are invited to find themselves represented in the parable as the elder son — responsible and obedient, it would seem, but failing in their solidarity with the redemptive purpose of God. Will they identify with God's will and, having done so, join repentant sinners at the table? Putting aside their own concerns with status and recognition (cf 14:7-14), will they accept as members of the family of God those whom God accepts? Or, refusing to embrace God's gracious calculus, which works to include those who (re)turn to him, will they exclude themselves from the family of God? The parable is open-ended, and so is the invitation.

5.5.7. *Kingdom Economics (16:1-31)*

Luke marks a shift of audience in 16:1, then almost immediately indicates its artificiality. The whole of the parabolic teaching of ch. 15 had been directed toward legal experts and Pharisees (15:1-3), and, in spite of Luke's designation of Jesus' audience as "the disciples" in 16:1, the Pharisees remain very much in view (16:14). This demonstrates again the degree to which the disciples are not yet portrayed as a distinctive group within the Lukan travel narrative.[256]

---

255. The clause, "we had to celebrate . . ." (v 32) employs one of Luke's favorite terms for expressing divine necessity, δεῖ (cf., e.g., 2:49; 4:43; 9:22; 11:42; et al.). He thus underscores a perspective that has already been asserted in vv 7 and 10.

256. See above on 9:51–19:48.

Teaching directed toward them can also be intended for a wider audience, just as teaching directed toward others — as in 16:14-31, to the Pharisees — can be communicated in the hearing of the disciples so as to provide a clear pattern of the behavior they are to avoid. Indeed, though the language of 12:1 is absent, the juxtaposition of teaching to the disciples and to the Pharisees in this chapter can be read as a similar warning to the disciples to steer clear of Pharisaic dispositions, which do not reflect insight into God's purpose.[257] Only with 17:1 does Jesus seem more deliberately to address the disciples in a way that segregates them from others, and even then Jesus' opposition to what might be regarded in Luke as a Pharisaic mind-set is not far from the surface.

Many have noted how the opening parable of ch. 16 is related to the parable of 15:11-32, especially in terms of vocabulary and style.[258] Both, for example, begin with a reference to "a certain person" (15:11; 16:1),[259] have central characters who "squander" property (15:13; 16:3) and encounter life-threatening choices (15:15-17; 16:3), narrate the surprising action of the "certain person" mentioned in the opening verse (15:20-24; 16:8), and so on. More consistently overlooked is the interesting parallel that develops between the younger son of 15:13-24 and Lazarus the beggar in 16:21-23. Although the prior autobiography of Lazarus is missing, both come to be portrayed as inhabitants of the cesspool of social status only to have their lots dramatically reversed. The structural similarities between chs. 15 and 16 remind Luke's audience that the immediate backdrop of Jesus' teaching to the disciples in ch. 16 is his portrayal of table fellowship as an appropriate means for including such outsiders as toll collectors and sinners in the community of the lost-but-found. In ch. 16, Jesus grounds this message about table fellowship more fundamentally in his overall teaching about possessions: Wealth should be used to welcome another cluster of outsiders, the poor who are incapable of reciprocating with invitations of their own or of helping to advance one's own status.

That is, the connection between ch. 16 and the preceding material is more organic than the aforementioned examples of linguistic and structural similarity might intimate. Already in 14:1-24, Pharisees and legal experts had been advised to engage in hospitality sans normal concerns with status main-

257. See above on 12:1-12. As will become clear in what follows, the problem of the Pharisees is a lack of openness with regarding to hospitality (combining motifs related to almsgiving and table fellowship, both rooted in the law); but this same problem surfaces in the early church according to Acts — cf. Acts 4:32–5:11; 10:1–11:18; Bartchy, "Community of Goods"; Esler, *Community and Gospel,* 71-109.

258. See, e.g., K. E. Bailey, *Poet and Peasant,* 109; Donahue, *Gospel in Parable,* 167-68; Austin, "Hypocritical Son," 307-10.

259. ἄνθρωπός τις.

tenance or advancement and without reference to the obligation of reciprocal invitations. In ch. 15, Jesus had defended himself in light of accusations brought against his table fellowship with the socially marginalized. Now, in ch. 16, in the context of specific references to table fellowship and hospitality (vv 4, 9, 19, 21, 24), Jesus weaves together the motifs of almsgiving (and, thus, possessions) and friendship in order to demonstrate further the comportment toward the poor expected of those whose lives are oriented around the kingdom of God.[260] The parable of 16:1-9 establishes the theme of this larger narrative section: *Faithfulness to God is demonstrated in the extension of hospitality to the poor. Such hospitality occasions the redistribution of wealth to those incapable of reciprocation, underscores the importance of the creation of friendship across social boundaries, and secures an eternal home.*[261] The instruction of vv 10-13 generalizes this theme, and vv 14-31 present the commitments and practices of the Pharisees as a dramatic counterexample to dispositions shaped by the kingdom.

5.5.7.1. Using Wealth to Make Friends (16:1-9)

1 *Then Jesus said to the disciples, "There was a rich man who had a manager, and charges were brought to him that this man was squandering his property.* 2 *So he summoned him and said to him, 'What is this that I hear about you? Give me an accounting of your management, because you cannot be my manager any longer.'* 3 *Then the manager said to himself, 'What will I do, now that my master is taking the position away from me? I am not strong enough to dig, and I am ashamed to beg.* 4 *I have decided what to do so that, when I am dismissed as manager, people may welcome me into their homes.'* 5 *So, summoning his master's debtors one by one, he asked the first, 'How much do you owe my master?'* 6 *He answered, 'A hundred jugs of olive oil.' He said to him, 'Take your bill, sit down quickly, and make it fifty.'* 7 *Then he asked another, 'And how much do you owe?' He replied, 'A hundred containers of wheat.' He said to him, 'Take your bill and make it eighty.'* 8 *And his master commended the dishonest manager because he had acted shrewdly; for the children of this age are more shrewd in dealing with their own generation than are the children of light.*

---

260. See Bekaert, "Literary Unity"; Moxnes, *Economy of the Kingdom.* Concerning possessions in Luke, see above, §11; also Green, *Gospel of Luke,* 112-17; Moxnes, *Economy of the Kingdom;* Pilgrim, *Good News;* Gillman, *Possessions;* Johnson, *Sharing Possessions;* Seccombe, *Possessions.*

261. *Pace* Donahue (*Gospel in Parable,* 162), who speaks for most when he observes of ch. 16 that, ". . . apart from a concern for material possessions, no thread emerges that gives it thematic unity."

9 And I tell you, make friends for yourselves by means of dishonest wealth so that when it is gone, they may welcome you into the eternal homes."

Luke marks a new narrative section by designating as Jesus' audience "the disciples." The practical consequence of this shift is that we understand that Jesus has completed his formal response to the Pharisees and legal experts (15:1-32). This does not mean, however, that Jesus has departed from the general *theme* of ch. 15. To the contrary, the parabolic instruction he now provides is closely tied to the preceding material, especially 14:1-24; 15:1-32 — all three having to do with intricately related issues of hospitality. Jesus extends that earlier teaching in this parable by concretizing it with respect to almsgiving and friendship.[262] In fact, the theme of this narrative section concerns the appropriate use of wealth to overstep social boundaries between rich and poor in order to participate in a form of economic redistribution grounded in kinship.

How is this message achieved? Three important interpretive issues intersect in this parable and its exposition within the Lukan narrative. First, the story Jesus narrates does not lend itself to an allegorical reading, whereby Luke's audience would be invited to find external referents (God? Jesus?) to correspond with the characters within the parable.[263] Instead, as elsewhere in the Lukan travel narrative, an example has been drawn simply and directly from everyday life, from taken-for-granted suppositions about "the way the world works."[264] Second, crucial to understanding this subsection of Jesus' message to his disciples is discerning its outer limits or boundaries, which, as Luke narrates it, is a fairly simple exercise. Since vv 4 and 9 stand in vivid parallel to one another — plan of action → nature of crisis → receiving hospitality — the relevance of v 9 must be taken into account in the reading of the parable itself. Verses 10-13 are also connected via common vocabulary, but not as integrally as v 9. Third, it is of great interest that the interpreter of

262. The problems attending this parable have attracted a plethora of interpretations; see the helpful survey in Ireland, "Recent Interpretation." Our own approach to this text will bypass most of the dark corridors of its history of study by focusing on its function in its narrative co-text (and not on its prehistory, on which see recently Parrott, "Dishonest Steward") and by refusing to engage in a referential or allegorical reading.

263. Interpretations that assume the need for locating references to characters outside the parable have faltered on attempts to correlate, e.g., "God" with "a rich man" (v 1), since the wealthy are negatively characterized in the Third Gospel; and "Jesus" with "his master/lord" (v 8), since this would entail having Jesus commend the manager for apparently criminal activity. See further below.

264. Cf. 11:5-8, 11-13; 18:2-5.

this text must stand, together with the text, at the crossroads of Jewish and wider Greco-Roman traditions. "Making friends," after all, borrows on Greco-Roman conceptualizations,[265] whereas the notion of almsgiving embedded in v 9 builds on more properly Jewish sensibilities.[266]

1-3 In Luke's narration, Jesus turns from addressing the concerns raised by the Pharisees and legal experts (15:1-2) to instructing his disciples. Only in hindsight do we realize that he has not thereby initiated a major thematic shift in his teaching.

The parable he introduces has two characters. The character of the first, a wealthy man, is little developed in Jesus' account. Given prior material on the wealthy in the Third Gospel, though, it is hard to be well disposed toward this man. Previously, the rich are introduced as those over whom Jesus pronounces misfortune (6:24), who find their security in their wealth (12:16), and who engage in reciprocal contracts with their social peers without regard for those of lower status (14:12; cf. 16:19-22!). The second is a "manager" — in the Roman context either a slave or a freedman who had access to his master's wealth and acted as his agent in business affairs. In this capacity, a manager would have enjoyed enviable status, so much so that persons were actually known to sell themselves, as a means of social promotion, to a wealthy man in order to administer his holdings.[267] The importance of this background information surfaces in the sense of crisis anticipated by this manager (vv 3-4). For him, loss of position as manager entails a forfeiture of social status, with the consequence that, initially, the only options he can entertain are manual labor and begging (v 3); these locate him prospectively among the "unclean and degraded" or even "expendable" of society (see Figure 1, p. 60). What is more, his imminent departure as manager signifies his loss of household attachment, hence his concomitant concern for a roof over his head (v 4).

His identification as manager is also crucial to the plot of Jesus' tale, with the report of his mismanagement and impending release driving this brief

---

265. See the helpful introductory survey in Garnsey and Saller, *Roman Empire*, 148-59.

266. Cf. Hamel, *Poverty and Charity;* Garrison, *Redemptive Almsgiving.* Fuks (*Social Conflict,* 52-189) illustrates the Greek concern for the poor, but his examples point generally to the fear among the wealthy of civil unrest among the poor. The typical attribution of poverty to laziness (or to other autobiographical roots) in the Greco-Roman world worked against more generous attitudes to the poor. Although concerns with autobiographical causation are not altogether absent from Jewish literature (cf., e.g., the laziness and/or wickedness of the poor in representative Wisdom texts), poverty is more typically regarded in OT legal and prophetic texts as a systemic issue (cf. the summary comments in Pleins, "Poor, Poverty: Old Testament").

267. See Thébert, "Slave," 156-57; Morel, "Craftsman," 223.

narrative forward. The precise connotation of "squandering"[268] is difficult to discern, though the use of the same verb in 15:13 suggests reckless irresponsibility in the present co-text as well. In any case, what is clearly in view is the manager's mismanagement of holdings that were not his to possess, but had been placed in his care by his master. The prospective release of the manager occasions a crisis, marked first by the question "What shall I do?"; similar questions are found in other situations of crisis in Luke-Acts (3:10-14; 12:17-18; Acts 2:37).

4-7 Having dismissed other options in soliloquy,[269] the manager hits upon an idea that is never explicitly outlined in Jesus' representation of the story. Instead, we learn his aim, to be welcomed into people's homes, and we are shown his course of action, reducing the financial obligations of his master's debtors. The connection between these two turns on the play on the word "receive" — translated as "welcome" in v 4 (so also v 9), "take" in vv 6 and 7.[270] Elsewhere in the Third Gospel, this verb is generally used with reference to hospitality, and this is the case in v 4.[271] Who will offer the manager hospitality? Those who, as it were, "receive" their amended loan agreements.

The nature of the manager's activity in vv 5-7 is much debated, though the simplest theory is also the most obvious.[272] The quantities involved in the

---

268. διασκορπίζω; cf. the discussion of alternative views in Parrott, "Dishonest Steward," 55: failing to achieve a profit? sloppy record keeping? outright theft?

269. On the significance of these options for the manager's future, see above on vv 1-3. Note the alliteration in v 3c — σκάπτειν οὐκ ἰσχύω, ἐπαιτεῖν αἰσχύνομαι — giving them an almost proverbial ring.

270. δέχομαι.

271. See 9:5, 48, 53; 10:8, 10.

272. On the general nature of debt-relationships assumed here, see above, §10. Arguing from mishnaic evidence, his own observations of twentieth-century Middle Eastern peasant culture, and the parallels between this parable and that in 15:11-32, K. E. Bailey (*Poet and Peasant,* 86-118) intimates that the manager places his master, a gracious and respectable man of the community, in a difficult position. In his own attempt to save face, the manager takes advantage of the mercy of the master by changing the contracts with his debtors without the master's knowledge. The master could go back to the debtors and explain that it was all a mistake, but instead chooses to ". . . keep silent, accept the praise that is even now being showered on him, and allow the clever steward to ride high on the wave of popular enthusiasm" (102). Bailey's interpretation suffers at a number of points: (1) in his focus on the manager's need to save face, Bailey fails to account for v 4: the explicit aim of the manager is to be received into people's homes after he has lost his job, not to receive the praise of the master; (2) his assumption about the character of the wealthy man flies in the face of the way the Third Evangelist has constructed his portrait of "the wealthy" thus far in the Gospel; (3) he depends on detailed correspondence between the activities described in the parable and mishnaic legislation, in spite of the much later provenance of the Mishnah; and (4), in his overall interpretation

591

renegotiation of debts are quite large (cf. Ezra 7:21-24),[273] reflecting the produce, respectively, of a considerable olive grove and of an acreage twenty to twenty-five times that of an ordinary family farm.[274] That this master has outstanding loan balances of these proportions marks him as a wealthy man indeed; similarly, these data indicate the enormity of the amount of the debt forgiven by the manager. What is more, given the stylized language of Jesus' narration ("one by one . . . the first . . . another . . ."), we may easily assume that the scenario painted in these two instances is representative of the many times it was repeated, with many debtors having their rather substantial debts similarly relaxed. By reducing their loan agreements so generously, the manager has done these debtors a significant favor; because he is still this wealthy man's manager, moreover, his agreements with these debtors are binding.[275] In this way, the manager has entered into his own patronal relationship with his master's debtors, apparently themselves also persons of

---

of Jesus' message, Bailey fails to notice the parallelism between vv 4 and 9 (in large part, of course, Bailey's interpretation is not and does not purport to be a reading of *the Lukan narrative,* for he is far more concerned with the world behind the text).

An alternative viewpoint is provided by Fitzmyer (2:1094-1111; cf. the summary in Donahue, *Gospel in Parable,* 165), whose fundamental problem is focused on the apparent commendation of dishonest practices in v 8. Attempting to resolve this issue, he observes that the manager is not actually "dishonest" (v 8), but had been hired to handle an unjust means of loaning money (i.e., taking τῆς ἀδικίας as an objective genitive). Rather than lend money and charge interest (forbidden in, e.g., Exod 22:24; Lev 25:35-37), a legal fiction was devised whereby the projected interest payment was written into the original loan. In vv 5-7, then, the manager is simply waiving this interest, his commission, not engaging in dishonest or illegal activity. (Derrett ["Fresh Light"] similarly posits that the manager is releasing debtors from interest charged against their loans in contravention to Jewish law against usury.) This interpretation is not a plausible one. First, in its attempt to circumvent the commendation of dishonesty in v 8, it assumes a problem where there is none. Given Luke's characterization of the wealthy thus far in his Gospel, it is not at all surprising that a rich man would approve of such behavior. Indeed, when we remember that Jesus is the narrator of this parable, we realize that (1) Jesus labels the manager as "dishonest," while (2) the rich man regards him as "shrewd." Second, as with Bailey's position, so with the theories of Fitzmyer and Derrett, there is the basic question of the relative antiquity of the materials, mishnaic and otherwise, concerning usury and agency on which the Lukan parable is alleged to depend for its meaning (see the summary in Parrott, "Dishonest Steward," 503). Finally, the Lukan text itself clearly holds the manager responsible for squandering property that did not belong to him, making attempts to rehabilitate the manager disingenuous.

273. βάτος (NRSV: "jug"), a loanword from Hebrew (בּת), refers to approximately 40 liters, or one-tenth of a κόρος (from Hebrew כֹּר; NRSV: "container"); cf. Fuchs, "βάτος."

274. Cf. Kloppenborg, "Dishonoured Master," 482.

275. Thébert ("Slave," 157-58) notes the de facto autonomy under which managers operated.

means. He has become their benefactor and, in return, can expect them to reciprocate by extending to him the hospitality of their homes. The manager has thus taken advantage of his now-short-lived status, using the lag time during which he was to make an accounting of his management (v 2) and his position to arrange for his future.

8-9   Point of view is important in these closing verses. The master commends the manager for his shrewdness, while the narrator of the parable, Jesus, identifies the manager as "dishonest." That is, the master does not commend his manager for his dishonesty, but for his prudence in business affairs.[276] With v 8b, Jesus' commentary on the parable begins, supporting immediately this construal of v 8a. "Children of this age," he observes, understand how the world works and use it to their benefit; why do "children of light" not understand the ways of the kingdom of God?

"This age" draws on a characterization of time divided into two aeons, the present epoch and the one to come (cf. 20:34-35). Collocated with "their own [i.e., "this"] generation" (cf., e.g., 7:31; 9:41; 11:29-32), "this age" is implicated in faithlessness and wickedness. That Jesus can speak of a manager as one who is commended by one of his own generation for his having prudently taken advantage of the systems of this world *and* as wicked is therefore not surprising. Analogous wisdom on the part of "children of light," on the other hand, would take its directives from the new aeon, the age to come.[277]

If they did understand the ways of the new aeon, how would this be manifest in their practices? Simply put, they would use "dishonest wealth" to "make friends" in order that they might be welcomed "into eternal homes" (v 9). "Wealth" (or mammon)[278] is characterized as "dishonest" in the same way that the manager was. Both belong to this aeon; indeed, in speaking of its demise, Jesus insinuates that mammon has no place in the age to come (cf. 12:33).

Jesus' counsel to "make friends" borrows on social conventions deeply

---

276. In the only other occurrence of φρόνιμος in Luke-Acts (12:42), the adjective is collocated with πιστός; φρονίμως is used only here in the NT. For the use of κύριος to signify "owner of the house," see 14:15-24. *Contra,* e.g., Jeremias, *Parables,* 45-46. As the NRSV makes plain by adding the possessive pronoun "his" before "master," the use of the first person singular pronoun by Jesus in v 9 makes it very difficult to identity ὁ κύριος in v 8 with Jesus.

277. Note the use of αἰών in v 8 and of αἰώνιος in v 9. "Sons of light" has close parallels in the QL (e.g., 1QS 1:9; 2:16; 1QM 1:3, 9, 11, 13), where it is typically set in opposition to "sons of darkness."

278. μαμωνᾶς (a transliteration of the Aramaic ממונא) refers here to possessions, property, or, more generally, wealth; in 16:10-13 it is represented more as an idolatrous power.

embedded in the Greco-Roman world, whereby friendship and economic considerations were inseparable. Friends in Roman antiquity might be "superior," "equal," or "lesser," depending on their relative resources.[279] Greater and lesser friends were actually involved in forms of patronage, though the term "friend" was employed to save "lesser friends" from the social embarrassment of being branded as clients. "Equal friends," on the other hand, were of analogous status and possessed equivalent resources. Using money to make friends, then, refers simply to the social reality: The exchange of money created, maintained, or solidified various forms of friendship. In vv 4-7, then, the manager used his master's wealth to gain friends who would repay him with hospitality.

It is precisely at this juncture that the analogy with vv 4-7 breaks down, however. Jesus counsels his disciples to make friends with mammon, to be sure, and this might take the form of giving to those in need or the more specific form of canceling debts (cf. 4:18-19; 6:35; 7:41-42; 11:4). *But Jesus provides no basis by which his followers might come to expect reciprocation from these friends.* This is due (1) to his earlier teaching that disciples should practice giving without expectation of return (6:32-35), and (2) to his expectation that the disciples would give to those who were incapable of reciprocation — that is, that they would give alms to the poor. Neither of these perspectives on giving can be ruled out; in the current co-text they are complementary. Like the former, the latter is commended within the larger Lukan narrative, where Jesus counsels the disposition of possessions (and hospitality) on behalf of the poor with the understanding that, while mammon will vanish, eternal treasure will have thus been secured (esp. 12:33; 14:12-14).[280] Taken on its own, this form of "making friends" would create a patron-client relationship, with the poor now indebted to serve and honor those who had provided for them. Such an understanding is undercut, though, by Jesus' related insistence that giving be done freely, with no strings attached, without expectation of return.[281] In this case, "almsgiving" has as its consequence genuine social solidarity between rich and poor, who act toward each other as "equal friends."

279. Pliny *Ep.* 7.3.2; 2.6.2; Seneca *Ep.* 94.14; Garnsey and Saller, *Roman Empire,* 149.

280. The subject of "welcome" in v 9 is not obvious — the recipients of alms? God (i.e., a form of divine passive)? The promise of "eschatological dwellings" (εἰς τὰς αἰωνίους σκηνάς [NRSV: "eternal homes] — cf. 9:33; Bühner, "σκηνή," 251), together with the parallels in 12:33; 14:14, supports the latter interpretation. See also Manson, *Sayings,* 293.

281. The possible interpretation of v 9 as counseling the construction of patron-client obligations is also undermined by subsequent teaching in vv 10-31.

5.5.7.2. The Rule of Wealth (16:10-13)

10 *"Whoever is faithful in a very little is faithful also in much; and whoever is dishonest in a very little is dishonest also in much.* 11 *If then you have not been faithful with the dishonest wealth, who will entrust to you the true riches?* 12 *And if you have not been faithful with what belongs to another, who will give you what is your own?* 13 *No slave can serve two masters; for a slave will either hate the one and love the other, or be devoted to the one and despise the other. You cannot serve God and Wealth."*[282]

Luke provides no textual markers to signal a break between vv 1-9 and 10-13. For purposes of discussion, we have separated vv 10-13 because of their generalizing quality ("Whoever is faithful . . .") and because of the important parallelism between vv 4 and 9. Nevertheless, the immediate co-text of these verses is critical for their interpretation — a reality that is underscored both by the lack of any such narrative boundary markers as change of scene or audience and by the impressive sharing of language between vv 1-9 and 10-13.[283] Thus, in spite of the aphoristic appearance of its content, the instruction contained in these verses should not be mistakenly identified as timeless proverbs. Instead, Luke records Jesus' self-conscious elaboration of motifs raised in the parable, especially stewardship and wealth.

10-11   Jesus first capitalizes on a series of appositions — faithful/dishonest, faithful/not faithful, little/much, dishonest wealth/true riches — whose connotations are determined by their immediate co-text in the parabolic teaching of vv 1-9 (esp. vv 8-9).[284] Hence, "faithful in a very little" is correlated with faithfulness with regard to "dishonest wealth," and the meaning of both expressions is grounded in the practices recommended in v 9. Faithfulness, then, is evidenced in the cancellation of debts and in almsgiving on behalf of the poor. These behaviors grow out of dispositions shaped by an orientation to the new aeon, the age to come, and so are rooted in a commitment toward solidarity across social lines. Lack of faithfulness, on the other hand, is related to dishonest practices — that is, practices that reflect a fundamental commitment to the present aeon (v 8).

"Dishonest wealth" is contrasted with "true riches" in a way that is reminiscent of 12:33, with its reference to securing "unfailing treasure in heaven" by selling possessions and giving alms (see also 16:9). Perhaps this

---

282. NRSV: "wealth."

283. Thus: ἀδικία (vv 8, 9), ἄδικος (vv 10, 11); κύριος (vv 3, 5, 8, 13); μαμωνᾶς (vv 9, 11, 13); οἰκονόμος (vv 1, 2, 3, 4, 8), οἶκος (v 4), οἰκέτης (v 13).

284. Hence, our discussion of these verses borrows heavily from our analysis of vv 8-9, above.

is enough to justify the translation of "the true (thing)" as "true riches." More needs to be said, however, since Jesus' language raises the question of the nature of Luke's dualism — an issue that surfaces again, immediately and even more prominently, in v 13 with regard to the opposition of two masters, God and Wealth. The term "the true (thing)" is used only here in Luke-Acts, but generally has the meaning "authentic." Philo actually uses the term to lexicalize the sort of wealth found in the heavens as opposed to "false wealth," and some have found a similar Platonism at work in Luke.[285] Antiquity knows many types of duality, though, with Plato's cosmological duality only one of them (and, by the first century C.E., his was a minority position).[286] The duality Luke sets up in vv 8-9 continues to shape the meaning of this text, and it is eschatological, not cosmological, in orientation. According to this perspective on history, the present aeon will be succeeded by an "age to come"; even in the present, then, faithfulness is determined by one's capacity to orient oneself around the coming aeon and, by extension, by one's capacity to reflect in one's practices the inbreaking kingdom of God. Even though "dishonest wealth" is a reality of the present age, one's use of this wealth can either be "dishonest" (i.e., determined by one's commitment to the present world order) or "faithful" (i.e., determined by the values of the new epoch).

12-13 Hence, in spite of the apparent inflexibility of the opposition of God and Wealth in v 13, this opposition cannot be understood in ontological categories, as though God and Wealth were forever locked in the battle between good and evil. In Jewish tradition, wealth (or "mammon")[287] is not inherently evil,[288] but, in the Lukan presentation, neither can one remain neutral in one's relationship to it. Wealth is either used faithfully — that is, in the service of God and thus in solidarity with and on behalf of those in need — or, as in v 13, it takes on a personified, cosmological status in which case its claims for service are as unyielding as they are perverse.[289] According to Luke, the rule of Wealth is manifest in theft and exploitation, hoarding, conspicuous consumption, and the more general disregard for outsiders and

---

285. ἀληθινός. See the helpful discussion in *TLNT,* 1:84 (where the relevant texts in Philo are cited [n. 80]). For Luke's alleged Platonism, see Johnson, 246.

286. Wright (*People of God,* 252-56) notes as many as ten varieties of duality and discusses briefly their attribution in first-century Judaism. D. B. Martin (*Corinthian Body,* 3-37) notes the need not only to understand Plato on his own terms, but also to ask how Plato's views fared at the hands of his interpreters in subsequent years, not least following the demise of his "school" in the early first century B.C.E. With respect to Plato's anthropological dualism, he observes that the influence of especially Stoicism had led to important modulations of Plato's views.

287. On μαμωνᾶς, see above on vv 8-9.

288. See Hauck, "μαμωνᾶς."

289. Cf. Davids, "Rich and Poor," 705.

persons of low status and need.[290] Interestingly, Luke's portrait intersects with Josephus's presentation of the Essenes: Because they despise riches, they participate in an admirable "community of goods," so that none can be found in a state of abject poverty or inordinate wealth.[291] That is, their understanding of the nature of wealth leads them into social solidarity — not the kind of social program envisioned by the Lukan narrative, but a form of social solidarity nonetheless.

Once the "masters" God and Wealth have been so clearly identified, the impossibility of serving them both becomes obvious. In the larger Greco-Roman world, of course, a slave could be owned by more than one master and clients could be and were shared among patrons. Jesus' teaching at this point, then, hardly reflects a generally accepted truth, but is specific to this co-text and to the identification of these masters. Because these two masters demand such diametrically opposed forms of service, since each grounds its demands in such antithetical worldviews, one cannot serve them both. Jesus underscores the impossibility of dual service through his use of contradictory terms of association (love, hate) and of honor and shame (devote, despise).[292]

Luke's reference to a household slave (NRSV: "slave")[293] in v 13 helps to draw the reader back into the parabolic material of vv 1-9, providing a co-text for making sense of v 12. The primary motif developed in vv 10-13 concerns faithfulness with regard to wealth, but here a second, closely related motif comes to expression. Countering any notion that he actually condoned the irresponsibility of the manager in vv 1-9, Jesus had already characterized him as "dishonest" (v 8). Given the world system he served, the manager had acted prudently, but even that world system is rejected in favor of the inbreaking kingdom. Jesus goes on now to draw from the parable the importance of a form of stewardship that is firmly rooted in the OT understanding of Yahweh as the true owner and conferrer of all land and property; these are given to human beings to manage, and it is to Yahweh that humans are and will be accountable. This perspective from the life of Israel, with its corollary that property and land are to be used for the good of all, is clearly reflected in Luke's position that the wealthy do not exist in isolation from others but already are to be forging relationships with the poor that signal the nature of salvation as eschatological reversal.[294]

290. See 11:39; 12:16-21; 14:12-14; 16:19-31; Moxnes, *Economy of the Kingdom*, 146.

291. Josephus *J.W.* 2.8.3 §§122-23; cf. 1QS 5:1-2; 6:18-20.

292. Again, it is of interest that Josephus uses καταφρονέω ("to treat with contempt") to describe the Essene disposition toward wealth (καταφρονηταὶ δὲ πλούτου; Josephus *J.W.* 2.8.3 §122).

293. οἰκέτης, used in Luke-Acts here and in Acts 10:7.

294. See, e.g., Gen 12:7; Exod 3:8; 32:13; Lev 20:24; 25; Deut 7:13; et al.; Gnuse, *Community and Property*, 3-9 (6); Merklein, "πλούσιος," 115-16.

5.5.7.3. Jesus' Polemic against the Pharisees, Lovers of Money (16:14-31)

14 *The Pharisees, who were lovers of money, heard all this, and they ridiculed him.* 15 *So he said to them, "You are those who justify your-selves in the sight of others; but God knows your hearts; for what is prized by human beings is an abomination in the sight of God.*

16 *Until John there were the law and the prophets;*[295] *since then the good news of the kingdom of God is proclaimed, and everyone is urged to enter it.*[296] 17 *But it is easier for heaven and earth to pass away, than for one stroke of a letter in the law to be dropped.*[297] 18 *Anyone who divorces his wife and marries another commits adul-tery, and whoever marries a woman divorced from her husband commits adultery.*

19 *"There was a rich man who was dressed in purple and fine linen and who feasted sumptuously every day.* 20 *And at his gate was tossed*[298] *a poor man named Lazarus, covered with sores,* 21 *who longed to satisfy his hunger with what fell from the rich man's table; even the dogs would come and lick his sores.* 22 *The poor man died and was carried away by the angels to be with Abraham. The rich man also died and was buried.* 23 *In Hades, where he was being tormented, he looked up and saw Abraham far away with Lazarus by his side.* 24 *He called out, 'Father Abraham, have mercy on me, and send Lazarus to dip the tip of his finger in water and cool my tongue; for I am in agony in these flames.'* 25 *But Abraham said, 'Child, remember that during your lifetime you received your good things, and Lazarus in like manner evil things; but now he is comforted here, and you are in agony.* 26 *Besides all this, between you and us a great chasm has been fixed, so that those who might want to pass from here to you cannot do so, and no one can cross from there to us.'* 27 *He said, 'Then, father, I beg you to send him to my father's house — 28 for I have five brothers — that he may bear witness to them,*[299] *so that they will not also come into this place of torment.'* 29 *Abraham replied, 'They have Moses and the prophets; they should listen to them.'* 30 *He said, 'No, father Abraham; but if someone goes to them from the dead, they will repent.'* 31 *He said to him, 'If they do not listen to Moses and the prophets, neither will they be convinced even if someone rises from the dead.' "*

295. NRSV: "The law and the prophets were in effect until John came."
296. NRSV: "tries to enter it by force."
297. The NRSV introduces a paragraph break here.
298. NRSV: "lay."
299. NRSV: "warn them."

In 16:1, following a defense of his ministry directed to the Pharisees and legal experts, Jesus had turned to address his disciples. In vv 14-15, however, not only does Jesus turn again to converse with the Pharisees, but Luke notes that they had never departed the scene. Instead, they have been eavesdropping on Jesus' discourse to his followers in vv 1-9, and well they should, since his message to the one group is closely aligned with his message to the other.[300] Given the substantive and illustrative materials Jesus brings together in this section, the identification of Pharisees as his primary audience is not surprising. Questions about the ongoing relevance of the law and the deployment of a story concerning the afterlife are clearly appropriate to historical Pharisaic sensibilities as these are known to us. Especially in this text, however, even more pivotal to Luke's portrayal of the Pharisees is his identification of them as "lovers of money." At this juncture, Luke has departed from what we know of the historical Pharisees, providing his own polemical evaluation of them in a narrative aside.[301] This is not to say that Luke has made an "error" in category, but that Luke means by "lovers of money" less, and more, than might first appear on the surface. As will become clear, the Lukan characterization of the Pharisees as "lovers of money" ties this narrative subsection thematically back into earlier material concerned with Pharisaic habits regarding wealth and hospitality (esp. 14:1-24; 15).

Verses 14-31 constitute one narrative unit, with a Pharisaic challenge to Jesus (v 14) opening the way to his counterchallenge (vv 15-31). No changes in audience are evident, nor are any fissures discernible in Jesus' address until 17:1.[302] Taken as a whole, this unit is tied together by a fundamental concern with wealth and its manifestations. Those who "love money" oppose Jesus (v 14); a wealthy man engages in conspicuous consumption without regard for a poor man, in spite of the fact that this beggar who resides at his gate is quite literally his "neighbor" (vv 19-21; cf. 10:29-37); and the rich and poor experience the eschatological reversal forecast in 6:20-24 (v 25). If wealth and its use provide the melody for this unit, its rather noticeable countermelody has to do with the law (and, more broadly, the Scriptures). As in the buildup to the parable of the compassionate Samaritan (i.e., 10:25-29), so here one finds concerns with the law juxtaposed with attempts at self-justification (vv 15-18); Jesus' practices vis-à-vis toll collectors, sinners, and

---

300. Cf. Green, *Gospel of Luke,* 104-5.

301. Historically, the Pharisees constituted a lay movement not known for the wealth of its constituents. The difficulty of attributing this epigraph to the Pharisees was highlighted in Manson, *Sayings,* 295-96. See the summary comments in Moxnes, *Economy of the Kingdom,* 1-5.

302. There, Jesus addresses again the disciples. This narrative arrangement suggests that the disciples, present in 16:1-13 and 17:1-10, are in the background but not offstage in 16:14-31.

other socio-religious undesirables have raised questions about his position on the contemporary relevance of the law (vv 16-17; cf. 15:1-2); and the wealthy are advised to heed "Moses and the prophets" (vv 29, 31). Comportment with regard to wealth and concerns with the relevance of the law — are these melody and countermelody; or components of one more complex theme? Clearly, they must be read together, as the story of Lazarus intimates. The wealthy man of Jesus' parable comes to realize too late that he has ignored the words of Moses and the prophets concerning the poor.

Hence, the hostility between Jesus and the Pharisees that blossoms in this text is ironic. Because in his choice of table companions Jesus oversteps Pharisaic concerns with purity and holiness, themselves rooted in their reading of the Scriptures, the Pharisees charge Jesus with relaxing the law. According to Jesus, in their "love of money," manifest in their concerns with status among persons of choice socio-religious status, the Pharisees have revealed their lack of commitment to God's purpose and have themselves transgressed the message of the Scriptures. According to Luke, then, Jesus is not abrogating the law,[303] but neither is he content with its treatment in the hands of the Pharisees. In the Lukan presentation, obedience to the ethical demands of the law is realized in the disposition of wealth on behalf of the needy (itself a manifestation of the command to love the neighbor, 10:25-37).[304]

14 "Hearing all these things" appears in the anterior position in the Greek text, drawing immediate attention to the fact that the Pharisees are *responding* to Jesus' preceding instruction. Are they reacting only to his message to his disciples (vv 1-9)? Should "all" be taken in a more inclusive sense, embracing also 15:1-32 (and, perhaps, even 14:1-24) — that is, teaching directed toward the Pharisees to which they have not yet had opportunity to respond in the Lukan narration? Although interesting, this question is not an urgent one. After all, Jesus' discourses in 14:1-24; 15:1-32; and 16:1-9 might be classified as variations on a theme: the opposition of concerns with status and purity on the one hand, hospitality and almsgiving on behalf of the poor on the other. Hence, whether the Pharisees are responding to one occasion of instruction or them all, the effect is essentially the same. Their grumbling (15:1-2) has evolved into ridicule. In mocking him, they disassociate themselves from him completely.[305] Their response is polemical, aimed at elimi-

---

303. *Contra* Moo ("Law," 460; following Blomberg, "Law"), who concludes that ". . . Luke's Jesus affirms the cessation of the authority of the OT, in some sense, in the age of the kingdom." Moo's view is grounded in a problematic reading of 16:16, itself based on categories introduced by Conzelmann *(Luke)* but foreign to Luke.

304. See the detailed discussion in Klinghardt, *Gesetz,* esp. 16-96.

305. Note that, previously, Jesus is found in the homes and at the table of Pharisees (7:36; 11:37; 14:1), but this practice is now discontinued for the rest of the Gospel.

nating any possibility that others will regard him as a legitimate agent of God and interpreter of the Scriptures. To the degree that an echo of Ps 22:7 can be heard, however, such scorn is ironic, self-defeating, for this is just the sort of behavior expected of those who resist God's righteous one.[306]

In an aside to his audience, Luke has inserted his characterization of the Pharisees as "lovers [or friends] of money." His readers may detect a subtle wordplay with v 9: rather than utilizing worldly wealth to "make friends," Pharisees are "friends" of money.[307] This need not be taken as an indication of the relative wealth of the Pharisees, but must be read against the contours of the developing Lukan narrative and in light of contemporary literature. Concerning the latter, both in Greco-Roman and Hellenistic Jewish circles one finds the polemical use of phrases like "lovers of money," often in tandem with statements about self-glory, in accusations against false teachers and false prophets.[308] In the contest between Jesus and the Pharisees regarding who has the authority to represent God's purpose, the significance of this material is transparent. The Pharisees are thus labeled as persons who are not to be trusted. When it is remembered that, in Roman antiquity, wealth had value proportional to one's ability to redeem it for the currency of status honor,[309] the sense of this Lukan label for the Pharisees becomes even more clear. He has repeatedly *shown* the Pharisees to be persons whose concerns with the maintenance and advancement of social standing negate any impulses toward care for the poor.[310] Now he *tells* his readers the same thing, summarizing in a single expression, "lovers of money," what he regards as the most essential and unrelenting description of the Pharisees. In ridiculing Jesus, the Pharisees attempt to marginalize him by publicly rejecting any claim he might make to divine authorization. They do this, according to the narrator, because they are lovers of money — that is, people who neglect the poor for the sake of their own community status, false teachers who reject God's purpose for themselves (cf. 7:29-30).

15 The subtle and ironic connection between the parabolic teaching in vv 1-9 and Jesus' allegations against the Pharisees continues. As "lovers of money" (v 14), Pharisees are implicated in the present world system, already characterized as "unjust" or "unrighteous" (NRSV: "dishonest") in

306. That such an echo is possible is supported by the fact that ἐκμυκτηρίζω, found in these psalmic texts, is used in the NT only here and in 23:35, where an allusion to Ps 22:7 (21:8, LXX) is obvious (cf. Green, *Death of Jesus*, 92).

307. φιλάργυροι; cf. 16:9: ποιήσατε φίλους ἐκ τοῦ μαμωνᾶ.

308. See the comments in Johnson, 249-50; Moxnes, *Economy of the Kingdom*, 6-9. Cf. Acts 20:33-34; 1 Thess 2:5-6; 1 Tim 6:5; 2 Tim 3:2; Tit 1:11; Philo *Praem.* 127; Dio *Discourses* 32:9-11; 35:1; 54:1-3; Epictetus *Discourses* 1, 9, 19-20; Lucian *Timon* 56.

309. See Green, "Good News," 64-65.

310. See esp. 11:39-43; 14:7-14; 15:1-2; and cf. 16:19-31.

Jesus' parable and subsequent teaching.[311] Though ensnared in an unjust world order, they nevertheless attempt "to justify" themselves. (Note again the connection with the parable of the compassionate Samaritan, esp. 10:29; cf. 18:9-14). Even this expression of concern with justice is perverted by its orientation toward securing the approval of humans rather than of God.[312] Jesus' reference to God as the one who "knows hearts,"[313] then, cannot be read as a judgment against the Pharisees as though their inner dispositions were at odds with their outer behavior. They are, for Luke, "lovers of money," and their behavior proves it; hence, both (inner) dispositions and (outer) behavior are condemned. As Jesus goes on to say, their status-seeking is nothing other than idolatry, manifesting the rule of Wealth (recall v 13!).[314] Instead, Jesus is calling into question a way of life embraced by the Pharisees, one that is focused on the quest for external approval[315] rather than on character and behavior that are valued by God. "God knows your hearts," then, should be read in parallel with the earlier statement about "the yeast of the Pharisees, that is, their hypocrisy" (see above on 12:1). Because their hearts are not oriented toward God's purpose, they are unreliable interpreters of his will — not least, as in the present case, with respect to the appropriate use of wealth.

16-18 Luke's record of Jesus charging the Pharisees with idolatry in v 15 becomes programmatic for our understanding of Jesus' teaching in vv 16-18 (and, then, vv 16-31). First, it provides Jesus with a base from which to demonstrate that his ministry is not a contravention of God's will as this is expressed in the Scriptures. Second, it sets up the need for Jesus to elucidate in what way the Pharisees are idolatrous. Although separable for purposes of discussion, these two issues are tightly interwoven in Jesus' instruction.

On what basis can Jesus carry on the kind of ministry that violates what the Pharisees regard as axiomatic concerning purity and holiness? This way of putting the question reminds us of the paradigmatic function of the

311. See our discussion, above, of the uses of ἀδικία in vv 8 and 9, and of ἄδικος in vv 10 and 11.

312. Cf. Brawley, *Jerusalem*, 124.

313. Cf. καρδιογνώστης ("one who knows the heart") in Acts 15:8; the concept is axiomatic in biblical literature (see esp. 1 Sam 16:7; also, e.g., Deut 8:2; 1 Kgs 8:39; LXX Pss 7:9; 43:21; 64:6; Jer 11:20; 17:9-10; et al.). Generally, it affirms God's omniscience as one who knows the innermost being of humans (cf. Behm, "καρδία," 613; Bauer, "Καρδιογνώστης").

314. βδέλυγμα has the more general meaning of "unclean" (Gen 43:32; 46:34; Exod 8:26), but it can carry the more specific sense of "idolatry" (cf. Deut 7:25; 12:31; 1 Kgs 11:6-8; 2 Kgs 23:4-14); cf. "the abomination of desolation" (τὸ βδέλυγμα τῆς ἐρημώσεως; Dan 9:27; 11:31; 12:11; Mark 13:14; Matt 24:15).

315. ὑψηλός can be used with its literal sense in Luke (Acts 13:17), but it is used figuratively here for "what is exalted."

indictment against Jesus in 15:1-2; the opposition Jesus now faces from the Pharisees is grounded in his association with socio-religious outsiders.[316] He justifies his practices by insisting that, beginning with John,[317] a new era had been introduced, and with it a fresh, expansive view of the reach of God's grace. The "good news" was described in Jesus' inaugural address as directed toward "the poor" — that is, those of low status, outcasts of all kinds (see above on 4:18-19). The proclamation of "the good news of the kingdom"[318] concerns the coming of the kingdom of God to displace other world systems. Not the least of these is the rule of Wealth (v 13), manifest in practices that separate the wealthy from those in need. As Luke has developed it, "kingdom of God" connotes a new world order where the marginalized are embraced in the redemptive purpose of God. Hence, its promulgation has as one of its primary effects the fact that "everyone is urged to enter it,"[319] and this is precisely the universalism to which the Pharisees have taken offense.[320] Thus, for Luke it is not that "the law and the prophets" belong to an old, now-bygone era, but that the Scriptures of Israel must be understood in light of the manifestation of God's purpose within the ministry of Jesus.[321]

Indeed, in vv 17-18 Jesus not only insists on the enduring validity of the law, but, with respect to the one example of divorce and adultery, he offers a surprisingly rigorous interpretation. Jesus places a man and woman on the same level with regard to adultery, and censures the practice whereby a husband divorces his wife in order to marry another. Especially in prohibiting remarriage and ruling out serial monogamy, Jesus' statement distinguishes itself from contemporary rabbinic teaching by its severity. On this issue he thus offers an interpretation that at once assumes the ongoing authority of the law (Deut 24:1-4), makes the Mosaic regulations more stringent than they appear in Deuteronomy, and challenges the relaxation of the law among his

316. See Klinghardt, *Gesetz*, 24-29.

317. That the new epoch begins with John is clear from the parallel use of εὐαγγελίζομαι in v 16 and in 3:18: even before the onset of Jesus' public ministry, John was "proclaiming the good news."

318. See the parallel language in 4:43; 8:1; cf. Acts 8:12.

319. For this rendering of βιάζομαι, see Cortés and Gatti, "Luke 16:16." Inexplicably, Spicq (*TLNT*, 1:289-91) summarizes the case for reading βιάζεται as a passive in its weakened sense, then offers a translation (as an active) that at least stands in tension with, if not outright contradicts, his earlier discussion.

320. Hence, Wilson (*Luke and the Law*, 43) is wrong to argue that the translation of v 16c (passive or active) is irrelevant to how one construes Jesus' understanding of the law in v 17. Verse 16c, with its affirmation of the universality of the gospel's reach, is the crux of the problem from the point of view of Luke's Pharisees. How can *all* be invited *and* the validity of the law be upheld?

321. Cf. Klinghardt, *Gesetz*, 16-96; Salo, *Luke's Treatment of the Law*, 136-50; Wilson, *Luke and the Law*, 43-51; more generally, Green, *Gospel of Luke*, 24-28.

contemporaries.[322] What is striking about this example is that Jesus' affirmation of the authority of the law is qualified by his (implicit) insistence that the law does not speak for itself and is susceptible to erroneous appropriation. Given the conflicted situation in which he finds himself with the Pharisees, it is not enough simply to affirm (or disaffirm) the abiding significance of the Scriptures. They are not set aside, but they must be interpreted appropriately, in relation to the inbreaking kingdom of God in Jesus' ministry.

How does all of this relate to Jesus' criticism of the Pharisees? The language of abomination (v 15) is key.[323] In Israel's Scriptures, the term "abomination" can be used to denote, among other things, idolatrous activity in general (e.g., Isa 1:13; 66:3), but also immoral financial dealings (Deut 25:16) and the act of remarrying a woman who has been divorced (Deut 24:4). Similarly, a Qumranic text, the Damascus Rule, observes that there are "three nets" with which Israel is snared, with each parading as a kind of righteousness or justice: "The first is fornication, the second is riches, and the third is profanation of the Temple." In the ensuing discussion, "fornication" is interpreted with reference to a lax interpretation of the Mosaic legislation on divorce (Deut 24:1-4), while "profanation of the temple" is correlated with, among other things, false prophecy and lack of insight into and commitment toward God's covenant.[324] As in the Damascus Rule, so in Jesus' invective, idolatry, wealth, and divorce are collocated as manifestations of pseudo-righteousness. Taken together, they are means by which the Pharisees have distanced themselves from the very law they thought to uphold. They seek to advocate and preserve the law's relevance, but they are unable to do so because they lack insight into God's design. The irony of Luke's portrayal of the Pharisees is underscored later in the narrative by the Pharisee at prayer in the temple (18:9-14). Thanking God that he is not like those who swindle, who are unjust, or who commit adultery, he uses the very categories that Jesus has used in his allegations against Pharisees (cf. 11:39; 16:15-18).[325]

19-31 Though these verses relate in discrete fashion a story parable, no boundaries separate them from the preceding material. As a consequence, vv 14-18 and vv 19-31 stand in the closest interpretive relationship, with the one subsection interpreting and being interpreted by the other.[326]

---

322. On the similar stringency at Qumran, see CD 4:14–5:10. For the later debate regarding acceptable grounds for divorce, see *m. Giṭ. in.* The School of Shammai insisted that the deuteronomic phrase, "an indecent thing" (Deut 24:1), connoted illicit sexual behavior, while the School of Hillel argued for a more expansive definition.

323. Johnson, 250, 255; cf. Wilson, *Luke and the Law,* 46.

324. CD 4:14–6:1; ET in Vermes, *Dead Sea Scrolls,* 86.

325. Moxnes, *Economy of the Kingdom,* 150. See below on 18:9-14.

326. The importance of the Lukan co-text to the meaning of this parable is underscored by the sometimes quite different interpretations offered by investigations that

19-22   The stage of Jesus' parable is set by the extravagant parallelism resident in the depictions of the two main characters. The social distance between the two is continued through to the end, symbolized first by the gate, then by the "distance" ("far away," v 23) and the "great chasm" fixed between them (v 26). The rich man is depicted in excessive, even outrageous terms, while Lazarus is numbered among society's "expendables," a man who had fallen prey to the ease with which, even in an advanced agrarian society, persons without secure landholdings might experience devastating downward mobility.[327]

Clothing is mentioned first. Wool was used to produce vestments that advertised the social status of those who wore them. The process by which wool was "fulled" in a basin with special clay in order to render the cloth brilliantly white was time-consuming and costly. Clothing colored with Tyrian purple dye was likewise a striking luxury. Though white garments indicated membership among the elite, they were regarded as modest when compared with clothing dyed purple. White garments underneath a purple robe — this was the sign of the highest opulence.[328] In contrast with the wealthy man, the clothes Lazarus wore receive no mention. Instead, we are told, he is covered with sores — a condition that undoubtedly marked him as unclean. The term used in his description suggests that Lazarus would even have been regarded as suffering from divine punishment.[329] In language familiar to us from the common theology of Job's friends, surely the wealthy man is blessed by God while Lazarus lives under the divine curse.

Food is mentioned second. Legends concerning King Agrippa II have it that, on a daily basis, he hosted a meal of banquet proportions;[330] this is precisely the picture Jesus paints of this wealthy man. In the story of the lost son (15:11-32), a feast is used to signal a special occasion, with a calf killed in order to feed as many as a hundred guests. Jesus has it that this was *daily* fare for this wealthy man,[331] and that in an economy where even the rich

---

adopt a tradition-historical approach. For example, Bauckham ("Rich Man and Lazarus") insists that the parable assumes neither that Lazarus was pious (and so did not "deserve" his heavenly reward) nor that the wealthy man was wicked (and so did not "deserve" his judgment). In the Lukan co-text, Lazarus is not portrayed as pious, but the rich man is condemned for not taking seriously his scriptural responsibility to use his wealth on behalf of the needy.

327. See Figure 1, p. 60; Lenski, *Power and Privilege,* 281-84.

328. Hamel, *Poverty and Charity,* 81; cf. 88 and, more generally, 64-65, 73; also Judg 8:26; Esth 8:15; Prov 31:32; Luke 7:25; Rev 18:12.

329. ἑλκόω; cf. the use of ἕλκος in Exod 9:10-11; Deut 28:35; Rev 16:2.

330. See Hamel, *Poverty and Charity,* 31.

331. See the comparable use of εὐφραίνω in 15:23; 16:19.

could afford to kill a calf only occasionally.[332] With what does Jesus compare this daily gala? Just as the younger son had longed to fill himself with food reserved for pigs (15:16), Lazarus longed to eat what was apparently scavenged by dogs from the food that fell from the wealthy man's plentiful table. These would have included morsels of food that fell from the table, to be sure, but also the loaves of bread that served as napkins and were then tossed from the table at the daily repast.[333] Although we may be tempted to think of the dogs of Jesus' story in sentimental terms, we should rather imagine pariahlike mongrels that roamed the outskirts of town in search of refuse.[334] These curs have not come to "lick his wounds" (as we would say), but to abuse him further and, in the story, to add one more reason for us to regard him as less than human, unclean, through-and-through an outcast.

Third, mention is made of their respective places of abode. The wealthy man has a gate, signifying his possession of an estate or house compound appropriate to his station.[335] Lazarus has no home, but has been thrown down[336] at the wealthy man's gate. This may mark him as a cripple (cf. Matt 8:6, 14; 9:2; Rev 2:22), a condition that would help to explain his tragic circumstances.

Consistent with this representation, throughout the ensuing parable, the wealthy man is generally an active agent, engaging in dialogue and making requests. Lazarus, on the other hand, is completely passive and is only the object of dialogue.

Interpreted against this mural, the fact that this poor, crippled man has a name at all is highly significant. The poor man's only claim to status is that he is named in the story; this alone raises the hope that there is more to his story than that of being subhuman.[337] The wealthy man, on the other hand, has no name;[338] perhaps this is Jesus' way of inviting his money-loving listeners to provide their own!

23-24 Jesus' comparison of these two characters in life continues in

---

332. Hamel, *Poverty and Charity,* 33. Hamel estimates that to have three-fourths pound of meat on the table on a daily basis, one must have the wealth necessary to pay thirty workers for a whole year.

333. See Jeremias, *Parables,* 184; Herzog, *Parables,* 118.

334. Firmage, "Zoology (Fauna)," 1143: "Today we commonly speak of the dog as 'man's best friend.' In the Bible, however, the dog is always spoken of in contempt." Cf. Ps 59:6, 14; 1 Kgs 14:11; Phil 3:2; Rev 22:15.

335. Cf. Acts 10:17; 12:13; Hengel, *Between Jesus and Paul,* 108: "the splendid house" (speaking of Mary's home in Acts 12); John 18:16.

336. ἐβέβλητο is a pluperfect passive.

337. This is true whether or not Luke's readers would have made anything of the etymology of Lazarus's name, "my God helps."

338. By way of filling in this perceived gap 𝔭[75] gives his name as Νευης; the tradition of interpretation gives him the name "Dives," from the Latin translation of "rich man."

death. Though for different reasons, both Romans and Jews valued proper burial, in the latter case so much that Romans were known to participate in funerary societies whose primary purpose was to guarantee suitable burial for its members. In Jewish tradition, to be refused burial, to be left exposed as carrion for scavenger animals (like dogs, v 21), was tantamount to bearing the curse of God.[339] It is not by chance that Jesus observes that the rich man received burial but provides no such detail in the case of Lazarus. The former is honored even in death; the latter receives the final disgrace.

Following death, however, the one whose only companions in life were scavenger dogs is transported by angels[340] to Abraham. Reference to "the bosom of Abraham" could refer to Lazarus' position of intimacy and honor at the heavenly banquet (cf. 13:28)[341] — no mean thing in light of the hunger he experienced in this life. Certainly it refers to paradisal bliss, to the care and comfort previously unknown to him.[342]

Both Lazarus and the wealthy man are apparently in Hades, though segregated ("far away") from each other. Thus, while Lazarus is in a blissful state, numbered with Abraham, the wealthy man experiences Hades as torment and agony. This portrait has many analogues in contemporary Jewish literature, where Hades is represented as the universal destiny of all humans, sometimes with the expected outcome of the final judgment already mapped through the separation of persons into wicked or righteous categories.[343]

---

339. Among Romans, ". . . to leave a corpse unburied had unpleasant repercussions on the fate of the departed soul" (Toynbee, *Death and Burial,* 43). On the value of proper burial in Jewish tradition, cf. Deut 29:26; Jer 8:1-2; 16:1-4; Ezek 29:5; Tob 1:16–2:10; Josephus *Ag. Ap.* 2.29 §211.

340. According to Davidson ("Angels," 11), the role attributed to the angels in this text is unprecedented in Jewish literature (until the second century C.E.).

341. Cf. John 13:23; Herzog, *Parables,* 121.

342. See *T. Abr.* 20:14: in the bosom of Abraham, ". . . there is no toil, no grief, no moaning, but peace, exultation and endless life" (ET in E. P. Sanders, "Testament of Abraham," 895). Cf. Hock, "Lazarus and Micyllus," 456.

343. See *1 Enoch* 22; *4 Ezra* 7:74-101; cf. the helpful summary in Bauckham, "Hades, Hell."

This parable is often taken as instruction on "the intermediate state" (cf. Cooper, *Body, Soul, and Life Everlasting,* 136-39), often with reference to the state of a disembodied soul; or as a manifestation of Luke's "individual eschatology" (Dupont, "Individuelle Eschatologie"; *contra* Carroll, *End of History,* 64-68). Although this text probably assumes an intermediate state (though this is denied by Dupont, "Individuelle Eschatologie," 47), (1) it does so largely in order to make use of the common motif of the "messenger to the living from the dead" (on which see Bauckham, "Rich Man and Lazarus," 236-44), only to deny the sending of a messenger; (2) the notion of the disembodied existence of a soul must be read into the story since the characters in Hades act as human agents with a corporeal existence; (3) *T. Abr.* 20:14 — where the bosom of Abraham and his descendants are already in paradise, yet Abraham is to be taken to paradise — bears witness to the lack

Amazingly, the wealthy man has not been humbled by his new and undoubtedly startling circumstances. Instead, he assumes that Abraham is still his "father" and that Lazarus, whom he knows by name but has never helped, is present with Abraham in order to carry out errands on behalf of a wealthy man like himself. Those who legitimately refer to Abraham as "father," however, are those whose lives reflect their repentance, their orientation toward God's redemptive aim (3:8). This makes the wealthy man's address as ironic as it is presumptuous. His audaciousness is only exacerbated by the long-standing tradition regarding Abraham as a model of hospitality to strangers,[344] a model that this wealthy man has manifestly not followed with regard to Lazarus. The final irony resides in a wordplay easily recognized in the Greek text: The one who now requests mercy (Greek: *eleos*) at the hand of Lazarus seems never to have contemplated the merciful act of almsgiving (*eleēmosynē*) on behalf of Lazarus.

25-26 The wealthy man's request is denied on two counts. First, on account of the eschatological reversal presaged by Jesus (6:20-24) and known in wider Jewish and Greco-Roman literature,[345] he is the victim of his own choices. Lazarus, who received no comfort, is now comforted; the wealthy, having received his consolation, will be consoled no more (cf. 1:53). Second, the gate that could have been transversed but was not, so that Lazarus was never the recipient of the wealthy man's hospitality (or even the food that fell or was thrown from his table), has now become fixed.[346] Consequently, in Abraham's speech, Abraham and Lazarus are classified as "us," sharply distinguishing them from the rich man and those like him ("you all").

27-31 Given the indifference that had characterized the comportment of this rich man in relation to Lazarus, we may be surprised at the concern he now shows. His concern, though, is characteristic of the rich, whose circle of compassion extends to "friends," "brothers," "relatives," and "rich neighbors" who are able to repay concern with concern, hospitality with hospitality (14:12-14). Even this show of sensitivity, then, is self-

---

of precision in statements about the afterlife; and (4) neither Luke nor other Christian writers (like Paul) seem to think that discussion of the fate of an individual negates a more thoroughgoing apocalyptic (corporate, future) eschatology.

344. See Gen 18:1-15; Philo *Abr.* 22-23 §§107-18; *T. Abr.* 20:15 (a Christian interpolation); Josephus *Ant.* 1.11.2 §196.

345. See esp. *1 Enoch* 96:4-8; 97:8-10; cf. Nickelsburg, "Riches, the Rich, and God's Judgment"; Hock, "Lazarus and Micyllus," 455-63; Bauckham, "Rich Man and Lazarus," 231-36.

346. Herzog (*Parables,* 121-26) is probably too optimistic about the possibility that the wealthy man is allowed to repent at this stage of the parable. Hades was not hell, as he correctly observes, but in Jewish literature it often did represent in prospect the outcome of the judgment.

indicting since it manifests how true to character this rich man has been and even now remains.

In his agony, the rich man asks for Lazarus to be sent as a witness[347] to his living brothers. The idea of the dead returning to visit the living was common in the ancient world, with some literary expressions of this idea oriented toward the return of the dead for the purpose of revealing his or her own fate or the fate of others in the next world. Against this background, Jesus' story is remarkable for its narration of the refusal to allow for such a return.[348] Lazarus is not permitted to return, nor are the wealthy man's brothers granted any warning from beyond the grave of the fate awaiting them. Abraham thus refuses to grant an apocalyptic revelation of the fate of the dead, insisting that the witness of Moses and the prophets should suffice. The wealthy man, accustomed to extra considerations, will not take No for an answer. Continuing to speak from his supposed position of privilege, the wealthy man insists that, for his family, more is needed, that a special envoy is required.

"Hearing" has a prominent role in Luke-Acts, where it either entails belief or is a necessary precursor to faith or repentance.[349] "To repent," especially in Acts, is often mentioned explicitly as the appropriate response to God's salvific work;[350] in the Gospel, it is sometimes portrayed as radical renunciation of one's possessions (e.g., 5:11, 28; 12:32-34; 14:25-33). "Repentance" in the present scene would necessitate that one take seriously the injustice of the coexistence of the wealthy and impoverished.

It is at this juncture that the "gate," mentioned at the outset of the story (v 20), may come to serve a second purpose. It was "in the gate [of the city]" that justice was to be served, not where the needy were to suffer from disregard. As Amos decried,

> For I know how many are your transgressions,
>   and how great are your sins —
> you who afflict the righteous, who take a bribe,
>   and push away the needy in the gate.
> . . . .
> Hate evil and love good,
>   and establish justice in the gate. . . . (5:12, 15)

---

347. For this sense of διαμαρτύρομαι, see its specialized usage in Acts for missionary proclamation — 2:42; 8:25; 10:42; 18:5; 20:21, 23, 24; 23:11; 28:23.

348. See the helpful summary in Bauckham, "Rich Man and Lazarus," 236-44.

349. See, e.g., 8:8-15, 18, 21; Acts 15:7-11.

350. See, e.g., 3:10-14; 15:3-10; Acts 2:38; 3:19; 5:31; 11:18; 17:30; 20:21; 26:20.

Of course, the Scriptures of Israel are replete with texts speaking to the axiomatic responsibility of the community of God's people to care for the poor.[351] As one who presumes to name Abraham as "father," this wealthy man should heed the Scriptures. So should his brothers.

And so should the Pharisees who have complained against Jesus' hospitality with social outcasts and ridiculed his teaching about the appropriate use of money on behalf of the poor — the very Pharisees to whom Jesus has directed this parable. This is his indictment against them: in neglecting the poor, they have disregarded the will of God so clearly expressed in the Scriptures.

5.5.8. Faithful Service (17:1-10)

17:1 *Jesus said to his disciples, "Occasions for stumbling are bound to come, but woe to anyone by whom they come!* 2 *It would be better for you if a millstone were hung around your neck and you were thrown into the sea than for you to cause one of these little ones to stumble.* 3 *Be on your guard! If another disciple sins, you must rebuke the offender, and if there is repentance, you must forgive.* 4 *And if the same person sins against you seven times a day, and turns back to you seven times and says, 'I repent,' you must forgive."*

5 *The apostles said to the Lord, "Give us faith!"*[352] 6 *The Lord replied, "If you had faith the size of a mustard seed, you could say to this mulberry tree, 'Be uprooted and planted in the sea,' and it would obey you.*

7 *"Who among you would say to your slave who has just come in from plowing or tending sheep in the field, 'Come here at once and take your place at the table'?* 8 *Would you not rather say to him, 'Prepare supper for me, put on your apron and serve me while I eat and drink; later you may eat and drink'?* 9 *Do you thank the slave for doing what was commanded?* 10 *So you also, when you have done all that you were ordered to do, say, 'We are worthless slaves; we have done only what we ought to have done!'"*

With 17:11, Luke will explicitly return to the travel motif, marking v 11 as the beginning of a new subsection within his larger narrative of Jesus' journey to Jerusalem (cf. 9:51–19:48). Consequently, vv 1-10 form the end of the

351. See the discussions, e.g., in Gnuse, *Community and Property;* Gordon, *Economic Problem,* chs. 1–4; Hengel, *Property and Riches,* ch. 2; N. F. Lohfink, *Option for the Poor.*

352. NRSV: "Increase our faith!"

lengthy section — concerned with the question, Who will participate in the kingdom? — that began in 13:10. Especially due to its location adjacent to prior accounts of Jesus' interaction with Pharisees, this pericope recapitulates Jesus' message to his followers: They are not to be like the Pharisees!

Luke designates the immediate recipients of Jesus' teaching as "his disciples" (v 1). This stands in contrast to the audience of 16:14-31, the Pharisees. The effect of such a contrast is mitigated by the fact that, in this section of the Third Gospel, Jesus seems to have made a practice of speaking to one audience in the presence of another.[353] Indeed, the content of his teaching to the disciples here takes its force in part from the probability that the narrator wants us to imagine Jesus always at center stage, with first the Pharisees (and scribes) and then the disciples moving into and out of the spotlight but never off the stage altogether. Each overhears instruction to the others, so that Jesus' fundamental message comes as point to his disciples, counterpoint to the Pharisees. On the one hand, this underscores a major thrust of Jesus' instruction: Avoid behaviors characteristic of the Pharisees. This message had come specifically to the fore in the earlier warning of 12:1 — "Beware of the yeast of the Pharisees" — a remark Jesus now echoes in v 3. On the other, that disciples and Pharisees receive parallel messages from Jesus shows that these two groups of recipients of Jesus' directives are not so far apart, at least not yet. Jesus remains open to the possibility that Pharisees will hear the word and respond in obedience, but is aware equally that the disciples, if they are to be his disciples, remain in need of formation.

On the surface, this narrative unit has the appearance of disparate sayings, thrown together with no discernible concern for thematic coherence. Read against the background provided by Jesus' alternating exchange with the Pharisees (and legal experts) and his disciples in this larger narrative section, however, the focus of this teaching becomes more clear. "Do not be like the Pharisees," Jesus is concerned to say. Earlier, his warning had taken the form of a saying about leaven and hypocrisy (12:1). Now, it comes in the form of critical reflections in relation to concrete commitments and practices usually identified with the Pharisees in Luke: lack of regard for the "little ones" and sinners in their midst, faithlessness, and a heightened, problematic concern for recognition and status.

1-4   The center of this paragraph, "Be on your guard!" (v 3a), is its theme, with Jesus providing two exemplars of the specific content of the warning. In vv 1-2, he draws out the meaning of the story of the wealthy man and Lazarus (16:19-31) for his disciples,[354] while in vv 3b-4 he relates the

353. See the discussion above at 9:51–19:48.
354. So Grundmann, 332.

611

message of the parable of the lost son (15:11-32) directly to the community of disciples.[355] What is striking about these correlations is that the parables on which Jesus' present instruction build were, in their Lukan co-texts, delivered as challenges to Pharisees and legal experts. That it is now specifically the disciples who are thus warned indicates that, at least during the journey to Jerusalem, the borders separating disciples and Pharisees remain relatively fluid. Although Jesus had pronounced blessing on "the poor" (6:20) and had just illustrated the eschatological reversal in the career of Lazarus (16:19-31), and although it is among the marginalized that Jesus has been declaring good news and issuing the call to discipleship, even lowly persons are apparently capable of the Pharisaic activities of "causing to stumble" and of segregating themselves from sinners.

The inevitability of occasions for stumbling[356] is grounded in the Lukan motif of hostility and opposition to the plan of God: All do not identify with and orient themselves around God's purpose.[357] The precise nature of the offensive behavior under critique here is left open, though the location of this saying in its wider Lukan co-text is suggestive. In the prior Lukan material, we may find referents to the phrase "little ones" in Lazarus, 16:19-31; the lost son, 15:11-32; and the poor, crippled, blind, and lame, 14:12-14 — in which case "cause to stumble" would refer to the injustice and indifference of inhospitality on behalf of those in need. "Millstone" refers to the heavy upper stone used for grinding flour in a large rotary mill driven by a mule or donkey.[358] With this language Jesus compares drowning favorably over against the fate of one who fails to show compassion and act justly on behalf of "the poor."[359] Recall the fate of the wealthy man in 16:24-28![360]

Disciples are to be on their guard against a mind-set that works against justice and compassion for the "little ones," but also against dispositions that obstruct the restoration of sinners to community. The NRSV reads "disciple"

355. Note the repeated motifs of "sin/sinner" (15:7, 10, 13-16, 18, 21, 30) and "repentance" (15:7, 10, 18-20).

356. "Occasions for stumbling" translates a term that is rare in Luke-Acts. σκάνδαλον/σκανδαλίζω appear only in 7:23; 17:1-2. In 7:23, the nature of Jesus' person and ministry is a potential stumbling block; here, offenses against brothers and sisters in the community of disciples are in view. In their two Lukan co-texts, these two senses coalesce around the centrality of the marginalized to Jesus' understanding and proclamation of the good news.

357. For the motif of hostility in Luke-Acts, cf., e.g., Tyson, "Conflict as a Literary Theme"; Kingsbury, *Conflict in Luke;* Green, *Gospel of Luke,* 22-49.

358. van der Toorn, "Mill, Millstone," 832.

359. Cf. Jer 51:63.

360. Cf. also 6:20, 24; 12:32-34.

for the Lukan term "brother [and sister],"[361] by which the Evangelist draws attention to kinship that has been severed by sin. Sin is an obstacle to full membership in the community of God's people, so repentance is necessary (cf. 15:8, 10). What Jesus counsels is, first, confrontation, and, second, readiness to forgive. Unlike the elder brother in the parable of the lost son (15:11-32), then, Jesus' followers are not to stand at a distance from the sinner, but to seek actively for his or her restoration. Elsewhere Luke speaks of the daily demands of discipleship (esp. 9:23); by collocating "daily" with forgiveness "seven times" he points to the need to forgive as a matter of course and "without limit."[362] To do so is not in any way extraordinary; rather, it is simply part of the daily life of those whose lives are oriented around the merciful God (cf. 6:36; 11:4).

5-6 The dual reference to Jesus as "Lord" comes at the hand of the narrator, but this perspective is consistent with the nature of the request for faith made by the apostles. Mention of the noun "faith" is perhaps striking in its infrequency thus far in the Third Gospel, but the five times it has appeared are telling. In each case, "faith" is not so much a possession as a disposition: Faith leads to faithful behavior; lack of faith leads to anxiety and fear (5:20; 7:9, 50; 8:25, 48). If for Luke faith manifests itself in faithfulness, then the request of Jesus' followers, "Give us faith,"[363] is tantamount to saying, "Make us faithful people!" Taking seriously the location of their request in immediate proximity to vv 1-4, we understand that the apostles thus look outside themselves for help so that they might comport themselves appropriately vis-à-vis "little ones" and "sinners." Implicit is the contrast that surfaced in 16:10-13, between those who align themselves with the inbreaking kingdom of God (and thus are regarded as faithful) and those whose lives are determined by the old aeon (and are thus regarded as unfaithful).

In his response Jesus contrasts the meager dimensions of the mustard seed with the deep- and strong-rooted sycamore, both proverbial in antiquity.[364] In this way he suggests that just a smidgen of faith would be sufficient to give rise to practices even more extraordinary than those he has just outlined. In addition, though, Jesus' reply casts doubt on whether his apostles have yet even this much faith.[365]

This is the first mention of the apostles since 9:10 (cf. 11:49). Luke

---

361. ἀδελφός is generic in this co-text. The use of "disciple" in this translation, though, masks Jesus' reference to the motif of kinship among those who hear and do the word of God (e.g., 8:1-21).

362. See Balz, "ἑπτάκις."

363. For προτίθημι as "provide" or "grant," see BAGD 719.

364. See Egelkraut, *Jesus' Mission,* 122.

365. Jesus' reply is in the form of a mixed conditional, with the apodosis an unreal conditional.

has generally been content to refer to the larger mass of disciples around Jesus. By raising doubt concerning the apostles' faith, the faith of those previously most identified with Jesus' mission, he raises perhaps even more sweeping questions about the wider circle of Jesus' followers. At least the apostles understand that it is to Jesus that they must turn for faith. By way of contrast, the Pharisees (and legal experts) murmur against his practices and scoff at his teaching (15:1-2; 16:14); indeed, as a group the Pharisees have repeatedly set their perception of faith and faithfulness in opposition to the person and ministry of Jesus.

7-10 As in, for example, 11:5-8, so here Jesus' parable takes the form of a lengthy question that expects a negative answer.[366] Also as in the parable in 11:5-8, Jesus is not so much inviting an allegorical reading of master-servant roles as drawing on a well-known reality of village life to teach something about faithfulness. Envisioned is a small landholder/farmer whose one slave performs the various outdoor and household duties that would be divided between slaves in a larger estate. The household, master/slave analogy has become a regular fixture of the Lukan narrative, providing the basis for important instruction on kinship, faithfulness, and status-seeking (e.g., 12:35-48; 16:1-9; cf. 22:24-27). In this instance, the parable turns on the observation that a slave who is simply completing his work does not by doing so place his master under any obligation to reward him in some way. That is, the absurdity Jesus outlines draws on a particular, taken-for-granted social script apparent to ancient readers but easily missed by many contemporary ones. In this script, "thanks" would not refer to a verbal expression of gratitude or social politeness, but to placing the master in debt to the slave.[367] In the master-slave relationship, does the master come to owe the slave special privileges because the slave fulfills his daily duties? Does the slave, through fulfilling his ordinary duties to the master, become his master's patron? Of course not! Similarly, "worthless slaves" (v 10) refers to slaves to whom no favor is due (and not to uselessness).[368]

In a message transparently designed to locate his disciples over against a Pharisaic mind-set, Jesus opposes any suggestion that obedience might be construed as a means to gain honor, or that one might engage in obedience

---

366. See Jeremias, *Parables,* 103.

367. For this sense of χάρις, as gratitude inspired by the act of one's benefactor, see *TLNT,* 3:503-4: "A person does not stop at merely feeling gratitude toward a benefactor but makes an effort to pay him *(sic)* back, as if paying off a debt by returning benefit for benefit." Cf. K. E. Bailey, *Through Peasant Eyes,* 121-22; Derrett, "Profitable Servant."

368. One need not follow all of the linguistic maneuvers Kilgallen ("Servants") makes in order to agree with his basic conclusion, that Jesus refers to "servants to whom no favor is due." Moulton notes that ἀχρεῖος is derived from χρή (MHT 2:287), which denotes "what is obliged" (cf. LSJ, 2004).

in order to receive a reward. Remembering those in need with justice and compassion, working for the restoration of the sinner into the community of God's family (vv 1-4) — practices of this nature are simply the daily fare of discipleship. Extraordinary in no way, neither do they provide the basis for status advancement within the community. Of course, Jesus' instructions cannot be taken simply as polemic against the Pharisees. After all, the disciples have already and will continue to show themselves lamentably adept at self-justification and honor-seeking (cf., e.g., 9:46-50; 22:24-27).

5.6. RESPONDING TO THE KINGDOM (17:11–19:27)

The interpretive role of this segment of Luke's travel narrative is heightened by its location in that narrative. In 19:28-48, Luke will narrate the finale of the long and meandering journey of Jesus from Galilee to Jerusalem. Hence, 19:28-48 serves a transitional role, bringing the travel section to its culmination (9:51–19:48) and preparing for the Lukan account of Jesus' brief career in Jerusalem (beginning in 20:1). The transitional function of this subsequent portion of the travel narrative gives the present narrative segment (17:11–19:27) the critical role of "thematic summary" and invitation to response. The journey motif has persisted since 9:51, helped along by only infrequent references to Jesus' travel. With 17:11 the number of journey markers increases dramatically. Here, as the travel section begins to draw to a close, the reality of the journey and the threads of its principal motifs are drawn together. As a result, terms that may appear innocent enough in their present location derive their meaning in large part from much larger, prior, narrative segments. For example, the possibilities for understanding references to "Samaria" and "Samaritan" (17:11, 16) are profoundly shaped by Samaritan-oriented material found earlier along the journey (9:52-54; 10:25-37); similarly, one may hear in the background of Jesus' depiction of the vocation of the Son of Man — "to seek out and to save the lost" (19:10) — thunderous echoes of the parabolic material of Luke 15.

In Luke's accounting, the traveling party that set out in 9:51-56 has made little progress. Only now are they "going through the region between Samaria and Galilee" (17:11). This is true even though, in narrative time, they had entered a Samaritan village long ago (9:52). The effect of this narrative strategy has been to concentrate attention on Jesus' interactions with his followers, the crowds, and Pharisees and legal experts on the way, rather than on any notion of an actual travelogue. Although Jesus' interactions with the various groups around him do not diminish in importance, the significance of the journey itself is elevated in the narrative unit before us. This happens, first, through the proportional increase in the sheer number of references to the journey (17:11; 18:31, 35; 19:1, 11). Moreover, the pace of the journey seems to be quickened: Jesus passes through the region between Samaria and Galilee, then, almost immediately, is approaching Jericho, enters Jericho, and, finally, is "near Jerusalem." At last, Jesus and his entourage seem actually to be traveling! Of critical import, too, is the repeated reminder that their destination is Jerusalem — the location of Jesus' destiny, where he will fulfill God's purpose for him (cf. 9:51-54; 13:31-35; 17:11, 25; 18:31).

As Jerusalem begins to loom larger on the horizon, Jesus is careful to interpret the significance of his arrival in the Holy City. In particular, he denies that his advent signals the eschatological arrival of the kingdom of God (19:11). This is true even if, in his presence and through his ministry, the kingdom of God and the salvation it portends are already present (e.g., 17:21; 19:10). Before the consummation of God's kingdom, before the coming of the Son of Man (17:22-37), the Son of Man "must endure much suffering and be rejected by this generation" (17:26; 18:30-33). Hence, contrary to the expectations of some, including his own followers (19:11), at this stage of the narrative, Jesus' arrival in Jerusalem marks the onset of his suffering and death. The approaching end of the journey thus raises expectations, but the resulting suspense, from Jesus' perspective, should be cast in terms of suffering, not the realization of the eschaton.

Of course, as Jesus is careful to intimate, suffering is not the last word, since death gives way to resurrection (18:33), and resurrection is a prelude to Jesus' return. Luke thus articulates an interlude between Jesus' rejection and enthronement on the one hand, and his return in royal authority on the other. This interlude consists of the "days of the Son of Man" (17:26), during which Jesus' followers are called to exercise faithfulness, so that when the Son of Man returns he will "find faith on earth" (17:8; cf. 12:35-39). Failing to understand the role of Jesus' rejection and death in God's plan, the disciples also misconstrue the timetable for the manifestation of God's kingdom. It is, after all, they who will long to see the eschatological denouement (17:22), and thus fail to comprehend either that Jesus' death is necessary or that they will participate in a mission itself characterized in part by rejection and death.[1] The possibility of ongoing faithfulness does not seem to be part of their vision.

The question of whether Jesus will find faith upon his return is therefore not a moot one, not least in the case of his own followers. This is disappointing, since one of the primary agenda of the journey narrative has been focused on the formation of disciples.[2] On this point, the protracted journey to Jerusalem seems to have been ineffectual. Indeed, at the close of the Galilean section of the Gospel, Luke had observed that the disciples did not understand his passion

---

1. Cf. Tannehill, *Narrative Unity,* 1:257-60.
2. Cf. above on 9:51–19:48.

prediction (9:45), employing words that seem frustratingly similar to Luke's observation at the close of the Jerusalem journey, again following a prophecy of his passion: "But they understood nothing about all these things; in fact, what he said was hidden from them, and they did not grasp what was said" (18:34).

"Faith on earth" is defined, in part, in identification with Jesus' suffering and death. According to Jesus, disciples are to "lose their life," not attempt to make it secure (17:33). Yet, against Jesus' own instruction, they show contempt for children, comporting themselves in a manner more characteristic of Pharisees (18:9-14, 15).[3] Like the crowds, they constitute themselves as an obstruction between Jesus and those to whom he came to show favor (cf. 18:15, 39; 19:3, 9), and consequently attract his rebuke (18:16). In spite of instruction along the road to Jerusalem, they do not yet comprehend the significance of the kingdom of God and fail to embrace fully the new view of the world that comes into focus in Jesus' proclamation. In spite of the abundance of Jesus' teaching on the matter, they have not yet grasped his criticism of conventional perspectives on honor and shame and his perspective on the meaning of suffering in relation to God's purpose. Because they have not adopted his view of the world, they cannot really understand Jesus' identity and mission, or grasp their impending role in his mission. Nor will they do so until the opening chapters of Acts, when they can review Jesus' teaching on the kingdom of God against the background of his suffering and resurrection (cf. Acts 1:3, 6-8).

If the disciples are not (yet) suitable examples of faithfulness, who are? Whose response to the kingdom of God in its present and future dimensions is instructive for discipleship? In an important sense, this is the focus of this larger narrative segment, and the list of candidates is instructive: a leper, Samaritan, foreigner (17:11-19); a widow who exemplifies God's "chosen ones who cry to him day and night" (18:1-8); a toll collector (18:9-14); infants, little children (18:15-17); and a toll collector and sinner (19:1-10).

The end-time destiny of persons is intimately related to, even determined by, the nature of their faith in the present. Luke 17:11–19:27 thus highlights the motif of division in response to the kingdom by setting it in eschatological perspective. In this respect, Jesus' question in 18:8b is programmatic: When he returns, will the Son of Man find faithfulness? This motif surfaces most transparently in the eschatological discourse of 17:22-37, where readiness is contrasted with self-absorption in the routines of life. Elsewhere in this narrative unit this contrast is cast in terms more familiar to Luke's readers. God intervenes on behalf of those in need, those living

---

3. For the irony of the disciples' misbehavior, see 17:3, and especially the discussion of 17:5-6, above.

on the socio-religious margins, the "little ones." These are the ones who have faith/act faithfully. Others, the self-possessed, those concerned with their own honor and position, those who look with contempt on those in need — these are the ones who will lose their lives in humiliation.[4] Coming as it does at the end of the travel narrative, this series of contrasts confronts Luke's audience with the need for clear choices in relationship to the nature of his mission and their identification with God's salvific purpose. The need for self-evaluation surfaces especially in Luke's presentation of Jesus' followers — who are apparently well intentioned, have participated in mission, and have been present for Jesus' instruction, but whose misunderstandings and practices continue to separate them from the very ones to whom divine benefaction is directed.

Finally, and not surprisingly, this narrative segment indicates a direct correlation between faith/faithfulness and proper identification of Jesus. The Samaritan leper addresses him as "Jesus, Master" (17:13) and recognizes the divine hand at work in Jesus (17:15-16). The blind man similarly discerns that Jesus is one through whom mercy is available (17:13; 18:38-39); his reference to Jesus as Son of David resonates with the words of Gabriel in his announcement to Mary of Jesus' birth (1:32-35). Zacchaeus joins the blind man, and both join the narrator, in naming Jesus as "Lord" (18:41; 19:8). These are all persons who come ready to receive from Jesus, whom they recognize in diverse ways as the agent of God's benefaction, the one through whom divine favor is operative.

5.6.1. Gratitude from a Foreign Leper (17:11-19)

11 *On the way to Jerusalem Jesus was going through the region between Samaria and Galilee.* 12 *As he entered a village, ten lepers approached him. Keeping their distance,* 13 *they called out, saying, "Jesus, Master, have mercy on us!"* 14 *When he saw them, he said to them, "Go and show yourselves to the priests." And as they went, they were made clean.* 15 *Then one of them, when he saw that he was healed, turned back, praising God with a loud voice.* 16 *He prostrated himself at Jesus' feet and thanked him. And he was a Samaritan.* 17 *Then Jesus asked, "Were not ten made clean? But the other nine, where are they?* 18 *Was none of them found to return and give praise to God except this foreigner?"* 19 *Then he said to him, "Get up and go on your way; your faith has made you well."*

---

4. Thus: a Pharisee who trusts in himself and asserts his own righteousness (18:9-14); the disciples (18:15) and the crowds (18:39; 19:3, 7) who separate Jesus from those who seek him; a ruler, the wealthy (18:18-30).

Earlier in the Third Gospel — specifically, during the recounting of his Galilean ministry (4:14–9:50) — accounts like the present one dotted the narrative landscape. There, such episodes communicated through their steady redundancy Jesus' competence in his role as Son of God; they also served to flesh out the nature of his role in the service of the divine purpose. This encounter with the ten lepers is in many ways reminiscent of those episodes, especially the account of Jesus cleansing the leper in 5:12-14. Even the motif of response, highlighted in the present scene, is typical of earlier miracle scenes. Descriptions of miracles in Luke's Gospel generally include the stage of response,[5] and this response is characteristically praise of God.[6] What distinguishes the present account from earlier, analogous reports is how Luke has held back from the reader a crucial aspect of the identity of the one leper who returns to express his gratitude. Only in v 16b does Luke drop the bombshell — "and he was a Samaritan" — on what had progressed as a rather routine, matter-of-fact account. That this is indeed pivotal to Luke's presentation is obvious from Jesus' subsequent reference to this one leper as a "foreigner" (v 18).

Of course, the Third Evangelist had prepared for this punch line earlier, in setting the scene for the encounter of Jesus and the ten lepers. Returning to the travel motif (see above), he notes that Jesus is "on the way to Jerusalem," "going through the region between Samaria and Galilee." The location thus pinpointed leaves ambiguous the sort of people with whom Jesus will come into contact, at the very least leaving open the possibility for interaction with Samaritans (as in 9:51-56).

The episode itself is structured in two parallel parts: approach + cry out (vv 12-13, 15-16) → a response from Jesus (vv 14a, 17-18) → statement of healing (from the narrator, v 14b; from Jesus, v 19).[7] This indicates the structural unity of this pericope, which is boundaried on the one side by the travel notice and on the other by Jesus' interaction with a different set of characters, the Pharisees.

As clear as these structural boundaries are, equally transparent are the socio-cultural boundaries contained within its perimeters and that help to give significance to this account. The first of these is leprosy, a disorder with social and spiritual ramifications that outstrip the difficulties of its physical presentation.[8] The boundary established by leprosy is marked in this pericope by

---

5. See M. H. Miller, "Character of Miracles," 50-55.

6. Cf., e.g., 5:25-26; 7:16; 13:13.

7. Cf. Blomberg, "Your Faith Has Made You Whole," 79-80. In his form-critical analysis, Bruners (*Reinigung der zehn Aussätzigen*, 56-122; esp. 69) develops this parallelism along slightly different lines.

8. Recall that "leprosy" denotes a wide range of skin maladies; the presence of true leprosy, Hansen's disease, in this historical context is unlikely.

the phrase "keeping their distance" (v 12). The second is the identification of at least one of these lepers as a Samaritan, a foreigner, employing language that draws a well-defined boundary between this person on the one hand, and Jesus and his (implied) entourage on the other. The first of these two barriers has been surmounted before, with the consequence that Luke's readers may well have already begun to place "lepers" in the category of "the poor" to whom good news is preached (cf. 4:18-19, 27; 5:12-14; 7:22). The second boundary is presented late in the narrative, as a surprise, where it will have the greatest effect.[9] First, Luke's readers are given a positive impression of this one leper who returns to Jesus in gratitude; he behaves appropriately, his response is prototypical. Only then does Luke report that he is an outsider. Impressed by his behavior, Luke's audience may have walked into a trap. Indeed, Luke has narrated this episode in a way that seems deliberately to challenge notions of the privileged position of the Jewish people within the redemptive economy of God.

This impression is supported by a further assumption that Luke has lodged in his reader's repertoire of the familiar. One may readily discern intertextual connections with earlier material in Luke, as we have seen (esp. 4:27; 5:12-14; 7:22). These connections, especially the brief summary of the Elijah-Naaman story in 4:27, also draw particular attention to the interplay between the present episode and the OT account of Naaman, himself a leprous foreigner (2 Kgs 5:1-19a).[10] Apart from the characterization of the diseased in each account, one may count among the common elements the Samaritan location, communication from a distance, a delayed cleansing (after departing from the agent of healing), a return, divine praise from the one healed, thanksgiving, and the status of the restored person as a foreigner. The point of this intertextuality is partially christological, indicating as before the connection between Jesus and God's prophetic messengers in the OT, but it is even more theological.[11] Jews are not the only ones who qualify for God's messianic blessings; outsiders may receive the benefits of salvation and, indeed, may prove to be more discerning about Jesus' identity and role within the divine plan than Jewish insiders.[12] Salvation comes to this former leper apart from normal concerns with physical ancestry and religious purity.

Finally, the interpretation of this episode is guided by the number of ways it refers, always implicitly, to the temple. Simply to mention Samaria and refer to a Samaritan, as this account does, brings to the fore the funda-

9. Sheeley, *Narrative Asides,* 105-6; cf. Tannehill, *Narrative Unity,* 1:118-19.
10. Cf. Bruners, *Reinigung der zehn Aussätzigen,* 103-18.
11. See C. A. Evans, "Luke's Ethic of Election," 74-76.
12. Note the studied contrast between this Samaritan leper and the Pharisees in vv 20-21! See Green, *Gospel of Luke,* 105.

mental point of division between Jews and Samaritans. This is the location of the divinely sanctioned place of worship: Jerusalem or Mount Gerizim? Sending the lepers to "the priests" (v 14) only exacerbates this problem, since Jesus does not specify to which priests they are to show themselves. Clearly, they must journey to a temple where they will undergo an inspection, then, presumably, offer the sacrifice appropriate to one who has been declared clean (see Lev 14:1-32). But to which temple? Jerusalem or Mount Gerizim? The act of giving praise to God itself (vv 15, 18) may invoke images of the temple cult. Against this backdrop, the act of the Samaritan is all the more startling. He does not travel to a temple,[13] but returns to Jesus. He recognizes that the restorative power of God is manifest in Jesus. In recounting his action thus, Luke indicates that the socio-religious divisions between Jew and Samaritan have been mediated in Jesus.[14] People who discern God at work through Jesus worship God at his feet.[15] In restoring to wholeness a Samaritan leper, Jesus has countered not only notions of acceptance based on ritual purity but also, and more importantly for this episode, conceptions of election grounded in nationality and genealogy. As the one in whom God's purpose is manifest and through whom God's salvific prerogative is available, Jesus is the instrument of healing in the midst of these long-standing and deeply rooted rifts.

11 Luke sets the scene by returning to the motif of the journey. In doing so, he explicitly mentions Jerusalem, Samaria, and Galilee, each of which has become encoded with more than simple geographical significance by this juncture in the narrative. Samaria had earlier been for Jesus a place of conflict and rejection (9:51-56), even if he had subsequently spoken in a disarmingly remarkable way about the capacity of a Samaritan to embody the mercy of God (10:25-37). Galilee, the location of Jesus' earlier public ministry, was the region wherein Jesus' ministry first gained shape; it was there, according to Luke, that Jesus' ministry began to actualize God's redemptive aim as status reversal. What does it mean that Jesus is now in the region between these two? On the one hand, Jesus is simply doing what pilgrims traveling from Galilee to Jerusalem might normally do — namely, take a circuitous route so as to bypass Samaritan territory. The bias toward this route was grounded in fundamental antipathies between Jew and Samaritan (see above, on 9:52-53), best summarized in the Samaritan rejection of Jerusalem as the center of God's dealing with humanity. On the other hand, additional possi-

---

13. At least, insofar as Luke has narrated the Samaritan's story, he does not travel to a temple. Even if one imagined that he did so after this encounter, Luke's point remains.

14. This prepares, proleptically, for Jesus' postresurrection words to his followers, ". . . you will be my witnesses in Jerusalem, in all Judea and Samaria, and to the end of the earth" (Acts 1:8).

15. See Hamm, "Samaritan Leper."

bilities present themselves. For example, Luke may be establishing the setting for Jesus to mediate between the largely positive response to Jesus by the Galilean populace and the rejection he suffered at the hands of the Samaritans. Luke may be indicating the possibility that status reversal, so much a part of his presentation of salvation thus far in the Gospel, extends to the Samaritans as well. And so on.

In the midst of such interpretive prospects are two points of clarity. First, Jesus is traveling to Jerusalem as more than a pilgrim. He has repeatedly prophesied that Jerusalem would be for him the place of destiny, the place wherein he would fulfill the divine purpose, and the place of his own execution. However else it is understood, then, this narrative unit should be seen in light of the overall purpose of God Jesus serves and to which this narrative points. Second, traveling "along the border between"[16] Galilee and Samaria renders ambiguous the identity of any persons Jesus might meet along the way. Without taking away from the pivotal, startling identification of one of these lepers as a Samaritan in v 16, this allows for the possibility of interaction with a non-Jew.

12-14 The geographical (and, thus, socio-religious) ambivalence of v 11 is continued in Luke's reference to "a village." Is it Galilean? Samaritan? This is unimportant for the moment, though this lingering vagueness may lull Luke's readers into false assumptions. Without evidence to the contrary, his audience will likely assume that the village is Jewish and, further, that the approaching lepers are likewise Jewish. A Jewish leper has been cleansed by Jesus before (5:12-14); within the Lukan narrative, then, this episode is proceeding along unremarkable lines.

What more can be said of the setting? First, as expected of lepers (cf. Lev 13:46; Num 5:2-3), these ten maintain their distance, even encountering Jesus outside the village.[17] Second, the narrative focus is so narrowly on Jesus that he appears to be traveling alone. Momentarily, he will speak as though his followers continue to be close at hand (see v 17), as they have been throughout his Jerusalem journey; for now, though, they are absent from view.

---

16. Luke's διὰ μέσον provides the only example of the locative use of διά + accusative in the NT (MHT 3:267), and has been corrected repeatedly in the manuscript tradition (e.g., διὰ μέσον, ἀνὰ μέσον). Apparently, "along the border between" is the sense. Conzelmann (*Luke*, 68-70) thinks it is strange that Samaria is placed first, whether one translates διὰ μέσον as "through the midst of" or "between," but this overlooks the importance of Samaria in this narrative unit.

17. The NRSV rendering of καὶ εἰσερχομένου αὐτοῦ, "as he entered," may suggest that the lepers are actually within the village perimeter. The genitive absolute is cast in the present tense, however; when read in this way — say, "while he was in the process of entering" — the location of the lepers is easily understood to be on the edge of town.

"Leprosy" was a term used to designate a number of skin diseases, so the fundamental problem of these ten was, in all likelihood, not a malady that was physically life-threatening. Instead, they were faced with a debilitating social disorder. Regarded as living under a divine curse and as ritually unclean (whether they were Jew or Samaritan, it does not matter), they were relegated to the margins of society.[18]

Because of the manifest status of these ten lepers as outcasts, their address to Jesus is startling. One might be tempted to regard their request for "mercy" as simply a request for financial assistance in light of their poverty (i.e., as "alms for the poor"). "To have compassion" could have this sense, and this nuance ought not to be ruled out in favor of, say, some spiritual benefit. On the other hand, the language of their request cannot easily be reduced to this interpretation,[19] and the appellation by which they name Jesus "Master" suggests that much more is at stake here. When used elsewhere in the Third Gospel, "Master" denotes one who has authority consistent with miraculous power, and this is its meaning here.[20] Of course, this begs the questions, (1) How did these ten lepers know Jesus by name, and (2) How did they know him to be an agent of miraculous power? Indeed, elsewhere this appellation is used of Jesus only by his disciples; how did these lepers come to such awareness? Here is a gap in the narrative that invites reflection on the part of its readers.[21] Perhaps these ten lepers should be counted among the many persons within the narrative who are typically regarded as outsiders, the marginalized, and yet who respond to Jesus in faithful ways (e.g., 7:1-10, 36-50; 19:1-10; 23:39-43). Such persons contrast sharply with those Jewish insiders who, one might expect, should perceive Jesus' identity and do not. What is clear is that, in naming him as master, these lepers place themselves in a position of subordination to him in the hope of receiving from him some form of benefaction. This benefaction, they seem to believe, will have its source in God; in effect, they request from Jesus a merciful visitation from God.[22]

Against the backdrop of the earlier Lukan account in 5:12-14, Jesus'

---

18. For discussion and bibliography, see above on 5:12-14.

19. ἐλεέω, "to have mercy," is related to the noun for "almsgiving," ἐλεημοσύνη, and in the LXX the notion of "having compassion" embraces the giving of alms (see *TLNT,* 1:473n.13). However, the expression "to give alms" seems to be lexicalized by a combination of the noun and such verbs as ποιέω and δίδωμι. For the use of ἐλεέω on behalf of one in financial difficulty, see MM 202.

20. ἐπιστάτης. Among the NT writers, only Luke employs this term. See 5:5; 8:24, 45; 9:33, 49; cf. Derrett, "Gratitude," 83.

21. On narrative gaps, see Iser, *Implied Reader,* passim.

22. Cf. 1:46-55, 58, 68, 72; 7:16. Mercy is generally regarded as a divine attribute in the LXX — see *TLNT,* 1:473-79, esp. 478.

reply appears uneventful, prosaic. As "health care consultants," priests functioned as "purity inspectors" to exclude persons or restore them to their social
roles; they were not themselves active in any therapeutic process.[23] In this
case, though Luke has not yet provided his audience with any notation about
their being cleansed, Jesus nevertheless refers the ten lepers to their priests,
who, presumably, would be able to confirm their cure. Jesus' prescribed course
of action raises two interesting interpretive possibilities. First, the intertextual
relationship between the current scene and the earlier cleansing of Naaman
in 2 Kgs 5:1-19a moves from possible echoes to probable. Naaman, too, had
been asked to act in anticipation of his cleansing (2 Kgs 5:10). Second, Jesus'
instruction begs the question, Which priests?[24] Does Jesus expect these persons to travel to Jerusalem? to Mount Gerizim? Again, the ambiguity allowed
by the setting of this scene in v 11 leaves open such options.

Acting on Jesus' directive, the lepers are cleansed. Luke uses the
normal word to describe the recovery from a leprous condition, "to be made
clean."[25] The same term appears in v 17, but other words are found in vv 15
and 19 — "to be healed" and "to be saved" — and all follow as a consequence of the request of the ten lepers for divine mercy. The collocation of
these terms both accents the benefit conferred and draws on the reality that,
in this social situation, the condition of leprosy was viewed in holistic terms
fully embracing human existence in its physical, spiritual, and psychosocial
unity. In this setting "cleansing" would denote forgiveness, physical recovery,
and restoration, and all of this as a gift of God to be recognized by the
community of God's people.

15-16 What distinguishes the one from the nine is that he "saw that
he was healed."[26] The emphasis placed on his observation recalls the important place of the "recovery of sight" in the Lukan narrative (e.g., 4:18), a
recovery that Luke develops in terms of both sight and insight.[27] Unlike the
other lepers, this one perceives that he has been the recipient of divine benefaction — and that at the hand of Jesus.[28] Of his three actions — praising God,
falling at Jesus' feet, and thanking Jesus — the first is expected within the
Lukan narrative, the second two quite extraordinary. Praising God following
a miracle is the appropriate response in the Third Gospel; indeed, this former
leper joins many in the narrative who witness God's mighty acts, then return

---

23. Avalos, *Illness and Health Care,* 365-67; cf. above, on 5:12-14.
24. Cf. Derrett, "Gratitude," 83.
25. καθαρίζω.
26. See Betz, "Cleansing," 315; Hamm, "Samaritan Leper," 274.
27. Cf. Hamm, "Sight to the Blind"; Culpepper, "Seeing the Kingdom of God."
28. In the NT, ἰάομαι is used with reference to extraordinary deeds performed by
persons with divine power (Leivestad, "ἰάομαι," 170).

praising God.[29] If praising God is anticipated, however, returning to Jesus in order to do so at first seems incongruous. In the Lukan presentation, persons do not typically act in this way; moreover, had not Jesus instructed this man along with the other nine to travel to the temple for purification rituals and restoration? Nothing in this account suggests that the leper's "return" ought to be understood as "repentance."[30] His coming back to Jesus does have the effect of marking Jesus as the deictic center of this episode, however, and this is important for our understanding of the former leper's further activity. "Falling at the feet" of someone is an act of submission by which one acknowledges another's authority; it signifies reverence,[31] just the sort of response one might make toward a person regarded as one's benefactor. Gratitude, too, is expected of those who have received benefaction.[32] Because the former leper recognizes Jesus as the agent of the inbreaking kingdom of God, there is nothing incongruous in his actions: Both praising God and honoring Jesus with gratitude follow immediately from Jesus' gracious answer to his request for the merciful visitation of God.

Only now does Luke provide in a narrative aside to his audience the momentous fact that the one leper who correctly discerned Jesus' identity and responded appropriately was a Samaritan. With this identification, Luke has pulled the rug from under any prejudgments concerning either who might receive divine benefits or who might correctly identify Jesus' role in the divine plan. A leprous Samaritan might be expected to fail under the onerous weight of wrong ancestry and loyalties, and of the divine curse that has left him at the margins of human interaction in a perpetual state of impurity. Yet this person made his request for mercy to Jesus as one with divine authority, perceived that, through Jesus' agency, he had been restored, and came back to honor him as his lord.

17-19   Only here in this pericope do we learn, implicitly, that Jesus was not traveling alone when he was approached by the ten lepers. From the larger co-text, of course, it is clear that Jesus is being accompanied by his disciples. Now Jesus' question assumes an audience, one consisting of more than the former leper to whom he will speak directly in v 19. By keeping Jesus' companions offstage, however, or at least in the background, Luke allows Jesus' queries to be aimed more pointedly at Luke's audience. We are

---

29. See 2:20; 5:25-26; 7:16-17; 13:13; 23:47; Acts 4:21; 11:18; 21:30; Hamm, "Samaritan Leper," 283.

30. ὑποστρέφω can be used by Luke to signify "repentance," but here it seems to have no more than its locative sense (*contra*, e.g., Betz, "Cleansing," 318).

31. See Josh 10:24; 1 Sam 25:24, 41; Luke 5:12; 7:38, 44-46; 8:35, 41; 10:39; Acts 4:35, 37; 5:2; 7:58; 10:25-26; 22:3.

32. This aspect of the account is helpfully highlighted in Derrett, "Gratitude."

candidly invited to feel the weight of his objections and to struggle with their implications.

The cleansing of the ten illustrates the validity of Jesus' earlier observation, that God's character is manifest in his provision of mercy even to the "ungrateful" (6:35-36). What separates the one from the nine, then, is not the nature of the salvific benefits received. Rather, the nine are distinguished by their apparent lack of perception and, then, by their ingratitude. They do not recognize that they have been healed. This may be because leprosy was as much or more a socio-religious stigma as a physical malady. For it to be effective, cleansing must reach more deeply than the surface of one's skin, and it may be precisely this added dimension of restoration that the nine fail to comprehend. More evident in the distinction between the behavior of the one and the nine, though, is the failure of the latter to recognize that they had received divine benefit *from Jesus*.[33]

In Jesus' words one reads one of the strongest possible endorsements of the Samaritan's behavior. He was right to come to Jesus and give praise to God. This implies not only that God is worthy of praise (a point already well established in the narrative), but also that the fitting location from which to offer such praise is at the feet of Jesus.[34] Worded differently, one appropriately gives praise to God via one's grateful submission to Jesus as master or lord, the "location," so to speak, of God's beneficence. Here, Luke's christology reaches impressive heights as he presents Jesus in the role of the temple — as one in whom the powerful and merciful presence of God is realized and before whom the God of the temple (whether in Jerusalem or Mount Gerizim!) can be worshiped.[35]

The irony of this narrative so taken up with issues of perception, divine benefaction, and worship surfaces again in v 18b, with Jesus' description of the one leper as a "foreigner." This term is found only here in the NT. Its etymology suggests its appropriateness as a label for one born to the wrong family. In terms of the rhetoric of the Lukan narrative, this former leper is thus classified as someone other than a child of Abraham, at least according to usual canons. The usage of this term in the context of temple worship in Jerusalem is also suggestive; there it was found on inscriptions that forbade "foreigners" from access to those areas of the temple available only to Jews.[36] Jesus' use of the term is thus ironic indeed, for he observes how this normally ostracized person has behaved in a manner appropriate to the authentic children of Abraham.[37]

---

33. Danker notes of the Samaritan, "He saw the Giver in the gift" (291).
34. Note the repetition of ὑποστρέφω in vv 15 and 18.
35. See the programmatic remarks in Hamm, "Samaritan Leper," 286-87.
36. ἀλλογενής — cf. BAGD 39.
37. Cf. 3:7-14.

The declaration, "your faith has saved you," appears three other times in the Third Gospel (7:50; 8:48; 18:42), employing a verb, "to save," that is capable of a wide array of connotations in the Greco-Roman world. In this co-text it is interesting that "salvation" was a semantic cousin of "benefaction,"[38] and thus had to do with the exercise of beneficent power in the provision of a variety of blessings, including the healing of physical malady.[39] Here, something more than healing must be intended, since (1) the efficacy of faith is mentioned and (2) all ten lepers experienced cleansing. The Samaritan was not only cleansed, but on account of faith gained something more — namely, insight into Jesus' role in the inbreaking kingdom. He is enabled to see and is thus enlightened, itself a metaphor for redemption.[40]

He has faith and responds faithfully to the mercy he has received. It is on this basis, and not because of his status as a Jew — measured either by physical ancestry and/or by ritual purity — that he receives salvation. As Luke has often done, then, here again he subverts first-century Jewish concerns with status and purity by moving away from issues of ascription (e.g., family heritage and inherited attributes) in favor of an expansive notion of the mercy and gracious initiative of God, held in tandem with faithful response to God.[41]

5.6.2. Faithfulness at the Coming of the Son of Man (17:20–18:8)

The eschatological focus of this narrative unit sets it apart from the surrounding co-text. Important ties remain, of course, since, for Luke, (1) the healing Jesus performed in 17:11-19 is a manifestation of the inbreaking kingdom of God, and (2) anticipation of the kingdom calls for faithful comportment in the present life, as in 18:9-30.[42]

Within this unit, Jesus addresses two audiences — the Pharisees (17:20-21) and his followers (17:22–18:8) — on a comparable topic. Nevertheless, Luke has left hints that instructions to Pharisees and disciples should be read together.[43] Jesus' words to the Pharisees — " 'Look, here it

---

38. Cf. Josephus *Life* 47 §244: ἐβόων ἅπαντες εὐεργέτην καὶ σωτῆρα τῆς χώρας αὐτῶν καλοῦντες; similarly, e.g., Herodotus 3.12.2.

39. See MM 620-22; Danker, *Benefactor;* Foester, "σῴζω and σωτηρία," 966-69; *TLNT,* 3:344-49.

40. Cf. Luke 9:45; 24:31; Acts 26:17-18.

41. On status issues in first-century Judaism, see the helpful discussion in Eilberg-Schwartz, *Savage in Judaism,* 195-216. Cf. Green, *Gospel in Luke,* 80-82; J. A. Sanders, "Ethics of Election."

42. On the eschatological significance of healing in Luke, see above on 4:18-19; 13:10-17. On the behaviors appropriate to eschatological anticipation, see, e.g., on 12:1–13:9.

43. Cf. Carroll, *End of History,* 72-76.

is!' or 'There it is!' " (v 21a) — for example, find their counterpart in the subsequent discourse aimed at the disciples in v 23a: " 'Look there!' or 'Look here!' " Moreover, the "coming" of the kingdom of God (17:20) parallels the "coming" of the Son of Man (18:8), forming an *inclusio* around this narrative section.[44] Most significantly, in the travel narrative the Third Evangelist has shown himself to be fond of juxtaposing instruction to Pharisees (and legal experts) and disciples, allowing his message to the one to complement or supplement his words to the other.[45] The episode in 17:11-19 has already underscored the import of discernment and faithful response, and these motifs remain at the fore in the present section, where Jesus' eschatological vision adds a sense of urgency. Even though the Pharisees' question in v 20 demonstrates their failure to understand the eschatological significance of Jesus' ministry, in Luke's narration their query is deemed relevant for the disciples too. They are still in the process of re-formation as disciples and are not immune from such longings and misreadings as are characteristic of Pharisees.

5.6.2.1. When Is the Kingdom? (17:20-21)

> 20 *Once Jesus was asked by the Pharisees when the kingdom of God was coming, and he answered, "The kingdom of God is not coming with observation;*[46] 21 *nor will they say, 'Look, here it is!' or 'There it is!' For, in fact, the kingdom of God is among you."*

Luke provides no particular setting for this dialogue except insofar as he has located it immediately adjacent to his account of the cleansing of the ten lepers and the faith of one. Given this interpretive co-text, it is difficult not to find a contrast between the Samaritan leper and these Pharisees: The former discerns the hand of God at work in Jesus' words, while the latter manifest no such awareness.

This is the first of several places in Luke-Acts where a request for clarity regarding the kingdom leads to the correction of misunderstanding about the eschatological timetable and, then, about the nature of God's dominion.[47] That it comes from the Pharisees is not surprising, since, thus far in the narrative, they have shown themselves inept in their capacity to under-

---

44. This does not mean, however, that "kingdom of God" and "Son of Man" are interchangeable phrases; see below. On their connection, see also 21:25-36; more broadly, Beasley-Murray, *Kingdom of God,* 219-312.

45. Recently, see the juxtaposition of teaching to Pharisees and to disciples in chs. 15–16.

46. NRSV: "things that can be observed."

47. See 19:11-27; 21:7-36; Acts 1:6; cf. Fusco, "Point of View," 1677-78; Carroll, *End of History,* 123-24.

stand the significance of the ministry of Jesus. Even if the Third Evangelist has been involved in a narrative reinterpretation of the kingdom of God in terms of its relationship to the presence of Jesus,[48] this perspective has thus far not been shared by the Pharisees. As will become immediately clear (see 17:22-37), however, the Pharisees are not alone in their failure to grasp Jesus' message about the character of God's reign.[49]

The question posed by the Pharisees is wrongheaded on two counts. First, it assumes that God's reign is exclusively a future entity. This sort of kingdom expectation is consistent with what we know of the eschatological understanding of the Pharisees in the first century, but it departs from the repeated teaching of Jesus in the Lukan narrative. There the emphasis has fallen on the kingdom of God already breaking into the world. Second, though more subtle, is the suggestion in Jesus' reply that the Pharisees are hoping to recognize the coming of God's dominion through scientific observation and assessment.[50] Sign-watching has already been denounced in Luke, not least when manifestations of the present work of God have not led to appropriate responses of repentance (cf. 11:16, 29-32). This is not because the arrival of the kingdom is devoid of evidence, but because this evidence is not self-interpreting and is often either misinterpreted or altogether overlooked. Although cast by Luke as keen observers of Jesus' activity, the Pharisees consistently measure his ministry against their own, fallacious canons. In light of this earlier emphasis, the possibility that Jesus' reply insinuates a nuance of hostility on the part of the Pharisees cannot be overlooked.[51]

If the temporal coming of God's kingdom cannot be determined through scientific analysis, neither can it be localized, as though it were inexorably associated with a particular place or nation (cf. Acts 1:6-8). Proclamation of the kingdom in the words and deeds of Jesus and his delegates may render present the saving power of God, but God's reign is cosmological in its implications and scope.[52]

---

48. Cf. 4:43; 6:20; 8:1; 9:2; 10:9-11; 11:20[!]; 12:32; Wolter, "Reich Gottes." On the kingdom in Luke-Acts, see also, e.g., Tannehill, "Kingdom"; O'Toole, "Kingdom of God"; Carroll, *End of History,* 80-87.

49. That is, the line between the Pharisees and disciples is not yet hard-and-fast in the Lukan narrative (cf. above, on 9:51–19:48) — a reality that is overlooked in attempts to paint the Pharisees as "insincere" in their request (so Gowler, *Portraits of the Pharisees,* 263-66).

50. For the use of παρατήρησις with reference, e.g., to the work of astronomers and physicians, see Riesenfeld, "τηρέω," 148-49.

51. This is suggested by the use of the cognate verb παρατηρέω in 6:7; 14:1; 20:20; Acts 9:24; cf. Carroll, *End of History,* 77.

52. That is, although the Lukan narrative does transform some aspects of traditional kingdom expectations, it does not exclude the OT notion of the universality of the rule of Yahweh (cf. Beasley-Murray, *Kingdom of God,* 20).

Having negated the wrongheaded assumptions of the Pharisees' question, Jesus turns to his own concise but constructive message concerning the nature of the kingdom. In doing so, he revisits the question of the kingdom's temporality and geography. He pronounces the kingdom as already active,[53] present even where it is unacknowledged — not least among these Pharisees.[54] Thus, Jesus reprimands the Pharisees in their kingdom-seeking for looking for the wrong thing and in the wrong way, and asserts that the kingdom is already operative, if only they would open their eyes to it. The kingdom of God is closely related to the person and activity of Jesus (cf. 11:20); failing to understand this, the Pharisees do not recognize (and cannot respond to) God's new world order.

5.6.2.2. Where Is the Kingdom? (17:22-37)

22 *Then he said to the disciples, "The days are coming when you will long to see one of the days of the Son of Man, and you will not see it.* 23 *They will say to you, 'Look there!' or 'Look here!' Do not go, do not set off in pursuit.* 24 *For as the lightning flashes and lights up the sky from one side to the other, so will the Son of Man be in his day.* 25 *But first he must endure much suffering and be rejected by this generation.* 26 *Just as it was in the days of Noah, so too it will be in the days of the Son of Man.* 27 *They were eating and drinking, and marrying and being given in marriage, until the day Noah entered the ark, and the flood came and destroyed all of them.* 28 *Likewise, just as it was in the days of Lot: they were eating and drinking, buying and selling, planting and building,*

---

53. Some have given Luke's present tense verb "to be" (ἐστιν) a future force; thus: "When the kingdom comes it will not have to be sought for it will be apparent, right there in your midst." So, recently, Nolland, 2:850, 853-54; cf. Mattill, *Last Things,* 190-203. Even Nolland is aware, though, that for the Lukan narrative "the kingdom of God had now already come in connection with the ministry of Jesus" (2:852). On this discussion, see the helpful comments by Maddox (*Purpose,* 134-36); Maddox observes that Luke's language emphasizes the unacknowledged and unexpected presence of the kingdom in the midst of the Pharisees. Even if the day of the Son of Man lies in the future (17:22-37), the kingdom is already present.

54. Attempts to read Luke's ἐντὸς ὑμῶν as a reference to the inward, spiritual dynamic of the kingdom of God (e.g., Caragounis, "Kingdom of God?" 423-24) find ready adherents in this age of psychology and individualism here in the West. But they falter especially on the grounds that (1) nowhere else in Luke-Acts is the dominion of God regarded as an inner, spiritual reality; and (2) the notion that the Pharisees contain within themselves the kingdom of God is inconsistent with the Lukan portrayal of persons from this Jewish group. For the usage of ἐντός + plural object with the sense "among," see the survey in Mattill, *Last Things,* 203-7. Cf. Lebourlier, *"Entos hymōn";* Maddox, *Purpose,* 134; Carroll, *End of History,* 79. An alternative translation is grammatically possible and makes sense within this co-text — namely, "within your purview" (cf. the related views of Darr, *Character Building,* 113-14; Beasley-Murray, *Kingdom of God,* 102-3).

29 *but on the day that Lot left Sodom, it rained fire and sulfur from heaven and destroyed all of them* 30 *— it will be like that on the day that the Son of Man is revealed.* 31 *On that day, anyone on the housetop who has belongings in the house must not come down to take them away; and likewise anyone in the field must not turn back.* 32 *Remember Lot's wife.* 33 *Those who try to make their life secure will lose it, but those who lose their life will keep it.* 34 *I tell you, on that night there will be two in one bed; one will be taken and the other left.* 35 *There will be two women grinding meal together; one will be taken and the other left."* 37 *Then they asked him, "Where, Lord?" He said to them, "Where the corpse is, there the vultures will gather."*

It is hardly coincidental that an inquiry from Pharisees (vv 20-21) leads immediately into instruction for the followers of Jesus. The move back and forth between Pharisees (along with legal experts) and disciples has been normal fare in chs. 15–17, highlighting the permeable quality of the perimeter separating the two. The Pharisees continue to be instructed by Jesus, for they may yet respond to his message; the disciples continue in their susceptibility to the miscalculations concerning the purpose of God otherwise characteristic of the Pharisees. If the Pharisees have failed to perceive the realization of God's redemptive project before their eyes in the ministry of Jesus, the disciples, too, will struggle with the divine timetable. Jesus' instruction, then, revolves around the question, What will it be like, the day when the Son of Man is revealed?[55] Here Jesus depicts that "day" as unmistakable, worldwide, sudden, inescapable, and, for those who are not prepared, calamitous.[56] The effect of Jesus' teaching is to punctuate the need for faithful readiness (cf. 12:35-49) with a pronounced sense of urgency.

Two structural features of this narrative unit help to give it meaning. First, one may recognize an inverted, conceptual parallelism, an A-B-C-B'-A' pattern:

A   Disciples will ask, "Where?" (vv 22-24)
  B   Jesus: repudiation and suffering (v 25)
    C   Readiness in anticipation of calamitous judgment (vv 26-30)
  B'   Disciples: abandonment of life (vv 31-35, esp. v 33)
A'   Disciples ask, "Where?" (v 37)

---

55. This question does not appear in this pericope, of course, but it is presumed in the repeated phrases, "so will the Son of Man be in his day" (v 24), "so too it will be in the days of the Son of Man" (v 26), and "it will be like that on the day that the Son of Man is revealed" (v 30).

56. See the discussion in Carroll, *End of History*, 88-94.

Recognition of this design is beneficial on three counts: (a) it helps to locate primary emphasis on the urgency of readiness (vv 26-30); (b) it interprets the character of that readiness by juxtaposing the rejection of Jesus (v 25) and the cost of discipleship (vv 31-35) in a way that is reminiscent of earlier teaching in Luke (e.g., 9:21-26); and (c), as we will see, it helps us to interpret the sense of the enigmatic proverb of v 37.

The second important organizational feature embedded in this narrative unit is the deliberate juxtaposition of the "day" and the "days," especially in the phrases "day of the Son of Man" and "days of the Son of Man." This emphasizes, first, that the career of the Son of Man embraces the present of Jesus' ministry and the life of the church as well as the eschaton, and more particularly it signifies that suffering and second coming (i.e., the apocalyptic "revealing" of the Son of Man — v 30), repudiation and vindication, are both integral to the divine purpose for Jesus.[57] The correlation of "day" and "days," second, recapitulates for the disciples one of Jesus' primary points to the Pharisees in vv 20-21 — namely, his message that the kingdom of God is already active even though God's project awaits a future consummation. Finally, Jesus thus indicates that, while living during the "days of the Son of Man," Jesus' followers must maintain faithful vigilance in light of the impending "day of the Son of Man."

22-24 Luke marks clearly a change of audience, from Pharisees (v 20) to disciples, but the topic of instruction remains the same. In fact, references to looking "here" and "there" in v 23 recall comparable references in v 21. This suggests that talk about the "days of the Son of Man" must be correlated with talk of the coming kingdom, and that the disciples (and not only the Pharisees) require instruction on the nature of the fulfillment of God's redemptive purpose.

As he had in vv 20-21, so here Jesus continues to emphasize the motif of perception, now with verbs of seeing and the analogy of lightning lighting up the sky.[58] Insofar as Luke has developed "sight" or "illumination" as an important soteriological term, Jesus' blunt statement, "you will not see," raises important interpretive questions. What will they not see? Why not? The analogy of vv 20-21 might suggest that their failure to see will be rooted in the nature of the kingdom, which "is not coming with observation" (v 20d). Such an interpretation would stand in irreconcilable tension with v 24, which emphasizes the ubiquity and unmistakable character of the Son of Man "in his day." Moreover, it misses the point of contrast in Jesus' teaching. For the

---

57. Kingsbury (*Conflict in Luke*, 73-78) notes that, in the use of "Son of Man" throughout his narrative, Luke ". . . emphasizes the twin features of repudiation and vindication."

58. Cf. the use of ὁράω (2x) in v 22, ἰδού (2x) in v 23, and λάμπω in v 24.

Pharisees he emphasizes the presence of God's project in response to their concern about its future. For these disciples on the other hand, who might be tempted to think in terms of the full realization of the kingdom in the present, Jesus emphasizes the future climax of God's purpose. What seems more probable, then, is that, in yearning "to see one of the days of the Son of Man," the disciples will have given expression to a wrongheaded anticipation — that is, they will not see what they are looking for because they are looking for the wrong thing.

Key to working out this puzzle is the relationship between the two phrases, "the days are coming" and "one of the days of the Son of Man." Reference to "coming days," found elsewhere in the Lukan narrative, is reminiscent of prophetic texts where this expression is used in anticipation of calamity and duress.[59] "One of the days of the Son of Man" refers to the time of the end, when the Son of Man will be revealed.[60] Consequently, Jesus is prophesying that, during the "coming days" of distress, the disciples will hunger for the final resolution. As they have repeatedly demonstrated, this is due to their incapacity or unwillingness to see the integral relation of suffering and rejection to God's salvific plan (see above, e.g., on 9:37-50). In other words, the disciples will long for the end in order that they might avoid the disquiet and pain of the present. Because of this, they might find reports of obscure appearances of the Son of Man alluring. Such reports stand in contrast, though, with Jesus' assurance that the revelation of the Son of Man at the end will be anything but obscure. Like lightning that lights up the whole sky so that all can see it, so prominent and pervasive will be the coming of the Son of Man.

25 The mistaken cravings of the disciples are addressed directly in this prediction of Jesus' suffering and rejection. According to the terms of this passion prediction, Jesus' commitment to the divine plan leads through suffering. Though divine necessity is stressed,[61] Jesus also makes clear that his

---

59. See 5:35; 19:43; 21:6; 23:29; cf. 10:12; 12:46; and, e.g., Amos 4:2; Jer 7:32; 16:14; Zech 14:1.

60. Marshall (658-59) outlines and helpfully discusses the interpretive options presented by this clause. The primary difficulty is that, in vv 26-30, "days of x" refers to the time preceding a terminal event; by way of analogy (as in v 26), then, we might expect "one of the days of the Son of Man" to refer to "one of the days during the period before the eschaton." Such a rendering in this instance would be nonsensical, however, since it would require Jesus to say something like, "During the days before the end you will long to see one of the days before the end, and will not see it." Cf. Conzelmann (*Luke,* 124), who thinks that Luke uses "days" because Luke views the eschaton as "a succession of events distinct from one another."

61. For Luke's use of δεῖ ("he *must* endure . . .") with reference to divine necessity, see, e.g., Cosgrove, "Divine Δεῖ"; Green, *Gospel of Luke,* 28-37.

repudiation will come because his fundamental orientation to the purpose of God stands in tension with the commitments of "this generation." The phrase "this generation" has appeared earlier in the Lukan narrative at 7:31, echoing the portrayal of the people of God in the Exodus material as stubborn, stiff-necked, and rebellious, as people who resist God's purpose and God's representatives.[62]

Within the narrative, Jesus' prophecy communicates to the disciples that the end will not precede the passion. Within Luke's own discourse situation, the passion of Jesus stands in the distant past, no longer as a necessary, anticipated chronological precursor to the revelation of the Son of Man. This does not strip it of meaning, however. Quite the contrary, it signifies, first, that Jesus' crucifixion did not constitute a rift in God's plan but was actually integral to it.[63] Moreover, it brings again into the foreground the ongoing status of suffering and rejection in the realization of God's purpose. For Luke-Acts, the *theologia crucis* is above all a narrative portrayal of the life of faithful discipleship as the way of the cross. Indeed, as Luke will repeatedly demonstrate in Acts, struggle and opposition do not contradict or impede but seem actually to promote the progress of the gospel: "It is through many persecutions that we must enter the kingdom of God" (Acts 14:22).[64]

26-30 The most prominent feature of this subunit is its parallelism, drawing an analogy between the "days of Noah" and the "days of Lot" on the one hand, and "days of the Son of Man" on the other. The text is remarkable for the way it lists two series of verbs — in the Greek text even more than in the NRSV, in staccato fashion, without conjunctions to interrupt their cadence — that describe in rhythmic repetition the activities of everyday life that are suddenly interrupted by something quite exceptional and cataclysmic.[65] God's judgment breaks inescapably, surprisingly, abruptly into the mundane of life. In spite of the proverbial wickedness of the people of Noah's day and of Lot's townspeople (cf., e.g., Gen 6:1-8; 18:16-21),[66] such concerns do not at all seem to occupy center stage here. Eating, drinking, marrying, and giving in marriage (v 27) — these are the stuff of everyday life and are not inherently wicked. To these are added commercial practices (v 28), again not problematic in themselves. Though not intrinsically evil, within their immediate co-text these practices are deemed as potential diversions. And this perspective is fully consistent with the portrayal of such everyday activities

---

62. See Exod 32:9; 33:3, 5; Deut 10:16; Luke 9:41; Acts 7:51-53.

63. Carroll, *End of History*, 93-94.

64. See the movement from Acts 6:1 to 6:7; and from 8:1-3 to 8:4. See further, Green, "Salvation to the End of the Earth," forthcoming.

65. Tannehill, *Sword of His Mouth*, 119.

66. Cf. Schlosser, "Luc xvii,26-30."

as eating and drinking and marrying, as well as of possessions, elsewhere in the Third Gospel: not inherently bad, but potential distractions from the necessity of one's fundamental orientation toward the purpose of God.[67] With these parallels from Israel's past, Jesus warns his followers about the dangers of the period before the end. This will be a time when life will be easily occupied with the everyday and the urgency of faith will easily be replaced with laxity.

31-35 Lest one gain the impression from vv 26-30 that such daily routines are intrinsically problematic, Jesus goes on to use them for illustrative purposes in a way that disallows any such understanding. This issue does not revolve around who has belongings, labors in the field, sleeps at night, or works at the grinding stone. What is at stake is not whether one is engaged fully in the routinization of life. Rather, the question is whether, in the midst of life, one maintains a single-minded orientation toward the aim of God and its realization at the eschaton.

"To remember" signifies more than a cognitive act in the biblical tradition, but is typically the precursory mental act leading to related activity.[68] The admonition, "Remember Lot's wife" (cf. Gen 19:26), then, both interprets her action as the manifestation of an unwillingness to relinquish everything at the time of judgment and serves to warn Jesus' followers against similarly misplaced values. Luke's audience may hear in the background Jesus' earlier instruction in 9:57-62.

Similarly, in the message of v 33, Luke's audience may hear echoes of Jesus' message concerning discipleship in 9:23-26. The faithfulness required by life lived in anticipation of judgment requires a reversal of the normal strategies deployed on behalf of life's preservation.[69] Life as constructed by identification with the present world, with its orientation toward the twin securities of status and possessions (cf. 12:1–13:9), attracts calamitous disaster at the end. Only those whose lives are built on the values of the kingdom of God, and whose case for respectable identity in the world is thus

---

67. Cf., e.g., 8:14; 12:19, 29, 45; 14:18-20.

68. "Remembering" is often portrayed as either a three-stage process (outside stimulus → mental process → behavioral response) or a two-stage process (mental process → behavioral response); cf. Gen 8:1; Num 10:9; Neh 9:17; Ezek 29:16; Wis 16:6-7; Green, *Death of Jesus,* 202-3.

69. Although περιποιέομαι is rare in the NT (17:33; Acts 20:28; 1 Tim 3:13), it is well known in the LXX and in nonbiblical Greek with the sense "to save a life." It is also often used in commercial contexts, "to acquire for oneself"; in light of Luke's pervasive concerns with possessions and the particular focus of this pericope on valuing possessions so much that one "turns back" at the judgment in order to get them (vv 31-32), it is not difficult to detect an astute play on the term here. For evidence of usage, see MM 507; *TLNT,* 3:100-101.

lost, will be ready for the end and, thus, for the form of human existence appropriate to the eschaton. From Jesus' eschatological perspective, this is no time for "business as usual."

In Jesus' infancy, Simeon had prophesied that Jesus would be the cause of division within Israel (2:34-35). Even though this prediction has already begun to be realized within the context of Jesus' ministry in Luke's Gospel, Jesus heralds the day of the Son of Man, the end, as a final division. Whether one is engaged in everyday pursuits is not the basis for judgment: Both are sleeping, both are grinding, but one is rescued while the other is caught up in the calamity of judgment. At stake is the nature of one's dispositions, one's commitments, one's attachments, one's ultimate loyalty.

37 Just as the Pharisees had inquired, "When?" so now the disciples inquire, "Where?" — this in spite of Jesus' instructions in vv 22-24. There he had informed them that the question of venue would be moot since the revelation of the Son of Man at the end will be a manifestly public affair, seen everywhere and by everyone. Jesus' proverbial reply may be redundant, but, in light of the disciples' slowness to understand, apparently it is necessarily so. Just as the presence of carrion is indicated by circling vultures, so will his presence at the end be clearly evident.[70]

5.6.2.3. Faithfulness in Anticipation (18:1-8)

1 *Then Jesus told them a parable about their need to pray always and not to lose heart.* 2 *He said, "In a certain city there was a judge who neither feared God nor had respect for people.* 3 *In that city there was a widow who kept coming to him and saying, 'Grant me justice against my opponent.'* 4 *For a while he refused; but later he said to himself, 'Though I have no fear of God and no respect for anyone,* 5 *yet because this widow keeps bothering me, I will grant her justice, lest she continue coming and end up doing violence to me!'"*[71] 6 *And the Lord said, "Listen to what the unjust judge says.* 7 *And will not God grant justice to his chosen ones who cry to him day and night? Will he delay long in helping them?* 8 *I tell you, he will quickly grant justice to them. And yet, when the Son of Man comes, will he find faith on earth?"*

70. This interpretation builds on the interpretive possibility encouraged by the inverted parallelism of this passage, which correlates v 37 with vv 22-24 (see above). Other readings are possible. For example, the disciples might be understood to be inquiring into the locality of those who are left at the final judgment (vv 33-34); in this instance, Jesus' reply would be that their whereabouts would be obvious in the same way that circling birds make obvious the location of corpses.

71. NRSV: "so that she may not wear me out by continually coming."

Jesus' parabolic teaching "about their need to pray always and not to lose heart" stands as the climax of this longer section on faithfulness at the coming of the Son of Man (17:20–18:8). Its narrative location provides this unit with a decidedly eschatological edge,[72] an emphasis that comes explicitly to the fore in vv 7-8. Verse 8 forms an *inclusio* with 17:20, indicating the concern of this larger narrative segment on the coming of the end. Together with v 7, v 8 also forms an *inclusio* with v 1, indicating the more narrow concern of this pericope with the nature of appropriate comportment in the present with respect to the eschaton.[73] Read against the horizon of 17:22-37, Jesus' teaching here is particularly oriented toward the necessity of tenacious, hopeful faith in the midst of present ordeal.

Jesus' message has two foci, associated with the two primary characters of the parable of vv 2-5.[74] On the one hand, based on an argument from lesser to greater, we hear in Jesus' words an affirmation of the faithfulness of God: He will assuredly act with dispatch on behalf of the elect. On the other, we see in the widow's action a model of perseverance in the midst of wrong. In fact, according to the Greek text of v 8, Jesus' question is not concerned with "faith" (in general) but with "*the* faith"[75] — that is, that manner of faith demonstrated by the widow in the antecedent parable. These two motifs — the certainty of God's justice and the call for resolute faithfulness in anticipation of that certainty — come in for development on account of the situation Jesus has anticipated in 17:22-25. This is the eventuality that his followers will encounter hostility, look for the deliverance that accompanies the consummation of the kingdom, and, not finding it, become disenchanted. Having anticipated this state of affairs, Jesus addresses it, first, by insisting that adversity is integral to the process by which God brings salvation (cf. 17:25, 32-34); and, second, by assuring his disciples that, despite delay, divine vindication is imminent (18:1-8).

72. Cf. Mattill, *Last Things,* 90-91.

73. Cf. Maddox, *Purpose,* 127; Donahue, *Gospel in Parable,* 181.

74. So also, e.g., Donahue, *Gospel in Parable,* 181-82; Carroll, *End of History,* 94-95; Blomberg, *Parables,* 272. The possibility of two foci is denied by some. Hedrick (*Parables,* 193, 201), e.g., insists that, structurally, the parable focuses on the judge, with the widow providing "merely the context and background for the judge's monologue" (193). His structural observations, together with the explicit charge on the part of Jesus, "Listen to what the unjust judge says" (v 6), are enough to disallow Schottroff's insistence (*Lydia's Impatient Sisters,* 101) that the sole focus of the parable is the widow (see further Seim, *Double Message,* 244). Hedrick is able to reach his conclusion, however, only by disengaging what he perceives to be the original parable from its Lukan co-text and interpretation. Verses 1 and 8, along with important socio-cultural considerations (see below), ensure that we also understand from Jesus' message the exemplary character of the widow in Jesus' instruction.

75. εὑρήσει τὴν πίστιν.

637

Throughout this pericope we may hear echoes of Sir 35:15b-25, where the figure of the widow also serves a prototypical function and God is portrayed as one whose justice is indubitable. This instance of intertextuality solidly grounds Jesus' portrait of God within Jewish tradition, but not without some innovation.[76] For example, the passage from Sirach develops the notion of divine vengeance against the unrighteous, a motif absent from Jesus' parabolic teaching in 18:1-8.[77] Moreover, the widow has an altogether more active role in the Lukan passage, evidencing her key role in Jesus' overall instruction.

In fact, it is in the interplay between Luke's interpretive introduction in v 1, Jesus' parting words concerning "faith on earth" (v 8b), and his characterization of the widow in vv 3 and 5 that we are able to discern the quality of life appropriate to Jesus' followers prior to the eschaton. In 11:2, they were advised to pray for the coming of the kingdom; because Jesus positions this widow as an archetype, the idea of "prayer" for the full realization of God's project is now expanded so as to signify also the active quest for justice. "Their whole existence is to be like that of the widow in relation to the unjust judge. . . . Praying and crying to God against injustices describes the whole life of believers: their efforts, their protests against injustice."[78]

1 Luke indicates the onset of this narrative unit with no changes of scene, topic, or character, thus intimating its immediate connection to the preceding account of Jesus' instruction. Jesus' audience remains the disciples, though his instruction is hardly privileged, since the Pharisees remain in the extended audience (though temporarily outside the narrator's focus — cf. 17:20-21; 18:9). The possibility of "losing heart" was raised implicitly in 17:22-37 — wherein anticipation of a delay in the fulfillment of God's eschatological purpose is coupled with the experience of opposition to provide a setting for a loss of eschatological perspective and the concomitant growth of a business-as-usual attitude. "Lose heart" may be too passive a way to understand Jesus' concern that his followers not begin to behave remissly;[79] in any case, it appears in this co-text as the opposite of "faith" (v 8a), itself manifest in deeds of faithfulness. As an antidote to laxity in one's discipleship, Jesus counsels continuous prayer; indeed, such prayer is advanced as a necessity[80] for his followers. He does not promote thereby a particular technology of prayer, as though one ought to pray for the same thing over and

76. See further the remarks in K. E. Bailey, *Through Peasant Eyes,* 127-28.
77. Cf. the similar exegesis of Isa 61:1-2 in Luke 4:18-19.
78. Schottroff, *Lydia's Impatient Sisters,* 102; cf. Donahue, *Gospel in Parable,* 184-85: "Luke understands continual prayer not simply as passive waiting but as the active quest for justice" (185).
79. For ἐγκακέω as "to behave remissly," see Freed, "Parable of the Judge," 40.
80. δεῖ.

over, as though through repetition one could wear God down so as to achieve one's objective. Rather, "prayer" in this co-text serves as a metonym for confidence in and openness to the benefaction of God.[81]

2-4a In Jesus' narration, the scene is set and an impasse reached almost in the same breath by focusing on the contrast between two main characters. This contrast is evident structurally in the Greek text: "a certain judge there was in a certain city . . . a widow there was in that city." Both characters appear as prototypes, then, and as occupants of different ends of the continuum of power and privilege. Presumably no more than a local magistrate (cf. 12:14, 58), this judge is nonetheless a male of notable status in his community. His characterization as one "who neither feared God nor had respect for people" is ambiguous, at least on the surface. He may thus appear to us as a judge ought to appear — unbiased, objective, neutral. Even a quality like impartiality is a matter of perspective, however, one that must be understood within a particular cultural context. In the one imagined by Jesus' parable, someone thus characterized is actually presented quite negatively. First, Jesus' valuation echoes analogous phrases employed in the wider Roman world as proverbial invectives. Within this world, the world of Luke, neither fearing God nor having regard for persons signified one's thorough wickedness.[82] In addition, elsewhere the Third Evangelist portrays those who "fear God" in positive fashion.[83] Second, when Jehoshaphat appointed judges throughout Judah his charge to them included the admonition to "let the fear of the LORD be upon you" (2 Chr 19:7); clearly this is an attribute not shared by the judge of this parable. Finally, even with appeals to divine and human impartiality dotting its pages (e.g., 2 Chron 19:4-7; Sir 35:15-16), the LXX gives no impression that the scales of divine justice are blind. The God who liberated Israel from Egypt is the God who directs his people to show special regard toward, *partiality* on behalf of, the oppressed among them — specifically for the alien, the orphan, and the widow.[84] In this respect, it is not accidental that Luke habitually portrays widows as persons of exemplary piety and/or as recipients of divine beneficence.[85]

As a widow, the second character of Jesus' parable has no intrinsic

---

81. Cf. Dunn, "Prayer," 624; see above on 11:1-13.

82. Freed ("Parable of the Judge," 42) draws special attention to Dionysius *Rom. Ant.* 10.10.7; Josephus *Ant.* 1.3.1; 10.5.2. In his attempt to paint the judge as a man of integrity, Hedrick (*Parables,* 195, 197) attempts to downplay the significance of these and other parallels; as he is well aware, though, Hedrick is not attempting here to read this parable in *the Lukan co-text,* where the judge is manifestly wicked (v 6).

83. Cf. Acts 10:2, 22, 35; 13:16, 26.

84. The texts are numerous — e.g., Lev 19:9-10; 23:22; Deut 14:28-29; 24:19-22; 26:12; cf. Jas 1:27; Lohfink, *Option for the Poor.*

85. See 2:37; 4:25-26; 7:11-17; 20:45–21:4; cf. Acts 6:1; 9:39-41.

standing in the community.[86] Inasmuch as the ancient court system belonged to the world of men, the fact that this woman finds herself before the magistrate indicates that she has no kinsman to bring her case to court; the fact that she must do so continuously suggests that she lacks the economic resources to offer the appropriate bribe necessary for a swift settlement. In the Scriptures of Israel and Jewish tradition, widowhood symbolized the ultimate state of vulnerability, status deprivation, and need; as the object of God's concern, they were also to be cared for within the community of God's people.[87] In spite of this, the scene Jesus paints is not atypical but develops the well-known topos of the widow who struggles with a corrupt judicial system for her rights.[88] Indeed, it is probably not too much to say that so much attention is given the divine concern for widows in the LXX precisely because this concern was so little evident among God's people. In Jesus' narrative, the widow's claim is unspecified, but it likely had to do with material resources being withheld from her.[89]

We are provided no information regarding why the judge refused to settle the widow's case; our only clue is Jesus' insight into his character: Neglect of a widow in her distress is entirely consistent with one who has neither fear of God nor regard for human beings.

More central to the parable as a whole is the astounding behavior of the widow. Perhaps it is expected that, having no man to plead her case, she will attend court on her own behalf. Having been slighted by the judge, though, her role should have been that of the helpless, hopeless victim. Like the hemorrhaging woman of 8:43-48, however, this woman assumes unusual responsibility for her own well-being, adopts a self-presentation of shocking initiative, and thus continually returns to the magistrate in her quest for justice.[90]

4b-6 As with some earlier parables (e.g., 15:11-32; 16:1-9), so this one turns on the introduction of soliloquy. How long the woman has sought a settlement from him is unclear[91] — long enough, though, for the judge to begin to feel badgered.[92] Interestingly, the judge's self-assessment is identical to Jesus' characterization of him, verifying that the action he proposes on behalf of this

---

86. See the summary in Ilan, *Jewish Women,* 147-51.

87. See Exod 22:1-4; Deut 10:16-18; Isa 1:16-17; Stählin, "χήρα," 444-48.

88. See Stählin, "χήρα," 434; Schottroff, *Lydia's Impatient Sisters,* 102-4.

89. Jeremias (*Parables,* 153; cf. K. E. Bailey, *Through Peasant Eyes,* 133-35) observes that, according to *b. Sanh.* 4b, "an authorized scholar may decide money cases sitting alone"; otherwise, three judges might be expected.

90. The use of the verb in the imperfect (ἤρχετο) refers to repeated or customary action.

91. ἐπὶ χρόνον designates an unspecified passage of time (BAGD 289).

92. The NRSV rendering of τὸ παρέχειν μοι κόπον as "bothering me" is weak, suggesting neither the duress the judge was under nor the level the widow's shocking behavior had reached in the judge's view; Johnson (270) suggests, "giving me such a beating."

widow is not motivated by his commitment to God's priorities nor by his concern for his standing in the community[93] nor by any residual altruism on his part. He is motivated, rather, by the woman's astonishing behavior. She is acting so out of station that, he muses, she may even be capable of assaulting him with more than words! The language Luke uses is startling, perhaps even humorous, borrowed as it is from the boxing ring,[94] for it invokes images of the almighty, fearless, macho judge cornered and slugged by the least powerful in society. Thus Jesus accents the astonishingly uncharacteristic initiative and persistence of an allegedly impotent woman in the face of injustice.

Luke's reference to Jesus as "Lord" is characteristic for the narrator, and it reminds his audience of Jesus' role as authoritative teacher. Jesus' charge to his followers to "listen" is reminiscent of his repeated emphasis on a form of hearing that leads to appropriate action (see esp. 8:1-21). The phrase "unjust judge" is also reminiscent of the analogous phrase in 16:8, a reminder that Jesus' followers may learn profound lessons about discipleship (oriented toward the coming age) from worldly examples (oriented to this age). In this instance, Jesus' followers may hear in the judge's words astonishment at the behavior of this woman. Directed to see her behavior in this light, they may learn from her the import of engaging in the quest for justice — even when that quest requires that one act outside the script provided by an unjust world.[95]

7-8 Jesus' subsequent commentary on the parable is closely tied to it by repetition of the motif of "granting justice."[96] This helps to solidify the double analogy he wishes to develop, from the unjust judge to God, and from the widow to God's elect, just as it helps to situate Jesus' appropriation of the parable within an eschatological frame.[97] First, Jesus adopts an argu-

---

93. Derrett ("Unjust Judge," 189-91) has been followed by some interpreters when he argues, on the basis of his rendering of ὑπωπιάζω as "to slander," that the judge acted in order to uphold his reputation in the community. The explicit denial of the judge's concern for public opinion in vv 2 and 4 speaks against this view, however.

94. ὑπωπιάζω, "to give a black eye [to someone]," is often granted a weaker sense, as in the NRSV: "she may . . . wear me out." Such a rendering is not otherwise attested, however (cf. MM 661), and seems to derive from the presumed unsuitability of this verb's usual rendering in this context.

95. Importantly, Jesus does not portray this widow as acting in a violent way, only in a way that departs from her culturally scripted role. The notion of violence derives from the judge, who may interpret her persistence as an act of violence against the system. See Schottroff, *Lydia's Patient Sisters,* 104.

96. See the use of ἐκδικέω/ἐκδίκησις in vv 3, 5, 7, and 8.

97. ἐκδικέω/ἐκδίκησις, used in the papyri with reference to "deciding a case" or "procuring justice for someone," can also be used in the LXX with reference to eschatological judgment (e.g., Hos 9:7; Mic 5:15; Falkenroth and C. Brown, "Punishment, Vengeance," 92-93).

ment from lesser to greater: If an unjust judge will finally grant justice, how much more will God! Importantly, this comparison comes after lengthy teaching in Luke wherein the gracious, attentive, beneficent character of God has become well established (e.g., 6:35-36; 11:1-13; 12:32). Second, the text introduces a straightforward analogy between the widow of the parable and God's "chosen ones who cry to him day and night." This is consistent with the portrayal of the widow Anna in 2:37, who worshiped in the temple with fasting and prayer "night and day" (cf. the characterization of exemplary widows in 1 Tim 5:5 as those who continue in prayer "night and day"). It is also congruous with the correspondence drawn between Israel (who called out to God and was delivered; cf. Deut 26:5-9) and the alien, the orphan, and the widow (for whom Israel was to care even as they had been shown divine care — e.g., Deut 24:21-22). The idea of "the elect" (i.e., God's chosen ones) is traditional in the OT and early Christianity.[98] Here, Luke designates as the elect those who adopt the manner of this widow caught in unjust circumstances; on the strength of this metaphor, "crying out to God" (v 7) must be correlated with practices consistent with the dogged pursuit of justice (vv 2-5).

Jesus' message in 17:22-37 admits the same reality as that portended by the parable — namely, that God's people will be the objects of unjust actions within an unjust world. In light of that eventuality, vv 7-8a maintain both the certainty and the imminence of vindication.[99] This emphasis serves a critical purpose for Luke, underscoring the necessity of faithful constancy — the sort of faithfulness exhibited by the widow of Jesus' parable. This faith has been narratologically expounded with reference to its pursuit of justice, its fundamental orientation and expectant openness to God's beneficence, and its astonishing persistence. With this, Jesus' eschatological teaching has come full circle since 17:20-21. Having begun with a question about the eschatological timetable from the Pharisees, Jesus has repeatedly — and now finally — insisted on changing the terms of the discussion and, therefore, of end-time speculation. The question is not When? or Where? but, given the present

---

98. See, e.g., Deut 4:37; 7:7; 1 Chr 16:13; Pss 77:31; 88:3; 105:6; Isa 43:20; Rom 8:33; Col 3:12; 1 Pet 1:1; et al.

99. The meaning of v 7b is much disputed — cf. Catchpole, "Son of Man's Search," 92-101; Marshall, 674-75. On the basis of the polysemy of μακροθυμέω, some have taken v 7b to refer to God's patience with the elect. Thus, e.g., Nolland, 2:865: "He [will indeed show himself] long-suffering with them" (cf. Johnson, 268, 270). But the plausibility of this rendering is mitigated generally by the co-text, which does not otherwise concern God's patience with the elect, and more specifically by v 8a, which functions well as providing an immediate and negative answer to the question of v 7b, "Will he delay long?" See the parallel thought in Sir 35:19.

activity of God and its promised, certain consummation, How will people respond?

The urgency of Jesus' question about faithfulness resides in the fact that it finds its sharpest expression in a discourse aimed at his own disciples, and even more so because Luke relates Jesus' question without reference to a particular group of people: Will this sort of faith be found *on earth?* In this way, Jesus' warning about persistence in the face of wrong speaks at all times, everywhere, to all, until the coming of the Son of Man.

5.6.3. How to Enter the Kingdom (18:9–19:27)

This narrative segment has the closest ties to the foregoing material — including such specific connections as a continued focus on the motif of prayer (18:1-8, 9-14) and an overall increase in the frequency of travel notices (18:31, 35; 19:1, 11); as well as the more general, thematic concern with fitness for the kingdom. Indeed, Luke provides no textual markers to suggest that the narrative has taken a significant turn with 18:9. However, 18:8 forms an *inclusio* with 17:20; the whole of 17:20–18:8 is set off from surrounding material by its eschatological focus (to which Jesus will return in 19:11-27); and, having broached the question of faithful comportment with regard to the present and impending work of God in 17:20–18:8, Jesus turns to this issue in earnest in this new section.

Apart from the aforementioned travel notices, Luke provides little in 18:9–19:27 by way of narrative structure. The result is that this segment of the Gospel is characterized by a pronounced episodic feel that may mask the important thematic connections between each scene. An important ribbon tying all of this material together is the motif of division, between those who have faith/act faithfully and others, the self-possessed, those concerned with their own honor and position, those who look with contempt on those in need and actually position themselves as a barrier between the needy and the compassionate God at work in Jesus' ministry.

The basic issue is this: Who recognizes God as the gracious benefactor? Who are those who not only come to God openhandedly in trust and expectation, but also behave accordingly, with graciousness, toward others. Coming as it does at the end of the travel narrative, the series of contrasts developed in this narrative segment confronts Luke's audience with the need for clear choices in relationship to the nature of Jesus' mission and their identification with God's salvific purpose. The need for self-evaluation and appropriate response is rendered urgent, too, by Luke's portrait of the disciples. The last we hear of them in this narrative segment concerns their lack of understanding (18:31-34), after which they fade temporarily into the background. The general lack of distinction between these followers and others who witness Jesus' ministry is disconcerting.

5.6.3.1. A Parable concerning the Self-possessed (18:9-14)

9 *He also told this parable to some who relied on*[100] *themselves because*[101] *they were righteous and regarded others with contempt:* 10 *"Two men went up to the temple to pray, one a Pharisee and the other a toll*[102] *collector.* 11 *The Pharisee, standing by himself, was praying thus, 'God, I thank you that I am not like other people: thieves, rogues, adulterers, or even like this toll collector.* 12 *I fast twice a week; I give a tenth of all my income.'* 13 *But the toll collector, standing far off, would not even look up to heaven, but was beating his breast and saying, 'God, be merciful to me, a sinner!'* 14 *I tell you, this man went down to his home justified rather than the other; for all who exalt themselves will be humbled, but all who humble themselves will be exalted."*

Having developed something of the nature of the kingdom, the Third Evangelist begins with this narrative segment to emphasize more pointedly the nature of fitness for the kingdom of God. The interrelatedness of this pericope to the preceding is easily discerned, however. First, v 9 contains nothing to suggest a change of scene. Second, although the designation of the audience of Jesus' parable seems to assume an expanded audience, the disciples — toward whom the discourse of 17:22–18:8 had been oriented — seem also to be present. This again suggests that the borders separating Jesus' followers from others remain porous at this juncture. Moreover, it warns against the facile identification of "some who relied on themselves" (v 9) as Pharisees.[103]

Finally, this and the immediately preceding pericope (vv 1-8) ostensibly have to do with prayer — "ostensibly" since, in each case, much more is at stake than prayer when defined modestly as a "practice." In these pericopae, prayer is metonymic for a person's dispositions and practices; that is, Jesus uses prayer to speak to the issue of what sort of people, with what sort of character and commitments as well as behaviors, are fit for the kingdom of God. Given the Lukan theme of reversal, it is noteworthy but not surprising that, again in both pericopae, a person of low social rank is found to be worthy of emulation by Jesus' followers.

The primary structural feature shaping our reading of this unit is the point-for-point polarization between the two characters of the parable. This

---

100. NRSV: "trusted in."

101. NRSV: "that."

102. NRSV: "toll"; also in vv 11 and 13.

103. *Contra*, e.g., Downing, "Pharisee and Toll-collector," 86; Darr, *Character Building*, 114; Neale, *None but the Sinners*, 114.

contrast begins already in the way the parable is framed, then continues through the parable itself and into the conclusion Jesus draws from it:[104]

The Pharisee	The Toll Collector
"some who relied on themselves because they were righteous and regarded others with contempt" (v 9)	"others" regarded with contempt (v 9; cf. v 11)
"one a Pharisee" (v 10)	"the other a toll collector" (v 10)
"standing by himself" (v 11a)	"standing far off" (v 13a)
thanks God for his state of righteousness (vv 11b-12)	addresses God in humility as a sinner with a request for reconciliation (v 13b)
returned home without justification (v 14a)	returned home justified (v 14a)
"all who exalt themselves will be humbled" (v 14b)	"all who humble themselves will be exalted" (v 14b)

Insofar as Luke's audience will identify themselves with one or the other of these characters, then, Luke has structured this account so as to render the choices starkly and to ensure that the toll collector will be viewed, however paradoxically, as the positive model.

9 The connection of this parable to the former one is marked by Luke's "also."[105] In an important sense this connective ties both this parable and indeed this whole narrative segment (18:9–19:27) to Jesus' message concerning the kingdom. Having developed the nature of the kingdom of God, Luke now recounts material concerning fitness for it.

As with 15:1-2; 18:1, so this verse provides as a literary frame the interpretive context within which the ensuing parabolic material takes its meaning. The lack of any detail concerning Jesus' audience, together with the fact that the disciples have been present in the foregoing (17:22), tells against any attempt on our part to specify further against whom Jesus relates this parable. This is important since our tendency is often to fill in gaps such as these, and to do so in ways that ensure that others, not us, are indicted by Jesus' words.

The "some" to whom the parable is aimed are characterized by parallel

---

104. So also Neale, *None but the Sinners*, 169-70.
105. εἶπεν δὲ καί.

statements.[106] First, having become convinced of their own righteousness, they have come to depend on themselves.[107] They are self-possessed, able, at least in their own minds, to live honorably before God quite apart from divine mercy. On the other hand, they disdain others,[108] their concerns with holiness manifested in the exclusion of others from their circles. We may be tempted to think that Luke has in mind legal experts and Pharisees, and not without good reason. After all, they have repeatedly been shown to be persons who, distinguishing themselves from others, exalt themselves.[109] But lines cannot be drawn so easily, with disciples always in danger of Pharisaic behavior (see 12:1-2) and, in fact, having already demonstrated comparable self-possession (see 9:46-50).[110] Luke's frame, then, is not designed so much around identifying as the culprit a particular Jewish group as to identify a *habitus,* a set of dispositions and commitments that generate practices, perceptions, and attitudes that are set in opposition to the way of the kingdom of God. While the Pharisees, especially when they appear in tandem with the scribes, are often identified as possessed by this way of life, within Luke-Acts this is not true of them always nor of them exclusively. Luke's purpose is not to condemn a particular group but to warn against a particular way of comporting oneself in light of the present and impending reign of God.

10 Jesus sets the parable in the courts of the temple in Jerusalem.[111] The temple is known as a place of prayer,[112] and the scene Jesus paints is consistent either with public prayer (as a part of daily temple service) or with prayer in public.[113] The temple has a function over and above its import as a place of prayer. This is its role as a "cultural center" — that is, that place in Jewish society where the world is ordered through its layout of courts that segregate Jews and Gentiles, men and women, priests and nonpriests, clean and unclean; and thus the divinely legitimated hub that mirrors as well as communicates and sustains the boundaries of social relations and experiences

---

106. τούς, then, is modified by both of the ensuing accusative, plural, masculine participles.

107. This way of understanding πέποιθα + ἐπί is suggested by Sand, "πείθω."

108. ἐξουθενέω appears in Luke-Acts elsewhere only in 23:11; Acts 4:11.

109. Cf., e.g., 10:29; 11:37-44; 14:1-14; 15:1-2; 16:14-17.

110. In fact, one of the significant aims of Luke's own rhetoric seems to be to address just such tendencies among Christians of his own discourse situation. See Beck, *Christian Character,* 127-44.

111. That it is the Jerusalem temple is clear from the topographical designations "up" and "down," denoting the relatively higher elevation of Jerusalem and the temple (vv 10, 14); cf. 2:22, 42, 51; Acts 3:1; et al. It is not possible to be more specific about the whereabouts of the location of these two men within the walls of the temple.

112. Cf. 1:9; 19:46; 24:53; Acts 2:46; 3:1; 22:17.

113. See K. E. Bailey, *Through Peasant Eyes,* 144-47; Bailey emphasizes that "private devotions" are not in view here.

of fictive kinship among the Jewish people.[114] The socio-religious distinctions that form the core of the potency of the temple in Lukan thought come immediately to expression in what follows.

The social polarization foregrounded in v 9 is concretized with the introduction of two men who serve as ideal characters in the parable. Pharisees are well known within the Third Gospel. Heretofore, their primary role has been as persons who inspect Jesus' faithfulness to the law; insofar as he has repeatedly interpreted the law in ways that depart from conventions shared by the Pharisees, they are often cast as his antagonists. In addition, Pharisees appear as persons concerned with self-promotion.[115] Even if those "who relied on themselves because they were righteous" cannot be taken as an exclusive or general designation of the Pharisees in Luke's Gospel, it is thus not surprising that a Pharisee represents such persons here. Toll collectors, too, are well known to Luke's readers. They are regularly found among those who respond positively to the good news, even if they are regarded as outsiders by the pious.[116] Hence, although it is easy to find this toll collector in the company of the repugnant "others" of v 9 (and v 11; cf. 5:29), Luke's readers are predisposed to give him at least the benefit of the doubt. Indeed, in light of the appearance of Pharisees and toll collectors on opposite sides of the purpose of God in 7:29-30, it is difficult to anticipate an alternative outcome in the scene Jesus has prepared.

11-12   Jesus' portrayal of this Pharisee operates at two levels. On the one hand, he is engaged in and admits to behavior characteristic of Pharisees: praying, fasting, and tithing (5:33; 11:42). In and of themselves, these are admirable practices for which scriptural warrant is easily found.[117] Fasting might be undertaken for any of a variety of pious purposes — for example, to ready oneself for service, to prepare oneself for communication with God, as a sign of repentance, and so on. Scriptural charges concerning fasting and tithing would only have been a baseline to a Pharisee like this, however. He did not limit fasting to the prescribed days, but fasted twice a week; similarly, he did not struggle with which items of produce required a tithe, but gave a tenth of everything.[118] It is crucial to remember that such ardent behavior as

---

114. The idea of "culture center" is borrowed from Geertz, *Local Knowledge,* esp. 122-23. This Lukan perspective on the temple is developed in Green, "Demise of the Temple," esp. 509-11.

115. See the summary remarks in Green, *Gospel of Luke,* 72-74.

116. See 3:12; 5:27-32; 7:29, 34; 15:1-2. On toll collectors more generally, see on 3:12.

117. On fasting, cf., e.g., Lev 16:29-31; Deut 9:9; 2 Sam 1:12; 12:16-23; Esth 4:16; Dan 9:3. On tithing, e.g., Lev 27:30-33; Num 18:21-32; Deut 14:22-27.

118. On fasting, cf. Böhl, "Fasten." The Pharisee could tithe what he himself produced, as the law required; the problem arose when procuring produce in the marketplace, produce on which he could be sure a tithe had been rendered. Although Scripture does not resolve this conundrum, the Pharisee did so by tithing on *every*thing. Cf. Westerholm, *Jesus,* 53-55.

this would have served as an important boundary marker, signifying conformity not only to Torah but also to the forms of Torah-interpretation specific to this Pharisee's community. This helps to set him apart from those "other people" named in his prayer.

We turn, secondly, to the content of the Pharisee's prayer, which, within its Lukan co-text, can only be understood ironically. Of course, drawing distinctions — whether as "separatists" or as those who "specify" the correct interpretation of Torah — is endemic to Pharisaic identity historically. So it is neither surprising nor necessarily a negative thing to see this Pharisee separate himself from persons who do not take Torah seriously. (Vice lists within the NT epistolary literature — e.g., 1 Cor 5:10-11; 6:9-10 — serve much the same function.) Indeed, it is fully appropriate that he thank God that he has been spared from a corrupt life.[119] What is striking is (1) that the Pharisee's prayer begins like a thanksgiving psalm, but never enumerates the divine actions for which one is thankful.[120] For God's acts, the Pharisee has substituted his own. (2) It is also telling that this Pharisee seems to place himself (and presumably those with similar practices) in one camp and *all others* in the category of thieves, rogues, and adulterers. With this list, he seems to have caricatured every form of possible sin — robbery, reprobation, and immorality[121] — and declared all other humans as guilty of them.

(3) Moreover, this Pharisee physically separates himself from others in the temple,[122] then, in public prayer, maintains the honor of his own piety at the expense of the toll collector, whom he regards as embodying the very essence of "otherness." (4) Finally, we must not overlook the reality that in Luke's narration even Pharisees must count themselves among the "others"

---

119. At this level of interpretation, Neale (*None but the Sinners,* 173-75) and Hedrick (*Parables,* 224-25) are justified in finding no fault in the Pharisee's prayer. See the parallels in 1QH 7:34; *b. Ber.* 28b.

120. Cf., e.g., Psalms 30; 92; 118; 136; 138; 1QH.

121. So Hedrick, *Parables,* 220-21: "robbery — violent theft of property; reprobate — impious as to religious obligations; adultery — sins of the flesh, i.e., immorality" (221).

122. The function of πρὸς ἑαυτόν in the phrase σταθεὶς πρὸς ἑαυτὸν ταῦτα προσηύχετο is ambiguous: "standing by himself, praying these things" or "standing, praying these things to/concerning himself"? Hedrick (*Parables,* 217) collects lexical information in favor of the former, then adopts the latter, motivated apparently by his attempt to rehabilitate this Pharisee. The former also parallels more clearly the stance of the toll collector in v 13, an important factor given the pervasiveness of this parallelism in this text. The possibility that we are to imagine the Pharisee praying to himself rather than to God is voided by the actual content of the prayer, "God, I thank you. . . ." Soliloquy is introduced elsewhere with the preposition ἐν. See K. E. Bailey, *Through Peasant Eyes,* 147-48.

from whom this Pharisee distances himself! In 11:39, Jesus indicts them for rapacity; in 11:42; 16:15 he questions their commitment to justice; and in 16:18 he charges them with relaxing the laws of divorce so that they leave themselves open to charges of adultery (see above on these texts). Pharisees, in other words, have been censured for doing exactly what this Pharisee is now doing — namely, asserting their own righteousness (16:15).

13-14   The polarity begun in v 9 continues, with Jesus' narration of the toll collector matching that of the Pharisee point-for-point, type and anti-type (see above). Like the Pharisee, the toll collector stands apart from others in the temple, but it quickly becomes obvious that their actions are differently motivated. Within his social world, the toll collector is a person of low status, a deviant; he has no place among the others, nor does he attempt to seize a place by asserting his honor. Averting his eyes, beating his breasts — these are demonstrations of humility and shame[123] that are consistent with his request for divine favor. Some have puzzled over the lack of any explicit reference to repentance in the toll collector's prayer.[124] The motif of repentance may reside in the act of "beating his breast" (cf. *Jos. An.* 10:15). It is not at all clear, however, that the toll collector *needs* to repent of specific wrongdoing. As 3:12 discloses, within Luke-Acts the vocation of a toll collector is not intrinsically sinful, irrespective of the labels provided toll collectors by others (v 11!). Like Peter (5:8), so the toll collector recognizes his state of unworthiness before God and confesses his need for reconciliation.[125]

According to Luke, Jesus' reading of this parable treats these two men in a way that idealizes one quality in each. One claims superior status for himself by comparing himself with and separating himself from others; the other makes no claims to status at all, but acknowledges his position as a sinner who can take refuge only in the beneficence of God. Convinced of his righteousness, dependent on his own acts of piety, one asks for and receives nothing from God. The other comes to God in humility and receives that for which he asks, compassion and restoration. Like other "sinners" in the Third Gospel, he finds himself included among God's people (5:29-32; 7:29, 34; 15:1-2). The connection between this parable and Jesus' earlier discourse with the Pharisees about status-seeking, where the proverb about exaltation and humiliation is first heard, is unmistakable (14:7-11).

123. See 23:48; Josephus *Ant.* 7.10.5 §252; Ezra 9:6; *1 Enoch* 13:5; *Jos. As.* 10:15.
124. Hedrick (*Parables,* 226-27), e.g., casts doubt on the exemplary character of the toll collector precisely on these grounds: He wants mercy without repentance.
125. The NRSV translates the imperative of ἱλάσκομαι as, "Be merciful . . . !" Both from the standpoint of lexical semantics and in light of the presence of the praying toll collector in the temple, we should think more broadly of reconciliation.

5.6.3.2. Receiving Children, Receiving the Kingdom (18:15-17)

15 *People were bringing even infants to him that he might touch them; and when the disciples saw it, they sternly ordered them not to do it.* 16 *But Jesus called for them and said, "Let the little children come to me, and do not stop them; for the kingdom of God consists of such as these.*[126] 17 *Truly I tell you, whoever does not receive the kingdom of God as a little child will never enter it."*

Polarity regarding status honor has just occupied Jesus, and he closes his parabolic teaching with a reaffirmation of value-transposition effective through his ministry (18:9-14; cf. 1:46-55; 14:11). Immediately following are two episodes that serve as striking exemplars of that message of reversal, the first (18:15-17) treating the blessedness of those of the most humble status, the second (18:18-30) concerned with a person of elevated rank. Luke narrates no change of scene in either v 15 or v 18; though new characters are introduced in each, there is no hint that the interactions Luke recounts occur before a different audience than that assumed in v 9. In fact, the active presence of the disciples (v 15) verifies that the disciples were present for Jesus' parable about the Pharisee and toll collector, and that they have thus far failed to internalize its message.

In Roman antiquity, babies were susceptible to adverse conditions of all kinds, resulting in a high mortality rate among children. Jesus' touch, then, as in former scenes, will have communicated divine blessing, perhaps even healing.[127] The disciples' reaction to those seeking such beneficence and Jesus' subsequent response to the disciples turn on two motifs already woven into the fabric of the Third Gospel: a cultural script concerning the status of children in the Greco-Roman world and the significance of hospitality.

Although it is easy to romanticize about children with respect to this pericope, such qualities as "innocence," "openness to the future," and "trusting" are not the first ones that come to mind when reviewing general perceptions of children in the first century.[128] We have already noted the high mortality rate about young children; added to this is the simple observation that children were viewed as "not adults." They might be valued for their present or future contribution to the family business, especially in an agricultural context, but otherwise they possessed little if any intrinsic value as human beings. Luke's phrase "even infants" draws attention to the particular vulner-

126. NRSV: "for it is to such as these that the kingdom of God belongs."
127. See 5:13; 6:19; 7:14; 8:44-47.
128. See Rawson, ed., *Family in Ancient Rome; idem, Marriage, Divorce, and Children;* Garnsey and Saller, *Roman Empire,* 136-41; what follows is indebted to the summary in Green, *Gospel of Luke,* 118.

ability of the smallest of children, perhaps accounting for the widespread practice of infanticide and child abandonment — and, thus, for the suitability of the infant as a particularly effective example of the lowliness accented in vv 9-14.[129] "Little children," on the other hand, translates a term used for household slaves and children, those maintained in a relationship of subordination in a Greco-Roman household.[130] Against this cultural horizon, the response of the disciples is easily understood, even justifiable. Why should Jesus' time be taken up with persons of such little importance, especially when a "ruler" was waiting in the wings (v 18)? On the other hand, Jesus has already called into question this way of constructing human relations — explicitly in 9:46-48, most recently in 18:9-14.

Hospitality has also played an important role in the Lukan narrative (e.g., 7:36-50), and it is central to this pericope. As Jesus makes clear in his response to the disciples, in denying children access to Jesus, the disciples have refused to welcome children. Yet, "receiving the kingdom" is intimately tied to "receiving little children." That is, the wording of v 17 masks an ellipsis: "Whoever does not receive the kingdom of God as *one receives* a little child will never enter it."[131] "Receiving little children" is tantamount to granting them hospitality, performing for them actions (washing of feet, kiss of greeting, and anointing the head — 7:44-46) normally reserved for those of equal or higher status. That is, Jesus is asking his followers to embrace a topsy-turvy system of values and to extend respectful service to that social group most often overlooked.

The rationale for such behavior is straightforward. It grows out of a transformed sense of the way the world works, one based on the power of the kingdom of God to deconstruct those worldly systems and values that stand in opposition to God's project. In this light, the action of the disciples is all the more self-indicting. Jesus "rebukes" whatever contests God's redemptive purpose;[132] as they rebuke those bringing children to Jesus, the disciples find themselves contesting the divine purpose, demonstrating their complete incomprehension concerning the nature of God's project. Here Jesus' teaching

129. So Schneider, 2:366-67. βρέφος, for "infant," also appears in 2:12, 16; Acts 7:19.

130. Bühner, "παῖς," 5.

131. Actually, with respect to Luke's ὡς, three interpretive possibilities present themselves: (1) "as one receives a little child"; (2) "as though one were a little child"; and (3) "as a little child receives it." The first is supported by the emphasis throughout this pericope on hospitality to children; it also conforms to the message of 9:48. The first two would be virtually identical in effect, since both assume self-humility. The third must be read into the text, since children otherwise have no active role in this passage.

132. ἐπιτιμάω; cf. 4:35, 39, 41; 8:24; 9:21, 42, 55.

on the kingdom is concerned with who is included[133] and how its leaders ought to function.[134] Failing to understand how the inbreaking kingdom undermines and supplants conventional canons of honor and status, the disciples fail to grasp God's concern for those held in lowest regard, fail to comport themselves with humility so as to share that concern, and fail to function as Jesus' agents. Having refused to extend respectful service to the socially marginalized, having misconstrued the nature of the kingdom, how will they ever enter it?

5.6.3.3. The Problem of Power and Wealth (18:18-30)

18 *A certain ruler asked him, "Good Teacher, what must I do to inherit eternal life?"* 19 *Jesus said to him, "Why do you call me good? No one is good but God alone.* 20 *You know the commandments: 'You shall not commit adultery; You shall not murder; You shall not steal; You shall not bear false witness; Honor your father and mother.'"* 21 *He replied, "I have kept all these since my youth."* 22 *When Jesus heard this, he said to him, "There is still one thing lacking. Sell all that you own and distribute the money to the poor, and you will have treasure in heaven; then come, follow me."* 23 *But when he heard this, he became sad; for he was very rich.* 24 *Jesus looked at him and said, "How hard it is for those who have wealth to enter the kingdom of God!* 25 *Indeed, it is easier for a camel to go through the eye of a needle than for someone who is rich to enter the kingdom of God."*

26 *Those who heard it said, "Then who can be saved?"* 27 *He replied, "What is impossible for mortals is possible for God."*

28 *Then Peter said, "Look, we have left what is ours[135] and followed you."* 29 *And he said to them, "Truly I tell you, there is no one who has left house or wife or brothers or parents or children, for the sake of the kingdom of God,* 30 *who will not get back very much more in this age, and in the age to come eternal life."*

The beginning of this narrative unit is stamped by the introduction of "a certain ruler," who remains present throughout the entire scene;[136] only in v 31 does the setting change, with Jesus sequestering the disciples for a rare

---

133. The translation of τῶν γὰρ τοιούτων is difficult; here it is regarded as a genitive of material.

134. Cf. Tannehill, "Kingdom," 20-21.

135. NRSV: "our homes."

136. Note in v 23, the ruler's negative response to the call to discipleship does not result in his departure; in fact, Jesus addresses him directly in v 24.

moment of private instruction. Luke narrates Jesus' interchange with the wealthy ruler immediately adjacent to the incident with the children, providing no textual markers to suggest a shift in scene. Though this contributes to the episodic feel of this larger section of the Lukan Gospel, we would be mistaken to think that the location of this narrative unit lacked purpose or significance. As we noted earlier, the juxtaposition of "little children" and a wealthy ruler ties these two incidents (vv 15-17, 18-30) together as an apt illustration of the principle of status transposition Jesus articulates in v 14 (cf. 1:51-53; 2:34; 6:20-26; et al.).

In addition to their sharing the theme of status reversal, this and the preceding pericope are joined by a common interest in the kingdom of God and, more generally, in soteriology and discipleship. Luke draws together several soteriological images in vv 18-30: "eternal life" (vv 18, 31 — which, then, serve as an *inclusio* for this narrative unit), "treasure in heaven" (v 22), "[entering] the kingdom of God" (vv 24 [2x], 29), and "being saved" (v 26). In the current scene, the movement from one metaphor to the next is significant for the way it shapes what is essentially a concern with future salvation on the part of the ruler (v 18) into a message about the presence of salvation and its demands (cf. 17:20-21), together with the future implications of present commitments and practices. In this way, "inheriting eternal life" is correlated with "entering the kingdom," the immediate concern of Jesus' interaction with the disciples concerning the status of children in this world and the next (vv 15-17).

The makeup of Jesus' audience, its size and diversity, has unraveled slowly, to include Pharisees in 17:20, disciples in 17:22, some with confidence in their own righteousness in 18:9, and people bringing children in 18:15. Now, we discover, that audience also included a wealthy ruler. This means that he, like the others, has been privy to Jesus' instruction — not least concerning the humiliation of the self-possessed and the place of those of lowest status, children, in the kingdom of God. Given his own status as a wealthy ruler, then, it is not without good reason that he inquires concerning how he might gain eternal life, even if the nature of his question and the shape of his response indicate how little he has understood of Jesus' message thus far. In this, he is not alone: Note the response of "those who heard" in v 26: like him, they continue to work under the values of the old world system, failing to account for the radical quality of Jesus' teaching on the power of the kingdom of God to overturn the value systems of this world.

Finally, the location of this pericope is important for the way it portrays the disciples. In the previous scene, we were left with a charge against the disciples that seemed devastating. In spite of their best (and, given normal protocols, justifiable) intentions, they were found actually working against God's purposes. Their conventional concerns with status and propriety would seem to have disqualified them from entry into the kingdom of God. Here, Luke recounts their rehabilitation, at least partially, as they are reminded of their basic commitments and identity. They are those who had answered the call to discipleship by leaving all. They had left their old lives in order to embrace new life as defined within the ministry of Jesus.

In some ways, then, this is an unsuccessful story, especially when read as an account of a quest or as a call narrative. The wealthy ruler comes searching but at the moment of discovery turns away. Jesus calls one to discipleship who does not embrace life with Jesus. This does not mean that this scene is without positive significance, however. Luke uses the interaction between Jesus and the ruler to help define again the particularity of the community oriented toward Jesus, a community of those who embody the values of the kingdom of God. They are those who distance themselves from the status conventions of this world, who find their devotion in God and not in "what they have," who undertake a radical disposition of their possessions on behalf of the poor, and who follow Jesus in discipleship (vv 22, 28-29). They are the ones who, having entered the kingdom, will inherit life eternal.

18-19 Without intervening information regarding a change of setting, Luke introduces "a certain ruler." Consequently, we are to imagine this man as having been present for Jesus' instruction thus far, and, then, that his question is motivated by it. If one must receive the kingdom of God as one receives a child (v 17), how might a ruler gain eternal life? This question is all the more pressing within the Lukan narrative, where "rulers" are usually portrayed negatively, as those of elevated social status, more often than not related to the synagogue.[137]

Our estimation of his address is mixed. On the one hand, it is nearly identical to that of the legal expert in 10:25. "Teacher" is a title of respect in the Lukan narrative, and is often used by those outside the circle of Jesus' followers who hope to learn from or receive something from Jesus.[138] The question of "doing" is not itself problematic within the Third Gospel, since for Luke one's dispositions, one's commitments and attitudes, are intimately related to one's practices (cf., e.g., 3:7-14; 8:1-21; 10:25-28). Indeed, Deuteronomy 6:16-25 develops the relationship between obedience to the law and inheritance, and apocalyptic Judaism had amplified the notion of "inheritance," initially a reference to the land of promise, so as to embrace the life

---

137. See 1:51, which announces that the powerful are brought down from their thrones. For ἄρχων (and compounds) with respect to synagogue leadership, cf. 8:41, 49; 13:14; Acts 13:15; 18:8, 17. On status issues, see 14:1. The term is used for a magistrate in 12:58. That a religious "ruler" is meant here is supported in vv 20-21. Cf. Klinghardt, *Gesetz*, 132-35.

138. διδάσκαλος; cf. 6:40; 7:40; 8:49; 9:38; 10:25; et al.

of the coming age (cf. Dan 12:2). Apart from the suggestion that the ruler sees salvation predominantly in future terms, then, his question must thus far be evaluated positively.

In comparison with 10:25, the one added element in the ruler's question is the modifier, "good," and it is to this that Jesus takes offense. This is because, in spite of Jesus' preceding instruction on issues of status and honor (vv 14-17), in addressing him as "Good Teacher" the ruler is engaged in a word game deeply rooted in concerns with status. According to this linguistic system, one commendation deserves another. Thus, even in the way the ruler addresses Jesus he signifies his commitment to a particular set of conventions, his identity within a particular social group, and his understanding of the speech event he has initiated.[139] Jesus' counterstatement concerning God's goodness thus not only echoes an important scriptural motif[140] but also serves notice that the terms of this interaction will not be set by the standard values to which the ruler has already paid homage.

20-22 Particularly if this "ruler" is not only a person of elevated social status but one who exercises his leadership within the context of the synagogue, the commandments Jesus lists are unremarkable. Jesus himself asserts his awareness that the ruler will have known the commandments, so the ruler's record of obedience seems almost assumed and in any case passes without challenge.[141] Such synopses of the Ten Commandments typically are not meant to be remarkable in Jewish contexts, but generally serve to provide a baseline from which one might articulate more precisely how they are to be understood within particular communities. That is, what is remarkable about such lists of the Commandments as this one is not the lists themselves but their interpretation, especially with regard to elements added to them. In this way they serve apologetic functions, distinguishing the particular character of a given community of interpretation.[142]

Jesus thus introduces these five commandments not in order to induct the ruler into their realm of influence, but to initiate him into a discussion of their particular appropriation within the community of Jesus' followers. These five commandments all have to do with kinship and community relations. The middle of the five concerns material possessions, but even it, when understood within the context of the experience of Exodus and formation of Israel as the people of God, must be understood as a signifier of

---

139. That address forms carry such significance, see Fasold, *Sociolinguistics,* 1-38. See also K. E. Bailey, *Through Peasant Eyes,* 162. For other possible interpretations, see Fitzmyer, 2:1197-99; Salo, *Luke's Treatment of the Law,* 153.

140. See, e.g., 1 Chr 16:34; 2 Chr 5:13; Pss 25:8; 34:8; 53:6; 72:1; et al.

141. The possibility of such faithfulness vis-à-vis the law is asserted, e.g., in 1:6; Acts 23:1; Phil 3:6.

142. See the important discussion in Klinghardt, *Gesetz,* 124-35.

human relationships, for within its historical and scriptural context, the admonition against stealing is essentially an affirmation of the priority of the community of God's people: Do not take for yourself what Yahweh has provided for the whole people of God.[143] This provides the point from which Jesus can launch his own interpretation of obedience to the will of God, so that his charge concerning the disposition of material goods on behalf of the poor must be understood (1) as an interpretive expansion of the Ten Commandments that (2) serves as a behavioral definition of the community of Jesus' followers. Jesus' use of the table of commandments from Deut 5:16-20 (cf. Exod 20:12-16), then, is apologetic; it defines the community of those who will "inherit eternal life."

This interpretation is supported by the linguistic connections between this pericope and the Lukan summary of the early community of disciples in Acts 4:32-35.[144] It is also consistent with the practice of the disciples (cf. 5:1, 28; 18:28) and above all with Jesus' repeated assertion that no one can be his disciple apart from the abdication of one's possessions (cf. 12:32-34; 14:33).[145] Jesus' message does not foreground poverty as an ascetic ideal; he does not counsel simple renunciation. Rather, the disposition of one's material goods is for the sake of the poor. Such an act is pregnant with significance. First, it embraces the biblical concern for the poor (e.g., Exod 23:11; Lev 19:9-16; Deut 15:1-18; et al.). Second, it participates in the orientation of Jesus' Spirit-anointed ministry toward "the poor" — those who live on the margins of society for reasons of economic destitution and/or status deprivation (see above on 4:18-19). Third, it signifies a thoroughgoing rejection of concerns with status honor and the predominant system of giving and receiving tied to enhancing one's honor in the community and to augmenting one's power over others. Such giving as that counseled by Jesus must be without expectation of return since its recipients are those incapable of reciprocation.[146] Fourth, it denotes identification with Jesus, who possesses no home and for whom hospitality is never assured (9:58).

In short, Jesus' answer to the ruler's question takes seriously how wealth is intricately spun together with issues of status, power, and social privilege.[147] His answer has the dual effect of defining the commitments and behaviors characteristic of the community of his followers and of undercutting completely the social conventions that governed the ruler's life and commu-

143. See Gnuse, *You Shall Not Steal*.
144. See the use of διάδος in v 22 and Acts 4:35; and of τὰ ἴδια in v 28 and in Acts 4:32.
145. See above, §11.
146. So Moxnes, *Economy of the Kingdom*, 119, 156. On models of reciprocity and economic exchange operative in Luke's world, see above, §10.
147. See Green, *Gospel of Luke*, 113-17.

nity. The kingdom of God calls for including the marginalized in one's circle of kin, for the abolition of status disjunctions, for giving without expectation of return — deviant behavior all, behavior that would lead to the ruler's loss of social standing *and* to his capacity to identify with the poor for whom the good news has come (cf. 4:18-19)

23-27   Luke records two responses to Jesus' teaching — by the ruler and by the standers-by — as well as Jesus' own commentary on the impossibility of his message. The ruler, faced with the wholesale rejection of his understanding of God and of the world, responds with deep sadness. "Those who heard" Jesus' teaching respond with inquisitive protest, "Then who can be saved?"[148] Both responses emanate from a common theology that posits a causal relationship between divine blessing and the possession of power, privilege, and material possessions. The literature of Israel and of Judaism provides ample evidence of the ongoing struggle concerning the relation of poverty and divine blessing;[149] there one hears important witnesses to a biographical understanding of poverty and wealth, as though these conditions were the consequence of laziness and industriousness, wickedness and righteousness, respectively.[150] This is not the only voice, of course, and one can point to both legal and prophetic texts that portray issues of poverty and wealth in systemic terms. As the book of Job testifies, however, conventional thinking is hard to escape. What is more, within the world Luke portrays, those in charge of the interpretation of Scripture are typically those of elevated status who rule over the synagogue and/or temple, and who find in this common theology a source of legitimation.

Jesus is not unaware of the pervasiveness of a theology that runs counter to his own. Indeed, he recognizes its potency when he affirms how hard it is for those with wealth to enter the kingdom of God. What is remarkable is that this theology grips not only the very rich, like the ruler of this encounter (v 23), but any who have wealth![151] This is reminiscent of John's teaching, wherein wealth is construed as having an extra cloak or additional food to share (3:10-11). The phrases "to enter the kingdom" and "to enter through the eye of a needle"[152] are set in parallel[153] in order to underscore

148. Luke provides no basis in the text for identifying those who thus respond to Jesus; cf. v 9a.

149. Cf. Pleins, "Poor, Poverty: Old Testament."

150. See esp. Deuteronomy 28 and Proverbs.

151. Luke uses χρῆμα here and in Acts 4:37; 8:18, 20; 24:26.

152. K. E. Bailey (*Through Peasant Eyes,* 165-66) puts to rest all attempts to mollify the starkness of this proverbial saying; he also draws attention to a rabbinic parallel that trades on the impossibility of "an elephant going through the eye of a needle" (*b. Ber.* 55b).

153. Both use the verb εἰσέρχομαι.

the sheer impossibility of pulling away from the gravity of wealth in order to embrace a world order in which status distinctions are irrelevant on account of the prevenient extension of God's graciousness to everyone. As Jesus has already stressed, wealth has the capacity to summon constancy that contests fidelity to God, just as it leads to practices of violence against the poor that run counter to the orientation of the good news to the poor (see above on 16:13).

"Entering the kingdom of God" stands as a synonym to "being saved" in this exchange only in an ironic way, since these two expressions, used by different persons, also derive from different worldviews. "Entering the kingdom," we have just learned, has to do with humbling oneself to the point of showing deference to the lowest in society, children — this, at least, is how Jesus uses the phrase (vv 14, 17). When "those who heard" use the term "to be saved," they indicate their failure to understand this interpretation of salvation in terms of status reversal. They have not escaped the grips of the rule of mammon. Nor can they, according to Jesus, apart from divine assistance.

28-30 The possibility of salvation, theoretical in v 27, is now exemplified concretely in the lives of the disciples. As their spokesperson (cf. 9:20, 33), Peter recalls that he and the others have done precisely what Jesus had asked of the ruler (see 5:11, 28). Note the parallelism:

"Sell all that you own and . . . follow me" (v 22).
"We have left what is ours and followed you" (v 28).

This constitutes a critical affirmation of the disciples, whose faithfulness was on the dock on account of the roadblock they had constructed against those bringing children to Jesus in vv 15-17. To be sure, it is not an unqualified endorsement; after all, it comes from the disciples themselves[154] and is modulated almost immediately in the private interaction Luke records in vv 31-34. Nevertheless, it serves to distinguish the disciples from the wealthy ruler whose response to the call to follow Jesus is negative. Luke's narration indicates the importance of their initial resolution to embrace a new way of life and demonstrates the necessity of ongoing resocialization as they come to embody ever more radically the conditions of that new life.

Jesus' response to the disciples does not so much agree with their self-assessment as assure them that this is precisely what constitutes discipleship and qualifies one for eternal life. Again, setting aside the priority of household and kin does not come as a consequence of serving an ascetic ideal, but is a corollary of the reorientation of life around the new world order present

---

154. The disciples have not yet proven themselves to be reliable commentators.

in Jesus' ministry.[155] Within this co-text, the "many times more" promised must relate to the new family within which "those who hear the word of God and do it" (8:21) are embraced. Not only this, but those who so orient their lives in the present are promised life in the age to come. With this, Jesus' message has returned to the point of the ruler's question at the outset of this scene.

The ruler, still present despite his negative response to the call of discipleship, has now heard the answer to his question twice. Those who would inherit life in the future must enter the kingdom of God in the present — following Jesus as he adopts the unconventional construction of human relationships peculiar to God's salvific project, valuing the poor as though they were one's own family.

5.6.3.4. The Enigma of Jesus' Suffering (18:31-34)

> 31 Then he took the twelve aside and said to them, "See, we are going up to Jerusalem, and everything that is written about the Son of Man by the prophets will be accomplished. 32 For he will be handed over to the Gentiles; and he will be mocked and insulted and spat upon. 33 After they have flogged him, they will kill him, and on the third day he will rise again." 34 But they understood nothing about all these things; in fact, what he said was hidden from them, and they did not grasp what was said.

In its focus on private instruction to the disciples and especially in its thematic intertwining of christology and discipleship, this paragraph is reminiscent of 9:1-50 (cf. §12). Temporally, it is related directly to the preceding interaction among Jesus, the wealthy ruler, and Jesus' followers. Although Jesus' words are now restricted to the disciples (cf. 9:10, 28), once the connection from christology to discipleship is made by reading this paragraph against the horizon of its local co-text, in terms of emphasis they correspond directly to his public instruction in vv 9-30.

Jesus' discourse first underscores the divine necessity being served in the journey to Jerusalem and in the events that will ensue there. Luke put his readers on notice concerning the importance of Jerusalem to the divine plan early on by locating the beginning of his narrative in the Holy City (see §3). The centrality of Jerusalem has been in plain view since the transfiguration account (9:31) and onset of the journey narrative (9:51, 53); more recent notices have ensured that we continue to correlate realization of the divine

---

155. That orientation to the purpose of God relativizes even the claims of one's family, see 8:19-21; 9:57-62; 12:51-53; 14:25-26.

purpose with arrival in Jerusalem (e.g., 17:11, 22; et al.). In addition to the Jerusalem motif, the motif of divine necessity is signaled with reference to "everything that is written . . . by the prophets" (cf. 24:25, 27),[156] coupled with a verb of fulfillment.[157] This serves less to pinpoint particular texts requiring or finding fulfillment in Jesus' passion, and more to characterize the Scriptures of Israel as giving witness to the purpose of God brought to culmination in the career of Jesus.[158] It is as Son of Man that Jesus fulfills the divine plan; here, as elsewhere in Luke, this title serves to hold together as one the shape of Jesus' ministry, his suffering, and his vindication.[159]

In the synopsis that follows, "everything that is written" turns out to be a detailed portrait of Jesus' rejection, his abuse and humiliation, and his vindication in resurrection. Compared to the earlier passion prediction in 9:22, this one is remarkable for its failure to mention the responsibility of the Jewish leadership in Jesus' suffering and death. It may be that one should read their agency in the passive verb, "handed over," though this could just as easily be a reference to God's agency (or to Judas's — cf. 6:16). More likely is that Luke is gradually constructing a composite picture of Jesus' passion; hence, since 9:22 had established the central role of the Jewish leadership in Jerusalem in Jesus' death, Gentile culpability may now be emphasized.[160] In the background of this contemptuous catalogue one may hear echoes of Isa 50:6[161] — a reference to the Servant of Yahweh whose divine vocation entailed a paradigmatic move from repudiation to vindication.

The detail with which Jesus refers to his impending suffering underscores one of the primary properties of execution among the Romans — namely, the humiliation of those condemned to death.[162] Indeed, the gestures

156. That is, "through the agency of [διά]" the prophets.

157. Namely, τελέω — cf. 2:39; 12:50; 22:37; Acts 13:29.

158. Cf. Jervell, "Center of Scripture"; Green, *Gospel of Luke,* ch. 2. One would be hard pressed to locate particular Scriptures, though the transposition Jesus anticipates in this text is reminiscent of the "careers" of the Righteous Sufferer and, more particularly, of the Servant of Yahweh — cf. Green, "God's Servant," esp. 12-28.

159. Cf. Kingsbury, *Conflict in Luke,* 73-78; Bock, "Son of Man."

160. Büchele, *Tod Jesu,* 136; cf. Carroll and Green, *Death of Jesus,* 194-98. For the role of Gentiles, see also Acts 2:23 (where διὰ χειρὸς ἀνόμων refers to the agency of the Romans); 4:24-28. μαστιγόω, in v 33, refers to the Roman practice of scourging prior to crucifixion — cf. Josephus *J.W.* 2.14.9 §§306-8.

161. For linguistic parallels, cf. 18:32-33 (ἐμπτυσθήσεται + μαστιγώσαντες) and Isa 50:6 (μάστιγας + ἐμπτυσμάτων).

162. Cf. Green, "Crucifixion," 198; more fully, Hengel, *Crucifixion.* "Crucifixion" is not specifically in view in this prediction, though references to the Gentiles' flogging and killing Jesus point clearly in this direction. That the detail in v 32 has primarily a metaphorical role in this co-text is intimated both by the analogous attention to detail in v 29, and by the fact that not all of the accusations predicted find a counterpart in the

Jesus outlines are not life-threatening but are designed to disgrace the victim thoroughly. The significance of this observation in the present co-text is obvious: In his suffering and resurrection, Jesus was to embody the fullness of salvation interpreted as status reversal; his death was the center point of the divine-human struggle over how life is to be lived, in humility or self-glorification (cf. v 14). Jesus' interpretation of his own career follows closely that expected of his followers: suffering the shame of leaving home and family for the sake of the kingdom, they would be rewarded with eternal life in the age to come (18:28-30).

What is remarkable is that the disciples have begun the journey of discipleship (cf. 18:28), but remain oblivious to the nature of God's plan. Their incognizance is emphasized in its threefold assertion by the narrator in v 34, itself closely modeled on the parallel in 9:45. Their behavior in vv 15-17 is enough to demonstrate that they have yet fully to internalize the values of the kingdom of God, values that subvert and supplant conventional perspectives on honor and shame. Consequently, they are kept from understanding the significance of Jesus' message concerning faithfulness and concerning himself; they are unable to comprehend the integration of suffering and shame, vindication and blessing in the divine purpose.[163]

5.6.3.5. The Irony of Blindness (18:35-43)

35 *As he approached Jericho, a blind man was sitting by the roadside begging.* 36 *When he heard a crowd going by, he asked what was happening.* 37 *They told him, "Jesus of Nazareth is passing by."* 38 *Then he shouted, "Jesus, Son of David, have mercy on me!"* 39 *Those who were in front sternly ordered him to be quiet; but he shouted even more loudly, "Son of David, have mercy on me!"* 40 *Jesus stood still and ordered the man to be brought to him; and when he came near, he asked him,* 41 *"What do you want me to do for you?" He said, "Lord, let me see again."* 42 *Jesus said to him, "Receive your sight; your faith has saved you."* 43 *Immediately he regained his sight and followed him, glorifying God; and all the people, when they saw it, praised God.*

This is the last of the Lukan narratives of healing within the Third Gospel[164] and the only narrative account of Jesus actually proclaiming "recovery of

---

Lukan passion account. Jesus is "handed over to the Gentiles" (23:1, 11, 14) and "mocked/insulted" (23:11, 36; cf. vv 35, 39), but is neither "flogged" (though cf. 23:16, 22) nor spat upon (cf. Mark 14:65).

163. See the discussion above, on 9:43b-45.

164. It is not, however, the last healing miracle in the Gospel; cf. 22:51.

sight to the blind" (4:18; cf. 7:22); its primary importance, however, resides in its role as an exemplary narrative. Set in its present co-text, Luke's account of the healing of the blind man epitomizes (1) the soteriological significance of the healing work of Jesus on behalf of "the poor" as a manifestation of the now-active kingdom of God,[165] (2) the comportment befitting those who desire the benefits of the good news of the kingdom, and (3) the continuing resistance of some to the topsy-turvy values of the kingdom, which accord privilege to the least, the last, and the left-out of society. People who fail to grasp the correlation of shame and suffering with divine vindication (cf. vv 14, 31-34) — that is, those who fail to comprehend that the divine plan is oriented to salvation as status reversal — will hardly anticipate the gift of salvation and discipleship to such social refuse as a blind beggar. Nevertheless, in the Lukan economy, it is precisely such marginalized persons as this beggar who are most apt to come to Jesus with openness to and expectation of divine benefaction. It is in just such a way that one demonstrates one's suitability for the kingdom — the concern of this larger narrative section (18:9–19:27).

Jesus has appeared to be relatively stationary as he has focused attention first on one, then on another, cluster of persons within the larger audience of the discourse that began in 17:20. Following the passion prediction of 18:31-34, however, he is now again on the move toward Jerusalem. Indeed, with this reference to Jericho, Luke indicates that the lengthy journey begun in 9:51 is nearing its end. Because Jerusalem is the ultimate destination, because suffering and death had come to be associated with Jerusalem, and because Jericho is located only *ca.* 20 kilometers from Jerusalem, this and the events Luke records in ch. 19 are bathed with a heightened urgency that gives them added christological significance.

35-37 Travel is marked repeatedly as Luke sets the stage for Jesus' encounter with a blind man: "he approached," "roadside," and "going by." This is an acute reminder of the journey motif operative from 9:51–19:48, the travel narrative during which Luke attempts to clarify Jesus' identity and, especially, to articulate clearly the nature of discipleship within the context of Jesus' proclamation of the good news.

The stage is set with reference to three characters: the crowd, the blind man, and Jesus. Once again (cf. vv 9, 26), Luke does not indicate the makeup of the crowd following Jesus; the disciples have faded into the background, as though their failure to internalize the orientation of his mission to those of lowest status (vv 15-17) and to comprehend his words concerning the divine purpose (v 34) have rendered them indistinguishable from others who have joined the parade around Jesus. Now distant from Galilean environs, Jesus is

165. So Busse, *Wunder,* 332-34.

known as "the Nazarene" — a reference to his hometown;[166] apparently, even here his reputation is such so as to attract a crowd (cf. 9:52; 19:37) and the attention of a blind beggar.

Luke's spotlight finds this blind beggar. In terms of power and privilege, such a person would belong to that five or ten percent of the population known as "expendables" (see Figure 1, p. 60), for whom society as a whole had no need. Forced by his physical malady to live off the charity of others, this man would have had no attachments to possessions or kin; his existence would have been an embarrassment (cf. 16:3), marginal to the daily lives of others, and, if not for the premium placed on almsgiving in Jewish circles, short-lived.[167] He is thus manifestly one of "the poor," as this is understood within the Lukan narrative.[168] Because of this identification, and especially because Luke has underscored the efficacy of the good news in providing recovery of sight for the blind (4:18-19; 7:21-22), the simple news that "Jesus is passing by" such a person may be enough to give Luke's readers an inkling of the outcome of the scene the Evangelist has begun to paint.

38-39   The blind man's reaction is reminiscent of that of the lepers in 17:11-17, and of God's "chosen ones" in 18:7;[169] this again raises expectations that Jesus will act on his behalf. Since he is a beggar, his request for mercy may mean no more than a plea for alms.[170] He addresses Jesus, however, as "Son of David." How he gained this insight into Jesus' identity is unknown to the reader, though in naming Jesus thus this poor man joins the ranks of those who have insight far beyond the expected, especially in view of the status of these persons as peripheral to the community of God's people (e.g., 7:1-10 [Gentile centurion], 36-50 [a sinner from the city]; 17:11-17 [a foreigner/Samaritan]). Jesus' status as "Son of David," correlated earlier with the title "Son of God," is crucial to his identity within the Lukan narrative. It was established in the birth narrative (1:27, 32-35; 2:4), and will come to the foreground again in the speeches of Acts; this, however, is its first public declaration. As the long-awaited Davidide, Jesus would reestablish the throne of David, deliver Israel from its enemies, and reign forever.[171] When read

166. ὁ Ναζωραῖος has long puzzled interpreters on account of its orthography (see the discussion in Schaeder, "Ναζαρηνός, Ναζωραῖος"), though this has not kept most from concluding that the noun is derived from the name of the city of Nazareth. Wise ("Nazarene," 573-74) has recently found linguistic support for this derivation in 1QIsaᵃ.

167. On almsgiving, see above on 11:41; Moxnes, *Economy of the Kingdom,* 113-23; more generally, Garrison, *Redemptive Almsgiving.*

168. See above on 4:18-19; 14:13, 21; more generally, Green, "Good News."

169. βοάω — cf. above on 18:7.

170. See above on 17:13; cf. Acts 3:1-10.

171. Cf. 1:32-35; 2 Sam 7:12-16; Psalm 89; *Psalms of Solomon* 17–18; 1QM 11:1-18; 4QFlor 1:11-14; 4QpIsaᵃ 3:18-21; 8–10; 4QTest 9-13; 2 Esdr 12:31-32.

against the backdrop of such expectations, the notion of extending mercy to an "expendable" like this beggar might seem out of place; read in view of the interpretive horizons of the Lukan narrative, however, and especially within the immediate co-text of this episode, such a request is not at all surprising.

Everything depends on whether one understands the nature of the kingdom of God as this has been rendered present in Jesus' career.[172] This beggar seems to comprehend Jesus' orientation to the needy and makes his plea accordingly. Others, identified only as "those in front," see things differently. It may be that we are to think of "in front" spatially — that is, those in front of the others. A different, less benign reading is not only possible but perhaps preferable. "In front" may refer to those regarded as leaders — spatially first perhaps, but only because of their claims to being first in status.[173] Whether these persons are disciples (cf. 9:52; 18:15) or not is unclear. What is transparent is that "those in front" regard this blind beggar as outside the perimeters of Jesus' ministry, marginal to human society as normally configured, and so outside the boundaries of God's grace. Indeed, they dismiss him in the same way that Jesus dismisses those who oppose the will of God.[174]

Like the widow faced with a recalcitrant judge (vv 1-8), the blind beggar refuses to act according to role. Rather than comport himself as the helpless and hopeless in the face of opposition from those of superior status, he persists in his cries for help, even increasing the volume of his plea. Such is his confidence that he has understood correctly the significance of the arrival of Jesus of Nazareth along his roadside.

40-43 The shift from "Son of David" to "Lord" gives us insight into how the blind beggar understands the nature of Jesus' ministry. The latter is a term appropriate for one's benefactor. According to this blind beggar, then, as Son of David Jesus is the one through whom divine blessing is manifest. What is more, he is sure that the everlasting kingdom being established via Jesus' mission (cf. 1:32-35) accords privilege to "lifting up the lowly" (1:52) and constitutes good news to "the poor" (cf. 4:18-19). Although blind, within

---

172. Cf. Strauss, *Davidic Messiah,* 306-7; Bauer, "Son of David," 767-68.

173. προάγω is susceptible to either interpretation. Johnson (284) thinks in terms of "leaders," but he immediately identifies these persons as Pharisees (as in 19:39). This is due to the lack of nuance in his understanding of the Pharisees in the Lukan narration; for him, Luke paints the Pharisees always and everywhere as hostile to Jesus. Luke is not monochromatic in his portrait of the Pharisees, however; in fact, it is not outside the realm of probability that "those in front" are not Pharisees but *Jesus' own followers!* After all, in 9:52 Jesus' followers are those who go before Jesus, and they have recently demonstrated their tendencies toward controlling who has access to Jesus (18:15-17).

174. ἐπιτιμάω — cf. 4:35, 39, 41; 8:24; 9:42, 55; 17:3; 18:15.

the Lukan narrative of Jesus' public ministry, this man possesses almost unparalleled insight (cf. 7:1-10; 17:11-17).

Jesus' response to the request for sight is a speech act — fulfilling literally one of the phrases Jesus uses to interpret the significance of his anointing by the Spirit: "to proclaim . . . recovery of sight to the blind" (4:18), and signifying his authority to act on God's behalf. Given the correlation of the titles "Son of God" and "Son of David" in the annunciation to Mary (1:32-35), we are thus able to see how accurately the blind beggar has construed Jesus' identity. As Son of David and Son of God, Jesus possesses divine authorization and the requisite status to wield divine power in a way that does not detract from people recognizing the handiwork of God (see v 43) but does legitimate Jesus in his redemptive role within the divine plan.[175]

Additionally, Jesus points to the efficacy of the blind beggar's faith, expressed both in his openness to and expectation of divine benefaction through Jesus' agency and in his persistence in the fact of obstruction.[176] On the expression "your faith has saved you," see above on 7:50.

What is the significance of "saved" (v 42) in this co-text? That the blind beggar receives the capacity to see is clearly meant, and Luke underscores Jesus' competence to heal with the adverb "immediately."[177] Insofar as his marginal status in his community has been grounded in his physical malady, the "saving" of this man must also mark at least the potential of the reversal of his station in the community. He is not returned by Jesus to his community, however (cf., e.g., 8:38-39), but instead follows Jesus in discipleship; in this way, this man, formerly existing outside ordinary circles of friend and family, is identified within the community of God's people and particularly with the "kin group" made up of Jesus and his band of followers (cf. 8:19-21). Still further, located in proximity to vv 15-30, with its concern with soteriology, for this man to be "saved" affirms that he has entered the kingdom of God; although he has neither family nor possessions of which to dispose (cf. 18:22, 28-30), he has already gained "very much more in this age, and in the age to come eternal life" (v 30).

Luke records one other consequence of Jesus' speech act: the formerly blind man and all the people give honor to God. As is typical in Lukan accounts of healing, people attribute restorative power to God, even while recognizing Jesus as the one through whom that power is manifest.[178] Jesus is thus identified as the authorized agent of God — in the language of this pericope, "Son of David."

---

175. See Thiselton, "Christology in Luke."
176. Cf. Theissen, *Miracle Stories,* 52-53.
177. Luke habitually uses παραχρῆμα to emphasize the instantaneous nature of a miracle — cf. 1:64; 4:39; 5:25; 8:44, 47, 55; 13:13; Acts 3:7; 5:10; 12:23; 13:11; 16:26.
178. Cf., e.g., 5:26; 7:16; Acts 10:38; Kee, *Miracle,* 203-4.

5.6.3.6. Who Is a Son of Abraham? (19:1-10)

1 *He entered Jericho and was passing through it.* 2 *Look,*[179] *a man was there named Zacchaeus; he was a ruler among toll collectors*[180] *and was rich.* 3 *He was trying to see who Jesus was, but could not on account of the crowd, for*[181] *he was short in stature.* 4 *So he ran ahead and climbed a sycamore tree to see him, because he was going to pass that way.* 5 *When Jesus came to the place, he looked up and said to him, "Zacchaeus, hurry and come down; for I must stay at your house today."* 6 *So he hurried down and was happy to welcome him.* 7 *All who saw it began to grumble and said, "He has gone to be the guest of one who is a sinner."* 8 *Zacchaeus stood there and said to the Lord, "Look, half of my possessions, Lord, I give*[182] *to the poor; and if I have defrauded anyone of anything, I pay back*[183] *four times as much."* 9 *Then Jesus said to him, "Today salvation has come to this house, because he too is a son of Abraham.* 10 *For the Son of Man came to seek out and to save the lost."*

Geographically as well as thematically, Jesus' encounter with Zacchaeus is firmly integrated into the foregoing material. In 18:35, Jesus was approaching Jericho; now, having entered the city, he is passing through it on his way to Jerusalem. The divine purpose he serves thus moves more and more into the forefront, such that Jesus can even assert that sharing a meal with Zacchaeus is a divine necessity.[184]

Numerous connections secure the Zacchaeus episode within its immediate co-text, underscoring the degree to which the significance of this scene is forcibly constrained by its narrative location. Zacchaeus is like others on comparable quests who are faced with obstacles (18:3-4, 15, 39); Zacchaeus, like a widow, a toll collector, children, and a blind beggar, is a person of low social status (ch. 18); and so on.[185] By far the most impressive parallels are between the accounts of the rich ruler (18:18-30) and of Zacchaeus. Both are "rulers." According to his self-evaluation, the first keeps the commandments, while Zacchaeus is, according to popular opinion, a "sinner." The ruler is

179. "Look" is missing from the NRSV.

180. Or, perhaps, "a leading toll collector"; NRSV: "chief tax collector."

181. NRSV: "on account of the crowd he could not, because."

182. NRSV: "I will give."

183. NRSV: "I will pay back."

184. See the use of δεῖ in v 5; also the centrality of table fellowship with toll collectors and sinners to Jesus' mission in 5:29-32.

185. See, e.g., O'Hanlon, "Story of Zacchaeus," 9-11; Neale, *None but the Sinners,* 181-82; O'Toole, "Literary Form," 112.

counseled to sell all he has and give to the poor; Zacchaeus sells half of his possessions and gives the proceeds to the poor. Both are wealthy. In the first interaction, Jesus is asked, "Who then can be saved?" while at the conclusion of the second, Jesus asserts, "Today salvation has come to this house." Such points of contact serve to orient our reading of 19:1-10 to the correlation of status and suitability for the kingdom.

Such issues come into focus in a different way within the parameters of this narrative unit by the repetition of keywords and motifs. First is the use of the verb "to seek" — used of Zacchaeus in v 3 and of Jesus in v 10: Who is seeking whom? We discover at the outset that Zacchaeus is on a quest[186] to see who Jesus is, only to learn in the end that, in accordance with his divine mission, Jesus has been on a quest for Zacchaeus, to bring him salvation. Second is the terminology of "seeing," the importance of which is intimated not only by its frequency in this account[187] but also by the preceding concern with blindness and recovery of sight in 18:35-43 — all read in relation to the larger Lukan concern with blindness and sight as metaphors appertaining to salvation.[188] Importantly, even we, Luke's readers, are encouraged to see! Third is the use of vertical imagery in the first half of the episode: Zacchaeus was "short in stature" (v 3; though see below), who climbed up a tree, then came down after Jesus looked up and instructed Zacchaeus to come down (vv 4-6). Such imagery speaks to Zacchaeus's devotion to his quest and serves also as a metaphor associated with matters of status honor (cf. 1:52).

In a paradoxical way, this narrative unit provides a notable illustration of "good news to the poor" — laying stress both on the bearer of this good news (christology and mission) and on appropriate response to the beneficence of God. As such, this unit constitutes an important and carefully crafted rhetorical exercise on the part of the Third Evangelist. Employing categories fully developed in the prior narrative in incongruous, even oxymoronic juxtaposition — "ruler," "toll collector," "wealthy," and "sinner" — Luke articulates by means of this account a pivotal element of his narrative theology. Here, Luke dismisses the usual, stereotypical categories by which one's status before God is predetermined, including even those surprising ones that might have been suggested in Luke's narration. Following a close reading of chs. 1–18, Luke's audience might assume that the wealthy and those who rule are out, sinners and toll collectors are in. What, then, are we to make of someone who is all of these things? In his characterization of Zacchaeus, Luke pulls the rug from under every cliché, every formula by which people's status before

186. On the description of this account as a "quest" story, see Tannehill, "Story of Zacchaeus"; O'Toole, "Literary Form."

187. ἰδού — vv 2 and 8; ὁράω — vv 3, 4, and 7; ἀναβλέπω — v 5.

188. See Hamm, "Sight to the Blind"; Culpepper, "Seeing the Kingdom of God."

God might be calculated. After the dust settles, two complementary assertions remain: (1) the salvific agency of Jesus on behalf of those routinely excluded and (2) the determination of one's inclusion in the family of God on the basis of the single query, Do you conduct yourself as a child of Abraham? (cf. 3:7-14).

1-2 Luke sets this scene with an important geographical reference to Jericho, located proximate to Jerusalem (about 20 kilometers away). Jesus is on the move,[189] bringing the chronologically lengthy journey to Jerusalem to a close. As might be expected, this pericope, together with the closely related parable to follow (vv 11-27), serves as the climax of the travel section, building on its primary motifs and characterizing appropriate response to Jesus' message.

Apart from Jesus himself, the primary character in this episode is Zacchaeus, introduced in v 2. He is characterized in four ways. He is a Jew,[190] a ruler, a toll collector, and wealthy. In English translations, Zacchaeus is usually referred to as a "chief toll collector," taking Luke's expression as a job description,[191] a kind of "district manager"[192] with other toll collectors working as his subordinates. The term itself is without parallel in contemporary Greek texts,[193] so it is not clear that a job title is intended. By way of analogy with other Lukan texts, however, it is clear that Zacchaeus is thus presented as a person of advanced status, even if only among other toll collectors. More specifically, as a "ruler" in the Greco-Roman world Zacchaeus would have enjoyed relative power and privilege, though from the perspective of the Lukan narrative we would anticipate his opposing the mission of Jesus.[194] That Zacchaeus is wealthy is emphasized within the narrative by its being enumerated separately, as a quality distinct from that of the others. Within the larger Greco-Roman world, possessing wealth was an ambiguous characteristic. Although wealth was required if one were to reach the upper echelons of nobility, how one got one's wealth was equally determinative. Zacchaeus's fortune was not "landed wealth" but was the consequence of his own entrepreneurial activity; hence, it would not have

189. See "entered," "passing through," "to pass that way" (vv 1, 4).

190. At least, his name portends his identity as a Jew — cf. 2 Macc 10:19; Fitzmyer, 2:1223.

191. ἀρχιτελώνης, then, is usually rendered on analogy with ἀρχισυνάγωγος — cf. 8:49; 13:14; Acts 13:15; 18:8, 17.

192. Gillman, *Possessions,* 89.

193. See Michel, "τελώνης," 98, 105.

194. See 1:51, which announces that the powerful are brought down from their thrones. For ἄρχων (and compounds) with respect to synagogue leadership, cf. 8:41, 49; 13:14; Acts 13:15; 18:8, 17. On status issues, see 14:1. The term is used for a magistrate in 12:58.

qualified him for enviable status.[195] Within the Lukan narrative, such ambiguity dissipates rapidly, since the wealthy are thus far repeatedly cast in a negative light.[196] Most recently, Jesus had remarked on the impossibility of the wealthy entering the kingdom of God (18:24-25).

On the other hand, Zacchaeus is a toll collector. Within the Greco-Roman world, he would have belonged to a circle of persons almost universally despised.[197] Within the Third Gospel, however, toll collectors are consistently portrayed in a positive light — as persons who respond well to the good news, as Jesus' companions, even as persons of exemplary piety.[198]

Thus, the presentation of Zacchaeus is mixed. Those who have been following Luke's narrative closely will understand already how Luke has interpreted such terms as "ruler," "toll collector," and "wealthy" in ways that depart from standard social conventions. Working with interpretive protocols provided by the Third Evangelist, however, Luke's audience may well be perplexed by the collocation of terms used to characterize Zacchaeus. If we have learned from Luke how to classify people as helpers and opponents of God merely by reference to such features, we will be bewildered by this opening portrait of Zacchaeus.

3-6   Any lingering, negative valuations of Zacchaeus from v 2 will likely be mitigated by Luke's description of this leading toll collector as a man on a quest. He is not interested merely in "seeing Jesus" but wants to know "who Jesus is" (cf. 10:21-22). He goes to extraordinary lengths to fulfill his quest, even enduring the probable shame of climbing a tree despite his adult male status and position in the community as a wealthy "ruler," however notorious. That he goes to such lengths is illustrative of his eagerness, to be sure, but is also a consequence of the crowd, which has positioned itself as a barrier to his endeavor.

English translations often find an explanation for Zacchaeus's inability to see Jesus in his shortness. This is problematic for two reasons. First, it may be that the Greek text is better represented with a reference not to his shortness of stature but to his relative youth.[199] This would account for his treatment as an insignificant person for whom the crowd would not make room. Even

---

195. See Badian, *Publicans;* Garnsey and Saller, *Roman Empire,* 43-51.

196. See 1:53; 6:24; 12:13-21; 14:12-14; 16:19-31; 18:18-30; cf. 20:45–21:4.

197. On toll collectors, see above on 3:12.

198. See 3:12; 5:27-32; 7:29; 15:1-2; 18:9-14.

199. As Moulton ("New Testament Greek," 91-92) observes, for ἡλικία there is a strong presumption in favor of "age" or "term of life." BAGD (345) lists a number of texts in which the translation "stature" is alleged, but on closer inspection these are not universally relevant. Lucian *Verae historiae* 1.40 refers to "size," but others (e.g., Josephus *Ant.* 2.9.6 §230; Plutarch *Lives: Philopoemen* 11.2; et al.) refer to age or maturity. J. Schneider ("ἡλικία," 942) concludes that, in the NT, Luke 19:3 "... is the only passage where the word indisputably means 'stature'." Why this is indisputable is not clear.

if smallness of stature is understood, however, this is no necessary obstacle to seeing a parade. People of regal status need not also be tall in order to have a view! Second, the phrase "on account of the crowd" has a causative force.[200] Thus, it is not simply that Zacchaeus cannot see over the crowd; rather, the crowd itself is present as an obstacle to him. On account of their negative assessment of Zacchaeus (cf. v 7), the people refused him the privilege of seeing Jesus as he passed by. Whether short or young, then, Zacchaeus is presented as a person of diminutive status in Jericho, thus rendering him as a member of the unenviable association of the lowly in ch. 18, along with a widow, a toll collector, children, and a blind beggar.[201]

Zacchaeus's persistence in the face of opposition from the crowd is rewarded by Jesus. Hoping to see Jesus, Zacchaeus is seen by him (cf. v 10). What is more, Jesus insists that the nature of his mission renders it imperative that he share Zacchaeus's hospitality.[202] His instructions to Zacchaeus are met with immediate and exact obedience,[203] and with joy. "Stay at your house" and "welcome" are unmistakable references to hospitality. This signifies from Jesus' point of view that he hopes, in the context of a shared meal, to forge a relationship with Zacchaeus in which the unifying dynamic is the good news of the kingdom.[204] In this respect, Jesus' use of the term "today" is highly suggestive, since elsewhere in Luke's narrative it is used to communicate the immediacy of salvation.[205] Because of the association of "joy" with news of divine intervention and salvation, that Zacchaeus welcomes Jesus with joy (NRSV: "happy") signifies genuine receptivity on the part of Zacchaeus, intimating that he is one who embraces the values and claims of the kingdom of God.[206]

7-10 According to the Third Evangelist, the crowd assesses the unfolding situation in a way that departs radically from the stance Zacchaeus has taken (v 6) and from the position Jesus will assume (vv 9-10). In place of Zacchaeus's "joy," they respond with "grumbling," labeling Zacchaeus a sinner and, by extension, calling Jesus' status into question on account of his willingness to receive hospitality from a sinner. The response of "grumbling" in light of Jesus' table companions is nothing new in the Third Gospel (see

200. For the causative use of ἀπό, see 21:26; 22:45; 24:41; Acts 12:14; 20:11; 22:11; BDF §210.1.

201. Cf. W. P. Loewe, "Lk 19:1-10," 325; Kariamadam, *Zacchaeus Story,* 17.

202. δεῖ — cf. 2:49; 4:43; 13:16; et al.

203. σπεύσας κατάβηθι . . . σπεύσας κατέβη.

204. On the importance of meals in the potential creation of kinship, see Moxnes, "Meals," 161-63. See 5:27-32; 15:1-2.

205. σήμερον — cf. 2:11; 4:21; Kariamadam, *Zacchaeus Story,* 23.

206. For the motif of joy, see, e.g., 1:14; 20:10; 6:23; 8:13; 10:17, 20; 15:5, 7, 10, 32. ὑποδέχομαι appears in Luke-Acts here and in 10:38; Acts 17:7.

5:30; 15:2);[207] such a reaction demonstrates how Jesus' mission runs counter to expected social norms. What is striking is that previously those who grumbled were identified as legal experts and Pharisees, while in the present text this response is attributed to "everyone who saw it." Who are included in this undifferentiated "crowd" (v 3), this "all"? Because of previous references one is tempted to think immediately of Pharisees. The line between Pharisees and others, including disciples, has become increasingly hard to discern, however, with the consequence that no such distinctions are possible here (cf. 18:9-14, 15-17). In spite of Jesus' repeated attempts throughout the journey (9:51–19:27) to address disciples and Pharisees, and indeed all who would listen, on issues of status and membership among God's people, his message seems thus far to have fallen universally on deaf ears.

The reference to Zacchaeus as a "sinner" marks him immediately as marginal to the community as one who does not follow its standards. Because Luke tells us nothing explicitly about Jewish practices in Jericho, it is difficult to delineate Zacchaeus's offenses; his vocation as a toll collector may be reason enough to have stigmatized him in this way. What follows in vv 8-10 is a reply, first from Zacchaeus and then from Jesus, to the accusation against him. Zacchaeus answers first, not with reference to behaviors or commitments that might mark him as acceptable according to standards developed heretofore — for example, fasting, praying, tithing (cf. 18:11-12), or even his choice of a different line of work! Instead, he responds in a way that suggests his inside knowledge of the messages of John (esp. 3:10-14) and Jesus regarding economic justice[208] and almsgiving. That is, he lists behaviors appropriate to those who have oriented themselves around the kingdom of God.[209]

The verbs in Zacchaeus's speech are in the present tense: "I give . . . I pay back." They have often been interpreted as examples of the "futuristic present" or as having the nuance of "present resolve."[210] In this case, Luke would be portraying Zacchaeus as responding not to those who defame him in v 7, but to the message of Jesus. Verse 8 would refer to his repentance, while vv 9-10 would refer to his being saved (usually understood in a spiritual sense).

It is fully consistent with the progression of the Lukan narrative to this point, however, to take these verbs as present progressives: "My customary

207. Luke 5:30 has the onomatopoeic γογγύζω, while 15:2 and 19:7 read the compound διαγογγύζω.

208. Fourfold restitution is by almost any reckoning excessive; cf. Exod 22:1; Lev 6:5; Num 5:6-7; 2 Sam 12:6.

209. On almsgiving, see esp. 16:9 and the negative example of 16:19-31; cf. Moxnes, *Economy of the Kingdom*.

210. Recently, see, e.g., Neale, *None but the Sinners,* 187; Tannehill, "Story of Zacchaeus," 203; Hamm, "Luke 19:8"; cf. Watson, "Zacchaeus," 283-85.

practice is to give half of what I have to the poor, etc."[211] Luke's narrative mentions nothing of Zacchaeus's need for repentance,[212] act of repentance, or faith; nor of Jesus' summons to repentance; nor does he in any other way structure this episode as a "story of conversion."[213] According to this reading, Zacchaeus does not resolve to undertake new practices but presents for Jesus' evaluation his current behaviors regarding money. He even joins the narrator in referring to Jesus as "Lord." Jesus' reference to "salvation" (v 9), then, signifies Zacchaeus's vindication and restoration to the community of God's people; he is not an outsider, after all, but has evidenced through his economic practices his kinship with Abraham (cf. 3:7-14). Zacchaeus thus joins the growing roll of persons whose "repentance" lies outside the narrative, who appear on the margins of the people of God, and yet who possess insight into and a commitment to the values of Jesus' mission that are exemplary.[214]

What are we to make of Zacchaeus's failure to disinvest himself completely of his possessions? The urgency of this question derives from the many parallels between the rich ruler, who was instructed to sell everything and give to the poor (18:22), and Zacchaeus, who distributes only half of his possessions to the poor. Here it is crucial to remember that, for Luke, almsgiving is neither charity in the modern sense nor an ascetic ideal; rather, it has to do with including in one's circle of kin those who are unable to reciprocate (e.g., 14:12-14), to "make friends" via giving without expectation of return (cf. 6:35-36; 16:9). Unlike the rich ruler, Zacchaeus does not employ his wealth so as to procure honor and friends; rather, he is a social outcast who puts his possessions in the service of the needy and of justice.[215] Such a person would indeed be eager to welcome Jesus, anointed by the Spirit to bring "good news to the poor" (4:18-19), with joy! (On faith and possessions in Luke, see §11.)

Zacchaeus's response to those who slandered him is followed by Jesus' twofold riposte. First, he insists that Zacchaeus is a son of Abraham. This is not a reference to his bloodline, for Luke has repeatedly indicated that one's birthright is no grounds for any particular privilege in the divine economy. Rather, since the Lukan narrative has redefined status as a "child of Abraham" with reference to lowly position and faithful practices, Jesus' assertion vindicates Zacchaeus as one who embodies the qualities of those fit for the kingdom of God.[216]

211. Cf., e.g., Godet, 2:217; White, "Vindication for Zacchaeus?"; Ravens, "Zacchaeus."

212. Nor can this be inferred from his vocation — cf. 3:12.

213. *Contra* Hamm, "Luke 19:8"; cf. O'Toole, "Literary Form"; also White, "Vindication for Zacchaeus?"

214. Cf. 7:1-10, 36-50; 17:11-17; 18:35-43; see Green, *Gospel of Luke,* 105.

215. See Green, "Good News," 71-72.

216. Hence, Luke's logic consists in two related syllogisms, as follows: (1) Chil-

"Salvation" thus refers to restoration to the community of God's people, a reality marked for Zacchaeus by Jesus' presence in his house. Note the parallel statements —

"I must stay at your house today" (v 5)
"Today salvation has come to this house" (v 9) —

an identification of salvation with Jesus also witnessed in 2:30. This reversal relates not only to Zacchaeus but also to his household (which, with him as householder, would also have suffered the ostracism he had experienced). Anticipated here are the accounts of household conversion in the narrative of Acts (e.g., 10:1–11:18; 16:25-34; 18:1-11).

Having spoken on Zacchaeus' behalf, vindicating him before his townspeople, Jesus goes on to defend his own coming to Zacchaeus's house. His characterization of his charge as Son of Man recalls his parabolic teaching in 15:1-32. There, he was indicted for having table fellowship with those toll collectors and sinners who had responded positively to his message; there, he insisted that his table practices were consonant with God's response to the recovery of the lost. Another form of intertextuality is important here, one that reaches beyond the Lukan narrative to Ezekiel 34, where Yahweh and David seek out the lost of Israel, those mistreated at the hands of Israel's leaders, and shepherd them. In seeking hospitality with one spurned as a socio-religious outcast, then, Jesus is simply fulfilling the divine will.

5.6.3.7. Those Who Refuse the King (19:11-27)

11 *As they were listening to this, he went on to tell a parable, because he was near Jerusalem, and because they supposed that the kingdom of God was to appear immediately.* 12 *So he said, "A nobleman went to a distant country to get royal power for himself and then return.* 13 *He summoned ten of his slaves, and gave them ten pounds, and said to them, 'Do business with these until I come back.'* 14 *But the citizens of his country hated him and sent a delegation after him, saying, 'We do not want this man to rule over us.'* 15 *When he returned, having received royal power, he ordered these slaves, to whom he had given the money, to be summoned so that he might find out what they had*

---

dren of Abraham are those whose lives (dispositions and behaviors) are oriented toward God. Zacchaeus's life is oriented toward God. Therefore, Zacchaeus is a child of Abraham. (2) Salvation is for the children of Abraham. Zacchaeus is a child of Abraham. Therefore, salvation is for Zacchaeus.

gained by trading. 16 *The first came forward and said, 'Lord, your pound has made ten more pounds.'* 17 *He said to him, 'Well done, good slave! Because you have been trustworthy in a very small thing, take charge of ten cities.'* 18 *Then the second came, saying, 'Lord, your pound has made five pounds.'* 19 *He said to him, 'And you, rule over five cities.'* 20 *Then the other came, saying, 'Lord, here is your pound. I wrapped it up in a piece of cloth,* 21 *for I was afraid of you, because you are a harsh man; you take what you did not deposit, and reap what you did not sow.'* 22 *He said to him, 'I will judge you by your own words, you wicked slave! You knew, did you, that I was a harsh man, taking what I did not deposit and reaping what I did not sow?* 23 *Why then did you not put my money into the bank? Then when I returned, I could have collected it with interest.'* 24 *He said to the bystanders, 'Take the pound from him and give it to the one who has ten pounds.'* 25 *(And they said to him, 'Lord, he has ten pounds!')* 26 *'I tell you, to all those who have, more will be given; but from those who have nothing, even what they have will be taken away.* 27 *But as for these enemies of mine who did not want me to be king over them —— bring them here and slaughter them in my presence.' "*

Luke's introductory clause, "as they were listening to this" (v 11), counsels against making any significant structural separation after v 10 and demands that we grapple with the relation of the parabolic teaching in vv 12-27 to the preceding account of Jesus' encounter with Zacchaeus (vv 1-10). Because in v 11 Luke has provided for his audience an interpretive frame by which to make sense of the ensuing parable, this is not difficult. The Lukan emphasis on the presence of salvation, *today* (vv 5, 9), raises questions about the eschatological timetable, just as it had, for example, in 17:11-21.[217] Historically, such concerns would only have been exacerbated by the relative proximity of Jesus' entourage to Jerusalem; within the Lukan narrative, high hopes have been vested in the arrival in Jerusalem too (cf., e.g., 9:31, 51).

On the one hand, then, Jesus' discourse has a backward referent and is concerned with the nature of appropriate eschatological outlook, as this subject has been broached thus far in the Third Gospel. In this respect, Jesus underscores the certainty of the "appearance" of the kingdom, but characteristically shifts the focus from the question of *when* to the issue of *faithful-*

---

217. See also Acts 1:6, where Luke's οὖν indicates how integrally related to the former words of Jesus the question of the restoration of the kingdom to Israel is. Jesus' discourse concerning baptisms with water and the Spirit (on the end-time significance of the outpouring of the Spirit, cf., e.g., Isa 44:3; Ezek 36:26-27; Joel 2:28-32; *T. Lev.* 18:11) and teaching on God's imperial rule have given rise to the query.

ness in anticipation.[218] His message thus accords privilege to how one responds to the "heir apparent" of the parable, noting how this response serves to qualify (or disqualify) one from participation in his dominion. (In fact, the language of royal rule weaves its way through the whole of Jesus' parabolic teaching.)[219] On the other, insofar as this section is located near the close of the journey narrative that has designated Jerusalem as its destination (9:51–19:48), and insofar as Luke's introduction to the parable anticipates entry into Jerusalem (v 11), it also has a forward referent. That is, this text helps to interpret the significance of Jesus' arrival in the city, as well as the events that will unfold in the closing chapters of the Third Gospel and in the opening of Acts.

This dual focus, forward- and backward-looking, is important because of the disciples' continuing incapacity to comprehend the nature of Jerusalem as a place of hostility and suffering and, thus, the place of rejection within the divine purpose (most recently, 18:31-34). Looking forward to unfolding events, Jesus' teaching portends again the eventuality of malice so as to demonstrate that the rejection he would undergo had come as no surprise. Jesus was first to meet death, not the consummation of the kingdom, in Jerusalem. Looking backward to preceding chapters of Luke's narrative, Jesus' message emphasizes that such rejection can never be the whole story, that the kingdom is sure to come, and that the process of waiting for the full realization of the kingdom was to serve as an opportunity for faithfulness (cf. 12:35-48).[220]

As with many of the Lukan parables, this one draws its significance in part from its realism and in part from its transparent points of contact with the larger narrative. Particularly as Luke has staged this parable, with the introductory rationale in v 11, the parable both helps to interpret and is inter-

---

218. *Contra* Conzelmann (*Luke,* 113), who rightly emphasizes Luke's concern with "readiness," but reads into this passage the motif of "a long time." Maddox (*Purpose,* 49-50, 105-6) is closer to the mark with his view that Luke's primary concern is not with *when* the kingdom will come but with *who* will qualify to be admitted to it.

219. Thus, βασιλεία (vv 11, 12, 15); βασιλεύω (vv 14 and 27), ἐξουσία (v 17; elliptical in v 19).

220. See Carroll, *End of History,* 99-100; cf. Strauss, *Davidic Messiah,* 307-11. An interesting alternative view is argued by L. T. Johnson, "Lukan Kingship Parable." For him, the parable has nothing to do with the eschaton, but is concerned only to interpret the ensuing narrative, wherein Jesus is immediately proclaimed as king (19:37-38). This interpretation is attractive but improbable (see the decisive remarks in Carroll, *End of History,* 100-103); after all, to proclaim Jesus as king is not equivalent to the realization of the kingdom (ἀναφαίνω, v 11); the parable demands a journey to a place far off where the nobleman will receive his rule, then return — an aspect of the parable that can easily be taken to refer to Jesus' exaltation and its interpretation in Acts (e.g., 2:30-36; 5:30-31), but which has no role at all to play in Johnson's reading.

675

preted by its surrounding co-text. This does not mean that the parable depends straightforwardly on an allegorical interpretation for its meaning. In fact, such a reading would be highly problematic, since, if one were to identify Jesus simply with the nobleman, it would portray Jesus in terms of harshness and exploitative practices. That a nobleman might be characterized thus is realistic on historical grounds. Within the parable, not only is his infamy first articulated by one of his slaves but, more importantly, it seems to be embraced by the nobleman himself (vv 22-23). Such qualities do not comport well with the Lukan picture of Jesus thus far in the narrative! If an allegorical interpretation of the parable is improbable, this means that charges of anti-Semitism raised against the parable are also untenable, since one could then not simply equate "the citizens of his country" with "the Jews."[221]

On the one hand, within the Third Gospel, Jesus has often used recognizably realistic anecdotes in order to score important points about the nature of God, the kingdom, and faithful comportment among those oriented toward the purpose of God, without insisting on point-for-point, allegorizing correspondence (e.g., 11:5-8; 16:1-9; 18:1-8). The realism of the present scene is suggested by the parallels between the journey of this nobleman and that of Archelaus to Rome in 4 B.C.E., seeking confirmation of his kingship; as recounted by Josephus, after Archelaus set out, a delegation was sent to protest his appointment, and, when he returned with royal power, he exacted judgment on his enemies.[222] Such realism is important for how this parable functions in this context, where it helps to clarify the nature of royal authority and response to the heir to the throne; within the present co-text, it demonstrates that the orientation of the kingdom of God to those of marginal status (e.g., 18:15-17, 35-43) does not preclude but demands the coming of judgment on those who refuse the nature of God's rule.[223]

On the other, especially given the regal motifs that have punctuated the narrative so fully in chs. 1–2 and most recently in 18:35-43, and that will become so prominent in the Lukan narrative following this parable, it is impossible not to read this parable about a king as a commentary on its co-text. Read within the Lukan narrative, however, the nobleman who becomes king serves as an analogy for Jesus primarily in a parodic or ironic way. It is true, of course, that Jesus is of noble birth; he is a Davidide and, conceived through the intervention of the Holy Spirit, he is the Son of God (1:27, 32-35; 2:4). The parody resident in the narrative identification of Jesus and the nobleman of this parable lies elsewhere, in the construction of Jesus' kingship and kingdom within the Gospel of Luke. In fact, the kingdom of God as this has

---

221. *Contra,* e.g., J. T. Sanders, "Parable of the Pounds."
222. Josephus *J.W.* 2.2.2 §16; 2.6.1 §80; 2.7.3 §111; cf. Jeremias, *Parables,* 59.
223. Cf. Tiede, *Prophecy and History,* 79.

been articulated by Jesus may seem harsh and arbitrary to any who have oriented their lives around the quest for status grounded in wealth and around legal interpretations that lead to perpetual separation from the needy. The affirmation of Zacchaeus recounted in the immediately adjacent scene (vv 1-10) overturns normally accepted standards of right and wrong, in and out, for example. And it is in this ironic sense that this Lukan parable takes an important christological turn. The question put forward by Jesus' parable is a pressing one. Those who abhor the nobleman and reject his claim to the throne — are they rebels or patriots? The slave who blew the whistle on the character and practices of the nobleman — is his action noteworthy (though tragic) or blameworthy (on account of his unwillingness to respond faithfully with what was entrusted to him by his lord)? Or, to change the terms of the discourse: Is Jesus really the heir apparent? Is this really the nature of God's imperial rule? Those who hear the parable are left to take sides.[224]

11 As in 18:1, 9, the sense of a parable is forcibly constrained by an initial interpretive frame. Sundered from its co-text, the parable of vv 12-27 is perhaps susceptible to a variety of interpretations;[225] understood within the Lukan narrative, however, such polysemy is significantly restricted.

The construction of Luke's transition to the parable ties Jesus' teaching in vv 12-27 closely to the preceding scene.[226] Luke envisions no change of scene at all, so that Jesus moves directly from his pronouncement vis-à-vis Zacchaeus (vv 9-10) to the story of a nobleman (v 12). The "they [who] supposed that the kingdom of God was to appear immediately" of whom Luke speaks in v 11 can only refer ambiguously to the crowds who were following Jesus and who had gathered to see him in Jericho. His disciples are included, as are others. According to recent events, the identification of disciples in Jesus' audience is particularly apropos, since Jesus had anticipated that they would be concerned with seeing the coming of the kingdom (17:20-37) and because of their ongoing miscomprehensions regarding the nature of the events awaiting Jesus in Jerusalem (18:31-34).

The connection of the parable to the foregoing is likely solidified by Jesus' affirmation concerning the presence of salvation in his ministry and the possible interpretation of that presence as signifying the arrival of the kingdom of God in its fullness. Indeed, Jesus has presaged the consummation of God's purpose in Jerusalem, and Luke has repeatedly emphasized the role of Jerusalem not only as the journey's end but also as the place of divine destiny (cf. 9:31, 51, 53; 13:22, 33-34; 17:11; 18:31-34). How Jerusalem (and the events that would ensue there) are related to the realization of the kingdom is therefore

---

224. So Weinert, "Parable of the Throne Claimant," 510.
225. See, e.g., Jeremias, *Parables,* 58-63; Herzog, *Parables,* 150-68.
226. Luke introduces this new discourse with a genitive absolute.

more than a matter of curiosity. Added to this is the supposition among some (again, their identity is not clear, though the disciples must be included)[227] that eschatological hopes were on the verge of fulfillment. In this co-text, then, "kingdom of God" refers to the end-time scenario, the reality of God's dominion in peace and justice at the eschaton, and its "appearance" is tantamount to its "coming."[228]

12-14 Luke's "so" emphasizes what the "because" of v 11 had already made clear — namely, that Jesus' parable takes its meaning from its immediate co-text.[229]

The parable's main character is a claimant to the throne whose description as "noble" marks him as one of lofty position on the scale of power and privilege on account of his birthright (see Figure 1, p. 60).[230] The need to travel to a distant country in order to secure his dominion would not seem odd in the Roman world, where rule was parceled out centrally from Rome to those who would serve as client-kings and governors;[231] here it contrasts with the immediacy of the kingdom assumed by some in v 11.

Slaves were often employed with doing business on behalf of the urban elite, supervising the sale and purchase of merchandise, handling loans, and the like; the adept might function with such autonomy and manage their own business affairs so astutely that, upon manumission, they were able to replicate for themselves financial structures analogous to those of their former master.[232] "To do business" may be too weak a translation for the practices assumed by the text; "turning a profit" refers to exploitation in the service of managing profitably the capital at one's disposal.[233] In this unfolding scenario, the amount of that capital, one "pound," is relatively small, roughly four months' wages for a day laborer.

If this nobleman has slaves at his disposal, he also has enemies. In 1:71, "all who hate us" is paralleled with "our enemies," pointing to the identity of those who repudiate the nobleman's status with the "enemies" mentioned in v 27. In this co-text, "to hate" is not a description of personal

---

227. Since the last reference to their lack of understanding (18:31-34), the disciples have faded into the crowds; for the moment, they have no separate identity as characters within the narrative.

228. ἀναφαίνω, then, substitutes for the more usual ἔρχομαι (e.g., 11:2; 17:20).

229. In v 11, διά is followed by parallel rationales: because (1) he was near Jerusalem, and (2) some supposed. . . . οὖν is used in v 12.

230. See the discussion in *TLNT,* 2:93-96, esp. 93.

231. See above on Archelaus; also, of Herod, Josephus *Ant.* 14.14.1-4 §§370-85.

232. Thébert, "Slave," 156-59.

233. πραγματεύομαι is used in v 13; the compound διαπραγματεύομαι in v 15; see *TLNT,* 3:150-51.

affect, but a rejection of his claim to the throne; their "hate" is realized in their petition that he not be allowed to have authority over them.

The basis for this attempt to have his claim vetoed is not discussed. The grounds by which Jesus' proclamation of the kingdom has been rejected are easier to discern from within the Lukan narrative. They have to do with the nature of the kingdom he proclaims and promises — its orientation toward persons who live on the periphery of respectable society and his tendencies toward interpreting the purpose of God as this is manifest in the Scriptures of Israel accordingly (see 4:18-19).

15-23 In spite of the attempt of his enemies to intervene against his appointment, the nobleman returns having been installed as ruler. The reckoning begins, and will occupy the rest of the parable.

Turning first to the slaves, having instructed them to turn a profit, he now asks whether they have done so. Of the ten entrusted with a pound each, the first two receive commendation and reward for their conformity to the nobleman's stated expectations.[234] In a deliberate echo of 16:10, trustworthiness "in a very small thing" is made to signify faithfulness to the master and readiness for greater responsibility, in this case, a share in the nobleman's authority (cf. 22:28-30).

The faithfulness of these two slaves is tied into the larger Lukan narrative in significant ways. Perhaps most obviously, in 12:35-48 Jesus variously envisions slaves and managers given responsibility before the master departs; there issues of alertness and faithful allegiance are at center stage. Also of importance is the reply of the second slave, "your pound has made five pounds," employing a term, "to make," that Luke often uses in contexts having to do with the bearing of fruit appropriate to the faithful disciple — that is, with faith expressed in the practices generated on account of one's fidelity to the will of God.[235]

A third slave[236] had refused the instructions of his master; rather than using his pound to exploit the market and turning a profit, he had taken the money out of circulation. He attributes his nonaction to his fear, characterizing the nobleman as a difficult, severe man.[237] Using metaphors borrowed from agriculture and commerce, moreover, he depicts his master as a fraud whose exploitative business practices contravene conventional procedures and writ-

---

234. The first is more developed, including the interjection εὖγε ("Great!" — based on the adverb εὖ, "well"); the second likely presupposes the language of the first.

235. ποιέω — cf. already in 3:7-14; also, e.g., 6:46; 8:19-21.

236. Luke actually refers to "the other." Is this one representative of the remaining eight, so that of the ten only two were found faithful? Or are all three mentioned in this account representative of the range of responses the nobleman elicited from his slaves?

237. αὐστηρός is used in the NT only in vv 21-22.

ten law.[238] Repeating the slave's words, the nobleman seems to accept this assessment of himself; in any case, he does nothing to contradict it. Instead, he uses the slave's own words to query the slave's response: Even collecting interest (which a Jew was forbidden to do,[239] but what is that to one already charged with expropriation?) would have been preferable to nonaction.

24-27 The end of the parable is focused primarily on judgment for those who prove themselves unfaithful to the nobleman or reject his kingdom altogether. The prospect of unfaithfulness is remarkable since it involves a master/servant relationship. Like the others, this third slave referred to the nobleman as "lord," signifying the nature of his allegiance and obligation to him, which he then flatly contradicts by his noncompliance. The severity of the judgment he receives is difficult to assess, though the standers-by (v 25) respond to a perceived unfairness. What is evident is the basis of judgment, made especially clear by the deliberate echo of 8:18: Those who hear and heed the instructions of the master will receive more, while those who hear but do not heed will lose what little they have. In this parable, "more" turns out to be not only more in terms of the original distribution of money, but also a share in the newly secured imperial rule.

"Enemies of mine" refers not to persons like this disobedient slave, but to the subjects of the realm who refuse to show allegiance to their ruler and, indeed, who oppose his claim to the throne (v 27; for the relation of "hate" and "enemy," see 1:71). As one kingdom displaces another, judgment follows for those who continue to show fealty to the old (Jer 39:5-7; 1 Sam 15:32-33; cf. Luke 12:46).

5.7. JESUS ARRIVES IN JERUSALEM (19:28-48)

The journey to Jerusalem, begun in 9:51, comes at last to its finale. With this segment of the narrative, Luke is especially concerned to build a bridge from a lengthy section concerned above all with the formation of disciples along the way to his accounts of Jesus' instruction in the city itself (20:1–21:38) and of the progression of events leading from Jesus' suffering and death (22:1–23:56) to his exaltation (24:1-53). Serving this concern with transition is a dual focus on Jesus' identity and the division precipitated by his arrival in Jerusalem.

(1) Christology and Discipleship. Given the great concern of the travel narrative overall with the resocialization of Jesus' followers within the new

---

238. This point is well made by C. F. Evans (671-72), who refers to Aelian *Varia Historia* 3.46; Plato *Laws* 8.844e; 11.913c; 12.941c; et al.

239. Cf. Exod 22:25; Lev 25:35-38; Deut 23:19-20.

community gathered around Jesus, the lack of interest in discipleship here may be surprising. However, following Luke's presentation of the disciples' incapacity to comprehend God's plan in 18:31-34, the disciples have receded more and more into the background. Indeed, at this juncture whatever had earlier distinguished the twelve from the others has been blurred. Luke's reference to "two of the disciples" (v 29) leaves open the question whether these are from the twelve, and his depiction of "the whole multitude of the disciples" (v 37) is reminiscent of the mass of Jesus' followers and hangers-on in 6:17-19. This gradual deemphasis on the disciples is matched in the narrative by a crescendoing preoccupation with christology. Begun already in 18:35-43 with the acclamation of Jesus as the "Son of David" and continuing with the parabolic material in 19:11-27 is Luke's renewed interest in portraying Jesus as the Davidic Messiah, a king. This itself recalls the birth narrative, where Jesus' identity was first broached so definitely by God's spokesperson, Gabriel (e.g., 1:32-35). And this emphasis moves even more into the limelight here, above all with the acclamation of Jesus as "the king who comes in the name of the Lord" (v 38).

(2) Division in Israel. Early on, Simeon had foretold that Jesus would be the cause of division within Israel (2:34-35), and Luke has narrated the realization of this prophecy in both the Galilean and journey sections of the Third Gospel. The strength of the presentation of this motif in this narrative section is unprecedented, however. Division comes to the fore, first, in the different responses elicited by Jesus' entry into Jerusalem: Some praised God for all the powerful deeds they had seen while others insist that Jesus silence his followers (vv 37-40). Second, in his oracle concerning Jerusalem, Jesus observes that Jerusalem had failed to recognize both the things that make for peace and the time of divine visitation (vv 42, 44). Finally, the Jewish leadership in Jerusalem and the people divide in their respective responses to Jesus, with the leaders looking for a way to execute Jesus (vv 47-48). With this, the opposition against Jesus has reached rare heights (though cf. 6:11; 13:31). Even this has been foretold, and related to Jesus' advent in Jerusalem (9:22, 44; 17:25; 18:31-33).

(3) Salvation to All. Soteriology, so important throughout the travel narrative (and, indeed, the theme of Luke-Acts as a whole), is not altogether absent from this narrative section, even if it is less explicit than has been the norm. As will become clear, the entrance of the king into Jerusalem has soteriological implications as it raises interpretive questions about the nature of his dominion. Of interest, too, is Jesus' oracle concerning the destruction of Jerusalem, a statement that portends not only the end of the city itself but perhaps more importantly the end of its socio-religious role as the dominant "cultural center" within the world of the narrative. "Culture centers" are active centers of social order that ". . . consist in the point or points in a

society where its leading ideas come together·with its leading institutions to create an arena in which the events that most vitally affect its members' lives take place."[1] Within the Lukan narrative, the Jerusalem temple is seen to serve a world-ordering function, particularly as its architecture provides a series of segregating zones that extend out from the temple mount to determine social relations and the experience of fictive kinship between Jew and Samaritan, Jew and Gentile, male and female, and so on.[2] If Jerusalem is utterly destroyed (with no stone left on another, v 44), then its socio-religious role is also decimated. If Jerusalem is no longer the center of the world, then the status distinctions it embodied and propagated are no longer definitive. In this light, the citation of Isa 56:7 in v 46, "My house shall be a house of prayer," sans the Isaianic phrase "for all peoples," is telling, for it runs counter to the eschatological vision of all peoples coming to Jerusalem to worship Yahweh[3] and paves the way for a mission that is centrifugal rather than centripetal (cf. Acts 1:8).

5.7.1. Going Up to Jerusalem (19:28-40)

28 *After he had said this, he went on ahead, going up to Jerusalem.*

29 *When he had come near Bethphage and Bethany, at the place called the Mount of Olives, he sent two of the disciples,* 30 *saying, "Go into the village ahead of you, and as you enter it you will find tied there a colt that has never been ridden. Untie it and bring it here.* 31 *If anyone asks you, 'Why are you untying it?' just say this, 'The Lord needs it.' "* 32 *So those who were sent departed and found it as he had told them.* 33 *As they were untying the colt, its owners asked them, "Why are you untying the colt?"* 34 *They said, "The Lord needs it."* 35 *Then they brought it to Jesus; and after throwing their cloaks on the colt, they set Jesus on it.* 36 *As he rode along, people kept spreading their cloaks on the road.* 37 *As he was now approaching the path down from the Mount of Olives, the whole multitude of the disciples began to praise God joyfully with a loud voice for all the deeds of power that they had seen,* 38 *saying,*

> *"Blessed is the king*
> *who comes in the name of the Lord!*
> *Peace in heaven,*
> *and glory in the highest heaven!"*

---

1. Geertz, *Local Knowledge,* 122-23.
2. See Knipe, "Temple," 122; Green, "Demise of the Temple."
3. See, e.g., McKnight, *Light among the Gentiles,* 47-48; Jeremias, *Jesus' Promise,* 57-62.

39 Some of the Pharisees in the crowd said to him, "Teacher, order your disciples to stop." 40 He answered, "I tell you, if these were silent, the stones would shout out."

By this juncture in the Third Gospel, Jerusalem has been vested with monumental significance. It is foremost the place of destiny, the goal to which Jesus has been headed on account of his submission to the divine plan (e.g., 9:31, 51; 13:31-35; 18:31-34). Luke's narration of Jesus' entry into Jerusalem is punctuated by a mélange of geographical markers; in fact, narrative time is slowed considerably and dramatic tension intensified by references to each stage of this final leg of the journey, marking the progression of Jesus as he draws closer and closer to Jerusalem. Additionally, because of Jerusalem's status as the Holy City — location of the temple, abode of God, nexus between human and divine, inviolable territory[4] — the question of the relationship between Jesus and Jerusalem is inevitable. Repeatedly, Jesus has run afoul of representatives from Jerusalem (5:17) and others who challenged his understanding of the Scriptures and of the nature of salvation. How will Jesus, who has claimed legitimacy as an interpreter of the divine will, fare in relation to Jerusalem — the city, the temple, and its leadership, to whom, in the eyes of most, God has granted divine authority? Jesus' entry, according to the Lukan narration, does not shy away from this confrontation. To the contrary, by painting Jesus with such regal, messianic hues, Luke sets the stage for subsequent challenges to Jesus' base of authority and, ultimately, for his demise (vv 39-40; cf. 20:2).

Luke depicts Jesus' entry in four scenes (vv 28-48), the first two concerned with the acquisition of a colt for the short trip from the Mount of Olives to the city and the trip itself (vv 28-40). These two serve a common theme — namely, Jesus' royal personage. As will become evident, the whole process from obtaining a colt to the crowds' proclaiming Jesus king is wrapped in the interpretive cloth of eschatological expectation and scriptural allusion (esp. Psalm 118 and Zech 9:9). These work together to certify Jesus' messianic status. What is more, Luke's account has important points of contact with a type scene or pattern known from Maccabean literature and from Josephus.[5] In analogous scenes, the person who enters the city does not do so in order to claim kingship; rather, entry presupposes an already achieved victory. This is important because it suggests that Jesus is not about to assert his royal status. This accords well with his acclamation as king even before his birth

---

4. See Knipe, "Temple," 107-12.

5. Catchpole ("Triumphal Entry," 319-21) refers to literary accounts of the "triumphal entries" of Alexander, Apollonius, Judas Maccabaeus, Jonathan Maccabaeus, Simon Maccabaeus, Antigonus, Marcus Agrippa, Archelaus, and "Alexander's 'double.'"

(1:32-35), and with an interpretation of the preceding chapters of the Lukan narrative as developing the nature of Jesus' kingship and, therefore, of his kingdom. What Luke is about to narrate, then, assumes the portrait of Jesus already established, with its soteriological emphasis on good news to those living on the margins of acceptable society (4:18-19).

28-34 Verse 28 is transitional, signaling the continuation of the journey motif following the brief respite recounted in vv 1-27, and imprinting upon the ensuing events the importance of Jerusalem (see above). Bethphage, then Bethany, then the Mount of Olives serve as milestones, marking with unprecedented detail the advance of Jesus toward his destiny. Luke has focused his narrative lens so narrowly on Jesus that he appears at first to be traveling alone, so that we are left to assume that his followers and the crowds are present on the road too (cf. vv 29b, 36-37). The Mount of Olives is mentioned twice (vv 29, 37), emphasizing both the proximity of Jesus to his destination[6] and the eschatological associations of the mountain with relation to the advent of the Messiah.[7]

Luke provides no basis for speculation about the identity of the two disciples sent to secure a colt, nor does he even hint that these messengers belong to the twelve (see "the whole multitude of the disciples," v 37), nor does he identify which village (Bethphage? Bethany? another?) is envisioned. This shortage of descriptive data contrasts sharply with the wealth of detail provided with respect to the colt, and this encourages exploration of the significance of those particulars.

First, the colt is tied and must be untied (mentioned five times!) — a possible echo of Gen 49:11, which speaks of a coming ruler who would tie a colt to a vine. The presence of such an echo would contribute to the royal reverberations of this scene,[8] though this instance of intertextuality would also comprise an important element of parody: The ruler of the Genesis text is characterized by extraordinary opulence, whereas the colt Jesus rides must be borrowed. Such an emphasis comports well with the larger Lukan motif of a kingdom oriented toward the least and the lost, and the picture of Jesus as one who has "nowhere to lay his head" (9:58). Second, the colt is one "that has never been ridden" (v 30). This is likely a paraphrastic way of drawing out the sense of Zech 9:9 LXX, which refers to the king's advent on a "new colt," since a new colt is one that would

---

6. Josephus gives the distance from the Mount of Olives to Jerusalem in *J.W.* 20.8.6 §169 as five stadia (*ca.* 3,035 feet) and in *Ant.* 5.2.3 §70 as six (*ca.* 3,642 feet).

7. The latter is grounded in Zech 14:4 (cf. Str-B 1:840-42; Josephus *J.W.* 2.13.15 §§261-63). The possibility of a scriptural echo in this co-text is advanced by the thematically related use of Zech 9:9 here (see below). Cf. Rese, *Alttestamentliche Motive,* 196-97.

8. Harvey, *Constraints of History,* 124.

not yet have been broken for riding.[9] Third, Jesus' instructions anticipate that the disciples will need a rejoinder for some who ask why they are untying the colt. In fact, its owners (Greek: "lords") do raise this question, and the disciples respond with the words Jesus had given them beforehand, "The Lord needs it." In this way, the claim of Jesus (as lord) supersedes the rights of ownership,[10] just as the requirements of a king supplant those of his subjects (cf. 1 Sam 8:10-18).[11] In these ways, the details of Luke's narration prove to be laden with royal significance, preparing for the more explicit affirmation of Jesus' kingly status in what follows.

Within the Lukan narrative, Jesus is progressing to Jerusalem, not moving back and forth. Hence, his instructions concerning what the disciples will find and what they are to do, combined with the narrator's conclusion, "those who were sent . . . found it just as he had told them," must point to Jesus' customary prophetic omniscience and not to his having made prior arrangements. Moreover, the close connection between prophecy and fulfillment in this episode draws attention to the fidelity of Jesus' revelatory word (cf. 2:20).

35-36 Thus far, Jesus has been making pilgrimage to Jerusalem on foot. That he now rides a colt, for only the last mile of the journey, intimates the symbolic character of this act.[12] The most obvious interpretation is provided by Zech 9:9: as the triumphant, victorious, yet humble king, Jesus comes riding on a colt.[13] Within Israel's history, too, the heirs of David rode to their coronation.[14] The spreading of outer garments onto the pathway is appropriate to the greeting of a royal figure as well.[15]

With the arrival of the colt, the disciples Jesus had sent had carried out all of the instructions he had given them. This means that, in setting Jesus on the colt, etc., they are taking their own initiative in acclaiming him as the Davidic Messiah. Thus they join Peter, who had earlier affirmed Jesus' messiahship (9:20). Whether they, like Peter, fail fully to understand the implications of Jesus' royal status is not yet clear. For the moment, though, Jesus' acquiescence to their actions confirms that they are right to regard him as king.

---

9. In addition, Catchpole ("Triumphal Entry," 324) refers to the rabbinic instruction that no one should use the animal on which a king rides (*Sanh.* 2.5).

10. This point is more obvious in the Greek text, where one reads κύριος in vv 31 and 33 (plural; NRSV: "owners"), 34.

11. See the related discussion of ἀγγαρεύω/ἀγγαρεία in *TLNT,* 1:23-25.

12. Cf. Harvey, *Constraints of History,* 121.

13. The strength of this echo is assisted by the use of ἐπιβιβάζω.

14. See 2 Sam 18:9; 19:26; 1 Kgs 1:32-40; J. A. Sanders, "Luke's Entrance Narrative," 142; Fernández Marcos, "La unción de Salomón"; Strauss, *Davidic Messiah,* 314.

15. See 2 Kgs 9:13; Str-B 1:844-45.

37-38 The Mount of Olives is located to the east of Jerusalem, across the Kidron Valley; hence, Luke's reference to the path down from the mountain is topographically realistic at the same time that it signifies Jesus' closeness (just over half a mile) to the city and temple. As in 6:17-19, the distinction between "the whole multitude of disciples" and the "people" is, qualitatively, not great. Both acclaim Jesus as king through their actions and/or words.

Psalm 118, quoted in v 38, was used in preexilic Israel as a hymn of royal entry on the occasion of an annual ritual of reenthronement. Later, it was used in the Feast of Tabernacles (or Booths), when palm branches would have been used celebratively in preparation for the building of booths. The absence of palm branches, along with the manifest presence of other royal meanings accruing to the Lukan account, indicate that Luke has in mind something other than the importance of Psalm 118 in times of festival celebrations. (Indeed, throughout Luke's account, Jesus has been portrayed as more than an ordinary pilgrim coming into Jerusalem.) Instead, in its Lukan co-text, Psalm 118 reverts to its earlier significance as a psalm of royal entry.[16]

The psalm is cited by the crowd of disciples in v 38, though with the addition of the words "the king" (Ps 118:26). This addendum likely has its origin in the language of Zech 9:9, though the acclamation of Jesus as king also resonates with the similar acclamation of Jehu in 2 Kgs 9:13: "Jehu is king!" (a text that reports how cloaks were spread before Jehu in a way analogous to Luke's report in vv 35-36). The phrase "one who comes" is reminiscent of the language used of Jesus in 3:15-17; 7:19-20, with the result that, in this way too, his ministry and person evidence messianic tones. Moreover, the conspicuous use of Zech 9:9-10 and Ps 118:26 in this co-text clears the way for us to find reverberations of a less explicit sort. Thus, the notion of *praising God* echoes the opening and much of the substance of Psalm 118; doing so *joyfully* may reflect Zech 9:9 and Ps 118:15; and the motif of *peace* in v 38a is made all the more sonorous by the collocation of peace and royal dominion in Zech 9:10.

This is not to say that the Evangelist has drawn these motifs only from OT precursors, for this is manifestly not the case. Praising God for his wondrous works is typically associated with Jesus' miraculous deeds in Luke-Acts,[17] and joy is regularly associated with divine intervention.[18] Jesus' "powerful deeds" appear repeatedly in Luke-Acts, and the Evangelist habitually interprets them theocentrically: In them we discern God at work through Jesus, who is thus identified as the divinely authorized and empowered agent

16. J. A. Sanders, "Luke's Entrance Narrative," 143-48.
17. Cf., e.g., 7:16; 13:17; 17:15; 18:43.
18. Cf. 1:14; 2:10; 6:23; 8:13; 10:17, 20; 13:17; 19:6.

of salvation.[19] Much of the content of v 37b is fully explicable in terms of the Lukan narrative as a whole, then. However, if one does not have to see the Scriptures of Israel as the primary wellhead from which these motifs flow, this does not mean that their interpretation in this co-text is not assisted by the reverberations identified above. The critical issue is not to authenticate origins, but to hear and appreciate the wealth of resonances — some from within the Lukan narrative, others from the intertextual relations of this text with Psalm 118 and Zechariah 9.[20]

The disciples' words, "Blessed is the king who comes in the name of the Lord," echo the Scriptures of Israel, as we have seen, but also the words of Jesus in 13:35. Those earlier words of Jesus were cast in the form of a conditional promise, as if to say, "If Israel will repent and greet with blessing the one who comes in the name of the Lord, then Israel will experience the advent of salvation."[21] The connection between that text and the present one, then, is not a happy one. This is because it is the crowd of Jesus' disciples, and not Jerusalem itself, that greets Jesus thus. As will become immediately evident (vv 41-44), the obduracy of Jerusalem persists, with the result that they have not recognized the coming of Jesus as the coming of salvation.[22]

The motif of peace contains an obvious echo of 2:14, and its significance is tied to a comparison of the two. In the former peace is said to be "on earth," while in the latter peace is "in heaven." The former proclaims that the divine intervention evident in the birth of Jesus has brought peace in the sense of manifesting God's redemptive purpose and inviting humanity to share in salvation. In light of the actual response to this invitation narrated thus far in the Third Gospel, however, "peace on earth" remains an intended future, a prospect that continues to invite positive response. "Peace in heaven," then, refers to the divine intention, the reality of God's reconciling presence, its full manifestation on earth interrupted by opposition to Jesus.[23]

39-40   That God's salvific purpose attracts opposition as well as support is evidenced by the response of "some of the Pharisees." This is the last reference to Pharisees in the Third Gospel, and these Pharisees exemplify all who set themselves over against the divine plan. They are those who, in v 14, "do not want this man to rule over us"; who "do not recognize the time of God's visitation" (v 44). This is not the universal response of the Pharisees,[24]

---

19. See 4:14, 18-19, 36; 5:17; 6:19; 7:16, 18-23; 8:13; 10:13, 19; Acts 2:22; 10:38.

20. Green and Hays, "Use of the Old Testament," 228-29; Green, "Beginning," 78-79.

21. See above on 13:34-35.

22. *Pace* C. A. Evans ("Prophecy and Polemic," 178-79), who thinks 13:35 must refer to the parousia, since it is not fulfilled by the inhabitants of Jerusalem in 19:37-38.

23. Cf. Godet, 2:230; Caird, 216; Brawley, *Centering on God,* 122, 137.

24. καί τινες τῶν Φαρισαίων; *contra* many scholars, e.g., Darr, *Character Building,* 115.

but those who do resist the acclamation of Jesus as king are emblematic of the Jewish leadership in Jerusalem who will seek and engineer Jesus' execution. From a narratological vantage point, then, these Pharisees put the reader on notice that the euphoria of this moment will be short-lived.

"Teacher" is an address used for Jesus by those outside the circle of his followers, by those who seek something from Jesus but have not fully formed their opinion of him.[25] Their request of Jesus ("rebuke them!") betrays their view that the disciples are acting in opposition to the will of God.[26] Accordingly, their lack of comprehension concerning the divine purpose, and particularly of Jesus' status before God, is exposed. Given the convictions concerning divine revelation and human obedience to God espoused by such persons earlier in the narrative, however, it is easy to see how the royalist claims made concerning Jesus in this scene would challenge the views and authority of the religious establishment, whom the Pharisees in this instance represent. Here we see the commencement of an historic clash of worldviews, of profoundly different understandings of God, salvation, and religious authority.

Thus far, messianic claims have been made on Jesus' behalf. With his reply, Jesus embraces them, and in doing so he implicitly affirms the people who made them for their insight. Indeed, "stones" would pick up the chorus of joyful praise were these people silenced, signaling the cosmic repercussions of the consummation of God's salvific plan signified in this event.[27] The tragic irony of Jesus' reply resides in the reality that Jerusalem's inhabitants should be welcoming their king with words of acclamation, not leaving the joyful chorus to inanimate stones.

5.7.2. Weeping over Jerusalem (19:41-44)

41 *As he came near and saw the city, he wept over it,* 42 *saying, "If you, even you, had only recognized on this day the things that make for peace! But now they are hidden from your eyes.* 43 *Indeed, the days will come upon you, when your enemies will set up ramparts around you and surround you, and hem you in on every side.* 44 *They will crush*

---

25. See 7:40; 10:25; 11:45; 18:18; Gowler, *Portraits of the Pharisees,* 273.

26. This is the implication of their use of the verb ἐπιτιμάω — cf. 4:35, 39, 41; 8:24; et al.

27. The notion of stones replacing human beings is also found in 3:8. For the motif of creation responding with joy, see, e.g., Ps 96:11-13; Isa 55:12. Some have found here an allusion to Hos 2:11, but the motif of judgment against the Chaldeans found there does not correspond well either with this joyous occasion or with the prediction of judgment for Jerusalem in vv 41-44. Kinman ("Joy or Judgment," 234) also rejects the judgment motif in this scene on syntactical grounds.

you to the ground, you and your children within you, and they will not
leave within you one stone upon another; because you did not recognize
the time of your visitation from God."

The stage is set for Jesus' prophetic lament and judgment in two ways. There is, first, his drawing near to the city of Jerusalem. Luke has employed the verb "to come near," like a litany,[28] using it repeatedly to slow the pace of the narrative and to dramatize the long-awaited arrival of Jesus, Israel's regal prophet, at the center of the Jewish world. Second, and even more crucial, is the failure of Jerusalem to receive its king with praise and blessing, registered in vv 28-40. This failure attracts more than the retort from Jesus recorded in v 40, however, but leads to a prophetic threat oracle.

This oracular form has three components: the address or summons, the indictment, and the threat or announcement of a verdict.[29] The address or summons is implicit in the combination of Luke's note that Jesus "saw the city" and the repetition of the personal pronoun "you."[30] Clearly, Jesus' oracle is delivered against Jerusalem. Just as clearly, his prophetic utterance is not a happy one, nor vindictive, but full of sorrow as he mourns the fate of the city.[31] The power and pathos of the oracle are served by its structure in the Greek text, with verbs of warfare and violence appearing at the beginning and the pronoun "you" at the close of each clause.

Jesus' indictment against Jerusalem boils down to one charge: its failure to recognize God's purposeful, salvific activity on its behalf. In this respect, the response of those Pharisees mentioned in v 39 is interpreted as proleptic for the response of Jerusalem itself. Indeed, as Luke will narrate, even if for only a moment, the leaders and populace will join together in their rejection of Jesus (see 23:13, 18, 21, 23). One can perhaps hear in the background the words of v 14: "We do not want this man to rule over us."

The one charge against Jerusalem takes two forms: (1) their failure to recognize "on this day the things that make for peace" (v 42a) and (2) their failure to "recognize the time of your visitation from God" (v 44b). These statements are closely related, just as divine visitation and peace were collocated in the Song of Zechariah (1:68-75). "Visitation" can refer to God's coming to bring salvation (as it does in 1:68; 7:16), but also for judgment. That the former was the hope in this instance is clear from the larger Lukan narrative (e.g., 2:38) and from the desire for peace expressed

28. ἐγγίζω — cf. 18:35, 40; 19:29, 37, 41.

29. So Borg, "Luke 19:42-44," 104-5.

30. A form of σύ is found 12 times in this text; accounting for the appearance of verbs in the second person raises this count (in the NRSV) to 15.

31. For the prophetic lament, see, e.g., Jer 9:1; 13:17; 14:17; Amos 5:1-3; et al.

in v 42a.[32] "Peace" in Luke has no connection to harmony with the Roman Empire or with the temple leadership, nor does it refer to subjective or individualistic tranquility. Peace, rather, is a soteriological term — shalom, peace and justice, the gift of God that embraces salvation for all in all of its social, material, and spiritual realities. Within this co-text (see "this day"), "the things required for peace" must include both the king (who brings, establishes, and perpetuates peace) and the responses of welcome and blessing by which people are to greet this king.[33] Jesus, however, anticipates his rejection — and thus the refusal of peace — in Jerusalem. As a consequence,[34] divine visitation will be experienced not as redemption but as judgment (cf. 10:8-15).[35] What is more, Luke's "now" (v 42b) indicates that Jerusalem, in its failure to recognize the significance of Jesus' advent at its gates, has reached a point of no return. Its lack of openness to the salvific intervention of God has resulted in Jerusalem's incapacity to see his handiwork.

In this co-text, not least in view of the narrative to follow in Acts, it is important to underscore that Jerusalem's ignorance and obduracy cannot be transferred to Israel as a whole or even, for that matter, to all of Jerusalem's inhabitants.[36] Throughout Luke-Acts, "Jerusalem" functions above all as a cipher for its role as a cultural center (see above on 19:28-48), so mention of the city relates primarily to the temple system and the leadership that draws its legitimacy from the temple. This system — represented in the temple's concern with the correlation of the concepts of holiness and relative purity and the consequent segregation along status lines of Gentile from Jew, male from female, and the like — and those who follow it are self-legitimating and, according to Luke, closed to the nature of the kingdom of God proclaimed and served by Jesus. Even when the opportunity to reassess the nature of God's activity among them, along with the centrality of Jesus' ministry to the divine will, is presented to them, those related to the temple in Jerusalem will continue in their resistance (cf. Acts 2–7). Jesus' insistence on the ignorance

32. On the syntax of the uncompleted conditional clause of v 42a, see BDF §482.

33. See the discussions in Swartley, "Politics or Peace"; and *TLNT,* 1:424-38 (esp. 430).

34. Tiede (*Prophecy and History,* 82) observes the connection between Luke's clause, "because you did not know," and the judgment oracles of Jeremiah (e.g., 22:8-9; 23:38; 38:20, LXX).

35. Comparison of the present co-text with 10:8-15 underscores both the correlation of Jesus' ministry with the presence of the kingdom of God and the significance of hospitality as welcoming the kingdom-messenger and embracing the purpose of God. For the phrase (τὸν καιρὸν τῆς ἐπισκοπῆς), cf. Jer 6:15; 10:15 (ἐν καιρῷ ἐπισκοπῆς).

36. On other grounds, Kinman ("Lucan Eschatology") argues that the prospective destruction of Jerusalem does not signify for Luke the demise of Israel in God's purpose.

of Jerusalem in this scene (vv 42a, 44b) prepares for the subsequent possibility of forgiveness (cf. 23:34; Acts 3:17; 13:27), but this possibility will not be realized in the case of those who continue to cling to the power structures supported by the temple ideology.

By way of pronouncing sentence upon Jerusalem, Jesus strings together five images of military conquest and destruction (vv 43-44a). The opening words, "the days will come upon you," are borrowed from prophetic oracles of judgment.[37] Moreover, Jesus' promise of the conquest and full-scale destruction of the city represents a collage of OT texts. These images are reminiscent of Israel's own past when Jerusalem was razed under Nebuchadnezzar, as this calamity is represented within the Scriptures.[38] Those connections urge an analogous interpretation of the Jerusalem that failed to recognize the entry of Jesus as "the time of your visitation from God." In effect, in narrating this prophetic oracle of judgment, Luke is engaged in a struggle of meaning. Unlike some of the Pharisees, who see the acclamation of Jesus as the Davidic Messiah as contrary to God's design (v 39), Luke has it that Jerusalem's rejection of Jesus is reminiscent of its historic betrayal of the covenant that led to the first destruction of Jerusalem and the exile. As Israel of old fell to its enemies on account of divine judgment for its unfaithfulness, so Jerusalem will be judged for its inconstancy.

5.7.3. Preparation of the Temple for Teaching (19:45-48)

45 *Then he entered the temple and began to drive out those who were selling things there;* 46 *and he said, "It is written,*

'My house shall be a house of prayer';

but you have made it a den of robbers."

47 *Every day he was teaching in the temple. The chief priests, the scribes, and the leaders of the people kept looking for a way to kill him;* 48 *but they did not find anything they could do, for all the people were spellbound by what they heard.*

Given the lengthy, dramatic buildup to this moment, Luke's account of Jesus' arrival in Jerusalem is surprisingly terse. For this same reason, however, it is laden with interpretive significance. (1) In the Lukan narration, this is the first time Jesus has been in the temple since he was 12 years old. Then, he asserted the divine necessity of his being in his Father's house — claiming the temple as the abode of God and prefiguring his own teaching ministry in it (see above on

---

37. See, e.g., Isa 39:6; Hos 9:7; Amos 4:2; Zech 14:1; et al.
38. See esp. Isa 29:3; 37:33; Jer 6:6, 15; 10:15; 52:4-5; Ezek 4:1-3; 21:22; Dodd, "Fall of Jerusalem."

2:41-51). (2) Since 9:51, the Third Gospel has been preoccupied with the motif of the journey, one of the primary emphases of which has been the journey's end in Jerusalem. In Jerusalem, Jesus was to meet his death as he served and fulfilled the divine purpose. (3) The city of Jerusalem and the Jerusalem temple are virtually equated in Lukan thought, so that Luke can record Jesus' arrival in the city as Jesus' entry into the temple.[39] Not surprisingly, then, Luke can move directly from a prophetic threat oracle against the city (vv 41-44) to his dramatic, symbolic act of censure and recovery in vv 45-46.

As a geographical location, Jerusalem and the temple constitute profoundly important social products that reflect and configure ways of understanding the world Luke is portraying.[40] For this reason a record of the confrontation between Jesus and the temple as it was understood and interpreted by the chief priests, scribes, and leaders of the people (v 47) is essential to the Lukan narrative. How could Jesus carry on his interpretive enterprise, reforming Jewish conceptions of God's salvation, and not deal with the Jerusalem temple? In fact, the setting of the temple ties these two paragraphs together, with Jesus' denunciation of the temple in vv 45-46 leading into Luke's summary statement concerning Jesus' instruction in the temple in vv 47-48.[41] The one act sets the stage for the other; or, better, in his prophetic critique of the temple, Jesus recovers the temple for its legitimate use — namely, revelatory teaching concerning the purpose of God even now coming to fruition. To reclaim the temple for its legitimate use, however, is to brand as illegitimate its utilization by the temple hierarchy, and thus to attract opposition.

45-46 The type scene relating the entry of a ruler (see above on 19:28-40) reaches its conclusion with cultic activity, either positive (e.g., the offering of sacrifices) or negative (e.g., the expulsion of the idolatrous).[42] Luke's narration follows this pattern well, with Jesus entering the Court of Gentiles,[43] the outer court of the temple, where he engages in what Luke describes as a brief, small-scale, but highly symbolic censuring of the temple system. The narrator actually describes Jesus' action as "driving out" objectionable people, in the same way that he "drove out" demons,[44] as though the merchandisers were similarly profane and oppressive.[45] What was the

---

39. See Bachmann, *Jerusalem und der Tempel;* Brawley, *Luke-Acts,* 123-24.

40. For this understanding of geographical space, see, e.g., Pred, *Human Geographies;* Soja, *Postmodern Geographies;* and Werlen, *Society, Action and Space.*

41. See Chance, *Jerusalem,* 57-58; Brawley, *Luke-Acts,* 123.

42. See Catchpole, "Triumphal Entry," 319-21.

43. This is the most likely location of those concerned with changing money and the merchandising of sacrificial animals — cf. Sanders, *Jesus and Judaism,* 67.

44. ἐκβάλλω — cf. 9:40, 49; 11:14-20; 13:32.

45. See Acts 10:38, where the devil is said "to oppress" people.

impetus behind Jesus' action? The sacrificial system itself does not come under criticism, so it is difficult to imagine that his concern focused simply on the changing of money and selling of birds that were necessary precursors to the offering of sacrifice.[46] The rationale for Jesus' action comes rather in the material borrowed from Isa 56:7 and Jer 7:11 in v 46,[47] a mixed citation that juxtaposes two contradictory ways of construing of the temple.

The temple, for Jesus, is properly used as a "house of prayer." This is a function it carries in 1:10, 13; 2:29-32, 37; 18:9-14; 24:53; Acts 3:1; 22:17, though allusion to such texts suggests additional, far-reaching considerations. First is the typically Lukan collocation of prayer and divine revelation in the temple, particularly revelation concerned with the nature and present outworking of the divine plan in human affairs (esp. 1:8-20; 2:25-32, 37-38; Acts 22:17-21). Prayer in other contexts is likewise revelatory, especially with regard to the identity of Jesus, his status before God and divine mission (e.g., 3:21-22; 4:42-44; 9:18-20; 10:21-24).[48] Had the temple been employed genuinely as a "house of prayer," would Jerusalem have failed to recognize the time of God's visitation (v 44)? Second is the characterization of prayer in 18:1-8, 9-14 as the persistent pursuit of justice and the humble openness to God that spurns self-aggrandizement. Had the temple been utilized genuinely as a "house of prayer," would its leaders not understand the nature of the inbreaking kingdom of God, and thus recognize "the things that make for peace" (v 42)?

Instead, the temple has served as a "cave for bandits." The phrase itself is borrowed from Jer 7:3-20. There, the use of the words "this is the temple of the Lord" as a mantra to warrant iniquitous practices is condemned (v 4), along with the use of the temple as a sanctuary for those who have committed such violent acts as oppression of the poor (vv 5-10). For Jeremiah, then, as well as for Luke's first-century readers, a "den of robbers" recalls the caves to which "people of violence" retreat in order to escape justice.[49] Such persons were known for their violence as well as rapacity,[50] which makes "robbers" an apt, albeit burlesque description of the Jewish leaders, whose economic power is grounded in the socio-religious significance of the temple. Legitimated by their exclusive capacity to handle holy paraphernalia and/or

---

46. This point is well made in principle by Sanders, *Jesus,* 61-65: "The business arrangements around the temple were *necessary* if the commandments were to be obeyed" (65). Sanders rightly rejects interpretations that focus on "outward practices" versus the "condition of the heart"; in the Lukan co-text, this has no place at all.

47. Luke uses a form of γράφω to introduce scriptural citations in 2:23; 3:4; 4:4, 8, 10, 17; 7:27; 10:26; 19:46; 20:17, 28; 22:37.

48. See Crump, *Jesus the Intercessor.*

49. Cf. Josephus *Ant.* 14.15.4 §415; 14.15.5 §421.

50. See *TLNT,* 2:390.

authoritative position as legal scholars, they distanced themselves from and even violated the needy, and in other ways demonstrated their antagonism to the ways of God surfacing in the ministry of Jesus and those who would follow him.[51] And, taking refuge in the temple, they use the abode of God to justify their practices.

It is no wonder, then, that Jesus' citation of Isa 56:7 stops short of embracing the role of the temple as a house of prayer *for all people.* Used by its leadership to demarcate lines of separation between those of acceptable status, insiders and outsiders, the temple would not have this function. Instead, ironically, it is in the temple that divine revelation concerning the universal mission for the salvation of all peoples would come (2:25-32; Acts 22:17-21). In the Lukan vision, Gentiles would not come to the temple to find Yahweh; rather, the Lord goes out, through his witnesses, to the Gentiles (cf. Acts 1:8).

47-48 Following its censure and reclamation, the temple becomes an important site for Jesus' ministry of teaching — itself an attempt further to orient the temple around its true significance as a place of "good news for the poor."[52] The content of his instruction is not specified in this summary statement. From a retrospective position, we may imagine that his message is similar to that in 4:16-30, since that synagogal sermon is programmatic for Jesus' message and typical of his teaching thus far in the Gospel. In this case, Jesus' teaching in the temple would consist of his use of the Scriptures of Israel to announce the dawning of eschatological salvation in his person and ministry. If one accounts for the teaching events Luke goes on to record during the tenure of Jesus' ministry in Jerusalem, this picture is not substantively altered, even though the record Luke provides is one-sided in its concentration on the hostility Jesus' message engenders.[53]

Just as Simeon had prophesied (2:34-35), Jesus' message is the cause of division within Israel, here recounted as a fundamental division between the people and the Jewish leadership in Jerusalem. Luke refers to "all the people," inviting us to imagine masses of people representing all of Israel gathered in Jerusalem and supportive of Jesus. Opposite them is the triumvirate — the chief priests, scribes, and the leaders — that is, the Jewish leadership in Jerusalem who constitute the sanhedrin,[54] all of whom are closely identified

---

51. See, e.g., 20:45–21:4; Acts 3:1–4:22. It is ironic, then, that Jesus is arrested as though he were a bandit (λῃστής — 22:52).

52. See also 21:37; 22:53; cf. 20:1, 28, 39; also Acts 5:19-21.

53. Cf. Bachmann, *Jerusalem und der Tempel,* 261-89; he emphasizes Jesus' concern in his temple teaching with proper interpretation of the law.

54. Cf. 22:66; 24:20; Josephus *Ag. Ap.* 2.21 §§184-87; Schürer, *Jewish People,* 2:212-13. For the responsibility of the Jewish leadership in Jerusalem for Jesus' death, see Carroll and Green, *Death of Jesus,* 194-99; Weatherly, *Jewish Responsibility.*

with the temple.[55] (For more detail on these groups, see above on 9:22.) Unlike Zacchaeus, who sought Jesus' identity (19:3), they seek his execution (cf. 6:11; 11:53-54).[56] For the present, the support of the crowds frustrates their quest (cf. 20:19-20; 22:2).

55. *Contra* J. H. Elliott ("Temple Versus Household," 220), who does not see the relation of the scribes to the temple. Cf. Schwartz, *Jewish Background,* 89-101; Sanders, *Judaism,* 170-82.

56. See the parallel use of ζητέω.

6. TEACHING IN THE JERUSALEM TEMPLE (20:1–21:38)

The buildup to this point in the narrative has been long (9:51–19:48) and dramatic, with Luke carefully marking the progress of Jesus and his entourage during the last leg of their journey before their arrival in Jerusalem.[1] Once he has arrived, Jesus' first order of business is to reclaim the temple for its legitimate use, as a center of revelatory teaching concerned with the purpose of God now coming to fruition (19:45-48). Luke's summary in v 47 — "every day he was teaching in the temple" — is born out in the presentation of Jesus the teacher in this new narrative section. Indeed, 20:1 forms an *inclusio* with 21:37-38, with both statements divulging the collocation of narrative elements so central to these two chapters: Jesus' teaching, the people as the recipients of his message, and the temple setting in which the whole is cast. Adding to this emphasis are the multiple references to Jesus as a teacher (20:21, 28, 39; 21:7) and to his teaching activity (20:1, 9, 21; 21:29, 37).

Throughout 20:1–21:38, "the people" have two key roles to play. They are, first, the recipients of Jesus' instruction. Even when Luke specifically refers to the disciples (20:45), they are "in the hearing of all the people." Second, they serve as a buffer between Jesus and his opponents, their very presence indicating such support for Jesus that they frustrate those with hostile aspirations against him (esp. 20:6, 19, 26).

This allusion to confrontation actually introduces the leitmotif of this section of Luke's Gospel — namely, conflict surrounding the question, Who has legitimate authority? The issue of legitimacy is two-pronged, having to do with the justification of a particular person or group to wield authority as well as with the setting of limits on appropriate behavior (or the determination

---

1. Cf. 17:11; 18:31, 35; 19:1, 28, 29, 41, 45.

of practices deemed acceptable).[2] This, in turn, raises two related questions: Who has divinely appointed authority? and, What actions can be said to fall within the parameters of divinely authorized behavior? The groups Luke mentions in this segment of the Third Gospel — chief priests, scribes, elders, Sadducees, and rich people — might differ, even dramatically, among themselves on some points, but all draw their legitimation from their relationship to the temple. In the Judaism Luke thus portrays, high politics and high worship originate from the same impulse, the Jerusalem temple. Given this state of affairs, juxtaposed with the nature of the kingdom of God proclaimed by Jesus, Jesus cannot afford a laissez-faire attitude toward the temple, but must engage it directly. Jesus' message, in the end, is deeply, intimately involved in this central construction of divine legitimation within Judaism[3] — hence, the temple's crucial importance as the setting for Jesus' instruction.

The reasoning of this narrative segment proceeds on the basis of this common understanding of the essential prominence of the temple as sacred space that establishes the order of the world and provides the axial point around which social life is aligned. (1) First, Luke narrates a series of accounts concerned fundamentally with conflict between Jesus and those associated with the Jerusalem temple (20:1-40). Next, Luke recounts how Jesus (2a) counters with a scriptural argument regarding the unsurpassed authority of the Son of David who is also Lord of all (20:41-44), after which he (2b) dislegitimizes those whose authority is rooted in the use of Scripture and the temple system to tyrannize and oppress the weak of society (20:45–21:4). In Luke's narration, this leads (3) to Jesus' forecast of calamity and destruction as the old world order gives way to the new (21:5-38).

6.1. CONFLICT WITH THE JERUSALEM LEADERSHIP (20:1–21:4)

This first major segment of Luke's narrative of Jesus' teaching ministry in the Jerusalem temple (see above on 20:1–21:38) has conflict as its primary focus, with the legitimation of authority serving as the subject of this conflict. Three constellations of characters are routinely spotlighted. The first is Jesus himself, whose practice (once he reached Jerusalem) was to teach regularly in the temple.[1] The second is a composite of the chief priests, scribes, elders, Sadducees, and the wealthy. Although distinguishable historically, and although

2. See Seymour-Smith, *Anthropology,* 166.
3. For this way of conceptualizing the issues, see esp. Geertz, *Local Knowledge,* 124, 143, 146.
1. Cf. 20:1, 21, 28, 39.

Luke himself provides some basis for the further differentiation of each in the ensuing narrative, with respect to the focal point of this narrative segment, their individual characteristics fade into the background. What remains is twofold: their association with the temple (and the status accorded to them as a consequence of this association) and their hostility toward Jesus. Third are "the people"; though they seem to initiate nothing in this succession of scenes, we would be mistaken to regard them merely as a backdrop or stage prop. They receive Jesus' teaching and thus, at least in principle, represent Israel as potential followers of Jesus. More explicit is Luke's placement of the people as an obstacle to the malicious machinations of the Jerusalem leadership. Although they desire to arrest Jesus and to hand him over to the governor (20:19, 20, 26), their intentions are frustrated by the people.

Jesus' counterarguments, wherein he calls his opponents into question for their unfaithfulness and illegitimate practices of leadership, are spoken to the people (20:9-19; 20:45–21:4). This serves at least three purposes. First (20:9-19), Jesus engages in self-interpretation that validates his authority, at least indirectly, at the same time that it publicly queries the status of those who oppose him. Second (20:45–21:4), as in earlier co-texts (e.g., 12:1-4), Jesus exploits the stereotypical qualities of his detractors in order to delineate negative behavioral patterns for his disciples. This is a reminder that the line between those who follow Jesus and those who resist his ministry is not easily sustained, for his followers are always in danger of lapsing into values and behaviors more suited to the old world order than the new. Third, with only minimal effort, Luke's own audience may begin to identify with "the people" who make up Jesus' auditors. Consequently, we may hear his arguments as though they were addressed to us, as though we need to grapple personally with his message.

We may discern in this seriation of encounters a definite progression. Jesus bests his detractors (20:1-40; see esp. vv 26, 40), then goes on the offensive in order to assert the basis of his own authority (20:41-44).[2] Having established by means of scriptural exegesis his own authority, he then denounces his opponents as persons whose lives are oriented away from the purpose of God and who therefore will be condemned (20:45–21:4).

6.1.1. The Question of Jesus' Authority (20:1-8)

20:1 *One day, as he was teaching the people in the temple and telling the good news, the chief priests and the scribes came with the elders* 2 *and said to him, "Tell us, by what authority are you doing these*

---

2. Jesus' status before God has already been asserted, parabolically, in 20:13; for "my beloved son," cf. 3:22.

things? Who is it who gave you this authority?" 3 *He answered them,* *"I will also ask you a question, and you tell me:* 4 *Did the baptism of* *John come from heaven, or was it of human origin?"* 5 *They discussed* *it with one another, saying, "If we say, 'From heaven,' he will say,* *'Why did you not believe him?'* 6 *But if we say, 'Of human origin,' all* *the people will stone us; for they are convinced that John was a* *prophet."* 7 *So they answered that they did not know where it came* *from.* 8 *Then Jesus said to them, "Neither will I tell you by what* *authority I am doing these things."*

Following the summary statement of 19:47-48, this first episode in the Lukan account of Jesus' ministry in the Jerusalem temple has an ominous ring to it. This is because Luke presents it as an archetype of expected activity in the temple,[3] under the general rubric of how Jesus' opponents sought to kill him. Jesus is present in the temple to proclaim "good news" to the people, but the Jerusalem leadership interrupts him with hostile intentions.[4] This will be Luke's focus. The strategy of the leaders is transparent. Accosting Jesus before the people, they seek to portray him as an outsider, not one to be held in high regard or trusted. Because status is a product of one's claim to a certain position *together with* public affirmation of that claim, these Jerusalem leaders attempt to shame him publicly by casting doubt on his authority base.[5] In what follows, Jesus will turn the opposition "unauthorized/authorized," introduced by his interlocutors, against them, dislegitimating their authority while presenting himself as *the* authoritative teacher.[6]

1-2 Following the summary in 19:47-48, almost all of the details of the setting Luke introduces are redundant. This has the dual effect of emphasizing the duplicated elements (teaching + the people + in the temple + delineation of Jewish leaders), and of drawing special attention to a new component (evangelizing). Jesus has reclaimed the temple for its legitimate use as a center of revelatory instruction concerned with the salvific purpose of God now materializing. The people, representing Israel, are the recipients of that teaching. Standing in opposition are the chief priests, legal experts, and elders,[7] representative of the Jerusalem sanhedrin, whose collective authority originates in the

---

3. The phrase ἐν μιᾷ τῶν ἡμερῶν (v 1) suggests that Jesus' ministry in the temple is carried out over several days, with Luke choosing to relate only a representative range of objections Jesus encountered by those who sought his execution.

4. For the use of ἐπέστησαν to mark an interruption (v 1), see Giblin, *Destruction of Jerusalem*, 61.

5. Cf. Tyson, *Images of Judaism*, 85; Dawsey, "Confrontation in the Temple," 159-60; *idem*, "Luke's Positive Perception," 11.

6. See Brawley, *Centering on God*, 196; Chance, *Jerusalem*, 58.

7. See above on 9:22; 19:47.

purity of their birthright (in the case of the priests), in their education (in the case of scribes), in their good fortune in having been born into Jerusalem families of high status, and above all in their proximity and relationship to the Jerusalem temple (see above on 20:1–21:38). Indeed, by the way he has staged this dispute Luke is careful to remind his audience of the leaders' advantage in the challenge and riposte that constitutes this scene; within the temple they serve and represent their authority must seem irrefutable. This is not the case with Jesus. Even if this moment was foreshadowed early in his life (2:41-51), in Jerusalem Jesus is a relatively unknown quantity.

Far from being intimidated by his surroundings, Jesus apparently regards the temple setting ("my Father's house," 2:49) as the appropriate place to unveil the divine plan. "To bring good news" is reminiscent of his message from the beginning and is intimately related to the inbreaking kingdom of God in Jesus' ministry and, thus, to the presence of eschatological redemption for those marginal to society-at-large (cf. 4:18-19, 43; 7:22; 8:1; 9:6; 16:16). Those peripheral people to whom the good news has been directed in Jesus' ministry would have included some (e.g., lepers) excluded from the boundaries of the temple due to their ritual uncleanness. Moreover, the scandal of Jesus' "good news" has repeatedly resided in its proclivity to accord privilege to those occupying low positions on the scales of power and privilege — positions far removed from persons like these chief priests, legal experts, and elders. "Chief priests," for example, gained their titles not by OT regulation but by their central connection to Jerusalem and their association with the administration and oversight of temple affairs.[8] The question they put to Jesus, then, is not an innocent one, nor can one consider the character of Jesus' instruction in the temple as naive. Luke brings into focus a war of worlds — fundamentally different visions of God's purpose, the character of leadership, and the nature of Israel's redemption.

Luke's audience knows already of Jesus' authority (4:32, 36; 5:24), signaled by his divine Sonship and grounded in his experience of the Spirit (1:35; 3:21-22; 4:18-19); so do the people, earlier seen welcoming him into Jerusalem as though he were a king (19:29-40). Now, however, his authority — its nature and its source[9] — is in question. As we have seen, such a protest gains its potency from the setting in which it is spoken. Jesus is not a priest. He has no official role in the temple. On what basis can he engage in actions (19:45-46) and proclamation (20:1) that counter the "reality"[10] of the temple

---

8. Most priests lived away from Jerusalem and commuted to the Holy City only when their priestly courses were due to serve (see above on 1:8). Cf. Hurst and Green, "Priest, Priesthood."

9. Plummer, 456.

10. By "reality," we mean reality as this has been culturally configured; cf. Berger and Luckmann, *Social Construction of Reality*.

as this has been propagated by the temple leadership and taken for granted within Israel?[11]

3-6 Although the initial question concerning the nature and source of authority was open-ended, Jesus' counterquestion narrows the choices to two: divine or human origin (cf. Acts 5:38-39). Here, "origin" refers to authorization and empowerment. His reference to "the baptism of John," itself a cipher for the whole of John's message,[12] serves three interrelated purposes. First, there is simply the importance of John and his ministry to the eschatological coming of redemption.[13] Indeed, already within the narrative how one has responded to John serves as a barometer of one's orientation to the divine purpose (7:29-30). Second, there is the more particular issue of the nature of John's ministry. As the Jerusalem leaders are aware (v 6), John is presented within the Third Gospel above all as a prophet (1:76; 7:26) — whose prophetic ministry originated with Yahweh, whose message was concerned with a social renewal and transformation set in opposition to Roman and Jewish leadership alike, and whose call for a repentance-baptism was linked to his radical questioning of the ethnic basis for one's status within the people of God.[14] From the standpoint of the authority base of the Jerusalem leadership represented here, then, John's baptism was indeed threatening. Third, John's role was largely to prepare the way for Jesus, prophet of God presaging Son of God (1:16-17, 32-35, 68-76; 3:16). Thus, if one were to allow that John's message originated with God, this would be tantamount to admitting that Jesus' ministry was itself sanctioned by God.

Such logic is not lost on the Jerusalem leadership. Luke portrays them as reasoning among themselves concerning the implications of the choices left them by Jesus' question,[15] though one may also hear in this private session echoes of earlier episodes where the thoughts of persons hostile to Jesus were brought to light through Jesus' ministry (e.g., 2:34-35; 5:21; 6:7-8). If they attribute divine origin to John's message, they will stand self-condemned — both because, in the past, they rejected his message[16] and because, now, they

---

11. Although he provides insufficient warrant for his thesis that Luke envisions a "process" of cleansing the temple through Jesus' action against the merchandisers and his teaching, Dawsey ("Confrontation in the Temple," esp. 158-60) has helpfully seen the association of these two kinds of action in Jesus' temple ministry. Both the symbolic action in the temple and Jesus' teaching are included in the ταῦτα of the question posed by the Jerusalem leaders.

12. See §8.

13. See §1.

14. See above on 3:1-20; also §8.

15. On the use of συλλογίζομαι for "logical reasoning," see Mussies, "Sense of συλλογίζεσθαι."

16. The response of the Jerusalem leadership to John is not narrated by Luke, though, in light of this information that they did not believe him, we may now understand

refuse to accept the divine character and origin of Jesus' ministry, prophesied by John. If they fail to acknowledge the divine origin of John's message, on the other hand, they will fall victim to mob action (cf. Acts 5:26). Such a stoning, instituted by the people, would have no legal warrant, though it may be that the people would thus be accusing the Jerusalem leadership of blasphemy.[17] That this prospect is noted by members of the sanhedrin is an indication of the yawning chasm between themselves and those they were allegedly to have led. For their part, in their assessment of John as a prophet, the people[18] distinguish themselves sharply from the Jerusalem leadership and align themselves with the point of view shared by unimpeachable spokespersons for God — the Spirit-filled Zechariah and the Spirit-anointed Jesus (1:67 → 1:76; 4:18-19 → 7:26).

7-8 Finally, Luke narrates answers to the questions raised in vv 2 and 4. When the Jerusalem leadership claims ignorance, Luke's audience may hear in the background Jesus' earlier indictment of Jerusalem concerning its ignorance of the time of the divine visitation (19:44). In this ironic way, these members of the sanhedrin stand self-condemned for their lack of openness to divine intervention. Equally transparent in their response to Jesus, though, is the system of values they serve. In this case, their answer serves as nothing more than pandering, an attempt to manipulate continued favor and elevated status within Israel.

Jesus' reply builds on the notion of *quid quo pro* established in vv 2-3: "Tell us," they demand; "you tell me," Jesus replies. Jesus uses their own words in his counterquestion, and he now repeats their question verbatim in his refusal to answer. This is not the whole story, however, for in referring to John he has laid implicit claim to divine authorization for himself. Moreover, in vv 9-19 he will address parabolically the nature and source of his authority at the same time that he discloses the reason for the forfeiture of divine authority on the part of the Jerusalem leadership. In the interim, however, the attempt of the Jerusalem leaders to shame Jesus has backfired.

---

the programmatic character of 7:30. There, we are told, by refusing baptism the Pharisees and legal experts rejected the divine purpose — a judgment that now seems fitting for the Jerusalem leadership as well.

17. Blasphemy might involve insulting those who act on God's behalf (see the survey in Bock, "Jesus' Blasphemy," 184-86). In this case, the penalty appropriate for a false prophet, stoning (Deut 13:1-13), would be extended to those who deny the legitimacy of a true one.

18. Luke uses the same phrase in v 6 and in 19:48: ὁ λαὸς ἅπας. This points to the thoroughgoing disjunction that currently exists between the people and their leadership, and urges a reading of "the people" as representative of Israel, the covenant people (cf. 1:10, 17, 21, 68, 77; 2:32; 7:16; et al.). This is not to say, however, that reference to "the people" always and necessarily brings into focus the attitudes and actions of all Israel. See the nuanced discussion in Brawley, *Luke-Acts,* 133-54.

6.1.2. Jerusalem's Unfaithful Leadership (20:9-19)

> 9 *He began to tell the people this parable: "A man planted a vineyard, and leased it to tenants, and went to another country for a long time.* 10 *When the season came, he sent a slave to the tenants in order that they might give him his share of the produce of the vineyard; but the tenants beat him and sent him away empty-handed.* 11 *Next he sent another slave; that one also they beat and insulted and sent away empty-handed.* 12 *And he sent still a third; this one also they wounded and threw out.* 13 *Then the owner of the vineyard said, 'What shall I do? I will send my beloved son; perhaps they will respect him.'* 14 *But when the tenants saw him, they discussed it among themselves and said, 'This is the heir; let us kill him so that the inheritance may be ours.'* 15 *So they threw him out of the vineyard and killed him. What then will the owner of the vineyard do to them?* 16 *He will come and destroy those tenants and give the vineyard to others." When they heard this, they said, "Heaven forbid!"* 17 *But he looked at them and said, "What then does this text mean:*
>
> *'The stone that the builders rejected*
>   *has become the cornerstone'?*
>
> 18 *Everyone who falls on that stone will be broken to pieces; and it will crush anyone on whom it falls."* 19 *When the scribes and chief priests realized that he had told this parable against them, they wanted to lay hands on him at that very hour, but they feared the people.*

Luke proceeds to recount Jesus' parabolic teaching with no break in the narrative other than the repeated note that Jesus' audience is "the people" (cf. v 1). With no change in setting or audience, Luke thus intimates the immediate relationship between this subsection and his account of Jesus' exchange with the Jerusalem leadership in vv 1-8. Before, Jesus had refused to reveal the nature and source of his authority, but now he does so in a parabolic way. What is more, to the Jerusalem leaders Jesus' message is all too clear, with the result that they perceive in his message the dislodging of their own base of authority. In their lack of fecundity before God and their defiant response to divine accountability, they have participated in forms of behavior that shatter the boundaries of divinely authorized practices.

Even if Jesus' primary audience is "the people" (representative of Israel), according to v 19 the main target of Jesus' parable is the Jerusalem leadership. This underscores the status of this and other encounters in this series (vv 1-44) as programmatic for Luke's presentation of Jesus' ministry in the temple, but not representative of the content of Jesus' teaching. Jesus is proclaiming the good news in the temple (v 1); though this proclamation serves as necessary backdrop, however, it is never fully articulated in this larger narrative segment (20:1–21:38). Instead, Luke accords privilege to the hostility occasioned by this disclosure of good news. That is, in proclaiming the good news of God's redemptive initiative, Jesus is in the process of restoring the temple to its legitimate purpose as a place of revelation and justice (see above on 19:45-46). Hostility arises when the Jerusalem leadership, whose authority is tied to the temple, refuses to embrace the function of the temple proposed by Jesus.

Understood against this interpretive horizon, the scene comprised of vv 9-19 serves a crucial role. Its importance rests, first, in the fact that Luke's account of Jesus' parabolic teaching has the form of a brief narrative embedded in a larger narrative, with the one interpreting and being interpreted by the other. Although the significance of Jesus' parable in this instance is not forcibly constrained in the same way that one finds with the use of interpretive frames in 18:1, 9; 19:11, its immediate relationship to the surrounding narrative is nonetheless obvious and consequential. The meaning of the parable is intertwined with the larger Lukan narrative by (1) the designation of the owner of the vineyard's son as "my beloved son," echoing God's own affirmation of Jesus (v 13; 3:22); (2) the analogous desire to kill the son/Jesus by the tenants/Jerusalem leadership (vv 14, 19; 19:47); (3) the similar motifs of judgment, including the image of the "stone" (v 18; 19:44); and especially (4) the recognition by the people and the Jerusalem leadership that events in the world of the parable have existential significance with reference to realities in their own world (vv 16b, 19).[19] These connections may have the effect of leading readers to an understanding of the parable and larger narrative in relation to each other that exceeds what they might understand of either in isolation.[20] Thus, Jesus' parabolic teaching actually pushes the narrative forward, underscoring such narrative needs as (1) the rejection and death of Jesus, the "beloved son" (v 13); (2) judgment falling on those who reject the Lord's emissaries, the Jewish leadership thinly disguised as tenants of a vineyard (vv 16 and 19); and (3) the transfer of leadership to "others," clearly designated in the ensuing narrative as Jesus and the apostles (22:28-30; cf. Acts 1:1-11).

Jesus' parabolic instruction draws its meaning, second, from its intertextual relationship with Isaiah 5:1-7.[21] Read in light of the parabolic identification of Israel with the vineyard in the Isaianic text, the Lukan parable

19. See Tannehill, *Narrative Unity,* 1:192; Brawley, *Text to Text,* 35.

20. Brawley, *Text to Text,* 33.

21. Note: the analogous use of the vineyard, as well as the verbal associations in τὸν ἀγαπητόν (v 13 → Isa 5:1), τί οὖν ποιήσει (v 15 → Isa 5:4-5), and ὁ κύριος τοῦ ἀμπελῶνος (v 15 → Isa 5:7). This relationship is denied by, e.g., Weatherly, *Jewish Responsibility,* 73; Doran, "Luke 20:18," 65-66. See, however, e.g., Giblin, *Destruction of Jerusalem,* 66-67; Kimball, "Luke 20:9-19"; Brawley, *Text to Text,* 28-30; Tyson, *Images of Judaism,* 81-82.

presents a shortened version of God's dealing with Israel in which the narrative of Luke-Acts participates. The planting of the vineyard, the choice of tenants, the attempt to hold the tenants accountable, the sending of a succession of servants to collect — these all have their analogues in aspects of the story of God's relationship with Israel preceding the narrative of Luke-Acts. The Third Evangelist, then, picks up the story at the point of the owner's decision to send his "beloved son," paralleled within the Lukan narrative by the pervasive motif of the purpose of God that intervenes in history in a definitive way with the advent of the Son of God. Continuing the analogy into the future, Jesus' parabolic teaching provides a proleptic announcement of judgment and transfer of authority, yet to be narrated by the Evangelist.

The Lukan parable also departs from its Isaianic subtext in a crucial way. In Isaiah 5, the owner of the vineyard pronounces judgment on the vineyard, not on the tenants; that is, God is said to deliver Israel itself over to destruction. This is not the case here, so that Jesus' message cuts short expectations provided by the Isaianic script — expectations that may lie behind the strongly negative response of the people in Luke, "Heaven forbid!" (v 16). Destruction of Jerusalem (cf. 19:41-44) does not mark the annihilation of Israel, just as destruction of the "tenants" does not mark the demolition of the vineyard. In the temple, Jesus has attempted to reorient Israel around the redemptive purpose of God; this purpose is resisted by the temple leadership, and the consequences of their defiance are their own devastation and the transfer of leadership to others, Jesus and his apostles.[22]

9-12 As vv 1-8 made clear, the question of legitimate authority is decisive within this narrative segment. Jesus takes his case to "the people," Israel,[23] in order to expose the illegitimate authority of the Jerusalem leadership that stands in opposition to his announcement of the good news. Even though the parable is spoken to the people, then, its brunt is reserved for Jerusalem's legal experts and chief priests (v 19).

The beginning of the parable is notable for its realism, but the interpretive co-text in which the parable as a whole is set disallows any notion that it ought to be interpreted in the Third Gospel as a commentary on agricultural processes or socio-political relations between urban elite and peasants reduced to tenancy. (For the interpretive horizons provided by the co-text, see above.) One aspect of Jesus' parable that does depend directly on its depiction of agribusiness is crucial, however; this is the "contract" between vineyard owner and tenant implicit in the parable. This establishes the basis for the motif of accountability for the harvest central to the parable, and adds significance to the obstinacy of the tenants.

---

22. See Tyson, *Images of Judaism,* 82, 86-87; Brawley, *Text to Text,* 38-41.
23. On ὁ λαός, see above on v 6.

The metaphorical use of "vineyard" to refer to Israel is well documented in Israel's Scriptures, especially in Isa 5:1-7 (which serves as a subtext of this parable; see above).[24] The inscription of Jesus' parable into the traditional use of this imagery is important, since biblical usage of this symbol typically focuses dually on God's construction and destruction of Israel, the vineyard.

Identification of Israel as the vineyard suggests a comparable metaphorical referent for the sequence of slaves sent to hold the tenants accountable before God, and one is easily found. In the world of commerce in Greco-Roman antiquity, a slave often functioned as a virtual stand-in for his master with regard to leased properties;[25] this already points to the identification of slaves with God's spokespersons, the prophets, in Jesus' parable. In fact, the term "slave" is often applied to the prophets in Israel's Scriptures,[26] and, as in Jesus' parable, the standard fortune of Israel's prophets is rejection.[27] The consequent imagery of humiliation and rejection of the prophets in this text is especially poignant on account of Jesus' earlier indictment of legal experts as persons implicated in the historical rejection of the prophets in Israel (11:47-51) and the more immediate reference to John, a prophet, whom the Jerusalem leadership failed to acknowledge (vv 4-7).

Neither is it difficult to see in the parables' tenants a metaphorical reference to the Jerusalem leadership. Indeed, it is already known for its rejection of John as a prophet of God (vv 3-7) and desire to kill Jesus (cf. vv 14, 19; 19:47). Moreover, as Luke will relate, the Jerusalem leadership read themselves into the parable in precisely this way (v 19).

It has been suggested that, read in light of social-historical concerns, the thrice-repeated beating, insulting, and turning away of the slaves is tantamount to a challenge on the part of the tenants regarding the ownership of the vineyard.[28] Refusing his claim to a share in the harvest, the tenants are denying his title to the vineyard. This would underscore what is already clear in the parable — namely, how far the Jerusalem leadership has departed their divinely authorized roles, so much so that they have refused to hold themselves and the form of their own leadership practices accountable to the God in relation to whom they claim legitimation.

The focal point of this accountability, fruitfulness, is familiar to readers of the Third Gospel. Since 3:7-9 Luke has constructed a narrative that places a premium on behaviors, "fruit," that demonstrate one's fundamental orientation

---

24. See also, e.g., Ps 80:8-13; Isa 27:2-5; Jer 2:21; Ezek 15:6; 19:10-14; Hos 10:1.
25. See Thébert, "Slave."
26. E.g., 1 Kgs 14:18; 15:29; 2 Kgs 9:7; 10:10; 14:24; Isa 20:3; 44:26; et al.
27. See 13:33-34; Acts 7:52; also 1 Kgs 22:27; 2 Chr 16:10; Neh 9:26; Jer 2:30; et al.
28. See Derrett, *Law in the New Testament*, 289-306.

to God's purpose (cf., e.g., 6:43-45; 8:1-21). Fecundity, obedience to God, is the outworking of faithful dispositions, and this — not one's birthright nor religious training nor relation to the administration of temple affairs — qualifies one as a member of the people of God. This Lukan emphasis articulates with the parable of the vineyard in Isaiah 5, where Israel is judged for its bad fruit — bloodshed instead of justice, a cry instead of righteousness; in Luke's account, we find no indication of fruitfulness at all, apart from acts of violence[29] and resistance to the divine prerogative in the life of Israel.

13-16a   As if the equanimity of the vineyard owner had not already been established, the parable now demonstrates it further.[30] Soliloquy is prominent in other Lukan parables; as in those cases, so in this one internal monologue provides a turning point in the parable as a course of action is decided.[31] If a slave might function as a stand-in for his master, how much more might a lord's son, particularly since the notion of "agency" was intrinsic to that of sonship. The son would have the full authority of his father, the owner of the vineyard, and, as heir, would also represent the father's interests.[32] Reference to "my beloved son" emphasizes within the parable the lengths to which the owner is willing to go in leaving open the possibility that his tenants will be faithful. Within the larger narrative of Luke, this phrase helps to interpret Jesus' parable as a microcosm of the ancient and developing story of the relationship between Israel and God, since for the Lukan narrative "my beloved son" is none other than Jesus of Nazareth (3:22).

On the still larger canvass, "my beloved son" is reminiscent of the Genesis account of Abraham and his son Isaac (e.g., Gen 22:2); here, however, the nature of the possible echoes is difficult to tie down. Luke has already inscribed the advent of Jesus into the ancient promises of God to Abraham, so reverberations of the Abrahamic material in this co-text serve at least to remind us that the story of Jesus continues the story begun with Abraham.[33] The potential of two additional echoes of the Abraham-Isaac material surfaces a further interpretive possibility. First, willingness to place the beloved son in harm's way recalls the sacrifice of Isaac, to which Jewish tradition accorded covenantal significance.[34]

29. See above on 19:45-46.

30. See Giblin, *Destruction of Jerusalem,* 69: "Herein lies the principal element of exaggeration in this parable."

31. Cf. 12:17-19; 15:17-19; 16:3-4.

32. Harvey, *Constraints of History,* 161-62.

33. On the importance of the Abrahamic material to Luke, see above, §2; Dahl, "Abraham."

34. References to Isaac as the "loved" or the "only" son are found in the Genesis account of the offering of Isaac (ch. 22). For reflection on the sacrificial and covenant-making significance of the Aqedah, cf. Philo *Abr.* 32-36 §§167-207; *Jub.* 17:15; Martin-Schard, "Isaac," 469.

Second, subsequent reference to the "inheritance" to be claimed upon the death of the beloved son (v 14) recalls Isaac's role as heir of the Abrahamic promise.[35] Taken together, these two resonances portend competing purposes at work in this co-text. For their part, the tenants/Jerusalem leaders imagine that by killing the heir/Jesus, the Abrahamic promises will fall to them (in spite of their lack of Abraham-like faithfulness! — cf. 3:7-9). On the other hand, previous and contemporary Jewish interpretation of the story of Abraham and Isaac suggests, to the contrary, that the act of handing the beloved son over to his death will have the effect of securing the divine covenant ("inheritance") for the people of God.

In the Lukan narrative, the act of "discussing among themselves" is typical of those who oppose the redemptive purpose of God at work in Jesus.[36] This detail only serves further to mark the tenants as persons who are thoroughly hostile to the vineyard owner. Following such characterization, Jesus' narration of the slaying of the beloved son is expected, almost anticlimactic.

Returning to the substructure of this account in Isaiah, Jesus inquires of "the people" — just as Isaiah had inquired of the "inhabitants of Jerusalem and people of Judah" (Isa 5:3-4) — what the owner's response might be. In Isaiah 5, total devastation of the vineyard is outlined. Jesus interrupts his story before it reaches such an end, however. The vineyard itself remains intact; the problem, for him, is not the vineyard but those who tend it — not Israel but its leadership in Jerusalem. The latter are to be destroyed and replaced by "others." Again, it is not Israel itself that will be destroyed, for the people of God will receive new leadership. The identity of these "others" is not specified here, though it will be later: Jesus and the apostles (22:28-30; cf. Acts 1:1-11).

16b-18 What lies behind the strongly negative reaction, "Heaven forbid"?[37] For those weaned on the vineyard imagery of the OT,[38] or for those who have learned simply to take for granted the centrality of Jerusalem for the people of God, the answer is self-evident. Surely the destruction of Jerusalem marks the obliteration of Israel as well! But this misses the careful distinction drawn in the parable between vineyard and tenants, and thus between Israel and its leaders.[39]

---

35. Cf. Gen 15:7; 21:10; 22:17; Johnson, 305. On the motif of inheritance, see above on 10:25.

36. διαλογίζομαι/διαλογισμός — cf. 2:35; 5:22; 6:8; et al.

37. That is, μὴ γένοιτο — literally, "May it never be!" — found only here in Luke-Acts, but common in Epictetus, frequently following rhetorical questions in Paul (cf. Rom 3:4, 6, 31; 6:2, 15; 7:7, 13; 9:14; 11:1, 11; et al.), and read occasionally in the LXX (e.g., Gen 44:7, 17; Deut 24:16; et al.) (Dunn, *Romans,* 132).

38. See above on vv 9-12; the vineyard image regularly holds in tandem divine establishment and destruction of the vineyard.

39. Cf. Chance, *Jerusalem,* 67-68.

Another, complementary possibility presents itself when it is recognized that Jesus' citation of Ps 118:22 and use of stone-imagery in vv 17-18 comprise his response to the negative reaction of the people.[40] As we noted earlier (see above on 19:38), Luke's use of Psalm 118 harkens to use of the psalm in the annual rite of reenthronement of the king. As such, the psalm speaks to the saving acts of Yahweh, but also recognizes the place of humiliation and rejection in the divine plan. The people have been quick to acclaim Jesus as king (19:38), but, like the disciples within the Lukan narrative, seem not to understand that, in the divine economy, regal status embraces humiliation and death, nor that exaltation is preceded by shame.

By inquiring of the people, "What does this text mean?" then, Jesus is pointing first to scriptural warrant for (and thus to the divine necessity of) the sequence of events outlined in the parable, including the demise of the son; and second to the certainty that the death of the son would not be the last word, but a prelude to exaltation (cf., e.g., Acts 4:11; 5:30-31). Third, Jesus justifies the destruction of the obstinate, violent tenants, and, in doing so, fourth, warns the people to distance themselves from the tenants, their own leadership, so that they might not be similarly judged for their part in the death of the owner's son.[41] All of this is accomplished by grouping together scriptural citation and allusion around the catchword "stone" (Ps 118:22; Isa 8:14-15; Dan 2:34-35, 44-45).[42] This interpretive move yields a stone that is rejected but vindicated,[43] and that is efficacious for judgment. Remembering that this parable has as its audience "the people" (v 9), it serves as an admonition for them to accept the one who would be rejected by the Jerusalem leadership.[44]

19 The force of Jesus' parable is not lost on the legal experts and chief priests,[45] who recognize that Jesus has thus identified them as the tenants who oppose God, and that he has thus driven further the wedge between themselves and the people over whom they have held sway.[46] Ironically, they

---

40. The use of ἐμβλέπω helps to focus the attention of the people (and of Luke's audience) on the exegesis to follow.

41. Doran ("Luke 20:18") helpfully underscores the motif of threat or warning resident in Jesus' parable, but his attempt to find the boast of a warrior or the image of holy war in the background of v 18 is problematic — cf. Giblin, *Destruction of Jerusalem,* 70-72.

42. See Kimball, "Luke 20:9-19," 88-89.

43. κεφαλὴν γωνίας most likely refers to a foundation stone, not a capstone (*contra* Jeremias, "λιθός," 274-76; *idem,* "κεφαλὴν γωνίας"); the cornerstone bore the weight of two walls and was thus critical for the stability of an edifice (see Fitzmyer, 2:1282).

44. See Weatherly, *Jewish Responsibility,* 74.

45. For details on these groups of people, see above at 9:22; 19:47-48.

46. Even more than the NRSV, the Greek text accentuates the immediacy of the reaction of the Jerusalem leaders, locating the words "the scribes and chief priests wanted to lay hands on him . . ." at the head of the sentence for emphasis.

know already their distance from the people, who have acknowledged in the case of Jesus a status before God that they have refused to grant. Fearing the whiplash of public opinion, they are constrained from taking Jesus into custody. The phrase "to lay hands [on someone]" has the nuance here of arresting someone, or seizing someone as a prelude to arrest.[47] In this case, arresting Jesus would serve to interrupt his influence among the people, and perhaps even lead to his execution (cf. 19:47; 22:2).

6.1.3. The Question of Caesar's Authority (and the Priority of the Temple) (20:20-26)

> 20 *So they watched him and commissioned agents*[48] *who pretended to be righteous,*[49] *in order to trap him by what he said, so as to hand him over to the jurisdiction and authority of the governor.* 21 *So they asked him, "Teacher, we know that you are right in what you say and teach, and you show deference to no one, but teach the way of God in accordance with truth.* 22 *Is it lawful for us to pay tribute*[50] *to the emperor, or not?"* 23 *But he perceived their craftiness and said to them,* 24 *"Show me a denarius. Whose image and inscription*[51] *does it bear?" They said, "The emperor's."* 25 *He said to them, "Then give to the emperor the things that are the emperor's, and to God the things that are God's."* 26 *And they were not able in the presence of the people to trap him by what he said; and being amazed by his answer, they became silent.*

Although this encounter regarding Jewish obligation to Caesar might be read as a discrete episode, Luke presents it as the consequence of Jesus' relating the parable of the vineyard. From one vantage point, this unit helps to establish the pattern of interaction that characterizes episodes in ch. 20: (1) the Jerusalem leadership attempt to trap Jesus with a question designed to undermine his message before the people; (2) Jesus eludes the snare, and in doing so, silences his opponents, turning their unspoken allegations against them.[52]

---

47. See the use of ἐπιβάλλω in 21:12; Acts 4:3; 5:18; 21:27.
48. NRSV: "sent spies."
49. NRSV: "honest."
50. NRSV: "taxes."
51. NRSV: "whose head and whose title."
52. See Dawsey, "Confrontation in the Temple," 161. Owen-Ball ("Rabbinic Rhetoric," 4) observes that the exchange between Jesus and his questioners follows a pattern of interrogation found in rabbinical literature soon after the first century C.E.: "(1) an outsider puts a hostile question to the rabbi; (2) the rabbi responds with a counter-question; (3) by answering the counterquestion the outsider becomes vulnerable; and (4) the rabbi

From another, this episode is the continuation and, indeed, the climax of the extended, first encounter between the Jerusalem leadership and Jesus begun in 20:1-2. Luke's note about the desire to arrest Jesus shared by the chief priests and legal experts, and his subsequent observation that they sent agents in an attempt to entrap him, suggests the passing of story time; nevertheless, at the level of the narrative, from vv 1-26, one event leads to the next in rapid succession as the central issue of Jesus' authority, its basis and extent, is examined by the Jerusalem authorities. Recognizing how Jesus had undermined their magisterial status before the people (v 19; cf. 11:53), the chief priests and legal experts respond in two ways: first, they set up a surveillance operation in order to monitor Jesus closely and, second, rather than face further public embarrassment, they enlist persons to act as agents on their behalf. The consequent portrait is almost vaudevillian, as some among the most respected in Jerusalem — persons who wield the momentous power accompanying their advanced status, persons whose words and deeds have seemed to bear the imprimatur of God — are reduced to the shadows of furtive activity.

Key to the interpretation of this scene is the place of Roman tribute in Jewish life. As a form of tax, it was relatively insignificant, requiring an annual payment of one denarius, a day's wage, per adult male.[53] Its symbolic connotations are of profound importance, however. (1) Of course, for those who lived close to the margins of economic subsistence, even the relatively modest requirements of the tribute only added to the already weighty burden of financial obligations external to the family.[54] (2) Tribute itself was a perennial reminder and acknowledgment of Jewish subjugation to a foreign overlord. From within the Lukan narrative, this recalls the elevated interest in the Roman census — to which the Third Evangelist devotes remarkable attention (2:1-7); we may recall that the primary purpose of the census was for the assessment of Roman tribute, and that Luke sets the birth of Jesus in apposition with Roman overlordship. (3) Failure to pay the tribute was tantamount to disavowal of Roman rule, and this during a period when Roman policy provided no quarter for sedition. It is hardly surprising that, in their presentation of Jesus to Pilate later in the Lukan narrative, the Jewish leaders recall this episode (23:2).

---

makes use of the opening provided by the vulnerable answer to refute the outsider's challenge." Although Owen-Ball's analysis focuses on the Markan account, the Lukan more closely fits this pattern.

53. The question of exactly who was subject to this "head tax" remains the subject of debate. If "tribute" also includes the land tax, the amount due would be somewhat higher; T. E. Schmidt ("Taxes," 804-5) estimates that, in Judea, the average adult male worked about three weeks per year in order to fulfill the national assessment for tribute to Rome.

54. See the general comments on economic obligations on the peasant family, above, §10.

(4) Historically, the Jerusalem sanhedrin was responsible for collecting Roman tribute, a fact that raises a series of relevant considerations. Although some might indict the Jerusalem leadership for compromising Jewish fidelity to Yahweh by exacting from the Jewish populace a sign of loyalty to Rome, clearly others believed that tribute to Rome was a small price to pay for Roman dispensation allowing the continuation of the temple cult and all it represented. As long as fidelity to the temple was preserved, compromises of a smaller order were justifiable. Such thinking placed the higher priority on the main-tenance of the temple as the abode of God and center of Jewish identity. Within the Lukan narrative, then, the question about the legality (according to Mosaic law) of paying tribute to the emperor is also a question about the authority of the sanhedrin to serve as Rome's agent in Judea. Much more, it is a question about Jesus' fidelity to the temple, the Holy Place, the nexus between human and divine, inviolable territory.[55] Jesus had already undermined the authority of the chief priests and legal experts, charging them with behaving in ways that opposed the purpose of God and that denied their legitimacy as Israel's leaders. What is the reach of Jesus' insolence? Will he go so far as to call into question the priority of the temple itself?

Much more is at stake in this encounter than might at first appear, then. The character of Jesus' message is on the line, as is the compass of his authority. In fact, two additional features of Luke's narration locate the primary emphasis of this scene on the issue of Jesus' authority. First, this scene is boundaried by dual references to the attempt "to trap [Jesus] by what he said" (vv 20, 26). Given this convergence of language,[56] it is notable that the context of the intended entrapment changes in focus. The objective of the first is to find a basis to charge Jesus before the governor, while the second is specifically concerned with snaring Jesus "in the presence of the people."[57] The resulting portrait has Jesus in a vice between Pilate and the people. If Jesus answers one way, he stands condemned by Rome as a dissident; if the other, he depletes his capital with the populace.[58] Because it is precisely his popularity that continues to hold at bay the malicious stratagems of the Jerusalem leadership against him, either way Jesus seems bound for execution. Second, there is the notable juxtaposition of the explicit "jurisdiction and authority of the governor" (v 20) and the implicit authority of Jesus the "teacher" (v 21), called upon to adjudicate

55. See Knipe, "Temple," 107-12.

56. Verse 20: ἐπιλάβωνται αὐτοῦ λόγου; v 26: ἐπιλαβέσθαι αὐτοῦ ῥήματος.

57. This is clearer in the Greek text, where "in the presence of the people" comes after "by what he said," so that the emphasis falls even more solidly on the failure to cause Jesus to mispeak in public and thus undermine his popular support.

58. Cf. Bruce, "Render to Caesar," 251.

between the potentially competing claims of Caesar and, via the Mosaic law, God.

20-22   The unspecified "they" of v 20 has as its antecedent the scribes and chief priests of v 19, indicating that the disappointment of their immediate desire to take him into custody has not left them without options. "To watch" has the nuance of monitoring behavior,[59] as though their response was to set up a surveillance operation. Shamed before the very people over whom they were to have provided leadership, the Jerusalem leaders are reduced to covert activity against Jesus, and to the use of agents who might represent their hostile intent.[60] "Agents who pretended to be righteous" is a difficult phrase to represent in translation.[61] "Agents" is used in the LXX with reference to "lying in ambush,"[62] while "to pretend to be righteous" refers to the behavior of those characterized by godless maliciousness. The closest analogue in the LXX is the reference to a captain who, pretending to be peaceably disposed, entered Jerusalem and killed great numbers of people (2 Macc 5:25).[63] Although "pretense" may call to mind the idea of "hypocrisy," in its usual modern sense of deliberate duplicity, "hypocrisy" has no place in Luke's characterization of the agents sent to snare Jesus. Read against the backdrop of earlier scenes, "pretending to be righteous" refers instead to doomed attempts at self-justification — that is, righteousness as this is measured with reference to popular status and acclaim rather than with reference to conformity to the way of God (see 10:29; 16:15; 18:9-14). These agents come to Jesus not in order to play a role given them, but because the form of righteousness served by their superiors demands that Jesus and his influence be removed from the temple.

Luke's characterization of the chief priests and legal experts and their agents stands in stark contrast to their characterization of Jesus in v 21. Their form of righteousness can only be a pretense since it is grounded in concerns with status honor and public opinion. He, on the other hand, is known foremost as a "teacher"[64] whose message is unconcerned with popular opinion but conforms to divine truth. The three phrases — "you are right . . . you show

---

59. παρατηρέω — cf. 6:7; 14:1. For this motif, cf. 11:53-54.

60. ἀποστέλλω has a more restricted sense than πέμπω in this co-text, then, and signifies "to commission" or "to authorize."

61. For the syntactical features — including the use of the accusative of object in tandem with a predicate accusative and the use of the reflexive pronoun in the accusative with the infinitive — cf. MHT 2:147; BDF §§157.2, 406.1.

62. ἐγκάθετος — cf. Job 19:12; 31:9.

63. ὑποκρίνομαι appears in the NT only in v 20. In Sir 32:15; 33:2; 2 Macc 6:21, 24; 4 Macc 6:15, 17, the verb refers to activity apart from or in opposition to the law of God. For the notion of "godless maliciousness," see Giesen, "ὑπόκρισις, ὑποκρίνομαι."

64. See the threefold use of διδάσκαλος/διδάσκω in v 21.

no deference . . . [you] teach the way of God in accordance with the truth"
— emphasize through their redundancy Jesus' nonnegotiable, noncompromis-
ing orientation to the will of God.[65] Of course, coming from the agents of the
Jerusalem leadership, this portrait of Jesus is ironic. Even if those who follow
Jesus, in and outside the narrative, know this portrait to be accurate, the
purpose of these agents in presenting it is not to honor Jesus but to trick him.
By drawing attention to his lack of deference, apparently his questioners wish
to draw Jesus into a position of indifference even to Caesar! Will his temerity
extend so far? If so, then he will have transgressed a law the penalty for which
not even popular opinion can protect him. Of course, Luke's audience knows
already that, by according privilege to children (for example) and social
outcasts, Jesus has already undermined the widespread system of deference
and social obligation that locates at its zenith the one to whom all are obligated,
the one of highest status, the emperor.[66]

It is difficult to overlook the implicit contrast established by the
agency of chief priests and legal experts (v 20), whose teaching and interpretive function are well known throughout the Lukan narrative, and the
use of the appellation "teacher" for Jesus. Within the Lukan narrative,
"teacher" is used by those who are outside the circle of Jesus' disciples,
generally by those who want something from Jesus, who have yet to
determine what to make of him, and most recently by those who oppose
the attribution of divine authority to him.[67] In this co-text, his instruction
stands in contrast to those whose authority to interpret the ways of God is
generally without question, whose status vis-à-vis the temple has practically
provided them a magisterium-like function. In this way, too, the attribution
to Jesus by his opponents of the appellation "teacher" must be understood
ironically.

On the tribute[68] and the seemingly impossible situation presented Jesus
with the question of the payment of tribute, see the introduction to this pericope
(above). The intensity of the question posed to Jesus would have been palpable
in the world Luke narrates. Following the Roman census in 6 C.E., some
Palestinian Jews embraced anew the theocratic ideals of their tradition and
espoused their conviction that the payment of tribute to Caesar was incongru-

---

65. For ὀρθῶς, see 7:43; 10:29. The words οὐ λαμβάνεις πρόσωπον ("you do not
lift up the face") is unknown in classical or Hellenistic Greek, though cf. Lev 19:5; Ps
82:2; Lam 4:16; Fitzmyer, 115, 1295 (who regards it as a Septuagintalism); cf. Acts 10:34.
For "the way of God," see above, 1:6, 79; 3:4; Deut 8:6; 10:12-13.

66. See Carroll and Green, *Death of Jesus*, 179-80.

67. See 7:40; 10:25; 11:45; 18:18, 39.

68. φόρος may refer to "tax" in a general way, but its usage in this co-text, with
reference to the emperor and to the denarius (the coin appropriate to payment of tribute),
suggests the more narrow sense of "tribute."

ous with fidelity to the one God, the sole ruler of Israel.[69] The question of congruity between faithful life in the covenant and payment of the tribute, therefore, was a real one.[70] Jesus' message of the kingdom — which we are to assume he has been proclaiming in the temple[71] — and his own acclamation as "king" at his arrival into Jerusalem (19:29-40) also press the question about the relation of the imperial rule of God present in Jesus' ministry and the terms of life under Rome.

23-25   The seemingly impossible position in which Jesus finds himself is somewhat mollified by his prophetic insight into the cunning[72] of his interlocutors. Although we are thus informed that Jesus is aware of the treachery of the flattery with which he has been addressed, it is not clear if or how this recognition might have shaped his response.

Insofar as those who have put the question of tribute payment to Jesus are agents of chief priests and legal experts, Jesus' request for a denarius is itself significant. Together with the elders, chief priests and scribes constituted the Jerusalem sanhedrin,[73] the sanhedrin collected the tribute on Rome's behalf, and the tribute was calculated in terms of and paid by the denarius.[74] By requesting from them a denarius, then, Jesus exposes the nature of the question, since it is clear that they, who possess denarii, also possess their own answer to the question they have posed. What is more, in the discourse that immediately follows, Jesus in essence charges them, together with the sanhedrin, with being about the business of Rome rather than about the business of God (cf. 2:49).[75]

In all probability, the denarius in question in this scene bore the image of Tiberius and the inscription, "Tiberius Caesar, son of the divine Augustus."[76] Key to understanding Jesus' response are, first, a reconstruction of the basis for his judgment in torah (as would be expected in the interrogation of a Jewish teacher), and, second, the connotation of the verb translated in the NRSV as "give." With regard to the scriptural foundations of Jesus' answer, likely candidates are found in Gen 1:26 (the creation of human beings in the divine image) and a cluster of passages concerned with the inscription of the

---

69. See the discussion in Hengel, *Zealots,* 134-40; Bruce, "Render to Caesar," 254-57.

70. For this use of ἔξεστιν (i.e., with reference to what is lawful within the covenant), see 6:2, 4, 9; 14:3; Acts 16:21.

71. See "good news" in v 1; cf. 4:43; 8:1-3.

72. πανουργία is found only here in Luke-Acts; in the NT it has a consistently negative connotation — cf. 1 Cor 3:19; 2 Cor 4:2; 11:3; Eph 4:14.

73. See above on 9:22; cf. 20:1.

74. See Hart, "Coin," 241.

75. See Dawsey, "Confrontation in the Temple," 160-62.

76. The evidence has been reviewed in Hart, "Coin."

divine law on the human person (cf. Exod 13:9; Prov 7:3; Jer 31:33).[77] The net effect of the reasoning grounded in this form of intertextuality is Jesus' fundamental emphasis on human beings as creatures who not only owe their very being to God but who also experience the fullness of their humanity in relation to God and in obedience to the way of God. On the second point, the verb "to give" is in this instance better understood as "to give back, "to return," or even "to pay what one owes,"[78] so that the sense is something like, "Give to Caesar what is his already, etc."

By this point in the interchange, Jesus has distanced himself significantly from the sort of Yes/No answer anticipated by the original question, "Is it lawful . . . , or not?" He has not escaped the issue, however, by dividing the world into two spheres, one belonging to the emperor and the other to God. Such dichotomous thinking would be entirely alien to ancient anthropology. Instead, while not denying the possibility of obedience to Caesar, Jesus asserts the prior and more fundamental claim of God on all human beings, on human existence itself. One may hear in the background the earlier words of Jesus, "No slave can serve two masters. . . . You cannot serve God and Wealth" (16:13). Whatever role the Empire might have, it, like Wealth, finds its appropriate function within and subservient to God's universal dominion. As a corollary, whatever demands the Empire might attempt to exact from its subjects, they are relativized by the antecedent claims of the kingdom of God. When these come into conflict — as they certainly do in the narrative Luke has written — one must choose which dominion one will serve. Serving as Rome's tribute-gatherer and comporting itself so as to win public favor (cf. 20:45–21:4; rather than the favor of God), the Jerusalem leadership appears to have sided with the Empire, against the purpose and rule of God. As in Jesus' adjacent parabolic teaching, they, like the tenants, fail to give the Lord what is due him (vv 9-19).

26 At the outset of this scene, we were informed of the intent of these agents of the Jewish leadership in Jerusalem to trap Jesus in order that he might be arrested by Pilate. Now Luke reports that they had attempted to trap Jesus in the presence of the people. These are not contradictory but speak pointedly to the nature of the snare laid for Jesus: If Jesus is a king (19:29-40), then he must be a rival ruler who would prohibit the payment of tribute to the Roman overlord; if he allows payment, then he is no king after all. According to the first scenario, Jesus would be marked a rebel and would be executed accordingly; according to the second, he would lose face with the crowd that has applauded and supported him. Jesus' answer has shown the logic of their trap to be faulty, but this leads only to their wonderment and silence, not to their understanding or repentance.

77. See Giblin, "Things of God," 521-23; and esp. Owen-Ball, "Rabbinic Rhetoric," 10-11.

78. ἀποδίδωμι — cf. 4:20; 7:42; 10:35; Lev 6:4.

6.1.4. The Question of Moses' Authority (20:27-40)

27 *Some Sadducees, those who say there is no resurrection, came to him* 28 *and asked him a question, "Teacher, Moses wrote for us that if a man's brother dies, leaving a wife but no children, the man shall marry the widow and raise up children for his brother.* 29 *Now there were seven brothers; the first married, and died childless;* 30 *then the second* 31 *and the third married her, and so in the same way all seven died childless.* 32 *Finally the woman also died.* 33 *In the resurrection, therefore, whose wife will the woman be? For the seven had married her."*

34 *Jesus said to them, "Those who belong to this age marry and are given in marriage;* 35 *but those who are considered worthy of a place in that age and in the resurrection from the dead neither marry nor are given in marriage.* 36 *Indeed they cannot die anymore, because they are like angels and are children of God, being children of the resurrection.* 37 *And the fact that the dead are raised Moses himself showed, in the story about the bush, where he speaks of the Lord as the God of Abraham, the God of Isaac, and the God of Jacob.* 38 *Now he is God not of the dead, but of the living; for to him all of them are alive."* 39 *Then some of the scribes answered, "Teacher, you have spoken well."* 40 *For they no longer dared to ask him another question.*

The coalition formed by the chief priests, scribes, and elders mentioned in v 1 is not coterminous with the Sadducees of this encounter, but there is enough overlap to include this episode among the accounts concerned fundamentally with conflict between Jesus and the Jerusalem leadership (vv 1-40). At one level, it may be possible to understand the Sadducees' question as a sincere attempt to learn from Jesus. Within this co-text, however, it can hardly be read as anything but a further attempt to ensnare Jesus by embarrassing him before the people. The artificiality of the question is suggested, moreover, by its absurdity; compare, for example, the later Jewish text in which a rabbi is asked whether, following the resurrection, persons will need to undergo ritual cleansing on account of Jewish legislation pertaining to corpse impurity.[79]

At the outset, Luke provides in a narrative aside information concerning the Sadducees necessary to understand the unfolding scene — namely, that they "say there is no resurrection."[80] In fact, resurrection-belief, mentioned six times in this pericope (vv 27, 33, 35, 36, 37, 38), becomes vital in the encounter between Jesus and his latest interlocutors. Recognition of the central

79. *b. Nid.* 70b.
80. See Sheeley, *Narrative Asides,* 106.

focus on resurrection, however, should not mask that this is only a means for grappling with the more basic question of the nature of Jesus' authority. In fact, the staging of this scene indicates that the real issue at stake is one of scriptural faithfulness, and then authority to interpret Scripture faithfully. Thus, Jesus' identity as "teacher" is juxtaposed with the authority of Moses (vv 28, 37, 39), and the position of the Sadducees is evidently contrasted with that of the legal experts, who side with Jesus on the question of the resurrection. The Sadducees, known for their emphasis on the Torah, attempt to set Jesus up; appealing to Moses, they concoct a scenario that, in essence, requires Jesus to answer the question, Do you follow Moses? The Sadducees are not the only ones to cite Moses, however; so does Jesus. The baseline of Jesus' answer may be surprising to his audience but harmonious with a central element of the larger Lukan perspective on Israel's Scriptures.[81] In a crucial sense, he turns the question away from *obedience* to Moses to one of *understanding* Moses. Who interprets Moses (and the Scriptures) faithfully?

In this scene, then, Luke presents a battle over the Scriptures.[82] The Scriptures are not for Jesus self-interpreting, but must be read from the right perspective. As he lays it out, this perspective is an eschatological one, one that takes into account the presently unfolding purpose of God, and that generates in the present both faithful interpretation and faithful response. This latter emphasis helps to explain why, at the end of this pericope, the scribes can appear to side with Jesus, only immediately to be soundly censured in the subsequent narrative. As Jesus will go on to argue, they may be correct in their resurrection-belief, but fail deplorably in their understanding of scriptural teaching concerning the Messiah as well as in the structure of their values and behaviors (20:41–21:4).

27-28 The Third Evangelist has located Jesus in the temple, where he brings "good news" to the people (v 1), then narrates a series of encounters wherein Jesus' authority is questioned by the leading people of Jerusalem (vv 1-40). Members of the sanhedrin and their agents have been shamed and confounded into silence (vv 19, 26), leaving an opening for some Sadducees to engage Jesus in discussion. This is our first introduction to the Sadducees in the Third Gospel, but from an historical perspective this is not surprising. Sadducees, after all, exercised their aristocratic influence in the Holy City. Surprisingly little is known of them,[83] undoubtedly owing to their loss of position following the destruction of the Jerusalem temple. Josephus observes that they had the confidence only of the wealthy,[84] and this comports

81. See Green, *Gospel of Luke,* 28, 74-75.
82. See Tyson, *Images of Judaism,* 89-90.
83. See the survey in Porton, "Sadducees."
84. Josephus *Ant.* 13.10.6 §298.

well with their appearance in the Third Gospel at this juncture. Luke has and will continue to represent Jesus in controversial encounters with those of highest status in the city, and this would include the Sadducees. In a narrative aside, Luke draws attention to one of the qualities for which this group was well known, both in the Lukan narrative and otherwise — namely, their rejection of the notion of a resurrection.[85] Also of importance is the Sadducean emphasis on Torah, on display here in the reference to Moses, the intimation that Moses wrote "for us," and the fusion of Deut 25:5 and Gen 38:8 in their representation of the legislation concerning levirate marriage.[86] With their reference to Jesus as "teacher," the Sadducees position themselves with others who have come to Jesus as outsiders, typically who are trying to make up their minds about him or, more recently, who oppose him.[87]

According to Deut 25:5, together with the examples of Judah and Tamar (Gen 38:6-11) and of Ruth and Boaz (Ruth 3:9–4:10), a woman whose husband died childless was required to be married by one of the deceased man's brothers.[88] The purpose of the levirate marriage ordinance, exploited by the Sadducees in this episode, was to continue the name of the deceased, to give him, in a sense, an afterlife. Also of import in what follows is the view of marriage institutionalized in this legislation, for it exhibits a profoundly patriarchal understanding of marriage, in which the woman was "taken"[89] by the man and was essential to his need for progeny.[90]

29-33 The scenario formulated by the Sadducees draws on the Mosaic legislation for its particulars, and thus functions rhetorically on two fronts. First, the story is inscribed in the sacred texts that, presumably, Jesus must honor; if he does not, then he shows himself to be defiant in the face of Moses. Second, the puzzle placed before Jesus advances two competing notions of "life after death."[91] There is, on the one hand, the persistence of life through one's progeny, guaranteed by ordinances governing levirate marriage. On the other, there is the resurrection. Belief in "immortality through pos-

---

85. Their rejection of this doctrine provides the primary impetus for their role in Luke-Acts — cf. Acts 4:1; 5:17; 23:6-8; Schwankl, *Sadduzäerfrage,* 337. See also, e.g., Josephus *Ant.* 18.1.4 §16; *War* 2.8.14 §165.

86. For a discussion of the text forms used, see Kimball, *Jewish Exposition,* 166-67.

87. See 7:40; 10:25; 11:45; 18:18, 39; 19:21.

88. For levirate marriage in the Second Temple period, see the discussion in Ilan, *Jewish Woman,* 152-57.

89. See the use of λαμβάνω in the idiom "to take a wife" (for "to marry") in vv 28, 29, and 31.

90. See Seim, *Double Message,* 213-19.

91. Note the Greek text in v 28, which uses the compound ἐξανίστημι ("to raise up") in parallel with ἀνάστασις ("resurrection") in v 33.

terity" is upheld by Moses, it is alleged, and this renders the idea of resurrection absurd; therefore, from a Sadducean point of view, Torah excludes belief in the afterlife.

34-36 Jesus' rejoinder comes in two parts — the first in vv 34-36 and the second in vv 37-38. The first has to do with the nature of resurrection-belief and the perspective from which one might understand God's purpose; the second has to do with Torah.

Fundamental to Jesus' first point is his contrast between two sorts of people, two aeons, and two forms of practice vis-à-vis marriage. Thus:

the sons	of this age	marry and consent to marriage
those considered worthy	of a place in that age and	neither marry nor consent to marriage; nor can they die anymore, for they are like the angels;
	in the resurrection from the dead	and they are sons of God, being sons of the resurrection.

The phrase "those who belong to this age" refers literally to "the sons of this age" (v 34), and this contrasts strikingly with (again, translating more literally) those who are "sons of God" and "sons of the resurrection" (v 36). The Third Gospel often depicts persons, both male and female, as "sons of . . . ," not as a matter of literal descent but as a way of denoting their character, their dispositions, their behavior.[92] One sort of person is thus oriented toward "this age," with its concerns for status honor, relationships of debt and reciprocity, and the like (cf. 16:8-9). (Indeed, earlier in the Third Gospel, the present age is characterized as faithless and wicked — cf., e.g., 7:31; 9:41; 11:29-32; 16:8-9.) The other group consists of "those who are considered worthy of a place in that age. . . ." The apposition of the two expressions "this age" and "that age" assumes a division of time into two aeons, the present age and the age to come. The nature of the age to come is clearly demarcated through its collocation in vv 35-36 with the ideas of resurrection and the cessation of death, and with its relationship to God. That the latter group "are considered worthy" signifies their apathy toward self-promotion and self-justification (cf. 10:29; 16:15; 18:9); their "worth" is not measured by comparison with others in a perpetual tug-of-war for honor and prestige in the agonistic culture of "this world," but is granted by God. On what basis? Earlier, "children of God" were understood to be those whose dispositions are marked by mercy, giving without expectation of return, love of enemies (6:35-36); here, people are marked as "children of God" by virtue of their being "children of the

92. Cf., e.g., 3:7-9; 10:6; 16:8.

resurrection."[93] They are those considered worthy of a place in the resurrection on account of their adopting the values and behaviors characteristic of the age to come (cf. 16:8-9).

Although typically represented as passive verbs, the instances of the two verbs translated "are given in marriage" (NRSV) actually appear in the middle voice: "to allow oneself to be married."[94] The focus shifts from a man "taking a wife" (vv 28, 29, 31) to include the woman's participation in the decision to marry. This is important because the basic concern here is with a reorientation of human relations *through a reorientation of eschatological vision.* One sort of person is aligned with the needs of the present age; such persons participate in the system envisioned and advocated by the Sadducees, itself rooted in the legislation governing levirate marriage, with women given and taken, even participating in their own objectification as necessary vehicles for the continuation of the family name and heritage. The other draws its ethos from the age to come, where people will resemble angels insofar as they no longer face death.[95] Absent the threat of death, the need for levirate marriage is erased. The undermining of the levirate marriage ordinance is itself a radical critique of marriage as this has been defined around the necessity of procreation. No longer must women find their value in producing children for patrimony. Jesus' message thus finds its interpretive antecedent in his instruction about family relations of all kinds: Hearing faithfully the good news relativizes all family relationships (cf., e.g., 8:1-3, 19-20).

Jesus thus underscores the absurdity of the Sadducees' question by undermining its major premises. The scenario they had painted has failed, first, in its perception of the nature of the age to come. Second, it fails to account for the reality that the age to come impinges already on life in the present.

37-38 The second half of Jesus' rejoinder engages the Sadducees more directly on exegetical grounds. Because they accord privilege to the Torah, he himself also turns to Moses in order to provide scriptural warrant

---

93. Cf. Schwankl, *Sadduzäerfrage,* 450-51.

94. In v 34, γαμίσκονται; in v 35, γαμίζονται.

95. This is the only appearance of ἰσάγγελος in the Greek Bible. With the use of γάρ, Luke indicates that the basis for comparison with angels is the one shared property that they never die. Though Luke does not develop it here, this is a further, subtle critique of the Sadducees, who also rejected the existence of angels (cf. Acts 23:8). The words οὐδὲ ἀποθανεῖν ἔτι δύνανται may suggest comparison with the Hellenistic notion of "immortality (of the soul)" (ἀθανασία) (cf. Schwankl, *Sadduzäerfrage,* 448-49; Fitzmyer, 2:1305). Caution is suggested, however, by (1) the general anthropological monism of the Second Temple period (*pace* Philo, who is hardly representative even of the Neoplatonists — cf. D. B. Martin, *Corinthian Body,* 1-37; Wright, *People of God,* 254-55); and (2) the specific references to resurrection (of the dead) in this pericope.

for resurrection-belief. Drawing on Exod 3:6, 15, he (1) notes that when God was speaking to Moses he was still the God of the long-dead patriarchs Abraham, Isaac, and Jacob; (2) infers the absurdity that God would broadcast a covenant relationship with persons whose existence had expired; (3) concludes that Abraham, Isaac, and Jacob must therefore still be alive; and (4) deduces that, in relating the story about the bush, Moses himself attested resurrection-belief. At the close of this argument, Jesus uses a clause, "for to him all of them are alive," meant to serve as a basis for his argumentation. His phrasing is reminiscent of 4 Macc 7:19; 16:25, where it is claimed that the martyrs "live to God" as the patriarchs do. The present tense rules out the suggestion that, in the faithfulness with which they face death, they prove that their lives are lived for God. Instead, in some sense, these texts affirm, these persons are given life by God.[96] Luke has already provided insight into the nature of resurrection life in his earlier reference to Lazarus, who was carried away by angels to Abraham (who *is* still alive[!]; see above, on 16:22-23).[97]

39-40 Although this encounter has been narrowly focused on the Sadducees and Jesus, Jesus is still in the temple. This implies that the Sadducees and Jesus have been involved in the familiar challenge-response convention by which Jesus' authority as an interpreter of God's purpose is on trial. What Luke now emphasizes, however, is the presence of "some of the scribes" as bystanders. Like the Sadducees, they refer to Jesus as "teacher," signifying their position on the outside of Jesus' circle of disciples, even though their response indicates their support of his rejoinder to the Sadducees. This is an important reminder that, even if we may not be won over by the logic of Jesus' exegesis in vv 37-38, by the interpretive norms of his day it was impressive.

These legal experts may have aligned themselves with the Pharisees (or perhaps they are Pharisees — Luke does not specify further their affiliations) over against the Sadducees regarding belief in the resurrection. Their support of Jesus at this juncture portends the support Jesus' witnesses will garner from Pharisees in the Acts of the Apostles (cf., e.g., Acts 23:6-10). Accord on this one issue does not make disciples of these scribes, however. They may interpret the Scriptures correctly on the question of resurrection, but they do not understand the Scriptures as they relate to the Messiah (see below, 20:41-44). Nor have they learned to orient their lives around the coming

---

96. See the discussion in Kimball, *Jesus' Exposition*, 173-75.
97. *Contra* Fitzmyer (2:1301-2), Luke gives us no reason to think in terms of the "immortality of the soul." In fact, one finds little support in the NT as a whole for a body-soul dualism, and the Lazarus-story provides no room for the existence of a disembodied soul after death (see above).

age. Instead, continuing to seek the public eye in order to advance their prestige, they do violence to those among the most vulnerable of society (see below, 20:45–21:4).

Hence, Luke can only conclude that Jesus had silenced his opponents, not that the Jewish leadership in Jerusalem had become so disoriented by his message that they were ready to repudiate their long-standing commitments and embrace the kind of faithfulness determined by the inbreaking kingdom of God.

6.1.5. The Question of the Messiah's Authority (20:41-44)

41 *Then he said to them, "How can they say that the Messiah is David's son? 42 For David himself says in the book of Psalms,*
'The Lord said to my Lord,
"Sit at my right hand,
43 until I make your enemies your footstool." '
44 David thus calls him Lord; so how can he be his son?"

Since v 1, Luke has portrayed Jesus teaching the people in the temple in the presence of the Jewish leadership in Jerusalem. Thus far, the Third Evangelist has been clear about the intended recipients of Jesus' message; however, with Jesus' opponents silenced and Jesus on the offensive, it is now less obvious to whom this section of Jesus' teaching is directed. Given the nature of the challenge-riposte type of exchange characteristic of this major section (i.e., from vv 1-44), it seems likely that the "them" of v 41 is the people, and the "they" of v 41 is comprised of the legal experts last mentioned in v 39.[98] Accordingly, in this pericope Jesus is not only asserting something of christological significance but is also calling into question the authority of the legal experts to interpret Scripture. Even if they agree with Jesus regarding the resurrection (v 39), this must not be taken as an indication that they have fully aligned themselves with Jesus or that they are to be trusted more generally.

The exegetical issue on which Jesus' question turns is the potential contradiction between two biblical texts.[99] The first reference constitutes an allusion to OT texts providing for the identification of the Messiah as a Davidide (e.g., 2 Sam 7:12-14).[100] The other is an almost word-for-word

98. The antecedent of these pronouns is debated, often with appeal made to their identity in the Second Gospel. Mark's reference to "the scribes" does not settle the issue within the Lukan narrative, however. Burger (*Jesus als Davidssohn,* 114-16) goes further to suggest that the presence of these pronouns allows for the presence of such christological questions within the early church.

99. Cf. Juel, *Messianic Exegesis,* 142-43.

100. See further above on 1:32-35.

citation of Ps 110:1,[101] which, according to Jesus, renders problematic any identification of a Son of David with the Messiah. In the psalm, at least according to the MT, Yahweh speaks to the king, presumably from the perspective of the priest. In later Judaism, however, Psalm 110 was used with reference to the vindication of the pious and to assist in the legitimation of persons, especially rulers.[102] In Jesus' reading of the psalm, David himself prophesies that Yahweh speaks to the Messiah who, David says, is "my Lord." Since normal conventions would have the son showing honor to his father rather than vice versa, it would be problematic to portray David, who thus honors the Messiah, as the father of the Messiah.

On the other hand, the Third Evangelist has affirmed that, as Messiah, Jesus is indeed "Son of David," especially in the birth narratives (1:27, 32-35; 2:4) but also subsequently (see 3:31; 18:38-39; cf. 19:38). Hence, within the Lukan narrative, Jesus' puzzle cannot be resolved by denying that the Messiah is a Davidide; rather, "Son of David" must not be the "ultimate category" for understanding the identity of the Messiah in Luke's narrative.[103] At stake in Jesus' query, then, is how best to make sense of the Messiah's relationship to David.[104]

In fact, Jesus provides no immediate resolution of the enigma he poses, though he does hint through his exegetical riddle that the better category for making sense of the Messiah is "Lord" (cf. 2:11). "Sit at my right hand" refers to the ascription of honor (cf. 1 Kgs 2:9), but the present text leaves open-ended how this might take place. Similarly, the reference to "enemies" in the psalmic citation (v 43) cannot be overlooked in this hostile co-text (ch. 20), even if it is not yet clear how Jesus' enemies, the Jewish leadership attached to the Jerusalem temple, will be subdued before Jesus. Only in Luke's second volume, in the Pentecost address of Peter (esp. Acts 2:34-36), do we learn how Jesus will be honored as "Lord." His exaltation to the right hand of God and installation as "Lord" come via his resurrection and ascension, which together constitute his divine vindication.[105]

6.1.6. The Despotic Authority of Jerusalem's Leadership (20:45–21:4)

45 *In the hearing of all the people he said to the disciples,* 46 *"Beware of the scribes, who like to walk around in long robes, and love to be greeted with respect in the marketplaces, and to have the best seats in*

---

101. The Lukan text departs from the LXX only by omitting the definite article before the first κύριος.

102. See the survey in Hay, *Glory at the Right Hand,* 19-33.

103. Bock, *Proclamation,* 132.

104. See the use of πῶς in v 41: "In what way. . . ?"

105. For the import of Psalm 110 in early christological reflection, see Hengel, *Between Jesus and Paul,* 78-96.

the synagogues and places of honor at banquets. 47 *They devour widows' houses and for the sake of appearance say long prayers. They will receive the greater condemnation."*

21:1 *He looked up and saw rich people putting their gifts into the treasury;* 2 *he also saw a poor widow put in two small copper coins.* 3 *He said, "Truly I tell you, this poor widow has put in more than all of them;* 4 *for all of them have contributed out of their abundance, but she out of her poverty has put in all she had to live on."*

It is not enough to indicate that the scribes, or legal experts, are inadequate as interpreters of Scripture (vv 41-44). As the juxtaposition of 20:41-44 and 20:45–21:4 indicates, failure to interpret Scripture faithfully is bundled together with failure to respond faithfully to Scripture. Having silenced his opponents in public exchange (20:1-40), Jesus has gone on the offensive against them, and the ultimate charge he can lay against them is their participation in behaviors and their perpetuation of a system that victimizes widows, counted among the weakest members of society, whom both law and leadership were to protect.

Luke has set these two moments of instruction to the disciples in one scene, indicating their intimate affinity.[106] The one is adjacent to the other, of course, but they are also bound together with respect to theme; by repetition of the term "widow" (20:47; 21:2-3) and reference to her livelihood ("houses" — 20:47; "all she had to live on" — 21:4); and by the staging of 21:1-4 as an example of the teaching of 20:45-47.[107] The analogy that Luke develops is helped along by the correlation of honor/public image (20:46-47) and wealth (21:1, 4) throughout the Third Gospel.[108]

Crucial to the interpretation of this scene is the identification of its two main groups of characters, each of which functions here to symbolize opposing kinds of people. First, there are legal experts, whom Luke repeatedly casts in roles hostile to Jesus.[109] From an historical point of view, scribes can be located throughout Palestine — some associated with the Pharisees (cf. Acts 23:9), some likely drawn from the priesthood, and so on.[110] Since they were interpreters of the law, their positions among the people were pivotal. Like some other sources within Second Temple Judaism, Luke seems to present them as persons of elevated social status alongside the leading priests in

106. Green, "Good News," 66.
107. Thus 21:1 begins, ἀναβλέψας δὲ εἶδεν.
108. See Moxnes, *Economy of the Kingdom.*
109. Cf. 6:1-11; 7:29-30; see above on 9:22.
110. See Schwartz, *Jewish Background,* 89-101; E. P. Sanders, *Judaism,* 170-82. That is, since priests were on active duty at the temple only two weeks out of the year, they served also as interpreters of the law for the people.

725

Jerusalem.[111] On the opposite end of the scale of power and privilege were widows (see Figure 1, p. 60), the weakest, most defenseless people in society, "persons without any prospects of fending for themselves."[112] Pivotal for this scene, then, is that those who interpret God's law on behalf of Israel, and the temple system that was to be the embodiment of God's presence for Israel, are set in opposition to those on whose behalf God has expressed particular care.

It is also of significance, though, that the disciples are warned about the behavior of the scribes — not simply to undermine the public authority of these legal experts, but to warn the disciples not to embrace this way of comporting themselves in the community of God's people.

45-46 Since 20:1, Jesus has been teaching the people in the presence of the Jerusalem leadership. The shift here is therefore deliberate and consequential. Now he teaches the disciples in the hearing of the people. This means that Jesus will continue in a public way to undermine the authority of the Jerusalem leadership, but also that the disciples are in need of specific instruction. In a way reminiscent of 12:1 ("Beware of the yeast of the Pharisees . . ."), Jesus admonishes his followers to "watch out"[113] lest they be lured into similar behavior (cf. 22:24!).

The four phrases used in 20:46 to characterize the teachers of the law are all ways of indicating claims to advanced social position through nonverbal behavior.[114] Each illuminates the attempt of the teachers of the law to lay claim to exalted social status. An outer garment is clearly intended in the first clause, and it may be that, by the first century, "robe" could refer to the festive garment worn to celebrate the Sabbath,[115] but this is uncertain. In the LXX "robe" refers especially to the outer garment by which a person is noted for his or her status.[116] Moreover, elsewhere in the Third Gospel (as throughout Roman Palestine)[117] clothes signify social status (cf. 7:25; 8:26-35; 16:19). Thus, teachers of the law are portrayed as those who enjoy parading around in clothes signifying their eminence.

The other three descriptive phrases —

---

111. See, e.g., Sir 38:24–39:11; *Jub.* 4:17-25.

112. Seim, *Double Message,* 230; cf. Ilan, *Jewish Women,* 147-48. See 2:37; 4:25-26; 7:12; Acts 6:1; 9:39. From the standpoint of Israel's Scriptures, partiality was expected on behalf of the widow — see above on 18:2-4a.

113. συνέχω, also used in 12:1.

114. That is, they are all forms of paralinguistic social deixis; cf. Levinson, *Pragmatics,* 54-94.

115. στολή. So Rengstorf, "Die στολαί."

116. E.g., Gen 41:14, 41-42; Esth 6:8; 1 Chr 15:27; 2 Chr 5:12; 1 Macc 6:15.

117. Cf. Hamel, *Poverty and Charity,* 73-93.

and love

> to be greeted with respect in the marketplaces,
> and to have the best seats in the synagogues,
> and   places of honor at banquets —

continue Jesus' critique of the public behavior of the legal experts. Each phrase parallels the other, with the result that three major public arenas are mentioned — the marketplace as social center, the synagogue, and the banquet room — together with symbols of honor relevant to each. "Best seats" and "places of honor" translate parallel Greek terms, both signifying the location of the seats reserved for the "first" among the gathered assembly.[118] Interestingly, each is paralleled elsewhere in Luke's Gospel. In 11:43, the Pharisees are condemned for loving the best seat in the synagogue and salutations in the marketplace; in 14:7-11, Jesus warns his fellow guests against choosing seats of honor, lest a more distinguished guest arrive.[119] In short, legal experts are portrayed as those who enjoy being treated as persons of status, as though they were wealthy benefactors.[120]

47 The relationship between kinship distance and economic exchange almost guarantees Jesus' further indictment of the legal experts.[121] Distancing themselves from the population-at-large by their concerns with public honor, they manifest no concern for widows. Refusing any relationship to these who are representative of society's most vulnerable, they actually do violence against them. How they "devour" the houses of widows is not made clear,[122] though the related material in 18:1-3 and the adjacent material in 21:1-4 recommend attention to systemic injustice on the part of the scribes. The "long prayers" of the legal experts may be nothing more than a pretext[123] for showing concern for the very widows whom they defraud, or may be related to the show of piety among those hoping to elevate their honor within the temple (cf. 18:9-14).

---

118. πρωτοκαθεδρία and πρωτοκλισία.

119. Luke 14:7-11 repeatedly underscores issues of status (cf. πρωτοκλισία — vv 7, 8; ἔντιμος — v 8; φίλος — v 10; ἀνώτερος — v 10; τότε ἔσται σοι δόξα ἐνώπιον πάντων τῶν συνανακειμένων σοι — v 10; ὑψόω — v 10) and shame (cf. αἰσχύνη — v 9; ἔσχατος — v 10; ταπεινόω — v 11), suggesting a concern with those who by their actions claim unwarranted honor.

120. Green, "Good News," 66-67.

121. This relationship is suggested by Sahlins, *Stone Age Economics;* for details, see above on §10.

122. See the summary of suggested options in Witherington, *Women in the Ministry of Jesus,* 17: taking advantage of their hospitality (cf. *T. Mos.* 7:6)? unscrupulous business practices?

123. For πρόφασις as "pretext," see *TLNT,* 3:204-6.

Jesus' pronouncement of judgment on such persons is subtly ironic: Seeking abundance in the public arena of status honor, they will instead receive abundance in the area of divine condemnation. Insofar as Jesus and the Jerusalem leadership have been ensconced in a struggle over who has authority to interpret Scripture faithfully and to lead the people, this indictment against the scribes is devastating.

1-4 The second half of the scene Luke paints is often taken as a counterexample, pitting the concern with status honor evident among legal experts over against the sacrificial generosity of the widow. This may be the case, but the points of contact between 20:45-47 and 21:1-4 (see above), and especially the characterization of the scribes as though they were wealthy benefactors, suggests a quite different reading. In this case, just as Jesus indicts the religious leadership for consuming the homes of widows, so now he laments the travesty of a religious system that has as its effect the devouring of this widow's livelihood. Note that in no way does Luke suggest that Jesus finds the widow's action exemplary or praiseworthy. How could he, when the religious system was supposed to care for such as these (cf. Acts 6:1-6), not render them utterly destitute? Jesus' mission is to bring good news to the poor, including this widow, not to impoverish the poor even further (see above on 4:16-30).

Accordingly, Luke's readers are invited to draw an analogy between the scribes of 20:45-47 and the wealthy of 21:1, 4, and between the widows of 20:47 and the widow of 21:2, 4. The former make a show of their piety, but give out of such abundance that, their gifts notwithstanding, they are able to continue lives of opulence that do not intersect in meaningful ways with the impoverished. Both the wealthy and the poor widow give to the temple treasury, located in the Court of Women in the Jerusalem temple.[124] Her gift, however, is spelled out as consisting of two lepta, 132 of which would have constituted a day's wage for the day laborer[125] — a puny amount, to be sure, but one that encompasses her entire means of support.[126] Thus does Luke contrast their wealth with her poverty, their superabundance with her deficiency.[127]

And thus does Luke draw attention to a system, the temple treasury itself, set up in such a way that it feeds off those who cannot fend for themselves. What is worse, because it is the *temple* treasury, it has an inherent

124. γαζοφυλάκιον; cf. 2 Esdr 20:38; 22:44; 1 Macc 14:49; Balz, "γαζοφυλάκιον."

125. See Schwank, "λεπτόν."

126. For this use of βίος, see 8:43; 15:12, 30.

127. Thus: πλούσιος stands in contrast with πενιχρός and πτωχός (synonyms in this co-text), and περισσεύω finds its antonym in ὑστέρημα.

claim to divine legitimation. How could it be involved in injustice? It is God's own house! This widespread assumption about the temple only highlights the necessity of Jesus' criticism of the temple, a criticism already begun in 19:41-48.[128] Because it has fallen into the hands of those who use it for injustice, Jesus must comport himself and his message over against the temple and its leadership in prophetic judgment.

6.2. THE COMING OF THE END: DEVASTATION, REDEMPTION, READINESS (21:5-38)

5 *When some were speaking about the temple, how it was adorned with beautiful stones and gifts dedicated to God, he said,* 6 *"As for these things that you see, the days will come when not one stone will be left upon another; all will be thrown down."*

7 *They asked him, "Teacher, when will these things[1] be, and what will be the sign that these things are[2] about to take place?"* 8 *And he said, "Beware that you are not led astray; for many will come in my name and say, 'I am he!' and, 'The time is near!' Do not go after them.*

9 *"When you hear of wars and insurrections, do not be terrified; for these things must take place first, but the end will not follow immediately."* 10 *Then he said to them, "Nation will rise against nation, and kingdom against kingdom;* 11 *there will be great earthquakes, and in various places famines and plagues; and there will be dreadful portents and great signs from heaven.*

12 *"But before all this occurs, they will arrest you and persecute you; they will hand you over to synagogues and prisons, and you will be brought before kings and governors because of my name.* 13 *This will give you an opportunity to testify.* 14 *So make up your minds not to prepare your defense in advance;* 15 *for I will give you words and a wisdom that none of your opponents will be able to withstand or contradict.* 16 *You will be betrayed even by parents and brothers, by relatives and friends; and they will put some of you to death.* 17 *You will be hated by all because of my name.* 18 *But not a hair of your head will perish.* 19 *By your endurance you will gain your lives.[3]*

20 *"When you see Jerusalem surrounded by armies, then know that*

---

128. Indeed, this scene highlights the aptness of Jesus' earlier characterization of the temple in the hands of the Jerusalem leadership as "a den of robbers" (19:46).

1. NRSV: "this."
2. NRSV: "this is."
3. NRSV: "souls."

its desolation has come near. 21 Then those in Judea must flee to the mountains, and those inside the city must leave it, and those out in the country must not enter it; 22 for these are days of vengeance, as a fulfillment of all that is written. 23 Woe to those who are pregnant and to those who are nursing infants in those days! For there will be great distress on the earth and wrath against this people; 24 they will fall by the edge of the sword and be taken away as captives among all nations; and Jerusalem will be trampled on by the Gentiles, until the times of the Gentiles are fulfilled.

25 "There will be signs in the sun, the moon, and the stars, and on the earth distress among nations confused by the roaring of the sea and the waves. 26 People will faint from fear and foreboding of what is coming upon the world, for the powers of the heavens will be shaken. 27 Then they will see 'the Son of Man coming in a cloud' with power and great glory. 28 Now when these things begin to take place, stand up and raise your heads, because your redemption is drawing near."

29 Then he told them a parable: "Look at the fig tree and all the trees; 30 as soon as they sprout leaves you can see for yourselves and know that summer is already near. 31 So also, when you see these things taking place, you know that the kingdom of God is near. 32 Truly I tell you, this generation will not pass away until all things have taken place. 33 Heaven and earth will pass away, but my words will not pass away.

34 "Be on guard so that your hearts are not weighed down with dissipation and drunkenness and the worries of this life, and that day catch you suddenly,⁴ 35 like a trap. For it will come upon all who live on the face of the whole earth. 36 Be alert at all times, praying that you may have the strength to escape all these things that will take place, and to stand before the Son of Man."

37 Every day he was teaching in the temple, and at night he would go out and spend the night on the Mount of Olives, as it was called. 38 And all the people would get up early in the morning to listen to him in the temple.

Throughout this larger section (20:1–21:37), Luke has presented a representative day (20:1: "one day"), with Jesus teaching the people of Israel and attracting opposition from their leaders in the temple precincts. Although Luke characterizes Jesus' message as "good news" (20:1), we hear almost nothing of the content of that proclamation, but instead are given access to the hostile encounters for which his "good news" provides the immediate impetus. At

---

4. NRSV: "unexpectedly."

stake is the question of legitimate authority: Does Jesus bear the divine imprimatur or does the Jerusalem leadership? In 20:1–21:4, Luke's portrait has had two major foci: (1) to certify that Jesus' authority comes from God and thus that he is able to interpret the will of God faithfully for the people and (2) to show in a public forum that the Jerusalem leaders do not enjoy divine sanction as evidenced in their participation in unwarranted behavior — namely, using their attachment to the temple to sustain and augment their positions of power and privilege. Jesus had entered Jerusalem seeking to reclaim the temple for its proper use. His efforts at reform and message of the salvation of God on behalf of "the poor" (cf. 4:18-19) have been rebuffed, however, with the result that he first censures those who refuse to hold themselves accountable to God (20:9-19) and use their positions and the temple system to tyrannize and oppress society's most vulnerable (20:45–21:4), and he now pronounces the destruction of the temple — indeed, the cosmic calamity soon to come as the old world gives way to the new (21:5-38).

The immediate difficulty confronting the interpreter of Jesus' lengthy discourse is its elusive focus. Does Jesus speak of the destruction of the temple or of the End? In fact, Jesus speaks of both, but not in a way that marks the fall of the temple as the onset of the consummation of God's purpose in history. Jesus does interpret the fall of Jerusalem as an eschatological event, but not in immediate relation to the coming of the eschaton.[5] With such temporal markers as "near" (vv 8, 20, 28, 31), "first" (v 9), and "before" (v 12), Luke points to the temporal priority of the fall of Jerusalem and to the necessity of delay following the destruction of the city and prior to the coming of the End, yet maintains an emphasis on the imminence of the eschaton.[6]

Having set the stage for Jesus' discourse (vv 5-7), structurally, Luke portrays Jesus first summarizing his instruction (vv 8-11),[7] then proceeding to lay out the progress of events[8] in chronological order: persecution and witness (vv 12-19); the fall of Jerusalem, leading to the "times of the Gentiles" (vv 20-24); and heavenly signs and earthly distress, leading to the coming of

5. In their attempt to indicate that the fall of Jerusalem does not signal the End, Geiger (*Die lukanischen Endzeitreden,* 249) and Carroll (*End of History,* 111) go too far in divorcing the destruction of Jerusalem from eschatology. See the discussion in Maddox, *Purpose,* 120-21, 123 (who overstates the case in the other direction, however).

6. Cf. Fusco, "Luke's Eschatological Discourse," 87; Nicol, "Luke 21," 69-70; Carroll, *End of History,* 109-10; Maddox, *Purpose,* 120-21.

7. So Carroll, *End of History,* 112.

8. The progression of events is repeatedly underscored by the use of "these things are about to take place" or related phrases in vv 7 (2x), 9, 12, 28, 31, and 36. Giblin (*Destruction of Jerusalem,* 79) is representative in his attempt to lay out the structure of this discourse with reference to such phrases as "he said" (vv 8, 10, 29); cf., however, Fusco, "Luke's Eschatological Discourse," 74-84.

the Son of Man (vv 25-28). This sequence of events in its entirety provides the context and impetus for readiness (vv 29-36). Finally, Luke provides a narrative conclusion to the whole of Jesus' instruction in the temple (vv 37-38).

Thematically, Jesus' discourse underscores the faithful hand of God in the series of events to unfold and the call for a concomitant human faithfulness. Divine faithfulness is bundled together with the trustworthiness of Jesus' prophecy in the assertion of divine necessity (v 9), in the language of fulfillment (vv 22, 24), in the elaborate use of OT language and motifs to describe the coming events (see below), in the affirmation of the permanence of Jesus' words (v 33), in the assurance that the suffering of the faithful does not lie outside the divine field of vision (v 18), in the promise of salvation (using a variety of metaphors — vv 19, 27, 28, 31, 36), and, indeed, in the reality that, prior to their coming to fruition, these events had been foretold by God's anointed royal prophet, Jesus.[9] The motif of human faithfulness, on the other hand, surfaces in Jesus' explicit directives to maintain alertness (vv 8, 34, 36), in Jesus' promise of empowered witness in the face of persecution (vv 12-17), and in Jesus' calls for endurance and prayer (vv 19, 36).

Within the narrative of Luke-Acts, Jesus' eschatological discourse functions in part as a proleptic announcement of the experience of both Jesus himself and his followers in the days and years ahead.[10] For example,

- vv 8-11 promise great earthquakes, famine, and heavenly portents — cf. 23:45; Acts 2:1-4, 19-20; 4:31; 11:28; 16:26;
- vv 12-19 promise being delivered over to prisons — fulfilled in the career of Jesus in chs. 22–23, and a frequent experience of the witnesses in Acts (e.g., Acts 4:3; 5:18-19; 8:3; 12:4; 16:23; cf. Luke 22:33); this includes their being led before "kings and governors" (cf. 23:1-17; Acts 9:15-16; 12:1; 23:24, 26; 25:13; 26:30); and
- vv 12-19 portend that persecution will provide the opportunity to bear witness — a prediction that finds fulfillment, e.g., in Acts 3:15; 4:33; 5:32; 20:26; 26:22.

9. This last point is of particular importance for Luke's audience, who knows that the events Jesus has thus outlined have already begun to find their fulfillment.

10. Cf. Korn, *Geschichte Jesu,* 201-3; Carroll, *End of History,* 117-19; Chance, *Jerusalem,* 120-21; Rapske, *Roman Custody,* 398-401. Rapske notes that vv 12-19 find their "pre-eminent fulfillment in the experience of Paul in Acts" (399). Of course, the narrative of Acts reaches its conclusion prior to the fall of Jerusalem and the destruction of the temple, which was to take place after the onset of persecution; moreover, with the close of Acts, the coming of the Son of Man remains an unfulfilled promise, the fulfillment of which is expected after the razing of Jerusalem and the completion of "the times of the Gentiles" (v 24).

What is the significance of these points of contact between Jesus' eschatological discourse and the subsequent Lukan narrative? (1) At a rudimentary level, these data indicate the narrative unity of Luke-Acts, indicating how both of the Lukan volumes serve the one divine purpose and relate its fulfillment through Jesus and his followers. (2) The immediate fulfillment of prophecies *within* the narrative underscores for characters within Luke-Acts and for readers outside of it that Jesus is a trustworthy prophet; hence, they (we) can trust that even those prophesied events that have not yet been realized will take place. (3) The travesties surrounding Jesus' passion, as well as the persecutions experienced subsequently by Jesus' followers, are not accidents of history, but were themselves known beforehand by God; far from denying the presence of the sovereign and gracious hand of God, then, these adversities are actually embraced within the divine plan to bring salvation to the world. (4) This, then, underscores the purpose of God at work in persecution, and urges Luke's audience to follow the examples of Jesus and his followers in Luke-Acts as they use the arena of rejection and hate as the occasion for faithful witness.[11]

5-7 Luke sets the stage for the discourse to follow. He provides no easy transition from the previous narrative unit (20:45–21:4) to this one, though the setting clearly remains the temple (cf. vv 27-28). Luke has staged this scene with greater attention to theme, so that the antagonism between Jesus and the Jewish leadership associated with the temple inevitably raises the question of the temple itself.

The Jerusalem temple admired by those with Jesus was the project of Herod the Great, who in 20/19 B.C.E. began a reconstruction of the temple that essentially doubled its size and otherwise reflected his own aggrandizing character. Pilgrims pouring into the city from the rustic environs of Palestine and the wider diaspora could not help but be impressed, even overwhelmed, by its sheer size and magnificence, by the brilliance of the gold plates that covered its façade, and by the white marble that adorned its upper reaches.[12] What is more, its splendor as an architectural feat would have been for the faithful more than matched by the awe it inspired as the abode of God and socio-religio-political center of the Jewish universe. Jesus' emphatic prediction of total annihilation (leaving no "stone upon stone"), echoing his earlier words in 19:44 as well as prophetic oracles of judgment in the OT,[13] must have been stunning on both accounts.

Who was speaking about the temple? Who questioned Jesus about his

---

11. This motif is highlighted in Cassidy, *Society and Politics*.
12. For offerings that add to the temple's splendor, see 2 Macc 3:2; 9:16.
13. For "the days are coming," see, e.g., Isa 39:6; Hos 9:7; Amos 4:2; Zech 14:1; et al.

prophecy? The clearest antecedent for the pronoun "they," supplied by Luke, is in 20:45: the disciples, in the hearing of the people. This makes sense of important aspects of Jesus' answer, wherein he refers to "you" in a way that seems to require a reference to his followers. However, this would dictate our identification of the disciples as those who address Jesus as "teacher" in v 7 — an identification that is problematic since it would place disciples in the larger category of persons in the Third Gospel, those who refer to Jesus as "teacher," who have not determined to follow Jesus, and who are undecided about his person and ministry.[14] This may represent Luke's subtle attempt to show the degree to which the disciples have in fact faded into the crowds since the end of the journey to Jerusalem.[15] Or it may be that the question in v 7 was raised by persons from the people gathered to hear Jesus in the temple (see 20:1; 21:37-38), among whom are the disciples. In any case, the line between the disciples and the Jewish people more generally is all but undiscernible, and the setting of Jesus' eschatological discourse is a public one.

The question raised comes in two parts, the second developing the sense of the first. Reference to "these things" refers transparently to the destruction of the temple,[16] but, in light of evidence for the correlation in the Second Temple period of the motifs of the destruction (and possible rebuilding) of the temple and of the coming of the eschaton,[17] reference to "these things" may accommodate eschatological connotations as well. In any case, in his response Jesus speaks of both the fall of the temple and the coming of the End, though without associating these two events so closely, and certainly without portraying them as occupying the same eschatological moment. In this co-text, "sign" has less the sense of "proof" (cf. 1:18; 11:29) than of "portent" or even "omen."[18]

8-11 At the outset of his eschatological discourse, Jesus provides a prospective summary of the remaining address (vv 12-36), indicating the relation of the destruction of Jerusalem to the End, and, most importantly, calling for discernment in the face of false, but seductive, interpretations of the events to come.[19] Reference to the fall of Jerusalem in these verses is indirect, localized in Jesus' reference to "wars and insurrections" (v 9). "The

14. Cf. 7:40; 8:49; 9:38; 10:25; 11:45; 12:13; 18:18; 19:39; 20:21, 28, 29.

15. That is, following their disappointing behavior in, e.g., 18:15-17, 34.

16. Thus, the NRSV translates ταῦτα as "this"; cf. Geiger, *Die lukanischen Endzeitreden,* 168-69.

17. See McKelvey, *New Temple;* Sanders, *Jesus and Judaism,* 77-90; Green, *Death of Jesus,* 278-81.

18. See *TLNT,* 3:249-52.

19. πλανάω is sometimes used in the LXX for seduction, e.g., to idolatry or disobedience — cf. Deut 4:19; 11:28; 30:17; Ezek 14:11; 44:10-15. For its use in relation to the end time, see also *T. Lev.* 10:2; 16:1.

End" (v 9) appears in apposition to "the time," with both referring to the eschaton.[20]

Jesus' explicit denial that the end time would come immediately after the fall of Jerusalem (v 9b) — effectively driving a temporal and, thus, hermeneutical, wedge between these two events — is an important interpretive move on his part. This is because such calamities as those he summarizes are grounded in scriptural texts[21] and serve as the stuff of speculation about the woes heralding the coming of the Messiah and/or the eschatological epoch.[22] Hence, it might seem quite natural to expect news of the advent of the Messiah or the nearness of "the time" (v 8) in the context of the coming afflictions. Given the apocalyptic responses of some, not least at Qumran, it might even have seemed natural to see the dawning of the eschatological rule as a summons to engage in violence to help overthrow the false powers — in this case, Jerusalem or Rome — that is, to see the eschatological finale as an opportunity to engage in the "last battle." This is exactly what happened in the 60s C.E., when messianic leaders recruited revolutionary forces against Rome.[23] Jesus explicitly warns his audience to resist such interpretations. They are not to follow after those making such claims, but neither are they to respond in terror. They are, instead, "to watch," to exercise their faith in such a way that they have insight into what God is doing.[24]

Jesus constructs his warning on two pillars. First, those who come genuinely "in [his] name" are those who comport themselves as he has — welcoming children and casting out demons, for example (9:48-49; cf. 10:17) — and who attract persecution (21:12, 17; cf. 6:22) as he will (chs. 22–23). Those who come in the name of Jesus, then, will not make extravagant claims about themselves (just as he has not); moreover, they will proclaim the message of repentance and forgiveness (cf. 24:47), not the timing of the eschaton (just as he does not; cf. Acts 1:6-7). In this way, Jesus provides in advance criteria for discerning false prophets.[25] Second, terror is an inappropriate response because the phenomena Jesus describes, however chaotic or unruly they might seem, are actually embraced within the divine purpose.[26]

12-19 Following the prospective summary in vv 8-11, Jesus begins

---

20. That is, neither ὁ τέλος nor ὁ καίρος, both used absolutely, can refer simply to the destruction of the temple; cf. vv 25-28; Acts 1:6-7.

21. Cf., e.g., 2 Chr 15:6; Isa 5:13-14; 19:2; Ezek 39:19-22; et al.

22. See the survey of the data in Allison, *End of the Ages,* 5-25.

23. See the summary in Heard, "Revolutionary Movements," 689-91.

24. βλέπω; cf. 8:18; Müller, "βλέπω," 222.

25. On the larger problematic of distinguishing true and false prophets, see, e.g., Deut 18:21-22; Jer 28:9; Matt 7:15-23; 1 Cor 12:1-3; 2 Thess 2:3-4; 1 John 2:18-20, 22; 4:1-3; 2 John 7; *Didache* 11. See Aune, *Prophecy,* 87-88, 222-29.

26. See the use of δεῖ in v 9.

to provide a sketchy timetable of events, with those outlined in this subunit having temporal priority. "Before all this occurs," then, introduces those things that would take place before the calamities related to the destruction of the temple (vv 6, 9) and, thus, before the woes associated with the end time.

"Persecution" is the heading under which this material can be gathered — persecution resulting from the identification of Jesus' followers first with his message and then, consequently, with his fate. Simeon and John had predicted that Jesus would be the cause of division within Israel (2:34-35; 3:17); now Jesus anticipates that his followers would be caught up in this division as people side with or against the purpose of God coming to expression among those who identify with "the name" (vv 12b, 17; cf. 6:22; 9:21-26).[27] The apposition of both "kings and governors" and "synagogues and prisons" portends the persecution of Jesus' followers among Jews as well as among Gentiles. In the book of Acts, it is before Jerusalem officials, a Herodian king, and Roman governors, as well as local authorities, that the first witnesses, and especially Paul, are arraigned.[28] In the Roman world, persons might be imprisoned for a variety of ends, including the precautionary imprisonment of persons to ensure their appearance at a trial but also as a form of punishment.[29] Among local Jewish communities, synagogues exercised religious disciplinary acts in order to eliminate alien elements.[30]

The coming resistance is, according to Jesus, not limited to that exacted by official bodies within Judaism and the realm of Rome, but would extend as well to one's own kin. The inventory of those who would betray the faithful is reminiscent of the list in 14:12, including those with whom, under normal conventions, one would share relationships of mutual trust and reciprocity. The coming of the kingdom, however, renders normal conventions obsolete, with the result that the faithful have repeatedly been called upon to redraw kinship lines, to find their familial attachments with those "who hear the word of God and do it" (esp. 8:21; cf. 18:29). Of course, it is precisely this disregard for normal conventions, this embracing of the purpose of God as it unfolds in and overtakes the present world order, that leads to the despising of Jesus' disciples among those who fail to recognize or serve God's redemptive project. Marked as deviants by their behavior, they will find themselves detested, shunned, by those who uphold the accepted protocols of their social world.

In the midst of his talk of persecution, Jesus provides three counter-

27. Cf. Acts 4:17-18; 5:28, 40-41; 9:15-16; 15:26; 21:13.
28. Cf., e.g., Acts 4:1-22; 5:17-40; 9:22-25; 18:12; 23:33–24:27; 25:1–26:32.
29. See the survey of the data in Rapske, *Roman Custody,* 10-20.
30. See Schürer, *Jewish People,* 431; cf. Mark 13:9; John 9:22; 12:42; 16:2; 2 Cor 11:24.

measures, all grounded in his assurance of ongoing divine presence. First, he interprets persecution as opportunity for witness (vv 13-15). The terseness of v 13 leaves room for ambiguity of meaning, with the two best options being: (1) When Jesus' followers find themselves in situations like those portended, this is a testimony (= proof) to them that events are unfolding as he had predicted; and (2) When the disciples find themselves on trial, they should see this as an occasion to bear witness to the faith (so the NRSV).[31] Within this co-text, the latter option is preferable, both because vv 14-15 would then follow more easily from v 13 (see the "therefore" or "so" in v 14) and because Acts presents Jesus' followers in the act of bearing witness while on trial.[32] The promise of "words and a wisdom" recalls the earlier pledge of inspired witness in 12:11-12, except that in the earlier text Jesus promises not wisdom but Spirit-empowerment; collated, these two texts anticipate the description of Stephen, who in Acts 6:10 speaks with wisdom and the Spirit. Jesus' followers, then, are not to be like trained orators, who practice their speeches in advance[33] but will nevertheless speak with power (cf. Acts 4:13). Moreover, Jesus thus portends his continual presence with the disciples even as they face the tribunal, following his death; only with the onset of Acts do we understand fully that he will be present to the community of his followers by means of the Holy Spirit poured out among them. That this witness cannot be withstood or contradicted finds ready fulfillment in Acts 4:14; 6:10, as well. This, however, does not guarantee that the testimony of Jesus' witnesses will win the day, only that the resistance they attract and even the executions they undergo are not to be perceived as testimony against the truth or vitality of their witness or the authenticity of their understanding of God's purpose. This is a pivotal message for Jesus' disciples, who thus far have been unable to correlate humiliation and suffering with the divine purpose (e.g., 9:44-50; 18:31-34).

Second, he insists that "not a hair of your head will perish" (v 18). As a proverb, this expression is used elsewhere to ensure complete physical safety (see Acts 27:34).[34] In close proximity to v 16b, which portends the execution of some, it can hardly have that meaning here. The parallel saying in 12:7 ("even the hairs of your head are all counted"), which also appears in a parallel co-text, compels a reading of this expression as a guarantee that nothing happens apart from divine purview. Its proximity to v 17 suggests,

---

31. The difficulty derives especially from the use of μαρτύριον, for which the meaning is usually "evidence" or "proof," rather than "act of bearing testimony" (as in μαρτυρία). See, however, the use of μαρτύριον in Acts 4:33. Other options have been championed, too; see the discussion in C. F. Evans, 742.

32. See Cassidy, *Society and Politics*.

33. προμελετάω — cf. BAGD 708.

34. Cf. 1 Sam 14:45; 2 Sam 14:11; 1 Kgs 1:52.

further, that Jesus promises that persecution, even death, does not spell the end of life for the faithful. Nevertheless, it is often the case in Acts that Jesus' followers are rescued from even life-threatening hostility (e.g., Acts 5:19-26; 12:6-11; 14:19-20), though manifestly this is not always the case — either with Jesus or with his followers (cf. chs. 22–23; Acts 7:54–8:1; 12:1-2).

Third, Jesus instructs his followers to endure (v 19). "Endurance" should not be mistaken for passive waiting or the placid exercise of patience; after all, Jesus has just noted that persecution provides the occasion for witness, and he earlier collocates "endurance" with the faithful bearing of fruit (8:15; cf. 18:1-8). As in the LXX, the endurance Jesus counsels is intertwined with a hope that has God as its object and as its expected outcome divine intervention.[35] In this case, one may hear another echo of Jesus' earlier eschatological teaching, wherein his disciples are ensured that persecution can lead to the death of the body, but not the cessation of one's life (12:4-5). Whether persecution leads to acquittal or to death, then, the lives of the faithful will be preserved.[36]

20-24 In a sense, it is only here that Jesus begins to take up directly the question raised in v 7, concerning the sign that the destruction of the temple is imminent. The omen Jesus furnishes is hardly spectacular: "When you see Jerusalem surrounded by armies . . ." describes only what one might expect in the context of a military operation whose objective was the defeat of a walled city like Jerusalem. Nevertheless, with v 20 a new stage in the progress of events has been reached. The first focused on persecution for those who identified with Jesus and his message (vv 12-19); following this is the fall of the Holy City.[37] This narrative sequence alone is enough to hint at a causal relationship between these two series of events, as if the text were implying that the city would be overrun on account of its resistance against Jesus and his followers and, thus, its rejection of God's purpose. What is only suggested by the narrative sequence is ardently promoted in Jesus' ensuing prognostications.

First, the scene Jesus paints is reminiscent of his earlier words in 19:43-44, where it was self-evident that divine judgment would come upon the city on account of its failure to recognize and accept the salvific visitation of God. Second, Jesus draws the details for his portrait predominantly from the LXX, with the result that he produces a virtual collage of scriptural texts that draws the anticipated destruction of Jerusalem and the temple into an

35. ὑπομονή; cf. *TLNT,* 3:418-19.

36. Given the proximity of Jesus' dialogue with the Sadducees in 20:27-40, it is not difficult to find here an implicit reference to the resurrection.

37. The wider focus on Jerusalem, rather than simply on the temple, underscores the role given the city and its leadership by the active presence of the temple in its midst. Above all else, Jerusalem drew its significance from its role as cultic center.

interpretive relationship with the fall of the city at the time of the Exile.[38] Indeed, Luke writes that the razing of the city is "a fulfillment of all that is written" (v 22). Third, he actually describes the season of Jerusalem's fall as "days of vengeance" (v 22), using a scriptural phrase denoting divine judgment.[39] Fourth, the scene Jesus imagines, with Jerusalem "trampled on by the Gentiles" (v 24), recalls the role of the nations as Yahweh's instrument of judgment against Israel.[40] Clearly, the anticipated fall of Jerusalem is portrayed as divine judgment for its unfaithfulness before Yahweh (cf. 20:9-18).

Will its destruction mark the end of Jerusalem's role within the divine purpose? On this, Luke is not altogether straightforward. On the one hand, within the OT, "the days of *vengeance* against unfaithful Israel anticipated the *vindication* of God in which Israel is restored."[41] In this case, "the times of the Gentiles" would mark a temporary season in which the Gentiles would occupy center stage in God's purpose, after which the spotlight would return to Jerusalem. On the other hand, with v 25 Jesus' eschatological discourse turns not to consider the place of Israel in God's plan but to the end time, marked by the coming of the Son of Man. Indeed, in this co-text Luke introduces no explicit motif of restoration.[42] In this case, "the times of the Gentiles" would mark a temporary season that would give way to the consummation of God's purpose in the eschatological fulfillment. At the outset of Acts, the question of the place of Israel in God's eschatological aim remains unanswered (Acts 1:6-8); there, as here, the focus is shifted from speculation about Israel to mission among the Gentiles.[43]

"Times of the Gentiles," then, has a dual reference in this co-text. It manifestly relates to the role of the Gentiles as God's agents in the prophesied destruction and subsequent occupation of Jerusalem. More than this, however, it portends the proclamation of the good news among the Gentiles.

25-28 From the "sign" (implicit) of the pending destruction of the temple (v 20), Jesus' eschatological discourse turns to the "signs" (explicit) of the coming of the End. As Luke presents it, then, this is the third stage in

---

38. The scriptural echoes are legion; see esp. Dodd, "Fall of Jerusalem."

39. Cf. Jer 5:29; Hos 9:7; Ezek 9:1; Sir 5:7; et al.

40. E.g., Ezek 39:23; Dan 2:44; 8:13-14; Zech 12:3; 1 Macc 3:45; et al.

41. Tiede, *Prophecy and History,* 93; with reference, e.g., to Zech 12:3; 1 Macc 3; 4:11; *2 Bar.* 68:1-5; cf. Acts 3:21; Chance, *Jerusalem,* 133-38.

42. Tiede *(Prophecy and History)* speaks of "an elusive hint of an end to Jerusalem's subjection when 'the times of the Gentiles are fulfilled' (21:24)" (89; cf. 92-95).

43. In the Acts passage, Jesus' reply does not negate the hope of Israel (Mußner, "Idee der Apokatastasis"; Legrand, "Gabriel and Politics"; Fusco, "Point of View"), even if that hope is clarified in relation to a Spirit-empowered mission outside the ethnic and geographical borders of Israel.

the timetable Jesus sketches: cosmic signs leading to the advent of the Son of Man and the coming of redemption. The images Jesus employs are reminiscent of those found in v 11, again marking vv 8-11 as a prospective summary of the discourse as a whole; by means of this intertextuality we are also reminded that the ordeals Jesus enumerates are marked with eschatological importance. This interpretation is highlighted by the use of scriptural texts as a reservoir from which to draw the meaning-laden details for this eschatological portrait. Thus, the OT is the source for this mural's astral phenomena ("signs in the sun, the moon, and the stars . . . the powers of the heavens will be shaken" — vv 25-26),[44] distress and confusion among the nations (v 25),[45] the roaring of the sea (v 25),[46] and the fear of the people (v 26).[47] It is of no little consequence that, especially when read against the background of their OT precursors, these images portend the advent of the Day of the Lord and, so, portray the coming of the Son of Man as a theophany. Jesus' eschatological discourse thus distinguishes the fall of Jerusalem and the coming of the End, denoting them as two separate phases in the realization of the divine plan. How far they are to be separated temporally, however, is not specified; earlier, Jesus had simply said, "the end will not follow immediately" (v 9).

Throughout his Gospel, Luke repeatedly identifies Jesus as the Son of Man and, more recently, has laid the groundwork for his readers to anticipate the coming of Jesus as Son of Man.[48] Luke 21:27 portrays the most exalted picture yet, however. On the one hand, here we may hear echoes of Jesus' parable about the heir to the throne who, having received regal power, returns to reward and punish the country's citizens (19:11-27). On the other, drawing explicitly on the language of Dan 7:13 — with its analogy between the coming of God "in the clouds" (e.g., Isa 19:1; Ps 18:2-3) and the coming of the Son of Man — this Lukan text depicts the return of Jesus as a theophany.[49] (See Acts 1:9-11, where it is said of Jesus, who had been taken out of sight in a cloud, that he "will come in the same way" — i.e., in a cloud.)

Although the nations will respond with perplexity, people will faint (or even die)[50] in fear, and the heavenly powers will be shaken at the onset of these portents, Jesus advises a different course of action for his followers. Their response should be one of confidence, standing with raised heads,

44. Cf., e.g., Isa 13:11, 13; Ezek 32:7-8; Joel 2:10, 30-31.
45. Cf., e.g., Isa 8:22; 13:4.
46. Cf., e.g., Isa 5:30; 17:12; Jonah 5:30.
47. Cf., e.g., Isa 13:6-11.
48. Cf. 9:26; 11:30; 12:8, 40; 17:22, 24, 26, 30; 18:8.
49. See Beasley-Murray, *Kingdom of God,* 331: "And, of course, the basic text for the parousia, Dan 7:13, is itself part of a theophanic vision, of which the feature of the coming in the clouds is a clear reminder. . . ."
50. ἀποψύχω, as in 4 Macc 15:18, "to die."

assured that the Day of the Lord is for them a day of redemption. The parallel statements, "your redemption is drawing near" (v 28) and "the kingdom of God is near" (v 31), help to qualify the nature of the object of Jesus' prophecy. In the birth narrative, "redemption" was used with reference to God's intervention on behalf of Israel and Jerusalem (1:68; 2:38). Without detracting from the validity of the anticipation expressed there, it remains true (1) that Jerusalem had failed to welcome the salvific coming of Yahweh (9:41-44) and (2) that the Third Evangelist, like any narrator, is capable of establishing narrative expectations only then to provide for them new significance, new possibilities for fulfillment. In the current text, the "you" in "your redemption" clearly refers to those who are faithful, those who have embraced the project of God unveiled in Jesus' ministry and oriented themselves around the divine purpose, and not to Jerusalem specifically. Although Jerusalem and its people — and, indeed, all of Israel — are not necessarily excluded from the coming redemption, the eschatological act of salvation of which Jesus speaks is good news for those who respond to Jesus as Lord with faithful endurance.[51]

29-36 Jesus moves from prophetic discourse to pastoral exhortation concerning faithful life in light of the events he has anticipated. "These things taking place" in v 31 stands in parallel with "all these things that will take place" in v 36, signifying that constant readiness and prayer are applicable not only in the midst of persecution or at the time of the siege of Jerusalem, but in all seasons preceding the eschaton.[52] The brief parable of vv 29-30 is illustrative of parabolic teaching in the Third Gospel — drawing its significance less from point-for-point allegory, more from lessons from the experienced world. The fig tree is a particularly apt illustration for Jesus' purpose, since the fig loses its leaves during the winter season; the change of seasons is definitively marked, then, by the appearance of new leaves on previously bare branches. Of course, Jesus is concerned with more than the proper discernment of the times; as in previous instruction, he is interested in perception that leads to appropriate action (e.g., 10:13-15; 11:29-32). Even if the End has been delayed, it has not been delayed indefinitely, and his disciples need to maintain constant readiness. The heavy emphasis Luke's presentation has placed on faithful living in light of the sequence of events by which God's purpose comes to fruition suggests that his audience has not been living in expectation of the parousia. Accordingly, Luke intimates that the arrival of the eschaton has not been delayed indefinitely, that the delay is itself incorporated into the eschato-

---

51. *Contra,* e.g., Chance (*Jerusalem,* 136-37), who does not allow the narrator to open up narrative possibilities that are then reinterpreted and/or reoriented.

52. See Crump, *Jesus the Intercessor,* 170-71.

logical timetable, and, therefore, that vigilant, expectant faith rules out a business-as-usual orientation toward life.[53]

Throughout much of the Third Gospel, the motif of the kingdom of God has been developed in relation to the present ministry of Jesus.[54] Other texts, however, have pointed to an additional aspect of the kingdom, the consummation of God's dominion at the End (e.g., 11:2; 14:15; 17:20; 19:11). The notion of the nearness of the kingdom (v 31) builds on those texts, with Jesus teaching that the totality of prophesied events — persecutions, the fall of Jerusalem, and cosmic signs — point toward the arrival of the kingdom not only in present history but also in its fullness at the end of history. Within the Lukan narrative, this message is undergirded by the pervasive emphasis on the conflict that arises as people side with or against the unfolding purpose of God.

Verses 32-33 contain assertions that may only after close examination seem to fit well within this co-text. In the Third Gospel, "this generation" (and related phrases) has regularly signified a category of people who are resistant to the purpose of God.[55] Verse 32, then, long a centerpiece in eschatological debate,[56] actually has less to say about the eschatological timetable and more to say about the motif of conflict related to the presence and expected culmination of the kingdom of God. "This generation" refers in Luke's narrative not to a set number of decades or to people living at such-and-such a time, but to people who stubbornly turn their backs on the divine purpose. Jesus' followers can expect hostility and calamity until the very End, Jesus teaches, for the old world, "this generation," does not easily give way to the new. Again, then, Jesus underscores how humiliation and suffering need not be taken as incongruous with his teaching regarding the inbreaking reign of God, but may be taken as signs of the realization of God's kingdom (see Acts 14:22). Nor should the tribulations Jesus has enumerated detract from confidence in his word; in language that recalls OT assurances of the certainty and permanence of Yahweh's word,[57] Jesus affirms the certainty and permanence of his own prophetic instruction.

Because his followers are able to read the signs (vv 29-31), because they have been made aware of the inexorable presence of resistance to the

53. See Fusco, "Luke's Eschatological Discourse," 87; Carroll, *End of History,* esp. 116, 166; Chance, *Jerusalem,* 91-95; Maddox, *Purpose,* e.g., 121-23.

54. See esp. Wolter, "Reich Gottes."

55. See 7:31; 9:41; 11:29-32, 50-51; 16:8; 17:25.

56. See the surveys in Mattill, *Last Things,* 97-104; Maddox, *Purpose,* 111-15. The list of proposals they dismiss (i.e., those that identify "this generation" with, e.g., "the Jewish people," "the human race," "the generation of Luke and his audience," et al.) does not include what may be within the Lukan co-text the most obvious sense, however.

57. See, e.g., Pss 102:25-27; 119:89, 160; Isa 40:8; 55:10-11; et al.

way of God prior to the End (v 32), because they may hold with conviction to the immutability of Jesus' word (v 33), they are to respond with faithful vigilance. As in previous uses of the admonition "be on guard,"[58] so in this one we must assume that Jesus summons his followers to watchfulness in the very areas where their inclinations place them most at risk. Implicated in practices reminiscent of those of the Pharisees and scribes, they had to be warned repeatedly about avoiding such influence and behavior. Now, Jesus perceives that the delay in the advent of the End may bring its own temptations to faithlessness and a business-as-usual orientation to life (cf., e.g., 8:13-14; 12:45-46; 17:24). In order to counter this, Jesus alerts his audience to the reality that the End will be sudden,[59] unexpected (v 35: "like a trap"), and ubiquitous ("upon all"). Eschatological testing is to be met, then, with constant alertness and prayer (cf. 22:40, 46);[60] such a response will allow people to stand (see v 28) as those found faithful (see 18:8) before the Son of Man who comes in power to bring judgment and redemption (see vv 27-28).

37-38   These verses form an *inclusio* with 20:1, marking the narrative closure not only of Jesus' eschatological discourse but also of Luke's narration of the teaching of Jesus in the temple. They underscore the temple context in which Jesus' teaching has taken place, as well as the overwhelmingly positive response of "the people" ("all"!) to Jesus.

Verses 37-38 function as narrative closure but also as summary, suggesting that we are to understand that this exemplary "day" of teaching (20:1) was characteristic of Jesus' ongoing teaching ministry in the temple ("every day," 21:37). They also serve as a transition to the Lukan account of Jesus' suffering and death (chs. 22–23) — first, by highlighting the support Jesus enjoys among the people, a form of support that continues to hold the hostile plans of his enemies at bay (see 19:47-48; 20:19; 22:2); and, second, by identifying Jesus' custom of teaching by day in the temple, then departing each night to the Mount of Olives (→ 22:39). It is only with 22:1 that we discover that Jesus has arrived in Jerusalem at the time of Unleavened Bread and Passover, but his daily movements are already indicative of this fact. This is because lodging in the city would become scarce at festival times, forcing pilgrims into outlying areas each evening.

---

58. συνέχω — cf. 12:1; 17:3; 20:45.

59. αἰφνίδιος, used in the NT only here and in 1 Thess 5:3.

60. As elsewhere in Luke-Acts, prayer here would seem to involve both discernment of the divine aim (which, in Luke, is regularly mediated through prayer) and orientation of oneself around that purpose.

7. THE SUFFERING AND DEATH OF JESUS (22:1–23:56)

Luke's narrative of Jesus' suffering and death is inexorably linked to the earlier chapters of the Third Gospel by the development of numerous motifs,[1] the most pervasive and important of which is the motif of conflict. Conflict, too, has been a primary force driving the narrative plot forward to this point. Jesus, according to Simeon, was to be the cause of division within Israel (2:34); as Luke has narrated it, division has surfaced as the divine purpose has been disclosed, first in the ministry of John (who was subsequently imprisoned [see 3:18-20] and beheaded [see 9:7-9]), then in the ministry of Jesus. The propagation of the "good news" has attracted both allies and opposition, with some persons working to embrace and serve the divine project, others to reject and obstruct it.[2]

Jerusalem, the primary setting for the Lukan narrative of Jesus' passion, has been a place of conflict for Jesus — both in anticipation (e.g., 13:31-35) and in reality (19:29–21:38). Because, according to Jesus' own predictions, Jerusalem is the site of his demise (cf. 18:31-33), his continued presence in the Holy City speaks strongly against his safety. Jerusalem, after all, is the abode of the Jewish leadership, repeatedly positioned against the purpose of God as this has been articulated by Jesus and, thus, against Jesus himself (e.g., 19:45-48; 20:9-19). Temporally, the setting for Jesus' death is a time of festival — of Unleavened Bread and of Passover. This contributes to the drama of the ensuing episodes by locating Jesus' death squarely within the highly charged

---

1. This is highlighted in recent study, e.g., by Karris, *Luke: Artist and Theologian;* Senior, *Passion of Jesus;* Matera, *Passion Narratives,* 150-220; Tyson, *Death of Jesus;* Carroll and Green, *Death of Jesus,* 60-81; and, to a lesser degree, Neyrey, *Passion according to Luke.*

2. See Green, *Gospel of Luke,* 22-49; for the motif of conflict, see Kingsbury, *Conflict in Luke;* Tyson, "Conflict as a Literary Theme"; *idem, Death of Jesus.*

environment of Israel's celebration of its own identity, with pilgrims swarming the city, and with the Roman leadership, normally resident in Caesarea (on the coast of the Mediterranean), also present.

By the opening of the passion account, Luke has constructed a series of oppositions of pivotal importance. On the one hand is Jesus, aligned with God, together with Jesus' disciples and "the people," who are supportive of Jesus. On the other are the Jewish leaders in Jerusalem, as well as the devil. Luke's narration has repeatedly established the important place of "the people" as a buffer between Jesus and his opposition (cf. 19:47-48; 20:19) — a barrier that must now be breached if the Jerusalem leadership is to have its way with him. One need not look far for hints that this barrier is penetrable, since those closest to Jesus, the disciples, have been known to falter in their understanding and support of Jesus (e.g., 9:46-50; 18:15-17, 31-34); indeed, we have known for some time that one of them would become a traitor (6:17). Moreover, Jesus had only just predicted with reference to his followers, "You will be betrayed even by parents and brothers, by relatives and friends; and they will put some of you to death" (21:16). If this is the destiny of the followers, what of the one whom they follow?

In fact, the Lukan account of Jesus' passion and death is in part the story of unholy alliances made and unmade, as this barrier is repeatedly, if only temporarily, breached. Satan and the Jerusalem leadership are allied in their opposition to Jesus (22:53), and it is through diabolic influence that one of the twelve, Judas, sides with the leadership against Jesus (22:3-6, 47-48). Judas is not alone, however. In their anxiety over relative honor and status at the table (22:24), all of the disciples participate in behavior reminiscent of that of the Jewish leadership (e.g., 20:45–21:4). Peter comes dangerously close to siding with Jesus' opponents, and he ends up denying his Lord three times (22:54-60). If Luke narrates the inconstancy of the disciples, though, he also recounts their eventual separation from those who oppose Jesus — first in the case of Peter (22:61-62), then in the case of the others (23:49). The only exception is Judas, whose place among the twelve must be filled by another (Acts 1:15-26).

The crowds (or the people) have by their support of Jesus frustrated the malicious plans of the temple leadership (22:1-6), but their support also wavers. First, "a crowd" interrupts Jesus on the Mount of Olives (22:47); in narrative time, several moments pass before Luke identifies the crowd as consisting of "the chief priests, the officers of the temple police, and the elders" (22:52), leaving us to think, however momentarily, that the crowds had not only wavered in their support of Jesus but had actually turned on him. Indeed, this is exactly what they come to do. In 23:4 the chief priests appear with "the crowds" of other Jewish authorities (22:52), then, without advance warning; and in 23:14 the chief priests, the leaders, *and* "the people" are said

745

to have brought Jesus to Pilate for judgment. This alliance of leadership and people continues through the trial of Jesus before Pilate up to Jesus' execution, when he requests divine forgiveness for all involved in his death (23:13-34). In fact, Luke seems purposely to have left open as a possible reading of his account our identification of the people of Jerusalem, together with their leaders, as persons physically responsible for the crucifixion of Jesus (see the ambiguous "they" in 23:26, 33-34).[3] Again, however, Luke also narrates how the people of Jerusalem distance themselves from their leadership — first in 23:27, where a number of Jerusalem's "daughters" mourn on Jesus' behalf; then in 23:35, where the people adopt a notably benign posture in comparison with the scornful demeanor of their leaders; and in 23:48, where "all the crowds" respond to Jesus' death with sorrow. (In Acts 2:22-40; 3:12-26, the people of Jerusalem, held responsible for Jesus' death, are invited to repent and participate in the salvation available through Jesus.)

Here resides the great irony of the conflict that weaves its way through the Third Gospel and reaches its climax in the Lukan passion narrative: Those who oppose Jesus believe themselves to be serving God, yet unwittingly serve a diabolic aim. Throughout his ministry, Jesus has, from their perspective, departed from the demands of Torah and set himself over against what had become not only unquestioned but also unquestionable practices by which one demonstrates one's obedience to Yahweh. Again from their perspective, Jesus' attempt to claim the temple for an alternative agenda was perverse; his teaching had resulted in the dislegitimation of the temple authorities and even the relativizing of the temple itself within the divine plan. The charges on which the Jewish leadership have him arraigned before Pilate essentially involve his identification as a false prophet who, on account of his popular following, poses a threat to Rome (23:1-5). Throughout his ministry, Jesus has been involved in a war of interpretation: Who understands and serves the divine aim, really? Who interprets and embodies the divine word, really? Because both Jerusalem authorities and Jesus see themselves as acting on behalf of the divine will, the actions that unfold in chs. 22–23 are indeed tragic. They are, nonetheless, the fullest manifestation of the competing aims at work in the Gospel narrative, previously seen best in the temptation of Jesus in the wilderness (4:1-13).[4]

The making and unmaking of unholy alliances are symptomatic of how, in the face of hostility, people can be tested in their commitments. This is particularly true on account of the evidence Luke provides for the presence

---

3. Cf. Acts 2:36; 3:12-15; 10:39. This is denied by Weatherly, *Jewish Responsibility,* 65-68; R. E. Brown, *Death of the Messiah,* 1:856-59 (though he includes the Jewish leaders and the people in the forgiveness proffered in 23:34! [2:973]).

4. Thus, the importance of 4:13: "When the devil had finished every test, he departed from him until an opportune time."

of Satan behind and through those who oppose the redemptive aim of God.[5] One is immediately reminded of Jesus' eschatological discourse, just delivered (21:5-36), with its admonitions to prayer and faithful vigilance. Luke's readers are thus encouraged to find in Jesus an exemplar of proper response in the face of trial and persecution. He is the model for disciples to follow.[6]

Contrary to what many have argued, however, this does not mean that Luke wants to present Jesus to the church as the prototypical martyr. It is true that Luke presents Jesus' comportment in the midst of persecution as exemplary, and Luke seems to allow the disciples a view into at least part of the events surrounding his passion. They remain with Jesus until he is taken; following this, Luke's angle of vision renders them invisible throughout most of the passion, though they reappear as witnesses to the crucifixion scene (23:49). Manifestly, there are martyrological features in Luke's portrait of Jesus' passion and death, but Jesus is far more than a martyr.[7] Within the passion narrative, Luke underscores the character of Jesus' death as the death of one who was righteous, like the Suffering Righteous One and the Servant of Yahweh,[8] and as the death of a prophet.[9] Additionally, the cross is linked to Jesus' entire career as Son of Man,[10] to his identity as the Royal Messiah, Son of God,[11] and to his characterization as the servant-benefactor who brings healing and salvation.[12] All of this is grounded in divine necessity, foreordained by God and foretold in the Scriptures.[13]

---

5. Cf. 23:3, 28, 31, 53; 23:44-45.

6. This is emphasized in Matera, *Passion Narratives,* 198-200; Senior, *Passion of Jesus,* 173-77, 179; Carroll and Green, *Death of Jesus,* 74-77.

7. The martyrological interpretation of Jesus' death in Luke is supported by Dibelius, *From Tradition to Gospel,* 201-2; Conzelmann, *Luke,* 81, 83-90; Talbert, 212-14; *idem,* "Martyrdom"; R. E. Brown, *Death of the Messiah,* 1:31-32; et al. Against this view, see, e.g., Matera, *Passion Narratives,* 150-52; Untergaßmair, *Kreuzweg und Kreuzigung Jesu,* 156-71; Beck, "Imitatio Christi"; Green, "Mount of Olives," 39-41; and the collection of essays in Sylva, ed., *Reimaging the Death.*

8. See, e.g., 22:51; 23:4, 14, 15, 20, 22, 41, 47; Büchele, *Tod Jesu,* 76-96; Carroll and Green, *Death of Jesus,* 72-74; Green, "Mount of Olives"; *idem,* "God's Servant."

9. See 22:13; 23:27-30; Matera, *Passion Narratives,* 205-6; Senior, *Passion of Jesus,* 169-71.

10. See 22:22, 48, 69.

11. See 22:29-30, 42-44, 67-71; 23:3, 11, 34-35, 37-39, 46; Matera, *Passion Narratives,* 213-14; Carroll and Green, *Death of Jesus,* 70-72; Senior, *Passion of Jesus,* 166-69.

12. See 22:27, 51; 23:34-35, 39, 43; Carroll and Green, *Death of Jesus,* 70-74; Fitzmyer, *Luke the Theologian,* 203-33; Garrett, "Jesus' Death," esp. 13-15. This does not mean that Luke has invested his theology of the cross with the sort of atonement theology one finds, say, in Paul; on this issue, see the survey and programmatic remarks in Green, "Salvation to the End of the Earth," forthcoming.

13. See 22:22, 37; 23:46; and the numerous allusions to Scripture — e.g., in 23:9, 33, 34, 36.

As in the Third Gospel as a whole, so in the passion narrative Jesus' identity is grasped by the most unlikely of people.[14] Simon, previously unknown within the narrative, becomes a surrogate disciple (23:26-27), while women from the city mourn on Jesus' behalf (23:27-28). A condemned-and-crucified criminal comprehends Jesus' righteousness and status as heir to the kingdom (23:40-43), and a Gentile centurion recognizes Jesus as the Righteous One (23:47). Not known to us within the Lukan narrative as a disciple, Joseph of Arimathea nevertheless expresses his exemplary piety in his care for Jesus' corpse (23:50-53).

As much as Luke's passion narrative is christologically oriented, it is also *theo*logically grounded. This is obvious insofar as the motif of conflict is central to chs. 22–23, since for Luke conflict is centered on how people respond to the divine aim; it is also evident from the repeated emphasis on the passion as the fulfillment of the divine aim (e.g., 22:22). But God is present in even more significant ways in the passion account. He is the faithful God to whom Jesus prays and who sends angelic fortitude to his son on the Mount of Olives (22:42-43). He is the one to whom, even in the face of death, Jesus can make requests and surrender his life (23:34, 46), and he is the one whom Jesus trusts for vindication (22:16, 18; 23:43).

7.1. THE LAST SUPPER (22:1-38)

Although the emphasis on the plot against Jesus that opens this narrative unit is now familiar (see 19:47-48; 20:19; 22:1-2), structurally the previous section on Jesus' ministry of teaching in the temple has come to an end (see the *inclusio,* 20:1 → 21:37-38). With 22:1 we enter a new phase of Luke's account of Jesus in Jerusalem. Because of his predictions of suffering and execution in Jerusalem and at the hands of the Jewish leadership centered in Jerusalem (e.g, 9:21-22; 18:31-33), and because of the hostility Jesus has already attracted in Jerusalem and from those very leaders (19:45–20:44), a dark sense of foreboding has begun to engulf the narrative. With this narrative unit, we realize that the divinely appointed time of destiny is fast approaching, that Jesus' death is just around the corner.

One of the most easily overlooked yet more significant of the literary features of the narrative section thus begun is its sheer length and attention to detail. It was not enough for Luke simply to report that Jesus ran afoul of the Jewish and Roman leadership and was killed. Quite the contrary, he has already been laying the groundwork for his readers to understand the centrality of humiliation and suffering to the unfolding of the divine purpose, and now

14. See, e.g., 7:37-50; 17:11-19; 19:1-10.

he turns to this task in earnest. Content and form unite, forcefully constraining how Jesus' looming demise might be understood.[1]

As the heading for this section, "the last supper," suggests, crucial for understanding both the form and content of vv 1-38 is its orientation around a meal. Meals have had a pivotal role to play in the Third Gospel thus far, and the current section takes its meaning in part from those earlier episodes — not least with regard to eschatological orientation (cf., e.g., 13:22-30; 14:15).[2] What makes this narrative unit distinctive even against that rich background is, first, the literary form, the "farewell discourse," within which it is cast. Second, Luke accents the identification of this meal as a Passover,[3] and uses the meal scene explicitly to point to the relationship between the Passover and the kingdom.

(1) As has often been the case in Lukan meal scenes, this one shares several points of contact with Greco-Roman symposia — for example, the setting is at a table; wisdom is conveyed by a chief figure (Jesus), sometimes in dialogical exchange; and concern over relative status is registered.[4] Even more central to our interpretation of vv 1-38, however, is how its material follows the recognizable pattern of the farewell discourse, widespread in Greco-Roman and Jewish (including Christian) sources. Like other literary forms, this one is somewhat elastic, but typical ingredients included a reference to approaching death; the gathering of family or disciples; a review of the figure's life; exhortation; predictions or prophecies; blessings, prayers, and/or warnings; and death and burial.[5] The farewell discourse Luke narrates does not actually begin until v 14 (then continues through v 38), and his recounting of the topos of death and burial is delayed. Nevertheless, vv 1-13 are preparatory to the meal, and the literary form of the farewell discourse is flexible enough to be capable of being assimilated into other literary co-texts.[6] In particular, Luke would not be the first to recount a farewell discourse within a meal scene displaying symposia-like

1. Jesus' death is mentioned directly, predicted, and/or interpreted repeatedly in vv 1, 4, 15, 19, 20, 21, 22, 33, and 37.

2. On the meal motif in Luke, see, e.g., Moxnes, "Meals"; Neyrey, "Ceremonies"; Karris, *Luke: Artist and Theologian,* esp. 47-78; D. E. Smith, "Table Fellowship"; Bösen, *Jesusmahl;* et al.

3. The Passover context of this meal is explicitly mentioned six times — vv 1, 7, 8, 11, 13, and 15.

4. On the symposium, see the brief discussion earlier, at 5:27-39. On these and other symposia-related topoi at the Lukan Last Supper, see Nelson, *Leadership,* 52-56.

5. See Paschal, "Farewell Discourse," 229-30; Nelson, *Leadership,* 97-119. Kurz ("Luke 22:14-38") argues that Luke has imitated biblical farewell addresses for Greco-Roman readers.

6. Narratives are particular adept in their capacity to incorporate literary forms of all kinds — cf. Bakhtin, "Heteroglossia," 214-17.

qualities.[7] The material Luke recounts, then, follows an identifiable configuration, including the gathering of friends, prediction of death, exhortation, review of life, promises and prophecies, and warnings and prayer.

Literary forms are more than patterns of oral and written speech, but
they emerge in particular social settings and serve particular communicative
ends.[8] Most obviously in this case, the farewell discourse is a potent means
of focusing the instruction of Jesus to his disciples — those within the narrative and outside it. "The life of the departing person serves both as a model
to the community and as a legitimizing figure for the teaching. The context
of the last or departing words of a respected person gives added moral power
to these teachings."[9] Accordingly, we would expect Luke's narrative of Jesus'
farewell discourse to draw together important threads of his teaching. This is
exactly what happens, as Jesus interprets his death within the purpose of God,
within Israel's history, within the context of hostility and betrayal, and with
respect to his disciples as he actualizes a new covenant and exemplifies his
servant role among them in his death. Sharing the spotlight is the discipleship
motif — with the narrative highlighting how Satan's influence lies behind the
faltering of the disciples (vv 3-6, 31-34) and pointing to continued struggle
and misunderstanding among Jesus' followers (vv 24, 38); yet Luke portrays
two disciples as taking on Jesus' role as "table servant" (vv 8-13), and Jesus
portends not only the constancy of the disciples in the face of diabolic testing
(v 28) but also their capacity to share regal authority (vv 29-30). Additionally,
the farewell discourse emerges in contexts of monumental transition, and this
is clearly the case here, as Jesus collapses the horizons between Passover and
kingdom (vv 15-16, 29-30) and warns his disciples in urgent terms of the
fundamental change in the welcome they will receive while engaged in the
missionary task (see "from now on," v 36).

(2) At the same time, the Passover focus of this narrative segment is
inescapable, in the same way that Luke's account is striking for its correlation
of Passover and kingdom. The Passover places its stamp on the meaning of
the kingdom, while the Passover finds itself fulfilled in the kingdom. All of
this raises sharply the question, What kind of kingdom? not least with respect
to the kingdom Jesus is said to confer on the disciples in vv 29-30. One might
reply that the whole of the Third Gospel has been oriented in part around
answering that question, but the apposition of Passover and kingdom in this
co-text urges that we understand how deeply Luke's patterns are rooted in
Israel's self-identity vis-à-vis God in the exodus cycle. This is not the first

---

7. So Kloppenborg, "Death of Jesus," 108-11 (with reference, e.g., to Plato
Phaedo; Plutarch *Anthony* 75-77; *Cato Minor* 66-72).

8. Cf. J. L. Bailey, "Genre Analysis," 200-203.

9. Paschal, "Farewell Discourse," 230; cf. Nelson, *Leadership,* 105-6.

time the Lukan narrative has capitalized on exodus motifs (cf., e.g., 1:68-79; 9:28-36), and the Passover emphasis here suggests at least four points of interpretive contact:[10] (1) the interpretive significance of exodus as liberation for the marginalized and oppressed; (2) the importance of sacrifice in relation to deliverance and covenant; (3) the importance of Yahweh's leadership of Israel in the exodus from Egypt as an anticipation of Israel's acknowledgment of his kingship (and the subsequent articulation of this motif in the phrase "kingdom of God");[11] and (4) the ritual celebration of Passover not only as a way of appropriating anew liberation and divine covenant but also of anticipating new exodus. From Jesus' viewpoint in the Lukan narrative, what Passover celebrates in Israel's past it appropriates anew for each generation of God's people and anticipates by way of future deliverance — all of this is wrapped up in and brought to completion through the death of Jesus (interpreted, then, in sacrificial terms), in the consummation of the divine purpose in the eschatological banquet of the kingdom of God.

7.1.1. Conspiracy (22:1-6)

> 22:1 *Now the festival of Unleavened Bread, which is called the Passover, was near.* 2 *The chief priests and the scribes were looking for a way to put Jesus to death, for they were afraid of the people.*
>
> 3 *Then Satan entered into Judas called Iscariot, who was one of the twelve;* 4 *he went away and conferred with the chief priests and officers of the temple police about how he might betray him to them.* 5 *They were greatly pleased and agreed to give him money.* 6 *So he consented and began to look for an opportunity to betray him to them when no crowd was present.*

Luke's narration of Jesus' period of teaching in the Jerusalem temple was boundaried by twin summaries forming an *inclusio* around that segment of the Third Gospel (20:1 → 21:37-38) and by parallel notices about the plot of the Jerusalem leadership against Jesus (19:47-48; 22:1-6). This new segment in the Lukan account is thus demarcated by reiteration of the motif of the plot against Jesus, in addition to the temporal reference in v 1. What differentiates this plot announcement from earlier ones is (1) *its position* following Luke's

---

10. For a more wide-ranging discussion of the relationship between the Passover and the Last Supper, see Barth, *Das Mahl*, 20-51 (available in English in abridged form in Barth, *Lord's Supper*, 7-27). See also Nelson, *Leadership*, 57-59.

11. Beasley-Murray (*Kingdom of God*, 3-62) argues that the concept of God's dominion, though absent linguistically from exodus materials, is nonetheless traceable to Israel's relationship to Yahweh in the exodus — especially insofar as Yahweh served as Deliverer and Leader.

narration of impassioned hostility on the part of the Jerusalem leadership against Jesus and his message, together with Jesus' emphatic rejection of their legitimacy and his prediction of the temple's destruction (chs. 20–21); and (2) *the introduction of means* by which the Jerusalem leadership might overcome the obstacle that has heretofore frustrated their machinations against Jesus.

The design of the leaders has been stymied by popular support for Jesus. Luke introduces his narrative of Jesus' death by indicating in two ways how they were able to move forward. First, utilizing two sets of parallel phrases, he points to human stratagems: (1) The chief priests and scribes want to know "how they might kill him," then Judas confers with the chief priests and officers "how he might betray him to them" (vv 2, 4).[12] (2) They were afraid of the people, and Judas sought to betray him apart from the crowd (vv 2, 6). More is at work than human schemes, however. Second, Luke credits Satan with providing necessary intervention, thus exposing the cosmic proportions of this conflict.

Though Luke's account does not appear to build on particular scriptural texts, it does contain echoes of a constellation of passages concerning the career of the Suffering Righteous. The righteousness of Jesus is a central emphasis within the Lukan narrative of Jesus' suffering and death. Here, this motif is grounded in the inscription of this opening unit in biblical texts relating the gathering of wicked forces, in the guise of both friends and enemies, against the righteous one.[13]

1-2 One of the three great pilgrim feasts (together with Weeks/Pentecost and Booths), Passover was celebrated in the spring, on the fourteenth day of the seventh month of the Jewish year (14 Nisan). Unleavened Bread and Passover had originally been separate feasts, but by the time of Jesus they had long been merged, with Unleavened Bread beginning on 15 Nisan and lasting for seven days (cf. Lev 23:4-8). Passover celebrates the basic act of divine liberation of Israel from Egypt, while Unleavened Bread commemorates how the Israelites ate only unleavened bread on the eve of the exodus (Exod 12; 23:15; 34:18). That Luke locates his account temporally with the approach of Passover/Unleavened Bread is significant in at least two ways. First, during Passover the number of people in Jerusalem swelled considerably, to include hundreds of thousands;[14] since the festival of Passover/Unleavened Bread

12. τὸ πῶς ἀνέλωσιν αὐτόν (v 2); τὸ πῶς αὐτοῖς παραδῷ αὐτόν (v 4). Cf. S. Brown, *Apostasy and Perseverance,* 92.

13. Cf., e.g., Pss 10:8; 31:13; 37:32; 41:9; 43:2; 52:3-6; 55:12-14, 20-21; 71:10; 86:14; 109:2-5. For this motif, see Ruppert, *Jesus als der leidende Gerechte?*

14. Few take seriously Josephus's estimate of 2,700,000 in the city (*J.W.* 6.9.3 §§425-26). Sanders (*Judaism,* 126-28) suggests as many as 500,000; Jeremias (*Eucharistic Words,* 42) would have us reckon with "a number well over 100,000 celebrants."

embodied themes of national liberation, the gathering of such a large crowd during the Roman period could provide the occasion for civil disturbance.[15] Second, the emphasis Luke gives to this temporal setting (underscoring his interest in the exodus motif) suggests an association between Passover, the celebration of national deliverance, and the death of Jesus, with the former foreshadowing the significance of the latter in God's redemptive plan.[16]

The plot against Jesus is by now familiar (see above), as are the key players mentioned here — representatives of two of the three groups forming the Sanhedrin.[17] Their active role in Jesus' passion was anticipated in Jesus' first passion prediction, 9:22. "Chief priests" belonged to the entourage of the high priest, enjoying the high status that came with their positions of leadership in temple affairs. Scribes served as legal experts, interpreting the law for the people, and were vested with elevated status of their own. Luke's characterization of them as "afraid of the people" evidences the dichotomy between the Jewish leadership and those whom they were to have led.[18] Their search to do away with Jesus had become a constant preoccupation,[19] made necessary because of the possibility of public outcry or riot.[20] We may also hear a murmur of Luke's incriminating portrayal of the chief priests and scribes as persons concerned with public rather than divine opinion (cf. 16:15).

3-6 What is needed is a way beyond the impasse provided by the popular support Jesus has from the people. This is provided by Satan, already known within the Third Gospel as the chief opponent of God's aim and, therefore, of God's Son.[21] Although Satan's influence has hardly been lacking from the Lukan narrative,[22] the Evangelist has nonetheless provided a linguistic connection between 4:13 and 22:6. In this way he hints that the "opportune time" for which Satan was waiting had begun to take shape, and that the propitious moment Judas seeks for his betrayal of Jesus will coincide with the implementation of Satan's own scheme.[23] Satan, it is said, "enters" Judas,

15. Josephus reports episodes of unrest at the time of Passover that led to military action in *J.W.* 2.1.3 §§10-13; 2.12.1 §§224-27.

16. Cf. Senior, *Passion of Jesus,* 42-43; Matera, *Passion Narratives,* 156.

17. These two are joined by the elders in the Jewish Council in Jerusalem.

18. Recall that Simeon had promised that Jesus would bring division in Israel (2:34-35). For this dichotomy, cf. 7:29-30; 19:36-40, 47-48; 20:19. For Jesus' popular support, cf., e.g., 4:42; 5:1, 15; 7:16; 18:43; 20:37-38.

19. See the use of ζητέω in the imperfect. ἀναιρέω has the sense "to kill" or "to do away with," here and in Acts 2:23; 5:33; 9:23-24, 29; 16:27.

20. The γάρ clause thus modifies τὸ πῶς . . . rather than ζητέω; cf. Marshall, 787.

21. For σατανᾶς, cf. 10:18; 11:18; 13:16; 22:31; Acts 5:3; 26:18. Luke refers to διάβολος in 4:2, 3, 6, 13; 8:12; 10:38; 13:10.

22. The importance of Satan within the Lukan narrative is demonstrated by Garrett, *Demise of the Devil.*

23. καιρός (4:13); εὐκαιρία (22:6).

probably reflecting the worldview explicated more fully in a Qumranic text: "And in the hand of the Angel of Darkness is total dominion over the sons of deceit; they walk on paths of darkness. Due to the Angel of Darkness all the sons of justice stray, and all their sins, their iniquities, their failings and their mutinous deeds are under his dominion . . . and all the spirits of their lot cause the sons of light to fall."[24] This gives what in the Third Gospel had earlier appeared to be a struggle among humans and human institutions an even more profound and cosmic dimension. It also leaves room for human volition on the part of Judas,[25] who in conference with the temple leadership contracts to betray Jesus in exchange for money. Judas may be influenced by Satan, but he has also fallen victim to the "rule of mammon," which works against the dominion of God — an important motif in Luke-Acts (cf. 16:13-15). Luke underscores the tragedy of this scene by reminding his readers that Judas belonged to the circle of the twelve (cf. 6:16).[26]

Except in rare instances, Roman soldiers were not allowed in the temple, with the result that the temple maintained its own guard. That the officers of the temple[27] join the chief priests in conference with Judas underscores how Luke wants to portray the interests of the temple in conflict with Jesus (cf. chs. 20–21).[28] In the Third Gospel, "to rejoice" (v 5; NRSV: "greatly pleased") is typically used to signify responses to divine, salvific activity;[29] its usage here is yet one more indication of how the Jerusalem leaders, whose joy is thus perverse, are misguided in their commitments.

7.1.2. Preparation for Passover (22:7-13)

7 *Then came the day of Unleavened Bread, on which the Passover lamb had to be sacrificed.* 8 *So Jesus sent Peter and John, saying, "Go and prepare the Passover meal for us that we may eat it."* 9 *They asked him, "Where do you want us to make preparations for it?"* 10 *"Listen," he said to them, "when you have entered the city, a man carrying a jar of water will meet you; follow him into the house he enters* 11 *and say to the owner of the house, 'The teacher asks you, "Where is the guest room, where I may eat the Passover with my disciples?"'* 12 *He will show you a large room upstairs, already furnished. Make prepa-*

24. 1QS 3:20-24 (see 4:13–4:26); ET in Martínez, *Dead Sea Scrolls*, 6. Cf. Luke 8:30, 32-33; Acts 5:3; *Mart. Isa.* 3:11; 5:11, where Beliar dwells in the hearts of Manasseh and his court, with the result that the king has Isaiah sawed in two with a tree saw.

25. See S. Brown, *Apostasy and Perseverance*, 82-97; Senior, *Passion of Jesus*, 47.

26. For ἀριθμός as an expression for a disciple, cf. Acts 6:7; 11:21; 16:5.

27. For this use of στρατηγοί, see Schürer, *Jewish People*, 2:277-79.

28. See also Karris, *Luke: Artist and Theologian*, 53.

29. χαίρω — cf., e.g., 8:13; 10:17; 13:17; 19:37.

rations for us there." 13 So they went and found everything as he had told them; and they prepared the Passover meal.

Luke moves immediately from the approaching day (v 1) to its arrival (v 7). In these seven verses, the phrase "the Passover"[30] and the notion of "preparation" each appear four times — easily demarcating the focus of this narrative unit. During the Hellenistic period, the celebration of Passover was no longer constituted by a simple meal shared in great haste (cf. Exod 12:11), but took on the look of a banquet, with couches or pillows on which to recline, wine to drink, and so on.[31] "Preparations," then, would have involved the purchase of an unblemished lamb and the other food necessary for the meal, the sacrifice of the lamb in the temple, roasting the lamb, and the arrangement of the room (already furnished — v 12).

Luke's account holds in tandem two compulsions. The first is the requirement that the lamb be sacrificed at the right time. Strictly speaking, the Passover lamb was sacrificed on the eve of "the day of Unleavened Bread" (and not the day itself), but Luke apparently follows acceptable practice in equating the two.[32] More significant is Luke's attribution of the timing of sacrifice to divine necessity — a necessity rooted in Scripture (cf. Exod 12:6, 21; Deut 16:1-7), but portrayed by Luke in such a way that one may be reminded of the progression of events related to Jesus' death according to divine necessity.[33] The requirements of Torah and the divine purpose concerning Jesus coalesce, so that the necessity of the Passover sacrifice parallels and anticipates the necessity of Jesus' suffering.[34]

Working in concert with the divine necessity of the timetable governing the sacrifice of the Passover lambs is, second, Jesus' own initiative in the preparation of the Passover meal. Whereas vv 1-6 might suggest that the Lukan narrative of Jesus' passion will recount what happened to him, here we find immediate evidence that Jesus is himself an active agent in the events beginning to unfold. He is no helpless victim but actually sets into motion a chain of events that will lead to his segregation from the crowds (and, thus, to the very condition for which Judas was seeking [v 6]). In an account echoing the preparations made for his entry into Jerusalem (19:28-34), Jesus demonstrates flawless foresight; in both accounts, Luke highlights Jesus' prophetic status, noting that his disciples "found it/everything as he had told them."

---

30. τὸ πάσχα, depending on context, can refer to the Passover lamb, the Passover meal, or the festival of Passover.

31. See Barth, *Lord's Supper,* 10-11.

32. See v 1; Josephus *J.W.* 5.3.1 §99; cf. *Ant.* 2.15.1 §317.

33. δεῖ. See, e.g., 9:22; 13:33; 22:22, 37; 24:7, 26, 44; Acts 1:16; 17:2-3. On this motif in Luke, see Büchele, *Tod Jesu,* 175-76; Lohse, "Lukas als Theologe," 150-53.

34. Green, "Preparation for Passover," 312.

Two features of Jesus' instructions call for special mention. The first has to do with the explicit contrast established between Judas (vv 3-6) on the one hand, and Peter and John on the other. All belong to the circle of the twelve, but whereas the former becomes an agent of Satan to betray Jesus in exchange for money, the latter are presented as exemplary disciples. Their portrayal as table servants (cf. 12:37; 17:7-10; 22:24-27) anticipates their roles as leaders in the book of Acts (3:1, 3, 11; 4:13, 19; 8:14).[35] Second, through Jesus' self-description as a "teacher" requiring a room to gather with his disciples to eat the Passover, read in light of the expectation that the Passover would be celebrated in family units (Exod 12:3-4), Luke presents the gathering of a fictive kin group. Jesus is thus seen as the head of a "household" that includes his closest followers.[36]

7.1.3. Teaching at the Passover Table (22:14-38)

Luke narrates the scene at the table as a relatively seamless discourse among Jesus and the apostles. This is accomplished by his utilization of the literary form of the farewell address (see above at vv 1-28), set within a Passover meal constructed along the lines of a Greco-Roman symposium.[37] Sharing a meal has more generally a community-building or boundary-making function,[38] and this function is escalated in this scene in two ways. First, it is explicitly designated as a Passover meal — typically shared among a family or a fictive kin group. Second, Jesus interprets the character of this meal as a foundational, covenant-making event. Given the nature of this meal, it is not surprising to see how Jesus holds together his own identity and fate with that of his disciples. He exercises his authority as a table servant (vv 17-20, 27), and so should they (vv 24-30). The course of his life is dotted with trials (including ordeals in which apostles are implicated in betrayal and denial — vv 21-23, 28, 31-34); likewise, times of distress and hostility for the disciples are menacing (vv 31-38). Jesus is certain, however, and he assures his audience, that the events about to unfold serve a deeper purpose than the whims or tactics of human agents. Behind them stands the purpose of God, predetermined and evident in the Scriptures of Israel (vv 21, 37).

---

35. See Schürmann, "Dienst des Petrus und Johannes."

36. For this motif in Luke, cf., e.g., 8:19-21.

37. Borrowing elements from the Greco-Roman symposium in the portrayal of a Passover meal would not be artificial in this historical context. Barth (Lord's Supper, 10) notes that, from the beginning of the Hellenistic era, the Passover evolved into a "Greek festive meal, a so-called symposium."

38. See, e.g., Moxnes, "Meals," 160-63; Douglas, "Deciphering a Meal."

7.1.3.1. Celebration and Fulfillment of Passover (22:14-20)

14 *When the hour came, he took his place at the table, and the apostles with him.* 15 *He said to them, "I have eagerly desired to eat this Passover with you before I suffer;* 16 *for I tell you, I will not eat it until it is fulfilled in the kingdom of God."* 17 *Then he took a cup, and after giving thanks he said, "Take this and divide it among yourselves;* 18 *for I tell you that from now on I will not drink of the fruit of the vine until the kingdom of God comes."* 19 *Then he took a loaf of bread, and when he had given thanks, he broke it and gave it to them, saying, "This is my body, which is given for you. Do this in remembrance of me."* 20 *And he did the same with the cup after supper, saying, "This cup that is poured out for you is the new covenant in my blood."*

The signal importance of this scene is indicated by how Luke has conscientiously marked the time leading up to this moment, the gathering of Jesus and the apostles for the Passover.[39] Here, and in the closely related, immediately adjacent exchange (vv 21-23), Jesus interprets his impending death. Jesus' double reference to the coming kingdom (vv 16, 19) speaks to the epochal character of this scene, too, as does the specific naming of Jesus' table companions as "apostles." "Apostles" is not a term used often in the Third Gospel, and here it is used with specific reference to the representative function of those who join Jesus in the Passover. Thus, when Jesus interprets his death with reference to "you," he speaks to the apostles as well as to the people of God (cf. vv 29-30).

Luke explicitly and emphatically refers to this meal as a Passover[40] and it is worth inquiring into the significance of this designation. By the Second Temple Period, the Passover itself had evolved from the hurried meal described in Exodus 12–13, just as it has evolved since (and in a variety of sometimes disparate ways). According to the sources available to us,[41] we can imagine an order of celebration as follows:

---

39. Cf. v 1 ("the festival . . . was near"), v 7 ("then came the day"), v 14 ("the hour came"). Elsewhere, as here, Luke has drawn attention to a moment of special significance with the use of ὥρα — cf., e.g., 1:10; 2:38; 7:21; 10:21; et al. Quesnell ("Women") urges that Luke's narration of the Lord's Supper includes more participants than Jesus and the apostles. Given the restrictions on the size of a Passover meal and the dearth of anything but circumstantial evidence, this otherwise attractive thesis cannot be supported.

40. Vv 1, 7, 8, 11, 13, and 15.

41. In addition to Exodus 12–13, cf. Philo *Quaest. Exod.* 1; *m. Pesaḥim.* See Higgins, *Lord's Supper,* 45-47; G. D. Kilpatrick, *Eucharist,* 40-41.

- The head of the family pronounces a blessing over the first cup; the cup is shared, followed by herbs dipped in a sauce.
- After the second cup is readied, the youngest son asks why this night is different from other nights, why unleavened bread is eaten on this night, etc. In reply, the head of the family tells the story of the exodus and delivers an exposition on Deut 26:5-11; the meal is interpreted as a present act of remembrance of and thanksgiving for God's past liberation of an oppressed people, a celebration of God's faithfulness leading to hope in the future deliverance of God's people. This is followed by the singing of the first part of the Hallel, either Psalm 113 or Psalms 113–114, and the drinking of the second cup.
- The head of the family takes unleavened bread, blesses it, breaks it, and hands it to the others. This is followed by the meal itself.
- There follow two more cups of wine, along with the singing of the second part of the Hallel (Psalms 114–118 or Psalms 115–118).

Points of contact between the Passover celebration and the Lukan scene are obvious, and we can readily see that Luke's scene draws on the meaning of Passover just as it contributes to a reinterpretation of Passover.[42] Especially critical is that the celebration of Passover assumes that the meal is not self-interpreting; why this particular food is eaten requires exposition. Similarly, within the Lukan text, the introduction of every detail is followed by an explanation, either in terms of the coming kingdom or Jesus' impending death.[43] *Interpretation* is therefore at center stage in this narrative unit, and Jesus makes use of key elements of the media available to him in the Passover to give significance to his suffering.

14-16 In a way consistent with the presentation of meals elsewhere in his narrative, as well as with the practice of Passover in the Hellenistic period, Luke has Jesus recline at the table.[44] More generally, this suggests a festive occasion, a symposium, where issues of status are symbolized in where one is positioned around the tables.[45] As the head of this gathering (cf. v 11), Jesus would presumably have taken his place at the head table (with the tables configured roughly in the form of a horseshoe); the relative honor attributed to his table companions by their placement around the tables will surface as an item of controversy in v 24.

At present, however, the apostles are "with him." Their presence at

42. G. D. Kilpatrick (*Eucharist,* 42) observes that vv 15-18 are both like and unlike the Passover celebration; cf. Marshall, *Last Supper,* 83-84.
43. See J. H. Petzer, "Luke 22:19b-20," 251.
44. ἀναπίπτω; cf. 11:37; 14:10; 17:7.
45. See above, at 5:27-39, for a brief discussion of the symposium.

this juncture should not be undervalued — both because being "with" Jesus signifies for Luke the substance of discipleship during Jesus' ministry (so much so that "being with Jesus" becomes one of the key credentials for apostolic office — so Acts 1:21),[46] and because the apostles have been remarkably absent from the focal point of Luke's narrative since the arrival of Jesus and his entourage in Jerusalem in 19:29-40. In fact, toward the end of the journey, Jesus' followers had become increasingly obtuse in their understanding of Jesus' mission (18:15-17, 34), and, for the duration of Jesus' teaching ministry in Jerusalem (chs. 20–21), they have scarcely been mentioned. Only rarely does Luke use the term "apostles";[47] here, he does not do so with respect to their "being sent" (as the term implies; cf. 9:1-10), but instead draws on their identification as commissioned representatives who will provide authorized leadership for God's people.[48]

Introducing the meal, Jesus speaks passionately of the fundamental transition he is about to experience in his career. His deep desire[49] to share this Passover is motivated by his recognition of this impending change, denoted by his suffering.[50] Following this meal, he announces, he will not again partake in a Passover until the Passover is fulfilled in the kingdom of God.[51] On the one hand, this underscores Jesus' conviction that death is not the last word, for he thus anticipates a renewal of fellowship around the table. On the other, as we have already noted, the celebration of Passover had a field of vision that encompasses past, present, and future, so that the feast anticipated eschatological deliverance, a second exodus, so to speak. This is also true of Jesus' meals in the Third Gospel, for Jesus practiced table fellowship in anticipation of the completion of God's purpose and spoke of the coming eschatological banquet in which his own meal practices would be the norm.[52] Read in this light, Jesus' words in v 16 anticipate the fulfillment of the salvific vision resident in his own practices at the table, as well as, then, the vision

46. Cf. 6:17; 7:11; 8:1, 22; 9:10; Green, *Gospel of Luke,* 108.

47. For Jesus' "inner circle," only in 6:13; 9:10; 17:5; 22:14; 24:10. Cf. 11:49.

48. See above on 6:12-13.

49. ἐπιθυμίᾳ ἐπεθύμησα, "with desire I have desired"; for comparable constructions, cf. Gen 31:30; Acts 5:28; 23:14.

50. For the absolute use of πάσχω with reference to Jesus' death, cf. 24:46; Acts 1:3; 3:18; 17:3; Wilckens, *Missionsreden,* 117.

51. That it is "the Passover" that will be fulfilled in the kingdom is clear from Luke's use of αὐτό; *contra* Neyrey, *Passion according to Luke,* 14. Some interpreters have followed Jeremias (*Eucharistic Words,* 207-18) in his view that Jesus vows not to participate even in the meal set at the table in this scene. This view seems contradicted by Jesus' eagerness to share this meal with his apostles, stated emphatically in vv 11 and 15. *Contra* Jeremias on this point, see further Patsch, *Abendmahl,* 131-39.

52. Cf. Isa 2:2-4; 25:6-9; 32:12; 55:1-2; 65:13; Luke 12:35-37; 13:28-29; 14:15; Wainwright, *Eucharist and Eschatology,* 18-25.

of liberation grounded in the celebration of Passover. Even if the kingdom of God has in the Lukan narrative a predominantly present referent, identifying the presence of the kingdom in the mission of Jesus, this saying joins a minority of others in the Third Gospel in referring to the kingdom in its future consummation.[53]

It might be supposed that the fulfillment of which Jesus speaks comes earlier than the eschaton, that the postresurrection meals with Jesus and, then, the celebratory meals dotting the landscape of the narrative of Acts function in this way.[54] According to this view, the kingdom of God is no longer a future expectation, since Jesus' exaltation served as his enthronement as king (Acts 2:31-36) — after which Jesus is said to have eaten with his followers (24:28-43; Acts 1:4;[55] 10:41), and numerous other fellowship meals are recorded.[56] The language Luke uses to describe these postresurrection meals is not peculiarly eucharistic, however, but is only suggestive of ordinary meals within Jewish piety (which language is borrowed within the Lukan presentation of the last supper). Moreover, Acts does not record the consummation of the kingdom of God — which, then, remains a future reality (cf. 21:31).[57] However, far from detracting from the importance of meals in Acts, this eschatological perspective heightens their relevance. They do not constitute the "fulfillment of Passover," but should nevertheless draw into the present and

53. See above on 21:31.

54. So, e.g., Neyrey, *Passion according to Luke,* 13-14; Barth, *Abendmahl,* 42-44; cf. Marshall, *Last Supper,* 79-80; Wainwright, *Eucharist and Eschatology,* 37-42.

55. Συναλιζόμενος has been taken as a form of συναλίζω ("to gather"; cf. Hatch, "Acts 1:4"); as a misspelling or variant of συναυλίζομαι ("to stay with"; cf. Cadbury, "Lodging," 310-17); and as a form of συναλίζομαι ("to eat together"; cf. Bowen, "συναλιζόμενος"; Wilcox, *Semitisms,* 106-9). Συναλίζω is doubtful here, for the plural form would have been expected. "To eat with" fits well in this context (*contra* Cadbury, "Lodging," 310-17) as a continuation of the table fellowship enjoyed by Jesus and his disciples in the Third Gospel (cf. Luke 24:36-48; Acts 10:41), and was understood in many older versions (Latin, Armenian, Coptic, Arabic, Ethiopic, Syriac; cf. Bowen, "συναλιζόμενος," 248-49). And a derivation from ἅλας builds on the association of "eating salt together" and friendship in Greco-Roman antiquity (e.g., Aristotle *Nic. Ethics* 8.3.8 §1156b:24). Although this form is not otherwise documented before the end of the second century, Wilcox argues that it reflects the use of the rare, poetic, Hebrew םחל ("to eat," "to feast"; *Semitisms,* 106-9).

56. On the importance of meals in Acts, see Esler, *Community and Gospel,* 71-109. Nowhere in the book of Acts does Luke refer to "the Lord's Supper"; "the breaking of the bread" (Acts 2:42, 46; 20:7; 27:35; cf. Luke 24:30) refers simply to "fellowship meals" that were continuous with Jesus' own table practices with his followers and others (see Green, *Death of Jesus,* 210-12).

57. See the programmatic comments in Carroll, *End of History,* 80-86. Certainly, Acts never equates the eschatological kingdom with the church (cf. Acts 1:3, 6-8; 8:12; 14:22; 19:8; 20:25; 29:23, 31).

continued experience of God's people the significance of meal sharing as this has been developed in the ministry of Jesus: times of celebration and eschatological anticipation, characterized by a reversal of normal status-oriented concerns and conventions.

17-18   The basic perspective outlined in vv 15-16 — namely, that this is Jesus' last meal, that this moment constitutes a crisis in the career of Jesus, to be followed ultimately by the eschatological sharing of food and drink in the kingdom — is continued and reinforced, with "eating this Passover (meal)" paralleled by "a cup"/"the fruit of the vine." The idiom "fruit of the vine" is also found in Deut 22:9; Isa 32:12, and echoes the language of the blessing pronounced over the cup: "Blessed are you, Lord our God, king of the universe, who has created the fruit of the vine" (*m. Bek.* 6:1).

The setting dictates that the cup Jesus takes is one of the four used in the Passover. It may be the first, the one with which the meal begins, but in the context of the Passover celebration Jesus' interpretive words in v 18 are more appropriate to the second cup. Here, his intimations of impending death and coming kingdom (on which see above, vv 15-16) would push the meaning of the Passover in a christological direction. Instead of the expected focus on the historic deliverance enacted by God in Israel's past, Jesus portends his own death and vindication, and the eschatological advent of God's dominion. If, as seems probable, Jesus' instructions to his disciples to share a common cup are unconventional,[58] this would underscore all the more the solidarity of those gathered, with regard both to the meal and to what it signifies.

19-20[59]   Jesus follows generally the order of the Passover celebration, but lingers over the bread and cup in order to charge them with interpretive significance that draws on yet departs from the meaning of Passover. Interestingly, though sacrificial images are present in these verses (see below), Jesus evokes no direct comparison between the Passover lamb and himself, preferring instead to interpret the bread and cup.[60] Nor does Luke portray the manner of his death with reference to the breaking of the bread, an act that is merely preparatory to the distribution of the bread and devoid of symbolic significance.[61] If the breaking of the bread bears no metaphorical weight, this is not true of its distribution, however. "Giving one's body" is potent as an image for giving one's life (in battle) for the sake of one's people.[62] The

---

58. Cf. Schürmann, *Paschamahlbericht,* 60-61.

59. Verses 19b-20 are omitted in D it, and, until recently, this "shorter text" was regarded as original by those who found here an example of a "Western noninterpolation" (e.g., NA[25], RSV, et al.). For our arguments supporting the originality of the "long text" (i.e., including 22:19b-20), see Green, *Death of Jesus,* 35-42.

60. Cf. 1 Cor 5:7.

61. So Marshall, *Last Supper,* 86.

62. So Nolland, 3:1054 (with reference, e.g., to Thucydides 2.43.2).

sequence Luke describes with reference to the bread — took + gave thanks + broke + gave — is reminiscent of Jesus' actions in the feeding of the multitudes in 9:16.[63] It is remarkable that the feeding miracle is also set in a co-text in which kingdom proclamation and messianic suffering figure prominently (9:1-27). The Scriptures employ the image of "the cup" both with reference to participation in salvation[64] and, especially, with reference to divine judgment.[65] Similarly, "blood poured out" signals violent death.[66] Jesus, then, is not enacting (or teaching his followers how to reenact) his death through his actions;[67] rather, he is interpreting through his words the significance of this Passover and, thus, of his death.

Jesus follows up the bread word with instruction to "Do this in remembrance of me." The notion of "remembrance" is pivotal to the celebration of Passover[68] and cannot be limited, as it often is in English usage, to the idea of cognitive recall of a prior occurrence. In the biblical tradition, cognitive (or affective) recall is often triggered by verbal communication for that purpose, and this provides the impetus for some response or action. In a related sense, "remembrance" is often employed with the sense of "the effect of the recollection of the past for present or future benefit."[69] With the repeated celebration of Passover as precursor, and with this linguistic background for the understanding of remembrance, we may understand Jesus as instructing his followers not only to continue sharing meals together, but to do so in a way that their fellowship meals recalled the significance of his own life and death in obedience to God on behalf of others. This recollection should have the effect of drawing forth responses reminiscent of Jesus' own table manners — his openness to outsiders, his comportment as a servant, his indifference toward issues of status honor, and the like — so that these features of his life would come to be embodied in the community of those who call him Lord. "A meal in memory of Jesus is one which celebrates and prolongs his lifestyle of justice and of serving the Father's food to all."[70]

63. In 9:16, however, Luke used εὐλογέω rather than εὐχαριστέω.
64. For example, Pss 23:5; 116:13.
65. For example, Ps 75:8; Isa 51:17, 22; Jer 25:15-28; Ezek 23:31-34.
66. For example, Gen 9:6; Isa 59:87; Ezek 18:10.
67. See the emphatic discussion in Barth, *Lord's Supper,* 12-26.
68. Cf. Exod 12:14; Deut 16:3; *m. Pesaḥ.* 10:5; Barth, *Lord's Supper,* 12-13.
69. See the survey in Green, *Death of Jesus,* 201-3. ἀνάμνησις/ἀναμιμνήσκω may be used for human remembering in a merely intellectual sense in Gen 41:9; Job 24:20. Far more frequent are references to "remembering" as a two- or three-stage process (outside stimulus + cognitive process + response, or cognitive process + response) — cf. Neh 9:17; Ezek 29:16; Wis 16:6-7; 1 Cor 4:16-17; et al. For the notion of "remember" as "the effect of the recollection of the past for present or future benefit," cf. Num 5:15; 1 Kgs 17:18; Ezek 33:13-16; et al. See Jones, "Ἀνάμνησις," 185-86.
70. Karris, *Luke: Artist and Theologian,* 68; cf. Senior, *Passion of Jesus,* 63-64.

If "the cup" is a metaphorical referent to divine judgment, the train of thought thus initiated is helped along by the reference to "blood poured out," which signals violent death and sacrifice.[71] The phraseology of v 20 ("new covenant in my blood") goes further, alluding to two OT texts that indicate Jesus' interpretation of his death as an effective, covenantal sacrifice. The language of "new covenant" is drawn from Jer 31:31-34; there, as in the portrayal of the ministry of Jesus in the Third Gospel, the eschatological work of God is developed with reference to the forgiveness of sins.[72] Indeed, throughout Luke-Acts, Jesus is presented as the Savior who grants forgiveness of sins. Setting the cup-word within the larger framework of Luke's presentation of Jesus' ministry disallows any notion of a "new covenant" discontinuous with the old, for Luke has emphasized the continuity between the ancient purpose of God and its fulfillment in the coming of Jesus. Similarly, in a number of Qumranic texts, the phrase "new covenant" functions as a cipher for a renewal of the covenant in conjunction with those whom God has called.[73] Additionally, in the phrase "covenant in my blood," one may hear an allusion to Exod 24:8, the covenant sacrifice that, in targumic texts, is interpreted as having been effective as an atoning sacrifice for the people by which they were brought into covenant with Yahweh.[74] By means of this allusion, a typological relationship is drawn between the covenant sacrifice of Exod 24:8 and the death of Jesus, so that Jesus' death is said to atone for the sins of the people and thus to enable their participation in the renewed, eschatological covenant with God.[75]

"Covenant" is fundamentally a relational term, pointing in this case to the bond of fidelity and love between God and humanity. The "you" with whom Jesus thus renews the divine covenant refers to the apostles who have joined him at the table, but it is precisely here that Luke's rationale for designating them in this co-text as "apostles" (rather than "disciples") comes

71. For this use of ἐκχέω/ἐκχύννω, cf., e.g., Gen 4:10-11; 9:6; Lev 4:18, 25, 30; Deut 19:10; Isa 53:12.

72. For the motif of forgiveness in Luke-Acts, cf. 1:77; 3:3; 5:20, 21, 23, 24; 6:37; 7:42, 43, 47, 48, 49; 11:4; 12:10; 17:3, 4; 23:34; 24:47; Acts 2:38; 5:31; 8:22; 13:38; 26:18.

73. Cf., e.g., 1QpHab 2:1-4; 1Q28b 3:25-26; 5:21-22; 1Q34 3:ii:5-6; 1QH 13:12; CD 6:19; 8:21; 19:34; 20:12.

74. Thus, *Targum Onqelos:* "And Moses took the blood and sprinkled it on the altar to atone for the people, and he said, 'Behold, this [is] the blood of the covenant which the Lord has decreed with you according to all these words' "; *Targum Pseudo-Jonathan:* "And Moses took half of the blood which was in the bowls and sprinkled it on the altar to atone for the people and said, 'Behold, this is the blood of the covenant which the Lord has decreed with you according to all these words.' " One may also hear in the background Zech 9:11, though this would hardly exclude the allusion to the covenant sacrifice in Exodus (cf. Moo, *Passion Narratives,* 302).

75. See Pesch, *Abendmahl,* 95.

into sharp focus. As "apostles," they are chosen to represent and to lead Israel (cf. 6:12-16; 22:29-30); hence, this covenant is extended beyond Jesus' immediate table partners to all who embrace "good news to the poor" (see above on 4:18-19).

It is remarkable that this Lukan text attributes such far-reaching significance to the death of Jesus, since the notion of the cross's substitutionary role is completely missing in the missionary sermons in Acts and otherwise present only in Paul's farewell address (Acts 20:28). Elsewhere, Luke emphasizes more pointedly (and pervasively) the salvific role of Jesus' exaltation.[76]

7.1.3.2. A Betrayer at the Table (22:21-23)

21 *But see, the one who betrays me is with me, and his hand is on the table.* 22 *For the Son of Man is going as it has been determined, but woe to that one by whom he is betrayed!"* 23 *Then they began to ask one another, which one of them it could be who would do this.*

Luke signals no break in the narrative as Jesus moves from the interpretation of his death as a covenantal sacrifice for the apostles and, by extension, for the people of God, to the interpretation of his death in relation to tragic betrayal. Jesus' words regarding his own actions in vv 15-20 are in this way set in stark contrast to the activity of Judas, just as, earlier, Judas was contrasted with Peter and John (vv 3-13). A distinction of a different sort is made between what Jesus' audience is able to grasp and what Luke's audience already comprehends. We have known of the prospect of betrayal, as well as the identity of the betrayer, since 6:16; moreover, we were made privy to the influence of Satan on Judas and to the contract he made with Jesus' enemies (22:3-6). In narrating this scene, however, the Third Evangelist shows no interest in naming the betrayer, and his identity is unknown to those at the table. Luke leaves the apostles to discuss[77] among themselves who it might be; this is troubling, since it suggests that any one of them is capable of breaking faith with Jesus. This is another example of Luke's portrayal of Jesus as one possessing prophetic insight and foresight.

The introduction of a betrayer in v 21 is pregnant with significance. First, it is stunning simply that the inner circle of Jesus' followers, those who constitute the kin group with whom he has chosen to share Passover, includes a betrayer (cf. 21:16). Though Luke does little linguistically to point his audience in this direction, we may nonetheless hear reverberations of the

---

76. See Green, "Salvation to the End of the Earth," forthcoming.

77. συζητέω can be rendered "to discuss" (24:15) or "to dispute" (Acts 6:9; 9:29; cf. the use of συζήτησις in Acts 15:2, 7; 28:29).

tragedy detailed with respect to the suffering righteous, including the travesty of treachery by a table intimate (Ps 41:9). Second, although "hand" often has the transferred sense of "power,"[78] this term has also been used in references to those who stand over against Jesus, those seeking his demise.[79] That such a person is present even at Passover with Jesus is illustrative of the openness of his practices of table fellowship, but is also reminiscent of his earlier warning: Sharing table fellowship with Jesus, even listening to his teachings — these are no guarantee of entry into eschatological redemption (13:22-30). Even under the influence of Satan, Judas is culpable for his actions, which contradict the way of life embraced by those who serve the divine purpose.[80]

In fact, v 22 is a transparent affirmation of the larger biblical notion of dual causation, a refusal to collapse the tension between divine sovereignty and human responsibility. Even if the scheme to do away with Jesus is a necessary aspect of the plot Luke has developed, it is not a sufficient cause of Jesus' death. Just as the Scriptures of Israel give expression to divine purpose, so does Luke's unfolding narration of Jesus and his passion disclose the salvific plan set into motion long ago by God.[81] In this co-text, Jesus' affirmation of the underlying aim of God provides reassurance that the tragic events unfolding would come as no surprise to God, but were actually foreseen by God and factored into his redemptive calculus. Read in light of Jesus' table talk thus far (vv 15-18), and against the backdrop of Jesus' most recent Son of Man saying (21:27), Jesus' words here also point beyond his execution; his death is not the full realization of the divine plan, only a necessary component of it, for Jesus' execution will be followed by vindication and royal dominion.

7.1.3.3. Service and Regal Authority (22:24-30)

24 *A dispute also arose among them as to which one of them was to be regarded as the greatest.* 25 *But he said to them, "The kings of the Gentiles lord it over them; and those in authority over them have themselves called*[82] *benefactors.* 26 *But not so with you; rather the greatest among you must become like the youngest, and the leader like one who serves.* 27 *For who is greater, the one who is at the table or*

78. See Lohse, "χείρ," 426-27, 430-31.
79. See 9:44; 20:19; 21:12; 24:7.
80. For this rendering of Jesus' "woe," see 6:24-26; 11:42-45; 17:1; Senior, *Passion of Jesus,* 65.
81. On Luke's use of ὁρίζω, see also Acts 2:23; 10:42; 17:26, 31. Luke uses a constellation of vocabulary to develop his emphasis on the divine plan — cf. O'Toole, *Unity,* 23-28; Green, *Gospel of Luke,* 28-37; Senior, *Passion of Jesus,* 35-39.
82. NRSV: "are called."

the one who serves? Is it not the one at the table? But I am among
you as one who serves.

28 *"You are those who have stood by me in my trials;* 29 *and I confer*
on you, just as my Father has conferred on me, a kingdom, 30 *so that*
you may eat and drink at my table in my kingdom, and you will sit on
thrones ruling[83] *the twelve tribes of Israel.*

Although Luke presents what may appear to be a new topic of conversation, in fact little has changed as the scene at the table unfolds into this interchange among those gathered with Jesus at the Passover table. In v 23 they had inquired among themselves "which one of them" would betray Jesus; now they inquire "which one of them" was the greatest.[84] Although one of the twelve will "betray" Jesus, Luke suggests in this ironic way that all twelve of them "betray" his basic kingdom message with its immediate implications for issues of status and position. The character of the meal Luke has narrated comes into new focus here, with a central concern of the Greco-Roman banquet or symposium (i.e., status honor) intersecting with typical ingredients of the farewell discourse (i.e., review of one's life, exhortation, and appointment of a successor[s]).[85] (For the literary forms utilized here, see above on vv 1-38.) If Jesus' prophecy concerning the inclusion of a betrayer among his table intimates was stunning (vv 21-23), so too is the behavior of the others gathered around him. A woe had been pronounced over the betrayer because of his departure from a fundamental orientation around the values of the kingdom; so, too, do the other apostles now insinuate by means of their behavior that their commitments remain surprisingly unreconstructed. Jesus' message on his own self-giving, presented so passionately in vv 15-20, seems to have fallen on deaf ears.

Even this dispute is transformed into a profound pedagogical moment, however, with Jesus seizing the opportunity to articulate two forms of reversal. Perhaps the most noticeable comes in the relationship between vv 24-27 and vv 28-30,[86] with its emphasis on the disciples' ultimate faithfulness and their participation in Jesus' royal leadership — in spite of their current failure. This

---

83. NRSV: "judging."

84. V 23: τὸ τίς . . . αὐτῶν; v 24: τὸ τίς αὐτῶν.

85. For elements of farewell addresses, including references to the character of one's own mission and example, exhortation to those gathered, and the appointment of successors, see the chart in Kurz, "Luke 22:14-38," 262-63. For parallels, see esp. Paul's farewell address in Acts 20:17-35.

86. Nelson ("Unitary Character") argues for the unitary character of vv 24-30 on the basis of language, structure, form, progression of thought, and symbolism. Neyrey (*Passion according to Luke*, 25) notes that Luke has carefully woven vv 28-30 into its narrative co-text with respect to the major motifs of meal, kingdom, and leadership.

transposition is possible, however, only because of the first, found in v 27, wherein Jesus redefines the relationship between authority and status. That is, Jesus can speak of the leadership roles of the apostles only after having transformed the conventional relationship between the benevolent performance of leadership and the reception of elevated status.[87] Jesus wants his disciples to lead, but in a wholly unconventional way.[88] Throughout, it is easy to hear echoes of earlier Lukan texts concerning meals and status honor (e.g., 14:7-14) and reversal (e.g., 1:51-53; 14:11; 18:14).

Luke's emphasis on reversal and ultimate faithfulness raises the question about Judas. Is he included in the prospect of Israel's leadership? At this juncture, Luke is astonishingly silent on this matter; indeed, it is only with the onset of Acts (1:15-26) that we can be confident that Judas is not included among those who, ultimately, have exercised enduring fidelity.

24   The dispute[89] Luke records may seem out of place following Jesus' interpretive words at the Passover feast (vv 15-20), but the greater shock may be that the disciples thus present themselves as persons so out of step with Jesus' overall teaching. In staging this scene Luke has borrowed elements from the Greco-Roman symposium (see above on vv 1-38; and esp. 5:27-39), with its hyperconcern with the demarcation of relative status through the proper allocation of seating arrangements. Luke has noted the proclivity of Pharisees and legal experts to concern themselves with such conventions (14:7; 20:46), but he has also recorded how Jesus counseled his followers against mimicking the behavior patterns of the Pharisees and scribes (12:1; 20:46). Moreover, prior to the journey to Jerusalem, Jesus had brought a small child into the midst of the disciples in order to teach them that "the least among all of you is the greatest" (9:46-48). If, in contracting with the chief priest and legal experts, Judas had positioned himself over against the divine project, then so do the apostles as they squabble over relative position.

25-27   The first reversal of this narrative unit comes to the fore as Jesus uses normal social protocols from the Greco-Roman world in order to insist that standard categories will not do. In a parabolic way, the disciples' concern with status honor is collocated with the behavior of Gentile kings and others in authority. Luke calls no special attention to singularly wicked kings or to persons who are particularly abusive in their exercise of authority. He seems to have in mind, instead, the normal routine of kings exercising their rule and of those for whom the use of authority is itself a means for gaining

---

87. So Moxnes, "Patron-Client Relations," 261: "There is, then, a break with the patron-client relationship at its most crucial point: a service performed or a favor done shall *not* be transformed into status and honor."

88. So Nelson, "Flow of Thought"; Tiede, "Kings of the Gentiles."

89. φιλονεικία appears only here in the NT.

status honor. It is at this point that comparison with the apostles is pertinent: they want to be acclaimed as benefactors.[90] The problem to which Luke points may be illustrated with reference to cities in the Roman world. The Emperor himself modeled what was expected of the wealthy elite in every locale — namely, the practice of generous benefaction. Rather than pay taxes, the wealthy contributed time and money in the service of the cities and towns. This form of benefaction was not managed centrally, as though wealth would be distributed where needs were generally agreed. Instead, gifts were made at the whim of givers. What is more, though private involvement of this kind was necessitated by deficiencies in the city treasury, it was to the advantage of the wealthy that the city's finances be kept in this weakened condition. Private benefaction was the primary means by which the wealthy were legitimated as those most deserving of public office and prestige in the community. In order to provide leadership, wealth was required, so only the wealthy could provide leadership and thus enjoy the honor and self-advancement reserved for those who gave so "generously."[91] This pattern pervaded the world, so that the giving of gifts brought with it obligations for service and honor.[92] The concern in this text, then, is not with abuses of the system by which leadership was exercised and legitimated, but with the nature of the system itself.

Jesus' negative instruction, "but not so with you," is so cryptic that it might easily be misunderstood.[93] Jesus is not teaching that his followers cannot be rulers or benefactors, but that their manner of ruling and benefaction must be utterly transformed. According to Jesus, disciples are, like God, to give without expectation of return, even to the wicked and the ungrateful (6:35-36). Indeed, in Acts Peter is said to have conferred "a benefit" in the healing of the lame man,[94] and Jesus' ministry is summarized as one of "benefaction."[95] Crucial to Jesus' argument here is the apposition of "greatest" (3x), "kings," "those in authority," "leader," and "one at the table," with "youngest" and

---

90. Cf. Tannehill, "Kingdom," 21. Accordingly, καλοῦνται is understood in its middle rather than passive sense.

91. Garnsey and Saller, *Roman Empire,* 33.

92. On benefactors and benefaction, see Danker, *Benefactor;* J. H. Elliott, "Patronage"; Moxnes, "Patron-Client Relations"; *TLNT,* 2:107-13.

93. Indeed, Lull ("Servant-Benefactor") argues that Jesus indicts his followers because they are not acting as benefactors — i.e., that Jesus presents the benefactor as a positive model worthy of emulation. Winter (*Seek the Welfare,* 40), though referring uncritically to Lull's work, observes that Jesus' prohibition is not against benefaction but against the style of benefaction of those in authority in the Gentile world. *Contra* Lull, see Nelson, "Flow of Thought."

94. Acts 4:9: εὐεργεσία.

95. See Acts 10:38: "doing good" (εὐεργετέω).

"one who serves" (3x). In this co-text, "youngest" refers to those of least status, and "service" is given concrete expression as "service at the table" — as it is often represented in the Lukan narrative.[96] The form of leadership appropriate to Jesus' community, then, is one that is unconcerned with the accrual of status honor but itself reflects the humility of table servants and of those who occupy the bottom rung of social power and privilege, the young.

Jesus' question in v 27, "Who is greater?" echoes the query at the center of the dispute among the apostles in v 24. He follows his parabolic instruction with the contrasting character of his own life. The answer to his question is self-evident (cf. 17:7-10): the one who sits at the table is the person of higher status. He does not deny, then, that some will lead, and so on; after all, he has been portrayed within the Lukan narrative as lord and king. He insists, rather, that his status as lord and king, as greatest, is expressed in the shape of his service, which is so integral to his character that it will determine the manner of his comportment with the faithful even in the eschaton (12:35-38). So also must it be the defining quality of the apostles — who, then, are to turn from their obsession with their own status to a comparable attentiveness to the needs of others.

28-30 How can Jesus confer regal authority on persons who have just demonstrated their failure to embody his message? As v 28 highlights, Jesus' overall evaluation of his apostles is positive; indeed, v 28 should be read as Jesus' reminder to his disciples that, not only the manner of his life (v 27), but even the past shape of their own lives with him contradicts their present behavior. In 9:57-62, for example, Jesus had outlined in a pro-grammatic way the depth of commitment that must accompany those seeking discipleship. Here, Jesus affirms that his apostles have manifested that depth; they have a history of demonstrating continued fidelity even in the midst of ordeals.[97] "Trials" is used in 4:13 and 8:12-13 with reference to diabolic attack and, when it is remembered that the divine aim in Luke-Acts has as its ultimate competitor the purpose of Satan (4:1-13), it is easy to regard all of the hostility against Jesus as an expression of the cosmic struggle against the fulfillment of the divine purpose in the work of Jesus.[98] The motif of enduring

---

96. See 4:39; 8:3(?); 10:40; 12:37; 17:8; Acts 1:17, 25; 6:1, 2, 4; 11:29; 12:25; 19:22; 20:24; 21:19.

97. The appearance of διαμένω in the perfect tense, together with the absence of the apostles' enduring any difficulties with Jesus since the onset of the passion narrative, speaks against Conzelmann's notion that v 28 points to the endurance of Jesus' followers only after the renewed activity of Satan in v 3 (*Luke,* 83; also, 80-81).

98. Cf. Acts 20:19, where the "trials" experienced by Paul presumably include plots against him, persecutions, and imprisonments (so Neyrey, *Passion according to Luke,* 26).

fidelity in the midst of testing was developed earlier in Jesus' parabolic teaching in 8:12-15.

In the Lukan birth narrative and more recently, Jesus has been portrayed as a king (e.g., 1:32-35; 19:11-40), and in his parabolic teaching he anticipated giving the faithful a share in his regal authority (esp. 19:17, 19). Accordingly, Jesus now rewards faithful endurance on the part of the apostles by granting them positions of leadership. Just as Jesus exercises regal power through his identification with the divine purpose, so are there limitations on the nature of the apostles' power. The text speaks, first, of a sharing of Jesus' royal authority, not a complete reallocation of it. This is signified by the first of the two purpose clauses of v 30: "so that you may eat and drink at my table in the kingdom." Even if he bestows a kingdom, it is still *his* kingdom. Jesus' reference to the eschatological banquet that will mark the end time[99] does not disallow the exercise of leadership on the part of the apostles prior to the eschaton, but does portend that Jesus' promises will not be consummated until the End.[100] This reading takes seriously (1) the analogy of Jesus' kingship and that of the apostles, since Jesus is king from birth but must await his enthronement until his exaltation (cf. 1:32-35; 2:11; Acts 2:32-36), as well as (2) one of the typical functions of the farewell discourse — namely, to provide for a transfer of leadership. Of course, that Jesus confers upon the apostles a kingdom does not suggest that they are thus chosen to receive special honor — an interpretation that would contradict Jesus' instruction in vv 24-27 and stand in tension with Jesus' earlier comment that the Father is pleased to give the kingdom to the whole of Jesus' "flock" (12:32).

Second, although the verb Luke uses may suggest a judiciary function for the apostles, the notion of "regal authority" (v 29) and the presence in Israel's past of "judges" whose role was actually "ruling" encourages Jesus' identification of the apostles as empowered leaders.[101] Indeed, it is again here that we see the significance of Luke's identification of Jesus' followers at the table as "apostles," whose appointment is an anticipation of the restoration of Israel as God's people and who, therefore, are commissioned to govern the renewed people of God.[102]

99. See 12:37; 13:22-30.

100. See, however, Nelson, "Luke 22:29-30." He argues against the present fulfillment of Jesus' promises.

101. For this use of κρίνω, cf. Judg 3:10; 10:1-2; 12:7; et al.; also Ps 2:10; 2 Chr 15:5; 1 Macc 9:73.

102. Cf. Chance, *Jerusalem*, 80-81.

7.1.3.4. Pending Trials (22:31-38)

31 *"Simon, Simon, listen! Satan has demanded to sift all of you like wheat,* 32 *but I have prayed for you that your own faith may not fail; and you, when once you have turned back, strengthen your brothers and sisters."*[103] 33 *And he said to him, "Lord, I am ready to go with you to prison and to death!"* 34 *Jesus said, "I tell you, Peter, the cock will not crow this day, until you have denied three times that you know me."*

35 *He said to them, "When I sent you out without a purse, bag, or sandals, did you lack anything?" They said, "No, not a thing."* 36 *He said to them, "But now, the one who has a purse must take it, and likewise a bag. And the one who has no sword must sell his cloak and buy one.* 37 *For I tell you, this scripture must be fulfilled in me, 'And he was counted among the lawless'; and indeed what is written about me is being fulfilled."* 38 *They said, "Lord, look, here are two swords." He replied, "It is enough."*

Luke signals no break in Jesus' instruction, but continues to recount Jesus' table talk following the meal. In spite of the initial, more specific address to Simon (v 31), Jesus' audience remains the apostles who have eaten the Passover with him. This is indicated by the use of the second-person-plural pronoun (v 31; NRSV: "all of you") and the narrator's introduction to vv 35-38 ("he said to *them*"), and has important repercussions for how we construe Jesus' intercessory prayer (v 32). Intercession is required because of coming turmoil. Trials to come are understood in two, interrelated ways. On the one hand, they are grounded in the aim of Satan to frustrate the divine purpose (vv 31-34). On the other, they have their expression very much in terms of human activity — specifically in the inhospitality, even riotous responses, the disciples will receive as they continue their missionary activity (vv 35-38). Not even this is sufficient ultimately to frustrate God's redemptive purpose. Peter and the others will temporarily succumb, but they will recover; what is more, far from thwarting the divine will, the events now unfolding are actually caught up in God's intention.

Throughout this entire scene, Luke's literary model has been the farewell discourse (see above on vv 1-38), and the current exchange provides no exceptions. The *Testaments of the Twelve Patriarchs* (testamentary literature from the second century B.C.E.) contain a number of predictions concerning satanic attacks on the heirs of the leader, as well as prognostications about the eventual success of those whom Satan assaults.[104] Additionally, vv 35-38

---

103. NRSV: "brothers."
104. See *T. Ben.* 3:3; *T. Reub.* 2:1-2; *T. Dan* 5:6, 10-12; *T. Lev.* 18:12; *T. Iss.* 7:7; Neyrey, *Passion according to Luke,* 36-37.

include Jesus' prophecy about coming affliction and exhortation regarding appropriate action — both standard fare in farewell speeches.

31-32 In 6:14, while listing the apostles, Luke had informed us that Jesus had given Simon the name "Peter" (cf. 5:3), and it is by this latter name that "Simon Peter" (5:8) has since been known within the Lukan narrative.[105] Reversion to the former name, together with its doubling in v 31, may signal for Luke's readers that Peter's identity and vocation as an apostle are at stake in the coming conflict, that Peter's faithfulness will be endangered.[106] Judas, influenced by Satan (v 3), had already "turned aside to go to his own place" (Acts 1:25); if this is true for Judas, and if even Peter's faithfulness is imperiled, then Luke's readers ought also to take seriously how their faith is at risk on account of the stratagems of Satan (cf. 8:12).

Jesus uses an image of Satan that is reminiscent of his role in Job 1–2, a heavenly official whose aim is to distinguish genuine from fraudulent integrity — or, in the imagery of Jesus' words, to sift the wheat from the chaff.[107] Within Luke-Acts (as in Job), Satan is not only the accuser, as though his only aim were to detect faithlessness; rather, he inspires faithlessness. He is the one who supplies occasions for failure, who is active in resisting God's plan and God's people.[108] Reference to Satan thus intimates that the temporary loss of steadfastness Luke will narrate on the part of the apostles is due to something more than human frailty. Having experienced initial success with Judas (v 3), Satan now turns to attack[109] the other apostles, to crush their faith.[110] That Jesus is aware of this plan is an added indication of his omniscience within the Lukan narrative.

How can human beings withstand the onslaught of Satan? Jesus provides two answers, the primary one being his own intercession on behalf of Peter;[111] secondarily, because Jesus' prayer on behalf of Peter will be effica-

---

105. See 8:45, 51; 9:20, 28, 32, 33; 12:41; 18:28; 22:8.

106. Cf. Senior, *Passion of Jesus*, 77; Matera, *Passion Narratives*, 165.

107. The connection to Job is denied by Neyrey, *Passion according to Luke*, 33; but cf. Crump, *Jesus the Intercessor*, 154-55.

108. Cf., e.g., 4:1-13; 8:12-13; 13:16; Acts 10:38; 13:8-10; Zech 3:1; Garrett, *Demise of the Devil*.

109. ἐξαιτέομαι appears nowhere else in the Greek Bible. The closest parallel may be *T. Ben.* 3:3: ἐὰν τὰ πνεύματα τοῦ βελίαρ εἰς πᾶσαν πονηρίαν τοῦ θλίβειν ἐξαιτήσωνται ὑμᾶς. . . . Stählin ("ἐξαιτέω") suggests the nuance, "to demand the surrender of."

110. That Satan's aim is to destroy their faith (and not simply to tempt them or to catch them in unfaithful behavior) is shown by the purpose of Jesus' prayer: ἵνα μὴ ἐκλίπῃ (ἐκλείπω — "to cease, to end, to fail") ἡ πίστις σου.

111. This is emphasized by Crump, *Jesus the Intercessor*, 154-62: "Thus *the perseverance of the disciples' faith, the survival of Satanic trials, is shown to be founded upon the intercession of the earthly Jesus*" (157).

cious, Peter will be able to strengthen the others. Although Jesus' words portend the efficacy of his prayer,[112] Peter will nonetheless experience temporary failure. He will need "to turn back," according to Jesus, who uses a verb that commonly appears in Luke-Acts with reference to repentance.[113] Of special interest is the analogous description of turning from the influence and domain of Satan to that of God in Acts 26:18. Similarly, in the *Testament of Benjamin,* Benjamin predicts of his heirs that, though the spirits of Beliar will demand to afflict them, those spirits will be unable to dominate them (3:3).

Even if the focus of Jesus' instruction has been toward Peter, all of the apostles are present in this scene; so too, even if the focus of his intercessory prayer has been on Peter, the others do not lie outside his prayerful concern.[114] Precisely what is envisioned by Peter's strengthening of his brothers and sisters is not clear, either here or in the subsequent Lukan narrative.[115] Clearly, Peter is later portrayed as the emerging leader of the Christian community, and in Acts 1:15-26 he exercises leadership in helping the community in its discernment of God's will in the Scriptures and in proposing action.[116]

33-34 The somber tone of the preceding verses is shattered by Peter's bravado as he announces his resolute faithfulness. He even addresses Jesus as "Lord," thus punctuating his readiness to endure affliction on behalf of Jesus with an affirmation of his uncompromising allegiance. The content of his response to Jesus is ironic — both because Jesus had announced the prospect of prison (21:12) and because Peter will in fact go to prison (Acts 4:1-22; 5:17-21; 12:3-11) and even face death (Acts 5:33; 12:1-4) on account of his unyielding fidelity to Jesus. At present, however, Peter is ill prepared for such ordeals, and Jesus again demonstrates his prescience by predicting

---

112. For the use of δέομαι/δέησις to signify petitionary prayer, see 1:13; 2:37; 5:12; 8:28, 38; 9:38, 40; 10:2; 21:36; Acts 1:14; 4:31; 8:22, 24 (intercessory prayer), 34; 10:2; 21:39; 26:3. Although prayer is a central motif in Luke-Acts (cf., e.g., Ott, *Gebet und Heil;* Trites, "Prayer Motif"; O'Brien, "Prayer in Luke-Acts"; Smalley, "Spirit, Kingdom and Prayer"; Plymale, *Prayer Texts;* Crump, *Jesus the Intercessor*), we are not normally informed about the content of Jesus' prayers (cf., though, 10:21-22; 22:42; 23:34, 46). This underscores the role of Jesus as one who intercedes on behalf of his followers — a motif developed in Crump, *Jesus the Intercessor.*

113. ἐπιστρέφω — see 17:4; Acts 3:19; 9:35; 11:21; 14:15; 15:19; 26:18, 20.

114. This, however, is not to say that Luke's language encourages us to understand that Jesus thus indicates that the content of his prayer has focused on them all — *contra* Crump, *Jesus the Intercessor,* 158-62. It is not clear why Crump needs to affirm that Jesus had prayed for all the apostles while praying "something extra for Peter," nor how this interpretation makes sense of either the second-person-singular pronoun in v 32 as opposed to the second-person-plural pronoun in v 31, or the specific instructions to Peter in v 32.

115. Cf. Schneider, "Stärke deine Brüder!"

116. Cf. Acts 1:14-15. See Johnson, *Decision Making,* 60-62.

Peter's failure publicly to acknowledge Jesus. This will happen very soon, "this day."[117]

Jesus' words portend that Peter will behave in ways that contradict the criteria for authentic discipleship: Rather than deny himself, rather than lose his life for the sake of Jesus (9:23-24), Peter will seek to save his life by denying Jesus. Even this can be forgiven, however, assuming that there is subsequent repentance. Jesus himself had earlier observed that "whoever denies me before others will be denied before the angels of God. And everyone who speaks a word against the Son of Man will be forgiven . . ." (12:9-10).[118] Following the fulfillment of Jesus' prophecy (vv 54-60), Luke records dramatically Peter's contrition (vv 61-62). Interest in this prediction-realization sequence should not blind us to the subtle hint of Peter's grasp of Jesus' role in God's salvific plan already in the present co-text, however. In spite of repeated efforts on Jesus' part to articulate the fact and necessity of his forthcoming suffering and death within his divine vocation, this is the first time that one of Jesus' followers has perceived that Jesus is about to die! If Peter is aware of this, perhaps he has also begun to grasp Jesus' instructions concerning the significance of his demise and, indeed, that it is through suffering that God's purpose is brought to completion.

35-38 The dialogue between Jesus and Peter in the presence of those at the table is broadened to include the other apostles. Jesus' words recall his instructions to those sent out in pairs in 9:2-3; 10:3-4 — and with them there is a recollection of Jesus' promise and their experience of divine provision and hospitality along the missionary journey. Even if Jesus has attracted hostility within the Lukan narrative, the apostles have been spared from want thus far. This state of affairs is about to undergo a radical shift, however, marked by Jesus words, "but now. . . ." Although the vocabulary is not identical, similar temporal innovations are marked in 1:48; 5:10; 12:52; and 22:18 (see also 22:69; Acts 18:6).[119] In times to come, the apostles can no longer depend on a warm welcome, but must prepare themselves for hostility, even of a violent sort.[120]

Mention of the need to purchase a sword adds to this picture a metaphorical reference to the coming reality. The possibility that Jesus' followers are literally to respond to hostility with a sword — that is, with violence — is negated in 22:49-51 (see above on 6:20-38), and elsewhere in the Third

---

117. Recalling that, in Jewish reckoning, the "day" is marked from evening to evening, we may understand Jesus to be intimating that only a few hours remain — following supper, but before the crowing of the rooster, typically to mark dawn.

118. The only uses of ἀπαρνέομαι in Luke-Acts are in 12:9; 22:34, 61. The simple ἀρνέομαι is used in 9:23 (as well as in 12:9; 22:57).

119. The phrase ἀπὸ τοῦ νῦν appears in these texts; v 36 reads ἀλλὰ νῦν.

120. See esp. Lampe, "Two Swords."

Gospel "sword" has been used as an image of animosity (12:51-53; cf. 2:34-35). In v 38, then, the apostles manifest their dullness when they suppose that Jesus opposes his own extensive and emphatic teaching by encouraging them actually to possess (or to purchase) weaponry.[121] His words, "It is enough!" are an expression of his exasperation.[122]

Verse 37 is in fact closely connected to Jesus' instructions regarding the transformation of the times, from hospitality to hostility. The opening clause, "for I tell you," advances a causal relationship: The times are changing *because* "this scripture" is being fulfilled in Jesus.[123] With an actual citation of Scripture, and the combination of references to "scripture," "it is necessary," and the language of fulfillment (2x), Luke emphatically articulates the realization of the divine purpose.[124] At the very least, this must be read as an affirmation that the ordeals Jesus anticipates for his disciples are not surprising to God but are the sequelae of the realization of God's purpose with respect to Jesus.[125]

Jesus' citation of Isa 53:12, together with the emphasis on his personal destiny, associates Jesus with the Servant of Yahweh in his being "reckoned among the lawless." Many readers of Luke assume that this is a prediction fulfilled in the manner of Jesus' execution, crucified alongside two "criminals" (23:32-33, 39).[126] Because this is the only appearance of the term "lawless" in the Third Gospel, this interpretation cannot be ruled out, even though Luke provides no linguistic basis for this association.[127] Given the use of "lawless" for a person who transgresses the law — that is, a "sinner" — a more arresting interpretation seems likely, however. A well-known motif within the Third Gospel is Jesus' friendship with sinners, and this is typically bundled together with the hostility he attracts on account of those associations (e.g., 7:34, 39;

---

121. Neyrey (*Passion according to Luke,* 39) compares the previous passion predictions in 9:44-45 and 18:31-34 with that in 22:37-38 in order to provide structural evidence for taking v 38a as a statement of the disciples' misunderstanding (cf. 9:45; 18:34).

122. Cf. the analogous expression in Deut 3:26: "Enough from you!"

123. See Moo, *Passion Narratives,* 132.

124. For this motif, see Green, *Gospel of Luke,* 24-37.

125. δεῖ, τελέω, and τέλος ἔχω emphatically point to the realization of divine necessity. The two phrases ἐν ἐμοῖ and τὸ περὶ ἐμοῦ designate the destiny of Jesus as the locus of the fulfillment of that purpose.

126. Cf., e.g., Büchele, *Tod Jesu,* 44; Lohse, *Geschichte des Leidens und Sterbens,* 93; Rese, *Alttestamentliche Motive,* 135-36; Bock, *Proclamation,* 138.

127. The Isaianic citation reads ἄνομος, while in 23:32-33, 39 Luke employs κακοῦργος; cf. Moo, *Passion Narratives,* 135-37. Improbable is the view of Neyrey (*Passion according to Luke,* 42-43; so also the earlier work of Minear, "Luke 22.36"); he argues that Jesus thus relates himself to the apostles, who are "lawless" on account of their possession of two swords. This position does not account for the γάρ clause in v 37, nor does it indicate who will count Jesus among the "lawless" apostles in a way that fulfills the Isaianic text.

15:1-2; 19:7-10). It is more probably in this sense that Jesus is "numbered with the lawless." This view is supported not only by the importance of this motif for Luke, but also by the probability that, as is the case in the Isaianic co-text, so here it is Jesus' adversaries who do the reckoning (cf. v 52; 23:1-5).[128] That is, as the use of the continuous present ("is being fulfilled") suggests, to be "numbered among the lawless" is the consequence of Jesus' mission throughout the Lukan narrative, since his enemies among the Jewish leadership interpret his activities as lying outside the boundaries of Torah; moreover, because of the opposition he thus attracts, Jesus is also responsible for disturbing the fragile peace between Rome and Jerusalem — and this constitutes from the Roman perspective an infraction of imperial law.[129]

Thus, the form and focus of Jesus' life, a life lived in harmony with the divine plan, are inseparable from the death he anticipates. Those who follow him can expect no less, so that they must ready themselves for the hostility they will face. The apostles do not yet understand this (hence v 38), but they will. In his second volume, Luke goes on to record how Jesus' witnesses receive both hospitality and hostility, often in the same city (e.g., Acts 16:11-40).

7.2. JESUS ON THE MOUNT OF OLIVES (22:39-46)

39 *He came out and went, as was his custom, to the Mount of Olives; and the disciples followed him.* 40 *When he reached the place, he said to them, "Pray that you may not come into the time of trial."* 41 *Then he withdrew from them about a stone's throw, knelt down, and prayed,* 42 *"Father, if you are willing, remove this cup from me; yet, not my will but yours be done."* 43 *Then an angel from heaven appeared to him and gave him strength.* 44 *In his anguish he prayed more earnestly, and his sweat became like great drops of blood falling down on the ground.*[1] 45 *When he got up from prayer, he came to the disciples and found them sleeping because of grief,* 46 *and he said to them, "Why are you sleeping? Get up and pray that you may not come into the time of trial."*

128. So also Senior, *Passion of Jesus,* 80-81.
129. Cf., then, the ironic use of ἄνομος in Acts 2:23.
1. The NRSV (following p[69vid.75] ℵ[1] A B T W et al.) places vv 43-44 in double brackets, indicating that these verses are regarded as a later addition to the Lukan text (for this view, cf. Metzger, *Textual Commentary,* 177; Ehrman and Plunkett, "Angel and Agony"). For the originality of these verses (supported by ℵ[*.2] D 0171 et al.), see Green, "Mount of Olives," 35-36; and the more lengthy discussion in R. E. Brown, *Death of Jesus,* 180-84.

The boundaries of this scene are clearly marked by the *inclusio* of vv 40 and 46, where Jesus instructs his followers to pray lest they "come into the time of trial." This is true even though Luke's account of Jesus' arrest in vv 47-53 is closely tied to the present scene, with Jesus' struggle in prayer equipping him for the "composed and masterful" role he will fill at his arrest.[2] In fact, Jesus' struggle on the Mount of Olives is presented by Luke as the watershed in the passion narrative, the critical point at which faithfulness to the divine will is embraced definitively in the strenuousness of prayer.[3]

Thematically, this scene focuses narrowly on the efficacy of prayer in the midst of trial, with Jesus presented as an example to be emulated by his disciples. The parallel instructions to pray (vv 40, 46) combined with the threefold reference to Jesus' act of praying (vv 41-45) thus serve a parenetic function: As Jesus prays in the face of "testing," so should the disciples.[4] When reviewed against the backdrop of Jesus' own teaching on prayer (11:1-13), the Lukan portrait of Jesus as one who practices what he preaches is only strengthened. As in that co-text, so here he addresses God as "Father" and relates prayer to deliverance in the midst of diabolic testing (11:2, 4).[5] Later, Luke will portray the early believers remarking similarly of Paul, "Let the Lord's will be done" (Acts 21:14). This emphasis disallows any interpretation of Jesus' actions motivated by some dark "death wish" or sense of masochism. On the Mount of Olives Jesus prayerfully declares his fundamental orientation around the will of God; if this leads to calamity and death, so be it.

Neither is it appropriate to attribute a martyrological interpretation to this Lukan scene.[6] To be sure, echoes of martyr accounts from Second Temple Jewish texts can be discerned — for example, in the references to supernatural conflict, the cup, angelic intervention, blood and sweat, and so on.[7] But these elements are hardly unique to martyrological scenes, and Jesus' struggle in prayer and request concerning the removal of "the cup" suggest a portrait of

2. R. E. Brown (*Death of the Messiah*, 192) speaks of the "composed and masterful Jesus" in both prayer and arrest (cf. Neyrey, "Absence of Jesus' Emotions"), but this view overlooks Luke's portrait of Jesus on the Mount of Olives as a genuine struggle against πειρασμός; see below.

3. See Barbour, "Gethsemane"; Beck, "Imitatio Christi," esp. 47; Green, "Mount of Olives," 38.

4. See Holleran, *Synoptic Gethsemane*, 214; Matera, *Passion Narratives*, 167-69; Green, "Mount of Olives," 38-39.

5. 11:4: μὴ εἰσενέγκῃς εἰς πειρασμόν; 22:40, 46: μὴ εἰσελθεῖν [εἰσέλθητε] εἰς πειρασμόν. Cf. Beck, "Imitatio Christi," 38; R. E. Brown, *Death of the Messiah*, 178.

6. Though cf., e.g., Dibelius, *From Tradition to Gospel*, 201-2; Conzelmann, *Luke*, 81, 83-90; Talbert, 212-14; Ford, *My Enemy Is My Guest*, 118-20; et al. See further above, on 22:1–23:56.

7. These and other motifs are catalogued in Green, "Mount of Olives," 39-41; see also R. E. Brown, *Death of the Messiah*, e.g., 183-84, 187-88.

Jesus that falls short of the superhuman bravado characteristic of Jewish martyrological scenes. More suggestive are the points of contact with the tradition of the Isaianic Servant of Yahweh, the presence of which is easily monitored in relationship to the Lukan interpretation of Jesus' death.[8] More particularly, within the current scene one may trace features reminiscent of Servant material — especially the emphasis on suffering as an outworking of the divine will, submissive obedience to the divine will on the part of the one chosen for this fate, and the offering of aid via a divine messenger.[9]

If Luke's scene of Jesus on the Mount of Olives marks a critical moment in the larger narrative, this is because of the consequence invested in this moment. Within this scene, what is at risk is signaled by intimations of cosmic struggle. The English phrase "time of trial" may mask the diabolic grounds of the trial here in view, but this is underscored both by the use of the term elsewhere in Luke[10] and by the already plentiful evidence within the passion account of satanic machinations (vv 3, 28, 31). Additionally, references to the divine will and the motif of angelic intervention highlight the eschatological and cosmic repercussions of this scene. As we cast the interpretive net more broadly, it is also important to recall that the whole of the Lukan narrative concerns the disclosure and realization of the divine will — divine activity that calls for people to align themselves with respect to God's purpose. Jesus has repeatedly asserted the divine necessity of his suffering; now faced with the imminent prospect of his ordeal, will he continue along the path of submission to his Father? Luke sketches this scene so as to underscore Jesus' unreserved allegiance to God. Insofar as the disciples' behavior and commitment contrast with that of Jesus, Luke also employs this scene pedagogically: The way to remain triumphant (measured as persistent obedience to the divine will) in the time of trial is through persistent, earnest, submissive prayer.

39 The narrator ties this scene into the previous narrative in two ways — first, by marking the close of Jesus' farewell discourse (vv 14-38) with Jesus' departure from the location of the meal, and, second, by drawing attention to Jesus' habit of retiring to the Mount of Olives (see 21:37). Luke signals his particular interest throughout this scene on Jesus by noting only that "*he* came out," employing a term used elsewhere in the Lukan narrative for Jesus' "going" in fulfillment of his divine vocation.[11] Only in a kind of

8. Cf., e.g., 22:19-20, 21-38 (esp. 37); 23:4, 9, 14, 15, 22, 33-34, 35, 37; Acts 3:13-15; 8:26-39; V. Taylor, *Passion Narrative,* 69-72; Green, "God's Servant."

9. Cf. Isa 41:10; 42:1, 6; 49:5; 50:4-7, 9; 52:13–53:12; Seccombe, "Luke and Isaiah," 258; Larkin, "Old Testament Background"; Green, "Mount of Olives," 41-42.

10. πειρασμός — cf. esp. 4:13; 8:12-13.

11. πορεύομαι thus appears in its third-person-singular form; for the metaphorical use of this term, cf. 9:51; 13:22; 22:22.

postscript do we learn that the disciples follow Jesus, underscoring the interest in the narrative on their continuing presence (cf. 23:49) while allowing for a narrow focalization on Jesus; this is consistent with Luke's portrait of discipleship thus far primarily as being "with" Jesus.[12] Mountains have served as places of prayer before (6:12; 9:28), but the Mount of Olives is no ordinary locality, vested as it is in Zech 14:4 with eschatological significance.

40-41   The use of the definite article, "*the* place," suggests that Jesus has journeyed to a particular, identifiable locale, but Luke draws no further attention to its description. Nor does he invest much detail in his portrait of Jesus' removing himself from his followers; "about a stone's throw" is the rough equivalent of "over yonder."[13] What is emphasized, instead, is the prayer motif — first by Jesus' instructions to his followers and then by his own kneeling to pray. The juxtaposition of these two references to prayer, together with the motif of "following Jesus" noted in v 39, suggests the narrator's intent to portray Jesus and the disciples in parallel, showing how each responds in the face of diabolic offensive.[14] As in 21:36, so here and in the parallel in v 46, Jesus explains that one may faithfully persevere in times of testing through prayer.[15] Especially when compared with 18:11, 13, where both Pharisee and toll collector stand to pray, Jesus' posture begs for comment. Occasionally found in the LXX and in Acts, kneeling for prayer draws special attention to submissiveness in prayer as well as to the urgency or intensity of the prayer itself.[16]

42-44   Within the Third Gospel, "time of testing" carries with it already the notion of diabolic assault, and this motif is underscored both by Luke's report of the content of Jesus' prayer and by the appearance of a strengthening angel. Conceptually, one may hear in this prayer reverberations of Jesus' testing in the wilderness (4:1-13), where the nature of Jesus' obedience was at stake. Indeed, it is here on the Mount of Olives that the motif of conflict reaches one of its highest points, with the opposing purposes of God and Satan coalescing in one scene. There is a certain irony in this, since, if Jesus embraces the cup in obedience to the divine purpose, he will also accept the fate willed for him by Satan;[17] only as the story unfolds does it become clear that Jesus' death represents not the greatest of the devil's achievements but actually his demise.

12. On the motifs of being "with" and "following" Jesus, cf. 6:17; 7:11; 8:1, 22, 38; 9:10, 23; 22:11, 14, 33, 38; Acts 1:21.

13. For this and comparable colloquialisms, see Thucydides 5.65.2; Gen 21:16.

14. For this use of πειρασμός, see the parallel usages in 4:13; 8:12-13; for satanic presence in the passion account, see 22:3, 31.

15. Crump, *Jesus the Intercessor,* 168.

16. Cf. Acts 7:60; 9:40; 20:36-37; 21:5; Schönweiss, "Prayer," 862.

17. Crump, *Jesus the Intercessor,* 168-69.

Before, Jesus was tempted in his role as "Son of God," and it is as "Son" that he now prays, addressing God as "Father." With this name Jesus addresses and refers to God throughout the Lukan narrative (e.g., 2:49; 10:21-22; 22:29), and he teaches his followers to do the same (11:2). Jesus thus confirms God's sovereignty, but also indicates his obedience to God.[18] This latter emphasis comes to the fore, too, in the structure of Jesus' prayer, with his request boundaried on both ends by references to the divine will:

A "Father, if you are *willing,*
    B remove this cup from me;
A′ yet, not my *will* but yours be done."

As recent, prior usage has made transparent, the "cup" is a metaphor for calamity and death (see above on vv 19-20). Faced with the looming reality of his ordeal, Jesus' desire is that God "remove this cup." Importantly, however, even in making this request Jesus affirms that his future is in the hands of God; if Jesus is to bypass suffering and death, it will be because God introduces an alternative route for the realization of his purpose. God's will and Jesus' submission to it are thus paramount in Jesus' words.

Whether Jesus required angelic assistance is not clarified within the narrative. What is clear is that the presence of the angel empowers Jesus to engage in even more ardent prayer. God's response to Jesus' prayer is to provide strength for the ordeal, not to remove the cup (cf. Isa 42:6; Sir 4:28). Thus strengthened, Jesus is portrayed like an athlete, so earnestly engaged in the contest that he sweats profusely.[19] Angels appear often in the Lukan narrative, providing messages and assistance for God's people,[20] and the picture of the divine messenger who strengthens or fights on behalf of the faithful is known in Daniel.[21] Against whom or what does Jesus contest in prayer? Some have found Jesus in a struggle with himself, lest he fail this

18. In the Greco-Roman world, one of the prominent ingredients of the concept of "sonship" was obedience to one's father (Harvey, *Constraints of History,* 159). On these motifs in Luke, see Mowery, "God the Father," 124-28.

19. The image Luke employs is of sweat dripping so profusely that it was like (ὡσεί) drops of blood, not that Jesus was actually "sweating blood." Luke's portrait thus gives no basis for interpretations that focus on the blood of Jesus on the Mount of Olives — e.g., that of Ford (*My Enemy Is My Guest,* 118): "his redemptive blood begins to flow in the garden." For examples of Luke's fondness for simile, see, e.g., 3:22; 10:18; 11:44; 22:31; et al. For the picture of "wrestling in prayer," cf. Col 4:12.

20. Note in this instance that the angel appears "from heaven"; cf. 1:26; 2:9; 12:8-9, 11; 15:10; Acts 5:19; 8:26; 10:3; 12:7, 23; 27:23.

21. Cf. Dan 3:24; 10:17-19, 20–11:1; 12:1.

test of virtue and give in to irrational, unbridled passion.[22] Luke has emphasized rather (1) the import of struggling against satanic opposition and (2) Jesus' present engagement in a decisive contest the outcome of which is in the hands of God. Hence, "strenuousness of prayer is demanded by the energy with which Satan is pressing his suit."[23]

45-46   Three times Luke refers to Jesus' prayer (vv 41, 44, 45), the final time to mark its completion. In parallel fashion, Luke had described Jesus as kneeling to pray and under physical stress while praying, but now he observes that Jesus arose from prayer. In these two ways, the Third Evangelist marks the end of the contest, the certainty with which Jesus has discerned the divine will, and the resolve with which he has embraced his divine vocation. The disciples have at best been on the periphery during Jesus' prayer-struggle, but they are now again included in the scene. Their behavior stands in stark contrast both to Jesus' initial instructions (v 40) and to Jesus' own behavior, but Luke's portrait of their failure is not a damning one. First, he excuses their behavior by attributing it to grief. Insofar as Jesus himself was enabled to engage in the struggle with angelic help, it is perhaps not surprising that the disciples were thus overcome. Second, Jesus repeats his instructions to "pray that you may not come into the time of trial," so that we must assume that their failure on the Mount of Olives was neither final nor fatal. They (and with them, Luke's own audience) will be given future opportunity to "pray always and not to lose heart" (18:1), to "be alert at all times, praying that you may have the strength to escape all these things that will take place, and to stand before the Son of Man" (21:36).

7.3. JESUS CONFRONTS THE ARRESTING PARTY (22:47-53)

47 *While he was still speaking, suddenly a crowd came, and the one called Judas, one of the twelve, was leading them. He approached Jesus to kiss him;* 48 *but Jesus said to him, "Judas, is it with a kiss that you are betraying the Son of Man?"* 49 *When those who were around him saw what was coming, they asked, "Lord, should we strike with the sword?"* 50 *Then one of them struck the slave of the high priest and cut off his right ear.* 51 *But Jesus said, "No more of this!" And he*

22. See esp. Neyrey, "Absence of Jesus' Emotions"; he concludes that "Jesus . . . is not a victim, out of control, subject to irrational passion; on the contrary, he is portrayed as practicing virtue, singleheartedly searching for God's will and being manfully [*sic*] obedient to God" (171). *Contra* Neyrey on this point, see Green, "Mount of Olives," 32-33.

23. Beck, "Imitatio Christi," 39; cf. R. E. Brown, *Death of the Messiah,* 188-89.

touched his ear and healed him. 52 *Then Jesus said to the chief priests, the officers of the temple police, and the elders who had come for him, "Have you come out with swords and clubs as if I were a bandit? 53 When I was with you day after day in the temple, you did not lay hands on me. But this is your hour, and the power of darkness!"*

Luke's narration of the arrival of a posse to "lay hands" on Jesus (v 53) is tightly stitched into its co-text — so much so that (1) Jesus is still addressing his disciples when a "crowd" arrives, and (2) one must wait for the next narrative unit for the actual arrest of Jesus (v 54). The relative coherence of the present scene is nonetheless important for interpretive reasons. First, we may understand vv 47-53 as a concrete manifestation of the "time of trial" Jesus had anticipated in vv 40 and 46. Second, not (directly) from the narrator and not from the arresting party itself, but only from Jesus do we discover the motivation of the crowd that approaches. This underscores the degree to which Jesus' prayer-struggle in vv 39-46 has led to his understanding of the divine purpose and prepared him for this encounter. Apart from any apparent source of information other than prophetic insight, he knows why Judas has come, and the crowd of Jewish officials with him.

A brief examination of the method of Luke's narration is instructive. As though he were working with an adjustable lens, he dramatizes this scene with clear, sharp changes in focusing — moving quickly from the crowd to Judas, then gradually to allow the crowd greater definition. Indeed, only as the scene unfolds are we allowed access to the identity of those who make up the crowd, and this is important for Luke's narrative rhetoric since it portends all the more the turning of every imaginable force against Jesus and the divine purpose. Luke's account also highlights the control Jesus exercises in this scene. Apart from his followers, who refer to him as "lord," no one speaks in this narrative other than Jesus, and he speaks primarily to disclose the motivations of Judas and the Jewish officials who have come out against him. With these words, together with the reprimand his disciples receive from him, Jesus demonstrates that, in spite of appearances, he is the true master of the unfolding circumstances that will lead eventually to the judgment against him.

47-48 The participial "while he was still speaking" relates this scene to the former one both temporally and hermeneutically. Jesus had just arisen from prayer and begun to instruct his disciples about the need to pray in anticipation of the "time of trial." That time had now come, so it is enlightening to see how Jesus and his disciples respond in its context. Jesus, who had struggled in prayer, comes to this encounter in a state of composed mastery; his disciples, who have been sleeping rather than praying, face the ordeal with agitation and miscomprehension.

Luke's introduction of the arresting party is subtle. He names those who appear simply as a "crowd."[1] Given the largely positive or, at worst, generally neutral role of crowds within the Lukan narrative, at this early juncture in this scene we might be tempted to imagine that Jesus is being enveloped by his supporters. Indeed, "crowds" have included those who support him (e.g., 14:25; 18:36), and the "crowd" has functioned as a buffer between Jesus and his opponents (e.g., 13:14, 17; 22:6). Luke has also used the term "crowd" in a negative way (19:3), however, and some among the supportive crowds have opposed him (19:39). Nevertheless, our sense of the crowds in Luke is generally positive, a reading that in this case Luke will counter only in stages. In fact, the present "crowd" begins to be defined, first, by its association with Judas.

Luke's account has left open at what point Judas departed the company of Jesus and the apostles in order to take up his role as betrayer. He had been present at the meal earlier in the evening (v 21), but his actions are not otherwise recorded. If his sudden appearance apart from Jesus and his band is unforeseen, the nature of his activity is not. Since his first introduction we have known Judas as a traitor (6:17) — a travesty marked again by his identification as "one of the twelve." Earlier in the Third Gospel, the "kiss" was a sign of genuine openness to Jesus and reception of his message (7:38, 45), so it is not surprising that Luke records Jesus interrupting Judas's attempt to kiss him. Here, as in vv 21-22, Judas's treachery is thus portrayed as a betrayal of intimacy (cf. 21:16).

Judas may be cast as a leader of this crowd and may have taken the initiative to greet Jesus, but it is Jesus who now acts to seize the initiative from Judas and those with him. Even if we do not yet understand the nature of these unfolding events, Jesus does. With prophetic insight, using language that echoes the earlier predictions of the suffering of the Son of Man (esp. 9:44; 22:21-22; cf. 22:4, 6), Jesus identifies Judas's perfidious intention.

49-51   The nature of the crowd that has appeared with Judas on the Mount of Olives is qualified further by the anxious response of Jesus' followers;[2] that is, they act as though a hostile throng had come into view. Earlier, they had misinterpreted Jesus' words about the sword (vv 34, 38); having slept rather than prepared themselves for this moment in prayer, they now misconstrue who is in charge of this progression of events. Seeing "what will be," they are unable to visualize how God's purpose might be served by betrayal and arrest. These misconceptions coalesce in an impetuous attempt

1. ὄχλος.
2. That "those who were around him" refers to Jesus' disciples is clear from their address of him as "Lord," a form of address used with regularity by the narrator and only otherwise by those who follow Jesus.

at resistance. The question, "Lord, should we strike with the sword?" only underscores their obtuseness, for they name Jesus as their master but neither effectively discern the relevance of his life message for this happenstance nor even wait for his response. Jesus' reply is a sharp admonishment, calling attention to how far his followers have overstepped themselves.[3]

The crowd is further defined by the mention of "the slave of the high priest," presumably the high priest's personal representative functioning as a leader of the posse whom Judas had served as guide.[4] His presence in the crowd again points to its hostile makeup.

That Jesus heals the ear of such a person emphasizes the depth of the apostles' misunderstanding of his message. In a general sense, Jesus' divine mission embraces healing, and Luke's description of Jesus' act on behalf of the slave draws on language now familiar to readers of Luke's accounts of the miraculous.[5] More important, though, is Jesus' teaching with regard to love of enemy, including the doing of good on behalf of one's foes (6:27-36). This act of healing on behalf of one whose life was not threatened manifests the character of Jesus' message throughout the Gospel, just as it also antici- pates Jesus' dying request that his enemies be forgiven (23:34). Additionally, it prepares for the emphasis in the Roman hearings on the innocence of Jesus (23:1-22); he is no "bandit" (see v 52).

52-53 Finally, after the aforementioned hints about the makeup of the crowd, Luke names its members explicitly. In doing so, he draws together representatives from earlier passion predictions and from among those who have conspired against Jesus — chief priests, officers of the temple police, and elders (esp. vv 2, 4; cf. Acts 4:1, 5). Jesus' reference to "bandits" is ironic. By counteracting the violence done by his apostles, he has proven that he is not a person of violence.[6] They, on the other hand, have come with weapons, ready for violence, proving the appropriateness of Jesus' earlier character- ization of the Jewish leadership as "brigands" who withdraw into the temple in order to camouflage their violent deeds (see above on 19:46; see also, e.g., 20:47). Reference to teaching in the temple recalls the heightening conflict generated by Jesus' proclamation of the good news in the temple and his interactions with those whose authority rested in the temple system (chs. 20–21). There, their hostile intentions were held at bay by the support of the

---

3. For the translation of ἐᾶτε ἕως τούτου, "Let that be enough!" see the comments in R. E. Brown, *Death of the Messiah*, 1:280.

4. See G. Schneider, "Verhaftung," 202. The importance of this figure among the arresting party is suggested by the definite article, ὁ δοῦλος.

5. For the use of ἅπτω in healing contexts, see, e.g., 4:40; 7:14; 14:4; Theissen, *Miracle Stories*, 62, 92-93. For ἰάομαι, see 5:17; 6:18, 19; 7:7; 8:47; 9:2, 11, 42; 14:4; 17:15.

6. That is, a λῃστής; cf. *TLNT*, 2:390.

crowds (cf. 19:47-48; 20:1, 19), but now those who oppose Jesus have become the "crowd" that comes out to put an end to Jesus' ministry. Through this slow metamorphosis of the image of the "crowd," from a presumably neutral or even positive entity (v 47) to this most hostile of forces, Luke may be raising the question of how the previously supportive crowds, the people of Israel themselves, will come to look upon the arrest of Jesus (ch. 23).

Whatever subtlety Luke has employed with the crowd-motif is set aside in his record of Jesus' final words before his arrest. "Your hour" refers to the hour of the arrest (cf. 20:19), but this is cast in diabolic terms. As Luke will later record, "darkness" is symbolic of the authority of Satan (Acts 26:18); correlating "your hour" and "the power of darkness," Luke casts the temple authorities as instruments of Satan. This helps further to explain the collusion between Judas and the temple leadership: They share the bond of diabolic influence (22:3).

7.4. PETER AND JESUS AT THE HIGH PRIEST'S MANSION (22:54-65)

> 54 Then they seized him and led him away, bringing him into the high priest's house. But Peter was following at a distance. 55 When they had kindled a fire in the middle of the courtyard and sat down together, Peter sat among them. 56 Then a servant-girl, seeing him in the firelight, stared at him and said, "This man also was with him." 57 But he denied it, saying, "Woman, I do not know him." 58 A little later someone else, on seeing him, said, "You also are one of them." But Peter said, "Man, I am not!" 59 Then about an hour later still another kept insisting, "Surely this man also was with him; for he is a Galilean." 60 But Peter said, "Man, I do not know what you are talking about!" At that moment, while he was still speaking, the cock crowed. 61 The Lord turned and looked at Peter. Then Peter remembered the word of the Lord, how he had said to him, "Before the cock crows today, you will deny me three times." 62 And he went out and wept bitterly.
> 63 Now the men who were holding Jesus began to mock him and beat him; 64 they also blindfolded him and kept asking him, "Prophesy! Who is it that struck you?" 65 They kept heaping many other insults on him.

Since the scene on the Mount of Olives, Luke has maintained a narrow focus on activity and interchange surrounding Jesus, consistently locating him as the deictic center of the narrative. This continues in the current scene, with the result that, at least temporarily and with only one exception, neither the fate nor the whereabouts of Jesus' followers are on the horizon of Luke's interests following the arrest. Peter is mentioned of course, but his role in the narrative is primarily related to demonstrating that Jesus is truly a prophet. After all, Jesus had foretold the primary events of this scene — both Peter's threefold denial before the crowing of the cock (v 34 → vv 56-61) and his own maltreatment (esp. 18:32; cf. 20:10-11 → 22:63-65). Not least in light of Luke's reference to Jesus' earlier prediction as "the word of the Lord" (v 61), which recalls the designation of prophetic speech earlier in the Gospel and in the OT (e.g., 3:2; Hos 1:1; Joel 1:1), the cruel game Jesus' captors play with him can only be understood by Luke's audience as ironic: It is to a genuine prophet that they address the demand, "Play the prophet!"

This means that, throughout this scene, Luke has given special care to the issue of staging.[1] First, he locates both Jesus and Peter geographically in the high priest's mansion — that is, in the courtyard of the high priest's quarters. Then, having established Jesus' role as a prophet by narrating the precise fulfillment of his prediction concerning Peter, he clears the stage of Peter so that the narrative focus might remain centrally on Jesus. This means not only that Jesus was the object of Peter's denial, but also that he was witness to Peter's failure. This underscores all the more the portrait Luke paints of Jesus' resolve, his assurance concerning the unfolding of the divine plan, as he faces abuse at the hands of the Jewish leadership.

Even if this scene is only secondarily concerned with Peter, it nonetheless contributes to Luke's characterization of this one who would exercise leadership in the opening chapters of Acts.[2] This scene recounts Peter's failure, but it is not absolute.[3] Indeed, Jesus had interpreted Peter's actions in this episode as grounded in satanic promptings in advance (v 31), and had assured Peter of his own intercession on Peter's behalf, guaranteeing him recovery (v 32). What is more, in spite of the mistaken bravado Peter exerts in v 33, in the end he finds himself where he had begun, recognizing that he is a sinful person (5:8). In Acts 4–5 Luke will go on to recount Peter's boldness in the face of prison and death when he again finds himself in the presence of the Jewish authorities.

54-55 Only after Jesus has finished his discourse to "the chief priests, the officers of the temple police, and the elders" (vv 52-53) are they allowed to arrest him. This highlights Jesus' command of the situation, in spite of appearances to the contrary. Luke's account thus also designates these Jewish

1. See Soards, "Luke 22,61," 518; *idem,* "Literary Analysis," 115.
2. Cf. Brawley, *Centering on God,* 139-47, esp. 141-42, 144; Dietrich, *Petrusbild,* esp. 154-57.
3. See 12:4-5, 9-10.

leaders as the "they" who arrest Jesus, lead him away, bring him into the high priest's estate, kindle a fire in the high priest's courtyard, and who, eventually, abuse Jesus in the courtyard. The portrait of Peter at this point is ambiguous: he follows, as a disciple, but he does so "at a distance" — the position of the unfaithful friend in the tradition of the Suffering Righteous (cf. Ps 38:11).[4] Moreover, although Peter's sitting "among them" by the fire prepares for and allows his recognition "in the firelight" by the servant-girl in v 56, it also isolates Peter in the company of Jesus' enemies inside the courtyard of their leader, the high priest.

56-60a   Jesus had predicted Peter's threefold denial in v 34; now Luke recounts the fulfillment of Jesus' prophecy in dramatic fashion punctuated by its staccatolike style. In quick succession, Peter denies that he knows Jesus (v 57, echoing v 34),[5] that he is associated with Jesus' followers (v 58), and finally his association with Jesus from the beginning of the ministry in Galilee (vv 59-60). Luke adds to the intensity of this scene, first, by noting the passing of time between each confrontation, allowing Peter opportunity to reconsider his position and to reflect on Jesus' earlier teaching regarding the importance of acknowledging Jesus before others and the promise of divine provision in the midst of examinations such as the one he is experiencing (e.g., 9:23-26; 12:4-12; 21:12-19). Although the pacing of these three denials may be prolonged by these time references at one level, however, there is no sluggishness at the level of the narrative presentation of these encounters, where one denial follows rapidly on the other.

Second, as we have already intimated, Luke records an escalation in the substance of Peter's denial. At one level, with the first exchange, Peter's denial is complete; in disavowing personal knowledge of Jesus, he has done precisely what Jesus had predicted. That he was pressed to this testimony by a servant-girl — that is, by one of only peripheral status in the Mediterranean world — contributes further to Peter's shame. What more can Peter deny? He goes on to denounce his relationship to his fellow disciples, thus marking how his disavowal of Jesus is expressed in his loss of kinship with Jesus' followers. Finally, the reference to Peter's Galilean origins[6] recalls Peter's first encounter with Jesus on the shore of the lake, his having left everything to follow Jesus, his receiving the name "Peter" from Jesus, and his participation with Jesus from the very outset of his ministry in Galilee. Thus, everything central to Peter's construction of his new identity since becoming a follower of Jesus he has now thrust aside. Just as the first denial had taken up the language of

---

4. Cf. Ruppert, *Der leidende Gerechte,* 85-96.

5. 22:34: με ἀπαρνήσῃ εἰδέναι; 22:57: ἠρνήσατο . . . οὐκ οἶδα αὐτόν.

6. Luke does not indicate how Peter was recognized as a Galilean, but possibilities include his dialect, his accent, and/or his clothing.

Jesus' prediction, so the latter two have linguistic connections within Luke 22. It is ironic that Peter had boldly proclaimed that he was ready to go *with* Jesus to prison and death (v 33), then denies that he was *with* Jesus at all (vv 59-60);[7] and, before the inquiry, that Peter's words, "I am not!" (v 58), contrast so pointedly with Jesus' own words, "I am" (v 70; see below).[8]

Mention of Galilee may bring into consideration other reverberations from the Lukan narrative. Galilee has been associated with its ruler, Herod, known for his execution of John and desire to see Jesus (cf. 3:2; 9:7-9); might this prepare for the trial scene (23:6-12)? In addition, Jesus had earlier been informed about "the Galileans whose blood Pilate had mingled with their sacrifices" (13:1-2); how might memory of the fate of these other Galileans in Jerusalem shape apprehensions about the unfolding narrative of this Galilean in Jerusalem?

60b-62 Peter has scarcely gotten the third and final denial out of his mouth when the cock crows; in this way, Luke underscores how Peter's behavior fulfills Jesus' prophecy in v 34.[9] The sound of the rooster may confirm Jesus' status as a prophet, but Peter's memory is jogged not by the rooster but by the Lord's actions: turning and looking at Peter. The verb "to turn" appears in the Third Gospel when Jesus chides or admonishes his audience,[10] as he does here. In the present co-text, Jesus thus prompts Peter's memory, and this has two immediate repercussions. First, it allows Luke to certify that Jesus is an authentic prophet, whose word is "the word of the Lord,"[11] and whose prediction is fulfilled exactly as he had pronounced it.[12] In fact, for the narrator, this is an important christological moment, which he highlights by employing the designation "Lord" twice in immediate proximity. The juxtaposition of these two phrases, "the Lord" and "the word of the Lord," indicates that Luke thinks of Jesus as more than a prophet who speaks on behalf of Yahweh. He is rather one who possesses divine agency, who speaks and acts for God with divine authority. Second, memory moves Peter to action — in this case, to the sort of lament known earlier in Luke as an acknowledgment of one's own sinfulness or a precursor to the reversal that comes with divine restoration (6:21; 7:13, 38;

---

7. 22:33: μετὰ σοῦ . . . ; 22:59: καὶ οὗτος μετ᾽ αὐτοῦ ἦν.

8. 22:58: οὐκ εἰμί; 22:70: ὑμεῖς λέγετε ὅτι ἐγώ εἰμι.

9. Thus, Luke's use of παραχρῆμα. Attempts to discover the timing of this and related events on this night of Jesus' passion by determining the time of the "cock crow" lie outside the narrator's interests and are probably doomed to failure; as Cicero observes, "Is there any time, night or day, that cocks do not crow?" (*De divinatione* 2.26.56; R. E. Brown, *Death of the Messiah,* 1:607).

10. See 7:9, 44; 9:55; 10:23; 14:25; 23:28.

11. See above, the introduction to this narrative unit.

12. For this criterion for determining genuine prophecy, see Deut 18:22.

8:52). "Weeping" marks the beginning of Peter's "turning" (cf. v 32), even if, on account of his particular focus on Jesus, Luke now dismisses Peter from the scene.[13]

63-65 Peter's threefold denial is not the only part of this scene grounded in Jesus' predictive word. In his passion predictions, Jesus had repeatedly anticipated his abuse — and had specifically forecast his being mocked (18:32) and, in a parabolic text, had noted how a delegate from the vineyard owner was beaten (20:10-11).[14] What is more, the OT speaks of the abuse of the prophets (1 Kgs 22:24-28; Jer 28:10-16), and Jesus had repeatedly spoken of the fate of the rejected prophets (4:24; 6:22-23; 11:47-51; 13:33-35; 20:9-18). In these ways, the scene of Jesus' abuse at the hands of the Jewish leaders works together with the account of Peter's denial to portray Jesus as a prophet (i.e., as at least a prophet — cf. 7:16; 9:8, 19), to indicate his solidarity with God's agents who speak on God's behalf and are rejected. This picture is furthered in an ironic way by the game Jesus' captors play with him, asking him to exercise prophetic insight (cf. 7:39) in order to identify who is striking him. All of this prepares for Jesus' indictment before Pilate as a false prophet (see on 23:2, 5, 14).

Who abuses Jesus thus? Luke names "the men who were holding Jesus," a phrase whose antecedent is the arresting party itself, described in v 52: "the chief priests, the officers of the temple police, and the elders." The personal role of the Jewish leadership in this ignominious affair clearly marks their culpability in the actions taken against Jesus.[15] Although the Greek text may be accurately represented by the NRSV's reference to the "many other insults" heaped upon Jesus, Luke's readers may hear something of even greater significance. Insofar as Jesus has just been referred to as "Lord" by the narrator (v 61), the verb "to blaspheme" may connote not only disrespect and slander, but blasphemy in the more weighty, religious sense of denigrating

---

13. Fitzmyer (2:1465) sees in Luke's words "[Peter] went out," Luke's narration of Peter's abandoning Jesus, but this overlooks how often Luke moves characters on and off the stage for purposes of focusing.

14. ἐμπαίζω is used in the Third Gospel in 14:29; 19:32; 23:11, 36, as well as in 22:63. For δέρω, see, in addition to v 63, 12:47-48; 20:10-11.

15. *Contra* G. Schneider (*Verleugnung,* 98-99), whose view that the role of the Jerusalem sanhedrin is lessened in the Lukan scene overlooks the fact that "the men who were holding Jesus" can refer only to those who came out to arrest him (vv 52-53). Although the arresting party is not the sanhedrin formally gathered, the arresting party manifestly includes members of the sanhedrin. Even more problematic is the view of Neyrey, *Passion according to Luke,* 70; he erroneously equates "Israel" with these Jewish leaders who abuse Jesus ("Luke's account presents Israel's rejection of God's prophet") — a mistake Luke himself does not make. See the discussion in Weatherly, *Jewish Responsibility,* 60-61.

THE GOSPEL OF LUKE

the power of God.[16] In this case, Luke would be describing this whole scene as blasphemous, indicating that those who oppose Jesus in this way have actually set themselves up in opposition to God.

7.5. THE TRIAL OF JESUS (22:66–23:25)

If the scene on the Mount of Olives (22:39-46) constitutes the watershed in the passion narrative, the critical point at which Jesus unreservedly embraces faithfulness to the divine will even in the face of impending death, the narrative unit focused on Jesus' trial comprises the ascendancy of what Jesus had termed "your hour and the power of darkness" (22:53). It is here that the Jewish leaders are able, however temporarily, to win the people of Israel gathered in Jerusalem away from Jesus' leadership, and thus to overwhelm Pilate and, in spite of his protestations concerning Jesus' innocence, to gain from Pilate a sentence of execution by crucifixion. Even if the act of crucifixion must await the subsequent narrative section (23:26-49), the actions Luke will narrate there are only the aftermath of decisions made here. Ironically, as Jesus, the narrator, and Luke's audience are aware, even these decisions, as heinous and tragic as they may be, are only the outworking of the ancient divine purpose.

Indeed, Luke has provided his audience with a double irony: In calling for Jesus' execution, the Jewish leaders think that they are acting on God's behalf by doing away with one who, in their view, opposes God's purpose, but in opposing Jesus they are actually opposing the very divine purpose they had thought to serve; yet, their instrumentality in Jesus' crucifixion, thus ironically conceived in opposition to the divine plan, actually serves that plan! From this morass of aims and counteraims will come the perspective taken within the speeches in Acts — namely, that the Jewish leaders may have unwittingly served the divine plan but are nonetheless culpable for their actions.[1]

The narrative unit concerned with Jesus' trial has four scenes: the hearing before the sanhedrin (22:66-71), the hearing before Pilate (23:1-5), the hearing before Herod (23:6-12), and the sentencing of Jesus (23:13-25). Although Jesus appears in each scene, following his understated and enigmatic response to the Jewish council (22:68-70) and to Pilate (23:3), he falls silent

---

16. βλασφημέω may have the nuance of "slander" or "defame," or the more particularly religious sense of dishonoring God. Hofius ("βλασφημία," 220) observes that these two renderings are interconnected in the scene in which Jesus is ridiculed: The mockery of Jesus is also the mockery of God. See also Johnson, 358; R. E. Brown, *Death of the Messiah*, 1:583.

1. See, e.g., Matera, "Death of Jesus"; Matera notes that this perspective is developed in order to call the Jewish leaders and the Jews in Jerusalem to repentance.

and is a passive participant in his own trial and sentencing. Otherwise, the single constant in this narrative unit is the active presence of the Jewish leadership. They are obviously and necessarily central in the first hearing, but also appear as Jesus' accusers before Pilate (23:2, 5) and Herod (23:10); when Jesus is returned to Pilate, they are again present, calling for Jesus' demise (23:13). Luke describes the Jerusalem leadership variously, calling them "elders" in 22:66 and "leaders" in 23:13, and otherwise parsing this company as chief priests (22:66; 23:4, 10), scribes (22:66; 23:10), and "the crowds" (23:4; cf. 22:47). Especially against the backdrop of Rome's attempt to exonerate Jesus (23:4, 14-15, 22), it is evident that Jesus' death is the consequence of the relentless and overpowering presence of the Jewish leadership. This is underscored particularly by Luke's climactic observation, "their voices prevailed" (23:23).[2] The motif of the power of their persistence is also developed in the variety of ways Luke adds texture to the nature of their accusations: they were "insistent" (23:5), they accused him "vehemently" (23:10), they "all" shouted "together" (23:10), and they "kept urgently demanding with loud shouts" (23:23).

As Luke paints it, even the resolute activity of the Jewish leaders against Jesus was not enough to assure his crucifixion. Also required was the complicity of the Jews in Jerusalem, heretofore aligned with Jesus (e.g., 19:48; 21:37-38; 22:2, 6). Though their participation is temporary and qualified, the people too are set against Jesus and call for his death (23:13, 18-25).[3]

2. "It is not Roman justice but the desire of the Jewish people — especially their leaders — that prevails" (Carroll and Green, *Death of Jesus,* 73).

3. *Contra,* e.g., Cassidy (*Jesus, Politics, and Society,* 70-71; *idem,* "Luke's Audience," 150-52), who denies that Luke in any way infers that the Jewish people as a whole were involved. He discounts the relevance of v 13, arguing that Pilate has called "the people" forward in order to counter the perspective and demands of the chief priests. Similarly, Chance ("Jewish People," 55-56; cf. *idem, Jerusalem,* 70) insists that, though "the people" are on the stage in 23:13-16, Pilate is concerned to address only the Jewish leaders. Tiede (*Prophecy and History,* 112; followed by Chance, "Jewish People," 59) avers the "double bind of the people" — namely, having come to Pilate in Jesus' defense, if they were to cry out in his defense they would only give substance to the charge of sedition brought against him. However, even if the "you" in 23:14 evidently refers to the Jewish assembly in 23:1 (as Chance rightly notes), Pilate seems to make no distinction between the Jewish people and their leaders, and, indeed, demonstrates his concern with leaders and people by calling them together in 23:13 (*contra* Chance). Nor do the people come of their own accord, as Cassidy and Tiede seem to require, nor does Luke give any hint whatsoever in this co-text that the people are motivated in some way that would distinguish them from their leaders. Nor elsewhere in the Third Gospel does Luke provide insight into the potential self-direction of the people — who seem, then, perpetually in need of leadership. What is more, Luke acknowledges that "they all shouted out together" (23:18; and not, "some of them shouted" or "the leaders shouted"), a reaction that carries with it, then, the strong intimation that the people have returned to the chief priests and their allies for leadership.

This heightening of Jewish responsibility for Jesus' death should not be taken as an attempt on the part of the Third Evangelist to exonerate the Romans, however. Although Rome, in the persons of Herod and Pilate, might witness correctly to Jesus' innocence, Luke's position is decidedly not pro-Roman. Otherwise, Pilate would not have allowed this miscarriage of justice, but would have freed Jesus as he twice intended (23:16, 22).[4] What is more, although Pilate and Herod side against the Jewish leaders in declaring Jesus innocent, these Roman rulers side with the chief priests and their allies in their refusal to recognize Jesus' true identity as the ruler over the people of God.[5]

While making his final entry into Jerusalem, Jesus had been hailed as king. Upon entering Jerusalem, he had taken steps to restore the temple to its proper role within the divine plan and had won the support of the people (19:29-48). These incidents had given rise to questions from the chief priests, the scribes, and the elders concerning Jesus' authority (ch. 20) and, in an important sense, this is the focus of this new round of questions and charges. Now the Jewish assembly labels Jesus as a false prophet (see 23:2, 5, 8, 14),[6] an offense punishable by death according to Deuteronomy 13. They then represent this charge to the Roman governor in a way that explicitly raises the threat of Jesus to the Roman Empire, parlaying their allegation against Jesus as a false prophet into messianic and royal terms.[7] The question to which Pilate is steered concerns Jesus' kingship, since execution (by crucifixion) was the fate of persons implicated in sedition. This is not mere political maneuvering on the part of the chief priests and their allies, however; in their own hearing they had put to Jesus the question whether he was the Messiah, the Son of God, and in this way they provide indirect testimony to what Luke's audience already knows. This is that Jesus is more than a prophet. He is the regal prophet, the Messiah, the Son of God (cf. esp. 1:32-35; 4:16-30).

7.5.1. The Hearing before the Sanhedrin (22:66-71)

66 *When day came, the assembly of the elders of the people, both chief priests and scribes, gathered together, and they brought him to their council.* 67 *They said, "If you are the Messiah, tell us." He replied, "If I tell you, you will not believe;* 68 *and if I question you, you will not answer.* 69 *But from now on the Son of Man will be seated at the*

---

4. See the parallel problem in the trials of Paul, Acts 25:25-27; 26:30-32.
5. See Acts 4:26-28; cf. Tyson, *Death of Jesus,* 127; Carlson, "Jewish People," 83.
6. Cf. Strobel, *Stunde der Wahrheit.*
7. See Carroll and Green, *Death of Jesus,* 174-75.

*right hand of the power of God." 70 All of them asked, "Are you, then,
the Son of God?" He said to them, "You say that I am." 71 Then they
said, "What further testimony do we need? We have heard it ourselves
from his own lips!"*

Although each of the four scenes of this section concerned with Jesus' trial
(22:66–23:25) is carefully woven into the other in order to achieve a coherent
account, the hearing before the Jewish leadership is particularly poignant for
the way it brings together two important elements of the Lukan narrative.
First, the mention of elders, chief priests, and scribes cannot help but recall
the first passion prediction, proclaiming the divine necessity that these very
persons would reject the Son of Man (9:22; cf. 17:25). The narrator thus draws
attention to the realization of the divine purpose in Jesus' passion. Second,
since 19:47 the chief priests, scribes, and leaders of the people (or some
comparable alliance) have been seeking to do away with Jesus (cf. 20:19;
22:2); the present scene recounts the culmination of their hostility toward him,
together with their formal rejection of any legitimate status he might have as
God's agent. In the conjunction of these two narrative elements resides a tragic
irony,[8] as the purpose of God is brought to completion by the very ones who
have most adamantly resisted that purpose. More specifically, the Jewish
leaders are provided all of the evidence they need to recognize Jesus as the
Messiah, the Son of God;[9] but, failing to believe (as he has prophesied, v 67),
ironically they interpret this evidence at his expense.

Fundamentally, the issue at stake is the same as has pervaded the
presentation of the Jewish leadership in the Third Gospel. Who interprets the
will of God correctly? Who legitimately exercises the authority of God? Who
will rule the people of God? Almost from the beginning of Jesus' Galilean
ministry, the legal experts (including those from Jerusalem, 5:17) have involved themselves in the task of monitoring Jesus' behavior to determine its
conformity with official norms. Since his arrival in Jerusalem, Jesus' authority
has been in question on account of his attempts at restoring the temple to its
legitimate role in God's design. In fact, from 19:45 to 21:38 Luke has portrayed
Jesus as a regal figure whose exercise of authority has been aimed at displacing
the authority of the temple establishment, and who has won the support of
the people. With him now in custody, it is no surprise that the Jewish assembly
is concerned with only one issue — namely, his identity and status before
God.[10] The degree to which Luke has prepared for this scene by reports of

8. The irony of this scene is developed in detail by Heil, "Luke 22:66-71."
9. Cf. Strauss, *Davidic Messiah*, 320-21.
10. See Matera, "Jesus before the ΠΡΕΣΒΥΤΕΡΙΟΝ," 525-27; Carlson, "Jewish
People," 92.

the crescendo of hostility toward Jesus on the part of those who now gather against him helps to explain the substance of the interchange Luke recounts. It also explains its brevity: The messianic question has been well anticipated in the larger narrative, so no buildup is necessary in the context of the hearing itself.

66 Luke apparently envisions Jesus' having been held in the courtyard of the high priest throughout the night, then brought to the chambers of the Jewish council the following morning.[11] This pattern is replicated in Acts, where witnesses are arrested and held in custody for a morning hearing (Acts 4:1-5; 5:17-21; 22:30). Those gathered have appeared before in the Lukan narrative, in Jesus' first passion prediction (9:22) and as Jesus' opponents.[12]

67-70 After the specific mention of the high priest in v 54, it may be surprising that, in the Lukan narration, the questions of Jesus come from the Jewish council as a whole (v 67: "they"; v 70: "all of them"). This is not because Luke is ignorant of the high priest's role as convener of and spokesperson for the council (cf. Acts 5:27-28; 23:1-5); rather, from the Lukan perspective, the whole of the temple establishment is joined in solidarity against Jesus. (This emphasis will be highlighted [23:1], then mollified [23:50-51] later in the narrative.)

The first question put to Jesus, regarding his messiahship, is suspiciously similar in form to the temptations posed by the devil much earlier in the narrative (4:3, 9); given the collocation of "Messiah" and "Son of God" in 1:32-35, the council's first question and the requests of the devil ("If you are the Son of God . . .") are also comparable in substance. Insofar as the activity of the Jewish leadership in Jerusalem has already been interpreted as diabolic (see above on v 53), this connection is not surprising. For Luke's audience, it has been made abundantly clear that Jesus is the Messiah (e.g., 2:11, 26; 4:41; 9:20; 20:41-44), even though Jesus has not himself affirmed his messianic status. It is nonetheless ironic that the sanhedrin has thus pre-

---

11. ἀπάγω is often used with reference to taking prisoners to justice — cf. Schneider, *Verleugnung,* 109-10. Luke's τὸ συνέδριον might refer to "the council itself" (cf. Acts 4:5; 5:21, 27; 22:30; 23:1, 15, 20, 28; 24:20), but it may be used to designate a place in Acts 4:15; 5:34, 41; 6:12, 15; 23:6. The presence of both εἰς (i.e., "into a place") and αὐτῶν (i.e., "their [the elders']" sanhedrin) speaks in favor of the latter sense.

12. For discussion, see above on 9:22. Neyrey (*Passion according to Luke,* esp. 71, 75) wrongly sees these persons as representatives of all Israel; Neyrey regularly overlooks the care with which Luke typically segregates the view of the people vis-à-vis Jesus from those of their leaders. Luke's τὸ πρεσβυτέριον τοῦ λαοῦ could be taken as a reference to a group of "elders" alongside the chief priests and scribes (cf. 9:22; 20:1; cf. 22:52), but in the only other two uses of the noun, Acts 22:5 and 1 Tim 4:14, τὸ πρεσβυτέριον designates the whole (Jewish) council. Moreover, "chief priests" and "legal experts" are joined in v 66 by τε καί, whereas τὸ πρεσβυτέριον τοῦ λαοῦ has no connective.

sented Jesus with a request the effect of which would operate at two levels simultaneously: In seeking evidence by which to condemn Jesus, the Jewish council is unwittingly requesting confirmation of his messianic status that would invite appropriate responses of support and faithfulness.[13]

Jesus' response takes the grammatical form of a future-more-vivid conditional sentence, indicating his conviction that the Jewish leadership will almost certainly not believe him or answer his questions.[14] That they will not answer Jesus has already been indicated in earlier dialogue in the temple (ch. 20). In particular, when Jesus asks concerning the legitimacy of John's baptism, they refused to answer him in a straightforward way (20:1-8). Added to this now is Jesus' expectation that, even if faced with direct evidence of Jesus' messiahship, the Jewish leaders would be incapable of belief (cf. Acts 13:40-41). Constrained in their own unreconstructed, self-legitimating views of God's purpose, they are incapable of grasping the truth that the ministry of Jesus is nothing less than the drawing near of the redemptive purpose of God. Since Jesus' entry into Jerusalem they have demonstrated their resistance to Jesus and their inability to discern in his advent the salvific visitation of God (see 19:41-48), and now Jesus pronounces them intractable in their unbelief.

Jesus qualifies his answer with reference to the Son of Man. The phrase "from now on"[15] appears repeatedly in the Lukan narrative to demarcate a new beginning. Previously, the Son of Man title has been developed in conjunction with portents of the rejection and humiliation of Jesus, with relatively brief intimations of vindication.[16] Standing before the sanhedrin, Jesus now experiences the indignity he had predicted (esp. vv 63-65). In this context, however, Jesus asserts that wrapped up in the culmination of his ignominy is the promise of status reversal. Dishonor will give way to highest honor![17] Indeed, drawing on the enthronement images of Ps 110:1, Jesus proleptically announces his reign at God's right hand. Since Luke has repeatedly portrayed Jesus as a reliable prophet (including prophecies of humiliation, now being fulfilled), Luke's audience may with good reason anticipate that Jesus' exaltation will take place shortly — an expectation that is met within the narrative

13. Heil, "Luke 22:66-71," 277; cf. Tyson, *Death of Jesus,* 125-26.

14. Cf. Jer 38:15, a parallel that adds to the portrayal of Jesus in this co-text as a prophet.

15. ἀπὸ τοῦ νῦν — cf. 1:48; 5:10; 12:52; 22:18; Acts 18:6.

16. See 6:22; 7:34; 9:22, 26, 44, 58; 17:24-25; 18:31-33. See Acts 7:56. Kingsbury (*Conflict in Luke,* 73-78) observes that the designation "Son of Man" functions for the Third Evangelist to hold in tandem the two features of Jesus' career, repudiation and vindication.

17. The notion that the Son of Man will sit in judgment, while present in 9:26; 12:8, is altogether lacking in Jesus' response, which is focused more narrowly on the experience of exaltation — cf. R. E. Brown, *Death of the Messiah,* 1:504.

(see Acts 1:6-11; 2:33-36). Why does Jesus speak of "the power of God"? On the one hand, this associates Jesus with divine power, in sharp contrast to the "power" being exercised by the Jewish leadership before whom he speaks — namely, "the power of darkness," diabolic power (cf. v 53; Acts 26:18). On the other, the ministry of Jesus has already been characterized as the arena in which the power of God is exercised (e.g., 4:36; 5:17), and it is this power that Jesus will assign to his followers for their work as witnesses upon his exaltation (cf. Acts 1:8; 2:33).

Of course, unlike Luke's readers, those of the Jewish council do not have the benefit of the interpretive strategies provided by the Lukan narrative; hence, they hear Jesus' words somewhat differently. For them, the enthrone-ment language Jesus borrows from Ps 110:1 is reminiscent of the similar imagery of Ps 2:6-7, in which the anointed of Yahweh is enthroned on Zion and designated son of God. For them, then, Jesus' initial, antagonistic response (vv 67-68) gives way to an apparent admission that he is the Lord's Anointed One, the Messiah.[18] This gives rise to their question, "Are you, then, the Son of God?" — which, from the Lukan perspective, is virtually the same question as before.[19] What is again ironic is that the Jerusalem leaders thus correctly infer Jesus' status, but this leads to their rejection rather than belief. Jesus boldly answers that they have properly assessed his identity, but goes further to draw the sanhedrin into this same admission. That is, Jesus turns their accusation of him into an unwitting confession![20]

71 Luke's account of the hearing before the sanhedrin has included testimony from only one person, Jesus, but this is enough. Just as Jesus had predicted of his followers that being brought to trial would provide them the opportunity to testify (21:12-13), so it is in his own case. Earlier, Jesus' opponents had hoped to catch Jesus in his own words (11:53-54); now their hopes have come to pass.[21] Dramatically clear is that the sanhedrin now has enough evidence — to embrace Jesus as God's emissary or to repudiate his claim. Their response authenticates Jesus' words regarding their eventual unbelief, uttered in v 67b. Had Jesus not just said, "If I tell you, you will not believe"?

18. So Strauss, *Davidic Messiah,* 320-21.

19. On the virtual equation of the titles "Christ" and "Son of God," see 1:31-32; 4:31; Acts 9:20-21; *contra,* e.g., Senior, *Passion of Jesus,* 104; R. E. Brown, *Death of the Messiah,* 1:493.

20. Recognition of the irony at work in this scene leads to this rendering of Jesus' reply, ὑμεῖς λέγετε ὅτι ἐγώ εἰμι, as an affirmation — cf. Fitzmyer, 2:1463 ("He stresses that they are actually saying it, even if they do not believe it"), 1468 (guardedly); R. E. Brown, *Death of the Messiah,* 1:493; Heil, "Luke 22:66-71," 281. Others (e.g., Tyson, *Death of Jesus,* 127) think that Jesus' reply is ambiguous at best.

21. 11:54: τι ἐκ τοῦ στόματος αὐτοῦ; 22:71: ἀπὸ τοῦ στόματος αὐτοῦ; cf. 20:20.

7.5.2. The Hearing before Pilate (23:1-5)

> 23:1 *Then the assembly rose as a body and brought Jesus before Pilate.* 2 *They began to accuse him, saying, "We found this man perverting our nation, forbidding us to pay taxes to the emperor, and saying that he himself is the Messiah, a king."* 3 *Then Pilate asked him, "Are you the king of the Jews?" He answered, "You say so."* 4 *Then Pilate said to the chief priests and the crowds, "I find no basis for an accusation against this man."* 5 *But they were insistent and said, "He stirs up the people by teaching throughout all Judea, from Galilee where he began even to this place."*

As with the previous scene, this stage of Jesus' trial is tightly woven into Luke's narrative fabric. Although some have observed little relationship between the examination of Jesus before the sanhedrin (22:66-71) and the charges brought against Jesus,[22] a narrative analysis suggests the contrary. First, because the Jewish leadership, since Jesus' entry into Jerusalem in ch. 19, have been building a case against Jesus, and because their hostility toward Jesus has been so fully documented, Luke was able to present a more truncated account of their hearing than is now possible with Pilate. Heretofore, Luke has neither narrated an earlier encounter between Jesus and Pilate nor indicated explicitly how Pilate might be predisposed toward Jesus (cf. 3:1; 13:1). With the introduction of Pilate as jurist, then, it is necessary to provide in this scene some form of concrete indictment against Jesus. Second, in fact, the form of their indictment sums up the perspective of the Jewish leadership vis-à-vis Jesus. Luke's readers may know the charges enumerated by the Jewish assembly to be at best distorted representations of Jesus' ministry, but, from the perspective of the Jerusalem elite, they are plausible interpretations nonetheless.[23] In the scene before Pilate, then, we have a précis of the case against Jesus that had earlier been summarized even more succinctly in the question regarding Jesus' messiahship (22:67). This case is presented in a fashion that draws together Jewish concern with the identification of false prophets (Deuteronomy 13) and Roman apprehension regarding rebellion and civil disturbance.[24] Third, in the previous scene, Jesus turns the accusation brought

---

22. So, e.g., Tyson, *Death of Jesus,* 129.

23. So G. Schneider, "Political Charge," 408; Carroll and Green, *Death of Jesus,* 73. D. Schmidt ("Luke's Innocent Jesus") rightly argues that vv 2 and 5 represent "Luke's summary of how the chief priests and scribes understood Jesus" (111), but his overall argument does not account for the negative characterization of the Jerusalem leadership within the Lukan narrative; they misunderstand and misrepresent Jesus' ministry because they have aligned themselves against the redemptive purpose of God.

24. Cf. Rapske, *Roman Custody,* 41-44.

against him by the Jerusalem leadership into a confession of his messianic status, and he will do the same with Pilate's query. Though the sanhedrin and Pilate each deny him that status, this leads to divergent courses of action with regard to Jesus — one to decide against Jesus, the other to declare him guiltless.[25]

In addition, this scene has been anticipated in at least three ways. At the more implicit level, Pilate has been mentioned in the narrative on account of his execution of Galilean pilgrims in Jerusalem (13:1). This report may be otherwise unattested, but it is consistent with what is otherwise known of Pilate historically.[26] Given this reputation, what might Luke's audience anticipate of this encounter between Pilate and this Galilean pilgrim? Additionally, while Jesus was teaching in the temple he was asked concerning paying tribute to Caesar in a ploy to "hand him over to the jurisdiction and authority of the governor" (20:20-26); that scene helps to set the stage for this one (see v 2b). More explicitly, Jesus had foreseen his being "handed over to the Gentiles" as a prelude to his suffering and death (18:32). Here, then, is the culmination of the divine necessity that has dominated the Lukan narrative of Jesus' ministry. Later, Luke will ground this interpretation further in Psalm 2 (Acts 4:25-26).

The picture Luke paints is at once congruent with his narrative and historically believable.[27] That is, his account coheres with traditional Roman trial proceedings: accusations were made, charges formulated, opportunity for defense given, and judgment rendered. As we have already intimated, the charges brought against Jesus are likewise intelligible against the backdrop of Jewish and Roman history. These points add to the verisimilitude of Luke's account.

Study of the trial of Jesus in Luke is replete with distinctions between the "religious" character of the scene before the sanhedrin (22:66-71) and the "political" character of the present one, but such distinctions are the consequence of a gross anachronism. Similarly, it cannot be said that Luke has recounted this scene before Pilate in order to demonstrate that Jesus constituted no threat toward Rome.[28] To the contrary, as we have repeatedly seen in the Lukan narrative, the Jewish authorities exercise a political leadership that is religiously legitimated; hence, to undermine their religious views is to subvert

25. "Innocent" may be too strong a word to describe the result of Pilate's interrogation at this juncture. For example, Andriscus (149-148 B.C.E.), having been imprisoned as a royal pretender, was later released as harmless (Diodorus Siculus 32.15.3-4).

26. See above on 3:1; 13:1.

27. Cf. Acts 25:16; Sherwin-White, *Roman Society,* 24-26; Brandon, *Trial of Jesus,* 119-20.

28. *Contra,* e.g., Matera, *Passion Narratives,* 177: "Jesus' message has not been political; there is no danger to Rome" — to cite only one of many examples of this view.

their politics. The same is true for the Roman Empire — both as Luke has presented it and as is evident from Roman propaganda (see above, e.g., on 2:1-20). The "peace of Rome" was a consequence of divine sanction, so that the Roman ethos itself possessed a religious quality. To deviate from Roman social order was not only to invoke shame on oneself, then, but to violate the sacred. The "household" that was the Roman Empire was instituted and validated by the gods. The charges on which Jesus was presented to Rome's representative, Pilate, urge that Jesus had run afoul of the religio-political order, the world as it had been determined to be by the gods.[29]

What aim does this scene serve for Luke? If in this scene Pilate finds no basis for an accusation against Jesus, this is not because Jesus and his message constitute no threat to Rome; rather, one can conclude from this only that Pilate has thus far been unable to discern any such threat. To this degree, the sanhedrin proves to be more discerning than Rome; both deny Jesus' royal claim, but Rome alone regards him therefore as harmless. Against the backdrop of the Lukan narrative, this can only be regarded as a manifestation of Roman arrogance. Clearly, Pilate's actions cannot be construed as in any way supportive of Jesus or benign in his case, for otherwise Pilate would have followed through on his dismissal of charges by dismissing his prisoner. Hence, the purpose of this scene cannot be primarily to have Rome establish Jesus' innocence. Rather, it is, first, to indicate the religio-political nature of the charges brought against Jesus, and especially to establish the pattern for the ensuing stages of the trial: The Jewish leadership presses its case against Jesus in spite of Roman reticence to act against him, leading eventually to Jesus' execution.

1-2   The transition from the first phase of the trial of Jesus to the second is marked by the physical movement of the sanhedrin as they transfer Jesus to Pilate's custody (cf. 18:32). Luke's phrase "as a body" signifies the solidarity with which the assembly of the elders (22:66) acts.[30] The verbs "to lead" and "to accuse" are both at home in the judicial context Luke presents.[31]

Grammatical and co-textual evidence urges that, in fact, only one charge is brought against Jesus — namely, "We found this man perverting

---

29. See Green, *Gospel of Luke,* 119-21; Carroll and Green, *Death of Jesus,* 176-81.

30. For this view of ἅπαν τὸ πλῆθος αὐτῶν, see Acts 23:7; Büchele, *Tod Jesu,* 27; Chance, "Jewish People," 51. *Contra,* e.g., Matera ("Jesus before Pilate," 538), who thinks that Luke understands τὸ πλῆθος to include the people of Israel together with their rulers. τὸ πλῆθος may refer to "the people" in Luke-Acts, but when it does, a further signifier is required — e.g., 1:10; 6:17; in 23:1, the only modifier is αὐτῶν, which finds its antecedent in 22:66. On the relation of πλῆθος in v 1 to ὄχλοι in v 4, see below.

31. ἄγω + ἐπί is sometimes used under the influence of legal terminology — cf. Acts 18:12; Borse, "ἄγω." Of the 23 instances of κατηγόρεω in the NT, 22 have a juridical sense: "to bring charges" — cf., e.g., Acts 22:30; 24:2; Balz, "κατηγορέω."

our nation" (v 2).[32] The other two — "He forbids us to pay taxes to the emperor" and "He says that he himself is the Messiah, a king" — are then elaborations of the one charge, which is subsequently twice repeated:

v 2: This man perverts our nation
v 5: He stirs up the people
v 14: He perverts the people

Reference to "leading astray" or "perverting" constitutes a formal allegation against Jesus as a false prophet, rooted in Deuteronomy 13. Indeed, using the same verb, Luke recounts in Acts 13:6-8 that "a Jewish false prophet . . . tried *to turn* the proconsul *away* from the faith." Similarly, the LXX records allegations against Moses and Elijah — two prophets with whom Jesus is identified in the Lukan narrative — as persons who had attempted "to lead astray" (Exod 5:4: "my people"; 1 Kgs 18:17: "Israel").[33] The Jewish leaders take a comparable view, insisting that Jesus has attempted to lead Israel[34] astray. From their vantage point, this would mean that Jesus lacked divine sanction for his ministry, that he did not speak on behalf of Yahweh, and that his attempts at reform in the temple were not only wrongheaded but even treasonous against the way of the Lord; in Pilate's ears, "leading the people astray" would likely have been commensurate with rebellion and civil unrest. (See the analogous scene involving Paul in Acts 17:5-9.)

In order to articulate more fully the ramifications of their fundamental charge against Jesus for this Roman official, the Jewish assembly interprets for Pilate two aspects of Jesus' earlier teaching. The first has to do with payment of tribute to Caesar. Although typically present in English translations (as in the NRSV), the pronoun "us" does not appear in the Greek text; it seems, then, that the sanhedrin represents Jesus as one who teaches the nonpayment of tribute as a general policy. The question of tribute was raised in 20:20-26 for the purpose of trapping Jesus so as to hand him over to Pilate. Earlier, we saw that failure to pay the annual tribute was tantamount to disavowal of Roman rule, and that it was on this point of payment that Jesus had resisted a straightforward Yes/No answer. For Jesus, the demands of the Empire are relativized by the prior claims of the kingdom of God; when these claims come into conflict, one must choose which dominion one

32. The two participial phrases, καὶ κωλύοντα φόρους διδόναι and καὶ λέγοντα ἑαυτὸν χριστὸν βασιλέα εἶναι — are thus subordinate to the main charge, διαστρέφοντα; note the use of καὶ . . . καί to signify parallelism (BDF §444.3) as well as the parallel infinitives. Cf. Büchele, *Tod Jesu,* 28; Schneider, "Political Charge," 407-8.

33. See Stanton, "Jesus of Nazareth"; Carlson, "Jewish People," 92.

34. For the use of τὸ ἔθνος with reference to Israel, see 7:5; Acts 10:22; 24:2, 10; 26:4; 28:19.

will serve. According to this interpretive matrix, the Jewish council, in foregrounding this issue and assuming in their accusation the unwavering legitimacy of Caesar's claim, have failed to acknowledge the priority of God's dominion.

Second, the Jewish assembly adds substance to their accusation against Jesus as one who leads the people astray by announcing that he claims divine authority to rule the people. This is fully consonant with Luke's portrayal of Jesus as one who is more than a prophet, as one who would "reign over the house of Jacob" (1:33; cf. 2:11). Moreover, in 22:66-70 the Jewish leadership hear in Jesus' words an apparent admission that he is the Lord's Anointed One, the Messiah (see above). Although they are unwilling to grant him this status, they do find it an adroit means by which to allow Jesus to incriminate himself. Because the term "Messiah" is more at home in a Jewish setting, they translate this phrase along royal lines, as "king," for their Roman audience (cf. 9:20; 19:38; 22:29). The result is nothing less than the charge of sedition, claiming to be a king in opposition to Caesar (cf. Acts 17:7).

That these charges originate with the Jerusalem elite is important, since they have been characterized negatively in the Lukan narrative. Beginning already with Mary's Song, it has been clear that the eschatological, salvific work of God would involve bringing down such rulers as these (1:52), and Jesus' ministry in Jerusalem has attracted virtually unmitigated hostility from the Jewish leadership. From the point of view of Luke's readers, the views of such persons are clearly not to be trusted; yet, their indictments are not without substance. Jesus is the Messiah, but, rather than accepting his messianic status and responding in faith, they use it against him. Jesus did relativize payment of the Roman tribute, but disallowed payment only insofar as embracing the purpose of God might oppose participating thus in the political economy. And he had come to lead the people, to restore Israel as God's people, but his vision of God's agenda stood in direct confrontation with that of the Jerusalem elite. It is no wonder that they would regard his ministry as one of perversion.

3-4 Although he will return to the primary charge brought against Jesus in v 14, in the Lukan narration Pilate now seizes on this last issue, formulating the charge in terms of Jesus' royal status. Given the opportunity to answer the question whether he was "king of the Jews," Jesus replies in a way that is reminiscent of his answer to the sanhedrin in 22:70. Here, as there, Jesus turns the question posed to him into an ironic affirmation about him — ironic because even though the question assesses Jesus' identity correctly, it is an identity not granted by those who ask it. Why Pilate's response is to dismiss the charges — for example, because he regards Jesus as innocent (in the judicial sense) or, say, a harmless eccentric — is not evident at this juncture.[35] In either case, neither Pilate nor the Jerusalem authorities regard Jesus as the one who rules God's people.[36]

Who constitutes "the crowds" present for Pilate's pronouncement, and who will immediately raise their voices against Jesus (v 5)? Within this co-text, the only plausible candidates are members of the Jewish sanhedrin, the assembly who had brought Jesus before Pilate (22:66; 23:1). No one else has been introduced into this stage of the hearing. Moreover, this usage comports well with the most recent appearance of the term "crowd" in 22:47-54, where the "crowd" consisted of the Jewish leaders and their guard.[37]

5 Unsatisfied with the outcome of the hearing before Pilate, the Jewish leaders renew their accusations — pressing their case even more urgently,[38] summarizing again the primary charge against Jesus (see above), and underscoring the scope of the unrest attendant upon Jesus' ministry. "To stir up"[39] is set in parallel with "to turn away" in v 2 in order to heighten the impression of civic turmoil incited by Jesus. Also adding to this effect is the reference to the scope of Jesus' ministry — extending from Galilee, throughout Judea,[40] and including Jerusalem itself. The phrase "even to this place" likely refers to the temple, thus drawing attention to Jesus' objectionable teaching in the temple (19:45–21:38) and especially to his success in swaying the crowds from the influence of the Jerusalem elite. The reference to Galilee is congruent with Jesus' Galilean origins, but here it functions especially as a bridge to the next scene (vv 7-12).

Thus begins the steady crescendo of hostility toward Jesus that will mark the trial of Jesus before Roman officials in vv 1-20. In the face of Roman unwillingness to act against Jesus, the Jewish leaders grow increasingly adamant, almost to the point of inciting a riot. Luke's point is clear: It is not Jesus who leads the people astray, but rather the Jewish leaders who stir up the people.[41]

7.5.3. *The Hearing before Herod (23:6-12)*

6 *When Pilate heard this, he asked whether the man was a Galilean.* 7 *And when he learned that he was under Herod's jurisdiction, he sent him off to Herod, who was himself in Jerusalem at that time.* 8 *When*

35. αἴτιος (cf. αἰτία) refers to "cause" — cf. vv 14 and 22; Acts 13:28; 19:40.

36. Carlson, "Jewish People," 93.

37. See above on 22:66–23:25; also Via, "According to Luke," 130; Weatherly, *Jewish Responsibility,* 63-64; Chance, "Jewish People," 51-54.

38. ἐπισχύω appears only here in the NT.

39. ἀνασείω appears only here in Luke-Acts.

40. "Judea" in this instance probably refers more broadly to "the land of the Jews," as in 4:44; 7:17; cf. Acts 10:37.

41. Cf. G. Schneider, "Political Charge," 408.

Herod saw Jesus, he was very glad, for he had been wanting to see him for a long time, because he had heard about him and was hoping to see him perform some sign. 9 He questioned him at some length, but Jesus gave him no answer. 10 The chief priests and the scribes stood by, vehemently accusing him. 11 Even Herod with his soldiers treated him with contempt; having mocked him and put an elegant robe on him, he sent him back to Pilate.[42] *12 That same day Herod and Pilate became friends with each other; before this they had been enemies.*

Often regarded as a curious interlude within the Lukan passion account, this scene before Herod actually underscores two pivotal motifs. The first is Rome's aversion to acting with justice in the case of Jesus.[43] For no apparent reason other than pressure from the Jewish leadership, Herod joins his soldiers in scorning Jesus and then returns Jesus to Pilate. The second is the central role of the scribes and chief priests (cf. 22:66) in the case against Jesus. The void of evidence against him is again filled by their accusations, this time communicated "insistently" or "vehemently." This representative of Rome, though he had longed to see Jesus, does not respond to Jesus in faith and is therefore counted among "the many prophets and kings" who desired to perceive the revelation of God, but prove incapable of seeing or hearing (10:24). Spurning Jesus, Herod aligns himself with those who neither recognize nor acknowledge Jesus' true status.

This scene has been anticipated in a variety of ways, none more important than the appearance of Herod throughout the Third Gospel. In 3:1, he was presented as the tetrarch of Galilee — an introduction that leads quickly to a description of his opposition to and imprisonment of John (3:19-20). On account of the parallelism between John and Jesus established in the opening chapters of the narrative, Herod's hostility toward John does not bode well for Jesus. Hence, after Herod admits that he had John beheaded, we can hardly assume that his desire to see Jesus, registered in 9:7-9, was a matter of mere curiosity. Indeed, Herod's next appearance in the narrative comes in a report about his desire to kill Jesus (13:31), with the result that, upon the introduction of a trial scene focused on interaction between Herod and Jesus, one might expect a climactic confrontation.[44] In other ways, too, this scene has been anticipated — for example, by the

42. NRSV: "and mocked him; then he put an elegant robe on him, and sent him back to Pilate."

43. So also Darr, *Character Building,* 166. Some interpreters (e.g., Matera, "Jesus before Pilate," 545; Soards, "Jesus before Herod," 349, 361, 362-63; R. E. Brown, *Death of the Messiah,* 1:760-86) regard the primary purpose of this scene as establishing Jesus' innocence. However, no mention is made of Jesus' innocence in this pericope (on Brown's attempt to argue otherwise, see below on v 11), though cf. v 15.

44. So Tyson, *Death of Jesus,* 134. On the characterization of Herod in Luke-Acts, see esp. Darr, *Character Building,* 127-68.

promises of mockery (with reference to Jesus, 18:32) and of being brought before "kings and governors" (with reference to the disciples, 21:12-13).[45]

6-7 Luke marks the transition from the first phase of the hearing before Pilate to Jesus' encounter with Herod by having Pilate focus on the question of domain. The Jewish leaders had raised the issue of Jesus' Galilean origins (v 5), and this leads to the introduction of Herod, known to us as tetrarch of Galilee (3:1). It may be that Luke envisions Jesus' case as coming under the legal authority of Herod rather than Pilate,[46] but the co-text suggests another reading. Unable to find reason to condemn Jesus himself, Pilate sends him to Herod for further examination (cf. Acts 25:23-27), perhaps thinking that the tetrarch of Galilee will have insight in a case involving a Galilean. The verb "to send" may therefore add to the legal tone of this scene, but is not used as a technical term for the ceding of jurisdiction to Herod.[47]

8-9 The encounter between Jesus and Herod is striking for its introduction of a dual contrast. Superficially, the lengthy questioning of Herod contrasts with Jesus' silence. More substantively, Herod's desire to see (mentioned three times in v 8), and his having heard about Jesus, stands in contrast with what appears to be a complete lack of response on Jesus' part. Having finally seen Jesus, Herod hears nothing from him. In his earlier representation in the Lukan narrative, Herod is aligned against those who serve the divine aim (3:18-20; 9:7-9; 13:31). To this portrait is now added his desire for a sign, an aspiration that was negatively evaluated in 11:16, 29-30. "Seeing" and "hearing" are often used in their metaphorical sense in the Third Gospel,[48] and they operate on this level here, too, as Herod devotes his encounter with Jesus to sign-seeking and interrogation, and so fails to see and hear the revelation of Jesus' identity and status before God available only to those who follow Jesus in discipleship (10:23-24).

According to analogous scenes in both Greco-Roman and Jewish literature, Jesus' silence before Herod is startling. In Greco-Roman literature, philosophers brought before tyrants exercise self-control and showcase their teaching, just as in the LXX prophets brought before kings deliver divine

---

45. Against the backdrop of 21:12-19, Buck ("Jesus before Herod") argues that this scene has parenetic value, showing disciples through Jesus' example how to face their accusers; see, however, 12:11-12; 21:14-15, where disciples are to speak whatever the Spirit (or the Lord) gives them to speak.

46. Cf. Acts 23:34. According to Sherwin-White (*Roman Society,* 28-31; cf. R. E. Brown, *Death of the Messiah,* 1:764-65), "One does not expect a governor of the late Republic and early Principate, when faced by a malefactor, to bother about the very fine question whether his *imperium* allowed him to deal with a man who was *in* but not *of* his province" (28-29).

47. ἀναπέμπω — used in vv 7, 11, and 15. In any case, Herod would not have been Pilate's superior, as a more technical usage of the verb would presume.

48. See above, e.g., on 4:18-19.

oracles of judgment against the ruler.[49] This literary backdrop highlights Jesus' silence, but to what end? For Greco-Roman readers, Jesus' behavior may have been seen as an expression of admirable self-control, perhaps even nobility; for readers of the LXX, his silence is reminiscent of the Servant of Yahweh with whom he is thus identified (Isa 53:7).[50]

10   The use of the pluperfect ("stood by")[51] reminds Luke's readers that the chief priests and scribes have not been absent during the encounter between Jesus and Herod. Though only now mentioned, these opponents of Jesus have been pressing their case unyieldingly, now the more vehemently.[52] These members of the Jewish council (22:66; cf. 9:22), together with their verbal opposition against Jesus, are the constant in the formula of Jesus' trial, the catalyst for the actions taken against him.

11-12   From a narratological perspective, when one event precedes another, the first is assumed in some sense to cause the second;[53] hence, the contempt now shown Jesus is portrayed by Luke not so much as the consequence of Herod's independent judgment but rather as the result of the compelling influence of the sanhedrin (v 10). The Jewish leaders are the force behind the events of Jesus' trial. In describing the actions of Herod and his soldiers, Luke strings together three participles — "to reject contemptuously," "to mock," and "to clothe [with a brilliant robe]." The third has sometimes been separated from the others and interpreted quite differently, as though "contempt" and "mockery" might give way to a declaration of innocence and nobility.[54] It is unlikely, however, that, without further notice, the third would depart so significantly from the first two, and so more likely that the coordination of these three actions marks a dramatic accumulation of actions similar in nature.[55] The color of the robe is not specified, but its "brilliance" suggests opulence, royal splendor, and elevated social rank. Hence, whatever more specific significance one might give this act,[56]

49. These scenes are discussed in Darr, *Character Building,* 151-58.

50. Cf. Acts 8:32-33; Moo, *Passion Narratives,* 148-51; Marcus, "Role of Scripture," 215; Soards, "Silence of Jesus." The lack of linguistic parallels between the Isaianic and Lukan texts is not as important as is the presence of multiple points of contact between Luke's portrayal of Jesus in his passion and the Isaianic Servant of the Lord (see, e.g., Green, "God's Servant"; Seccombe, "Luke and Isaiah").

51. εἰστήκεισαν.

52. For κατηγορέω, see above on v 2; for εὐτόνως, see also Acts 18:28.

53. See, e.g., Chatman, *Story and Discourse,* 45-48; Prince, *Narratology,* 11-12.

54. So, e.g., R. E. Brown, *Death of the Messiah,* 1:774.

55. Cf. Dupriez, *Literary Devices,* 9-12.

56. On the meaning of ἐσθῆτα λαμπράν, see *TLNT,* 2:364-65. Hamel (*Poverty and Charity,* 83-86) and R. E. Brown (*Death of the Messiah,* 1:775-76) think that the robe signifies "purity" or "innocence," but this is based on a reading of λαμπρός as "white" rather than "brilliant." See the parallels in Acts 10:30 (ἐν ἐσθῆτι λαμπρᾷ); 12:21 (ἐσθῆτα βασιλικήν); cf. Luke 24:4.

clearly it points to Jesus' ironic mockery. Though Herod and the guards regard Jesus as little more than riffraff, they place on him the clothing that Luke and his readers will understand actually befits his station. Adding to the pathos of this scene is the king's lowering of himself to the level of his own guards in order to participate in this show of contempt.

It is transparently important for Luke that Herod and Pilate be seen as "friends" at the close of this scene, for this is a remark that seems otherwise out of place. In what since have they become friends? The best commentary is provided in Acts, where it is said that Herod and Pilate "gathered together" in opposition against "your holy servant Jesus" (Acts 4:26-27). They are thus joined in their hostility against Jesus.[57]

7.5.4. The Sentencing of Jesus (23:13-25)

> 13 *Pilate then called together the chief priests, the leaders, and the people,* 14 *and said to them, "You brought me this man as one who was perverting the people; and here I have examined him in your presence and have not found this man guilty of any of your charges against him.* 15 *Neither has Herod, for he sent him back to us. Indeed, he has done nothing to deserve death.* 16 *I will therefore have him flogged and release him."*
>
> 18 *Then they all shouted out together, "Away with this fellow! Release Barabbas for us!"* 19 *(This was a man who had been put in prison for an insurrection that had taken place in the city, and for murder.)* 20 *Pilate, wanting to release Jesus, addressed them again;* 21 *but they kept shouting, "Crucify, crucify him!"* 22 *A third time he said to them, "Why, what evil has he done? I have found in him no ground for the sentence of death; I will therefore have him flogged and then release him."* 23 *But they kept urgently demanding with loud shouts that he should be crucified; and their voices prevailed.* 24 *So Pilate gave his*

---

57. Some interpreters regard this "friendship" as a sign that Jesus' passion brings reconciliation (e.g., Matera, *Passion Narratives,* 158; Karris, *Luke: Artist and Theologian,* 85) or as evidence that "Jesus went about doing good" (Soards, "Jesus before Pilate," 363; with reference to Acts 10:38). It is hard to imagine, however, that Luke would, temporarily, so completely capitulate on his characterization of these rulers as to present them as models of the effect of Jesus' ministry. Others think that Luke's trial scene stands in tension with Acts 4:26-27, since in the former Rome's representatives confirm Jesus' innocence while in the latter they are portrayed as Jesus' enemies. This tension is mitigated by the scene of mockery, by Pilate's willingness to whip Jesus, by Pilate's and Herod's failure to perceive and/or acknowledge Jesus' true identity, and by Pilate's continued participation in Jesus' passion in spite of his inability to substantiate the charges brought against him.

verdict that their demand should be granted. 25 *He released the man they asked for, the one who had been put in prison for insurrection and murder, and he handed Jesus over as they wished.*

As Luke tells it, this final phase of Jesus' trial is punctuated by the threefold attempt of Pilate to effect Jesus' release set over against heightening efforts on the part of the Jewish people and their leaders to have Jesus executed. The first interchange comes in vv 13-19, the second in vv 20-21, and the third in vv 22-23, with the whole scene achieving its denouement with Pilate acquiescing to their demand (vv 24-25). Twice, Luke reports in Pilate's direct speech that he had been unable to find any basis for a death sentence in the case of Jesus, so he offers to have Jesus flogged prior to releasing him (vv 14-16, 22); a third instance is reported in summary fashion (v 20). The Jews and their leaders, on the other hand, "shouted out together" (v 18) and "kept shouting" (v 21), "urgently demanding with loud shouts" (v 23) until "their voices prevailed" (v 23). Here, then, is the tale of two opposing wills: Pilate's desire to release Jesus (v 20) on the one hand, the desire of the Jewish people and their leaders to see him crucified on the other (see "demand"/"ask" in vv 23-25); in the end, their will is granted (v 25).[58]

The effect of Luke's narrative strategy is to focus attention on the innocence of Jesus and the determination of the Jews to have Jesus executed. Pilate, and with him Rome, is not thereby declared blameless in these goings-on, however. Read in the context of his own declarations of innocence, Pilate's attempt to have Jesus flogged can be read as nothing less than a bid to assuage the Jewish people; indeed, this concern eventuates in his final decision to release a murdering insurrectionist while handing Jesus over to be crucified.

Controlling this scene are two strong contrasts,[59] charted through the repeated use of the term "release" (vv 17, 18, 20, 22, 25). The first is between Pilate and the Jewish people and their leaders. The second is between Jesus, repeatedly declared innocent by the Roman governor, and Barabbas, imprisoned for an offense, insurrection, for which crucifixion was the fitting punishment. Pilate wants to release one who is not guilty, the one whom they want crucified. They want Pilate to release one who is guilty, one for whom crucifixion is reserved. Later in the Lukan narrative, Peter will articulate the terms of this account even more starkly: "You handed over and rejected Jesus in the presence of Pilate, though he had decided to release him. . . . You

---

58. θέλω/θέλημα — vv 20 and 25; αἰτέω/αἴτημα — vv 23, 24, and 25. Within the larger Lukan narrative, it is difficult not to set this marked interest in volition within the larger framework of the divine will at work in and through these events — cf., e.g., 24:25-27; Acts 3:17-18.

59. Cf. Senior, *Passion of Jesus,* 117.

rejected the Holy and Righteous One and asked to have a murderer given to you . . ." (Acts 3:13-14).

13-16 With Jesus having been returned to him by Herod, Pilate calls together a kind of town meeting in order to announce his judgment in this case. The term "leaders" refers to the sanhedrin, present since 22:66;[60] the additional mention of the chief priests (who would have been included among "the leaders") underscores their central responsibility for the events unfolding. For the first time in the trial narrative, "the people" are brought together with the Jerusalem elite. In spite of attempts by some to deny the participation of the Jewish people in Jesus' passion, Luke is emphatic in his insistence that "they all shouted out together, 'Away with this fellow!' " (v 18); in Acts, the Jewish people in Jerusalem will also be held responsible for Jesus' death.[61] Pilate's reference to all those gathered as the company that had brought charges against Jesus indicates the point of view Pilate is now testing — namely, that the Jewish leaders in fact speak on behalf of the people as a whole. Luke's presentation of the residents of Jerusalem and their leaders in this way serves two immediate purposes. First, for Pilate, this larger audience serves to test the political will of the people, and thus the political feasibility of whatever verdict he might choose.[62] Second, as Luke will relate, the Jewish people and their leaders who reject Jesus are the same persons who align themselves with Barabbas, a known felon; by thus calling into question the commitments of the Jews in Jerusalem, Luke provides an indirect rationale for their spurning of Jesus.

Pilate summarizes the indictment brought against Jesus with reference to the one charge first enunciated in v 2 (also v 4). Readers of the LXX will recognize in the language of "perverting the people" an attempt to brand Jesus as a "false prophet" (see above on vv 1-2), though from a Roman perspective "turning the people away" will likely have been heard as a reference to revolutionary activity. "To examine" adds a forensic tone to the declaration of Jesus' innocence.[63] Pilate adds to his own judgment that of Herod, though

---

60. For ἄρχοντες, see 14:1; 23:35; 24:20; Acts 3:17; 4:5, 8; 13:27.

61. See Acts 2:23; 3:13-14, 17; 4:27; 10:39; 13:27-28. This is not the same thing as saying that all of Israel crucified Jesus, however, since Luke typically speaks more narrowly of the Jews in Jerusalem, and especially of their leaders. Cassidy ("Luke's Audience," 151-52) tries to argue that the Jewish people were called together to counter their leaders, while Chance ("Jewish People," 59) thinks that, in light of the charges brought against Jesus, the people were impotent to act against Jesus lest by doing so they prove that he was leading a rebellion. These views overlook the Lukan portrayal of the people gathered before Pilate in a near frenzied state, participating in moblike behavior, as they call for Jesus' crucifixion and demand the release of an insurrectionist. See further the discussion in Weatherly, *Jewish Responsibility,* 78.

62. Luke thus indicates that Rome might employ such political considerations in the maintenance of peace; cf. Bammel, "Trial," 430-31.

63. ἀνακρίνω — cf. Acts 4:9; 12:19; 24:8; 28:18; cf. ἀνάκρισις in Acts 25:26.

we are left to wonder how the mere fact that Herod returned Jesus to Pilate ("us," employing the royal plural) indicates the nature of Herod's verdict. (Perhaps Pilate recognized in Jesus' "elegant robe" [v 11] the signs of mockery, that in his encounter with Jesus Herod had found nothing in which to invest serious concern?)

Pilate introduces the notion of capital punishment. That he denies its applicability in the case of Jesus should not mask the fact that the possibility of Jesus' being executed has not heretofore been mentioned directly in the trial narrative. Readers of the LXX will recognize that, in branding Jesus as a false prophet, the sanhedrin had introduced the death penalty in an indirect way (see Deuteronomy 13), but Pilate's words serve to underscore the importance of his decision and to prepare for the shouts of the Jewish people and their leaders as they demand Jesus' crucifixion. "To flog" refers to a lesser, disciplinary action,[64] offered here as an alternative to capital punishment — not because Jesus has been found guilty of any charge but in order for Pilate to win and/or maintain favor with the Jewish people and their leaders in Jerusalem.

18-19 The prospect of Jesus' release meets with immediate and unanimous resistance.[65] The participation of the people in this rejection of Jesus may be surprising in light of his popularity among the people in chs. 20–21, but it has been prefigured in 4:16-30 and 19:11-27 (esp. 19:14).[66] They offer two alternatives. First, they shout, "Away with this fellow!" using language descriptive of the demise of the Servant of Yahweh, cited in Acts 8:33 (Isa 53:8). In this co-text, their words call for Jesus' death.[67] Second, they demand the release of Barabbas — identified immediately in a narrative aside as one imprisoned for rebellion and murder. The importance of this information is marked by its repetition in v 25b. Since no attempt is made to vitiate Barabbas's guilt, his primary function in the narrative is as a foil for Jesus' innocence.

Luke indicates Pilate's willingness to release Jesus on account of his innocence, but he provides no customary or legal basis for the possible release of Barabbas.[68] Rather, in the Lukan narrative, the Jewish people and their leaders seem on their own to have extended the idea of release in this new

---

64. παιδεύω. Cf. Bammel, "Trial," 441. On the use of corporal punishment in Jewish and Roman practice, see Pobee, *Persecution and Martyrdom*, 10-11.

65. μαμπληθεί ("all together") is used only here in the NT; it indicates the solidarity of Jewish leaders and Jerusalem residents in this scene.

66. So Carroll and Green, *Death of Jesus*, 65.

67. Cf. Acts 21:36; 22:22.

68. This void is filled by later scribes who inserted v 17 into the Lukan narrative: "Now he was obliged to release someone for them at the festival." The basis for the so-called *privilegium Paschale* is discussed in Bammel, "Trial," 427; R. E. Brown, *Death of the Messiah*, 1:814-20. It is of no apparent interest to the Third Evangelist.

direction. By thus aligning themselves with the seditious Barabbas over against the innocent Jesus, the Jewish people indirectly malign their own character.

20-21 Luke summarizes Pilate's second attempt to have Jesus released. The use of the phrase "a third time" in v 22 suggests that Pilate's second address would have taken much the same form as his first and third. The words of those assembled become more focused, however. For the first time, they call for Jesus' crucifixion.

As a means of execution, crucifixion was particularly heinous.[69] This had as much to do with the public humiliation accompanying crucifixion as with the act itself. Bound or nailed to a stake, tree, or cross, the victim faced death with all organs intact and with relatively little blood loss. As a consequence, death came slowly, sometimes over several days, as the body succumbed to shock or asphyxiation. No standard form of crucifixion was universally practiced, though a summary outline of Roman practice is possible. Crucifixion included a flogging beforehand, with victims often required to carry their own crossbeams to the site of execution, where they were nailed or bound to the cross with arms extended, raised up, and perhaps seated on a small wooden peg. Even among the Romans this procedure was subject to variation. In his account of the siege of Jerusalem by the Romans, for example, Josephus observes how hundreds of Jews were "scourged and subjected to torture of every description . . . and then crucified opposite the city walls." Free to fulfill their whims in the hope of persuading those Jews remaining in the city to surrender their positions, "the soldiers out of rage and hatred amused themselves by nailing their prisoners in different positions. . . ."[70]

Josephus's account reminds us that crucifixion was reserved by the Romans especially for those who resisted the authority of Roman occupation. Naked and fastened to a tree, stake, or cross, located typically at major crossroads, the victim was subjected both to a particularly abhorrent form of capital punishment and to optimum, savage ridicule. The corpse of the crucified was typically left on the tree to rot or as food for scavenging birds. In this way the general populace were granted a somber reminder of the fate of those daring to assert themselves against Rome.

22-23 Luke notes that the scene played out by Pilate and the Jews he had assembled repeats itself yet a third time. The language employed by the governor is almost identical to that in vv 14-16, with the important exception that, now, Pilate wonders whether Jesus has done any "evil thing" at all. The contrast between Pilate and the Jewish leaders is pressed by the

69. On what follows, see esp. Hengel, *Crucifixion;* also Green, "Death of Jesus," 147-48; *idem,* "Crucifixion."

70. Josephus *J.W.* 5.11.1 §§449-51.

repeated use of the verb "to find"[71] in vv 2, 4, 14, and 22: They "found this man perverting our nation," but he finds Jesus guilty of nothing. The intensity of this emphasis on Jesus' innocence is important for Luke's overall portrayal of Jesus as the righteous one who suffers and will be vindicated. Equally important for Luke's narrative is the intensity of Jewish resistance[72] to Pilate's plan to flog and release Jesus. The Jewish people in Jerusalem and their leaders, having rejected Jesus, demand that he be crucified; their voices — raised in crescendo in vv 18, 21, and 23 — finally prove to be stronger than Pilate's own resolve (v 20a). The effect Luke achieves has Pilate acting ultimately in order to assuage a riotous mob, to preserve peace rather than to promote justice.

24-25 The verb "to give a verdict" generally refers to pronouncing an edict, but in its other two usages in the Greek Bible it is used as it is here, in co-texts insinuating a miscarriage of justice.[73] The verb translated by the NRSV as "to ask" is actually the same as the verb in v 23, "to demand" (see the cognate in v 24, "demand"); this repetition correlates with "their wish" in v 25c to emphasize the volition of the Jews in Jerusalem and their leaders in calling for Jesus' execution and Barabbas' release.[74] The travesty of this decision is accentuated by the evident guilt of Barabbas, whose crimes warranted death by crucifixion, and by the manifest political expediency that has governed Pilate's actions. The potency of Jewish pressure groups in Roman legal cases involving Jesus' followers will be noted in Acts 24:27; 25:9.

7.6. THE CRUCIFIXION OF JESUS (23:26-49)

At the outset of the Lukan narrative, Simeon had prophesied that Jesus would be the cause of division within Israel. That prophecy may seem to have been jeopardized as the lengthy account of Jesus' trial came to an end (22:66–23:25); in the final scene before Pilate, Jewish people had joined Jerusalem leadership in calling for Jesus' crucifixion. The ambiguous "they" of v 26 ("As they led him away . . .") signifies the solidarity of Rome, Jewish leaders, and Jewish people in opposition against Jesus. The hostility against Jesus seems not divided but unanimous. Immediately, however, Luke begins to show the segregation caused as people respond differently to the condemned Jesus.

71. εὑρίσκω.
72. Luke uses the imperfect of ἐπίκειμαι to signify the menacing press of the people.
73. ἐπικρίνω — cf. 2 Macc 4:47; 3 Macc 4:2.
74. This is emphasized in Neyrey, *Passion according to Luke,* 83.

Most poignantly, v 35 notes that "the people stood by, watching" at the scene of the crucifixion, while "the leaders scoffed at him." The leaders and soldiers scorn Jesus (vv 35-36), but after his death the crowds "return home, beating their breasts" (v 48).

Remarkably, as has been the case throughout the Third Gospel, so in the climactic scene of Jesus' death, sympathy toward Jesus or even recognition of and appropriate response to him are attributed to relative outsiders. *Simon of Cyrene,* whose relative anonymity marks him as someone other than a member of the powerful in Jerusalem, carries the cross behind Jesus and so provides a reminder of the nature of discipleship (v 26); *women* mourn Jesus (v 27); a *criminal* acknowledges Jesus' innocence as well as his own need for Jesus' beneficence (vv 40-42); and a *Gentile centurion* affirms the faithfulness of Jesus as the Suffering Righteous One (v 47). At one level, with his depiction of these persons, Luke takes the measure of the separation between those who align themselves with Jesus and those who resist him; at another, Luke demonstrates how, both in life and in death, Jesus' ministry is oriented toward and embraced by those living beyond the margins of the religious inner circle.

In another sense, Luke's account of the crucifixion of Jesus presses the issue of Jesus' identity. Jesus emerges as more than a hapless victim; he is ever in control and his trust in God never wavers. Even under the burden of a death sentence he continues his prophetic role (vv 28-31), intercedes on behalf of those who dishonor and execute him (v 34), promises Paradise to a criminal (v 43), and, with his dying breath, offers up his life to God (v 46). Words of mockery repudiate his identity as Savior, but only because those who speak them fail miserably to understand the nature of his salvific mission. They call upon Jesus to save himself (vv 35, 39), but Jesus had earlier announced, "Those who want to save their life will lose it, and those who lose their life for my sake will save it" (9:24). At his own crucifixion, he offers forgiveness and plays the role of Savior (vv 34, 43). In this way Luke affirms what has been underscored again and again in the narrative — namely, the way of the regal prophet includes rejection and death. It is through suffering that Jesus fulfills the divine purpose. From the cross Jesus twice addresses God in familial terms as Father, confirming that he regards his passion as fully congruent with his status as God's Son.[1]

Even in this scene, focused so narrowly on the cross, Luke's theocentrism emerges as a crucial ingredient. Indeed, God is explicitly mentioned five times ("God" — vv 35, 40, 47; "Father" — vv 34, 46), each time as a reminder that it is God's plan that is being worked out in Jesus' life and death, that it is the divine beneficence that is available through his ministry. From

1. On this and other motifs, see Carroll, "Luke's Crucifixion Scene."

the Lukan perspective, the centurion rightly gives glory to God, who manifests his saving purpose in Jesus (v 47).

7.6.1. On the Way to the Crucifixion (23:26-31)

> 26 *As they led him away, they seized a man, Simon of Cyrene, who was coming from the country, and they laid the cross on him, and made him carry it behind Jesus. 27 A great number of the people followed him, and among them were women who were beating their breasts and wailing for him. 28 But Jesus turned to them and said, "Daughters of Jerusalem, do not weep for me, but weep for yourselves and for your children. 29 For the days are surely coming when they will say, 'Blessed are the barren, and the wombs that never bore, and the breasts that never nursed.' 30 Then they will begin to say to the mountains, 'Fall on us'; and to the hills, 'Cover us.' 31 For if they do this when the wood is green, what will happen when it is dry?"*

Luke lingers over that phase of Jesus' passion concerned with his physical movement from the place of decision to that of crucifixion. Executions were typically located outside the city walls,[2] but Luke is more interested with what transpired along the way than with route or distance. His foremost concern is in indicating how short-lived was the solidarity of the Jewish people with their Jerusalem leaders in opposition to Jesus. The appearance of Simon, absent from the goings-on in the city, reminds us that the mob shouting for Jesus' execution in vv 13-25 did not include all of Israel. Even those who follow Jesus to the place of his execution appear in something other than an antagonist role. In fact, Luke unveils their changing attitude toward Jesus first by having them follow Jesus, then stand apart from their leaders (v 35), and finally join the women in acts of sorrow (v 48). In the present scene, then, the women who mourn represent in a proleptic way the responses of "the people."

Beyond this, with Jesus now condemned to death, Luke turns immediately to the interpretation of the event now pending. On the one hand, in his portrayal of Simon, Luke reminds his audience of cross-bearing as integral to discipleship (cf. 9:23; 14:27). On the other, by insisting that the mourning of these "daughters of Jerusalem" is misplaced, Jesus indicates that his death has meaning beyond itself. It helps to introduce "the last days,"[3] days of judgment and peril when even catastrophic death will seem like a merciful gift. Rather than mourn for Jesus, whose impending death is grounded in the

---

2. See the discussion in R. E. Brown, *Death of the Messiah*, 2:912.
3. See Soards, "Jesus' Speech."

redemptive plan of God, mourning ought to be directed to Jerusalem, whose failure to recognize the time of God's gracious visitation has led it to reject the Messiah (cf. 19:41-44). Jesus announces judgment, therefore, but also the hope of repentance.

26 Who is it that led Jesus away? At best, Luke's "they" is ambiguous, and some have argued that Luke thus intimates to his readers, against all historical probability, that the Jewish people and their leaders are responsible for the actual act of crucifixion.[4] At the end of the trial scene, however, all involved are aligned in opposition to Jesus — Rome and Jerusalem — so that Luke's "they" signifies the concord of Rome, Jewish leaders, and Jewish people in their hostility toward Jesus. "Cross" could be used for the "crossbeam," and it was the latter that was carried by the condemned to the place of execution. Why Jesus requires assistance from Simon is not stated by Luke, who seems more interested in providing a reminder of the implications of Jesus' faithfulness to God's purpose for those who want to follow him in discipleship:

9:23: If any want to become my followers, let them . . . take up their cross daily and follow me.
14:27: Whoever does not carry the cross and follow me cannot be my disciple.
23:26: They laid the cross on him, and made him carry it behind Jesus.[5]

Given the care with which Luke often introduces characters, Simon's introduction is remarkably indirect. Although "Simon" is a Greek name, Cyrene, capital of the Roman province of Cyrenaica (Libya) in North Africa, was a center of Jewish population,[6] and Luke will later mention the presence in Jerusalem of devout Jews from Cyrene (Acts 2:10) and a Cyrenian synagogue (Acts 6:9); hence, Simon may well have been Jewish. At the same time, he is described as "coming from the country," an enigmatic phrase that is clear on one crucial point

---

4. So, e.g., Neyrey, *Passion according to Luke,* 120; Matera, *Passion Narratives,* 181. *Contra,* e.g., Weatherly, *Jewish Responsibility,* 65-68; R. E. Brown, *Death of Jesus,* 1:856-59.

5. Many interpreters have found in Simon a model of discipleship (e.g., Büchele, *Tod Jesu,* 42, 67; Karris, *Luke: Artist and Theologian,* 92). If he were to function this way for Luke, however, we might have expected a more thorough characterization of him. In fact, the linguistic connections among these parallels is minimal, though they share obvious conceptual relations (cf. Green, *Death of Jesus,* 87). Beck ("Imitatio Christi," 33; cf. Senior, *Passion of Jesus,* 121) writes, "By the use of the words τὸν σταυρὸν φέρειν ὄπισθεν τοῦ Ἰησοῦ the reader is reminded of the implications for others of what happens to Jesus."

6. Josephus *Ag. Ap.* 2.4-5 §§41-54; *Ant.* 14.7.2 §114; 1 Macc 15:23; 2 Macc 2:23.

— namely, that Simon had not participated in the riotous scene associated with Jesus' trial and condemnation. Luke thus immediately reminds his audience that Jewish hostility leading to Jesus' sentencing was not universal.

27 Luke envisions one group of people following Jesus to the place of crucifixion.[7] The women are numbered among them and, as we will see, they are representative of the larger crowd. Elsewhere in the Third Gospel, the verb "to follow" may be used with reference to discipleship;[8] but, within this immediate co-text, this more nuanced sense finds little support. "The people" thus portrayed have moved dramatically from the antagonism that characterized them in the previous scene, but they are not yet "disciples." Nor are the women who mourn Jesus depicted as disciples, though their sympathies are transparently with Jesus.[9] Drawing on the imagery of Zech 12:10-14, Luke portrays them as mourning for Jesus in anticipation of his death.[10] In this way, these women anticipate the response of the people following Jesus' death (v 48).

28-31 The phrase "daughters of Jerusalem" represents stock language from the LXX,[11] signifying "those who inhabit Jerusalem" (cf. 13:34). Hence, although Jesus directs his oracle to those who mourn him, these women are representative of the larger population of the city. Important for understanding Jesus' response are several intertextual connections, most of which are internal to the Third Gospel. (1) This scene is immediately reminiscent of the aftermath of Peter's denial of Jesus in 22:61-62. There, as here, Jesus "turned," an action that is often a precursor to his chiding or admonishing his audience.[12] In addition, Peter weeps in recognition of his failure, just as Jesus now calls upon these representatives of Jerusalem to weep in light of their failure to align themselves with Jesus when he most needed their support.[13]

---

7. Brawley (*Luke-Acts,* 140) correctly observes that one article controls the two genitives — τοῦ λαοῦ καὶ γυναικῶν — but overinterprets v 27 when he observes, "The entire crowd of the people mourns the fate of Jesus." That Luke portrays no division between the people and the women, see also Weatherly, *Jewish Responsibility,* 79-80; *contra* Soards, "Jesus' Address," 79.

8. ἀκολουθέω — cf. 5:11, 27, 28; 9:11, 23, 49, 57, 59, 61; 18:22; et al.

9. *Contra,* e.g., Untergaßmair, *Kreuzweg und Kreuzigung Jesu,* 144; Neyrey, *Passion according to Luke,* 111.

10. The connection to Zech 12:10-14 (noted, e.g., by Büchele, *Tod Jesu,* 43) is denied by most interpreters (Moo [*Passion Narratives,* 221] is representative), primarily because an allusion to the Zechariah text would be expected following Jesus' death rather than before it. However, this is equally true of the mourning of these women, since κοπετός and θρῆνος belong to scenes of burial (Stählin, "κοπετός," 845-46).

11. Cf. Cant 2:7; 3:5, 10; 5:8, 9, 16, 17; 8:4; Mic 4:8; Zeph 3:14; Zech 9:9.

12. See 7:9, 44; 9:55; 10:23; 14:25.

13. Ascough ("Rejection and Response," 356-59) notes how Peter's denial and repentance parallel and anticipate the rejection of Jesus by the people and their repentance.

(2) Other Lukan texts in which people "beat their breasts" and "weep" (6:21, 25; 7:13, 38; 8:52; 22:62) suggest, on the one hand, that these women are indeed weeping for the wrong reason, but also that weeping in light of one's own sorrowful condition is a precursor to God's redemptive intervention. Thus far, these persons do not understand Jesus' identity or place within the divine purpose, else they would recognize the travesty that awaits them on account of their repudiation of God's redemptive agent. Were they more perceptive, they would ally themselves with Jesus in weeping for the doomed city (19:41).

(3) Jesus' oracle draws and builds on his earlier prophecies concerning Jerusalem in 13:34-35; 19:41-44; 21:20-24, emphasizing the causal relationship between the rejection of Jesus and the judgment on Jerusalem. The nature of the calamity Jesus envisions is accentuated by the reversal of the usual state of blessedness in v 29. Children are generally seen as expressions of divine favor, but in the coming catastrophe it is better to be barren.[14] Jesus' prophecy also draws on the language of Hos 10:8: "They shall say to the mountains, Cover us, and to the hills, Fall on us." In its co-text, the Hosean text portends a destruction grounded in the substitution of faithfulness to God with idolatry. Echoing Hosea, Jesus anticipates that those who have rejected God's salvific purpose by rejecting Jesus and his divinely ordained mission will articulate a similar death wish. The proverb of v 31 joins scriptural witness to certify the disastrous proportions of the coming judgment. The "they" of v 31 refers most simply to those who rejected Jesus; if they treated Jesus in this way, how will they be treated for instigating his execution?[15] Jesus' proverb, together with the expression "the days are surely coming,"[16] intimates the certainty and imminence of judgment. Luke's readers may also recall, however, that destruction is not the final act in God's plan. The calamity of divine judgment, for those who align themselves with the purpose of God, is a sign that redemption is near (21:28).[17]

---

14. Cf. *2 Apoc. Bar.* 10:6, with reference to the afflictions of Zion: "Blessed is he who was not born, or he who was born and died" (ET in Klijn, "2 (Syriac Apocalypse of) Baruch," 624). For similar thought in Greco-Roman literature, see Marshall, 864. For the more typical association of children with divine blessing, see above on 1:7.

15. Without more by way of culture-specific information, any more precise rendering of this aphorism will always be suspect. A widely held view has it that God is the subject throughout this proverb: If God did not spare Jesus, how much more will the impenitent nation be the object of divine judgment? However, Luke does not portray God as the subject of the act of crucifixion. See the discussion in Fitzmyer, 2:1498-99; R. E. Brown, *Death of the Messiah,* 2:925-27.

16. This phrase, reminiscent of OT prophecy, is used elsewhere in the Lukan narrative in predictions of calamity and judgment — see above on 17:22.

17. See Soards, "Jesus' Address," 242-44.

Taken together, these observations indicate that Jesus' words to the "daughters of Jerusalem" do constitute an oracle of judgment sealing the fate of Jerusalem. This, however, is not the whole story, for the inhabitants of the city are counseled to mourn on behalf of the city. Their fate is not inevitably tied to its destruction; rather, they have opportunity again to respond to Jesus with repentance.[18]

7.6.2. Jesus Crucified and Mocked (23:32-43)

32 *Two others also, who were criminals, were led away to be put to death with him.* 33 *When they came to the place that is called The Skull, they crucified Jesus there with the criminals, one on his right and one on his left.* 34 *Then Jesus said, "Father, forgive them; for they do not know what they are doing."*[19] *And they cast lots to divide his clothing.* 35 *And the people stood by, watching; but the leaders scoffed at him, saying, "He saved others; let him save himself if he is the Messiah of God, his chosen one!"* 36 *The soldiers also mocked him, coming up and offering him sour wine,* 37 *and saying, "If you are the King of the Jews, save yourself!"* 38 *There was also an inscription over him, "This is the King of the Jews."*

39 *One of the criminals who were hanged there kept deriding him and saying, "Are you not the Messiah? Save yourself and us!"* 40 *But the other rebuked him, saying, "Do you not fear God, since you are under the same sentence of condemnation?* 41 *And we indeed have been condemned justly, for we are getting what we deserve for our deeds, but this man has done nothing wrong."* 42 *Then he said, "Jesus, remember me when you come into your kingdom."* 43 *He replied, "Truly I tell you, today you will be with me in Paradise."*

Though the actual act of Jesus' crucifixion is passed over sans any of the heinous detail, Luke does fix the spotlight on its immediate aftermath. Three emphases are closely intertwined in the scene painted by the Evangelist. First, and perhaps most readily apparent, is the division of this account into three phases of mockery. Here, persons of diminishing status — the religious

18. For this emphasis, see also Karris, *Luke: Artist and Theologian,* 93-94; Senior, *Passion of Jesus,* 121-26. The judgment motif is emphasized by Untergaßmair, *Kreuzweg und Kreuzigung Jesu,* 38-39; Neyrey, *Passion according to Luke,* 108-28.

19. The NRSV (following 𝔭⁷⁵ ℵ¹ B D* W Θ et al.) places v 34a in brackets, thus indicating the view of the editors that Jesus' prayer is not original to the Third Gospel. For a defence of its authenticity (supported by ℵ*·² [A] C D² L Ψ et al.), see Green, *Death of Jesus,* 91-92; and more, recently, Crump, *Jesus the Intercessor,* 79-85; R. E. Brown, *Death of the Messiah,* 2:975-81.

leaders, the Roman soldiers, and an executed criminal — turn their derisive attention on Jesus, scoffing at him, mocking him, and blaspheming him. The humiliation and repudiation of Jesus are underscored in many ways in this co-text, but none more dishonoring than his being spurned by a criminal, by one whose place in mainstream society had already been categorically dismissed.

Second, and of even greater importance to the Lukan narrative, is Luke's presentation of contrasting responses to Jesus. The brief unanimity that characterized the opposition against him in the trial scene (vv 13-25) had already begun to erode in the previous scene (vv 26-31), but now the Evangelist introduces an expansive rift between those who are scandalized by the cross and those who are not.[20] Aligning himself with Jesus most transparently is the second criminal, who recognizes Jesus' innocence and trusts in his potent beneficence (vv 40-42). Less intelligible is the posture of "the people" vis-à-vis Jesus (v 35). Though Luke's portrait ensures that they are not participants in the scorning of Jesus, he does not yet present them as positively disposed toward him. Aligned over against Jesus are the Jewish leaders, and with them the Roman soldiers. Both see his crucifixion as an irrefutable denial of his regal status. Filled with interpretive potential is the solidarity of Jewish leaders and Roman soldiers with a justly condemned criminal (v 39). Even the words with which these three groups express their contempt are comparable, and their shared hostility against Jesus invites the interpretation that they are all evildoers. This interpretation is furthered by the points of contact between the challenges put to Jesus by the devil, by the sanhedrin, and now by the Jewish leaders, Roman guards, and this justly condemned criminal.[21]

Third, one finds evidence, even here in Jesus' must vulnerable moments at the end of his life, that he is the Savior (cf. 2:11). The verb "to save" is used repeatedly in this scene (4x) with respect to Jesus' alleged incapacity "to save himself." What is striking is that Jesus' inability (unwillingness?) to save himself does not render him impotent to save others (cf. 9:24). From the cross, he asks God to extend forgiveness even to those responsible for his crucifixion, then promises salvation to one of those crucified with him.

It is at the intersection of these three emphases that we are able to grapple with the central affirmation of this account. From the mouths of Jesus' opponents, we hear repeatedly what we know to be true — namely, that Jesus'

---

20. Cf. Neyrey, *Passion according to Luke*, 129-33, 136.

21. 4:3: εἰ υἰὸς εἶ τοῦ θεοῦ . . .

 4:9: εἰ υἰὸς εἶ τοῦ θεοῦ . . .

22:67: εἰ σὺ εἶ ὁ Χριστός . . .

23:35: εἰ οὗτός ἐστιν ὁ Χριστὸς τοῦ θεοῦ . . .

23:37: εἰ σὺ εἶ ὁ βασιλεὺς τῶν Ἰουδαίων . . .

23:39: οὐχὶ σὺ εἶ ὁ Χριστός . . .

royal status and his role as Savior are interconnected. What we know, but they do not, however, is that royal identity and salvation are further collocated in the Third Gospel with the necessity of Jesus' suffering (e.g., 9:22; 17:25; 18:31-32). They see his suffering and death as a denial of his divine vocation. Even from the cross, though, Jesus can refer to God as his Father, he can proffer forgiveness, and he can promise Paradise. Evidently, he understands his death as consistent with the divine plan, not as a repudiation of his status and ministry. Indeed, from the Lukan perspective, the crucifixion seals the identity of Jesus as the Messiah and king who accomplishes the divine purpose precisely as the suffering one.[22] Herein is the irony that determines the role of this pericope within Luke's narrative.

32-34   The narrow focus of Luke's narrative lens becomes clear when he mentions the other two who were led to the place of execution. Their stories are unknown to us. We hear only that they are "criminals" — that is, "good-for-nothing's" or "evildoers." Their precise crime cannot be determined, though their punishment, crucifixion, marks them as a threat to the state, perhaps dangerous and violent men.[23] Though some interpreters have found in their presence with Jesus at the crucifixion a fulfillment of the Isaianic reference in 22:37, this is not likely.[24] Instead, the introduction of these criminals prepares for their exchange regarding Jesus in vv 39-41.

The stage is further set with reference to "The Skull," the very name of which has gruesome connotations. It may have received its identity on account of the shape of the hill or rock spur on which crucifixions were held.[25] It was the nature of this form of Roman execution that it be held in a public place to ensure maximum traffic and, therefore, maximum deterrent value for people subjected to foreign rule. On the practice of crucifixion, see above on v 21.

Responding first to Jesus' crucifixion is Jesus himself. In his mind, his horrible and humiliating condition in no way jeopardizes his relationship with God, whom he thus continues to address with the characteristic appellation, "Father." Even in the midst of his passion, he affirms the beneficence of God — not only for himself but now also for those responsible for his crucifixion.[26] In this co-text, the "them" for whom Jesus intercedes includes

---

22. Brawley, *Centering on God,* 51; cf. Carroll, "Luke's Crucifixion Scene," 114-16.

23. κακοῦργος; cf. *TLNT,* 2:241-43; Hengel, *Crucifixion,* 46-50.

24. See, e.g., Büchele, *Tod Jesu,* 44; Karris, *Luke: Artist and Theologian,* 95. For the interpretation of 22:37, see above. Note that ἄνομος is used in 22:37, κακοῦργος here, so that Luke provides no linguistic tag for this identification.

25. See Corbo, "Golgotha."

26. See 2:49; 10:21-22; 11:2; 22:42; Mowery, "God the Father," 126; Brawley, *Centering on God,* 116-17.

both Jews and Romans — that is, those who have found concord in their opposition to Jesus.[27] Jesus' petition manifests the motif of forgiveness, important in Luke's understanding of Jesus' ministry and the salvific message proclaimed in Luke and Acts.[28] Also achieving importance in the speeches in Acts is the notion of the ignorance of those responsible for Jesus' demise, a point underscored earlier in 12:48, and rooted in the Pentateuch, which holds out the possibility of atonement for those who sin unwittingly.[29] In death, Jesus continues his redemptive ministry, even putting into practice his own instruction regarding love for one's enemies: "Pray for those who abuse you" (6:27-28).

Drawing as it does on Ps 22:18, Luke's note that "they cast lots to divide his clothing" similarly speaks to the reality that Jesus' abominable fate is neither a surprise to God nor a contradiction of the divine purpose. To be stripped of clothing signified gross indignity and the loss of personal identity.[30] Contrast this with the regal clothes placed on Jesus in v 11! Hence, even if, historically, the executioners had the right to share the minor possessions of their victim,[31] Luke's purpose in including this detail would not have been merely to represent historical events or to add to the verisimilitude of his account. It was, rather, to underscore at the same time the utter humiliation experienced by Jesus and the divine foresight of even this incident.

35-37 Jesus' own analysis from the cross is that the divine plan continues to unfold, irrespective of appearances to the contrary. This viewpoint is not shared by all, however, and Luke records in these verses the first two of three phases of mockery. Importantly, "the people" only "stand by, watching," and are segregated from their leaders at this stage of the narrative.

The rare verb Luke uses to describe the activity of the rulers, "to scoff," urges the view that Luke is borrowing from Ps 22:7 in his portrayal;[32] the psalm speaks of one whose status is less than human, "a worm," scorned, despised, and mocked. This is the very picture painted by Luke. The verb used to describe the response of the soldiers, "to mock," is used in Jesus'

---

27. See above on v 26; cf. C. A. Evans, "Prophecy and Polemic," 183; R. E. Brown, *Death of the Messiah,* 2:972-73.

28. Cf. esp. 1:77; 7:47-50; Acts 2:38; 5:31; 10:43.

29. See Lev 5:17-19; Num 15:25-31; Derrett, *New Resolutions,* 92-93; C. A. Evans, "Prophecy and Polemic," 183. For the motif of ignorance, see Acts 3:17; 13:27; 14:16; 17:30; 26:9.

30. Cf. Hamel, *Poverty and Charity,* 73: "In Jewish eyes, especially since the time they had been exposed to Greek mores, to be naked was to lack human status" (with reference to *Jub.* 3:31).

31. So Sherwin-White, *Roman Society,* 46.

32. ἐκμυκτηρίζω appears in the NT only in 16:14; 23:35. For οἱ ἄρχοντες, see v 13.

prediction of his passion in 18:32; the actions of these Romans[33] parallels that of the sanhedrin in 22:63 and of Herod and his soldiers in 23:11. The words of these two groups are also comparable, though the party of Jewish leaders refers to Jesus as "Messiah of God," whereas the Romans speak of him as "the King of the Jews." Each thus uses culturally appropriate language.

The Jewish leaders also speak of Jesus as God's "chosen one," using language borrowed from Isa 42:1 and used messianically in this period.[34] In doing so, they echo one of God's own ways of referring to Jesus, "my Chosen One" (9:35).[35] Ironically, then, these Jewish leaders refer to Jesus correctly, and even employ language that draws together the identity of Jesus as the Servant of Yahweh and as the Messiah, language that leaves the door open for the identification of a Messiah who suffers.[36] All of the requisite categories are present in their words, but they cannot collate them in any way other than to repudiate Jesus' salvific role. For them, self-deliverance is the criterion for his genuineness, in spite of the fact that the psalm on which their behavior is modeled recognizes God as the one who delivers (Psalm 22).

To their words, the soldiers add the offer of "sour wine." As a form of mockery, this action is reminiscent of Ps 69:21, where the gift of vinegar to drink is noted as an insult. They provide for him a beverage befitting their true evaluation of his status: cheap wine, a burlesque gift for a king.[37]

38 The use of a placard or other medium for communicating to the populace the impetus for execution, and thus to deter similar behavior, has historical basis. In this instance, Jesus is depicted as having made a claim to the throne, thus threatening the sovereignty of the emperor.[38] Luke's agenda is not narrowly focused on getting the details right, however. Locating his reference to the inscription in this co-text, he adds the official witness of Roman rule to the voices sneering at Jesus. Pilate had already rejected the view that Jesus was king of the Jews (vv 3-4), and so had Herod (see above on v 11). The inscription is thus, from the Roman perspective, false, yet it constitutes for Luke and his audience an ironic affirmation of the truth of Jesus' regal identity.

---

33. Ascough ("Rejection and Response," 363) thinks that these soldiers are Jewish. In support of this view, one might refer to 22:52; however, the change from "Messiah of God" to "King of the Jews" in vv 36-37 tells against it.

34. See, e.g., *1 Enoch* 39:6-8; 45; 48:6-10 (cf. Ps 2:2); 49 (cf. Isa 42:1); 51:52; 6219663 (cf. Isa 52:13–53:12); *Apocalypse of Abraham* 30–31 (31:1); Schrenk, "ἐκλεκτός," 184-85.

35. 9:35: ὁ ἐκλελεγμένος; 23:35: ὁ ἐκλεκτός.

36. Cf. Strauss, *Davidic Messiah*, 266-67.

37. So R. E. Brown, *Death of the Messiah*, 2:997; similarly, Brawley, *Text to Text*, 54: "The soldiers are mocking Jesus as a king — carnival king, and they offer him sour wine instead of the superior beverage appropriate for a king."

38. See Bammell, "The *titulus*"; Harvey, *Constraints of History*, 13.

39-43 In this third phase of the scene of mockery, Luke exhibits his interest in those crucified with Jesus (vv 32-33).[39] One of them joins Rome and the Jerusalem elite in "deriding him." His challenge to Jesus parallels theirs, though Luke takes an additional step, indicating that, like the Jewish leaders before him (22:65), this criminal "blasphemes" Jesus. "To blaspheme" may refer to the casting of insults, but one may hear deeper echoes of a more religious sort, as if Luke were saying that, in denigrating Jesus, this criminal (and with him, perhaps, all those who mock Jesus on the cross) is denigrating the power of God.[40] What is more, though Luke's audience will immediately recognize that this criminal has aligned himself with Jesus' opponents, he presumes to identify himself and the other crucified man with Jesus: Save yourself, *and us!*

The irony of this situation is not lost on the second criminal, who rebukes the first just as Jesus had rebuked evil spirits (e.g., 4:35, 41). The mistake of the first is threefold: (1) Rather than fearing God, he maligns God's instrument of salvation. (2) He assumes that Jesus is guilty when, in fact, he is innocent. (3) In his sarcasm, he fails to recognize that this Suffering Righteous One will be delivered not from but through death, and that he will continue to exercise his role as Savior. What is more, in admitting his own guilt, the second criminal distances himself from Jesus (as had Peter in 5:8), thus presenting himself, according to the Lukan calculus, as a candidate for divine beneficence. Indeed, his request, "remember me," echoes words repeatedly addressed to Yahweh, whose memory is a source of divine blessing in keeping with his covenant.[41] Like other marginalized persons in the Third Gospel, the second criminal, this religious and social outsider, thus exercises astounding insight into the status and identity of Jesus.[42] Indeed, quite apart from any recorded introductions, he knows Jesus' name and refers to him by name, Jesus — the name given by divine fiat in conjunction with Jesus' status as the Davidic Messiah (1:31-35), a name spoken by others seeking restoration (17:13; 18:38).[43]

The interaction between the second criminal and Jesus is important above all for the way it demonstrates an evaluation of Jesus' passion that counters the views of his detractors in vv 35b-39. This criminal, whose reliability as a hermeneut is ratified by Jesus' gracious response to him, is the first to recognize that Jesus' death is not a contradiction of his messiahship, his role as Savior; he

---

39. κρεμάννυμι, "to hang," is used with reference to crucifixion (e.g., "hanging on a tree") in Acts 5:30; 10:39.

40. For this use of βλασφημέω, see above on 22:65.

41. Cf. Ps 115:12; Judg 16:28; 1 Sam 1:11, 19; et al.; *TLNT,* 2:491-92.

42. Cf., e.g., 7:1-10, 36-50; 8:43-48; 19:1-10.

43. Or by demoniacs — cf. 4:34; 8:28.

is the first to recognize that Jesus' crucifixion is a precursor to his enthronement (cf. Acts 5:30-31), and thus he anticipates in his request Jesus' kingly rule. "Paradise" refers to "God's garden," an eschatological image of new creation.[44] Jesus' promise of Paradise "today" is in keeping with Luke's understanding of the immediacy of salvation (cf. 4:21; 19:9) and underscores a central aspect of Luke's perspective on Jesus' death: God's plan comes to fruition through, not in spite of, the crucifixion of Jesus, so that Jesus is able to exercise his regal power of salvation in death as in life.[45]

7.6.3. The Death of Jesus (23:44-49)

44 *It was now about noon, and darkness came over the whole land until three in the afternoon,* 45 *while the sun's light failed; and the curtain of the temple was torn in two.* 46 *Then Jesus, crying with a loud voice, said, "Father, into your hands I commend my spirit." Having said this, he breathed his last.* 47 *When the centurion saw what had taken place, he praised God and said, "Certainly this man was righteous."[46]* 48 *And when all the crowds who had gathered there for this spectacle saw what had taken place, they returned home, beating their breasts.* 49 *But all his acquaintances, including the women who had followed him from Galilee, stood at a distance, watching these things.*

The culmination of an extraordinarily detailed passion account, the death of Jesus is paralleled only by his birth with regard to interpretive attention. This is not to say that Luke lingers long over the actual event of Jesus' crucifixion (recounted in only three words, v 33), or rehearses much the exact nature of his death (v 46). Rather, Jesus' death is interpreted, first, by its numerous proleptic announcements in the Third Gospel (e.g., 9:22; 17:25; 18:32-33; 20:9-19; et al.), and then by the phenomena accompanying it. Echoes of Israel's Scriptures add depth to that interpretation.

Crucial to our reading of this scene, then, is appropriate scrutiny of what happens before and after Jesus' expiration, recognizing that, in narratives, the linear placement of events points not simply to correlation but more specifically to causation.[47] That is, we must attend fully to the staging of the

44. For relevant texts and discussion, see Charlesworth, "Paradise."

45. See further, Fitzmyer, *Luke the Theologian,* 203-33; on the place of Jesus' death in Lukan soteriology, see further Green, "Salvation to the End of the Earth," forthcoming.

46. NRSV: "innocent."

47. See, e.g., Chatman, *Story and Discourse,* 45-48; Prince, *Narratology,* 11-12.

scene of Jesus' death so as to appreciate how the darkness and rending of the temple veil (vv 44-45) prepare for and lead into Jesus' outcry and death (v 46), which then prompts the series of responses outlined in vv 47-49.[48] In this case, the portents in vv 44-45 signify the cosmic stage on which Jesus' final hours are played out.[49] The "power of darkness" is particularly formidable, but does not nullify the presence of God, who responds to the escalation of hostility against his Son by rending the curtain of the temple. Jesus himself recognizes the interminable presence of God, the Father to whom he now commits his life in death. Finally, the Evangelist reports the effects of Jesus' death on the centurion, on the gathered crowds, and on Jesus' own followers. These three are related by the common motif of "witness" (see "saw" [2x], "spectacle," and "watching" in vv 47-49), though not all see equally well. Building on the metaphorical importance of "sight" employed throughout the Gospel (see above on 4:18-19), Luke pictures the centurion as seeing *and really seeing* — that is, as recognizing more fully than the rest the significance attributed the death of Jesus within the Lukan narrative. He exercises insight into Jesus' own identity, and realizes in Jesus' presence, even in Jesus' dying moment, the presence of God. The crowds express remorse, and this prepares for their repentance and faith in the early chapters of Acts. Luke thus has both Gentile and Jewish reactions to the death of Jesus, signifying in a limited but proleptic way the fulfillment of Simeon's vision that the coming of Jesus would effect God's salvation for all peoples, Jew and Gentile (2:30-32). More puzzling is the stance of "those who knew Jesus," who at least witness "these things," even if they do so from afar.

Relegated to the background of this scene are those whose hostility toward Jesus led to his rejection, crucifixion, and ongoing ridicule. Their place is taken instead by the "rule of darkness" with which, in their malevolence toward Jesus, they had aligned themselves. At one level, the demise of Jesus may seem to spell the triumph of darkness. Already in this scene, however, Luke has begun to demonstrate that rejection of Jesus by the Jewish leadership, in alliance with diabolic power (22:53), leads not to the squelching of the divine purpose but to the widening of the mission to embrace others.[50]

44-45 The scene of Jesus' death is set in three ways. First, Luke introduces into the passion account for the first time explicit measurements

---

48. In discourse analysis "staging" refers to the observation that what comes before prepares for and is assumed by what comes after (Brown and Yule, *Discourse Analysis*, 133-34).

49. Büchele (*Tod Jesu*, 52) regards the darkness and the rending of the temple veil as apocalyptic signs rooted in Joel 3:4 LXX: wonders in heaven, signs on the earth. Cf. Tyson, *Death of Jesus*, 108; Matera, "Death of Jesus," 475.

50. This pattern will be repeated in Acts — e.g., 13:44-49; 14:1-18; 18:2-6; 28:17-29. On the perspective sketched here, see Green, "Demise of the Temple."

of time. The effect of timekeeping is to slow the pace of the narrative down even further, to raise the gravity of the events now unfolding, and to invite interpretive probing of what happens in this particular time period. Second, he introduces again the motif of darkness, specifically through his mention of a three-hour period of the sun's failing. In Greco-Roman literature it was not unusual for the death of great persons to be accompanied by extraordinary signs,[51] but such parallels do not explain fully the function of this darkness for Luke. "Darkness" is collocated elsewhere in the narrative with diabolic enmity against God's purposes and thus against Jesus.[52] Moreover, darkness has eschatological significance related to the last days or Day of the Lord in Joel 2:30-31, a text that is paralleled elsewhere in the Scriptures (e.g., Amos 8:9; Zeph 1:15) and cited in Acts 2:20. If darkness points to the "last days,"[53] it is also of importance that, for Luke, the "last days" are associated with the mission to "all people" (Acts 2:17-21); darkness, then, anticipates and gives way to the universal spread of the light of God (cf. Acts 26:18).

Finally, Luke observes that "the curtain of the temple was torn in two." This has been a notoriously difficult phrase to interpret,[54] though it is clear from the use of the divine passive that Luke imagines the veil being rent by God. It is, then, the divine response to the hostility against Jesus. Luke generally has a positive view toward the temple, presenting it as a center of teaching and pious observance, and as a place of divine revelation.[55] At the same time, however, Luke has presented Jesus as God's agent to reform the temple, to return it to its rightful role in God's purpose (see above on 19:45-48), then recounted how Jesus' attempts at renewal were spurned by the temple leadership. In addition, Luke has indicated how the temple has functioned, problematically, as a sacred symbol of socio-religious power serving to legitimate the segregation of Jew and Gentile, priest and lay, male and female, and so on.[56] The rending of the temple veil, then, does not symbolize the destruction of the temple for Luke; though the collapse of the Holy City, and

51. See the examples in R. E. Brown, *Death of the Messiah,* 2:1043 — e.g., "Indeed, Pliny (*Natural History* 2.30; #97) mentions this death [of Julius Caesar] to exemplify a wide expectation: 'portentous and long eclipses of the sun, such as when Caesar the dictator was murdered.' "

52. See 1:78-19; 22:53; Acts 26:18; cf. the additional references to satanic activity in the passion account — 22:3, 28, 31, 40, and 46.

53. So, e.g., Matera, "Death of Jesus," 475.

54. The options are conveniently listed in Nolland, 3:1157.

55. See Green, "Demise of the Temple," 511-14. For positive assessments of the temple in Lukan theology, see, e.g., Bachmann, *Jerusalem und der Tempel;* Sylva, "Meaning and Function"; Weinert, "Meaning of the Temple"; *idem,* "Jerusalem's Abandoned House."

56. See Green, "Demise of the Temple," 509-11.

with it the temple, has already been prophesied by Jesus (e.g., vv 28-31), the temple is still standing and Jesus' followers continue to relate to it in the early chapters of Acts. What is signified is God's turning away from the temple in order to accomplish his purposes by other means. Luke portrays the rending of the temple veil as a symbol of the destruction of the symbolic world surrounding and emanating from the temple, neutralizing the centrality of the temple in preparation for the centrifugal mission of Jesus' followers — not *to* Jerusalem, but *from* it, and to the "end of the earth" (Acts 1:8).

46 It is important to remember that, in the midst of darkness (vv 44-45a), God is still present. Jesus' death does not contradict but actually helps to fulfill the divine purpose. This is signified by the tearing of the temple curtain in v 45b, and is evidenced in Jesus' final words from the cross. If God's presence is not in doubt, neither is Jesus' relationship to him. As he normally does in the Third Gospel, Jesus addresses God as "Father" (see above on vv 32-34). The words of his prayer are borrowed from Ps 31:5, a text in which the Suffering Righteous One entrusts himself to God's care. Employing this psalm, Jesus manifests his own faith in the sovereign God whom, he believes, will rescue him from the hands of his enemies. In light of the coupling of death and resurrection in Jesus' passion predictions (esp. 9:22; 18:31-33), we may hear in Jesus' prayer his faith in the God who raises from the dead.[57]

47-49 The persons whom Luke now mentions share in common their role as witnesses to Jesus' death.[58] The first two responses, that of the centurion and the crowds, are set in parallel:

When the centurion	When all the crowds . . .
saw what had taken place,	saw what had taken place,
he praised God and said . . .	they returned home, beating their breasts.

What did they see? On this Luke is not very explicit, though his use of the singular, "what had taken place" (compare "these things" in v 49), might suggest that he is thinking narrowly of Jesus' prayer and death, read as one event (v 46b).[59] Even if this is not the case, however, Luke has nonetheless provided a further instance of the revelatory character of Jesus' prayer. As in

---

57. Cf. Acts 2:27-28, 31; Neyrey, *Passion according to Luke,* 146-54. Jesus' entrusting his "spirit" need not be read as a reference to the separation of his body and spirit in death. Such a reading owes more to a Cartesian anthropology than to that shared by Luke's contemporaries (cf. D. B. Martin, *Corinthian Body,* 3-37). πνεῦμα refers to "life (in its totality)."

58. ὁράω — vv 47, 49; θεωρία/θεωρέω — v 48.

59. So Crump, *Jesus the Intercessor,* 89-90.

earlier scenes (e.g., 3:21-22; 9:18-20, 28-36), so here, Jesus' prayer results in persons having insight into his status before God.[60]

Roman soldiers have been portrayed in various ways in the Lukan narrative. Although some have been involved in Jesus' crucifixion, others had responded positively to the good news (Luke 3:10-14); in addition, earlier, a centurion was cast as an example of faith even to Israel (Luke 7:1-10; cf. Acts 10:1-4). Almost certainly a Gentile,[61] this centurion exercises extraordinary insight into Jesus' status, rivaled only by that of the second criminal, who had recognized that, in spite of Jesus' current position on a Roman cross, Jesus was capable of saving him (vv 42-43). The designation of Jesus as "righteous" plays off several related motifs. First, we are reminded of Jesus' innocence, repeatedly testified in the trial scene. Second, we are reminded of Luke's identification of Jesus with the Suffering Righteous One of the Scriptures of Israel.[62] Third, and more specifically, Luke thus identifies Jesus as the Isaianic Servant of Yahweh. This last point is made clear by two considerations: (1) the presence of other echoes of the Servant material in the Lukan passion account, and (2) the comparable use of "righteous" in conjunction with Jesus' death in Acts 3:13-14, in a co-text where the allusion to Isa 52:13–53:12 is indisputable. Again, then, Luke has brought into close proximity the dual identification of Jesus as Messiah and Servant, so as to articulate the suffering role of the Messiah.[63] Whether or not this Gentile centurion had access to all the interpretive clues available to Luke's audience and thus could discern the depth of his own christological statement, it is nevertheless clear that, in his response to Jesus' death, he recognizes the salvific hand of God at work in Jesus. This is, after all, the nuance given the phrase "to praise God" elsewhere in the Lukan narrative.[64]

The aforementioned parallelism between the centurion and the crowd affirms that their response, too, must be read in a positive light. These are the Jewish people who, earlier, had joined the Jewish council in demanding Jesus' execution, and then, shortly afterward, had begun to distance themselves from their leaders (vv 27, 35). "To return" may signify "repentance," but it is more likely that Luke portrays the people as returning from the place of crucifixion

---

60. This stands in obvious contrast with Herod, who hears about what has taken place but never grasps who Jesus is — cf. 9:7, 9; 23:8.

61. Cf. Josephus *J.W.* 18.3.5 §84.

62. See esp. Psalms 22 and 31, employed in the portrayal of Jesus' passion in Luke 23. Cf. Wisdom 2, 4-5. On the translation of δίκαιος as "righteous," rather than (merely) "innocent," see Karris, "Luke 23:47"; Beck, "Imitatio Christi," 40-46; Green, "God's Servant," 19-21.

63. For echoes of Servant texts, see, e.g., 22:37, 39-46; 23:9, 35. Cf. Green, "God's Servant," 18-23; Strauss, *Davidic Messiah,* 331-32.

64. δοξάζω — see 2:20; 5:25-26; 7:16; 13:13; 17:15; 18:43.

to the city.[65] "Beating their breasts" suggests sorrow or mourning, with the result that Luke has framed the scene of execution with acts of grief (Jerusalem's daughters — v 27; the gathered crowds — v 48). Linguistic parallels invite further comparison between the humble, justified tax collector (18:9-14) and these crowds (23:48).

"All his acquaintances" is a probable reference to the disciples and likely includes the apostles themselves, whose whereabouts have been unknown since the arrest (22:47-53). Nevertheless, Luke draws particular attention only to the presence of women disciples, indicating that they had followed him from Galilee (see 8:1-3).[66] They will provide the required continuity of memory following the resurrection (cf. 23:55; 24:6). As eyewitnesses, these persons will have an important role to fill in the book of Acts, but their characterization in this scene is not altogether positive. Like Peter in 22:54, they are distanced from Jesus; by analogy, the question remains, Will they remain faithful (as he did not!)? Comparison is also invited with Ps 38:11, where the Suffering Righteous One complains, "My friends and companions stand aloof from my affliction, and my neighbors stand far off." It is crucial to the Lukan narrative that they have at least to this degree remained "with" Jesus,[67] but their geographical remoteness indicates a weakened discipleship that is as yet unwilling to identify too closely with Jesus in his humiliation and death.[68] Their comportment vis-à-vis the cross of Christ creates a renewed sense of narrative tension that begs to be resolved: How will they respond to Jesus' death? What will be the future of God's purpose now that Jesus has died?

7.7. THE BURIAL OF JESUS (23:50-56)

> 50 *Now there was a good and righteous man named Joseph, who, though a member of the council,* 51 *had not agreed to their plan and action. He came from the Jewish town of Arimathea, and he was waiting expectantly for the kingdom of God.* 52 *This man went to Pilate and asked for the body of Jesus.* 53 *Then he took it down, wrapped it in a linen cloth, and laid it in a rock-hewn tomb where no one had ever been laid.* 54 *It was the day of Preparation, and the sabbath was beginning.* 55 *The women who had come with him from Galilee fol-*

65. ὑποστρέφω is not a synonym for μετανοέω in the Lukan narrative, though a double entente is possible here as well as in 2:20; 17:15, 18. See, however, v 56.

66. The phrase αἱ συνακολουθοῦσαι αὐτῷ, in the feminine, applies not to the whole of the group watching from afar, but specifically to the women.

67. On the importance of being "with" Jesus for the Lukan understanding of discipleship, see 6:17; 7:11; 8:1, 22; 9:10; 22:11, 14, 28, 39; cf. Acts 1:21.

68. See Tannehill, *Narrative Unity,* 1:272.

lowed, and they saw the tomb and how his body was laid. 56 Then they returned, and prepared spices and ointments. On the sabbath they rested according to the commandment.

Jewish people may have joined with the Jewish leadership in rejecting Jesus and calling for his execution (vv 13-25), Jesus may have presaged the inevitable destruction of Jerusalem (vv 28-31), and God may have invalidated the sacred authority of the temple by tearing the veil of the temple (v 45), but the sum of these factors is not for Luke a blanket condemnation of Judaism. Jesus' advent effects a division in Israel (cf. 2:34-35), not a complete repudiation of the ancient people of God. Immediately following Jesus' death, then, Luke portrays the Jewish people expressing remorse for his ignominious end (v 48). Adding to this picture is now the presentation of a Jewish man — indeed, one of the Jerusalem elite! — as one whose exemplary piety was available for telling and showing. Moreover, women disciples, in their decision to delay an important service to Jesus' corpse on account of the approaching Sabbath, act in accordance with the Mosaic law. Here at the end of Jesus' life, we find reminiscences of the beginning (chs. 1–2), with Jewish faithfulness on full display.

Luke's interest is not only to underscore the congruity between devout Judaism and the story of Jesus, however. Also emphasized in this transitional scene is the honor Jesus receives at the hands of Joseph of Arimathea and anticipated in the women's preparation of spices and ointments — honor far surpassing anything expected of an executed criminal in either Roman or Jewish tradition. It is probably not too much to say that Luke's account is shaped thematically so as to indicate that Israel expresses its faithfulness most fully when it is oriented toward Jesus, God's redemptive agent.[1]

50-53 Luke expends extraordinary detail in his characterization of Joseph, undoubtedly because, in the Greek text, he first allows an astounding incongruity: Joseph is "a council member," but he is also "a good and righteous man." Since it is the council that rejected Jesus and handed him over to Pilate, led the riotous call for Jesus' execution, and mocked him on the cross, how could Joseph be "righteous"? The paradox is only heightened when it is remembered that the centurion had just employed the same word, "righteous,"[2] with reference to Jesus (v 47). The resolution to this puzzle comes in a play on the word "plan," which, in Greek, is cognate with the word for "council member."[3] Even though he was a member of the council,

---

1. For this emphasis in the Lukan writings, see Green, *Gospel of Luke,* 68-75.

2. δίκαιος.

3. βουλή, βουλευτής. This explains why Luke uses this term for "council member" rather than the vocabulary used to describe the Jewish leadership in Jerusalem earlier in the passion narrative.

he did not agree with its counsel. This may help to recall for Luke's readers that the story of Luke-Acts is, in large part, the tale of two competing purposes — that of God and that which opposes God.[4] Like Elizabeth and Zechariah, Simeon and Anna, Joseph is aligned with God's purpose (cf. 1:5-6; 2:25, 37). Joseph's Jewishness is further accented by the explicit report that he hailed from a Judean town (v 51), just as his exemplary piety is emphasized by his comportment with regard to the kingdom of God. He does not yet participate in it,[5] but, like Simeon and others in Jerusalem, is awaiting it (cf. 2:25, 38).

Luke is not content simply to speak about Joseph's piety, but goes on to demonstrate it. Burying the deceased, in Jewish tradition, was a means of fulfilling the obligation to share with those in need. To be refused burial, conversely, was a fate interpreted under the heading of divine curse.[6] Typically, preparation for burial entailed washing, anointing, and clothing the body. The warm climate in ancient Palestine dictated a speedy burial, with spices and ointments used not for purposes of embalming but in order to counter the stench of decomposition. The tomb imagined by Luke's account (v 53) was fashioned by quarrying into the side of a rock face. Such a tomb might have included a forecourt before a cave, the mouth of which could be covered by a large, disk-shaped stone set in a groove cut in the rock beneath it (cf. 24:2). The entrance would lead into the burial chamber with a stone step and central pit of sufficient height to allow persons to stand in order to prepare a corpse for interment on one of the stone benches carved into the rock along the sides of the chamber. Joseph's apparent possession of such a tomb, like his membership in the Jerusalem council, evidences his elite status.[7]

Burial, though also a matter of honor and obligation in the Roman world, was typically denied persons sentenced to death as a pronounced form of dishonor. The first-century Alexandrian Jew Philo does report cases on the eve of festive occasions where the crucified were removed and given to their relatives for burial. More generally, in light of the instructions regarding burial in Deut 21:22-23, Jewish practice was, when possible, always to provide

4. For this emphasis, see Green, *Gospel of Luke,* 22-49.

5. *Contra,* e.g., Karris, *Luke: Artist and Theologian,* 114; Bauernfield, *Apostelgeschichte,* 175. They apparently regard Joseph already as a disciple of Jesus. That Joseph is not regarded by Luke as a follower of Jesus is suggested by the report in Acts 13:29, to the effect that the inhabitants of Jerusalem and their leaders were responsible for burying Jesus (cf. John 19:31; *Gos. Pet.* 6:21).

6. See, e.g., Deut 28:26; Jer 8:1-2; 16:1-4; Ezek 29:5; Tob 1:16–2:10; Josephus *Ag. Ap.* 2.29 §211.

7. Because the tomb is new, this is even more the case, since the practice of "second burial" allowed for the repeated use of tombs. The body was placed on a sand-covered stone bench; after a twelve-month period of decomposition, the bones were collected and placed in an ossuary.

burial.[8] That Jesus was buried at all, then, is unusual though not wholly unexpected. More surprising is the honor given his corpse since, even among Jews, the executed were provided only the ignominious burial suited to the condemned.[9] Jesus, by way of contrast, was wrapped in a linen cloth and shown the honor of a new tomb;[10] similarly, in vv 55-56, women prepare the ointments and spices to complete an honorable burial process.

54-56 This subunit of the Lukan account is marked by the dual reference to the approaching Sabbath (vv 54, 56b). The purpose of this *inclusio* is twofold — first, to avoid any hint that these disciples of Jesus were engaged in Sabbath-breaking; and, second, to provide a bridge between the scenes of crucifixion and resurrection appearance by mandating the return of these women following the Sabbath. As at his birth (e.g., 2:21-24), so in his burial, the law is fulfilled.

Luke's introduction of the women follows closely the wording of v 49 in mentioning their Galilean origins (see 24:6) and in describing their primary role as one of observing.[11] This provides a further link between the scenes of execution, burial, and resurrection, as well as intimates the continuity between the Jesus of Galilee and the resurrected Jesus.

---

8. Philo *Flacc.* 10.83-84. For Roman and Jewish practices, see R. E. Brown, *Death of the Messiah,* 2:1207-11; Green, "Burial," 88-90.

9. See 1 Kgs 13:21-22; Jer 26:23; Josephus *Ant.* 5.1.14 §44; 4.8.6 §202.

10. Cf. 19:30: "a colt that has never been ridden"; 23:53: "a rock-hewn tomb where no one had ever been laid."

11. ὁράω is used in v 49 (also v 47), θεωρέω in v 55 (also v 48).

8. THE EXALTATION OF JESUS (24:1-53)

Among the central moments in Jesus' career Luke has led his readers to anticipate, three remain: his ascension, his baptism with the Spirit, and his return in glory. The third will not be narrated by the Third Evangelist, though even in the Acts of the Apostles he will continue to nurture expectation of Jesus' return.[1] The second will occupy the Evangelist in the book of Acts, especially in Acts 2. The first is in focus here. Jesus' ascension has been envisioned most explicitly in the narrator's analysis of Jesus' turn to Jerusalem, from whence he would "be taken up" (9:51), and earlier, in the transfiguration scene, wherein Jesus is said to have spoken with Moses and Elijah concerning his "exodus" (9:31). Repeated contemplation of Jesus' impending enthronement has also portended the vindication and exaltation he would experience in his resurrection and ascension. Chapter 24 of Luke thus narrates the climax of the Third Gospel, even if it does not constitute the conclusion of the Lukan narrative.

Indeed, taken together, Luke 24 and Acts 1 provide the transition in the Lukan narrative from the story of Jesus to the story of his witnesses. To this end, the Evangelist has incorporated into the final chapter of the Gospel both retrospective summaries and interpretations of the Third Gospel and prospective intimations of the shape of the story to come.[2] A comparison of the closing verses of Luke 24 and Acts 1:4-11 highlights immediately Luke's use of internal repetition to weave tightly together his two volumes into a continuous narrative.[3] Both record:

1. See, e.g., Acts 1:11; Carroll, *End of History*.
2. So also Tannehill, *Narrative Unity*, 1:277.
3. Previous scholarship was fascinated with the dissimilarities between these accounts, which constituted the raw materials for interpolation theories and tradition-historical inquiry. More recently, scholars have viewed these differences (1) against the background of Luke's interest in repetition and variation (cf. Mussies, "Variation"), and

- an appearance of Jesus to his followers
- Jesus' eating in front of/with the disciples
- the directive to remain in Jerusalem
- the prospective fulfillment of the Father's promise
- the description of disciples as "witnesses"
- the universal scope of the mission
- an account of the ascension

Retrospective synopses occur in vv 6-7, 14, 18b-21, and 44, the burden of which is that, between Jesus' earlier proclamation and the Scriptures of Israel, the disciples (should) possess already the interpretive tools necessary to make sense of the suffering and death of Jesus. Heretofore, the disciples had been unable to correlate Jesus' status before God and divinely ordained mission with his passion (e.g., 9:44-45; 18:31-34; cf. 24:18-21), with the consequence that the centrality of Jesus' crucifixion to the divine purpose must now be emphasized again, and definitively. Importantly, the necessity of the death of the Messiah will serve subsequently as a central component of the missionary preaching of Jesus' witnesses (e.g., Acts 3:18; 17:2-3); this points to the efficacy of these final lessons reported in Luke 24, as angels and Jesus recall for Jesus' disciples his own teaching about his suffering and as Jesus "opens their minds to understand the scriptures" concerning messianic suffering (vv 45-46).

In spite of the degree to which Luke 24 brings closure to the Third Gospel,[4] other narrative threads within the Gospel are left hanging, including the most basic: the fulfillment of God's purpose to bring salvation in all its fullness to all people. Luke 24 also leaves open-ended the problem of Israel's response to God's gracious visitation, the repeated but as-yet-unfulfilled promise of the baptism with/gift of the Holy Spirit, and the anticipated parousia. These suggest the degree to which the Lukan Gospel is incomplete in itself, the degree to which it requires the addition of a second volume, the Acts of the Apostles. It is no coincidence, then, that each of these narrative threads is taken up again in Acts 1:1-11, with the result that Luke will invite his audience to contemplate in what ways his second volume might resolve these narrative needs. Luke 24, and especially vv 47-49, anticipates the ever-widening mission to "all nations" — anticipated in, but hardly broached since, the birth narra-

---

(2) in the light of the distinctive narrative purposes of these accounts, on the analogy, e.g., of the telling and retelling of the story of Cornelius in 10:1–11:18 and the multiple accounts of Saul's Damascus Road experience in 9:1-19; 22:1-21; 26:9-23 (where discrepancies also occur). What serves to close the narrative in Luke 24 is refashioned to open new possibilities in Acts 1.

4. This is emphasized by Parsons, *Departure of Jesus,* 65-113; *idem,* "Narrative Closure."

tives (chs. 1–2). The final words of Jesus to which Luke makes us privy identify the disciples as "witnesses" and instruct them to remain in Jerusalem for the Father's promise; for what purpose and to whom will they be witnesses (cf. 12:11; 20:12-13)? At the close of the Gospel, they respond to his instruction obediently, remaining in the Jerusalem temple. What comes next? In such ways as these, Luke entices his audience to "turn the page," as it were, to move from volume one to volume two in anticipation of the report and aftermath of the disciples' being "clothed with power."

Understanding and obedience are not the first responses of Jesus' followers, however. Encountering the empty tomb leads first to perplexity (v 4) and amazement (v 12); the women's description of the empty tomb and angelic message is met with cynicism and unbelief (v 11). The two disciples on the road to Emmaus are clueless concerning the meaning of Jesus' death, disappointed by this presumed dashing of their hopes (vv 13-21), and astounded by reports of the empty tomb (v 22). Even in the presence of the risen Jesus, though filled with joy, some were disbelieving and wondering (v 41). It is as if they lacked the interpretive categories for rendering recent events in a meaningful way. The nature of these responses is testimony to the inherent ambiguity of these events. The cross and empty tomb — these are not self-interpreting, but require elucidation.[5] In ch. 24, then, Luke highlights the necessity of interpretation while at the same time indicating the sources and contours of valid interpretation.

What are these sources and contours?[6] Luke makes use, first, of internal repetition — that is, repetition within the Gospel itself, drawing attention to the consistency between what Jesus predicted would happen to him in his role as Son of Man and what in fact has now taken place. Jesus' own words as God's regal prophet are thus key to discerning the unfolding of God's purpose. Second, Luke makes use of external repetition, indicating in his summaries of Jesus' instruction that what the disciples have taken as confusing events leading to and including Jesus' demise are actually continuous with the Scriptures of Israel. Through his portrayal of Jesus as teacher, through the employment of the vocabulary of interpretation,[7] and through his depiction of the prophetic pattern of Jesus' life, Luke presents Jesus as the one who both interprets and actualizes in his own life the Scriptures. From this flow important corollaries: (1) Jesus' passion is not a contradiction of his status or mission, but its fulfillment; he is the rejected prophet, the suffering Messiah who, according to the Scriptures, brings God's purpose to realization. (2) The

---

5. Schubert ("Structure and Significance," 167-68) emphasizes how the empty tomb has little value as a means of revelation in Luke's account.

6. See Schubert, "Structure and Significance"; Bock, *Proclamation;* Koet, *Five Studies,* 56-72.

7. See, e.g., συζητέω, διανοίγω, διερμηνεύω, ὁμιλέω; Koet, *Five Studies,* 65-70.

resurrection and ascension of Jesus are likewise grounded in Scripture, and so constitute God's vindication of Jesus. Indeed, Luke 24 is in part a narrative affirmation that "everything written" is coming to fruition. (3) Just as these events in Jesus' life do not carry within themselves their own interpretation, so also the Scriptures of Israel are not self-interpreting. By means of the resurrection, Jesus' perspective on and use of the Scriptures are shown to be authorized by God, over against the interpretations of his opponents among the Jerusalem leadership (see chs. 20–23). God's purpose as revealed in the Scriptures, then, is best understood in light of its fulfillment in Jesus' career. (4) Jesus' role is not only that of a hermeneut for his followers. He must also enable them properly to read the Scriptures.[8]

The Evangelist has set this series of scenes in and around Jerusalem. The significance of this setting is suggested by the fact that the Third Gospel thus begins and ends in the Holy City and by the importance given Jerusalem as the place of destiny for Jesus earlier in the narrative. The first three scenes are set in a single day (vv 1, 13, 36), with the fourth less clearly tied temporally to the others.[9]

8.1. THE EMPTY TOMB (24:1-12)

> 24:1 *But on the first day of the week, at early dawn, they came to the tomb, taking the spices that they had prepared.* 2 *They found the stone rolled away from the tomb,* 3 *but when they went in, they did not find the body of the Lord Jesus.*[1] 4 *While they were perplexed about this, suddenly two men in dazzling clothes stood beside them.* 5 *The women were terrified and bowed their faces to the ground, but the men said to them, "Why do you look for the living among the dead? He is not here, but has risen.* 6 *Remember how he told you, while he was still in Galilee,* 7 *that the Son of Man must be handed over to sinners,*

---

8. See Koet, *Five Studies,* 70-71.

9. For many interpreters, vv 50-53 stand in tension with the testimony of Acts, that the resurrection appearances extended over forty days (1:3). For example, Moule ("Ascension") theorizes that Luke came across the tradition of forty days only after completing his Gospel, and Wilson ("Ascension," 271) conjectures that by the time he wrote Acts 1:3 Luke had forgotten what he had written previously. In fact, this tension is more apparent than real, since vv 50-53 are only loosely connected in a chronological sense to the preceding material. As Dillon has noted, ". . . Luke is not primarily interested [in Luke 24] in the external time-framework of the paschal happenings, but in their inner unity and totality" (*Eyewitnesses,* 181).

1. Apparently on the strength of its omission in the Western text, the NRSV omits "of the Lord Jesus." The phrase is included in p[75] ℵ A B C W Θ f[1] f[13] et al.

and be crucified, and on the third day rise again." 8 Then they remem-
bered his words, 9 and returning from the tomb, they told all this to
the eleven and to all the rest. 10 Now it was Mary Magdalene, Joanna,
Mary the mother of James, and the other women with them who told
this to the apostles. 11 But these words seemed to them an idle tale,
and they did not believe them. 12 But Peter got up and ran to the tomb;
stooping and looking in, he saw the linen cloths by themselves; then
he went home, amazed at what had happened.

Activity in this episode revolves around an incongruity that serves well the
role of this scene as a bridge from the scenes of Jesus' death and burial to the
appearance stories to follow. Functioning as the deictic center of this account
is the tomb. The women come to the tomb and enter it, then return from it
(vv 1-2, 8), as does Peter (v 12). Moreover, Luke is careful throughout this
episode to record a series of cognitive, affective, and behavioral responses to
what happens at the tomb. Yet, the tomb is ill suited for its role since, by this
point in the narrative, it has become irrelevant. As the angels declare of Jesus,
"He is not here, but has risen" (v 5).

The theme of incongruity Luke weaves into the story line of this scene
serves a further function. It also underscores the import of Jesus' earlier
teaching regarding how he would fulfill his divine role in his passion, how
his suffering was neither a contradiction of his status before God nor the last
word in God's plan for him. The Evangelist has repeatedly noted the incapacity
of the disciples to grasp this truth (e.g., 9:44-45; 18:31-34), but now he signals
a breakthrough on the part of the women. If the male disciples continue in
their obtuseness, and thus lack of faith, at least Peter responds to the witness
of the women by going to the tomb. His behavior portends at least the
possibility of a more full understanding of Jesus' message on their part.

It cannot be overlooked, though, that the move from perplexity to clarity
on the part of the women disciples is enabled by the angelic call to remember
Jesus' words. The empty tomb is little more than a mystery apart from its place
in the sum of Jesus' ministry; only in light of his appraisal of the divine plan is
interpretation conceivable. And it is precisely here that the parallel between the
women and Peter breaks down. Both come to and enter the tomb, both find Jesus'
corpse missing, and both return from the tomb. Only the women receive
heavenly communication about these goings-on, however, so only they receive
insight into their significance. Peter's "amazement" may represent an advance
on the women's original bewilderment, but it is not yet faith or even comprehension. As Luke has it, events require interpretation,[2] and the key to interpretation is Jesus' own articulation of the purpose of God.

2. See Dillon, *Eyewitnesses,* 19-20; Schubert, "Structure and Significance," 167-68.

1-3 This scene is closely tied to that of the burial of Jesus (23:50-56) by numerous elements, including temporal markers (from Sabbath to the first day of the week), the desire of the women to complete Jesus' honorable burial with spices, and the preparation of those spices. In the earlier scene Luke was careful to note that the women "saw the tomb and how his body was laid," with the result that, as they now return to the tomb, they can hardly expect anything other than an undisturbed corpse. In this way he preserves the element of astonishment when the body is found missing. Indeed, this point of the account is heightened by the double use of the verb "to find": they *found* the stone rolled away from the tomb, but did not *find* the corpse. Who are these women? How was the stone removed? Luke's account neglects such detail, for he wants to move quickly to the pivotal discovery of an empty tomb.

On the architecture of the tomb envisioned here, see above on 23:50-53.

The use of the prepositional phrase "of the Lord Jesus" is a subtle intimation of the news to come when the significance of the appearances of Jesus cascades onto his followers. His identity and status before God have not in any way been negated or diminished by his shameful rejection and ignominious execution. The name "Lord Jesus" will be repeated in Acts 1:21; 4:33; 8:16, and in Acts 2:32-36 Peter will develop the logic of Jesus' lordship by referring to Jesus' exaltation by God.

4-7 The designation of Jesus as Lord in v 3 is available to Luke's audience, but not to the women, who then are lacking in interpretive resources. Expecting a corpse to anoint, they can only respond to its absence with bewilderment.[3] Resolution for the puzzle with which they are faced comes in the form of an angelophany, to which they respond, typically, with fear and reverence.[4] The angels address the women as though the latter were persons on a quest — though, in comparison with other quest stories in the Third Gospel, this one is unusual. In such stories generally, persons approach Jesus in the hope of human restoration (e.g., 5:17-26; 7:1-10; 17:12-19; 19:1-10).[5] These women come looking for Jesus, but they want to minister to him, and, as they quickly discover, because they lack understanding, they are looking in the wrong place. The angels first admonish them, employing language that is reminiscent of Jesus' rejoinder to the Sadducees in 20:38: God is not the God of the dead but of the living! That is, in spite of their devout intentions

---

3. ἀπορέω — use in Luke-Acts only here and in Acts 25:20.

4. That the words "two men" designate angels is evident from v 23: "a vision of angels." For parallel use of ἀνήρ, see Acts 1:10; 10:30; cf. Dan 8:15: ὡς ὅρασις ἀνθρώπου. For ἀστράπτω and related terms, cf. 9:29; 10:18; 11:36; 17:24; its usage in this co-text is consistent with the imagery of an angelophany. ἐσθής is used similarly in Acts 1:10; 10:30. For responses of fear in such co-texts, see above on 1:12. For "bowing the face," see Dan 10:9, 15.

5. See Tannehill, *Narrative Unity,* 111-27.

in coming to anoint Jesus' body, these women have failed to grasp Jesus' message about the resurrection and, thus, have not taken with appropriate gravity the power of God.

The antidote for this miscalculation is remembrance. The women are addressed as persons who had themselves received Jesus' teaching in Galilee,[6] and the angel's message fuses Jesus' predictions during the Galilean phase of his ministry (9:22, 44). Thus they are reminded that the career of the Son of Man blends the two motifs of suffering and vindication, and that in doing so he fulfills the divine will.[7] Two innovations in this Son of Man saying indicate the different narrative placements of the Galilean sayings and of this one. First, the term "crucified" is used, rather than "killed," reflecting the actual form of execution. Second, those responsible for Jesus' death are labeled as "sinners"; from the heavenly perspective, the repudiation and killing of Jesus was an evil act. Importantly, the women are given no commission, but are themselves treated as recipients of Jesus' words and summoned simply to authentic understanding. Their reception of the resurrection message ". . . confirms their discipleship and the instruction they have received as disciples."[8]

8-10 The response of the women to the angelic message is reminiscent of Peter's response in 22:61:

"Then Peter remembered the word of the Lord . . ."
"Then they remembered his words. . . ."

In both cases Jesus' prophecy is the content of the memory, and in both cases "to remember" consists of more than cognitive evocation. "To remember" includes as well the nuance of understanding or insight, and is the threshold of response apropos what is recalled.[9] The women are not instructed to bear witness to what they had experienced and the new insight they now shared, but they do so spontaneously (cf. Acts 4:20). Luke underscores the faithfulness

6. This is underscored in Rigato, "Luke 24:6-8," 96. R. J. Dillon (*Eyewitnesses,* 38) thinks that Luke's ὑμῖν refers not so much to the women as to Luke's audience, but Luke's ὑμῖν (v 6) must be read in parallel with πρὸς αὐτάς in v 5; consequently, Luke's audience will understand themselves as the addressees of the angels' instruction only to the degree that they are able to identify with these women disciples.

7. As in 9:22, 44, this passion-and-resurrection saying uses the term δεῖ to signify what is necessary according to the divine plan. For this perspective on Luke's use of the phrase "Son of Man," see esp. Kingsbury, *Conflict in Luke,* 73-78.

8. Seim, *Double Message,* 151; cf. Witherington, *Women in the Earliest Churches,* 130-31.

9. See Leivestad, "μιμνῄσκομαι," 430; *TLNT,* 2:491-93, 495; Plevnik, "Eyewitnesses," 91-98.

of their testimony by noting that they announced "all these things" — that is, what they had observed, what they had been told, and the new significance they attributed to Jesus' passion and the absence of his corpse. Only now does Luke provide names of some previously hidden in their anonymity among "the women who had followed him from Galilee" (23:49, 55), and two of them are known to Luke's audience as exemplary disciples (cf. 8:1-3).[10] In this way, the credibility of their testimony would seem to have been secured: A complete report ("all this") is given by persons who have participated fully (since Galilee) in Jesus' mission. Specifying these names also allows the following apposition of the women disciples (who have seen the empty tomb, heard the angels, and possess new insight) with the male disciples:

Mary Magdalene, Joanna,	the eleven[11] (also known as apostles — v 10)
Mary the mother of James, and the other women	and all the rest[12]

Reference to "the others" and to "all the rest" signals the preeminence of Mary Magdalene, Joanna, Mary the mother of James, and the eleven apostles within the community.[13]

11-12 The gap between male and female disciples widens, as the faithful account of the women falls on the cynical and unbelieving ears of the men. Nothing more than useless chatter[14] — this is how their announcement is evaluated and discarded. This can be explained in at least two ways. First, the earlier situation of the women disciples is being repeated in the case of their male counterparts; failing to grasp Jesus' teaching regarding his suffering and resurrection, they cannot make sense of the news shared with them.[15] At the same time, however, Luke's "all this" (v 8) cannot but include the message they had received from the angels, so that the men were given access to the significance of recent events. The dismissive response of the men is therefore

10. Mary Magdalene and Joanna are mentioned in 8:1-3, but this is the first time Mary, the mother of James, is mentioned. Her identification in relation to a male, in spite of the faithfulness she has exercised, is typical for this period.

11. That is, the twelve sans Judas, whose defection will be addressed in Acts 1:15-26.

12. Cf. Acts 1:12-15.

13. See the suggestive comments in Plevnik, "The Eleven."

14. λῆρος, used only here in the NT. Although this noun belongs to the technical vocabulary of medicine where it denotes the delirium caused by high fever, Spicq (*TLNT*, 2:387) observes that the sense of this term in the Lukan co-text derives from its usage in "familiar, sarcastic conversation."

15. Cf. Conzelmann, *Luke,* 93-94n.2.

better explained with reference to the fact that those doing the reporting are women in a world biased against the admissibility of women as witnesses.[16]

Against this backdrop, Peter's response — to retrace the steps the women had taken in vv 1-3[17] — must be evaluated all the more positively. As has happened previously in the passion account (cf. 22:31-34, 54b, 61-62), he is segregated from the others. Even he does not reach the level of insight shared by the women, however. In the Third Gospel, "to be amazed" is a characteristic response to the extraordinary, but it is neither tantamount to faith nor does it portend the eventuality of genuine perception or faith.[18] Unlike the women, he returns home with no new message to share.

8.2. ENCOUNTER ON THE ROAD TO EMMAUS (24:13-35)

13 *Now on that same day two of them were going to a village called Emmaus, about seven miles from Jerusalem,* 14 *and talking with each other about all these things that had happened.* 15 *While they were talking and discussing, Jesus himself came near and went with them,* 16 *but their eyes were kept from recognizing him.* 17 *And he said to them, "What are you discussing with each other while you walk along?" They stood still, looking sad.* 18 *Then one of them, whose name was Cleopas, answered him, "Are you the only stranger in Jerusalem who does not know the things that have taken place there in these days?"* 19 *He asked them, "What things?" They replied, "The things about Jesus of Nazareth, who was a prophet mighty in deed and word before God and all the people,* 20 *and how our chief priests and leaders handed him over to be condemned to death and crucified him.* 21 *But we had hoped that he was the one to redeem Israel. Yes, and besides all this, it is now the third day since these things took place.* 22 *Moreover, some women of our group astounded us. They were at*

16. Cf. Seim, *Double Message,* 156-57; Witherington, *Women in the Earliest Churches,* 132 (though this position is nuanced in Witherington, *Women in the Ministry of Jesus,* 135-36n.88). Ilan (*Jewish Women,* 163-66) observes cases where women were called upon to provide testimony in court, but also provides documentation that the testimony of women was avoided whenever possible. According to Josephus (*Ant.* 4.8.15 §219), women were disqualified on account of their giddiness and impetuosity (κουφότης καὶ θράσος; cf. λῆρος in 24:11).

17. The status of v 12 has been subjected to extensive debate, though most interpreters today regard it as authentic — cf. the discussion in Ross, "Luke 24:12"; Neirynck, "Empty Tomb Stories," 172-75; *idem,* "Luke 24,12" (in response to Dauer, "Lk 24,12").

18. Cf., e.g., 2:18; 4:25; 8:25; 11:38; 20:26.

the tomb early this morning, 23 *and when they did not find his body there, they came back and told us that they had indeed seen a vision of angels who said that he was alive.* 24 *Some of those who were with us went to the tomb and found it just as the women had said; but they did not see him."* 25 *Then he said to them, "Oh, how foolish you are, and how slow of heart to believe all that the prophets have declared!* 26 *Was it not necessary that the Messiah should suffer these things and then enter into his glory?"* 27 *Then beginning with Moses and all the prophets, he interpreted to them the things about himself in all the scriptures.*

28 *As they came near the village to which they were going, he walked ahead as if he were going on.* 29 *But they urged him strongly, saying, "Stay with us, because it is almost evening and the day is now nearly over." So he went in to stay with them.* 30 *When he was at the table with them, he took bread, blessed and broke it, and gave it to them.* 31 *Then their eyes were opened, and they recognized him; and he vanished from their sight.* 32 *They said to each other, "Were not our hearts burning within us while he was talking to us on the road, while he was opening the scriptures to us?"* 33 *That same hour they got up and returned to Jerusalem; and they found the eleven and their companions gathered together.* 34 *They were saying, "The Lord has risen indeed, and he has appeared to Simon!"* 35 *Then they told what had happened on the road, and how he had been made known to them in the breaking of the bread.*

The significance and focus of this account are determined considerably by its narrative location. At one level, the Emmaus story is embedded into the Lukan passion- and empty-tomb episodes,[1] and indeed, the whole of Luke's account of Jesus' ministry, by retrospective summary (vv 19-24), consistency of characters ("two of them," v 13), geographical references (with Jerusalem as the point of reference — vv 13, 33), temporal continuity ("that same day," v 13) and emphasis on the "third day" (vv 13, 21, 33), and the emphasis on the fulfillment of prophecy (vv 6-7, 25-26, 44-46). Even more organic to the progression of Lukan interests, however, is the central role of this pericope in the development of the theme of perception and response. In ch. 24, despite the clarity of Jesus' prophecies, the empty tomb leads to mixed evaluations, with only the women disciples exercising needed insight. Peter's trip to the tomb raises the possibility for broader understanding, but this prospect is obstructed by disbelief (vv 1-12). The possibility of insight for Jesus' followers is strengthened, however, by the intervention of Jesus in the Emmaus scene,

1. Cf. DeLeers, "The Road to Emmaus," 100-101.

for he opens the Scriptures and, in doing so, opens the eyes of additional disciples. Though Luke does not record it, his account assumes an additional appearance episode, so that the voices of the Emmaus travelers join that of the women, and they add to their testimony the witness of Simon: "The Lord has risen indeed!" Possibility (vv 1-12) thus gives way to probability (vv 13-35), and probability to actuality (vv 36-49) and resolution (vv 50-53) — that is, to fresh understanding and obedience. In this way, Jesus' followers are indeed prepared to serve as "witnesses of these things" (v 48), and this they will do with the opening of Luke's second volume, the book of Acts.

Not surprisingly, then, the Emmaus account is structured in such a way as to call particular attention to the progression from lack of recognition to full recognition and to the means by which insight is gained, and thus to underscore the women's earlier affirmation that Jesus is alive. For example, Luke's account shares points of contact with episodes of divine encounter in Genesis, but departs from them in its interest in the deliberation over the meaning of Jesus' passion.[2] Additionally, numerous studies have pointed to the similarities between this account and Luke's narrative of Philip's encounter with the Ethiopian Eunuch (Acts 8:26-40), which also concentrates on issues of meaning, and particularly on the interpretive interplay between the Scriptures and the ministry of Jesus.[3] Finally, the following inverted parallelism is discernible —

    The Journey from Jerusalem (vv 14-15)
        Appearance, "Obstructed Eyes," Lack of Recognition (v 16)
            Interaction (vv 17-18)
                Summary of "the things" (vv 19-21)
                    Empty Tomb and Vision (vv 22-23a)
                        Jesus Is Alive (v 23b)
                    Empty Tomb, but No Vision (v 24)
                Interpretation of "the things" (vv 25-27)
            Interaction (vv 28-30)
        "Opened Eyes," Recognition, and Disappearance (vv 31-32)
    The Journey to Jerusalem (vv 33-35) —

and this sketches the import of disclosure and perception to the Lukan agenda. Other motifs are present, of course, but these serve the larger theme

2. Cf., e.g., Gen 16:7-15; 18:1-33. These and other parallels are discussed in Legrand, "Christ the Fellow Traveller," 33-36.

3. Cf., e.g., D'Sa, "Emmaus Narrative"; Gibbs, "Luke 24:13-33 and Acts 8:26-39"; Grassi, "Emmaus Revisited"; B. P. Robinson, "Emmaus Story," 483-84; Rosica, "Road to Emmaus"; *idem,* "Two Journeys of Faith."

of this account. *(1) The Journey:* In light of the importance of the journey motif to the Lukan enterprise (see above on 9:51–19:48), repeated references to travel in this pericope are all the more noticeable.[4] At the outset of the journey to Jerusalem and at its close, the disciples had proven themselves extraordinarily intractable in their lack of perception (9:45; 18:34), in spite of Jesus' attempts to enlighten them "on the way." Now that Luke pictures these disciples "on the road" with Jesus again, the query is raised, What will be the effect of *this* journey on their obduracy?

(2) Hospitality and Table Fellowship: Again in light of the Lukan narrative as a whole, the revelatory significance afforded the moment of sharing the table cannot be overlooked.[5] Echoes of Luke's account of Jesus' last meal with his disciples (22:19-20) have caused some to see in the Emmaus episode eucharistic overtones.[6] This view rests on a problematic rendering of the phrase "the breaking of the bread" (see below, v 35) and an exaggerated view of the Third Evangelist's interest in the eucharist;[7] neither does it take seriously enough that the closest parallels to Jesus' activity at the table at the close of this "third day" are in the miraculous feeding episode (9:12-17) and not in the Last Supper.[8] Not coincidentally, the feeding of the thousands itself possesses revelatory significance within the Lukan narrative, leading from misconception to correct perception of Jesus' identity as Messiah (9:7-20).

(3) Scriptural Fulfillment: From the standpoint of the Lukan narrative, the key to making sense of the death of Jesus lies in construing it within the matrix of "the scriptures" (vv 25-27, 32). This draws attention both to Luke's perspective on the prophetic role of the Scriptures and to the necessity of interpreting them faithfully.

Evident above all, then, is the need for revelation, which comes for Luke not so much via angelic intervention (though this is hardly out of the

---

4. "Going" (v 13), "came near" (v 15), "went" (v 15), "walking along" (v 17), "came near" (v 28), "going" (v 28), "walked" (v 28), "going on" (v 28), "went" (v 29), "on the road" (v 32), "got up and returned" (v 33), and "on the road" (v 35). Cf. also travel to and from the tomb — vv. 22-24. On this motif in vv 13-35, see, e.g., B. P. Robinson, "Emmaus Story," 481-82; Karris, "Luke 24:13-35," 57-58; Just, *Ongoing Feast,* 58; R. J. Dillon, *Eyewitnesses,* 89-90.

5. Just (*Ongoing Feast,* e.g., 219) regards this as the climax of the account. On this motif, see also, e.g., Karris, "Luke 24:13-35," 58-59; B. P. Robinson, "Emmaus Story," 485-87.

6. For example, Osborne, *Resurrection Narratives,* 123-24; Just, *Ongoing Feast.*

7. This is emphasized by B. P. Robinson, "Emmaus Story," 487-93; and, on different grounds, by Green, *Death of Jesus,* 211-12.

8. To suggest, as many do, that 9:12-17 is designed to echo the eucharistic practices of the early church and, so, to portend the Last Supper account in 22:19-20, only begs the question whether Luke highlights the eucharist in his narrative. The presumption of unity of eucharistic practice in the apostolic era rests on surprisingly little data.

question! — v 23), but through a hermeneutical process of comprehending the purpose of God in the correlation of Jesus' career with the Scriptures of Israel. What has happened with Jesus can be understood only in light of the Scriptures, yet the Scriptures themselves can be understood only in light of what has happened with Jesus. These two are mutually informing. And before the disciples will be able to recognize the risen Lord (vv 3, 5, 34), they must grasp especially the nexus between suffering and messiahship.[9]

13-16 Luke immediately inscribes this scene into the preceding one in two ways. The first is a temporal marker, referring back to both the "first day of the week" (v 1) and, thus, the day on which the women reported their experiences at the empty tomb.[10] Second, the Evangelist singles out "two of them" from among the larger company of disciples. This means of identifying the travelers is of importance since it characterizes these two as persons from among those who earlier discounted the women's testimony as nothing more than meaningless chatter. The retrospective quality of this introduction is also served by Luke's identification of the substance of their discussion: "all these things that had happened." The combination of words Luke uses, "carrying on social discourse" and "contemplating,"[11] emphasizes the polysemy of recent events, and suggests that the sense of Jesus' death and burial, together with the news of the empty tomb, was difficult to fathom. As will become clear (v 21), the interpretive problematic consists in the apparent incongruity between Jesus' messianic career and its conclusion at the Place of the Skull.

What is the significance of the journey from Jerusalem to Emmaus?[12] Because the earlier pilgrimage of Jesus and his followers had revelatory significance (see above on 9:51–19:48), Luke's audience might be led by the reference to this journey[13] to anticipate divine disclosure. In the interim, however, the departure of these two disciples constitutes a physical representation of the division Luke had narrated in v 11. Dismissal of the women's witness points to a fissure in the company of disciples, just as the departure of these two persons from Jerusalem marks the beginnings of the drift away from high hopes and the community of discipleship.[14]

---

9. Cf. DeLeers, "The Road to Emmaus," 104-5; Gibbs, "Luke 24:13-35 and Acts 8:26-39," 20-22; Rosica, "Road to Emmaus," 127; *idem,* "In Search of Jesus"; Strauss, *Davidic Messiah,* 256.

10. This emphasis is continued in vv 21 and 33.

11. ὁμιλέω and συζητέω; Koet (*Five Studies,* 58-60) relates συζητέω to scriptural interpretation.

12. Luke does not otherwise mention this village, and its location is disputed (see the summary in Riesner, "Archeology and Geography," 43). Its importance here is grounded in its proximity to Jerusalem (vv 13, 33).

13. πορεύομαι.

14. For this latter point, cf. R. H. Smith, *Easter Gospels,* 113.

The Greek text is emphatic: Jesus *himself* joined them on the journey,[15] underscoring the parallel between this journey and that of the middle section of Luke's Gospel, as well as raising hopes that the earlier witness of the women will be corroborated by means of this encounter. These hopes are immediately dashed, however, by now-familiar words; just as in 9:44-45; 18:31-34, where the disciples had failed to embrace Jesus' repeated disclosure of God's purpose, where they had failed to grasp the topsy-turvy construction of the new world order determined by God's reign that had been the substance of Jesus' teaching, so now these disciples are incapable of recognizing Jesus.[16] Reference to their "eyes" is reminiscent of the correlation of "sight" with comprehension, faith, and salvation elsewhere in the Gospel.[17]

17-19a   Having joined them, Jesus engages in an initial interaction that sets the stage for two related but different perspectives on "the things that have taken place ... in these days" (v 18; cf. v 14) — theirs (vv 19b-24) and his (vv 25-27). "In these days" suggests that their concern is with the immediate past and that the nature of their outlook on it is foreshadowed by their gloomy comportment.[18] Referring to Jesus as a "stranger" or "foreigner,"[19] Cleopas manifests what Luke has already informed us concerning — namely, the travelers' inability to recognize their new companion.[20] Cleopas falls victim to a subtle irony in Luke's narration: He and his companion do not know the identity of this fellow traveler, yet they are astonished that he does not know of recent events;[21] in fact, Jesus is the only one who is genuinely "in the know." This, combined with Cleopas's astonished reference to Jesus as the "only" uninformed person in Jerusalem, portends the public character of the events to which he refers, but also the widespread ignorance regarding their meaning.

19b-24   Three times we have encountered reference to "(these) things" (vv 13, 18, 19). Only now are they specified in a brief précis of Jesus' career, with particular attention drawn to the apparent incongruity between his prophetic ministry and his death at the hand of the Jerusalem leadership, and to the puzzle of the empty tomb.

---

15. καὶ αὐτὸς Ἰησοῦς.

16. *Contra* views that the passive form of κρατέω assumes Luke's use of a "divine passive," see the discussion above on 9:43b-45; also Tannehill, *Narrative Unity,* 1:282.

17. Cf. 1:78-79; 2:30; 6:39-42; 10:23; 11:34; 18:35-42; 19:42. See above on 4:18-19.

18. σκυθρωπός appears only here in Luke-Acts; cf. Matt 6:16.

19. παροικέω; the reference could be to someone living as a resident alien in Jerusalem or to someone who had journeyed to Jerusalem as a pilgrim.

20. Cleopas is mentioned only here in the NT. The absence of a second name has fueled speculation — Cleopas's wife? son? Simon? — cf. Fitzmyer, 2:1563.

21. ἐπιγινώσκω — v 16; γινώσκω — v 18.

The appellation "Jesus of Nazareth" is generally used with reference to Jesus in his capacity as a miracle worker,[22] and this corresponds to his characterization here as "a prophet mighty in deed and word." Luke's audience can scarcely but be reminded of the beginnings of Jesus' public ministry in Nazareth, when he proclaimed in his hometown that he had been anointed by the Spirit for a ministry in which miraculous activity and teaching would be given equal weight.[23] The description of Jesus as "mighty" or "powerful" is also reminiscent of the Nazareth address, since it is there that Jesus is presented as the Spirit-endowed agent of God (cf. Isa 11:2) whose ministry would be the exercise of divine power.[24] Thus far, this synopsis of Jesus' ministry intimates the high degree of correspondence between the perspective of Jesus' companions on the road and that of the narrator.

Clearly, Jesus' presentation by Cleopas and his companion is designed to reflect traditions about the prophet-like-Moses; indeed, in Acts 7:22 Stephen will describe Moses in parallel words: "powerful in his words and deeds." The phrase, "before God and all the people" likewise echoes Moses' epitaph in Deut 34:10-12. Furthermore, Jesus was expected "to redeem Israel," just as, later in the narrative, we will hear that God sent Moses in order to redeem the people (Acts 7:22). In their perspective, then, Jesus was the prophet-like-Moses, a viewpoint obviously shared by the Third Evangelist — who develops Jesus' prophetic and Mosaic identity and claims him as Israel's liberator.[25] Nor does Luke deny the validity of their hope specifically for Israel's redemption.[26]

What is lacking in their interpretation of Jesus' significance, however, is the understanding that, as God's prophet, Jesus must fulfill the destiny of the prophets: rejection, suffering, and death. They thus misunderstand the prophetic pattern in the Scriptures that Jesus fulfills. What is more, even

22. See 4:34; 18:37; Acts 2:22; 3:6; 4:10; 10:38. Cf. Acts 6:14; 26:9.
23. 4:18-19; cf. Acts 1:1; Achtemeier, "Lucan Perspective," 550-59; Green, "Daughter of Abraham," 645-46.
24. Cf. 4:14, 36; 5:17; 6:19; 8:46; 10:13; 19:37. Cf. the giving of power to the disciples — 9:1; 10:19; 24:49; Acts 1:8.
25. On Jesus' prophetic and Mosaic identity, cf., e.g., 7:16, 39; 11:49-51; 13:33-34; 22:64; Acts 3:12-26. On the association of Jesus with Israel's redemption, see, e.g., 1:68; 2:38.
26. See Acts 1:6. At the onset of Acts, Jesus' followers remain interested in the restoration of Israel (ἀποκαθιστάνω; cf., e.g., Ps 16:5; Jer 15:19; 16:15; 23:8; 24:6; Ezek 16:55; 17:23; Hos 11:1). Clearly, the question of Israel remains outstanding as Acts opens. Mary, Zechariah, Simeon, Anna — all are Spirit-endowed characters in Luke 1–2 as they portend a political salvation, and they are in no way censured or judged to be unreliable (*contra* Tannehill, *Narrative Unity,* 1:35). At the close of the Third Gospel, though, the question remains, What are the ramifications for Israel's restoration of the rejection of Jesus by the Jewish leadership in Jerusalem?

though they regard Jesus as a prophet, they have failed to take with appropriate seriousness his prophecies regarding his own suffering, death, and resurrection. They juxtapose "the people" over against "chief priests and leaders," just as Luke has done with almost unflagging consistency since Jesus' arrival in Jerusalem (e.g., 19:47-48; 22:2; 23:35),[27] but they fail to see beyond his crucifixion to the possibility of his continuing to serve as Israel's redeemer.

Their incomprehension runs deeper, too. Against the backdrop of the Lukan birth narratives, it is not enough to think of Jesus as a "prophet." The one who would redeem Israel is the Savior who is a messianic figure in the lineage of David. Jesus is a prophet, but he is more; he is God's regal prophet. What Jesus must clarify for his traveling companions, then, is the correlation of suffering and messiahship,[28] for the scandal of the cross has become for them an occasion for stumbling (cf. 7:23).

Having completed their sketch of Jesus' career and demise, Jesus' companions on the road summarize with greater fullness the scene recounted by Luke in vv 1-12. Their synopsis is important on four counts. (1) With their use of the expression "the third day," they recall Jesus' prophecies (9:22; 13:32; 18:33; cf. 24:7), affirming again though unknowingly his reliability as a prophet. In this way, they intimate that all the raw materials for making sense of recent events are available to them, but they are as yet unable to construct a faithful interpretation. (2) They mention only that they were "astounded" by the women, thus portraying themselves more positively than had the Evangelist (v 11). In actuality, by continuing to reflect on the significance of recent events (vv 14-15), they had already begun to distance themselves from their initial, dismissive reaction to the women's report. (3) Whereas Luke had mentioned only Peter, Cleopas and his friend relate that "some" went to the tomb and verified that it was empty, as the women had said. This suggests greater openness on the part of the disciples than the earlier report might have allowed, so narrowly focused as it was on the response of Peter. It is not unusual for Luke's lens to be so tightly focused on one or more characters that the presence of others is missed.[29] (4) Nevertheless, as in the earlier scene, so now what distinguishes the women from the others who visited the tomb is illumination. The former had a vision of angels, while the latter "did not

27. Luke's compressed account actually designates the Jewish leadership as the agents of Jesus' crucifixion. This form of abbreviation focuses on the culpability of the Jewish leadership, but it does not signify that Luke thinks of the Romans as being uninvolved in the crucifixion, any more than it suggests that Luke does not think of the Jewish people as participating in Jesus' condemnation. See above on 23:13-25, 26.

28. Cf. R. H. Smith, *Easter Gospels,* 116; Strauss, *Davidic Messiah,* 255-56; Rosica, "In Search of Jesus."

29. Cf., e.g., 16:1, 14.

see." And, as Luke has developed the metaphor, "seeing" is a prerequisite for the affirmation that Jesus is alive.[30]

25-27 Having communicated the disciples' perspective on "the things about Jesus of Nazareth," Luke now turns to Jesus' response. "Foolish" does not have the sense of "moronic" but of "obtuse"[31] — that is, Jesus calls attention to the lack of understanding of his companions. This is not to say, however, that they are simply lacking cognitive input. "Slow of heart" calls attention to their failure to orient themselves fully around Jesus' teaching, not to their need merely for remedial education. "Heart" refers here as in the LXX to the inner commitments, the dispositions and attitudes, of a person that determine his or her life.[32] Failure of insight comes from failure to embrace the ways of God.

The central question, then, is found in v 26: "Was it not necessary that the Messiah should suffer these things and then enter into his glory?" From the perspective of his followers, the answer is, clearly and categorically, No! According to Jesus, the perspective of the Scriptures is different. Hence, according to Luke's summary of Jesus' instruction in v 27, Jesus brings into interpretive interplay "the things about himself" (i.e., "the things" outlined in vv 19b-24) and "all the scriptures." "Moses and all the prophets" may refer to "all the scriptures," but this expression may as easily refer to Moses as the first of the prophets and all of those raised up after him by God. Their prophetic careers, together with the Scriptures, all point forward to the realization of the divine purpose in God's Messiah. They are also in need of interpretation.

Which texts does Jesus exegete for his companions? We are not told, but the implication with which Luke leaves us is that it does not matter. The pattern exemplified by Moses and the prophets is consummated in a Messiah who suffers. Likewise, all of the Scriptures have their fulfillment in a Messiah who suffers. With what logic does Jesus demonstrate the necessity of the Messiah's suffering? We are not told. In fact, heretofore, we have been told consistently that it is the Son of Man or the prophets who "must suffer." Yet, in the remainder of the Lukan narrative, it is the Messiah who "must suffer."[33] This shift is without direct and explicit precedent in the OT, for which "a suffering Messiah" would be an oxymoron, and it is here that Jesus' hermeneutical innovation best surfaces. By correlating the unremarkable demise of

30. For the import of the metaphor of sight in Luke, see, e.g., Culpepper, "Seeing the Kingdom of God"; Hamm, "Sight to the Blind." Also, see above on 4:18-19.

31. ἀνόητος is used only here in Luke-Acts, though cf. Rom 1:14; Gal 1:1, 3; Tit 3:3.

32. Cf. Sand, "καρδία."

33. For the Son of Man, cf. 9:22, 44; 17:25; 18:31-34; 22:22; for the prophet, cf. 4:24; 13:33-34; for the Messiah, cf. 24:26, 46; Acts 3:18; 17:3; 26:23.

the prophets — unremarkable since suffering and rejection were their presumed destiny — with messiahship, he is able to assert that the Scriptures presage the eschatological king who would suffer before entering his glory.[34] In God's economy, the high status of God's anointed one is not the antithesis of humility or humiliation. Rather, in his suffering and resurrection, Jesus embodied the fullness of salvation interpreted as status reversal; his death was the center point of the divine-human struggle over how life is to be lived, in humility or self-glorification. Though anointed by God, though righteous before God, though innocent, he is put to death. Rejected by people, he is raised up by God — with both activities subsumed under the one divine purpose.

28-32 Luke reminds his audience that this journey had a destination, a village (Emmaus — v 1). By calling attention to its proximity, he allows for the possibility that Jesus will be separated from these disciples who have conversed with him but who do not yet recognize him. In this way, and by mentioning the nearness of nightfall, the Evangelist raises the level of suspense in this account. Will they come to recognize him? Will they gain insight into the significance of this particular day, this day to which they have referred as "the third" (v 21), this day of fulfillment? Will the impasse be overcome? Seemingly at the last moment, they extend hospitality to Jesus — an act pregnant with possibilities in the Third Gospel where meals have so often been the site for revelatory discourse and the prospect of genuine fellowship characteristic of the kingdom of God. Also in keeping with other meal scenes in the Gospel of Luke, once he is at the table, Jesus' role shifts. He is no longer the honored guest but the host of the meal, and it is in this role that he distributes the bread.[35]

The series of actions — took bread, blessed and broke it, and gave it to them — is most reminiscent of his similar actions in 9:16 in the account of the miraculous feeding.[36] Importantly, that earlier meal had a revelatory function. Prior to the feeding, Luke records misconceptions about Jesus' identity, including the possibility that Jesus is a prophet; Herod could not determine who Jesus was, but was perplexed and desired to see him (9:7-9). Afterward, Peter acknowledges that Jesus is the Messiah. Thus far, Jesus' companions have been unable to see, having blocked eyes, and had responded with sadness and astonishment; will they now be able to see Jesus? to identify

---

34. So Strauss, *Davidic Messiah,* 257.

35. Cf. 5:29-39; 10:38-42; 11:27-28; 14:1-24; 19:1-27; Koenig, *New Testament Hospitality,* 90-91.

36. Not only are the actions set in parallel (9:16; 24:30); in addition, both meals are set in the evening (9:12; 24:29), and those present "reclined" (κατακλίνω — 9:14-15; 24:30). See also 22:19, though in this instance Jesus "gives thanks" rather than "blesses."

him as the Messiah, in spite of his ignominious end? This is precisely what Luke narrates. The prior condition of the disciples is reversed: "Their eyes were opened and they recognized him." This language parallels their subsequent description of Jesus' talking while "on the road": "He was opening the scriptures to us."[37] This coincidence helps to identify the crucial function of scriptural interpretation for the new insight of the disciples, even if the revelatory moment is "the breaking of the bread" (see the apposition of these two moments again in v 35).

Jesus' disappearance stands in parallel with his drawing near in v 15 (cf. Acts 8:30, 39), so that center stage is again occupied by the dialogue between these two disciples. The difference between the beginning and the end is remarkable. Earlier, they were puzzling over recent events, but they are now able to articulate the reality of the divine presence among them, transforming them, as they had the Scriptures interpreted to them during the journey.[38]

33-35 The chronological integrity of the Emmaus episode is preserved with Luke's opening reference to "that same hour" — toward evening (v 29), but on the same day that the women first found the tomb empty (vv 1-3), the "third day" since Jesus' crucifixion (vv 7, 21). Given the nature of the journey from Jerusalem — melancholic, with hopes dampened — the return to Jerusalem is bursting with significance. Luke thus exemplifies the import of Jesus' resurrection for the formation of community, as well as charts the reversal of emotions depicted in this scene. "The eleven and their companions" refers to the circle of twelve sans Judas — presumably women and men (vv 9-10), those gathered in the opening chapter of Acts (cf. Acts 1:12-26). Like the women before them, these disciples from Emmaus received no particular commission, but respond spontaneously to their newly found insight by returning immediately to the community of disciples in order to bear witness to Jesus' resurrection.

Arriving in Jerusalem, however, they discover that Jesus has also appeared to Simon, so that others have become convinced of the resurrection.[39] Like the narrator (v 3), the circle of disciples refers to Jesus as "Lord," signifying their conversion to the belief that the heinousness of his crucifixion

---

37. διανοίγω is used in vv 31 ("open the eyes") and in vv 32 and 45 ("interpret the scriptures" — cf. Koet, *Five Studies*, 60-62).

38. If we understand "heart" in a way comparable to its usage in v 25, and understand "burning" in a figurative sense, connoting the divine presence (e.g., Exod 3:2; Deut 4:11; 9:15; et al.; cf. Johnson, 397), Luke's expression could be construed in this way. Similarly, Koenig (*New Testament Hospitality,* 116) speaks of the disciples' recollection of "an earlier stage of repentance."

39. The identity of the speakers in v 34 is ambiguous in English, but not in Greek (λέγοντας, rather than λέγοντες [though the latter is read in D]).

is no contradiction of his status as the one through whom the gracious bene-faction of God would continue to be made available (cf. v 21). Luke's account includes a yawning gap — namely, this reference to an appearance to Simon, otherwise unmentioned in ch. 24. It is left to us to fill in what has not been narrated, though we must still inquire into why Luke has drawn special attention to Simon. Undoubtedly, this is to indicate Simon's full rehabilitation following his denial of Jesus and repentance (22:55-62) and thus to legitimate Simon not merely as an authentic "witness of the resurrection" (Acts 1:22) but as leader of the community of witnesses (cf. 22:31-34).[40]

The effect of the arrival of these travelers, then, is to substantiate further the report that Jesus is alive. This they do, holding in tandem Jesus' interpretive activity "on the road" and his being made known to them "in the breaking of the bread" in their narration.[41] This assures the dual importance of both hermeneutical activity and participation in ongoing table fellowship with Jesus. The "breaking of the bread" refers to the meal itself,[42] and thus provides a bridge from table fellowship during Jesus' ministry to the celebrative meals characteristic of the early church in Acts (e.g., Acts 2:46). Given the back-ground in Jesus' own table practices for occasions of "breaking bread" in Acts, we might anticipate that these meals would signify the coming near of salvation, and this is certainly the case.[43]

8.3. THE APPEARANCE TO THE DISCIPLES (24:36-49)

36 *While they were talking about this, Jesus himself stood among them and said to them, "Peace be with you." 37 They were startled and terrified, and thought that they were seeing a ghost. 38 He said to them,*

40. Cf. R. H. Smith, *Easter Gospels,* 121.

41. ἐξηγέομαι — cf. Acts 10:8; 15:12, 14; 21:19; and the comparable use of διηγέομαι in 1:1; 8:39; 9:10; Acts 9:27; 12:17.

42. That is, "the breaking of the bread," which signals the beginning of the meal, is metonymic for the meal as a whole (cf. Lake and Cadbury, *English Translation,* 28; for a survey of options, see B. P. Robinson, "Emmaus Story," 484). Parallel phrases are found in Acts 2:42, 46; 20:7; 27:35. The idea of "eucharist" for this phrase is supported by Marshall (*Last Supper,* 126-30). His view is based on the problematic identification of κοινωνία with "common meal" rather than with the more probable "sharing of posses-sions," however. Moreover, in spite of the presence of comparable language in Acts 27:33-36, he doubts that "a Christian sacrament" is being described in this text. Pesch (*Apostelgeschichte,* 1:130) thinks that "the breaking of the bread" refers to both a common meal and to the Lord's Supper, but adduces no evidence in support of this double meaning.

43. Cf. esp. the co-texts in which "the breaking of bread" appears in Acts 20:7; 27:35. This motif is emphasized by Wanke *(Emmauserzählung),* who, however, exaggerates Luke's interest in the presence of Jesus at the meal.

"Why are you frightened, and why do doubts arise in your hearts?
39 *Look at my hands and my feet; see that it is I myself. Touch me and
see; for a ghost does not have flesh and bones as you see that I have."*
40 *And when he had said this, he showed them his hands and his feet.*
41 *While in their joy they were disbelieving and still wondering, he said
to them, "Have you anything here to eat?"* 42 *They gave him a piece
of broiled fish,* 43 *and he took it and ate in their presence.*

44 *Then he said to them, "These are my words that I spoke to you
while I was still with you — that everything written about me in the
law of Moses, the prophets, and the psalms must be fulfilled."* 45 *Then
he opened their minds to understand the scriptures,* 46 *and he said to
them, "Thus it is written, that the Messiah is to suffer and to rise from
the dead on the third day,* 47 *and that repentance for forgiveness of
sins*[1] *is to be proclaimed in his name to all nations, beginning from
Jerusalem.* 48 *You are witnesses of these things.* 49 *And see, I am sending upon you what my Father promised; so stay here in the city until
you have been clothed with power from on high."*

Jesus' prophecies of suffering and resurrection, beginning in 9:22, established
explicitly the story line of his career that reaches its culmination in this scene
as Jesus manifests himself not only to selected individuals (vv 31, 34) but to
the whole company of his followers. The climactic status of this scene is
secure even if the response of Jesus' disciples is less than ideal; only with vv
50-53 do fear, amazement, and doubt (vv 37, 41) give way to worship, great
joy, and obedience. In the meantime, the Evangelist places a premium on
"seeing."[2] Additionally, Luke has cast this scene in terms reminiscent of
angelophanies (see esp. 1:11-13). Initial points of contact with accounts of
angelic appearances signal the wonder of this moment, while points of contrast
indicate the reality of Jesus' resurrection. On the one hand, then, the narrative
rules out any notion of the resuscitation of a corpse; on the other, it excludes
interpretations of the resurrection as merely an ethereal event. Luke's narrative
affirms a resurrected Jesus over against these other options for the afterlife
current in the Hellenistic world.

If this scene affirms the authenticity of Jesus' prophecy of what was
to take place on "the third day" (cf. vv 7, 21, 46), and thus reviews Jesus'
past words in light of present events, it also builds a bridge to the future. In
fact, it is worth reflecting on the various ways in which the substance of this

1. NRSV: "repentance and forgiveness of sins."
2. Sight-related and similar verbs are found in vv 37, 39 (3x, 4x in the NRSV),
40, and 43, helping to interpret the substance of the "these things" to which Jesus followers
will serve as witnesses (v 48).

interaction brings to the surface concerns raised earlier in the Lukan narrative but not yet resolved. Among these, the most prominent is clearly Simeon's anticipation that the advent of Jesus marked salvation for the Gentiles (2:32). We may see in Jesus' ministry throughout the Gospel of Luke how the way has been paved for such a mission — particularly with reference to Jesus' offer of restoration to people living at the margins of Jewish life — but this does not mask the fact that he has interacted only rarely with non-Jews. How will this narrative need be resolved? Luke's answer is clear: Jesus' disciples, now cast in the role of "witnesses," will take up this portfolio. Less obvious, but no less critical, is the question of empowerment for ministry. Luke's perspective has been that the kingdom of God is brought near in the ministry of Jesus, and that Jesus' ministry has been conducted in the sphere of the Holy Spirit. Through what means might Jesus' followers now serve as agents of God's beneficence, continuing the works of healing and proclamation befitting the commencement of God's reign? Jesus has anticipated this need. Couched in the language of the "Father's promise" is his own commitment to empower them with the Holy Spirit. Of course, the Gospel of Luke closes before either of these narrative concerns is resolved, indicating the degree to which the Third Gospel is incomplete in itself and requires the Acts of the Apostles for the progression of the story.

Before the story can continue, however, a grave impediment must be surmounted. This is the failure of Jesus' followers to apprehend fully the meaning of their own acclamation in v 34, "The Lord has risen indeed!" Their response to the appearance of Jesus among them (vv 36-37) demonstrates the unreconstructed nature of their worldviews, their lack of acceptance of the whole of Jesus' teaching concerning how the divine purpose would be fulfilled in him. In this scene, then, Jesus undertakes to unveil the truth (i.e., the actuality and meaning) of his resurrection in three ways — the first two oriented toward underscoring the materiality of his continued existence (vv 38-43), and the latter concerned with its scriptural significance (vv 44-49).

36-37 Luke carefully stitches this scene into the previous one, indicating chronological and thematic continuity with the clause, "while they were talking about these things." The set of characters is also constant, and includes what is evidently the whole company of Jesus' followers who have thus far remained in Jerusalem (cf. vv 9-10; Acts 1:12-14, 15). "These things" have to do superficially with evidences of the risen Lord, but more profoundly with the coherence between the pattern provided by Moses and all the prophets, the prophetic witness of the Scriptures to the Messiah who suffers and enters into his glory, the ministry of Jesus as this has been focused on table fellowship, and the experience of the resurrected Jesus (v 35). During their discussion of these things, these followers see what they take to be an appari-

853

tion, a phantom;[3] apparently they recognize the one before them as Jesus, but are not ready to accept that he could have any form other than an intangible one. Here at the outset, the shape of Luke's account might pass for that of an angelophany (cf. v 5; also the appearance of Gabriel to Zechariah in 1:11-13).[4]

Jesus' greeting, "peace," is expected in a Semitic context (cf. 10:5), and communicates the wish for communal well-being, *shalom*. Within the Third Gospel, "peace" is metonymic for "salvation,"[5] so that, in this co-text, Jesus' greeting takes on an enlarged meaning. The Emmaus travelers imagined that his rejection and crucifixion had rendered Jesus incapable of serving as Israel's redeemer; here, following his death, though, he communicates or transmits continued salvation to those gathered.

With these conflicting responses — the conveyance of *shalom* versus trepidation, even panic — the stage is set.

38-43 Jesus' response to his followers intimates the high stakes of the encounter Luke relates. "Frightened"[6] earlier described Zechariah, whose reaction to the divine messenger was limited (see 1:12, 18-20). "Doubt" is typical of Jesus' opponents, or of Jesus' disciples at those moments when they most fail to embody his message.[7] "Heart" has already been used in vv 25 and 32, reminding Luke's audience of the importance in these scenes of the need for the inner commitments of these persons to be reshaped in light of the resurrection of Jesus. They must be wholly transformed — in disposition and attitude, cognition and affect, as well as practices and behavior — but they continue to lack the categories for rendering this new experience of Jesus in a meaningful way. As with Jesus' companions on the road to Emmaus, they are obtuse, slow of heart (v 25).

As an initial remedy, Jesus offers two proofs of his own materiality as evidence of his resurrected existence. Negating two among the several possible categories for imagining the afterlife — one barbaric, the other more sophisticated — Luke first shows that Jesus' disciples do not mistake him for a cadaver brought back to life (v 37), then certifies that neither is Jesus an "immortal soul" free from bodily existence. Like the rich man and Lazarus in Jesus' tale in 16:19-31, so Jesus is now represented as alive beyond the grave as an embodied person. Jesus' affirmation is emphatic — "It is I myself!" "It is really me!" — intimating continuity between these phases of

3. πνεῦμα is thus used with reference to "the disembodied spirit [or soul])" — cf. v 39. See the interpretive φάντασμα in D.

4. ἔμφοβος appears here and in v 5; πτοέομαι appears elsewhere in Luke-Acts only in 21:9.

5. Cf. 1:79; 2:14, 29; 7:50; 8:48; 10:5-7; 19:38.

6. ταράσσω, used in the passive voice to express the reaction of terror in the face of astonishing phenomena.

7. See the usage of διαλογισμός in 2:35; 5:22; 6:8; 9:46-47.

Jesus' life, before crucifixion and after resurrection.[8] This is demonstrated, first, with reference to his hands and feet, flesh and bones, and, second, by his capacity to eat food.[9] Repeated references to "seeing"[10] and the important notation that Jesus ate "in their presence" signifies that the *apologia* being provided here is for the sake of the authentic witness upon which the disciples would subsequently be called to give (cf. v 48).

Nestled between these two demonstrations of materiality is a transparent indication that such exhibitions are insufficient for producing the desired effects. This is consistent with the emphasis throughout ch. 24 on the inherent ambiguity of "facts" and, thus, the absolute necessity of interpretation. Not even incontrovertible evidence of Jesus' embodied existence is capable of producing faith; resolution will come only when scriptural illumination is added to material data.[11] Prior to this, the disciples respond as others do to extraordinary events, with wonder, but the combination of "disbelief and wonder," paralleling earlier responses in vv 11-12, intimates how little their apprehension of Jesus' message concerning his death and resurrection has progressed. Luke attributes their disbelief to joy.[12] This may seem surprising insofar as "joy" is typically a positive response to divine activity in the Gospel,[13] but an affective response of this nature is crucial for indicating the absence of a more sinister motivation for their disbelief. What they were experiencing was simply too good to be true. Later, "disbelief resulting from joy" will be replaced by "great joy" in association with praise and obedience (vv 50-53).

44-49   If one were to think of the stories of Israel, Jesus, and the early church as in some sense distinct, in these verses one would find the seam wherein they are sown together into one cloth. Jesus first inscribes his own

---

8. ἐγώ εἰμι αὐτός; cf. Hendrickx, *Resurrection Narratives*, 90-91.

9. Cf. 8:55; Bede, *Homilies*, 2:84 (though Bede denies that Jesus, in his immortal state, *needed* "natural sustenance"); O'Toole, *Interpreting the Resurrection*, 47-48 ("bodily reality").

Some interpreters have located in vv 42-43 a further instance of "table fellowship" in Luke-Acts — e.g., Dumm, "Luke 24:44-49 and Hospitality"; O'Toole, *Interpreting the Resurrection*, 49-50; R. J. Dillon, *Eyewitnesses*, 200-201. Although Luke later summarizes the postresurrection period with reference to Jesus' sharing table fellowship with his followers (Acts 1:4; 10:40-41), he provides no evidence here that Jesus ate *with* anyone. His concern is rather that Jesus ate *in front of* (ἐνώπιον) his followers. Such concerns as (renewed) fellowship and inclusivity often associated with table fellowship in Luke-Acts, therefore, ought not to be read into this text.

10. ὁράω — v 39 (2x); θεωρέω — v 39; cf. δείκνυμι (i.e., "allow to see") — v 40.

11. Cf. R. J. Dillon, *Eyewitnesses*, 198-99.

12. The word order in Greek makes this clear: ἔτι δὲ ἀπιστούντων αὐτῶν ἀπὸ τῆς χαρᾶς. For causative ἀπό, see 21:26; 22:45b; BDF §210.1.

13. See 1:14, 44, 47, 58; 2:10; 8:13; et al.; cf. Barton, *Spirituality*, 74-77.

story, the story of the Messiah who suffers and is raised, into the scriptural story, and then inscribes the story of the early church into both his own story and that of the Scriptures. He underscores the truth of the resurrection (i.e., its actuality and its significance within the divine plan), and ensures that the disciples grasp fully how the past, present, and future of God's activity belong to one great mural of salvation.[14] In this way, the Evangelist assures the capacity of his followers to serve as effective "witnesses." In this climax of the risen Lord's revelation to his disciples, then, we find the key point of transition into the book of Acts.[15]

Jesus' opening words correspond roughly to the angels' message to the women at the tomb (vv 6-7) and Jesus' utterance on the Emmaus journey (vv 25-27). Included among the parallel elements are the following: (1) continuity of message before and after the crucifixion and resurrection, (2) the necessity of messianic suffering, (3) the promise of resurrection on the third day, and (4) the emphasis on fulfillment. "Divine purpose," a pervasive Lukan motif,[16] surfaces in Luke's terminology — "it is necessary" and "fulfilled"[17] — and in the all-encompassing reference to the Scriptures. The latter is highlighted by the unusual reference to "the psalms" alongside "the law of Moses and the prophets,"[18] a consequence of the important role of the psalms in Luke's interpretation of Jesus' passion. Not only Isaiah (cf. 22:37), then, but all of the Scriptures speak of Jesus and have their consummation in him. Equally reminiscent of the Emmaus episode is Luke's observation that Jesus "opened their minds to understand the scriptures" (vv 31-32, 45); this parallelism accentuates again how the career of Jesus and the message of the Scriptures are mutually informative.

Jesus' interpretation of the Scriptures moves in three directions, designated by parallel verbs in the infinitive: (1) "the Messiah is *to suffer*" and (2) "*to rise* from the dead on the third day," and (3) "repentance for forgiveness of sins is *to be proclaimed* in his name to all nations, beginning from Jerusalem."[19] "To suffer" is regularly used by Luke to denote the totality of Jesus' passion.[20] The collocation of this verb with its subject, "Messiah,"

---

14. See Green, "Internal Repetition."

15. Tannehill, *Narrative Unity,* 1:294; cf. Korn, *Geschichte Jesu,* 128-70.

16. See, e.g., Cosgrove, "Divine Δεῖ"; du Plooy, "God's Design"; Squires, *Plan of God;* Green, *Gospel of Luke,* 22-49.

17. δεῖ, πληρόω.

18. Cf. the prologue to Sirach ("the Law and the Prophets and the other books of our ancestors"); also 4QMMT 95 ("the book of Moses and the words of the prophets and of David" — ET in Martínez, *Dead Sea Scrolls,* 79).

19. This structure is difficult to represent in English, but obvious in Greek: οὕτως γέγραπται παθεῖν . . . ἀναστῆναι . . . κηρυχθῆναι. . . .

20. Cf. 22:15; 24:26; Acts 1:3; 3:18; 17:3.

makes both a christological statement and a statement about the nature of life before God (see above on vv 25-27). That with which the disciples have regularly struggled — namely, the correlation of Jesus' divine status and mission with the prospect of his suffering — comes to the fore in this concise slogan in order to indicate how the consummation of God's purpose revolutionizes normal social conventions. Status before God does not come through lording it over others, or by the clever, agonistic machinations ordinarily governing social interaction, but through the rejection of such values in one's commitments and practices.

If the Scriptures, and Jesus' own words, are fulfilled in his crucifixion, then should his disciples not also expect that the repeated prophecy of his being raised "on the third day" (cf. 9:22; 18:33) would also be realized? And if this is so, why do the disciples think of him as a phantom and respond to him with fear and disbelief?

Which Scriptures portend messianic suffering and resurrection? One would be hard-pressed to locate specific texts that make these prognostications explicit. Even to attempt to do so would be wrongheaded, however. The point of Jesus' words is not that such-and-such a verse has now come true, but that the truth to which all of the Scriptures point has now been realized! Even so, Luke does provide direct hints for the scriptural basis of the reversal Jesus has experienced in his life, death, and resurrection, by drawing above all on the psalms and Isaiah in his presentation of Jesus' passion. Similarly, the proclamation of repentance for forgiveness of sins to all nations is scripturally based, with the Lukan narrative suggesting in this respect the pivotal importance of Isa 49:6. Simeon borrows from this text in Luke 2:32, Paul cites it in Acts 13:47, and it is echoed again in Acts 1:8 (cf. Acts 26:23; 28:28). This scriptural background manifestly portends the mission to all peoples.[21]

Jesus' words "beginning from Jerusalem" contain a perhaps subtle but vital transformation of normal orientation. One would normally have considered Jerusalem to be the center point to which the nations would come (i.e., a centripetal orientation for the universal mission);[22] this is reversed in Jesus' missionary cartography, which envisions instead a centrifugal missionary movement. Already the effects of the rending of the temple veil at Jesus' death (23:45) are being felt.

Otherwise, Jesus' words echo material from earlier in the Gospel and point forward to the Acts of the Apostles. The act of "proclaiming" binds the work of the disciples to that for which Jesus was Spirit-anointed (4:18), while

21. Betori (Luke 24:47") emphasizes that the mission to "all nations" does not have its point of departure from Jerusalem, but actually begins in the Holy City.
22. Cf. McKnight, *Light among the Nations,* 47-48; Jeremias, *Jesus' Promise,* 57-62

the message "repentance for the forgiveness of sins" corresponds to the word broadcast by John (3:3). "Repentance" will be a key term describing the appropriate response to the offer of salvation in Acts,[23] and connotes the (re)alignment of one's life — that is, dispositions and behaviors — toward God's purpose.[24] Forgiveness has been throughout the Gospel and will continue to be in Acts central to the content and experience of salvation.[25] Since these disciples are to continue Jesus' ministry, perhaps it is not surprising that they are to proclaim the salvific message "in his name." In fact, what is done in the "name" of Jesus surfaces as an important motif in Acts. Luke will portray a community very much oriented around Jesus (1:1, 21-22) — with salvation offered to "everyone who calls on the name of the Lord" (= Jesus; cf. 2:21, 36), and people directed to be baptized "in the name of Jesus Christ" (2:38), appropriating the blessings available through and signaling their allegiance to him. Subsequently in Acts Christians heal (3:6, 16; 4:10, 30; 19:13), preach (4:12; 5:28, 40), and are baptized (8:16; 10:48; 19:5) in the name of Jesus; suffer for his name (5:41; 9:16; 21:13); and are those "who call upon the name" of Jesus (9:14, 21; 22:16).

The missiological role of the disciples is summarized in the words, "You are witnesses of these things." In this co-text, the referent of "these things" should probably be understood broadly to include the suffering and resurrection of the Messiah as well as their significance in relation to the Scriptures and to the ongoing proclamation of the early church (i.e., the substance of vv 44-47).[26] In Acts, Jesus' followers serve precisely in this capacity.[27]

How are they enabled to serve thus? First, Luke underscores that they have been transformed (their eyes opened) in their understanding of God's purposes as these are centered in Jesus' crucifixion and resurrection. Second, Luke notes that they will be "clothed with power from on high."[28] Luke thus draws a direct connection between their service as "witnesses" and their reception of the Holy Spirit.[29]

---

23. For example, Acts 2:38; 3:19; 5:31; 8:22.

24. Cf. Green, *Gospel of Luke,* 107-8.

25. See esp. on 4:18-19; also 1:77; 3:3; 5:20-21, 23-24; 7:47-49; 11:4; 12:10; 17:3-4; 23:34; Acts 2:38; 5:31; 8:22; 10:43; 13:38; 26:18.

26. So R. J. Dillon, "Easter Revelation," 254.

27. Cf. 1:8; 2:32; 3:15; 5:32; 10:39, 41; 13:31.

28. This is the only figurative use of ἐνδύω in Luke-Acts (cf. 8:27; 12:22; 15:22; Acts 12:21), though it is more common in Paul (e.g., Gal 3:27; Rom 13:12). Cf. LXX Pss 34:26; 92:1; 108:18; 131:9, 16, 18.

29. This is emphasized by numerous interpreters — e.g., Shelton, *Mighty in Word,* 116-17. This is not to say, however, that the gift of the Spirit is *only* for the empowerment of witness — cf., e.g., M. Turner, "Spirit and Power"; *idem,* "Spirit of Prophecy"; Shepherd, *Narrative Function,* 149.

Earlier in the Lukan narrative, Jesus had commissioned his followers for missionary activity, having given them the requisite "power and authority" (9:1-2). In the present, as he commissions them as witnesses, he announces to them that they will receive "what my Father promised." The nature of this promise will become immediately clear in the opening of Acts (1:4-5, 8; 2:33), where parallel language is used. It is the Holy Spirit who will empower them for their role as witnesses. At this juncture, however, the nature of this promise is less obvious. One important clue comes in 11:1-13, where Jesus teaches his followers to address God as "Father," as well as depicts the Holy Spirit as the Father's greatest gift. The connection between Spirit-empowered ministry and the inbreaking kingdom of God also makes 12:32 relevant: "It is your Father's good pleasure to give you the kingdom." Jesus thus portrays God as the gracious Lord, whose benefaction is to be manifest especially in the gift of the Spirit.[30] Amazingly, however, it is not the Father who will dispense the Spirit, but Jesus himself. This recalls the words of John in Luke 3:16, and his message finds parallels later in Acts 1:5; 11:16. This repetition shows that Luke saw the realization of John's prophecy in the post-ascension activity of Jesus, at Pentecost and in the ensuing Christian mission.

Jesus' parting words raise, at least momentarily, a note of suspense. This is because he instructs his followers to remain in the city until they have been empowered. Luke's audience knows that the company of disciples has already begun to splinter, with the departure of two of their number to Emmaus already recounted (v 13). Will the disciples be obedient to Jesus' words and remain in Jerusalem? Will they receive the Father's promise and be empowered for witness?

8.4. THE ASCENSION OF JESUS (24:50-53)

50 Then he led them out as far as Bethany, and, lifting up his hands, he blessed them. 51 While he was blessing them, he withdrew from them and was carried up into heaven. 52 And they worshiped him, and returned to Jerusalem with great joy; 53 and they were continually in the temple blessing God.[1]

30. Cf. Sieber, "Promise of My Father," 276-77. Menzies (*Empowered for Witness*, 171-72), however, thinks that the notion of "the promise of the Father" derives from the reference to the gift of the Spirit in Joel 2:38-42 (Acts 2:17-21); he does not spell out how the link is made between "God says" in Acts 2:17 and the more specific reference to God as "Father" in our phrase.

1. This final scene is plagued by numerous text-critical problems, and the NRSV text represents current scholarly consensus. For recent discussion, see Zwiep, "Text."

Whereas Luke's account of Jesus' ascension is integrally related to its co-text, the temporal relationship between it and the preceding scenes is equivocal. Linguistically, Jesus' appearance among the disciples in v 36 is paired with his departure in v 51.[2] Jerusalem continues to be the primary point of reference,[3] as it has been throughout ch. 24. Only here do we learn that the disciples have responded appropriately to Jesus, whose true identity and status they at last recognize. And, of course, the Evangelist has been preparing his audience for Jesus' departure from as far back in the narrative as the transfiguration scene (9:31: "they were speaking of his exodus"; see also 9:51: "When the days drew near for him to be taken up"). In spite of these points of integration, however, this concluding scene does not share with previous encounters in ch. 24 Luke's concern to mark carefully the chronology of his account. Discovery of the empty tomb, the Emmaus episode, and the appearance of Jesus to his apostles — each of these is explicitly located temporally on the same day, "the first day of the week" (v 1), the "third day" following the crucifixion (vv 7, 21; cf. 33, 36). The connective at v 50 lacks this degree of clarity: "And he led . . ." (NRSV: "Then he led . . .").[4] One may have the impression that the ascension, too, took place late on Sunday evening, but Luke's account leaves open other possibilities — which he will exploit more fully at the beginning of his second volume (Acts 1:1-11).

Jesus' role as leader of the community is immediately affirmed by the use of the verb "to lead out." His companions would include the three women named in v 10, along with "the other women," the eleven apostles, and "all the rest" (vv 9-10); in Acts 1:12-15, this company is said to encompass some 120 persons, including Mary the mother of Jesus and Jesus' brothers. Located on the Mount of Olives, about three kilometers from Jerusalem, Bethany was the site from which Jesus' triumphal entry had originated (19:29-40). That it would also serve as the locale of Jesus' final exaltation is therefore fitting (cf. Acts 1:9-12).

Jesus' final act closely parallels the behavior of priests in Lev 9:22 and especially Sir 50:20-22,[5] suggesting to some interpreters that Luke closes his Gospel with reference to a priestly Jesus.[6] If this view were supported by the narrative, it is certainly of interest that Jesus would thus function as a priest *outside* of the temple, and, indeed, outside of Jerusalem. It cannot be over-

2. ἔστη — v 36; διέστη — v 51.

3. "He led them out . . . they returned to Jerusalem . . . in the temple" (vv 50, 52, 53).

4. ἐξήγαγεν δέ. . . .

5. See Lohfink, *Himmelfahrt Jesu*, 167-69.

6. Cf., e.g., van Stempvoort, "Ascension." For some, this includes the possible identification of Jesus with reference to speculation regarding a priestly messiah, in spite of Luke's manifest interest in a specifically *Davidic* Messiah.

looked, however, that Luke otherwise demonstrates no interest in portraying Jesus in priestly garb, so that an alternative explanation for these parallels seems advisable.[7] Jesus' blessing his disciples is important enough to be mentioned twice in rapid succession (vv 50, 51), and it occurs just prior to his final departure. This suggests that the pronouncement of blessing is modeled on the leave-taking of such personages as Moses (Deuteronomy 33) and Abraham (Genesis 49), with the echoes of Sirach emphasizing the stature of Jesus.[8] The disciples are thus assured of divine favor.

In addition, insofar as Jesus' blessing marks the finale of his earthly sojourn with his followers, the import of Jesus' instruction in vv 44-49 is immediately heightened. They are now seen more clearly to constitute his "last words," which have preeminence precisely because they are "last."[9] As a consequence, the directive to engage in a mission as witnesses "to all nations" receives the strongest possible legitimation — as do those who receive this commission, provided they respond to Jesus in obedience.

Jesus' departure is accomplished via a dual movement, away and up. Although for some this raises immediate questions regarding the cosmology of Luke's account,[10] it is important to appreciate fully the socio-theological significance of the image envisioned here. "Into heaven" signifies both the finality of Jesus' departure (until the parousia) and Jesus' glorified status. The abode of God, heaven, was "up," so, in the "universe" of his day, one went "up" to meet God.[11] In this account, movement "upward" signifies in a visible and concrete way the elevated status of Jesus.[12] The glory and regal power anticipated of Jesus (9:26, 32, 51; 19:12) is now made visible to his fol-

---

7. Parsons ("Narrative Closure," 205-6) discounts this criticism because, he says, the priestly motif is employed by the narrator in order to assist with narrative closure. Such reasoning hardly stands up to close scrutiny, since either it depends on circular reasoning (a priestly motif exists because we find it here) or it urges that we sunder Luke's literary strategy from his christological agenda. See the rejection of the priestly interpretation in R. J. Dillon, *Eyewitnesses*, 222.

8. So R. J. Dillon, *Eyewitnesses*, 223; Nolland, 3:1227.

9. Cf. Paschal, "Farewell Discourse," 230.

10. See the discussion between Dunn and Gooding: Dunn, "Demythologizing"; *idem*, "Ascension"; Gooding, "Demythologizing Old and New"; *idem*, "Demythologizing the Ascension."

11. For example, on a mountain — cf., e.g., Luke 6:12; 9:28; 22:39-46; Acts 1:12.

12. That is, *contra* those who simply dismiss this account of the ascension as reflective of a three-storied universe that (most) ancients thought actually existed (cf., though, the heliocentric universe of Aristarchus; and the argument in Houtman, *Hemel*, 195-219, that ancient Israel had no unified cosmology with heaven resting on pillars), it must be recognized that every view of the world is socially constructed and embraced because of its having achieved legitimated status within the community for which it has meaning (cf. Berger and Luckmann, *Social Construction of Reality*).

lowers;[13] they are thus provided with incontrovertible evidence that Jesus' humility and humiliation on the cross, far from disqualifying divine sanction of his mission, are actually embraced by God. God's verdict reverses and supersedes the verdict of those who rejected, condemned, and executed Jesus.[14]

At this juncture in the narrative, the ascension of Jesus functions in at least two additional ways. First, Luke draws a connection between the going of Jesus and the coming of the Spirit. It is as a consequence of his royal, exalted status that Jesus is able to commit to his followers the Holy Spirit (v 49; cf. Acts 2:32-33). Theologically for Luke, then, the ascension is the prelude to the outpouring of the Spirit and consequent mission of the church.[15] Second, with the ascension Luke addresses the problem of continuity in God's salvation-historical design.[16] This coherence can be articulated along two lines: (1) between Jesus of Nazareth and Jesus, Lord and Christ: The Jesus who suffered and died is the same who is carried up into heaven to exercise royal power; and (2) between the ministry of Jesus and the mission of the early church (cf. Acts 1:1-11).

The disciples' response is fourfold. First, they worship Jesus, behaving in a way almost without parallel in the Third Gospel. Typically, evidence of divine activity, even when it is manifested in Jesus' ministry, leads people to worship God.[17] This is exactly what happens in v 53, a second response of the disciples, when they "bless God" — that is, render to God thankful praise for the manifestation of his salvific purpose.[18] The only possible precursor to worship of Jesus in the Gospel of Luke comes in 17:16, where a foreign leper, cleansed by Jesus, demonstrates his reverence and gratitude by falling at Jesus' feet.[19] This is prefaced by Luke's note that the leper "saw" that he had been healed — that is, exercised insight into the beneficent presence of God in Jesus' mission. Of further interest is the fact that, in Luke-Acts, worship is denied images, the devil, and mere mortals, and allowed only in the case of God.[20] Their worship of Jesus signifies that the disciples have, at last, recognized Jesus for who he is.

---

13. Chance, *Jerusalem,* 64-65: "How better to describe the witnessing of the enthronement than to allow the apostles to witness objectively Jesus' coronation through a heavenly ascension?" (65). Cf. Giles, "Ascension," 50; Korn, *Geschichte Jesu,* 168; Lohfink, *Himmelfahrt,* 242-50; Maile, "Ascension."

14. Cf. Davies, *He Ascended,* 63.

15. Cf. Vanhoozer, *Biblical Narrative,* 253-54.

16. Cf. Korn, *Geschichte Jesu,* 175-89.

17. Cf., e.g., 5:26; 7:16; 13:13; 17:15; 18:43.

18. For this use of εὐλογέω, see 1:42, 64; 2:28; 13:35; 19:38.

19. προσκυνέω may be translated "to worship," but usually carries the sense "to prostrate oneself as an act of veneration."

20. Cf. 4:7; Acts 7:43; 8:27; 10:25; 24:11.

Third, the company of Jesus' followers returns to Jerusalem and remains in the temple.[21] Recognition of the importance of such behavior rests on the memory that this is exactly what Jesus instructed them to do: "stay here in the city until you have been clothed with power from on high" (v 49). The disciples respond to the ascension of Jesus by remembering Jesus' words and heeding them. Their constant presence in the temple compares them favorably with Anna, whose exemplary piety was exhibited in her worshipful presence in the temple "night and day" (2:37).

Finally, their earlier joy, which produced astonishment and disbelief (v 41), has given way to "great joy" — the sort of exhilaration generally associated with disclosures of divine redemption in the Third Gospel. Indeed, the two motifs found here, blessing God and eschatological joy, as well as the aforementioned piety and obedience, are characteristic of the disciples at the close of the Lukan narrative just as they were on display at the beginning. Joy and praise were associated with the birth of Jesus, and those known for their faithfulness to God lived in hope of divine redemption and blessed God at the news of the advent of a Savior.[22] At the close of the Gospel, the faithful continue to wait, now for the Holy Spirit who will empower them for service as agents of this same salvation.

---

21. On the continuing import of the temple, see Acts 2:46; 3:1; 5:42, though, with the progression of the narrative, the temple will be cast more and more in a negative light.
22. Cf. 1:14, 28, 41, 44, 46-47, 58, 64, 68; 2:10, 13-14, 20, 28, 38.

INDEX OF SUBJECTS

INDEX OF MODERN AUTHORS

870

873

INDEX OF SCRIPTURE REFERENCES

884

905

INDEX OF EARLY EXTRABIBLICAL LITERATURE

924